The Routledge Anthology of Restoration and Eighteenth-Century Drama

The Routledge Anthology of Restoration and Eighteenth-Century Drama brings together the work of key playwrights—including many important women writers for the stage—from 1660 to 1800, divided into three main sections:

- Restoring the Theatre: 1660–1700
- Managing Entertainment: 1700–1760
- Entertainment in an Age of Revolutions: 1760–1800

Each of the 20 plays featured is accompanied by an extraordinary wealth of print and online supplementary materials, including primary critical sources, commentaries, illustrations and reviews of productions.

Taking in the spectrum of this period's dramatic landscape—from Restoration tragedies and comedies to ballad operas and popular forms of stage spectacle—*The Routledge Anthology of Restoration and Eighteenth-Century Drama* is an essential resource for students and teachers alike.

Kristina Straub is Professor of English at Carnegie Mellon University.

Misty Anderson is Professor of English and Adjunct Professor of Theatre at the University of Tennessee, Knoxville.

Daniel O'Quinn is Professor in the School of English and Theatre Studies at the University of Guelph.

The Routledge Anthology of Restoration and Eighteenth-Century Drama

Edited by Kristina Straub, Misty Anderson, and Daniel O'Quinn

LONDON AND NEW YORK

First published 2017
by Routledge
2 Park Square, Milton Park, Abingdon, Oxon OX14 4RN

and by Routledge
711 Third Avenue, New York, NY 10017

Routledge is an imprint of the Taylor & Francis Group, an informa business

British Library Cataloguing-in-Publication Data
A catalogue record for this book is available from the British Library

Library of Congress Cataloging-in-Publication Data
Names: Straub, Kristina, 1951– author editor. | Anderson, Misty G., 1967– author editor. | O'Quinn, Daniel, 1962– author editor.
Title: The Routledge Anthology of Restoration and Eighteenth-Century Drama / Kristina Straub, Misty Anderson, and Daniel O'Quinn.
Description: Milton Park, Abingdon, Oxon; New York: Routledge, 2017.
Identifiers: LCCN 2016025687| ISBN 9781138915411 (hardback) | ISBN 9781138915428 (pbk.) | ISBN 9781315690247 (ebook)
Subjects: LCSH: English drama—Restoration, 1660–1700. | English drama—eighteenth century.
Classification: LCC PR1265 .R68 2017 | DDC 822/.408 – dc23
LC record available at https://lccn.loc.gov/2016025687

ISBN: 978-1-138-91541-1 (hbk)
ISBN: 978-1-138-91542-8 (pbk)
ISBN: 978-1-315-69024-7 (ebk)

Typeset in Bembo and Trade Gothic
by Florence Production, Stoodleigh Court, Stoodleigh, Devon, UK

Visit the companion website: www.routledge.com/cw/Straub

Contents

Detailed Contents: Print and Online Content

All shaded items are available as part of the *Anthology*'s online supplement, at **www.routledge.com/cw/Straub**

Image Acknowledgments

Acknowledgments

The editors of this anthology and sourcebook have many debts to individuals and institutions. We want to thank the undergraduate, graduate, and post-graduate research assistants who helped us with the seemingly endless tasks of transcribing and editing: Leslie Allin, Kerri Considine, Mark Kaethler, Rachael MacLean, Sarah White, Pierce Williams, and Zane Vorhes-Grip were indefatigable. Kerri Considine deserves additional thanks as the force behind the biographical index. In addition we want to thank the Folger Shakespeare Library, the Lewis Walpole Library, the National Portrait Gallery in Washington, D.C., the National Portrait Gallery in London, the National Library of Australia, the British Library, the British Museum, the Victoria and Albert Museum, and the Yale Center for British Art for permission to use the many fascinating and beautiful images and texts from their collections. We owe a special debt of gratitude to Chris Caldwell of the University of Tennessee Library; he provided invaluable assistance in finding and making available usable texts for many of the plays in this anthology. We thank the EEBO Text Creation Partnership for the use of many of their online texts, and also wish to thank the Georgetown Library, and especially Scott Taylor, for providing us with a copy of the Crewe manuscript for *The School for Scandal*. Thanks to Jack Lynch for permitting us to use many texts from his wonderful site *Electronic Texts* (andromeda.rutgers.edu/~jlynch/Texts/).

The students in Misty Anderson's satire and graduate theatre classes contributed to the project by reading drafts of these editions and making valuable suggestions. Thanks to the English Departments at Carnegie Mellon, University of Tennessee, and the University of Guelph and the many colleagues who support our work and daily lives: Andreea Ritivoi, Richard Purcell, Jon Klancher, Jennifer Schacker, Judith Welch, Michell Elleray, and Lori Irvine. Daniel O'Quinn has received generous support from the Social Sciences and Humanities Research Council for many years and this project benefitted from their commitment to fund graduate research assistants.

We also thrive as eighteenth-centuryists because of the vibrant communities of the American and Canadian Societies for Eighteenth Century Studies and the many friends and colleagues who support our work: Ros Ballaster, Janine Barchas, Michael Burden, Tita Chico, Ashley Cohen, Brian Corman, Laura Engel, Marilyn Francus, Marcie Frank, Lisa Freeman, Jacqueline Langille, Susan Lanser, Fiona Ritchie, Joseph Roach, Laura Rosenthal, Gillian Russell, Stuart Sherman, David Francis Taylor, James Anderson Winn, and Eugenia Zurakowski.

We are grateful for the patience, love, and support of our families, particularly Bailey and Evie Clark, Suzanne S. Currey, Carol Goldburg, John and Trevor Tirro, and Eli, Gabriel, and Jo-Ann Seamon.

Our editors at Routledge, Ben Piggot and Kate Edwards, have been patient with our questions and generous with their time. Finally, our most profound thanks go to each other. We have answered each other's questions, cheered each other on, and put up with each other's occasional work panics since Fall of 2014 when we began this project. This book has been shaped by all three of us: Kristina began with the original conception of an historically grounded, performance-based anthology, but the architecture of book and online supplement was jointly conceived. Misty envisioned the section on actors' biographies. We have worked together with phone calls and endless streams of email messages. We literally could not have made this book without each other, and though separated by miles, we have learned from and supported each other, often laughed together, and found friendship as a real byproduct of this scholarly work.

A Note on the Texts

In most cases, the editors have worked from first editions of plays, correcting them against at least one later edition. Sheridan's *School For Scandal*, which was not published in a version authorized by Sheridan during his lifetime, is the exception to that rule. Daniel O'Quinn created his edition from the Crewe manuscript, a presentation copy made by Sheridan for his mistress, Frances Anne Crewe. The editors are grateful to Georgetown University Library for providing us with a copy of this manuscript. We have retained original spellings and punctuation except when textual clarity was compromised. We have modernized capitalization except in instances when capitalization carries nuance in the original. We hope that students will notice how these practices in language usage change over the course of the volume, from 1660–1800. Original stage directions have been adhered to as closely as possible. In a few instances we have moved a direction in the text to clarify its relationship to a speech, and have occasionally added a dash to indicate when a directed speech begins after an aside. Our general goal was to deliver as strong a sense as we can of Restoration and eighteenth-century readers' experiences with these texts.

ICONS

The following icons are used throughout the book to indicate what type of content is being presented:

 Playscript

 Image

 Article (newspaper piece or review)

 Commentary

 Document (official court or government papers)

 Essay (book chapter extract or journal article)

 Lyrics

 Poem

Introduction

Performing Drama, Performing Culture

THEATRICAL PERFORMANCE for audiences from 1660 into the nineteenth century defined their culture even more than Shakespearean drama now defines the Elizabethan age for modern readers. Shakespeare's plays are performed constantly today in theatres (including a reconstructed version of his Globe), movie houses and a wide variety of digital entertainment platforms, and read with varying degrees of duty and delight in classrooms throughout the English-speaking world. But many students in modern theatre and literature departments have little experience with reading—let alone seeing—the plays that were such an important cultural force in this long, formative period in the history of European modernity. The Long Eighteenth is the super-sized century in which gender, class, sexuality, race and so many social institutions and practices—empirical science, the nation-state, and a capitalist economy, to name a few—began to take on recognizably modern forms. This book presents new and old students of this period not just with the texts of these plays, but with resources for understanding their performative contexts and impact: the experiences that London audiences brought with them into the theatre, the experiences that they had while there, and the two-way flow between theatrical and cultural politics.

London theatres grew, beginning with their re-opening after the Commonwealth period in 1660, into hot connective points in the relays of information, politics, and the tangled web of thoughts and feelings we call culture that shaped modernity. As the century went on, theatres were part of a growing public culture that thrived in the newly opened urban leisure spaces of London. Parks and buildings dedicated to the consumption of music, art, and the social pleasures of seeing and being seen opened and flourished. Coffee houses served a wide social range of male clientele with newspapers and pamphlets as well as coffee and chocolate. Shopping became a pastime as well as a necessity for men and women who could afford to examine printed goods at pamphlet shops, silks, lace, and brocades at the milliner's, and jewelry and snuff boxes at the toy shops of London. Summers brought fairs that featured theatrical entertainment as well as tumblers, boxers, rope dancers, animal acts, and puppet shows for a broad audience. As the century went on, entertainment grew into the money-making business it is today, and London's theatres were central to that growth.

The plays in this volume were performed in professional theatres centered in London and Dublin,[1] but also in provincial theatres across Britain and its colonial holdings in North America and the Caribbean. The resort of Bath, especially, was an increasingly vibrant theatrical town in the second half of the century. Outside the brick and mortar theatres, strolling acting troupes set up shop in barns and taverns, despite their questionable legal status as "rogues and vagabonds"—people without the legal protection of belonging to a permanent household.[2] During times such as the summer months when the urban theatres were closed—which they were less and less often as the London entertainment business grew—actors, along with other entertainers, performed at the traditional festive and mercantile fairs such as Southwark and Bartholomew. Despite a cultural and religious heritage that resisted theatre, plays were performed in the American colonies almost as soon as there were towns to support audiences for them, and British Caribbean and Indian colonies also had their theatres.[3] Theatrical performance grew with the imperial and colonial nation-state of Britain and was part of the process by which people came to know themselves as Britons.

The availability of cheap print editions of most plays almost as soon as they were performed in a London or Dublin theatre added to the range and extent of theatricality as a part of British social life. As scholars such as Benedict Anderson have argued,[4] reading practices supported a modern sense of national identity and patriotism. Plays—as texts to be read as well as performed—joined newspapers, novels, sermons, and other relatively inexpensive print genres in the process by which Britons read themselves into a sense of belonging to a nation. In the case of plays, especially, we have reason to believe that this reading was not always silent and individual, but often oral, social, and performative. Amateur theatricals were a part of household and even neighborhood leisure-time amusements, as evidenced in the personal letters and diaries of writers such as Frances Burney and Jane Austen. Some wealthy aristocrats even built elaborate permanent theatres as part of their estates in which well-born amateurs tried out their theatrical chops, sometimes with the assistance of a professional or two supplementing their regular income from commercial theatre. Theatricality permeated British literate culture and even reached those who could not read as many servants and lower-status artisans benefited from cheap tickets, accompanying their employers to the theatre, or invitations to fill out the audience at amateur events.

In London and Dublin, especially, theatres were hubs for the performance of British sociability as well as plays. "Sociability," however, does not always reference harmonious or even civil interactions. Theatres brought together people from diverse social and economic backgrounds in ephemeral but important moments of what Victor Turner has called "communitas," the sense of belonging to a cohesive group that is engendered, however temporarily, by the shared purpose and enjoyment of a performance.[5] But it was also the site of disagreements—between audiences, playwrights, actors, and theatre managers in all possible combinations—over politics, personalities, and what should or should not be performed on a public stage. Three factors contributed to the ongoing social drama that was British theatre in the long eighteenth century: the mixed and contentious status of theatrical professionals as representatives of the stage, the diversity of theatre audiences, and the wild variety of entertainment genres that grew out of the on-going task of appealing to that diversity.

PERFORMERS

Theatrical professionals were, at the opening of the theatres in 1660, a mixed lot. Initially, the managers who were commissioned by the Crown to run the licensed theatres in London were indisputably gentlemen, men of birth and fairly high social standing, if not wealth. The ranks of the performers, however, drew from different walks of life men and women who sought the excitement and income of a career on the boards. English actors had never claimed a particularly high social status, whatever their recognition as artists. The forces of anti-theatricality that succeeded in nearly shutting down the stage in the seventeenth century had amplified already existing accusations of immorality and bad social and sexual behavior. To make matters more difficult for the managers, the hiatus in public theatrical performance, beginning with the onset of the English Civil War and only ending in 1660, meant that a new generation of performers had to be trained, and a new generation of theatre-goers had to be enticed into the pleasures of theatre-going. Even Londoners who did not hold with the anti-theatrical biases of the Commonwealth were no longer in the habit of going to the theatre, as in Shakespeare's London. At this moment, actresses first stepped on the stages of the English public theatres. When Charles II decreed, upon his re-opening of the theatres in 1660, that women could play female characters for the first time in English theatrical history, there was no existent pipeline of women performers waiting to take advantage of the expanding opportunities created by the exploding popularity of this novelty. The first actresses were working and servant-class women who often plied the trade of prostitute as well as thespian. The shady reputations of these early actresses did not improve the already questionable social status of the players as a whole.

When, after the Actors' Rebellion of 1695, actors moved into management (see Part 1 "Restoring the Theatre: 1660–1700"), even the gentlemanly status of the manager was drawn into question. The social and moral role of the theatres was clearly read as powerful; the vehemence with which it is critiqued by anti-theatrical polemicists attests as much to its cultural importance as the celebratory prose of its defenders. But the low social status of the theatrical professional, the taint of questionable sexual morality, and a socially precarious lifestyle that often lent itself to alcoholism and casual violence did not inspire strong confidence in the moral character of this institution's personnel. This is not to say, however, that all actors were drunken, brawling louts, and that actresses were all whores. Thomas Betterton, who took over the management of the Theatre Royal in 1695, was well respected as a man as well as an artist, and was one of the first of many actors buried in Westminster Abbey. Colley Cibber, his successor as actor/manager, went on to become poet laureate of England. Early actresses worked hard to achieve a high level of professionalism and could even make a fair living on the stage, although never a salary commensurate with their male peers.[6] But even Betterton was taunted for his alleged promiscuity, and Cibber was the butt of many jokes that questioned his social and sexual status. The point is that if the theatre was to become an important force for the state and for state-sanctioned ideology—and it did—it had to struggle continuously to establish its credibility as a voice for British culture. It is important to note, however, that by the 1790s, the statesman Edmund Burke recognized the moral influence of the theatre as potentially more powerful than the most devoutly heard sermon: "Indeed the theatre is a better school of moral sentiments than churches, where the feelings of humanity are thus outraged."[7]

As Burke's somewhat reluctant testimony suggests, this struggle was fought and at least partially won over the course of the long eighteenth century. The actor and theatre manager David Garrick, who acted at and managed the Theatre Royal at Drury Lane between 1747 and 1776, was instrumental in establishing the gentlemanly status of the actor, as was Thomas Sheridan in Dublin. The latter famously faced down poorly behaved upper-class male audience members on the grounds of his own gentle status, a cultural performance that was reported and discussed throughout the British Isles. Garrick hobnobbed with not only a wide range of artists and literary figures, but many of the socially high-ranking aristocracy. He did much to reform the behavior of the players and to turn the playhouses into places where some degree of refinement was, at least, desirable if not always displayed, and acting into a career that demanded professionalism and a more stable way of living. By mid century, actresses such as Frances Abbington entered into London circles of feminine sociability for acting and looking like ladies off as well as on the stage. (Abbington was well known for her fashion sense and well-born ladies sought her styling advice.) By the last decades of the century, Sarah Siddons, the greatest tragic actress of her day and like many actresses, a working mother, proudly and strategically claimed the moral and social high ground of maternal and wifely duty. While actresses still carried questionable sexual reputations (as they sometimes do today), they joined with men to embrace the higher status of this professionalism.

Another modern development in which actors and actresses were deeply implicated is the phenomenon of celebrity. David Garrick and Frances Abbington were two of a significant handful of actors who were as celebrated for their personalities off the stage as they were for their most famous theatrical roles. As theatre historian and performance theorist Joseph Roach has argued, the Restoration period saw the emergence of "It," an ineffable quality of personal appeal that commands not only interest but "public intimacy," the desire to know and feel close to the famous person.[8] The fascination of "It" contributed to the formation of a public culture of fandom: celebrity performers drew audiences into the theatres, but they also created the demand for actors' faces reproduced in print and visual texts, as well as porcelain figurines, snuffboxes, cups, pitchers, bowls, and a variety of objects that allowed fans to bring their celebrities home.

The celebrity of performers is an important part of a larger social process, namely the role of the theatre in the making of an increasingly modern culture and nation. What kind of institution was the theatre and what was its relation to the state and the body politic? The big London theatres were licensed by the state, and were, beginning with Charles II, a venue for the display of political as well as aesthetic performances. The presence of British royalty at the theatre was as much a part of what audiences came to see as the performances on the stage, and was noted dutifully in the newspapers after performances, as were the plays as the century went on. From their opening in 1660, however, the theatres were also a commercial enterprise needing to attract audiences. As such, they were part of the emergent capitalist culture that would be theorized in 1776 by Adam Smith's *Wealth of Nations*, both a description of and a rationale for market capitalism. Operating on the cusp between state authority and a market economy, theatres were subject to government control and the demands of a diverse audience. In the decade spanning the 1720s and 1730s, for example, audiences delighted in the political satires of the playwright and theatre manager Henry Fielding, which turned an irreverent gaze on the prime minister of England, Robert Walpole, as did the smash-hit musical of the century, John Gay's *The Beggar's Opera*, a few years earlier. In 1737, however, Parliament passed the Licensing Act, which subjected the performance of any new plays in the licensed London theatres to the approval of the Lord Chamberlain. While theatre professionals found many ways to work around this strict government control—by putting on entertainments that were not, strictly speaking, plays, and inviting audiences to enjoy a concert and a "dish of chocolate" while, incidentally, watching a "free" play—this act institutionalized the British government's strong interest and role in the shaping of commercial theatre as it evolved over the century. It also suggests just how important a social institution the theatre came to be in the formation of British culture and the body politic.

AUDIENCES

An observer in London in the 1660s might have had a hard time believing in the cultural power and reach of British theatre later in the eighteenth century. A generation used to the theatres of Shakespeare had died by then, and another generation had grown up without the habit of theatre-going. Nonetheless, many town dwellers, such as the Restoration diarist Samuel Pepys, seem to have been addicted to their theatre-going, while for others, especially those visiting London from the country (like Margery Pinchwife in *The Country Wife*), a trip to the theatre was a rare treat. In the Restoration period, the theatres promoted themselves by staging plays, especially comedies, that made theatre-going seem fashionable, the thing to do. This self-promotion was quickly taken up as nostalgia in the early eighteenth century, as writers such as John Dennis looked back on a mythic Restoration audience organized around the King and his witty, male courtiers:

> That Reign was a Reign of Pleasure, even the entertainments of their Closet were all delightful. Poetry and Eloquence were then their Studies, and that human, gay, and sprightly Philosophy, which qualify'd them to relish the only reasonable

> pleasures which man can have in the World, and those are Conversation and Dramatick Poetry. . . . The discourse, which now every where turns upon Interest, rolled then upon Manners and Humours of Men . . . free from Fear and Taxes, and by reason of that plenty which overflowed among them, they were in the happiest condition in the World, to attain to that knowledge of Mankind, which is requisite for the judging of Comedy.[9]

Whatever the actual numbers of people in the playhouses when they first re-opened in 1660, going to the theatre became in the cultural imagination "what one did" when "seeing the Town," that is, London. The growth of this city supported the growth of theatres. London's population growth is part of a spike in England's over-all population, which went from 5 to 9 million between 1700 and 1800; about 1 in 10 of the total population lived in London by the century's end. Even in the Restoration period London had achieved the status of "the Town" (with the capitalized "T" seen in many plays in this volume) and a cultural magnet for both genders and all classes of people. For the traditional ruling class of England, the landed gentry whose estates comprised the wealthy agribusinesses of the period, London was a place one visited to do business but also, increasingly, to socialize, to see and be seen, and to bring one's marriageable daughters into "good" society. Plays were among the regular amusements that these families consumed while on a visit to London during "the season." As London's social and leisure culture flourished, offering not only plays but musical concerts, lectures on esoteric as well as topical subjects, "scientific" demonstrations, exhibits of mechanical and natural curiosities, and pleasure gardens such as Vauxhall and Ranelagh, the landed gentry began establishing permanent residences in London on the fashionable west end of the city, which increased the theatre's wealthy clientele and enabled a longer season.

With these families came servants—maids of all sorts, cooks, footmen, butlers, and coachmen—to support a fashionable London lifestyle, and servants are a significant part of the London population—and the theatre audience—by the second half of the century. It was a common practice among well-to-do families to send a servant to "hold their place" when the theatres opened; the posh theatre-goer could then make a fashionably late entrance, upon which the servant, usually a footman, was relegated to another place in the theatre. Until manager David Garrick did away with the practice, the footmen had their own gallery in the Theatre Royal at Drury Lane, a free privilege that they used (or abused) to articulate a raucous and to many annoying collective voice at the plays. In addition to servants, many apprentices (young men and women working for artisans and other tradesmen in order to learn a trade), yeoman craftsmen, and, of course, master artisans could afford seats in the pit. In sum, a pretty broad demographic cross-section of the British population comprised the audience.

Changes in the traditions of rural life and agriculture, such as the practice of enclosing common lands for the recreation and revenue of estate owners, which rendered those resources off-limits to the working rural poor, resulted in an increasingly mobile labor force. Many displaced workers went to London, drawn by the promise of urban employment created by growing markets in trade and business. Many found work supporting the lifestyle and amusements of those who could afford servants and the goods, services, and amusements of the London markets for consumables, including entertainment. Others, frustrated by a glutted market for displaced laborers, resorted to petty crime and prostitution to support themselves, and whores and pickpockets were a much-noted part of London public life. Hierarchies of status based on birth and wealth were no less important in this London public than in an older, rural, more feudally organized England, but the certainty and stability that a rural, agricultural England gave to those hierarchies eroded in the context of an economic market that increasingly allowed for more mobility across traditional status lines. Inter-class relations, stabilized through generations by Britons' sense of social place in the rural scenarios of estate and village, had to be negotiated anew in urban spaces of public leisure and amusement, and the theatres were the largest and most consistently patronized of those spaces. Men and women, as well as different classes, mixed socially in the theatres, and gendered as well as classed relationships were formed and reformed with a variety and novelty that was noted, loved, and feared by many social observers and commentators of the period. As early as 1679, Samuel Pepys worried that the increasingly mixed audience reflected the "vanity and prodigality of the age,"[10] code for the lower ranks having enough leisure and wealth to engage in the same pastimes as their "betters."

London theatres, as a result, were sites of both conflict and the formation of new social relations between different kinds of people. Audiences were not docile spectators in the eighteenth century. The theatres were well-lit spaces conducive to the chatting, flirting, and sometimes fighting of audience members before, after—and during—performances. The later years of the period saw substantial expansions in theatre size, allowing for larger crowds. In addition to interacting with each other, audiences were also not shy about communicating their approval or disapproval to the entertainers on the stage. The former could take the form of clapping, "huzzahing," or calling for a performer to repeat a favorite speech or song—multiple times, if the audience so pleased. The latter was expressed by making noise—lots of it—by hissing, booing, yelling insults, and the infamous cat-call. Less noisy but equally effective expressions of disapproval could involve throwing objects at the performers: dried peas on the stage could put a quick end to dances, and even less savory projectiles, such as rotten fruit and offal, were highly effective expressions of audience displeasure. From at least as early as 1722, armed militia were hired to stand guard in the playhouse on performance days, to contain squabbles between audience members and to quash audience assaults on actors, managers, and, most damagingly, on the playhouse itself. *The London Stage, 1660–1800*, a list of performances in the London theatres and a wealth of information for any student of this period, records rioting serious enough to call for military interventions in 1712, 1722, 1735, 1737, 1738, 1744, 1745, 1750, 1755, 1763, 1766, and 1791.[11] By mid century, these riots had taken on aspects of social ritual, beginning with the "ladies" being "asked to leave" the playhouse and proceeding to the breakage of chandeliers and glass, the tearing of curtains and costumes, and the "ripping up" of the benches in the pit. Even the disruptive (and expensive) violence of audiences solidified into somewhat predictable social ritual. Gradually, the frequency of audience violence subsided into a more quiescent form of spectatorship, but as we can see with the Old Price riots of 1809, when audience violence disrupted performances for three months in response to a rise in ticket prices at the newly rebuilt Covent Garden Theatre, nineteenth-century theatre-goers were still far from the polite, silent audience who sit quietly in the dark.

Theatre audiences were, like the performers, part of a long process of negotiating new social rituals and new social identities within the changing economies and societies of Britain and, as the empire grew, its colonial extensions. Domestically, these negotiations involved forging new social relations and identities responsive to more fluid and less static definitions of social status, and an increasing emphasis on gender difference as a structural principle of social order and behavior. Family relations based on affective as well as blood connection slotted men and women into binary roles that, in turn, mapped onto social behaviors and institutions. (Asking "the ladies" to leave before the "gentlemen" tore up the playhouse is symptomatic of this new order asserting itself even in the most chaotic moments of social life within the theatre.) As Britain grew into its role of colonial and imperial empire, the theatre also served as a means of negotiating imaginary relations between what the English saw as central—themselves—and peripheral—anybody else. From visits from the "Indian Kings" in the Restoration[12] to the pantomime performances of *Omai* at the end of the period, theatrical performances and audiences incorporated into the relatively safe space of entertainment and spectacle embodied concepts of racial, ethnic, and religious differences. Theatrical performance produced even as it responded to the expanding variety of experience brought into British consciousness by colonial exploration, conquest, and trade—including the trafficking of human bodies in the African slave trade. In the British theatres, human variety was performed on the stage and in the audience, alongside performances that presented visions of national, even patriotic cohesion and unity. By late in the century, after-pieces, short performances played after the main piece, such as *The Fairy Prince*, an allegory of royal succession, increasingly celebrated the Royal Family and the British state, and throughout the century audiences were as inclined to join in enthusiastic singing of "Rule Britannia" and "Britons Strike Home" as they were to hiss and cat-call the performers.

THE ENTERTAINMENTS

The human variety performed in the audience correlates with the variety of performance genres within the playhouses. In order to draw the large and diverse audiences needed to support commercial theatres, managers delivered many different kinds of performances. As Richard Leveridge, the composer and theatre manager, wrote in the 1720s, "As Diversion is the Business of the Stage, 'tis Variety best contributes to that Diversion."[13] Theatres had to appeal to a wide range of different literacies and aesthetics. The broad, physical comedy performed in a farce might be effectively paired with a word-rich, witty comedy or an expensively produced music- and dance-rich spectacle. Sentimental scenes of reconciled lovers in the main play might be followed by a comic hornpipe or a contortionist's act. The trick, for the canny theatre manager, was to hit a balance between different parts of the evening's entertainment that would appeal to all of the diverse segments of the theatre-going public without overly annoying any one part.

Opera's history in the London theatres is perhaps the most dramatic example of an entertainment form that polarized audiences. Italian opera was introduced to the British in the seventeenth century and was almost immediately patronized by the cosmopolitan aristocracy, a group who sent its young men to Europe and generally spoke several European languages. At the same time, "semi-operatic" plays in English, such as Henry Purcell's *The Fairy Queen*, delivered hybrid mixes of distinctively English plays embellished with music, dance, and spectacular scenery and special effects for a much wider appeal. Italian opera was supported by the patronage of the elite and, beginning with George Frederick Handel's career during the reign of Queen Anne (1702–1714), the Royal Family. Under the reign of George I, Anne's successor, Handel composed music for grand state occasions as well as operas. The importation of Italian singers for this demanding, specialized form of singing soon became, however, a lightening rod for complaints from the public, especially against the high-handed female divas and, worse, the Italian castrati, male sopranos castrated at an early age to preserve their high voices. Aesthetic differences were argued between different status groups in terms of gendered and sexualized moral categories, with theatrical professionals attempting to mediate between them by finding an impossible balance of entertainments that would appeal to all. David Garrick, as late as the 1750s, incorporated Italian singers into English operas in semi-operatic works such as *The Fairies*. But variety, produced by different understandings of what British theatre should be, could become itself an object of critique. "Shakespearianus" could write of Garrick in a 1755 review of *The Fairies*, "All Parties agree in applauding and encouraging his unwearied Endeavours to entertain the Publick; and though Variety may be very agreeable to them, yet he ought not to gratify it at the Expence of an Author, whose Memory is certainly dear to them."[14] One can see Garrick caught in the tension named by "Shakespearianus" between an audience addicted to variety and spectacle and at the same time supportive of a nationalistic theatrical agenda that, especially after David Garrick's Shakespeare Jubilee in 1769, cohered around the figure of William Shakespeare. Theatrical professionals leveraged the British public's support for national unity against the disruptive diversity of audience tastes and demands in the face of almost nonstop European wars.

WHAT'S IN THIS BOOK

The editors of this volume present students of drama and literature with texts, visual and print, that convey multiple senses of performance: the plays that were performed on the stage, the performative responses of the audiences, and the cultural performances outside the playhouse that informed and sometimes reflected experiences within. We have tried to reconstruct as much as possible how audiences over the long eighteenth century experienced going to the playhouse, reading plays, and reading about plays and the theatre.

The student will find plays, such as *The Country Wife* and *School for Scandal*, that are well-known in twentieth- and twenty-first-century revivals and for their place in the English and theatrical canon. They will also find an example of Shakespearean adaptation, a distinctive feature of this period during which many different versions of Shakespeare's plays were almost constantly on the stage, and this author went from being a good writer to the iconic English Bard. They will find pantomimes that theatre scholars have only recently begun to study as a prominent part of the theatre-goer's experience. We have privileged performance over reading experience, in some cases choosing to present students with the most frequently performed versions of a play, as opposed to the version that conforms to scholarly models of authenticity. For example, *The Tempest* adaptation in this book is from a print edition that captures the most performed version of the play, not the one closest to Shakespeare or even the original adaptation by William Davenant and John Dryden.

In some cases, we give students a play that was not regularly performed but is worth their notice because of the social and political contexts it foregrounds. Aphra Behn, for example, is one of the most popular playwrights of the Restoration, but we have chosen not to present her most frequently published and performed play, *The Rover*, but a play that actually failed in its first performance and has been given little attention since: *The Widdow Ranter*. This seemingly counter-intuitive choice allows students a window into the Restoration's imaginings of ethnic, racial, and cultural otherness at an early moment in British colonialism, as well as a displaced performance of rebellion that speaks as richly to the aftermath of the English Civil Wars as to the rebellion of Nathanial Bacon in colonial Virginia. It also makes a helpful point of comparison with performances of the 1790s, well into British colonial imperialism and well past the French Revolution of 1789.

With each play we have provided students with additional print documents, and images that will help students tap into performances within and without the playhouses. We have tried to call attention to developments in the physical spaces, craft, and technologies of theatres over the long eighteenth century. Theatres generally grew larger, with greater audiences over the course of this period, and the semi-thrust stages of the Restoration retreated to increase seating capacity and place actors further and further behind today's familiar proscenium arch. This change in stage configuration also allowed for increasingly spectacular and complicated scenery and stage effects. The history of the physical playhouse frames how we might think of the performance of a Restoration *Tempest* very differently from how we imagine a late eighteenth-century play such as *Inkle and Yarico* on the stage. Acting styles, too, changed from the more declamatory methods of the Restoration, with actors assuming relatively static postures and expressing emotion through voice and hand gestures, to the more active and "realistic" acting style famously attributed to the actor/manager Garrick in the mid-eighteenth century. The theatre increasingly cultivated physicality in performance as well as oratory, as is also suggested by the emergence of the first great modern clown, Joseph Grimaldi, at the turn into the nineteenth century.

Another element of theatrical performance that this volume highlights is the many and complex ways in which different literacies in this period inform each other: the literacy of embodied and spoken performance in the theatre and the growing print literacy of audiences during this period shape and respond to each other. We include, whenever possible, how people would have encountered plays in the realm of print as well as the stage. Plays were usually printed immediately after a first performance, allowing them to circulate farther and longer than their original run. From around 1700 on, playbills and, more importantly, newspaper ads told the public what to expect on specific nights at the theatre, providing veritable anthologies of entertainments, from hornpipes and ballets to farces and plays. Actors became a feature in these documents as favorite performers' names became advertising ploys to bring people into the playhouse and the modern phenomenon of celebrity began to flourish. After 1750, theatrical reviews featured in daily and weekly newspapers, and Garrick, like several canny managers before him, capitalized on this phenomenon by cultivating relationships with newspaper editors and writers such as Henry Bate to manage how his audiences read about as well as physically experienced his theatre.[15] Events in the theatre were both precipitated by advance editorializing about a performance and replayed multiple times in the press after a performance. Novels such as Frances Burney's run-away hit novel, *Evelina or a Young Lady's Entrance into the World* (1778) gained popularity through their vivid recreations of London leisure activities and spaces, among which time spent at the theatre was a major feature.

Eighteenth-century British theatres, then, were hubs for a rich array of all kinds of performances—political, social, cultural, aesthetic—in both embodied and print forms. We can convey only a slight sample of this performative world within the covers of a textbook, hence, the need for an online supplement that we hope readers will use to expand their sense of this formative period in modern performance culture. Each play in the book is accompanied by print and visual texts that will contribute to that sense, and the reader will find additional contextual materials in the online supplement.

The plays in this book are good reads, but we also hope that students will go beyond the text on the page to imagine and perhaps even experience for themselves, through staging exercises and reader's theatre, the affective intensity of these texts brought to embodied and spoken life. What we hope to offer is, beyond a sampling of plays that are key to understanding a period when so much that is modern came into being, a peek into the fascinating social world that formed in and around the London theatres.

Notes

1 This volume focuses on London performances and contexts but for information about the important Dublin theatre, see Helen Burke, "Acting in the Periphery: The Irish Theatre" in Jane Moody and Daniel O'Quinn, Eds. *The Cambridge Companion to British Theatre, 1730–1830* (219–232). Cambridge, UK: Cambridge University Press, 2007. Also, La Tourette Stockwell, *Dublin Theatres and Theatre Customs* (1637–1820). New York: B. Blum, 1968.

2 Archaic law even in the eighteenth century, the law allowed the arrest of individuals without a permanent attachment to a business or household and could be evoked at the whim of town officials and magistrates.

3 Kathleen Wilson, *A New Imperial History: Culture, Identity, and Modernity in Britain and the Empire, 1660–1840*. Cambridge, UK: Cambridge University Press, 2004.

4 *Imagined Communities: Reflections on the Origin and Spread of Nationalism*. London; New York: Verso, 1991.

5 "Are there Universals of Performance in Myth, Ritual, and Drama?" *By Means of Performance: Intercultural Studies of Theatre and Ritual*. Eds. Richard Schechner and Willa Appel. Cambridge and New York: Cambridge University Press, 1990.

6 Helen E. M. Brooks, *Actresses, Gender, and the Eighteenth-Century Stage: Playing Women*. Houndsmills, Basingstoke: Palgrave Macmillan, 2015, 16–41.

7 *Reflections on the Revolution in France*. Ed. L.G. Mitchell. Oxford: Oxford University Press, 1993, 81.

8 *It*. Ann Arbor, MI: University of Michigan Press, 2007, 1–21.

9 John Dennis, "Epistle Dedicatory" to *The Comical Gallant: or the Amours of Sir John Falstaffe*. A Comedy. As it is Acted at the Theatre Royal in Drury-lane. By his Majesty's Servants. London: A. Baldwin, 1702.

10 *The Diary of Samuel Pepys*. Eds. Robert Lathum and William Matthews. Berkeley, CA: University of California Press, 1970. Vol. 9, 2.

11 Terrance M. Freeman, *Dramatic Representations of British Soldiers and Sailors on the London Stage, 1660–1800: Briton's Strike Home*. Studies in British History, Volume 36. Lewiston/Queenston/Lampeter: The Edwin Mellon Press, 1995, 35–37.

12 Joseph Roach, *Cities of the Dead: Circum-Atlantic Performance*. New York: Columbia University Press, 1996, 8.

13 'Preface' to *The Comic Masque of Pyramus and Thisbe*. As it is Perform'd at the Theatre in Lincoln's-Inn Fields.

14 *London Evening Post*, February 18, 1755.

15 See Stuart Sherman, "Garrick among the Media: The '*Now* Performer' Navigates the News." *PMLA*, 126.4 (October 2011): 966–82 for an account of Garrick's relationship with Bate as newspaper editor.

A Biographical Dictionary of Stage Personnel

Abington, Frances (née Barton 1737–1815) was born into humble circumstances and apprenticed in the theatre company at Drury Lane under David Garrick. After working in Ireland Mrs. Abington eventually returned to Drury Lane, although she and Garrick would quarrel throughout his remaining time as manager. Garrick called her "the worst of bad women," but her box office appeal is reflected in Tom Davies' account of her appearance as Charlotte in *The West Indian*, "It is impossible to conceive that more gaiety, ease, humour, elegance, and grace could have been assumed by any actress than by Mrs. Abington in this part." Under Sheridan's management, she played her most famous role, Lady Teazle, a part that Sheridan wrote with her personality and comic gifts in mind.

Aickin, Francis (?–1805) and his younger brother James Aickin both performed on London stages in similar roles, even appearing together at times (as they did in *The West Indian*). Both began their careers in Ireland, and both eventually moved to Drury Lane. Francis had a falling out with David Garrick, and in 1774 he moved to Covent Garden, while James continued to perform at Drury Lane as well as at the Haymarket. Toward the end of his career, Francis focused on villain types for his characters, earning the nickname, "Tyrant Aickin."

Aickin, James (?–1803) See Aickin, Francis. Toward the end of his career, James earned the nickname, "belly," for his increasing girth.

Angel, Edward (?–1673) was a talented mimic and actor known for low comedy roles and for playing female parts. Angel probably played Stephano in John Dryden and Sir William Davenant's adaptation of *The Tempest*.

Baddeley, Robert (1733–1794) reportedly worked as a cook for Samuel Foote before he made his first appearance as Sir William Wealthy in Foote's *The Minor*. He became a member of the company at Drury Lane and developed a reputation for low comedy and for being somewhat of a dandy. In 1763 he eloped with Sophia Snow (see Sophia Baddeley), and introduced her to the stage. In 1770 Baddeley got into a duel with George Garrick, David Garrick's brother, over Sophia's rumored amorous exploits and Baddeley's casual attitude about them. His best known role was Moses in *The School for Scandal*, a role he originated and which he played over 200 times.

Baddeley, Sophia (née Snow 1745?–1786) was born into a family of musicians. Her father Valentine Snow was a serjeant-trumpeter to George II and theatrical musician and her grandfather Moses Snow was the royal musician. In 1763 she eloped with Robert Baddeley. She was well known for her singing voice, her beauty, and her vibrant personality. She was reputed to have had several affairs, precipitating her husband's duel with George Garrick, after which they separated. Sophia continued her affairs as well as appearances onstage, sometimes even with Robert, as she did in *The West Indian* in 1771. Her strongest roles, such as Polly Peachum in *The Beggar's Opera* and music in Garrick's *Jubilee*, involved singing.

Bannister Jr., John (1760–1836) was the congenial son of singer and comic actor Charles Bannister. Early in his career Bannister was coached by David Garrick; he worked at Drury Lane and later at Haymarket, often appearing with his father in comic roles until Charles retired in 1799. In 1781 both father and son appeared in *Beggar's Opera Metamorphosed*, taking female roles (Charles played Polly, John played Jenny Diver). Bannister married Elizabeth Harper, and they appeared together in *Inkle and Yarico*. After his father's retirement, Bannister often took roles his father had played, and he earned an even greater reputation. He played at Drury Lane, but was also a staple of the summer season at the Haymarket.

Bannister, Elizabeth (née Harper 1757–1849) was a singer and actress who often appeared at the Haymarket. In 1783 she married John Bannister (see above). She primarily played comic and comic opera roles.

Barry, Ann Street (1733–1801) was the daughter of a prominent apothecary in Bath. After being jilted at the age of 17, she went on the stage where she began a long career of playing primarily tragic roles. In 1754 she married, much against her family's wishes, the actor William Dancer, who played Lear against her Cordelia. She was celebrated for her beauty and passionate delivery rather than for nuanced acting. By the time Dancer died in 1759, she was known to be the mistress of Spranger Barry, her manager at the Crow Street Theatre in Dublin, whom she later married. In 1767, she and Barry joined David Garrick's company at Drury Lane when the Dublin theatre failed. After her second husband died, she remarried a barrister and would-be actor, Thomas Crawford, but supported herself, acting until her retirement on a comfortable income after her last performance in 1797.

Barry, Elizabeth (c.1658–1713) one of the best known English actresses of the period, was taken under the wing of Sir William Davenant at a young age, her father having been financially ruined. Accounts indicate she was not initially a very good actress, and it is anecdotally reported that the Earl of Rochester took it upon himself to train her for a wager. Barry and Rochester became lovers, and she had a daughter by him in 1677. Barry returned to the stage in 1678, and over the next few years her talent and reputation flourished. She became a leading lady at the Duke's Company by 1680, often playing opposite Betterton, and staying on when it became the United Company in 1682. The playwright Thomas Otway became enamoured of her, and wrote the part of Belvidera in *Venice Preserved* for her. Barry was romantically linked to several other men (a fact that distressed Otway), including Sir George Etherege. Among her many popular roles were Mrs. Loveit in *The Man of Mode* and Olivia in *The Plain Dealer.* In 1694 Christopher Rich's handling of the finances at the United Company caused several of the older actors, including Barry and Betterton, to leave and create their own company at Lincoln's Inn Fields. She continued to dominate the stage, and it is during this period that she originated the role of Mrs. Marwood in *The Way of the World.* She did not retire until 1710. By all accounts, Barry was passionate, occasionally ruthless, but in all an excellent actress.

Barry, Spranger (bap. 1717–1777) was born to a Dublin silversmith and apprenticed to that trade, but turned to the theatre and was impressive enough to play the tragic role of Othello in his twenties. He played in Dublin alongside a young David Garrick, with whom, despite efforts at collaboration, he had a life-long rivalry.

Bates, William (?–1813?) was a comic actor who played low comedy and harlequin characters. He was also interested in scenery and stage machinery. Among his London roles, he played Silvertongue in *The Belle's Stratagem.* In 1793 he travelled to America, where he performed in Annapolis, Maryland, Philadelphia, Boston, and Providence.

Bellamy, George Anne (1731?–1788) was born in Ireland, the illegitimate daughter of a minor actress and an Irish Baron. Her father sent her to France for a convent education, where she converted to Catholicism. She acted at Covent Garden as early as 1741 and played over the course of her career at both London theatres, and in Dublin and Edinburgh. While not considered a great actress, she was valued for her beauty and her ability at playing tender, passionate love scenes. She was Juliet to Garrick's Romeo in the 12-night battle between the latter two and Spranger Barry and Susanna Cibber in the same roles at the two competing London playhouses. She lived an extravagant and financially precarious life, cohabitating serially with at least three men, one the actor West Digges, and bearing three illegitimate children. Her memoirs, *An Apology for the Life of George Anne Bellamy*, was published in six volumes in 1785.

Betterton, Mary (née Saunderson c.1637–1712) was one of the earliest professional actresses on the English stage. Her first recorded performance was in Sir William Davenant's *The Siege of Rhodes* in its 1661 expanded two-part version. She married Thomas Betterton in 1662, and continued to perform, becoming a leading lady in the Duke's Company. She, along with her husband, taught and trained court performers for the masque *Calisto*; Mary's primary job was to teach the Princesses Anne (later Queen) and Mary. When Anne Bracegirdle's father met with financial difficulties in the late 1660s, the Betterton took her in and treated her as their own child. Betterton continued to train and mentor young actresses throughout her life. In 1676 she created the role of Bellinda in *The Man of Mode.* She received high praise for her portrayal of Lady Macbeth, a role in which Colley Cibber commended her by noting that not even Elizabeth Barry could surpass her performance. By 1694 she retired from the stage.

Betterton, Thomas (baptized 1635–1710) was baptized in London, reportedly the son of an undercook for Charles II and Frances Flowerdew. He began acting with Thomas Killigrew's company in 1660 and quickly gained reputation, becoming known, by the end of his life, as the best actor between Richard Burbage, Shakespeare's contemporary, and David Garrick. He probably originated the role of Dorimant in *The Man of Mode*. Later, after taking over the management of the United Company, he gained the role of Anthony in *All For Love*. He played a staggering 200+ roles over the course of his career and was an actor of great range and effectiveness, especially known for his voice. His body was reported to be rather clumsy and static in performance. He married the actress Mary Saunders and though childless, they lived respectably with two adopted daughters, one of whom became the famous actress Anne Bracegirdle. After a long and successful career as actor and theatre manager, he was buried in Westminster Abbey.

Blurton, James (1756–?) was a dancer who made his first appearance at Covent Garden at age 11. He primarily danced in pantomimes, at both Covent Garden and Drury Lane. He played the title character in *Omai* in 1785.

Bowman, Elizabeth (née Watson 1677?–1707?) was taken in by the Bettertons when her father died shortly after encountering financial difficulties. She married actor John Bowman, performing after as Mrs. John Bowman. She was involved with the complaints against Christopher Rich and the formation of the United Company in 1694. She performed consistently at Lincoln's Inn Fields with Betterton's company, including her role as Mrs. Fainall in *The Way of the World*, although she was not as popular as Elizabeth Barry or Anne Bracegirdle.

Bowman, John (1651?–1739) began his career with the Duke's Company acting at the Dorset Garden theatre. Bowman was both a singer and actor, and reportedly had a close association with the King. He generally played either the fop character or the sympathetic friend. In 1692 he married Elizabeth Watson. One of his most famous roles was Petulant in *The Way of the World*. Later in life he took up father characters, including Priuli in *Venice Preserv'd*.

Bowen, William (1666–1718) had joined the United Company at Drury Lane by 1689, although his early career is uncertain. He began playing primarily comic roles, and later worked up to larger parts. His friend William Congreve wrote Sir Joseph in *The Old Bachelor* for him. When the United Company split in 1694 he joined Betterton, but was not made a sharer in the company, in part due to their disagreements and Betterton's fear of rebellion. In 1700 he played Witwoud in *The Way of the World*, the third part written specifically for him by Congreve. In the fall of that same year he left the stage, allegedly convinced by Jeremy Collier's writings that the theatre was immoral (although a more likely explanation has to do with a salary dispute). This did not last, and Bowman was back on the stage four months later. He performed in both London and Dublin for several years, simultaneously taking on different government positions. Bowen was charged more than once for murder, and spent some time in and out of prison. His last recorded appearance was in 1717, and in 1718 he was fatally wounded in a duel by the actor James Quin.

Bowtell, Elizabeth (née Ridley?) joined the King's Company after she married Barnaby Bowtell around 1669. She was known for her breeches roles, including Benzayda in *Conquest of Granada* and Margery Pinchwife in *The Country Wife*. Her most famous role, however, was as Queen Statira in *The Rival Queens*, in which she played opposite Elizabeth Barry. Reportedly, in the heat of an onstage fight (anecdotally attributed to an offstage quarrel), Barry so forcefully thrust a blunted stage dagger at Bowtell that it pierced her stays. Bowtell worked consistently and was successful during her career until she retired in 1690.

Bracegirdle, Anne (c.1663–1748) was an actress and singer born in Northamptonshire to a coachman and his wife. At an early age, she was adopted by Thomas and Mary Betterton, who mentored her development as an actress. She played Semernia in *The Widdow Ranter* and was well known for her attractions in breeches roles. In 1692 she was the victim of an attempted kidnapping by one Captain Hill and Lord Mohun; the latter subsequently murdered the actor William Mountfort, whom Mohun thought was her lover. She went on to become a leading attraction in the United Company and later at Lincoln's Inn Fields, with the Bettertons and Elizabeth Barry. She played a wide range of roles, including Millamant in *The Way of the World* in 1700. Feeling displaced by the rising star of Anne Oldfield, she left the stage after a final performance in 1707. She was buried in Westminster Abbey.

Bridgewater, Roger (?–1754) began at the Drury Lane company playing dramatic roles. In 1731 he played Thorowgood in the premiere of *The London Merchant*. When Theophilus Cibber rebelled against the company at Drury Lane and left for the Haymarket, Bridgwater remained at Drury Lane until 1734, when he joined John Rich at Covent Garden, where he continued to play dramatic roles. One of his recurring roles later in his career was Falstaff in both parts of *Henry IV*, a role he played until it became too strenuous for his failing health.

Bright, George (?) had his first known appearance in London at the Dorset Garden theatre in 1679 with the Duke's Company. He specialized in fops, servants, and comic dullards. Bright joined Betterton when the United Company split in 1694, and played Waitwell in the premiere of Congreve's *The Way of the World*. When the attacks against the stage's immorality began in earnest, Bright was one of the actors who bore the brunt of the authorities' ire, leading him into dire financial straits, from which he never quite recovered.

Bulkley, Mary (née Wilford 1748–1792) began her career as a dancer. She married George Bulkley in 1767, and performed at Covent Garden from 1761 until 1781. In 1782 she worked briefly in the company at Drury Lane, and then worked in Edinburgh and, in the summers, at the Haymarket. She originated many roles, including

Miss Hardcastle in *She Stoops to Conquer* and Julia in *The Rivals*. In 1788 Bulkley married Captain Ebenezer Barrisford, and subsequently performed under the name Mrs. Barrisford.

Bullock Jr., Christopher (c.1690–1722) was the eldest son of actor William Bullock. One of his early roles was Whisper in *The Busie Body* in the premiere. In 1714 Bullock and his father joined John Rich's company at Lincoln's Inn Fields. He often played fops and comic servants, but played young lovers and serious roles as well. In 1717 he married actress Jane Rogers and, when John Rich came into financial straits, Bullock and Theophilus Keene took over management of the troupe at Lincoln's Inn Fields.

Bullock, Hildebrand (?–1733) was the second son of actor William Bullock. By 1715 he had joined his father and his older brother Christopher at Lincoln's Inn Fields, primarily playing smaller comic roles. In 1715 Bullock married dancer Anne Russell. After Christopher died in 1722, Bullock was more often mentioned on playbills. He played Jemmy Twitcher in the premiere of *The Beggar's Opera* at Lincoln's Inn Fields.

Bullock, William (c.1667–1742) was the patriarch of a family of theatrical talent. Bullock's first recorded London performance was in a skirt role in *The Mock-Marriage*, and he and his sons would continue to play female roles throughout their careers. He generally played in comedy and farce, usually the roles of fops, country bumpkins, coarse fathers, comic Irish or Scotsmen, hotheads, or old ladies. He played Sir Tunbelly Clumsey in the premiere of *The Relapse* at Drury Lane, and later played Sir Jealous Traffick in the premiere of *The Busie Body*, in which he was joined by his son Christopher. He was a well regarded comedian, and Richard Steele consistently praised his on-stage antics. In 1712 Bullock joined John Rich at Lincoln's Inn Fields, where Bullock remained throughout the rest of his career. Almost all of the Bullock clan played at Lincoln's Inn Fields; Bullock was joined by his sons Christopher (and his wife Jane), Hildebrand, and William, and his daughter Henrietta Maria. Bullock continued acting throughout his life, outliving all three of his sons, although the frequency with which he appeared onstage lessened considerably after 1734.

Burden, Kitty (née White?) first appeared onstage at Covent Garden in 1757. She married Mr. Burden around the same time she played Lucy in the premiere of Samuel Foote's *The Minor*. She tended to play the young female roles in comedies. She primarily performed at Covent Garden or at the Haymarket with Foote, although she did perform in Dublin for a few seasons from time to time.

Butler, Elizabeth (?–1748) had her first recorded appearance on the London stage at Drury Lane in 1726. She played several important roles for the company at Drury Lane, including Millwood in the premiere of *The London Merchant*. In 1733 she followed Theophilus Cibber to the Haymarket and then returned again to Drury Lane (along with other actors who had seceded with Cibber), continuing to play lead roles. In 1742, after some difficulties in a failed attempt to take over management of Drury Lane along with

Cibber and Mills, Butler joined the troupe at Lincoln's Inn Fields, until she retired from the stage in 1743.

Cartwright, William (c.1606–1686) was the son of an Elizabethan actor. He worked as a bookseller during the Commonwealth period, but on at least one occasion was engaged in furtive theatrical endeavors. After theatrical activity was again made legal, Cartwright joined a company at the Red Bull theatre, eventually becoming part of Thomas Killigrew's King's Company. He moved to the new Drury Lane theatre with the company in 1673, and played many major roles during this period, including Abenamar in *The Conquest of Granada* and Sir Jasper Fidget in the premiere of *The Country Wife*. After Thomas Killigrew and his son Charles struggled over management of the company, the Lord Chamberlain placed Cartwright, along with Hart, Mohun, and Kynaston, in control (although Hart gained primary control not long after this). He stayed on when the King's Company and the Duke's Company became the United Company in 1682, although he did not perform much at this point, and retired after the 1684–1685 season.

Cautherley, Samuel (?–1805) was rumored to be the son of David Garrick. He began his career as a child at Drury Lane, and Garrick acted as a mentor to him. Evidently the young Cautherley was a handsome boy but not very smart, and Garrick attempted to send him to school before he decided to return him to the stage in 1760. He played sporadically before being sent away again by Garrick in 1763, returning to Drury Lane in 1765. Cautherley was often criticized in the press, in spite of Garrick's assistance. During this time, he played Charles Dudley in the premiere of *The West Indian*, along with a string of strong supporting and occasional lead roles he obtained with Garrick's help. He and Garrick had a falling out, possibly due to Cautherley's resentment over his own lack of success. Whatever the reason, Cautherley's last recorded performance was in 1775.

Centlivre, Susanna (1669?–1723) was a self-educated playwright and actress. She wrote some of the most enduring comedies of the eighteenth century and was able, as her career matured, to support herself with the proceeds of her plays. See the headnote to *The Busie Body*.

Chapman, Thomas (c.1683–1747) primarily played comic roles, although he did try his hand at more serious parts (and was reportedly not very good in them). He often played at Lincoln's Inn Fields in the mid–late 1720s, and by the 1727–1728 season was engaged in a very busy schedule there. He played the Beggar in the premiere of Gay's *The Beggar's Opera*. He kept up this rigorous schedule at Lincoln's Inn Fields, and later he also performed at Covent Garden. In 1730 he took on the management of his own playhouse, a venture that lasted into the 1740s. He also appeared in the summers at Bartholomew Fair.

Charke, Charlotte (née Cibber 1713–1760) was the daughter of the famous actor/manager and Poet Laureate of England, Colley Cibber and his wife, the singer/actress Catherine Cibber. She married Richard Charke, a musician and composer in 1730, a marriage that failed, leaving Charke alone to raise their daughter. Over the course of her acting career, she played Lucy in *The London Merchant* and Marplot in *The Busybody*, and was known, especially while working for Henry Fielding at the Haymarket Theatre, for her breeches acting. She cross-dressed off the stage as well as on, travelling as Mr. Brown with her companion Mrs. Brown for a stint as a strolling player. Over the course of her life, recorded in the autobiographical *A Narrative of the Life of Mrs. Charlotte Charke*, she acted, sold sausages, worked as a valet for a dissolute nobleman and as a waiter in a tavern, and ran a puppet theatre. A headstrong and rebellious young woman, she alienated her father through her defiant and often foolish behavior and by parodying him in Fielding's satirical plays. She wrote two plays and a novel, *The History of Henry Dumont*, in addition to her autobiography, and died in poverty after a life of bad luck and poor decision making.

Cibber, Colley (1671–1757) was an actor, manager, playwright, poet, and autobiographer. He created the role of Lord Foppington in *The Relapse*, based on the character of *Sir Novelty Fashion*, which he originated in his play, *Love's Last Shift*. In his life, and in his autobiography, Cibber integrated the theatrical fop into his personal style and self-presentation. Born to a well-known sculptor, Cibber was drawn early into acting and played a wide range of roles, although he was generally better received in comic parts. He moved into management in 1709 when he led his fellow actors from Christopher Rich's Drury Lane for the Queen's Theatre in the Haymarket. He returned to Drury Lane where he became the stable third of a changing triumvirate of actors/managers until he retired in 1733. As manager, he was central to the shaping of theatrical culture in London in the 1720s, making only the one enormous error of turning down John Gay's *The Beggar's Opera*, one of the most popular plays of the eighteenth century. As playwright, he wrote successful comedies that mixed sentiment with comedy; his adaptation of Shakespeare's *Richard III* was the version most frequently performed in the eighteenth century, and it has survived even into the twentieth. In 1730 he was named Poet Laureate of England, a post he owed more to his ardent support of the Hanoverian monarchy and his importance to the theatrical world than to his poetic talent. In 1740, he published a lengthy, lively autobiography that is a goldmine of information for anyone who is interested in the history of the theatre.

Cibber, Jane (née Johnson 1706–1733) was the first wife of Theophilus Cibber, son of Colley Cibber, in 1725. She was well received as an actress, playing young female roles in both comedies and tragedies, including Maria in the premiere of *The London Merchant*.

Cibber, Susannah Maria (1714–1766) was a celebrated singer and actress, the sister of the composer Thomas Arne. In addition to performing in plays, she was a favorite of Handel's and performed in his oratorios. In 1734 she married Theophilus Cibber, joining his company at Drury Lane, where she drew the attention and gained the mentorship of Colley Cibber. Her career flourished, but her profligate husband prostituted her to a gentleman, William Sloper, an affair that caused a scandal when Theophilus accused the pair of adultery in a lawsuit that he won, but with so small a sum in damages as to suggest that no one was fooled by Theophilus's claims. He sued again when Sloper and Cibber, by now in love with each other and the parents of a daughter, ran off with each other to begin a long and apparently happy life together. Humiliated by her husband in the press, Susanna rehabilitated her career in the premier of Handel's *Messiah* in Dublin, and returned to London's Covent Garden in 1742. By the end of her career, she was celebrated as an actress as well as singer and was buried in Westminster Abbey.

Cibber, Theophilus (1703–1758) son of Colley Cibber, attended Winchester College and joined his father's acting company at the age of seventeen. He showed great initial promise as an actor and, with his father's support, might have followed in the latter's footsteps as actor/manager, had it not been for his financial extravagance, marital infidelity, and habitually alienating behavior towards his theatrical associates. (See Susannah Maria Cibber, above, for an example.) He nonetheless made some positive marks on London theatre, introducing *The London Merchant* and originating the role of George Barnwell in 1735. He sustained a precarious career as actor and writer until 1758 when Benjamin Victor, manager of the Dublin Theatre, invited him to join that company. The ship in which Cibber was sailing was caught in a storm and Cibber was one of the many passengers drowned.

Clarke, Mrs. (Nathaniel?) (?) was probably the wife of actor Nathaniel Clarke, and played at many different venues during the late 1720s to the late 1740s. She was Jenny Diver in the premiere of *The Beggar's Opera* and Lady Kingcall in the premiere of *The Author's Farce.*

Clarke, Thomas (?) was a member of the King's Company by the 1670–1671 season. He played Dollabella in the premiere of *All for Love* at Drury Lane in 1677. He was considered talented, but Colley Cibber thought him difficult to work with as his career continued.

Clive, Kitty (1711–1785) was born to an Irish lawyer and his wife in Kilkenny. In 1728, she joined the company under Cibber at Drury Lane, where she flourished in musical comedy roles, including not the first, but one of the more famous Pollys of *The Beggar's Opera*. Her marriage to George Clive, a barrister, was brief and produced no children, and Clive's biography shows remarkable independence and initiative. For example, left without employment in the 1740s, Clive took her case to the public in *The Case of Mrs. Clive*, a pamphlet that raised public sympathy and support and led to a lucrative benefit performance sponsored by the Prince and Princess of Wales. Her career stabilized under Garrick's management at Drury Lane, and she continued to play roles such as Lady Wishfort in *The Way of the World* and wrote one successful farce, *The Rehearsal, or Bays in Petticoats*. She became friends with Horace Walpole, and in her mature years moved in social circles that went beyond the theatrical community, finally retiring on a well-managed income in 1769.

Corey, Katherine (née Mitchell c.1635–?) was one of the first women to act in the public theatre after the Restoration. Although we know little of her early career, Dol

Common in *The Alchemist* was probably one of her early roles, and it was a popular role for her later on as well. Samuel Pepys called her "Doll Common," and appears to have approved of her skills. In 1668, while performing in *Catiline* with the King's Company, Mrs. Corey found herself caught in a squabble between two court ladies. According to Pepys's report, Lady Harvy was offended by Mrs. Corey's acting of Semponia, and had her imprisoned. Another court lady, Lady Castlemayne, had her released, but an angry Lady Harvy had people hiss at her and throw oranges when she performed again. She was very active as an actress, primarily playing nurses, serving women, governesses, mothers, scolds, and bawds. In 1689 Mrs. Corey played Mrs. Flirt in the premiere of *The Widdow Ranter*, in 1675 she played Lucy in the premiere of *The Country Wife*, and in 1677 she played Octavia in *All for Love*.

Cross, Letitia (c.1677–1737) began acting at a young age. In 1696 she played Miss Hoyden in the premiere of *The Relapse*. She often played roles similar to this, and it is possible that Vanbrugh tailored this part to her talents. She played Miranda in the premiere of *The Busie Body*. Not long after this she ran into some disagreement with the managers at Drury Lane, causing her young male admirers to send a letter to the managers threatening to riot if her roles were given to anyone else.

Currer, Elizabeth (?) joined the Duke's Company by 1673–1674 season. She became a regular speaker of prologues and epilogues, and in 1679 Aphra Behn wrote the prologue for *The Feign'd Curtizans* for her in which she spoke the lines, "Who says this Age a Reformation wants,/When Better Currer's Lovers all turn Saints?/In vain, alas, I flatter, swear and vow,/You'll scarce do any thing for Charity now:/Yet I am handsom still, still young and mad." In 1682 she joined the United Company, and played the title role in *The Widdow Ranter* in 1689.

David, Thomas Dibble (?–1795) took the stage name Davis, and primarily played smaller roles in comedies and farces. He often played at Covent Garden, and he began also working with Samuel Foote's company at the Haymarket in the summer of 1760, when he played Loader in the premiere of *The Minor*.

Davis, Mary (1651–1708) was more commonly known as "Moll" Davis, and was a dancer, singer, and actress. She earned high praise from Samuel Pepys, and eventually attracted the interest of Charles II, who made her his mistress. This turn of events tempered Pepys's admiration. She played Ariel in *The Tempest* in 1667. A great beauty, she was the subject of more than one painting by Lely and Kneller.

De Loutherbourg, Phillipe Jacques (1740–1812) was born in Strasbourg, the son of a Polish miniature painter, and was educated at the University of Strasbourg. Rejecting a career in the Lutheran ministry, he became a painter and a member of the French Academy in 1767. In 1771 he settled in London, working until 1785 for a substantial salary to produce and manage scenery and special effects at Drury Lane Theatre under David Garrick's management. In addition, he opened the "Eidophusikon," a miniature mechanical theatre that created moving spectacles replicating natural phenomena and fantastical scenes such as *Paradise Lost*'s Satan arraying his troops in hell.

Delpini, Carlo Antonio (1740–1828) was known for his work as a clown in pantomimes and harlequinades. He performed at all the patent houses, and often also worked behind the scenes, arranging the machinery and spectacle for the shows. In addition, he worked at Hughes's Royal Circus and at other London amphitheatres. He played the Clown in *Omai*.

Dibdin, Charles (bap.1745–1814) was the son of a silversmith who died in this actor/composer/writer's childhood. At nine he sang as a chorister at Winchester Cathedral, and by 1760 he was singing in the chorus at Drury Lane Theatre. His break-out role as a singer/actor was as Ralph in Isaac Bickerstaff's *The Maid of the Mill* in 1765 and the two collaborated on *The Padlock*, in which Dibdin played the character of Mungo. He carried on a sometimes precarious, sometimes prosperous career as a character actor, singer, and composer of popular songs. After a falling out with Garrick at Drury Lane at the end of 1775, Dibdin struck out as a freelance composer/performer whose songs of patriotic sentiment featured British sailors and soldiers. He also wrote and published two novels and an autobiography.

Dibdin, Charles Isaac Mungo (1768–1833) was born to Charles Dibdin and Harriet Pitt, an actress. Estranged from his father from an early age, he debuted as a child at Drury Lane marching in the procession of Shakespeare's characters in *The Jubilee*. He was apprenticed to a pawnbroker at 14, but returned to the Royal Theatre to perform in a one-man show. From then, he was known as Dibdin the Younger. His most successful and stable period came as manager of the Sadler's Wells Theatre where he established a reputation for delivering the spectacles that audiences would flock to, including an aquatic theatre in which he could stage naval battles and the dramatic rescue of drowning children by Newfoundland dogs. As the appetite for spectacle waned, Dibdin fell into debt, sold his shares in Sadler's Wells, and wrote songs and pantomimes for the Surrey Theatre.

Dodd, James William (1740?–1796) was known for his work playing fops, coxcombs, and silly gentlemen. In 1765 David Garrick brought him on at Drury Lane, where he quickly established a London reputation for his work and focused on comedies of manners and sentimental comedies. He began a long affair with the actress Mary Bulkley in 1769, which cost him some of his favor in London public opinion (they were both then married to other people). Dodd originated the role of Sir Benjamin Backbite in *The School for Scandal* in 1777.

Doggett, Thomas (c.1670?–1721) began his career in Dublin before becoming a strolling player. He appeared as Solon in *The Marriage-Hater Match'd* in 1692, and the favorable reviews of this role led to his being known by the nickname "Solon." In 1696 he played Lory in *The Relapse*, but apparently it did not suit him; he quickly relinquished the role to Pinkethman. He switched companies several times, and would return to strolling from time to time as well. In 1709 he joined Wilks and Cibber in theatrical management, first at the Queen's Theatre and then at Drury Lane. Under their management the company at Drury Lane flourished, although a falling out between Doggett and Wilks over the actor Barton Booth's role in the company would eventually divide the triumvirate (and Booth would eventually replace Doggett in the company management).

Dubellamy, Charles Clementine (?–1793) was the stage name of singer/actor John Evans. He was considered handsome and praised for his singing voice. He often played at Covent Garden and, later, summers at the Haymarket. In 1773 he played Hastings in the premiere of *She Stoops to Conquer.*

Edwin, John (1749–1790) began his professional London career at the Haymarket with Samuel Foote, gaining a reputation for his work as a comic actor. Later, he became one of Covent Garden's best known comic actors. He played the original Silvertongue in Cowley's *The Belle's Stratagem* and Trudge in *Inkle and Yarico.* He also played Otaheitian in *Omai.*

Egerton, Mrs. (née Ambrose?) began her career in Ireland, and first appeared in London at Drury Lane in 1761 (as "Miss Ambrose"). Sometime later that year she married a Mr. Kelf, and by November appeared on playbills in Dublin as "Mrs. Kelf." In the fall of 1770 she joined David Garrick's company at Drury Lane, now performing under the name "Mrs. Egerton." In 1771 she originated the role of Mrs. Fulmer in *The West Indian.*

Egleton, Mrs. (formerly Mrs. Giffard? –c.1734) performed primarily at Lincoln's Inn Fields. She married actor John Egleton sometime in 1721 and began acting under the name "Mrs. Egleton." In 1728 she played Lucy Lockit in the premiere of *The Beggar's Opera.*

Estcourt, Richard (1668–1712) was an actor, dramatist, and lyricist. His first play, *The Fair Example: or The Modish Citizens*, premiered at Drury Lane in 1703. While Colley Cibber was hesitant about his acting prowess, Christopher Rich at Drury Lane apparently found him to be valuable as a comic actor and mimic. In 1708 he joined Cibber and Wilks as a deputy manager of Drury Lane. He played Sir Francis Gripe in the premiere of *The Busie Body* in 1709.

Esten, Harriet Pye (née Bennett 1765?–1865) turned to the stage possibly in order to support her children when her husband James Esten suffered financial difficulties and was forced to flee to France. She began performing in the provinces and in Ireland before finally being engaged at Covent Garden in 1789. Esten won the lease to the Edinburgh Theatre over Stephen Kemble in 1792, although she left the management of the theatre to her mother and returned to Covent Garden (she would eventually turn the lease over to Kemble). She played Miss Wooburn in the premiere of *Every One Has His Fault* in 1793.

Farren, Elizabeth (1759–1762?–1829) was the daughter of George and Margaret Farren, who managed a touring acting company out of Liverpool. Margaret appeared to have given her daughter a good education, excellent skills at sociability, and a proper sense of feminine decorum that made her an admired but respectable celebrity after her London debut as Kate Hardcastle in *She Stoops to Conquer.* She was celebrated for her beauty, singing voice, and social decorum off the stage, and the friendship of Emily Fitzgerald, Duchess of Leinster, brought her into social circles that included Edward Smith Stanley, twelfth earl of Derby. Lord Derby was married to a notoriously adulterous wife, and he and Farren married after her death. Before then, Farren, who continued to live with her mother and decorously received the earl's social visits with her, was accepted in aristocratic circles as a better alternative than the scandalous wife. In the 1780s, she played Lady Teazle in *School for Scandal* at Drury Lane and starred in aristocratic theatre at Richmond House, where she mixed with royalty and the cream of British society. She retired promptly upon her marriage to the Earl in 1797.

Farren, William (1754–1795) made his Drury Lane debut in 1775, probably thanks to his friendship with the actor Richard Yates, and he continued on there through the 1783–1784 season. He began by playing strong supporting roles, but built his repertoire over the years to include some lead roles. He originated the role of Careless in the 1777 premiere of *The School for Scandal.* While at Drury Lane he began playing occasionally at Covent Garden, and after he left Drury Lane he joined that company and remained there until his death. While at Covent Garden he played Lord Norland in the premiere of *Every One Has His Fault* in 1789. Although he was reported to be a solid actor rather than a strong one, his work was versatile; he played roles in comedy, tragedy, and farce.

Fawcett, John (1768–1837) was the son of the actor and singer John Fawcett. Although his father attempted to prevent him from following in his footsteps, the young Fawcett eventually made his way to the stage, beginning in the provinces. Fawcett started his career by insisting on playing tragedies, but was reportedly not very good, and Tate Wilkinson, the theatrical manager in York, determined to move him into comedy. Afterward he primarily played low comedy parts, including rustics and eccentric characters. In 1791 he was engaged at Covent Garden, taking over the roles of the comic actor John Edwin who had recently died. In 1793 he played Mr. Placid in *Every One Has His Fault.* He took comic roles at the Haymarket during the summer, and also worked later in his career as a stage manager at Covent Garden and as a dramatist, primarily writing pantomimes.

Fearon, James (1746–1789) had his London stage debut in 1771 at the Haymarket, and he continued to work with Samuel Foote there in the summers through 1777, playing many supporting roles in comedies and light farces. He began working at Covent Garden in 1774, and in 1780 he played Porter in the premiere of Hannah Cowley's *The Belle's Stratagem.* Over the years he expanded his repertoire to include a wide variety of roles.

Fenton, Lavinia (née Beswick 1708–1760) rose to acclaim after her successful portrayal of Polly Peachum in the original run of *The Beggar's Opera*. She worked at the Haymarket and at Lincoln's Inn Fields. Fenton received much attention in the press for her natural style of singing after her performances as Polly, most of it positive but some gleefully and negatively satirical.

Foote, Samuel (1721–1777), actor and playwright, was the son of a lawyer, magistrate, and MP for Tiverton and his well-born wife. He attended Worcester College, Oxford, but was dismissed for poor conduct. Under the tutelage of Charles Macklin, Foote debuted at the Haymarket in 1744 and played a variety of roles, including Lord Foppington in *The Relapse*, though without finding stable employment at any theatre. His fortunes changed when he rented the Haymarket in 1746 and, working around the Licensing Act and the hours of the regular London theatres, presented *The Diversions of a Morning, or a Dish of Chocolate*, a satirical review that took off many of the most famous contemporary actors, gratis, following a concert and refreshments for which the audience ostensibly paid. Foote had found his forte in topical satire, and *The Minor*, *The Nabob*, and many other popular plays followed, satirizing everything from Methodism and the entrepreneurial class making their fortunes in India, to his fellow actors. He also put on shows with life-size puppets that made fun of many London celebrities. In 1766, Foote lost a leg in a riding accident provoked by a dare from his aristocratic patrons, but he used the incident to his advantage, gaining a patent for the Haymarket Theatre and his first stable, theatrical house. The ill-will he created through his satirical performances caught up with him when he mocked Elizabeth Chudleigh, duchess of Kingston. Reprisals took the form of accusations of homosexuality laid against Foote by Chudleigh and the publisher William Jackson, followed by the charge of homosexual assault by one of Foote's servants. Foote was acquitted, but the experience of prolonged and vicious attacks broke his health and spirit and his career took a sharp downturn, ending in his death. He is buried, though without a marker, in Westminster Abbey.

Forster, Ann (née Field ?–1789) began her career as Ann Field at Drury Lane, where she played from 1777 until her death. Described by Anthony Pasquin as as "timid nymph," one of her best-known roles was Ariel in *The Tempest* (her debut role at Drury Lane). In 1786 she married William Forster, and began performing under the name Mrs. Forster. During her time at the Haymarket between 1787 and 1788, she played Patty in the 1787 *Inkle and Yarico*.

Freeman, John (?) began acting in Dublin, and had joined the Duke's Company in London by 1680. In 1689 he played Colonel Wellman in the premiere of *The Widdow Ranter*. In 1695 Freeman went with Thomas Betterton to Lincoln's Inn Fields, and later moved to the Queen's Theatre in Haymarket. He played diverse roles in a career that spanned 35 years.

Gardner, William (?–1790) had his first recorded London appearance at Drury Lane in the summer of 1761 (when rented by Samuel Foote). That winter he joined the company at Covent Garden, where he continued regularly for eleven seasons and played many minor roles. His few larger roles included Sir Charles Marlow in the premiere of *She Stoops to Conquer* in 1773. He was also with Foote at the Haymarket, where he played more substantial roles.

Garrick, David (1717–1779) was the son of an army officer and pupil of the author and lexicographer, Samuel Johnson. His first performance was as a substitute for Richard Yates' Harlequin in a pantomime, a fact that he often suppressed. He played the blackface role of Aboan in Thomas Southerne's *Oroonoko* anonymously to test audience reaction to his acting skills, but his break-out London debut was in the role of Richard III at Covent Garden, by which he first impressed the public with his active, expressive acting style, very different from the more static, declamatory style that was dominant in the early eighteenth century. He played a variety of roles with great success in London and Dublin, taking on the management of Drury Lane in 1747, a position he held until 1776. His acting inspired future generations of English actors, and he did much to bring respectability to the acting profession and social decorum to the theatre. He was also masterful at managing public relations, both for himself and his theatre. Garrick built upon a growing investment in Shakespeare as British poet, promoting the image of the author as iconic both through the performance of his plays (though rarely unadapted) and events such as the Shakespeare Jubilee of 1769 on the 250th anniversary of Shakespeare's death, which, though rained out, had a long afterlife in *The Jubilee* at Drury Lane Theatre.

George, Georgina (?–1835) began singing as "Miss George" in concerts around Oxford in 1780. She joined the company at the Haymarket in 1783, and played there on and off throughout her career. She performed at Drury Lane for several seasons in the mid 1780s and was known for her singing voice. In 1787 she played Wowski in *Inkle and Yarico* at the Haymarket.

Goodman, Cardell (1653–?) joined Thomas Killigrew's King's Company in 1673, and began by playing bit parts in burlesques. One of his noted roles was Mariamne, a female cinder wench, in Thomas Duffett's burlesque of Settle's *The Empress of Morocco.* All the characters in this production were in blackface, and the image of Goodman as a blackface Mariamne graced the frontispiece of the 1673 edition of Duffett's piece. In 1677 he played Alexas in the premiere of Dryden's *All for Love.* He had money problems for most of his early life, and was consistently entangled in legal issues due to criminal activity such as alleged highway robbery. Although he did go to prison on more than one occasion, he usually got off very lightly or was eventually pardoned.

Green, Jane (née Hippisley 1719–1791) probably began her career at Drury Lane appearing in benefit shows for her father the comedian John Hippisley. She joined the company at Goodman's Fields in 1740, playing young female characters in both comedies and tragedies. In 1747 she joined David Garrick at Drury Lane for several seasons. In 1754 she began performing at Covent Garden, where she stayed until the end of the

1779–1780 season and transitioned to more mature roles. She played Mrs. Hardcastle in the premiere of Goldsmith's *She Stoops to Conquer* in 1773, and was the original Mrs. Malaprop in Sheridan's *The Rivals* in 1775.

Griffin, Philip (?) was in the King's Company by the 1671–1672 season, and was involved in disagreements with Charles Killigrew over the company's management. In 1677 he played Serapion in *All for Love*. In 1682 he remained with the company when it became the United Company.

Gwyn, Eleanor (Nell) (1651?–1687) was one of the early actresses of the Restoration who compounded her celebrity by becoming royal mistress to Charles II. Samuel Pepys reports that she was better at comic than serious roles (Pepys, 8.91, 594). Of obscure and probably poor origins, Gwynn established her financial and social position at court and the careers of her two illegitimate sons by Charles with an irreverent charm that added to the appeal of the court. Prior to becoming a royal mistress, she was alleged to be the lover of first the actor Charles Hart, and second Charles Sackville, Lord Buckhurst.

Haines, Joseph (?–1701) was especially skilled at satiric, comic roles and was well known for his witty and sometimes offensive prologues and epilogues. He is famous for having spoken some of the former from the back of an ass. He led an irregular and debt-ridden private life but played successfully both in London and at the court of Louis XIV in France, as well as other venues on the continent. He played Sparkish in *The Country Wife* and may have choreographed the dances in *The Tempest*. He was lover to Pepys' favorite, Mrs. Knepp.

Hall, John (?–1734) joined John Rich's Company at Lincoln's Inn Fields by the end of 1714, and remained there until his death in 1734, although he would occasionally perform in Edinburgh and also at other locations such as fairs. In 1728 he played the original Lockit in *The Beggar's Opera*. He was called "Fat" Hall in one advertisement due to his size.

Hallam, William (1712?–1758?) was the son of actors Mr. and Mrs. Thomas Hallam. Other actors in the family include William's sister, Ann, and three of his four brothers, Lewis, Adam, and George. Because there were so many Hallams working on London stages at the same time it is often difficult to know which Hallam was meant in the playbills. William worked at Goodman's Fields, the Haymarket, and Covent Garden, and also as a strolling player. He played the Poet in *The Author's Farce* in its 1730 premiere. It is likely he was joined by at least one of his brothers, probably Lewis, in this show—the playbill lists a "Hallam" in addition to "W. Hallam." William and Lewis Hallam left England in 1752 with many of their acting family to perform in Williamsburg, Virginia, establishing the first fully professional theatre in the American colonies. This same family helped, with John Moody, to establish professional theatre in Kingston, Jamaica.

Harris, Henry (c.1634–1704) was with the Duke's Company from at least 1660. Although he was listed as a scene painter in these early documents, most of his career was as an actor. Harris had court connections, allowing him to seek the position "engraver of seals," and also became a friend to the diarist Samuel Pepys. In 1667 he played Ferdinand in *The Tempest*. When Sir William Davenant died Harris and Betterton took over the management of the Duke's Company and began acting there when the company moved to the new theatre in Dorset Gardens. He played Medley in the premiere of *The Man of Mode* in 1676. Harris retired from the stage before the Duke's Company and the King's Company joined in 1682.

Hart, Charles (c.1630–1683) acted as a boy before the closing of the theatres in 1642. When the theatres re-opened he returned to the stage, joining the King's Company. He would briefly manage the company in the mid 1670s. In 1674 the company began performing at the new Drury Lane theatre, and it was here that Hart performed Mr. Horner in the premiere of *The Country Wife* in 1675 and Marc Antony in *All for Love* in 1677. He was known to be a lover of Nell Gwynn, the actress who went on to be one of Charles II's mistresses. Hart and Gwynn parted ways in 1677, the same year as *All For Love*'s first performances. When the King's Company and the Duke's Company united in 1682, Hart played an instrumental role in the merger. Hart was considered a talented actor, especially in tragic roles.

Hartley, Elizabeth (née White 1750?–1824) took the name of a Mr. Hartley to whom she was mistress but whom she never married. She made her London debut at Covent Garden in 1772 after performing in Edinburgh and Bristol. In 1780 she originated the role of Lady Frances Touchwood in *The Belle's Stratagem*.

Hippisley, John (1696–1748) was trained by the actor John Rich as a harlequin and performed with his company at Lincoln's Inn Fields and later at Covent Garden. Hippisley played a great number of roles over the years, excelling in skirts roles, dialect roles, bumpkins, clowns, rascals, and eccentric old gentlemen. He also played at fairs and elsewhere around London, and he managed the Bristol theatre for a time as well. In 1728 he originated the role of Peachum in *The Beggar's Opera*.

Holliday, Elizabeth (?) played Mrs. Coaxer in the premiere of *The Beggar's Opera* in 1728. She played first at Lincoln's Inn Fields, then at Covent Garden, until she transferred to Drury Lane in 1734, where she remained for the rest of her career. In 1737 she married the actor William Mills the second, and after the 1737–1738 season, regularly appeared as "Mrs. Mills."

Hopkins, Elizabeth (née Barton 1731–1801) married the actor William Hopkins in 1731, and began her acting career touring the provinces with her husband. When her husband was engaged as a prompter at Drury Lane, Mrs. Hopkins followed him and made her London debut there. She remained busy at Drury Lane throughout her career. In 1771 she played Lady Rusport in the premiere of Richard Cumberland's *The West Indian*. By the 1780s she transitioned from playing younger (often tragic) women to playing older roles: the stage mother, the old eccentric, and the dowager.

Hopkins, Priscillia (1758–1854) was the daughter of the prompter William Hopkins and actress Elizabeth Hopkins. She became part of the company at Drury Lane in 1775. In 1777 she played Maria at the first performance of *The School for Scandal*. She married actor William Brereton in 1777, and worked under the name Mrs. Brereton at Drury Lane for eight years. Her husband's mental health declined until he was restrained at Hoxton asylum. After his death in 1787 she married actor John Philip Kemble, after which she appeared in playbills as "Mrs. Kemble."

Inchbald, Elizabeth (1753–1821) was born to the Catholic Simpson family and aspired early on to become an actress, despite a chronic stammer. She worked as an actress for seventeen years, overcoming this impediment, though she never achieved critical acclaim in this profession. She married Joseph Inchbald in 1772, probably to avoid the sexual aggression that would have been directed at a very pretty, unprotected woman in the theatre. She did not remarry after his death. She began writing for the theatre, and she performed, in her first piece to be produced, a farce called *The Mogul's Tale* in 1784. From this time on, she became a prolific and popular playwright who, with wise financial management, was able to shift from acting to full-time writing by 1789. Her play *A Lover's Vows*, an adaptation of August Kotzebue's *Child of Love*, is the famously scandalous play in Jane Austen's novel, *Mansfield Park*. In 1791 her novel *A Simple Story* was well received, and she went on to a distinguished career as a critic and editor with the 25-volume *The British Theatre* (1806–9), a seven-volume *Collection of Farces and Afterpieces* (1809), and the ten-volume *Modern Theatre* in 1811. She moved in the radical political circles of the 1790s and was friends with Thomas Holcroft and William Godwin, though her investment in personal respectability made her break with the latter over his marriage to Mary Wollstonecraft.

James, Elizabeth (?) was an actress and singer. Although records are sparse for her appearances, she appeared in several pieces by John Dryden. In 1675 she played Alithea in the premiere of William Wycherley's *The Country Wife*. A manuscript poem of Rochester dated 1678 refers to her as "a damn'd daub'd Picture upon the Ale house Wall/So James is ill painted, and Expos'd to all."

Jevon, Thomas (1652–1688) was a dancing master and actor known for low comic parts. A member of the Duke's Company, *The Biographica Dictionary of Actors* remarks that he was "cast in serious roles at a playwright's peril." He played Young Bellair in *The Man of Mode* in 1676. When the Duke's Company joined with the King's Company to become the United Company Jevon stayed on, continuing to play low comic parts. He also wrote the play *The Devil of a Wife; or, The Comical Transformation*, which was adapted by Charles Coffey into the ballad opera, *The Devil to Pay*.

Johnson, Benjamin (1665–1742) began his career as a scene painter before becoming a strolling player and eventually joining Christopher Rich's company at Drury Lane in 1695. He usually played comic roles. In 1696 he played Coupler in the premiere of *The Relapse*. Johnson began playing at Drury Lane after Cibber, Wilks, and Doggett took over in 1710, although, reportedly, Cibber arranged matters so as to take over Johnson's roles.

Jones, Inigo (1573–1652) was an architect and theatre designer who, in collaboration with Ben Jonson, as librettist, created the elaborate and spectacular court masques of James I, and later Charles I. After he and Jonson parted company, he assumed primary creative control over the court masques. While Charles II did not revive the custom of the masque, Jones' former collaborator, William Davenant, carried into the newly re-opened theatres of the 1660s many of the former's design innovations, such as the proscenium arch, side flats, and back shutters, insuring the architect's influence on theatre design throughout the eighteenth century.

Jordan, Dorothy (1761–1816) was born Phillips in London to Frances Bland, an Irish captain, and Grace Phillips, an actress. Bland capitulated to family wishes and left his family in Ireland to marry a more suitable woman in 1774. Dorothy Phillips debuted at Smock Alley Theatre in Dublin under the management of Richard Daly, who exploited her both sexually and financially. She fled Dublin for Tate Wilkerson's York company and it was Wilkerson who gave her the name Jordan. She entered into the protection of Richard Ford, a major share-holder at Drury Lane, and lived with him as a wife, bearing him three children, until she caught the attention of Prince William Henry, duke of Clarence, and later William IV of England. She lived with the Duke from 1790 to 1811, bearing him ten children, when he announced his intention to break with her and marry for money. Jordan had not, despite the duke's support for the years of their liaison, left off acting, and she continued to play a wide variety of roles, although the fame of Sarah Siddons in tragic roles often cast Jordan in the part of the comic rather than tragic actress. She specialized in youthful, romping roles such as Hoyden in *The Relapse* and Margery in Garrick's *Country Girl*. In the 1790s, she originated the role of Angela in Matthew Gregory Lewis's gothic thriller, *Castle Spectre*.

Kean, Edmund (1787–1833) was born to Ann Carey, an actress and part-time prostitute, and endured a difficult childhood working for strolling acting companies. He achieved success at Drury Lane for the quickness of his movement and intensity of his facial expressions, and much like Garrick, was notable for his dark, expressive eyes. He was particularly celebrated for his Shakespearean roles. He made a successful American tour, but his career was dogged by alcoholism and illness.

Kemble, Charles (1775–1854) was born into the acting family that also produced Sarah Siddons and John Philip Kemble. He was well-known for his Shakespearean roles and played Macbeth against his sister's famous Lady Macbeth.

Kemble, Elizabeth (née Satchell 1762?–1841) was an actress and singer who debuted at Covent Garden in 1780. In 1781 she played Adelaide in the premiere of *The Count of Narbonne*. After a rough start, Adelaide became her most famous role, and established her reputation. In 1783 she married the actor Stephen George Kemble. Her husband was discharged from Covent Garden in 1784, and the pair then played the provinces.

In 1787 they joined the company at the Haymarket. She was the original Yarico in George Colman the Younger's *Inkle and Yarico*. She was praised both for her acting and for her voice; her style was often described as "simple" and "unaffected."

Kemble, John Philip (1757–1823) was brother to Charles Kemble and Sarah Siddons and was known for his good looks, athletic build, and his careful, almost scholarly approach to the performance of Shakespeare. He played successfully at Drury Lane, where he also served as acting manager, and at Covent Garden.

Kennedy, Agnes (née Holmes c.1759–1832) began her stage career in York with Tate Wilkinson. She married actor Thomas Kennedy before 1779, when she was announced as "Mrs. Kennedy" at the Haymarket when she played Amelia in *The English Merchant*. She performed mostly in the provinces with her husband until the 1784–1785 season, when they were both engaged at Covent Garden. There, they appeared together in *Omai* (Thomas played Harlequin, while Agnes played Oediddee).

Kennedy, Thomas (c.1750–1808) began performing in Dublin at a very young age with his parents, who were also actors. In 1760 he went with them to Drury Lane, where he made his London debut, and then played in the provinces. Sometime before 1779 he married Agnes Holmes and appeared with her in *Omai* (see above). He played at Covent Garden for a few seasons, but spent most of the rest of his career in the provinces.

Kent, Mary (?) was the wife of Thomas Kent, an actor at Drury Lane. She was first listed in the playbills at Drury Lane in 1692. She remained with her husband at Drury Lane with Christopher Rich's company after the breakup of the United Company in 1695. In 1696 she played Young Fashion in *The Relapse*, a breeches role she would reprise later in her career. She performed in William Pinktheman's theatre in Greenwich beginning in 1710, playing larger roles than she had been granted at Drury Lane. Kent also worked with the puppeteer Powell when he visited London and performed at Punch's theatre in St. Martin's Lane. She joined John Rich's company at Lincoln's Inn Fields in 1715, and remained there through the 1718–1719 season.

King, Thomas (1730–1805) was the son of a London merchant who, apprenticed to a solicitor, ran away to join a company of strolling players at the age of 17. He gained minor roles at Drury Lane early in his career, but spent nine productive years in Dublin working for Thomas Sheridan. Returning to Drury Lane, he played the role of Sir Peter Teazle in *School for Scandal*. He was the plant in Garrick's audience for the "Ode to Shakespeare" at the 1769 Stratford Jubilee, who opposed the manager's celebration of the Bard, and he was often used by Garrick to soothe a ruffled audience because of his general popularity. He recommended a young Sarah Siddons to Garrick, and he also had a lively career in the resort theatres of Bristol and Sadler's Wells.

Knepp, Mrs. (?–1681) was an actress, singer, dancer, and a recurrent figure in the diary of Samuel Pepys. Many details about her life, including her first name, cannot be verified.

Mrs. Knepp had joined the King's Company by 1666, having first encountered Samuel Pepys sometime the year before. According to his diary they carried on a flirtation for some time, even after Pepys's wife began demanding he avoid her company. In 1675 she played Lady Fidget in the premiere of *The Country Wife*. She later became the mistress of actor Joseph Haines, and died giving birth to his stillborn child.

Knight, Frances Maria (?) was a member of the United Company until it broke up in 1695. During this period she played Madam Surelove in *The Widdow Ranter* in 1689. In 1692 Mrs. Knight played a role in the trial of Captain Hill and Lord Mohun over the murder of William Mountfort. She remained with Christopher Rich at Drury Lane after the 1695 breakup and became one of the leading ladies of tragedy within the company. She later left to join John Rich's company.

Knott, Mr. (?) was an actor and dancer who played some harlequin roles at the Haymarket in the summers of 1729–1730. He played Monsieur Pantomime in the premiere of *The Author's Farce* in 1730.

Kynaston, Edward (bap. 1643–1712) began playing female parts for William Davenant in 1660. Although women had begun playing these roles, the scarcity of actresses left work for a skillful and beautiful young actor, and the theatre-goer Samuel Pepys thought him beautiful and convincing as a stage woman. He also played male roles and was Harcourt in Wycherley's *The Country Wife*.

Lacy, James (1696–1774) was an actor and theatrical manager. He joined John Rich at the company at Lincoln's Inn Fields by 1724. In 1728 he played Robin of Bagshot in the premiere of *The Beggar's Opera* along with his first wife, who played Dolly Trull. In the 1730s he played at every London theatre with the exception of Drury Lane and played several roles for Henry Fielding, including Witmore in the premiere of *The Author's Farce*. He worked with Fielding in his booth at Bartholomew Fair in 1734 and got into trouble after the Licensing Act of 1737 by attempting to produce plays illegally. By 1744, he was the manager of Drury Lane and had a disagreement with Garrick that caused Garrick to leave. By 1747 Lacy, who needed Garrick's acting and managerial skills, sought a reconciliation, and the two became co-managers who turned the flagging business of Drury Lane into a successful endeavor.

Lacy, Mrs. James (?) was James Lacy's first wife and performed in London from the late 1720s to the late 1730s. She was Dolly Trull in the premiere of *The Beggar's Opera*. Like her husband, she also worked with Henry Fielding at Bartholomew Fair.

Leigh, Anthony (?–1692) first appears in the London records when the Lord Chamberlain ordered him arrested in 1671 for performing plays without a license. He and his wife appeared in the Duke's Company and later with the United Company. He played Old Bellair in *The Man of Mode*, and was known for playing important comic roles and for delivering prologues and epilogues.

Leigh, Elinor (née Dixon?) worked with the Duke's Company and later with the United Company. She married actor Anthony Leigh some time around 1671. She probably played Lady Woodvil in the original production of *The Man of Mode.* After the death of her husband she joined Thomas Betterton at Lincoln's Inn Fields, where she played Lady Wishfort in the premiere of *The Way of the World.*

Leoni, Michael (c.1750–1797), or Myer Lyon, was the hazzan or cantor in the Great Synagogue of London who became famous as a tenor in Thomas Arne's *Artaxerxes* and in Richard Brinsley Sheridan's *The Duenna.* His celebrated performance as Don Carlos in Sheridan's comic opera was crucial to its success.

Lewes, Charles Lee (1740–1803), who originated the role of Young Marlowe in *She Stoops to Conquer* at Covent Garden Theatre in 1773, was born to a well educated hosier and his well-born wife. He was a reliable supporting and comic actor. His farewell benefit performance in 1803 was Lisardio in Centlivre's *The Wonder.*

Lewis, William Thomas (c.1746–1811), the son of actors, began appearing onstage as a child, primarily as a strolling actor in Ireland. He began his London career at Covent Garden in 1773, where he would remain for 35 seasons, playing over 194 roles, primarily in comedies. In 1780 he originated the role of Doricourt in *The Belle's Stratagem,* and in 1793 he played Sir Robert Ramble in the premiere of *Every One Has His Fault.* He worked as the deputy manager of Covent Garden from 1782–1803.

Linley, Elizabeth (1754–1792) singer and writer, was the daughter of the musician Thomas Linley. Celebrated for her beauty and voice, Linley was the object of very public romantic obsessions. Her engagement to the wealthy and elderly Walter Long was broken off, perhaps because of Long's embarrassment over Samuel Foote's *The Maid of Bath,* which made a spectacle of Linley's romantic relationship difficulties. Thomas Matthews, a friend of her father's, pursued her to the point of forcing her to flee into France under the protection of Richard Brinsley Sheridan, who persuaded her into a secret and probably invalid marriage. Sheridan later fought two duels with Matthews, and was severely wounded. Linley was returned to her family's protection and the relationship between the two cooled when Sheridan began affairs with other women. Eventually, however, Sheridan managed to convince father and daughter and he married Linley in 1773, an event that ended her singing career and began a long and ultimately unhappy marriage, during which she aided Sheridan as a writer and editor and later as wife and supporter to Sheridan the politician.

Long, Jane (?) was one of the original actresses in Sir William Davenant's Duke's Company. She began in smaller roles, and also occasionally played breeches roles. In 1667 she played Hippolyto in Davenant and Dryden's *The Tempest.*

Love, Mrs. James (née L'Amour? c.1719–1807) was the wife of James Love (the stage name used by James Dance) and performed with him in Ireland and Scotland before they moved to London in 1762. She and her husband joined David Garrick at Drury Lane, where Mrs. Love only played sporadically. In 1769 she played Margery Jarvis in Garrick's *Jubilee*, and in 1771 she played Lucy in *The West Indian*. She remained at Drury Lane for a while after her husband's death in 1774, and had more roles in this period. She also acted at the Haymarket during the summers beginning in 1774.

Lydall, Edward (?) is recorded as one of a group of "lewd fellows" whipped for acting as a "rogue and a vagabond" in 1655. He was reported to have been a "Papist" at that time. When he played Dorilant in the premiere of *The Country Wife*, he was more respectably established with the King's Company at Drury Lane.

Macklin, Charles (1699?–1797) was an actor and playwright born in humble circumstances in Dublin. He joined touring companies in Wales, the Midlands, Bristol, and Bath until an exodus of actors from John Highmore's poor management at Drury Lane created an opening for Macklin from 1733–34. By 1734 he had made a place under Charles Fleetwood at Drury Lane as a reliable supporting actor. In 1735, he nearly lost everything when, in a fit of temper, he ran the actor Thomas Hallam through the eye when the latter claimed a wig that Macklin thought belonged to him. Macklin successfully undertook his own defense at the Old Bailey, an experience that may have given him a taste for litigation, which he pursued throughout his career, successfully defending in court his right to the plays he authored and his livelihood as a performer. He was back at Drury Lane by 1736. The 1740–41 season saw Macklin's most famous performance: Shylock in Shakespeare's *Merchant of Venice*. Instead of playing the role in a broad, comic vein, Macklin reportedly observed the clothing and manners of the Jewish inhabitants of the London ghettoes and turned in a darkly realistic Shylock that changed forever the way that character was performed. By 1753, acrimonious relations with the rising star manager Garrick led Macklin to announce his retirement. He established a tavern cum lecture hall, "the British Inquisition," featuring a meal, a lecture from Macklin, and a public debate, but the venture soon left Macklin bankrupt. Shortly after, Macklin wrote his most successful play, *Love a la Mode*, followed by another success, *The Man of the World*. Finances necessitated that he return to acting, however, in a new *Macbeth* in 1773. Macklin's staging of the play was a success, but his performance was not. His subsequent appeal to the audience, protesting the alleged unfairness of the newspaper reviewers, led to a riot at his next performance as Shylock, and he was thereafter dismissed. He sued the conspirators who incited the riot and won before no less a judge than Lord Mansfield. But his career afterwards was sadly marked by age and ill health. He shares credit with Garrick for bringing to bear on acting scientific principles of observation and adherence to observed realities.

Mara, Madame (1749–1833) was the most accomplished German operatic soprano of the late eighteenth century. After a full career in the Prussian court, she sang to much acclaim in Paris and eventually came to London in 1784. She played a prominent role in the Handel Commemoration of that year and continued to sing on the operatic stage in London until 1802.

Martin, Mrs. (?) was one of two Mrs. Martins working in London between 1729 and 1733 and probably a younger relative of the Mrs. Martin who worked in John Rich's company and starred in the premiere of *The Beggar's Opera.* She played at the Haymarket theatre, and in 1730 played Mrs. Novel in the premiere of *The Author's Farce.*

Martin, Mrs. (?) was the other of two Mrs. Martins working in London between 1729 and 1733 (see above). She began her career in Ireland before joining John Rich's company at Lincoln's Inn Fields, and she would remain with his company for 22 years. In 1728 she played Mrs. Peachum and Diana Trapes in *The Beggar's Opera.*

Martyr, Margaret (née Thornton ?–1807) had her first London appearance in 1779 at Covent Garden, and she remained with the company there consistently from 1780 through the 1803–1804 season. She married Captain Martyr in 1780. In 1785 she played Oberea in *Omai.* She often played breeches roles, and appeared in comic operas and pantomimes.

Mattocks, Isabella (née Hallam 1746–1826) was the youngest child of actor Lewis Hallam. She began acting at a very early age, and appeared in many roles over the years, primarily at Covent Garden. In 1780 she played Mrs. Racket in *The Belle's Stratagem,* and in 1793 she played Mrs. Placid in *Every One Has His Fault.*

Messink, James (1721–1789) was a machinist and scene painter who also performed as an actor, singer, and wire-dancer. He often worked at Covent Garden and the Haymarket. In 1767 David Garrick brought him to Drury Lane, where he was integral to the success of Garrick's *Jubilee,* devising the procession along with its elaborate costumes, scenery, and stage machinery, as well as appearing in the pageant. Messink also appears to have had a hand in the formation of a theatre company in Calcutta.

Mills, John (?–1736) was a member of Christopher Rich's company at Drury Lane from 1695, and consistently worked as a strong supporting actor. In 1696 he played Sir John Friendly in the premiere of *The Relapse.* He married actress Margaret sometime before the birth of their son William in 1701. In 1706 he went with Owen Swiney to the Queen's Theatre, but ultimately returned to Drury Lane, where he would remain versatile and reliable actor for the rest of his career. In 1709 he played Charles in the premiere of *The Busie Body.*

Mills, Margaret (?–1717) was the wife of actor John Mills, and she worked at Drury Lane from at least 1696 through the early 1700s. She played Scentwell in the premiere of *The Busie Body* in 1709.

Mills, William (1701–1750?) was the son of actors Margaret and John Mills, and began performing, probably under the mentorship of his father, as a young man. He started in small roles at Drury Lane, eventually working up to larger parts. He married dancer and actress Theodosia Tenoe in 1727, and after she passed away he married actress Elizabeth Holliday. In 1731 he played Trueman in the premiere of *The London Merchant.*

He briefly played at the Haymarket in 1733–1734 when he participated in Theophilus Cibber's rebellion against the Drury Lane company, but he returned the following year. Throughout his time at Drury Lane he played a wide variety of roles and was reportedly a serviceable, if not striking, actor.

Milward, William (1702–1742) was an actor who began his career acting with John Rich's company at Lincoln's Inn Fields (and later at Covent Garden) and occasionally the Haymarket. In 1728 he played the Player in the premiere of *The Beggar's Opera.* Milward first appeared at Drury Lane in 1734, and would remain there for the rest of his career. He was praised as a skillful actor.

Misdale, Mr. (?) played Canker in the premiere of *The Minor.* Not much else is known about this actor.

Mohun, Michael (1616?–1684) was a former boy-actor of female characters long before the Restoration. Michael Mohun managed the King's Company with Hart and John Lacy, under Thomas Killigrew. He also played Pinchwife in *The Country Wife.*

Moody, John (1727–1812) was the stage name used by James Cochran. Moody was an Irish actor who pioneered a number of modes of ethnic performance in the Georgian period. In his highly acclaimed performance as Major O'Flaherty in *The West Indian* and his role in David Garrick's *The Jubilee,* he set many of the parameters for the stage Irishman—honest, impetuous, and quick with his fists. He was also responsible for many of the first blackface/West Indian dialect roles on the London stage. Having founded a successful theatre company in Kingston, Jamaica in the wake of the Jacobite rebellion, he was the original Kingston in David Garrick's *High Life Below Stairs* and he provided Mungo's dialect for Charles Dibdin's *The Padlock.* All of these aspects of Moody's career, including his Jacobite exile, would have been intelligible to the audiences of the time.

Morgan, Henrietta Maria (?) began her career playing primarily at Lincoln's Inn Fields, where, in 1728, she played Mrs. Slammekin in the premiere of *The Beggar's Opera* in which her husband Robert played Ben Budge. The Morgans played at many different patent houses, as well as at summer fairs and provincial theatres.

Morgan, Robert (?) See entry for Henrietta Maria Morgan.

Morton, Mary (1756–1800) Mary Morton (née Dayes) was an actress and singer who played eleven successful seasons at Covent Garden. She played a wide variety of roles, primarily in comedies and ballad operas. In 1780 she played Miss Ogle in the premiere of *The Belle's Stratagem.*

Mullart, Elizabeth (?–1745) performed with her husband William Mullart at fairs, at the Haymarket, and at the other patent houses in London. In 1730 she played Mrs. Moneywood and the Goddess of Nonsense in the premiere of *The Author's Farce,* along with her husband as Luckless. Like her husband, she joined John Rich's troupe at Covent Garden in 1734 and remained there for the rest of her career.

Mullart, William (?–1742) played regularly at fairs, at the Haymarket, and at the patent houses in London. See entry for Elizabeth Mullart.

Munden, Joseph Shepherd (1758–1832) spent the early part of his career as a strolling player in the provinces. He made his debut at Covent Garden in 1790, and played there until 1811, appearing in hundreds of productions. In 1793 he played Mr. Harmony in the premiere of *Every One Has His Fault*. He left Covent Garden after a disagreement with the management, and in 1813 he joined the troupe at Drury Lane for the rest of his career. He was considered an actor of talent, generally played smaller supporting roles to high praise, and played many varied roles over the course of his career.

Pack, George (?) began his career in London at Lincoln's Inn Fields as a singer and actor. Between 1705 and 1710 he performed at Drury Lane and at the Queen's Theatre, and then remained at Drury Lane until the new Lincoln's Inn Fields theatre opened in 1714, when he joined John Rich's company there. In 1709 he originated the role of Marplot in *The Busie Body*. At Lincoln's Inn Fields he often sang in between acts and would wear skirts for comic songs. In 1722 he played Marplot again at Lincoln's Inn Fields, announcing that it was "the last Time he will Act on any Stage." After this, he opened a tavern that he named "The Busy Body," which had a sign showing him as his favorite character of Marplot.

Packer, John Hayman (1730–1806) made his London debut at Covent Garden in 1758 and was taken on by David Garrick at Drury Lane. He worked at Drury Lane throughout his career, more than 45 seasons total. In 1771 he played Captain Dudley in the premiere of *The West Indian* and in 1777 he originated the role of Snake in *The School for Scandal*. He also played in the provinces during the summers. He was thought of as a solid actor and played many roles over the years.

Palmer, John (1744–1798) later known as "Plausible Jack," was the brother of William and Robert L. Palmer. He worked on and off again with David Garrick at Drury Lane and also with Samuel Foote at the Haymarket in the 1760s. When a different John Palmer (called "Gentleman Palmer" and unrelated to "Plausible Jack") became ill and subsequently died in 1768, "Plausible Jack" Palmer took many of his roles. In 1776 he began playing at the Haymarket in the summers along with his brother Robert. In 1777 he played Joseph Surface in *The School for Scandal*, a role Sheridan wrote specifically for him and attuned to his personality. In the 1780s he began a protracted and ultimately failed attempt to open his own theatre: The Royalty Theatre. He was a popular success during his long career, although personally he was reported to be unfaithful and brutal to his wife.

Palmer, William (?–1798) was the brother of actors John ("Plausible Jack") Palmer and Robert L. Palmer. In 1785–1786 he played at Covent Garden, where he appeared as Don Struttolando in *Omai*.

Parsons, William (1736–1795) began his acting career first in amateur theatricals in London and then as a strolling player. He made his debut at Drury Lane in 1762, and remained at Drury Lane for 32 seasons. In 1769 he played the Ostler in Garrick's *Jubilee.* In 1771 he played Varland in the premiere of *The West Indian*, and originated the role of Crabtree in the *The School for Scandal* in 1777. He also played occasionally at the Haymarket during this time; in 1787 he played Sir Christopher Curry in *Inkle and Yarico.* Parsons played over two hundred roles and was well respected as an actor. He was known for playing old men, a niche he began filling in his late thirties. He also played country clowns.

Pope, Elizabeth (c.1740–1797) See entry for Elizabeth Younge.

Pope, Jane (1744–1818) was the daughter of the barber and wigmaker for the Theatre Royal at Drury Lane, and she spent much of her career at that theatre under the management of David Garrick. As a child, she played in Garrick's novelty *Lilliput*, and she originated Mrs. Candour in *The School for Scandal* as well as playing one of the century's many Pollys in *The Beggar's Opera.* She earned a respectable income and was able to retire comfortably in 1808.

Powell, George (1658?–1714) was the son of an actor and began his career in 1686–1687. He played Friendly in *The Widdow Ranter*, and in midcareer played Aboan in *Oroonoko* and Worthy in *The Relapse.* He had a propensity for drunkenness and violence, and was often in trouble with the law. Famously, he disrupted a performance of *The Relapse* by going on drunk and carrying his assault on Amanda's virtue to near conclusion.

Powell, Mary (?) had married actor George Powell by 1686. From 1695 through 1714 she appeared regularly on London stages, at first with Christopher Rich's company at Drury Lane and sometimes at Dorset Garden, and later also at the Queen's Theatre. In 1695 she played the Nurse in the premiere of *The Relapse.*

Prince, Mrs. (?) was an actress and singer who performed at Lincoln's Inn Fields from 1696–1704. In 1700 she played Mincing in the premiere of *The Way of the World.*

Pritchard, Hannah (1709–1768) was born Hannah Vaughan and married William Pritchard, an engraver, sometimes actor, and theatre administrator in 1730. They had three daughters and ran a thriving costume business for the theatre, in addition to their acting careers. She played at Drury Lane, the Haymarket, and Bartholomew Fair, but the date on which her acting career began is unclear. In 1740, she had her first major triumph as Rosalind in *As You Like It* at Drury Lane. In 1748, she first played against Garrick at Drury Lane, commencing a long and celebrated professional partnership. Pritchard was a versatile actress, gifted in a variety of roles.

Quick, John (1748–1831) began his career in the provinces before joining Samuel Foote at the Haymarket in the summer of 1766. He joined the company at Covent Garden in 1767, where he built his reputation as a comedian. In 1773 he played Tony Lumpkin in *She Stoops to Conquer*, a role that enhanced that reputation. In 1780 he played the original Hardy in *The Belle's Stratagem*, and in 1793 he performed as Mr. Solus in the premiere of *Every One Has His Fault*.

Rich, John (1692–1761) was the son of Christopher Rich, theatre manager, who passed his patent on to his son when he died, when Christopher was 22. For 47 years, John Rich managed first Lincoln's Inn's Fields and then Covent Garden Theatre. He developed the art of pantomime, contributed to the growing sophistication of stage effects and scenery, and became the most accomplished comic dancer on the English stage. Under the stage name Lun, Rich drew on Italian *commedia dell'arte*, dancing Harlequin in tight, crossed trousers and a black vizard mask. While Drury Lane introduced dance in serious, high-art forms, Rich answered in comic replies, *Mars and Venus, or the Mouse Trap*, for Drury Lane's *The Loves of Mars and Venus*. His 1723 *The Necromancer* opened the door to a string of pantomimical hits. Rich had equal success as a manager, putting on John Gay's *The Beggar's Opera* after Colley Cibber turned it down. It proved to be one of the most successful and long-lived plays of the century and lives on today in modern productions and adaptations, including Brecht's *The Threepenny Opera*. He held his own against Garrick at Drury Lane, and advanced the technologies of theatrical spectacle.

Robinson, Anastasia (1692–1755) was one of Handel's most valued singers. She started her career as a soprano but illness meant that she ended her career singing contralto roles. Handel composed the role of Cornelia in *Giulio Cesare in Egitto* (1724) with her in mind. She originated key roles in a range of other Handel operas.

Robson, Thomas (1737–1813) the stage name used by Thomas Robson Brownhill, had a 30-year career and played in London and the provinces. He was in the company at Covent Garden for six seasons beginning in 1776. During this time he played Courtall in the premiere of Hannah Cowley's *The Belle's Stratagem*.

Rogers, Jane (?–1718) remained with Christopher Rich at Drury Lane when Thomas Betterton led many actors away, probably because she was in competition for parts with Anne Bracegirdle, who went with Betterton. Rogers played Amanda in the premiere of *The Relapse* in 1696. She had an affair with the actor Robert Wilks, and they had a daughter, also named Jane, who married actor Christopher Bullock. She was one of the leading players in Rich's company by the end of the seventeenth century. In 1714 she joined John Rich at Lincoln's Inn Fields, where she remained for the rest of her career.

Rowson, Elizabeth (?–1790) was a dancer, singer, and actress who worked occasionally at Covent Garden, playing mostly in pantomimes and in comedy roles. In 1785 she played Columbine in *Omai*.

Rutter, Margaret (?) began acting in the early 1660s. Little else is known about her.

Sallé, Mme. Francis (?) was the wife of dancer Francis Sallé, and appeared in the premiere of *The Beggar's Opera* as Molly Brazen.

Sandford, Samuel (?) developed a popular reputation for playing villains during the Restoration. In one memorable performance he accidentally stabbed actor George Powell with a real dagger (rather than a fake one), and he had at least one arrest for disorderly conduct off the stage. In 1689 he played Dareing in the premiere of *The Widdow Ranter.* Anthony Aston describes him as "Round-shoulder'd, Meagre-fac'd, Spindle-shanked, Splay-footed, with a sour Countenance, and long lean Arms."

Saunders, Margaret (1686–c.1745) performed primarily with the company at Drury Lane and sometimes at the Queen's Theatre. In 1709 she played Patch in the premiere of *The Busie Body.*

Shuter, Edward (1728?–1776) was a talented comic actor and singer whose origins are obscure. He was not well educated and probably came from the classes doing menial labor. He made his London debut at Covent Garden Theatre in 1745. His roles covered a wide comic range and included Filch in *The Beggar's Opera.* His broad, comic style suited him well for Rich's Covent Garden Theatre, which emphasized dancing, physicality, comedy, and spectacle. His propensity for alcohol and a dissolute lifestyle often got in the way of his professionalism.

Siddons, Sarah (1755–1831) born Kemble, was sister to John Philip and is considered the greatest actress of the century, perhaps even of British acting history. She was given a gentile education and served as maid and then companion to Lady Mary Greatheed for two years, but followed her early inclinations by marrying William Siddons, an actor, and performing in provincial theatres where she drew enough positive notice for David Garrick to send first Thomas King and then William Henry Bate, his journalist friend, to scout her. Invited to play at Drury Lane in 1775, she debuted disastrously as Portia in *The Merchant of Venice* and was let go by the end of the season. From 1776–1782, she rebuilt her confidence and reputation playing in provincial theatres, but it was at John Palmer's theatre at Bath that she began her career as iconic tragic actress. Asked to return to Drury Lane, she famously brought her "three reasons" for leaving Bath onto the stage with her for her last performance: her three children. As an actress, Siddons built an almost unprecedented personal image of the respectable and devoted wife and mother that fused with her powerfully pathetic stage presence to make her into the feminine icon for her age. Numerous images of Siddons, including Sir Joshua Reynolds' painting of her as *The Tragic Muse*, contributed to her iconic status. She was a hard-working actress who suffered considerable personal tragedy, including an unhappy marriage and the early deaths of her children. Her performance of Lady Macbeth, in which she initiated the stage action of putting down the candle the character traditionally carried, and washing her hand in the air, knitted her iconic status with that of Shakespeare, the British "God of our Idolatry," as Garrick called him.

Simpson, Thomas (?) was a member of the United Company by 1688. When the company split in 1695, he remained at Drury Lane with Christopher Rich. Simpson played Bull in the premiere of *The Relapse* in 1696.

Smith, Charles (1701?–1775) was an actor, singer, and dancer who first performed at Lincoln's Inn Fields and later at Covent Garden. In 1728 he played the original Wat Dreary in the premiere of *The Beggar's Opera*, a role he would return to many times during his career.

Smith, William (?–1695) started out as a barrister before joining Sir William Davenant's Duke's Company and becoming one of its leading actors. Samuel Pepys praised Smith's acting in his diary. In 1676 he played Sir Fopling Flutter in the premiere of *The Man of Mode*. From 1677–1682 he co-managed the company with Thomas Betterton, and was intimately involved when the two companies merged to form the United Company. In addition to the many roles he played over the years, Smith also spoke prologues and epilogues.

Stuart, Ann (?–1809) performed at Covent Garden in the 1780s and 1790s. In 1780 she played Kitty Willis in the premiere of *The Belle's Stratagem*. She primarily played maids and minor roles.

Underhill, Cave (1634–1713) One of the original members of Sir William Davenant's Duke's Company in 1660, he was a popular comic actor and often spoke prologues and epilogues. In 1667 he played Trincalo in *The Tempest* (after which he was sometimes nicknamed "Trincalo"). After the King's and Duke's company joined he remained with the United Company. In 1689 he played Timerous Cornet in *The Widdow Ranter*. Unhappy with Christopher Rich, he joined Thomas Betterton at Lincoln's Inn Fields in 1695. In 1700 he played Sir Willfull Witwoud there in the premiere of *The Way of the World*.

Verbruggen, John Baptista (?–1708) was a member of the United Company by 1688. It is possible that he also performed under the name "Mr. Alexander" in these early years. If so, then it might have been Verbruggen who played Hazard in the premiere of *The Widdow Ranter* in 1689. In 1694 Verbruggen married Susanna Mountfort, the widow of actor William Mountfort. When Thomas Betterton left the United Company with many of the older actors, Verbruggen initially remained with Christopher Rich at Drury Lane, where he played many roles including Loveless in the premiere of *The Relapse*. In 1697, however, he joined the rival company at Lincoln's Inn Fields, and in 1700 he originated the role of Mirabell in *The Way of the World*.

Verbruggen, Susanna (née Percival c.1667–1703) was born around 1667 into an acting family. She married the actor William Mountfort in 1686 and they had several children. In 1692, William Mountfort was murdered during one of his wife's pregnancies by a gentleman who mistakenly thought him the lover of Anne Bracegirdle, an actress with whom he was in love. Susanna remarried a young John Verbruggen in 1694, and it was under the name Verbruggen that she played some of her most famous roles. She was popular in breeches parts and comic roles. She also frequently spoke prologues and epilogues. In 1696 she played Berinthia in the premiere of *The Relapse*. She is described in a contemporary account as a "fine, fair Woman, plump, full-featured" and, surprisingly, given her popularity in breeches roles, as having "thick legs and thighs, corpulent and large posteriers."

Vernon, Joseph (c.1731–1782) made his London debut singing at Drury Lane in 1750. Indeed, Drury Lane would be his theatrical home throughout his career, and he played a number of acting and singing roles over the years. In 1769 he played the Ballad Singer in *The Jubilee.*

Walker, Thomas (1698–1744) was taken on at Drury Lane in the late 1710s after Barton Booth saw him perform. In late summers he played at fairs. In 1721 he joined John Rich's company at Lincoln's Inn Fields, where, in 1728, he played his most famous role: Macheath in the premiere of *The Beggar's Opera.* Walker was not originally slated to play Macheath, but when actor James Quin refused the role it fell to him even though he was not a trained singer. He was, however, highly successful in the part. He continued to act at Lincoln's Inn Fields, Covent Garden, and later at Goodman's Fields.

Weaver, John (1673–1760) was a dancing master, theatrical dancer, and choreographer who contributed greatly to the development of dance in Britain by introducing the pantomime, a theatrical performance form based on *commedia dell'arte* happily exploited by John Rich, and by bringing dance into a more regular and scientific status through step notation, historical writing, and even including anatomy instruction in his teaching of the art form. He preceded Rich in introducing the pantomime at Drury Lane in 1703 and between 1717 and 1721 he composed and danced in three serious and two grotesque or comic dances at that theatre. His serious pantomimes, such as *The Loves of Mars and Venus* and *Perseus and Andromeda*, inspired comic answers from Rich at Covent Garden.

Webb, Mrs. Richard (?–1793) was a popular comedienne and actress who appeared primarily at Covent Garden and the Haymarket from the late 1770s until her death in 1793. In 1793 she played Miss Spinster in *Every One Has His Fault.*

Whitfield, John (1752–1814) began his career in the provinces before appearing in London at Covent Garden in 1774. Whitfield and his wife moved to Drury Lane for David Garrick's final season as manager, but moved to Covent Garden, where he played Villiers in the premiere of *The Belle's Stratagem* in 1780. He then joined the company at Drury Lane in 1786 before finally returning to Covent Garden in 1798. He often played youthful beaux, sentimental lovers, and gallant officers. His larger roles were typically in comedies, but he played both comic and tragic roles.

Wilks, Robert (c.1665–1732) was born near Dublin, received a good education, and was forced to join the forces of King William when war broke out in Ireland. Though he did not see active combat, the war disrupted regular theatres, which meant that his debut as Othello at Smock Alley Theatre in 1691 in celebration of the Stuart defeat, was at least partially amateur. Wilks stayed on at Smock Alley for two years before he was engaged (and underpaid) by Christopher Rich at Drury Lane, so he returned to Dublin where he successfully played, among other roles, Dorimant in *The Man of Mode*. He came back to Drury Lane in 1699 in the role of Harry Wildair in his friend George Farquhar's *Constant Couple* and continued to play nearly daily even after he joined Thomas Dogget and Colley Cibber in the management of Drury Lane in 1709.

Williams, Joseph (c.1663–?) began his career by appearing with the Duke's Company, often at Dorset Gardens. He later performed with the United Company at both Drury Lane and Dorset Gardens. In 1689 he played Bacon in the premiere of *The Widdow Ranter*. Although he initially planned to join Thomas Betterton when he broke away from the company in 1695, Williams ended up remaining with Christopher Rich at Drury Lane.

Willis, Elizabeth (c.1669–1739) had joined Thomas Betterton's company at Lincoln's Inn Fields (and later at the Queen's Theatre) by 1697, where she performed the role of Foible in the premiere of *The Way of the World* in 1700. Later in her career she moved back and forth between different companies, performing at Lincoln's Inn Fields, Drury Lane, and the Queen's Theatre. She also performed in late summer fairs.

Woodward, Henry (1714–1777) was a versatile actor and pantomimist who succeeded John Rich in the latter line as "Lun Jr." He was born and apprenticed to a tallow chandler, but joined John Rich's troupe in Lincoln's Inn Fields in 1729, playing the roles of the Beggar and Filch in *The Beggar's Opera*. He performed regularly in all the licensed London theatres over the course of his career, as well as performing in Dublin and in summer stints at Southwark and Bartholomew Fairs; Young Bellair in *The Man of Mode*, Sparkish in *The Country Wife*, Witwoud in *The Way of the World*, and Marplot in *The Busie Body* were among his many roles. Though he specialized in playing dissolute characters, he led an unusually sober and disciplined life for an actor of the era, saved his money, and maintained a respectable reputation. He ventured into management of the ill-fated Crow Street Theatre in Dublin, his one serious financial misstep. In addition to conventional roles, he was well known and well paid for his dancing and comic skills as Harlequin, and he wrote successfully in a satirical vein, mocking his colleagues Susanna Maria Cibber and Kitty Clive, as well as taking a swipe at Italian opera, in *The Beggar's Pantomime, or, the Contending Columbines*. After the death of his wife, George Anne Bellamy became his companion, and she nursed him in his final illness until his death.

Wroughton, Richard (1748–1822) made his first stage appearance as a young man at Covent Garden in 1768, and he remained in the Covent Garden company until 1786, playing a variety of roles. In 1780 he played Sir George Touchwood in the premiere of *The Belle's Stratagem*. Dissatisfied with management, he moved to Drury Lane for the 1787–1788 season, and remained there for a decade. He also managed the theatre at Sadler's Wells from 1784 until his retirement in 1798. He later returned to the stage and briefly served as manager at Drury Lane. Wroughton played well over two hundred roles during his 37 years on the London stage.

Yates, Mary Ann (1728–1787) née Graham, debuted inauspiciously in Dublin in 1753, and her success as the leading tragedienne between Susanna Maria Cibber and Sarah Siddons did not come until after her marriage to Richard Yates at Drury Lane Theatre under David Garrick's management. She was best known for pathetic parts in she-tragedies, but she also played roles as diverse as Mrs. Marwood in *The Way of the World* and Cleopatra in *All For Love*. She was an active and able businesswoman as well as actress, who partnered with her husband in management and negotiated aggressively for the highest possible salaries.

Yates, Richard (1706?–1796), actor and theatre manager, debuted at Henry Fielding's Haymarket Theatre in the 1736–37 season. He specialized in low comic parts, especially Shakespeare's clowns, and played the Ghost of Gaffer Thumb in Fielding's *Tragedy of Tragedies*. He was also a skilled dancer as Harlequin. A serviceable actor, he played many supporting roles, though given his leanings towards physical comedy, he must have been an odd fit as Trueman in *The London Merchant*. He played all the licensed London theatres and married Mary Ann Graham, whose career as a tragic actress by far overshadowed Yates. He and his wife collaborated with James and Frances Brooke in managing the King's Theatre that specialized in opera, and he also built and managed the playhouse at Birmingham.

Younge, Elizabeth (c.1740–1797) became one of Garrick's principle leading ladies after the retirement of Hannah Pritchard in 1768. She played Cleopatra, Perdita, Jane Shore, and other major tragic roles at Drury Lane. In 1778–79, she moved to Covent Garden and played there until 1797. See also Elizabeth Pope.

Part 1
Restoring the Theatre: 1660–1700

OVERVIEW

John Dryden and William Davenant, *The Tempest or The Enchanted Island*
William Wycherley, *The Country Wife*
George Etherege, *The Man of Mode*
John Dryden, *All For Love*
Aphra Behn, *The Widdow Ranter*
John Vanbrugh, *The Relapse*

THE PERIOD OF BRITISH HISTORY that we call the Restoration could be characterized by practically all the alternative meanings listed under the verb "restore" in the *Oxford English Dictionary*. Following the bloody English Civil Wars (1642–1651) and the Interregnum period of parliamentary and dictatorial rule, the time between 1660 and 1700 was about recompense (to the victors), repair (of damaged state infrastructure and a social fabric torn by conflict), reinstatement (of a mixed government by parliament and the monarchy), and bringing back (of King Charles II, heir to the throne, from exile). The theatres, which had been officially closed and mostly silent during two civil wars and the period of rule by the Commonwealth of England and the Protectorate, under Oliver Cromwell, were integral to the social processes of re-establishing the hereditary monarchy and the patching up of war-torn English society. In this period, in highly specific ways that were new to the relationship between theatre and the social and political culture with which it is always connected, performances within the space of the licensed London theatres resonate with the cultural performances of politics, governance, and national identity.

Less than 40 years after the reign of Elizabeth I and the vibrant London theatres of Shakespeare in the English Renaissance, Elizabeth's successors, James I and then Charles

I, attempted to force an England used to a strong parliament and riven by religious differences into a monarchically governed state unified under a single religion. The result was a series of wars that resulted in the trial of Charles I for treason and his spectacularly public execution in front of Whitehall Palace in 1649. A tradition of anti-theatricality, rooted in dissenting Protestantism, almost completely eradicated public theatre during the Commonwealth and Protectorate. When the Protectorate weakened and then failed under the governance of Cromwell's son, and Charles' son, Charles II, returned from his exile in France, one of his first actions was to license two London theatres, the Duke of York's Men under William Davenant's management in Lincoln's Inn Fields, and the King's Company, first at the Red Bull and then at the Theatre Royal at Drury Lane, under Thomas Killigrew. Davenant and Killigrew had both fought on the Royalist side in the Civil Wars, and the theatres they ran were spaces that sought to restore the glory of monarchy through fictions of strong male heroism, wit, and homosociality, with sumptuous spectacles and costuming. (The King and members of his court even lent their gorgeous, ceremonial garb to actors performing make-believe kings and courtiers.) Charles himself was a regular at the theatres, which became spaces for performing royal power as well as plays. The playhouse was not only a place to see actors perform; it was a space for social performance by the audience. Aside from the flirting, *bon mots*, and ogling that took place among the audience, elite young men also showed off their finest clothes by paying to sit on the stage during the play's action. The theatres were not, however, the exclusive domain of the elite. As Henry Misson notes in 1698, many people from different walks of life who could afford a ticket went to the theatre:

> The Pit is an Amphitheatre, fill'd with Benches without Backboards, and adorn'd and cover'd with green Cloth. Men of Quality, particularly the younger Sort, some Ladies of Reputation and Virtue, and abundance of Damsels that haunt for Prey, sit all together in this Place, Higgledy-piggledy, chatter, toy, play, hear, hear not. Farther up, against the Wall, under the first Gallery and just opposite to the Stage, rises another Amphitheatre, which is taken by persons of the best Quality, among whom are generally very few Men. The Galleries, whereof there are only two Rows, are fill'd with none but ordinary People, particularly the Upper one.[1]

In this socially heterogeneous space, both audience and actors perform different social identities as well as collective expressions of what it meant to be British.

Women, as we can see from Misson's description, were important to audience performance; they were also, literally, major players in stage performance as well. When Charles re-established the London theatres he also changed them forever by allowing women to act professionally. This change did not happen all at once; a pipeline of actresses did not stand ready to take their parts. Very quickly, however, the novelty and titillation of women acting drew audiences and motivated women to seek a living in the theatre. Actresses, initially, were not clearly distinguishable from the "Damsels who hunt for prey" in the audience. Many had made their living as prostitutes before they became actresses (as was the case of the famous Nell Gwyn) and to be an actress was to step into a sexual market in which the female performer almost automatically became the goods. It would be a mistake, however, to reduce these early actresses to opportunistic prostitutes; in a society in which women were limited in their work choices outside the space of home and family, acting provided a new venue for female professionalism and actresses could make a living from their artistic as well as sexual skills.

The presence of sexually available women in the pit and on the stage conduced to making the theatre a venue for masculine sexual display by the audience as much, perhaps more than, the actors on stage. The King took a starring role in this display. Charles not only patronized the theatres, but took many of its most attractive actresses as mistresses (including the above-mentioned Gwyn). The publicly displayed virility and sexual promiscuity of the monarch did nothing to endear him to many on the losing side of the Civil Wars, the anti-theatrical dissenting Protestants, and it was not exactly embraced whole-heartedly by his less hostile, but more sober Anglican supporters, but it did contribute to the personal charisma that made the British public want to know their king as a man as well as a monarch, a feature of celebrity that performance theorist Joseph Roach calls "public intimacy," the desire to know and feel close to a public figure. As Roach argues, Charles had "It," the star quality that gives its possessor the power to fascinate and even create love in people, including those whom the "It" person has never met.[2] Many of Charles' courtiers, such as John Wilmot, the Earl of Rochester (the model for Etherege's Dorimant in *The Man of Mode*) contributed to the performance of a masculine elite surrounding Charles and sharing in his personal and sexual charisma. If the heroic Antony embodies elements of that charisma in tragedy, so does the witty hero of Restoration comedy.

Charles needed all the star power he could muster. He faced a daunting task in re-establishing English stability and prosperity after devastating civil wars. He was not helped by an outbreak of bubonic plague in London in 1665, nor a fire the next year that burned down most of the traditional, walled city of London. Charles' monarchy was not wealthy, and he depended (secretly) on financial support from the Catholic French monarchy. He weathered serious challenges to his authority, especially the Exclusion Crisis that nearly outlawed the hereditary succession of his Catholic brother, James. When Charles died in 1685, James's reign as a Catholic king over a Protestant nation was intolerable, however, and in 1688, William of Orange and his consort Mary "invaded" England by invitation, taking over the English throne and sending James into exile in France. For the last decade of the century, the theatres had lost their royal "star," but their potential as a venue for social exchange and the expression of political power was established and would be fulfilled over the long eighteenth century. Playhouses, with, by the mid-eighteenth century, the periodical press, constitute the social media of the long eighteenth century.

This is not to claim, however, that the Restoration theatres did not have a seamier side or that they did not undergo financial and administrative struggles. The glamour and sexual appeal of the actresses could easily turn to exploitation and even violence. In 1665 the actress Rebecca Marshal petitioned the King for protection from "one Mark Trevor of the Temple Esq." who "several times barbarously and insolently affronted" the actress "as well upon the stage as off." Her court deposition continued to complain that:

> the said Trevor assaulted her violently in a coach and, after many horrid oaths and threats that he would be revenged of her for complaining to my Lord Chamberlain formerly of him, pursued her with his sword in his hand; and when by flight she had secured herself in a house, he continued his abusive language and broke the windows of the adjoining house.[3]

The early theatre historian Wright complained that "the playhouses are so extremely pestered with vizard masks[4] and their trade, (occasioning continual quarrels and abuses) that many of the more civilized parts of the town are uneasy in the company and shun the theatre as they would a house of scandal."[5] Actors were subject to "punishment" at the hands of affronted male audience members if they were perceived as encroaching upon gentlemanly prerogatives, such as carrying a sword or sleeping with a desirable actress. The playhouse could be a violent space as well as a space of sociability and celebrity.

The London theatres were also just finding their financial legs. The two companies, the King's and the Duke's, merged in 1683 when the King's Company failed financially. Mismanagement after the original regimes of Killigrew and Davenant led the manager of the United Company, Christopher Rich, to squeeze his actors financially to the point of rebelling and establishing their own theatre under the management of the actor Thomas Betterton in 1695, when, again, two playhouses competed for audiences in the London entertainment industry.

Music, dance, and spectacular scenery and stage effects were risky but essential investments in the theatres' imperative to draw in paying customers. Experimental mixings of opera with English plays, such as Henry Purcell's remix of Shakespeare's *A Midsummer Night's Dream, The Fairy Queen,* featured impressive special effects, but were too expensive to sustain for more than a few performances, as John Downes reports:

> *The Fairy Queen,* made into an opera, from a Comedy of Mr. Shakespeare's: This in Ornaments was Superior to the other Two [*King Arthur* and *The Prophetess*]; especially in Cloaths, for all the Singers and Dancers, Scenes, Machines and Decorations, all most profusely set off; and excellently perform'd, chiefly the Instrumental and Vocal part Compos'd by the said Mr. Purcel, and Dances by Mr. Priest. The Court and Town were wonderfully satisfy'd with it; but the Expenses in setting it out being so great, the Company got very little by it.[6]

Other musical adaptations of Shakespeare were more durable. Downes reports on:

> the tragedy of Macbeth, altered by Sir William Davenant; being dressed in all its finery, as new clothes, new scenes, machines, as flyings for the witches; with all the singing and dancing in it . . .. It being excellently performed, being in the nature of an opera, it recompensed double the expense; it proves still a lasting play.[7]

Except for the short time in which the King's Company played at the Red Bull, the playhouses themselves were not the open-roofed structure of Shakespeare's Globe. Davenant's theatre, with capacity for scenic design and expanded space for the audience, set the template for Christopher Wren's design for the Theatre Royal in Drury Lane and many eighteenth-century theatres to follow. Colley Cibber, the eighteenth-century actor and manager of Drury Lane Theatre between 1711 and 1732, describes the Theatre Royal prior to 1696:

> It must be observed then that the area or platform of the old stage projected about four foot forwarder, in a semi-oval figure, parallel to the benches of the pit; and that the former lower doors of entrance for the actors were brought down between the two foremost (and then only) pilasters; in the pace of which doors now the two stage boxes are fixed. That where the doors of entrance now are, there formerly stood two additional side-wings, in front to a full set of scenes, which had then almost a double effect in their loftiness and magnificence.
>
> By this original form, the usual station of the actors, in almost every scene was advanced at least ten foot nearer to the audience than they now can be; because, not only from the stage's being shortened in front, but likewise from the additional interposition of those stage boxes, the actors (in respect to the spectators that fill them) are kept so much more backward from the main audience than they used to be. But when the actors are in possession of that forwarder space to advance upon, the voice was then more in the centre of the house so that the most distant ear had scarce the least doubt of difficulty in hearing what fell from the weakest utterance: all objects were thus drawn nearer to the sense; every painted scene was stronger; every grand scene and dance more extended; every rich or fine-coloured habit had a more lively lustre; nor was the minutest motion of a feature (properly changing with the passion or humour it suited) ever lost, as they frequently must be in the obscurity of too great a distance. And how valuable an advantage the facility of hearing distinctly is to every well-acted scene, every common spectator is a judge.[8]

This stage was a compromise between the thrust stage of the Elizabethan theatre and the nineteenth-century recessed stage with proscenium arch, which allowed actors close contact with the audience while also facilitating impressive scenery and special effects—such as the flying chariot used by Hecate in *Macbeth*—in the background. An evening at the theatre started in the late afternoon to take advantage of natural daylight, but theatres were lit by candles (a consistently large figure in theatre budgets throughout the century) augmented with reflective surrounds and lanterns. While footlights and lighting over the stage brightened the performance space, the pit, gallery, and boxes were also well-lit during performances, facilitating social performances by audiences who were often as interested in looking at and hearing each other as they were engaged by the players. Writing of an evening at the playhouse on February 18, 1667, Samuel Pepys reports on giving up on a play in the face of the more proximate performance of the audience around him:

> To the King's House to The Maid's Tragedy; but vexed all the while with two talking ladies and Sir Charles Sedley, yet pleased to hear their discourse, he being a stranger. And one of the ladies would and did sit with her mask on, all the play and being exceedingly witty as ever I hear woman, did talk most pleasantly with him; but was, I believe, a virtuous woman and of quality. He would fain know who she was, but she would not tell; yet did give him many pleasant hints of her knowledge of him, by that means setting his brains at work to find out who she was, and did give him leave to use all means to find out who she was but pulling off her mask. He was mighty witty and she also, making sport of him very inoffensively, that a more pleasant rencontre I never heard. By that means lost the pleasure of the play wholly, to which now and then Sir Charles Sedley's exceptions against both words and pronouncing them were very pretty.[9]

Aristocratic performances by courtiers such as Sedley, a notorious libertine and a prominent figure in Charles' court, and the glittering spectacle and repartee of the women who may or may not be part of the King's court themselves, augmented the celebrity of Charles and his court and made the theatre the place to be, regardless of the play. Pepys grumpily notes that even those who could barely afford the lowest price of admission was there, as he writes on January 1, 1669 of a visit to the Duke of York's playhouse:

> Here a mighty company of citizens, prentices and others; and it makes me observe that when I began first to be able to bestow a play on myself, I do not remember that I saw by half of the ordinary prentices and mean people in the pit at 2 s 6 d a piece, as now. . . . So much the vanity and prodigality of the age is to be observed in this particular.[10]

This last sentence, from the addicted play-goer and lover-of-all-things-theatre Pepys, points to the ambiguities of the theatres' social function and meaning. The playhouses were both centers of sociability and dangerous sites of contact between different classes and both genders with the potential for social conflict as well as sexual misbehavior. The rowdiness and even violence with which eighteenth-century audiences often "performed" their point of view on actors, plays, managers, playwrights, and anything else they had an opinion about grew from a Restoration playhouse that was playground and venue for social connection between many different kinds of people, from aristocrat to orange girl, the young woman who sold fruit—and herself—as the audience watched—or didn't watch—the plays.

While the people who wrote the plays for this mixed audience were all, of course, better educated and of higher social standing than the servants in the galleries or the lower artisans in the pit, playwrights, too, were a heterogeneous group. The demand for new plays was met by talent that crossed both status and gender lines. While many held claim to gentlemanly status, John Dryden, the poet laureate and author of *All For Love* and many other heroic tragedies and several adaptations of Shakespeare's plays, importantly opened a space in the culture of Restoration theatre for the professional writer—regardless of social status—as the best authority on what is good and not good in dramatic literature. His prefatory writing to his plays jumpstarted the tradition of English literary criticism that would thrive over the course of the centuries to follow. Women, too, stepped up to the demand for new plays, one of the most successful being Aphra Behn, the author of *The Widdow Ranter* as well as many popular and much-performed plays, novels, and poetry. Women were not only integral to the performance of plays, but writers such as Behn, Mary Pix, and Catherine Trotter played major roles in shaping the archive of Restoration dramatic texts.

The plays themselves were also a diverse mix of word-rich tragedy and comedy as well as spectacular "operas"—the term applied to a wide variety of shows heavy on music, dance, scenery, and special effects. Italian opera of the kind that we associate with the term was also introduced during the Restoration, and would become a strong competitor for ticket sales among aristocratic audience members later in the early eighteenth century. Initially, Davenant's company at Lincoln's Inn Fields specialized in spectacle and music, while Killigrew's featured the witty comedies that we associate so strongly with Restoration theatre today. The demand for plays that exploded with the restoration of the theatres meant that the works of Ben Jonson, William Shakespeare, and other playwrights of the Renaissance and early seventeenth-century were divided up between the companies and formed substantial parts of the repertoire. Adaptation was rampant; Restoration theatre professionals had no compunction about re-fitting old plays, especially Shakespeare's, to meet new audiences' tastes and demands. (Hence the spectacular, "operatic" *Tempest* in this volume.)

This productive if sometimes contentious contrast between formally elaborate performances that appealed to the audience's sensory experience (and love for blank verse) and the more colloquial, informal humor of bantering characters that we see in plays such as *The Country Wife* and *The Man of Mode* attracted a broad range of audiences for a broad range of reasons. Pepys, for example, an amateur musician, was as passionate about the music of the stage as he was about the plays themselves, often pushing himself to learn a new piece of music he had recently heard in the theatre. Music with lyrics was printed and sold, a complement to the performances on the stage. The plays themselves were usually printed within a few days of their first production, and contributed to the cultivation of an audience of readers as well as listeners and observers.

The long partnership between the publication and performance industries begins in the Restoration, and although theatre reviews would not become an important part of daily or weekly newspapers until the middle of the eighteenth-century, the dramatic criticism of playwrights such as Dryden as well as the symbiotic relationship between the performance and printing of plays, and the relays between print text and performance, reading and sensory experience, began functioning in the Restoration like the firings between synapses of a great, social brain. The print industry responded to a growing market during this period, creating an archive of documents—from plays themselves to theatrical biographies and histories as well as visual prints—that can help us access across three centuries the ephemeral performances that are the beating pulse of any theatre.

Notes

1 *Memoirs and Observations in his Travels over England.* Translated by John Ozell. London: De. Browne, 1719, 219–20.
2 *It.* Ann Arbor, MI: University of Michigan Press, 2007.
3 David Thomas and Arnold Hare, *Theatre in Europe: A Documentary History. Restoration and Georgian England, 1660–1788.* Cambridge: Cambridge University Press, 1989, 185–6.
4 Prostitutes.
5 Thomas and Hare, 189.
6 *Roscius Anglicanus.* Ed. Montague Summers. Bronx, NY: Benjamin Blom, 1968, 42–43.
7 Downes, 33.
8 *An Apology for the Life of Mr Colley Cibber, written by himself.* Ed. R. W. Lowe. New York: AMS Press, 1966, vol. 2, 84–6.
9 *The Diary of Samuel Pepys.* Eds. Robert Lathum and William Matthews. Berkeley, CA: University of California Press, 1970. February 18, 1667. Vol. 8, 71–2.
10 Pepys, vol. 9, 2.

1. *The Tempest*

***THE TEMPEST, OR THE ENCHANTED ISLAND*. A COMEDY. AS IT IS NOW ACTED AT HIS HIGHNESS THE DUKE OF YORK'S THEATRE. JOHN DRYDEN AND WILLIAM DAVENANT. FIRST PERFORMED 16 MAY1674 (?) AND FIRST PUBLISHED 1674.**

1.1 *THE TEMPEST, OR THE ENCHANTED ISLAND.* A COMEDY. AS IT IS NOW ACTED AT HIS HIGHNESS THE DUKE OF YORK'S THEATRE.[1]

John Dryden and William Davenant

First Performed 16 May 1674 and First Published 1674.

THIS VERSION OF SHAKESPEARE'S *The Tempest* is the one with which Restoration and eighteenth-century audiences would have been most familiar. It is an operatic production, generally attributed to Thomas Shadwell but probably the work of several hands, of a drastically adapted version of the play by Sir William Davenant and John Dryden that was first performed in 1667 and published in 1670. "Shadwell's" operatic version, which includes the concluding masque of Neptune, was first published and performed in 1674 and enjoyed multiple revivals until William Macready's production of the Shakespeare play effectively replaced it, well into the nineteenth century.

The Dryden/Davenant adaptation of Shakespeare's *Tempest* added the doubling of characters, most notably Miranda's sister, Dorinda, her lover Hippolito, a man who has never seen a woman (usually played as a breeches part by an actress), and Caliban's sister Sycorax. The "Shadwell" version also gives Ariel a fairy lover, Milcha, with whom he sings duets. Samuel Pepys, that avid diarist and theatre-goer of the Restoration, saw this play multiple times in 1667, repeatedly commenting on his pleasure in its "variety":

> To the Duke of York's house, to the play, 'The Tempest,' which we have often seen but yet I was pleased again, and shall be again to see it, it is so full of variety, and particularly this day I took pleasure to learn the tune of the seaman's dance, which I have much desired to be perfect in, and have made myself so.
>
> (*Diary*, Feb 3, 1668)

Pepys's comments suggest that "variety" contributed to the Dryden/Davenant play's popularity. It had comedy, romance, tragedy, monsters, fairies, spectacle—and music. That the talented amateur musician Pepys took great pleasure (and pride) in learning the music is a telling detail that speaks to the importance of music in public and private life, in professional and amateur performance, and to the theatre in particular. Musicians consumed large and ever-growing portions of theatre budgets as the century went on, and the "Shadwell" opera expanded on the Shakespeare play's original feature of song and dance with special effects, spectacle, and the music of the age's best composers.

Dryden's and Davenant's version of the play used approximately one third of Shakespeare's lines; the operatic adaptation used slightly less Shakespeare but added more music and spectacle. Given the reverence with which we treat Shakespeare's plays today, this playing fast and loose with the Bard seems a bit like turning *War and Peace* into musical comedy, but it is important to recall that Shakespeare and his plays did not begin receiving this sort of reverence until well into the second half of the eighteenth century. David Garrick, the actor/manager of Drury Lane Theatre, launched a promotional campaign the likes of which no playwright had seen before to place Shakespeare on the top shelf of British national treasures.[2] His Shakespeare Jubilee in 1769 featured horse races, fireworks, choral performances, a parade of Shakespeare's characters, and an ode to Shakespeare written and performed by Garrick—just about every kind of entertainment except a Shakespeare play. It put Stratford-Upon-Avon on the map as the birthplace of Shakespeare, and while the Jubilee itself was a rained-out mess, it became the subject of theatrical spectacle in London for many years after. (You will find the script and production materials for *The Jubilee* in the third section of this volume.) As scholars and editors became increasingly concerned to nail down textually "the real Shakespeare," Garrick started a campaign to make his plays central to the British theatrical repertoire and was known for his own, spectacular performances of Hamlet, Macbeth, Benedick, and many other choice Shakespearian roles.

Yet Garrick himself capitalized on the market for song, dance, and spectacle by turning two of Shakespeare's plays, *A Midsummer Night's Dream* and *The Tempest*, into operas, complete with Italian castrati singers. As late as the 1750s, an enthusiasm for Shakespeare and operatic spectacle were not mutually exclusive. Garrick's *The Fairies* was moderately successful in ticket sales and reception, in part because the manager cast some very talented child actors in the roles of the fairies, thereby tapping into a growing fashion for singing, dancing children as theatrical spectacle. The operatic *Tempest* he produced in 1756 was a short, three-act mash-up of Shakespeare and the Dryden/Davenant play with chaste, romantic duets and musical celebrations of matrimony replacing the neo-classical spectacle of Neptune. This play flopped, probably for a number of reasons, but its failure seems to have ended Garrick's attempt to wed Shakespeare with opera, and he produced a spoken *Tempest* that is a shortened version of Shakespeare's play within a year of the failed opera. This version held the stage at Drury Lane until after Garrick's death, but the "Shadwell" opera continued to draw audiences and critical praise from theatre professionals as astute as Elizabeth Inchbald, the actress, playwright, and editor of *The British Stage*. As performed on the stage, then, this operatic *Tempest* deserves our attention as it did that of the audiences who made it such an important part of eighteenth-century theatrical history.

Preface to *The Enchanted Island*

The writing of prefaces to plays, was probably invented by some very ambitious poet, who never thought he had done enough: perhaps by some ape of the French eloquence, which uses to make a business of a letter of gallantry, an examen[3] of a farce; and in short, a great pomp and ostentation of words on every trifle. This is certainly the talent of that nation, and ought not to be invaded by any other. They do that out of gaiety, which would be an imposition upon us.

We may satisfie our selves with surmounting them in the scene, and safely leave them those trappings of writing, and flourishes of the pen, with which they adorn the borders of their plays, and which are indeed no more than good landskips[4] to a very indifferent picture. I must proceed no farther in this argument, lest I run my self beyond my excuse for writing this. Give me leave therefore to tell you, reader, that I do it not to set a value on any thing I have written in this play, but out of gratitude to the memory of Sir William Davenant, who did me the honour to joyn me with him in the alteration of it.

It was originally Shakespear's: a poet for whom he had particularly a high veneration, and whom he first taught me to admire. The play itself had formerly been acted with success in the Black-Friers:[5] and our excellent Fletcher[6] had so great a value for it, that he thought fit to make use of the same design, not much varied, a second time. Those who have seen his Sea-Voyage, may easily discern that it was a copy of Shakespear's Tempest: the storm, the desart Island, and the woman who had never seen a man, are all sufficient testimonies of it. But Fletcher was not the only poet who made use of Shakespear's plot: Sir John Suckling,[7] a profess'd admirer of our author, has follow'd his footsteps in his Goblins; his Regmella being an open imitation of Shakespear's Miranda; and his spirits, though counterfeit, yet are copied from Ariel. But Sir William Davenant, as he was a man of quick and piercing imagination, soon found that somewhat might be added to the design of Shakespear, of which neither Fletcher nor Suckling had ever thought: and therefore to put the last hand to it, he design'd the counter-part to Shakespear's plot, namely, that of a man who had never seen a woman; that by this means those two characters of innocence and love might the more illustrate and commend each other. This excellent contrivance he was pleas'd to communicate to me, and to desire my assistance in it. I confess that from the very first moment it so pleas'd me, that I never writ any thing with more delight. I must likewise do him that justice to acknowledge, that my writing received daily his amendments, and that is the reason why it is not so faulty, as the rest which I have done, without the help or correction of so judicious a friend. The comical parts of the sailors were also his invention, and for the most part his writing, as you will easily discover by the style. In the time I writ with him I had the opportunity to observe somewhat more nearly of him than I had formerly done, when I had only a bare acquaintance with him: I found him then of so quick a fancy, that nothing was propos'd to him, on which he could not suddenly produce a thought extreamly pleasant and surprising: and those first thoughts of his, contrary to the old Latin proverb, were not always the least happy.[8] And as his fancy was quick, so likewise were the products of it remote and new. He borrowed not of any other; and his imaginations were such as could not easily enter into any other man. His corrections were sober and judicious: and he corrected his own writings much more severely than those of another man, bestowing twice the time and labour in polishing, which he us'd in invention. It had perhaps been easie enough for me to have arrogated more to my self than was due, in the writing of this play, and to have pass'd by his name with silence in the publication of it, with the same ingratitude which others have us'd to him, whose writings he hath not only corrected, as he has done this, but has had a greater inspection over them, and sometimes added whole scenes together, which may as easily be distinguish'd from the rest, as true gold from counterfeit by the weight. But besides the unworthiness of the action which deterred me from it (there being nothing so base as to rob the dead of his reputation) I am satisfi'd I could never have receiv'd so much honour, in being thought the author of any poem, how excellent soever, as I shall from the joyning my imperfections with the merit and name of Shakespear and Sir William Davenant.

Decemb. 1. 1669.
JOHN DRYDEN.

Prologue to the *Tempest*, or *The Enchanted Island*.

As when a tree's cut down, the secret root
Lives under ground, and thence new branches shoot;
So, from old Shakespear's honour'd dust, this day
Springs up and buds a new reviving play.
Shakespear, who (taught by none) did first impart
To Fletcher wit, to labouring Johnson[9] art.
He monarch-like gave those his subjects law,
And is that nature which they paint and draw.
Fletcher reach'd that which on his heights did grow,
Whilst Johnson crept and gather'd all below.
This did his love, and this his mirth digest:
One imitates him most, the other best.
If they have since out-writ all other men,
'Tis with the drops which fell from Shakespear's pen.
The storm which vanish'd on the neighb'ring shore,
Was taught by Shakespear's Tempest first to roar.
That innocence and beauty which did smile
In Fletcher, grew on this enchanted isle.
But Shakespear's magick could not copy'd be,
Within that circle none durst walk but he.

I must confess 'twas bold, nor would you now,
That liberty to vulgar wits allow,
Which works by magick supernatural things:
But Shakespear's pow'r is sacred as a king's.
Those legends from old priest-hood were receiv'd,
And he then writ, as people then believ'd.
But, if for Shakespear we your grace implore,
We for our theatre shall want it more:
Who by our dearth of youths[10] are forc'd t'employ
One of our women to present a boy.
And that's a transformation, you will say
Exceeding all the magick in the play.
Let none expect in the last act to find,
Her sex transform'd from man to woman-kind.
What ere she was before the play began,
All you shall see of her is perfect man.
Or if your fancy will be farther led,
To find her woman, it must be a bed.

Dramatis Personae.[11]

Alonzo Duke of *Savoy,* and usurper of the dukedom of *Mantua.*
Ferdinand his son.
Prospero right Duke of *Millain.*
Antonio his brother, usurper of the dukedom.
Gonzalo a noble man of *Savoy.*
Hippolito, one that never saw woman, right heir of the dukedom of *Mantua.*
Stephano Master of the ship.
Mustacho his mate.
Trincalo boatswain.
Ventoso a mariner.
Several mariners.
A cabbin-boy.
Miranda }
Dorinda } (daughters to *Prospero*) that never saw man.
Ariel an aiery spirit, attendant to *Prospero.*
Several spirits guards to *Prospero.*
Caliban
Sycorax his sister } two monsters of the isle.

Act I. Scene I.

[*The front of the stage is open'd, and the band of 24 violins, with the harpsicals*[12] *and thurbos*[13] *which accompany the voices, are plac'd between the pit and the stage. While the overture is playing, the curtain rises, and discovers a new frontispiece, joyn'd to the great pylasters,*[14] *on each side of the stage. This frontispiece is a noble arch, supported by large wreathed columns of the Corinthian order; the wreathing of the columns are beautif'd with roses wound round them, and several cupids flying about them. On the cornice, just over the capitals, sits on either side a figure, with a trumpet in one hand, and a palm in the other, representing Fame. A little farther on the same cornice, on each side of a compass-pediment,*[15] *lie a lion and a unicorn, the supporters of the royal arms of England. In the middle of the arch are several angels, holding the King's arms, as if they were placing them in the midst of that compass-pediment. Behind this is the scene, which represents a thick cloudy sky, a very rocky coast, and a tempestuous sea in perpetual agitation. This tempest (suppos'd to be rais'd by magick) has many dreadful objects in it, as several spirits in horrid shapes flying down amongst the sailors, then rising and crossing in the air. And when the ship is sinking, the whole house is darken'd, and a shower of fire falls upon 'em. This is accompanied with lightning, and several claps of thunder, to the end of the storm. Enter* Mustacho *and* Ventoso.]

VENTOSO. What a sea comes in?

MUSTACHO. A hoaming[16] sea! We shall have foul weather.

[*Enter* Trincalo.

TRINCALO. The scud[17] comes against the wind, 'twill blow hard.

[*Enter* Stephano.

STEPHANO. Bosen!

TRINCALO. Here, Master, what say you?

STEPHANO. Ill weather! Let's off to sea.

MUSTACHO. Let's have sea room enough, and then let it blow the Devil's head off.

STEPHANO. Boy! Boy!

[*Enter* Cabin-boy.

BOY. Yaw, yaw, here, Master.

STEPHANO. Give the pilot a dram of the bottle.

[*Exeunt* Stephano *and* Boy. *Enter* mariners *and pass over the stage.*

TRINCALO. Bring the cable to the capstorm.[18]

[*Enter* Alonzo, Antonio, Gonzalo.

ALONZO. Good Bosen have a care; where's the Master? Play the men.

TRINCALO. Pray keep below.

ANTONIO. Where's the Master, Bosen?

TRINCALO. Do you not hear him? You hinder us: keep your cabin, you help the storm.

GONZALO. Nay, good friend be patient.

TRINCALO. Aye, when the sea is: hence; what care these roarers for the name of Duke; to cabin; silence; trouble us not.

GONZALO. Good friend, remember whom thou hast aboard.

TRINCALO. None that I love more than my self: you are a counseller, if you can advise these elements to silence, use your wisdom: if you cannot, make your self ready in the cabin for the ill hour. Cheerly good hearts! Out of our way, Sirs. [*Exeunt* Trincalo *and* mariners.

GONZALO. I have great comfort from this fellow! Methinks his complexion is perfect gallows; stand fast, good fate, to his hanging; make the rope of his destiny our cable, for our own does little advantage us; if he be not born to be hang'd we shall be drown'd. [*Exit.*

[*Enter* Trincalo *and* Stephano.

TRINCALO. Up aloft, lads. Come, reef[19] both top-sails.

STEPHANO. Make haste, let's weigh, let's weigh, and off to sea.

[*Exit* Stephano. *Enter two* mariners *and pass over the stage.*

TRINCALO. Hands down! Man your main-capstorm.

[*Enter* Mustacho *and* Ventoso *at the other door.*

MUSTACHO. Up aloft! And man your steere-capstorm.

VENTOSO. My Lads, my hearts of gold, get in your capstorm-bar. Hoa up, hoa up, &c. [*Exeunt* Mustacho *and* Ventoso. *Enter* Stephano.

STEPHANO. Hold on well! Hold on well! Nip[20] well there; Quarter-Master, get's more nippers. [*Exit* Stephano.

[*Enter two* mariners *and pass over again.*

TRINCALO. Turn out, turn out, all hands to capstorm.

You dogs, is this a time to sleep? Lubbord.[21]

Heave together, lads. [Trincalo *whistles. Exeunt* Mustacho *and* Ventoso.

MUSTACHO. [*Within*] Our vial's[22] broke.

VENTOSO. [*Within*] 'Tis but our vial-block has given way. Come heave, lads! We are fix'd again. Heave together bullyes.[23]

[*Enter* Stephano.

STEPHANO. Cut down the hammocks! Cut down the hammocks! Come, my lads: Come bullyes, chear up! Heave lustily. The anchor's a peek.[24]

TRINCALO. Is the anchor a peek?

STEPHANO. Is a weigh! Is a weigh!

TRINCALO. Up aloft, my lads, upon the fore-castle![25] Cut the anchor, cut him.

[*All within*] Haul catt[26], haul catt, &c. haul catt, haul: haul, catt, haul. Below.

STEPHANO. Aft, aft! And loose the misen[27]!

TRINCALO. Get the misen-tack aboard. Haul aft misen-sheet!

[*Enter* Mustacho.

MUSTACHO. Loose the main top-sail!

STEPHANO. Let him alone, there's too much wind.

TRINCALO. Loose fore-sail! Haul aft both sheets! Trim her right afore the wind. Aft! aft! lads, and hale up the misen here.

MUSTACHO. A mackrel-gale,[28] Master.

STEPHANO. [*Within*] Port hard, port! The wind veers forward, bring the tack aboard port is. Starboard, star-board, a little steady; now steady, keep her thus, no nearer you cannot come, till the sails are loose.

[*Enter* Ventoso.

VENTOSO. Some hands down: the guns are loose. [*Exit* Mustacho.

TRINCALO. Try the pump, try the pump! [*Exit* Ventoso.

[*Enter* Mustacho *at the other door.*

MUSTACHO. O Master! Six foot water in hold.

STEPHANO. Clap the helm hard awether! Flat, flat, flat in the fore-sheet there.

TRINCALO. Over-haul your fore-boling.[29]

STEPHANO. Brace in the lar-board.[30] [*Exit.*

TRINCALO. A curse upon this howling, [*a great cry within*] They are louder than the weather.

[*Enter* Antonio *and* Gonzalo.

Yet again, what do you here? Shall we give o'r, and drown? Ha' you a mind to sink?

GONZALO. A pox o' your throat, you bawling, blasphemous, uncharitable dog.

TRINCALO. Work you then and be poxt.

ANTONIO. Hang, Cur, hang, you whorson insolent noise-maker, we are less afraid to be drown'd than thou art.

TRINCALO. Ease the fore-brace a little. [*Exit.*

GONZALO. I'll warrant him for drowning, though the ship were no stronger than a nut-shell, and as leaky as an unstaunch'd wench.

[*Enter* Alonzo *and* Ferdinand.

FERDINAND. For my self I care not, but your loss brings a thousand deaths to me.

ALONZO. O name not me, I am grown old, my son; I now am tedious to the world, and that, by use, is so to me: but, *Ferdinand*, I grieve my subjects' loss in thee: Alas! I suffer justly for my crimes, but why thou shouldest – O Heaven! [*A cry within*] Hark, farewell, my son! A long farewell!

[*Enter* Trincalo, Mustacho, *and* Ventoso.

TRINCALO. What, must our mouths be cold then?

VENTOSO. All's lost. To prayers, to prayers.

GONZALO. The Duke and Prince are gone within to prayers. Let's assist them.

MUSTACHO. Nay, we may e'en pray too; our case is now alike.

ANTONIO. Mercy upon us! We split, we split.

GONZALO. Let's all sink with the Duke, and the young Prince. [*Exeunt. Enter* Stephano, Trincalo.

TRINCALO. The ship is sinking. [*A new cry within.*

STEPHANO. Run her ashore!

TRINCALO. Luff! Luff![31] Or we are all lost! There's a rock upon the starboard bow.

STEPHANO. She strikes, she strikes! All shift for themselves. [*Exeunt.*

Scene II.

[*In the midst of the shower of fire the scene changes. The cloudy sky, rocks, and sea vanish; and when the lights return, discover that beautiful part of the island, which was the habitation of* Prospero; *'tis compos'd of three walks of cypress-trees, each side-walk leads to a cave, in one of which* Prospero *keeps his daughters, in the other* Hippolito*: the middle-walk is of a great depth, and leads to an open part of the island. Enter* Prospero *and* Miranda.]

PROSPERO. Miranda! Where's your sister?

MIRANDA. I left her looking from the pointed rock, at the walk's end, on the huge beat of waters.

PROSPERO. It is a dreadful object.

MIRANDA. If by your art, my dearest Father, you have put them in this roar, allay 'em quickly.

PROSPERO. I have so order'd, that not one creature in the ship is lost:
I have done nothing but in care of thee,
My daughter, and thy pretty sister:
You both are ignorant of what you are,
Not knowing whence I am, nor that I'm more
Than *Prospero*, master of a narrow cell,
And thy unhappy father.

MIRANDA. I ne'r endeavour'd to know more than you were pleas'd to tell me.

PROSPERO. I should inform thee farther.

MIRANDA. You often, Sir, began to tell me what I am,
But then you stopt.

PROSPERO. The hour's now come;
Obey, and be attentive. Canst thou remember a time before we came into this cell? I do not think thou canst, for then thou wert not full three years old.

MIRANDA. Certainly I can, Sir.

PROSPERO. Tell me the image then of any thing which thou dost keep in thy remembrance still.

MIRANDA. Sir, had I not four or five women once that tended me?

PROSPERO. Thou hadst, and more, *Miranda*: what see'st thou else in the dark back-ward, and abyss of time?
If thou remembrest ought e're thou cam'st here, then, how thou cam'st thou may'st remember too.

MIRANDA. Sir, that I do not.

PROSPERO. Fifteen years since, *Miranda*, thy father was the Duke of *Millan*, and a prince of power.

MIRANDA. Sir, are not you my father?

PROSPERO. Thy mother was all virtue, and she said, thou wast my daughter, and thy sister too.

MIRANDA. O Heavens! What foul play had we, that we hither came, or was't a blessing that we did?

PROSPERO. Both, both, my Girl.

MIRANDA. But, Sir, I pray proceed.

PROSPERO. My brother, and thy uncle, call'd *Antonio*, to whom I trusted then the manage of my state, while I was wrap'd with secret studies: That false Uncle having attain'd the craft of granting suits, and of denying them; whom to advance, or lop, for over-topping, soon was grown the ivy which did hide my princely trunk, and suck'd my verdure out: thou attend'st not.

MIRANDA. O good Sir, I do.

PROSPERO. I thus neglecting worldly ends, and bent to closeness, and the bettering of my mind, wak'd in my false brother an evil nature:
He did believe he was indeed the Duke, because he then did execute the outward face of sovereignty. Do'st thou still mark me?

MIRANDA. Your story would cure deafness.

PROSPERO. This false Duke needs would be absolute *Millan*, and confederates with *Savoy's* Duke, to give him tribute, and to do him homage.

MIRANDA. False man!

PROSPERO. This Duke of *Savoy* being an enemy,
To me inveterate, strait grants my brother's suit.
And on a night
Mated to his design, *Antonio* opened the gates of *Millan*, and i'th' dead of darkness, hurri'd me thence with thy young sister, and thy crying self.

MIRANDA. But wherefore did they not that hour destroy us?

PROSPERO. They durst not, Girl, in *Millan*, for the love my people bore me; in short, they hurri'd us away to *Savoy*, and thence aboard a bark at *Nissa's* Port: bore us some leagues to sea, where they prepar'd a rotten carkass of a boat, not rigged, no tackle, sail, nor mast; the very rats instinctively had quit it.

MIRANDA. Alack! What trouble was I then to you?

PROSPERO. Thou and thy sister were two cherubins, which did preserve me: you both did smile, infus'd with fortitude from Heaven.

MIRANDA. How came we ashore?

PROSPERO. By Providence divine,

Some food we had, and some fresh water, which a nobleman of *Savoy*, called *Gonzalo*, appointed master of that black design, gave us; with rich garments, and all necessaries, which since have steaded much: and of his gentleness (knowing I lov'd my books) he furnish'd me from mine own library, with volumes which I prize above my dukedom.

MIRANDA. Would I might see that man.

PROSPERO. Here in this Island we arriv'd, and here have I your tutor been. But by my skill I find, that my mid-heaven doth depend on a most happy star, whose influence if I now court not, but omit, my fortunes will ever after droop: here cease more questions, thou art inclin'd to sleep: 'tis a good dulness, and give it way; I know thou canst not chuse. [*She falls asleep.*

Come away my Spirit: I am ready now, approach.

My *Ariel,* come.

[*Enter* Ariel.

ARIEL. All hail, great Master, grave Sir, hail, I come to answer thy best pleasure, be it to fly, to swim, to shoot into the fire, to ride on the curl'd clouds; to thy strong bidding, task *Ariel* and all his qualities.

PROSPERO. Hast thou, Spirit, perform'd to point the tempest that I bad thee?

ARIEL. To every article.

I boarded the Duke's ship, now on the beak, now in the waste, the deck, in every cabin; I flam'd amazement, and sometimes I seem'd to burn in many places on the top-mast, the yards, and bore-sprit;[32] I did flame distinctly. Nay once I rain'd a shower of fire upon 'em.

PROSPERO. My brave Spirit!

Who was so firm, so constant, that this coil did not infect his reason?

ARIEL. Not a soul,

But felt a feaver of the mind, and play'd some tricks of desperation; all, but mariners, plung'd in the foaming brine, and quit the vessel: the Duke's Son, *Ferdinand,* with hair upstairing (more like reeds than hair) was the first man that leap'd; cry'd, Hell is empty, and all the devils are here.

PROSPERO. Why that's my Spirit;

But was not this nigh shore?

ARIEL. Close by my Master.

PROSPERO. But, *Ariel,* are they safe?

ARIEL. Not a hair perish'd.

In troops I have dispers'd them round this isle.

The Duke's son I have landed by himself, whom I have left warming the air with sighs, in an odd angle of the isle, and sitting, his arms he folded in this sad knot.

PROSPERO. Say how thou hast dispos'd the mariners of the Duke's ship, and all the rest of the fleet?

ARIEL. Safely in harbour

Is the Duke's ship, in the deep nook, where once thou called'st

Me up at midnight to fetch dew from the

Still vext *Bermoothes*,[33] there she's hid,

The mariners all under hatches stow'd,

Whom, with a charm, join'd to their suffer'd labour,

I have left asleep, and for the rest o'th' fleet

(Which I disperst) they all have met again,

And are upon the *Mediterranean* float,

Bound sadly home for *Italy*;

Supposing that they saw the Duke's ship wrack'd,

And his great person perish.

PROSPERO. *Ariel,* thy charge

Exactly is perform'd, but there's more work:

What is the time o'th' day?

ARIEL. Past the mid-season.

PROSPERO. At least two glasses: the time 'tween six and now must by us both be spent most preciously.

ARIEL. Is there more toyl? Since thou dost give me pains, let me remember thee what thou hast promis'd, which is not yet perform'd me.

PROSPERO. How now, Moodie?

What is't thou canst demand?

ARIEL. My liberty.

PROSPERO. Before the time be out? No more.

ARIEL. I prethee!

Remember I have done thee faithful service,

Told thee no lies, made thee no mistakings,

Serv'd without or grudge, or grumblings:

Thou didst promise to bate me a full year.

PROSPERO. Dost thou forget

From what a torment I did free thee?

ARIEL. No.

PROSPERO. Thou dost, and think'st it much to tread the ooze

Of the salt deep:
To run against the sharp wind of the north,
To do my business in the veins of the earth,
When it is bak'd with frost.

ARIEL. I do not, Sir.

PROSPERO. Thou ly'st, malignant thing! Hast thou forgot the foul witch *Sycorax*, who with age and envy was grown into a hoop? Hast thou forgot her?

ARIEL. No Sir.

PROSPERO. Thou hast; where was she born? Speak, tell me.

ARIEL. Sir, in Argier.

PROSPERO. Oh, was she so! I must
Once every month recount what thou hast been, which thou forgettest. This damn'd witch *Sycorax* for mischiefs manifold, and sorceries too terrible to enter human hearing, from *Argier* thou know'st was banish'd: but for one thing she did, they would not take her life: is not this true?

ARIEL. Aye, Sir.

PROSPERO. This blew-ey'd hag was hither brought with child,
And here was left by th' sailors, thou, my slave,
As thou report'st thy self, wast then her servant,
And 'cause thou wast a spirit too delicate
To act her earthy and abhorr'd commands;
Refusing her grand hests, she did confine thee,
By help of her more potent ministers,
(In her unmitigable rage) into a cloven pine,
Within whose rift imprison'd, thou didst painfully
Remain a dozen years; within which space she dy'd,
And left thee there; where thou didst vent thy
Groans, as fast as mill-wheels strike.
Then was this isle (save for two brats, which she did
Litter here, the brutish *Caliban*, and his twin sister,
Two freckl'd hag-born whelps) not honour'd with
A humane shape.

ARIEL. Yes! *Caliban* her son, and *Sycorax* his sister.

PROSPERO. Dull thing, I say so; he, that *Caliban*, and she, that *Sycorax*, whom I now keep in service. Thou best know'st what torment I did find thee in, thy groans did make the wolves howl, and penetrate the breasts of even angry bears, it was a torment to lay upon the damn'd, which *Sycorax* could ne'r again undo: It was my art, when I arriv'd, and heard thee, that made the pine to gape and let thee out.

ARIEL. I thank thee, Master.

PROSPERO. If thou more murmurest, I will rend an oak,
And peg thee in his knotty entrails, till thou
Hast howl'd away twelve winters more.

ARIEL. Pardon, Master.
I will be correspondent to command, and be
A gentle spirit.

PROSPERO. Do so, and after two days I'll discharge thee.

ARIEL. Thanks, my great Master. But I have yet one request.

PROSPERO. What's that, my Spirit?

ARIEL. I know that this day's business is important, requiring too much toyl for one alone. I have a gentle spirit for my Love, who twice seven years has waited for my freedom: let it appear, it will assist me much, and we with mutual joy shall entertain each other. This I beseech you grant me.

PROSPERO. You shall have your desire.

ARIEL. That's my noble Master. *Milcha*!

[Milcha *flies down to his assistance.*

MILCHA. I am here, my Love.

ARIEL. Thou art free! Welcome, my dear! What shall we do? Say, say, what shall we do?

PROSPERO. Be subject to no sight but mine, invisible to every eye-ball else. Hence with diligence, anon thou shalt know more.

[*They both fly up and cross in the air.*

Thou hast slept well my Child. [*To* Miranda.

MIRANDA. The sadness of your story put heaviness in me.

PROSPERO. Shake it off; come on, I'll now call *Caliban*, my slave, who never yields us a kind answer.

MIRANDA. 'Tis a creature, Sir, I do not love to look on.

PROSPERO. But as 'Tis, we cannot miss him; he does make our fire, fetch in our wood, and serve in offices that profit us: what hoa! Slave! *Caliban*! Thou earth thou, speak.

CALIBAN. [*Within*] There's wood enough within.

PROSPERO. Thou poisonous slave, got by the Devil himself upon thy wicked dam, come forth.

[*Enter* Caliban.

CALIBAN. As wicked dew, as e'r my mother brush'd with raven's feather from unwholesome fens, drop on you both: a south-west blow on you, and blister you all o'r.

PROSPERO. For this be sure, to night thou shalt have cramps, side-stitches, that shall pen thy breath up; urchins[34] shall prick thee till thou bleed'st: thou shalt be pinch'd as thick as honey-combs, each pinch more stinging than the bees which made 'em.

CALIBAN. I must eat my dinner: this island's mine by *Sycorax* my mother, which thou took'st from me. When thou cam'st first, thou stroak'st me, and mad'st much of me, wouldst give me water with berries in't, and teach me how to name the bigger light, and how the less, that burn by day and night; and then I lov'd thee, and shew'd thee all the qualities of the isle, the fresh-springs, brine-pits, barren places, and fertile. Curs'd be I, that I did so: all the charms of *Sycorax,* toads, beetles, bats, light on thee, for I am all the subjects that thou hast. I first was mine own lord; and here thou stay'st me in this hard rock, whiles thou dost keep from me the rest o'th' island.

PROSPERO. Thou most lying slave, whom stripes may move, not kindness: I have us'd thee (filth that thou art) with humane care, and lodg'd thee in mine own cell, till thou didst seek to violate the honour of my children.

CALIBAN. Oh ho, Oh ho, would't had been done: thou didst prevent me, I had peopl'd else this isle with *Calibans.*

PROSPERO. Abhor'd Slave!
Who ne'r would any print of goodness take, being capable of all ill: I pity'd thee, took pains to make thee speak, taught thee each hour one thing or other; when thou didst not (Savage) know thy own meaning, but wouldst gabble, like a thing most brutish, I endow'd thy purposes with words which made them known: but thy wild race (though thou didst learn) had that in't, which good natures could not abide to be with: therefore wast thou deservedly pent up into this rock.

CALIBAN. You taught me language, and my profit by it is, that I know to curse: the red botch rid you for learning me your language.

PROSPERO. Hag-seed hence!
Fetch us in fewel, and be quick
To answer other business: shrugst thou (malice)
If thou neglectest, or dost unwillingly what I command,
I'll wrack thee with old cramps, fill all thy bones with
Aches, make thee roar, that beasts shall tremble
At thy din.

CALIBAN. No prethee!
I must obey. His art is of such power,
It would controul my dam's god, *Setebos,*
And make a vassal of him.

PROSPERO. So Slave, hence. [*Exeunt* Prospero *and* Caliban *severally.*

[*Enter* Dorinda.

DORINDA. Oh Sister! What have I beheld?

MIRANDA. What is it moves you so?

DORINDA. From yonder rock,
As I my eyes cast down upon the seas,
The whistling winds blew rudely on my face,
And the waves roar'd! At first I thought the war
Had been between themselves, but straight I spy'd
A huge great creature.

MIRANDA. O you mean the ship.

DORINDA. Is't not a creature then? It seem'd alive.

MIRANDA. But what of it?

DORINDA. This floating ram did bear his horns above;
All ty'd with ribbands, ruffling in the wind;
Sometimes he nodded down his head a while,
And then the waves did heave him to the moon;
He clamb'ring to the top of all the billows,
And then again he curtsy'd down so low,
I could not see him: till, at last, all side-long
With a great crack his belly burst in pieces.

MIRANDA. There all had perish'd,
Had not my father's magick art reliev'd them.
But, Sister, I have stranger news to tell you;
In this great creature there were other creatures,
And shortly we may chance to see that thing,
Which you have heard my father call, a man.

DORINDA. But what is that? For yet he never told me.

MIRANDA. I know no more than you: but I have heard

My father say we women were made for him.

DORINDA. What, that he should eat us, Sister?

MIRANDA. No sure, you see my father is a man, and yet
He does us good. I would he were not old.

DORINDA. Me thinks indeed it would be finer, if we two
Had two young fathers.

MIRANDA. No Sister, no, if they were young, my father
Said, that we must call them brothers.

DORINDA. But pray how does it come, that we two are not brothers then, and have not beards like him?

MIRANDA. Now I confess you pose me.

DORINDA. How did he come to be our father too?

MIRANDA. I think he found us when we both were little, and grew within the ground.

DORINDA. Why could he not find more of us? Pray, Sister, let you and I look up and down one day, to find some little ones for us to play with.

MIRANDA. Agreed; but now we must go in. This is the hour
Wherein my father's charm will work,
Which seizes all who are in open air:
Th' effect of his great art I long to see,
Which will perform as much as magick can.

DORINDA. And I, methinks, more long to see a man.

Act II. Scene I.

[*The scene changes to the wilder part of the island, 'tis compos'd of divers sorts of trees, and barren places, with a prospect of the sea at a great distance.*]

[*Enter* Stephano, Mustacho, Ventoso.

VENTOSO. The runlet[35] of brandy was a loving runlet, and floated after us out of pure pity.

MUSTACHO. This kind bottle, like an old acquaintance, swam after it. And this scollop-shell is all our plate now.

VENTOSO. 'Tis well we have found something since we landed.
I prethee fill a soop,[36] and let it go round.
Where hast thou laid the runlet?

MUSTACHO. I'th' hollow of an old tree.

VENTOSO. Fill apace,
We cannot live long in this barren island, and we may
Take a soop before death, as well as others drink
At our funerals.

MUSTACHO. This is prize-brandy, we steal custom, and it costs nothing. Let's have two rounds more.

VENTOSO. Master, what have you sav'd?

STEPHANO. Just nothing but my self.

VENTOSO. This works comfortably on a cold stomach.

STEPHANO. Fill's another round.

VENTOSO. Look! *Mustacho* weeps. Hang losses, as long as we have brandy left. Prithee leave weeping.

STEPHANO. He sheds his brandy out of his eyes: he shall drink no more.

MUSTACHO. This will be a doleful day with old *Bess*. She gave me a gilt nutmeg at parting. That's lost too. But, as you say, hang losses. Prithee fill again.

VENTOSO. Beshrew thy heart for putting me in mind of thy wife,
I had no thought of mine else, Nature will shew it self,
I must melt. I prithee fill again, my wife's a good old jade,
And has but one eye left: but she'll weep out that too,
When she hears that I am dead.

STEPHANO. Would you were both hang'd for putting me in thought of mine.

VENTOSO. But come, Master, sorrow is dry! There's for you again.

STEPHANO. A mariner had e'en as good be a fish as a man, but for the comfort we get ashore: O for an old dry wench now I am wet.

MUSTACHO. Poor heart! That would soon make you dry again: but all is barren in this isle: here we may lie at hull[37] till the wind blow nore and by south, ere we can cry, a sail, a sail, at sight of a white apron. And therefore here's another soop to comfort us.

VENTOSO. This isle's our own, that's our comfort, for the Duke, the Prince, and all their train are perished.

MUSTACHO. Our ship is sunk, and we can never get home again: we must e'en turn salvages,[38] and the next that catches his fellow may eat him.

VENTOSO. No, no, let us have a government; for if we live well and orderly, Heav'n will drive shipwracks ashore to make us all rich; therefore let us carry good consciences, and not eat one another.[39]

STEPHANO. Whoever eats any of my subjects, I'll break out his teeth with my scepter: for I was Master at sea, and will be Duke on land: you *Mustacho* have been my Mate, and shall be my Vice-Roy.

VENTOSO. When you are Duke, you may choose your Vice-Roy; but I am a free subject in a new plantation, and will have no Duke without my voice. And so fill me the other soop.

STEPHANO. [*Whispering*] *Ventoso*, dost thou hear, I will advance thee, prithee give me thy voice.

VENTOSO. I'll have no whisperings to corrupt the election; and to show that I have no private ends, I declare aloud that I will be Vice-Roy, or I'll keep my voice for my self.

MUSTACHO. *Stephano*, hear me, I will speak for the people, because there are few, or rather none in the isle to speak for themselves. Know then, that to prevent the farther shedding of Christian blood, we are all content *Ventoso* shall be Vice-Roy, upon condition I may be Vice-Roy over him. Speak good people, are you well agreed? What, no man answer? Well, you may take their silence for consent.

VENTOSO. You speak for the people, *Mustacho*? I'll speak for 'em, and declare generally with one voice, one and all; that there shall be no Vice-Roy but the Duke, unless I be he.

MUSTACHO. You declare for the people who never saw your face! Cold iron shall decide it. [*Both draw.*

STEPHANO. Hold, loving subjects: we will have no civil war during our reign: I do hereby appoint you both to be my Vice-Roys over the whole island.

BOTH. Agreed! Agreed!

[*Enter* Trincalo *with a great bottle, half drunk.*

VENTOSO. How! *Trincalo* our brave Bosen!

MUSTACHO. He reels: can he be drunk with sea-water?

TRINCALO. [*Sings.*
I shall no more to sea, to sea,
Here I shall die ashore.
This is a very scurvy tune to sing at a man's funeral,
But here's my comfort. [*Drinks.*
[*Sings.*
The Master, the Swabber, the Gunner, and I,
The Surgeon, and his Mate,
Lov'd *Mall*, *Meg*, and *Marrian*, and *Margery*,
But none of us car'd for *Kate*.
For she had a tongue with a tang,
Wou'd cry to a sailor, go hang:
She lov'd not the savour of tar nor of pitch,
Yet a tailor might scratch her where ere she did itch.
This is a scurvy tune too, but here's my comfort again. [*Drinks.*

STEPHANO. We have got another subject now; welcome, welcome into our dominions!

TRINCALO. What subject, or what dominions? Here's old sack,[40] boys: the king of good fellows can be no subject.
I will be Old *Simon* the King.

MUSTACHO. Hah, old Boy! How didst thou scape?

TRINCALO. Upon a butt of sack, Boys, which the sailors
Threw overboard: but are you alive, hoa! For I will
Tipple with no ghosts till I'm dead: thy hand *Mustacho*,
And thine *Ventoso*; the storm has done its worst:
Stephano alive too! Give thy Bosen thy hand, Master.

VENTOSO. You must kiss it then, for, I must tell you, we have chosen him Duke in a full assembly.

TRINCALO. A Duke! Where? What's he Duke of?

MUSTACHO. Of this island, man. Oh *Trincalo*, we are all made, the island's empty; all's our own, Boy; and we will speak to his Grace for thee, that thou may'st be as great as we are.

TRINCALO. You great? What the Devil are you?

VENTOSO. We two are Vice-Roys over all the island; and when we are weary of governing, thou shalt succeed us.

TRINCALO. Do you hear, *Ventoso*, I will succeed you in both your places before you enter into 'em.

STEPHANO. *Trincalo,* sleep and be sober; and make no more uproars in my country.

TRINCALO. Why, what are you, Sir, what are you?

STEPHANO. What I am, I am by free election, and you *Trincalo*, are not your self; but we pardon your first fault, because it is the first day of our reign.

TRINCALO. Umph, were matters carried so swimmingly against me, whilst I was swimming, and saving my self for the good of the people of this island.

MUSTACHO. Art thou mad, *Trincalo*? Wilt thou disturb a settled government, where thou art a meer stranger to the laws of the country?

TRINCALO. I'll have no laws.

VENTOSO. Then civil war begins. [Ventoso, Mustacho *draw*.

STEPHANO. Hold, hold, I'll have no blood shed,
My subjects are but few; let him make a rebellion
By himself; and a rebel, I Duke *Stephano* declare him:
Vice-Roys, come away.

TRINCALO. And Duke *Trincalo* declares, that he will make open war where ever he meets thee or thy Vice-Roys [*Exit* Stephano, Mustacho, Ventuso.

[*Enter* Caliban *with wood upon his back.*

TRINCALO. Hah! Whom have we here?

CALIBAN. All the infections that the sun sucks up from fogs, fens, flats, on *Prospero* fall, and make him by inch-meal a disease: his spirits hear me, and yet I needs must curse, but they'll not pinch, fright me with urchin shows, pitch me i'th' mire, nor lead me in the dark out of my way, unless he bid 'em: but for every trifle he sets them on me; sometimes like baboons they mow and chatter at me, and often bite me; like hedgehogs then they mount their prickles at me, tumbling before me in my barefoot way. Sometimes I am all wound about with adders, who with their cloven tongues hiss me to madness. Hah! Yonder stands one of his spirits to torment me.

TRINCALO. What have we here, a man, or a fish?
This is some monster of the isle, were I in *England*,
As once I was, and had him painted;
Not a holy-day fool there but would give me
Six-pence for the sight of him; well, if I could make
Him tame, he were a present for an emperour.
Come hither, pretty Monster, I'll do thee no harm.
Come hither!

CALIBAN. Torment me not;
I'll bring thee wood home faster.

TRINCALO. He talks none of the wisest, but I'll give him
A dram o'th' bottle, that will clear his understanding.
Come on your ways, Master Monster, open your mouth.
How now, you perverse Moon-calf! What,
I think you cannot tell who is your friend!
Open your chops, I say. [*Pours wine down his throat.*

CALIBAN. This is a brave god, and bears celestial liquor, I'll kneel to him.

TRINCALO. He is a very hopeful monster; Monster, what say'st thou, art thou content to turn civil and sober, as I am? For then thou shalt be my subject.

CALIBAN. I'll swear upon that bottle to be true; for the liquor is not earthly: did'st thou not drop from Heaven?

TRINCALO. Only out of the moon, I was the man in her when time was. By this light, a very shallow monster.

CALIBAN. I'll shew thee every fertile inch i'th' isle, and kiss thy foot: I prithee be my god, and let me drink. [*Drinks again.*

TRINCALO. Well drawn, Monster, in good faith.

CALIBAN. I'll shew thee the best springs, I'll pluck thee berries,
I'll fish for thee, and get thee wood enough:
A curse upon the tyrant whom I serve, I'll bear him no more sticks, but follow thee.

TRINCALO. The poor monster is loving in his drink.

CALIBAN. I prithee let me bring thee where crabs grow,
And I with my long nails, will dig thee pignuts,
Shew thee a jay's nest, and instruct thee how to snare
The marmazet;[41] I'll bring thee to cluster'd filberds;
Wilt thou go with me?

TRINCALO. This monster comes of a good natur'd race;
Is there no more of thy kin in this island?

CALIBAN. Divine, here is but one besides my self;
My lovely sister, beautiful and bright as the full moon.

TRINCALO. Where is she?

CALIBAN. I left her clambring up a hollow oak,

And plucking thence the dropping honey-combs.
Say, my King, shall I call her to thee?
TRINCALO. She shall swear upon the bottle too.
If she proves handsome she is mine: here, Monster,
Drink again for thy good news; thou shalt speak
A good word for me. [*Gives him the bottle.*
CALIBAN. Farewell, old Master, farewell, farewell.
[*Sings*] No more dams I'll make for fish,
Nor fetch in firing at requiring,
Nor scrape trencher, nor wash dish,
Ban, Ban, *Cackaliban*
Has a new master, get a new man.
Heigh-day! Freedom, freedom!
TRINCALO. Here's two subjects got already, the monster,
And his sister: well, Duke *Stephano,* I say, and say again,
Wars will ensue, and so I drink. [*Drinks.*
From this worshipful monster, and Mistress, Monster his sister,
I'll lay claim to this island by alliance:
Monster, I say thy sister shall be my spouse:
Come away, Brother Monster, I'll lead thee to my butt,
And drink her health. [*Exeunt.*

Scene II.

[*Cypress trees and cave.*]

[*Enter* Prospero *alone.*

PROSPERO. 'Tis not yet fit to let my daughters know I kept
The infant Duke of *Mantua* so near them in this isle,
Whose father dying, bequeath'd him to my care;
Till my false brother (when he design'd t'usurp
My dukedom from me) expos'd him to that fate
He meant for me. By calculation of his birth
I saw death threatning him, if, till some time were
Past, he should behold the face of any woman:
And now the danger's nigh: *Hippolito*!

[*Enter* Hippolito.

HIPPOLITO. Sir, I attend your pleasure.
PROSPERO. How I have loved thee from thy infancy,
Heav'n knows, and thou thy self canst bear me witness,
Therefore accuse not me for thy restraint.
HIPPOLITO. Since I knew life, you've kept me in a rock,
And you this day have hurri'd me from thence,
Only to change my prison, not to free me.
I murmur not, but I may wonder at it.
PROSPERO. O gentle Youth, Fate waits for thee abroad,
A black star threatens thee, and death unseen
Stands ready to devour thee.
HIPPOLITO. You taught me not to fear him in any of his shapes:
Let me meet death rather than be a prisoner.
PROSPERO. 'Tis pity he should seize thy tender youth.
HIPPOLITO. Sir, I have often heard you say, no creature liv'd
Within this isle, but those which man was lord of;
Why then should I fear?
PROSPERO. But here are creatures which I nam'd not to thee, Who share man's sovereignty by Nature's laws,
And oft depose him from it.
HIPPOLITO. What are those creatures, Sir?
PROSPERO. Those dangerous enemies of men call'd women.
HIPPOLITO. Women! I never heard of them before.
What are women like?
PROSPERO. Imagine something between young men and angels:
Fatally beauteous, and have killing eyes,
Their voices charm beyond the nightingales,
They are all enchantment, those who once behold 'em,
Are made their slaves for ever.
HIPPOLITO. Then I will wink and fight with 'em.
PROSPERO. 'Tis but in vain,
They'll haunt you in your very sleep.

HIPPOLITO. Then I'll revenge it on 'em when I wake.

PROSPERO. You are without all possibility of revenge,
They are so beautiful, that you can ne'r attempt,
Nor wish to hurt them.

HIPPOLITO. Are they so beautiful?

PROSPERO. Calm sleep is not so soft, nor winter suns,
Nor summer shades so pleasant.

HIPPOLITO. Can they be fairer than the plumes of swans?
Or more delightful than the peacock's feathers?
Or than the gloss upon the necks of doves?
Or have more various beauty than the rainbow?
These I have seen, and without danger wondred at.

PROSPERO. All these are far below 'em: Nature made
Nothing but woman dangerous and fair:
Therefore if you should chance to see 'em,
Avoid 'em straight, I charge you.

HIPPOLITO. Well, since you say they are so dangerous,
I'll so far shun 'em as I may with safety of the
Unblemish'd honour which you taught me.
But let 'em not provoke me, for I'm sure I shall
Not then forbear them.

PROSPERO. Go in and read the book I gave you last.
Tomorrow I may bring you better news.

HIPPOLITO. I shall obey you, Sir. [*Exit* Hippolito.

PROSPERO. So, so; I hope this lesson has secur'd him,
For I have been constrain'd to change his lodging
From yonder rock where first I bred him up,
And here have brought him home to my own cell,
Because the shipwrack happen'd near his mansion.
I hope he will not stir beyond his limits,
For hitherto he hath been all obedience.
The planets seem to smile on my designs,
And yet there is one sullen cloud behind,
I would it were disperst.

[*Enter* Miranda *and* Dorinda.

How, my daughters! I thought I had instructed
Them enough: Children! Retire;
Why do you walk this way?

MIRANDA. It is within our bounds, Sir.

PROSPERO. But both take heed, that path is very dangerous.
Remember what I told you.

DORINDA. Is the man that way, Sir?

PROSPERO. All that you can imagine is ill there,
The curled lion, and the rugged bear,
Are not so dreadful as that man.

MIRANDA. Oh me, why stay we here then?

DORINDA. I'll keep far enough from his den, I warrant him.

MIRANDA. But you have told me, Sir, you are a man;
And yet you are not dreadful.

PROSPERO. *I* Child! But *I* am a tame man; old men are tame
By nature, but all the danger lies in a wild
Young man.

DORINDA. Do they run wild about the woods?

PROSPERO. No, they are wild within doors, in chambers,
And in closets.[42]

DORINDA. But, Father, I would stroak 'em and make 'em gentle, then sure they would not hurt me.

PROSPERO. You must not trust them, Child: no woman can come
Near 'em, but she feels a pain, full nine months.
Well, *I* must in; for new affairs require my
Presence: be you, *Miranda*, your sister's guardian.

[*Exit* Prospero.

DORINDA. Come, Sister, shall we walk the other way?
The man will catch us else: we have but two legs,
And he perhaps has four.

MIRANDA. Well, Sister, though he have; yet look about you,
And we shall spy him ere he comes too near us.

DORINDA. Come back, that way is towards his den.

MIRANDA. Let me alone; I'll venture first, for sure he can
Devour but one of us at once.

DORINDA. How dare you venture?

MIRANDA. We'll find him sitting like a hare in's form,[43]
And he shall not see us.

DORINDA. Aye, but you know my father charg'd us both.

MIRANDA. But who shall tell him on't? We'll keep each
Other's counsel.

DORINDA. *I* dare not for the world.

MIRANDA. But how shall we hereafter shun him, if we do not know him first?

DORINDA. Nay, *I* confess *I* would fain see him too. I find it in my nature, because my father has forbid me.

MIRANDA. Aye, there's it, Sister, if he had said nothing, I had been quiet. Go softly, and if you see him first, be quick, and beckon me away.

DORINDA. Well, if he does catch me, I'll humble my self to him,
And ask him pardon, as I do my father,
When I have done a fault.

MIRANDA. And if I can but scape with life, I had rather be in pain nine months, as my father threatn'd, than lose my longing. [*Exeunt. The scene continues, enter* Hippolito.

HIPPOLITO. *Prospero* has often said, that Nature makes
Nothing in vain: why then are women made?
Are they to suck the poison of the earth,
As gaudy colour'd serpents are? I'll ask that
Question, when next I see him here.

[*Enter* Miranda *and* Dorinda *peeping*.

DORINDA. O Sister, there it is, it walks about like one of us.

MIRANDA. Aye, just so, and has legs as we have too.

HIPPOLITO. It strangely puzzles me: yet 'tis most likely
Women are somewhat between men and spirits.

DORINDA. Heark! It talks, sure this is not it my father meant,
For this is just like one of us: methinks I am not half
So much afraid on't as I was; see, now it turns this way.

MIRANDA. Heaven! What a goodly thing it is?

DORINDA. I'll go nearer it.

MIRANDA. O no, 'tis dangerous, Sister! I'll go to it.
I would not for the world that you should venture.
My father charg'd me to secure you from it.

DORINDA. I warrant you this is a tame man, dear Sister,
He'll not hurt me, I see it by his looks.

MIRANDA. Indeed he will! But go back, and he shall eat me first: Fie, are you not asham'd to be so much inquisitive?

DORINDA. You chide me for't, and wou'd give your self.

MIRANDA. Come back, or I will tell my father.
Observe how he begins to stare already.
I'll meet the danger first, and then call you.

DORINDA. Nay, Sister, you shall never vanquish me in kindness.
I'll venture you, no more than you will me.

PROSPERO. [*Within*] *Miranda*, Child, where are you!

MIRANDA. Do you not hear my father call? Go in.

DORINDA. 'Twas you he nam'd, not me; I will but say my prayers,
And follow you immediately.

MIRANDA. Well, Sister, you'll repent it. [*Exit* Miranda.

DORINDA. Though I die for't, I must have th'other peep.

HIPPOLITO. [*Seeing her*] What thing is that? Sure 'tis some infant of the sun, dress'd in his father's gayest beams, and comes to play with birds: my sight is dazl'd, and yet I find I'm loth to shut my eyes.
I must go nearer it – but stay a while;
May it not be that beauteous murderer, woman,
Which I was charg'd to shun? Speak, what art thou?
Thou shining vision!

DORINDA. Alas, I know not; but I'm told I am a woman;
Do not hurt me, pray, fair thing.

HIPPOLITO. I'd sooner tear my eyes out, than consent to do you any harm; though I was told a woman was my enemy.

DORINDA. I never knew what 'twas to be an enemy, nor can I ere prove so to that which looks like you: for though I have been charg'd by him (whom yet I never disobey'd) to shun your presence, yet I'd rather die than lose it; therefore I hope you will not have the heart to hurt me: though I fear you are a man, that dangerous thing of which I have been warn'd. Pray tell me what you are?

HIPPOLITO. I must confess, I was inform'd I am a man,
But if I fright you, I shall wish I were some other creature.
I was bid to fear you too.

DORINDA. Ay me! Heav'n grant we be not poison to each other!
Alas, can we not meet but we must die?

HIPPOLITO. I hope not so! For when two poisonous creatures,
Both of the same kind, meet, yet neither dies.
I've seen two serpents harmless to each other,
Though they have twin'd into a mutual knot:
If we have any venome in us, sure, we cannot be more
Poisonous, when we meet, than serpents are.
You have a hand like mine, may I not gently touch it? [*Takes her hand.*

DORINDA. I've touch'd my father's and my sister's hands,
And felt no pain; but now, alas! There's something,
When I touch yours, which makes me sigh: just so
I've seen two turtles mourning when they met;
Yet mine's a pleasing grief; and so me thought was theirs;
For still they mourn'd, and still they seem'd to murmur too,
And yet they often met.

HIPPOLITO. Oh Heavens! I have the same sense too: your hand
Methinks goes through me; I feel at my heart,
And find it pleases, though it pains me.

PROSPERO. [*Within*] *Dorinda*!

DORINDA. My father calls again; ah, I must leave you.

HIPPOLITO. Alas, I'm subject to the same command.

DORINDA. This is my first offence against my father,
Which he, by severing us, too cruelly does punish.

HIPPOLITO. And this is my first trespass too: but he hath more
Offended truth than we have him:
He said our meeting would destructive be,
But I no death but in our parting see.
[*Exeunt several ways.*

Scene III.

[*A wild island.*]

[*Enter* Alonzo, Antonio, Gonzalo.

GONZALO. Beseech your Grace be merry; you have cause, so have we all, of joy, for our strange 'scape: then wisely, good Sir, weigh our sorrow with our comfort.

ALONZO. Prithee peace, you cram these words into my ears, against my stomach; how can I rejoyce, when my dear son, perhaps this very moment, is made a meal to some strange fish?

ANTONIO. Sir, he may live, I saw him beat the billows under him, and ride upon their backs; I do not doubt he came alive to land.

ALONZO. No, no, he's gone; and you and I, *Antonio*, were those who caus'd his death.

ANTONIO. How could we help it?

ALONZO. Then, then we should have help'd it, when thou betrayedst thy brother *Prospero*, and *Mantua*'s infant sovereign to my power; and when I, too ambitious, took by force another's right; then lost we *Ferdinand*; then forfeited our navy to this tempest.

ANTONIO. Indeed we first broke truce with Heaven; you to the waves an infant prince expos'd, and on the waves have lost an only son; I did usurp my brother's fertile lands, and now am cast upon this desart isle.

GONZALO. These, Sirs, 'tis true, were crimes of a black dye, but both of you have made amends to Heav'n by your late voyage into *Portugal*; where, in defence of Christianity, your valour has repuls'd the Moors of *Spain*.

ALONZO. O name it not *Gonzalo*;
No act but penitence can expiate!
Must we teach Heaven what price to set on murder! What rate on lawless power, and wild ambition! Or dare we traffick with the powers above, and sell by weight a good deed for a bad?
[*A flourish of Musick.*[44]

GONZALO. Musick! And in the air! Sure we are shipwrack'd on the dominions of some merry devil!

ANTONIO. This isle's inchanted ground; for I have heard swift voices flying by my ear, and groans of lamenting ghosts.

ALONZO. I pull'd a tree, and blood pursu'd my hand.
Heaven deliver me from this dire place, and all the after actions of my life shall mark my penitence and my bounty. [*Musick again louder.*
Hark, the sounds approach us. [*The stage opens in several places.*

ANTONIO. Lo the earth opens to devour us quick.
These dreadful horrors, and the guilty sense of my foul treason, have unmann'd me quite.

ALONZO. We on the brink of swift destruction stand;
No means of our escape is left.

[*Another flourish of voices under the stage.*

ANTONIO. Ah! What amazing sounds are these we hear!

GONZALO. What horrid masque will the dire fiends present?

[*Sing under the stage.*

1. DEVIL. Where does the black fiend Ambition reside,
With the mischievous Devil of Pride?

2. DEVIL. In the lowest and darkest caverns of Hell
Both Pride and Ambition does dwell.

1. DEVIL. Who are the chief Leaders of the damned Host?

3. DEVIL. Proud monarchs, who tyrannize most.

1. DEVIL. Damned princes there
The worst of torments bear;

3. DEVIL. Who in earth all others in pleasures excel,
Must feel the worst torments of Hell.

[*They rise singing this chorus.*

ANTONIO. Oh Heav'ns! What horrid vision's this?
How they upbraid us with our crimes!

ALONZO. What fearful vengeance is in store for us!

1. DEVIL. Tyrants by whom their subjects bleed,
Should in pains all others exceed;

2. DEVIL. And barb'rous monarchs who their neighbours invade,
And their crowns unjustly get;
And such who their brothers to death have betray'd,
In Hell upon burning thrones shall be set.

3. DEVIL. – In Hell, in Hell with flames they shall reign,

CHOR. And for ever, for ever shall suffer the pain.

ANTONIO. Oh my soul; for ever, for ever shall suffer the pain.

ALONZO. Has Heav'n in all its infinite stock of mercy
No overflowings for us? Poor miserable, guilty men!

GONZALO. Nothing but horrors do encompass us!
For ever, for ever must we suffer!

ALONZO. For ever we shall perish! O dismal words, for ever!

1. DEVIL. Who are the pillars of the tyrant's court?

2. DEVIL. Rapine and murder his crown must support!

3. DEVIL. His cruelty does tread
On orphans' tender breasts, and brothers dead!

2. DEVIL. Can Heav'n permit such crimes should be
Attended with felicity?

1. DEVIL. No tyrants their scepters do easily bear,
In the midst of their guards they their consciences fear.

2. DEVIL. Care their minds when they wake unquiet will keep,

CHOR. And we with dire visions disturb all their sleep.

ANTONIO. Oh horrid sight! How they stare upon us!
The Fiends will hurry us to the dark mansion.
Sweet Heav'n, have mercy on us!

1. DEVIL. Say, say, shall we bear these bold mortals from hence?

2. DEVIL. No, no, let us show their degrees of offence.

3. DEVIL. Let's muster their crimes up on every side,
And first let's discover their pride.

[*Enter* Pride.

PRIDE. Lo here is Pride who first led them astray,
And did to ambition their minds then betray.

[*Enter* Fraud.

FRAUD. And Fraud does next appear,
Their wandring steps who led,
When they from Vertue fled,
They in my crooked paths their course did steer.

[*Enter* Rapine.

RAPINE. From Fraud to force they soon arrive,
Where Rapine did their actions drive.

[*Enter* Murder.

MURDER. There long they could not stay;
Down the steep hill they run,
And to perfect the mischief which they had begun,
To Murder they bent all their way.

CHORUS OF ALL. Around, around we pace,
About this cursed place;
While thus we compass in
These mortals and their sin. [*Devils vanish.*
ANTONIO. Heav'n has heard me, they are vanish'd!
ALONZO. But they have left me all unmann'd.
I feel my sinews slacken with the fright;
And a cold sweat trills down o'r all my limbs,
As if I were dissolving into water.
Oh, *Prospero*, my crimes 'gainst thee sit heavy on my heart!
ANTONIO. And mine 'gainst him and young *Hippolito*.
GONZALO. Heav'n have mercy on the penitent.
ALONZO. Lead from this cursed ground;
The seas in all their rage are not so dreadful.
This is the region of despair and death.
GONZALO. Shall we not seek some food?
ALONZO. Beware all fruit, but what the birds have pecked. The shadows of the trees are poisonous too: a secret venom slides from every branch! My conscience does distract me! O my son! Why do I speak of eating or repose, before I know thy fortune?

[*As they are going out, a devil rises just before them, at which they start, and are frighted.*

ALONZO. O Heavens! Yet more apparitions!

[*Devil sings.*

Arise, arise! Ye subterranean winds,
More to disturb their guilty minds.
And all ye filthy damps and vapours rise,
Which use t'infect the Earth, and trouble all the skies,
Rise you, from whom devouring plagues have birth:
You that i' th' vast and hollow womb of Earth,
Engender earthquakes, make whole countreys shake,
And stately cities into desarts turn;
And you who feed the flames by which Earth's entrails burn.
Ye raging winds, whose rapid force can make
All but the fix'd and solid centre shake:
Come drive these wretches to that part o' th' isle,
Where Nature never yet did smile:
Cause fogs & storms, whirlwinds & earthquakes there:
There let 'em houl and languish in despair.
Rise and obey the pow'rful Prince o' th' Air.

[*Two winds rise, ten more enter and dance. At the end of the dance, three winds sink, the rest drive* Alonzo, Antonio, Gonzalo *off.*

Act III. Scene I.

[*Enter* Ferdinand, *and* Ariel *and* Milcha *invisible.*]

ARIEL'S SONG

Come unto these yellow sands,
And then take hands,
Curtsy'd when you have, and kiss'd;
The wild waves whist.
Foot it featly here and there,
And sweet sprights the burthen bear.
Hark! Hark!
Bow waugh, the watch-dogs bark,
Bow waugh. Hark! Hark! I hear
The strain of strutting Chanticleer,
Cry, cock a doodle do.

FERDINAND. Where should this musick be? I'th' air, or earth? It sounds no more, and sure it waits upon some god i' th' island; sitting on a bank, weeping against the Duke; my father's wrack'd; this musick hover'd on the waters, allaying both their fury and my passion with charming airs. Thence I have follow'd it (or it hath drawn me rather) but 'tis gone: no, it begins again.

MILCHA. [*Sings.*
Full fathom five thy father lies,
Of his bones is coral made:
Those are pearls that were his eyes,
Nothing of him that does fade,
But does suffer a sea-change
Into something rich and strange:
Sea nymphs hourly ring his knell;
Hark! Now I hear 'em, ding dong bell.

FERDINAND. This mournful ditty mentions my drown'd father. This is no mortal business, nor a sound which the earth owns . . . I hear it now before me; however I will on and follow it.

[*Exit* Ferdinand *following* Ariel.

Scene II.

[*The Cypress-trees and Cave. Enter* Prospero *and* Miranda.]

PROSPERO. Excuse it not, *Miranda*, for to you (the elder, and I thought the more discreet) I gave the conduct of your sister's actions.

MIRANDA. Sir, when you call'd me thence, I did not fail to mind her of her duty to depart.

PROSPERO. How can I think you did remember hers, when you forgot your own? Did you not see the man whom I commanded you to shun?

MIRANDA. I must confess I saw him at a distance.

PROSPERO. Did not his eyes infect and poison you?
What alteration found you in your self?

MIRANDA. I only wondred at a sight so new.

PROSPERO. But have you no desire once more to see him?
Come, tell me truly what you think of him?

MIRANDA. As of the gayest thing I ever saw, so fine that it appear'd more fit to be belov'd than fear'd, and seem'd so near my kind, that I did think I might have call'd it sister.

PROSPERO. You do not love it?

MIRANDA. How is it likely that I should, except the thing had first lov'd me?

PROSPERO. Cherish those thoughts; you have a gen'rous soul;
And since I see your mind not apt to take the light
Impressions of a sudden love, I will unfold
A secret to your knowledge.
That creature which you saw, is of a kind which
Nature made a prop and guide to yours.

MIRANDA. Why did you then propose him as an object of terrour to my mind? You never us'd to teach me any thing but god-like truths, and what you said, I did believe as sacred.

PROSPERO. I fear'd the pleasing form of this young man
Might unawares possess your tender breast,
Which for a nobler guest I had design'd;
For shortly, my *Miranda*, you shall see another of this kind,
The full blown flower, of which this youth was but the
Op'ning bud. Go in, and send your sister to me.

MIRANDA. Heav'n still preserve you, Sir. [*Exit* Miranda.

PROSPERO. And make thee fortunate.

[*Enter* Dorinda.

PROSPERO. O, come hither, you have seen a man to day,
Against my strict command.

DORINDA. Who I? Indeed I saw him but a little, Sir.

PROSPERO. Come, come, be clear. Your sister told me all.

DORINDA. Did she? Truly she would have seen him more than I,
But that I would not let her.

PROSPERO. Why so?

DORINDA. Because, methought, he would have hurt me less
Than he would her. But if I knew you'd not be angry
With me, I could tell you, Sir, that he was much to blame.

PROSPERO. Hah! Was he to blame?
Tell me, with that sincerity I taught you, how you became so bold to see the man?

DORINDA. I hope you will forgive me, Sir, because I did not see him much till he saw me. Sir, he would needs come in my way, and star'd, and star'd upon my face; and so I thought I would be reveng'd of him, and therefore I gaz'd on him as long; but if I ere come near a man again –

PROSPERO. I told you he was dangerous; but you would not be warn'd.

DORINDA. Pray be not angry, Sir, if I tell you, you are mistaken in him; for he did me no great hurt.

PROSPERO. But he may do you more harm hereafter.

DORINDA. No, Sir, I'm as well as ever I was in all my life,
But that I cannot eat nor drink for thought of him.
That dangerous man runs ever in my mind.

PROSPERO. The way to cure you, is no more to see him.

DORINDA. Nay pray, Sir, say not so, I promis'd him
To see him once again; and you know, Sir,
You charg'd me I should never break my promise.

PROSPERO. Wou'd you see him who did you so much mischief?

DORINDA. I warrant you I did him as much harm as he did me;
For when I left him, Sir, he sigh'd so as it griev'd
My heart to hear him.
PROSPERO. Those sighs were poisonous, they infected you:
You say, they griev'd you to the heart.
DORINDA. 'Tis true; but yet his looks and words were gentle.
PROSPERO. These are the day-dreams of a maid in love.
But still I fear the worst.
DORINDA. O fear not him, Sir,
PROSPERO. You speak of him with too much passion; tell me
(And on your duty tell me true, *Dorinda*)
What past betwixt you and that horrid creature?
DORINDA. How, horrid, Sir? If any else but you should call it so, indeed I should be angry.
PROSPERO. Go to! You are a foolish girl; but answer to what I ask, what thought you when you saw it?
DORINDA. At first it star'd upon me, and seem'd wild,
And then I trembled, yet it look'd so lovely, that when
I would have fled away, my feet seem'd fasten'd to the ground,
Then it drew near, and with amazement ask'd
To touch my hand; which, as a ransom for my life,
I gave: but when he had it, with a furious gripe
He put it to his mouth so eagerly, I was afraid he
Would have swallow'd it.
PROSPERO. Well, what was his behaviour afterwards?
DORINDA. He on a sudden grew so tame and gentle,
That he became more kind to me than you are;
Then, Sir, I grew I know not how, and touching his hand
Again, my heart did beat so strong, as I lack'd breath
To answer what he ask'd.
PROSPERO. You have been too fond, and I should chide you for it.
DORINDA. Then send me to that creature to be punish'd.
PROSPERO. Poor Child! Thy passion, like a lazy ague
Has seiz'd thy blood, instead of striving, thou humour'st
And feed'st thy languishing disease: thou fight'st
The battels of thy enemy, and 'tis one part of what
I threatn'd thee, not to perceive thy danger.
DORINDA. Danger, Sir?
If he would hurt me, yet he knows not how:
He hath no claws, nor teeth, nor horns to hurt me,
But looks about him like a callow-bird
Just straggl'd from the nest: pray trust me, Sir,
To go to him again.
PROSPERO. Since you will venture,
I charge you bear your self reserv'dly to him,
Let him not dare to touch your naked hand,
But keep at distance from him.
DORINDA. This is hard.
PROSPERO. It is the way to make him love you more;
He will despise you if you grow too kind.
DORINDA. I'll struggle with my heart to follow this,
But if I lose him by it, will you promise
To bring him back again?
PROSPERO. Fear not, *Dorinda*;
But use him ill, and he'll be yours for ever.
DORINDA. I hope you have not couzen'd me again.
[*Exit* Dorinda.
PROSPERO. Now my designs are gathering to a head.
My spirits are obedient to my charms.
What, *Ariel*! My servant *Ariel*, where art thou?

[*Enter* Ariel.

ARIEL. What wou'd my potent Master? Here I am.
PROSPERO. Thou and thy meaner fellows your last service
Did worthily perform, and I must use you in such another
Work: how goes the day?
ARIEL. On the fourth, my Lord, and on the sixth, you said our work should cease.
PROSPERO. And so it shall;
And thou shalt have the open air at freedom.
ARIEL. Thanks, my great Lord.
PROSPERO. But tell me first, my Spirit,
How fares the Duke, my brother, and their followers?

ARIEL. Confin'd together, as you gave me order,
In the lime grove which weather-fends your cell;
Within that circuit up and down they wander,
But cannot stir one step beyond their compass.
PROSPERO. How do they bear their sorrows?
ARIEL. The two Dukes appear like men distracted, their
Attendants brim-full of sorrow mourning over 'em;
But chiefly, he you term'd the good *Gonzalo*:
His tears run down his beard, like winter drops
From eaves of reeds, your vision did so work 'em,
That if you now behold 'em, your affections
Would become tender.
PROSPERO. Do'st thou think so, Spirit?
ARIEL. Mine would, Sir, were I humane.
PROSPERO. And mine shall:
Hast thou, who art but air, a touch, a feeling of their
Afflictions, and shall not I (a man like them, one
Who as sharply relish passions as they) be kindlier
Mov'd than thou art? Though they have pierc'd
Me to the quick with injuries, yet with my nobler
Reason 'gainst my fury I will take part;
The rarer action is in virtue than in vengeance.
Go, my *Ariel*, refresh with needful food their
Famish'd bodies. With shows and cheerful
Musick comfort 'em.
ARIEL. Presently, Master.
PROSPERO. With a twinkle, *Ariel*. But stay, my spirit;
What is become of my slave *Caliban*,
And *Sycorax* his sister?
ARIEL. Potent Sir!
They have cast off your service, and revolted
To the wrack'd mariners, who have already
Parcell'd your island into governments.
PROSPERO. No matter, I have now no need of 'em.
But, Spirit, now I stay thee on the wing;
Haste to perform what I have given in charge:
But see they keep within the bounds I set 'em.
ARIEL. I'll keep 'em in with walls of adamant,
Invisible as air to mortal eyes,
But yet unpassable.
PROSPERO. Make haste then. [*Exeunt severally.*

Scene III.

[*Wild island. Enter* Alonzo, Antonio, Gonzalo.

GONZALO. I am weary, and can go no further, Sir.
ALONZO. Old Lord, I cannot blame thee, who am my self seiz'd
With a weariness to the dulling of my spirits: [*They sit.*
Even here I will put off my hope, and keep it no longer
For my flatterers: he is drown'd whom thus we
Stray to find.
I'm faint with hunger, and must despair
Of food. [*Musick without.*
What! Harmony again, my good friends, heark!
ANTONIO. I fear some other horrid apparition.
Give us kind keepers, Heaven I beseech thee!
GONZALO. 'Tis chearful musick, this, unlike the first.

[Ariel *and* Milcha *invisible, sing.*

Dry those eyes which are o'r flowing,
All your storms are over-blowing:
While you in this isle are biding,
You shall feast without providing:
Every dainty you can think of,
Ev'ry wine which you would drink of,
Shall be yours; all want shall shun you,
Ceres' blessing so is on you.
ALONZO. This voice speaks comfort to us.
ANTONIO. Wou'd 'twere come; there is no musick in a song
To me, my stomach being empty.
GONZALO. O for a heavenly vision of boyl'd,
Bak'd, and roasted!

[*Dance of fantastic spirits, after the dance, a table furnish'd with meat and fruits is brought in by two spirits.*

ANTONIO. My Lord, the Duke, see yonder.

A table, as I live, set out and furnish'd
With all varieties of meats and fruits.

ALONZO. 'Tis so indeed, but who dares taste this feast,
Which fiends provide, perhaps, to poison us?

GONZALO. Why that dare I; if the black Gentleman be so ill-natur'd, he may do his pleasure.

ANTONIO. 'Tis certain we must either eat or famish;
I will encounter it, and feed.

ALONZO. If both resolve, I will adventure too.

GONZALO. The Devil may fright me, yet he shall not starve me. [*Two spirits descend, and flie away with the table.*

ALONZO. Heav'n! Behold, it is as you suspected: 'tis vanish'd.
Shall we be always haunted with these fiends?

ANTONIO. Here we shall wander till we famish.

GONZALO. Certainly one of you was so wicked as to say grace:
This comes on't, when men will be godly out of season.

ANTONIO. Yonder's another table, let's try that – [*Exeunt.*

[*Enter* Trincalo *and* Caliban.

TRINCALO. Brother Monster, welcome to my private palace.
But where's thy sister, is she so brave a lass?

CALIBAN. In all this isle there are but two more, the daughters of the tyrant *Prospero*; and she is bigger than 'em both. O here she comes; now thou may'st judge thy self, my Lord.

[*Enter* Sycorax.

TRINCALO. She's monstrous fair indeed. Is this to be my spouse? Well, she's heir of all this isle (for I will geld Monster). The *Trincalos*, like other wise men, have anciently us'd to marry for estate more than for beauty.

SYCORAX. I prithee let me have the gay thing about thy neck, and that which dangles at thy wrist. [Sycorax *points to his bosens whistle, and his bottle.*

TRINCALO. My dear Blobber-lips; this, observe my Chuck, is a badge of my sea-office; my fair Fuss, thou dost not know it.

SYCORAX. No, my dread Lord.

TRINCALO. It shall be a whistle for our first babe, and when the next shipwrack puts me again to swimming, I'll dive to get a coral[45] to it.

SYCORAX. I'll be thy pretty child, and wear it first.

TRINCALO. I prithee, sweet Baby, do not play the wanton, and cry for my goods e'r I'm dead. When thou art my widow, thou shalt have the Devil and all.

SYCORAX. May I not have the other fine thing?

TRINCALO. This is a sucking-bottle for young *Trincalo*.

CALIBAN. Shall she not taste of that immortal liquor?

TRINCALO. Umph! That's another question: for if she be thus flipant in her water, what will she be in her wine?

[*Enter* Ariel *(invisible) and changes the bottle which stands upon the ground.*

ARIEL. There's water for your wine. [*Exit* Ariel.

TRINCALO. Well! Since it must be so. [*Gives her the bottle. She drinks.*
How do you like it now, my Queen that must be?

SYCORAX. Is this your heavenly liquor? I'll bring you to a river of the same.

TRINCALO. Wilt thou so, Madam Monster? What a mighty prince shall I be then? I would not change my dukedom to be great Turk *Trincalo*.

SYCORAX. This is the drink of frogs.

TRINCALO. Nay, if the frogs of this island drink such, they are the merriest frogs in Christendom.

CALIBAN. She does not know the virtue of this liquor:
I prithee let me drink for her.

TRINCALO. Well said, Subject Monster. [Caliban *drinks.*

CALIBAN. My Lord, this is meer water.

TRINCALO. 'Tis thou hast chang'd the wine then, and drunk it up,
Like a debauch'd fish as thou art. Let me see't,
I'll taste it my self. Element! Meer element! As I live.
It was a cold gulp, such as this, which kill'd my famous
Predecessor, old *Simon* the King.

CALIBAN. How does thy honour? Prithee be not angry, and I will lick thy shoe.

TRINCALO. I could find in my heart to turn thee out of my dominions for a liquorish monster.

CALIBAN. O my Lord, I have found it out; this must be done by one of *Prospero*'s spirits.

TRINCALO. There's nothing but malice in these devils, I would it had been holy-water for their sakes.

SYCORAX. 'Tis no matter, I will cleave to thee.

TRINCALO. Lovingly said, in troth: now cannot I hold out against her. This wife-like virtue of hers has overcome me.

SYCORAX. Shall I have thee in my arms?

TRINCALO. Thou shalt have Duke *Trincalo* in thy arms:
But prithee be not too boistrous with me at first;
Do not discourage a young beginner.
[*They embrace.*
Stand to your arms, my Spouse,
And subject monster;

[*Enter* Stephano, Mustacho, *and* Ventuso.

The enemy is come to surprise us in our quarters.
You shall know, Rebels, that I'm marri'd to a witch,
And we have a thousand spirits of our party.

STEPHANO. Hold! I ask a truce! I and my Vice-Roys
(Finding no food, and but a small remainder of brandy)
Are come to treat a peace betwixt us,
Which may be for the good of both armies,
Therefore *Trincalo* disband.

TRINCALO. Plain *Trincalo*, methinks I might have been a duke in your mouth; I'll not accept of your embassy without my title.

STEPHANO. A title shall break no squares betwixt us:
Vice-Roys, give him his style of Duke, and treat with him,
Whilst I walk by in state.

[Ventoso *and* Mustacho *bow, whilst* Trincalo *puts on his cap.*

MUSTACHO. Our Lord and Master, Duke *Stephano*, has sent us
In the first place to demand of you, upon what
Ground you make war against him, having no right
To govern here, as being elected only by
Your own voice.

TRINCALO. To this I answer, that having in the face of the world
Espous'd the lawful Inheritrix of this island,
Queen *Blouze* the first, and having homage done me,
By this hectoring[46] spark her brother, from these two
I claim a lawful title to this island.

MUSTACHO. Who, that Monster? He a Hector?

CALIBAN. Lo! How he mocks me, wilt thou let him, my Lord?

TRINCALO. Vice-Roys! Keep good tongues in your heads,
I advise you, and proceed to your business.

MUSTACHO. First and foremost, as to your claim that you have answer'd.

VENTOSO. But second and foremost, we demand of you,
That if we make a peace, the butt also may be
Comprehended in the treaty.

TRINCALO. I cannot treat with my honour, without your submission.

STEPHANO. I understand, being present, from my embassadors, what your resolution is, and ask an hour's time of deliberation, and so I take our leave; but first I desire to be entertain'd at your butt, as becomes a prince, and his embassadors.

TRINCALO. That I refuse, till acts of hostility be ceas'd.
These rogues are rather spies than embassadors;
I must take heed of my butt. They come to pry
Into the secrets of my Dukedom.

VENTOSO. *Trincalo* you are a barbarous prince, and so farewell. [*Exeunt* Stephano, Mustacho, Ventoso.

TRINCALO. Subject Monster! Stand your sentry before my cellar; my Queen and I will enter, and feast our selves within. [*Exeunt.*

[*Enter* Ferdinand, Ariel *and* Milcha *(invisible).*

FERDINAND. How far will this invisible musician conduct
My steps? He hovers still about me, whether
For good or ill, I cannot tell, nor care I much;
For I have been so long a slave to chance, that
I'm as weary of her flatteries as her frowns,
But here I am –

ARIEL. Here I am.

FERDINAND. Hah! Art thou so? The spirit's turn'd an eccho:
This might seem pleasant, could the burthen of my
Griefs accord with any thing but sighs.
And my last words, like those of dying men,
Need no reply. Fain I would go to shades, where
Few would wish to follow me.

ARIEL. Follow me.

FERDINAND. This evil spirit grows importunate,
But I'll not take his counsel.

ARIEL. Take his counsel.

FERDINAND. It may be the Devil's counsel. I'll never take it.

ARIEL. Take it.

FERDINAND. I will discourse no more with thee,
Nor follow one step further.
ARIEL. One step further.
FERDINAND. This must have more importance than an eccho.
Some spirit tempts to a precipice.
I'll try if it will answer when I sing
My sorrows to the murmurs of this brook.
[*He sings*] Go thy way.
ARIEL. Go thy way.
FERDINAND. Why should'st thou stay?
ARIEL. Why should'st thou stay?
FERDINAND. Where the winds whistle, and where the streams creep,
Under yon willow-tree, fain would I sleep.
Then let me alone,
For 'tis time to be gone.
ARIEL. For 'tis time to be gone.
FERDINAND. What cares or pleasures can be in this isle?
Within this desart place
There lives no humane race;
Fate cannot frown here, nor kind fortune smile.
ARIEL. Kind Fortune smiles, and she
Has yet in store for thee
Some strange felicity.
Follow me, follow me,
And thou shalt see.
FERDINAND. I'll take thy word for once;
Lead on Musician. [*Exeunt and return.*

Scene IV.

[*Scene changes, and discovers* Prospero *and* Miranda.]

PROSPERO. Advance the fringed curtains of thine eyes, and say what thou seest yonder.

MIRANDA. Is it a spirit?
Lord! How it looks about! Sir, I confess it carries a brave form.
But 'tis a spirit.

PROSPERO. No, Girl, it eats and sleeps, and has such senses as we have. This young gallant, whom thou see'st, was in the wrack; were he not somewhat stain'd with grief (beauty's worst canker) thou might'st call him a goodly person; he has lost his company, and strays about to find 'em.

MIRANDA. I might call him a thing divine, for nothing natural I ever saw so noble.

PROSPERO. It goes on as my soul prompts it: Spirit, fine Spirit. I'll free thee within two days for this.

FERDINAND. She's sure the mistress, on whom these airs attend. Fair Excellence, if, as your form declares, you are divine, be pleas'd to instruct me how you will be worship'd; so bright a beauty cannot sure belong to humane kind.

MIRANDA. I am, like you, a mortal, if such you are.

FERDINAND. My language too! O Heavens! I am the best of them who speak this speech, when I'm in my own Country.

PROSPERO. How, the best? What wert thou if the Duke of *Savoy* heard thee?

FERDINAND. As I am now, who wonders to hear thee speak of *Savoy*: he does hear me, and that he does I weep, my self am *Savoy*, whose fatal eyes (e're since at ebb) beheld the Duke my father wrack'd.

MIRANDA. Alack for pity.

PROSPERO. At the first sight they have chang'd eyes, dear *Ariel*,
I'll set thee free for this – young, Sir, a word.
With hazard of your self you do me wrong.

MIRANDA. Why speaks my father so urgently?
This is the third man that e're I saw, the first whom
E're I sigh'd for, sweet Heaven move my father
To be inclin'd my way.

FERDINAND. O! If a virgin! And your affection not gone forth,
I'll make you Mistress of *Savoy*.

PROSPERO. Soft, Sir! One word more.
They are in each other's powers, but this swift
Bus'ness I must uneasie make, lest too light
Winning make the prize light – one word more.
Thou usurp'st the name not due to thee, and hast
Put thy self upon this island as a spy to get the Government from me, the lord of it.

FERDINAND. No, as I'm a man.

MIRANDA. There's nothing ill can dwell in such a temple,
If the evil spirit hath so fair a house,
Good things will strive to dwell with it.
PROSPERO. No more. Speak not you for him, he's a traitor.
Come! Thou art my pris'ner and shalt be in
Bonds. Sea-water shalt thou drink, thy food
Shall be the fresh-brook-muscles, wither'd roots,
And husks, wherein the acorn crawl'd; follow.
FERDINAND. No, I will resist such entertainment
Till my enemy has more power.

[*He draws, and is charm'd from moving.*

MIRANDA. O dear Father! Make not too rash a trial
Of him, for he's gentle and not fearful.
PROSPERO. My child my tutor! Put thy sword up traitor,
Who mak'st a show, but dar'st not strike: thy
Conscience is posses'd with guilt. Come from
Thy ward, for I can here disarm thee with
This wand, and make thy weapon drop.
MIRANDA. Beseech you Father.
PROSPERO. Hence: hang not on my garment.
MIRANDA. Sir, have pity,
I'll be his surety.
PROSPERO. Silence! One word more shall make me chide thee,
If not hate thee: what, an advocate for an
Impostor? Sure thou think'st there are no more
Such shapes as his?
To the most of men this is a *Caliban*,
And they to him are angels.
MIRANDA. My affections are then most humble;
I have no ambition to see a goodlier man.
PROSPERO. Come on, obey:
Thy nerves are in their infancy again, and have
No vigour in them.
FERDINAND. So they are:
My spirits, as in a dream, are all bound up:
My father's loss, the weakness which I feel,
The wrack of all my friends, and this man's threats,
To whom I am subdu'd, would seem light to me,
Might I but once a day through my prison behold this maid:
All corners else o'th' earth let liberty make use of:
I have space enough in such a prison.
PROSPERO. It works: come on.
Thou hast done well, fine *Ariel*: follow me.
Heark what thou shalt more do for me.
[*Whispers* Ariel.
MIRANDA. Be of comfort!
My father's of a better nature, Sir, than he appears by speech: this is unwonted
Which now came from him.
PROSPERO. Thou shalt be as free as mountain winds:
But then exactly do all points of my command.
ARIEL. To a syllable. [*Exit* Ariel.
PROSPERO. [*To* Miranda] Go in that way, speak not a word for him:
I'll separate you. [*Exit* Miranda.
FERDINAND. As soon thou may'st divide the waters
When thou strik'st 'em, which pursue thy bootless blow,
And meet when 'tis past.
PROSPERO. Go practise your philosophy within,
And if you are the same you speak your self,
Bear your afflictions like a prince – that door
Shews you your lodging.
FERDINAND. 'Tis in vain to strive, I must obey. [*Exit* Ferdinand.
PROSPERO. This goes as I would wish it.
Now for my second care, *Hippolito*.
I shall not need to chide him for his fault,
His passion is become his punishment.
Come forth, *Hippolito*.

[*Enter* Hippolito.

HIPPOLITO. [*Entring*] 'Tis Prospero's voice.
PROSPERO. *Hippolito*! I know you now expect I should severely chide you: you have seen a woman in contempt of my commands.
HIPPOLITO. But, Sir, you see I am come off unharm'd;
I told you, that you need not doubt my courage.
PROSPERO. You think you have receiv'd no hurt.
HIPPOLITO. No, none, Sir.
Try me again, when e're you please I'm ready:
I think I cannot fear an army of 'em.
PROSPERO. [*Aside*] *How much in vain it is to bridle Nature!*
Well! What was the success of your encounter?
HIPPOLITO. Sir, we had none, we yielded both at first,
For I took her to mercy, and she me.
PROSPERO. But are you not much chang'd from what you were?

HIPPOLITO. Methinks I wish and wish! For what I know not,
But still I wish – yet if I had that woman,
She, I believe, could tell me what I wish for.

PROSPERO. What wou'd you do to make that woman yours?

HIPPOLITO. I'd quit the rest o'th' world, that I might live alone with
Her, she never should be from me.
We two would sit and look till our eyes ak'd.

PROSPERO. You'd soon be weary of her.

HIPPOLITO. O, Sir, never.

PROSPERO. But you'd grow old and wrinkl'd, as you see me now,
And then you will not care for her.

HIPPOLITO. You may do what you please, but, Sir, we two can never possibly grow old.

PROSPERO. You must, *Hippolito*.

HIPPOLITO. Whether we will or no, Sir, who shall make us?

PROSPERO. Nature, which made me so.

HIPPOLITO. But you have told me her works are various;
She made you old, but she has made us young.

PROSPERO. Time will convince you,
Mean while be sure you tread in honour's paths,
That you may merit her, and that you may not want
Fit occasions to employ your virtue, in this next
Cave there is a stranger lodg'd, one of your kind,
Young, of a noble presence, and as he says himself,
Of princely birth, he is my pris'ner and in deep
Affliction: visit, and comfort him; it will become you.

HIPPOLITO. It is my duty, Sir. [*Exit* Hippolito.

PROSPERO. True, he has seen a woman, yet he lives; perhaps I took the moment of his birth amiss, perhaps my art it self is false: on what strange grounds we build our hopes and fears, man's life is all a mist, and in the dark, our fortunes meet us.
If fate be not, then what can we foresee,
Or how can we avoid it, if it be?
If by free-will in our own paths we move,
How are we bounded by decrees above?
Whether we drive, or whether we are driven,
If ill 'tis ours; if good the act of Heaven. [*Exit* Prospero.

[*Scene, a Cave. Enter* Hippolito *and* Ferdinand.

FERDINAND. Your pity, noble youth, doth much oblige me,
Indeed 'twas sad to lose a father so.

HIPPOLITO. Aye, and an only father too, for sure you said
You had but one.

FERDINAND. [*Aside*] *But one father! He's wondrous simple!*

HIPPOLITO. Are such misfortunes frequent in your world,
Where many men live?

FERDINAND. Such we are born to.
But, gentle Youth, as you have question'd me,
So give me leave to ask you, what you are?

HIPPOLITO. Do not you know?

FERDINAND. How should I?

HIPPOLITO. I well hop'd I was a man, but by your ignorance
Of what I am, I fear it is not so:
Well, *Prospero*! This is now the second time
You have deceiv'd me.

FERDINAND. Sir, there is no doubt you are a man:
But I would know of whence?

HIPPOLITO. Why, of this world, I never was in yours.

FERDINAND. Have you a father?

HIPPOLITO. I was told I had one, and that he was a man, yet I have bin so much deceived, I dare not tell't you for a truth; but I have still been kept a prisoner for fear of women.

FERDINAND. They indeed are dangerous, for since I came I have beheld one here, whose beauty pierc'd my heart.

HIPPOLITO. How did she pierce, you seem not hurt.

FERDINAND. Alas! The wound was made by her bright eyes,
And festers by her absence.
But to speak plainer to you, Sir, I love her.

HIPPOLITO. Now I suspect that love's the very thing, that I feel too! Pray tell me, truly, Sir, are you not grown unquiet since you saw her?

FERDINAND. I take no rest.

HIPPOLITO. Just, just my disease.
Do you not wish you do not know for what?

FERDINAND. O no! I know too well for what I wish.

HIPPOLITO. There, I confess, I differ from you, Sir:
But you desire she may be always with you?

FERDINAND. I can have no felicity without her.

HIPPOLITO. Just my condition! Alas, gentle Sir:
I'll pity you, and you shall pity me.

FERDINAND. I love so much, that if I have her not, I find I cannot live.

HIPPOLITO. How! Do you love her?
And would you have her too? That must not be:
For none but I must have her.

FERDINAND. But perhaps we do not love the same:
All beauties are not pleasing alike to all.

HIPPOLITO. Why are there more fair women, Sir,
Besides that one I love?

FERDINAND. That's a strange question. There are many more besides that beauty which you love.

HIPPOLITO. I will have all of that kind, if there be a hundred of 'em.

FERDINAND. But noble youth, you know not what you say.

HIPPOLITO. Sir, they are things I love, I cannot be without 'em:
O, how I rejoyce! More women!

FERDINAND. Sir, if you love you must be ty'd to one.

HIPPOLITO. Ty'd! How ty'd to her?

FERDINAND. To love none but her.

HIPPOLITO. But, Sir, I find it is against my nature.
I must love where I like, and I believe I may like all,
All that are fair: come; bring me to this woman,
For I must have her.

FERDINAND. – [*Aside*] *His simplicity*
Is such, that I can scarce be angry with him. –
Perhaps, sweet Youth, when you behold her,
You will find you do not love her.

HIPPOLITO. I find already I love, because she is another woman.

FERDINAND. You cannot love two women both at once.

HIPPOLITO. Sure 'tis my duty to love all who do resemble
Her whom I've already seen. I'll have as many as I can,
That are so good, and angel-like, as she I love.
And will have yours.

FERDINAND. Pretty Youth, you cannot.

HIPPOLITO. I can do any thing for that I love.

FERDINAND. I may, perhaps, by force restrain you from it.

HIPPOLITO. Why do so if you can. But either promise me
To love no woman, or you must try your force.

FERDINAND. I cannot help it, I must love.

HIPPOLITO. Well you may love, for *Prospero* taught me friendship too: you shall love me and other men if you can find 'em, but all the angel-women shall be mine.

FERDINAND. I must break off this conference, or he will
Urge me else beyond what I can bear.
Sweet Youth! Some other time we will speak
Further concerning both our loves; at present
I am indispos'd with weariness and grief,
And would, if you are pleas'd, retire a while.

HIPPOLITO. Some other time be it; but, Sir, remember
That I both seek and much intreat your friendship,
For next to women, I find I can love you.

FERDINAND. I thank you, Sir, I will consider of it.
[*Exit* Ferdinand.

HIPPOLITO. This stranger does insult, and comes into my
World to take those heavenly beauties from me,
Which I believe I am inspir'd to love,
And yet he said he did desire but one.
He would be poor in love, but I'll be rich:
I now perceive that *Prospero* was cunning;
For when he frighted me from woman-kind,
Those precious things he for himself design'd.
[*Exit*.

Act IV. Scene I.

[*Cypress trees and cave. Enter* Prospero, *and* Miranda.]

PROSPERO. Your suit has pity in't, and has prevail'd.
Within this cave he lies, and you may see him:
But yet take heed; let prudence be your guide;
You must not stay, your visit must be short.
[*She's going.*
One thing I had forgot; insinuate into his mind
A kindness to that youth, whom first you saw;
I would have friendship grow betwixt 'em.

MIRANDA. You shall be obey'd in all things.

PROSPERO. Be earnest to unite their very souls.

MIRANDA. I shall endeavour it.

PROSPERO. This may secure *Hippolito* from that dark danger which my art forebodes; for friendship does provide a double strength t'oppose th'assaults of fortune. [*Exit* Prospero.

[*Enter* Ferdinand.

FERDINAND. To be a pris'ner where I dearly love, is but a double tye; a link of fortune joyn'd to the chain of love; but not to see her, and yet to be so near her, there's the hardship; I feel my self as on a rack, stretch'd out, and nigh the ground, on which I might have ease, yet cannot reach it.

MIRANDA. Sir! My Lord! Where are you?

FERDINAND. Is it your voice, my Love? Or do I dream?

MIRANDA. Speak softly, it is I.

FERDINAND. O heavenly Creature! Ten times more gentle than your father's cruel, how, on a sudden, all my griefs are vanish'd!

MIRANDA. How do you bear your prison?

FERDINAND. 'Tis my palace while you are here, and love and silence wait upon our wishes; do but think we chuse it, and 'tis what we would chuse.

MIRANDA. I'm sure what I would.
But how can I be certain that you love me?
Look to't; for I will die when you are false.
I've heard my father tell of maids, who dy'd,
And haunted their false lovers with their ghosts.

FERDINAND. Your ghost must take another form to fright me,
This shape will be too pleasing: do I love you?
O Heav'n! O Earth! Bear witness to this sound,
If I prove false –

MIRANDA. Oh hold, you shall not swear;
For Heav'n will hate you if you prove forsworn.

FERDINAND. Did I not love, I could no more endure this undeserved captivity, than I could wish to gain my freedom with the loss of you.

MIRANDA. I am a fool to weep at what I'm glad of: but I have a suit to you, and that, Sir, shall be now the only trial of your love.

FERDINAND. Y'ave said enough, never to be deny'd, were it my life; for you have far o'rebid the price of all that humane life is worth.

MIRANDA. Sir, 'tis to love one for my sake, who for his own deserves all the respect which you can ever pay him.

FERDINAND. You mean your father: do not think his usage can make me hate him; when he gave you being, he then did that which cancell'd all these wrongs.

MIRANDA. I meant not him, for that was a request, which if you love, I should not need to urge.

FERDINAND. Is there another whom I ought to love?
And love him for your sake?

MIRANDA. Yes such a one, who, for his sweetness and his goodly shape (if I, who am unskill'd in forms, may judge) I think can scarce be equall'd: 'tis a youth, a stranger too as you are.

FERDINAND. Of such a graceful feature, and must I for your sake love?

MIRANDA. Yes, Sir, do you scruple to grant the first request I ever made? He's wholly unacquainted with the world, and wants your conversation. You should have compassion on so meer a stranger.

FERDINAND. Those need compassion whom you discommend, not whom you praise.

MIRANDA. Come, you must love him for my sake: you shall.

FERDINAND. Must I for yours, and cannot for my own?
Either you do not love, or think that I do not:
But when you bid me love him, I must hate him.

MIRANDA. Have I so far offended you already,
That he offends you only for my sake?
Yet sure you would not hate him, if you saw

Him as I have done, so full of youth and beauty.

FERDINAND. – [*Aside*] *O poison to my hopes!* –
When he did visit me, and I did mention this
Beauteous creature to him, he did then tell me
He would have her.

MIRANDA. Alas, what mean you?

FERDINAND. It is too plain: like most of her frail sex, she's false,
But has not learnt the art to hide it;
Nature has done her part, she loves variety:
Why did I think that any woman could be innocent,
Because she's young? No, no, their nurses teach them
Change, when with two nipples they divide their
Liking.

MIRANDA. I fear I have offended you, and yet I meant no harm;
But if you please to hear me – [*A noise within.*
Heark, Sir! Now I am sure my father comes, I know
His steps; dear Love, retire a while, I fear
I've stay'd too long.

FERDINAND. Too long indeed and yet not long enough: Oh jealousie!
Oh Love! How you distract me?
[*Exit* Ferdinand.

MIRANDA. He appears displeas'd with that young man, I know
Not why; but, till I find from whence his hate proceeds,
I must conceal it from my father's knowledge,
For he will think that guiltless I have caus'd it;
And suffer me no more to see my Love.

[*Enter* Prospero.

PROSPERO. Now I have been indulgent to your wish,
You have seen the prisoner?

MIRANDA. Yes.

PROSPERO. And he spake to you?

MIRANDA. He spoke; but he receiv'd short answers from me.

PROSPERO. How like you his converse?

MIRANDA. At second sight
A man does not appear so rare a creature.

PROSPERO. – [*Aside*] *I find she loves him much because she hides it.*
Love teaches cunning even to innocence. –
Well go in.

MIRANDA. [*Aside*] *Forgive me, truth, for thus disguising thee; if I can make him think I do not love the stranger much, he'll let me see him oftner.* [*Exit* Miranda.

PROSPERO. Stay! Stay – I had forgot to ask her what she has said
Of young *Hippolito*:

[*Enter* Hippolito *and* Dorinda.

Oh! Here he comes! And with him
My *Dorinda*. I'll not be seen, let
Their loves grow in secret. [*Exit* Prospero.

HIPPOLITO. But why are you so sad?

DORINDA. But why are you so joyful?

HIPPOLITO. I have within me all, all the various musick of
The woods. Since last I saw you, I have heard brave news!
I'll tell you, and make you joyful for me.

DORINDA. Sir, when I saw you first, I through my eyes drew
Something in, I know not what it is;
But still it entertains me with such thoughts
As makes me doubtful whether joy becomes me.

HIPPOLITO. Pray believe me;
As I'm a man, I'll tell you blessed news.
I have heard there are more women in the world,
As fair as you are too.

DORINDA. Is this your news? You see it moves not me.

HIPPOLITO. And I'll have 'em all.

DORINDA. What will become of me then?

HIPPOLITO. I'll have you too.
But are not you acquainted with these women?

DORINDA. I never saw but one.

HIPPOLITO. Is there but one here?
This is a base poor world, I'll go to th'other;
I've heard men have abundance of 'em there.
But pray where is that one woman?

DORINDA. Who, my sister?

HIPPOLITO. Is she your sister? I'm glad o'that: you shall help me to her, and I'll love you for't. [*Offers to take her hand.*

DORINDA. Away! I will not have you touch my hand.
– [*Aside*] *My father's counsel which enjoyn'd reservedness,*
Was not in vain, I see.

HIPPOLITO. What makes you shun me?

DORINDA. You need not care, you'll have my sister's hand.

HIPPOLITO. Why, must not he who touches hers, touch yours?
DORINDA. You mean to love her too.
HIPPOLITO. Do not you love her?
Then why should not I do so?
DORINDA. She is my sister, and therefore I must love her:
But you cannot love both of us.
HIPPOLITO. I warrant you I can.
Oh that you had more sisters!
DORINDA. You may love her, but then I'll not love you.
HIPPOLITO. O but you must;
One is enough for you, but not for me.
DORINDA. My sister told me she had seen another;
A man like you, and she lik'd only him;
Therefore if one must be enough for her,
He is that one, and then you cannot have her.
HIPPOLITO. If she like him, she may like both of us.
DORINDA. But how if I should change and like that man?
Would you be willing to permit that change?
HIPPOLITO. No, for you lik'd me first.
DORINDA. So you did me.
HIPPOLITO. But I would never have you see that man;
I cannot bear it.
DORINDA. I'll see neither of you.
HIPPOLITO. Yes, me you may, for we are now acquainted;
But he's the man of whom your father warn'd you:
O! He's a terrible, huge, monstrous creature,
I am but a woman to him.
DORINDA. I will see him.
Except you'll promise not to see my sister.
HIPPOLITO. Yes, for your sake I must needs see your sister.
DORINDA. But, she would eat me; therefore take heed.
HIPPOLITO. I heard that she was fair, and like you.
DORINDA. No, indeed, she's like my father, with a great beard,
'Twould fright you to look on her,
Therefore that man and she may go together,
They are fit for no body but one another.
HIPPOLITO. [*Looking in*] Yonder he comes with glaring eyes, fly! Fly! Before he sees you.
DORINDA. Must we part so soon?
HIPPOLITO. Y'are a lost woman if you see him.
DORINDA. I would not willingly be lost, for fear you
Should not find me. I'll avoid him. [*Exit* Dorinda.
HIPPOLITO. She fain would have deceived me, but I know her
Sister must be fair, for she's a woman;
All of a kind that I have seen are like to one
Another: all the creatures of the rivers and
The woods are so.

[*Enter* Ferdinand.

FERDINAND. O! Well encounter'd, you are the happy man!
Y'have got the hearts of both the beauteous women.
HIPPOLITO. How! Sir? Pray, are you sure on't?
FERDINAND. One of 'em charg'd me to love you for her sake.
HIPPOLITO. Then I must have her.
FERDINAND. No, not till I am dead.
HIPPOLITO. How dead? What's that? But whatsoe'r it be, I long to have her.
FERDINAND. Time and my grief may make me die.
HIPPOLITO. But for a friend you should make haste; I ne'r ask'd
Any thing of you before.
FERDINAND. I see your ignorance;
And therefore will instruct you in my meaning.
The woman, whom I love, saw you and lov'd you.
Now, Sir, if you love her you'll cause my death.
HIPPOLITO. Be sure I'll do it then.
FERDINAND. But I am your friend;
And I request you that you would not love her.
HIPPOLITO. When friends request unreasonable things,
Sure th'are to be deny'd: you say she's fair,
And I must love all who are fair; for, to tell
You a secret, Sir, which I have lately found
Within my self; they all are made for me.
FERDINAND. That's but a fond conceit: you are made for one, and one for you.
HIPPOLITO. You cannot tell me, Sir,
I know I'm made for twenty hundred women.
(I mean if there so many be i'th' world)
So that if once I see her I shall love her.
FERDINAND. Then do not see her.
HIPPOLITO. Yes, Sir, I must see her.
For I wou'd fain have my heart beat again,
Just as it did when I first saw her sister.
FERDINAND. I find I must not let you see her then.
HIPPOLITO. How will you hinder me?

FERDINAND. By force of arms.
HIPPOLITO. By force of arms?
My arms perhaps may be as strong as yours.
FERDINAND. He's still so ignorant that I pity him, and fain
Would avoid force: pray, do not see her, she was
Mine first; you have no right to her.
HIPPOLITO. I have not yet consider'd what is right, but, Sir,
I know my inclinations are to love all women:
And I have been taught that to dissemble what I
Think is base. In honour then of truth, I must
Declare that I do love, and I will see your woman.
FERDINAND. Wou'd you be willing I should see and love your
Woman, and endeavour to seduce her from that
Affection which she vow'd to you?
HIPPOLITO. I wou'd not you should do it, but if she should
Love you best, I cannot hinder her.
But, Sir, for fear she shou'd, I will provide against
The worst, and try to get your woman.
FERDINAND. But I pretend no claim at all to yours;
Besides you are more beautiful than I,
And fitter to allure unpractis'd hearts.
Therefore I once more beg you will not see her.
HIPPOLITO. I'm glad you let me know I have such beauty.
If that will get me women, they shall have it
As far as ere 'twill go: I'll never want 'em.
FERDINAND. Then since you have refused this act of friendship,
Provide your self a sword; for we must fight.
HIPPOLITO. A sword, what's that?
FERDINAND. Why such a thing as this.
HIPPOLITO. What should I do with it?
FERDINAND. You must stand thus, and push against me,
While I push at you, till one of us fall dead.
HIPPOLITO. This is brave sport;
But we have no swords growing in our world.
FERDINAND. What shall we do then to decide our quarrel?
HIPPOLITO. We'll take the sword by turns, and fight with it.
FERDINAND. Strange ignorance! You must defend your life,
And so must I: but since you have no sword,
Take this; for in a corner of my cave
[*Gives him his sword.*
I found a rusty one; perhaps 'twas his who keeps
Me pris'ner here: that I will fit:
When next we meet, prepare your self to fight.
HIPPOLITO. Make haste then, this shall ne'r be yours again.
I mean to fight with all the men I meet, and
When they are dead, their women shall be mine.
FERDINAND. I see you are unskillful; I desire not to take
Your life, but, if you please, we'll fight on
These conditions; he who first draws blood,
Or who can take the other's weapon from him,
Shall be acknowledg'd as the conquerour,
And both the women shall be his.
HIPPOLITO. Agreed,
And ev'ry day I'll fight for two more with you.
FERDINAND. But win these first.
HIPPOLITO. I'll warrant you I'll push you. [*Exeunt severally.*

Scene II.

[*The wild island. Enter* Trincalo, Caliban, Sycorax.

CALIBAN. My Lord, I see 'em coming yonder.
TRINCALO. Whom?
CALIBAN. The starv'd Prince, and his two thirsty subjects,
That would have our liquor.
TRINCALO. If thou wert a monster of parts, I would make thee
My Master of Ceremonies, to conduct 'em in.
The Devil take all dunces, thou hast lost a brave
Employment by not being a linguist, and for want
Of behaviour.
SYCORAX. My Lord, shall I go meet 'em? I'll be kind to all of 'em,
Just as I am to thee.
TRINCALO. No, that's against the fundamental laws of my dukedom: you are in a high place, Spouse, and must give good example. Here they come, we'll put on the gravity of statesmen, and be very dull, that we may be held wise.

[*Enter* Stephano, Ventoso, Mustacho.

VENTOSO. Duke *Trincalo*, we have consider'd.
TRINCALO. Peace, or war?
MUSTACHO. Peace, and the butt.
STEPHANO. I come now as a private person, and promise to live peaceably under your government.
TRINCALO. You shall enjoy the benefits of peace; and the first fruits of it, amongst all civil nations, is to be drunk for joy: *Caliban*, skink[47] about.
STEPHANO. [*Aside*] *I long to have a rowse*[48] *to her Grace's health, and to the Haunse in Kelder, or rather Haddock in Kelder,*[49] *for I guess it will be half fish.*
TRINCALO. Subject *Stephan*, here's to thee; and let old quarrels be drown'd in this draught. [*Drinks.*
STEPHANO. Great Magistrate, here's thy sisters' health to thee. [*Drinks to* Caliban.
SYCORAX. He shall not drink of that immortal liquor,
My Lord, let him drink water.
TRINCALO. O Sweet Heart, you must not shame your self to day.
Gentlemen Subjects, pray bear with her good huswifry:
She wants a little breeding, but she's hearty.

MUSTACHO. *Ventoso*, here's to thee. Is it not better to pierce the butt, than to quarrel and pierce one another's bellies?
VENTOSO. Let it come, Boy.
TRINCALO. Now wou'd I lay greatness aside, and shake my heels, if I had but musick.
CALIBAN. O my Lord! My mother left us in her will a hundred spirits to attend us, devils of all sorts, some great roaring devils, and some little singing sprights.
SYCORAX. Shall we call? And thou shalt hear them in the air.
TRINCALO. I accept the motion: let us have our mother-in-law's legacy immediately.
CALIBAN. [*Sings.*
We want musick, we want mirth,
Up, Dam, and cleave the earth,
We have now no lords that wrong us,
Send thy merry sprights among us.
TRINCALO. What a merry tyrant am I, to have my musick and pay nothing for't?

[*A table rises, and four spirits with wine and meat enter, placing it, as they dance, on the table: the dance ended, the bottles vanish, and the table sinks again.*

VENTOSO. The bottle's drunk.
MUSTACHO. Then the bottle's a weak shallow fellow, if it be drunk first.
TRINCALO. *Stephano*, give me thy hand,
Thou hast been a rebel, but here's to thee, [*Drinks.*
Prithee why should we quarrel? Shall I swear
Two oaths? By bottle, and by butt I love thee:
In witness whereof I drink soundly.
STEPHANO. Your Grace shall find there's no love lost,
For I will pledge you soundly.
TRINCALO. Thou hast been a false rebel, but that's all one;
Pledge my Grace faithfully.
Caliban,
Go to the butt, and tell me how it sounds:
Peer *Stephano*, dost thou love me?
STEPHANO. I love your Grace, and all your princely family.
TRINCALO. 'Tis no matter if thou lov'st me; hang my family:

Thou art my friend, prithee tell me what
Thou think'st of my princess?

STEPHANO. I look on her, as on a very noble princess.

TRINCALO. Noble? Indeed she had a witch to her mother, and the witches are of great families in *Lapland*, but the Devil was her father, and I have heard of the Mounsor *De-Viles* in *France*; but look on her beauty, is she a fit wife for Duke *Trincalo*? Mark her behaviour too, she's tippling yonder with the serving-men.

STEPHANO. An please your Grace, she's somewhat homely, but that's no blemish in a princess. She is virtuous.

TRINCALO. Umph! Virtuous! I am loth to disparage her;
But thou art my friend, canst thou be close?

STEPHANO. As a stopt bottle, an't please your Grace.

[*Enter* Caliban *again with a bottle.*

TRINCALO. Why then I'll tell thee, I found her an hour ago under an elder-tree, upon a sweet bed of nettles, singing Tory, Rory, and Ranthum, Scantum, with her own natural brother.

STEPHANO. O Jew! Make love in her own tribe?

TRINCALO. But 'tis no matter, to tell thee true, I marri'd her to be a great man, and so forth: but make no words on't, for I care not who knows it, and so here's to thee again, give me the bottle, *Caliban*! Did you knock the butt? How does it sound?

CALIBAN. It sounds as though it had a noise within.

TRINCALO. I fear the butt begins to rattle in the throat and is departing: give me the bottle. [*Drinks.*

MUSTACHO. A short life and a merry, I say. [Stephano *whispers* Sycorax.

SYCORAX. But did he tell you so?

STEPHANO. He said you were as ugly as your mother, and that he marri'd you only to get possession of the island.

SYCORAX. My mother's devils fetch him for't.

STEPHANO. And your father's too, hem! Skink about his Grace's health again. O if you will but cast an eye of pity upon me –

SYCORAX. I will cast two eyes of pity on thee, I love thee more than haws, or black-berries, I have a hoard of wildings[50] in the moss, my brother knows not of 'em; but I'll bring thee where they are.

STEPHANO. *Trincalo* was but my man when time was.

SYCORAX. Wert thou his god, and didst thou give him liquor?

STEPHANO. I gave him brandy and drunk sack my self; wilt thou leave him, and thou shalt be my princess?

SYCORAX. If thou canst make me glad with this liquor.

STEPHANO. I warrant thee we'll ride into the country where it grows.

SYCORAX. How wilt thou carry me thither?

STEPHANO. Upon a hackney-devil of thy mother's.

TRINCALO. What's that you will do? Hah! I hope you have not betray'd me? How does my Pigs-nye? [*To* Sycorax.

SYCORAX. Be gone! Thou shalt not be my lord, thou say'st I'm ugly.

TRINCALO. Did you tell her so – hah! He's a rogue, do not believe him, Chuck.

STEPHANO. The foul words were yours: I will not eat 'em for you.

TRINCALO. I see if once a rebel, then ever a rebel. Did I receive thee into grace for this? I will correct thee with my royal hand. [*Strikes* Stephano.

SYCORAX. Dost thou hurt my love? [*Flies at* Trincalo.

TRINCALO. Where are our guards? Treason! Treason! [Ventuso, Mustacho, Caliban *run betwixt.*

VENTOSO. Who took up arms first, the prince or the people?

TRINCALO. This false traitor has corrupted the wife of my bosom. [*Whispers* Mustacho *hastily.*
Mustacho, strike on my side, and thou shalt be my Vice-Roy.

MUSTACHO. I'm against rebels! *Ventoso*, obey your Vice-Roy.

VENTOSO. You a Vice-Roy? [*They two fight off from the rest.*

STEPHANO. Hah! Hector Monster! Do you stand neuter?

CALIBAN. Thou would'st drink my liquor, I will not help thee.

SYCORAX. 'Twas his doing that I had such a husband, but I'll claw him. [Sycorax *and* Caliban *fight,* Sycorax *beating him off the stage.*

TRINCALO. The whole nation is up in arms, and shall I stand idle? [Trincalo *beats off* Stephano *to the door. Exit* Stephano.
I'll not pursue too far,
For fear the enemy should rally again and surprise my butt in the cittadel; well, I must be rid of my Lady, *Trincalo*, she will be in the fashion else; first cuckold her husband, and then sue for a separation, to get alimony. [*Exit.*

Scene III.

[*The cypress-trees and cave. Enter* Ferdinand, Hippolito *(with their swords drawn).*]

FERDINAND. Come, Sir, our cave affords no choice of place,
But the ground's firm and even: are you ready?
HIPPOLITO. As ready as your self, Sir.
FERDINAND. You remember on what conditions we must fight?
Who first receives a wound is to submit.
HIPPOLITO. Come, come, this loses time; now for the
women, Sir. [*They fight a little,* Ferdinand *hurts him.*
FERDINAND. Sir, you are wounded.
HIPPOLITO. No.
FERDINAND. Believe your blood.
HIPPOLITO. I feel no hurt, no matter for my blood.
FERDINAND. Remember our conditions.
HIPPOLITO. I'll not leave, till my sword hits you too. [Hippolito *presses on,* Ferdinand *retires and wards.*
FERDINAND. I'm loth to kill you, you are unskillful, Sir.
HIPPOLITO. You beat aside my sword, but let it come as near
As yours, and you shall see my skill.
FERDINAND. You faint for loss of blood, I see you stagger,
Pray, Sir, retire.
HIPPOLITO. No! I will ne'r go back –
Methinks the cave turns round, I cannot find –
FERDINAND. Your eyes begin to dazle.
HIPPOLITO. Why do you swim so, and dance about me?
Stand but still till I have made one thrust.
[Hippolito *thrusts and falls.*
FERDINAND. O help, help, help!
Unhappy man! What have I done?
HIPPOLITO. I'm going to a cold sleep, but when I wake,
I'll fight again. Pray stay for me. [*Swounds.*
FERDINAND. He's gone! He's gone! O stay, sweet lovely Youth!
Help, help!

[*Enter* Prospero.

PROSPERO. What dismal noise is that?
FERDINAND. O see, Sir, see!
What mischief my unhappy hand has wrought.
PROSPERO. Alas! How much in vain doth feeble art endeavour
To resist the will of Heaven? [*Rubs* Hippolito.
He's gone for ever; O thou cruel son of an
Inhumane father! All my designs are ruin'd
And unravell'd by this blow.
No pleasure now is left me but revenge.
FERDINAND. Sir, if you knew my innocence –
PROSPERO. Peace, peace,
Can thy excuses give me back his life?
What *Ariel*! Sluggish spirit, where art thou?

[*Enter* Ariel.

ARIEL. Here, at thy beck, my Lord.
PROSPERO. Aye, now thou com'st, when fate is past and not to be
Recall'd. Look there, and glut the malice of
Thy nature, for as thou art thy self, thou
Canst not be but glad to see young virtue
Nipt i'th' blossom.
ARIEL. My Lord, the *Being* high above can witness I am not glad; we airy spirits are not of a temper
So malicious as the earthy,
But of a nature more approaching good.
For which we meet in swarms, and often combat
Betwixt the confines of the air and earth.
PROSPERO. Why did'st thou not prevent, at least foretell,
This fatal action then?
ARIEL. Pardon, great Sir,
I meant to do it, but I was forbidden
By the ill genius of *Hippolito*,
Who came and threaten'd me if I disclos'd it,
To bind me in the bottom of the sea,
Far from the light some regions of the air,
(My native fields) above a hundred years.
PROSPERO. I'll chain thee in the north for thy neglect,
Within the burning bowels of Mount *Heila*,
I'll singe thy airy wings with sulph'rous flames,
And choak thy tender nostrils with blew smoak,
At ev'ry hick-up of the belching mountain,
Thou shalt be lifted up to taste fresh air,
And then fall down again.

ARIEL. Pardon, dread Lord.
PROSPERO. No more of pardon than just Heav'n intends thee
Shalt thou e'r find from me: hence! Fly with speed,
Unbind the charms which hold this murtherer's
Father, and bring him, with my brother, streight
Before me.
ARIEL. Mercy, my potent Lord, and I'll outfly thy thought. [*Exit* Ariel.
FERDINAND. O Heavens! What words are those I heard?
Yet cannot see who spoke 'em: sure the woman
Whom I lov'd was like this, some aiery vision.
PROSPERO. No, Murd'rer, she's, like thee, of mortal mould,
But much too pure to mix with thy black crimes;
Yet she had faults, and must be punish'd for 'em.
Miranda and *Dorinda*! Where are ye?
The will of Heaven's accomplish'd: I have
Now no more to fear, and nothing left to hope,
Now you may enter.

[*Enter* Miranda *and* Dorinda.

MIRANDA. My Love! Is it permitted me to see you once again?
PROSPERO. You come to look your last; I will
For ever take him from your eyes.
But, on my blessing, speak not, nor approach him.
DORINDA. Pray, Father, is not this my sister's man?
He has a noble form; but yet he's not so excellent
As my Hippolito.
PROSPERO. Alas, poor Girl, thou hast no man: look yonder;
There's all of him that's left.
DORINDA. Why, was there ever any more of him?
He lies asleep, Sir, shall I waken him?

[*She kneels by* Hippolito, *and jogs him.*

FERDINAND. Alas! He's never to be wak'd again.
DORINDA. My Love, my Love! Will you not speak to me?
I fear you have displeas'd him, Sir, and now
He will not answer me, he's dumb and cold too,
But I'll run streight, and make a fire to warm him. [*Exit* Dorinda *running.*

[*Enter* Alonzo, Gonzalo, Antonio. Ariel *(invisible).*

ALONZO. Never were beasts so hunted into toils,
As we have been pursu'd by dreadful shapes.
But is not that my son? O *Ferdinand*!
If thou art not a ghost, let me embrace thee.
FERDINAND. My Father! O sinister happiness! Is it
Decreed I should recover you alive, just in that
Fatal hour when this brave youth is lost in death,
And by my hand?
ANTONIO. Heaven! What new wonder's this?
GONZALO. This isle is full of nothing else.
PROSPERO. You stare upon me as
You n'er had seen me; have fifteen years
So lost me to your knowledge, that you retain
No memory of *Prospero*?
GONZALO. The good old Duke of *Millain*!
PROSPERO. I wonder less, that thou, *Antonio*, know'st me not,
Because thou did'st long since forget I was thy brother,
Else I never had been here.
ANTONIO. Shame choaks my words.
ALONZO. And wonder mine.
PROSPERO. For you, usurping Prince, [*To* Alonzo]
Know, by my art, you shipwrack'd on this isle,
Where, after I a while had punish'd you, my vengeance
Wou'd have ended, I design'd to match that son
Of yours, with this my daughter.
ALONZO. Pursue it still, I am most willing to't.
PROSPERO. So am not I. No marriages can prosper
Which are with murderers made; look on that corps,
This, whilst he liv'd, was young *Hippolito*, that
Infant Duke of *Mantua*, Sir, whom you expos'd
With me; and here I bred him up, till that blood-thirsty
Man, that *Ferdinand* –
But why do I exclaim on him, when Justice calls
To unsheath her sword against his guilt?
ALONZO. What do you mean?
PROSPERO. To execute Heaven's laws.
Here I am plac'd by Heav'n, here I am Prince,

Though you have dispossess'd me of my *Millain*.
Blood calls for blood; your *Ferdinand* shall die,
And I, in bitterness, have sent for you,
To have the sudden joy of seeing him alive,
And then the greater grief to see him die.

ALONZO. And think'st thou I, or these will tamely stand,
To view the execution? [*Lays hand upon his sword*.

FERDINAND. Hold, dear Father! I cannot suffer you
T' attempt against his life, who gave her being
Whom I love.

PROSPERO. Nay then appear my guards – I thought no more to
Use their aids; (I'm curs'd because I us'd it)

[*He stamps, and many Spirits appear.*

But they are now the ministers of Heaven,
Whilst I revenge this murder.

ALONZO. Have I for this found thee, my Son, so soon again,
To lose thee? *Antonio*, *Gonzalo*, speak for pity.

FERDINAND. [*To* Miranda] Adieu my fairest Mistress.

MIRANDA. Now I can hold no longer; I must speak.
Though I am loth to disobey you, Sir,
Be not so cruel to the man I love,
Or be so kind to let me suffer with him.

FERDINAND. Recall that pray'r, or I shall wish to live,
Though death be all the mends that I can make.

PROSPERO. This night I will allow you, *Ferdinand*, to fit
You for your death, that cave's your prison.

ALONZO. Ah, *Prospero*! Hear me speak. You are a father,
Look on my age, and look upon his youth.

PROSPERO. No more! All you can say is urg'd in vain,
I have no room for pity left within me.
Do you refuse? Help, *Ariel*, with your fellows
To drive 'em in; *Alonzo* and his son bestow in
Yonder cave, and here *Gonzalo* shall with
Antonio lodge. [*Spirits drive 'em in, as they are appointed*.

[*Enter* Dorinda.

DORINDA. Sir, I have made a fire, shall he be warm'd?

PROSPERO. He's dead, and vital warmth will ne'r return.

DORINDA. Dead, Sir, what's that?

PROSPERO. His soul has left his body.

DORINDA. When will it come again?

PROSPERO. O never, never!
He must be laid in earth, and there consume.

DORINDA. He shall not lie in earth, you do not know
How well he loves me: indeed he'll come again;
He told me he would go a little while,
But promis'd me he would not tarry long.

PROSPERO. He's murder'd by the man who lov'd your sister.
Now both of you may see what 'tis to break
A father's precept; you would needs see men, and by
That sight are made for ever wretched.
Hippolito is dead, and *Ferdinand* must die
For murdering him.

MIRANDA. Have you no pity?

PROSPERO. Your disobedience has so much incens'd me, that
I this night can leave no blessing with you.
Help to convey the body to my couch,
Then leave me to mourn over it alone. [*They bear off the body of* Hippolito.

[*Enter* Miranda*, and* Dorinda *again.* Ariel *behind'em.*

ARIEL. I've been so chid for my neglect by *Prospero*,
That I must now watch all, and be unseen.

MIRANDA. Sister, I say again, 'twas long of you
That all this mischief happen'd.

DORINDA. Blame not me for your own fault, your
Curiosity brought me to see the man.

MIRANDA. You safely might have seen him, and retir'd, but
You wou'd needs go near him, and converse, you may
Remember my father call'd me thence, and I call'd you.

DORINDA. That was your envy, Sister, not your love;
You call'd me thence, because you could not be
Alone with him your self; but I am sure my
Man had never gone to Heaven so soon, but
That yours made him go. [*Crying.*

MIRANDA. Sister, I could not wish that either of 'em shou'd

Go to Heaven without us, but it was his fortune,
And you must be satisfi'd?

DORINDA. I'll not be satisfi'd: my father says he'll make
Your man as cold as mine is now, and when he
Is made cold, my father will not let you strive
To make him warm again.

MIRANDA. In spight of you mine never shall be cold.

DORINDA. I'm sure 'twas he that made me miserable,
And I will be reveng'd. Perhaps you think 'tis
Nothing to lose a man.

MIRANDA. Yes, but there is some difference betwixt
My *Ferdinand*, and your *Hippolito*.

DORINDA. Aye, there's your judgment. Yours is the oldest
Man I ever saw except it were my father.

MIRANDA. Sister, no more. It is not comely in a daughter,
When she says her father's old.

DORINDA. But why do I stay here, whilst my cold Love
Perhaps may want me?
I'll pray my father to make yours cold too.

MIRANDA. Sister, I'll never sleep with you again.

DORINDA. I'll never more meet in a bed with you,
But lodge on the bare ground, and watch my Love.

MIRANDA. And at the entrance of that cave I'll lie,
And eccho to each blast of wind a sigh.

[*Exeunt severally, looking discontentedly on one another.*

ARIEL. Harsh discord reigns throughout this fatal isle,
At which good angels mourn, ill spirits smile;
Old *Prospero*, by his daughters robb'd of rest,
Has in displeasure left 'em both unblest.
Unkindly they abjure each other's bed,
To save the living, and revenge the dead.
Alonzo and his son are pris'ners made,
And good *Gonzalo* does their crimes upbraid.
Antonio and *Gonzalo* disagree,
And wou'd, though in one cave, at distance be.
The seamen all that cursed wine have spent,
Which still renew'd their thirst of government;
And, wanting subjects for the food of pow'r,
Each wou'd to rule alone the rest devour.
The monsters *Sycorax* and *Caliban*,
More monstrous grow by passions learn'd from man.
Even I not fram'd of warring elements,
Partake and suffer in these discontents.
Why shou'd a mortal by enchantments hold
In chains a spirit of aetherial mold?
Accursed magick we our selves have taught,
And our own pow'r has our subjection wrought! [*Exit.*

Act V. Scene I.

[*Enter* Prospero *and* Miranda.]

PROSPERO. You beg in vain; I cannot pardon him,
He has offended Heaven.

MIRANDA. Then let Heaven punish him.

PROSPERO. It will by me.

MIRANDA. Grant him at least some respite for my sake.

PROSPERO. I by deferring justice should incense the Deity
Against my self and you.

MIRANDA. Yet I have heard you say, the powers above are slow in punishing, and shou'd not you resemble them?

PROSPERO. The argument is weak, but I want time
To let you see your errours; retire, and, if you love him,
Pray for him. [*He's going.*

MIRANDA. And can you be his judge and executioner?

PROSPERO. I cannot force *Gonzalo* or my brother, much
Less the father to destroy the son; it must
Be then the monster *Caliban*, and he's not here;
But *Ariel* strait shall fetch him.

[*Enter* Ariel.

ARIEL. My potent Lord, before thou call'st, I come,
To serve thy will.

PROSPERO. Then, Spirit, fetch me here my salvage slave.

ARIEL. My Lord, it does not need.

PROSPERO. Art thou then prone to mischief, wilt thou be thy self the executioner?

ARIEL. Think better of thy aiery minister, who,
For thy fake, unbidden, this night has flown
O'r almost all the habitable world.

PROSPERO. But to what purpose was all thy diligence?

ARIEL. When I was chidden by my mighty Lord for my
Neglect of young *Hippolito,* I went to view
His body, and soon found his soul was but retir'd,
Not sally'd out: then I collected
The best of simples[51] underneath the moon,
The best of balms, and to the wound apply'd
The healing juice of vulnerary[52] herbs.
His only danger was the loss of blood, but now
He's wak'd, my Lord, and just this hour
He must be dress'd again, as I have done it.
Anoint the sword which pierc'd him with this
Weapon-salve, and wrap it close from air till
I have time to visit him again.

PROSPERO. Thou art my faithful servant.
It shall be done, be it your task, *Miranda,* because your
Sister is not present here, while I go visit your
Dear *Ferdinand,* from whom I will a while conceal
This news, that it may be more welcome.

MIRANDA. I obey you, and with a double duty, Sir: for now
You twice have given me life.

PROSPERO. My Ariel, follow me. [*Exeunt severally.*

[Hippolito *discovered on a couch,* Dorinda *by him.*

DORINDA. How do you find your self?

HIPPOLITO. I'm somewhat cold, can you not draw me nearer
To the sun? I am too weak to walk.

DORINDA. My Love, I'll try. [*She draws the chair nearer the audience.*
I thought you never would have walk'd again,
They told me you were gone away to Heaven;
Have you been there?

HIPPOLITO. I know not where I was.

DORINDA. I will not leave till you promise me you
Will not die again.

HIPPOLITO. Indeed I will not.

DORINDA. You must not go to Heav'n unless we go together;
For I've heard my father say, that we must strive
To be each other's guide, the way to it will else
Be difficult, especially to those who are so young.
But I much wonder what it is to die.

HIPPOLITO. Sure 'tis to dream, a kind of breathless sleep,
When once the soul's gone out.

DORINDA. What is the soul?

HIPPOLITO. A small blew thing, that runs about within us.

DORINDA. Then I have seen it in a frosty morning run
Smoaking from my mouth.

HIPPOLITO. But dear Dorinda
What is become of him who fought with me?

DORINDA. O, I can tell you joyful news of him,
My father means to make him die to day,
For what he did to you.

HIPPOLITO. That must not be, my dear *Dorinda*; go and beg your father, he may not die; it was my fault he hurt me, I urg'd him to it first.

DORINDA. But if he live, he'll never leave killing you.

HIPPOLITO. O no! I just remember when I fell asleep, I heard him calling me a great way off, and crying over me as you wou'd do; besides we have no cause of quarrel now.

DORINDA. Pray how began your difference first?

HIPPOLITO. I fought with him for all the women in the world.

DORINDA. That hurt you had was justly sent from Heaven
For wishing to have any more but me.

HIPPOLITO. Indeed I think it was, but I repent it: the fault
Was only in my blood, for now 'tis gone, I find
I do not love so many.

DORINDA. In confidence of this, I'll beg my father, that he
May live; I'm glad the naughty blood, that made
You love so many is gone out.

HIPPOLITO. My Dear, go quickly, lest you come too late.

[*Exit* Dorinda.

Enter Miranda *at the other door, with* Hippolito*'s sword wrapt up.*

HIPPOLITO. Who's this who looks so fair and beautiful, as
Nothing but *Dorinda* can surpass her? O!
I believe it is that angel, woman,
Whom she calls sister.

MIRANDA. Sir, I am sent hither to dress your wound;
How do you find your strength?

HIPPOLITO. Fair Creature, I am faint with loss of blood.

MIRANDA. I'm sorry for't.

HIPPOLITO. Indeed and so am I, for if I had that blood, I then should find a great delight in loving you.

MIRANDA. But, Sir, I am another's, and your love is given already to my sister.

HIPPOLITO. Yet I find that, if you please, I can love still a little.

MIRANDA. I cannot be unconstant, nor shou'd you.

HIPPOLITO. O my wound pains me.

MIRANDA. I am come to ease you. [*She unwraps the sword.*

HIPPOLITO. Alas! I feel the cold air come to me,
My wound shoots worse than ever. [*She wipes and anoints the sword.*

MIRANDA. Does it still grieve you?

HIPPOLITO. Now methinks there's something laid just upon it.

MIRANDA. Do you find no ease?

HIPPOLITO. Yes, yes, upon the sudden all the pain
Is leaving me: sweet Heaven, how I am eas'd!

[*Enter* Ferdinand *and* Dorinda *to them.*

FERDINAND. [*To* Dorinda] Madam, I must confess my life is yours,
I owe it to your generosity.

DORINDA. I am o'rjoy'd my father lets you live, and proud
Of my good fortune, that he gave your life to me.

MIRANDA. How? Gave his life to her!

HIPPOLITO. Alas! I think she said so, and he said he ow'd it
To her generosity.

FERDINAND. But is not that your sister with *Hippolito*?

DORINDA. So kind already?

FERDINAND. I came to welcome life, and I have met the
Cruellest of deaths.

HIPPOLITO. My dear *Dorinda* with another man?

DORINDA. Sister, what bus'ness have you here?

MIRANDA. You see I dress *Hippolito.*

DORINDA. Y'are very charitable to a stranger.

MIRANDA. You are not much behind in charity, to beg a pardon
For a man, whom you scarce ever saw before.

DORINDA. Henceforward let your surgery alone, for I had
Rather he should die, than you should cure his wound.

MIRANDA. And I wish *Ferdinand* had dy'd before
He ow'd his life to your entreaty.

FERDINAND. [*To* Hippolito] Sir, I'm glad you are so well recover'd, you
Keep your humour still to have all women.

HIPPOLITO. Not all, Sir, you except one of the number,
Your new Love there, *Dorinda.*

MIRANDA. Ah *Ferdinand*! Can you become inconstant?
If I must lose you, I had rather death should take
You from me, than you take your self.

FERDINAND. And if I might have chosen, I would have wish'd
That death from *Prospero*, and not this from you.

DORINDA. Aye, now I find why I was sent away,
That you might have my sister's company.

HIPPOLITO. *Dorinda*, kill me not with your unkindness,
This is too much, first to be false your self,
And then accuse me too.

FERDINAND. We all accuse each other, and each one denies their guilt,
I should be glad it were a mutual errour.
And therefore first to clear my self from fault,
Madam, I beg your pardon, while I say I only love
Your sister. [*To* Dorinda.

MIRANDA. O blest word!
I'm sure I love no man but *Ferdinand.*

DORINDA. Nor I, Heav'n knows, but my *Hippolito.*

HIPPOLITO. I never knew I lov'd so much, before I fear'd
Dorinda's constancy; but now I am convinc'd that
I lov'd none but her, because none else can
Recompence her loss.

FERDINAND. 'twas happy then you had this little trial.
But how we all so much mistook, I know not.

MIRANDA. I have only this to say in my defence: my father sent
Me hither, to attend the wounded stranger.

DORINDA. And *Hippolito* sent me to beg the life of *Ferdinand*.

FERDINAND. From such small errours, left at first unheeded,
Have often sprung sad accidents in love:
But see, our fathers and our friends are come
To mix their joys with ours.

[*Enter* Prospero, Alonzo, Antonio, Gonzalo.

ALONZO. [*To* Prospero] Let it no more be thought of, your purpose,
Though it was severe was just. In losing *Ferdinand*
I should have mourn'd, but could not have complain'd.

PROSPERO. Sir, I am glad kind Heaven decreed it otherwise.

DORINDA. O wonder!
How many goodly creatures are there here!
How beauteous mankind is!

HIPPOLITO. O brave new world that has such people in't!

ALONZO. [*To* Ferdinand] Now all the blessings of a glad father
Compass thee about,
And make thee happy in thy beauteous choice.

GONZALO. I've inward wept, or should have spoke ere this.
Look down, sweet Heaven, and on this couple drop
A blessed crown, for it is you chalk'd out the
Way which brought us hither.

ANTONIO. Though penitence forc'd by necessity can scarce
Seem real, yet, dearest Brother, I have hope
My blood may plead for pardon with you, I resign
Dominion, which 'tis true I could not keep,
But Heaven knows too I would not.

PROSPERO. All past crimes I bury in the joy of this
Blessed day.

ALONZO. And that I may not be behind in justice, to this
Young Prince I render back his dukedom,
And as the Duke of *Mantua* thus salute him.

HIPPOLITO. What is it that you render back, methinks
You give me nothing.

PROSPERO. You are to be lord of a great people,
And o're towns and cities.

HIPPOLITO. And shall these people be all men and women?

GONZALO. Yes, and shall call you Lord.

HIPPOLITO. Why then I'll live no longer in a prison, but
Have a whole cave to my self hereafter.

PROSPERO. And that your happiness may be compleat,
I give you my *Dorinda* for your wife, she shall
Be yours for ever, when the priest has made you one.

HIPPOLITO. How can he make us one? Shall I grow to her?

PROSPERO. By saying holy words you shall be joyn'd in marriage to each other.

DORINDA. I warrant you those holy words are charms.
My father means to conjure us together.

PROSPERO. [*To his daughter*] My *Ariel* told me, when last night you quarrell'd,
You said you would for ever part your beds;
But what you threaten'd in your anger, Heaven Has turn'd to prophecy.
For you, *Miranda*, must with *Ferdinand*,
And you, *Dorinda*, with *Hippolito* lie in
One bed hereafter.

ALONZO. And Heaven make those beds still fruitful in
Producing children, to bless their parents'
Youth, and grandsire's age.

MIRANDA. [*To* Dorinda] If children come by lying in a bed, I wonder you
And I had none between us.

DORINDA. Sister it was our fault, we meant like fools
To look 'em in the fields, and they it seems
Are only found in beds.

HIPPOLITO. I am o'rjoy'd that I shall have *Dorinda* in a bed,
We'll lie all night and day together there,
And never rise again.

FERDINAND. [*Aside to him*] Hippolito! You yet are ignorant of your great happiness, but there is somewhat, which for your own and fair Dorinda's sake I must instruct you in.

HIPPOLITO. Pray teach me quickly how men and women in your world make love, I shall soon learn,
I warrant you.

[*Enter* Ariel *driving in* Stephano, Trincalo, Mustacho, Ventuso, Caliban, Sycorax.

PROSPERO. Why that's my dainty *Ariel*, I shall miss thee,
But yet thou shalt have freedom.

GONZALO. O look, Sir, look the Master and the sailors –
The Bosen too – my prophecy is out, that if
A gallows were on land, that man could n'er
Be drown'd.

ALONZO. [*To* Trincalo] Now Blasphemy, what not one oath ashore?
Hast thou no mouth by land? Why star'st thou so?

TRINCALO. What more dukes yet? I must resign my dukedom; but 'tis no matter, I was almost starv'd in't.

MUSTACHO. Here's nothing but wild sallads without oyl or vinegar.

STEPHANO. The Duke and Prince alive! Would I had now our gallant ship again, and were her Master, I'd willingly give all my island for her.

VENTOSO. And I my viceroy-ship.

TRINCALO. I shall need no hangman, for I shall e'en hang
My self, now my friend Butt has shed his
Last drop of life. Poor Butt is quite departed.

ANTONIO. They talk like mad men.

PROSPERO. No matter, time will bring 'em to themselves, and
Now their wine is gone they will not quarrel.
Your ship is safe and tight, and bravely rigg'd,
As when you first set sail.

ALONZO. This news is wonderful.

ARIEL. Was it well done, my Lord?

PROSPERO. Rarely, my Diligence.

GONZALO. But pray, Sir, what are those mishapen creatures?

PROSPERO. Their mother was a witch, and one so strong
She would controul the moon, make flows
And ebbs, and deal in her command without
Her power.

SYCORAX. O *Setebos*! These be brave sprights indeed.

PROSPERO. [*To* Caliban] Go, Sirrah to my cell, and as you hope for pardon, trim it up.

CALIBAN. Most carefully. I will be wise hereafter.
What a dull fool was I to take those drunkards
For gods, when such as these were in the world?

PROSPERO. Sir, I invite your Highness and your train
To my poor cave this night; a part of which
I will employ in telling you my story.

ALONZO. No doubt it must be strangely taking, Sir.

PROSPERO. When the morn draws, I'll bring you to your ship,
And promise you calm seas and happy gales.
My *Ariel*, that's thy charge: then to the elements
Be free, and fare thee well.

ARIEL. I'll do it Master.

PROSPERO. Now to make amends
For the rough treatment you have found to day,
I'll entertain you with my magick art:
I'll, by my power, transform this place, and call
Up those that shall make good my promise to you.

[*Scene changes to the rocks, with the arch of rocks, and calm sea. Musick playing on the rocks.*

PROSPERO. Neptune, and your fair Amphitrite, rise;
Oceanus, with your *Tethys* too, appear;
All ye Sea-Gods, and Goddesses, appear!
Come, all ye *Tritons*; all ye *Nereides*, come,
And teach your sawcy elements to obey:
For you have princes now to entertain,
And unsoil'd beauties, with fresh youthful lovers.

[Neptune, Amphitrite, Oceanus *and* Tethys *appear in a chariot drawn with sea horses; on each side of the chariot, sea gods and goddesses,* Tritons *and* Nereides.

ALONZO. This is prodigious.

ANTONIO. Ah! What amazing objects do we see?

GONZALO. This art doth much exceed all humane skill.

SONG.

AMPHITRITE.
My Lord: Great Neptune, for my sake,
Of these bright beauties pity take:
And to the rest allow
Your mercy too.
Let this inraged element be still,
Let Aeolus obey my will:
Let him boystrous prisoners safely keep
Till those arrive upon their wish'd for shore.

NEPTUNE.
So much my Amphitrite's love I prize,
That no commands of hers I can despise.
Tethys no sorrows now shall wear,
Oceanus no wrinkles on his brow,
Let your serenest looks appear!
Be calm and gentle now.

NEPTUNE. & AMPHITRITE.
Be calm, ye great parents of the flouds and the springs
While each Nereide and Triton plays, revels, and sings.

OCEANUS.
Confine the roaring winds, and we
Will soon obey you cheerfully.

CHORUS OF TRITONS AND NEREIDES.
Tie up the winds, and we'll obey,
Upon the flouds, we'll sing and play,

[Here the dancers mingle with the singers.

And celebrate a Halcyon day.

NEPTUNE.
Great Nephew Aeolus make no noise,
Muzle your roaring boys. [*Aeolus* appears.

AMPHITRITE.
Let 'em not bluster to disturb our ears,
Or strike these noble passengers with fears.

NEPTUNE.
Afford 'em only such an easie gale,
As pleasantly may swell each sail.

AMPHITRITE.
While fell sea monsters cause intestine jars,
This empire you invade with foreign wars.

NEPTUNE.
But you shall now be still,
And shall obey my Amphitrites' will.
You I'll obey, who at one stroke can make,
[*Aeolus* descends.
With your dread trident the whole earth to quake.
Come down, my Blusterers, swell no more,
Your stormy rage give o'r.
[*Winds* from the four corners appear.
Let all black tempests cease –
And let the troubled ocean rest:
Let all the sea enjoy as calm a peace
As where the Halcyon builds her quiet nest.
To your prisons below,
Down down you must go:
You in the earth's entrals your revels may keep;
But no more till I call shall you trouble the deep.
[*Winds* fly down.
Now they are gone, all stormy wars shall cease:
Then let your Trumpeters proclaim a peace.

AMPHITRITE.
Tritons, my Sons, your trumpets sound,
And let the noise from neighbouring shores rebound.
Sound a calm.
Sound a calm.

CHORUS.
Sound a calm.
a calm.
Sound a calm.

[Here the *Tritons*, at every repeat of sound a calm, changing their figure and postures, seem to sound their wreathed trumpets made of shells. A Symphony of musick, like trumpets, to which four *Tritons* dance.

NEPTUNE.
See, see, the heavens smile, all your troubles are past,
Your joys by black clouds shall no more be o'rcast.

AMPHITRITE.
On this barren isle ye shall lose all your fears,
Leave behind all your sorrows, and banish your cares.
And your loves and your lives shall in safety enjoy;

BOTH.
No influence of stars shall your quiet destroy.

CHORUS OF ALL.
And your loves, &c.
No influence, &c.

[Here the dancers mingle with the singers.

OCEANUS.
We'll safely convey you to your own happy shore,
And yours and your countrey's soft peace we'll restore.

TETHYS.
To treat you blest lovers, as you sail on the deep
The Tritons and Sea-Nymphs their revels shall keep.
On the swift dolphins' backs they shall sing and shall play;

BOTH.
They shall guard you by night, and delight you by day.

CHORUS OF ALL.
On the swift, &c.
And shall guard, &c.

[Here the dancers mingle with the singers.

[A dance of twelve *Tritons*.

MIRANDA. What charming things are these?
DORINDA. What heavenly power is this?
PROSPERO. Now, my Ariel, be visible,
And let the rest of your aerial train
appear, and entertain 'em with a song;

[*Scene changes to the rising sun, and a number of aerial spirits in the air,* Ariel *flying from the sun, advances towards the pit.*

And then farewell my long lov'd *Ariel.*
ALONZO. Heav'n! What are these we see?
PROSPERO. They are spirits, with which the air abounds
In swarms. But that they are not subject
To poor feeble mortal eyes.
ANTONIO. O wondrous skill!
GONZALO. O power divine!

[Ariel *and the rest sing the following song.*

Where the bee sucks there suck I,
In a cowslip's bell, I lie;
There I couch when owls do cry.
On the swallow's wing I fly
After Summer merrily.
Merrily, merrily shall I live now
Under the blossom that hangs on the bough.

[*Song ended,* Ariel *speaks, hovering in the air.*

ARIEL. My Noble Master!
May theirs and your blest joys never impair.
And for the freedom I enjoy in air,
I will be still your *Ariel*, and wait
On aiery accidents that work for Fate.
What ever shall your happiness concern,
From your still faithful *Ariel* you shall learn.
PROSPERO. Thou hast been always diligent and kind!
Farewell my long lov'd Ariel, thou shalt find,
I will preserve thee ever in my mind.
Henceforth this isle to the afflicted be
A place of refuge, as it was to me;
The promises of blooming Spring live here,
And all the blessings of the ripening year.
On my retreat, let Heaven and Nature smile,
And ever flourish the *Enchanted Isle.* [*Exeunt.*

Epilogue.

Gallants, by all good signs it does appear,
That sixty seven's a very damning year,
For knaves abroad, and for ill poets here.

Among the muses there's a gen'ral rot,
The Rhyming Mounsieur and the Spanish Plot:
Defie or court, all's one, they go to pot.

The ghosts of poets walk within this place,
And haunt us actors wheresoe're we pass,
In visions bloodier than King Richard's was.

For this poor wretch, he has not much to say,
But quietly brings in his part o'th' play,
And begs the favour to be damn'd to day.

He sends me only like a sheriff's man here
To let you know the malefactor's near;
And that he means to die, en cavalier.

For if you shou'd be gracious to his pen,
Th' example will prove ill to other men,
And you'll be troubled with 'em all again.

1.2 DAVID GARRICK, "PROLOGUE" TO *THE TEMPEST. AN OPERA.*

DAVID GARRICK, "PROLOGUE." *The Tempest. An Opera. Taken from Shakespear. As it is Performed at the Theatre-Royal in Drury-Lane.* Volume 3. *Garrick's Adaptations of Shakespeare, 1744–1756. The Plays of David Garrick.* Eds. Harry William Pedicord and Fredrick Louis Bergmann. Carbondale and Edwardsville: Southern Illinois University Press, 1980. This prologue or, actually, dialogue, was spoken before the performance of David Garrick's three-act, operatic version of Shakespeare's play in 1756. It stages a debate between two Englishmen, one a lover of Shakespeare with a xenophobic hatred of the popular Italian opera and the French (with whom the British were upon the brink of war), the other more accepting of the important role that music played in the London theatres. Indeed, next to candles to light the playhouse, music before, during, and after plays took up a hefty part of theatre budgets. The prologue met with considerable heckling from the first night's audience and the opera failed after three performances as the last attempt by Garrick to turn a Shakespeare play into an opera.

Dialogue[53]

Wormwood & Heartly.

WORMWOOD. I say it is a shame, Mr. Heartly, and I am amazed that you let your good nature talk thus against the conviction of your understanding.

HEARTLY. You won't let me talk, sir; if you would but have patience and hear reason a little.

WORMWOOD. I wish I could, sir; but you put me out of all patience by having no reason to give me. I say that this frittering and sol-fa-ing our best poets is a damned thing. I have yet heard no reason to justify it, and I have no patience when I think of it.

HEARTLY. I see you have not—

WORMWOOD. What! are we to be quivered and quavered out of our senses? Give me Shakespear in all his force, rigor, and spirit! What! would you make an eunuch of him? No, Shakespear is for my money—

HEARTLY. Nay, but, dear sir, hear me in my turn, or the truth for which we are, or ought to be, so warmly fighting will slip thro' our fingers.

WORMWOOD. Will you hold it when you have it? I say, Mr. Heartly, while you let your good nature—

HEARTLY. And I say, Mr. WORMWOOD, while you are to be influenced and blown up by paragraphs in newspapers and insinuations in coffee houses, we can never come to a fair debate. They who write upon all subjects without understanding any, or will talk about music without ears or taste for it, are but very indifferent judges in our dispute.

WORMWOOD. Well, come on, Mr. Sol-fa. Let you and I fight it out—or to speak in the musical phrase, let us have a duette together. I'll clean up my pipes and have at you—hem—

HEARTLY. With all my heart, tho' I'm afraid you'll make it a solo, for you have not yet suffered the second part to come in.

WORMWOOD. Ho! play away, sir. I'll be dumb.

HEARTLY. Let us calmly consider this complaint of yours. If it is well founded, I will submit with pleasure; if not, you will—

WORMWOOD. Not submit with pleasure, I assure you. I never do.

HEARTLY. You will at least have this satisfaction, that the sentence which will be given, whether for or against you, will be as indisputable as it will be just.

WORMWOOD. I don't know what you mean. Nothing's indisputable that I please to contradict, and nothing's just that I please to call in question.

HEARTLY. Look round upon the court, and if you can reasonably except against any of the jury, I will give up the cause before trial.

WORMWOOD. Oh ho, what? You are bribing the court beforehand with your flattery, are you?

HEARTLY. There you are out again. Our countrymen in a body are no more to be flattered than bullied, which I hope their enemies (who can do both) will be convinced of before they have done with them. But I wander from the question. To the point: what are your objections to this night's entertainment?

WORMWOOD. I hate an opera.

HEARTLY. I dislike tie-wigs. But should I throw yours into the fire because I choose to wear a bag?

WORMWOOD. Woe be to your bag if you did.

HEARTLY. You hate music, perhaps?

WORMWOOD. Damnably, and dancing too.

HEARTLY. But why, pray?

WORMWOOD. They pervert nature. Legs are made for walking, tongues for speaking, and therefore capering and quavering are unnatural and abominable.

HEARTLY. You like Shakespear?

WORMWOOD. Like him! Adore him, worship him—no capering and quavering in his works.

HEARTLY. Have a care.

"The man that has not music in himself
Nor is not moved with concord of sweet sounds
Is fit for treason, stratagems, and spoils.
The motions of his spirit are dull as night.
Let no such man be trusted."[54]

WORMWOOD. Fit for treason! dull as night! not to be trusted— so you have proved me both a blockhead and a rebel. Don't provoke me, Mr. Heartly. Shakespear never writ such stuff as that. 'tis foisted in by some fiddler or other.

HEARTLY. You pay the fiddlers (as you call 'em) a very great compliment.

WORMWOOD. Did I? I am sorry for it. I did not mean it. Were I to pay 'em—crabstick's the word.

HEARTLY. For shame, Mr. Wormwood. Let me ask you a question: would you choose that your country shou'd be excelled in anything by your neighbors?

WORMWOOD. In manufactures? No—from the casting of cannon to the making of pins, from the weaving of velvets to the making of hopsacks—but your capering and quavering only spoil us and make us the jests, who should be the terrors of Europe.

HEARTLY. But English music, Mr. Wormwood—

WORMWOOD. English music or any music enervates the body, weakens the mind, and lessens the courage—

HEARTLY. Quite the contrary.

WORMWOOD. Prove that and I'll learn the gamut immediately; nay, bespeak me a pair of pumps and make one at the dancing academy of grown gentlemen.

HEARTLY. Let us suppose an invasion!

WORMWOOD. Ha, ha, ha!—an invasion. Music and an invasion! They are well coupled, truly!

HEARTLY. Patience, sir, I say, let us suppose ten thousand French landed.

WORMWOOD. I had rather suppose 'em at the bottom of the sea.

HEARTLY. So had I, but the ten thousand are upon the coast.

WORMWOOD. The devil they are! What then?

HEARTLY. Why, then I say, let but "Britons strike home!"[55] or "God save the King" be sounded in the ears of five thousand brave Englishmen with a Protestant Prince at the head of 'em, and they'll drive every Monsieur into the sea and make 'em food for sprats and mackrell.

WORMWOOD. Huzza! and so they will! 'Egad, you're in the right. I'll say no more. Britons strike home. You have warmed me and pleased me; you have converted me. I'll get a place in the house and be as hearty as the best of 'em for the music of old England! Sprats and mackrells! that's good. Excellent! I thank you for it. Music for ever. Britains strike home! God save the King!

HEARTLY. The last thing I have to say will touch you as nearly, Mr. Wormwood.

WORMWOOD. You have touched me already. Say no more; I am satisfied. I shall never forget sprats and mackrells.

HEARTLY. We may boast, sincerely boast of many excellent English composers, and would not you permit your countrymen to have the same encouragement of foreigners?

WORMWOOD. Encouragement! Why, I'll encourage 'em myself, man.

HEARTLY. Where can they show their talents unless upon the English stages? And if the managers of them will not give us a few nights to encourage English music, our musical countrymen,

Mr. Wormwood, wou'd be of the number of those persons of merit who are undeservedly neglected in this kingdom.

WORMWOOD. But they shan't. I'll support 'em. I'll nevermore hearken to your club speeches and your dissertations. I see my error. But I'll make amends. Let us meet after it is over and take a bottle to sprats and mackrells, eh, Master Heartly, at the Shakespear. I'll be with you. Britons strike home!

Exit singing.

HEARTLY. Mr. Wormwood is now as much too violent in his zeal as he was before in his prejudice. We expect not, ladies and gentlemen, that this night's performance shou'd meet with success merely because it is English; you would be as incapable of conceiving as we of urging such false and contracted notions. Yet on the other hand, let not our musical brethren be cast off because fashion, caprice, or manners too refined may have given you prejudices against 'em. Music is the young sister of poetry and can boast her charms and accomplishments. Therefore suffer not the younger be turned out of doors while the elder is to be warmly and deservedly cherished.

If worthy you'll protect her, tho' distressed;
'Tis the known principle of a British breast;
Those to befriend the most who're most
oppressed.

1.3 ELIZABETH INCHBALD, "PREFACE" TO *THE TEMPEST*

ELIZABETH INCHBALD, "PREFACE" TO *The Tempest* from *The British Theatre: or A Collection of Plays, which are acted at the Theatres Royal, Drury-Lane, Covent-Garden, and Haymarket. Printed under the Authority of the Managers, from the Prompt books. With Biographical and Critical Remarks by Mrs. Inchbald.* Vol. V. London: Longman, Hurst, Rees, Orme, and Brown, n.d.. Inchbald (1753–1821) was both an actress and a very successful playwright. The publisher Longman asked her to write prefaces to the 25-volume *The British Theatre* (1806–1809) from which this preface comes.

The Tempest; or, *The Enchanted Island; A Play in Five Acts; By William Shakespeare. Adapted to the Stage, with Additions from Dryden and Davenant, by J. P. Kemble. As Performed under the Authority of the Managers from the Prompt Book. With Remarks by Mrs. Inchbald.* 3–5.

Shakespeare had now written more than thirty plays, and, like other hackneyed authors, he began to be weary of his employment. But he had a resource in fancy, to which others apply in vain. Tired of the same dull round of forming men and women, he said—"Let there be spirits, fairies, goblins, and monsters." At his word, these supernatural things had dramatic existence. . .. it would never have become a favourite on the stage, without the aid of Dryden's alteration. The human beings in the original drama had not business enough on the scene, to make human beings anxious about them: and the preternatural characters were more wonderful than pleasing; for, whilst an auditor or a reader pours forth his praise before the Creator of Caliban, he loathes the creature.

Ariel, opposed to this monster, is one of those happy contrasts, which Shakespeare deals in; yet, this airy and mild spirit cannot charm an audience, except by singing. Nor could the love scenes produce much sympathy, but from the artlessness of the objects concerned. Ignorance of what their own sensations mean, is the charm which alone elevates those pleasing characters, above the common order of insipid lovers.

. . . This drama does *not* interest the passions. Less variety might have engaged them; but here genius has been too much expanded. Exercised on fewer objects, its force had been concentrated, and more effectual.

The senses are, indeed, powerfully engaged by the grandeur of the spectacle in a London theatre—and the senses highly gratified, are sometimes mistaken, by the possessor himself—for the passions.

1.4 JOHN PETER SIMON, *THE INCHANTED ISLAND: BEFORE THE CELL OF PROSPERO*

John Peter Simon, *The Inchanted Island: Before the Cell of Prospero* (engraving, 1797): This image of act I, scene II, is an engraving by Simon (1764?–c. 1810) based on a painting by Henry Fuseli (1741–1825) that hung in the famous Shakespeare Gallery financed and promoted by John Boydell (1720–1804). Fuseli did numerous interpretive paintings of Shakespeare scenes, particularly those with supernatural or fantastic themes. By permission of the Folger Shakespeare Library. ART File S528t2 no. 112.

1.5 WILLIAM HOGARTH, *SCENE FROM THE TEMPEST*

William Hogarth, *Scene from Shakespeare's The Tempest*, circa 1735: Hogarth (1697–1764) was a highly successful painter and print maker who brought satirical and topical subjects to a growing audience for the visual arts, which he cultivated through the production of affordable print copies of his paintings. This painting does not seem to be taken from a staging, but rather reflects Hogarth's vision of Shakespeare's characters, including a Caliban who does not even notice the dove upon which he treads.

Notes

1 This edition is based on the 1674 "operatic" version of the Davenant and Dryden play. A 1670 edition preceded this edition. There are significant differences between the 1670 and 1674 versions; most significantly, the latter includes the splashy masque of Neptune, and omits a good bit of dialogue, mostly between the sailors and the two monsters. In addition, scene I in Act II of the 1670 edition becomes scene III in Act II of the 1674 version; scene II in Act II becomes scene I in Act III; scene III in Act II becomes scene I in Act II; and scenes IV and V become Scene II in Act II. While the 1670 edition is the closest to Shakespeare's play and undoubtedly represents best what came from the pen of the playwrights, the 1674 version dominated productions of this play for most of the Restoration and well into the eighteenth century. Similar editions followed it during the Restoration, in 1676, 1690, and 1695, all of which were consulted in editing this text. Edition of 1670 printed by J.M. for Henry Herringman; 1674 and 1676 edition also printed by J.M. for Henry Herringman.

2 For a history of Shakespeare's rise to the status of national poet in Britain see Michael Dobson, *The Making of the National Poet: Shakespeare, Adaptation, and Authorship, 1660–1769.* Oxford and New York: Clarendon Press, 1992. For the story of the 1769 Jubilee see Christian Deelman, *The Great Shakespeare Jubilee.* New York: Viking Press, 1964.

3 Examination.

4 Landscapes.

5 The indoor Elizabethan theatre in which many of Shakespeare's plays were originally acted.

6 John Fletcher (1579–1625), a prolific English playwright and contemporary of Shakespeare.

7 Sir John Suckling (Bap. 1609–1641?), poet and playwright. Dryden references his play *The Goblins* (1638–1641).

8 The Roman poet, Horace (65 BCE to 8 BCE), counseled writers in his *Ars Poetica* to keep their work and revise it before giving it to other readers.

9 Ben Jonson (1572–1637), another poet and playwright roughly contemporary with Shakespeare. Some of his plays, like Shakespeare's, were regularly adapted and performed in the Restoration and into the eighteenth century.

10 Charles II lifted the prohibition against women actors in the English theatre in 1660. The result was the sky-rocketing popularity of female performers and the decline of boy actors playing female characters, the dominant practice in Shakespeare's theatre. Casting women actors in male roles allowed them to wear the close-fitting pants fashionable for aristocratic men at the time, revealing their legs, and drawing audiences to see this new spectacle. Hence, the stage went from boys playing women to women playing boys.

11 There is no cast list, but Ferdinand may have been played by the versatile Henry Harris. Stephano may have been played by Edward Angel and Trincalo by the comic actor Cave Underhill. Ariel was played by Mary "Moll" Davis and Hippolito by Jane Long.

12 Harpsichords.

13 A large, stringed instrument of the lute family.

14 A square or rectangular column.

15 A wide, usually triangular structure over the entrance to a classical building, often ornamented with relief sculptures.

16 A word apparently coined by Dryden or Davenant in this play, possibly meaning "humming."

17 Dirt or refuse.

18 Mechanism for rolling up a sail.

19 Roll up.

20 To secure a rope by cross-turns.

21 Referring to the left-hand side of the ship, from the point of view facing toward the stern; the opposite of starboard.

22 Unidentified, but almost certainly sailor's language.

23 A term of comradeship used between men.

24 Come loose, so as to be seen.

25 Short, raised deck at the front of a ship.

26 Ship.
27 Principal sail on the mast of the ship.
28 A strong wind.
29 Unidentified, but almost certainly sailor's language.
30 See note 18 above.
31 To steer the ship nearer to the wind.
32 A boom extending out from the stem of the ship.
33 Part of a ship's rigging.
34 This word can mean elves or goblins; it can also refer to porcupines.
35 A little stream.
36 A bucket; pail.
37 To drift.
38 Savages.
39 The comic discussion that follows about setting up a government, and who should lead it, would have had strong resonances, for Restoration audiences, of the English Civil Wars and the Interregnum period immediately preceding the restoration of the English monarchy in 1660. This conversation between drunken, plebian characters parodies the establishment of several forms of government in England after the execution of Charles I during the English Commonwealth period.
40 A class of white wines from Spain and the Canary Islands.
41 A small monkey.
42 A private space used for solitary activities, such as reading, writing, or personal prayer.
43 In its usual place.
44 Shakespeare included a masque in his version of *The Tempest*, following a fashion in the Elizabethan court for staging elaborate spectacles with music and dance, often with classical or allegorical themes. The masque died out after the Restoration (1660), but elements of its spectacle and stage effect were continued in the English semi-operas, such as Henry Purcell's *The Fairy Queen*, of the period.
45 Coral was sometimes smoothed and given an ornamental shape to be used to soothe teething babies.
46 Bullying.
47 Pour the wine.
48 Praise, ceremonially or formally given.
49 A traditional toast to pregnant women.
50 Crab apples.
51 Medicines composed of only one herb or plant.
52 Curative.
53 The "Dialogue" was performed to a mixed reception and is not printed in the 1756 edition of the play.
54 *Merchant of Venice*, V, i, 83–86, 88.
55 From Vanbrugh's *The Provoke'd Wife*, IV, i.

2. *The Country Wife*

THE COUNTRY-WIFE. A COMEDY, ACTED AT THE THEATRE ROYAL. WILLIAM WYCHERLEY. FIRST PERFORMED 12 JANUARY 1675 (?) AND FIRST PUBLISHED 1675.

2.1 *THE COUNTRY-WIFE*, A COMEDY, ACTED AT THE THEATRE ROYAL.[1]

William Wycherley

First Performed 12 January 1675 and First Published 1675

THE COUNTRY WIFE WAS PUBLISHED in 1675, but its first performance date is uncertain. It has been given as early as 1672 and as late as the 1674/75 theatre season. It consolidated the literary reputation that William Wycherley had begun to establish with his *Love in a Wood*, first performed in 1671. Wycherley epitomizes the changing fortunes and varying scenes of life associated with the Restoration gentleman libertine. Born in India and educated in France, Wycherley was at some points of his life Catholic and at others Protestant. He served in the British navy, gained and lost the favor of Charles II, and at one point was the lover of Charles' mistress, Barbara Villiers, the Duchess of Cleveland. Known for his straightforward manner and honesty, he was known as "Manly Wycherley," a reputation consolidated by his later play, *The Plain Dealer* (1676).

The play's performance history depends on the fortunes of its main character's sexual exploits with changing audience tastes and morals. Charles Hart, who probably played the first Horner, was typically associated with virile lover/hero roles, and the his character in the first performances of this play were likely to have been made attractive by that actor's charisma. Its frank sexuality was controversial from the beginning, however, as Wycherley himself noted by having a character in *The Plain Dealer* comment that *The Country Wife* had "quite taken away the reputation of poor china itself, and sullied the most innocent and pretty furniture of a lady's chamber" and refer to him as that "beastly author" (II, i.). It played fairly regularly, however, until the 1740s; its last eighteenth-century performance was in 1753, followed by a 171-year hiatus when it re-emerged to become one of the most performed and popular Restoration comedies of the twentieth century. In 1766 it was sanitized by David Garrick into *The Country Girl*, a popular vehicle for actresses, such as Peg Woffington and Dorothy Jordan, known for their feminine attractions in breeches.

As can be seen from Wycherley's ironic self-criticism in *The Plain Dealer*, the famous (or infamous) china scene has drawn the most laughter and the most virulent criticism of the play. Porcelain was not manufactured in Europe until the 1730s, and chinaware produced in China (and later, Japan) was the object of fashionable obsession by those who could afford it in the Restoration. Consumer gratification—focused narrowly on porcelain imported from Asia—parallels sexual gratification in social as well as dramatic performances of the Restoration Court.

The political and social importance of libertine display has been well established in the history and criticism of this period and is clearly communicated in plays such as *The Man of Mode*. The sexual charisma of Charles II—proudly reported by John Dryden to have "scattered his maker's image through the land"—and courtiers such as John Wilmot, Earl of Rochester (whose pornographic poetry is included in this volume) were key to the performance of royal and courtly power. Charles' palace at Whitehall was decorated with enormous, lusciously colored portraits of the ladies of his court, not a few of which were his mistresses. These pink-and-white-fleshed, silk-gowned trophies say as much about the King's sexual as political power. Significantly, when the protestant William and Mary assumed the throne after the overthrow of Charles' Catholic brother, James, in the "Glorious Revolution" of 1688, Mary's decorating strategy unconsciously restaged the displacement of sexuality onto china by decking out Whitehall in a famous "China room" that displayed her extensive collection of porcelain. Daniel Defoe, writing in *A tour thro' the whole Island of Great Britain, 1724–27*, reports that Queen Mary

> brought in the custom or humour, as I may call it, of furnishing houses with china-ware, which increased to a strange degree afterwards, piling their china upon the tops of cabinets, scrutores, and every chimney-piece, to the tops of the ceilings, and even setting up shelves for their china-ware, where they wanted such places, till it became a grievance in the expence of it, and even injurious to their families and estates.
>
> (reprint G. D. Cole, ed. London, 1927, vol. I, p. 166)

The display of male sexual prowess was displaced by the display of buying power, a fashion much more readily imitated by a growing consumer public than the libertine high-jinks of Charles's male courtiers.[2] This displacement is playfully anticipated by Wycherley's china scene.

As Douglas Canfield has pointed out,[3] Wycherley also changed the cuckolding plot that was so popular a feature of Restoration comedy. Instead of cuckolding the "cits," the businessmen of London trade and government, Horner goes after the wives of men of his own class, effectively removing the theme of class conflict from the plot. Male libertine performance in this play hangs uneasily between the publicly enacted spectacle of aristocratic male dominance and private consumer gratification. *The Country Wife* reflects a cultural landscape of economic and political relationships caught between old social hierarchies of birth and status and emerging, modern markets of trade and sociability.

PROLOGUE, spoken by Mr. *Hart*.

Poets, like cudgel'd bullys, never do
At first, or second blow, submit to you;
But will provoke you still, and nev'r have done,
Till you are weary first, with laying on:
The late so bafled scribler of this day,
Though he stands trembling, bids me boldly say,
What we, before most playes are us'd to do,
For poets out of fear, first draw on you;
In a fierce prologue, the still pit[4] defie,
And e're you speak, like *Castril*,[5] give the lye;
But though our *Bayses'*[6] battels oft I've fought,
And with bruis'd knuckles, their dear conquests bought;
Nay, never yet fear'd odds upon the stage,
In prologue dare not hector[7] with the age,
But wou'd take quarter from your saving hands,
Though *Bayse* within all yielding countermands,
Says you confedrate wits no quarter give,
Ther'fore his play shan't ask your leave to live:
Well, let the vain rash Fop,[8] by huffing so,
Think to obtain the better terms of you;
But we the actors humbly will submit,
Now, and at any time, to a full pit;
Nay, often we anticipate your rage,
And murder poets for you, on our stage:
We set no guards upon our tyring-room,[9]
But when with flying colours, there you come,
We patiently you see, give up to you,
Our poets, virgins, nay our matrons too.

The Persons.

Mr. *Horner*,	Mr. *Hart*.
Mr. *Harcourt*,	Mr. *Kenaston*.[10]
Mr. *Dorilant*,	Mr. *Lydal*.
Mr. *Pinchwife*,	Mr. *Mohan*.
Mr. *Sparkish*,	Mr. *Haynes*.
Sir *Jasper Fidget*,	Mr. *Cartwright*.
Mrs. *Margery Pinchwife*,	Mrs. *Bowtel*.
Mrs. *Alithea*,	Mrs. *James*.

My Lady Fidget,	Mrs. *Knep.*
Mrs. *Dainty Fidget,*	Mrs. *Corbet.*
Mrs. *Squeamish,*	Mrs. *Wyatt.*
Old Lady Squeamish,	Mrs. *Rutter.*
Waiters, Servants, and *Attendants,*	
A BOY,	
A Quack,[11]	Mr. *Shotterel.*
Lucy, Alithea's Maid,	Mrs. *Cory.*

Act I.

[*The SCENE London. Enter* Horner, *and* Quack *following him at a distance.*]

HORNER. – [*Aside*] *A quack is as fit for a pimp, as a midwife for a bawd;*[12] *they are still but in their way, both helpers of Nature.* – Well, my dear Doctor, hast thou done what I desired?

QUACK. I have undone you for ever with the women, and reported you throughout the whole Town as bad as an *eunuch*, with as much trouble as if I had made you one in earnest.

HORNER. But have you told all the midwives you know, the orange wenches at the playhouses,[13] the city husbands,[14] and old fumbling keepers[15] of this end of the Town, for they'll be the readiest to report it.

QUACK. I have told all the chamber-maids, waiting women, tyre women,[16] and old women of my acquaintance; nay, and whisper'd it as a secret to'em, and to the whisperers of *Whitehall*;[17] so that you need not doubt 'twill spread, and you will be as odious to the handsome young women, as –

HORNER. As the small pox.[18] – Well –

QUACK. And to the married women of this end of the Town, as –

HORNER. As the great ones; nay, as their own husbands.

QUACK. And to the city dames as annis-seed *Robin*,[19] of filthy and contemptible memory; and they will frighten their children with your name, especially their females.

HORNER. And cry *Horner*'s coming to carry you away: I am only afraid 'twill not be believ'd; you told 'em it was by an *English – French* disaster, and an *English – French* chirurgeon, who has given me at once, not only a cure, but an antidote for the future, against that damn'd malady,[20] and that worse distemper, love, and all other women's evils.

QUACK. Your late journey into *France* has made it the more credible, and your being here a fortnight before you appear'd in publick, looks as if you apprehended the shame, which I wonder you do not: Well I have been hired by young gallants to bely 'em t'other way; but you are the first wou'd be thought a man unfit for women.

HORNER. Dear Mr. Doctor, let vain rogues be contented only to be thought abler men than they are, generally 'tis all the pleasure they have, but mine lyes another way.

QUACK. You take, methinks, a very preposterous way to it, and as ridiculous as if we operators in physick, shou'd put forth bills to disparage our medicaments, with hopes to gain customers.

HORNER. Doctor, there are quacks in love, as well as physick, who get but the fewer and worse patients, for their boasting; a good name is seldom got by giving it one's self, and women no more than honour are compass'd by bragging. Come, come Doctor, the wisest lawyer never discovers the merits of his cause till the tryal; the wealthiest man conceals his riches, and the cunning gamester his play; shy husbands and keepers like old rooks[21] are not to be cheated, but by a new unpractis'd trick; false friendship will pass now no more than false dice upon'em, no, not in the city.

[*Enter* Boy.

BOY. There are two ladies and a gentleman coming up.

HORNER. A pox, some unbelieving sisters of my former acquaintance, who I am afraid, expect their sense shou'd be satisfy'd of the falsity of the report. No – this formal fool and women!

[*Enter* Sir Jasper Fidget, Lady Fidget, *and* Mrs. Dainty Fidget.

QUACK. His wife and sister.

SIR JASPER. My coach breaking just now before your door, Sir, I look upon as an occasional reprimand to me Sir, for not kissing your hands Sir, since your coming out of *France* Sir; and so my disaster Sir, has been my good fortune Sir; and this is my wife, and sister Sir.

HORNER. What then, Sir?

SIR JASPER. My Lady, and sister, Sir. – Wife, this is Master *Horner.*

LADY FIDGET. Master *Horner,* Husband!

SIR JASPER. My Lady, my Lady *Fidget,* Sir.

HORNER. So, Sir.

SIR JASPER. Won't you be acquainted with her Sir? – [*Aside*] *So the report is true, I find by his coldness or aversion to the sex; but I'll play the wag with him.* – Pray salute my wife, my Lady, Sir.

HORNER. I will kiss no man's wife, Sir, for him, Sir; I have taken my eternal leave, Sir, of the sex already, Sir.

SIR JASPER. – [*Aside*] *Hah, hah, hah; I'll plague him yet.* – Not know my wife, Sir?

HORNER. I do know your wife, Sir, she's a woman, Sir, and consequently a monster, Sir, a greater monster than a husband, Sir.

SIR JASPER. A husband; how, Sir?

HORNER. So, Sir; but I make no more cuckholds, Sir. [*Makes horns.*[22]

SIR JASPER. Hah, hah, hah, *Mercury, Mercury.*[23]

LADY FIDGET. Pray, Sir *Jasper,* let us be gone from this rude fellow.

DAINTY FIDGET. Who, by his breeding, wou'd think, he had ever been in *France*?

LADY FIDGET. Foh, he's but too much a French fellow, such as hate women of quality and virtue, for their love to their husbands, Sr. *Jasper*; a woman is hated by'em as much for loving her husband, as for loving their money: But pray, let's be gone.

HORNER. You do well, Madam, for I have nothing that you came for: I have brought over not so much as a bawdy picture, new postures, nor the second part of the *Escole de Filles*;[24] Nor –

QUACK. Hold for shame, Sir; what d'ye mean? You'll ruine your self for ever with the sex – [*Apart to* Horner.

SIR JASPER. Hah, hah, hah, he hates women perfectly I find.

DAINTY FIDGET. What pity 'tis he shou'd.

LADY FIDGET. Ay, he's a base rude fellow for't; but affectation makes not a woman more odious to them, than virtue.

HORNER. Because your virtue is your greatest affectation, Madam.

LADY FIDGET. How, you sawcy Fellow, wou'd you wrong my honour?

HORNER. If I cou'd.

LADY FIDGET. How d'ye mean, Sir?

SIR JASPER. Hah, hah, hah, no he can't wrong your Ladyship's honour, upon my honour; he poor man – hark you in your ear – a meer eunuch.

LADY FIDGET. O filthy French Beast, foh, foh; why do we stay? Let's be gone; I can't endure the sight of him.

SIR JASPER. Stay, but till the chairs[25] come, they'll be here presently.

LADY FIDGET. No, no.

SIR JASPER. Nor can I stay longer; 'tis – let me see, a quarter and a half quarter of a minute past eleven; the Council will be sate, I must away: business must be preferr'd always before love and ceremony with the wise Mr. *Horner.*

HORNER. And the impotent Sir Jasper.

SIR JASPER. Ay, ay, the impotent Master *Horner,* hah, ha, ha.

LADY FIDGET. What leave us with a filthy man alone in his lodgings?

SIR JASPER. He's an innocent man now, you know; pray stay, I'll hasten the chairs to you. – Mr. *Horner* your Servant, I shou'd be glad to see you at my house; pray, come and dine with me, and play at cards with my wife after dinner, you are fit for women at that game; yet hah, ha – [*Aside*] *('Tis as much a husband's prudence to provide innocent diversion for a wife, as to hinder her unlawful pleasures; and he had better employ her, than let her employ her self.* – Farewell. [*Exit* Sir Jasper.

HORNER. Your Servant Sir. *Jasper.*

LADY FIDGET. I will not stay with him, foh –

HORNER. Nay, Madam, I beseech you stay, if it be but to see, I can be as civil to ladies yet, as they wou'd desire.

LADY FIDGET. No, no, foh, you cannot be civil to ladies.

DAINTY FIDGET. You as civil as ladies wou'd desire.

LADY FIDGET. No, no, no, foh, foh, foh. [*Exeunt* Lady Fidget *and* Dainty

QUACK. Now I think, I, or you your self rather, have done your business with the women.

HORNER. Thou art an ass, don't you see already upon the report and my carriage, this grave man of business leaves his wife in my lodgings, invites me to his house and wife, who before wou'd not be acquainted with me out of jealousy.

QUACK. Nay, by this means you may be the more acquainted with the husbands, but the less with the wives.

HORNER. Let me along, if I can but abuse the husbands, I'll soon disabuse the wives. Stay – I'll reckon you up the advantages, I am like to have by my stratagem: First, I shall I be rid of all my old acquaintances, the most insatiable sorts of duns, that invade our lodgings in a morning: and next, to the pleasure of making a new mistress, is that of being rid of an old one, and of all old debts; love when it comes to be so, is paid the most unwillingly.

QUACK. Well, you may be so rid of your old acquaintances; but how will you get any new ones?

HORNER. Doctor, thou wilt never make a good chymist, thou art so incredulous and impatient; ask but all the young fellows of the Town, if they do not lose more time like huntsmen, in starting the game, than in running it down; one knows not where to find 'em. Who will, or will not; women of quality are so civil, you can hardly distinguish love from good breeding, and a man is often mistaken; but now I can be sure, she that shews an aversion to me loves the sport, as those women that are gone, whom I warrant to be right: and then the next thing, is your women of honour, as you call 'em, are only chary of their reputations, not their persons, and 'tis scandal they wou'd avoid, not men: Now may I have, by the reputation of an eunuch, the privileges of one; and be seen in a ladies' chamber, in a morning as early as her husband; kiss virgins before their parents, or lovers; and may be in short the *pas par tout*[26] of the Town. Now Doctor.

QUACK. Nay, now you shall be the doctor; and your process is so new, that we do not know but it may succeed.

HORNER. Not so new neither, *probatum est*[27] Doctor.

QUACK. Well, I wish you luck and many patients whil'st I go to mine. [*Exit* Quack.

[*Enter* Harcourt*, and* Dorilant *to* Horner.

HARCOURT. Come, your appearance at the play yesterday, has I hope hardned you for the future against the women's contempt, and the men's raillery; and now you'll abroad as you were wont.

HORNER. Did I not bear it bravely?

DORILANT. With a most theatrical impudence; nay more than the wenches shew there, or a drunken vizard mask,[28] or a great belly'd actress;[29] nay, or the most impudent of creatures, an ill poet; or what is yet more impudent, a second-hand critick.

HORNER. But what say the ladies, have they no pity?

HARCOURT. What ladies? The vizard masks you know never pity a man when all's gone, though in their service.

DORILANT. And for the women in the boxes,[30] you'd never pity them, when 'twas in your power.

HARCOURT. They say, 'tis pity, but all that deal with common women shou'd be serv'd so.

DORILANT. Nay, I dare swear, they won't admit you to play at cards with them, go to plays with 'em, or do the little duties which other shadows of men are wont to do for 'em.

HORNER. Who do you call shadows of men?

DORILANT. Half men.

HORNER. What boys?

DORILANT. Ay, your old boys, old *beaux garcons*,[31] who like superannuated stallions are suffer'd to run, feed, and whinny with the mares as long as they live, though they can do nothing else.

HORNER. Well, a pox on love and wenching, women serve but to keep a man from better company; though I can't enjoy them, I shall you the more: good fellowship and friendship, are lasting, rational and manly pleasures.

HARCOURT. For all that give me some of those pleasures, you call effeminate too, they help to relish one another.

HORNER. They disturb one another.

HARCOURT. No, mistresses are like books; if you pore upon them too much, they doze you, and make you unfit for company; but if us'd discreetly, you are the fitter for conversation by 'em.

DORILANT. A mistress shou'd be like a little country retreat near the Town, not to dwell in constantly, but only for a night and away; to taste the Town the better when a man returns.

HORNER. I tell you, 'tis as hard to be a good fellow, a good friend, and a lover of women, as 'tis to be a good fellow, a good friend, and a lover of money: you cannot follow both, then choose your side; wine gives you liberty, love takes it away.

DORILANT. Gad, he's in the right on't.

HORNER. Wine gives you joy, love grief and tortures; besides the chirurgeon's wine makes us witty, love only sots: wine makes us sleep, love breaks it.

DORILANT. By the World he has reason, *Harcourt*.

HORNER. Wine makes –

DORILANT. Ay, wine makes us – makes us princes, love makes us beggars, poor rogues, y gad – and wine –

HORNER. So, there's one converted. – No, no, love and wine, oil and vinegar.

HARCOURT. I grant it; love will still be uppermost.

HORNER. Come, for my part I will have only those glorious, manly pleasures of being very drunk, and very slovenly.

[*Enter* Boy.

BOY. Mr. *Sparkish* is below, Sir.

HARCOURT. What, my dear Friend! A rogue that is fond of me, only I think for abusing him.

DORILANT. No, he can no more think the men laugh at him, than that women jilt him, his opinion of himself is so good.

HORNER. Well, there's another pleasure by drinking, I thought not of; I shall lose his acquaintance, because he cannot drink; and you know 'tis a very hard thing to be rid of him, for he's one of those nauseous offerers at wit, who like the worst fidlers run themselves into all companies.

HARCOURT. One, that by being in the company of men of sense wou'd pass for one.

HORNER. And may so to the short-sighted World, as a false jewel amongst true ones, is not discern'd at a distance; his company is as troublesome to us, as a cuckold's, when you have a mind to his wife's.

HARCOURT. No, the rogue will not let us enjoy one another, but ravishes our conversation, though he signifies no more to't, than Sir *Martin Mar-all*'s gaping, and auker'd thrumming upon the lute, does to his man's voice, and musick.[32]

DORILANT. And to pass for a wit in Town, shews himself a fool every night to us, that are guilty of the plot.

HORNER. Such wits as he, are, to a company of reasonable men, like rooks to the gamesters, who only fill a room at the table, but are so far from contributing to the play, that they only serve to spoil the fancy of those that do.

DORILANT. Nay, they are us'd like rooks too, snub'd, check'd, and abus'd; yet the rogues will hang on.

HORNER. A pox on 'em, and all that force Nature, and wou'd be still what she forbids 'em; affectation is her greatest monster.

HARCOURT. Most men are the contraries to that they wou'd seem; your bully you see, is a coward with a long sword; the little humbly fawning physician with his ebony cane, is he that destroys men.

DORILANT. The usurer, a poor rogue, possess'd of moldy bonds, and mortgages; and we they call spend-thrifts, are only wealthy, who lay out his money upon daily new purchases of pleasure.

HORNER. Ay, your errantest cheat, is your trustee, or executor; your jealous man, the greatest cuckhold; your Church-man, the greatest atheist; and your noisy pert rogue of a wit, the greatest fop, dullest ass, and worst company, as you shall see: for here he comes.

[*Enter* Sparkish *to them.*

SPARKISH. How is't, Sparks, how is't? Well Faith, *Harry*, I must railly thee a little, ha, ha, ha, upon the report in Town of thee, ha, ha, ha, I can't hold y faith; shall I speak?

HORNER. Yes, but you'll be so bitter then.

SPARKISH. Honest *Dick* and *Frank* here shall answer for me, I will not be extream bitter by the Universe.

HARCOURT. We will be bound in ten thousand pound bond, he shall not be bitter at all.

DORILANT. Nor sharp, nor sweet.

HORNER. What, not down right insipid?

SPARKISH. Nay then, since you are so brisk, and provoke me, take what follows; you must know, I was discoursing and raillying with some ladies yesterday, and they hapned to talk of the fine new signs in Town.[33]

HORNER. Very fine ladies I believe.

SPARKISH. Said I, I know where the best new sign is. Where, says one of the ladies? In *Covent-Garden*, I reply'd. Said another, in what street? In *Russel-street*, answer'd I. Lord says another, I'm sure there was nev'r a fine new sign there yesterday. Yes, but there was, said I again, and it came out of *France*, and has been there a fortnight.

DORILANT. A pox, I can hear no more, prethee.

HORNER. No hear him out; let him tune his crowd a while.

HARCOURT. The worst musick the greatest preparation.

SPARKISH. Nay faith, I'll make you laugh. It cannot be, says a third lady. Yes, yes, quoth I again. Says a fourth lady, –

HORNER. Look to't, we'll have no more ladies.

SPARKISH. No. – then mark, mark, now, said I to the fourth, did you never see Mr. *Horner*; he lodges in *Russel-street*, and he's a sign of a man, you know, since he came out of *France*, heh, hah, he.

HORNER. But the Devil take me, if thine be the sign of a jest.

SPARKISH. With that they all fell a laughing, till they bepiss'd themselves; what, but it does not move you, methinks? Well see one had as good go to law without a witness, as break a jest without a laughter on one's side. – Come, come Sparks,[34] but where do we dine, I have left at *Whitehall* an Earl to dine with you.

DORILANT. Why, I thought thou hadst lov'd a man with a title better, than a suit with a French trimming to't.

HARCOURT. Go to him again.

SPARKISH. No, Sir, a wit to me is the greatest title in the World.

HORNER. But go dine with your Earl, Sir, he may be exceptious; we are your friends, and will not take it ill to be left, I do assure you.

HARCOURT. Nay, faith he shall go to him.

SPARKISH. Nay, pray Gentlemen.

DORILANT. We'll thrust you out, if you wo'not, what disappoint any body for us.

SPARKISH. Nay, dear Gentlemen hear me.

HORNER. No, no, Sir, by no means; pray go Sir.

SPARKISH. Why, dear Rogues. [*They all thrust him out of the room.*

DORILANT. No, no.

ALL. Ha, ha, ha. [Sparkish *returns.*

SPARKISH. But, Sparks, pray hear me; what d'ye think I'll eat then with gay shallow fops, and silent coxcombs? I think wit as necessary at dinner as a glass of good wine, and that's the reason I never have any stomach when I eat alone. – Come, but where do we dine?

HORNER. Ev'n where you will.

SPARKISH. At *Chateline's.*

DORILANT. Yes, if you will.

SPARKISH. Or at the *Cock.*

DORILANT. Yes, if you please.

SPARKISH. Or at the *Dog* and *Partridg.*[35]

HORNER. Ay, if you have mind to't, for we shall dine at neither.

SPARKISH. Pshaw, with your fooling we shall lose the new play; and I wou'd no more miss seeing a new play the first day, than I wou'd miss setting in the wits' row; therefore I'll go fetch my mistress and away. [*Exit* Sparkish.

[*Manent* Horner, Harcourt, Dorilant*; Enter to them* Mr. Pinchwife.

HORNER. Who have we here, *Pinchwife?*

MR. PINCHWIFE. Gentlemen, your humble Servant.

HORNER. Well, *Jack*, by thy long absence from the Town, the grumness[36] of thy countenance, and the slovenlyness of thy habit; I shou'd give thee joy, shou'd I not, of marriage?

MR. PINCHWIFE. – [*Aside*] *Death does he know I'm married too? I thought to have conceal'd it from him at least.* – My long stay in the Country will excuse my dress, and I have a suit of law; that brings me up to Town, that puts me out of humour; besides I must give *Sparkish* to morrow five thousand pound to lye with my sister.

HORNER. Nay, you Country gentlemen rather than not purchase, will buy any thing, and he is a crackt title, if we may quibble: Well, but am I to give thee joy, I heard thou wert marry'd?

MR. PINCHWIFE. What then?

HORNER. Why, the next thing that is to be heard, is thou'rt a cuckold.

MR. PINCHWIFE. [*Aside*] *Insupportable name.*

HORNER. But I did not expect marriage from such a whoremaster as you, one that knew the Town so much, and women so well.

MR. PINCHWIFE. Why, I have marry'd no *London* wife.

HORNER. Pshaw, that's all one, that grave circumspection in marrying a wife, is like refusing a deceitful pamper'd *Smithfield* jade,[37] to go and be cheated by a friend in the Country.

MR. PINCHWIFE. – [*Aside*] *A pox on him and his simile.* – At least we are a little surer of the breed there, know what her keeping has been, whether soyl'd[38] or unsound.

HORNER. Come, come, I have known a clap[39] gotten in *Wales*, and there are cozens, justices, clarks, and chaplains in the Country, I won't say coach-men, but she's handsome and young.

MR. PINCHWIFE. – [*Aside*] *I'll answer as I shou'd do.* – No, no, she has no beauty, but her youth; no attraction, but her modesty, wholesome, homely, and huswifely, that's all.

DORILANT. He talks as like a grasier[40] as he looks.

MR. PINCHWIFE. She's too auker'd, ill-favour'd, and silly[41] to bring to Town.

HARCOURT. Then methinks you shou'd bring her, to be taught breeding.

MR. PINCHWIFE. To be taught; no, Sir, I thank you, good wives, and private souldiers shou'd be ignorant. – [*Aside*] *I'll keep her from your instructions, I warrant you.*

HARCOURT. [*Aside*] *The rogue is as jealous, as if his wife were not ignorant.*

HORNER. Why, if she be ill favour'd, there will be less danger here for you, than by leaving her in the Country; we have such variety of dainties that we are seldom hungry.

DORILANT. But they have alwayes coarse, constant, swinging stomachs in the Country.

HARCOURT. Foul feeders indeed.

DORILANT. And your hospitality is great there.

HARCOURT. Open house, every man's welcome.

MR. PINCHWIFE. So, so, Gentlemen.

HORNER. But prethee, why woud'st thou marry her? If she be ugly, ill-bred, and silly, she must be rich then.

MR. PINCHWIFE. As rich as if she brought me twenty thousand pound out of this Town; for she'll be as sure not to spend her moderate portion, as a *London* baggage wou'd be to spend hers, let it be what it wou'd; so 'tis all one: then because she's ugly, she's the likelyer to be my own; and being ill bred, she'll hate conversation; and since silly and innocent, will not know the difference betwixt a man of one and twenty, and one of forty.

HORNER. Nine – to my knowledge; but if she be silly, she'll expect as much from a man of forty nine, as from him of one and twenty: but methinks wit is more necessary than beauty, and I think no young woman ugly that has it, and no handsome woman agreeable without it.

MR. PINCHWIFE. 'Tis my maxim, he's a fool that marrys, but he's a greater that does not marry a fool; what is wit in a wife good for, but to make a man a cuckold?

HORNER. Yes, to keep it from his knowledge.

MR. PINCHWIFE. A fool cannot contrive to make her husband a cuckold.

HORNER. No, but she'll club with a man that can; and what is worse, if she cannot make her husband a cuckold, she'll make him jealous, and pass for one, and then 'tis all one.

MR. PINCHWIFE. Well, well, I'll take care for one, my wife shall make me no cuckold, though she had your help Mr. *Horner*; I understand the Town, Sir.

DORILANT. [*Aside*] *His help!*

HARCOURT. [*Aside*] *He's come newly to Town it seems, and has not heard how things are with him.*

HORNER. But tell me, has marriage cured thee of whoring, which it seldom does.

HARCOURT. 'Tis more than age can do.

HORNER. No, the word is, I'll marry and live honest; but a marriage vow is like a penitent gamester's oath, and entring into bonds, and penalties to stint himself to such a particular small sum at play for the future, which makes him but the more eager, and not being able to hold out, loses his money again, and his forfeit to boot.

DORILANT. Ay, ay, a gamester will be a gamester, whilst his money lasts; and a whoremaster, whilst his vigour.

HARCOURT. Nay, I have known 'em, when they are broke and can lose no more, keep a fumbling with the box in their hands to fool with only, and hinder other gamesters.

DORILANT. That had wherewithall to make lusty stakes.

MR. PINCHWIFE. Well, Gentlemen, you may laugh at me, but you shall never lye with my wife, I know the Town.

HORNER. But prethee, was not the way you were in better; is not keeping better than marriage?

MR. PINCHWIFE. A pox on't, the jades wou'd jilt me, I cou'd never keep a whore to my self.

HORNER. So then you only marry'd to keep a whore to your self; well, but let me tell you, women, as you say, are like souldiers, made constant and loyal by good pay, rather than by oaths and covenants, therefore I'd advise my friends to keep rather than marry; since too I find by your example, it does not serve one's turn, for I saw you yesterday in the eighteen penny place with a pretty country-wench.

MR. PINCHWIFE. [*Aside*] *How the Devil, did he see my wife then? I sate there that she might not be seen; but she shall never go to a play again.*

HORNER. What dost thou blush at nine and forty, for having been seen with a wench?

DORILANT. No Faith, I warrant 'twas his wife, which he seated there out of sight, for he's a cunning rogue, and understands the Town.

HARCOURT. He blushes, then 'twas his wife; for men are now more ashamed to be seen with them in publick, than with a wench.

MR. PINCHWIFE. [*Aside*] *Hell and damnation, I'm undone, since* Horner *has seen her, and they know 'twas she.*

HORNER. But prethee, was it thy wife? She was exceedingly pretty; I was in love with her at that distance.

MR. PINCHWIFE. You are like never to be nearer to her. Your Servant Gentlemen. [*Offers to go.*

HORNER. Nay, prethee stay.

MR. PINCHWIFE. I cannot, I will not.

HORNER. Come you shall dine with us.

MR. PINCHWIFE. I have din'd already.

HORNER. Come, I know thou hast not; I'll treat thee dear Rogue, thou sha't spend none of thy *Hampshire* money to day.

MR. PINCHWIFE. [*Aside*] *Treat me; so he uses me already like his cuckold.*

HORNER. Nay, you shall not go.

MR. PINCHWIFE. I must, I have business at home. [*Exit* Pinchwife.

HARCOURT. To beat his wife, he's as jealous of her, as a *Cheapside* husband of a *Covent-garden* wife.[42]

HORNER. Why, 'tis as hard to find an old whore-master without jealousy and the gout, as a young one without fear or the pox.

As gout in age, from pox in youth proceeds;
So wenching past, then jealousy succeeds:
The worst disease that love and wenching breeds.

Act II.

[Mrs. Margery Pinchwife, *and* Alithea: Mr. Pinchwife *peeping behind at the door.*]

MRS. PINCHWIFE. Pray, Sister, where are the best fields and woods, to walk in in *London?*

ALITHEA. A pretty question; why, Sister! *Mulberry Garden*, and St. *James's Park*; and for close walks the *New Exchange*.[43]

MRS. PINCHWIFE. Pray, Sister, tell me why my husband looks so grum here in Town? And keeps me up so close, and will not let me go a walking, nor let me wear my best gown yesterday?

ALITHEA. O he's jealous, Sister.

MRS. PINCHWIFE. Jealous, what's that?

ALITHEA. He's afraid you shou'd love another man.

MRS. PINCHWIFE. How shou'd he be afraid of my loving another man, when he will not let me see any but himself.

ALITHEA. Did he not carry you yesterday to a play?

MRS. PINCHWIFE. Ay, but we sate amongst ugly people, he wou'd not let me come near the gentry, who sate under us, so that I cou'd not see 'em: he told me none but naughty women sate there, whom they tous'd and mous'd; but I wou'd have ventur'd for all that.

ALITHEA. But how did you like the play?

MRS. PINCHWIFE. Indeed I was aweary of the play, but I lik'd hugeously the actors; they are the goodlyest proper'st men, Sister.

ALITHEA. O but you must not like the actors, Sister.

MRS. PINCHWIFE. Ay, how shou'd I help it, Sister? Pray, Sister, when my husband comes in, will you ask leave for me to go a walking?

ALITHEA. – [*Aside*] *A walking, hah, ha; Lord, a Country gentlewoman's pleasure is the drudgery of a foot-post; and she requires as much airing as her husband's horses.* –

[*Enter* Mr. Pinchwife *to them*]

But here comes your husband; I'll ask, though I'm sure he'll not grant it.

MRS. PINCHWIFE. He says he won't let me go abroad, for fear of catching the pox.

ALITHEA. Fye, the small pox you shou'd say.

MRS. PINCHWIFE. Oh my dear, dear Bud, welcome home; why dost thou look so fropish,[44] who has nanger'd thee?

MR. PINCHWIFE. You're a fool. [Mrs. Pinchwife *goes aside, & cryes.*

ALITHEA. Faith so she is, for crying for no fault, poor tender creature!

MR. PINCHWIFE. What you wou'd have her as impudent as your self, as errant a jilflirt, a gadder, a magpy, and to say all, a meer notorious Town-Woman?

ALITHEA. Brother, you are my only censurer; and the honour of your family shall sooner suffer in your wife there, than in me, though I take the innocent liberty of the Town.

MR. PINCHWIFE. Hark you Mistress, do not talk so before my wife, the innocent liberty of the Town!

ALITHEA. Why, pray, who boasts of any intrigue with me? What lampoon has made my name notorious? What ill women frequent my lodgings? I keep no company with any women of scandalous reputations.

MR. PINCHWIFE. No, you keep the men of scandalous reputations company.

ALITHEA. Where? Wou'd you not have me civil? Answer 'em in a box at the plays? In the drawing room at *Whitehall*? In St. *James's Park*? *Mulberry-garden*? Or –

MR. PINCHWIFE. Hold, hold, do not teach my wife, where the men are to be found; I believe she's the worse for your Town documents already; I bid you keep her in ignorance as I do.

MRS. PINCHWIFE. Indeed be not angry with her Bud, she will tell me nothing of the Town, though I ask her a thousand times a day.

MR. PINCHWIFE. Then you are very inquisitive to know, I find?

MRS. PINCHWIFE. Not I indeed, Dear, I hate *London*; our place-house in the Country is worth a thousand of't, wou'd I were there again.

MR. PINCHWIFE. So you shall I warrant; but were you not talking of plays, and players, when I came in? You are her encourager in such discourses.

MRS. PINCHWIFE. No indeed, Dear, she chid me just now for liking the player men.

MR. PINCHWIFE. – [*Aside*] *Nay, if she be so innocent as to own to me her liking them, there is no hurt in't* – Come my poor Rogue, but thou lik'st none better then me?

MRS. PINCHWIFE. Yes indeed, but I do, the player men are finer folks.

MR. PINCHWIFE. But you love none better then me?

MRS. PINCHWIFE. You are mine own Dear Bud, and I know you, I hate a stranger.

MR. PINCHWIFE. Ay, my Dear, you must love me only, and not be like the naughty Town women, who only hate their husbands, and love every man else, love plays, visits, fine coaches, fine clothes, fidles, balls, treates, and so lead a wicked Town-life.

MRS. PINCHWIFE. Nay, if to enjoy all these things be a Town-life, *London* is not so bad a place, Dear.

MR. PINCHWIFE. How! If you love me, you must hate *London*.

ALITHEA. The fool has forbid me discovering to her the pleasures of the Town, and he is now setting her agog upon them himself.

MRS. PINCHWIFE. But, Husband, do the Town-women love the player men too?

MR. PINCHWIFE. Yes, I warrant you.

MRS. PINCHWIFE. Ay, I warrant you.

MR. PINCHWIFE. Why, you do not, I hope?

MRS. PINCHWIFE. No, no, Bud; but why have we no player-men in the Country?

MR. PINCHWIFE. Ha – Mrs. Minx, ask me no more to go to a play.

MRS. PINCHWIFE. Nay, why, Love? I did not care for going; but when you forbid me, you make me as't were desire it.

ALITHEA. [*Aside*] *So 'twill be in other things, I warrant.*

MRS. PINCHWIFE. Pray, let me go to a play, Dear.

MR. PINCHWIFE. Hold your peace, I wo'not.

MRS. PINCHWIFE. Why, Love?

MR. PINCHWIFE. Why, I'll tell you.

ALITHEA. [*Aside*] *Nay, if he tell her, she'll give him more cause to forbid her that place.*

MRS. PINCHWIFE. Pray, why, Dear?

MR. PINCHWIFE. First, you like the actors, and the gallants may like you.

MRS. PINCHWIFE. What, a homely Country girl? No Bud, no body will like me.

MR. PINCHWIFE. I tell you, yes, they may.

MRS. PINCHWIFE. No, no, you jest – I won't believe you, I will go.

MR. PINCHWIFE. I tell you then, that one of the lewdest fellows in Town, who saw you there, told me he was in love with you.

MRS. PINCHWIFE. Indeed! Who, who, pray who was't?

MR. PINCHWIFE. [*Aside*] *I've gone too far, and slipt before I was aware; how overjoy'd she is!*

MRS. PINCHWIFE. Was it any *Hampshire* gallant, any of our neighbours? I promise you, I am beholding to him.

MR. PINCHWIFE. I promise you, you lye; for he wou'd but ruin you, as he has done hundreds: he has no other love for women, but that, such as he, look upon women like basilisks,[45] but to destroy 'em.

MRS. PINCHWIFE. Ay, but if he loves me, why shou'd he ruin me? Answer me to that: methinks he shou'd not, I wou'd do him no harm.

ALITHEA. Hah, ha, ha.

MR. PINCHWIFE. 'Tis very well; but I'll keep him from doing you any harm, or me either.

[*Enter* Sparkish *and* Harcourt.

But here comes company, get you in, get you in.

MRS. PINCHWIFE. But pray, Husband, is he a pretty gentleman, that loves me?

MR. PINCHWIFE. In baggage, in. [*Thrusts her in: shuts the door*] What all the lewd libertines of the Town brought to my lodging, by this easie coxcomb! S'death I'll not suffer it.

SPARKISH. Here *Harcourt*, do you approve my choice? Dear, little Rogue, I told you, I'd bring you acquainted with all my friends, the wits, and – [Harcourt *salutes her.*

MR. PINCHWIFE. Ay, they shall know her, as well as you your self will, I warrant you.

SPARKISH. This is one of those, my pretty Rogue, that are to dance at your wedding to morrow; and him you must bid welcome ever, to what you and I have.

MR. PINCHWIFE. [*Aside*] *Monstrous!*

SPARKISH. *Harcourt* how dost thou like her, Faith? Nay, Dear, do not look down; I should hate to have a wife of mine out of countenance at any thing.

MR. PINCHWIFE. Wonderful!

SPARKISH. Tell me, I say, *Harcourt*, how dost thou like her? Thou hast star'd upon her enough, to resolve me.

HARCOURT. So infinitely well, that I cou'd wish I had a mistress too, that might differ from her in nothing, but her love and engagement to you.

ALITHEA. Sir, Master *Sparkish* has often told me, that his acquaintance were all wits and raillieurs, and now I find it.

SPARKISH. No, by the Universe, Madam, he does not railly now; you may believe him: I do assure you, he is the honestest, worthyest, true hearted gentleman – A man of such perfect honour, he wou'd say nothing to a lady, he does not mean.

MR. PINCHWIFE. Praising another man to his mistress!

HARCOURT. Sir, you are so beyond expectation obliging, that –

SPARKISH. Nay, I gad, I am sure you do admire her extreamly, I see't in your eyes. – He does admire you Madam. – By the World, don't you?

HARCOURT. Yes, above the World, or, the most glorious part of it, her whole sex; and till now I never thought I shou'd have envied you, or any man about to marry, but you have the best excuse for marriage I ever knew.

ALITHEA. Nay, now, Sir, I'm satisfied you are of the society of the wits, and raillieurs, since you cannot spare your friend, even when he is but too civil to you; but the surest sign is, since you are an enemy to marriage, for that I hear you hate as much as business or bad wine.

HARCOURT. Truly, Madam, I never was an enemy to marriage, till now, because marriage was never an enemy to me before.

ALITHEA. But why, Sir, is marriage an enemy to you now? Because it robs you of your friend here; for you look upon a friend married, as one gone into a monastery, that is dead to the World.

HARCOURT. 'Tis indeed, because you marry him; I see Madam, you can guess my meaning: I do confess heartily and openly, I wish it were in my power to break the match, by Heavens. I wou'd.

SPARKISH. Poor *Frank!'*

ALITHEA. Wou'd you be so unkind to me?

HARCOURT. No, no, 'tis not because I wou'd be unkind to you.

SPARKISH. Poor *Frank*, no gad, 'tis only his kindness to me.

MR. PINCHWIFE. [*Aside*] *Great kindness to you indeed; insensible fop, let a man make love to his wife to his face.*

SPARKISH. Come dear *Frank*, for all my wife there that shall be, thou shalt enjoy me sometimes dear Rogue; by my honour, we men of wit condole for our deceased brother in marriage, as much as for one dead in earnest: I think that was prettily said of me, ha *Harcourt?* – But come *Frank*, be not melancholy for me.

HARCOURT. No, I assure you I am not melancholy for you.

SPARKISH. Prethee, *Frank*, dost think my wife that shall be there a fine person?[46]

HARCOURT. I cou'd gaze upon her, till *I* became as blind as you are.

SPARKISH. How, as *I* am! How!

HARCOURT. Because you are a lover, and true lovers are blind, stockblind.

SPARKISH. True, true; but by the World she has wit too, as well as beauty: go, go with her into a corner, and trye if she has wit, talk to her any thing, she's bashful before me.

HARCOURT. Indeed if a woman wants wit in a corner, she has it no where.

ALITHEA. Sir, you dispose of me a little before your time. – [*Aside to* Sparkish.

SPARKISH. Nay, nay, Madam let me have an earnest of your obedience, or – go, go, Madam – [Harcourt *courts* Alithea *aside.*

MR. PINCHWIFE. How, Sir, if you are not concern'd for the honour of a wife, I am for that of a sister;

he shall not debauch her: be a pander to your own wife, bring men to her, let'em make love before your face, thrust'em into a corner together, then leave 'em in private! Is this your Town wit and conduct?

SPARKISH. Hah, ha, ha, a silly wise rogue, wou'd make one laugh more then a stark fool, ha, ha: *I* shall burst. Nay, you shall not disturb 'em; I'll vex thee, by the World. [*Struggles with* Pinchwife *to keep him from* Harcourt *and* Alithea.

ALITHEA. The writings are drawn, Sir, settlements[47] made; 'tis too late, Sir, and past all revocation.

HARCOURT. Then so is my death.

ALITHEA. I wou'd not be unjust to him.

HARCOURT. Then why to me so?

ALITHEA. I have no obligation to you.

HARCOURT. My love.

ALITHEA. I had his before.

HARCOURT. You never had it; he wants you see jealousie, the only infallible sign of it.

ALITHEA. Love proceeds from esteem; he cannot distrust my virtue, besides he loves me, or he wou'd not marry me.

HARCOURT. Marrying you, is no more sign of his love, then bribing your woman, that he may marry you, is a sign of his generosity: marriage is rather a sign of interest, then love; and he that marries a fortune, covets a mistress, not loves her: But if you take marriage for a sign of love, take it from me immediately.

ALITHEA. No, now you have put a scruple in my head; but in short, Sir, to end our dispute, I must marry him, my reputation wou'd suffer in the world else.

HARCOURT. No; if you do marry him, with your pardon, Madam, your reputation suffers in the world, and you wou'd be thought in necessity for a cloak.

ALITHEA. Nay, now you are rude, Sir. – Mr. *Sparkish*, pray come hither, your friend here is very troublesom, and very loving.

HARCOURT. [*Aside to* Alithea] Hold, hold –

MR. PINCHWIFE. D'ye hear that?

SPARKISH. Why, d'ye think I'll seem to be jealous, like a Country bumpkin?

MR. PINCHWIFE. No, rather be a cuckold, like a credulous Cit.[48]

HARCOURT. Madam, you wou'd not have been so little generous as to have told him.

ALITHEA. Yes, since you cou'd be so little generous, as to wrong him.

HARCOURT. Wrong him, no man can do't, he's beneath an injury; a bubble,[49] a coward, a senseless idiot, a wretch so contemptible to all the World but you, that –

ALITHEA. Hold, do not rail at him, for since he is like to be my husband, I am resolv'd to like him: Nay, I think I am oblig'd to tell him, you are not his friend. – Master *Sparkish*, Master *Sparkish*.

SPARKISH. What, what; now dear Rogue, has not she wit?

HARCOURT. Not so much as I thought, and hoped she had. [*Speaks surlily*.

ALITHEA. Mr. *Sparkish*, do you bring people to rail at you?

HARCOURT. Madam –

SPARKISH. How! No, but if he does rail at me, 'tis but in jest I warrant; what we wits do for one another, and never take any notice of it.

ALITHEA. He spoke so scurrilously of you, I had no patience to hear him; besides he has been making love to me.

HARCOURT. [*Aside*] *True damn'd tell-tale-woman.*

SPARKISH. Pshaw, to shew his parts[50] – we wits rail and make love often, but to shew our parts; as we have no affections, so we have no malice, we –

ALITHEA. He said you were a wretch, below an injury.

SPARKISH. Pshaw.

HARCOURT. Damn'd, senseless, impudent, virtuous jade; well since she won't let me have her, she'll do as good, she'll make me hate her.

ALITHEA. A common bubble.

SPARKISH. Pshaw.

ALITHEA. A coward.

SPARKISH. Pshaw, pshaw.

ALITHEA. A senseless driveling idiot.

SPARKISH. How, did he disparage my parts? Nay, then my honour's concern'd, I can't put up that, Sir; by the World, Brother help me to kill him; – [*Aside. Offers to draw*] *I may draw now, since we have the odds of him: – 'tis a good occasion too before my mistress –*

ALITHEA. Hold, hold.

SPARKISH. What, what.

ALITHEA. [*Aside*] *I must not let'em kill the gentleman neither, for his kindness to me; I am so far from hating him, that I wish my gallant had his person and understanding: – Nay if my honour –*

SPARKISH. I'll be thy death.

ALITHEA. Hold, hold, indeed to tell the truth, the gentleman said after all, that what he spoke, was but out of friendship to you.

SPARKISH. How! Say, I am, I am a fool, that is no wit, out of friendship to me.

ALITHEA. Yes, to try whether I was concern'd enough for you, and made love to me only to be satisfy'd of my virtue, for your sake.

HARCOURT. [*Aside*] *Kind however.*

SPARKISH. Nay, if it were so, my dear Rogue, I ask thee pardon; but why wou'd not you tell me so, faith.

HARCOURT. Because *I* did not think on't, faith.

SPARKISH. Come, *Horner* does not come, *Harcourt*, let's be gone to the new play. – Come Madam.

ALITHEA. I will not go, if you intend to leave me alone in the box, and run into the pit, as you use to do.

SPARKISH. Pshaw, I'll leave *Harcourt* with you in the box, to entertain you, and that's as good; if I sate in the box, I shou'd be thought no judge, but of trimmings. – Come away *Harcourt*, lead her down. [*Exeunt* Sparkish, Harcourt, *and* Alithea.

MR. PINCHWIFE. Well, go thy wayes, for the flower of the true Town fops, such as spend their estates, before they come to'em, and are cuckolds before they're married. But let me go look to my own free-hold – How –

[*Enter my* Lady Fidget, Mistress Dainty Fidget, *and* Mistress Squeamish.

LADY FIDGET. Your Servant, Sir, where is your Lady? We are come to wait upon her to the new play.

MR. PINCHWIFE. New play!

LADY FIDGET. And my husband will wait upon you presently.

MR. PINCHWIFE. – [*Aside*] *Damn your civility* – Madam, by no means, I will not see Sir *Jasper* here, till I have waited upon him at home; nor shall my wife see you, till she has waited upon your Ladyship at your lodgings.

LADY FIDGET. Now we are here, Sir –

MR. PINCHWIFE. No, Madam.

DAINTY FIDGET. Pray, let us see her.

MRS. SQUEAMISH. We will not stir, till we see her.

MR. PINCHWIFE. – [*Aside*] *A pox on you all* – [*Goes to the door, and returns*] – She has lock'd the door, and is gone abroad.

LADY FIDGET. No, you have lock'd the door, and she's within.

DAINTY FIDGET. They told us below, she was here.

MR. PINCHWIFE. (Will nothing do?) – Well it must out then, to tell you the truth, Ladies, which I was afraid to let you know before, lest it might endanger your lives, my wife has just now the small pox come out upon her, do not be frighten'd; but pray, be gone Ladies, you shall not stay here in danger of your lives; pray get you gone Ladies.

LADY FIDGET. No, no, we have all had 'em.

MRS. SQUEAMISH. Alack, alack!

DAINTY FIDGET. Come, come, we must see how it goes with her, I understand the disease.

LADY FIDGET. Come.

MR. PINCHWIFE. [*Aside*] *Well, there is no being too hard for women at their own weapon, lying, therefore I'll quit the field.* [*Exit* Pinchwife.

MRS. SQUEAMISH. Here's an example of jealousy.

LADY FIDGET. Indeed as the World goes, I wonder there are no more jealous, since wives are so neglected.

DAINTY FIDGET. Pshaw, as the World goes, to what end shou'd they be jealous.

LADY FIDGET. Foh, 'tis a nasty World.

MRS. SQUEAMISH. That men of parts, great acquaintance, and quality shou'd take up with, and spend themselves and fortunes, in keeping little play-house creatures, foh.

LADY FIDGET. Nay, that women of understanding, great acquaintance, and good quality, shou'd fall a keeping too of little creatures, foh.

MRS. SQUEAMISH. Why, 'tis the men of qualities' fault, they never visit women of honour, and reputation, as they us'd to do; and have not so much as common civility, for ladies of our rank, but use us with the same indifferency, and ill breeding, as if we were all marry'd to 'em.

LADY FIDGET. She says true, 'tis an errant shame women of quality shou'd be so slighted; methinks, birth, birth, shou'd go for something; I have known men admired, courted, and followed for their titles only.

MRS. SQUEAMISH. Ay, one wou'd think men of honour shou'd not love no more, than marry out of their own rank.

DAINTY FIDGET. Fye, fye upon 'em, they are come to think cross breeding for themselves best, as well as for their dogs, and horses.

LADY FIDGET. They are dogs, and horses for't.

MRS. SQUEAMISH. One wou'd think if not for love, for vanity a little.

DAINTY FIDGET. Nay, they do satisfy their vanity upon us sometimes; and are kind to us in their report, tell all the World they lye with us.

LADY FIDGET. Damn'd rascals, that we shou'd be only wrong'd by 'em; to report a man has had a person, when he has not had a person, is the greatest wrong in the whole world, that can be done to a person.

MRS. SQUEAMISH. Well, 'tis an errant shame, noble persons shou'd be so wrong'd, and neglected.

LADY FIDGET. But still 'tis an erranter shame for a noble person, to neglect her own honour, and defame her own noble person, with little inconsiderable fellows, foh! –

DAINTY FIDGET. I suppose the crime against our honour, is the same with a man of quality as with another.

LADY FIDGET. How! No sure the man of quality is likest one's husband, and therefore the fault shou'd be the less.

DAINTY FIDGET. But then the pleasure shou'd be the less.

LADY FIDGET. Fye, fye, fye, for shame Sister, whither shall we ramble? Be continent in your discourse, or I shall hate you.

DAINTY FIDGET. Besides an intrigue is so much the more notorious for the man's quality.

MRS. SQUEAMISH. 'Tis true, no body takes notice of a private man, and therefore with him, 'tis more secret, and the crime's the less, when 'tis not known.

LADY FIDGET. You say true; y faith, I think you are in the right on't: 'tis not an injury to a husband, till it be an injury to our honours; so that a woman of honour loses no honour with a private person; and to say truth –

DAINTY FIDGET. So the little Fellow is grown a private Person – with her – [*Apart to* Squeamish.

LADY FIDGET. But still my dear, dear honour.

[*Enter* Sir Jasper, Horner, Dorilant.

SIR JASPER. Ay, my dear, dear of honour, thou hast still so much honour in thy mouth –

HORNER. [*Aside*] *That she has none elsewhere.*

LADY FIDGET. Oh, what d'ye mean to bring in these upon us?

DAINTY FIDGET. Foh, these are as bad as wits.

MRS. SQUEAMISH. Foh!

LADY FIDGET. Let us leave the room.

SIR JASPER. Stay, stay, faith to tell you the naked truth.

LADY FIDGET. Fye, Sir *Jasper*, do not use that word naked.

SIR JASPER. Well, well, in short I have business at *Whitehall*, and cannot go to the play with you, therefore wou'd have you go –

LADY FIDGET. With those two to a play?

SIR JASPER. No, not with t'other, but with Mr. *Horner*, there can be no more scandal to go with him, than with Mr. *Tattle*, or Master *Limberham*.[51]

LADY FIDGET. With that nasty fellow! No – no.

SIR JASPER. Nay, prethee Dear, hear me. [*Whispers to* Lady Fidget.

HORNER. Ladies. [Horner, Dorilant *drawing near* Squeamish, *and* Dainty.

DAINTY FIDGET. Stand off.

MRS. SQUEAMISH. Do not approach us.

DAINTY FIDGET. You herd with the wits, you are obscenity all over.

MRS. SQUEAMISH. And I wou'd as soon look upon a picture of *Adam* and *Eve*, without fig leaves, as any of you, if I cou'd help it, therefore keep off, and do not make us sick.

DORILANT. What a Devil are these?

HORNER. Why, these are pretenders to honour, as criticks to wit, only by censuring others; and as every raw, peevish, out-of-humour'd, affected, dull, tea-drinking, arithmetical fop sets up for a wit, by railing at men of sense, so these for honour, by railing at the Court, and ladies of as great honour, as quality.

SIR JASPER. Come, Mr. *Horner*, I must desire you to go with these ladies to the play, Sir.

HORNER. I! Sir.

SIR JASPER. Ay, ay, come, Sir.

HORNER. I must beg your pardon, Sir, and theirs, I will not be seen in women's company in publick again for the world.

SIR JASPER. Ha, ha, strange aversion!

MRS. SQUEAMISH. No, he's for women's company in private.

SIR JASPER. He – poor man – he! Hah, ha, ha.

DAINTY FIDGET. 'Tis a greater shame amongst lew'd fellows to be seen in virtuous women's company, than for the women to be seen with them.

HORNER. Indeed, Madam, the time was I only hated virtuous women, but now I hate the other too; I beg your pardon Ladies.

LADY FIDGET. You are very obliging, Sir, because we wou'd not be troubled with you.

SIR JASPER. In sober sadness he shall go.

DORILANT. Nay, if he wo'not, I am ready to wait upon the Ladies; and I think I am the fitter man.

SIR JASPER. You, Sir, no I thank you for that – Master *Horner* is a privileg'd man amongst the virtuous ladies, 'twill be a great while before you are so; heh, he, he, he's my wive's gallant, heh, he he; no pray withdraw, Sir, for as I take it, the virtuous ladies have no business with you.

DORILANT. And I am sure, he can have none with them: 'tis strange a man can't come amongst virtuous women now, but upon the same terms, as men are admitted into the great Turk's Seraglio; but Heavens keep me, from being an hombre[52] player with'em: but where is *Pinchwife* – [*Exit* Dorilant.

SIR JASPER. Come, come, Man; what avoid the sweet society of woman-kind? That sweet, soft, gentle, tame, noble creature woman, made for man's companion –

HORNER. So is that soft, gentle, tame, and more noble creature a spaniel, and has all their tricks, can fawn, lye down, suffer beating, and fawn the more; barks at your friends, when they come to see you; makes your bed hard, gives you fleas, and the mange sometimes: and all the difference is, the spaniel's the more faithful animal, and fawns but upon one master.

SIR JASPER. Heh, he, he.

MRS. SQUEAMISH. O the rude beast.

DAINTY FIDGET. Insolent brute.

LADY FIDGET. Brute! Stinking mortify'd rotten French weather, to dare –

SIR JASPER. Hold, an't please your Ladyship; for shame Master *Horner*, your mother was a woman – [*Aside*] *Now shall I never reconcile'em.* – Hark you, Madam, take my advice in your anger; you know you often want one to make up your droling pack of hombre players; and you may cheat him easily, for he's an ill gamester, and consequently loves play: besides you know, you have but two old civil gentlemen (with stinking breaths too) to wait upon you abroad, take in the third, into your service; the other are but crazy: and a lady shou'd have a supernumerary Gentleman-Usher,[53] as a supernumerary coach-horse, lest sometimes you shou'd be forc'd to stay at home.

LADY FIDGET. But are you sure he loves play, and has money?

SIR JASPER. He loves play as much as you, and has money as much as I.

LADY FIDGET. Then I am contented to make him pay for his scurrillity; money makes up in a measure all other wants in men. – [*Aside*] *Those whom we cannot make hold for gallants, we make fine.*

SIR JASPER. – [*Aside*] *So, so; now to mollify, to wheedle him.* – Master *Horner* will you never keep civil company, methinks 'tis time now, since you are only fit for them: Come, come, Man you must e'en fall to visiting our wives, eating at our tables, drinking tea with our virtuous relations after dinner, dealing cards to 'em, reading plays, and gazets to 'em, picking fleas out of their shocks[54] for 'em, collecting receipts,[55] new songs, women, pages, and footmen for 'em.

HORNER. I hope they'll afford me better employment, Sir.

SIR JASPER. Heh, he, he, 'tis fit you know your work before you come into your place; and since you are unprovided of a lady to flatter, and a good house to eat at, pray frequent mine, and call my wife Mistress, and she shall call you Gallant, according to the custom.

HORNER. Who I? –

SIR JASPER. Faith, thou sha't for my sake, come for my sake only.

HORNER. For your sake –

SIR JASPER. Come, come, here's a gamester for you, let him be a little familiar sometimes; nay, what if a little rude; gamesters may be rude with ladies, you know.

LADY FIDGET. Yes, losing gamesters have a privilege with women.

HORNER. I alwayes thought the contrary, that the winning gamester had most privilege with women, for when you have lost your money to a man, you'll lose any thing you have, all you have, they say, and he may use you as he pleases.

SIR JASPER. Heh, he, he, well, win or lose you shall have your liberty with her.

LADY FIDGET. As he behaves himself; and for your sake I'll give him admittance and freedom.

HORNER. All sorts of freedom, Madam?

SIR JASPER. Ay, ay, ay, all sorts of freedom thou can'st take, and so go to her, begin thy new employment; wheedle her, jest with her, and be better acquainted one with another.

HORNER. [*Aside*] *I think I know her already, therefore may venture with her, my secret for hers* – [Horner, *and* Lady Fidget *whisper.*

SIR JASPER. Sister *Cuz*, I have provided an innocent play-fellow for you there.

DAINTY FIDGET. Who he!

MRS. SQUEAMISH. There's a play-fellow indeed.

SIR JASPER. Yes sure, what he is good enough to play at cards, Blind-man's buff, or the fool with sometimes.

MRS. SQUEAMISH. Foh, we'll have no such play-fellows.

DAINTY FIDGET. No, Sir, you shan't choose play-fellows for us, we thank you.

SIR JASPER. Nay, pray hear me. [*Whispering to them.*

LADY FIDGET. But, poor Gentleman, cou'd you be so generous? So truly a man of honour, as for the sakes of us women of honour, to cause your self to be reported no man? No man! And to suffer your self the greatest shame that cou'd fall upon a man, that none might fall upon us women by your conversation; but indeed, Sir, as perfectly, perfectly, the same man as before your going into *France*, Sir; as perfectly, perfectly, Sir.

HORNER. As perfectly, perfectly, Madam; nay, I scorn you shou'd take my word; I desire to be try'd only, Madam.

LADY FIDGET. Well, that's spoken again like a man of honour, all men of honour desire to come to the test: but indeed, generally you men report such things of your selves, one does not know how, or whom to believe; and it is come to that pass, we dare not take your words, no more than your taylor's, without some staid servant of yours be bound with you; but I have so strong a faith in your honour, dear, dear, noble Sir, that I'd forfeit mine for yours at any time, dear Sir.

HORNER. No, Madam, you shou'd not need to forfeit it for me, I have given you security already to save you harmless, my late reputation being so well known in the World, Madam.

LADY FIDGET. But if upon any future falling out, or upon a suspition of my taking the trust out of your hands, to employ some other, you your self shou'd betray your trust, dear Sir; I mean, if you'll give me leave to speak obscenely, you might tell, dear Sir.

HORNER. If I did, no body wou'd believe me; the reputation of impotency is as hardly recover'd again in the World, as that of cowardise, dear Madam.

LADY FIDGET. Nay then, as one may say, you may do your worst, dear, dear, Sir.

SIR JASPER. Come, is your Ladyship reconciled to him yet? Have you agreed on matters? For I must be gone to *Whitehall*.

LADY FIDGET. Why, indeed, Sir *Jasper*, Master *Horner* is a thousand, thousand times a better man, than I thought him: Cosen *Squeamish*, Sister *Dainty*, I can name him now, truly not long ago you know, I thought his very name obscenity, and I wou'd as soon have lain with him, as have nam'd him.

SIR JASPER. Very likely, poor Madam.

DAINTY FIDGET. I believe it.

MRS. SQUEAMISH. No doubt on't.

SIR JASPER. Well, well – that your Ladyship is as virtuous as any she, – I know, and him all the Town knows – heh, he, he; therefore now you like him, get you gone to your business together; go, go, to your business, I say, pleasure, whilst I go to my pleasure, business.

LADY FIDGET. Come then dear Gallant.

HORNER. Come away, my dearest Mistress.

SIR JASPER. So, so, why 'tis as I'd have it. [*Exit* Sir Jasper.

HORNER. And as I'd have it.

LADY FIDGET. Who for his business, from his wife will run;

Takes the best care, to have her bus'ness done. [*Exeunt omnes*.

Act III.

[Alithea, *and* Mrs. Pinchwife.]

ALITHEA. Sister, what ailes you, you are grown melancholy?

MRS. PINCHWIFE. Wou'd it not make any one melancholy, to see you go every day fluttering about abroad, whil'st I must stay at home like a poor lonely, sullen bird in a cage?

ALITHEA. Ay, Sister, but you came young, and just from the nest to your cage, so that I thought you lik'd it; and cou'd be as chearful in't, as others that took their flight themselves early, and are hopping abroad in the open air.

MRS. PINCHWIFE. Nay, I confess I was quiet enough, till my husband told me, what pure lives, the *London* ladies live abroad, with their dancing, meetings, and junketings, and drest every day in their best gowns; and I warrant you, play at Nine Pins every day of the week, so they do.

[*Enter* Mr. Pinchwife.

MR. PINCHWIFE. Come, what's here to do? You are putting the Town pleasures in her head, and setting her a longing.

ALITHEA. Yes, after Nine Pins; you suffer none to give her those longings, you mean, but your self.

MR. PINCHWIFE. I tell her of the vanities of the Town like a confessor.

ALITHEA. A confessor! Just such a confessor, as he that by forbidding a silly oastler,[56] to grease the horses' teeth, taught him to do't.

MR. PINCHWIFE. Come Mistress *Flippant*, good precepts are lost, when bad examples are still before us; the liberty you take abroad makes her hanker after it; and out of humour at home, poor wretch! She desired not to come to *London*, I wou'd bring her.

ALITHEA. Very well.

MR. PINCHWIFE. She has been this week in Town, and never desired, till this afternoon, to go abroad.

ALITHEA. Was she not at a play yesterday?

MR. PINCHWIFE. Yes, but she ne'er ask'd me; I was my self the cause of her going.

ALITHEA. Then if she ask you again, you are the cause of her asking, and not my example.

MR. PINCHWIFE. Well, to morrow night I shall be rid of you; and the next day before 'tis light, she and I'll be rid of the Town, and my dreadful apprehensions: Come, be not melancholly, for thou sha't go into the Country after to morrow, Dearest.

ALITHEA. Great comfort.

MRS. PINCHWIFE. Pish, what d'ye tell me of the Country for?

MR. PINCHWIFE. How's this! What, pish at the Country?

MRS. PINCHWIFE. Let me alone, I am not well.

MR. PINCHWIFE. O, if that be all – what ailes my dearest?

MRS. PINCHWIFE. Truly I don't know; but I have not been well, since you told me there was a gallant at the play in love with me.

MR. PINCHWIFE. Ha –

ALITHEA. That's by my example too.

MR. PINCHWIFE. Nay, if you are not well, but are so concern'd, because a lew'd fellow chanc'd to lye, and say he lik'd you, you'll make me sick too.

MRS. PINCHWIFE. Of what sickness?

MR. PINCHWIFE. O, of that which is worse than the plague, jealousy.

MRS. PINCHWIFE. Pish, you jeer, I'm sure there's no such disease in our receipt-book at home.

MR. PINCHWIFE. No, thou never met'st with it, poor Innocent – [*Aside*] *well, if thou cuckold me, 'twill be my own fault – for cuckolds and bastards, are generally makers of their own fortune.*

MRS. PINCHWIFE. Well, but pray Bud, let's go to a play to night.

MR. PINCHWIFE. 'Tis just done, she comes from it; but why are you so eager to see a play?

MRS. PINCHWIFE. Faith Dear, not that I care one pin for their talk there; but I like to look upon the player-men, and wou'd see, if I cou'd, the gallant you say loves me; that's all dear Bud.

MR. PINCHWIFE. Is that all dear Bud?

ALITHEA. This proceeds from my example.

MRS. PINCHWIFE. But if the play be done, let's go abroad however, dear Bud.

MR. PINCHWIFE. Come have a little patience, and thou shalt go into the Country on Friday.

MRS. PINCHWIFE. Therefore I wou'd see first some sights, to tell my neighbours of. Nay, I will go abroad, that's once.

ALITHEA. I'm the cause of this desire too.

MR. PINCHWIFE. But now I think on't, who was the cause of *Horner*'s coming to my lodging to day? That was you.

ALITHEA. No, you, because you wou'd not let him see your handsome wife out of your lodging.

MRS. PINCHWIFE. Why, O Lord! Did the gentleman come hither to see me indeed?

MR. PINCHWIFE. No, no; – you are not cause of that damn'd question too, Mistress *Alithea*? – [*Aside*] *Well she's in the right of it; he is in love with my wife – and comes after her – 'tis so – but I'll nip his love in the bud; lest he should follow us into the Country, and break his chariot-wheel near our house, on purpose for an excuse to come to't; but I think I know the Town.*

MRS. PINCHWIFE. Come, pray Bud, let's go abroad before 'tis late; for I will go, that's flat and plain.

MR. PINCHWIFE. – [*Aside*] *So! The obstinacy already of a Town-wife, and I must, whilst she's here, humour her like one.* – Sister, how shall we do, that she may not be seen, or known?

ALITHEA. Let her put on her mask.

MR. PINCHWIFE. Pshaw, a mask makes people but the more inquisitive, and is as ridiculous a disguise, as a stage-beard; her shape, stature, habit will be known: and if we shou'd meet with *Horner*, he wou'd be sure to take acquaintance with us, must wish her joy, kiss her, talk to her, leer upon her, and the Devil and all; no I'll not use her to a mask, 'tis dangerous; for masks have made more cuckolds, than the best faces that ever were known.

ALITHEA. How will you do then?

MRS. PINCHWIFE. Nay, shall we go? The *Exchange* will be shut, and I have a mind to see that.

MR. PINCHWIFE. So – I have it – I'll dress her up in the suit, we are to carry down to her brother, little Sir *James*; nay, I understand the Town tricks: Come let's go dress her; a mask! No –

a woman mask'd, like a cover'd dish, gives a man curiosity, and appetite, when, it may be, uncover'd, 'twou'd turn his stomach; no, no.

ALITHEA. Indeed your comparison is something a greasie one: but I had a gentle gallant, us'd to say, a beauty mask'd, lik'd the sun in eclipse, gathers together more gazers, than if it shin'd out. [*Exeunt.*

[*The Scene changes to the new Exchange: Enter* Horner, Harcourt, Dorilant.

DORILANT. Engag'd to women, and not sup with us?

HORNER. Ay, a pox on 'em all.

HARCOURT. You were much a more reasonable man in the morning, and had as noble resolutions against 'em, as a widdower of a week's liberty.

DORILANT. Did I ever think, to see you keep company with women in vain.

HORNER. In vain! No – 'tis, since I can't love 'em, to be reveng'd on 'em.

HARCOURT. Now your sting is gone, you look'd in the box amongst all those women, like a drone in the hive, all upon you; shov'd and ill-us'd by 'em all, and thrust from one side to t'other.

DORILANT. Yet he must be buzzing amongst 'em still, like other old beetle-headed, lycorish[57] drones; avoid 'em, and hate'm as they hate you.

HORNER. Because I do hate 'em, and wou'd hate 'em yet more, I'll frequent 'em; you may see by marriage, nothing makes a man hate a woman more, than her constant conversation: In short, I converse with 'em, as you do with rich fools, to laugh at 'em, and use 'em ill.

DORILANT. But I wou'd no more sup with women, unless I cou'd lye with'em, than sup with a rich coxcomb, unless I cou'd cheat him.

HORNER. Yes, I have known thee sup with a fool, for his drinking, if he cou'd set out your hand that way only, you were satisfy'd; and if he were a wine-swallowing mouth 'twas enough.

HARCOURT. Yes, a man drinks often with a fool, as he tosses with a marker, only to keep his hand in ure;[58] but do the ladies drink?

HORNER. Yes, Sir, and I shall have the pleasure at least of laying 'em flat with a bottle; and bring as much scandal that way upon 'em, as formerly t'other.

HARCOURT. Perhaps you may prove as weak a brother amongst 'em that way, as t'other.

DORILANT. Foh, drinking with women, is as unnatural, as scolding with 'em; but 'tis a pleasure of decay'd fornicators, and the basest way of quenching love.

HARCOURT. Nay, 'tis drowning love, instead of quenching it; but leave us for civil women too!

DORILANT. Ay, when he can't be the better for 'em; we hardly pardon a man, that leaves his friend for a wench, and that's a pretty lawful call.

HORNER. Faith, I wou'd not leave you for 'em, if they wou'd not drink.

DORILANT. Who wou'd disappoint his company at *Lewis*'s, for a gossiping?

HARCOURT. Foh, wine and women good apart, together as nauseous as sack[59] and sugar: But hark you, Sir, before you go, a little of your advice, an old maim'd General, when unfit for action is fittest for counsel; I have other designs upon women, than eating and drinking with them: I am in love with *Sparkish*'s mistress, whom he is to marry to morrow, now how shall I get her?

[*Enter* Sparkish, *looking about.*

HORNER. Why, here comes one will help you to her.

HARCOURT. He! He, I tell you, is my rival, and will hinder my love.

HORNER. No, a foolish rival, and a jealous husband assist their rival's designs; for they are sure to make their women hate them, which is the first step to their love, for another man.

HARCOURT. But I cannot come near his mistress, but in his company.

HORNER. Still the better for you, for fools are most easily cheated, when they themselves are accessaries; and he is to be bubbled[60] of his mistress, as of his money, the common mistress, by keeping him company.

SPARKISH. Who is that, that is to be bubbled? Faith let me snack,[61] I han't met with a bubble since Christmas: gad; I think bubbles are like their brother woodcocks, go out with the cold weather.

HARCOURT. A pox, he did not hear all I hope. [*Apart to* Horner.

SPARKISH. Come, you bubbling Rogues you, where do we sup – Oh, *Harcourt*, my Mistress tells me, you have been making fierce love to her all the play long, hah, ha – but I –

HARCOURT. I make love to her?

SPARKISH. Nay, I forgive thee; for I think I know thee, and I know her, but I am sure I know my self.

HARCOURT. Did she tell you so? I see all women are like these of the *Exchange*, who to enhance the price of their commodities, report to their fond customers' offers which were never made 'em.

HORNER. Ay, women are as apt to tell before the intrigue, as men after it, and so shew themselves the vainer sex; but hast thou a mistress, *Sparkish*? 'tis as hard for me to believe it, as that thou ever hadst a bubble, as you brag'd just now.

SPARKISH. O your Servant, Sir; are you at your raillery, Sir? But we were some of us beforehand with you to day at the play: the wits were something bold with you, Sir; did you not hear us laugh?

HARCOURT. Yes, but I thought you had gone to plays, to laugh at the poet's wit, not at your own.

SPARKISH. Your Servant, Sir, no I thank you; gad I go to a play as to a Country-treat, I carry my own wine to one, and my own wit to t'other, or else I'm sure I shou'd not be merry at either; and the reason why we are so often lowder, than the players, is, because we think we speak more wit, and so become the poet's rivals in his audience: for to tell you the truth, we hate the silly rogues; nay, so much that we find fault even with their bawdy upon the stage, whilst we talk nothing else in the pit as lowd.

HORNER. But, why should'st thou hate the silly poets, thou hast too much wit to be one, and they like whores are only hated by each other; and thou dost scorn writing, I'm sure.

SPARKISH. Yes, I'd have you to know, I scorn writing; but women, women, that make men do all foolish things, make 'em write songs too; every body does it: 'tis ev'n as common with lovers, as playing with fans;[62] and you can no more help rhyming to your *Phyllis*, than drinking to your *Phyllis*.[63]

HARCOURT. Nay, poetry in love is no more to be avoided, than jealousy.

DORILANT. But the poets damn'd your songs, did they?

SPARKISH. Damn the poets, they turn'd 'em into Burlesque, as they call it; that Burlesque is a *hocus-pocus*-trick, they have got, which by the virtue of *hictius doctius, topsey turvey*,[64] they make a wise and witty man in the World, a fool upon the stage you know not how; and 'tis therefore I hate 'em too, for I know not but it may be my own case; for they'll put a man into a play for looking a squint: their predecessors were contented to make serving-men only their stage-fools, but these rogues must have gentlemen, with a pox to 'em, nay knights: and indeed you shall hardly see a fool upon the stage, but he's a knight; and to tell you the truth, they have kept me these six years from being a knight in earnest, for fear of being knighted in a play, and dubb'd a fool.

DORILANT. Blame 'em not, they must follow their copy, the Age.

HARCOURT. But why should'st thou be afraid of being in a play, who expose your self every day in the play-houses, and as publick places.

HORNER. 'Tis but being on the stage, instead of standing on a bench in the pit.

DORILANT. Don't you give money to painters to draw you like? And are you afraid of your pictures, at length in a play-house, where all your mistresses may see you.

SPARKISH. A pox, painters don't draw the small pox, or pimples in one's face; come damn all your silly authors what-ever, all books and book-sellers, by the World, and all readers, courteous or uncourteous.

HARCOURT. But, who comes here, *Sparkish*?

[*Enter* Mr. Pinchwife, *and his wife in man's clothes,* Alithea, Lucy *her Maid.*

SPARKISH. Oh hide me, there's my mistress too. [Sparkish *hides himself behind* Harcourt.

HARCOURT. She sees you.

SPARKISH. But I will not see her, 'tis time to go to *Whitehall*, and I must not fail the drawing room.[65]

HARCOURT. Pray, first carry me, and reconcile me to her.

SPARKISH. Another time, faith the King will have sup't.

HARCOURT. Not with the worse stomach for thy absence; thou art one of those fools, that think their attendance at the King's meals, as necessary as his physician's, when you are more troublesom to him, than his doctors, or his dogs.

SPARKISH. Pshaw, I know my interest, Sir, prethee hide me.

HORNER. Your Servant, *Pinchwife*, – what he knows us not –

MR. PINCHWIFE. [*To his Wife aside*] *Come along.*

MRS. PINCHWIFE. Pray, have you any ballads,[66] give me six-penny worth?

CLASP. We have no ballads.

MRS. PINCHWIFE. Then give me *Covent-garden-Drollery*,[67] and a play or two – Oh here's *Tarugo's Wiles*, and the *Slighted Maiden*,[68] I'll have them.

MR. PINCHWIFE. No, plays are not for your reading; come along, will you discover your self? [*Apart to her.*

HORNER. Who is that pretty youth with him, *Sparkish*?

SPARKISH. I believe his wife's brother, because he's something like her, but I never saw her but once.

HORNER. Extreamly handsom, I have seen a face like it too; let us follow 'em. [*Exeunt* Pinchwife, Mistress Pinchwife. Alithea, Lucy, Horner, Dorilant *following them*.

HARCOURT. Come, *Sparkish*, your mistress saw you, and will be angry you go not to her; besides I wou'd fain be reconcil'd to her, which none but you can do, dear Friend.

SPARKISH. Well that's a better reason, dear Friend; I wou'd not go near her now, for hers, or my own sake, but I can deny you nothing; for though I have known thee a great while, never go, if I do not love thee, as well as a new acquaintance.

HARCOURT. I am oblig'd to you indeed, dear Friend, I wou'd be well with her only, to be well with thee still; for these tyes to wives usually dissolve all tyes to friends: I wou'd be contented, she shou'd enjoy you a nights, but I wou'd have you to my self a dayes, as I have had, dear Friend.

SPARKISH. And thou shalt enjoy me a dayes, dear, dear Friend, never stir; and I'll be divorced from her, sooner than from thee; come along –

HARCOURT. [*Aside*] *So we are hard put to't, when we make our rival our procurer; but neither she, nor her brother, wou'd let me come near her now: when all's done, a rival is the best cloak to steal to a mistress under, without suspicion; and when we have once got to her as we desire, we throw him off like other cloaks.* [*Exit* Sparkish, *and* Harcourt *following him*.

[*Re-enter* Mr. Pinchwife, Mistress Pinchwife *in man's clothes*.

MR. PINCHWIFE. [*To* Alithea] Sister, if you will not go, we must leave you – [*Aside*] *The fool her gallant, and she, will muster up all the young santerers of this place, and they will leave their dear seamstresses to follow us;*[69] *what a swarm of cuckolds, and cuckold-makers are here?* – Come let's be gone Mistress *Margery*.

MRS. PINCHWIFE. Don't you believe that, I han't half my belly full of sights yet.

MR. PINCHWIFE. Then walk this way.

MRS. PINCHWIFE. Lord, what a power of brave signs are here! Stay – the Bull's-head, the Rams-head, and the Stags-head, dear –

MR. PINCHWIFE. Nay, if every husband's proper sign here were visible, they wou'd be all alike.

MRS. PINCHWIFE. What d'ye mean by that, Bud?

MR. PINCHWIFE. 'Tis no matter – no matter, Bud.

MRS. PINCHWIFE. Pray tell me; nay, I will know.

MR. PINCHWIFE. They wou'd be all bull's, stag's, and ram's heads. [*Exeunt* Mr. Pinchwife, Mrs. Pinchwife.

[*Re-enter* Sparkish, Harcourt, Alithea, Lucy, *at t'other door*.

SPARKISH. Come, dear Madam, for my sake you shall be reconciled to him.

ALITHEA. For your sake I hate him.

HARCOURT. That's something too cruel, Madam, to hate me for his sake.

SPARKISH. Ay indeed, Madam, too, too cruel to me, to hate my friend for my sake.

ALITHEA. I hate him because he is your enemy; and you ought to hate him too, for making love to me, if you love me.

SPARKISH. That's a good one, I hate a man for loving you; if he did love you, 'tis but what he can't help, and 'tis your fault not his, if he admires you: I hate a man for being of my opinion, I'll ne'er do't, by the World.

ALITHEA. Is it for your honour or mine, to suffer a man to make love to me, who am to marry you to morrow?

SPARKISH. Is it for your honour or mine, to have me jealous? That he makes love to you, is a sign you are handsome; and that I am not jealous, is a sign you are virtuous, that I think is for your honour.

ALITHEA. But 'tis your honour too, I am concerned for.

HARCOURT. But why, dearest Madam, will you be more concern'd for his honour, than he is himself; let his honour alone for my sake, and his, he, he, has no honour –

SPARKISH. How's that?

HARCOURT. But what, my dear Friend can guard himself.

SPARKISH. O ho – that's right again.

HARCOURT. Your care of his honour argues his neglect of it, which is no honour to my dear Friend here; therefore once more, let his honour go which way it will, dear Madam.

SPARKISH. Ay, ay, were it for my honour to marry a woman, whose virtue I suspected, and cou'd not trust her in a friend's hands?

ALITHEA. Are you not afraid to lose me?

HARCOURT. He afraid to lose you, Madam! No, no – you may see how the most estimable, and most glorious creature in the world, is valued by him; will you not see it?

SPARKISH. Right, honest *Frank*, I have that noble value for her, that I cannot be jealous of her.

ALITHEA. You mistake him, he means you care not for me, nor who has me.

SPARKISH. Lord, Madam, I see you are jealous; will you wrest a poor man's meaning from his words?

ALITHEA. You astonish me, Sir, with your want of jealousie.

SPARKISH. And you make me giddy, Madam, with your jealousie, and fears, and virtue, and honour; gad, I see virtue makes a woman as troublesome, as a little reading, or learning.

ALITHEA. Monstrous!

LUCY. Well to see what easie husbands these women of quality can meet with, a poor chamber maid can never have such lady-like luck; besides he's thrown away upon her, she'll make no use of her fortune, her blessing, none to a gentleman, for a pure cuckold, for it requires good breeding to be a cuckold. [*Behind.*

ALITHEA. I tell you then plainly, he pursues me to marry me.

SPARKISH. Pshaw –

HARCOURT. Come, Madam, you see you strive in vain to make him jealous of me; my dear Friend is the kindest creature in the world to me.

SPARKISH. Poor fellow.

HARCOURT. But his kindness only is not enough for me, without your favour; your good opinion, dear Madam, 'tis that must perfect my happiness: good Gentleman he believes all I say, wou'd you wou'd do so, jealous of me! I wou'd not wrong him nor you for the world.

SPARKISH. Look you there; hear him, hear him, and do not walk away so. [Alithea *walks carelessly, to and fro.*

HARCOURT. I love you, Madam, so –

SPARKISH. How's that! Nay – now you begin to go too far indeed.

HARCOURT. So much I confess, I say I love you, that I wou'd not have you miserable, and cast your self away upon so unworthy, and inconsiderable a thing, as what you see here. [*Clapping his hand on his breast, points at* Sparkish.

SPARKISH. No faith, I believe thou woud'st not, now his meaning is plain: but I knew before thou woud'st not wrong me nor her.

HARCOURT. No, no, Heavens forbid, the glory of her sex shou'd fall so low as into the embraces of such a contemptible wretch, the last of mankind – my dear Friend here – I injure him. [*Embracing* Sparkish.

ALITHEA. Very well.

SPARKISH. No, no, dear Friend, I knew it Madam, you see he will rather wrong himself than me, in giving himself such names.

ALITHEA. Do not you understand him yet?

SPARKISH. Yes, how modestly he speaks of himself, poor fellow.

ALITHEA. Methinks he speaks impudently of your self, since – before your self too, insomuch that I can no longer suffer his scurrilous abusiveness to you, no more than his love to me. [*Offers to go.*

SPARKISH. Nay, nay, Madam, pray stay, his love to you: Lord, Madam, has he not spoke yet plain enough?

ALITHEA. Yes indeed, I shou'd think so.

SPARKISH. Well then, by the World, a man can't speak civilly to a woman now, but presently she says, he makes love to her: Nay, Madam, you shall stay, with your pardon, since you have not yet understood him, till he has made an eclairisment of his love to you, that is what kind of love it is; answer to thy catechism: Friend, do you love my mistress here?

HARCOURT. Yes, I wish she wou'd not doubt it.

SPARKISH. But how do you love her?

HARCOURT. With all my soul.

ALITHEA. I thank him, methinks he speaks plain enough now.

SPARKISH. [*To* Alithea] You are out still. But with what kind of love, *Harcourt*?

HARCOURT. With the best, and truest love in the world.

SPARKISH. Look you there then, that is with no matrimonial love, I'm sure.

ALITHEA. How's that, do you say matrimonial love is not best?

SPARKISH. Gad, I went too far e're I was aware: but speak for thy self *Harcourt*, you said you wou'd not wrong me, nor her.

HARCOURT. No, no, Madam, e'en take him for Heaven's sake.

SPARKISH. Look you there, Madam.

HARCOURT. Who shou'd in all justice be yours, he that loves you most. [*Claps his hand on his breast.*

ALITHEA. Look you there, Mr. *Sparkish*, who's that?

SPARKISH. Who shou'd it be? Go on *Harcourt*.

HARCOURT. Who loves you more than women, titles, or fortune fools. [*Points at* Sparkish.

SPARKISH. Look you there, he means me still, for he points at me.

ALITHEA. Ridiculous!

HARCOURT. Who can only match your faith, and constancy in love.

SPARKISH. Ay.

HARCOURT. Who knows, if it be possible, how to value so much beauty and virtue.

SPARKISH. Ay.

HARCOURT. Whose love can no more be equall'd in the world, than that heavenly form of yours.

SPARKISH. No –

HARCOURT. Who cou'd no more suffer a rival, than your absence, and yet cou'd no more suspect your virtue, than his own constancy in his love to you.

SPARKISH. No –

HARCOURT. Who in fine loves you better than his eyes, that first made him love you.

SPARKISH. Ay – nay, Madam, faith you shan't go, till –

ALITHEA. Have a care, lest you make me stay too long –

SPARKISH. But till he has saluted you; that I may be assur'd you are friends, after his honest advice and declaration: come pray, Madam, be friends with him.

[*Enter* Master Pinchwife, Mistress Pinchwife.

ALITHEA. You must pardon me, Sir, that I am not yet so obedient to you.

MR. PINCHWIFE. What, invite your wife to kiss men? Monstrous! Are you not asham'd? I will never forgive you.

SPARKISH. Are you not asham'd, that I shou'd have more confidence in the chastity of your family, than you have; you must not teach me, I am a man of honour, Sir, though I am frank and free; I am frank, Sir –

MR. PINCHWIFE. Very frank, Sir, to share your wife with your friends.

SPARKISH. He is an humble, menial friend, such as reconciles the differences of the marriage-bed; you know man and wife do not alwayes agree, I design him for that use, therefore wou'd have him well with my wife.

MR. PINCHWIFE. A menial friend – you will get a great many menial friends, by shewing your wife as you do.

SPARKISH. What then, it may be I have a pleasure in't, as I have to shew fine clothes, at a play-house the first day, and count money before poor rogues.

MR. PINCHWIFE. He that shews his wife, or money, will be in danger of having them borrowed sometimes.

SPARKISH. I love to be envy'd, and wou'd not marry a wife, that I alone cou'd love; loving alone is as dull, as eating alone; is it not a frank age, and I am a frank person? And to tell you the truth, it may be I love to have rivals in a wife, they make her seem to a man still, but as a kept mistress; and so good night, for I must to *Whitehall*. Madam, I hope you are now reconcil'd to my friend; and so I wish you a good night, Madam, and sleep if you can, for to morrow you know I must visit you early with a canonical gentleman. Good night dear *Harcourt*. [*Exit* Sparkish.

HARCOURT. Madam, I hope you will not refuse my visit to morrow, if it shou'd be earlyer, with a canonical gentleman, than Mr. *Sparkish*'s?

MR. PINCHWIFE. This gentle-woman is yet under my care, therefore you must yet forbear your freedom with her, Sir. [*Coming between* Alithea *and* Harcourt.

HARCOURT. Must, Sir –

MR. PINCHWIFE. Yes, Sir, she is my sister.

HARCOURT. 'Tis well she is, Sir – for I must be her servant, Sir. Madam –

MR. PINCHWIFE. Come away Sister, we had been gone, if it had not been for you, and so avoided these lewd Rakehells, who seem to haunt us.

[*Enter* Horner, Dorilant *to them*.

HORNER. How now *Pinchwife*?

MR. PINCHWIFE. Your Servant.

HORNER. What, I see a little time in the Country makes a man turn wild and unsociable, and only fit to converse with his horses, dogs, and his herds.

MR. PINCHWIFE. I have business, Sir, and must mind it; your business is pleasure, therefore you and I must go different wayes.

HORNER. Well, you may go on, but this pretty young gentleman – [*Takes hold of* Mrs. Pinchwife.

HARCOURT. The lady –

DORILANT. And the maid –

HORNER. Shall stay with us, for I suppose their business is the same with ours, pleasure.

MR. PINCHWIFE. [*Aside*] *'Sdeath he knows her, she carries it so sillily, yet if he does not, I shou'd be more silly to discover it first.*

ALITHEA. Pray, let us go, Sir.

MR. PINCHWIFE. Come, come –

HORNER. [*To* Mrs. Pinchwife] Had you not rather stay with us? [*To* Mr. Pinchwife] Prethee *Pinchwife*, who is this pretty young gentleman?

MR. PINCHWIFE. One to whom I'm a guardian. – [*Aside*] *I wish I cou'd keep her out of your hands –*

HORNER. Who is he? I never saw any thing so pretty in all my life.

MR. PINCHWIFE. Pshaw, do not look upon him so much, he's a poor bashful youth, you'll put him out of countenance. Come away Brother. [*Offers to take her away.*

HORNER. O your brother!

MR. PINCHWIFE. Yes, my wife's brother; come, come, she'll stay supper for us.

HORNER. I thought so, for he is very like her I saw you at the play with, whom I told you, I was in love with.

MRS. PINCHWIFE. – [*Aside*] *O Jeminy! Is this he that was in love with me, I am glad on't I vow, for he's a curious fine gentleman, and I love him already too.* – [*To* Mr. Pinchwife] Is this he Bud?

MR. PINCHWIFE. Come away, come away. [*To his wife.*

HORNER. Why, what haste are you in? Why won't you let me talk with him?

MR. PINCHWIFE. Because you'll debauch him, he's yet young and innocent, and I wou'd not have him debauch'd for any thing in the world. – [*Aside*] *How she gazes on him! The Devil –*

HORNER. *Harcourt, Dorilant*, look you here, this is the likeness of that dowdey he told us of, his wife, did you ever see a lovelyer creature? The rogue has reason to be jealous of his wife, since she is like him, for she wou'd make all that see her, in love with her.

HARCOURT. And as I remember now, she is as like him here as can be.

DORILANT. She is indeed very pretty, if she be like him.

HORNER. Very pretty, a very pretty commendation – she is a glorious creature, beautiful beyond all things I ever beheld.

MR. PINCHWIFE. So, so.

HARCOURT. More beautiful than a poet's first mistress of imagination.

HORNER. Or another man's last mistress of flesh and blood.

MRS. PINCHWIFE. Nay, now you jeer, Sir; pray don't jeer me –

MR. PINCHWIFE. Come, come. – [*Aside*] *By Heavens she'll discover her self.*

HORNER. I speak of your sister, Sir.

MR. PINCHWIFE. Ay, but saying she was handsom, if like him, made him blush. – [*Aside*] *I am upon a wrack –*

HORNER. Methinks he is so handsom, he shou'd not be a man.

MR. PINCHWIFE. O there 'tis out, he has discovered her, I am not able to suffer any longer. [*To his wife*] Come, come away, I say –

HORNER. Nay, by your leave, Sir, he shall not go yet – *Harcourt, Dorilant*, let us torment this jealous rogue a little. [*To them.*

HARCOURT. How?

DORILANT. How?

HORNER. I'll shew you.

MR. PINCHWIFE. Come, pray let him go, I cannot stay fooling any longer; I tell you his sister stays supper for us.

HORNER. Do's she, come then we'll all go sup with her and thee.

MR. PINCHWIFE. No, now I think on't, having staid so long for us, I warrant she's gone to bed – [*Aside*] *I wish she and I were well out of their hands* – Come, I must rise early to morrow, come.

HORNER. Well then, if she be gone to bed, I wish her and you a good night. But pray, young Gentleman, present my humble service to her.

MRS. PINCHWIFE. Thank you heartily, Sir.

MR. PINCHWIFE. [*Aside*] *S'death, she will discover her self yet in spight of me. He is something more civil to you, for your kindness to his sister, than I am, it seems.*

HORNER. Tell her, dear sweet little Gentleman, for all your brother there, that you have reviv'd the love, I had for her at first sight in the play-house.

MRS. PINCHWIFE. But did you love her indeed, and indeed?

MR. PINCHWIFE. – [*Aside*] *So, so.* – Away, I say.

HORNER. Nay stay; yes indeed, and indeed, pray do you tell her so, and give her this kiss from me. [*Kisses her.*

MR. PINCHWIFE. [*Aside*] *O Heavens! What do I suffer; now 'tis too plain he knows her, and yet –*

HORNER. And this, and this – [*Kisses her again.*

MRS. PINCHWIFE. What do you kiss me for, I am no woman.

MR. PINCHWIFE. – [*Aside*] *So – there 'tis out.* – Come, I cannot, nor will stay any longer.

HORNER. Nay, they shall send your Lady a kiss too; here *Harcourt, Dorilant*, will you not? [*They kiss her.*

MR. PINCHWIFE. – [*Aside*] *How, do I suffer this? Was I not accusing another just now, for this rascally patience, in permitting his wife to be kiss'd before his face? Ten thousand ulcers gnaw away their lips.* – Come, come.

HORNER. Good night dear little Gentleman; Madam, goodnight; farewell *Pinchwife*. [*Apart to* Harcourt *and* Dorilant] Did not I tell you, I wou'd raise his jealous gall? [*Exeunt* Horner, Harcourt, *and* Dorilant.

MR. PINCHWIFE. So they are gone at last; stay, let me see first if the coach be at this door. [*Exit.*

[Horner, Harcourt, Dorilant *return.*

HORNER. What not gone yet? Will you be sure to do as I desired you, sweet Sir?

MRS. PINCHWIFE. Sweet Sir, but what will you give me then?

HORNER. Any thing, come away into the next walk. [*Exit* Horner, *hailing away* Mrs. Pinchwife.

ALITHEA. Hold, hold, – what d'ye do?

LUCY. Stay, stay, hold –

HARCOURT. Hold Madam, hold, let him present him[70], he'll come presently; nay, I will never let you go, till you answer my question. [Alithea, Lucy *struggling with* Harcourt, *and* Dorilant.

LUCY. For God's sake, Sir, I must follow 'em.

DORILANT. No, I have something to present you with too, you shan't follow them.

[Pinchwife *returns.*

MR. PINCHWIFE. Where? – How? – What's become of? Gone – whither?

LUCY. He's only gone with the gentleman, who will give him something, an't please your Worship.

MR. PINCHWIFE. Something – give him something, with a pox – where are they?

ALITHEA. In the next walk only, Brother.

MR. PINCHWIFE. Only, only; where, where? [*Exit* Pinchwife, *and returns presently, then goes out again.*

HARCOURT. What's the matter with him? Why so much concern'd? But dearest Madam –

ALITHEA. Pray, let me go, Sir, I have said, and suffer'd enough already.

HARCOURT. Then you will not look upon, nor pity my sufferings?

ALITHEA. To look upon 'em, when I cannot help 'em, were cruelty, not pity, therefore I will never see you more.

HARCOURT. Let me then, Madam, have my privilege of a banished lover, complaining or railing, and giving you but a farewell reason; why, if you cannot condescend to marry me, you shou'd not take that wretch my rival.

ALITHEA. He only, not you, since my honour is engag'd so far to him, can give me a reason, why I shou'd not marry him; but if he be true, and what I think him to me, I must be so to him; your Servant, Sir.

HARCOURT. Have women only constancy when 'tis a vice, and like fortune only true to fools?

DORILANT. Thou sha't not stir thou robust creature, you see I can deal with you, therefore you shou'd stay the rather, and be kind. [*To* Lucy, *who struggles to get from him.*

[*Enter* Pinchwife.

MR. PINCHWIFE. Gone, gone, not to be found; quite gone, ten thousand plagues go with 'em; which way went they?

ALITHEA. But into t'other walk, Brother.

LUCY. Their business will be done presently sure, an't please your Worship, it can't be long in doing I'm sure on't.

ALITHEA. Are they not there?

MR. PINCHWIFE. No, you know where they are, you infamous Wretch, eternal shame of your family, which you do not dishonour enough your self, you think, but you must help her to do it too, thou legion of bawds.

ALITHEA. Good Brother.

MR. PINCHWIFE. Damn'd, damn'd Sister.

ALITHEA. Look you here, she's coming.

[*Enter* Mistress Pinchwife *in man's clothes, running with her hat under her arm, full of oranges and dried fruit,* Horner *following.*

MRS. PINCHWIFE. O dear Bud, look you here what I have got, see.

MR. PINCHWIFE. *And what I have got here too, which you can't see.* [*Aside rubbing his forehead.*

MRS. PINCHWIFE. The fine Gentleman has given me better things yet.

MR. PINCHWIFE. [*Aside*] *Ha's he so? Out of breath and colour'd – I must hold yet.*

HORNER. I have only given your little Brother an orange, Sir.

MR. PINCHWIFE. [*To* Horner] Thank you, Sir. – [*Aside*] *You have only squeez'd my orange, I suppose, and given it me again; yet I must have a City-patience.*[71] – [*To his wife*] Come, come away –

MRS. PINCHWIFE. Stay, till I have put up my fine things, Bud.

[*Enter* Sir Jasper Fidget.

SIR JASPER. O Master *Horner*, come, come, the ladies stay for you; your mistress, my wife, wonders you make not more haste to her.

HORNER. I have staid this half hour for you here, and 'tis your fault I am not now with your wife.

SIR JASPER. But pray, don't let her know so much, the truth on't is, I was advancing a certain project to his Majesty, about – I'll tell you.

HORNER. No, let's go, and hear it at your house: Good night sweet little Gentleman; one kiss more, you'll remember me now I hope. [*Kisses her.*

DORILANT. What, Sir *Jasper*, will you separate friends? He promis'd to sup with us; and if you take him to your house, you'll be in danger of our company too.

SIR JASPER. Alas Gentlemen my house is not fit for you, there are none but civil women there, which are not for your turn; he you know can bear with the society of civil women, now, ha, ha, ha; besides he's one of my family; – he's – heh, heh, heh.

DORILANT. What is he?

SIR JASPER. Faith, my eunuch, since you'll have it, heh, he, he. [*Exit* Sir Jasper Fidget, *and* Horner.

DORILANT. I rather wish thou wert his, or my cuckold: *Harcourt*, what a good cuckold is lost there, for want of a man to make him one; thee and I cannot have *Horner*'s privilege, who can make use of it.

HARCOURT. Ay, to poor *Horner*, 'tis like coming to an estate at threescore, when a man can't be the better for't.

MR. PINCHWIFE. Come.

MRS. PINCHWIFE. Presently Bud.

DORILANT. Come let us go too: [*To* Alithea] Madam, your Servant. [*To* Lucy] Good night Strapper. –

HARCOURT. Madam, though you will not let me have a good day, or night, I wish you one; but dare not name the other half of my wish.

ALITHEA. Good night, Sir, for ever.

MRS. PINCHWIFE. I don't know where to put this here, dear Bud, you shall eat it; nay, you shall have part of the fine gentleman's good things, or treat as you call it, when we come home.

MR. PINCHWIFE. Indeed I deserve it, since I furnish'd the best part of it. [*Strikes away the orange.*

The Gallant treats, presents, and gives the ball;
But 'tis the absent cuckold, pays for all.

Act IV.

[*In* Pinchwife*'s house in the morning.* Lucy, Alithea *dress'd in new clothes.*]

LUCY. Well – Madam, now have I dress'd you, and set you out with so many ornaments, and spent upon you ounces of essence,[72] and pulvilio;[73] and all this for no other purpose, but as people adorn, and perfume a corps, for a stinking second-hand-grave, such or as bad I think Master *Sparkish*'s bed.

ALITHEA. Hold your peace.

LUCY. Nay, Madam, I will ask you the reason, why you wou'd banish poor Master *Harcourt* for ever from your sight? How cou'd you be so hard-hearted?

ALITHEA. 'twas because I was not hard-hearted.

LUCY. No, no; 'twas stark love and kindness, I warrant.

ALITHEA. It was so; I wou'd see him no more, because I love him.

LUCY. Hey day, a very pretty reason.

ALITHEA. You do not understand me.

LUCY. I wish you may your self.

ALITHEA. I was engag'd to marry, you see, another man, whom my justice will not suffer me to deceive, or injure.

LUCY. Can there be a greater cheat, or wrong done to a man, than to give him your person, without your heart, I shou'd make a conscience of it.

ALITHEA. I'll retrieve it for him after I am married a while.

LUCY. The woman that marries to love better, will be as much mistaken, as the wencher that marries to live better. No, Madam, marrying to increase love, is like gaming to become rich; alas you only lose, what little stock you had before.

ALITHEA. I find by your rhetorick you have been brib'd to betray me.

LUCY. Only by his merit, that has brib'd your heart you see against your word, and rigid honour; but what a Devil is this honour? 'tis sure a disease in the head, like the megrim, or falling-sickness, that alwayes hurries people away to do themselves mischief; men lose their lives by it: women what's dearer to 'em, their love, the life of life.

ALITHEA. Come, pray talk you no more of honour, nor Master *Harcourt*; I wish the other wou'd come, to secure my fidelity to him, and his right in me.

LUCY. You will marry him then?

ALITHEA. Certainly, I have given him already my word, and will my hand too, to make it good when he comes.

LUCY. Well, I wish I may never stick pin[74] more, if he be not an errant natural,[75] to t'other fine gentleman.

ALITHEA. I own he wants the wit of *Harcourt*, which I will dispense withall, for another want he has, which is want of jealousie, which men of wit seldom want.

LUCY. Lord, Madam, what shou'd you do with a fool to your husband, you intend to be honest, don't you? Then that husbandly virtue, credulity, is thrown away upon you.

ALITHEA. He only that could suspect my virtue, shou'd have cause to do it; 'tis *Sparkish*'s confidence in my truth, that obliges me to be so faithful to him.

LUCY. You are not sure his opinion may last.

ALITHEA. I am satisfied, 'tis impossible for him to be jealous, after the proofs I have had of him: jealousie in a husband, Heaven defend me from it, it begets a thousand plagues to a poor woman, the loss of her honour, her quiet, and her –

LUCY. And her pleasure.

ALITHEA. What d'ye mean, Impertinent?

LUCY. Liberty is a great pleasure, Madam.

ALITHEA. I say loss of her honour, her quiet, nay, her life sometimes; and what's as bad almost, the loss of this Town, that is, she is sent into the Country, which is the last ill usage of a husband to a wife, I think.

LUCY. – [*Aside*] *O do's the wind lye there?* – Then of necessity, Madam, you think a man must carry his wife into the Country, if he be wise; the Country is as terrible I find to our young English ladies, as a monastery to those abroad: and on my virginity, I think they wou'd rather marry a *London*-gaoler,[76] than a high sheriff of a county, since neither can stir from his employment: formerly women of wit married fools, for a great estate, a fine seat, or the like; but now 'tis for a pretty seat only in *Lincoln's Inn-fields*, St. *James's-fields*, or the *Pall-mall*.[77]

[*Enter to them* Sparkish, *and* Harcourt *dress'd like a parson.*

SPARKISH. Madam, your humble Servant, a happy day to you, and to us all.

HARCOURT. Amen. –

ALITHEA. Who have we here?

SPARKISH. My Chaplain faith – O Madam, poor *Harcourt* remembers his humble service to you; and in obedience to your last commands, refrains coming into your sight.

ALITHEA. Is not that he?

SPARKISH. No, fye no; but to shew that he nev'r intended to hinder our match has sent his brother here to joyn our hands: when I get me a wife, I must get her a Chaplain, according to the custom; this is his brother, and my Chaplain.

ALITHEA. His brother?

LUCY. [*Aside*] *And your Chaplain, to preach in your pulpit then* –

ALITHEA. His brother!

SPARKISH. Nay, I knew you wou'd not believe it; I told you, Sir, she wou'd take you for your brother *Frank*.

ALITHEA. Believe it!

LUCY. [*Aside*] *His brother! Hah, ha, he, he has a trick left still it seems* –

SPARKISH. Come my dearest, pray let us go to Church before the Canonical hour[78] is past.

ALITHEA. For shame, you are abus'd still.

SPARKISH. By the World 'tis strange now you are so incredulous.

ALITHEA. 'Tis strange you are so credulous.

SPARKISH. Dearest of my life, hear me, I tell you this is *Ned Harcourt* of *Cambridge*, by the World, you see he has a sneaking colledg look; 'tis true he's something like his Brother *Frank*, and they differ from each other no more than in their age, for they were twins.

LUCY. Hah, ha, he.

ALITHEA. Your Servant, Sir, I cannot be so deceiv'd, though you are; but come let's hear, how do you know what you affirm so confidently?

SPARKISH. Why, I'll tell you all; *Frank Harcourt* coming to me this morning, to wish me joy, and present his service to you: I ask'd him, if he cou'd help me to a parson; whereupon he told me, he had a brother in Town who was in orders, and he went straight away, and sent him, you see there, to me.

ALITHEA. Yes, *Frank* goes, and puts on a black-coat, then tells you, he is *Ned*, that's all you have for't.

SPARKISH. Pshaw, pshaw, I tell you by the same token, the midwife put her garter about *Frank*'s neck, to know 'em asunder, they were so like.

ALITHEA. *Frank* tells you this too.

SPARKISH. Ay, and *Ned*, there too; nay, they are both in a story.

ALITHEA. So, so, very foolish.

SPARKISH. Lord, if you won't believe one, you had best try him by your chamber maid there; for chamber-maids must needs know chaplains from other men, they are so us'd to'em.

LUCY. Let's see; nay, I'll be sworn he has the canonical smirk, and the filthy, clammy palm of a chaplain.

ALITHEA. Well, most reverend Doctor, pray let us make an end of this fooling.

HARCOURT. With all my soul, Divine, Heavenly Creature, when you please.

ALITHEA. He speaks like a chaplain indeed.

SPARKISH. Why, was there not, soul, divine, heavenly, in what he said?

ALITHEA. Once more, most impertinent Black-coat, cease your persecution, and let us have a conclusion of this ridiculous love.

HARCOURT. [*Aside*] *I had forgot, I must suit my stile to my coat, or I wear it in vain.*

ALITHEA. I have no more patience left, let us make once an end of this troublesome love, I say.

HARCOURT. So be it, Seraphick Lady, when your honour shall think it meet, and convenient so to do.

SPARKISH. Gad I'm sure none but a chaplain cou'd speak so, I think.

ALITHEA. Let me tell you Sir, this dull trick will not serve your turn, though you delay our marriage, you shall not hinder it.

HARCOURT. Far be it from me, Munificent Patroness, to delay your marriage, I desire nothing more than to marry you presently, which I might do, if you your self wou'd; for my noble, good-natur'd and thrice generous patron here wou'd not hinder it.

SPARKISH. No, poor man, not I faith.

HARCOURT. And now, Madam, let me tell you plainly, no body else shall marry you, by Heavens, I'll die first, for I'm sure I shou'd die after it.

LUCY. How his love has made him forget his function, as I have seen it in real parsons.

ALITHEA. That was spoken like a chaplain too, now you understand him, I hope.

SPARKISH. Poor man, he takes it hainously to be refus'd; I can't blame him, 'tis putting an indignity upon him not to be suffer'd, but you'll pardon me Madam, it shan't be, he shall marry us, come away, pray Madam.

LUCY. Hah, ha, he, more ado! 'tis late.

ALITHEA. Invincible stupidity, I tell you he wou'd marry me, as your rival, not as your chaplain.

SPARKISH. Come, come Madam. [*Pulling her away.*

LUCY. I pray Madam, do not refuse this Reverend Divine, the honour and satisfaction of marrying you; for I dare say, he has set his heart upon't, good Doctor.

ALITHEA. What can you hope, or design by this?

HARCOURT. I cou'd answer her, a reprieve for a day only, often revokes a hasty doom; at worst, if she will not take mercy on me, and let me marry her, I have at least the lover's second pleasure, hindring my rival's enjoyment, though but for a time.

SPARKISH. Come Madam, 'tis e'n twelve a clock, and my mother charg'd me never to be married out of the canonical hours; come, come, Lord here's such a deal of modesty, I warrant the first day.

LUCY. Yes, an't please your Worship, married women shew all their modesty the first day, because married men shew all their love the first day. [*Exeunt* Sparkish, Alithea, Harcourt, *and* Lucy.

[*The Scene changes to a bed chamber, where appear* Pinchwife, Mrs. Pinchwife.

MR. PINCHWIFE. Come tell me, I say.

MRS. PINCHWIFE. Lord, han't I told it an hundred times over.

MR. PINCHWIFE. – [*Aside*] *I wou'd try, if in the repetition of the ungrateful tale, I cou'd find her altering it in the least circumstance, for if her story be false, she is so too.* – Come how was't Baggage?

MRS. PINCHWIFE. Lord, what pleasure you take to hear it sure!

MR. PINCHWIFE. No, you take more in telling it I find, but speak, how was't?

MRS. PINCHWIFE. He carried me up into the house, next to the Exchange.

MR. PINCHWIFE. So, and you two were only in the room.

MRS. PINCHWIFE. Yes, for he sent away a youth that was there, for some dryed fruit, and China oranges.

MR. PINCHWIFE. Did he so? Damn him for it – and for –

MRS. PINCHWIFE. But presently came up the gentlewoman of the house.

MR. PINCHWIFE. O 'twas well she did, but what did he do whilest the fruit came?

MRS. PINCHWIFE. He kiss'd me an hundred times, and told me he fancied he kiss'd my fine sister, meaning me you know, whom he said he lov'd with all his soul, and bid me be sure to tell her so, and to desire her to be at her window, by eleven of the clock this morning, and he wou'd walk under it at that time.

MR. PINCHWIFE. [*Aside*] *And he was as good as his word, very punctual, a pox reward him for't.*

MRS. PINCHWIFE. Well, and he said if you were not within, he wou'd come up to her, meaning me you know, Bud, still.

MR. PINCHWIFE. – [*Aside*] *So – he knew her certainly, but for this confession, I am oblig'd to her simplicity.* – But what you stood very still, when he kiss'd you?

MRS. PINCHWIFE. Yes I warrant you, wou'd you have had me discover'd my self?

MR. PINCHWIFE. But you told me, he did some beastliness to you, as you call'd it, what was't?

MRS. PINCHWIFE. Why, he put –

MR. PINCHWIFE. What?

MRS. PINCHWIFE. Why he put the tip of his tongue between my lips, and so musl'd me – and I said, I'd bite it.

MR. PINCHWIFE. An eternal canker seize it, for a dog.

MRS. PINCHWIFE. Nay, you need not be so angry with him neither, for to say truth, he has the sweetest breath I ever knew.

MR. PINCHWIFE. The Devil – you were satisfied with it then, and wou'd do it again.

MRS. PINCHWIFE. Not unless he shou'd force me.

MR. PINCHWIFE. Force you, changeling![79] I tell you no woman can be forced.

MRS. PINCHWIFE. Yes, but she may sure, by such a one as he, for he's a proper, goodly strong man, 'tis hard, let me tell you, to resist him.

MR. PINCHWIFE. So, 'tis plain she loves him, yet she has not love enough to make her conceal it from me, but the sight of him will increase her aversion for me, and love for him; and that love instruct her how to deceive me, and satisfie him, all ideot as she is. Love, 'twas he gave women first their craft, their art of deluding; out of Nature's hands, they came plain, open, silly and fit for slaves, as she and Heaven intended 'em; but damn'd Love – well – I must strangle that little Monster, whilest I can deal with him. Go fetch pen, ink and paper out of the next room.

MRS. PINCHWIFE. Yes Bud. [*Exit* Mrs. Pinchwife.

MR. PINCHWIFE. – [*Aside*] *Why should women have more invention in love than men? It can only be, because they have more desires, more soliciting passions, more lust, and more of the Devil.* –

[Mrs. Pinchwife *returns*] Come, Minks,[80] sit down and write.

MRS. PINCHWIFE. Ay, dear Bud, but I can't do't very well.

MR. PINCHWIFE. I wish you cou'd not at all.

MRS. PINCHWIFE. But what shou'd I write for?

MR. PINCHWIFE. I'll have you write a letter to your lover.

MRS. PINCHWIFE. O Lord, to the fine Gentleman a letter!

MR. PINCHWIFE. Yes, to the fine Gentleman.

MRS. PINCHWIFE. Lord, you do but jeer; sure you jest.

MR. PINCHWIFE. I am not so merry, come write as I bid you.

MRS. PINCHWIFE. What, do you think I am a fool?

MR. PINCHWIFE. She's afraid I would not dictate any love to him, therefore she's unwilling; but you had best begin.

MRS. PINCHWIFE. Indeed, and indeed, but I won't, so I won't.

MR. PINCHWIFE. Why?

MRS. PINCHWIFE. Because he's in Town, you may send for him if you will.

MR. PINCHWIFE. Very well, you wou'd have him brought to you; is it come to this? I say take the pen and write, or you'll provoke me.

MRS. PINCHWIFE. Lord, what d'ye make a fool of me for? Don't I know that letters are never writ, but from the Country to *London*, and from *London* into the Country; now he's in Town, and I am in Town too; therefore I can't write to him you know.

MR. PINCHWIFE. – [*Aside*] *So, I am glad it is no worse, she is innocent enough yet.* – Yes you may when your husband bids you write letters to people that are in Town.

MRS. PINCHWIFE. O may I so! Then I'm satisfied.

MR. PINCHWIFE. Come begin – Sir – [*Dictates.*

MRS. PINCHWIFE. Shan't I say, Dear Sir? You know one says always something more than bare Sir.

MR. PINCHWIFE. Write as I bid you, or I will write Whore with this penknife in your face.

MRS. PINCHWIFE. Nay good Bud – Sir – [*She writes.*

MR. PINCHWIFE. Though I suffer'd last night your nauseous, loath'd kisses and embraces – write.

MRS. PINCHWIFE. Nay, why shou'd I say so? You know I told you, he had a sweet breath.

MR. PINCHWIFE. Write.

MRS. PINCHWIFE. Let me but put out, loath'd.

MR. PINCHWIFE. Write I say.

MRS. PINCHWIFE. Well then. [*Writes.*

MR. PINCHWIFE. Let's see what have you writ? Though I suffer'd last night your kisses and embraces – [*Takes the paper, and reads*] Thou impudent creature, where is nauseous and loath'd?

MRS. PINCHWIFE. I can't abide to write such filthy words.

MR. PINCHWIFE. Once more write as I'd have you, and question it not, or I will spoil thy writing with this, I will stab out those eyes that cause my mischief. [*Holds up the penknife.*

MRS. PINCHWIFE. O Lord, I will.

MR. PINCHWIFE. So – so – Let's see now! [*Reads*] Though I suffer'd last night your nauseous, loath'd kisses, and embraces; go on – yet I would not have you presume that you shall ever repeat them – So – [*She writes.*

MRS. PINCHWIFE. I have writ it.

MR. PINCHWIFE. On then – I then conceal'd my self from your knowledge, to avoid your insolencies – [*She writes.*

MRS. PINCHWIFE. So –

MR. PINCHWIFE. The same reason now I am out of your hands – [*She writes.*

MRS. PINCHWIFE. So –

MR. PINCHWIFE. Makes me own to you my unfortunate, though innocent frolick, of being in man's cloths. [*She writes.*

MRS. PINCHWIFE. So –

MR. PINCHWIFE. That you may for ever more cease to pursue her, who hates and detests you – [*She writes on.*

MRS. PINCHWIFE. So – h – [*Sighs.*

MR. PINCHWIFE. What do you sigh? – detests you – as much as she loves her husband and her honour –

MRS. PINCHWIFE. I vow Husband he'll ne'er believe, I shou'd write such a letter.

MR. PINCHWIFE. What he'd expect a kinder from you? Come now your name only.

MRS. PINCHWIFE. What, shan't I say your most faithful, humble Servant till death?

MR. PINCHWIFE. – [*Aside*] *No, tormenting Fiend; her stile I find wou'd be very soft.* – Come wrap it up now, whilest I go fetch wax and a candle;[81] and write on the back side, for Mr. *Horner.* [*Exit* Pinchwife.

MRS. PINCHWIFE. For Mr. *Horner* – So, I am glad he has told me his name; Dear Mr. *Horner,* but why should I send thee such a letter, that will vex thee, and make thee angry with me; – well I will not send it – Ay but then my husband will kill me – for I see plainly, he won't let me love Mr. *Horner* – but what care I for my husband – I won't so I won't send poor Mr. *Horner* such a letter – but then my husband – But oh – what if I writ at bottom, my husband made me write it – Ay but then my husband wou'd see't – Can one have no shift, ah, a *London* woman wou'd have had a hundred presently; stay – what if I shou'd write a letter, and wrap it up like this, and write upon't too; ay but then my husband wou'd see't – I don't know what to do – But yet y vads I'll try, so I will – for I will not send this letter to poor Mr. *Horner,* come what will on't. [*She writes, and repeats what she hath writ*] Dear, sweet Mr. *Horner* – *so* – my husband wou'd have me send you a base, rude, unmannerly letter – but I won't – *so* – and wou'd have me forbid you loving me – but I won't – *so* – and wou'd have me say to you, I hate you poor Mr. *Horner* – but I won't tell a lye for him – *there* – for I'm sure if you and I were in the Country at cards together, – *so* – I cou'd not help treading on your toe under the table – *so* – or rubbing knees with you, and staring in your face, 'till you saw me – *very well* – and then looking down, and blushing for an hour together – *so* – but I must make haste before my husband come; and now he has taught me to write letters: you shall have longer ones from me, who am

> Dear, dear, poor dear Mr. *Horner,* your most humble friend, and servant to command 'till death,
> *Margery Pinchwife.*

Stay I must give him a hint at bottom – *so* – now wrap it up just like t'other – *so* – now write for Mr. *Horner,* – But oh now, what shall I do with it? For here comes my husband.

[*Enter* Pinchwife.

MR. PINCHWIFE. – [*Aside*] *I have been detained by a sparkish coxcomb, who pretended a visit to me; but I fear 'twas to my wife.* – What, have you done?

MRS. PINCHWIFE. Ay, ay Bud, just now.

MR. PINCHWIFE. Let's see't, what d'ye tremble for; what, you wou'd not have it go?

MRS. PINCHWIFE. Here – [*Aside*] *No I must not give him that, so I had been served if I had given him this.* [*He opens, and reads the first letter.*

MR. PINCHWIFE. Come, where's the wax and seal?

MRS. PINCHWIFE. – [*Aside*] *Lord, what shall I do now? Nay then I have it* – Pray let me see't, Lord you think me so errand a fool, I cannot seal a letter, I will do't, so I will. [*Snatches the letter from him, changes it for the other, seals it, and delivers it to him.*

MR. PINCHWIFE. Nay, I believe you will learn that, and other things too, which I wou'd not have you.

MRS. PINCHWIFE. So, han't I done it curiously?[82] – [*Aside*] *I think I have, there's my letter going to Mr.* Horner*; since he'll needs have me send letters to folks.*

MR. PINCHWIFE. 'Tis very well, but I warrant, you wou'd not have it go now?

MRS. PINCHWIFE. Yes indeed, but I wou'd, Bud, now.

MR. PINCHWIFE. Well you are a good girl then, come let me lock you up in your chamber, 'till I come back; and be sure you come not within three strides of the window, when I am gone; for I have a spye in the street. [*Exit* Mrs. Pinchwife. Pinchwife *locks the door.*

At least, 'tis fit she think so, if we do not cheat women, they'll cheat us; and fraud may be justly used with secret enemies, of which a wife is the most dangerous; and he that has a handsome one to keep, and a frontier town, must provide against treachery, rather than open force – Now I have secured all within, I'll deal with the foe without with false intelligence. [*Holds up the letter. Exit* Pinchwife.

[*The Scene changes to* Horner*'s lodging.* Quack *and* Horner.

QUACK. Well Sir, how fadges[83] the new design; have you not the luck of all your brother Projectors,[84] to deceive only your self at last.

HORNER. No, good *Domine* Doctor, I deceive you it seems, and others too; for the grave matrons, and old ridgid husbands think me as unfit for love, as they are; but their wives, sisters and daughters, know some of 'em better things already.

QUACK. Already!

HORNER. Already, I say; last night I was drunk with half a dozen of your civil persons, as you call 'em, and people of honour, and so was made free of their society, and dressing rooms for ever hereafter; and am already come to the privileges of sleeping upon their pallats, warming smocks, tying shooes and garters, and the like Doctor, already, already Doctor.

QUACK. You have made use of your time, Sir.

HORNER. I tell thee, I am now no more interruption to 'em, when they sing, or talk bawdy, than a little squab[85] French page, who speaks no English.

QUACK. But do civil persons, and women of honour drink, and sing bawdy songs?

HORNER. O amongst friends, amongst friends; for your bigots in honour, are just like those in religion; they fear the eye of the World, more than the eye of Heaven, and think there is no virtue, but railing at vice; and no sin, but giving scandal: they rail at a poor, little, kept player, and keep themselves some young, modest pulpit comedian to be privy to their sins in their closets, not to tell 'em of them in their chappels.[86]

QUACK. Nay, the truth on't is, priests amongst the women now, have quite got the better of us lay confessors, physicians.

HORNER. And they are rather their patients, but –

[*Enter my* Lady Fidget*, looking about her.*

Now we talk of women of honour, here comes one, step behind the screen there, and but observe; if I have not particular privileges, with the women of reputation already, Doctor, already.

LADY FIDGET. Well *Horner*, am not I a woman of honour? You see I'm as good as my word.

HORNER. And you shall see Madam, I'll not be behind hand with you in honour; and I'll be as good as my word too, if you please but to withdraw into the next room.

LADY FIDGET. But first, my dear Sir, you must promise to have a care of my dear honour.

HORNER. If you talk a word more of your honour, you'll make me incapable to wrong it; to talk of honour in the mysteries of love, is like talking of Heaven, or the Deity in an operation of witchcraft, just when you are employing the Devil, it makes the charm impotent.

LADY FIDGET. Nay, fie, let us not be smooty;[87] but you talk of mysteries, and bewitching to me, I don't understand you.

HORNER. I tell you Madam, the word money in a mistress's mouth, at such a nick of time, is not a more disheartning sound to a younger brother,[88] than that of honour to an eager lover like my self.

LADY FIDGET. But you can't blame a lady of my reputation to be chary.

HORNER. Chary – I have been chary of it already, by the report I have caus'd of my self.

LADY FIDGET. Ay, but if you shou'd ever let other women know that dear secret, it would come out; nay, you must have a great care of your conduct; for my acquaintance are so censorious, (oh 'tis a wicked censorious World, Mr. *Horner*) I say, are so censorious, and detracting, that perhaps they'll talk to the prejudice of my honour, though you shou'd not let them know the dear secret.

HORNER. Nay Madam, rather than they shall prejudice your honour, I'll prejudice theirs; and to serve you, I'll lye with 'em all, make the secret their own, and then they'll keep it: I am a *Machiavel* in love, Madam.

LADY FIDGET. O, no Sir, not that way.

HORNER. Nay, the Devil take me, if censorious women are to be silenc'd any other way.

LADY FIDGET. A secret is better kept I hope, by a single person, than a multitude; therefore pray do not trust any body else with it, dear, dear Mr. *Horner*. [*Embracing him.*

[*Enter* Sir Jasper Fidget.

SIR JASPER. How now!

LADY FIDGET. – [*Aside*] *O my Husband – prevented – and what's almost as bad, found with my arms about another man – that will appear too much – what shall I say?* – Sir *Jasper*, come hither, I am trying if Mr. *Horner* were ticklish, and he's as ticklish as can be, I love to torment the confounded Toad; let you and I tickle him.

SIR JASPER. No, your Ladyship will tickle him better without me, I suppose, but is this your buying china, I thought you had been at the China House?

HORNER. – [*Aside*] *China-House, that's my cue, I must take it.* – A pox, can't you keep your impertinent wives at home? Some men are troubled with the husbands, but I with the wives; but I'd have you to know, since I cannot be your journey-man[89] by night, I will not be your drudge by day, to squire your wife about, and be your man of straw, or scare-crow only to pyes[90] and jays; that would be nibling at your forbidden fruit; I shall be shortly the hackney Gentleman-Usher[91] of the Town.

SIR JASPER. – [*Aside*] *Heh, heh, he, poor fellow he's in the right on't faith, to squire women about for other folks, is as ungrateful an employment, as to tell money for other folks;* – heh, he, he, ben't angry *Horner* –

LADY FIDGET. No, 'tis I have more reason to be angry, who am left by you, to go abroad indecently alone; or, what is more indecent, to pin my self upon such ill bred people of your acquaintance, as this is.

SIR JASPER. Nay, pr'ythee what has he done?

LADY FIDGET. Nay, he has done nothing.

SIR JASPER. But what d'ye take ill, if he has done nothing?

LADY FIDGET. Hah, hah, hah, Faith, I can't but laugh however; why d'ye think the unmannerly toad wou'd not come down to me to the coach, I was fain to come up to fetch him, or go without him, which I was resolved not to do; for he knows china very well, and has himself very good, but will not let me see it, lest I should beg some; but I will find it out, and have what I came for yet. [*Exit* Lady Fidget, *and locks the door, followed by* Horner *to the door.*

HORNER. [*Apart to* Lady Fidget] Lock the door Madam – So, she has got into my chamber, and lock'd me out; oh the impertinency of woman-kind! Well Sir *Jasper*, plain dealing is a jewel; if ever you suffer your wife to trouble me again here, she shall carry you home a pair of horns, by my Lord Mayor she shall; though I cannot furnish you my self, you are sure, yet I'll find a way.

SIR JASPER. [*Aside*] *Hah, ha, he, at my first coming in, and finding her arms about him, tickling him it seems, I was half jealous, but now I see my folly. Heh, he, he, poor* Horner.

HORNER. Nay, though you laugh now, 'twill be my turn e're long: Oh women, more impertinent, more cunning, and more mischievous than their monkeys,[92] and to me almost as ugly – now is she throwing my things about, and rifling all I have, but I'll get into her the back way, and so rifle her for it –

SIR JASPER. Hah, ha, ha, poor angry *Horner*.

HORNER. Stay here a little, I'll ferret her out to you presently, I warrant. [*Exit* Horner *at t'other door.*

SIR JASPER. Wife, my Lady *Fidget*, Wife, he is coming into you the back way. [Sir Jasper *calls through the door to his wife, she answers from within.*

LADY FIDGET. Let him come, and welcome, which way he will.

SIR JASPER. He'll catch you, and use you roughly, and be too strong for you.

LADY FIDGET. Don't you trouble your self, let him if he can.

QUACK. [*Behind*] This indeed, I cou'd not have believ'd from him, nor any but my own eyes.

[*Enter* Mrs. Squeamish.

MRS. SQUEAMISH. Where's this woman-hater, this toad, this ugly, greasie, dirty sloven?

SIR JASPER. So the women all will have him ugly, methinks he is a comely person; but his wants make his form contemptible to 'em; and 'tis e'en as my wife said yesterday, talking of him, that a proper handsome eunuch, was as ridiculous a thing, as a gigantick coward.

MRS. SQUEAMISH. Sir *Jasper*, your Servant, where is the odious beast?

SIR JASPER. He's within in his chamber, with my wife; she's playing the wag with him.

MRS. SQUEAMISH. Is she so, and he's a clownish[93] beast, he'll give her no quarter, he'll play the wag with her again, let me tell you; come, let's go help her – What, the door's lock't?

SIR JASPER. Ay, my wife lock't it –

MRS. SQUEAMISH. Did she so, let us break it open then?

SIR JASPER. No, no, he'll do her no hurt.

MRS. SQUEAMISH. [*Aside*] *No – But is there no other way to get into 'em, whither goes this? I will disturb'em.* [*Exit* Squeamish *at another door.*

[*Enter* Old Lady Squeamish.

OLD LADY SQUEAMISH. Where is this harlotry, this impudent baggage, this rambling Tomrigg?[94] O Sir *Jasper*, I'm glad to see you here, did you not see my vil'd grandchild come in hither just now?

SIR JASPER. Yes,

OLD LADY SQUEAMISH. Ay, but where is she then? Where is she? Lord Sir *Jasper* I have e'en ratled my self to pieces in pursuit of her, but can you tell what she makes here, they say below, no woman lodges here.

SIR JASPER. No.

OLD LADY SQUEAMISH. No – What does she here then? Say if it be not a woman's lodging, what makes she here? But are you sure no woman lodges here?

SIR JASPER. No, nor no man neither, this is Mr. *Horner*'s lodging.

OLD LADY SQUEAMISH. Is it so are you sure?

SIR JASPER. Yes, yes.

OLD LADY SQUEAMISH. So then there's no hurt in't I hope, but where is he?

SIR JASPER. He's in the next room with my wife.

OLD LADY SQUEAMISH. Nay if you trust him with your wife, I may with my Biddy, they say he's a merry harmless man now, e'en as harmless a man as ever came out of *Italy* with a good voice,[95] and as pretty harmless company for a lady, as a snake without his teeth.

SIR JASPER. Ay, ay poor man.

[*Enter* Mrs. Squeamish.

MRS. SQUEAMISH. I can't find'em – Oh are you here, Grandmother, I follow'd you must know my Lady *Fidget* hither, 'tis the prettyest lodging, and I have been staring on the prettyest pictures.

[*Enter* Lady Fidget *with a piece of china in her hand, and* Horner *following.*

LADY FIDGET. And I have been toyling and moyling, for the pretti'st piece of china, my Dear.

HORNER. Nay she has been too hard for me do what I cou'd.

MRS. SQUEAMISH. Oh Lord I'll have some china too, good Mr. *Horner*, don't think to give other people china, and me none, come in with me too.

HORNER. Upon my honour I have none left now.

MRS. SQUEAMISH. Nay, nay I have known you deny your china before now, but you shan't put me off so, come –

HORNER. This Lady had the last there.

LADY FIDGET. Yes indeed, Madam, to my certain knowledge he has no more left.

MRS. SQUEAMISH. O but it may be he may have some you could not find.

LADY FIDGET. What d'ye think if he had had any left, I would not have had it too, for we women of quality never think we have china enough.

HORNER. Do not take it ill, I cannot make china for you all, but I will have a rol-waggon[96] for you too, another time.

MRS. SQUEAMISH. [*To* Horner, *aside*] *Thank you dear Toad.*

LADY FIDGET. What do you mean by that promise?

HORNER. Alas she has an innocent, literal understanding. [*Apart to* Lady Fidget.

OLD LADY SQUEAMISH. Poor Mr. *Horner*, he has enough to do to please you all, I see.

HORNER. Ay Madam, you see how they use me.

OLD LADY SQUEAMISH. Poor Gentleman I pity you.

HORNER. I thank you Madam, I could never find pity, but from such reverend ladies as you are, the young ones will never spare a man.

MRS. SQUEAMISH. Come come, Beast, and go dine with us, for we shall want a man at Hombre after dinner.

HORNER. That's all their use of me Madam you see.

MRS. SQUEAMISH. Come Sloven, I'll lead you to be sure of you. [*Pulls him by the crevat.*

OLD LADY SQUEAMISH. Alas poor man how she tuggs him, kiss, kiss her, that's the way to make such nice women quiet.

HORNER. No Madam, that remedy is worse than the torment, they know I dare suffer any thing rather than do it.

OLD LADY SQUEAMISH. Prythee kiss her, and I'll give you her picture in little,[97] that you admir'd so last night, prythee do.

HORNER. Well nothing but that could bribe me, I love a woman only in effigie, and good painting as much as I hate them – I'll do't, for I cou'd adore the Devil well painted. [*Kisses* Mrs. Squeamish.

MRS. SQUEAMISH. Foh, you filthy Toad, nay now I've done jesting.

OLD LADY SQUEAMISH. Ha, ha, ha, I told you so.

MRS. SQUEAMISH. Foh, a kiss of his –

SIR JASPER. Has no more hurt in't, than one of my spaniels.

MRS. SQUEAMISH. Nor no more good neither.

QUACK. I will now believe any thing he tells me. [*Behind.*

[*Enter* Mr. Pinchwife.

LADY FIDGET. O Lord here's a man, Sir *Jasper*, my mask, my mask, I would not be seen here for the world.

SIR JASPER. What not when I am with you.

LADY FIDGET. No, no my honour – let's be gone.

MRS. SQUEAMISH. Oh Grandmother, let us be gone, make haste, make haste, I know not how he may censure us.

LADY FIDGET. Be found in the lodging of any thing like a man, away. [*Exeunt* Sir Jasper, Lady Fidget, Old Lady Squeamish, Mrs. Squeamish.

QUACK. What's here another Cuckold – he looks like one, and none else sure have any business with him. [*Behind.*

HORNER. Well, what brings my dear friend hither?

MR. PINCHWIFE. Your impertinency.

HORNER. My impertinency – why you gentlemen that have got handsome wives, think you have a privilege of saying any thing to your friends, and are as brutish, as if you were our creditors.

MR. PINCHWIFE. No Sir, I'll nev'r trust you any way.

HORNER. But why not, dear *Jack*, why diffide in me,[98] thou know'st so well.

MR. PINCHWIFE. Because I do know you so well.

HORNER. Han't I been always thy friend, honest *Jack*, always ready to serve thee, in love, or battle, before thou wert married, and am so still?

MR. PINCHWIFE. I believe so you wou'd be my second[99] now indeed.

HORNER. Well then dear *Jack*, why so unkind, so grum, so strange to me, come prythee kiss me dear Rogue, gad I was always I say, and am still as much thy servant as –

MR. PINCHWIFE. As I am yours Sir. What you wou'd send a kiss to my wife, is that it?

HORNER. So there 'tis – a man can't shew his friendship to a married man, but presently he talks of his wife to you, prythee let thy wife alone, and let thee and I be all one, as we were wont, what thou art as shye of my kindness, as a Lumbard-street alderman of a courtier's civility at Lockets.[100]

MR. PINCHWIFE. But you are over kind to me, as kind, as if I were your cuckold already, yet I must confess you ought to be kind and civil to me, since I am so kind, so civil to you, as to bring you this, look you there Sir. [*Delivers him a letter.*

HORNER. What is't?

MR. PINCHWIFE. Only a love letter Sir.

HORNER. From whom – how, this is from your wife – hum – and hum – [*Reads.*

MR. PINCHWIFE. Even from my wife Sir, am I not wondrous kind and civil to you, now too? – [*Aside*] *But you'll not think her so.*

HORNER. [*Aside*] *Ha, is this a trick of his or hers?*

MR. PINCHWIFE. The gentleman's surpriz'd I find, what you expected a kinder letter?

HORNER. No faith not I, how cou'd I.

MR. PINCHWIFE. Yes yes, I'm sure you did; a man so well made as you are must needs be disappointed, if the women declare not their passion at first sight or opportunity.

HORNER. But what should this mean? Stay, the postscript. – [*Reads aside*] *Be sure you love me whatsoever my husband says to the contrary, and let him not see this, lest he should come home, and pinch me, or kill my squirrel.* – [*Aside*] *It seems he knows not what the letter contains.*

MR. PINCHWIFE. Come nev'r wonder at it so much.

HORNER. Faith I can't help it.

MR. PINCHWIFE. Now I think I have deserv'd your infinite friendship, and kindness, and have shewed my self sufficiently an obliging kind friend and husband, am I not so, to bring a letter from my wife to her gallant?

HORNER. Ay, the Devil take me, art thou, the most obliging, kind friend and husband in the world, ha, ha.

MR. PINCHWIFE. Well you may be merry Sir, but in short I must tell you Sir, my honour will suffer no jesting.

HORNER. What do'st thou mean?

MR. PINCHWIFE. Does the letter want a comment? Then know Sir, though I have been so civil a husband, as to bring you a letter from my wife, to let you kiss and court her to my face, I will not be a cuckold Sir, I will not.

HORNER. Thou art mad with jealousie, I never saw thy wife in my life, but at the play yesterday, and I know not if it were she or no, I court her, kiss her!

MR. PINCHWIFE. I will not be a cuckold I say, there will be danger in making me a cuckold.

HORNER. Why, wert thou not well cur'd of thy last clap?

MR. PINCHWIFE. I wear a sword.

HORNER. It should be taken from thee, lest thou should'st do thy self a mischief with it, thou art mad, Man.

MR. PINCHWIFE. As mad as I am, and as merry as you are, I must have more reason from you e're we part, I say again, though you kiss'd, and courted last night my wife in man's clothes, as she confesses in her letter.

HORNER. [*Aside*] *Ha –*

MR. PINCHWIFE. Both she and I say you must not design it again, for you have mistaken your woman, as you have done your man.

HORNER. – [*Aside*] *Oh – I understand something now* – Was that thy wife? Why would'st thou not tell me 'twas she? Faith my freedom with her was your fault, not mine.

MR. PINCHWIFE. [*Aside*] *Faith so 'twas –*

HORNER. Fye, I'd never do't to a woman before her husband's face, sure.

MR. PINCHWIFE. But I had rather you should do't to my wife before my face, than behind my back, and that you shall never do.

HORNER. No – you will hinder me.

MR. PINCHWIFE. If I would not hinder you, you see by her letter, she wou'd.

HORNER. Well, I must e'en acquiesce then, and be contented with what she writes.

MR. PINCHWIFE. I'll assure you 'twas voluntarily writ, I had no hand in't you may believe me.

HORNER. I do believe thee, faith.

MR. PINCHWIFE. And believe her too, for she's an innocent creature, has no dissembling in her, and so fare you well Sir.

HORNER. Pray however present my humble service to her, and tell her I will obey her letter to a tittle, and fulfill her desires be what they will, or with what difficulty soever I do't, and you shall be no more jealous of me, I warrant her, and you –

MR. PINCHWIFE. Well then fare you well, and play with any man's honour but mine, kiss any man's wife but mine, and welcome – [*Exit* Mr. Pinchwife.

HORNER. Ha, ha, ha, Doctor.

QUACK. It seems he has not heard the report of you, or does not believe it?

HORNER. Ha, ha, now Doctor what think you?

QUACK. Pray let's see the letter – hum – for – dear – love you – [*Reads the letter.*

HORNER. I wonder how she cou'd contrive it! What say'st thou to't, 'tis an original.

QUACK. So are your cuckolds too originals: for they are like no other common cuckolds, and I will henceforth believe it not impossible for you to cuckold the Grand Signior amidst his guards of eunuchs, that I say –

HORNER. And I say for the letter, 'tis the first love letter that ever was without flames, darts, fates, destinies,[101] lying and dissembling in't.

[*Enter* Sparkish *pulling in* Mr. Pinchwife.

SPARKISH. Come back, you are a pretty brother-in-law, neither go to church, nor to dinner with your Sister Bride.

MR. PINCHWIFE. My sister denies her marriage, and you see is gone away from you dissatisfy'd.

SPARKISH. Pshaw, upon a foolish scruple, that our parson was not in lawful orders, and did not say all the common prayer, but 'tis her modesty only I believe, but let women be never so modest the first day, they'll be sure to come to themselves by night, and I shall have enough of her then; in the mean time, *Harry Horner*, you must dine with me, I keep my wedding at my Aunt's in the Piazza.

HORNER. Thy wedding, what stale maid has liv'd to despair of a husband, or what young one of a gallant?

SPARKISH. O your Servant Sir – this gentleman's sister then – no stale maid.

HORNER. I'm sorry for't.

MR. PINCHWIFE. [*Aside*] *How comes he so concern'd for her –*

SPARKISH. You sorry for't, why do you know any ill by her?

HORNER. No, I know none but by thee, 'tis for her sake, not yours, and another man's sake that might have hop'd, I thought –

SPARKISH. Another man, another man, what is his name?

HORNER. Nay, since 'tis past he shall be nameless. – [*Aside*] *Poor* Harcourt *I am sorry thou hast mist her* –

MR. PINCHWIFE. [*Aside*] *He seems to be much troubled at the match* –

SPARKISH. Prythee tell me – nay you shan't go Brother.

MR. PINCHWIFE. I must of necessity, but I'll come to you to dinner. [*Exit* Pinchwife.

SPARKISH. But *Harry*, what have I a rival in my wife already? But with all my heart, for he may be of use to me hereafter, for though my hunger is now my sawce, and I can fall on heartily without, but the time will come, when a rival will be as good sawce for a married man to a wife, as an orange to veal.

HORNER. O thou damn'd Rogue, thou hast set my teeth on edge with thy orange.

SPARKISH. Then let's to dinner, there I was with you again, come.

HORNER. But who dines with thee?

SPARKISH. My friends and relations, my Brother *Pinchwife* you see, of your acquaintance.

HORNER. And his wife.

SPARKISH. No gad, he'll ne'er let her come amongst us good fellows, your stingy Country coxcomb keeps his wife from his friends, as he does his little firkin[102] of ale, for his own drinking, and a gentleman can't get a smack on't, but his servants, when his back is turn'd, broach it at their pleasures, and dust it away, ha, ha, ha, gad I am witty, I think, considering I was married to day, by the World, but come –

HORNER. No, I will not dine with you, unless you can fetch her too.

SPARKISH. Pshaw, what pleasure can'st thou have with women now, *Harry*?

HORNER. My eyes are not gone, I love a good prospect yet, and will not dine with you, unless she does too, go fetch her therefore, but do not tell her husband, 'tis for my sake.

SPARKISH. Well I'll go try what I can do, in the mean time come away to my aunt's lodging, 'tis in the way to *Pinchwife*'s.

HORNER. The poor woman has call'd for aid, and stretch'd forth her hand Doctor, I cannot but help her over the pale out of the bryars. [*Exeunt* Sparkish, Horner, Quack.

[*The Scene changes to* Pinchwife*'s house.* Mrs. Pinchwife *alone leaning on her elbow. A table, pen, ink, and paper.*

MRS. PINCHWIFE. Well 'tis e'en so, I have got the *London* disease, they call love, I am sick of my husband, and for my gallant; I have heard this distemper, call'd a feaver, but methinks 'tis liker an ague, for when I think of my husband, I tremble, and am in a cold sweat, and have inclinations to vomit, but when I think of my gallant, dear Mr. *Horner*, my hot fit comes, and I am all in a feaver, indeed, and as in other feavers, my own chamber is tedious to me, and I would fain be remov'd to his, and then methinks I shou'd be well; ah poor Mr. *Horner*, well I cannot, will not stay here, therefore I'll make an end of my letter to him, which shall be a finer letter than my last, because I have studied it like any thing; O Sick, sick! [*Takes the pen and writes.*

[*Enter* Mr. Pinchwife *who seeing her writing, steales softly behind her, and looking over her shoulder, snatches the paper from her.*

MR. PINCHWIFE. What writing more letters?

MRS. PINCHWIFE. O Lord Budd, why d'ye fright me so? [*She offers to run out: he stops her, and reads.*

MR. PINCHWIFE. How's this! Nay you shall not stir Madam. Dear, dear, dear, Mr. *Horner* – very well – I have taught you to write letters to good purpose – but let's see't.

> First I am to beg your pardon for my boldness in writing to you, which I'd have you to know, I would not have done, had not you said first you lov'd me so extreamly, which if you do, you will never suffer me to lye in the arms of another man, whom I loath, nauseate, and detest – (now you can write these filthy words) but what follows – Therefore I hope you will speedily find some way to free me from this unfortunate match, which was never, I assure you, of my choice, but I'm afraid 'tis already too far gone; however if you love me, as I do you, you will try what you can do, but you must help me away before to morrow, or else alas I shall be for ever out of your reach, for I can defer no longer our – our – what is to follow our – speak what? Our journey into [*The letter concludes*]

the Country I suppose – Oh Woman, damn'd Woman, and Love, damn'd Love, their old Tempter, for this is one of his miracles, in a moment, he can make those blind that cou'd see, and those see that were blind, those dumb that could speak, and those prattle who were dumb before, nay what is more than all, make these dow-bak'd,[103] senseless, indocile animals, Women, too hard for us their politick lords and rulers in a moment; but make an end of your letter, and then I'll make an end of you thus, and all my plagues together. [*Draws his sword.*

MRS. PINCHWIFE. O Lord, O Lord you are such a passionate man, Budd.

[*Enter* Sparkish.

SPARKISH. How now what's here to do?

MR. PINCHWIFE. This fool here now!

SPARKISH. What drawn upon your wife? You shou'd never do that but at night in the dark when you can't hurt her, this is my sister in law is it not? Ay; faith e'en our Country *Margery*, one may know her. [*Pulls aside her handkercheife.* Come she and you must go dine with me, dinner's ready, come, but where's my wife, is she not come home yet, where is she?

MR. PINCHWIFE. Making you a cuckold, 'tis that they all do, as soon as they can.

SPARKISH. What the wedding day? No, a wife that designs to make a cully of her husband, will be sure to let him win the first stake of love, by the World, but come they stay dinner for us, come I'll lead down our *Margery*.

MRS. PINCHWIFE. No – Sir go, we'll follow you.

SPARKISH. I will not wag without you.

MR. PINCHWIFE. This coxcomb is a sensible torment to me amidst the greatest in the World.

SPARKISH. Come, come Madam *Margery*.

MR. PINCHWIFE. No, I'll lead her my way, [*Leads her to t'other door, and locks her in and returns*] what wou'd you treat your friends with mine, for want of your own wife? – [*Aside*] *I am contented my rage shou'd take breath* –

SPARKISH. I told *Horner* this.

MR. PINCHWIFE. Come now.

SPARKISH. Lord, how shye you are of your wife, but let me tell you Brother, we men of wit have amongst us a saying, that cuckolding like the small pox comes with a fear, and you may keep your wife as much as you will out of danger of infection, but if her constitution incline her to't, she'll have it sooner or later by the World, say they.

MR. PINCHWIFE. – [*Aside*] *What a thing is a cuckold, that every fool can make him ridiculous* – Well Sir – But let me advise you, now you are come to be concern'd, because you suspect the danger, not to neglect the means to prevent it, especially when the greatest share of the malady will light upon your own head, for –

How' sere the kind wife's belly comes to swell.
The husband breeds for her, and first is ill.

Act V.

[Mr. Pinchwife's *house. Enter* Mr. Pinchwife *and* Mrs. Pinchwife, *a table and candle.*]

MR. PINCHWIFE. Come, take the pen and make an end of the letter, just as you intended, if you are false in a tittle, I shall soon perceive it, and punish you with this as you deserve. [*Lays his hand on his sword*] Write what was to follow – let's see – "You must make haste and help me away before to morrow, or else I shall be for ever out of your reach, for I can defer no longer our" – What follows our? –

MRS. PINCHWIFE. Must all out then Budd? – Look you there then. [Mrs. Pinchwife *takes the pen and writes.*

MR. PINCHWIFE. Let's see – "For I can defer no longer our – wedding – your slighted *Alithea*." What's the meaning of this, my sister's name to't, speak, unriddle?

MRS. PINCHWIFE. Yes indeed Budd.

MR. PINCHWIFE. But why her name to't, speak – speak I say?

MRS. PINCHWIFE. Ay but you'll tell her then again, if you wou'd not tell her again.

MR. PINCHWIFE. I will not, I am stunn'd, my head turns round, speak.

MRS. PINCHWIFE. Won't you tell her indeed, and indeed.

MR. PINCHWIFE. No, speak I say.

MRS. PINCHWIFE. She'll be angry with me, but I had rather she should be angry with me than you

Budd; and to tell you the truth, 'twas she made me write the letter, and taught me what I should write.

MR. PINCHWIFE. Ha – I thought the stile was somewhat better than her own, but how cou'd she come to you to teach you, since I had lock'd you up alone?

MRS. PINCHWIFE. O through the key hole, Budd.

MR. PINCHWIFE. But why should she make you write a letter for her to him, since she can write her self?

MRS. PINCHWIFE. Why she said because – for I was unwilling to do it.

MR. PINCHWIFE. Because what – because.

MRS. PINCHWIFE. Because lest Mr. *Horner* should be cruel, and refuse her, or vain afterwards, and shew the letter, she might disown it, the hand not being hers.

MR. PINCHWIFE. – [*Aside*] *How's this? Ha – then I think I shall come to my self again – this changeling cou'd not invent this lye, but if she cou'd, why should she? She might think I should soon discover it – stay – now I think on't too,* Horner *said he was sorry she had married* Sparkish, *and her disowning her marriage to me, makes me think she has evaded it, for* Horner*'s sake, yet why should she take this course? But men in love are fools, women may well be so.* – But hark you Madam, your sister went out in the morning, and I have not seen her within since.

MRS. PINCHWIFE. A lack a day she has been crying all day above it seems in a corner.

MR. PINCHWIFE. Where is she, let me speak with her.

MRS. PINCHWIFE. – [*Aside*] *O Lord then he'll discover all* – Pray hold Budd, what d'ye mean to discover me, she'll know I have told you then, pray Budd let me talk with her first –

MR. PINCHWIFE. I must speak with her to know whether *Horner* ever made her any promise; and whether she be married to *Sparkish* or no.

MRS. PINCHWIFE. Pray dear Budd don't, till I have spoken with her, and told her that I have told you all, for she'll kill me else.

MR. PINCHWIFE. Go then, and bid her come out to me.

MRS. PINCHWIFE. Yes, yes Budd –

MR. PINCHWIFE. Let me see –

MRS. PINCHWIFE. [*Aside*] *I'll go, but she is not within to come to him, I have just got time to know of Lucy her maid, who first set me on work, what lye I shall tell next, for I am e'en at my wit's end* – [*Exit* Mrs. Pinchwife.

MR. PINCHWIFE. Well I resolve it, *Horner* shall have her, I'd rather give him my sister than lend him my wife, and such an alliance will prevent his pretensions to my wife sure, – I'll make him of kin to her, and then he won't care for her,

[Mrs. Pinchwife *returns.*

MRS. PINCHWIFE. O Lord Budd I told you what anger you would make me with my sister.

MR. PINCHWIFE. Won't she come hither?

MRS. PINCHWIFE. No no, alack a day, she's asham'd to look you in the face, and she says if you go in to her, she'll run away down stairs, and shamefully go her self to Mr. *Horner,* who has promis'd her marriage she says, and she will have no other, so she won't –

MR. PINCHWIFE. Did he so – promise her marriage – then she shall have no other, go tell her so, and if she will come and discourse with me a little concerning the means, I will about it immediately, go – [*Exit* Mrs. Pinchwife] His estate is equal to *Sparkish*'s, and his extraction as much better than his, as his parts are, but my chief reason is, I'd rather be of kin to him by the name of brother-in-law, than that of cuckold –

[*Enter* Mrs. Pinchwife.

Well what says she now? –

MRS. PINCHWIFE. Why she says she would only have you lead her to *Horner*'s lodging – with whom she first will discourse the matter before she talk with you, which yet she cannot do; for alack poor creature, she says she can't so much as look you in the face, therefore she'll come to you in a mask, and you must excuse her if she make you no answer to any question of yours, till you have brought her to Mr. *Horner,* and if you will not chide her, nor question her, she'll come out to you immediately.

MR. PINCHWIFE. Let her come; I will not speak a word to her, nor require a word from her.

MRS. PINCHWIFE. Oh I forgot, besides she says, she cannot look you in the face, though through a mask, therefore wou'd desire you to put out the candle. [*Exit* Mrs. Pinchwife.

MR. PINCHWIFE. I agree to all, let her make haste – there 'tis out. [*Puts out the candle*] – My case is something better, I'd rather fight with *Horner,* for not lying with my sister, than for lying with my wife, and of the two, I had rather find my sister too forward, than my wife; I expected no other from her free education, as she calls it, and her passion for the Town – well – wife and sister are names which make us expect love and duty, pleasure and comfort, but we find 'em plagues and torments, and are equally, though differently troublesome to their keeper; for we have as much ado to get people to lye with our sisters, as to keep 'em from lying with our wives.

[*Enter* Mrs. Pinchwife *masked, and in hoods and scarves, and a night gown*[104] *and petticoat of* Alithea*'s in the dark.*

What are you come Sister? Let us go then – but first let me lock up my wife. Mrs. *Margery* where are you?

MRS. PINCHWIFE. Here Budd.

MR. PINCHWIFE. Come hither, that I may lock you up, get you in. Come Sister where are you now? [*Locks the door.* Mrs. Pinchwife *gives him her hand, but when he lets her go, she steals softly on t'other side of him, and is led away by him for his Sister* Alithea.

[*The scene changes to* Horner*'s lodging.* Quack, Horner.

QUACK. What all alone, not so much as one of your cuckolds here, nor one of their wives! They use to take their turns with you, as if they were to watch you.

HORNER. Yes it often happens, that a cuckold is but his wife's spye, and is more upon family duty, when he is with her gallant abroad hindring his pleasure, than when he is at home with her playing the gallant, but the hardest duty a married woman imposes upon a lover is keeping her husband company always.

QUACK. And his fondness wearies you almost as soon as hers.

HORNER. A pox, keeping a cuckold company after you have had his wife, is as tiresome as the company of a Country squire to a witty fellow of the Town, when he has got all his money.

QUACK. And as at first a man makes a friend of the husband to get the wife, so at last you are fain to fall out with the wife to be rid of the husband.

HORNER. Ay, most cuckold-makers are true courtiers, when once a poor man has crack'd his credit for 'em, they can't abide to come near him.

QUACK. But at first to draw him in are so sweet, so kind, so dear, just as you are to *Pinchwife*, but what becomes of that intrigue with his wife?

HORNER. A pox he's as surly as an alderman that has been bit,[105] and since he's so coy, his wife's kindness is in vain, for she's a silly innocent.

QUACK. Did she not send you a letter by him?

HORNER. Yes, but that's a riddle I have not yet solv'd – allow the poor creature to be willing, she is silly too, and he keeps her up so close –

QUACK. Yes, so close that he makes her but the more willing, and adds but revenge to her love, which two when met seldom fail of satisfying each other one way or other.

HORNER. What here's the man we are talking of I think.

[*Enter* Mr. Pinchwife *leading in his wife masqued, muffled, and in her sister's gown.*

HORNER. Pshaw.

QUACK. Bringing his wife to you is the next thing to bringing a love letter from her.

HORNER. What means this?

MR. PINCHWIFE. The last time you know Sir I brought you a love letter, now you see a mistress, I think you'll say I am a civil man to you.

HORNER. Ay the Devil take me will I say thou art the civillest man I ever met with, and I have known some; I fancy, I understand thee now, better than I did the letter, but hark thee in thy ear –

MR. PINCHWIFE. What?

HORNER. Nothing but the usual question man, is she sound[106] on thy word?

MR. PINCHWIFE. What you take her for a wench and me for a pimp?

HORNER. Pshaw, wench and pimp, paw[107] words, I know thou art an honest fellow, and hast a great acquaintance among the ladies, and perhaps hast made love for me rather than let me make love to thy wife –

MR. PINCHWIFE. Come Sir, in short, I am for no fooling.

HORNER. Nor I neither, therefore prythee let's see her face presently, make her show man, art thou sure I don't know her?

MR. PINCHWIFE. I am sure you do know her.

HORNER. A pox why dost thou bring her to me then?

MR. PINCHWIFE. Because she's a relation of mine.

HORNER. Is she faith man, then thou art still more civil and obliging, dear Rogue.

MR. PINCHWIFE. Who desir'd me to bring her to you.

HORNER. Then she is obliging, dear Rogue.

MR. PINCHWIFE. You'll make her welcome for my sake I hope.

HORNER. I hope she is handsome enough to make her self welcome; prythee let her unmask.

MR. PINCHWIFE. Do you speak to her, she wou'd never be rul'd by me.

HORNER. Madam – [Mrs. Pinchwife *whispers to* Horner] She says she must speak with me in private, withdraw prythee.

MR. PINCHWIFE. –[*Aside*] *She's unwilling it seems I shou'd know all her undecent conduct in this business* – Well then I'll leave you together, and hope when I am gone you'll agree, if not you and I shan't agree Sir. –

HORNER. What means the fool? – If she and I agree 'tis no matter what you and I do. [*Whispers to* Mrs. Pinchwife, *who makes signs with her hand for him to be gone.*

MR. PINCHWIFE. In the mean time I'll fetch a parson, and find out *Sparkish* and disabuse him. You wou'd have me fetch a parson, would you not, well then – now I think I am rid of her, and shall have no more trouble with her – our sisters and daughters like usurers' money, are safest, when put out; but our wives, like their writings, never safe, but in our closets under lock and key. [*Exit* Mr. Pinchwife.

[*Enter* Boy.

BOY. Sir *Jasper Fidget* Sir is coming up.

HORNER. Here's the trouble of a cuckold, now we are talking of, a pox on him, has he not enough to do to hinder his wife's sport, but he must other women's too. – Step in here Madam. [*Exit* Mrs. Pinchwife.

[*Enter* Sir Jasper.

SIR JASPER. My best and dearest Friend.

HORNER. The old stile Doctor –
Well be short, for I am busie, what would
your impertinent wife have now?

SIR JASPER. Well guess'd y' faith, for I do come from her.

HORNER. To invite me to supper, tell her I can't come, go.

SIR JASPER. Nay, now you are out faith, for my Lady and the whole knot of the virtuous gang, as they call themselves, are resolv'd upon a frolick of coming to you to night in a masquerade,[108] and are all drest already.

HORNER. I shan't be at home.

SIR JASPER. Lord how churlish he is to women – nay prythee don't disappoint 'em, they'll think 'tis my fault, prythee don't, I'll send in the banquet and the fiddles, but make no noise on't, for the poor virtuous rogues would not have it known for the world, that they go a masquerading, and they would come to no man's ball, but yours.

HORNER. Well, well – get you gone, and tell 'em if they come, 'twill be at the peril of their honour and yours.

SIR JASPER. Heh, he, he – we'll trust you for that, farewell – [*Exit* Sir Jasper.

HORNER. Doctor anon you too shall be my guest.
But now I'm going to a private feast.

[*The scene changes to the Piazza of Covent Garden.* Sparkish, Pinchwife.

SPARKISH. But who would have thought a woman could have been false to me, by the world, I could not have thought it. [*With the letter in his hand.*

MR. PINCHWIFE. You were for giving and taking liberty, she has taken it only Sir, now you find in that letter, you are a frank person, and so is she you see there.

SPARKISH. Nay, if this be her hand – for I never saw it.

MR. PINCHWIFE. 'Tis no matter whether that be her hand or no, I am sure this hand at her desire led her to Mr. *Horner*, with whom I left her just now, to go fetch a parson to 'em at their desire too, to deprive you of her for ever, for it seems yours was but a mock marriage.

SPARKISH. Indeed she wou'd needs have it that 'twas *Harcourt* himself in a parson's habit, that married us, but I'm sure he told me 'twas his brother Ned.

MR. PINCHWIFE. O there 'tis out, and you were deceiv'd not she, for you are such a frank person – but I must be gone – you'll find her at Mr. *Horner*'s, go and believe your eyes. [*Exit* Mr. Pinchwife.

SPARKISH. Nay I'll to her, and call her as many crocodiles, syrens, harpies, and other heathenish names, as a poet would do a mistress, who had refus'd to hear his suit, nay more his verses on her.

But stay, is not that she following a torch[109] at t'other end of the Piazza, and from *Horner*'s certainly – 'tis so –

[*Enter* Alithea *following a torch, and* Lucy *behind.*

You are well met Madam, though you don't think so; what you have made a short visit to Mr. *Horner*, but I suppose you'll return to him presently, by that time the parson can be with him.

ALITHEA. Mr. *Horner*, and the parson Sir –

SPARKISH. Come Madam, no more dissembling, no more jilting, for I am no more a frank person.

ALITHEA. How's this.

LUCY. [*Aside*] *So 'twill work I see –*

SPARKISH. Cou'd you find out no easie Country fool to abuse? None but me, a gentleman of wit and pleasure about the Town, but it was your pride to be too hard for a man of parts, unworthy false woman, false as a friend that lends a man money to lose, false as dice, who undo those that trust all they have to 'em.

LUCY. [*Aside*] *He has been a great bubble*[110] *by his similes as they say –*

ALITHEA. You have been too merry Sir at your wedding dinner sure.

SPARKISH. What d'ye mock me too?

ALITHEA. Or you have been deluded.

SPARKISH. By you.

ALITHEA. Let me understand you.

SPARKISH. Have you the confidence, I should call it something else, since you know your guilt, to stand my just reproaches? You did not write an impudent letter to Mr. *Horner*, who I find now has club'd with you in deluding me with his aversion for women, that I might not forsooth suspect him for my rival.

LUCY. [*Aside to* Alithea] D'ye think the gentleman can be jealous now Madam –

ALITHEA. I write a Letter to Mr. *Horner*!

SPARKISH. Nay Madam, do not deny it, your brother shew'd it me just now, and told me likewise he left you at *Horner*'s lodging to fetch a parson to marry you to him, and I wish you joy Madam, joy, joy, and to him too, much joy, and to my self more joy for not marrying you.

ALITHEA. – [*Aside*] *So I find my brother would break off the match, and I can consent to't, since I see this gentleman can be made jealous.* – O *Lucy*, by his rude usage and jealousie, he makes me almost afraid I am married to him, art thou sure 'twas *Harcourt* himself and no parson that married us.

SPARKISH. No Madam I thank you, I suppose that was a contrivance too of Mr. *Horner*'s and yours, to make *Harcourt* play the parson, but I would as little as you have him one now, no not for the world, for shall I tell you another truth, I never had any passion for you, 'till now, for now I hate you, 'tis true I might have married your portion, as other men of parts of the Town do sometimes, and so your Servant, and to shew my unconcernedness, I'll come to your wedding, and resign you with as much joy as I would a stale wench to a new cully,[111] nay with as much joy as I would after the first night, if I had been married to you, there's for you, and so your Servant, Servant. [*Exit* Sparkish.

ALITHEA. How was I deceiv'd in a man!

LUCY. You'll believe then a fool may be made jealous now? For that easiness in him that suffers him to be led by a wife, will likewise permit him to be perswaded against her by others.

ALITHEA. But marry Mr. *Horner*, my brother does not intend it sure; if I thought he did, I would take thy advice, and Mr. *Harcourt* for my husband, and now I wish, that if there be any over-wise woman of the Town, who like me would marry a fool, for fortune, liberty, or title, first that her husband may love play, and be a cully to all the Town, but her, and suffer none but fortune to be mistress of his purse, then if for liberty, that he may send her into the Country under the conduct of some housewifely mother-in-law; and if for title, may the World give 'em none but that of cuckold.

LUCY. And for her greater curse Madam, may he not deserve it.

ALITHEA. Away impertinent – is not this my old Lady *Lanterlus*?

LUCY. Yes Madam. [*Aside*] *And here I hope we shall find Mr.* Harcourt – [*Exeunt* Alithea, Lucy.

[*The Scene changes again to* Horner*'s lodging.* Horner, Lady Fidget, Mrs. Dainty Fidget, Mrs. Squeamish, *a table, banquet, and bottles.*

HORNER. [*Aside*] *A pox they are come too soon – before I have sent back my new – mistress, all I have now to do, is to lock her in, that they may not see her –*

LADY FIDGET. That we may be sure of our welcome, we have brought our entertainment with us, and are resolv'd to treat thee, dear Toad.

DAINTY FIDGET. And that we may be merry to purpose, have left Sir *Jasper* and my old Lady *Squeamish* quarrelling at home at Baggammon.

SQUEAM. Therefore let us make use of our time, lest they should chance to interrupt us.

LADY FIDGET. Let us sit then.

HORNER. First that you may be private, let me lock this door, and that, and I'll wait upon you presently.

LADY FIDGET. No Sir, shut 'em only and your lips for ever, for we must trust you as much as our women.

HORNER. You know all vanity's kill'd in me, I have no occasion for talking.

LADY FIDGET. Now Ladies, supposing we had drank each of us our two bottles, let us speak the truth of our hearts.

DAINTY FIDGET AND MRS. SQUEAMISH. Agreed.

LADY FIDGET. By this brimmer, for truth is no where else to be found, (not in thy heart false man). [*Aside to* Horner.

HORNER. You have found me a true man I'm sure. [*Aside to* Lady Fidget.

LADY FIDGET. Not every way – [*Aside to* Horner. – But let us sit and be merry.

[Lady Fidget *sings*.

I.
Why should our damn'd tyrants oblige us to live
On the pittance of pleasure which they only give?
We must not rejoyce,
With wine and with noise.
In vain we must wake in a dull bed alone,
Whilst to our warm rival the bottle, they're gone.
Then lay aside charms,
And take up these arms.*

**The glasses.*

2.
'Tis wine only gives 'em their courage and wit,
Because we live sober to men we submit.
If for beauties you'd pass,
Take a lick of the glass,
'Twill mend your complections, and when they are gone,
The best red we have is the red of the grape.
Then Sisters lay't on.
And dam a good shape.

DAINTY FIDGET. Dear Brimmer, well in token of our openness and plain dealing, let us throw our masques over our heads.

HORNER. So 'twill come to the glasses anon.

MRS. SQUEAMISH. Lovely Brimmer, let me enjoy him first.

LADY FIDGET. No, I never part with a gallant till I've try'd him. Dear Brimmer that mak'st our husbands short-sighted.

DAINTY FIDGET. And our bashful gallants bold.

MRS. SQUEAMISH. And for want of a gallant, the butler lovely in our eyes, drink Eunuch.

LADY FIDGET. Drink thou representative of a husband, damn a husband.

DAINTY FIDGET. And as it were a husband, an old keeper.

MRS. SQUEAMISH. And an old grandmother.

HORNER. And an English bawd, and a French chirurgion.

LADY FIDGET. Ay we have all reason to curse 'em.

HORNER. For my sake Ladies.

LADY FIDGET. No, for our own, for the first spoils all young gallants' industry.

DAINTY FIDGET. And the others' art makes 'em bold only with common women.

MRS. SQUEAMISH. And rather run the hazard of the vile distemper amongst them, than of a denial amongst us.

DAINTY FIDGET. The filthy toads chuse mistresses now, as they do stuffs,[112] for having been fancy'd and worn by others.

MRS. SQUEAMISH. For being common and cheap.

LADY FIDGET. Whilst women of quality, like the richest stuffs, lye untumbled, and unask'd for.

HORNER. Ay neat, and cheap, and new often they think best.

DAINTY FIDGET. No Sir, the beasts will be known by a mistress longer than by a suit.

MRS. SQUEAMISH. And 'tis not for cheapness neither.

LADY FIDGET. No, for the vain fopps will take up druggets,[113] and embroider 'em, but I wonder at the depraved appetites of witty men, they use to be out of the common road, and hate imitation, pray tell me beast, when you were a man, why you rather chose to club with a multitude in a common house, for an entertainment, than to be the only guest at a good table.

HORNER. Why faith ceremony and expectation are unsufferable to those that are sharp bent,[114] people always eat with the best stomach at an ordinary,[115] where every man is snatching for the best bit.

LADY FIDGET. Though he get a cut over the fingers – but I have heard people eat most heartily of another man's meat, that is, what they do not pay for.

HORNER. When they are sure of their welcome and freedom, for ceremony in love and eating, is as ridiculous as in fighting, falling on briskly is all should be done in those occasions.

LADY FIDGET. Well then let me tell you Sir, there is no where more freedom than in our houses, and we take freedom from a young person as a sign of good breeding, and a person may be as free as he pleases with us, as frolick, as gamesome, as wild as he will.

HORNER. Han't I heard you all declaim against wild men.

LADY FIDGET. Yes, but for all that, we think wildness in a man, as desireable a quality, as in a duck, or rabbet; a tame man, foh.

HORNER. I know not, but your reputations frightned me, as much as your faces invited me.

LADY FIDGET. Our reputation, Lord! Why should you not think, that we women make use of our reputation, as you men of yours, only to deceive the World with less suspicion; our virtue is like the state-man's religion, the Quaker's word, the gamester's oath, and the great man's honour, but to cheat those that trust us.

MRS. SQUEAMISH. And that demureness, coyness, and modesty, that you see in our faces in the boxes at plays, is as much a sign of a kind woman, as a vizard-mask in the pit.

DAINTY FIDGET. For I assure you, women are least mask'd, when they have the velvet vizard on.

LADY FIDGET. You wou'd have found us modest women in our denyals only.

MRS. SQUEAMISH. Our bashfulness is only the reflection of the men's.

DAINTY FIDGET. We blush, when they are shame-fac'd.

HORNER. I beg your pardon Ladies, I was deceiv'd in you devilishly, but why, that mighty pretence to honour?

LADY FIDGET. We have told you; but sometimes 'twas for the same reason you men pretend business often, to avoid ill company, to enjoy the better, and more privately those you love.

HORNER. But why, wou'd you ne'er give a friend a wink then?

LADY FIDGET. Faith, your reputation frightned us as much, as ours did you, you were so notoriously lewd.

HORNER. And you so seemingly honest.

LADY FIDGET. Was that all that deterr'd you?

HORNER. And so expensive – you allow freedom you say.

LADY FIDGET. Ay, ay.

HORNER. That I was afraid of losing my little money, as well as my little time, both which my other pleasures required.

LADY FIDGET. Money, foh – you talk like a little fellow now, do such as we expect money?

HORNER. I beg your pardon, Madam, I must confess, I have heard that great ladies, like great merchants, set but the higher prizes upon what they have, because they are not in necessity of taking the first offer.

DAINTY FIDGET. Such as we, make sale of our hearts?

MRS. SQUEAMISH. We brib'd for our love? Foh.

HORNER. With your pardon, Ladies, I know, like great men in offices, you seem to exact flattery and attendance only from your followers, but you have receivers about you, and such fees to pay, a man is afraid to pass your grants; besides we must let you win at cards, or we lose your hearts; and if you make an assignation, 'tis at a goldsmith's, jeweller's, or China-house, where for your honour, you deposit to him, he must pawn his, to the punctual Cit, and so paying for what you take up, pays for what he takes up.

DAINTY FIDGET. Wou'd you not have us assur'd of our gallants' love?

MRS. SQUEAMISH. For love is better known by liberality, than by jealousie.

LADY FIDGET. – [*Aside*] *For one may be dissembled, the other not – but my jealousie can be no longer dissembled, and they are telling ripe.* – Come here's to our gallants in waiting, whom we must name, and I'll begin, this is my false Rogue. [*Claps him on the back.*

MRS. SQUEAMISH. How!

HORNER. So all will out now –

MRS. SQUEAMISH. Did you not tell me, 'twas for my sake only, you reported your self no man? [*Aside to* Horner.

DAINTY FIDGET. Oh Wretch! Did you not swear to me, 'twas for my love, and honour, you pass'd for that thing you do? [*Aside to* Horner.

HORNER. So, so.

LADY FIDGET. Come, speak Ladies, this is my false villain.

MRS. SQUEAMISH. And mine too.

DAINTY FIDGET. And mine.

HORNER. Well then, you are all three my false Rogues too, and there's an end on't.

LADY FIDGET. Well then, there's no remedy, Sister Sharers, let us not fall out, but have a care of our honour; though we get no presents, no jewels of him, we are savers of our honour, the jewel of most value and use, which shines yet to the World unsuspected, though it be counterfeit.

HORNER. Nay, and is e'en as good, as if it were true, provided the World think so; for honour, like beauty now, only depends on the opinion of others.

LADY FIDGET. Well Harry Common, I hope you can be true to three, swear, but 'tis no purpose, to require your oath; for you are as often forsworn, as you swear to new women.

HORNER. Come, faith Madam, let us e'en pardon one another, for all the difference I find betwixt we men, and you women, we forswear our selves at the beginning of an amour, you, as long as it lasts.

[*Enter* Sir Jasper Fidget, *and* Old Lady Squeamish.

SIR JASPER. Oh my Lady *Fidget*, was this your cunning, to come to Mr. *Horner* without me; but you have been no where else I hope.

LADY FIDGET. No, Sir *Jasper*.

OLD LADY SQUEAMISH. And you came straight hither Biddy.

MRS. SQUEAMISH. Yes indeed, Lady Grandmother.

SIR JASPER. 'Tis well, 'tis well, I knew when once they were thoroughly acquainted with poor *Horner*, they'd ne'er be from him; you may let her masquerade it with my wife, and *Horner*, and I warrant her reputation safe.

[*Enter* Boy.

BOY. O Sir, here's the gentleman come, whom you bid me not suffer to come up, without giving you notice, with a lady too, and other gentlemen –

HORNER. Do you all go in there, whil'st I send 'em away, and Boy, do you desire 'em to stay below 'til I come, which shall be immediately. [*Exeunt* Sir Jasper, Lady Squeamish, Lady Fidget, Mrs. Dainty, Mrs. Squeamish.

BOY. Yes Sir. [*Exit. Exit* Horner *at t'other door, and returns with* Mrs. Pinchwife.

HORNER. You wou'd not take my advice to be gone home, before your husband came back, he'll now discover all, yet pray my Dearest be perswaded to go home, and leave the rest to my management, I'll let you down the back way.

MRS. PINCHWIFE. I don't know the way home, so I don't.

HORNER. My man shall wait upon you.

MRS. PINCHWIFE. No, don't you believe, that I'll go at all; what are you weary of me already?

HORNER. No my life, 'tis that I may love you long, 'tis to secure my love, and your reputation with your husband, he'll never receive you again else.

MRS. PINCHWIFE. What care I, d'ye think to frighten me with that? I don't intend to go to him again; you shall be my husband now.

HORNER. I cannot be your husband, Dearest, since you are married to him.

MRS. PINCHWIFE. O wou'd you make me believe that – don't I see every day at *London* here, women leave their first husbands, and go, and live with other men as their wives, pish, pshaw, you'd make me angry, but that I love you so mainly.

HORNER. So, they are coming up – in again, in, I hear'em: [*Exit* Mrs. Pinchwife.
Well, a silly mistress, is like a weak place,[116] soon got, soon lost, a man has scarce time for plunder; she betrays her husband first to her gallant, and then her gallant, to her husband.

[*Enter* Pinchwife, Alithea, Harcourt, Sparkish, Lucy, *and a parson.*

MR. PINCHWIFE. Come, Madam, 'tis not the sudden change of your dress, the confidence of your asseverations, and your false witness there, shall perswade me, I did not bring you hither, just now; here's my witness, who cannot deny it, since you must be confronted – Mr. *Horner*, did not I bring this lady to you just now?

HORNER. [*Aside*] *Now must I wrong one woman for another's sake, but that's no new thing with me; for in these cases I am still on the criminal's side, against the innocent.*

ALITHEA. Pray, speak Sir.

HORNER. [*Aside*] *It must be so – I must be impudent, and try my luck, impudence uses to be too hard for truth.*

MR. PINCHWIFE. What, you are studying an evasion, or excuse for her, speak Sir.

HORNER. No faith, I am something backward only, to speak in women's affairs or disputes.

MR. PINCHWIFE. She bids you speak.

ALITHEA. Ay, pray Sir do, pray satisfie him.

HORNER. Then truly, you did bring that lady to me just now.

MR. PINCHWIFE. O ho –

ALITHEA. How Sir –

HARCOURT. How, *Horner*!

ALITHEA. What mean you Sir, I always took you for a man of honour?

HORNER. [*Aside*] *Ay, so much a man of honour, that I must save my mistress, I thank you, come what will on't.*

SPARKISH. So if I had had her, she'd have made me believe, the moon had been made of a Christmas pye.

LUCY. [*Aside*] *Now cou'd I speak, if I durst, and 'solve the riddle, who am the author of it.*

ALITHEA. O unfortunate woman! A combination against my honour, which most concerns me now, because you share in my disgrace, Sir, and it is your censure which I must now suffer, that troubles me, not theirs.

HARCOURT. Madam, then have no trouble, you shall now see 'tis possible for me to love too, without being jealous, I will not only believe your innocence my self, but make all the World believe it – [*Apart to* Horner] *Horner*, I must now be concern'd for this ladie's honour.

HORNER. And I must be concern'd for a ladie's honour too.

HARCOURT. This lady has her honour, and I will protect it.

HORNER. My lady has not her honour, but has given it me to keep, and I will preserve it.

HARCOURT. I understand you not.

HORNER. I wou'd not have you.

MRS. PINCHWIFE. What's the matter with 'em all. [Mrs. Pinchwife *peeping in behind.*

MR. PINCHWIFE. Come, come, Mr. *Horner*, no more disputing, here's the parson, I brought him not in vain.

HORNER. No Sir, I'll employ him, if this lady please.

MR. PINCHWIFE. How, what d'ye mean?

SPARKISH. Ay, what does he mean?

HORNER. Why, I have resign'd your sister to him, he has my consent.

MR. PINCHWIFE. But he has not mine Sir, a woman's injur'd honour, no more than a man's, can be repair'd or satisfied by any, but him that first wrong'd it; and you shall marry her presently, or – [*Lays his hand on his sword.*

[*Enter to them* Mrs. Pinchwife.

MRS. PINCHWIFE. O Lord, they'll kill poor Mr. *Horner*, besides he shan't marry her, whilest I stand by, and look on, I'll not lose my second husband so.

MR. PINCHWIFE. What do I see?

ALITHEA. My sister in my clothes!

SPARKISH. Ha!

MRS. PINCHWIFE. Nay, pray now don't quarrel about finding work for the parson, he shall marry me to Mr. *Horner*; for now I believe, you have enough of me. [*To* Mr. Pinchwife.

HORNER. Damn'd, damn'd loving Changeling.

MRS. PINCHWIFE. Pray Sister, pardon me for telling so many lyes of you.

HARCOURT. I suppose the riddle is plain now.

LUCY. No, that must be my work, good Sir, hear me. [*Kneels to* Mr. Pinchwife, *who stands doggedly, with his hat over his eyes.*

MR. PINCHWIFE. I will never hear woman again, but make 'em all silent, thus – [*Offers to draw upon his wife.*

HORNER. No, that must not be.

MR. PINCHWIFE. You then shall go first, 'tis all one to me. [*Offers to draw on* Horner, *stopt by* Harcourt.

HARCOURT. Hold –

[*Enter* Sir Jasper Fidget, Lady Fidget, Lady Squeamish, Mrs. Dainty Fidget, Mrs. Squeamish.

SIR JASPER. What's the matter, what's the matter, pray what's the matter Sir, I beseech you communicate Sir.

MR. PINCHWIFE. Why my wife has communicated Sir, as your wife may have done too Sir, if she knows him Sir –

SIR JASPER. Pshaw, with him, ha, ha, he.

MR. PINCHWIFE. D'ye mock me Sir, a cuckold is a kind of a wild beast, have a care Sir –

SIR JASPER. No sure, you mock me Sir – he cuckold you! It can't be, ha, ha, he, why, I'll tell you Sir. [*Offers to whisper.*

MR. PINCHWIFE. I tell you again, he has whor'd my wife, and yours too, if he knows her, and all the women he comes near; 'tis not his dissembling, his hypocrisie can wheedle me.

SIR JASPER. How does he dissemble, is he a hypocrite? Nay then – how – Wife – Sister is he an hypocrite?

OLD LADY SQUEAMISH. An hypocrite, a dissembler, speak young Harlotry, speak how?

SIR JASPER. Nay then – O my head too – O thou libinous Lady!

OLD LADY SQUEAMISH. O thou harloting, Harlotry, hast thou done't then?

SIR JASPER. Speak good *Horner*, art thou a dissembler, a rogue? Hast thou –

HORNER. Soh –

LUCY. I'll fetch you off, and her too, if she will but hold her tongue. [*Apart to* Horner.

HORNER. Canst thou? I'll give thee – [*Apart to* Lucy.

LUCY. [*To* Mr. Pinchwife] Pray have but patience to hear me Sir, who am the unfortunate cause of all this confusion, your wife is innocent, I only culpable; for I put her upon telling you all these lyes, concerning my mistress, in order to the breaking off the match between Mr. *Sparkish* and her, to make way for Mr. *Harcourt.*

SPARKISH. Did you so eternal Rotten-tooth? Then it seems my mistress was not false to me, I was only deceiv'd by you. Brother that shou'd have been, now man of conduct, who is a frank person now, to bring your wife to her lover – ha –

LUCY. I assure you Sir, she came not to Mr. *Horner* out of love, for she loves him no more –

MRS. PINCHWIFE. Hold, I told lyes for you, but you shall tell none for me, for I do love Mr. *Horner* with all my soul, and no body shall say me nay; pray don't you go to make poor Mr. *Horner* believe to the contrary, 'tis spitefully done of you, I'm sure.

HORNER. Peace, Dear Ideot. [*To* Mrs. Pinchwife.

MRS. PINCHWIFE. Nay, I will not peace.

MR. PINCHWIFE. Not 'till I make you.

[*Enter* Dorilant, Quack.

DORILANT. *Horner*, your Servant, I am the Doctor's guest, he must excuse our intrusion.

QUACK. But what's the matter Gentlemen, for Heaven's sake, what's the matter?

HORNER. Oh 'tis well you are come – 'tis a censorious World we live in, you may have brought me a reprieve, or else I had died for a crime, I never committed, and these innocent ladies had suffer'd with me, therefore pray satisfie these worthy, honourable, jealous Gentlemen – that – [*Whispers*.

QUACK. O I understand you, is that all – Sir *Jasper*, by Heavens and upon the word of a physician Sir, – [*Whispers to* Sir Jasper.

SIR JASPER. Nay I do believe you truly – pardon me my virtuous Lady, and dear of honour.

OLD LADY SQUEAMISH. What then all's right again.

SIR JASPER. Ay, ay, and now let us satisfie him too. [*They whisper with* Mr. Pinchwife.

MR. PINCHWIFE. An eunuch! Pray no fooling with me.

QUACK. I'll bring half the chirurgions in Town to swear it.

MR. PINCHWIFE. They – they'll swear a man that bled to death through his wounds died of an apoplexy.

QUACK. Pray hear me Sir – why all the Town has heard the report of him.

MR. PINCHWIFE. But does all the Town believe it.

QUACK. Pray inquire a little, and first of all these.

MR. PINCHWIFE. I'm sure when I left the Town he was the lewdest fellow in't.

QUACK. I tell you Sir he has been in *France* since, pray ask but these ladies and gentlemen, your friend Mr. *Dorilant*, Gentlemen and Ladies, han't you all heard the late sad report of poor Mr. *Horner*.

ALL LADIES. Ay, ay, ay.

DORILANT. Why thou jealous Fool do'st thou doubt it, he's an errant French capon.

MRS. PINCHWIFE. 'Tis false Sir, you shall not disparage poor Mr. *Horner*, for to my certain knowledge –

LUCY. O hold –

MRS. SQUEAMISH. Stop her mouth – [*Aside to* Lucy.

LADY FIDGET. Upon my honour Sir, 'tis as true. [*To* Pinchwife.

DAINTY FIDGET. D'y think we would have been seen in his company –

MRS. SQUEAMISH. Trust our unspotted reputations with him!

LADY FIDGET. This you get, and we too, by trusting your secret to a fool – [*Aside to* Horner.

HORNER. Peace Madam, [*Aside to* Quack] – well Doctor is not this a good design that carries a man on unsuspected, and brings him off safe. –

MR. PINCHWIFE. [*Aside*] *Well, if this were true, but my wife* – [Dorilant *whispers with* Mrs. Pinchwife.

ALITHEA. Come Brother, your wife is yet innocent you see, but have a care of too strong an imagination, lest like an overconcern'd timorous gamester, by fancying an unlucky cast, it should come, women and fortune are truest still to those that trust 'em.

LUCY. And any wild thing grows but the more fierce and hungry for being kept up, and more dangerous to the keeper.

ALITHEA. There's doctrine for all husbands Mr. *Harcourt*.

HARCOURT. I edifie Madam so much, that I am impatient till I am one.

DORILANT. And I edifie so much by example I will never be one.

SPARKISH. And because I will not disparage my parts I'll nev'r be one.

HORNER. And I alas can't be one.

MR. PINCHWIFE. But I must be one – against my will to a Country-Wife, with a Country-murrain[117] to me.

MRS. PINCHWIFE. [*Aside*] *And I must be a Country Wife still too I find, for I can't like a City one, be rid of my musty husband and do what I list.*

HORNER. Now Sir I must pronounce your wife innocent, though I blush whilst I do it, and I am the only man by her now expos'd to shame, which I will straight drown in wine, as you shall your suspicion, and the Ladies' troubles we'll divert with a ballet, Doctor where are your maskers?

LUCY. Indeed she's innocent Sir, I am her witness, and her end of coming out was but to see her sister's wedding, and what she has said to your face of her love to Mr. *Horner* was but the usual innocent revenge on a husband's jealousie, was it not Madam speak –

MRS. PINCHWIFE. – [*Aside to* Lucy *and* Horner] Since you'll have me tell more lyes – Yes indeed Budd.

MR. PINCHWIFE. For my own sake fain I wou'd all believe.
Cuckolds like lovers shou'd themselves deceive.
But–[*Sighs*] –
His honour is least safe, (too late I find)
Who trusts it with a foolish wife or friend.

[*A dance of Cuckolds.*

HORNER. Vain fopps, but court, and dress, and keep a puther,[118]
To pass for women's men, with one another.
But he who aims by women to be priz'd,
First by the men you see must be despis'd.

EPILOGUE

spoken by Mrs. Knep:[119]

Now you the Vigorous, who dayly here
O're vizard mask, in publick domineer,
And what you'd do to her if in place where;
Nay have the confidence, to cry come out,
Yet when she says lead on, you are not stout;
But to your well-drest brother straight turn round
And cry, pox on her *Ned*, she can't be sound:
Then slink away, a fresh one to ingage,
With so much seeming heat and loving rage,
You'd frighten listning actress on the stage:
Till she at last has seen you huffing come,
And talk of keeping in the tyreing-room,[120]
Yet cannot be provok'd to lead her home:
Next you *Fallstaffs* of fifty,[121] who beset
Your buckram maidenheads,[122] which your friends get;
And whilst to them, you of atchievements boast,
They share the booty, and laugh at your cost,
In fine, you Essens't Boyes,[123] both old and young,
Who wou'd be thought so eager, brisk, and strong,
Yet do the ladies, not their husbands, wrong:
Whose purses for your manhood make excuse,
And keep your Flanders mares[124] for shew, not use;
Encourag'd by our Woman's Man to day,
A *Horner*'s part may vainly think to play;
And may intreagues so bashfully disown
That they may doubted be by few or none,
May kiss the cards at Picquet, Hombre, –Lu,[125]
And so be thought to kiss the lady too;
But Gallants, have a care faith, what you do.
The World, which to no man his due will give,
You by experience know you can deceive,
And men may still believe you vigorous,
But then we women, –there's no cous'ning us.

FINIS.

2.2 JOHN WILMOT, EARL OF ROCHESTER, "THE IMPERFECT ENJOYMENT"

JOHN WILMOT, EARL OF ROCHESTER, "The Imperfect Enjoyment" in *The Works of John Wilmot, Earl of Rochester*. Ed. Harold Love. Oxford: Oxford University Press, 1999, 268–269. Wilmot, the second Earl of Rochester (1647–1680), the model for Dorimant in *The Man of Mode*, was the most celebrated of the libertine wits of Charles II's court. His poetry, which circulated in manuscript before its posthumous publication, often dealt frankly—to the point of pornography—with sexuality.

Naked she lay, clasped in my longing arms,
I filled with love, and she all over charms;
Both equally inspired with eager fire,
Melting through kindness, flaming in desire.
With arms, legs, lips close clinging to embrace,
She clips me to her breast, and sucks me to her face.
Her nimble tongue, love's lesser lightning, played
Within my mouth, and to my thoughts conveyed
Swift orders that I should prepare to throw
The all-dissolving thunderbolt below.
My fluttering soul, sprung with the pointed kiss,
Hangs hovering o'er her balmy brinks of bliss.
But whilst her busy hand would guide that part
Which should convey my soul up to her heart,
In liquid raptures I dissolve all o'er,
Melt into sperm, and spend at every pore.
A touch from any part of her had done 't:
Her hand, her foot, her very look's a cunt.
Smiling, she chides in a kind murmuring noise,
And from her body wipes the clammy joys,
When, with a thousand kisses wandering o'er
My panting bosom, "Is there then no more?"
She cries. "All this to love and rapture's due;
Must we not pay a debt to pleasure too?"
But I, the most forlorn, lost man alive,
To show my wished obedience vainly strive:
I sigh, alas! and kiss, but cannot swive.
Eager desires confound my first intent,
Succeeding shame does more success prevent,
And rage at last confirms me impotent.

Ev'n her fair hand, which might bid heat return
To frozen age, and make cold hermits burn,
Applied to my dear cinder, warms no more
Than fire to ashes could past flames restore.
Trembling, confused, despairing, limber, dry,
A wishing, weak, unmoving lump I lie.
This dart of love, whose piercing point, oft tried,
With virgin blood ten thousand maids has dyed,
Which nature still directed with such art
That it through every cunt reached every heart—
Stiffly resolved, 'twould carelessly invade
Woman or man, nor ought its fury stayed:
Where'er it pierced, a cunt it found or made—
Now languid lies in this unhappy hour,
Shrunk up and sapless like a withered flower.
Thou treacherous, base deserter of my flame,
False to my passion, fatal to my fame,
Through what mistaken magic dost thou prove
So true to lewdness, so untrue to love?
What oyster-cinder-beggar-common whore
Didst thou e'er fail in all thy life before?
When vice, disease, and scandal lead the way,
With what officious haste doest thou obey!
Like a rude, roaring hector[126] in the streets
Who scuffles, cuffs, and justles all he meets,
But if his king or country claim his aid,
The rakehell villain shrinks and hides his head;
Ev'n so thy brutal valor is displayed,
Breaks every stew,[127] does each small whore invade,
But when great Love the onset does command,
Base recreant to thy prince, thou dar'st not stand.
Worst part of me, and henceforth hated most,
Through all the town a common fucking post,
On whom each whore relieves her tingling cunt
As hogs on gates do rub themselves and grunt,
Mayst thou to ravenous chancres be a prey,
Or in consuming weepings waste away;
May strangury[128] and stone thy days attend;
May'st thou never piss, who didst refuse to spend
When all my joys did on false thee depend.
And may ten thousand abler pricks agree
To do the wronged Corinna right for thee.

2.3 DAVID GARRICK, "PREFACE" TO *THE COUNTRY GIRL*

DAVID GARRICK, "PREFACE" to *The Country Girl. A Comedy. Altered from Wycherly by David Garrick, Esq. Adapted for Theatrical Representation, as Performed at the Theatre-Royal, Drury-Lane. Regulated from the Prompt-Books, By Permission of the Managers*. London: John Bell, 1791. Garrick (1717–1779) was a celebrity actor, theatre manager and playwright. His adaptation of *The Country Wife* eliminates the original's frank sexuality and leaves little of its plot. Nonetheless, this sanitized adaptation proved a star vehicle for actresses such as Dorothy Jordan, who were popular for their playing of breeches roles, cross-dressed parts that allowed the actresses to show their legs.

This Comic Poet was born about the year 1640.—Like several of the Muse's ornaments, he was intended for the profession of the law—but the gay and seducing amusements of the town allured him from the severities of that study, and finding the production of Comedy the shortest step into favour and fashion, he commenced a Writer for the Stage.

The reign of the Second Charles was favourable thus far to literature, that the Court patronized what was believed the brightest talent among the people.—WYCHERLY came in for a full share of this distinction; and what has seldom happened from crowned heads, CHARLES in person condescended to visit the poet in a severe indisposition, under which he was reduced to the last extremity. His Majesty laid his commands upon him to go to the South of France, and liberally ordered him 500*l.* to defray his expences.—At his return, the Monarch told him that his opinion of him was so high, that his Son should be consigned to his tuition, and that as his governor he should receive an appointment of 1500*l.* per ann.

. . .

This Comedy is an alteration from the Country Wife of WYCHERLY. The usual taint of the time in which he wrote had so infected the whole mass, that Mr. GARRICK found himself reduced to the necessity of lopping off a limb (HORNER) to save the whole from putrefaction.

As it is here given, there is a considerable degree of sprightly dialogue, keen remark, and facility of invention.—If we except CONGREVE, WYCHERLY is equal to any of his followers; with them he has one common defect, that they are not sufficiently scrupulous as to tendency—and the spoiler of domestic peace unpunished riots in the perversion of legitimate principles, and the injury offered to the wise and the worthy.—A foible is without distinction punished as a vice, and the profligacy of the pleasing debauchee rewarded as a virtue.

It would be unpardonable if we were to close this article without observing, that the excellence of Mrs. JORDAN in the Country Girl is so powerful—every girlish trick so minutely and naturally delineated, that we pronounce the performance to be HER *chef d'oeuvre*, and assuredly the boast of modern acting.

2.4 DANIEL MAROT, *DESIGN FOR QUEEN MARY'S CHINA ROOM*

Daniel Marot (1661–1752), *Design for Queen Mary's china room.* Marot was a French designer and engraver. He was employed in designing interiors at the palace at Het Loo in Holland by William the Stadthouder and designed this china room for Mary, his queen, at Hampton Court Palace in London. Victoria and Albert Museum, London.

2.5 SIR PETER LELY, *DIANA KIRKE, LATER COUNTESS OF OXFORD*

Sir Peter Lely, *Diana Kirke, later Countess of Oxford* (ca. 1665).
Yale Center for British Art.

Notes

1. This text is based on the 1675 edition, printed for Thomas Dring, at the Harrow, at the Corner of Chancery-Lane in Fleet Street, London and corrected against a second edition of 1683, also printed by Dring.
2. In one famous instance, a naked Sir Charles Sedley is reported to have performed various sexual postures and movements on a balcony over a public street, topping off his performance by washing his penis in a glass of wine and drinking it off in a toast to the King.
3. Douglas Canfield, "Tupping Your Rival's Women: Cit-Cuckolding as Class Warfare in Restoration Comedy." In Katherine Quinsey, Ed. *Broken Boundaries: Women and Feminism in Restoration Drama* (113–28). Lexington, KY: University Press of Kentucky, 1996.
4. The audience seated on the main floor of the theatre. Though often mixed, this part of the audience was usually associated with the "cits," that is, the businessmen and respectable artisans of London.
5. A character, listed as "the angry Boy" from Ben Jonson's *The Alchemist* (first performed in 1610).
6. A categorical name for a poet, referencing the laurel or crown made of bay leaves that was associated with poetic achievement in classical Roman literature.
7. Bully.
8. A common cultural stereotype that features in much Restoration and eighteenth-century drama. The fop is a foolish man who pretends to wit and sophistication; he is generally over-concerned with his physical appearance, particularly his dress. The fop's sexuality tends to vacillate between simple disinterest in actual intercourse with women and an over-attraction to other men, though the identification of the fop with homosexuality becomes increasingly visible from the middle of the eighteenth century on.
9. The backstage area of the theatre where the actors dressed to go on stage. During the Restoration, it became fashionable for upper-class men to visit the tyring, or tiring, room in order to flirt—and sometimes engage in more serious sexual play—with the actresses while they dressed.
10. Edward Kynaston (see actors' biographical information).
11. A doctor, though probably not one with much reputation for integrity.
12. Procuress.
13. Working class women who sold fruit, especially oranges, were fixtures in the theatre, circulating among audience members to sell their wares. Often, they were prostitutes as well as fruit vendors.
14. A married man of the business and upper artisan classes who made his living, and often lived, within the older part of London identified with trade. This figure is commonly ridiculed on stage as a cuckold, a man whose wife has been seduced, usually by an upper-class man.
15. A old man who keeps a mistress.
16. Maids to ladies who assist their mistresses in dressing and, in the process, share gossip.
17. Street in London that was the center of government offices.
18. An inoculation against this disease was not developed until later in the eighteenth century. It was responsible for many deaths, but also left disfiguring scars upon its survivors.
19. A real person who died in 1651, aniseed Robin sold water flavored with that spice and was briefly married to a well known highwayman. Samuel Pepys refers to her as an hermaphrodite.
20. Venereal disease.
21. Practiced cheaters.
22. Horner holds two fingers up to his forehead to signify a cuckold, a husband whose wife has committed adultery and given him "horns."
23. Mercury was a common, but highly ineffective cure for venereal disease. It was also, of course, highly poisonous.
24. A pornographic novel.
25. Sedan chairs, carried by professional chairmen, were a common form of public transportation in London.
26. A person who may go anywhere.
27. A proven fact.
28. Some respectable women wore masks or vizards to the theatre (Alithea suggests it to Margery later in the play), but the vizards were primarily associated with prostitutes.

29 Actresses were associated with illicit sexual behavior, hence, with pregnancy out of wedlock. Given the need to make a living, many actresses performed while pregnant.
30 The boxes in the theatre were usually the domain of the upper classes. They were also highly visible places to show off one's fine clothes and beauty.
31 Attractive young men.
32 The title character of one of John Dryden's most successful comedies. He courts a mistress by miming playing on a lute while lip-syncing to his man's singing and playing. Of course, he is exposed as a fraud.
33 Many visitors to London commented on the finely painted signs that advertised businesses to potential customers.
34 Young men of fashionable appearance.
35 Given the dangers of fire from kitchens, very present to mind after the great fire that destroyed much of London in 1666, many Londoners dined or took food out from taverns and inns which became centers of sociability, especially among fashionable young men.
36 Gloominess, surliness.
37 Smithfield was a large, open public space in London, therefore a market for prostitutes to ply their trade.
38 Spoiled.
39 Case of venereal disease.
40 One who takes care of and feeds cattle to ready them for market.
41 Simple, without guile.
42 Cheapside and Covent Garden were both important markets in London. The former was associated with men of business, while the latter was established by 1670 as a market for fresh produce, many venders of which were women.
43 Mulberry Garden was a pleasure ground known for mulberry trees planted by James I. It was on the present site of Buckingham Palace. St. James's Park was opened to the public by Charles II and while fashionable, was also known as site of illicit sexuality. The New Exchange probably refers to the recently rebuilt Royal Exchange, an international center of trade, which burned down in the fire of 1666.
44 Peevish.
45 A mythical reptile whose very look was supposed to kill.
46 Good looking.
47 Financial agreements made before marriage.
48 Used contemptuously to refer to a male citizen of London as one who must work for a living, not a gentleman.
49 Victim of a scam.
50 Wit, intelligence.
51 Tag names for obsequious, sexually nonthreatening men.
52 Ombre, a card game.
53 Formal escort.
54 Pet lap dogs.
55 Recipes.
56 Stableman or groom at an inn.
57 Greedy, desiring.
58 Practice.
59 White wines, usually imported from Spain or the Canary Islands.
60 Cheated.
61 Share.
62 Fans were popular fashion accessories for women, who used them very expressively to flirt, express chagrin, etc.
63 A conventional name for a mistress.
64 Phrases used by jugglers while performing their tricks; the equivalent of "abracadabra."
65 The king's formal reception.

66 Songs, often sold by street hawkers, that were popular among lower, often illiterate classes. They frequently told traditional stories of romance and heroism.
67 A popular joke book.
68 Play titles.
69 The "santerers" (saunterers) and their "seamstresses" refer to the practice of fashionable young gentlemen hanging out in milliners' shops to flirt with the young women who worked there in a relatively public and unprotected space.
70 To give him a present.
71 The patience of a Cit who is being cuckolded by a gentleman.
72 Perfume.
73 Perfumed cosmetic powder for the face.
74 Pins were used to hold together items of clothing. As a lady's maid whose job was to help her employer dress, Lucy would be sticking in a lot of pins.
75 Simpleton.
76 Keeper of a jail.
77 All fashionable places of pleasure and leisure in London.
78 The Church of England prescribed the hours between which marriages could be legally performed.
79 This word could refer to a stupid or to a fickle person.
80 A sly and flirtatious young woman.
81 To seal the letter.
82 Cleverly.
83 Fits, suits—how goes the new design?
84 Those who form schemes by which to fool others.
85 Plump.
86 They condemn an actress or actor who is being kept for sexual services, but sin with an attractive young clergyman in secret.
87 Smutty.
88 Under the informal rules of primogeniture, the younger brother would not inherit a part of the estate, which would go, intact, to the oldest male child. Hence, younger brothers are perpetually short of money.
89 One who works for wages.
90 Mag pyes.
91 Hired escort.
92 Monkeys, like small dogs, were fashionable pets for ladies. They were also considered mischievous and were associated with hyper-sexuality.
93 Clumsy and awkward, like a country bumpkin.
94 A masculine young woman, the equivalent of the modern tomboy.
95 Reference to the Italian castrati, male singers who were castrated at birth in order to keep their high voices. Italian opera had recently been introduced in London.
96 A tall, slender vase of fairly large proportions, made of blue and white porcelain and imported from China.
97 A painted miniature.
98 Why distrust me?
99 A second represents the principal in a duel.
100 Lombard Street was associated with businessmen and men of finance. Aldermen were city officials, usually from the business and merchant classes, therefore not likely to be trusting of a Courtier, one of noble birth, whose wealth and prestige were inherited. Locket's was a fashionable eating establishment.
101 Conventional imagery of courtly love poetry (and letters).
102 Cask for liquids.
103 Half-baked.
104 An evening dress.
105 Fooled, tricked, cheated.

106 Healthy; that is, she does not have venereal disease.
107 Obscene, improper.
108 Masquerades were popular, albeit much criticized, forms of both public and private entertainment in which people disguised themselves in masks and costumes, often even disguising their voices in a "masquerade squeak." They were often seen as events that supported all kinds of illicit sexual encounters. See Terry Castle's *Masquerade and Civilization: The Carnivalesque in Eighteenth-Century Culture and Fiction* (Stanford, CA: Stanford University Press, 1986) for a study of this phenomenon throughout the long eighteenth century.
109 A young man or boy carrying a torch to light the way through dark London streets.
110 One who is cheated in a game of chance, in this case.
111 One who is cheated, as by a prostitute.
112 Textiles, fabric to be made into fashionable clothing.
113 Heavy wool cloth, sometimes blended with silk or linen.
114 Hungry.
115 A meal regularly available at a fixed price at an inn, public house or tavern.
116 A job or office with a government agency, usually gained through appointment, and sometimes an opportunity for embezzlement or graft.
117 Disease or pestilence.
118 Turmoil or disturbance.
119 Spoken by Charles Hart in the first, 1675 production.
120 Keeping as in keeping a mistress; the tyreing-room was the room in the theatre that the actresses used for dressing and getting ready for a performance. Gentlemen often visited there to flirt with and seduce them.
121 Reference to the hard-drinking, gluttonous, and whoring character in Shakespeare's *Henry IV*, parts 1 and 2.
122 "Buckram" is another reference to Shakespeare's Falstaff, who falsely claims battle with actually nonexistent "men in buckram."
123 Perfumed young men.
124 Slang term for an ugly woman.
125 Popular card games.
126 Bully.
127 Brothel.
128 Condition involving slow, painful urination.

3. *The Man of Mode*

***THE MAN OF MODE, OR, SIR FOPLING FLUTTER*. A COMEDY. ACTED AT THE DUKE'S THEATRE.[1] GEORGE ETHEREGE ESQ. FIRST PERFORMED 11 MARCH 1696 AND FIRST PUBLISHED 1676**

3.1 *THE MAN OF MODE, OR, SIR FOPLING FLUTTER. A COMEDY.*

Acted at the *Duke's Theatre.*[2] *George Etherege* Esq.

First Performed 11 March 1676 and First Published 1676

THE FIRST PERFORMANCE OF *The Man of Mode* in 1676 was before an audience that included Charles II and members of his Court. Various contemporary identifications were immediately made of its rakish male characters, Dorimant in particular, and the play was strongly associated with the group of male courtiers whose reputations surpassed even the King's for indulgence in libertine wit, sexuality, and all-around rowdy behavior: John Wilmot, Earl of Rochester, the Duke of Buckingham, and Sir Charles Sedley. Rochester, especially, was often identified with Dorimant, an identification that cleaned up the public image of the courtier most outrageous for his adventures in bi-sexuality, drunkenness, and public violence. The identification of Rochester with Dorimant also helped carry the "insider" joke of Loveit being played by Elizabeth Barry, an actress well known to be the Earl's mistress. The play enjoyed considerable popularity with the Court and was performed at Whitehall palace in 1685. In 1722, the critic and would-be playwright John Dennis would refer to it as "well receiv'd, and believ'd by the people of *England* to be the most agreeable Comedy for about Half a Century,"[3] but his praise for the play was defensive, a response to increasing attacks on its morality, specifically, the critique by Joseph Addison in a *Spectator* of 1711. The play was considered too immoral for public performance by the second half of the eighteenth century.

Etherege was himself known to be a friend and fellow libertine to the most notorious male wits of the court. Begun with birth into a respectable family, Etherege's life and career were shaped by strong royalist loyalties. His father had been part of the court of Henrietta Maria, queen of the ill-fated Charles I, and he followed his queen into exile in France when she fled England in 1644. Etherege was apprenticed as a law clerk in the 1650s, but after the return of Charles II to the English throne in 1660, he entered libertine court circles through his exchange of bawdy verses with Lord Buckhurst, to whom he dedicated his first play, *The Comical Revenge*, in 1664. His varying fortunes thereafter depended on the patronage of the Court (and his profligate spending habits).

Like many plays of the Restoration, *Man of Mode* featured the still excitingly innovative casting of women in spectacular female roles. Loveit and Bellinda are the desiring—and often at risk of ridicule and disgrace—partners in the sexual couplings of the libertine courtier, Dorimant. Harriet's "wild" wittiness and her imagined—though not performed on stage—role as his future wife grounds libertine performance in the stability of the English landed aristocracy. The female characters reflect something of the dangerous sexual charisma of women in the court of Charles II, in which the King's and courtiers' mistresses—including actresses—played a public and sometimes political role.

Dorimant and Sir Fopling Flutter perform different versions of an equally spectacular masculinity that echoes the public image of Charles' courtiers, in particular the notorious Earl of Rochester. Jeremy Webster has cannily labeled Rochester and his cronies, Buckingham and Sir Charles Sedley, performance artists of the Restoration because of their often very public displays of a highly stylized, sexualized, homosociality.[4] Dorimant's self-styling in the play's first scene is performed before the mixed "audience" of Orange Nan and the Shoemaker, reflecting the "street theatre" performed by Rochester and his cronies during the early years of the Restoration when the glamour of the newly returned King Charles licensed public displays of convivial, drunken licentiousness. Interestingly, however, Sir Fopling's comic spectacle of fashion and bad "wit" is often the masculine performance that is most remembered by the audience; Dennis' defense calls the play "Sir Fopling Flutter," and this role became the gold standard for the theatrical fop, the effeminate, self-absorbed comic type who would later grow into Lord Foppington in *The Relapse*. The play both celebrates and critiques the spectacular masculinity that, along with the spectacle of the actress, was on offer within the space of the theatre, both on the stage and in the audience.[5]

The Man of Mode was not performed during the early twentieth century's revival of Restoration comedies such as *The Country Wife*. It was first performed, after a hiatus since the eighteenth century, in 1971 and was, in its late twentieth-century versions, probably at least partial inspiration for the 2004 film, *The Libertine*, which drew on Rochester's verse and autobiography—both verifiable and apocryphal—to focus on the dark side of the Earl's spectacular masculinity, notably his alcoholism and venereal disease. Johnny Depp's performance nonetheless incorporates the charm and sexual charisma of Etherege's Dorimant as well as returning to Rochester's identity as English aristocrat, courtier, and loyalist politician.

TO HER ROYAL HIGHNESS THE DUCHESS.[6]

Madam,

Poets, however they may be modest otherwise, have always too good an opinion of what they write. The World when it sees this play dedicated to *Your Royal Highness*, will conclude, I have more than my share of that vanity. But, I hope, the honour I have of belonging to you, will excuse my presumption. 'tis the first thing I have produc'd in your service, and my duty obliges me to what my choice durst not else have aspir'd.

I am very sensible, *Madam*, how much it is beholding to your indulgence, for the success it had in the acting, and your protection will be no less fortunate to it in the printing; for all are so ambitious of making their court to you, that none can be severe to what you are pleas'd to favour.

This universal submission and respect is due to the greatness of your rank and birth; but you have other illustrious qualities, which are much more ingaging. Those wou'd but dazle, did not these really charm the eyes and understandings of all who have the happiness to approach you.

Authors on these occasions are never wanting to publish a particular of their patron's virtues and perfections; but *Your Royal Highness*'s are so eminently known, that did I follow their examples, I shou'd but paint those wonders here, of which every one already has the idea in his mind. Besides, I do not think it proper to aim at that in prose, which is so glorious a subject for verse; in which hereafter if I show more zeal than skill, it will not grieve me much, since I less passionately desire to be esteem'd a poet, than to be thought,

Madam,
Your Royal Highness's
Most humble, most obedient,
and most faithful Servant, *George Etherege.*

Prologue.
By Sir Car Scroope Baronet.[7]

Like dancers on the ropes[8] poor poets fare,
Most perish young, the rest in danger are;
This (one wou'd think) shou'd make our authors wary,
But gamester-like the giddy fools miscarry.
A lucky hand or two so tempts 'em on,
They cannot leave off play till they're undone.
With modest fears a muse does first begin,
Like a young wench newly entic'd to sin:
But tickl'd once with praise by her good will,
The wanton fool wou'd never more lie still.
'tis an old Mrs.[9] you'll meet here to night,
Whose charms you once have lookt on with delight.
But now of late such dirty drabs have known yee,
A muse o'th' better sort's asham'd to own yee.
Nature well drawn and wit must now give place
To gawdy nonsense and to dull grimace;[10]
Nor is it strange that you shou'd like so much
That kind of wit, for most of yours is such.
But I'm afraid that while to *France* we go,
To bring you home fine dresses, dance, and show;
The Stage like you will but more foppish grow.
Of foreign wares why shou'd we fetch the scum,
When we can be so richly serv'd at home?
For Heav'n be thankt 'tis not so wise an age,
But your own follies may supply the Stage.
Tho' often plow'd, there's no great fear the soil
Should barren grow by the too frequent toil;
While at your doors are to be daily found,
Such loads of dung-hill to manure the ground.

'Tis by your follies that we players thrive,
As the physicians by diseases live.
And as each year some new distemper reigns,
Whose friendly poison helps to increase their gains:
So among you, there starts up every day,
Some new unheard of fool for us to play.
Then for your own sakes be not too severe,
Nor what you all admire at home, damn here.
Since each is fond of his own ugly face,
Why shou'd you, when we hold it, break the glass?

Dramatis Personae.[11]

Gentlemen

Mr *Dorimant*
Mr *Medley*
Old *Bellair*
Young *Bellair*
Sir *Fopling Flutter*

Gentlewomen

Lady *Townley*
Emilia
Mrs. *Loveit*
Bellinda
Lady *Woodvil*, and *Harriet* her Daughter
Pert, and *Busy*, Waiting Women
A Shoomaker
An Orange-woman[12]
Three Slovenly Bullies
Two Chair-men[13]
Mr *Smirk, a Parson*
Handy, a Valet de Chambre
Pages, Footmen, &c

Act I.

[*A dressing room, a table covered with a toilet,*[14] *cloaths laid ready. Enter* Dorimant *in his gown and slippers, with a note in his hand made up, repeating verses.*]

DORIMANT. *Now for some ages had the pride of Spain,*
Made the sun shine on half the World in vain.[15]

[*Then looking on the note.*

For Mrs. Loveit.

What a dull insipid thing is a billet doux written in cold blood, after the heat of the business is over? It is a tax upon good nature which I have here been labouring to pay, and have done it, but with as much regret, as ever fanatick paid the Royal Aid, or Church Duties;[16] 'twill have the same fate I know that all my notes to her have had of late, 'twill not be thought kind enough. Faith women are i'the right when they jealously examine our letters, for in them we always first discover our decay of passion.—Hay! Who waits!

[*Enter* Handy.

HANDY. Sir.—

DORIMANT. Call a footman.

HANDY. None of 'em are come yet.

DORIMANT. Dogs! Will they ever lie snoring a bed till noon.

HANDY. 'Tis all one, Sir: if they're up, you indulge 'em so, they're ever poaching after whores all the morning.

DORIMANT. Take notice henceforward who's wanting in his duty, the next clap he gets, he shall rot for an example. What vermin are those chattering without?

HANDY. Foggy *Nan* the Orange Woman, and swearing *Tom* the Shoomaker.

DORIMANT. Go; call in that over-grown jade with the flasket of guts before her, fruit is refreshing in a morning. [*Exit* Handy.
It is not that I love you less
Than when before your feet I lay.

[*Enter* Orange Woman *and* Handy.

How now double tripe, what news do you bring?

ORANGE WOMAN. News! Here's the best fruit has come to Town t'year, Gad I was up before four a clock this morning, and bought all the choice i'the market.

DORIMANT. The nasty refuse of your shop.

ORANGE WOMAN. You need not make mouths at it, I assure you 'tis all cull'd ware.

DORIMANT. The citizens buy better on a holiday in their walk to *Totnam.*[17]

ORANGE WOMAN. Good or bad, 'tis all one, I never knew you commend any thing, Lord wou'd the ladies had heard you talk of 'em as I have done:

here bid your man give me an angel.[18] [*Sets down the fruit.*

DORIMANT. Give the bawd her fruit again.

ORANGE WOMAN. Well, on my conscience, there never was the like of you. God's my life, I had almost forgot to tell you, there is a young gentlewoman lately come to Town with her mother, that is so taken with you.

DORIMANT. Is she handsome?

ORANGE WOMAN. Nay, Gad there are few finer women I tell you but so, and a hugeous fortune they say. Here, eat this peach, it comes from the stone, 'tis better than any *Newington*[19] y'have tasted.

DORIMANT. This fine woman I'll lay my life [*Taking the peach*] is some awkward ill fashion'd Country Toad, who not having above four dozen of black hairs on her head, had adorn'd her baldness with a large white fruz,[20] that she may look sparkishly in the fore front of the King's box, at an old play.

ORANGE WOMAN. Gad, you'd change your note quickly if you did but see her.

DORIMANT. How came she to know me?

ORANGE WOMAN. She saw you yesterday at the *Change*,[21] she told me, you came and fool'd with the woman at the next shop.

DORIMANT. I remember there was a mask[22] observ'd me indeed. Fool'd did she say?

ORANGE WOMAN. Ay, I vow she told me twenty things you said too, and acted with head and with her body so like you—

[*Enter* Medley.

MEDLEY. *Dorimant* my Life, my Joy, my darling Sin; how dost thou.

ORANGE WOMAN. Lord what a filthy trick these men have got of kissing one another! [*She spits.*

MEDLEY. Why do you suffer this cart-load of scandal to come near you, and make your neighbours think you so improvident to need a bawd?

ORANGE WOMAN. Good now, we shall have it, you did but want him to help you; come pay me for my fruit.

MEDLEY. Make us thankful for it Huswife, bawds are as much out of fashion as Gentlemen Ushers;[23] None but old formal ladies use the one, and none but foppish old stagers[24] employ the other: Go, you are an insignificant brandy bottle.

DORIMANT. Nay, there you wrong her, three quarts of canary[25] is her business.

ORANGE WOMAN. What you please Gentlemen.

DORIMANT. To him, give him as good as he brings.

ORANGE WOMAN. Hang him, there is not such another heathen in the Town again, except it be the Shoomaker without.

MEDLEY. I shall see you hold up your hand at the bar next sessions for murder, Huswife; that Shoomaker can take his oath you are in fee with the doctors to sell green fruit to the gentry, that the crudities may breed diseases.

ORANGE WOMAN. Pray give me my money.

DORIMANT. Not a penny, when you bring the gentlewoman hither you spoke of, you shall be paid.

ORANGE WOMAN. The gentlewoman! The gentlewoman may be as honest as your sisters for ought as I know. Pray pay me, Mr. *Dorimant*, and do not abuse me so, I have an honester way of living, you know it.

MEDLEY. Was there ever such a resty[26] bawd?

DORIMANT. Some jade's tricks she has, but she makes amends when she's in good humour: come, tell me the lady's name, and *Handy* shall pay you.

ORANGE WOMAN. I must not, she forbid me.

DORIMANT. That's a sure sign she wou'd have you.

MEDLEY. Where does she live?

ORANGE WOMAN. They lodge at my house.

MEDLEY. Nay, then she's in a hopeful way.

ORANGE WOMAN. Good Mr. *Medley*, say your pleasure of me, but take heed how you affront my house, God's my life, in a hopeful way!

DORIMANT. Prithee, peace, what kind of woman's the mother?

ORANGE WOMAN. A goodly grave gentlewoman, Lord how she talks against the wild young men o' the Town; as for your part she thinks you an arrant devil, shou'd she see you, on my conscience she wou'd look if you had not a cloven foot.[27]

DORIMANT. Does she know me?

ORANGE WOMAN. Only by hearsay, a thousand horrid stories have been told her of you, and she believes 'em all.

MEDLEY. By the character, this should be the famous Lady *Woodvill*, and her daughter *Harriet*.

ORANGE WOMAN. The Devil's in him for guessing I think.

DORIMANT. Do you know 'em?

MEDLEY. Both very well, the mother's a great admirer of the forms and civilities of the last age.

DORIMANT. An antiquated beauty may be allow'd to be out of humour at the freedoms of the present. This is a good account of the mother, pray what is the daughter?

MEDLEY. Why, first she's an heiress vastly rich.

DORIMANT. And handsome?

MEDLEY. What an alteration a twelve-month may have bred in her I know not, but a year ago she was the beautifullest creature I ever saw; a fine, easie, clean shape, light brown hair in abundance; her features regular, her complexion clear and lively, large wanton eyes, but above all, a mouth that has made me kiss it a thousand times in imagination, teeth white and even, and pretty pouting lips, with a little moisture ever hanging on them, that look like the province rose fresh on the bush, 'ere the morning sun has quite drawn up the dew.

DORIMANT. Rapture, meer rapture!

ORANGE WOMAN. Nay, Gad he tells you true, she's a delicate creature.

DORIMANT. Has she wit?

MEDLEY. More than is usual in her sex, and as much malice. Then she's as wild as you wou'd wish her, and has a demureness in her looks that makes it so surprising.

DORIMANT. Flesh and blood cannot hear this and not long to know her.

MEDLEY. I wonder what makes her mother bring her up to Town, an old doating keeper[28] cannot be more jealous of his mistress.

ORANGE WOMAN. She made me laugh yesterday, there was a Judge came to visit 'em, and the old man she told me did so stare upon her, and when he saluted her smack'd so heartily; who wou'd think it of 'em?

MEDLEY. God a mercy judge.

DORIMANT. Do 'em right, the gentlemen of the long robe[29] have not been wanting by their good examples to countenance the crying sin o' the nation.

MEDLEY. Come, on with your trappings, 'tis later than you imagine.

DORIMANT. Call in the Shoomaker, *Handy*.

ORANGE WOMAN. Good Mr. *Dorimant* pay me, Gad I had rather give you my fruit than stay to be abus'd by that foul-mouth'd rogue; what you gentlemen say it matters not much, but such a dirty fellow does one more disgrace.

DORIMANT. Give her ten shillings, and be sure you tell the young gentlewoman I must be acquainted with her.

ORANGE WOMAN. Now do you long to be tempting this pretty creature. Well, Heavens mend you.

MEDLEY. Farewell Bogg.—[*Exit* Orange Woman *and* Handy] *Dorimant*, when did you see your *pis aller*[30] as you call her, Mrs. *Loveit*?

DORIMANT. Not these two days.

MEDLEY. And how stand affairs between you?

DORIMANT. There has been great patching[31] of late, much ado we make a shift to hang together.

MEDLEY. I wonder how her mighty spirit bears it.

DORIMANT. I'll enough on all conscience, I never knew so violent a creature.

MEDLEY. She's the most passionate in her love, and the most extravagant in her jealousie of any woman I ever heard of. What note is that?

DORIMANT. An excuse I am going to send her for the neglect I am guilty of.

MEDLEY. Prithee read it.

DORIMANT. No, but if you will take the pains, you may.

MEDLEY. [*Reads*] *I never was a lover of business, but now I have a just reason to hate it, since it has kept me these two days from seeing you. I intend to wait upon you in the afternoon, and in the pleasure of your conversation, forget all I have suffer'd during this tedious absence.*

This business of yours Dorimant has been with a vizard[32] at the playhouse, I have had an eye on you. If some malicious body shou'd betray you, this kind note wou'd hardly make your peace with her.

DORIMANT. I desire no better.

MEDLEY. Why, wou'd her knowledge of it oblige you?

DORIMANT. Most infinitely; next to the coming to a good understanding with a new mistress, I love a quarrel with an old one, but the Devil's in't, there has been such a calm in my affairs of late, I have not had the pleasure of making a woman so much as break her fan, to be sullen, or forswear her self these three days.

MEDLEY. A very great misfortune. Let me see, I love mischief well enough, to forward this business my self. I'll about it presently, and though I know the truth of what y'ave done, will set her a raving, I'll heighten it a little with invention, leave her in a fit o' the mother,[33] and be here again before y'are ready.

DORIMANT. Pray stay, you may spare your self the labour, the business is undertaken already by one who will manage it with as much address, and I think with a little more malice than you can.

MEDLEY. Who i'the Devil's name can this be!

DORIMANT. Why the vizard, that very vizard you saw me with.

MEDLEY. Does she love mischief so well, as to betray her self to spight another?

DORIMANT. Not so neither, Medley, I will make you comprehend the mystery; this masque for a farther confirmation of what I have been these two days swearing to her, made me yesterday at the playhouse make her a promise before her face, utterly to break off with Loveit; and because she tenders[34] my reputation, and wou'd not have me do a barbarous thing, has contriv'd a way to give me a handsome occasion.

MEDLEY. Very good.

DORIMANT. She intends about an hour before me, this afternoon, to make Loveit a visit, and (having the priviledge by reason of a profess'd friendship between 'em) to talk of her concerns.

MEDLEY. Is she a friend?

DORIMANT. Oh, an intimate friend!

MEDLEY. Better and better, pray proceed.

DORIMANT. She means insensibly to insinuate a discourse of me, and artificially raise her jealousie to such a height, that transported with the first motions of her passion, she shall fly upon me with all the fury imaginable, as soon as ever I enter, the quarrel being thus happily begun, I am to play my part, confess and justifie all my roguery, swear her impertinence and ill humour makes her intolerable, tax her with the next fop that comes into my head, and in a huff march away, slight her and leave her to be taken by whosoever thinks it worth his time to lie down before her.

MEDLEY. This vizard is a spark,[35] and has a genius that makes her worthy of your self, Dorimant.

[*Enter* Handy, Shoomaker, *and* Footman.

DORIMANT. You Rogue there, who sneak like a dog that has flung down a dish, if you do not mend your waiting, I'll uncase you,[36] and turn you loose to the Wheel of Fortune. *Handy*, seal this and let him run with it presently. [*Exit* Handy *and* Footman.

MEDLEY. Since y'are resolv'd on a quarrel, why do you send her this kind note?

DORIMANT. To keep her at home in order to the business. How now you drunken Sot? [*To the* Shoomaker.

SHOOMAKER. 'Zbud, you have no reason to talk, I have not had a bottle of sack of yours in my belly this fortnight.

MEDLEY. The *Orange Woman* says, your neighbours take notice what a heathen you are, and design to inform the bishop, and have you burn'd for an atheist.

SHOOMAKER. Damn her, Dunghill, if her husband does not remove her, she stinks so, the parish intend to indite him for a nusance.

MEDLEY. I advise you like a friend, reform your life, you have brought the envy of the World upon you, by living above your self. Whoring and swearing are vices too gentile for a shoomaker.

SHOOMAKER. 'Zbud, I think you men of quality will grow as unreasonable as the women; you wou'd ingross the sins o' the nation; poor folks can no sooner be wicked, but th' are rail'd at by their betters.

DORIMANT. Sirrah, I'll have you stand i'the pillory[37] for this libel.

SHOOMAKER. Some of you deserve it, I'm sure, there are so many of 'em, that our journeymen now adays instead of harmless ballads,[38] sing nothing but your damn'd lampoons.

DORIMANT. Our lampoons, you Rogue?

SHOOMAKER. Nay, Good Master, why shou'd not you write your own commentaries as well as *Caesar*?[39]

MEDLEY. The raskal's read, I perceive.

SHOOMAKER. You know the old proverb, ale and history.[40]

DORIMANT. Draw on my shooes, sirrah.

SHOOMAKER. Here's a shooe.

DORIMANT. Sits with more wrinkles than there are in an angry bully's forehead.

SHOOMAKER. 'Zbud, as smooth as your mistress's skin does upon her, so, strike your foot in home. 'Zbud[41] if e're a monsieur of 'em all make more fashionable ware, I'll be content to have my ears whip'd off with my own paring knife.

MEDLEY. And serv'd up in a ragoust,[42] instead of coxcombs to a company of French shoomakers for a collation.

SHOOMAKER. Hold, hold, damn 'em catterpillars, let 'em feed upon cabbage; come Master, your health this morning next my heart now.

DORIMANT. Go, get you home, and govern your family better; do not let your wife follow you to the alehouse, beat your whore, and lead you home in triumph.

SHOOMAKER. Zbud, there's never a man i'the Town lives more like a gentleman, with his wife, than I do. I never mind her motions, she never inquires into mine, we speak to one another civilly, hate one another heartily, and because 'tis vulgar to lie and soak together, we have each of us our several settle-bed.

DORIMANT. Give him half a crown.

MEDLEY. Not without he will promise to be bloody drunk.

SHOOMAKER. Tope's[43] the word i'the eye of the World for my master's honour, *Robin*.[44]

DORIMANT. Do not debauch my servants, Sirrah.

SHOOMAKER. I only tip him the wink, he knows an alehouse from a hovel. [*Exit* Shoomaker.

DORIMANT. My cloaths quickly.

MEDLEY. Where shall we dine to day?

[*Enter* Young Bellair.

DORIMANT. Where you will; here comes a good third man.

YOUNG BELLAIR. Your servant, Gentlemen.

MEDLEY. Gentle Sir; how will you answer this visit to your honourable mistress? 'Tis not her interest you shou'd keep company with men of sense, who will be talking reason.

YOUNG BELLAIR. I do not fear her pardon, do you but grant me yours, for my neglect of late.

MEDLEY. Though y'ave made us miserable by the want of your good company; to shew you I am free from all resentment, may the beautiful cause of our misfortune, give you all the joys happy lovers have shar'd ever since the World began.

YOUNG BELLAIR. You wish me in Heaven, but you believe me on my journey to Hell.

MEDLEY. You have a good strong faith, and that may contribute much towards your salvation. I confess I am but of an untoward constitution, apt to have doubts and scruples, and in love they are no less distracting than in religion; were I so near marriage, I shou'd cry out by fits as I ride in my coach, cuckold, cuckold, with no less fury than the mad fanatick does glory in *Bethlem*.[45]

YOUNG BELLAIR. Because religion makes some run mad, must I live an atheist?

MEDLEY. Is it not great indiscretion for a man of credit, who may have money enough on his word, to go and deal with Jews; who for little sums make men enter into bonds, and give judgments?[46] Preach no more on this text, I am determin'd, and there is no hope of my conversion.

DORIMANT. Leave your unnecessary fidling; a wasp that's buzzing about a man's nose at dinner, is not more troublesome than thou art. [*To* Handy *who is fidling about him.*

HANDY. You love to have your cloaths hang just, Sir.

DORIMANT. I love to be well dress'd, Sir: and think it no scandal to my understanding.

HANDY. Will you use the essence or orange flower water?

DORIMANT. I will smell as I do to day, no offence to the ladies' noses.

HANDY. Your pleasure, Sir.

DORIMANT. That a man's excellency should lie in neatly tying of a ribbond, or a crevat! How careful's Nature in furnishing the World with necessary coxcombs!

YOUNG BELLAIR. That's a mighty pretty suit of yours, *Dorimant.*

DORIMANT. I am glad 't has your approbation.

YOUNG BELLAIR. No man in Town has a better fancy in his cloaths than you have.

DORIMANT. You will make me have an opinion of my genius.

MEDLEY. There is a great critick, I hear, in these matters, lately arriv'd piping hot from *Paris*.

YOUNG BELLAIR. Sir *Fopling Flutter* you mean.

MEDLEY. The same.

YOUNG BELLAIR. He thinks himself the pattern of modern gallantry.

DORIMANT. He is indeed the pattern of modern foppery.

MEDLEY. He was yesterday at the play, with a pair of gloves up to his elbows, and a periwig more exactly curl'd then a lady's head newly dress'd for a ball.

YOUNG BELLAIR. What a pretty lisp he has!

DORIMANT. Ho; that he affects in imitation of the people of quality of *France*.

MEDLEY. His head stands, for the most part, on one side, and his looks are more languishing than a lady's when she lolls at stretch in her coach, or leans her head carelesly against the side of a box i'the playhouse.

DORIMANT. He is a person indeed of great acquir'd follies.

MEDLEY. He is like many others, beholding to his education for making him so eminent a coxcomb; many a fool had been lost to the World, had their indulgent parents wisely bestow'd neither learning nor good breeding on 'em.

YOUNG BELLAIR. He has been, as the sparkish word is, brisk upon the ladies already, he was yesterday at my Aunt *Townley*'s, and gave Mrs. *Loveit* a catalogue of his good qualities, under the character of a compleat gentleman, who according to Sir *Fopling*, ought to dress well, dance well, fence well, have a genius for love letters, an agreeable voice for a chamber, be very amorous, something discreet, but not over constant.

MEDLEY. Pretty ingredients to make an accomplish'd person.

DORIMANT. I am glad he pitch'd upon *Loveit*.

YOUNG BELLAIR. How so?

DORIMANT. I wanted a fop to lay to her charge, and this is as pat as may be.

YOUNG BELLAIR. I am confident she loves no man but you.

DORIMANT. The good fortune were enough to make me vain, but that I am in my nature modest.

YOUNG BELLAIR. Hark you *Dorimant*, with your leave, Mr. *Medley*, 'tis only a secret concerning a fair lady.

MEDLEY. Your good breeding, Sir, gives you too much trouble, you might have whisper'd without all this ceremony.

YOUNG BELLAIR. How stand your affairs with *Bellinda* of late? [*To Dorimant*.

DORIMANT. She's a little jilting baggage.

YOUNG BELLAIR. Nay, I believe her false enough, but she's ne'er the worse for your purpose; she was with you yesterday in a disguise at the play.

DORIMANT. There we fell out, and resolv'd never to speak to one another more.

YOUNG BELLAIR. The occasion?

DORIMANT. Want of courage to meet me at the place appointed. These young women apprehend loving, as much as the young men do fighting at first; but once enter'd, like them too, they all turn bullies straight.

[*Enter* Handy *to* Young Bellair.

HANDY. Sir, your man without desires to speak with you.

YOUNG BELLAIR. Gentlemen, I'll return immediately. [*Exit* Young Bellair.

MEDLEY. A very pretty fellow this.

DORIMANT. He's handsome, well bred, and by much the most tolerable of all the young men that do not abound in wit.

MEDLEY. Ever well dress'd, always complaisant, and seldom impertinent; you and he are grown very intimate I see.

DORIMANT. It is our mutual interest to be so; it makes the women think the better of his understanding, and judge more favourably of my reputation; it makes him pass upon some for a man of very good sense, and I upon others for a very civil person.

MEDLEY. What was that whisper?

DORIMANT. A thing which he would fain have known, but I did not think it fit to tell him; it might have frighted him from his honourable intentions of marrying.

MEDLEY. *Emilia*, give her her due, has the best reputation of any young woman about the Town; who has beauty enough to provoke detraction; her carriage is unaffected, her discourse modest, not at all censorious, nor pretending like the counterfeits of the age.

DORIMANT. She's a discreet maid, and I believe nothing can corrupt her but a husband.

MEDLEY. A husband?

DORIMANT. Yes, a husband; I have known many women make a difficulty of losing a maidenhead, who have afterwards made none of making a cuckold.

MEDLEY. This prudent consideration I am apt to think has made you confirm poor *Bellair* in the desperate resolution he has taken.

DORIMANT. Indeed the little hope I found there was of her in the state she was in, has made me by my advice, contribute something towards the changing of her condition.

[*Enter* Young Bellair.

Dear *Bellair*, by Heavens, I thought we had lost thee; men in love are never to be reckon'd on when we wou'd form a company.

YOUNG BELLAIR. *Dorimant*, I am undone, my man has brought the most surprising news i'the world.

DORIMANT. Some strange misfortune is befaln your love.

YOUNG BELLAIR. My father came to Town last night, and lodges i'the very house where *Emilia* lyes.

MEDLEY. Does he know it is with her you are in love?

YOUNG BELLAIR. He knows I love, but knows not whom, without some officious sot has betray'd me.

DORIMANT. Your Aunt *Townley* is your confidant, and favours the business.

YOUNG BELLAIR. I do not apprehend any ill office from her. I have receiv'd a letter, in which I am commanded by my father to meet him at my aunt's this afternoon; he tells me farther, he has made a match for me, and bids me resolve to be obedient to his will, or expect to be disinherited.

MEDLEY. Now's your time, *Bellair*, never had lover such an opportunity of giving a generous proof of his passion.

YOUNG BELLAIR. As how, I pray?

MEDLEY. Why, hang an estate, marry *Emilia* out of hand, and provoke your father to do what he threatens; 'tis but despising a coach, humbling your self to a pair of goloshoes,[47] being out of countenance[48] when you meet your friends, pointed at and pitied wherever you go, by all the amorous fops that know you, and your fame will be immortal.

YOUNG BELLAIR. I cou'd find in my heart to resolve not to marry at all.

DORIMANT. Fie, fie, that would spoil a good jest, and disappoint the well-natur'd Town of an occasion of laughing at you.

YOUNG BELLAIR. The storm I have so long expected, hangs o're my head, and begins to pour down upon me; I am on the rack,[49] and can have no rest till I'm satisfied in what I fear; where do you dine?

DORIMANT. At *Long's*, or *Lockets'*.[50]

MEDLEY. At *Long's* let it be.

YOUNG BELLAIR. I'll run and see *Emilia*, and inform my self how matters stand; if my misfortunes are not so great as to make me unfit for company, I'll be with you. [*Exit* Young Bellair.

[*Enter a* Footman *with a letter.*

FOOTMAN. Here's a letter, Sir. [*To* Dorimant.

DORIMANT. The superscription's right; for Mr. *Dorimant.*

MEDLEY. Let's see the very scrawl and spelling of a true-bred whore.

DORIMANT. I know the hand, the style is admirable, I assure you.

MEDLEY. Prithee read it.

DORIMANT. [*Reads*]

> *I told a you you dud not love me, if you dud, you wou'd have seen me again e're now; I have no money and am very mallicolly; pray send me a guynie to see the operies.*
>
> *Your Servant to Command,*
>
> *Molly.*

MEDLEY. Pray let the whore have a favourable answer, that she may spark it in a box, and do honour to her profession.

DORIMANT. She shall; and perk up i'the face of quality. Is the coach at the door?

HANDY. You did not bid me send for it.

DORIMANT. Eternal Blockhead! [Handy *offers to go out*] Hay, Sot –

HANDY. Did you call me, Sir?

DORIMANT. I hope you have no just exceptions to the name, Sir?

HANDY. I have sense, Sir.

DORIMANT. Not so much as a fly in winter:—How did you come, *Medley*?

MEDLEY. In a chair.

FOOTMAN. You may have a hackney coach[51] if you please, Sir.

DORIMANT. I may ride the elephant if I please, Sir; call another chair, and let my coach follow to *Long*'s.

Be calm, ye great Parents, &c. [*Exit singing.*

Act II. Scene I.

[*Enter my* Lady Townley, *and* Emilia.]

TOWNLEY. I was afraid, *Emilia*, all had been discover'd.

EMILIA. I tremble with the apprehension still.

TOWNLEY. That my brother should take lodgings i'the very house where you lie.

EMILIA. 'Twas lucky, we had timely notice to warn the people to be secret, he seems to be a mighty good humour'd old man.

TOWNLEY. He ever had a notable smerking way with him.

EMILIA. He calls me rogue, tells me he can't abide me; and does so bepat me.

TOWNLEY. On my word you are much in his favour then.

EMILIA. He has been very inquisitive I am told about my family, my reputation, and my fortune.

TOWNLEY. I am confident he does not i'the least suspect you are the woman his son's in love with.

EMILIA. What shou'd make him then inform himself so particularly of me?

TOWNLEY. He was always of a very loving temper himself; it may be he has a doating fit upon him, who knows.

EMILIA. It cannot be.

[*Enter* Young Bellair.

TOWNLEY. Here comes my nephew. Where did you leave your father?

YOUNG BELLAIR. Writing a note within; *Emilia*, this early visit looks as if some kind jealousie wou'd not let you rest at home.

EMILIA. The knowledge I have of my rival, gives me a little cause to fear your constancy.

YOUNG BELLAIR. My constancy! I vow—

EMILIA. Do not vow—our love is frail as is our life, and full as little in our power, and are you sure you shall out-live this day?

YOUNG BELLAIR. I am not, but when we are in perfect health, 'twere an idle thing to fright our selves with the thoughts of sudden death.

TOWNLEY. Pray what has pass'd between you and your father i'the garden?

YOUNG BELLAIR. He's firm in his resolution, tells me I must marry Mrs. *Harriet*, or swears he'll marry himself, and disinherit me. When I saw I could not prevail with him to be more indulgent, I dissembled an obedience to his will, which has compos'd his passion, and will give us time, and I hope opportunity to deceive him.

[*Enter* Old Bellair, *with a note in his hand.*

TOWNLEY. Peace, here he comes.

OLD BELLAIR. *Harry*, take this, and let your man carry it for me to Mr. *Fourbe*'s[52] chamber, my lawyer i'the Temple.[53] [*To* Emilia] Neighbour, a Dod I am glad to see thee here, make much of her sister, she's one of the best of your acquaintance; I like her countenance and her behaviour well, she has a modesty that is not common i'this age, a Dod, she has.

TOWNLEY. I know her value, Brother, and esteem her accordingly.

OLD BELLAIR. Advise her to wear a little more mirth in her face, a Dod she's too serious.

TOWNLEY. The fault is very excusable in a young woman.

OLD BELLAIR. Nay, a Dod, I like her ne're the worse, a melancholy beauty has her charms, I love a pretty sadness in a face which varies now and then, like changeable colours, into a smile.

TOWNLEY. Methinks you speak very feelingly, Brother.

OLD BELLAIR. I am but five and fifty, Sister, you know, an age not altogether unsensible! [*To* Emilia] Chear up Sweet Heart; I have a secret to tell thee, may chance to make thee merry, we three will make collation together anon, i'the mean time mum, I can't abide you, go, I can't abide you.

[*Enter* Young Bellair.

Harry, Come you must along with me to my Lady *Woodvill*'s. I am going to slip the boy at a mistress.

YOUNG BELLAIR. At a wife, Sir, you wou'd say.

OLD BELLAIR. You need not look so glum, Sir, a wife is no curse when she brings the blessing of a good estate with her, but an idle Town flurt, with a painted face, a rotten reputation, and a crasie fortune, a Dod is the Devil and all, and such a one I hear you are in league with.

YOUNG BELLAIR. I cannot help detraction, Sir.

OLD BELLAIR. Out, a pize o' their breeches, there are keeping fools enough for such flaunting baggages, and they are e'n too good for 'em. Remember night, [*To* Emilia] go y' are a rogue, y'are a rogue; fare you well; come, come, come along, Sir. [*Exit* Old and Young Bellair.

TOWNLEY. On my word the old man comes on apace; I'll lay my life he's smitten.

EMILIA. This is nothing but the pleasantness of his humour.

TOWNLEY. I know him better than you, let it work, it may prove lucky.

[*Enter a* Page.

PAGE. Madam, Mr. *Medley* has sent to know whether a visit will not be troublesome this afternoon?

TOWNLEY. Send him word, his visits never are so.

EMILIA. He's a very pleasant man.

TOWNLEY. He's a very necessary man among us women; he's not scandalous i'the least, perpetually contriving to bring good company together, and always ready to stop up a gap at ombre,[54] then he knows all the little news i'the Town.

EMILIA. I love to hear him talk o' the intrigues, let 'em be never so dull in themselves, he'll make 'em pleasant i'the relation.

TOWNLEY. But he improves things so much, one can take no measure of the truth from him. Mr. *Dorimant* swears a flea or a maggot is not made more monstrous by a magnifying glass, than a story is by his telling it.

EMILIA. Hold, here he comes.

[*Enter* Medley.

TOWNLEY. Mr. *Medley*.

MEDLEY. Your servant, Madam.

TOWNLEY. You have made your self a stranger of late.

EMILIA. I believe you took a surfeit of ombre last time you were here.

MEDLEY. Indeed I had my belly full of that tarmagant[55] Lady Dealer; there never was so unsatiable a carder,[56] an old gleeker[57] never lov'd to sit to't like her; I have plaid with her now at least a dozen times, till she'as worn out all her fine complexion, and her tour[58] wou'd keep in curl no longer.

TOWNLEY. Blame her not poor woman, she loves nothing so well as a black ace.

MEDLEY. The pleasure I have seen her in when she has had hope in drawing for a matadore.[59]

EMILIA. 'Tis as pretty sport to her, as perswading masks off is to you to make discoveries.

TOWNLEY. Pray where's your friend, Mr. *Dorimant*?

MEDLEY. Soliciting his affairs, he's a man of great imployment, has more mistresses now depending, than the most eminent lawyer in *England* has causes.

EMILIA. Here has been Mrs. *Loveit*, so uneasie and out of humour these two days.

TOWNLEY. How strangely love and jealousie rage in that poor woman!

MEDLEY. She cou'd not have pick'd out a devil upon earth so proper to torment her, has made her break a dozen or two of fans already, tare half a score points[60] in pieces, and destroy hoods and knots[61] without number.

TOWNLEY. We heard of a pleasant serenade he gave her t'other night.

MEDLEY. A Danish serenade with kettle drums, and trumpets.

EMILIA. Oh barbarous!

MEDLEY. What, you are of the number of the ladies, whose ears are grown so delicate since our operas, you can be charm'd with nothing but flute doux, and French hoboys.[62]

EMILIA. Leave your raillery, and tell us, is there any new wit come forth, songs or novels?

MEDLEY. A very pretty piece of gallantry, by an eminent author, call'd *the diversions of Bruxells*, very necessary to be read by all old ladies who are desirous to improve themselves at Questions and Commands, Blindman's Buff, and the like fashionable recreations.

EMILIA. Oh ridiculous!

MEDLEY. Then there is the Art of Affectation, written by a late Beauty of Quality, teaching you how to draw up your breasts, stretch up your neck, to thrust out your breech, to play with your head, to toss up your nose, to bite your lips, to turn up your eyes, to speak in a silly soft tone of a voice, and use all the foolish French words, that will infallibly make your person and conversation charming, with a short apologie at the latter end, in the behalf of young ladies, who notoriously wash, and paint,[63] though they have naturally good complexions.

EMILIA. What a deal of stuff you tell us?

MEDLEY. Such as the Town affords, Madam. The *Russians* hearing the great respect we have for foreign dancing, have lately sent over some of their best balladins,[64] who are now practising a famous ballet which will be suddenly danc'd at the *Bear-Garden*.[65]

TOWNLEY. Pray forbear your idle stories, and give us an account of the state of love, as it now stands.

MEDLEY. Truly there has been some revolutions in those affairs, great chopping and changing among the old, and some new lovers, whom malice, indiscretion, and misfortune, have luckily brought into play.

TOWNLEY. What think you of walking into the next room, and sitting down before you engage in this business?

MEDLEY. I wait upon you, and I hope (though women are commonly unreasonable) by the plenty of scandal I shall discover, to give you very good content, Ladies. [*Exeunt.*

Scene II.

[*Enter* Mrs. Loveit *and* Pert. Mrs. Loveit *putting up a letter, then pulling out her pocket glass, and looking in it.*]

LOVEIT. Pert.

PERT. Madam.

LOVEIT. I hate my self, I look so ill to day.

PERT. Hate the wicked cause on't, that base man

Mr. *Dorimant*, who makes you torment and vex your self continually.

LOVEIT. He is to blame indeed.

PERT. To blame to be two days without sending, writing, or coming near you, contrary to his oath and covenant; 'twas to much purpose to make him swear; I'll lay my life there's not an article but he has broken, talk'd to the vizards i'the pit, waited upon the ladies from the boxes to their coaches; gone behind the scenes, and fawn'd upon those little insignificant creatures, the players;[66] 'twas impossible for a man of his inconstant temper to forbear I'm sure.

LOVEIT. I know he is a devil, but he has something of the angel yet undefac'd in him, which makes him so charming and agreeable, that I must love him be he never so wicked.

PERT. I little thought, Madam, to see your spirit tam'd to this degree, who banish'd poor Mr. *Lackwit* but for taking up another lady's fan in your presence.

LOVEIT. My knowing of such odious fools, contributes to the making of me love *Dorimant* the better.

PERT. Your knowing of Mr. *Dorimant*, in my mind, shou'd rather make you hate all mankind.

LOVEIT. So it does, besides himself.

PERT. Pray, what excuse does he make in his letter?

LOVEIT. He has had business.

PERT. Business in general terms wou'd not have been a current excuse for another; a modish man is always very busie when he is in pursuit of a new mistress.

LOVEIT. Some fop has brib'd you to rail at him; he had business, I will believe it, and will forgive him.

PERT. You may forgive him any thing, but I shall never forgive him his turning me into ridicule, as I hear he does.

LOVEIT. I perceive you are of the number of those fools his wit had made his enemies.

PERT. I am of the number of those he's pleas'd to railly, Madam, and if we may believe Mr. *Wagfan*, and Mr. *Caperwell*, he sometimes makes merry with your self too, among his laughing companions.

LOVEIT. Blockheads are as malicious to witty men, as ugly women are to the handsome; 'tis their interest, and they make it their business to defame 'em.

PERT. I wish Mr. *Dorimant* wou'd not make it his business to defame you.

LOVEIT. Shou'd he, I had rather be made infamous by him, than owe my reputation to the dull discretion of those fops you talk of. Bellinda! [*Running to her.*

[*Enter* Bellinda.

BELLINDA. My Dear.

LOVEIT. You have been unkind of late.

BELLINDA. Do not say unkind, say unhappy!

LOVEIT. I cou'd chide you, where have you been these two days?

BELLINDA. Pity me rather my Dear, where I have been so tired with two or three Country Gentlewomen, whose conversation has been more unsufferable than a Country fiddle.

LOVEIT. Are they relations?

BELLINDA. No, Welch acquaintance I made when I was last year at St. *Winefred*'s, they have asked me a thousand questions of the modes and intrigues of the Town, and I have told 'em almost as many things for news that hardly were so, when their gowns were in fashion.

LOVEIT. Provoking creatures, how cou'd you endure 'em?

BELLINDA. – [*Aside*] *Now to carry on my plot, nothing but love cou'd make me capable of so much falshood; 'tis time to begin, lest Dorimant shou'd come before her jealousie has stung her;* [*Laughs, and then speaks on*] – I was yesterday at a play with 'em, where I was fain to shew 'em the living, as the man at Westminster does the dead;[67] that is Mrs. such a one, admired for her beauty, this is Mr. such a one, cry'd up for a wit; that is sparkish Mr. such a one, who keeps reverend Mrs. such a one, and there sits fine Mrs. such a one, who was lately cast off by my Lord such a one.

LOVEIT. Did you see *Dorimant* there?

BELLINDA. I did, and imagine you were there with him, and have no mind to own it.

LOVEIT. What shou'd make you think so?

BELLINDA. A lady mask'd in a pretty dishabillié[68] whom *Dorimant* entertain'd with more respect, than the gallants do a common vizard.

LOVEIT. [*Aside*] Dorimant *at the play entertaining a mask, Oh Heaven's!*

BELLINDA. [*Aside*] *Good.*

LOVEIT. Did he stay all the while?

BELLINDA. 'till the play was done, and then led her out, which confirms me it was you.

LOVEIT. Traytor!

PERT. Now you may believe he had business, and you may forgive him too.

LOVEIT. Ingrateful, perjur'd man!

BELLINDA. You seem so much concern'd my Dear, I fear I have told you unawares what I had better have conceal'd for your quiet.

LOVEIT. What manner of shape had she?

BELLINDA. Tall and slender, her motions were very gentile, certainly she must be some person of condition.

LOVEIT. Shame and confusion be ever in her face when she shows it.

BELLINDA. I should blame your discretion for loving that wild man, my Dear, but they say he has a way so bewitching, that few can defend their hearts who know him.

LOVEIT. I will tear him from mine, or die i'the attempt.

BELLINDA. Be more moderate.

LOVEIT. Wou'd I had daggers, darts, or poyson'd arrows in my breast, so I cou'd but remove the thoughts of him from thence.

BELLINDA. Fie, fie, your transports are too violent, my Dear. This may be but an accidental gallantry, and 'tis likely ended at her coach.

PERT. Shou'd it proceed farther, let your comfort be, the conduct Mr. *Dorimant* affects, will quickly make you know your rival; ten to one let you see her ruin'd, her reputation expos'd to the Town, a happiness none will envy her but your self, Madam.

LOVEIT. Who e're she be, all the harm I wish her, is, may she love him as well as I do, and may he give her as much cause to hate him.

PERT. Never doubt the latter end of your curse, Madam!

LOVEIT. May all the passions that are rais'd by neglected love, jealousie, indignation, spight, and thirst of revenge, eternally rage in her soul, as they do now in mine. [*Walks up and down with a distracted air.*

[*Enter a* Page.

PAGE. Madam, Mr. *Dorimant* –

LOVEIT. I will not see him.

PAGE. I told him you were within, Madam.

LOVEIT. Say you ly'd, say I'm busie, shut the door; say any thing.

PAGE. He's here, Madam.

[*Enter* Dorimant.

DORIMANT. *They taste of death who do at Heaven arrive,*
But we this Paradise approach alive.[69]

What, dancing the Galloping Nag[70] without a fiddle? [*To* Loveit. *Offers to catch her by the hand, she flings away and walks on*] I fear this restlessness of the body, Madam, [*Pursuing her*] proceeds from an unquietness of the mind. What unlucky accident puts you out of humour; a point ill-wash'd, knots spoil'd i'the making up, hair shaded awry, or some other little mistake in setting you in order?

PERT. A trifle in my opinion, Sir, more inconsiderable than any you mention.

DORIMANT. Oh Mrs. Pert, I never knew you sullen enough to be silent, come let me know the business.

PERT. The business, Sir, is the business that has taken you up these two days; how have I seen you laugh at men of business, and now to become a man of business your self!

DORIMANT. We are not masters of our own affections, our inclinations daily alter; now we love pleasure, and anon we shall doat on business; humane frailty will have it so, and who can help it?

LOVEIT. Faithless, inhumane, barbarous man –

DORIMANT. [*Aside*] *Good, now the alarm strikes* –

LOVEIT. Without sense of love, of honour, or of gratitude, tell me, for I will know, what devil mask'd she was, you were with at the play yesterday?

DORIMANT. Faith I resolv'd as much as you, but the devil was obstinate, and wou'd not tell me.

LOVEIT. False in this as in your vows to me, you do know!

DORIMANT. The truth is, I did all I cou'd to know.

LOVEIT. And dare you own it to my face? Hell and furies! [*Tears her fan in pieces.*

DORIMANT. Spare your fan, Madam, you are growing hot, and will want it to cool you.

LOVEIT. Horrour and distraction seize you, sorrow and remorse gnaw your soul, and punish all your perjuries to me – [*Weeps.*

DORIMANT. *So thunder breaks the clouds in twain,*
And makes a passage for the rain.[71] [*Turning to* Bellinda.

[*To* Bellinda] *Bellinda*, you are the devil that have rais'd this storm; you were at the play yesterday, and have been making discoveries to your dear.

BELLINDA. Y'are the most mistaken man i'the world.

DORIMANT. It must be so, and here I vow revenge; resolve to pursue, and persecute you more impertinently than ever any loving fop did his mistress, hunt you i'the *Park*, trace you i'the

Mail,[72] dog you in every visit you make, haunt you at the plays, and i'the drawing room, hang my nose in your neck, and talk to you whether you will or no, and ever look upon you with such dying eyes, till your friends grow jealous of me, send you out of Town, and the World suspect your reputation. [*In a lower voice*] At my Lady *Townley*'s when we go from hence. [*He looks kindly on* Bellinda.

BELLINDA. I'll meet you there.

DORIMANT. Enough.

LOVEIT. Stand off, you sha' not stare upon her so. [*Pushing* Dorimant *away*.

DORIMANT. Good! There's one made jealous already.

LOVEIT. Is this the constancy you vow'd?

DORIMANT. Constancy at my years! 'Tis not a vertue in season, you might as well expect the fruit the Autumn ripens, i'the Spring.

LOVEIT. Monstrous principle!

DORIMANT. Youth has a long journey to go, Madam, shou'd I have set up my rest at the first inn I lodg'd at, I shou'd never have arriv'd at the happiness I now enjoy.

LOVEIT. Dissembler, damn'd dissembler!

DORIMANT. I am so I confess, good nature, and good manners corrupt me. I am honest in my inclinations, and wou'd not, wer't not to avoid offence, make a lady a little in years believe I think her young, wilfully mistake Art for Nature; and seem as fond of a thing I am weary of, as when I doated on't in earnest.

LOVEIT. False man.

DORIMANT. True woman.

LOVEIT. Now you begin to show your self!

DORIMANT. Love gilds us over, and makes us show fine things to one another for a time, but soon the gold wears off, and then again the native brass appears.

LOVEIT. Think on your oaths, your vows and protestations. Perjur'd man!

DORIMANT. I made 'em when I was in love.

LOVEIT. And therefore ought they not to bind? Oh impious!

DORIMANT. What we swear at such a time may be a certain proof of a present passion, but to say truth, in love there is no security to be given for the future.

LOVEIT. Horrid and ingrateful, begone, and never see me more.

DORIMANT. I am not one of those troublesome coxcombs, who, because they were once well receiv'd, take the priviledge to plague a woman with their love ever after; I shall obey you, Madam, though I do my self some violence. [*He offers to go, and* Loveit *pulls him back*.

LOVEIT. Come back, you sha' not go. Cou'd you have the ill nature to offer it?

DORIMANT. When love grows diseas'd the best thing we can do is to put it to a violent death; I cannot endure the torture of a lingring and consumptive passion.

LOVEIT. Can you think mine sickly?

DORIMANT. Oh, 'tis desperately ill! What worse symptoms are there than your being always uneasie when I visit you, your picking quarrels with me on slight occasions, and in my absence kindly listning to the impertinences of every fashionable fool that talks to you?

LOVEIT. What fashionable fool can you lay to my charge?

DORIMANT. Why the very cock-fool of all those fools, Sir Fopling Flutter.

LOVEIT. I never saw him in my life, but once.

DORIMANT. The worse woman you, at first sight to put on all your charms, to entertain him with that softness in your voice, and all that wanton kindness in your eyes, you so notoriously affect, when you design a conquest.

LOVEIT. So damn'd a lie did never malice yet invent; who told you this?

DORIMANT. No matter; that ever I shou'd love a woman that can doat on a senseless caper, a tawdry French riband, and a formal cravat.

LOVEIT. You make me mad.

DORIMANT. A guilty conscience may do much, go on, be the Game-Mistress o' the Town, and enter all our young fops, as fast as they come from travail.[73]

LOVEIT. Base and scurrilous!

DORIMANT. A fine mortifying reputation 'twill be for a woman of your pride, wit, and quality!

LOVEIT. This jealousy's a meer pretence, a cursed trick of your own devising; I know you.

DORIMANT. Believe it and all the ill of me you can, I wou'd not have a woman have the least good thought of me, that can think well of *Fopling*; farewell, fall to, and much good may do you with your coxcomb.

LOVEIT. Stay, oh stay, and I will tell you all.

DORIMANT. I have been told too much already. [*Exit* Dorimant.

LOVEIT. Call him again.

PERT. E'n let him go, a fair riddance.

LOVEIT. Run I say, call him again, I will have him call'd.

PERT. The Devil shou'd carry him away first, were it my concern. [*Exit* Pert.

BELLINDA. H'as frighted me from the very thoughts of loving men; for Heav'n's sake, my dear, do not discover what I told you; I dread his tongue as much as you ought to have done his friendship.

[*Enter* Pert.

PERT. He's gone, Madam.

LOVEIT. Lightning blast him.

PERT. When I told him you desired him to come back, he smil'd, made a mouth at me, flung into his coach, and said –

LOVEIT. What did he say?

PERT. Drive away, and then repeated verses.

LOVEIT. Wou'd I had made a contract to be a witch when first I entertain'd this greater devil, monster, barbarian; I could tear my self in pieces. Revenge, nothing but revenge can ease me; plague, war, famine, fire, all that can bring universal ruin and misery on mankind, with joy I'd perish to have you in my power but this moment. [*Exit* Loveit.

PERT. Follow Madam, leave her not in this outragious passion. [Pert *gathers up the things.*

BELLINDA. H'as given me the proof which I desired of his love, but 'tis a proof of his ill nature too; I wish I had not seen him use her so.

I sigh to think that Dorimant may be,
One day as faithless, and unkind to me. [*Exeunt.*

Act III. Scene I.

[*SCENE* Lady Woodvil*'s lodgings. Enter* Harriet*, and* Busy *her woman.*]

BUSY. Dear Madam! Let me set that curl in order.

HARRIET. Let me alone, I will shake 'em all out of order.

BUSY. Will you never leave this wildness?

HARRIET. Torment me not.

BUSY. Look! There's a knot falling off.

HARRIET. Let it drop.

BUSY. But one pin, dear Madam.

HARRIET. How do I daily suffer under thy officious fingers?

BUSY. Ah the difference that is between you and my Lady *Dapper*? How uneasy she is if the least thing be amiss about her?

HARRIET. She is indeed most exact! Nothing is ever wanting to make her ugliness remarkable!

BUSY. Jeering people say so!

HARRIET. Her powdering, painting, and her patching never fail in publick to draw the tongues and eyes of all the men upon her.

BUSY. She is indeed a little too pretending.

HARRIET. That women should set up for beauty as much in spite of Nature, as some men have done for wit.

BUSY. I hope without offence one may endeavour to make one's self agreeable.

HARRIET. Not, when 'tis impossible. Women then ought to be no more fond of dressing than fools should be of talking; hoods and modesty, masques and silence, things that shadow and conceal; they should think of nothing else.

BUSY. Jesu! Madam, what will your mother think is become of you? For Heav'n's sake go in again.

HARRIET. I won't!

BUSY. This is the extravagant'st thing that ever you did in your life, to leave her and a gentleman who is to be your husband.

HARRIET. My husband! Hast thou so little wit to think I spoke what I meant when I over-joy'd her in the Country, with a low courtsy, and what you please, Madam, I shall ever be obedient.

BUSY. Nay, I know not, you have so many fetches.

HARRIET. And this was one, to get her up to *London*! Nothing else I assure thee.

BUSY. Well, the man, in my mind, is a fine man!

HARRIET. The man indeed wears his cloaths fashionably, and has a pretty negligent way with him, very courtly, and much affected; he bows, and talks, and smiles so agreeably as he thinks.

BUSY. I never saw any thing so gentile!

HARRIET. Varnish'd over with good breeding, many a blockhead makes a tolerable show.

BUSY. I wonder you do not like him.

HARRIET. I think I might be brought to endure him, and that is all a reasonable woman should expect in a husband, but there is duty i'the case – and like the haughty *Merab*, I

Find much aversion in my stubborn mind,
Which is bred by being promis'd and design'd.[74]

BUSY. I wish you do not design your own ruin! I partly guess your inclinations, Madam – that Mr. *Dorimant* –

HARRIET. Leave your prating, and sing some foolish song or other.

BUSY. I will, the song you love so well ever since you saw Mr. *Dorimant*.

SONG.

When first Amintas charm'd my heart,
My heedless sheep began to stray;
The wolves soon stole the greatest part,
And all will now be made a prey.

Ah, let not love your thoughts possess,
'Tis fatal to a shepherdess;
The dang'rous passion you must shun,
Or else like me be quite undone.

HARRIET. Shall I be paid down by a covetous parent for a purchase? I need no land; no, I'll lay my self out all in love. It is decreed –

[*Enter* Young Bellair.

YOUNG BELLAIR. What generous resolution are you making, Madam?

HARRIET. Only to be disobedient, Sir.

YOUNG BELLAIR. Let me join hands with you in that –

HARRIET. With all my heart, I never thought I should have given you mine so willingly. Here I *Harriet* –

YOUNG BELLAIR. And I *Harry* –

HARRIET. Do solemnly protest –

YOUNG BELLAIR. And vow –

HARRIET. That I with you –

YOUNG BELLAIR. And I with you –

BOTH. Will never marry –

HARRIET. A match!

YOUNG BELLAIR. And no match! How do you like this indifference now?

HARRIET. You expect I should take it ill I see!

YOUNG BELLAIR. 'Tis not unnatural for young women to be a little angry, you miss a conquest, though you wou'd slight the poor man were he in your power.

HARRIET. There are some it may be have an eye like *Bart'lomew*,[75] big enough for the whole Fair, but I am not of the number, and you may keep your ginger-bread.[76] 'Twill be more acceptable to the lady, whose dear image it wears, Sir.

YOUNG BELLAIR. I must confess, Madam, you came a day after the Fair.

HARRIET. You own then you are in love –

YOUNG BELLAIR. I do.

HARRIET. The confidence is generous, and in return I could almost find in my heart to let you know my inclinations.

YOUNG BELLAIR. Are you in love?

HARRIET. Yes, with this dear Town, to that degree, I can scarce endure the Country in landskapes and in hangings.

YOUNG BELLAIR. What a dreadful thing 'twould be to be hurried back to *Hampshire*!

HARRIET. Ah – name it not! –

YOUNG BELLAIR. As for us, I find we shall agree well enough! Wou'd we cou'd do something to deceive the grave people!

HARRIET. Could we delay their quick proceeding, 'twere well, a reprieve is a good step towards the getting of a pardon.

YOUNG BELLAIR. If we give over the game, we are undone! What think you of playing it on booty?[77]

HARRIET. What do you mean?

YOUNG BELLAIR. Pretend to be in love with one another! 'Twill make some dilatory excuses we may feign, pass the better.

HARRIET. Let us do't, if it be but for the dear pleasure of dissembling.

YOUNG BELLAIR. Can you play your part?

HARRIET. I know not what it is to love, but I have made pretty remarks by being now and then where lovers meet. Where did you leave their gravities?

YOUNG BELLAIR. I'th' next room! Your mother was censuring our modern gallant.

[*Enter* Old Bellair, *and* Lady Woodvil.

HARRIET. Peace! Here they come, I will lean against this wall, and look bashfully down upon my fan, while you like an amorous spark, modishly entertain me.

LADY WOODVIL. Never go about to excuse 'em, come, come, it was not so when I was a young woman.

OLD BELLAIR. A Dod, they're something disrespectful –

LADY WOODVIL. Quality was then consider'd, and not rally'd by every fleering[78] fellow.

OLD BELLAIR. Youth will have its jest, a Dod it will.

LADY WOODVIL. 'Tis good breeding now to be civil to none but players and *Exchange* women,[79] they are treated by 'em as much above their condition, as others are below theirs.

OLD BELLAIR. Out, a pize on 'em, talk no more, the rogues ha' got an ill habit of preferring beauty, no matter where they find it.

LADY WOODVIL. See your son, and my daughter, they have improv'd their acquaintance since they were within.

OLD BELLAIR. A Dod methinks they have! Let's keep back and observe.

YOUNG BELLAIR. Now for a look and gestures that may perswade 'em I am saying all the passionate things imaginable –

HARRIET. Your head a little more on one side, ease your self on your left leg, and play with your right hand.

YOUNG BELLAIR. Thus, is it not?

HARRIET. Now set your right leg firm on the ground, adjust your belt, then look about you.

YOUNG BELLAIR. A little exercising will make me perfect.

HARRIET. Smile, and turn to me again very sparkish!

YOUNG BELLAIR. Will you take your turn and be instructed?

HARRIET. With all my heart.

YOUNG BELLAIR. At one motion play your fan, roul your eyes, and then settle a kind look upon me.

HARRIET. So.

YOUNG BELLAIR. Now spread your fan, look down upon it, and tell[80] the sticks with a finger.

HARRIET. Very modish.

YOUNG BELLAIR. Clap your hand up to your bosom, hold down your gown; shrug a little, draw up your breasts, and let 'em fall again, gently, with a sigh or two, *&c.*

HARRIET. By the good instructions you give, I suspect you for one of those malitious observers who watch people's eyes, and from innocent looks, make scandalous conclusions.

YOUNG BELLAIR. I know some indeed, who out of meer love to mischief, are as vigilant as jealousy it self, and will give you an account of every glance that passes at a play, and i'th' Circle![81]

HARRIET. 'Twill not be amiss now to seem a little pleasant.

YOUNG BELLAIR. Clap your fan then in both your hands, snatch it to your mouth, smile, and with a lively motion fling your body a little forwards. So – now spread it; fall back on the sudden, cover your face with it, and break out into a loud laughter – take up! Look grave, and fall a fanning of your self – admirably well acted.

HARRIET. I think I am pretty apt at these matters!

OLD BELLAIR. A Dod I like this well.

LADY WOODVIL. This promises something.

OLD BELLAIR. Come! There is love i'th' case, a dod there is, or will be; what say you, young Lady?

HARRIET. All in good time Sir, you expect we should fall to, and love as game-cocks fight, as soon as we are set together, a Dod y'are unreasonable!

OLD BELLAIR. A Dod, Sirrah, I like thy wit well.

[*Enter a* Servant.

SERVANT. The coach is at the door, Madam.

OLD BELLAIR. Go, get you and take the air together.

LADY WOODVIL. Will not you go with us?

OLD BELLAIR. Out, a pize: A Dod I ha' business and cannot. We shall meet at night at my Sister *Townley*'s.

YOUNG BELLAIR. [*Aside*] *He's going to Emilia. I overheard him talk of a collation.* [*Exeunt.*

Scene II.

[*Enter* Lady Townley, Emilia, *and* Mr. Medley.]

LADY TOWNLEY. I pity the young lovers, we last talk'd of, though to say truth, their conduct has been so indiscreet, they deserve to be unfortunate.

MEDLEY. Y' have had an exact account, from the great Lady i'th' box down to the little orange wench.

EMILIA. Y' are a living libel, a breathing lampoon; I wonder you are not torn in pieces.

MEDLEY. What think you of setting up an Office of Intelligence for these matters? The project may get money.

LADY TOWNLEY. You would have great dealings with Country ladies.

MEDLEY. More than *Muddiman*[82] has with their husbands.

[*Enter* Bellinda.

LADY TOWNLEY. *Bellinda*, what has been become of you! We have not seen you here of late with your friend Mrs. *Loveit.*

BELLINDA. Dear creature, I left her but now so sadly afflicted.

LADY TOWNLEY. With her old distemper, jealousy!

MEDLEY. *Dorimant* has plaid her some new prank.

BELLINDA. Well, that *Dorimant* is certainly the worst man breathing.

EMILIA. I once thought so.

BELLINDA. And do you not think so still?

EMILIA. No indeed!

BELLINDA. Oh Jesu!

EMILIA. The Town does him a great deal of injury, and I will never believe what it says of a man I do not know, again for his sake!

BELLINDA. You make me wonder!

LADY TOWNLEY. He's a very well bred man.

BELLINDA. But strangely ill-natur'd.

EMILIA. Then he's a very witty man!

BELLINDA. But a man of no principles.

MEDLEY. Your man of principles is a very fine thing indeed.

BELLINDA. To be preferr'd to men of parts by women who have regard to their reputation and quiet. Well were I minded to play the fool, he shou'd be the last man I'd think of.

MEDLEY. He has been the first in many ladies' favours, though you are so severe, Madam.

LADY TOWNLEY. What he may be for a lover I know not, but he's a very pleasant acquaintance I am sure.

BELLINDA. Had you seen him use Mrs. *Loveit* as I have done, you wou'd never endure him more –

EMILIA. What, he has quarrel'd with her again!

BELLINDA. Upon the slightest occasion, he's jealous of Sir *Fopling*.

LADY TOWNLEY. She never saw him in her life but yesterday, and that was here.

EMILIA. On my conscience! He's the only man in Town, that's her aversion, how horribly out of humour she was all the while he talk'd to her!

BELLINDA. And some body has wickedly told him –

EMILIA. Here he comes.

[*Enter* Dorimant.

MEDLEY. *Dorimant*! You are luckily come to justify your self – here's a Lady –

BELLINDA. Has a word or two to say to you from a disconsolate person.

DORIMANT. You tender your reputation too much I know, Madam, to whisper with me before this good company.

BELLINDA. To serve Mrs. *Loveit*, I'll make a bold venture.

DORIMANT. Here's *Medley*, the very spirit of scandal.

BELLINDA. No matter!

EMILIA. 'Tis something you are unwilling to hear, Mr. *Dorimant*.

LADY TOWNLEY. Tell him, *Bellinda* whether he will or no!

BELLINDA. Mrs. *Loveit*! [*Aloud*.

DORIMANT. Softly, these are laughers, you do not know 'em.

BELLINDA. [*To* Dorimant *apart*] In a word y'ave made me hate you, which I thought you never could have done.

DORIMANT. In obeying your commands.

BELLINDA. Twas a cruel part you play'd! How could you act it?

DORIMANT. Nothing is cruel to a man who could kill himself to please you; remember five a clock to morrow morning.

BELLINDA. I tremble when you name it.

DORIMANT. Be sure you come.

BELLINDA. I sha'not.

DORIMANT. Swear you will!

BELLINDA. I dare not.

DORIMANT. Swear I say.

BELLINDA. By my life! By all the happiness I hope for –

DORIMANT. You will.

BELLINDA. I will.

DORIMANT. Kind.

BELLINDA. I am glad I've sworn, I vow I think I should ha' fail'd you else!

DORIMANT. Surprisingly kind! In what temper did you leave *Loveit*?

BELLINDA. Her raving was prettily over, and she began to be in a brave way of defying you, and all your works. Where have you been since you went from thence?

DORIMANT. I look'd in at the play.

BELLINDA. I have promis'd and must return to her agen.

DORIMANT. Perswade her to walk in the Mail this evening.

BELLINDA. She hates the place and will not come.

DORIMANT. Do all you can to prevail with her.

BELLINDA. For what purpose?

DORIMANT. Sir *Fopling* will be here anon, I'll prepare him to set upon her there before me.

BELLINDA. You persecute her too much, but I'll do all you'll ha' me.

DORIMANT. Tell her plainly, 'tis grown so dull a business [*Aloud*] I can drudge on no longer.

EMILIA. There are afflictions in love, Mr. *Dorimant*.

DORIMANT. You women make 'em, who are commonly as unreasonable in that as you are at play; without the advantage be on your side, a man can never quietly give over when he's weary?

MEDLEY. If you would play without being obliged to complaisance, *Dorimant*, you should play in publick places.

DORIMANT. Ordinaries[83] were a very good thing for that, but gentlemen do not of late frequent 'em; the deep play is now in private houses. [Bellinda *offering to steal away.*

LADY TOWNLEY. *Bellinda*, are you leaving us so soon?

BELLINDA. I am to go to the park with Mrs. *Loveit*, Madam – [*Exit* Bellinda.

LADY TOWNLEY. This confidence will go nigh to spoil this young creature.

MEDLEY. 'Twill do her good, Madam. Young men who are brought up under practising lawyers prove the abler council when they come to be call'd to the Bar themselves –

DORIMANT. The Town has been very favourable to you this afternoon, my Lady *Townley*, you use to have an embara's[84] of chairs and coaches at your door, an uproar of footmen in your hall, and a noise of fools above here.

LADY TOWNLEY. Indeed my house is the general rendevouze, and next to the play-house is the common refuge of all the young idle people.

EMILIA. Company is a very good thing, Madam, but I wonder you do not love it a little more chosen.

LADY TOWNLEY. 'Tis good to have an universal taste, we should love wit, but for variety, be able to divert our selves with the extravagancies of those who want it.

MEDLEY. Fools will make you laugh.

EMILIA. For once or twice! But the repetition of their folly after a visit or two grows tedious and unsufferable.

LADY TOWNLEY. You are a little too delicate, *Emilia*.

[*Enter a* Page.

PAGE. Sir *Fopling Flutter*, Madam, desires to know if you are to be seen.

LADY TOWNLEY. Here's the freshest fool in Town, and one who has not cloy'd you yet. Page!

PAGE. Madam!

LADY TOWNLEY. Desire him to walk up.

DORIMANT. Do not you fall on him, *Medley*, and snub him. Sooth him up in his extravagance! He will shew the better.

MEDLEY. You know I have a natural indulgence for fools, and need not this caution, Sir!

[*Enter* Sir Fopling Flutter*, with his* Page *after him.*

SIR FOPLING. *Page*! Wait without. [*To* Lady Townley] Madam, I kiss your hands, I see yesterday was nothing of chance, the bellès assemblès[85] form themselves here every day. [*To* Emilia] Lady your servant; *Dorimant*, let me embrace thee, without lying I have not met with any of my acquaintance, who retain so much of *Paris* as thou dost, the very air thou hadst when the Marquise mistook thee i'th' Tuilleries,[86] and cry'd Hey Chevalier, and then begg'd thy pardon.

DORIMANT. I would fain wear in fashion as long as I can, Sir, 'tis a thing to be valu'd in men as well as bawbles.

SIR FOPLING. Thou art a man of wit, and understands the Town: prithee let thee and I be intimate, there is no living without making some good man the confident of our pleasures.

DORIMANT. 'Tis true! But there is no man so improper for such a business as I am.

SIR FOPLING. Prithee! Why hast thou so modest an opinion of thy self?

DORIMANT. Why first, I could never keep a secret in my life, and then there is no charm so infallibly makes me fall in love with a woman as my knowing a friend loves her. I deal honestly with you.

SIR FOPLING. Thy humour's very gallant or let me perish, I knew a French count so like thee.

LADY TOWNLEY. Wit I perceive has more power over you than beauty, Sir *Fopling*, else you would not have let this Lady stand so long neglected.

SIR FOPLING. A thousand pardons Madam, [*To* Emilia] some civilities' due of course upon the meeting a long absent friend. The eclat[87] of so much beauty I confess ought to have charm'd me sooner.

EMILIA. The brilliance of so much good language, Sir, has much more power than the little beauty I can boast.

SIR FOPLING. I never saw any thing prettier than this high work on your Point D'espaigne –[88]

EMILIA. 'Tis not so rich as Point *De Venice*[89] –

SIR FOPLING. Not altogether, but looks cooler, and is more proper for the season. *Dorimant*, is not that *Medley*?

DORIMANT. The same, Sir.

SIR FOPLING. Forgive me, Sir, in this embara's of civilities, I could not come to have you in my arms sooner. You understand an equipage the best of any man in town, I hear.

MEDLEY. By my own you would not guess it.

SIR FOPLING. There are criticks who do not write, Sir.

MEDLEY. Our peevish poets will scarce allow it.

SIR FOPLING. Dam'em, they'll allow no man wit, who does not play the fool like themselves and show it! Have you taken notice of the gallesh[90] I brought over?

MEDLEY. O yes! 'T has quite another air, than th' English makes.

SIR FOPLING. 'Tis as easily known from an English tumbril,[91] as an Inns of Court-man[92] is from one of us.

DORIMANT. Truly there is a bell-air in galleshes as well as men.

MEDLEY. But there are few so delicate to observe it.

SIR FOPLING. The World is generally very grossier[93] here indeed.

LADY TOWNLEY. He's very fine.

EMILIA. Extream proper.

SIR FOPLING. A slight suit I made to appear in at my first arrival, not worthy your consideration, Ladies.

DORIMANT. The pantaloon is very well mounted.

SIR FOPLING. The tassels are new and pretty.

MEDLEY. I never saw a coat better cut.

SIR FOPLING. It makes me show long-wasted, and I think slender.

DORIMANT. That's the shape our ladies doat on.

MEDLEY. Your breech though is a handful too high in my eye Sir *Fopling*.

SIR FOPLING. Peace, *Medley*, I have wish'd it lower a thousand times, but a pox on't, 'twill not be.

LADY TOWNLEY. His gloves are well fring'd, large and graceful.

SIR FOPLING. I was always eminent for being bien ganté.[94]

EMILIA. He wears nothing but what are originals of the most famous hands in *Paris*.

SIR FOPLING. You are in the right, Madam.

LADY TOWNLEY. The suit.

SIR FOPLING. Barroy.

EMILIA. The garniture.[95]

SIR FOPLING. Le Gras –

MEDLEY. The shooes!

SIR FOPLING. Piccar!

DORIMANT. The perriwig!

SIR FOPLING. Chedreux.[96]

LADY TOWNLEY and EMILIA. The gloves!

SIR FOPLING. Orangerii![97] You know the smell, Ladies! Dorimant, I could find in my heart for an amusement to have a gallantry with some of our English ladies.

DORIMANT. 'Tis a thing no less necessary to confirm the reputation of your wit, than a duel will be to satisfie the Town of your courage.

SIR FOPLING. Here was a woman yesterday –

DORIMANT. Mistriss *Loveit*.

SIR FOPLING. You have nam'd her!

DORIMANT. You cannot pitch on a better for your purpose.

SIR FOPLING. Prithee! What is she?

DORIMANT. A person of quality, and one who has a rest of reputation enough to make the conquest considerable: besides I hear she likes you too!

SIR FOPLING. Methoughts she seem'd though very reserv'd, and uneasie all the time I entertain'd her.

DORIMANT. Grimace and affectation: you will see her i'th' Mail to night.

SIR FOPLING. Prithee, let thee and I take the air together.

DORIMANT. I am engag'd to Medley, but I'll meet you at Saint James's, and give you some information, upon the which you may regulate your proceedings.

SIR FOPLING. All the World will be in the park to night: Ladies, 'twere pity to keep so much beauty longer within doors, and rob the Ring of all those charms that should adorn it – Hey Page.

[*Enter* Page, *and goes out again.*

See that all my people be ready. *Dorimant* a Revoir. [*Exit* Sir Fopling.

MEDLEY. A fine mettl'd coxcomb.

DORIMANT. Brisk and insipid –

MEDLEY. Pert and dull.

EMILIA. However you despise him, Gentlemen, I'll lay my life he passes for a wit with many.

DORIMANT. That may very well be, Nature has her cheats, stum's[98] a brain, and puts sophisticate dulness often on the tastless multitude for true wit and good humour. *Medley*, come.

MEDLEY. I must go a little way, I will meet you i'the Mail.

DORIMANT. I'll walk through the garden thither, we shall meet anon and bow. [*To the women.*

LADY TOWNLEY. Not to night! We are engag'd about a business, the knowledge of which may make you laugh hereafter.

MEDLEY. Your servant, Ladies.

DORIMANT. A revoir, as Sir *Fopling* says – [*Exit* Medley *and* Dorimant.

LADY TOWNLEY. The old man will be here immediately.

EMILIA. Let's expect him i'th' garden –

LADY TOWNLEY. Go, you are a rogue.

EMILIA. I can't abide you. [*Exeunt.*

Scene III.

[*The Mall.* Harriet, Young Bellair, *she pulling him.*]

HARRIET. Come along.

YOUNG BELLAIR. And leave your mother.

HARRIET. *Busy* will be sent with a hue and cry after us; but that's no matter.

YOUNG BELLAIR. 'Twill look strangely in me.

HARRIET. She'll believe it a freak of mine, and never blame your manners.

YOUNG BELLAIR. What reverend acquaintance is that she has met?

HARRIET. A fellow-beauty of the last King's time,[99] though by the ruines you would hardly guess it. [*Exeunt.*

[*Enter* Dorimant *and crosses the stage.*

[*Enter* Young Bellair, *and* Harriet.

YOUNG BELLAIR. By this time your mother is in a fine taking.

HARRIET. If your friend Mr. *Dorimant* were but here now, that she might find me talking with him.

YOUNG BELLAIR. She does not know him but dreads him, I hear, of all mankind.

HARRIET. She concludes if he does but speak to a woman she's undone, is on her knees every day to pray Heav'n defend me from him.

YOUNG BELLAIR. You do not apprehend him so much as she does.

HARRIET. I never saw any thing in him that was frightful.

YOUNG BELLAIR. On the contrary, have you not observed something extream delightful in his wit and person?

HARRIET. He's agreeable and pleasant I must own, but he does so much affect being so, he displeases me.

YOUNG BELLAIR. Lord, Madam, all he does and says, is so easie, and so natural.

HARRIET. Some men's verses seem so to the unskilful, but labour i'the one, and affectation in the other to the judicious plainly appear.

YOUNG BELLAIR. I never heard him accus'd of affectation before.

[*Enter* Dorimant *and stares upon her.*

HARRIET. It passes on the easie Town, who are favourably pleas'd in him to call it humour. [*Exit* Young Bellair *and* Harriet.

DORIMANT. 'Tis she! It must be she, that lovely hair, that easie shape, those wanton eyes, and all those melting charms about her mouth, which *Medley* spoke of; I'll follow the lottery, and put in for a prize with my friend *Bellair.*
In love the victors from the vanquish'd fly;
They fly that wound, and they pursue that die.[100]

[*Exit* Dorimant *repeating.*

[*Enter* Young Bellair, *and* Harriet, *and after them* Dorimant *standing at a distance.*

YOUNG BELLAIR. Most people prefer *High Park*[101] to this place.

HARRIET. It has the better reputation I confess: but I abominate the dull diversions there, the formal bows, the affected smiles, the silly by-words, and amorous tweers,[102] in passing; here one meets with a little conversation now and then.

YOUNG BELLAIR. These conversations have been fatal to some of your sex, Madam.

HARRIET. It may be so, because some who want temper have been undone by gaming, must others who have it, wholly deny themselves the pleasure of play?

DORIMANT. Trust me, it were unreasonable, Madam. [*Coming up gently, and bowing to her.*

HARRIET. Lord! Who's this? [*She starts and looks grave.*

YOUNG BELLAIR. Dorimant.

DORIMANT. Is this the woman your father would have you marry?

YOUNG BELLAIR. It is.

DORIMANT. Her name?

YOUNG BELLAIR. Harriet.

DORIMANT. I am not mistaken, she's handsome.

YOUNG BELLAIR. Talk to her, her wit is better than her face; we were wishing for you but now.

DORIMANT. [*To* Harriet] Overcast with seriousness o' the sudden! A thousand smiles were shining in that face but now; I never saw so quick a change of weather.

HARRIET. [*Aside*] *I feel as great a change within; but he shall never know it.*

DORIMANT. You were talking of play, Madam, pray what may be your stint?[103]

HARRIET. A little harmless discourse in publick walks, or at most an appointment in a box barefac'd at the play-house; you are for masks, and private meetings; where women engage for all they are worth I hear.

DORIMANT. I have been us'd to deep play, but I can make one at small game, when I like my gamester well.

HARRIET. And be so unconcern'd you'll ha' no pleasure in't.

DORIMANT. Where there is a considerable sum to be won, the hope of drawing people in, makes every trifle considerable.

HARRIET. The sordidness of men's natures I know makes 'em willing to flatter and comply with the rich, though they are sure never to be the better for 'em.

DORIMANT. 'Tis in their power to do us good, and we despair not but at some time or other they may be willing.

HARRIET. To men who have far'd in this town like you, 'twould be a great mortification to live on hope; could you keep a Lent for a mistriss?

DORIMANT. In expectation of a happy Easter, and though time be very precious, think forty days well lost, to gain your favour.

HARRIET. Mr. *Bellair*! Let us walk, 'tis time to leave him; men grow dull when they begin to be particular.

DORIMANT. Y'are mistaken, flattery will not ensue, though I know y'are greedy of the praises of the whole Mail.

HARRIET. You do me wrong.

DORIMANT. I do not, as I follow'd you, I observ'd how you were pleased when the *fops* cry'd she's handsome, very handsome, by God she is, and whisper'd aloud your name, the thousand several forms you put your face into; then, to make your self more agreeable, how wantonly you play'd with your head, flung back your locks, and look'd smilingly over your shoulder at 'em.

HARRIET. I do not go begging the men's as you do the ladies' good liking with a sly softness in your looks, and a gentle slowness in your bows, as you pass by 'em – as thus Sir – [*Acts him*] Is not this like you?

[*Enter* Lady Woodvil *and* Busy.

YOUNG BELLAIR. Your mother, Madam. [*Pulls* Harriet. *She composes her self.*

LADY WOODVIL. Ah my Dear Child *Harriet.*

BUSY. Now is she so pleased with finding her agen, she cannot chide her.

LADY WOODVIL. Come away!

DORIMANT. 'Tis now but high Mail, Madam, the most entertaining time of all the evening.

HARRIET. I would fain see that *Dorimant*, Mother, you so cry out of, for a monster, he's in the *Mail* I hear.

LADY WOODVIL. Come away then! The plague is here, and you should dread the infection.

YOUNG BELLAIR. You may be misinform'd of the gentleman.

LADY WOODVIL. Oh no! I hope you do not know him. He is the prince of all the devils in the Town, delights in nothing but in rapes and riots.

DORIMANT. If you did but hear him speak, Madam!

LADY WOODVIL. Oh! He has a tongue they say would tempt the angels to a second fall.

[*Enter* Sir Fopling *with his equipage, six* Footmen, *and a* Page.

SIR FOPLING. Hey, Champaine, Norman, La Rose, la Fleur, La Tour, La Verdure. Dorimant –

LADY WOODVIL. Here, here he is among this rout, he names him; come away *Harriet*, come away. [*Exit* Lady Woodvil, Harriet, Busy *and* Young Bellair.

DORIMANT. This fool's coming has spoil'd all, she's gone, but she has left a pleasing image of her self behind, that wanders in my soul – it must not settle there.

SIR FOPLING. What reverie is this! Speak man.

DORIMANT. *Snatcht from my self how far behind*
Already I behold the shore![104]

[*Enter* Medley.

MEDLEY. *Dorimant*, a discovery! I met with *Bellair.*

DORIMANT. You can tell me no news Sir, I know all.

MEDLEY. How do you like the daughter?

DORIMANT. You never came so near truth in your life, as you did in her description.

MEDLEY. What think you of the mother?

DORIMANT. What ever I think of her, she thinks very well of me, I find.

MEDLEY. Did she know you?

DORIMANT. She did not, whether she does now or no, I know not. Here was a pleasant scene towards, when in came Sir *Fopling*, mustering up his equipage, and at the latter end nam'd me, and frighted her away.

MEDLEY. *Loveit* and *Bellinda* are not far off, I saw 'em alight at St. *James*'s.

DORIMANT. Sir *Fopling*, hark you, a word or two, [*Whispers*] Look you do not want assurance.

SIR FOPLING. I never do on these occasions.

DORIMANT. Walk on, we must not be seen together, make your advantage of what I have told you, the next turn you will meet the Lady.

SIR FOPLING. Hey – Follow me all. [*Exit Sir* Fopling *& his Equipage.*

DORIMANT. *Medley*, you shall see good sport anon between *Loveit* and this *Fopling*.

MEDLEY. I thought there was something toward by that whisper.

DORIMANT. You know a worthy principle of hers?

MEDLEY. Not to be so much as civil to a man who speaks to her in the presence of him she professes to love.

DORIMANT. I have encourag'd *Fopling* to talk to her to night.

MEDLEY. Now you are here she will go nigh to beat him.

DORIMANT. In the humor she's in, her love will make her do some very extravagant thing, doubtless.

MEDLEY. What was *Bellinda*'s business with you at my Lady *Townley*'s?

DORIMANT. To get me to meet *Loveit* here in order to an eclerismènt;[105] I made some difficulty of it, and have prepar'd this rancounter to make good my jealousy.

MEDLEY. Here they come!

[*Enter* Loveit, Bellinda*, and* Pert.

DORIMANT. I'll meet her and provoke her with a deal of dumb civility in passing by, then turn short and be behind her, when Sir *Fopling* sets upon her –

See how unregarded now
That piece of Beauty passes[106]–

[*Exit* Dorimant *and* Medley.

BELLINDA. How wonderful respectfully he bow'd!

PERT. He's always over-mannerly when he has done a mischief.

BELLINDA. Methoughts indeed at the same time he had a strange despising countenance.

PERT. The unlucky look he thinks becomes him.

BELLINDA. I was afraid you would have spoke to him, my Dear.

LOVEIT. I would have done first; he shall no more find me the loving fool he has done.

BELLINDA. You love him still!

LOVEIT. No.

PERT. I wish you did not.

LOVEIT. I do not, and I will have you think so: what made you hale me to this odious place, *Bellinda*?

BELLINDA. I hate to be hulch'd up[107] in a coach; walking is much better.

LOVEIT. Would we could meet Sir *Fopling* now.

BELLINDA. Lord! Would you not avoid him?

LOVEIT. I would make him all the advances that may be.

BELLINDA. That would confirm *Dorimant*'s suspicion, my Dear.

LOVEIT. He is not jealous; but I will make him so, and be reveng'd a way he little thinks on.

BELLINDA. – [*Aside*] *If she should make him jealous, that may make him fond of her again: I must disswade her from it.* – Lord! My Dear, this will certainly make him hate you.

LOVEIT. 'Twill make him uneasie though he does not care for me; I know the effects of jealousie on men of his proud temper.

BELLINDA. 'Tis a fantastick remedy, its operations are dangerous and uncertain.

LOVEIT. 'Tis the strongest cordial we can give to dying love, it often brings it back when there's no sign of life remaining: but I design not so much the reviving his, as my revenge.

[*Enter Sir* Fopling *and his Equipage.*

SIR FOPLING. Hey! Bid the coach-man send home four of his horses, and bring the coach to *White-Hall*,[108] I'll walk over the park – Madam, the honour of kissing your fair hands is a happiness I miss'd this afternoon at my Lady *Townley*'s!

LOVEIT. You were very obliging, Sir *Fopling*, the last time I saw you there.

SIR FOPLING. The preference was due to your wit and beauty. Madam, your Servant, there never was so sweet an evening.

BELLINDA. 'T has drawn all the rabble of the Town hither.

SIR FOPLING. 'Tis pity there's not an order made, that none but the beau monde should walk here.

LOVEIT. 'Twould add much to the beauty of the place: see what a sort of nasty fellows are coming.

[*Enter four ill-fashion'd fellows singing,*

'Tis not for kisses alone, &c.[109]

LOVEIT. Fo! Their perriwigs are scented with tobacco so strong –

SIR FOPLING. It overcomes our pulvilio[110] – methinks I smell the coffee-house they come from.

1 MAN. *Dorimant*'s convenient, Madam *Loveit.*

2 MAN. I like the oylie – buttock[111] with her.

3 MAN. What spruce prig is that?

1 MAN. A caravan,[112] lately come from *Paris.*

2 MAN. Peace, they smoak.[113]

There's something else to be done, &c. [*All of them coughing. Exit singing.*

[*Enter* Dorimant *and* Medley.

DORIMANT. They're ingag'd –

MEDLEY. She entertains him as if she lik'd him.

DORIMANT. Let us go forward – seem earnest in discourse and shew our selves. Then you shall see how she'll use him!

BELLINDA. Yonder's *Dorimant,* my Dear.

LOVEIT. I see him. – [*Aside*] *He comes insulting; but I will disappoint him in his expectation.* – [*To Sir* Fopling]

I like this pretty nice humour of yours, Sir *Fopling*: with what a loathing eye he look'd upon those fellows!

SIR FOPLING. I sat near one of 'em at a play to day, and was almost poison'd with a pair of cordivant[114] gloves he wears –

LOVEIT. Oh! Filthy cordivant, how I hate the smell! [*Laughs in a loud affected way.*

SIR FOPLING. Did you observe, Madam, how their crevats hung loose an inch from their neck, and what a frightful air it gave 'em.

LOVEIT. Oh I took particular notice of one that is alwaies spruc'd up with a deal of dirty sky-colour'd ribband.

BELLINDA. That's one of the walking flajolets[115] who haunt the Mail o'nights –

LOVEIT. Oh! I remember him! H' has a hollow tooth[116] enough to spoil the sweetness of an evening.

SIR FOPLING. I have seen the tallest walk the streets with a dainty pair of boxes, neatly buckl'd on.[117]

LOVEIT. And a little footboy at his heels, pocket-high, with a flat-cap – a durty face.

SIR FOPLING. And a snotty nose –

LOVEIT. Oh – odious, there's many of my own sex with that *Holborn* equipage[118] trigg[119] to *Grey's Inn-Walks;*[120] and now and then travail hither on a Sunday.

MEDLEY. She takes no notice of you.

DORIMANT. Damn her! I am jealous of a counter-plot!

LOVEIT. Your liveries[121] are the finest, Sir *Fopling* – Oh that page! That page is the prettily'st drest – they are all Frenchmen.

SIR FOPLING. There's one damn'd English blockhead among 'em, you may know him by his meine.

LOVEIT. Oh! That's he, that's he, what do you call him?

SIR FOPLING. Hey – I know not what to call him –

LOVEIT. What's your name?

FOOTMAN. *John Trott*, Madam!

SIR FOPLING. O unsufferable! *Trott, Trott, Trott*! There's nothing so barbarous as the names of our English servants. What countryman are you, Sirrah?

FOOTMAN. *Hampshire*, Sir.

SIR FOPLING. Then *Hampshire* be your name. Hey, *Hampshire*!

LOVEIT. O that sound, that sound becomes the mouth of a man of quality!

MEDLEY. *Dorimant*, you look a little bashful on the matter!

DORIMANT. She dissembles better than I thought she could have done.

MEDLEY. You have tempted her with too luscious a bait. She bites at the coxcomb.

DORIMANT. She cannot fall from loving me to that?

MEDLEY. You begin to be jealous in earnest.

DORIMANT. Of one I do not love –

MEDLEY. You did love her.

DORIMANT. The fit has long been over –

MEDLEY. But I have known men fall into dangerous relapses when they have found a woman inclining to another.

DORIMANT. *He guesses the secret of my heart! I am concern'd, but dare not show it, lest Bellinda should mistrust all I have done to gain her.* [*To himself.*

BELLINDA. [*Aside*] *I have watch'd his look, and find no alteration there. Did he love her, some signs of jealousy would have appear'd?*

DORIMANT. I hope this happy evening, Madam, has reconcil'd you to the scandalous Mail, we shall have you now hankering here again –

LOVEIT. Sir *Fopling*, will you walk –

SIR FOPLING. I am all obedience, Madam –

LOVEIT. Come along then – and let's agree to be malitious on all the ill-fashion'd things we meet.

SIR FOPLING. We'll make a critick on the whole Mail, Madam.

LOVEIT. *Bellinda*, you shall engage –

BELLINDA. To the reserve of our friends, my Dear.

LOVEIT. No! No! Exceptions –

SIR FOPLING. We'll sacrifice all to our diversion –

LOVEIT. All – all –

SIR FOPLING. All.

BELLINDA. All? Then let it be. [*Exit Sir* Fopling, Loveit, Bellinda, *and* Pert, *laughing*.

MEDLEY. Would you had brought some more of your friends, *Dorimant*, to have been witnesses of Sir *Fopling*'s disgrace and your triumph –

DORIMANT. 'Twere unreasonable to desire you not to laugh at me; but pray do not expose me to the Town this day or two.

MEDLEY. By that time you hope to have regain'd your credit.

DORIMANT. I know she hates *Fopling*, and only makes use of him in hope to work me on agen; had it not been for some powerful considerations which will be remov'd to morrow morning, I had made her pluck off this mask, and shew the passion that lyes panting under.

[*Enter a* Footman.

MEDLEY. Here comes a man from *Bellair*, with news of your last adventure.

DORIMANT. I am glad he sent him. I long to know the consequence of our parting.

FOOTMAN. Sir, my master desires you to come to my Lady *Townley*'s presently, and bring Mr. *Medley* with you. My Lady *Woodvill* and her daughter are there.

MEDLEY. Then all's well, *Dorimant* –

FOOTMAN. They have sent for the fiddles and mean to dance! He bid me tell you, Sir, the old lady does not know you, and would have you own your self to be Mr. *Courtage*. They are all prepar'd to receive you by that name.

DORIMANT. That foppish admirer of quality, who flatters the very meat at honourable tables, and never offers love to a woman below a Lady Grandmother.

MEDLEY. You know the character you are to act, I see!

DORIMANT. This is *Harriet*'s contrivance – wild, witty, lovesome, beautiful and young[122] – come along, *Medley* –

MEDLEY. This new woman would well supply the loss of *Loveit*.

DORIMANT. That business must not end so, before to morrow sun is set, I will revenge and clear it.

And you and Loveit to her cost shall find,
I fathom all the depths of Womankind.

[*Exeunt*.

Act IV. Scene I.

[*The Scene opens with the fiddles playing a country dance. Enter* Dorimant, Lady Woodvil, Young Bellair, *and* Mrs. Harriet, Old Bellair, *and* Emilia, Mr. Medley *and* Lady Townley; *as having just ended the dance*.]

OLD BELLAIR. So, so, so! A smart bout, a very smart bout, a Dod!

LADY TOWNLEY. How do you like *Emilia*'s dancing, Brother?

OLD BELLAIR. Not at all, not at all.

LADY TOWNLEY. You speak not what you think, I am sure.

OLD BELLAIR. No matter for that, go, bid her dance no more, it don't become her, it don't become her, tell her I say so; – [*Aside*] *a Dod I love her*.

DORIMANT. All people mingle now a days, Madam, and in publick places women of quality have the least respect show'd 'em. [*To* Lady Woodvil.

LADY WOODVIL. I protest you say the truth, Mr. Courtage.

DORIMANT. Forms and ceremonies, the only things that uphold quality and greatness, are now shamefully laid aside and neglected.

LADY WOODVIL. Well! This is not the women's Age, let 'em think what they will, lewdness is the business now, love was the bus'ness in my time.

DORIMANT. The women indeed are little beholding to the young men of this Age, they're generally only dull admirers of themselves, and make their court to nothing but their perriwigs and their crevats, and would be more concern'd for the disordering of 'em, tho' on a good occasion, than a young maid would be for the tumbling of her head or handkercher.[123]

LADY WOODVIL. I protest you hit 'em.

DORIMANT. They are very assiduous to show themselves at Court well dress't to the women of quality, but their bus'ness is with the stale mistresses of the Town, who are prepar'd to receive their lazy addresses by industrious old lovers, who have cast 'em off, and made 'em easy.

HARRIET. He fits my mother's humor so well, a little more and she'll dance a kissing dance with him anon.

MEDLEY. Dutifully observ'd, Madam.

DORIMANT. They pretend to be great criticks in beauty, by their talk you would think they lik'd no face, and yet can doat on an ill one, if it belong to a landress[124] or a tailor's daughter: they cry a woman's past her prime at 20, decay'd at four and 20, old and unsufferable at 30.

LADY WOODVIL. Unsufferable at 30! That they are in the wrong, Mr. Courtage, at five and 30, there are living proofs enough to convince 'em.

DORIMANT. Ay Madam! There's Mrs. Setlooks, Mrs. Droplip, and my Lady Lowd! Shew me among all our opening buds, a face that promises so much beauty as the remains of theirs.

LADY WOODVIL. The deprav'd appetite of this vicious Age tastes nothing but green fruit, and loaths it when 'tis kindly ripen'd.

DORIMANT. Else so many deserving women, Madam, would not be so untimely neglected.

LADY WOODVIL. I protest Mr. Courtage, a dozen such good men as you, would be enough to attone for that wicked Dorimant, and all the under debauchees of the Town. What's the matter there? [Harcourt, Emilia, Young Bellair, Medley, Lady Townley *break out into a laughter.*

MEDLEY. A pleasant mistake, Madam, that a lady has made, occasions a little laughter.

OLD BELLAIR. Come, come, you keep 'em idle! They are impatient till the fiddles play again.

DORIMANT. You are not weary, Madam?

LADY WOODVIL. One dance more! I cannot refuse you Mr. *Courtage*. [*They dance.*

EMILIA. You are very active, Sir. [*After the dance,* Old Bellair, *singing and dancing up to* Emilia.

OLD BELLAIR. A Dod, Sirrah; when I was a young fellow, I could ha' caper'd up to my woman's gorget.[125]

DORIMANT. You are willing to rest your self, Madam –

LADY TOWNLEY. We'll walk into my chamber and sit down.

MEDLEY. Leave us Mr. *Courtage*, he's a dancer, and the young ladies are not weary yet.

LADY WOODVIL. We'll send him out again.

HARRIET. If you do not quickly, I know where to send for Mr. *Dorimant*.

LADY WOODVIL. This girl's head, Mr. *Courtage*, is ever running on that wild fellow.

DORIMANT. 'Tis well you have got her a good husband, Madam, that will settle it. [*Exit* Lady Townley, Lady Woodvil *and* Dorimant.

OLD BELLAIR. [*To* Emilia] A Dod, sweet-heart be advis'd, and do not throw thy self away on a young idle fellow.

EMILIA. I have no such intention, Sir.

OLD BELLAIR. Have a little patience! Thou shalt have the man I spake of. A Dod, he loves thee, and will make a good husband, but no words –

EMILIA. But Sir –

OLD BELLAIR. No answer – out a pize! Peace! And think on't.

[*Enter* Dorimant.

DORIMANT. Your company is desir'd within, Sir.

OLD BELLAIR. I go! I go! Good Mr. *Courtage* – fare you well! Go! I'll see you no more. [*To* Emilia.

EMILIA. What have I done, Sir?

OLD BELLAIR. You are ugly, you are ugly! Is she not, Mr. *Courtage*?

EMILIA. Better words or I sha'nt abide you.

OLD BELLAIR. Out a pize – a Dod, what does she say! Hit her a pat for me there. [*Exit* Old Bellair.

MEDLEY. You have charms for the whole family.

DORIMANT. You'll spoil all with some unseasonable jest, *Medley*.

MEDLEY. You see I confine my tongue, and am content to be a bare spectator, much contrary to my nature.

EMILIA. Methinks, Mr. *Dorimant*, my Lady *Woodvil* is a little fond of you.

DORIMANT. Would her daughter were.

MEDLEY. It may be you may find her so! Try her, you have an opportunity.

DORIMANT. And I will not lose it! *Bellair*, here's a lady has something to say to you.

YOUNG BELLAIR. I wait upon her. Mr *Medley*, we have both business with you.

DORIMANT. Get you all together then. That demure curt'sy is not amiss in jest, [*To* Harriet] but do not think in earnest it becomes you.

HARRIET. Affectation is catching I find; from your grave bow I got it.

DORIMANT. Where had you all that scorn, and coldness in your look?

HARRIET. From Nature, Sir, pardon my want of art: I have not learnt those softnesses and languishings which now in faces are so much in fashion.

DORIMANT. You need 'em not, you have a sweetness of your own, if you would but calm your frowns and let it settle.

HARRIET. My eyes are wild and wandring like my passions, and cannot yet be ty'd to rules of charming.

DORIMANT. Women indeed have commonly a method of managing those messengers of love! Now they will look as if they would kill, and anon they will look as if they were dying. They point and rebate their glances, the better to invite us.

HARRIET. I like this variety well enough, but hate the set face that always looks as it would say come love me. A woman, who at plays makes the deux yeux[126] to a whole audience, and at home cannot forbear 'em to her monkey.

DORIMANT. Put on a gentle smile, and let me see, how well it will become you.

HARRIET. I am sorry my face does not please you as it is, but I shall not be complaisant and change it.

DORIMANT. Though you are obstinate, I know 'tis capable of improvement, and shall do you justice, Madam, if I chance to be at Court, when the critics of the circle pass their judgment; for thither you must come.

HARRIET. And expect to be taken in pieces, have all my features examin'd, every motion censur'd, and on the whole be condemn'd to be but pretty, or a beauty of the lowest rate. What think you?

DORIMANT. The women, nay, the very lovers who belong to the Drawing-room will malitiously allow you more than that; they always grant what is apparent, that they may the better be believ'd when they name conceal'd faults they cannot easily be disprov'd in.

HARRIET. Beauty runs as great a risque expos'd at Court, as wit does on the stage, where the ugly and the foolish, all are free to censure.

DORIMANT. – [*Aside*] *I love her, and dare not let her know it, I fear sh'as an ascendant o're me, and may revenge the wrongs I have done her sex.* – [*To her*] Think of making a party, Madam, love will engage.

HARRIET. You make me start! I did not think to have heard of love from you.

DORIMANT. I never knew what 'twas to have a settled ague yet, but now and then have had irregular fits.

HARRIET. Take heed, sickness after long health is commonly more violent and dangerous.

DORIMANT. – [*Aside*] *I have took the infection from her, and feel the disease now spreading in me* – [*To her*] Is the name of love so frightful that you dare not stand it?

HARRIET. 'Twill do little execution out of your mouth on me, I am sure.

DORIMANT. It has been fatal –

HARRIET. To some easy women, but we are not all born to one destiny, I was inform'd you use to laugh at love, and not make it.

DORIMANT. The time has been, but now I must speak –

HARRIET. If it be on that idle subject, I will put on my serious look, turn my head carelesly from you, drop my lip, let my eyelids fall, and hang half o're my eyes – thus while you buz a speech of an hour long in my ear, and I answer never a word! Why do you not begin?

DORIMANT. That the company may take notice how passionately I make advances of love! And how disdainfully you receive 'em.

HARRIET. When your love's grown strong enough to make you bear being laugh'd at, I'll give you leave to trouble me with it. Till then pray forbear, Sir.

[*Enter* Sir Fopling *and others in masques.*

DORIMANT. What's here, masquerades?[127]

HARRIET. I thought that foppery had been left off, and people might have been in private with a fiddle.

DORIMANT. 'Tis endeavour'd to be kept on foot still by some who find themselves the more acceptable, the less they are known.

YOUNG BELLAIR. This must be Sir *Fopling*.

MEDLEY. That extraordinary habit[128] shews it.

YOUNG BELLAIR. What are the rest?

MEDLEY. A company of French rascals, whom he pick'd up in *Paris*, and has brought over to be his dancing equipage on these occasions! Make him own himself; a fool is very troublesome when he presumes he is incognito.

SIR FOPLING. Do you know me? [*To* Harriet.

HARRIET. Ten to one but I guess at you?

SIR FOPLING. Are you women as fond of a vizard as we men are?

HARRIET. I am very fond of a vizard that covers a face I do not like, Sir.

YOUNG BELLAIR. Here are no masques you see, Sir, but those which came with you, this was intended a private meeting, but because you look like a gentleman, if you will discover your self and we know you to be such, you shall be welcome.

SIR FOPLING. Dear Bellair! [*Pulling off his mask.*

MEDLEY. Sir *Fopling*! How came you hither?

SIR FOPLING. Faith, as I was coming late from *White-Hall*, after the *King*'s Coucheé,[129] one of my people told me he had heard fiddles at my Lady *Townley*'s, and –

DORIMANT. You need not say any more, Sir.

SIR FOPLING. *Dorimant*, let me kiss thee.

DORIMANT. Hark you Sir Fopling? [*Whispers.*

SIR FOPLING. Enough, enough, Courtage. A pretty kind of young woman that, *Medley*, I observ'd her in the Mail more eveliè[130] than our English women commonly are, prithee what is she?

MEDLEY. The most noted coquetté[131] in town; beware of her.

SIR FOPLING. Let her be what she will, I know how to take my measures, in *Paris* the mode is to flatter the prudè,[132] laugh at the faux-prudè, make serious love to the demi-prudè, and only railly with the coquetté.[133] *Medley*, what think you?

MEDLEY. That for all this smattering of the mathematicks, you may be out in your judgment at tennis.

SIR FOPLING. What a Coque a Lasne[134] is this? I talk of women, and thou answer'st tennis.

MEDLEY. Mistakes will be for want of apprehension.

SIR FOPLING. I am very glad of the acquaintance I have with this family.

MEDLEY. My Lady truly is a good woman.

SIR FOPLING. Ah! *Dorimant*, Courtage I would say, would thou hadst spent the last winter in *Paris* with me. When thou wer't there La corneùs and Sallyes[135] were the only habitudes we had, a comedian would have been a boné fortune. No stranger ever pass'd his time so well as I did some months before I came over. I was well receiv'd in a dozen families, where all the women of quality us'd to come to a visit, I have intrigues to tell thee, more pleasant, than ever thou read'st in a novel.

HARRIET. Write 'em, Sir, and oblige us women! Our language wants such little stories.

SIR FOPLING. Writing, Madam, 's a mechanick part of wit! A gentleman should never go beyond a song or a billèt.

HARRIET. *Bussiè* was a gentleman.

SIR FOPLING. Who D'Ambois?

MEDLEY. Was there ever such a brisk blockhead?

HARRIET. Not D'Ambois, Sir, but Rubutin.[136] He who writ the Loves of France.

SIR FOPLING. That may be, Madam! Many gentlemen do things that are below 'em. Damn your authors, Courtage, women are the prettiest things we can fool away our time with.

HARRIET. I hope ye have weari'd your self to night at Court, Sir, and will not think of fooling with any body here.

SIR FOPLING. I cannot complain of my fortune there, Madam – *Dorimant* –

DORIMANT. Again!

SIR FOPLING. Courtage, a pox on't, I have something to tell thee. When I had made my court within, I came out and flung my self upon the matt under the state[137] i'th' outward room, i'th' midst of half a dozen beauties who were withdrawn to jeèr among themselves, as they call'd it.

DORIMANT. Did you know 'em?

SIR FOPLING. Not one of 'em by Heav'ns! Not I, but they were all your friends.

DORIMANT. How are you sure of that?

SIR FOPLING. Why we laugh'd at all the Town; spar'd no body but your self, they found me a man for their purpose.

DORIMANT. I know you are malitious to your power.

SIR FOPLING. And faith! I had occasion to shew it, for I never saw more gaping fools at a ball or on a birth-day.[138]

DORIMANT. You learn'd who the women were.

SIR FOPLING. No matter! They frequent the Drawing Room.[139]

DORIMANT. And entertain themselves pleasantly at the expence of all the fops who come there.

SIR FOPLING. That's their bus'ness, faith I sifted 'em, and find they have a sort of wit among them – Ah filthy. [*Pinches a tallow candle.*

DORIMANT. Look, he has been pinching the tallow candle.

SIR FOPLING. How can you breath in a room where there's grease frying! *Dorimant* thou art intimate with my Lady, advise her, for her own sake and the good company that comes hither, to burn wax lights.

HARRIET. What are these masquerades who stand so obsequiously at a distance?

SIR FOPLING. A set of Bulladins,[140] whom I pick'd out of the best in *France* and brought over, with a flutes deux or two, my servants; they shall entertain you.

HARRIET. I had rather see you dance your self, Sir *Fopling.*

SIR FOPLING. And I had rather do it – all the company knows it – but Madam –

MEDLEY. Come, come! No excuses Sir *Fopling.*

SIR FOPLING. By Heav'ns –

MEDLEY. Like a woman I find you must be struggl'd with before one brings you what you desire.

HARRIET. [*Aside to* Emilia] Can he dance?

EMILIA. And fence and sing too, if you'll believe him.

DORIMANT. He has no more excellence in his heels than in his head. He went to *Paris* a plain bashful English blockhead, and is return'd a fine undertaking *French fopp.*

MEDLEY. I cannot prevail.

SIR FOPLING. Do not think it want of complaisance, Madam.

HARRIET. You are too well bred to want that, Sir *Fopling.* I believe it want of power.

SIR FOPLING. By Heav'ns, and so it is. I have sat up so damn'd late and drunk so curs'd hard since I came to this lewd Town, that I am fit for nothing but low dancing now, a Corant, a Boreè, or a Minnuét:[141] but St. *Andrè*[142] tells me, if I will but be regular, in one month I shall rise agen. Pox on this debauchery. [*Endeavours at a caper.*

EMILIA. I have heard your dancing much commended.

SIR FOPLING. It had the good fortune to please in *Paris.* I was judg'd to rise within an inch as high as the Basqué[143] in an entry I danc'd there.

HARRIET. I am mightily taken with this fool, let us sit: here's a seat, Sir *Fopling.*

SIR FOPLING. At your feet, Madam; I can be no where so much at ease: by your leave, Gown.

HARRIET AND EMILIA. Ah! You'll spoil it.

SIR FOPLING. No matter, my cloaths are my creatures. I make 'em to make my court to you Ladies, Hey – Quon Comencè! [*Dance*]
[*To* John Trott, *the English Dancer*] English motions! I was forc'd to entertain[144] this fellow, one of my set miscarrying – Oh horrid! Leave your damn'd manner of dancing, and put on the French air: have you not a pattern before you – Pretty well! Imitation in time may bring him to something.

[*After the dance enter* Old Bellair, Lady Woodvil *and* Lady Townley.

OLD BELLAIR. Hey a Dod! What have we here, a mumming?

LADY WOODVIL. Where's my daughter – *Harriet.*

DORIMANT. Here, here, Madam! I know not but under these disguises there may be dangerous sparks, I gave the young Lady warning!

LADY WOODVIL. Lord! I am so oblig'd to you, Mr. *Courtage.*

HARRIET. Lord! How you admire this man!

LADY WOODVIL. What have you to except against him?

HARRIET. He's a fop.

LADY WOODVIL. He's not a *Dorimant,* a wild extravagant fellow of the times.

HARRIET. He's a man made up of forms and common places, suckt out of the remaining lees of the last age.

LADY WOODVIL. He's so good a man that were you not engag'd –

LADY TOWNLEY. You'll have but little night to sleep in.

LADY WOODVIL. Lord! 'Tis perfect day –

DORIMANT. [*Aside*] *The hour is almost come, I appointed Bellinda, and I am not so foppishly in love here to forget; I am flesh and blood yet.*

LADY TOWNLEY. I am very sensible, Madam.

LADY WOODVIL. Lord, Madam!

HARRIET. Look in what a struggle is my poor mother yonder?

YOUNG BELLAIR. She has much ado to bring out the complement?

DORIMANT. She strains hard for it.

HARRIET. See, see! Her head tottering, her eyes stairing, and her under-lip trembling –

DORIMANT. Now, now, she's in the very convulsions of her civility. –[*Aside*] *'Sdeath I shall lose Bellinda: I must fright her hence! She'll be an hour in this fit of good manners else.* – [*To* Lady Woodvil] Do you not know, Sir *Fopling,* Madam?

LADY WOODVIL. I have seen that Face – Oh Heav'n, 'tis the same we met in the Mail, how came he here?

DORIMANT. A fiddle in this Town is a kind of fop-call; no sooner it strikes up, but the house is besieg'd with an army of masquerades straight.

LADY WOODVIL. Lord! I tremble, Mr. *Courtage*! For certain *Dorimant* is in the company.

DORIMANT. I cannot confidently say he is not, you had best begon. I will wait upon you; your daughter is in the hands of Mr. *Bellair.*

LADY WOODVIL. I'll see her before me. *Harriet,* come away.

YOUNG BELLAIR. Lights! Lights!

LADY TOWNLEY. Light down there.

OLD BELLAIR. A Dod it needs not –

DORIMANT. Call my Lady *Woodvil*'s coach to the door quickly.

OLD BELLAIR. Stay, Mr. *Medley*, let the young fellows do that duty; we will drink a glass of wine together. 'Tis good after dancing! What mumming spark is that?

MEDLEY. He is not to be comprehended in few words.

SIR FOPLING. Hey! La Tower.

MEDLEY. Whither away, Sir *Fopling*?

SIR FOPLING. I have bus'ness with *Courtage*! –

MEDLEY. He'll but put the ladies into their coach and come up agen.

OLD BELLAIR. In the mean time I'll call for a bottle. [*Exit* Old Bellair.

[*Enter* Young Bellair.

MEDLEY. Where's Dorimant?

YOUNG BELLAIR. Stoln home! He has had business waiting for him there all this night, I believe, by an impatience I observ'd in him.

MEDLEY. Very likely, 'tis but dissembling drunkenness, railing at his friends, and the kind soul will embrace the blessing, and forget the tedious expectation.

SIR FOPLING. I must speak with him before I sleep!

YOUNG BELLAIR. *Emilia* and I are resolved on that business.

MEDLEY. Peace here's your father.

[*Enter* Old Bellair, *and* Butler *with a bottle of wine.*

OLD BELLAIR. The women are all gone to bed. Fill Boy! Mr. *Medley*, begin a health.

MEDLEY. To *Emilia*. [*Whispers.*

OLD BELLAIR. Out a pize! She's a rogue and I'll not pledge you.

MEDLEY. I know you well.

OLD BELLAIR. A Dod, drink it then.

SIR FOPLING. Let us have the new Bachique.

OLD BELLAIR. A Dod, that is a hard word! What does it mean, Sir?

MEDLEY. A catch, or drinking song.

OLD BELLAIR. Let us have it then.

SIR FOPLING. Fill the glasses round, and draw up in a body. Hey! Musick!

[*They sing.*

The pleasures of love and the joys of good wine,
To perfect our happiness wisely we joyn.
We to beauty all day
Give the soveraign sway,
And her favourite nymphs devoutly obey.
At the plays we are constantly making our court,
And when they are ended we follow the sport.
To the Mall and the Park
Where we love till 'tis dark;
Then sparkling champaigne
Puts an end to their reign;
It quickly recovers,
Poor languishing lovers,
Makes us frolick and gay, and drowns all our sorrow.
But alas! We relapse again on the morrow.
Let every man stand,
With his glass in his hand:
And briskly discharge at the word of command.
Here's a health to all those,
Whom to night we depose.
Wine and beauty by turns great souls should inspire.
Present all together; and now boys give fire –

OLD BELLAIR. A Dod, a pretty bus'ness and very merry.

SIR FOPLING. Hark you, Medley, let you and I take the fiddles, and go waken Dorimant.

MEDLEY. We shall do him a courtesy, if it be as I guess. For after the fatigue of this night, he'll quickly have his belly full: and be glad of an occasion to cry, take away, Handy.

YOUNG BELLAIR. I'll go with you, and there we'll consult about affairs, Medley.

OLD BELLAIR. [*Looks on his watch*] A Dod, 'tis six a clock.

SIR FOPLING. Let's away then.

OLD BELLAIR. Mr. *Medley*, my sister tells me you are an honest man. And a Dod I love you. Few words and hearty, that's the way with old *Harry*, old *Harry*.

SIR FOPLING. Light your Flambeux.[145] Hey.

OLD BELLAIR. What does the man mean?

MEDLEY. 'Tis day, Sir *Fopling*.

SIR FOPLING. No matter; our serenade will look the greater. [*Exit Omnes.*

Scene II.

[Dorimant*'s lodging, a table, a candle, a toilet, &c.* Handy *tying up linnen. Enter* Dorimant *in his gown, and* Bellinda.]

DORIMANT. Why will you be gone so soon?

BELLINDA. Why did you stay out so late?

DORIMANT. Call a chair, *Handy*! What makes you tremble so?

BELLINDA. I have a thousand fears about me: have I not been seen think you?

DORIMANT. By no body but my self and trusty *Handy*.

BELLINDA. Where are all your people?

DORIMANT. I have disperst 'em on sleeveless[146] errands. What does that sigh mean?

BELLINDA. Can you be so unkind to ask me? – Well – [*Sighs*] Were it to do again –

DORIMANT. We should do it, should we not?

BELLINDA. I think we should: the wickeder man you to make me love so well – will you be discreet now?

DORIMANT. I will –

BELLINDA. You cannot.

DORIMANT. Never doubt it.

BELLINDA. I will not expect it.

DORIMANT. You do me wrong.

BELLINDA. You have no more power to keep the secret, than I had not to trust you with it.

DORIMANT. By all the joys I have had, and those you keep in store –

BELLINDA. You'll do for my sake what you never did before –

DORIMANT. By that truth thou hast spoken, a wife shall sooner betray her self to her husband –

BELLINDA. Yet I had rather you should be false in this than in another thing you promis'd me.

DORIMANT. What's that?

BELLINDA. That you would never see *Loveit* more but in publick places, in the Park, at Court and plays.

DORIMANT. 'Tis not likely a man should be fond of seeing a damn'd old play when there is a new one acted.

BELLINDA. I dare not trust your promise.

DORIMANT. You may –

BELLINDA. This does not satisfy me. You shall swear you never will see her more.

DORIMANT. I will! A thousand oaths – by all –

BELLINDA. Hold – you shall not, now I think on't better.

DORIMANT. I will swear –

BELLINDA. I shall grow jealous of the oath, and think I owe your truth to that, not to your love.

DORIMANT. Then, by my love! No other oath I'll swear.

[*Enter* Handy.

HANDY. Here's a chair.

BELLINDA. Let me go.

DORIMANT. I cannot.

BELLINDA. Too willingly I fear.

DORIMANT. Too unkindly fear'd. When will you promise me again?

BELLINDA. Not this fortnight.

DORIMANT. You will be better than your word.

BELLINDA. I think I shall. Will it not make you love me less? [*Starting*] Heark! What fiddles are these? [*Fiddles without.*

DORIMANT. Look out, *Handy*!

[*Exit* Handy *and returns.*

HANDY. Mr. *Medley*, Mr. *Bellair*, and Sir *Fopling*. They are coming up.

DORIMANT. How got they in?

HANDY. The door was open for the chair.

BELLINDA. Lord! Let me fly –

DORIMANT. Here, here, down the back stairs. I'll see you into your chair.

BELLINDA. No, No! Stay and receive 'em: and be sure you keep your word and never see *Loveit* more. Let it be a proof of your kindness.

DORIMANT. It shall – *Handy*, direct her. Everlasting love go along with thee. [*Kissing her hand. Exit* Bellinda *and* Handy.

[*Enter* Young Bellair, Medley*, and* Sir Fopling.

YOUNG BELLAIR. Not a bed yet!

MEDLEY. You have had an irregular fit, *Dorimant.*

DORIMANT. I have.

YOUNG BELLAIR. And is it off already?

DORIMANT. Nature has done her part, Gentlemen, when she falls kindly to work, great cures are effected in little time, you know.

SIR FOPLING. We thought there was a wench in the case by the chair that waited. Prithee make us a confidence.

DORIMANT. Excuse me.

SIR FOPLING. Lè sagè,[147] *Dorimant* – was she pretty?

DORIMANT. So pretty she may come to keep her coach and pay parish duties if the good humour of the age continue.[148]

MEDLEY. And be of the number of the ladies kept by publick spirited men for the good of the whole Town.

SIR FOPLING. Well said, *Medley*. [Sir Fopling *dancing by himself.*

YOUNG BELLAIR. See Sir *Fopling* dancing.

DORIMANT. You are practising and have a mind to recover I see.

SIR FOPLING. Prithee *Dorimant*! Why hast not thou a glass hung up here? A room is the dullest thing without one!

YOUNG BELLAIR. Here is company to entertain you.

SIR FOPLING. But I mean in case of being alone. In a glass a man may entertain himself –

DORIMANT. The shadow of himself indeed.

SIR FOPLING. Correct the errours of his motions and his dress.

MEDLEY. I find Sir *Fopling* in your solitude, you remember the saying of the wise man, and study your self.

SIR FOPLING. 'Tis the best diversion in our retirements. *Dorimant*, thou art a pretty fellow, and wear'st thy cloaths well, but I never saw thee have a handsome crevat. Were they made up like mine, they'd give another aire to thy face. Prithee let me send my man to dress thee but one day. By Heav'ns an English man cannot tye a ribbon.

DORIMANT. They are something clumsy fisted –

SIR FOPLING. I have brought over the prettiest fellow that ever spread a toilet, he serv'd some time under *Merille* the greatest Genie in the World for a valet d' chambré.[149]

DORIMANT. What, he who formerly belong'd to the Duke of *Candale*? [150]

SIR FOPLING. The same, and got him his immortal reputation.

DORIMANT. Y'have a very fine Brandenburgh[151] on Sir *Fopling*.

SIR FOPLING. It serves to wrap me up, after the fatigue of a ball.

MEDLEY. I see you often in it, with your perriwig ty'd up.

SIR FOPLING. We should not always be in a set dress, 'tis more en Cavalier to appear now and then in a dissabilleé.[152]

MEDLEY. Pray how goes your business with *Loveit*?

SIR FOPLING. You might have answer'd your self in the Mail last night. *Dorimant*! Did you not see the advances she made me? I have been endeavouring at a song!

DORIMANT. Already!

SIR FOPLING. 'Tis my coup'd essay[153] in English, I would fain have thy opinion of it.

DORIMANT. Let's see it.

SIR FOPLING. Hey Page give me my song – *Bellair*, here, thou hast a pretty voice, sing it.

YOUNG BELLAIR. Sing it your self, Sir *Fopling*.

SIR FOPLING. Excuse me.

YOUNG BELLAIR. You learnt to sing in *Paris*.

SIR FOPLING. I did of *Lambert*[154] the greatest master in the World: but I have his own fault, a weak voice, and care not to sing out of a ruél.[155]

DORIMANT. A ruél is a pretty cage for a singing fop indeed.

YOUNG BELLAIR. [*Reads the song.*

How Charming Phillis is, how fair!
Ah that she were as willing,
To ease my wounded heart of care
And make her eyes less killing.
I sigh! I sigh! I languish now,
And love will not let me rest,
I drive about the Park, and bow
Still as I meet my dearest.

SIR FOPLING. Sing it, sing it man, it goes to a pretty new tune which I am confident was made by *Baptist*.[156]

MEDLEY. Sing it your self, Sir *Fopling*, he does not know the tune.

SIR FOPLING. I'll venture. [Sir Fopling *sings.*

DORIMANT. Ay marry! Now 'tis something. I shall not flatter you, Sir *Fopling*, there is not much thought in't, but 'tis passionate and well turn'd.

MEDLEY. After the French way.

SIR FOPLING. That I aim'd at – does it not give you a lively image of the thing? Slap down goes the glass,[157] and thus we are at it.

DORIMANT. It does indeed, I perceive, Sir *Fopling*, you'll be the very head of the sparks, who are lucky in compositions of this nature.

[*Enter* Sir Fopling*'s* Footman.

SIR FOPLING. *La Touer*, is the bath ready?

FOOTMAN. Yes, Sir.

SIR FOPLING. Adieu, don mes cheres. [*Exit* Sir Fopling.

MEDLEY. When have you your revenge on *Loveit*, *Dorimant*?

DORIMANT. I will but change my linen, and about it.

MEDLEY. The powerful considerations which hinder'd have bin remov'd then.

DORIMANT. Most luckily this morning, you must along with me, my reputation lyes at stake there.

MEDLEY. I am engag'd to *Bellair*.

DORIMANT. What's your business.

MEDLEY. Ma-tri-mony an't like you.

DORIMANT. It does not, Sir.

YOUNG BELLAIR. It may in time *Dorimant*, what think you of Mrs.[158] *Harriet*?

DORIMANT. What does she think of me?

YOUNG BELLAIR. I am confident she loves you.

DORIMANT. How does it appear?

YOUNG BELLAIR. Why she's never well but when she's talking of you, but then she finds all the faults in you she can. She laughs at all who commend you, but then she speaks ill of all who do not.

DORIMANT. Women of her temper betray themselves, by their over cunning. I had once a growing love with a lady, who would always quarrel with me when I came to see her, and yet was never quiet if I stay'd a day from her.

YOUNG BELLAIR. My father is in love with *Emilia*.

DORIMANT. That is a good warrant for your proceedings; go on and prosper, I must to *Loveit*. *Medley*, I am sorry you cannot be a witness.

MEDLEY. Make her meet Sir *Fopling* again in the same place, and use him ill before me.

DORIMANT. That may be brought about I think. I'll be at your aunt's anon, and give you joy, Mr. *Bellair*.

YOUNG BELLAIR. You had not best think of Mrs. *Harriet* too much, without church security there's no taking up there.

DORIMANT. I may fall into the snare too. But –

The wise will find a difference in our fate,
You wed a woman, I a good estate. [*Exeunt.*

Scene III.

[*Enter the chair with* Bellinda, *the men set it down and open it.* Bellinda *starting.*]

BELLINDA. Lord! Where am I? In the Mail? Whither have you brought me? [*Surpriz'd.*

1 CHAIRMAN. You gave us no directions, Madam?

BELLINDA. [*Aside*] *The fright I was in made me forget it.*

1 CHAIRMAN. We use to carry a lady from the Squire's hither.

BELLINDA. – [*Aside*] *This is Loveit, I am undone if she sees me.* – Quickly, carry me away.

1 CHAIRMAN. Whither, an't like your Honour?

BELLINDA. Ask no questions –

[*Enter* Loveit*'s* Footman.

FOOTMAN. Have you seen my Lady, Madam?

BELLINDA. I am just come to wait upon her –

FOOTMAN. She will be glad to see you, Madam. She sent me to you this morning, to desire your company, and I was told you went out by five a clock.

BELLINDA. [*Aside*] *More and more unlucky!*

FOOTMAN. Will you walk in, Madam?

BELLINDA. I'll discharge my chair and follow. [*Exit* Footman] Tell your Mrs. I am here. [*Gives the* Chairmen *money*] Take this! And if ever you should be examin'd, be sure you say, you took me up in the *Strand*, over against the *Exchange*, as you will answer it to Mr. *Dorimant*.

CHAIRMEN. We will an't like your Honour. [*Exit* Chairmen.

BELLINDA. Now to come off, I must on –

In confidence and lies some hope is left;
'Twere hard to be found out in the first theft.
[*Exit.*

Act V. Scene I.

[*Enter* Mrs. Loveit, *and* Pert *her Woman.*]

PERT. WELL! In my eyes Sir *Fopling* is no such despicable person.

LOVEIT. You are an excellent judge.

PERT. He's as handsome a man as Mr. *Dorimant*, and as great a gallant.

LOVEIT. Intolerable! Is't not enough I submit to his impertinences, but must I be plagu'd with yours too?

PERT. Indeed, Madam –

LOVEIT. 'Tis false, mercenary malice –

[*Enter her* Footman.

FOOTMAN. Mrs. Bellinda, Madam –

LOVEIT. What of her?

FOOTMAN. She's below.

LOVEIT. How came she?

FOOTMAN. In a chair, ambling Harry brought her.

LOVEIT. He bring her! His chair stands near *Dorimant*'s door, and always brings me from thence – run and ask him where he took her up; go, there is no truth in friendship neither. Women, as well as men, all are false, or all are so to me at least.

PERT. You are jealous of her too?

LOVEIT. You had best tell her I am. 'Twill become the liberty you take of late. This fellow's bringing of her, her going out by five a clock – I know not what to think.

[*Enter* Bellinda.

Bellinda, you are grown an early riser, I hear!

BELLINDA. Do you not wonder my Dear, what made me abroad so soon?

LOVEIT. You do not use to be so.

BELLINDA. The Country Gentlewomen I told you of (Lord! They have the oddest diversions!) would never let me rest till I promis'd to go with them to the markets this morning to eat fruit and buy nosegays.

LOVEIT. Are they so fond of a filthy nosegay?

BELLINDA. They complain of the stinks of the Town,[159] and are never well but when they have their noses in one.

LOVEIT. There are essences and sweet waters.

BELLINDA. O they cry out upon perfumes they are unwholesome, one of 'em was falling into a fit with the smell of these narolii.[160]

LOVEIT. Methinks in complaisance you shou'd have had a nosegay too.

BELLINDA. Do you think, my Dear, I could be so loathsome to trick my self up with carnations and stock-gilly flowers? I begg'd their pardon and told them I never wore any thing but orange flowers and tuberose. That which made me willing to go was, a strange desire I had to eat some fresh nectarens.

LOVEIT. And had you any?

BELLINDA. The best I ever tasted.

LOVEIT. Whence came you now?

BELLINDA. From their lodgings, where I crowded out of a coach, and took a chair to come and see you, my Dear;

LOVEIT. Whither did you send for that chair?

BELLINDA. 'Twas going by empty.

LOVEIT. Where do these Country Gentlewomen lodge I pray?

BELLINDA. In the *Strand* over against the Exchange.

PERT. That place is never without a nest of 'em, they are always as one goes by fleering in balconies or staring out of windows.

[*Enter* Footman.

LOVEIT. Come hither. [*To the* Footman; *whispers.*

BELLINDA. [*Aside*] *This fellow by her order has been questioning the chairmen! I threatn'd 'em with the name of Dorimant, if they should have told truth I am lost for ever.*

LOVEIT. In the *Strand* said you?

FOOTMAN. Yes Madam, over against the *Exchange.* [*Exit* Footman.

LOVEIT. She's innocent and I am much to blame.

BELLINDA. [*Aside*] *I am so frighted, my countenance will betray me.*

LOVEIT. *Bellinda*! What makes you look so pale?

BELLINDA. Want of my usual rest, and jolting up and down so long in an odious hackney.

[Footman *returns.*

FOOTMAN. Madam! Mr. *Dorimant*!

LOVEIT. What makes him here?

BELLINDA. [*Aside*] *Then I am betray'd indeed, h' has broke his word, and I love a man that does not care for me.*

LOVEIT. Lord! You faint, *Bellinda*!

BELLINDA. I think I shall! Such an oppression here on the sudden.

PERT. She has eaten too much fruit I warrant you.

LOVEIT. Not unlikely!

PERT. 'Tis that lyes heavy on her stomach.

LOVEIT. Have her into my chamber, give her some surfeit water,[161] and let her lye down a little.

PERT. Come, Madam! I was a strange devourer of fruit when I was young, so ravenous – [*Exit* Bellinda *and* Pert *leading her off.*

LOVEIT. Oh that my love would be but calm awhile! That I might receive this man with all the scorn and indignation he deserves.

[*Enter* Dorimant.

DORIMANT. Now for a touch of Sir *Fopling* to begin with. Hey – Page – give positive order that none of my people stir – let the cannile[162] wait as they should do – since noise and nonsense have such pow'rful charms,

I that I may successful prove,
Transform my self to what you love.[163]

LOVEIT. If that would do, you need not change from what you are, you can be vain and lowd enough.

DORIMANT. But not with so good a grace as Sir *Fopling*. Hey, *Hampshire* – oh – that sound, that sound becomes the mouth of a man of quality.

LOVEIT. Is there a thing so hateful as a senseless mimick?

DORIMANT. He's a great grievance indeed to all who like your self, Madam, love to play the fool in quiet.

LOVEIT. A ridiculous animal, who has more of the ape, than the ape has of the man in him.

DORIMANT. I have as mean an opinion of a sheer mimick as your self, yet were he all ape, I should prefer him to the gay, the giddy, brisk insipid noisy fool you doat on.

LOVEIT. Those noisy fools, however you despise 'em, have good qualities, which weigh more (or ought at least) with us women, than all the pernicious wit you have to boast of.

DORIMANT. That I may hereafter have a just value for their merit, pray do me the favour to name 'em.

LOVEIT. You'll despise 'em as the dull effects of ignorance and vanity! Yet I care not if I mention some. First, they really admire us, while you at best but flatter us well.

DORIMANT. Take heed! Fools can dissemble too –

LOVEIT. They may! But not so artificially as you – There is no fear they should deceive us! Then they are assiduous, Sir, they are ever offering us their service, and always waiting on our will.

DORIMANT. You owe that to their excessive idleness! They know not how to entertain themselves at home, and find so little welcome abroad, they are fain to fly to you who countenance 'em as a refuge against the solitude they would be otherwise condemn'd to.

LOVEIT. Their conversation too diverts us better.

DORIMANT. Playing with your fan, smelling to your gloves, commending your hair, and taking notice how 'tis cut and shaded after the new way –

LOVEIT. Were it sillier than you can make it, you must allow 'tis pleasanter to laugh at others, than to be laugh'd at our selves, though never so wittily. Then, though they want skill to flatter us, they flatter themselves so well, they save us the labour! We need not take that care and pains to satisfy 'em of our love, which we so often lose on you.

DORIMANT. They commonly indeed believe too well of themselves, and always better of you than you deserve.

LOVEIT. You are in the right, they have an implicit faith in us, which keeps 'em from prying narrowly into our secrets, and saves us the vexatious trouble of clearing doubts which your subtle and causeless jealousies every moment raise.

DORIMANT. There is an inbred falshood in women, which inclines 'em still to them, whom they may most easily deceive.

LOVEIT. The man who loves above his quality, does not suffer more from the insolent impertinence of his mistress, than the woman who loves above her understanding does from the arrogant presumptions of her friend.

DORIMANT. You mistake the use of fools, they are design'd for properties and not for friends, you have an indifferent stock of reputation left yet. Lose it all like a frank gamester on the square, 'twill then be time enough to turn rook, and cheat it up again on a good substantial bubble.[164]

LOVEIT. The old and the ill-favour'd are only fit for properties indeed, but young and handsome fools have met with kinder fortunes.

DORIMANT. They have, to the shame of your sex be it spoken, 'twas this, the thought of this made me by a timely jealousy, endeavour to prevent the good fortune you are providing for Sir *Fopling* – but against a woman's frailty all our care is vain.

LOVEIT. Had I not with a dear experience bought the knowledge of your falshood, you might have fool'd me yet. This is not the first jealousy you have feign'd to make a quarrel with me, and get a week to throw away on some such unknown inconsiderable slut, as you have been lately lurking with at plays.

DORIMANT. Women, when they would break off with a man, never want th' address to turn the fault on him.

LOVEIT. You take a pride of late in using of me ill, that the Town may know the power you have over me. Which now (as unreasonably as your self) expects that I (do me all the injuries you can) must love you still.

DORIMANT. I am so far from expecting that you should, I begin to think you never did love me.

LOVEIT. Would the memory of it were so wholly worn out in me, that I did doubt it too! What made you come to disturb my growing quiet?

DORIMANT. To give you joy of your growing infamy.

LOVEIT. Insupportable! Insulting devil! This from you, the only author of my shame! This from another had been but justice, but from you, 'tis a hellish and inhumane outrage. What have I done?

DORIMANT. A thing that puts you below my scorn, and makes my anger as ridiculous as you have made my love.

LOVEIT. I walk'd last night with Sir *Fopling*.

DORIMANT. You did, Madam, and you talk't and laught aloud ha, ha, ha – Oh that laugh, that laugh becomes the confidence of a woman of quality.

LOVEIT. You who have more pleasure in the ruine of a woman's reputation than in the indearments of her love, reproach me not with your self, and I defy you to name the man can lay a blemish on my fame.

DORIMANT. To be seen publickly so transported with the vain follies of that notorious fop, to me is an infamy below the sin of prostitution with another man.

LOVEIT. Rail on, I am satisfy'd in the justice of what I did, you had provok'd me to 't.

DORIMANT. What I did was the effect of a passion, whose extravagancies you have been willing to forgive.

LOVEIT. And what I did was the effect of a passion you may forgive if you think fit.

DORIMANT. Are you so indifferent grown?

LOVEIT. I am.

DORIMANT. Nay! Then 'tis time to part. I'll send you back your letters you have so often ask't for: I have two or three of 'em about me.

LOVEIT. Give 'em me.

DORIMANT. You snatch as if you thought I would not – there – and may the perjuries in 'em be mine, if ere I see you more. [*Offers to go, she catches him.*

LOVEIT. Stay!

DORIMANT. I will not.

LOVEIT. You shall.

DORIMANT. What have you to say?

LOVEIT. I cannot speak it yet.

DORIMANT. Something more in commendation of the fool. Death! I want patience, let me go.

LOVEIT. – [*Aside*] *I cannot. I can sooner part with the limbs that hold him.* – I hate that nauseous fool, you know I do.

DORIMANT. Was it the scandal you were fond of then?

LOVEIT. Y' had rais'd my anger equal to my love, a thing you ne're could do before, and in revenge I did – I know not what I did: – would you would not think on't any more.

DORIMANT. Should I be willing to forget it, I shall be daily minded of it, 'twill be a common place for all the Town to laugh at me, and *Medley*, when he is rhetorically drunk, will ever be declaiming on it in my ears.

LOVEIT. 'Twill be believ'd a jealous spite! Come, forget it.

DORIMANT. Let me consult my reputation, you are too careless of it. [*Pauses*] You shall meet Sir *Fopling* in the Mail again to night.

LOVEIT. What mean you?

DORIMANT. I have thought on it, and you must. 'Tis necessary to justify my love to the World: you can handle a coxcomb as he deserves, when you are not out of humour, Madam!

LOVEIT. Publick satisfaction for the wrong I have done you! This is some new device to make me more ridiculous!

DORIMANT. Hear me!

LOVEIT. I will not!

DORIMANT. You will be perswaded.

LOVEIT. Never.

DORIMANT. Are you so obstinate?

LOVEIT. Are you so base?

DORIMANT. You will not satisfy my love?

LOVEIT. I would die to satisfy that, but I will not, to save you from a thousand racks, do a shameless thing to please your vanity.

DORIMANT. Farewell false woman.

LOVEIT. Do! Go!

DORIMANT. You will call me back again.

LOVEIT. Exquisite fiend! I knew you came but to torment me.

[*Enter* Bellinda *and* Pert.

DORIMANT. *Bellinda* here! [*Surpriz'd.*

BELLINDA. [*Aside*] *He starts! And looks pale, the sight of me has toucht his guilty soul.*

PERT. 'Twas but a qualm as I said, a little indigestion; the Surfeit Water did it, Madam, mixt with a little Mirabilis.[165]

DORIMANT. I am confounded! And cannot guess how she came hither!

LOVEIT. 'Tis your fortune Bellinda ever to be here, when I am abus'd by this prodigy of ill nature.

BELLINDA. I am amaz'd to find him here! How has he the face to come near you?

DORIMANT. [*Aside*] *Here is fine work towards! I never was at such a loss before.*

BELLINDA. One who makes a publick profession of breach of faith and ingratitude! I loath the sight of him.

DORIMANT. There is no remedy, I must submit to their tongues now, and some other time bring my self off as well as I can.

BELLINDA. Other men are wicked, but then they have some sense of shame! He is never well but when he triumphs, nay! Glories to a woman's face in his villainies.

LOVEIT. You are in the right, *Bellinda*, but methinks your kindness for me makes you concern your self too much with him.

BELLINDA. It does indeed, my Dear! His barbarous carriage to you yesterday, made me hope you ne're would see him more, and the very next day to find him here again, provokes me strangely: but because I know you love him, I have done.

DORIMANT. You have reproach't me handsomely, and I deserve it for coming hither, but –

PERT. You must expect it, Sir! All women will hate you for my Lady's sake!

DORIMANT. Nay, if she begins too, 'tis time to fly! I shall be scolded to death else. – [*Aside to* Bellinda] I am to blame in some circumstances, I confess; but as to the main, I am not so guilty as you imagine. I shall seek a more convenient time to clear my self.

LOVEIT. Do it now! What impediments are here?

DORIMANT. I want time, and you want temper.

LOVEIT. These are weak pretences!

DORIMANT. You were never more mistaken in your life, and so farewell. [Dorimant *flings off.*

LOVEIT. Call a footman! *Pert*! Quickly, I will have him dogg'd.

PERT. I wish you would not for my quiet and your own.

LOVEIT. I'll find out the infamous cause of all our quarrels, pluck her mask off, and expose her bare-fac'd to the World.

BELLINDA. [*Aside*] *Let me but escape this time, I'll never venture more.*

LOVEIT. *Bellinda*! You shall go with me.

BELLINDA. I have such a heaviness hangs on me with what I did this morning, I wou'd fain go home and sleep, my Dear.

LOVEIT. Death! And eternal darkness. I shall never sleep again. Raging feavours seize the World, and make mankind as restless all as I am. [*Exit* Loveit.

BELLINDA. I knew him false and help'd to make him so. Was not her ruine enough to fright me from the danger? It should have been, but love can take no warning. [*Exit* Bellinda.

Scene II.

[Lady Townley's house. *Enter* Medley, Young Bellair, Lady Townley, Emilia *and* Chaplain.]

MEDLEY. Bear up, *Bellair*, and do not let us see that repentance in thine, we daily do in married faces.

LADY TOWNLEY. This wedding will strangely surprize my brother, when he knows it.

MEDLEY. Your nephew ought to conceal it for a time, Madam, since marriage has lost its good name, prudent men seldom expose their own reputations till 'tis convenient to justify their wives.

OLD BELLAIR. [*Without*] Where are you all there? Out, a Dod, will no body hear?

LADY TOWNLEY. My brother, quickly Mr. *Smirk*, into this closet,[166] you must not be seen yet. [*Goes into the closet.*

[*Enter* Old Bellair *and* Lady Townley*'s* Page.

OLD BELLAIR. Desire Mr. *Furb* to walk into the lower parlor, I will be with him presently – [*To* Young Bellair] Where have you been, Sir, you cou'd not wait on me to day?

YOUNG BELLAIR. About a business.

OLD BELLAIR. Are you so good at business? A Dod, I have a business too, you shall dispatch out of hand, Sir. Send for a parson, Sister; my Lady *Woodvil* and her daughter are coming.

LADY TOWNLEY. What need you huddle up things thus?

OLD BELLAIR. Out a pize, youth is apt to play the fool, and 'tis not good it should be in their power.

LADY TOWNLEY. You need not fear your son.

OLD BELLAIR. He has been idling this morning, and a Dod I do not like him. How dost thou do Sweet-heart? [*To* Emilia.

EMILIA. You are very severe, Sir, Marri'd in such haste!

OLD BELLAIR. Go too, thou'rt a rogue, and I will talk with thee anon. Here's my Lady *Woodvil* come.

[*Enter* Lady Woodvil, Harriet *and* Busy.

Welcome, Madam; Mr. *Furb*'s below with the writings.[167]

LADY WOODVIL. Let us down and make an end then.

OLD BELLAIR. Sister, shew the way. [*To* Young Bellair *who is talking to* Harriet] *Harry*, your business lyes not there yet! Excuse him till we have done Lady, and then a Dod he shall be for thee. Mr. *Medley* we must trouble you to be a witness.

MEDLEY. I luckily came for that purpose, Sir. [*Exit* Old Bellair, Medley, Young Bellair, Lady Townley *and* Lady Woodvil.

BUSY. What will you do, Madam?

HARRIET. Be carried back and mew'd up in the Country agen, run away here, any thing, rather than be married to a man I do not care for – Dear *Emilia*, do thou advise me!

EMILIA. Mr. *Bellair* is engag'd you know.

HARRIET. I do; but know not what the fear of losing an estate may fright him to.

EMILIA. In the desp'rate condition you are in, you should consult with some judicious man; what think you of Mr. *Dorimant*?

HARRIET. I do not think of him at all.

BUSY. She thinks of nothing else I am sure –

EMILIA. How fond your mother was of Mr. *Courtage*!

HARRIET. Because I contriv'd the mistake to make a little mirth, you believe I like the man.

EMILIA. Mr. *Bellair* believes you love him.

HARRIET. Men are seldome in the right when they guess at a woman's mind; would she whom he loves, lov'd him no better.

BUSY. [*Aside*] *That's e'n well enough on all conscience.*

EMILIA. Mr. *Dorimant* has a great deal of wit.

HARRIET. And takes a great deal of pains to shew it.

EMILIA. He's extremely well fashion'd.

HARRIET. Affectedly grave, or ridiculously wild and apish.

BUSY. You defend him still against your mother.

HARRIET. I would not were he justly rallied, but I cannot hear any one undeservedly rail'd at.

EMILIA. Has your woman learnt the song you were so taken with?

HARRIET. I was fond of a new thing, 'tis dull at second hearing.

EMILIA. Mr. *Dorimant* made it.

BUSY. She knows it, Madam, and has made me sing it at least a dozen times this morning.

HARRIET. Thy tongue is as impertinent as thy fingers.

EMILIA. You have provok'd her.

BUSY. 'Tis but singing the song and I shall appease her.

EMILIA. Prithee do.

HARRIET. She has a voice will grate your ears worse than a cat-call,[168] and dresses so ill, she's scarce fit to trick up a yeoman's daughter on a holyday.[169]

[Busy *sings.*

As Amoret with Phillis sat
One evening on the plain,
And saw the charming Strephon wait
To tell the Nymph his pain.

The threatning danger to remove
She whisper'd in her ear,
Ah Phillis, if you would not love,
This Shepherd do not hear.

None ever had so strange an art
His passion to convey
Into a listning virgin's heart
And steal her soul away.

Fly, fly betimes, for fear you give
Occasion for your fate.
In vain said she, in vain I strive,
Alas! 'Tis now too late.[170]

[*Enter* Dorimant.

DORIMANT. Musick so softens and disarms the mind.

HARRIET. That not one arrow does resistance find.[171]

DORIMANT. Let us make use of the lucky minute then.

HARRIET. [*Aside, turning from* Dorimant] *My love springs with my blood into my face, I dare not look upon him yet.*

DORIMANT. What have we here, the picture of celebrated beauty, giving audience in publick to a declar'd lover?

HARRIET. Play the dying fop, and make the piece compleat, Sir.

DORIMANT. What think you if the hint were well improv'd? The whole mystery of making love pleasantly design'd, and wrought in a suit of hangings?[172]

HARRIET. 'Twere needless to execute fools in effigie, who suffer daily in their own persons.

DORIMANT. [*To* Emilia *aside*] *Mrs. Bride, for such I know this happy day has made you.*

EMILIA. Defer the formal joy you are to give me, and mind your business with her –
[*Aloud*] Here are dreadful preparations, Mr. *Dorimant*, writings' sealing, and a parson sent for –

DORIMANT. To marry this Lady –

BUSY. Condemn'd she is, and what will become of her I know not, without you generously engage in a rescue.

DORIMANT. In this sad condition, Madam, I can do no less than offer you my service.

HARRIET. The obligation is not great, you are the common sanctuary for all young women who run from their relations.[173]

DORIMANT. I have always my arms open to receive the distressed. But I will open my heart and receive you, where none yet did ever enter – you have fill'd it with a secret, might I but let you know it –

HARRIET. Do not speak it, if you would have me believe it; your tongue is so fam'd for false-hood, 'twill do the truth an injury. [*Turns away her head.*

DORIMANT. Turn not away then; but look on me and guess it.

HARRIET. Did you not tell me there was no credit to be given to faces? That women now adays have their passions as much at will, as they have their complexions, and put on joy and sadness, scorn and kindness, with the same ease they do their paint and patches – are they the only counterfeits?

DORIMANT. You wrong your own, while you suspect my eyes, by all the hope I have in you, the inimitable colour in your cheeks is not more free from art, than are the sighs I offer.

HARRIET. In men who have been long harden'd in sin, we have reason to mistrust the first signs of repentance.

DORIMANT. The prospect of such a Heav'n will make me persevere, and give you marks that are infallible.

HARRIET. What are those?

DORIMANT. I will renounce all the joys I have in friendship and in wine, sacrifice to you all the interest I have in other women –

HARRIET. Hold – though I wish you devout, I would not have you turn fanatick – could you neglect these a while and make a journey into the Country?

DORIMANT. To be with you I could live there: and never send one thought to *London*.

HARRIET. What e're you say, I know all beyond *High-Park*'s a desart to you, and that no gallantry can draw you farther.

DORIMANT. That has been the utmost limit of my love – but now my passion knows no bounds, and there's no measure to be taken of what I'll do for you, from any thing I ever did before.

HARRIET. When I hear you talk thus in *Hampshire*, I shall begin to think there may be some truth inlarg'd upon.

DORIMANT. Is this all – will you not promise me –

HARRIET. I hate to promise! What we do then is expected from us, and wants much of the welcome it finds, when it surprizes.

DORIMANT. May I not hope?

HARRIET. That depends on you, and not on me, and 'tis to no purpose to forbid it. [*Turns to* Busy.

BUSY. Faith, Madam, now I perceive the gentleman loves you too, e'en let him know your mind, and torment your selves no longer.

HARRIET. Dost think I have no sense of modesty?

BUSY. Think, if you lose this, you may never have another opportunity.

HARRIET. May he hate me, (a curse that frights me when I speak it!) if ever I do a thing against the rules of decency and honour.

DORIMANT. [*To* Emilia] I am beholding to you for your good intentions, Madam.

EMILIA. I thought the concealing of our marriage from her, might have done you better service.

DORIMANT. Try her again –

EMILIA. What have you resolv'd, Madam? The time draws near.

HARRIET. To be obstinate and protest against this marriage.

[*Enter* Lady Townley *in haste.*

LADY TOWNLEY. [*To* Emilia] Quickly, quickly, let Mr. *Smirk* out of the closet. [Smirk *comes out of the closet.*

HARRIET. A parson! Had you laid him in here?

DORIMANT. I knew nothing of him.

HARRIET. Should it appear you did, your opinion of my easiness may cost you dear.

[*Enter* Old Bellair, Young Bellair, Medley, *and* Lady Woodvil.

OLD BELLAIR. Out a pize! The Canonical hour[174] is almost past; Sister, is the man of God come?

LADY TOWNLEY. He waits your leisure –

OLD BELLAIR. By your favour, Sir. A Dod, a pretty spruce fellow! What may we call him?

LADY TOWNLEY. Mr. *Smirk*! My Lady *Biggot*'s chaplain.

OLD BELLAIR. A wise woman! A Dod she is. The man will serve for the flesh as well as the spirit. Please you, Sir, to commission a young couple to go to bed together a God's name? – *Harry*.

YOUNG BELLAIR. Here Sir –

OLD BELLAIR. Out a pize. Without your mistriss in your hand!

SMIRK. Is this the gentleman?

OLD BELLAIR. Yes Sir!

SMIRK. Are you not mistaken, Sir?

OLD BELLAIR. A Dod, I think not, Sir.

SMIRK. Sure you are, Sir?

OLD BELLAIR. You look as if you would forbid the bains.[175] Mr. *Smirk*, I hope you have no pretention to the Lady!

SMIRK. Wish him joy, Sir! I have done him the good office to day already.

OLD BELLAIR. Out a pize, what do I hear?

LADY TOWNLEY. Never storm, Brother, the truth is out.

OLD BELLAIR. How say you, Sir! Is this your wedding day?

YOUNG BELLAIR. It is, Sir.

OLD BELLAIR. And a Dod it shall be mine too, [*To* Emilia] give me thy hand, Sweet-heart, What dost thou mean? Give me thy hand I say. [Emilia *kneels and* Young Bellair.

LADY TOWNLEY. Come come, give her your blessing, this is the woman your son lov'd, and is marry'd to.

OLD BELLAIR. Ha! Cheated! Cozen'd! And by your contrivance, Sister!

LADY TOWNLEY. What would you do with her? She's a rogue and you can't abide her.

MEDLEY. Shall I hit her a pat for you, Sir?

OLD BELLAIR. A Dod, you are all rogues, and I never will forgive you.

LADY TOWNLEY. Whither! Whither away?

MEDLEY. Let him go and cool awhile!

LADY WOODVIL. Here's a business broke out now, Mr. *Courtage*, I am made a fine fool of. [*To* Dorimant.

DORIMANT. You see the old gentleman knew nothing of it.

LADY WOODVIL. I find he did not. I shall have some trick put upon me if I stay in this wicked Town any longer. *Harriet*! Dear Child! Where art thou? I'll into the Country straight.

OLD BELLAIR. A Dod, Madam, you shall hear me first –

[*Enter* Loveit, *and* Bellinda.

LOVEIT. Hither my man dogg'd him! –

BELLINDA. Yonder he stands, my Dear.

LOVEIT. I see him. – [*Aside*] *And with him the face that has undone me! Oh that I were but where I might throw out the anguish of my heart, here it must rage within and break it.*

LADY TOWNLEY. Mrs. *Loveit*! Are you afraid to come forward?

LOVEIT. I was amaz'd to see so much company here in a morning, the occasion sure is extraordinary –

DORIMANT. [*Aside*] Loveit *and* Bellinda*! The Devil owes me a shame to day, and I think never will have done paying it.*

LOVEIT. Marry'd! Dear *Emilia*! How am I transported with the news?

HARRIET. I little thought *Emilia* was the woman Mr. *Bellair* was in love with – I'll chide her for not trusting me with the secret. [*To Dorimant.*

DORIMANT. How do you like Mrs. *Loveit*?

HARRIET. She's a fam'd Mrs. of yours I hear –

DORIMANT. She has been on occasion!

OLD BELLAIR. A Dod, Madam, I cannot help it. [*To* Lady Woodvil.

LADY WOODVIL. You need make no more apologies, Sir!

EMILIA. The old gentleman's excusing himself to my Lady *Woodvil*. [*To* Loveit.

LOVEIT. Ha, ha, ha! I never heard of any thing so pleasant.

HARRIET. She's extreamly overjoy'd at something. [*To* Dorimant.

DORIMANT. At nothing, she is one of those hoyting[176] ladies, who gayly fling themselves about, and force a laugh, when their aking hearts are full of discontent and malice.

LOVEIT. Oh Heav'n! I was never so near killing my self with laughing – Mr. *Dorimant*! Are you a brideman?

LADY WOODVIL. Mr. *Dorimant*! Is this Mr. *Dorimant*, Madam?

LOVEIT. If you doubt it, your daughter can resolve you, I suppose.

LADY WOODVIL. I am cheated too, basely cheated.

OLD BELLAIR. Out a pize, what's here more knavery yet!

LADY WOODVIL. *Harriet*! On my blessing come away I charge you.

HARRIET. Dear Mother! Do but stay and hear me.

LADY WOODVIL. I am betray'd and thou art undone I fear.

HARRIET. Do not fear it – I have not, nor never will do any thing against my duty – believe me! Dear Mother, do.

DORIMANT. I had trusted you with this secret, but that I knew the violence of your nature would ruin my fortune, as now unluckily it has: I thank you, Madam. [*To* Loveit.

LOVEIT. She's an heiress I know, and very rich.

DORIMANT. To satisfy you I must give up my interest wholly to my love, had you been a reasonable woman, I might have secur'd 'em both, and been happy –

LOVEIT. You might have trusted me with any thing of this kind, you know you might. Why did you go under a wrong name?

DORIMANT. The story is too long to tell you now, be satisfied, this is the business; this is the masque has kept me from you.

BELLINDA. [*Aside*] *He's tender of my honour, though he's cruel to my Love.*

LOVEIT. Was it no idle mistress then?

DORIMANT. Believe me a wife, to repair the ruines of my estate that needs it.

LOVEIT. The knowledge of this makes my grief hang lighter on my soul; but I shall never more be happy.

DORIMANT. Bellinda!

BELLINDA. Do not think of clearing your self with me, it is impossible – Do all men break their words thus?

DORIMANT. Th' extravagant words they speak in love; 'tis as unreasonable to expect we should perform all we promise then, as do all we threaten when we are angry – when I see you next –

BELLINDA. Take no notice of me, and I shall not hate you.

DORIMANT. How came you to Mrs. *Loveit*?

BELLINDA. By a mistake the chairmen made for want of my giving them directions.

DORIMANT. 'Twas a pleasant one. We must meet agen.

BELLINDA. Never.

DORIMANT. Never!

BELLINDA. When we do, may I be as infamous as you are false.

LADY TOWNLEY. Men of Mr. *Dorimant*'s character, always suffer in the general opinion of the World.

MEDLEY. You can make no judgment of a witty man from common fame, considering the prevailing faction, Madam –

OLD BELLAIR. A Dod, he's in the right.

MEDLEY. Besides 'tis a common errour among women, to believe too well of them they know, and too ill of them they don't.

OLD BELLAIR. A Dod, he observes well.

LADY TOWNLEY. Believe me, Madam, you will find Mr. *Dorimant* as civil a gentleman as you thought Mr. *Courtage*.

HARRIET. If you would but know him better –

LADY WOODVIL. You have a mind to know him better! Come away – You shall never see him more –

HARRIET. Dear Mother, stay –

LADY WOODVIL. I wo'not be consenting to your ruine –

HARRIET. Were my fortune in your power –

LADY WOODVIL. Your person is.

HARRIET. Could I be disobedient I might take it out of yours, and put it into his.

LADY WOODVIL. 'Tis that you would be at, you would marry this *Dorimant*.

HARRIET. I cannot deny it! I would, and never will marry any other man.

LADY WOODVIL. Is this the duty that you promis'd?

HARRIET. But I will never marry him against your will –

LADY WOODVIL. – [*Aside*] *She knows the way to melt my heart.* – [*To* Harriet] Upon your self light your undoing.

MEDLEY. [*To* Old Bellair] Come, Sir, you have not the heart any longer to refuse your blessing.

OLD BELLAIR. [*To* Emilia] A Dod, I ha'not – Rise and God bless you both – make much of her

Harry, she deserves thy kindness – A Dod Sirrah, I did not think it had been in thee.

[*Enter* Sir Fopling *and his* Page.

SIR FOPLING. 'Tis a damn'd windy day! Hey Page! Is my perriwig right?

PAGE. A little out of order, Sir!

SIR FOPLING. Pox o' this apartment, it wants an antichamber to adjust one's self in. Madam! I came from your house, and your servants directed me hither. [*To* Loveit.

LOVEIT. I will give order hereafter they shall direct you better.

SIR FOPLING. The great satisfaction I had in the Mail last night has given me much disquiet since.

LOVEIT. 'Tis likely to give me more than I desire.

SIR FOPLING. What the devil makes her so reserv'd? Am I guilty of an indiscretion, Madam?

LOVEIT. You will be of a great one, if you continue your mistake, Sir.

SIR FOPLING. Something puts you out of humour.

LOVEIT. The most foolish inconsiderable thing that ever did.

SIR FOPLING. Is it in my power?

LOVEIT. To hang or drown it, do one of 'em, and trouble me no more.

SIR FOPLING. So fierè serviteur,[177] Madam – *Medley*, where's *Dorimant*?

MEDLEY. Me thinks the Lady has not made you those advances to day she did last night, Sir *Fopling* –

SIR FOPLING. Prithee do not talk of her.

MEDLEY. She would be a bone[178] fortune.

SIR FOPLING. Not to me at present.

MEDLEY. How so?

SIR FOPLING. An intrigue now would be but a temptation to me to throw away that vigour on one which I mean shall shortly make my court to the whole sex in a ballet.

MEDLEY. Wisely consider'd, Sir *Fopling*.

SIR FOPLING. No one woman is worth the loss of a cut in a caper.

MEDLEY. Not when 'tis so universally design'd.

LADY WOODVIL. Mr. *Dorimant*, every one has spoke so much in your behalf, that I can no longer doubt but I was in the wrong.

LOVEIT. There's nothing but falsehood and impertinence in this World! All men are villains or fools; take example from my misfortunes. *Bellinda*, if thou would'st be happy, give thy self wholly up to goodness.

HARRIET. Mr. *Dorimant* has been your God Almighty long enough, 'tis time to think of another – [*To* Loveit.

LOVEIT. Jeer'd by her! I will lock my self up in my house, and never see the World again.

HARRIET. A nunnery is the more fashionable place for such a retreat, and has been the fatal consequence of many a belle passion.

LOVEIT. Hold heart! till I get home! Should I answer 'twould make her triumph greater. [*Is going out.*

DORIMANT. Your hand, Sir *Fopling* –

SIR FOPLING. Shall I wait upon you, Madam?

LOVEIT. Legion of Fools, as many Devils take thee. [*Exit* Loveit.

MEDLEY. *Dorimant*? I pronounce thy reputation clear – and hence forward when I would know any thing of woman, I will consult no other oracle.

SIR FOPLING. Stark mad, by all that's handsome! *Dorimant*, thou hast engag'd me in a pretty business.

DORIMANT. I have not leisure now to talk about it.

OLD BELLAIR. Out a pize, what does this man of mode do here agen?

LADY TOWNLEY. He'll be an excellent entertainment within, Brother, and is luckily come to raise the mirth of the company.

LADY WOODVIL. Madam, I take my leave of you.

LADY TOWNLEY. What do you mean, Madam?

LADY WOODVIL. To go this afternoon part of my way to *Hartly* –

OLD BELLAIR. A Dod you shall stay and dine first! Come we will all be good friends, and you shall give Mr. *Dorimant* leave to wait upon you and your daughter in the Country.

LADY WOODVIL. If his occasions bring him that way, I have now so good an opinion of him, he shall be welcome.

HARRIET. To a great rambling lone house, that looks as it were not inhabited, the family's so small; there you'll find my mother, an old lame aunt, and my self, Sir, perch'd up on chairs at a distance in a large parlour; sitting moping like three or four melancholy birds in a spacious vollary[179] – does not this stagger your resolution?

DORIMANT. Not at all, Madam! The first time I saw you, you left me with the pangs of love upon me, and this day my soul has quite given up her liberty.

HARRIET. This is more dismal than the Country! *Emilia*! pity me, who am going to that sad place. Methinks I hear the hateful noise of rooks already – kaw, kaw, kaw – there's musick in the worst cry in *London*! My Dill and Cowcumbers to pickle.[180]

OLD BELLAIR. Sister! knowing of this matter, I hope you have provided us some good chear.

LADY TOWNLEY. I have, Brother, and the fiddles too –

OLD BELLAIR. Let 'em strike up then, the young Lady shall have a dance before she departs. [*Dance.*

[*After the Dance.*

So now we'll in, and make this an arrant wedding day –

And if these honest Gentlemen rejoyce,
[To the Pitt.[181]
A Dod the boy has made a happy choice.
[Ex. Omnes.

The EPILOGUE by Mr *Dryden.*

Most modern wits, such monstrous fools have shown,
They seem'd not of Heav'n's making but their own.
Those nauseous Harlequins[182] in farce may pass,
But there goes more to a substantial ass!
Something of man must be expos'd to view,
That, Gallants, they may more resemble you:
Sir *Fopling* is a fool so nicely writ,
The ladies wou'd mistake him for a wit.
And when he sings, talks loud, and cocks; wou'd cry,
I vow methinks he's pretty company,
So brisk, so gay, so travail'd, so refin'd,
As he took pains to graft upon his kind.[183]
True fops help Nature's work, and go to school,
To file and finish God-a'mighty's fool.
Yet none Sir *Fopling* him, or him can call;
He's Knight o'th' Shire,[184] and represents ye all.
From each he meets, he culls what e're he can,
Legion's his name, a people in a man.
His bulky folly gathers as it goes,
And, rolling o're you, like a snow-ball growes.
His various modes from various fathers follow,
One taught the toss,[185] and one the new *French* wallow.[186]
His sword-knot, this; his crevat, this design'd,
And this, the yard long snake[187] he twirls behind.
From one the sacred perriwig he gain'd,
Which wind ne're blew, nor touch of hat prophan'd.
Another's diving bow he did adore,
Which, with a shog,[188] casts all the hair before:
'Till he with full decorum brings it back,
And rises with a water spaniel shake.
As for his songs (the ladies' dear delight)
Those sure he took from most of you who write.
Yet every man is safe from what he fear'd,
For no one fool is hunted from the herd.

3.2 JOHN WILMOT, EARL OF ROCHESTER, "A RAMBLE IN ST. JAMES PARK"

JOHN WILMOT, EARL OF ROCHESTER, *Poems on Several Occasions* [*1680?*] (Scholar Press, 1971): 14–19. RPO Edition: 2011. Adjacent to Whitehall Palace, St. James Park was landscaped by James I after his ascension to the throne in 1603 and became a site for keeping exotic animals. Upon his return from exile, Charles II, influenced by the formal gardens of the French, had the park re-landscaped in that style and opened the park to the public. It was notorious as a meeting place for sexual liasons.

A Ramble in St. James Park

John Wilmot, Earl of Rochester

Much Wine had past, with grave Discourse,
Of who Fucks who, and who do's worse;
Such as you usually do hear
From them that Diet at the *Bear*;[189]
When I, who still take care to see
Drunk'nness Reliev'd by Letchery,
Went out into St. *James*'s Park,
To cool my Head, and fire my Heart;
But though St. *James* has the Honour ont!
'Tis Consecrate to *Prick* and *Cunt*.
There, by a most Incestuous Birth,
Strange Woods Spring from the teeming Earth:
For they relate how heretofore
When Ancient *Pict*[190] began to Whore,
Deluded of his Assignation,[191]
(Jilting it seems was then in fashion.)
Poor pensive Lover in this place.
Wou'd Frig upon his Mothers Face;
Whence Rows of Mandrakes[192] tall did rise,
Whose Lewd tops Fuck'd the very Skies.
Each imitated Branch do's twine
In some Love Fold of *Aretine*:[193]
And nightly now beneath their Shade
Are Bugg'ries, Rapes, and Incests made,
Unto this All-sin-sheltring Grove,

Whores of the Bulk and the Alcove,[194]
Great Ladies, Chambermaids and Drudges,
The Rag-picker and Heires trudges;
Car-men, Divines, great Lords, and Taylers;
Prentices, Pimps, Poets, and Gaolers,
Foot-boys, fine Fops, do here arrive,
And here promiscuously they Swive.[195]
Along these hallow'd Walks it was
That I beheld *Corinna* pass;
Whoever had been by to see
The proud Disdain she cast on me,
Through Charming Eyes, he wou'd have Swore
She dropt from Heav'n that very Hour,
Forsaking the Divine Aboad
In scorn of some despairing God.
But mark what Creatures Women are,
How infinitely Vile and Fair.
Three Knights o' th' Elbow and the Slur,[196]
With wrigling Tails made up to her.
The first was of your *White-hall* Blades,[197]
Near Kin to the Mother of the Maids,
Grac'd by whose Favour he was able
To bring a Friend to the Waiters Table;[198]
Where he had heard Sir *Edward S—*
Say how the K— lov'd *Bansted* Mutton,[199]
Since when he'd ne're be brought to eat,
By's good will, any other Meat.
In this, as well as all the rest,
He ventures to do like the Best:
But wanting common Sence, th'Ingredient
In chusing well, not least expedient,
Converts Abortive Imitation
To universal Affectation;
So he not only eats and talks,
But feels and smells, sits down and walks,
Nay looks, and lives, and Loves by Rote,
In an old Tawdry Birth-day Coat.[200]
The Second was a *Grays-Inn-Wit*,[201]
A great Inhabiter of the Pit,[202]
Where Critick-like he sits and *Squints*,
Steals Pocket-handkerchiefs and *Hints*
From's Neighbour and the Comedy,

To Court and Pay his Landlady.
The Third a Ladies Eldest Son,
Within few Years of Twenty One,
Who hopes from his propitious Fate,
Against he comes to his Estate,
By these Two *Worthies* to be made
A most accomplish'd tearing *Blade*.
One in a strain 'twixt *Tune* and *Nonsense*,
Cries, *Madam, I have lov'd you long since,*
Permit me your fair Hand to Kiss:
When at her Mouth her Cunt says Yes.
In short without much more ado,
Joyful and pleas'd away she flew.
And with these Three confounded Asses
From Park to Hackney-Coach she passes.
So a Proud Bitch do's lead about
Of humble Curs the Amorous Rout,
Who most obsequiously do Hunt
The sav'ry Scent of Salt swoln Cunt.
Some Pow'r more patient now relate
The Scence of this surprizing Fate.
Gods! that a thing admir'd by me,
Shou'd taste so much of Infamy!
Had she pick'd out to rub her Arse on,
Some stiff-Prick'd Clown, or well-hung Parson,
Each Job[203] of whose Spermatick Sluce
Had fill'd her *Cunt* with whollsome Juice,
I the proceeding shou'd have prais'd,
In hope she had quencht a Fire I rais'd:
Such nat'ral freedoms are but Just,
There's something gen'rous in meer Lust;
But to turn Damn'd Abandon'd *Jade*,
When neither *Head* nor *Tail* perswade?
To be a *Whore* in understanding,
A Passive *Pot* for *Fools* to spend in,
The *Devil* plaid Booty sure with thee,[204]
To bring a Blot on Infamy.
But why was I, of all *Mankind*,
To so severe a Fate design'd?
Ungreatful! why this Treachery
To humble, fond, believing me?
Who gave you Priviledges above

The Nice Allowances of Love?
Did ever I refuse to bear
The meanest part your Lust cou'd spare?
When your lewd *Cunt* came spewing home,
Drench'd with the Seed of half the *Town*,
My Dram of Sperm was sup'd up after,
For the digestive Surfeit-Water.[205]
Full gorged at another time
With a vast *Meal* of Nasty Slime,
Which your devouring *Cunt* had drawn
From *Porters Backs*, and *Foot-mens* Brawn;
I was content to serve you up
My *Ballocks* full, for your *Grace Cup*;[206]
Nor ever thought it an Abuse,
While you had Pleasure for Excuse.
You that cou'd make my Heart away,
For Noise and Colours and betray
The Secrets of my tender Hours,
To such *Knight-Errant Paramours*,
When leaning on your faithless Breast,
Wrapt in security, and rest.
Soft Kindness all my pow'rs did move,
And reason lay dissolv'd in love.
May stinking *Vapour* choak your *Womb*,
Such as the *Men* you doat upon;
May your deprav'd Appetite,
That cou'd in whiffling *Fools* delight,
Beget such *Frenzies* in your *Mind*,
You may go Mad for the *North wind*.
And fixing all your hopes upon't,
To have him Bluster in your *Cunt*.
Turn up your longing Arse to th' Air,
And Perish in a wild despair.
But *Cowards* shall forget to Rant,
School-boys to Frig, old *Whores* to Paint:
The *Jesuits Fraternity*,
Shall leave the use of *Buggery*.
Crab-Lowse, inspir'd with Grace Divine,
From Earthly *Cod*, to *Heav'n* shall climb;
Physicians, shall believe in *Jesus*,
And disobedience cease to please us.
E're I desist with all my Power,

To plague this *Woman* and undo her.
But my Revenge will best be tim'd,
When she is *Marri'd* that is lim'd,[207]
In that most lamentable State,
I'll make her feel my Scorn, and Hate;
Pelt her with Scandals, Truth or Lies,
And her poor *Cur* with Jealousies.
Till I have torn him from her *Breech*,
While she whines like a *Dog-drawn Bitch*.[208]
Loath'd, and depriv'd, kickt out of *Town*,
Into some dirty hole alone,
To Chew the *Cud* of Misery,
And know she owes it all to me.

And may no Woman better thrive,
Who dares prophane the Cunt *I Swive.*

3.3 SIR RICHARD STEELE, *THE SPECTATOR*, NO. 65 (TUESDAY, MAY 15, 1711)

SIR RICHARD STEELE, *The Spectator*. Ed. Donald Bond. Vol. I. No. 65 (Tuesday, May 15, 1711). Oxford: The Clarendon Press 1965, 278–80. Steele was a literary and cultural critic who was also a successful playwright with *The Conscious Lovers* in 1722. He began writing *The Spectator* with Joseph Addison in 1711, and the periodical publication was an enduring model for cultural, social, and literary criticism throughout the century. Steele's agenda was to reform the theatre into a venue for moral instruction as well as entertainment and he contributed greatly to the shift from the witty, but morally careless comedies of the Restoration to the sentimental and moral comedies of the eighteenth century.

No. 65 Tuesday, May 15, 1711
Steele

. . . Demetri, teque, Tigelli,
Discipularum inter Jubeo plorare cathedras.[209]
Hor.

After having at large explained what Wit is, and described the false Appearances of it, all that Labour seems but an useless Enquiry, without some Time be spent in considering the Application of it. The Seat of Wit, when one speaks as a Man of the Town and the World, is the Play-house; I shall therefore fill this Paper with Reflections upon the Use of it in that Place. The Application of Wit in the Theatre has as strong an Effect upon the Manners of our Gentlemen, as the Taste of it has upon the Writing of our Authors. It may, perhaps, look like a very Presumptuous Work, tho' not Foreign from the Duty of a SPECTATOR, to tax the Writings of such as have long had the general Applause of a Nation: But I shall always make Reason, Truth, and Nature the Measures of Praise and Dispraise; if those are for me, the Generality of Opinion is of no Consequence against me; if they are against me, the General Opinion cannot long support me.

Without further Preface, I am going to look into some of our most Applauded Plays, and see whether they deserve the Figure they at present bear in the Imaginations of Men, or not.

In reflecting upon these Works, I shall chiefly dwell upon that for which each respective Play is most celebrated. The present Paper shall be employed upon Sir *Foplin Flutter*. The Received Character of this Play is, That it is the Pattern of Gentile Comedy. *Dorimant* and *Harriot* are the Characters of Greatest Consequence, and if these are Low and Mean, the Reputation of the Play is very Unjust.

I will take for granted, that a fine Gentleman should be honest in his Actions, and refined in his Language. Instead of this, our Hero, in this Piece, is a direct Knave in his Designs, and a Clown in his Language. Bellair is his admirer and Friend, in return for which, because he is forsooth a greater Wit than his said Friend, he thinks it reasonable to perswade him to Marry a young Lady, whose Virtue, he thinks, will last no longer than 'till she is a Wife, and then she cannot but fall to his Share, as he is an irresistible fine Gentleman. The Falshood to Mrs. *Loveit*, and the Barbarity of Triumphing over her Anguish for losing him, is another Instance of his Honesty, as well as his good Nature. As to his fine Language; he calls the Orange Woman, who, it seems, is inclined to grow Fat, *An Over-grown Jade, with a Flasket of Guts before her*; and salutes her with a pretty Phrase of, *How now, Double Tripe?* Upon the Mention of a Country Gentlewoman, whom he knows nothing of, (no one can imagine why) he *will lay his Life she is some awkard, ill-fashioned Country Toad, who not having above four Dozen of Hairs on her Head, has adorned her Baldness with a large white Fruz, that she may look Sparkishly in the Fore-front of the King's Box at an old Play*. Unnatural Mixture of senseless Common Place!

As to the Generosity of his Temper, he tells his poor Footman, *If he did not wait better*— he would turn him away, in the insolent Phrase of, *I'll Uncase you*.

Now for Mrs. *Harriot*: She laughs at Obedience to an absent Mother, whose Tenderness *Busie* describes to be very exquisite, for *that she is so pleased with finding* Harriot *again, that she cannot chide her for being out of the Way*. This Witty Daughter, and Fine Lady, has so little Respect for this good Woman, that she Ridicules her Air in taking Leave, and cries, *In what Struggle is my poor Mother yonder? See, See, her Head tottering, her Eyes staring, and her under Lip trembling*. But all this atoned for, because *she has more Wit than is usual in her Sex, and as much Malice, tho' she is as Wild as you would wish her, and has a Demureness in her Looks that makes it so surprising!* Then to recommend her as a fit Spouse for his Hero, the Poet makes her speak her Sense of Marriage very ingeniously. *I Think*, says she, *I might be brought to endure him, and that is all a reasonable Woman should expect in an Husband*. It is, methinks, unnatural that we are not made to understand how she that was bred under a silly pious old Mother, that would never trust her out of her Sight, came to be so Polite.

It cannot be denied, but that the Negligence of every thing, which engages the Attention of the sober and valuable Part of Mankind, appears very well drawn in this Piece: But it is denied, that it is necessary to the Character of a Fine Gentleman, that he should in that manner Trample upon all Order and Decency. As for the Character of *Dorimant*, it is more of a Coxcomb than that of *Foplin*. He says of one of his Companions,[210] that a good Correspondence between them is their mutual Interest. Speaking of that Friend, he declares, their being much together *makes the Women think the better of his Understanding, and judge more favourably of my Reputation. It makes him pass upon some for a Man of very good Sense, and me upon others for a very civil Person*.

This whole celebrated Piece is a perfect Contradiction to good Manners, good Sense, and common Honesty; and as there is nothing in it but what is built upon the Ruin of Virtue and Innocence, according to the Notion of Merit in this Comedy, I take the

Shoomaker to be, in reality, the fine Gentleman of the Play: For it seems he is an Atheist, if we may depend upon his Character as given by the Orange-Woman, who is her self far from being the lowest in the Play. She says of a fine Man, who is *Dorimant*'s Companion, There *is not such another Heathen in the Town, except the Shoe-maker.* His Pretention to be the Hero of the *Drama* appears still more in his own Description of his way of Living with his Lady. *There is,* says he, *never a Man in Town lives more like a Gentleman with his Wife than I do; I never mind her Motions; she never enquires into mine. We speak to one another civilly, hate on another heartily; and because it is Vulgar to Lye and Soak together, we have each of us our several Settle-Bed.* That of *Soaking together* is as good as if *Dorimant* had spoken it himself; and, I think, since he puts Humane Nature in as ugly a Form as the Circumstance will bear, and is a staunch Unbeliever, he is very much Wronged in having no part of the good Fortune bestowed in the last Act.

To speak plainly of this whole Work, I think nothing but being lost to a Sense of Innocence and Virtue can make any one see this Comedy, without observing more frequent Occasion to move Sorrow and Indignation, than Mirth and Laughter. At the same time I allow it to be Nature, but it is Nature in its utmost Corruption and Degeneracy.[211]

3.4 ANONYMOUS, *PORTRAIT OF JOHN WILMOT, EARL OF ROCHESTER*

Unknown Artist, *John Wilmot, 2nd Earl of Rochester*, circa 1665–1670. National Portrait Gallery, London.

Notes

1–2 This text is based on the first edition printed by *I. Macock*, for *Henry Herringman*, in London at the Sign of the *Blew Anchor* in the Lower Walk of the *New Exchange*, 1676. It was corrected against a 1684 edition.

3 See an excerpt from Dennis' lengthy defense of the play in the online supplement to this volume.

4 Jeremy W. Webster, *Performing Libertinism in Charles II's Court: Politics, Drama, Sexuality*. New York: Palgrave Macmillan, 2005, 1–36.

5 It was customary, in fact, for aristocratic young men of fashion to pay extra for seats upon the stage where they sat throughout a play's performance, literally becoming a part of theatrical spectacle.

6 Mary Modena, Duchess of York. In 1673, she was married to James, the openly Catholic brother of Charles II and the (short-lived) successor to the British throne after Charles' death in 1786.

7 Poet and courtier.

8 Rope dancing was a popular form of entertainment at fairs and, after plays, in the London theatres.

9 Mistress.

10 Showy staging and over-acting (as in making ridiculous faces in order to draw a laugh).

11 A list of actors was not published with the first editions of this play. The prompter John Downes records that the accomplished and renowned Thomas Betterton, thought to be the greatest English actor after Richard Burbage and before David Garrick, played Dorimant, and Elizabeth Barry, the mistress and protégée of the libertine courtier, John Wilmot, Earl of Rochester, was not the first, but one of the most successful Mrs. Loveits of the Restoration stage. Medley was played by Henry Harris, Fopling by the barrister-turned-actor and duelist, William Smith, Old Bellair by the well-known comic actor Anthony Leigh, and Young Bellair by Thomas Jevon, reported by *The Biographical Dictionary of Actors* as a "low comedian by nature" who "was cast in serious roles at a playwright's peril." Bellinda was played by Mary Betterton, Thomas' wife, Lady Woodvil by Elinor Leigh, Anthony's wife, and Emilia by Mrs. Timothy Twiford (her first known role).

12 Women who sell fruit, primarily oranges; they also worked as prostitutes in the theatres. As this character shows us, they could retail in gossip and enable gentlemen's access to other women.

13 Men who made their living by carrying paying customers in sedan chairs through the often muddy streets of London.

14 Articles needed for dressing and general personal grooming.

15 Opening verses of Edmund Waller, "Of a War with Spain, and a Fight at Sea."

16 The "fanatic" would be a religious dissenter, a Protestant who does not subscribe to the Church of England. The Royal and church duties were taxes that a dissenter would be unwilling to pay.

17 A lower to middle class neighborhood of London.

18 A gold coin worth about ten shillings.

19 A peach from Newington, Kent.

20 Short, curly wig.

21 The New Exchange, a fashionable place for strolling and shopping.

22 A woman wearing a mask. Masks were often associated with prostitutes, but they were also worn by respectable women for privacy.

23 Formal door keepers.

24 An old, experienced hand.

25 Wine from the Canary Islands.

26 Restive.

27 Like the Devil.

28 One who "keeps" a mistress.

29 Lawyers.

30 Last resort.

31 Patching in the sense of making up, but also a pun on the practice of women applying artificial beauty marks or patches to enhance their attractiveness.

32 A masked woman, often a prostitute.

33 An hysterical fit.

34 Is careful or "tender" of.
35 A beautiful, witty woman.
36 Strip you of your livery, or uniform.
37 A punishment for libel, among other crimes, involving stocks that held the prisoner's hands and sometimes feet so as to immobilize them in a public place where they could be subject to the punishing abuse of London street people.
38 Traditional songs, sold in print form and sung by hawkers in the streets.
39 A pun on "commentary" in the dual sense of treatise and satire.
40 "Truth is in ale as in history."
41 A contraction for "God's blood," an oath.
42 Ragout.
43 Drunk.
44 Robin is a common way of addressing a servant.
45 Bethlehem Hospital for the insane in London.
46 Securities.
47 Galoshes.
48 Embarrassed.
49 Tortured by anticipation.
50 Fashionable taverns, places to eat.
51 A coach available for hire, like a taxi cab today.
52 Echoes the French word "fourbe," to cheat.
53 Center of London's legal profession.
54 Fashionable card game.
55 Also spelled "termagant." A term applied to a violently quarrelsome and over-bearing person, usually a woman.
56 Card player.
57 Gleek was a card game.
58 Fake hair worn in front, at the forehead.
59 A high trump card.
60 Pieces of lace.
61 Ornamental ribbons or ties on a garment.
62 High-pitched flutes and French hautboys or oboes.
63 Use cosmetics on the face.
64 Theatrical dancers.
65 An arena in London where bears were baited—not a place of high theatrical culture.
66 Actors.
67 Many eminent people were buried in Westminster Abbey, which was, as now, a draw for sight-seers.
68 Revealing, usually low-cut dress.
69 First lines of Edmund Waller's "Of her Chamber."
70 A country dance.
71 Matthew Roydon, "An Elegy . . . for his Astophel."
72 A fashionable walk in St. James Park.
73 Travel. It was customary for fashionable young gentlemen to travel in Europe, primarily France and Italy to "finish" their educations.
74 1 Samuel. Merab was promised to King David, but married to Adriel. Based on Abraham Cowley's *Davideis*, Book III.
75 Bartholomew Cokes in Ben Jonson's play *Bartholomew Fair,* a play set during the annual fair by that name held in August. Cokes is a rabid consumer who wants to buy everything in sight.
76 Commonly sold at the fair.
77 As in a conspiracy against the others.
78 Grinning.
79 Actors and women who keep retail stalls in the New Exchange.

80 Count.
81 Circular path in Hyde Park.
82 Henry Muddiman (1629–1692) was the publisher of some early journals prefiguring modern newspapers and a writer about society news.
83 Taverns.
84 *Embarras*, an overabundance.
85 Gatherings of fashionable people.
86 Well-known gardens in Paris.
87 Brilliance.
88 A lace worked with gold or silver needlepoint, of Spanish origin.
89 A Venetian lace popular in the seventeenth century characterized by its floral rather than geometric patterns.
90 *Caleche*, a light carriage with a folding roof—essentially, an early version of a convertible.
91 A cart used for homely purposes, such as carrying dung.
92 Someone who works (such as a lawyer) as opposed to a true gentleman, who does not have to work for a living.
93 Crude.
94 Well-gloved.
95 Ornament or trimming added to clothes.
96 These are all names of famous French merchants.
97 Scented with orange.
98 Confuses the brain, as wine does.
99 Charles I, who was executed in 1649. His reign was followed by the Interregnum government; hence, there is a spread of over a decade between the last and the present king's reign.
100 Waller, "To a Friend, of the Different Success of their Loves"
101 Another name for Hyde Park, along with St. James, one of the fashionable public parks of London.
102 Leers.
103 Limit.
104 Waller, "Of Loving at First Sight."
105 *Eclaircissement.* Clarification.
106 Sir John Suckling, "Sonnet I."
107 Bundled into.
108 Whitehall Palace, the primary residence of the British monarchy until large portions were destroyed by fire in 1698.
109 From a popular song that came out the same year as the play.
110 Scented powder.
111 Copulation.
112 A ripe target for plunder.
113 They understand what we are saying.
114 A kind of leather made in Cordova, Spain.
115 Flutes—tall, thin people.
116 A decayed tooth that smells.
117 Overshoes.
118 Middle-class servants, attendants.
119 Trot.
120 The gardens at the Inns of Court in Holborn.
121 Your servants' uniforms.
122 Echoing lines in Waller's "Of the Danger his Majesty (Being Prince Escaped . . ."
123 A square of material worn by a woman around her neck and covering the upper part of her bosom.
124 Laundress.
125 To caper is to perform a high jump or kick in dance; Old Bellair would have kicked up to his partner's neckscarf.
126 Makes eyes at.

127 People wearing masques and fancy costumes that disguise their identities. Masquerades were a popular form of entertainment at public and private gatherings; masquerades also used their festive disguises to crash parties and other gatherings to which they had not been invited.
128 Costume.
129 Evening reception.
130 A mispronunciation of the French word *eveillee*, meaning sprightly.
131 The final e in this word is usually not accented—Medley is mocking Sir Fopling's bad French, of which we have a long example in the latter's next speech.
132 A person, usually female, who affects rigid moral standards, particularly in the realm of sexuality.
133 Different kinds of women who affect various levels of prudery; the coquette is a woman more interested in flirting than in serious romantic commitment.
134 Nonsense.
135 Mesdames Corneul and Selles, women of literary reputations.
136 Sir Fopling confuses the French author Roger de Rabutin, Comte de Bussy, with the character of Bussy d'Ambois, the hero of a play by George Chapman.
137 Canopy.
138 The King's birthday.
139 A reception at the King's Drawing Room.
140 Balladines.
141 Formal, stately dances.
142 A famous French dancing master.
143 The skirt of a coat.
144 Hire.
145 Torches.
146 Meaningless, useless.
147 The wise man.
148 That is, toleration for prostitution.
149 Valet to the Duke of Orleans.
150 A famous French courtier and general.
151 A coat usually worn in the morning, typically less formal than evening dress.
152 Casually dressed.
153 First effort.
154 Musician of Louis XIV's court.
155 *Ruelle*, a lady's bed chamber.
156 Another musician of Louis XIV's court.
157 The coach window.
158 A title of respect not confined to married women.
159 The sewage system of London was an open kennel, or trench, in the streets, from which waste flowed into the Thames. It must have been a strongly smelling place. Ladies would hold nosegays, small bouquets of flowers, to their noses to block the smell.
160 Essence of orange.
161 A medicinal drink for treating indigestion.
162 The rabble.
163 Waller, "To the Mutable Fair."
164 Dupe.
165 Spiced wine drink.
166 A small room, often off a bedroom, used for private tasks such as reading, writing, and praying; also useful as a hiding place in many comedies.
167 Financial agreements around the marriage.
168 A rude noise made by theatre audiences when the performance was disliked.
169 A working artisan's daughter on a holiday.
170 Song by either Sir Car Scroope or Sir Charles Sedley, two high-profile courtiers.
171 Waller, "Of My Lady Isabella, Playing on the Lute."

172 Tapestries to warm and decorate rooms.
173 John Wilmot, Earl of Rochester, on whom the character of Dorimant is based, notoriously kidnapped and married his wife.
174 The times when marriages could be legally performed, as determined by the Church.
175 Forbid the bans, or call off the marriage.
176 Romping, roughly playful.
177 "So haughty? Your servant, madam."
178 Good.
179 Aviary.
180 Street-vender's cry.
181 The general part of the audience where the middling classes usually sat.
182 The character of Harlequin was just gaining popularity on the London stage in pantomimes that would become one of the most popular—and criticized—forms of theatrical entertainment in the century.
183 To improve upon his kind.
184 Member of the British parliament.
185 Toss of the head.
186 Affected, rolling gait.
187 Tail of a wig.
188 Shake.
189 Eat at a well-known local tavern.
190 An ancient Celtic people who inhabited regions of what are now northern and eastern Scotland.
191 Disappointed by a lover who failed to meet him for sex.
192 A medicinal plant, the roots of which were alleged to have mystical healing powers and to resemble human legs.
193 Editions of sixteenth-century sonnets by Pietro Aretino were accompanied by illustrations of sexual postures.
194 The bulk and the alcove refer to women of the lowest and highest sort, respectively. "Bulk" could refer to a pile or heap of cargo, usually fish, and "bulk" also was a slang term for the assistant to one of the many pickpockets on the London streets. "Alcove" in this case probably refers to a secluded recess or nook in a garden to which a couple might go for privacy.
195 To swive is to copulate.
196 Gamblers. To slur was to cheat at the gaming table, particularly in dice games.
197 Whitehall was the home of the Restoration court. This courtier has gained entrance by being related to one of the Queen's maids of honor.
198 The table for those who wait on the King.
199 "Mutton" was slang for prostitutes. Sir Edward Sutton (d. 1695), a Gentleman Usher and Daily Waiter to the King, had remarked of Charles II's fondness for mutton, sheep's or lamb's meat, from Banstead Downs, Surrey.
200 Part of a fine suit, to be worn in honor of the king's or queen's birthday.
201 Gray's Inn was one of the Inns of Court, a center for legal training, and the workplace of many writers for the stage. Law clerks often made attempts at sophistication by composing amateur literary criticism.
202 Frequent theatregoer.
203 Thrust.
204 To play booty is to join with confederates in antagonizing or victimizing another, particularly while playing a game.
205 A remedy for indigestion or overdrinking.
206 *Ballocks*: testicles; *Grace Cup*: the final drink, after grace is said at the end of a meal.
207 To be limed was to be caught, as in a "limed bird." In this case, being caught probably means pregnant.
208 To "dog-draw" is to track an illegally wounded or killed game animal by using a dog to follow the scent.

209 *Motto*. Horace, *Satires*, I. 10. 90–91:
Demetrius and Tigellius, know your place;
Go hence, and whine among the school-boy race.

210 Bellair.

211 See John Dennis' *Defence of Sir Fopling Flutter* (in the online supplement).

---

4. *All for Love: or, the World Well Lost*

ALL FOR LOVE: OR, THE WORLD WELL LOST. **A TRAGEDY, AS IT IS ACTED AT THE THEATRE-ROYAL; AND WRITTEN IN IMITATION OF SHAKESPEARE'S STILE.[1] JOHN DRYDEN. FIRST PERFORMED 12 DECEMBER 1677 (?) AND FIRST PUBLISHED 1678**

4.1 *ALL FOR LOVE: OR, THE WORLD WELL LOST.* A TRAGEDY, AS IT IS ACTED AT THE THEATRE-ROYAL; AND WRITTEN IN IMITATION OF SHAKESPEARE'S STILE.[2]

John Dryden.

First Performed 12 December 1677 (?) and First Published 1678

ALL FOR LOVE'S FIRST PERFORMANCE and its first printing shortly after together constitute a cultural performance "about" the religious, moral, and political uncertainties of its first audiences and readers. John Dryden was at the most prosperous stretch of his writing career, having been appointed Poet Laureate in 1668 and Historiographer Royal in 1670. The play's long dedication to Thomas Osbourne, Earl of Danby, reflects the playwright's navigation of the complicated court politics of the 1670s, as does the lengthy preface; both were printed with the first edition and retained in all subsequent editions of the 1600s and can be read in the online supplement to this text.

While the Restoration of Charles II to the English throne had ended the rule of anti-monarchical, parliamentary government, the country—and the court—were still riven by religious and political divisions, and the government of Charles was struggling to survive both politically and financially. Danby was a key figure in managing both those divisions and precarious finances. While Danby was responsible for paying Dryden's salary, the poet in fact derived most of his income during this decade from his theatre work, not court patronage; Dryden's appeal to Danby had more to do with the latter's influence on court policies than with his control of the purse strings. Although Danby had inherited a dangerously chaotic treasury he was effective in restoring the monarchy to fiscal stability. His politics, however, cut against Charles' general tendency towards religious toleration. While the King was inclined to extend rights to dissenting Protestants and was sympathetic to Catholics, Danby supported a strictly Anglican body politic and was hostile towards Catholics and the French court, with whom Charles had lived in exile and retained cultural and financial ties. He was also, however, sexually involved with the king's politically powerful French mistress, Louise de Keroualle, the Duchess of Portland. *All For Love* plays on the political, religious, and personal ambivalences with which choices between power and pleasure, duty and love, were faced by the King and his ministers.

The preface, on the other hand, (also available in the online supplement) like so many of Dryden's prefaces, claims space for the poet as a professional aesthetician, as critic as well as playwright, pushing against the authority and power of courtly poets, particularly John Wilmot, Earl of Rochester (the model for Etherege's Dorimant in *The Man of Mode*) with whom Dryden was feuding. Dryden scathingly alludes to "Men of pleasant conversation, (at least esteem'd so) and indu'd with a trifling kind of fancy, perhaps help'd out with some smattering of Latin":

> [I]s not this a wretched affectation, not to be contented with what fortune has done for them, and sit down quietly with their estates, but they must call their wits in question, and needlessly expose their nakedness[3] to publick view?

The work of criticism, as well as poetry, Dryden claims for himself as a professional writer. The precedent that Dryden evokes in defiance of the courtly, libertine wit, is Shakespeare:

> [H]e who began dramatick poetry amongst us, untaught by any, and, as *Ben Johnson* tells us, without learning, should by the force of his own genius perform so much, that in a manner he has left no praise for any who come after him.

All For Love is not the first adaptation of a Shakespeare play, but it helped to establish Shakespeare—not the courtly, aristocratic gentleman poet—as model for the professional playwright.

The prefatory material, hence, evokes many of the public and courtly "dramas" that haunt this play: the Duchess's highly politicized romances ghost Cleopatra's dramatic performances of a woman desired by many; Dollabella's contradictory love for Cleopatra, despite his loyalty to Rome, Ventidius' hardline patriotism, and Antony's vacillations all resonate with the choices and ambivalences of political life in the 1670s. The ghost of Shakespeare haunts the performance of the professional playwright beginning to claim authority over the artistic and cultural work of the theatre.

We have little information about how it was first received, but it was a fairly popular play through the eighteenth century, with 123 performances before 1800. It was given a lavishly produced revival in 1718, and the role of Cleopatra was played by star actresses such as Anne Oldfield and Peg Woffington. The script, with its magnificent entrances and exotic dances, must have gratified the growing appetite for theatrical spectacle. The moral ambivalence of this text was not lost on spectators long after the intrigues of Charles' court were over, however, and the critic John Dennis in the early years of the eighteenth century accused the play of immorality, an opinion later shared by Samuel Johnson in his *Lives of the Poets*. Dryden's reputation as a poet remained high, however, throughout the long eighteenth century, and modern literary scholars see him as an important figure in the emergence of an English literary critical tradition as well as one of the most influential poets and playwrights of the Restoration.

PROLOGUE

What flocks of criticks hover here to day,
As vultures wait on armies for their prey,
All gaping for the carcass of a play!
With croaking notes they bode some dire event;
And follow dying poets by the scent.
Ours gives himself for gone; y'have watch'd your time!
He fights this day unarm'd; without his rhyme.
And brings a tale which often has been told;
As sad as Dido's;[4] and almost as old.
His heroe, whom you wits his bully call,
Bates of his mettle;[5] and scarce rants at all:
He's somewhat lewd; but a well-meaning mind;
Weeps much; fights little; but is wond'rous kind.
In short, a pattern, and companion fit,
For all thee keeping tonyes[6] of the pit.[7]
I cou'd name more; a wife, and mistress too;
Both (to be plain) too good for most of you:
The wife well-natur'd, and the mistress true.
Now, poets, if your fame has been his care;
Allow him all the candour you can spare.
A brave man scorns to quarrel once a day;
Like Hectors,[8] in at every petty fray,
Let those find fault whose wit's so very small,
They've need to show that they can think at all:
Errours like straws upon the surface flow;
He who would search for pearls must dive below.
Fops may have leave to level all they can;
As pigmies wou'd be glad to lopp a man.
Half-wits are fleas; so little and so light;
We scarce cou'd know they live; but that they bite.
But, as the rich, when tir'd with daily feasts,
For change, become their next poor tenant's guests;
Drink hearty draughts of ale, from plain brown bowls,
And snatch the homely rasher[9] from the coals:
So you, retiring from much better cheer,
For once, may venture to do penance here.
And since that plenteous autumn now is past,
Whose grapes and peaches have indulg'd your taste,
Take in good part from our poor poet's board,
Such rivell'd fruits as winter can afford.

Persons Represented.

Marc Antony	Mr. Hart.
Ventidius, his General	Mr. Mohun.
Dollabella, his friend	Mr. Clarke.
Alexas, the Queen's eunuch	Mr. Goodman.
Serapion, priest of *Isis*, servant to *Antony*	Mr. Griffin.
Another Priest	Mr. Coysh.
Servants to *Antony*	
Cleopatra, Queen of *Egypt*	Mrs. Boutell.
Octavia, *Antony's* wife	Mrs. Corey.
Charmion and *Iras*, Cleopatra's maids	
Antony's two little daughters	

Act I.

[*Scene: The Temple of Isis. Enter* Serapion, Myris*, Priests of Isis.*]

SERAPION. Portents and prodigies are grown so frequent,
That they have lost their name. Our fruitful *Nile*
Flow'd e're the wonted season, with a torrent
So unexpected, and so wondrous fierce,
That the wild deluge overtook the haste,
Ev'n of the hinds[10] that watch'd it: men and beasts
Were born above the tops of trees, that grew
On th' utmost margin of the water-mark.
Then, with so swift an ebb, the flood drove backward
It slipt from underneath the scaly herd:
Here monstrous *Phocae*[11] panted on the shore;
Forsaken *dolphins* there, with their broad tails,
Lay lashing the departing waves: hard by 'em,
Sea-horses[12] floundring in the slimy mud,
Toss'd up their heads, and dash'd the ooze about 'em.

[*Enter* Alexas *behind them.*

MYRIS. Avert these omens, Heav'n.

SERAPION. Last night, between the hours of twelve and one,
In a lone isle o'th' temple, while I walk'd,
A whirl-wind rose, that, with a violent blast,
Shook all the *dome*: the doors around me clap,
The iron wicket that defends the vault,
Where the long race of *Ptolemies*[13] is lay'd,
Burst open, and disclos'd the mighty dead.
From out each monument, in order plac'd,
An armed ghost start up: the Boy-King[14] last
Rear'd his inglorious head. A peal of groans
Then follow'd, and a lamentable voice
Cry'd, *Egypt* is no more. My blood ran back,
My shaking knees against each other knock'd;
On the cold pavement, down I fell intranc'd,
And so unfinish'd left the horrid scene.

ALEXAS. [*Showing himself*] And, dream'd you this? Or, did invent the story?
To frighten our *Egyptian* boys withal,
And train 'em up betimes in fear of priesthood?

SERAPION. My Lord, I saw you not,
Nor meant my words should reach your ears; but what
I utter'd was most true.

ALEXAS. A foolish dream,
Bred from the fumes of indigested feasts,
And holy luxury.

SERAPION. I know my duty:
This goes no farther.

ALEXAS. 'Tis not fit it should.
Nor would the times now bear it, were it true.
All southern, from you hills, the *Roman* camp
Hangs o'er us black and threatning, like a storm
Just breaking on our heads.
SERAPION. Our faint *Egyptians* pray for *Antony*;
But in their servile hearts they own *Octavius*.
MYRIS. Why then does *Antony* dream out his hours,
And tempts not Fortune for a noble day,
Which might redeem what *Actium*[15] lost?
ALEXAS. He thinks 'tis past recovery.
SERAPION. Yet the foe
Seems not to press the siege.
ALEXAS. O, there's the wonder.
Mecoenas and *Agrippa*, who can most
With *Caesar*[16] are his foes. His wife *Octavia*,
Driv'n from his house, solicits her revenge;
And *Dollabella*, who was once his friend,
Upon some private grudge, now seeks his ruine:
Yet still war seems on either side to sleep.
SERAPION. 'Tis strange that *Antony*, for some days past,
Has not beheld the face of *Cleopatra*;
But here, in *Isis*' temple, lives retir'd,
And makes his heart a prey to black despair.
ALEXAS. 'Tis true; and we much fear he hopes by absence
To cure his mind of love.
SERAPION. If he be vanquish'd,
Or make his peace, *Egypt* is doom'd to be
A *Roman* province; and our plenteous harvests
Must then redeem the scarceness of their soil.
While *Antony* stood firm, our *Alexandria*
Rival'd proud *Rome* (Dominion's other seat)
And fortune striding, like a vast *Colossus*,
Cou'd fix an equal foot of empire here.
ALEXAS. Had I my wish, these tyrants of all Nature
Who lord it o'er mankind, should perish, perish,
Each by the other's sword; but, since our will
Is lamely follow'd by our pow'r, we must
Depend on one; with him to rise or fall.
SERAPION. How stands the Queen affected?
ALEXAS. O, she dotes,
She dotes, *Serapion*, on this vanquish'd man,
And winds her self about his mighty ruins,
Whom would she yet forsake, yet yield him up,
This hunted prey, to his pursuers' hands,
She might preserve us all; but 'tis in vain–
This changes my designs, this blasts my counsels,
And makes me use all means to keep him here,
Whom I could wish divided from her arms
Far as the Earth's deep center. Well, you know
The state of things; no more of your ill omens,
And black prognosticks; labour to confirm
The people's hearts.

[*Enter* Ventidius, *talking aside with a gentleman of* Antony*'s*.

SERAPION. These *Romans* will o're-hear us.
But, who's that stranger? By his warlike port,
His fierce demeanor, and erected look,
He's of no vulgar note.
ALEXAS. O 'tis *Ventidius*,
Our Emp'ror's great Lieutenant in the East,
Who first show'd *Rome*, that *Parthia* could be conquer'd.
When *Antony* return'd from *Syria* last,
He left this man to guard the *Roman* frontiers.
SERAPION. You seem to know him well.
ALEXAS. Too well. I saw him in *Cilicia* first,
When *Cleopatra* there met *Antony*:
A mortal foe he was to us, and *Egypt*.
But, let me witness to the worth I hate,
A braver *Roman* never drew a sword.
Firm to his Prince; but, as a friend, not slave.
He ne'r was of his pleasures; but presides
O're all his cooler hours and morning counsels:
In short, the plainness, fierceness, rugged virtue
Of an old true-stampt *Roman* lives in him.
His coming bodes I know not what of ill
To our affairs. Withdraw, to mark him better;
And I'll acquaint you, why I sought you here,
And what's our present work.

[*They withdraw to a corner of the stage; and* Ventidius, *with the other, comes forward to the front*.

VENTIDIUS. Not see him, say you?
I say, I must and will.
GENTLEMAN. He has commanded,
On pain of death, none should approach his presence.
VENTIDIUS. I bring him news will raise his drooping spirits,
Give him new life.
GENTLEMAN. He sees not *Cleopatra*.
VENTIDIUS. Would he had never seen her.

GENTLEMAN. He eats not, drinks not, sleeps not, has no use
Of any thing, but thought; or, if he talks,
'Tis to himself, and then 'tis perfect raving:
Then he defies the World, and bids it pass;
Sometimes he gnaws his lip, and curses loud
The boy *Octavius*; then he draws his mouth
Into a scornful smile, and cries, take all,
The World's not worth my care.
VENTIDIUS. Just, just his nature.
Virtue's his path; but sometimes 'tis too narrow
For his vast soul; and then he starts out wide,
And bounds into a vice that bears him far
From his first course, and plunges him in ills:
But, when his danger makes him find his fault,
Quick to observe, and full of sharp remorse,
He censures eagerly his own misdeeds,
Judging himself with malice to himself,
And not forgiving what as man he did,
Because his other parts are more than man.
He must not thus be lost.

[Alexas *and the priests come forward.*

ALEXAS. You have your full instructions, now advance;
Proclaim your orders loudly.
SERAPION. *Romans*, *Egyptians*, hear the Queen's command.
Thus *Cleopatra* bids, let labor cease,
To pomp and triumphs give this happy day,
That gave the World a Lord: 'tis *Antony*'s.
Live, *Antony*; and *Cleopatra* live.
Be this the general voice sent up to Heav'n,
And every publick place repeat this eccho.
VENTIDIUS. [*Aside*] *Fine pageantry!*
SERAPION. Set out before your doors
The images of all your sleeping fathers,
With laurels crown'd; with laurels wreath your posts,
And strow with flow'rs the pavement; let the priests
Do present sacrifice; pour out the wine,
And call the gods to join with you in gladness.
VENTIDIUS. Curse on the tongue that bids this general joy.
Can they be friends of *Antony*, who revel
When *Antony*'s in danger? Hide, for shame,
You *Romans*, your great grandsires' images,
For fear their souls should animate their marbles,
To blush at their degenerate progeny.
ALEXAS. A love which knows no bounds to *Antony*,
Would mark the day with honours; when all Heaven
Labour'd for him, when each propitious star
Stood wakeful in his orb, to watch that hour,
And shed his better influence. Her own birth-day
Our Queen neglected, like a vulgar fate,
That pass'd obscurely by.
VENTIDIUS. Would it had slept,
Divided far from his; till some remote
And future age had call'd it out, to ruin
Some other prince, not him.
ALEXAS. Your Emperor,
Tho grown unkind, would be more gentle, than
T'upbraid my Queen for loving him too well.
VENTIDIUS. Does the mute sacrifice upbraid the priest?
He knows him not his executioner.
O, she has deck'd his ruin with her love,
Led him in golden bands to gaudy slaughter,
And made perdition pleasing: she has left him
The blank of what he was;
I tell thee, Eunuch, she has unmann'd him:
Can any *Roman* see, and know him now,
Thus alter'd from the lord of half mankind,
Unbent, unsinew'd made a woman's toy,
Shrunk from the vast extent of all his honours,
And crampt within a corner of the World?
O, *Antony*!
Thou bravest soldier, and thou best of friends!
Bounteous as Nature; next to Nature's God!
Could'st thou but make new worlds, so wouldst thou give 'em,
As bounty were thy being, rough in battle,
As the first *Romans*, when they went to war;
Yet, after victory, more pitiful,
Than all their praying virgins left at home!
ALEXAS. Would you could add to those more shining virtues,
His truth to her who loves him.
VENTIDIUS. Would I could not.
But, wherefore waste I precious hours with thee?
Thou art her darling mischief, her chief engine,
Antony's other fate. Go, tell thy Queen,
Ventidius is arriv'd, to end her charms.

Let your *Egyptian* timbrels[17] play alone;
Nor mix effeminate sounds with *Roman* trumpets.
You dare not fight for *Antony*; go pray,
And keep your coward's holy-day in temples.
[*Exeunt* Alexas, Serapion.

[*Re-enter the gentlemen of* Antony.

2 GENTLEMAN. The Emperor approaches, and commands,
On pain of death that none presume to stay.

1 GENTLEMAN. [*Going out with the other*] I dare not disobey him.

VENTIDIUS. Well, I dare.
But, I'll observe him first unseen, and find
Which way his humor drives: the rest I'll venture [*Withdraws.*

[*Enter* Antony, *walking with a disturb'd motion, before he speaks.*

ANTONY. They tell me 'tis my birth-day, and I'll keep it
With double pomp of sadness
'Tis what the day deserves, which gave me breath.
Why was I rais'd the Meteor of the World,
Hung in the skies, and blazing as I travell'd,
Till all my fires were spent; and then cast downward
To be trod out by *Caesar*?

VENTIDIUS. [*Aside*] *On my soul,*
'Tis mournful, wondrous mournful!

ANTONY. Count thy gains.
Now, *Antony*, wouldst thou be born for this?
Glutton of fortune, thy devouring youth
Has starv'd thy wanting age.

VENTIDIUS. [*Aside*] *How sorrow shakes him!*
So, now the tempest tears him up by th' roots,
And on the ground extends the noble ruin.

ANTONY. [*Having thrown himself down.*
Lye there, thou shadow of an emperor;
The place thou pressest on thy mother Earth
Is all thy empire now: now it contains thee;
Some few days hence, and then 'twill be too large,
When thou'rt contracted in thy narrow urn,
Shrunk to a few cold ashes; then Octavia,
(For *Cleopatra* will not live to see it)
Octavia then will have thee all her own,
And bear thee in her widow'd hand to *Caesar*;
Caesar will weep, the crocodile will weep,
To see his rival of the universe
Lie still and peaceful there. I'll think no more on't.
Give me some musick; look that it be sad:
I'll sooth my melancholy till I swell,
And burst my self with sighing –

[*Soft musick.*

'Tis somewhat to my humor. Stay, I fancy
I'm now turn'd wild, a commoner of Nature;
Of all forsaken, and forsaking all;
Live in a shady forest's *Sylvan* scene,
Stretch'd at my length beneath some blasted oak;
I lean my head upon the mossy bark,
And look just of a piece, as I grew from it:
My uncomb'd locks, matted like *mistletoe*,
Hang o're my hoary face; a murm'ring brook
Runs at my foot.

VENTIDIUS. Methinks I fancy
My self there too.

ANTONY. The herd come jumping by me,
And fearless, quench their thirst, while I look on,
And take me for their fellow-citizen,
More of this image, more; it lulls my thoughts.

[*Soft musick again.*

VENTIDIUS. [*Stands before him*] I must disturb him; I can hold no longer.

ANTONY. [*Starting up*] Art thou *Ventidius*?

VENTIDIUS. Are you *Antony*?
I'm liker what I was, than you to him
I left you last.

ANTONY. I'm angry.

VENTIDIUS. So am I.

ANTONY. I would be private: leave me.

VENTIDIUS. Sir, I love you.
And therefore will not leave you.

ANTONY. Will not leave me?
Where have you learnt that answer? Who am I?

VENTIDIUS. My Emperor; the man I love next Heaven:
If I said more, I think 'twere scarce a sin;
Y'are all that's good, and good-like.

ANTONY. All that's wretched.
You will not leave me then?

VENTIDIUS. 'Twas too presuming
To say I would not; but I dare not leave you:
And, 'tis unkind in you to chide me hence
So soon, when I so far have come to see you.

ANTONY. Now thou hast seen me, art thou satisfy'd?

For, if a friend, thou hast beheld enough;
And, if a foe, too much.

VENTIDIUS. [*Weeping*] Look, Emperor, this is no common dew.
I have not wept this forty years; but now
My mother comes afresh into my eyes;
I cannot help her softness.

ANTONY. By Heav'n, he weeps, poor good old man, he weeps!
The big round drops course one another down
The furrows of his cheeks. Stop 'em, *Ventidius*,
Or I shall blush to death: they set my shame,
That caus'd 'em, full before me.

VENTIDIUS. I'll do my best.

ANTONY. Sure there's contagion in the tears of friends:
See, I have caught it too. Believe me, 'tis not
For my own griefs, but thine – Nay, Father.

VENTIDIUS. Emperor.

ANTONY. Emperor! Why, that's the style of victory,
The conqu'ring soldier, red with unfelt wounds,
Salutes his General so: but never more
Shall that sound reach my ears.

VENTIDIUS. I warrant you.

ANTONY. *Actium, Actium*! Oh –

VENTIDIUS. It sits too near you.

ANTONY. Here, here it lies; a lump of lead by day,
And, in my short distracted nightly slumbers,
The hag that rides my dreams –

VENTIDIUS. Out with it; give it vent.

ANTONY. Urge not my shame.
I lost a battle.

VENTIDIUS. So has *Julius* done.

ANTONY. Thou favour'st me, and speak'st not half thou think'st;
For *Julius* fought it out, and lost it fairly:
But *Antony* –

VENTIDIUS. Nay, stop not.

ANTONY. *Antony*.
(Well, thou wilt have it) like a coward fled,
Fled while his soldiers fought; fled first, *Ventidius*.
Thou long'st to curse me, and I give thee leave.
I know thou com'st prepar'd to rail.

VENTIDIUS. I did.

ANTONY. I'll help thee – I have been a man, *Ventidius*.

VENTIDIUS. Yes, and a brave one; but –

ANTONY. I know thy meaning.
But, I have lost my reason, have disgrac'd
The name of Soldier, with inglorious ease.
In the full vintage of my flowing honours,
Sate still, and saw it prest by other hands.
Fortune came smiling to my youth, and woo'd it,
And purple greatness met my ripen'd years.
When first I came to empire, I was born
On tides of people, crouding to my triumphs;
The wish of nations; and the willing World
Receiv'd me as its pledge of future peace;
I was so great, so happy, so belov'd,
Fate could not ruine me; till I took pains
And work'd against my Fortune, chid her from me,
And turn'd her loose; yet still she came again.
My careless days, and my luxurious nights,
At length have weary'd her, and now she's gone,
Gone, gone, divorc'd for ever. Help me, Soldier,
To curse this madman, this industrious fool,
Who labour'd to be wretched: prithee curse me.

VENTIDIUS. No.

ANTONY. Why?

VENTIDIUS. You are too sensible already
Of what y'have done, too conscious of your failings,
And, like a scorpion, whipt by others first
To fury, sting your self in mad revenge.
I would bring balm and pour it in your wounds,
Cure your distemper'd mind, and heal your fortunes.

ANTONY. I know thou would'st.

VENTIDIUS. I will.

ANTONY. Ha, ha, ha, ha.

VENTIDIUS. You laugh.

ANTONY. I do, to see officious love
Give cordials to the dead.

VENTIDIUS. You would be lost then?

ANTONY. I am.

VENTIDIUS. I say, you are not. Try your fortune.

ANTONY. I have to th'utmost. Dost thou think me desperate,
Without just cause? No, when I found all lost
Beyond repair, I hid me from the World,
And learnt to scorn it here; which now I do
So heartily, I think it is not worth
The cost of keeping.

VENTIDIUS. *Caesar* thinks not so:
He'll thank you for the gift he could not take.
You would be kill'd, like *Tully*,[18] would you? Do,
Hold out your throat to *Caesar*, and die tamely.
ANTONY. No, I can kill my self; and so resolve.
VENTIDIUS. I can die with you too, when time shall serve;
But fortune calls upon us now to live,
To fight, to conquer.
ANTONY. Sure thou dream'st, *Ventidius*.
VENTIDIUS. No, 'tis you dream; you sleep away your hours
In desperate sloth, miscall'd *Philosophy*.
Up, up, for honour's sake; twelve legions wait you,
And long to call you Chief: by painful journeys,
I led 'em, patient, both of heat and hunger,
Down from the *Parthian* marches, to the *Nile*.
'Twill do you good to see their sun-burnt faces,
Their skar'd cheeks and chopt hands; there's virtue in 'em,
They'll sell those mangled limbs at dearer rates
Than yon trim bands can buy.
ANTONY. Where left you them?
VENTIDIUS. I said, in lower *Syria*.
ANTONY. Bring 'em hither;
There may be life in these.
VENTIDIUS. They will not come.
ANTONY. Why did'st thou mock my hopes with promis'd aids
To double my despair? They're mutinous.
VENTIDIUS. Most firm and loyal.
ANTONY. Yet they will not march
To succour me. Oh trifler!
VENTIDIUS. They petition
You would make hast to head 'em.
ANTONY. I'm besieg'd.
VENTIDIUS. There's but one way shut up: How came I hither?
ANTONY. I will not stir.
VENTIDIUS. They would perhaps desire
A better reason.
ANTONY. I have never us'd
My soldiers to demand a reason of
My actions. Why did they refuse to march?
VENTIDIUS. They said they would not fight for *Cleopatra*.
ANTONY. What was't they said?
VENTIDIUS. They said they would not fight for *Cleopatra*.
Why should they fight, indeed, to make her conquer,
And make you more a slave? To gain you kingdoms,
Which, for a kiss, at your next midnight feast,
You'll sell to her? Then she new names her jewels,
And calls this diamond such or such a tax,
Each pendant in her ear shall be a province.
ANTONY. *Ventidius*, I allow your tongue free license
On all my other faults; but, on your life,
No word of *Cleopatra*: she deserves
More worlds than I can lose.
VENTIDIUS. Behold, you pow'rs,
To whom you have intrusted humankind;
See *Europe*, *Africk*, *Asia*, put in balance,
And all weigh'd down by one light worthless woman!
I think the gods are *Antony*'s, and give
Like prodigals, this nether World away,
To none but wastful hands.
ANTONY. You grow presumptuous.
VENTIDIUS. I take the priviledge of plain love to speak.
ANTONY. Plain love! Plain arrogance, plain insolence:
Thy men are cowards; thou an envious traitor;
Who, under seeming honesty, hast vented
The burden of thy rank o'reflowing gall.
O that thou wert my equal; great in arms.
As the first *Caesar* was, that I might kill thee
Without a stain to honour!
VENTIDIUS. You may kill me;
You have done more already, call'd me traitor.
ANTONY. Art thou not one?
VENTIDIUS. For showing you your self,
Which none else durst have done; but had I been
That name, which I disdain to speak again,
I needed not have sought your abject fortunes,
Come to partake your fate, to die with you.
What hindred me t'have led my conqu'ring eagles
To fill *Octavius*'s bands? I could have been
A traitor then, a glorious happy traitor,
And not have been so call'd.
ANTONY. Forgive me, Soldier:
I've been too passionate,
VENTIDIUS. You thought me false;
Thought my old age betray'd you: kill me, Sir;

Pray kill me; yet you need not, your unkindness
Has left your sword no work.
ANTONY. I did not think so;
I said it in my rage: prithee forgive me:
Why did'st thou tempt my anger, by discovery
Of what I would not hear?
VENTIDIUS. No Prince but you,
Could merit that sincerity I us'd,
Nor durst another man have ventur'd it;
But you, e're love misled your wandring eyes,
Were sure the chief and best of human race,
Fram'd in the very pride and boast of Nature,
So perfect, that the gods who form'd you, wonder'd
At their own skill, and cry'd, a lucky hit
Has mended our design. Their envy hindred,
Else you had been immortal, and a pattern,
When Heav'n would work for ostentation sake,
To copy out again.
ANTONY. But *Cleopatra* –
Go on; for I can bear it now.
VENTIDIUS . No more.
ANTONY. Thou dar'st not trust my passion; but thou may'st:
Thou only lov'st; the rest have flatter'd me.
VENTIDIUS. Heav'ns blessing on your heart for that kind word.
May I believe you love me? Speak again.
ANTONY. Indeed I do. Speak this, and this, and this. [*Hugging him.*
Thy praises were unjust; but I'll deserve 'em,
And yet mend all. Do with me what thou wilt,
Lead me to victory, thou know'st the way.
VENTIDIUS. And, will you leave this –
ANTONY. Prithee do not curse her,
And I will leave her; though, Heav'n knows, I love
Beyond life, conquest, empire; all, but honour,
But I will leave her.
VENTIDIUS. That's my Royal Master.
And, shall we fight?
ANTONY. I warrant thee, old Soldier,
Thou shalt behold me once again in iron,
And at the head of our old troops, that beat
The *Parthians*, cry aloud, come follow me.
VENTIDIUS. O now I hear my Emperor! In that word
Octavius fell. Gods, let me see that day,
And if I have ten years behind, take all;
I'll thank you for th' exchange.
ANTONY. Oh *Cleopatra*!
VENTIDIUS. Again?
ANTONY. I've done: in that last sigh she went.
Caesar shall know what 'tis to force a lover,
From all he holds most dear.
VENTIDIUS. Methinks you breathe
Another soul: your looks are more divine;
You speak a heroe, and you move a god.
ANTONY. O, thou hast fir'd me; my soul's up in arms,
And mans each part about me: once again,
That noble eagerness of fight has seiz'd me;
That eagerness with which I darted upward
To *Cassius*'s camp:[19] In vain the steepy hill.
Oppos'd my way; in vain a war of spears
Sung round my head; and planted all my shield:
I won the trenches, while my foremost men
Lagg'd on the plain below.
VENTIDIUS. Ye Gods, ye Gods,
For such another hour.
ANTONY. Come on, my Soldier!
Our hearts and arms are still the same: I long
Once more to meet our foes; that thou and I,
Like Time and Death, marching before our troops,
May taste fate to 'em; mow 'em out a passage,
And entring where the foremost squadrons yield,
Begin the noble harvest of the field. [*Exeunt.*

Act II.

[*Enter* Cleopatra, Iras, *and* Alexas.]

CLEOPATRA. What shall I do, or whither shall I turn?
Ventidius has o'rcome, and he will go.
ALEXAS. He goes to fight for you.
CLEOPATRA. Then he would see me e're he went to fight
Flatter me not: if once he goes, he's lost:
And all my hopes destroy'd.

ALEXAS. Does this weak passion
Become a mighty Queen?
CLEOPATRA. I am no Queen;
Is this to be a Queen, to be besieg'd
By yon insulting *Roman*; and to wait
Each hour the victor's chain? These ills are small;
For *Antony* is lost, and I can mourn
For nothing else but him. Now come, *Octavius*,
I have no more to lose; prepare thy bands;
I'm fit to be a captive: *Antony*
Has taught my mind the fortune of a slave.
IRAS. Call reason to assist you.
CLEOPATRA. I have none.
And none would have: my love's a noble madness.
Which shows the cause deserv'd it. Moderate sorrow
Fits vulgar love; and for a vulgar man:
But I have lov'd with such transcendent passion,
I soar'd, at first, quite out of reason's view,
And now am lost above it – No, I'm proud
'Tis thus, would *Antony* could see me now;
Think you he would not sigh? Though he must leave me,
Shure he would sigh; for he is noble-natur'd,
And bears a tender heart: I know him well.
Ah, no, I know him not; I knew him once,
But now 'tis past.
IRAS. Let it be past with you:
Forget him, Madam.
CLEOPATRA. Never, never, Iras.
He once was mine; and once, though now 'tis gone,
Leaves a faint image of possession still.
ALEXAS. Think him unconstant, cruel, and ungrateful.
CLEOPATRA. I cannot: if I could, those thoughts were vain;
Faithless, ungrateful, cruel, though he be,
I still must love him.

[*Enter* Charmion.

Now, what news my *Charmion*?
Will he be kind? And will he not forsake me?
Am I to live, or die? Nay, do I live?
Or am I dead? For when he gave his answer,
Fate took the word, and then I liv'd, or dy'd.
CHARMION. I found him, Madam –
CLEOPATRA. A long speech preparing?
If thou bring'st comfort, haste, and give it me;
For never was more need.
IRAS. I know he loves you.
CLEOPATRA. Had he been kind, her eyes had told me so,
Before her tongue could speak it: now she studies,
To soften what he said; but give me death,
Just as he sent it, *Charmion*, undisguis'd,
And in the words he spoke.
CHARMION. I found him then
Incompass'd round, I think, with iron statues,
So mute, so motionless his soldiers stood,
While awfully he cast his eyes about,
And ev'ry leader's hopes or fears survey'd:
Methought he look'd resolv'd, and yet not pleas'd.
When he beheld me struggling in the crowd,
He blush'd, and bade, make way.
ALEXAS. There's comfort yet.
CHARMION. *Ventidius* fixt his eyes upon my passage,
Severely, as he meant to frown me back,
And sullenly gave place: I told my message.
Just as you gave it, broken and disorder'd;
I numbred in it all your sighs and tears,
And while I mov'd your pitiful request,
That you but only beg'd a last farewell,
He fetch an inward groan, and ev'ry time
I nam'd you, sigh'd, as if his heart were breaking,
But shun'd my eyes, and guiltily look'd down;
He seem'd not now that awful *Antony*
Who shook an arm'd assembly with his nod,
But making show as he would rub his eyes,
Disguis'd and blotted out a falling tear.
CLEOPATRA. Did he then weep? And, was I worth a tear?
If what thou hast to say be not as pleasing,
Tell me no more, but let me die contented.
CHARMION. He bid me say, he knew himself so well,
He could deny you nothing, if he saw you;
And therefore –
CLEOPATRA. Thou would say, he wou'd not see me?
CHARMION. And therefore beg'd you not to use a power,
Which he could ill resist; yet he should ever
Respect you as he ought.
CLEOPATRA. Is that a word
For *Antony* to use to *Cleopatra*?
Oh that faint word, respect! How I disdain it!
Disdain my self, for loving after it!

He should have kept that word for cold *Octavia*.
Respect is for a wife: am I that thing,
That dull insipid lump, without desires,
And without pow'r to give 'em?

ALEXAS. You misjudge;
You see through love, and that deludes your sight:
As, what is strait, seems crooked through the water;
But I, who bear my reason undisturb'd,
Can see this *Antony*, this dreaded man,
A fearful slave, who fain would run away,
And shuns his master's eyes: if you pursue him,
My life on't, he still drags a chain along,
That needs must clog his flight.

CLEOPATRA. Could I believe thee! –

ALEXAS. By ev'ry circumstance I know he loves.
True, he's hard prest, by interest and by honour;
Yet he but doubts, and parleys, and casts out
Many a long lookt for succour.

CLEOPATRA. He sends word,
He fears to see my face.

ALEXAS. And would you more?
He shows his weakness who declines the combat;
And you must urge your fortune. Could he speak
More plainly? To my ears, the message sounds
Come to my rescue, *Cleopatra*, come;
Come, free me from *Ventidius*; from my tyrant:
See me, and give me a pretence to leave him.
I hear his trumpets. This way he must pass.
Please you, retire a while; I'll work him first,
That he may bend more easie.

CLEOPATRA. You shall rule me;
But all, I fear, in vain.

[*Exit with* Charmion *and* Iras.

ALEXAS. I fear so too!
Though I conceal'd my thoughts, to make her bold:
But, 'tis our utmost means, and fate befriend it. [*Withdraws.*

[*Enter Lictors with Fasces;*[20] *one bearing the eagle: then enter* Antony *with* Ventidius, *follow'd by other commanders.*

ANTONY. *Octavius* is the minion of blind chance,
But holds from virtue nothing.

VENTIDIUS. Has he courage?

ANTONY. But just enough to season him from coward.
O, 'tis the coldest youth upon a charge,
The most deliberate fighter! If he ventures
(As in *Illyria* once they say he did
To storm a town) 'tis when he cannot choose,
When all the World have fixt their eyes upon him;
And then he lives on that for seven years after,
But, at a close revenge he never fails.

VENTIDIUS. I heard, you challeng'd him.

ANTONY. I did, *Ventidius*.
What think'st thou was his answer? 'Twas so tame, –
He said he had more ways than one to die;
I had not.

VENTIDIUS. Poor!

ANTONY. He has more ways than one;
But he would choose 'em all before that one.

VENTIDIUS. He first would choose an ague, or a fever:

ANTONY. No: it must be an ague, not a fever;
He has not warmth enough to die by that.

VENTIDIUS. Or old age, and a bed.

ANTONY. Ay, there's his choice.
He would live, like a lamp, to the last wink,
And crawl upon the utmost verge of life:
O *Hercules*! Why should a man like this,
Who dares not trust his fate for one great action,
Be all the care of Heaven? Why should he lord it
O're fourscore thousand men, of whom, each one
Is braver than himself?

VENTIDIUS. You conquer'd for him:
Philippi knows it: there you shar'd with him.
That empire, which your sword made all your own.[21]

ANTONY. Fool that I was, upon my eagle's wings
I bore this wren, till I was tir'd with soaring,
And now he mounts above me.
Good heav'ns, is this, is this the man who braves me?
Who bids my age make way: drives me before him,
To the World's ridge, and sweeps me off like rubbish?

VENTIDIUS. Sir, we lose time; the troops are mounted all.

ANTONY. Then give the word to march:
I long to leave this prison of a town,

To join thy legions; and, in open field,
Once more to show my face. Lead, my Deliverer.

[*Enter* Alexas.

ALEXAS. Great Emperor,
In mighty arms renown'd above mankind,
But, in soft pity to th' opprest, a god:
This message sends the mournful *Cleopatra*
To her departing Lord.

VENTIDIUS. Smooth Sycophant!

ALEXAS. A thousand wishes, and ten thousand prayers,
Millions of blessings wait you to the wars,
Millions of sighs and tears she sends you too,
And would have sent
As many dear embraces to your arms,
As many parting kisses to your lips;
But those, she fears, have weary'd you already.

VENTIDIUS . [*Aside*] *False Crocodyle!*

ALEXAS. And yet she begs not now, you would not leave her,
That were a wish too mighty for her hopes,
Too presuming for her low fortune, and your ebbing love,
That were a wish for her more prosperous days,
Her blooming beauty, and your growing kindness.

ANTONY. – [*Aside*] *Well, I must man it out.* – What would the Queen?

ALEXAS. First, to these noble warriors, who attend,
Your daring courage in the chase of fame,
(Too daring, and too dang'rous for her quiet)
She humbly recommends all she holds dear,
All her own cares and fears, the care of you.

VENTIDIUS. Yes, witness *Actium.*

ANTONY. Let him speak, *Ventidius.*

ALEXAS. You, when his matchless valour bears him forward,
With ardor too heroick, on his foes
Fall down, as she would do, before his feet;
Lye in his way, and stop the paths of death;
Tell him, this god is not invulnerable,
That absent *Cleopatra* bleeds in him;
And, that you may remember her petition,
She begs you wear these trifles, as a pawn,
Which, at your wisht return, she will redeem.

[*Gives jewels to the commanders.*

With all the wealth of *Egypt*:
This, to the great *Ventidius* she presents,
Whom she can never count her enemy,
Because he loves her Lord.

VENTIDIUS. Tell her I'll none on't;
I'm not asham'd of honest poverty:
Not all the diamonds of the East can bribe
Ventidius from his faith. I hope to see
These, and the rest of all her sparkling store,
Where they shall more deservingly be plac'd.

ANTONY. And who must wear 'em then?

VENTIDIUS. The wrong'd *Octavia.*

ANTONY. You might have spar'd that word.

VENTIDIUS. And he that bribe.

ANTONY. But have I no remembrance?

ALEXAS. Yes, a dear one:
Your slave, the Queen–

ANTONY. My Mistress.

ALEXAS. Then your Mistress,
Your Mistress would, she says, have sent her soul,
But that you had long since; she humbly begs
This ruby bracelet, set with bleeding hearts,
(The emblems of her own) may bind your arm. [*Presenting a bracelet.*

VENTIDIUS. Now, my best Lord, in honour's name, I ask you,
For manhood's sake, and for your own dear safety,
Touch not these poison'd gifts,
Infected by the sender, touch 'em not,
Myriads of bluest plagues lye underneath 'em,
And more than aconite[22] has dipt the silk.

ANTONY. Nay, now you grow too cynical, *Ventidius.*
A lady's favours may be worn with honour.
What, to refuse her bracelet! On my soul,
When I lye pensive in my tent alone,
'Twill pass the wakeful hours of winter nights,
To tell these pretty beads upon my arm,
To count for every one a soft embrace,
A melting kiss at such and such a time;
And now and then the fury of her love.
When – and what harm's in this?

ALEXAS. None, none my Lord,
But what's to her, that now 'tis past for ever.

ANTONY. [*Going to tie it*] We soldiers are so awkward – help me tie it.

ALEXAS. In faith, my Lord, we courtiers too are awkward
In these affairs: so are all men indeed;
Ev'n I, who am not one. But shall I speak?

ANTONY. Yes, freely.

ALEXAS. Then, my Lord, fair hands alone
Are fit to tie it; she, who sent it, can.
VENTIDIUS. Hell, death; this eunuch *Pandar*[23] ruins you.
You will not see her?

[Alexas *whispers an attendant, who goes out.*

ANTONY. But to take my leave.
VENTIDIUS. Then I have wash'd an *Aethiope*.[24] Y'are undone;
Y'are in the toils; y'are taken; y'are destroy'd:
Her eyes do *Caesar*'s work.
ANTONY. You fear too soon.
I'm constant to my self: I know my strength;
And yet she shall not think me barbarous, neither.
Born in the depths of *Africk*: I'm a *Roman*.
Bred to the rules of soft humanity.
A guest, and kindly us'd, should bid farewell.
VENTIDIUS. You do not know
How weak you are to her, how much an infant:
You are not proof against a smile or glance;
A sigh will quite disarm you.
ANTONY. See, she comes!
Now you shall find your error. Gods, I thank you:
I form'd the danger greater than it was,
And, now 'tis near, 'tis lessen'd.
VENTIDIUS. Mark the end yet.

[*Enter* Cleopatra, Charmion *and* Iras.

ANTONY. Well, Madam, we are met.
CLEOPATRA. Is this a meeting?
Then, we must part?
ANTONY. We must.
CLEOPATRA. Who says we must?
ANTONY. Our own hard fates.
CLEOPATRA. We make those fates our selves.
ANTONY. Yes, we have made 'em; we have lov'd each other
Into our mutual ruin.
CLEOPATRA. The gods have seen my joys with envious eyes;
I have no friends in Heaven; and all the World,
(As 'twere the bus'ness of Mankind to part us)
Is arm'd against my love: ev'n you your self with the rest; you, you are arm'd against me.
ANTONY. I will be justify'd in all I do
To late posterity, and therefore hear me.
If I mix a lie
With any truth, reproach me freely with it;
Else, favor me with silence.
CLEOPATRA. You command me,
And I am dumb.
VENTIDIUS. I like this well: he shows authority.
ANTONY. That I derive my ruin
From you alone –
CLEOPATRA. O heav'ns! I ruin you!
ANTONY. You promis'd me your silence, and you break it
E're I have scarce begun.
CLEOPATRA. Well, I obey you.
ANTONY. When I beheld you first, it was in *Egypt*,
E're *Caesar* saw your eyes; you gave me love,
And were too young to know it, that I settled
Your father in his throne, was for your sake,
I left the acknowledgment for time to ripen.
Caesar stept in, and with a greedy hand
Pluck'd the green fruit, e'er the first blush of red
Yet cleaving to the bough. He was my lord,
And was, beside, too great for me to rival,
But, I deserv'd you first, though he enjoy'd you.
When after, I beheld you in *Cilicia*,
An enemy to *Rome*, I pardon'd you.
CLEOPATRA. I clear'd my self –
ANTONY. Again you break your promise.
I lov'd you still, and took your weak excuses,
Took you into my bosom, stain'd by *Caesar*,
And not half mine: I went to *Egypt* with you,
And hid me from the bus'ness of the World,
Shut out enquiring nations from my sight,
To give whole years to you.
VENTIDIUS. [*Aside*] *Yes, to your shame be't spoken.*
ANTONY. How I lov'd
Witness ye days and nights, and all your hours,
That danc'd away with down upon your feet,
As all your bus'ness were to count my passion.
One day past by, and nothing saw but love;
Another came, and still 'twas only love:
The suns were weary'd out with looking on,
And I untir'd with loving.
I saw you ev'ry day, and all the day;
And ev'ry day was still but as the first:
So eager was I still to see you more.
VENTIDIUS. 'Tis all too true.
ANTONY. *Fulvia*, my wife, grew jealous,
As she indeed had reason; rais'd a war
In *Italy* to call me back.

VENTIDIUS . But yet
You went not.
ANTONY. While within your arms I lay,
The World fell mouldring from my hands each hour,
And left me scarce a grasp (I thank your love for't.)
VENTIDIUS. Well push'd: that last was home.
CLEOPATRA. Yet may I speak?
ANTONY. If I have urg'd a falshood, yes, else, not.
Your silence says I have not. *Fulvia* dy'd;
(Pardon, you gods, with my unkindness dy'd.)
To set the World at peace, I took *Octavia*,
This *Caesar*'s sister; in her pride of youth
And flow'r of beauty did I wed that Lady,
Whom blushing I must praise, because I left her.
You call'd; my love obey'd the fatal summons:
This rais'd the *Roman* arms; the cause was yours,
I would have sought by land, where I was stronger;
You hindered it: yet, when I fought at sea,
Forsook me fighting; and (Oh stain to honour!
Oh lasting shame!) I knew not that I fled;
But fled to follow you.
VENTIDIUS. What haste she made to hoist her purple sails!
And to appear magnificent in flight,
Drew half our strength away.
ANTONY. All this you caus'd.
And, would you multiply more ruins on me?
This honest man, my best, my only friend,
Has gather'd up the shipwreck of my fortunes;
Twelve legions I have left, my last recruits,
And you have watch'd the news, and bring your eyes
To seize them too. If you have ought to answer,
Now speak, you have free leave.
ALEXAS. [*Aside*] *She stands confounded:*
Despair is in her eyes.
VENTIDIUS. Now lay a sigh i'th' way, to stop his passage:
Prepare a tear, and bid it for his legions;
'Tis like they shall be sold.
CLEOPATRA. How shall I plead my cause, when you, my Judge
Already have condemn'd me? Shall I bring
The love you bore me for my advocate?
That now is turn'd against me, that destroys me;
For, love once past, is, at the best, forgotten;
But oftner sours to hate: 'twill please my Lord
To ruine me, and therefore I'll be guilty.
But, could I once have thought it would have pleas'd you,
That you would pry, with narrow searching eyes
Into my faults, severe to my destruction:
And watching all advantages with care,
That serve to make me wretched? Speak, my Lord,
For I end here. Though I deserve this usage,
Was it like you to give it?
ANTONY. O you wrong me,
To think I sought this parting, or desir'd
To accuse you more than what will clear my self,
And justifie this breach.
CLEOPATRA. Thus low I thank you.
And since my innocence will not offend,
I shall not blush to own it.
VENTIDIUS. After this
I think she'll blush at nothing.
CLEOPATRA. You seem griev'd,
(And therein you are kind) that *Caesar* first
Enjoy'd my love, though you deserv'd it better:
I grieve for that, my Lord, much more than you;
For, had I first been yours, it would have sav'd
My second choice: I never had been his,
And ne'r had been but yours. But *Caesar* first,
You say, possess'd my love. Not so, my Lord;
He first possess'd my person; you my love:
Caesar lov'd me; but I lov'd *Antony*.
If I endur'd him after, 'twas because
I judg'd it due to the first name of men;
And, half constrain'd, I gave, as to a tyrant,
What he would take by force.
VENTIDIUS. O syren! Syren!
Yet grant that all the love she boasts were true,
Has she not ruin'd you? I still urge that,
The fatal consequence.
CLEOPATRA. The consequence indeed,
For I dare challenge him, my greatest foe,
To say it was design'd: 'tis true, I lov'd you,
And kept you far from an uneasie wife,
(Such *Fulvia* was.)
Yes, but he'll say, you left *Octavia* for me; –
And, can you blame me to receive that love,
Which quitted such desert, for worthless me?
How often have I wish'd some other *Caesar*,

Great as the first, and as the second young,
Would court my love to be refus'd for you!

VENTIDIUS. Words, words; but *Actium*, Sir, remember *Actium*.

CLEOPATRA. Ev'n there, I dare his malice. True, I counsel'd
To fight at sea; but I betray'd you not.
I fled; but not to the enemy. 'Twas fear;
Would I had been a man, not to have fear'd,
For none would then have envy'd me your friendship,
Who envy me your love.

ANTONY. We're both unhappy:
If nothing else, yet our ill fortune parts us.
Speak; would you have me perish, by my stay?

CLEOPATRA. If as a friend you ask my judgment, go;
If as a lover, stay. If you must perish:
'Tis a hard word; but stay.

VENTIDIUS. See now th' effects of her so boasted love!
She strives to drag you down to ruine with her:
But, could she 'scape without you, oh how soon
Would she let go her hold, and haste to shore,
And never look behind!

CLEOPATRA. Then judge my love by this.
[*Giving* Antony *a writing.*
Could I have born
A life or death, a happiness or woe
From yours divided, this had giv'n me means.

ANTONY. By *Hercules*, the writing of *Octavius*!
I know it well; 'tis that prescribing hand,
Young as it was, that led the way to mine,
And left me but the second place in murder.–
See, see, *Ventidius*! Here he offers *Egypt*,
And joins all *Syria* to it as a present,
So, in requital, she forsake my fortunes,
And join her arms with his.

CLEOPATRA. And yet you leave me!
You leave me, *Antony*; and yet I love you.
Indeed I do: I have refus'd a kingdom,
That's a trifle:
For I could part with life; with any thing,
But only you. O let me die, but with you!
Is that a hard request?

ANTONY. Next living with you,
'Tis all that Heav'n can give.

ALEXAS. [*Aside*] *He melts; we conquer.*

CLEOPATRA. No: you shall go: your int'rest calls you hence;
Yes, your dear interest pulls too strong, for these
Weak arms to hold you here. – [*Takes his hand.*
Go; leave me, Soldier;
(For you're no more a lover:) leave me dying:
Push me all pale and panting from your bosome,
And, when your march begins, let one run after
Breathless almost for joy; and cry, she's dead:
The soldiers shout; you then perhaps may sigh,
And muster all your *Roman* gravity;
Ventidius chides; and strait your brow clears up.
As I had never been.

ANTONY. Gods, 'tis too much; too much for man to bear!

CLEOPATRA. What is't for me then,
A weak forsaken woman? And a lover? –
Here let me breath my last: envy me not
This minute in your arms: I'll die apace:
As fast as e'er I can; and end your trouble.

ANTONY. Die! Rather let me perish: loos'nd Nature
Leap from its hinges. Sink the props of Heav'n,
And fall the skies to crush the Nether World.
My eyes, my soul; my all! – [*Embraces her.*

VENTIDIUS. And what's this toy
In balance with your fortune, honour, fame?

ANTONY. What is't, *Ventidius*? It out-weighs 'em all;
Why, we have more than conquer'd *Caesar* now:
My Queen's not only innocent, but loves me.
This, this is she who drags me down to ruin!
'But, could she 'scape without me, with what haste
Would she let slip her hold, and make to shore,
And never look behind!
Down on thy knees, blasphemer as thou art,
And ask forgiveness of wrong'd innocence.

VENTIDIUS. I'll rather die, than take it. Will you go?

ANTONY. Go! Whither? Go from all that's excellent!
Faith, honour, virtue, all good things forbid,
That I should go from her, who sets my love
Above the price of kingdoms. Give, you gods,
Give to your boy, your *Caesar*,
This rattle of a globe to play withal,
This gew-gaw World, and put him cheaply off:

I'll not be pleas'd with less than *Cleopatra*.
CLEOPATRA. She's wholly yours. My heart's so full of joy,
That I shall do some wild extravagance
Of love in publick; and the foolish World,
Which knows not tenderness, will think me mad.
VENTIDIUS. O Women! Women! Women! All the gods
Have not such pow'r of doing good to man,
As you of doing harm. [*Exit.*
ANTONY. Our men are arm'd.
Unbar the gate that looks to *Caesar*'s camp;
I would revenge the treachery he meant me;
And long security makes conquest easie.
I'm eager to return before I go;
For, all the pleasures I have known, beat thick
On my remembrance: how I long for night!
That both the sweets of mutual love may try,
And once triumph o'er *Caesar* e're we die.
[*Exeunt.*

Act III.

[*At one door, enter* Cleopatra, Charmion, Iras, *and* Alexas, *a train of* Egyptians: *at the other,* Antony *and* Romans. *The entrance on both sides is prepar'd by musick; the trumpets first sounding on* Antony's *part: then answer'd by timbrels, &c. on* Cleopatra's. Charmion *and* Iras *hold a laurel wreath betwixt them. A dance of Egyptians. After the ceremony,* Cleopatra *crowns* Antony.]

ANTONY. I thought how those white arms would fold me in,
And strain me close, and melt me into love;
So pleas'd with that sweet image, I sprung forwards,
And added all my strength to every blow.
CLEOPATRA. Come to me, come my Soldier, to my arms,
You've been too long away from my embraces;
But, when I have you fast, and all my own,
With broken murmurs, and with amorous sighs,
I'll say, you were unkind, and punish you,
And mark you red with many an eager kiss.
ANTONY. My brighter *Venus*!
CLEOPATRA. O my greater *Mars*!
ANTONY. Thou joinst us well, my Love!
Suppose me come from the *Phlegraean* plains,[25]
Where gasping gyants lay, cleft by my sword:
And mountain tops par'd off each other blow,
To bury those I slew: receive me, Goddess:
Let *Caesar* spread his subtle nets, like *Vulcan*,[26]
In thy embraces I would be beheld
By Heav'n and Earth at once:
And make their envy what they meant their sport
Let those who took us blush; I would love on
With awful state, regardless of their frowns,
As their superior god.
There's no satiety of love, in thee;
Enjoy'd, thou still art new; perpetual Spring
Is in thy arms; the ripen'd fruit but falls,
And blossoms rise to fill its empty place;
And I grow rich by giving.

[*Enter* Ventidius, *and stands apart.*

ALEXAS. O, now the danger's past, your General comes.
He joins not in your joys, nor minds your triumphs,
But, with contracted brows, looks frowning on,
As envying your success.
ANTONY. Now, on my soul, he loves me; truly loves me;
He never flatter'd me in any vice,
But awes me with his virtue: ev'n this minute
Methinks he has a right of chiding me.
Lead to the temple: I'll avoid his presence;
It checks too strong upon me.
[*Exeunt the rest.*

[*As* Antony *is going,* Ventidius *pulls him by the robe.*

VENTIDIUS. Emperor.
ANTONY. [*Looking back*] 'Tis the old argument; I pr'ythee spare me.
VENTIDIUS. But this one hearing, Emperor.
ANTONY. Let go
My robe; or, by my father *Hercules* –.

VENTIDIUS. By *Hercules* his father, that's yet greater,
I bring you somewhat you would wish to know.
ANTONY. Thou see'st we are observ'd; attend me here,
And I'll return. [*Exit.*
VENTIDIUS. I'm waning in his favour, yet I love him;
I love this man, who runs to meet his ruin;
And, sure the gods, like me, are fond of him:
His virtues lye so mingled with his crimes,
As would confound their choice to punish one,
And not reward the other.

[*Enter* Antony.

ANTONY. We can conquer,
You see, without your aid.
We have dislodg'd their troops,
They look on us at distance, and, like curs
Scap'd from the lions paws, they bay far off,
And lick their wounds, and faintly threaten war.
Five thousand *Romans* with their faces upward,
Lye breathless on the plain.
VENTIDIUS. 'Tis well: and he
Who lost 'em, could have spar'd ten thousand more,
Yet if, by this advantage, you could gain
An easier peace, while *Caesar* doubts the chance
Of arms! –
ANTONY. O think not on't, *Ventidius*;
The boy pursues my ruin, he'll no peace:
His malice is considerate in advantage;
O, he's the coolest murderer, so stanch,[27]
He kills, and keeps his temper.
VENTIDIUS. Have you no friend
In all his army, who has power to move him,
Mecaenas, or *Agrippa* might do much.
ANTONY. They're both too deep in *Caesar's* interests,
We'll work it out by dint of sword, or perish.
VENTIDIUS. Fain I would find some other.
ANTONY. Thank thy love.
Some four or five such victories as this,
Will save thy farther pains.
VENTIDIUS. Expect no more; *Caesar* is on his guard:
I know, Sir, you have conquer'd against odds;
But still you draw supplies from one poor town,
And of *Egyptians*: he has all the World,
And, at his back, nations come pouring in,
To fill the gaps you make. Pray think again.
ANTONY. Why dost thou drive me from my self, to search
For foreign aids? To hunt my memory,
And range all o'er a waste and barren place
To find a friend? The wretched have no friends –
Yet I had one, the bravest youth of *Rome*,
Whom *Caesar* loves beyond the love of women;
He could resolve his mind, as fire does wax,
From that hard rugged image, melt him down,
And mould him in what softer form he pleas'd.
VENTIDIUS. Him would I see; that man of all the World:
Just such a one we want.
ANTONY. He lov'd me too.
I was his soul; he liv'd not but in me:
We were so clos'd within each other's breasts,
The rivets were not found that join'd us first.
That does not reach us yet: we were so mixt,
As meeting streams, both to our selves were lost;
We were one mass; we could not give or take,
But from the same; for he was I, I he.
VENTIDIUS. [*Aside*] *He moves as I would wish him.*
ANTONY. After this,
I need not tell his name: 'twas *Dollabella*.
VENTIDIUS. He's now in *Caesar*'s camp.
ANTONY. No matter where,
Since he's no longer mine. He took unkindly
That I forbad him *Cleopatra*'s sight;
Because I fear'd he lov'd her: he confess'd
He had a warmth, which, for my sake, he stifled;
For 'twere impossible that two, so one,
Should not have lov'd the same. When he departed,
He took no leave; and that confirm'd my thoughts.
VENTIDIUS. It argues that he lov'd you more than her,
Else he had staid; but he perceiv'd you jealous,
And would not grieve his friend: I know he loves you.
ANTONY. I should have seen him then ere now.
VENTIDIUS. Perhaps
He has thus long been lab'ring for your peace.
ANTONY. Would he were here.

VENTIDIUS. Would you believe he lov'd you?
I read your answer in your eyes; you would.
Not to conceal it longer, he has sent
A messenger from *Caesar*'s camp, with letters.
ANTONY. Let him appear.
VENTIDIUS. I'll bring him instantly.

[*Exit* Ventidius, *and re-enters immediately with* Dollabella.

ANTONY. 'Tis he himself, himself, by holy friendship! [*Runs to embrace him.*
Art thou return'd at last, my better half?
Come, give me all my self.
Let me not live,
If the young bridegroom, longing for his night,
Was ever half so fond.
DOLLABELLA. I must be silent; for my soul is busie
About a noble work: she's new come home,
Like a long absent man, and wanders o'er
Each room, a stranger to her own, to look
If all be safe.
ANTONY. Thou hast what's left of me,
For I am now so sunk from what I was,
Thou find'st me at my lowest water-mark.
The rivers that ran in, and rais'd my fortunes,
Are all dry'd up, or take another course:
What I have left is from my native spring;
I've still a heart that swells, in scorn of fate.
And lifts me to my banks.
DOLLABELLA. Still you are Lord of all the World to me.
ANTONY. Why, then I yet am so; for thou art all.
If I had any joy when thou wert absent,
I grudg'd it to my self; methought I robb'd
Thee of thy part. But, oh my *Dollabella*!
Thou hast beheld me other than I am.
Hast thou not seen my morning chambers fill'd
With scepter'd slaves, who waited to salute me:
With eastern monarchs, who forgot the sun,
To worship my uprising? Menial kings
Ran coursing up and down my palace-yard,
Stood silent in my presence, watch'd my eyes,
And, at my least command, all started out
Like racers to the gaol.[28]
DOLLABELLA. Slaves to your fortune.
ANTONY. Fortune is *Caesar*'s now; and what am I?
VENTIDIUS. What you have made your self; I will not flatter.
ANTONY. Is this friendly done?
DOLLABELLA. Yes, when his end is so, I must join with him;
Indeed I must, and yet you must not chide:
Why am I else your friend?
ANTONY. Take heed, young man,
How thou upbraid'st my love: the Queen has eyes,
And thou too hast a soul. Canst thou remember
When, swell'd with hatred, thou beheld'st her first
As accessary to thy brother's death?
DOLLABELLA. Spare my remembrance; 'twas a guilty day,
And still the blush hangs here.
ANTONY. To clear her self,
For sending him no aid, she came from *Egypt*.
Her gally down the silver *Cydnos*[29] row'd,
The tackling silk, the streamers wav'd with gold,
The gentle winds were lodg'd in purple sails:
Her nymphs, like *nereids*,[30] round her couch, were plac'd;
Where she, another sea-born *Venus*, lay.
DOLLABELLA. No more: I would not hear it.
ANTONY. O, you must!
She lay, and leant her cheek upon her hand,
And cast a look so languishingly sweet,
As if, secure of all beholders' hearts,
Neglecting she could take 'em: boys, like cupids,
Stood fanning, with their painted wings, the winds
That played about her face: but if she smil'd,
A darting glory seem'd to blaze abroad:
That men's desiring eyes were never weary'd;
But hung upon the object: to soft flutes
The silver oars kept time; and while they played,
The hearing gave new pleasure to the sight;
And both to thought: 'twas Heav'n or somewhat more;
For she so charm'd all hearts, that gazing crowds
Stood panting on the shore, and wanted breath
To give their welcome voice.
Then, *Dollabella*, where was then thy soul?
Was not thy fury quite disarm'd with wonder?
Didst thou not shrink behind me from those eyes,

And whisper in my ears? Oh, tell her not
That I accus'd her with my brother's death!

DOLLABELLA. And should my weakness be a plea for yours?
Mine was an age when love might be excus'd,
When kindly warmth, and when my springing youth
Made it a debt to Nature. Yours –

VENTIDIUS. Speak boldly.
Yours, he would say; in your declining age,
When no more heat was left but what you forc'd,
When all the sap was needful for the trunk,
When it went down, then you constrain'd the course,
And robb'd from Nature, to supply Desire;
In you (I would not use so harsh a word)
But 'tis plain dotage.

ANTONY. Ha!

DOLLABELLA. 'Twas urg'd too home.
But yet the loss was private that I made;
'twas but my self I lost: I lost no legions;
I had no World to lose, no people's love.

ANTONY. This from a friend?

DOLLABELLA. Yes, *Antony*, a true one;
A friend so tender, that each word I speak
Stabs my own heart, before it reach your ear.
O, judge me not less kind because I chide:
To *Caesar* I excuse you.

ANTONY. O ye gods!
Have I then liv'd to be excus'd to *Caesar*?

DOLLABELLA. As to your equal.

ANTONY. While I wear this, he never shall be more.

DOLLABELLA. I bring conditions from him.

ANTONY. Are they noble?
Methinks thou shouldst not bring 'em else; yet he
Is full of deep dissembling; knows no honour,
Divided from his int'rest. Fate mistook him;
For Nature meant him for an usurer,[31]
He's fit indeed to buy, not conquer kingdoms.

VENTIDIUS. Then, granting this,
What pow'r was theirs who wrought so hard a temper
To honourable terms!

ANTONY. It was my *Dollabella*, or some god.

DOLLABELLA. Nor I; nor yet *Mecaenas*, nor *Agrippa*:
They were your enemies; and I a friend
Too weak alone; yet 'twas a *Roman*'s deed.

ANTONY. 'Twas like a *Roman* done: show me that man
Who has preserv'd my life, my love, my honour;
Let me but see his face.

VENTIDIUS. That task is mine,
And, Heav'n thou know'st how pleasing. [*Exit* Ventidius.

DOLLABELLA. You'll remember
To whom you stand oblig'd?

ANTONY. When I forget it,
Be thou unkind, and that's my greatest curse.
My Queen shall thank him too.

DOLLABELLA. I fear she will not.

ANTONY. But she shall do't: the Queen, my *Dollabella*!
Hast thou not still some grudgings of thy fever?

DOLLABELLA. I would not see her lost.

ANTONY. When I forsake her,
Leave me, my better Stars; for she has truth
Beyond her beauty. *Caesar* tempted her,
At no less price than kingdoms, to betray me;
But she resisted all: and yet thou chid'st me
For loving her too well. Could I do so?

DOLLABELLA. Yes there's my reason.

[*Re-enter* Ventidius, *with* Octavia, *leading* Antony*'s two little daughters*.

ANTONY. [*Starting back*] Where?–*Octavia* there!

VENTIDIUS. What, is she poyson to you? A disease?
Look on her, view her well; and those she brings:
Are they all strangers to your eyes? Has Nature
No secret call, no whisper they are yours?

DOLLABELLA. For shame, my Lord, if not for love, receive 'em
With kinder eyes. If you confess a Man,
Meet 'em, embrace 'em, bid 'em welcome to you.
Your arms should open, ev'n without; your knowledge,
To clasp 'em in; your feet should turn to wings,
To bear you to 'em; and your eyes dart out,
And aim a kiss ere you could reach the lips.

ANTONY. I stood amaz'd to think how they came hither.

VENTIDIUS. I sent for 'em; I brought 'em in, unknown
To *Cleopatra*'s guards.

DOLLABELLA. Yet are you cold?

OCTAVIA. Thus long I have attended for my welcome;

Which, as a stranger, sure I might expect,
Who am I?
ANTONY. *Caesar*'s sister.
OCTAVIA. That's unkind!
Had I been nothing more than *Caesar*'s sister,
Know, I had still remain'd in *Caesar*'s camp;
But your *Octavia*, your much injur'd wife,
Though banish'd from your bed, driv'n from your house,
In spite of *Caesar*'s sister, still is yours.
'Tis true, I have a heart disdains your coldness,
And prompts me not to seek what you should offer;
But a wife's virtue still surmounts that pride:
I come to claim you as my own; to show
My duty first, to ask, nay beg, your kindness:
Your hand, my Lord; 'tis mine, and I will have it. [*Taking his hand.*
VENTIDIUS. Do, take it, thou deserv'st it.
DOLLABELLA. On my soul,
And so she does: she's neither too submissive,
Nor yet too haughty; but so just a mean,
Shows, as it ought, a wife and *Roman* too.
ANTONY. I fear, *Octavia*, you have begg'd my life.
OCTAVIA. Begg'd it, my Lord?
ANTONY Yes, begg'd it, my Ambassadress,
Poorly and basely begg'd it of your brother.
OCTAVIA. Poorly and basely I could never beg;
Nor could my brother grant.
ANTONY. Shall I, who, to my kneeling slave, could say,
Rise up, and be a king; shall I fall down
And cry, forgive me, *Caesar*? Shall I set
A man, my equal, in the place of *Jove*,
As he could give me being? No; that word,
Forgive, would choke me up,
And die upon my tongue.
DOLLABELLA. You shall not need it.
ANTONY. I will not need it. Come, you've all betray'd me:
My friend too! To receive some vile conditions
My wife has bought me, with her prayers and tears;
And now I must become her branded slave:
In every peevish mood she will upbraid
The life she gave: if I but look awry,
She cries, I'll tell my brother.
OCTAVIA. My hard fortune
Subjects me still to your unkind mistakes.
But the conditions I have brought are such
You need not blush to take: I love your honour,
Because 'tis mine; it never shall be said
Octavia's husband was her brother's slave.
Sir, you are free; free, ev'n from her you loath;
For, tho' my brother bargains for your love,
Makes me the price and cement of your peace,
I have a soul like yours; I cannot take
Your love as alms, nor beg what I deserve.
I'll tell my brother we are reconcil'd;
He shall draw back his troops, and you shall march
To rule the East: I may be dropt at *Athens*;
No matter where, I never will complain,
But only keep the barren name of Wife,
And rid you of the trouble.
VENTIDIUS. Was ever such a strife of sullen honour!
Both scorn'd to be oblig'd.
DOLLABELLA. Oh, she has toucht him in the tender'st part;
See how he reddens with despight[32] and shame
To be out-done in generosity!
VENTIDIUS. See how he winks! How he dries up a tear,
That fain would fall!
ANTONY. *Octavia*, I have heard you, and must praise
The greatness of your soul;
But cannot yield to what you have propos'd:
For I can ne'er be conquer'd but by love;
And you do all for duty. You would free me,
And would be dropt at *Athens*; was't not so?
OCTAVIA. It was, my Lord.
ANTONY. Then I must be oblig'd
To one who loves me not, who, to her self,
May call me thankless and ungrateful Man:
I'll not endure it, no.
VENTIDIUS. I'm glad it pinches there.
OCTAVIA. Would you triumph o'er poor *Octavia*'s virtue?
That pride was all I had to bear me up;
That you might think you ow'd me for your life,
And ow'd it to my duty, not my love.
I have been injur'd, and my haughty soul
Could brook but ill the man who slights my bed.
ANTONY. Therefore you love me not.
OCTAVIA. Therefore, my Lord,
I should not love you.
ANTONY. Therefore you wou'd leave me?
OCTAVIA. And therefore I should leave you – if I could.

DOLLABELLA. Her soul's too great, after such injuries,
To say she loves; and yet she lets you see it.
Her modesty and silence plead her cause.
ANTONY. Oh, *Dollabella*, which way shall I turn?
I find a secret yielding in my soul;
But *Cleopatra*, who would die with me,
Must she be left? Pity pleads for *Octavia*;
But does it not plead more for *Cleopatra*?
VENTIDIUS. Justice and pity both plead for *Octavia*;
For *Cleopatra*, neither.
One would be ruin'd with you; but she first
Had ruin'd you: the other, you have ruin'd,
And yet she would preserve you.
In every thing their merits are unequal.
ANTONY. Oh, my distracted soul!
OCTAVIA. Sweet Heav'n compose it.
Come, come, my Lord, if I can pardon you,
Methinks you should accept it. Look on these;
Are they not yours? Or stand they thus neglected
As they are mine? Go to him, Children, go;
Kneel to him, take him by the hand, speak to him;
For you may speak, and he may own you too,
Without a blush; and so he cannot all
His children: Go, I say, and pull him to me,
And pull him to your selves, from that bad woman.
You, *Agrippina*, hang upon his arms;
And you, *Antonia*, clasp about his waste:[33]
If he will shake you off, if he will dash you
Against the pavement, you must bear it, Children;
For you are mine, and I was born to suffer.

[*Here the children go to him, &c.*

VENTIDIUS. Was ever sight so moving! Emperor!
DOLLABELLA. Friend!
OCTAVIA. Husband!
BOTH CHILDREN. Father!
ANTONY. I am vanquish'd: take me,
Octavia; take me, Children; share me all. [*Embracing them.*
I've been a thriftless debtor to your loves,
And run out much, in riot, from your stock;
But all shall be amended.
OCTAVIA. O blest hour!
DOLLABELLA. O happy change!
VENTIDIUS. My joy stops at my tongue;
But it has found two channels here for one,
And bubbles out above.

ANTONY. This is thy triumph; lead me where thou wilt;
Ev'n to thy brother's camp. [*To* Octavia.
OCTAVIA. All there are yours.

[*Enter* Alexas *hastily.*

ALEXAS. The Queen, my Mistress, Sir, and yours –
ANTONY. 'Tis past. *Octavia*, you shall stay this night; To morrow,
Caesar and we are one.

[*Exit leading* Octavia, Dollabella *and the children follow.*

VENTIDIUS. There's news for you; run,
My officious Eunuch,
Be sure to be the first; haste forward:
Haste, my dear Eunuch, haste. [*Exit.*
ALEXAS. This downright fighting fool, this thick-scull'd hero,
This blunt unthinking instrument of death,
With plain dull virtue, has out-gone my wit:
Pleasure forsook my early'st infancy,
The luxury of others robb'd my cradle,
And ravish'd thence the promise of a man:
Cast out from Nature, disinherited
Of what her meanest children claim by kind;
Yet, greatness kept me from contempt: that's gone.
Had *Cleopatra* follow'd my advice,
Then he had been betray'd, who now forsakes.
She dies for love; but she has known its joys:
Gods, is this just, that I, who knows no joys,
Must die, because she loves?

[*Enter* Cleopatra, Charmion, Iras, *train.*

Oh, Madam, I have seen what blasts my eyes!
Octavia's here!
CLEOPATRA. Peace with that raven's note.
I know it too; and now am in
The pangs of death.
ALEXAS. You are no more a queen;
Egypt is lost.
CLEOPATRA. What tell'st thou me of *Egypt*?
My Life, my Soul is lost! *Octavia* has him!
O fatal name to *Cleopatra*'s love!
My kisses, my embraces now are hers;
While I – but thou hast seen my rival; speak,
Does she deserve this blessing? Is she fair,
Bright as a goddess? And is all perfection
Confin'd to her? It is. Poor I was made
Of that coarse matter which, when she was finish'd,
The gods threw by, for rubbish.

ALEXAS. She's indeed a very miracle.
CLEOPATRA. Death to my hopes, a miracle!
ALEXAS. [*Bowing*] A miracle;
I mean of goodness; for in beauty, Madam,
You make all wonders cease.
CLEOPATRA. I was too rash:
Take this in part of recompence. But, oh, [*Giving a ring.*
I fear thou flatter'st me.
CHARMION. She comes! She's here!
IRAS. Flee, Madam, *Caesar*'s sister!
CLEOPATRA. Were she the sister of the thund'rer *Jove*,
And bore her brother's lightning in her eyes,
Thus would I face my rival.

[*Meets* Octavia *with* Ventidius. Octavia *bears up to her. Their trains come up on either side.*

OCTAVIA. I need not ask if you are *Cleopatra*,
Your haughty carriage –
CLEOPATRA. Shows I am a Queen:
Nor need I ask you who you are.
OCTAVIA. A *Roman*:
A name that makes, and can unmake a Queen.
CLEOPATRA. Your Lord, the man who serves me, is a *Roman*.
OCTAVIA. He was a *Roman*, till he lost that name
To be a slave in *Egypt*; but I come
To free him thence.
CLEOPATRA. Peace, peace, my Lover's *Juno*.
When he grew weary of that houshold-clog,[34]
He chose my easier bonds.
OCTAVIA. I wonder not
Your bonds are easie; you have long been practis'd
In that lascivious art: he's not the first
For whom you spread your snares: let *Caesar* witness.
CLEOPATRA. I lov'd not *Caesar*; 'twas but gratitude
I paid his love: the worst your malice can,
Is but to say the greatest of mankind
Has been my slave. The next, but far above him,
In my esteem, is he whom law calls yours,
But whom his love made mine. [Octavia *coming up close to her.*
OCTAVIA. I would view nearer
That face, which has so long usurp'd my right,
To find th' inevitable charms, that catch
Mankind so sure, that ruin'd my dear Lord.
CLEOPATRA. O, you do well to search; for had you known
But half these charms, you had not lost his heart.
OCTAVIA. Far be their knowledge from a *Roman* lady,
Far from a modest wife. Shame of our Sex,
Dost thou not blush, to own those black endearments
That make sin pleasing?
CLEOPATRA. You may blush, who want 'em: if bounteous Nature, if indulgent Heav'n
Have giv'n me charms to please the bravest man;
Should I not thank 'em? Should I be asham'd,
And not be proud? I am, that he has lov'd me;
And, when I love not him, Heav'n change this face
For one like that.
OCTAVIA. Thou lov'st him not so well.
CLEOPATRA. I love him better, and deserve him more.
OCTAVIA. You do not; cannot: you have been his ruine.
Who made him cheap at *Rome*, but *Cleopatra*?
Who made him scorn'd abroad, but *Cleopatra*?
At *Actium*, who betray'd him? *Cleopatra*.
Who made his children orphans? And poor me
A wretched widow? Only *Cleopatra*.
CLEOPATRA. Yet she who loves him best is *Cleopatra*.
If you have suffer'd, I have suffer'd more.
You bear the specious title of a Wife,
To gild your cause, and draw the pitying World
To favour it: the World condemns poor me;
For I have lost my honour, lost my fame,
And stain'd the glory of my royal house,
And all to bear the branded name of Mistress.
There wants but life, and that too I would lose
For him I love.
OCTAVIA. Be't so then; take thy wish. [*Exit cum suis.*
CLEOPATRA. And 'tis my wish,
Now he is lost for whom alone I liv'd.
My sight grows dim, and every object dances,
And swims before me, in the maze of death.
My spirits, while they were oppos'd, kept up;
They could not sink beneath a rival's scorn:
But now she's gone they faint.
ALEXAS. Mine have had leisure
To recollect their strength, and furnish counsel,
To ruine her; who else must ruine you.

CLEOPATRA. Vain Promiser!
Lead me, my *Charmion*; nay, your hand too, *Iras*:
My grief has weight enough to sink you both.
Conduct me to some solitary chamber,
And draw the curtains round;
Then leave me to my self, to take alone
My fill of grief:
There I till death will his unkindness weep:
As harmless infants moan themselves asleep.
[*Exeunt.*

Act IV.

[*Enter* Antony, Dollabella.]

DOLLABELLA. Why would you shift it from your self, on me?
Can you not tell her you must part?
ANTONY. I cannot,
I could pull out an eye, and bid it go,
And t'other should not weep. Oh, *Dollabella,*
How many deaths are in this word depart!
I dare not trust my tongue to tell her so:
One look of hers, would thaw me into tears,
And I should melt till I were lost again.
DOLLABELLA. Then let *Ventidius;*
He's rough by nature.
ANTONY. Oh, he'll speak too harshly;
He'll kill her with the news: thou, only thou.
DOLLABELLA. Nature has cast me in so soft a mould,
That but to hear a story feign'd for pleasure
Of some sad lover's death, moistens my eyes,
And robs me of my manhood. – I should speak
So faintly; with such fear to grieve her heart,
She'd not believe it earnest.
ANTONY. Therefore; therefore
Thou only, thou art fit: think thy self me,
And when thou speak'st (but let it first be long)
Take off the edge from every sharper sound,
And let our parting be as gently made
As other loves begin: wilt thou do this?
DOLLABELLA. What you have said, so sinks into my soul,
That, if I must speak, I shall speak just so.
ANTONY. I leave you then to your sad task: farewell.
I sent her word to meet you. [*Goes to the door, and comes back.*
I forgot;
Let her be told, I'll make her peace with mine:
Her crown and dignity shall be preserv'd,
If I have pow'r with *Caesar.* – O, be sure
To think on that.
DOLLABELLA. Fear not, I will remember.
[Antony *goes again to the door, and comes back.*
ANTONY. And tell her, too, how much I was constrain'd;
I did not this, but with extreamest force:
Desire her not to hate my memory,
For I still cherish hers; – insist on that.
DOLLABELLA. Trust me, I'll not forget it.
ANTONY. Then that's all. [*Goes out, and returns again.*
Wilt thou forgive my fondness this once more?
Tell her, tho' we shall never meet again,
If I should hear she took another love,
The news would break my heart. – now I must go;
For every time I have return'd, I feel
My soul more tender; and my next command
Would be to bid her stay, and ruine both.
[*Exit.*
DOLLABELLA. Men are but children of a larger growth,
Our appetites as apt to change as theirs,
And full as craving too, and full as vain;
And yet the soul, shut up in her dark room,
Viewing so clear abroad, at home sees nothing;
But, like a mole in earth, busie and blind,
Works all her folly up, and casts it outward
To the World's open view: thus I discover'd,
And blam'd the love of ruin'd *Antony;*
Yet wish that I were he, to be so ruin'd.

[*Enter* Ventidius *above.*

VENTIDIUS. Alone? And talking to himself?
Concern'd too?

Perhaps my guess is right; he lov'd her once,
And may pursue it still.

DOLLABELLA. O friendship! Friendship!
Ill canst thou answer this; and reason, worse:
Unfaithful in th' attempt; hopeless to win;
And, if I win, undone: mere madness all.
And yet th' occasion's fair. What injury,
To him, to wear the robe which he throws by?

VENTIDIUS. None, none at all. This happens as I wish,
To ruine her yet more with *Antony*.

[*Enter* Cleopatra, *talking with* Alexas, Charmion, Iras *on the other side.*

DOLLABELLA. She comes! What charms have sorrow on that face!
Sorrow seems pleas'd to dwell with so much sweetness;
Yet, now and then, a melancholy smile
Breaks loose, like lightning, in a winter's night,
And shows a moment's day.

VENTIDIUS. If she should love him too! Her Eunuch there!
That *Porcpisce*[35] bodes ill weather. Draw, draw nearer,
Sweet Devil, that I may hear.

ALEXAS. Believe me; try [Dollabella *goes over to* Charimon *and* Iras; *seems to talk with them.*
To make him jealous; jealousie is like
A polisht glass held to the lips when life's in doubt:
If there be breath, 'twill catch the damp and show it.

CLEOPATRA. I grant you jealousie's a proof of love,
But 'tis a weak and unavailing med'cine;
It puts out the disease, and makes it show,
But has no pow'r to cure.

ALEXAS. 'Tis your last remedy, and strongest too:
And then this *Dollabella*, who so fit
To practice on? He's handsome, valiant, young,
And looks as he were laid for Nature's bait
To catch weak women's eyes.
He stands already more than half suspected
Of loving you: the least kind word, or glance,
You give this youth, will kindle him with love:
Then, like a burning vessel set adrift,
You'll send him down amain before the wind,
To fire the heart of jealous *Antony*.

CLEOPATRA. Can I do this? Ah no; my love's so true,
That I can neither hide it where it is,
Nor show it where it is not. Nature meant me
A wife, a silly harmless houshold dove,
Fond without art; and kind without deceit;
But fortune, that has made a mistress of me,
Hast thrust me out to the wide World, unfurnish'd
Of falshood to be happy.

ALEXAS. Force your self.
Th' event will be, your lover will return
Doubly desirous to possess the good
Which once he fear'd to lose.

CLEOPATRA. I must attempt it;
But oh with what regret!

[*Exit* Alexas. *She comes up to* Dollabella.

VENTIDIUS. So, now the scene draws near; they're in my reach.

CLEOPATRA. [*To* Dollabella] Discoursing with my women! Might not I
Share in your entertainment?

CHARMION. You have been
The subject of it, Madam.

CLEOPATRA. How; and how?

IRAS. Such praises of your beauty!

CLEOPATRA. Mere poetry.
Your *Roman* wits, your *Gallus* and *Tibullus*,
Have taught you this from *Citheris* and *Delia*.[36]

DOLLABELLA. Those *Roman* wits have never been in *Egypt*,
Citheris and *Delia* else had been unsung:
I, who have seen – had I been born a poet,
Should choose a nobler name.

CLEOPATRA. You flatter me.
But, 'tis your Nation's vice: all of your country
Are flatterers, and all false. Your friends like you.
I'm sure he sent you not to speak these words.

DOLLABELLA. No, Madam; yet he sent me –

CLEOPATRA. Well, he sent you –

DOLLABELLA. Of a less pleasing errand.

CLEOPATRA. How less pleasing?
Less to your self, or me?

DOLLABELLA. Madam, to both;
For you must mourn, and I must grieve to cause it.

CLEOPATRA. You, *Charmion*, and your fellow, stand at distance.

– [*Aside*] *Hold up, my spirits.* – Well, now your mournful matter;
For I'm prepar'd, perhaps can guess it too.

DOLLABELLA. I wish you would; for 'tis a thankless office
To tell ill news: and I, of all your sex,
Most fear displeasing you.

CLEOPATRA. Of all your sex,
I soonest could forgive you, if you should.

VENTIDIUS. Most delicate advances! Woman! Woman!
Dear damn'd, inconstant sex!

CLEOPATRA. In the first place,
I am to be forsaken; is't not so?

DOLLABELLA. I wish I could not answer to that question.

CLEOPATRA. Then pass it o'er, because it troubles you:
I should have been more griev'd another time.
Next, I'm to lose my kingdom.–Farewell, *Egypt*.
Yet, is there any more?

DOLLABELLA. Madam, I fear
Your too deep sense of grief has turn'd your reason.

CLEOPATRA. No, no, I'm not run mad; I can bear fortune:
And love may be expell'd by other love,
As poysons are by poysons.

DOLLABELLA. – You o'erjoy me, Madam,
To find your griefs so moderately born.
You've heard the worst; all are not false, like him.

CLEOPATRA. No; Heav'n forbid they should.

DOLLABELLA. Some men are constant.

CLEOPATRA. And constancy deserves reward, that's certain.

DOLLABELLA. Deserves it not; but give it leave to hope.

VENTIDIUS. I'll swear thou hast my leave. I have enough:
But how to manage this! Well, I'll consider. [*Exit*.

DOLLABELLA. I came prepar'd,
To tell you heavy news; news, which I thought,
Would fright the blood from your pale cheeks to hear:
But you have met it with a cheerfulness
That makes my task more easie; and my tongue,
Which on another's message was employ'd,
Would gladly speak its own.

CLEOPATRA. Hold, *Dollabella*.
First tell me, were you chosen by my Lord?
Or sought you this employment?

DOLLABELLA. He pick'd me out; and, as his bosom-friend,
He charg'd me with his words.

CLEOPATRA. The message then
I know was tender, and each accent smooth,
To mollify that rugged word *depart*.

DOLLABELLA. Oh, you mistake: he chose the harshest words,
With fiery eyes, and with contracted brows,
He coined his face in the severest stamp:
And fury shook his fabrick like an earthquake;
He heav'd for vent, and burst like bellowing *Aetna*,
In sounds scarce human, "Hence, away for ever:
Let her be gone, the blot of my renown,
And bane of all my hopes:
Let her be driv'n as far as men can think
From Man's commerce: She'll poyson to the center."

[*All the time of this speech,* Cleopatra *seems more and more concern'd, till she sinks quite down.*

CLEOPATRA. Oh, I can bear no more!

DOLLABELLA. Help, help: oh Wretch! Oh cursed, cursed Wretch!
What have I done?

CHARMION. Help, chafe her temples, Iras.

IRAS. Bend, bend her forward quickly.

CHARMION. Heav'n be prais'd,
She comes again.

CLEOPATRA. Oh, let him not approach me.
Why have you brought me back to this loath'd being,
Th' abode of falshood, violated vows,
And injur'd love? For pity, let me go;
For, if there be a place of long repose,
I'm sure I want it. My disdainful Lord
Can never break that quiet; nor awake
The sleeping soul, with hollowing in my tomb
Such words as fright her hence, unkind, unkind.

DOLLABELLA. [*Kneeling*] Believe me, 'tis against my self I speak,
That sure deserves belief; I injur'd him:
My friend ne'er spoke those words. Oh, had you seen
How often he came back, and every time
With something more obliging and more kind,
To add to what he said; what dear farewells;

How almost vanquisht by his love he parted,
And lean'd to what unwillingly he left:
I, traitor as I was, for love of you,
(But what can you not do, who made me false!)
I forg'd that lie; for whose forgiveness kneels
This self-accus'd, self-punish'd criminal.

CLEOPATRA. With how much ease believe we what we wish!
Rise, *Dollabella*; if you have been guilty,
I have contributed, and too much love
Has made me guilty too.
Th' advance of kindness which I made, was feign'd,
To call back fleeting love by jealousie;
But 'twould not last. Oh, rather let me lose
Than so ignobly trifle with his heart.

DOLLABELLA. I find your breast fenc'd round from human reach,
Transparent as a rock of solid crystal;
Seen through, but never pierc'd. My Friend, my Friend!
What endless treasure hast thou thrown away,
And scatter'd, like an infant, in the ocean,
Vain sums of wealth which none can gather thence.

CLEOPATRA. Could you not beg
An hour's admittance to his private ear?
Like one who wanders through long barren wilds,
And yet foreknows no hospitable inn.
Is near to succour hunger,
Eats his fill, before his painful march:
So would I feed a while my famish'd eyes
Before we part; for I have far to go,
If death be far, and never must return.

[Ventidius, *with* Octavia, *behind.*

VENTIDIUS. From hence you may discover –
Oh, sweet, sweet!
Would you indeed? The pretty hand in earnest?

[Dollabella *takes her hand.*

DOLLABELLA. I will, for this reward. –Draw it not back,
'Tis all I e'er will beg.

VENTIDIUS. They turn upon us.

OCTAVIA. What quick eyes has guilt!

VENTIDIUS. Seem not to have observ'd 'em, and go on.

[*They enter.*

DOLLABELLA. Saw you the Emperor, *Ventidius*?

VENTIDIUS. No.
I sought him; but I heard that he was private,
None with him, but *Hipparchus* his freedman.[37]

DOLLABELLA. Know you his bus'ness?

VENTIDIUS. Giving him instructions,
And letters, to his brother *Caesar.*

DOLLABELLA. Well,
He must be found.

[*Exeunt* Dollabella *and* Cleopatra.

OCTAVIA. Most glorious impudence!

VENTIDIUS. She look'd methought
As she would say, take your old man, *Octavia*;
Thank you, I'm better here.
Well, but what use
Make we of this discovery?

OCTAVIA. Let it die.

VENTIDIUS. I pity *Dollabella*; but she's dangerous:
Her eyes have pow'r beyond *Thessalian* charms[38]
To draw the moon from Heav'n; for eloquence,
The sea-green syrens taught her voice their flatt'ry;
And, while she speaks, night steals upon the day,
Unmark'd of those that hear: then she's so charming,
Age buds at sight of her, and swells to youth:
The holy priests gaze on her when she smiles;
And with heav'd hands forgetting gravity,
They bless her wanton eyes: Even I who hate her,
With a malignant joy behold such beauty;
And, while I curse, desire it. *Antony*
Must needs have some remains of passion still,
Which may ferment into a worse relapse,
If now not fully cur'd. I know, this minute,
With *Caesar* he's endeavouring her peace.

OCTAVIA. You have prevail'd: – but for a farther purpose. [*Walks off.*
I'll prove[39] how he will relish this discovery.
What, make a strumpet's peace! It swells my heart:
It must not, shall not be.

VENTIDIUS. His guards appear.
Let me begin, and you shall second me.

[*Enter* Antony.

ANTONY. *Octavia*, I was looking you, my Love:[40]

What, are your letters ready? I have giv'n
My last instructions.
OCTAVIA. Mine, my Lord, are written.
ANTONY. *Ventidius*! [*Drawing him aside.*
VENTIDIUS. My Lord?
ANTONY. A word in private.
When saw you *Dollabella*?
VENTIDIUS. Now, my Lord,
He parted hence; and *Cleopatra* with him.
ANTONY. Speak softly. 'Twas by my command he went,
To bear my last farewell.
VENTIDIUS. It look'd indeed
Like your farewell. [*Aloud.*
ANTONY. More softly. – My farewell?
What secret meaning have you in those words
Of my farewell? He did it by my order.
VENTIDIUS. Then he obey'd your order. [*Aloud*] I suppose
You bid him do it with all gentleness,
All kindness, and all – love.
ANTONY. How she mourn'd,
The poor forsaken creature!
VENTIDIUS. She took it as she ought; she bore your parting
As she did *Caesar*'s, as she would another's,
Were a new love to come.
ANTONY. Thou dost belie her;
Most basely, and maliciously belie her. [*Aloud.*
VENTIDIUS. I thought not to displease you; I have done.
OCTAVIA. [*Coming up*] You seem disturb'd, my Lord.
ANTONY. A very trifle.
Retire, my Love.
VENTIDIUS. It was indeed a trifle.
He sent –
ANTONY. No more. Look how thou disobey'st me;
Thy life shall answer it. [*Angrily.*
OCTAVIA. Then 'tis no trifle.
VENTIDIUS. 'Tis less; a very nothing: you too saw it,
As well as I, and therefore 'tis no secret.
[*To* Octavia.
ANTONY. She saw it!
VENTIDIUS. Yes: she saw young *Dollabella* –
ANTONY. Young *Dollabella*!
VENTIDIUS. Young, I think him young,
And handsome too; and so do others think him.
But what of that? He went by your command,
Indeed 'tis probable, with some kind message;
For she receiv'd it graciously; she smil'd:
And then he grew familiar with her hand,
Squeez'd it, and worry'd it with ravenous kisses;
She blush'd, and sigh'd, and smil'd, and blush'd again;
At last she took occasion to talk softly,
And brought her cheek up close, and lean'd on his:
At which, he whisper'd kisses back on hers;
And then she cry'd aloud, that constancy
Should be rewarded.
OCTAVIA. This I saw and heard.
ANTONY. What woman was it, whom you heard and saw
So playful with my friend!
Not *Cleopatra*?
VENTIDIUS. Ev'n she, my Lord!
ANTONY. My *Cleopatra*?
VENTIDIUS. Your *Cleopatra*;
Dollabella's *Cleopatra*?
Every man's *Cleopatra*.
ANTONY. Thou liest.
VENTIDIUS. I do not lie, my Lord.
Is this so strange? Should mistresses be left,
And not provide against a time of change?
You know she's not much used to lonely nights.
ANTONY. I'll think no more on't.
I know 'tis false, and see the plot betwixt you.
You needed not have gone this way, *Octavia*.
What harms it you that *Cleopatra*'s just?
She's mine no more. I see; and I forgive:
Urge it no farther, Love.
OCTAVIA. Are you concern'd
That she's found false?
ANTONY. I should be, were it so;
For, tho 'tis past, I would not that the World
Should tax my former choice: that I lov'd one
Of so light note; but I forgive you both.
VENTIDIUS. What has my age deserv'd, that you should think
I would abuse your ears with perjury?
If Heav'n be true, she's false.
ANTONY. Tho Heav'n and Earth
Should witness it, I'll not believe her tainted.
VENTIDIUS. I'll bring you then a witness
From Hell to prove her so. Nay, go not back;

[*Seeing* Alexas *just entring, and starting back.*

For stay you must and shall.

ALEXAS. What means my Lord?
VENTIDIUS. To make you do what most you hate; speak truth.
You are of *Cleopatra*'s private counsel,
Of her bed-counsel, her lascivious hours;
Are conscious of each nightly change she makes,
And watch her, as *Chaldeans* do the moon,[41]
Can tell what signs she passes through, what day.
ALEXAS. My Noble Lord.
VENTIDIUS. My most Illustrious Pander,
No fine set speech, no cadence, no turn'd periods,
But a plain home-spun truth, is what I ask:
I did, my self, o'er hear your Queen make love
To *Dollabella*. Speak; for I will know,
By your confession, what more past betwixt 'em;
How near the bus'ness draws to your employment;
And when the happy hour.
ANTONY. Speak truth, *Alexas*, whether it offend
Or please *Ventidius*, care not: justifie
Thy injur'd Queen from malice: dare his worst.
OCTAVIA. [*Aside*] *See how he gives him courage! How he fears*
To find her false! And shuts his eyes to truth,
Willing to be misled!
ALEXAS. As far as love may plead for woman's frailty,
Urg'd by desert and greatness of the lover;
So far (divine *Octavia*!) may my Queen
Stand ev'n excus'd to you, for loving him,
Who is your Lord: so far, from brave *Ventidius*,
May her past actions hope a fair report.
ANTONY. 'Tis well, and truly spoken: mark, *Ventidius*.
ALEXAS. To you, most noble Emperor, her strong passion
Stands not excus'd, but wholly justifi'd.
Her beauty's charms alone, without her crown,
From *Ind* and *Meroe* drew the distant vows[42]
Of sighing kings; and at her feet were laid
The scepters of the earth, expos'd on heaps,
To choose where she would reign:
She thought a *Roman* only could deserve her;
And, of all *Romans*, only *Antony*.
And, to be less than wife to you, disdain'd
Their lawful passion.
ANTONY. 'Tis but truth.
ALEXAS. And yet, tho' love, and your unmatch'd desert,
Have drawn her from the due regard of honour,
At last, Heav'n open'd her unwilling eyes
To see the wrongs she offer'd fair *Octavia*,
Whose holy bed she lawfully usurpt,
The sad effects of this unprosperous war,
Confirm'd those pious thoughts.
VENTIDIUS. – [*Aside*] *O, wheel you there?* –
Observe him now; the man begins to mend,
And talk substantial reason. Fear not, Eunuch,
The Emperor has giv'n thee leave to speak.
ALEXAS. Else had I never dar'd to offend his ears
With what the last necessity has urg'd
On my forsaken Mistress; yet I must not
Presume to say her heart is wholly alter'd.
ANTONY. No, dare not for thy life, I charge thee dare not,
Pronounce that fatal word.
OCTAVIA. [*Aside*] *Must I bear this? Good Heav'n, afford me patience.*
VENTIDIUS. On, sweet Eunuch; my dear Half Man, proceed.
ALEXAS. Yet *Dollabella*
Has lov'd her long. He, next my god-like Lord,
Deserves her best; and should she meet his passion,
Rejected, as she is, by him she lov'd –
ANTONY. Hence, from my sight; for I can bear no more:
Let Furies drag thee quick to Hell; each torturing hand
Do thou employ, till *Cleopatra* comes,
Then join thou too, and help to torture her.

[*Exit* Alexas, *thrust out by* Antony.

OCTAVIA. 'Tis not well,
Indeed, my Lord, 'tis much unkind to me,
To show this passion, this extreme concernment
For an abandon'd, faithless prostitute.
ANTONY. Octavia, leave me: I am much disorder'd.
Leave me, I say.
OCTAVIA. My Lord?
ANTONY. I bid you leave me.
VENTIDIUS. Obey him, Madam: best withdraw a while,
And see how this will work.

OCTAVIA. Wherein have I offended you, my Lord,
That I am bid to leave you? Am I false,
Or infamous? Am I a *Cleopatra*?
Were I she,
Base as she is, you would not bid me leave you;
But hang upon my neck, take slight excuses,
And fawn upon my falshood.

ANTONY. 'Tis too much,
Too much, *Octavia*; I am prest with sorrows
Too heavy to be born; and you add more:
I would retire, and recollect what's left
Of man within, to aid me.

OCTAVIA. You would mourn
In private, for your Love, who has betray'd you;
You did but half return to me: your kindness
Linger'd behind with her. I hear, my Lord,
You make conditions for her,
And would include her treaty. Wondrous proofs
Of love to me!

ANTONY. Are you my friend, *Ventidius*?
Or are you turn'd a *Dollabella* too,
And let this Fury loose?

VENTIDIUS. Oh, be advis'd,
Sweet Madam, and retire.

OCTAVIA. Yes, I will go; but never to return.
You shall no more be haunted with this fury.
My Lord, my Lord, love will not always last,
When urg'd with long unkindness, and disdain;
Take her again whom you prefer to me;
She stays but to be call'd. Poor cozen'd man!
Let a feign'd parting give her back your heart,
Which a feign'd love first got; for injur'd me,
Tho my just sense of wrongs forbid my stay,
My duty shall be yours.
To the dear pledges of our former love,
My tenderness and care shall be transferr'd,
And they shall cheer, by turns, my widow'd nights:
So, take my last farewell; for I despair
To have you whole, and scorn to take you half. [*Exit*.

VENTIDIUS. I combat Heav'n, which blasts my best designs:
My last attempt must be to win her back;
But oh, I fear in vain. [*Exit*.

ANTONY. Why was I fram'd with this plain honest heart,
Which knows not to disguise its griefs, and weakness,
But bears its workings outward to the World?
I should have kept the mighty anguish in,
And forc'd a smile at *Cleopatra*'s falshood:
Octavia had believ'd it, and had staid;
But I am made a shallow-forded stream,
Seen to the bottom: all my clearness scorn'd,
And all my faults expos'd! – See, where he comes

[*Enter* Dollabella.

Who has prophan'd the sacred name of Friend,
And worn it into vileness!
With how secure a brow, and specious form
He gilds the secret Villain! Sure that face
Was meant for honesty; but Heav'n mis-match'd it,
And furnish'd treason out with Nature's pomp,
To make its work more easie.

DOLLABELLA. O, my Friend!

ANTONY. Well, *Dollabella*, you perform'd my message?

DOLLABELLA. I did, unwillingly.

ANTONY. Unwillingly?
Was it so hard for you to bear our parting?
You should have wisht it.

DOLLABELLA. Why?

ANTONY. Because you love me.
And she receiv'd my message, with as true,
With as unfeign'd a sorrow, as you brought it?

DOLLABELLA. She loves you, ev'n to madness.

ANTONY. Oh, I know it.
You, *Dollabella*, do not better know
How much she loves me. And should I
Forsake this Beauty? This all-perfect Creature?

DOLLABELLA. I could not, were she mine.

ANTONY. And yet you first
Perswaded me: how come you alter'd since?

DOLLABELLA. I said at first I was not fit to go;
I could not hear her sighs, and see her tears,
But pity must prevail: and so, perhaps,
It may again with you; for I have promis'd
That she should take her last farewell: and, see,
She comes to claim my word.

[*Enter* Cleopatra.

ANTONY. False *Dollabella*!

DOLLABELLA. What's false, my Lord?

ANTONY. Why, *Dollabella*'s false;
And *Cleopatra*'s false; both false and faithless.
Draw near, you well-join'd Wickedness, you Serpents,
Whom I have, in my kindly bosom, warm'd
Till I am stung to death.

DOLLABELLA. My Lord, have I
Deserv'd to be thus us'd?

CLEOPATRA. Can Heav'n prepare
A newer torment? Can it find a curse
Beyond our separation?

ANTONY. Yes, if Fate
Be just, much greater: Heav'n should be ingenious
In punishing such crimes. The rolling stone,[43]
And gnawing vulture,[44] were slight pains, invented
When *Jove* was young, and no examples known
Of mighty ills; but you have ripen'd sin
To such a monstrous growth, 'twill pose the gods
To find an equal torture. Two, two such,
Oh there's no farther name, two such – to me,
To me, who lock'd my soul within your breasts,
Had no desires, no joys, no life, but you;
When half the globe was mine, I gave it you
In dowry with my heart; I had no use,
No fruit of all, but you: a friend and mistress
Was what the World could give. Oh, *Cleopatra*!
Oh, *Dollabella*! How could you betray
This tender heart, which with an infant-fondness.
Lay lull'd betwixt your bosoms, and there slept
Secure of injur'd faith?

DOLLABELLA. If she has wrong'd you,
Heav'n, Hell, and you revenge it.

ANTONY. If she wrong'd me,
Thou wouldst evade thy part of guilt; but swear
Thou lov'st not her.

DOLLABELLA. Not so as I love you.

ANTONY. Not so! Swear, swear, I say; thou dost not love her;

DOLLABELLA. No more than friendship will allow.

ANTONY. No more?
Friendship allows thee nothing: thou art perjur'd.–
And yet thou didst not swear thou lov'dst her not;
But not so much, no more. Oh trifling Hypocrite,
Who dar'st not own to her thou dost not love,
Not own to me thou dost! *Ventidius* heard it;
Octavia saw it.

CLEOPATRA. They are enemies.

ANTONY. *Alexas* is not so: he, he confest it.
He, who, next Hell, best knew it, he avow'd it.
[*To* Dollabella] Why do I seek a proof beyond your self?
You whom I sent to bear my last farewell,
Return'd to plead her stay.

DOLLABELLA. What shall I answer?
If to have lov'd be guilt, then I have sinn'd;
But if to have repented of that love
Can wash away my crime, I have repented.
Yet, if I have offended past forgiveness,
Let not her suffer: she is innocent.

CLEOPATRA. Ah, what will not a woman do who loves!
What means will she refuse, to keep that heart
Where all her joys are plac'd! 'Twas I encourag'd,
'Twas I blew up the fire that scorch'd his soul,
To make you jealous; and by that regain you.
But all in vain; I could not counterfeit:
In spight of all the dams, my love broke o'er,
And drown'd my heart again: Fate took th' occasion;
And thus one minute's feigning has destroy'd
My whole life's truth.

ANTONY. Thin cobweb arts of falshood;
Seen, and broke through at first.

DOLLABELLA. Forgive your mistress.

CLEOPATRA. Forgive your friend.

ANTONY. You have convinc'd your selves,
You plead each other's cause: what witness have you,
That you but meant to raise my jealousie?

CLEOPATRA. Our selves, and Heav'n.

ANTONY. Guilt witnesses for guilt. Hence, love and friendship;
You have no longer place in human breasts,
These two have driv'n you out: avoid my sight;

I would not kill the man whom I lov'd;
And cannot hurt the woman; but avoid me,
I do not know how long I can be tame;
For, if I stay one minute more to think
How I am wrong'd, my justice and revenge
Will cry so loud within me, that my pity
Will not be heard for either.

DOLLABELLA. Heav'n has but
Our sorrow for our sins; and then delights
To pardon erring Man: sweet mercy seems
Its darling attribute, which limits justice;
As if there were degrees in infinite;
And infinite would rather want perfection
Than punish to extent.

ANTONY. I can forgive
A foe; but not a mistress, and a friend:
Treason is there in its most horrid shape,
Where trust is greatest: and the soul resign'd
Is stabb'd by its own guards: I'll hear no more;
Hence from my sight for ever.

CLEOPATRA. How? For ever,
I cannot go one moment from your sight,
And must I go for ever?
My joys, my only joys are center'd here:
What place have I to go to? My own kingdom?
That I have lost for you: or to the *Romans*?
They hate me for your sake: or must I wander
The wide World o'er, a helpless, banish'd woman,
Banish'd for love of you; banish'd from you?
I, there's the banishment! Oh hear me; hear me,
With strictest justice: for I beg no favour:
And if I have offended you: then kill me,
But do not banish me.

ANTONY. I must not hear you.
I have a fool within me takes your part;
But honour stops my ears.

CLEOPATRA. For pity hear me!
Wou'd you cast off a slave who follow'd you,
Who crouch'd beneath your spurn? – He has no pity!
See, if he gives one tear to my departure;
One look, one kind farewell: Oh iron heart!
Let all the gods look down, and judge betwixt us,
If he did ever love!

ANTONY. No more: *Alexas*!

DOLLABELLA. A perjur'd Villain!

ANTONY. Your *Alexas*; yours. [*To* Cleopatra.

CLEOPATRA. O 'twas his plot: his ruinous design
To engage you in my love by jealousie.
Hear him; confront him with me; let him speak.

ANTONY. I have; I have.

CLEOPATRA. And if he clear me not –

ANTONY. Your Creature! One who hangs upon your smiles!
Watches your eye to say or to unsay
Whate'er you please! I am not to be mov'd.

CLEOPATRA. Then must we part? Farewell, my cruel Lord,
Th'appearance is against me; and I go
Unjustifi'd, for ever from your sight.
How I have lov'd, you know; how yet I love,
My only comfort is, I know my self:
I love you more, ev'n now you are unkind,
Than when you lov'd me most; so well, so truly,
I'll never strive against it; but die pleas'd
To think you once were mine.

ANTONY. Good Heav'n, they weep at parting.
Must I weep too? That calls 'em innocent.
I must not weep; and yet I must, to think
That I must not forgive –
Live; but live wretched, 'tis but just you shou'd,
Who made me so: live from each other's sight:
Let me not hear you meet: set all the earth,
And all the seas, betwixt your sunder'd loves:
View nothing common but the sun and skies:
Now, all take several ways;
And each your own sad fate with mine deplore;
That you were false, and I could trust no more. [*Exeunt severally*.

Act V.

[*Enter* Cleopatra, Charmion, Iras.]

CHARMION. Be juster, Heav'n: such virtue punish'd thus,
Will make us think that Chance rules all above,
And shuffles, with a random hand, the lots
Which Man is forc'd to draw.

CLEOPATRA. I cou'd tear out these eyes, that gain'd his heart,
And had not pow'r to keep it. O the curse
Of doting on, ev'n when I find it dotage!
Bear witness, gods, you heard him bid me go;
You whom he mock'd with imprecating vows
Of promis'd faith – I'll die, I will not bear it.
You may hold me. – [*She pulls out her dagger, and they hold her.*
But I can keep my breath; I can die inward,
And choke this love.

[*Enter* Alexas.

IRAS. Help, O *Alexas* help!
The Queen grows desperate, her soul struggles in her,
With all the agonies of love and rage,
And strives to force its passage.

CLEOPATRA. Let me go.
Art thou there, Traitor! – O
O, for a little breath, to vent my rage!
Give, give me way, and let me loose upon him.

ALEXAS. Yes, I deserve it, for my ill-tim'd truth.
Was it for me to prop
The ruins of a falling Majesty?
To place my self beneath the mighty flaw,
Thus to be crush'd, and pounded into atoms,
By its o'erwhelming weight? 'Tis too presuming
For subjects, to preserve that wilful pow'r
Which courts its own destruction.

CLEOPATRA. I wou'd reason
More calmly with you. Did not you o'er-rule,
And force my plain, direct, and open love
Into these crooked paths of jealousie?
Now, what's th' event? *Octavia* is remov'd;
But *Cleopatra*'s banish'd. Thou, thou, Villain,
Has push'd my boat, to open sea; to prove,
At my sad cost, if thou canst steer it back.
It cannot be; I'm lost too far; I'm ruin'd:
Hence, thou Impostor, Traitor, Monster, Devil. –
I can no more: thou, and my griefs, have sunk
Me down so low, that I want voice to curse thee.

ALEXAS. Suppose from shipwrack'd seaman near the shore,
Dropping and faint, with climbing up the cliff,
If, from above, some charitable hand
Pull him to safety, hazarding himself
To draw the other's weight; wou'd he look back
And curse him for his pains? The case is yours;
But one step more, and you have gain'd the height.

CLEOPATRA. Sunk, never more to rise.

ALEXAS. *Octavia*'s gone, and *Dollabella* banish'd.
Believe me, Madam, *Antony* is yours.
His heart was never lost; but started off
To jealousie, love's last retreat and covert:
Where it lies hid in shades, watchful in silence,
And list'ning for the sound that calls it back,
Some other, any man ('tis so advanc'd)
May perfect this unfinish'd work, which I
(Unhappy only to my self) have left
So easie to his hand.

CLEOPATRA. Look well thou do't; else –

ALEXAS. Else, what your silence threatens – *Antony*
Is mounted up the *Pharos*;[45] from whose turret,
He stands surveying our *Egyptian* gallies,
Engag'd with *Caesar*'s fleet: now death, or conquest.
If the first happen, fate acquits my promise:
If we o'ercome, the Conqueror is yours.

[*A distant shout within.*

CHARMION. Have comfort, Madam: did you mark that shout?

[*Second shout nearer.*

IRAS. Hark; they redouble it.

ALEXAS. 'Tis from the port.
The loudness shows it near: good news, kind Heavens.

CLEOPATRA. *Osiris* make it so.

[*Enter* Serapion.

SERAPION. Where, where's the Queen?
ALEXAS. How frightfully the holy Coward stares!
As if not yet recover'd of th' assault,
When all his gods, and what's more dear to him,
His offerings were at stake.
SERAPION. O horror, horror!
Egypt has been; our latest hour is come:
The Queen of Nations from her ancient seat,
Is sunk for ever in the dark abyss:
Time has unrowl'd her glories to the last,
And now clos'd up the volume.
CLEOPATRA. Be more plain:
Say, whence thou com'st, (though fate is in thy face,
Which from thy haggard eyes looks wildly out,
And threatens ere thou speak'st.)
SERAPION. I came from *Pharos*;
From viewing (spare me and imagine it)
Our land's last hope, your navy. –
CLEOPATRA. Vanquish'd?
SERAPION. No.
They fought not.
CLEOPATRA. Then they fled.
SERAPION. Nor that. I saw,
With Antony, your well appointed fleet
Row out; and thrice he wav'd his hand on high,
And thrice with cheerful cries they shouted back:
'Twas then, false fortune, like a fawning strumpet,
About to leave the bankrupt Prodigal,
With a dissembling smile would kiss at parting,
And flatter to the last; the well-tim'd oars
Now dipt from every bank, now smoothly run
To meet the foe; and soon indeed they met,
But not as foes. In few, we saw their caps
On either side thrown up; the *Egyptian* gallies
(Receiv'd like friends) past through, and fell behind
The *Roman* rear: and now, they all come forward,
And ride within the port.
CLEOPATRA. Enough, *Serapion*:
I've heard my doom. This needed not, you gods:
When I lost *Antony*, your work was done;
'Tis but superstitious malice. Where's my Lord?
How bears he this last blow?
SERAPION. His fury cannot be express'd by words:
Thrice he attempted headlong to have fallen
Full on his foes, and aim'd at *Caesar*'s galley:
With-held, he raves on you; cries, he's betray'd
Should he now find you. –
ALEXAS. Shun him, 'seek your safety,
Till you can clear your innocence.
CLEOPATRA. I'll stay.
ALEXAS. You must not, haste you to your monument,
While I make speed to *Caesar*.
CLEOPATRA. *Caesar*! No,
I have no business with him.
ALEXAS. I can work him.
To spare your life, and let this madman perish.
CLEOPATRA. Base fawning Wretch! Wouldst thou betray him too?
Hence from my sight, I will not hear a traitor;
'Twas thy design brought all this ruine on us;
Serapion, thou art honest; counsel me:
But haste, each moment's precious.
SERAPION. Retire; you must not yet see *Antony*.
He who began this mischief,
'Tis just he tempt the danger: let him clear you;
And, since he offer'd you his servile tongue,
To gain a poor precarious life from *Caesar*,
Let him expose that fawning eloquence,
And speak to *Antony*.
ALEXAS. O Heavens! I dare not,
I meet my certain death.
CLEOPATRA. Slave, thou deserv'st it.
Not that I fear my Lord, will I avoid him;
I know him noble: when he banish'd me,
And thought me false, he scorn'd to take my life;
But I'll be justifi'd, and then die with him.
ALEXAS. O pity me, and let me follow you.
CLEOPATRA. To death, if thou stir hence. Speak, if thou canst,
Now for thy life, which basely thou wou'dst save;
While mine I prize at this. Come, good *Serapion*.

[*Exeunt* Cleopatra, Serapion, Charmion, Iras.

ALEXAS. O that I less cou'd fear to lose this being,
Which, like a snow-ball, in my coward hand,
The more 'tis grasp'd, the faster melts away.
Poor reason! What a wretched aid art thou!
For still in spight of thee,

These two long lovers, soul and body, dread
Their final separation. Let me think:
What can I say, to save my self from death?
No matter what becomes of *Cleopatra*.
ANTONY. [*Within*] Which way? Where?
VENTIDIUS. [*Within*] This leads to th' monument.
ALEXAS. Ah me! I hear him; yet I'm unprepar'd:
My gift of lying's gone;
And this Court-Devil, which I so oft have rais'd,
Forsakes me at my need. I dare not stay;
Yet cannot far go hence. [*Exit.*

[*Enter* Antony *and* Ventidius.

ANTONY. O happy *Caesar*! Thou hast men to lead:
Think not 'tis thou hast conquer'd *Antony*;
But *Rome* has conquer'd *Egypt*. I'm betray'd.
VENTIDIUS. Curse on this treach'rous train!
Their soil and Heav'n infect 'em all with baseness:
And their young souls come tainted to the World
With the first breath they draw.
ANTONY. Th' original Villain sure no god created;
He was a bastard of the sun, by *Nile*
Ap'd into man: with all his mother's mud
Crusted about his soul.
VENTIDIUS. The Nation is
One universal traitor; and their Queen
The very spirit and extract of 'em all.
ANTONY. Is there yet left
A possibility of aid from valour?
Is there one god unsworn to my destruction?
The least unmortgag'd hope? For, if there be,
Methinks I cannot fall beneath the fate
Of such a boy as *Caesar*.
The World's one half is yet in *Antony*;
And, from each limb of it that's hew'd away,
The soul comes back to me.
VENTIDIUS. There yet remain
Three legions in the town. The last assault
Lopt off the rest: if death be your design;
(As I must wish it now) these are sufficient
To make a heap about us of dead foes,
An honest pile for burial.
ANTONY. They're enough.
We'll not divide our stars; but side by side
Fight emulous: and with malicious eyes
Survey each other's acts: so every death
Thou giv'st, I'll take on me, as a just debt,
And pay thee back a soul.
VENTIDIUS. Now you shall see I love you. Not a word
Of chiding more. By my few hours of life,
I am so pleas'd with this brave *Roman* fate,
That I wou'd not be *Caesar*, to out-live you.
When we put off this flesh, and mount together,
I shall be shown to all th' etherial crowd;
Lo, this is he who dy'd with *Antony*.
ANTONY. Who knows but we may pierce through all their troops,
And reach my veterans yet? 'Tis worth the tempting,
T' o'er-leap this gulf of fate,
And leave our wand'ring destinies behind.

[*Enter* Alexas, *trembling*.

VENTIDIUS. See, see, that Villain;
See *Cleopatra* stampt upon that face,
With all her cunning, all her arts of falshood!
How she looks out through those dissembling eyes!
How he sets his count'nance for deceit;
And promises a lie, before he speaks!
Let me dispatch him first. [*Drawing*.
ALEXAS. O, spare me, spare me.
ANTONY. Hold; he's not worth your killing. On thy life,
(Which thou mayst keep, because I scorn to take it)
No syllable to justifie thy Queen;
Save thy base tongue its office.
ALEXAS. Sir she's gone,
Where she shall never be molested more
By love, or you.
ANTONY. Fled to her *Dollabella*!
Die, Traitor, I revoke my promise, die. [*Going to kill him*.
ALEXAS. O hold, she is not fled.
ANTONY. She is: my eyes
Are open to her falshood; my whole life
Has been a golden dream, of love and friendship.
But, now I wake, I'm like a merchant, rows'd
From soft repose, to see his vessel sinking,
And all his wealth cast o'er. Ingrateful Woman!
Who follow'd me, but as the swallow summer,
Hatching her young ones in my kindly beams,
Singing her flatt'ries to my morning wake;
But, now my winter comes, she spread her wings,
And seeks the spring of *Caesar*.

ALEXAS. Think not so:
Her fortunes have, in all things, mixt with yours.
Had she betray'd her naval force to *Rome*,
How easily might she have gone to *Caesar*,
Secure by such a bribe!
VENTIDIUS. She sent it first,
To be more welcome after.
ANTONY. 'Tis too plain;
Else wou'd she have appear'd, to clear her self.
ALEXAS. Too fatally she has; she could not bear
To be accus'd by you; but shut her self
Within her monument: look'd down, and sigh'd;
While, from her unchang'd face, the silent tears
Dropt, as they had not leave, but stole their parting.
Some undistinguish'd words she inly murmur'd;
At last, she rais'd her eyes; and, with such looks
As dying *Lucrece* cast, –[46]
ANTONY. My heart forbodes. –
VENTIDIUS. All for the best: go on.
ALEXAS. She snatch'd her ponyard,[47]
And, ere we cou'd prevent the fatal blow,
Plung'd it within her breast: then turn'd to me,
Go, bear my Lord (said she) my last farewell;
And ask him if he yet suspect my faith.
More she was saying, but death rush'd betwixt.
She half pronounc'd your name with her last breath,
And bury'd half within her.
VENTIDIUS. Heav'n be prais'd.
ANTONY. Then art thou innocent, my poor dear Love?
And art thou dead?
O those two words! Their sound shou'd be divided:
Hadst thou been false, and dy'd; or hadst thou liv'd,
And hadst been true –. But innocence and death!
This shows not well above. Then what am I,
The murderer of this truth, this innocence!
Thoughts cannot form themselves in words so horrid
As can express my guilt!
VENTIDIUS. Is't come to this? The gods have been too gracious:
And thus you thank 'em for't.
ANTONY. Why stay'st thou here?
Is it for thee to spy upon my soul,
And see its inward mourning? Get thee hence;
Thou art not worthy to behold, what now
Becomes a *Roman* emperor to perform.
[*To* Alexas.
ALEXAS. [*Aside*] *He loves her still:*
His grief betrays it. Good! The joy to find
She's yet alive, compleats the reconcilement.
I've sav'd my self, and her. But, oh! The Romans*!*
Fate comes too fast upon my wit.
Hunts me too hard, and meets me at each double.
[*Exit.*
VENTIDIUS. Wou'd she had dy'd a little sooner tho,
Before *Octavia* went; you might have treated:
Now 'twill look tame, and wou'd not be receiv'd.
Come, rouze your self, and let's die warm together.
ANTONY. I will not fight: there's no more work for war.
The bus'ness of my angry hours is done.
VENTIDIUS. Caesar is at your gates.
ANTONY. Why, let him enter,
He's welcome now.
VENTIDIUS. What lethargy has crept into your soul?
ANTONY. 'Tis but a scorn of life, and just desire
To free my self from bondage.
VENTIDIUS. Do it bravely.
ANTONY. I will; but not by fighting. O, *Ventidius*!
What shou'd I fight for now? My Queen is dead.
I was but great for her; my pow'r, my empire,
Were but my merchandise to buy her love;
And conquer'd kings, my factors.[48] Now she's dead,
Let *Caesar* take the World, –
An empty circle, since the jewel's gone
Which made it worth my strife: my being's nauseous;
For all the bribes of life are gone away.
VENTIDIUS. Wou'd you be taken?
ANTONY. Yes, I wou'd be taken;
But, as a *Roman* ought, dead, my *Ventidius*:
For I'll convey my soul from *Caesar*'s reach,
And lay down life my self. 'Tis time the World
Shou'd have a lord, and know whom to obey.

We two have kept its homage in suspence,
And bent the globe on whose each side we trod,
Until it was dented inwards: Let him walk
Alone upon't; I'm weary of my part.
My torch is out; and the World stands before me
Like a black desert, at the approach of night:
I'll lay me down, and stray no farther on.

VENTIDIUS. I cou'd be griev'd,
But that I'll not out-live you: choose your death;
For, I have seen him in such various shapes,
I care not which I take: I'm only troubled
The life I bear, is worn to such a rag,
'Tis scarce worth giving. I cou'd wish indeed
We threw it from us with a better grace;
That, like two lions taken in the toils,
We might at last thrust out our paws, and wound
The hunters that enclose us.

ANTONY. I have thought on't.
Ventidius, you must live.

VENTIDIUS. I must not, Sir.

ANTONY. Wilt thou not live, to speak some good of me?
To stand by my fair fame, and guard th' approaches
From the ill tongues of men?

VENTIDIUS. Who shall guard mine,
For living after you?

ANTONY. Say, I command it.

VENTIDIUS. If we die well, our deaths will speak themselves,
And need no living witness.

ANTONY. Thou hast lov'd me,
And fain I wou'd reward thee: I must die;
Kill me, and take the merit of my death
To make thee friends with *Caesar*.

VENTIDIUS. Thank your kindness.
You said I lov'd you; and, in recompence,
You bid me turn a traitor: did I think
You wou'd have us'd me thus? That I shou'd die
With a hard thought of you?

ANTONY. Forgive me, *Roman*.
Since I have heard of *Cleopatra*'s death,
My reason bears no rule upon my tongue,
But lets my thoughts break all at random out:
I've thought better; do not deny me twice.

VENTIDIUS. By Heav'n, I will not.
Let it not be t' out-live you.

ANTONY. Kill me first,
And then die thou: for 'tis but just thou serve
Thy friend, before thy self.

VENTIDIUS. Give me your hand.
We soon shall meet again. Now farewell, Emperor. [*Embrace*.
Methinks that word's too cold to be my last:
Since death sweeps distinctions, farewell, Friend.
That's all. –
I will not make a bus'ness of a trifle:
And yet I cannot look on you, and kill you;
Pray turn your face.

ANTONY. I do: strike home sure.

VENTIDIUS. Home, as my sword will reach. [*Kills himself*.

ANTONY. O, thou mistak'st;
That wound was none of thine: give it me back:
Thou robb'st me of my death.

VENTIDIUS. I do indeed;
But, think 'tis the first time I e'er deceiv'd you;
If that may plead my pardon. And you, Gods,
Forgive me, if you will; for I die perjur'd,
Rather then kill my friend. [*Dies*.

ANTONY. Farewell. Ever my leader, ev'n in death!
My Queen and thou have got the start of me,
And I'm the lag of honour. – Gone so soon?
Is death no more? He us'd him carelessly,
With a familiar kindness: ere he knock'd,
Ran to the door, and took him in his arms,
As who shou'd say, y' are welcome at all hours,
A friend need give no warning. Books had spoil'd him;
For all the learn'd are cowards by profession.
'Tis not worth
My farther thought: for death, for ought I know,
Is but to think no more. Here's to be satisfi'd.
[*Falls on his sword*.
I've mist my heart. O unperforming hand!
Thou never cou'dst have err'd in a worse time.
My fortune jades me to the last; and death,
Like a great man, takes state, and makes me wait
For my admittance –. [*Trampling within*.
Some perhaps from *Caesar*:
If he shou'd find me living, and suspect
That I played booty with my life! I'll mend

My work, ere they can reach me. [*Rises upon his knees.*

[*Enter* Cleopatra, Charmion, Iras.

CLEOPATRA. Where is my Lord? Where is he?
CHARMION. There he lies,
And dead *Ventidius* by him.
CLEOPATRA. My fears were prophets; I am come too late.
O that accurs'd *Alexas*! [*Runs to him.*
ANTONY. Art thou living?
Or am I dead before I knew? And thou
The first kind ghost that meets me?
CLEOPATRA. Help me seat him.
Send quickly, send for help. [*They place him in a chair.*
ANTONY. I am answer'd.
We live both. Sit thee down, my *Cleopatra*:
I'll make the most I can of life, to stay
A moment more with thee.
CLEOPATRA. How is it with you?
ANTONY. 'Tis as with a man
Removing in a hurry; all pack'd up,
But one dear jewel that his haste forgot;
And he, for that returns upon the spur:
So I come back, for thee.
CLEOPATRA. Too long, you Heav'ns, you have been cruel to me;
Now show your mended faith, and give me back
His fleeting life.
ANTONY. It will not be, my love.
I keep my soul by force.
Say but thou art not false.
CLEOPATRA. 'Tis now too late
To say I'm true: I'll prove it, and die with you,
Unknown to me, *Alexas* feign'd my death:
Which, when I knew, I hasted to prevent
This fatal consequence. My fleet betray'd
Both you and me.
ANTONY. And *Dollabella*. –
CLEOPATRA. Scarce esteem'd before he lov'd; but hated now.
ANTONY. Enough: my life's not long enough for more.
Thou sayst thou wilt come after: I believe thee;
For I can now believe whate'er thou sayst,
That we may part more kindly.
CLEOPATRA. I will come:
Doubt not, my life, I'll come, and quickly too:
Caesar shall triumph o'er no part of thee.
ANTONY. But grieve not, while thou stay'st
My last disastrous times:
Think we have had a clear and glorious day;
And Heav'n did kindly to delay the storm
Just till our close of ev'ning. Ten years love,
And not a moment lost, but all improv'd
To th' utmost joys: what ages have we liv'd?
And now to die each other's; and, so dying,
While hand in hand we walk in groves below,
Whole troops of lovers' ghosts shall flock about us,
And all the train be ours.
CLEOPATRA. Your words are like the notes of dying swans,
Too sweet to last. Were there so many hours
For your unkindness, and not one for love?
ANTONY. No, not a minute. – This one kiss – more worth
Than all I leave to *Caesar*. [*Dies.*
CLEOPATRA. O, tell me so again,
And take ten thousand kisses, for that word.
My Lord, my Lord: speak, if you yet have being;
Sigh to me, if you cannot speak; or cast
One look: Do any thing that shows you live.
IRAS. He's gone too far, to hear you;
And this you see, a lump of sensless clay,
The leavings of a soul.
CHARMION. Remember Madam,
He charg'd you not to grieve.
CLEOPATRA. And I'll obey him.
I have not lov'd a *Roman* not to know
What should become of his wife; his Wife, my *Charmion*;
For 'tis to that high title I aspire,
And now I'll not die less. Let dull *Octavia*
Survive, to mourn him dead: my nobler fate
Shall knit our spousals with a tie too strong
For *Roman* laws to break.
IRAS. Will you then die?
CLEOPATRA. Why shou'dst thou make that question?
IRAS. *Caesar* is most merciful.
CLEOPATRA. Let him be so
To those that want his mercy: my poor Lord
Made no such cov'nant with him to spare me
When he was dead. Yield me to *Caesar*'s pride?
What, to be led in triumph through the streets,
A spectacle to base *plebeian* eyes;
While some dejected friend of *Antony*'s,
Close in a corner, shakes his head, and mutters

A secret curse on her who ruin'd him?
I'll none of that.

CHARMION. Whatever you resolve,
I'll follow ev'n to death.

IRAS. I only fear'd
For you; but more shou'd fear to live without you.

CLEOPATRA. Why, now 'tis as it shou'd be. Quick, my friends,
Dispatch; ere this, the town's in *Caesar*'s hands:
My Lord looks down concern'd, and fears my stay,
Lest I shou'd be surpriz'd;
Keep him not waiting for his love too long.
You, *Charmion*, bring my crown and richest jewels,
With 'em, the wreath of victory I made
(Vain augury!) for him who now lies dead;
You, *Iras*, bring the cure of all our ills.

IRAS. The aspicks,[49] Madam?

CLEOPATRA. Must I bid you twice?

[*Exeunt* Charmion *and* Iras.

'Tis sweet to die, when they wou'd force life on me,
To rush into the dark abode of death,
And seize him first; if he be like my love,
He is not frightful sure.
We're now alone, in secrecy and silence;
And is not this like lovers? I may kiss
These pale, cold lips; *Octavia* does not see me;
And, oh! 'Tis better far to have him thus,
Than see him in her arms. – O welcome, welcome.

[*Enter* Charmion, Iras.

CHARMION. What must be done?

CLEOPATRA. Short ceremony, Friends:
But yet it must be decent. First, this laurel
Shall crown my hero's head: he fell not basely,
Nor left his shield behind him. Only thou
Cou'dst triumph o'er thy self; and thou alone
Wert worthy so to triumph.

CHARMION. To what end
These ensigns of your pomp and royalty?

CLEOPATRA. Dull, that thou art! Why, 'tis to meet my love;
As when I saw him first, on *Cydnos* bank,
All sparkling, like a goddess; so adorn'd,
I'll find him once again: my second spousals
Shall match my first, in glory. Haste, haste, both,
And dress the bride of *Antony*.

CHARMION. 'Tis done.

CLEOPATRA. Now seat me by my Lord. I claim this place;
For I must conquer *Caesar* too, like him,
And win my share o'th' World. Hail, you dear relicks
Of my immortal love!
O let no impious hand remove you hence;
But rest for ever here: let *Egypt* give
His death that peace, which it deny'd his life.
Reach me the casket.

IRAS. Underneath the fruit the aspick lies.

CLEOPATRA. [*Putting aside the leaves*] Welcome, thou kind deceiver!
Thou best of thieves; who, with an easie key,
Do'st open life, and unperceiv'd by us,
Ev'n steal us from our selves: discharging so
Death's dreadful office, better than himself,
Touching our limbs so gently into slumber,
That death stands by, deceiv'd by his own image,
And thinks himself but sleep.

SERAPION. [*Within*] The Queen, where is she?
The town is yielded, *Caesar*'s at the gates.

CLEOPATRA. He comes too late to invade the rights of death.
Haste, bare my arm, and rouze the serpent's fury. [*Holds out her arm and draws it back.*
Coward flesh –
Woud'st thou conspire with *Caesar*, to betray me,
As thou wert none of mine? I'll force thee to't,
And not be sent by him,
But bring my self, my soul to *Antony*. [*Turns aside, and then shows her arm bloody*]
Take hence; the work is done.

SERAPION. [*Within*] Break open the door,
And guard the traitor well.

CHARMION. The next is ours.

IRAS. Now, *Charmion*, to be worthy
Of your great Queen and Mistress. [*They apply the aspicks.*

CLEOPATRA. Already, Death I feel thee in my veins;
I go with such a will to find my Lord,
That we shall quickly meet.
A heavy numbness creeps through every limb,
And now 'tis at my head: my eye-lids fall,
And my dear Love is vanish'd in a mist.

Where shall I find him, where? O turn me to him,
And lay me on his breast. – *Caesar*, thy worst;
Now part us, if thou caust. [*Dies.*

[Iras *sinks down at her feet, and dies;* Charmion *stands behind her chair, as dressing her head.*

[*Enter* Serapion, *two* priests, Alexas *bound, Egyptians.*

TWO PRIESTS. Behold, *Serapion*, what havock death has made!
SERAPION. 'Twas what I fear'd.
Charmion, is this well done?
CHARMION. Yes, 'tis well done, and like a Queen, the last
Of her great Race: I follow her. [*Sinks down; Dies.*
ALEXAS. 'Tis true,
She has done well: much better thus to die,
Than live to make a holy-day[50] in *Rome.*
SERAPION. See, see how the lovers sit in state together,
As they were giving laws to half mankind.
Th' impression of a smile left in her face,
Shows she dy'd pleas'd with him for whom she liv'd,
And went to charm him in another World.
Caesar's just entring; grief has now no leisure.
Secure that villain, as our pledge of safety
To grace th' imperial triumph. Sleep, blest Pair,
Secure from humane chance, long ages out,
While all the storms of fate fly o'er your tomb;
And fame, to late posterity, shall tell,
No lovers liv'd so great, or dy'd so well.

EPILOGUE.

Poets, like disputants, when reasons fail,
Have one sure refuge left and that's to rail;
Fop, Coxcomb, Fool, are thunder'd through the pit;
And this is all their equipage[51] of wit.
We wonder how the Devil this diff'rence grows,
Betwixt our fools in verse, and yours in prose?
For, 'faith, the quarrel rightly understood,
'Tis Civil War with their own flesh and blood.
The thread-bare author hates the gawdy coat;
And swears at the gilt coach, but swears a foot:
For 'tis observ'd of every scribbling man,
He grows a fop as fast as e'er he can;
Prunes up, and asks his oracle the glass,
If pink or purple best become his face.
For our poor wretch, he neither rails nor prays;
Nor likes your wit just as you like his plays;
He has not yet so much of Mr. Bays.[52]
He does his best; and, if he cannot please,
Wou'd quietly sue out his writ of ease.[53]
Yet, if he might his own grand jury call,
By the fair Sex he begs to stand or fall.
Let Caesar's pow'r the men's ambition move,
But grace you him who lost the World for love.
Yet if some antiquated lady say,
The last age is not copy'd in his play;
Heav'n help the man who for that face must drudge,
Which only has the wrinkles of a judge.
Let not the young and beauteous join with those;
For shou'd you raise such numerous hosts of foes,
Young wits and sparks he to his aid must call;
'Tis more than one man's work to please you all.

4.2 JOHN WILMOT, EARL OF ROCHESTER, "A SATYR ON CHARLES II"

JOHN WILMOT, EARL OF ROCHESTER, "A Satyr." *The Works of John Wilmot Earl of Rochester.* Ed. Harold Love. Oxford: Oxford University Press, 1999, 86–87. (See note on "The Imperfect Enjoyment.") Rochester's "Satyr" was circulated in manuscript, finding its way to the King and earning the courtier/poet a period of exile from court.

A Satyr on Charles II

In th' isle of Britain, long since famous grown
For breeding the best cunts in Christendom,
There reigns, and oh! long may he reign and thrive,
The easiest King and best-bred man alive.
Him no ambition moves to get renown
Like the French fool,[54] that wanders up and down
Starving his people, hazarding his crown.

Peace is his aim, his gentleness is such,
And love he loves, for he loves fucking much.

Nor are his high desires above his strength:
His scepter and his prick are of a length;
And she may sway the one who plays with th' other,
And make him little wiser than his brother.[55]
Poor Prince! thy prick, like thy buffoons at Court,
Will govern thee because it makes thee sport.
'Tis sure the sauciest prick that e'er did swive.[56]
The proudest, peremptoriest[57] prick alive.
Though safety, law, religion, life lay on 't,
'Twould break through all to make its way to cunt.
Restless he rolls about from whore to whore,
A merry monarch, scandalous and poor.

To Carwell,[58] the most dear of all his dears,
The best relief of his declining years,
Oft he bewails his fortune, and her fate:
To love so well, and be beloved so late.
For though in her he settles well his tarse,
Yet his dull, graceless bollocks hand an arse.

This you'd believe, had I but time to tell ye
The pains it costs to poor, laborious Nelly,[59]
Whilst she employs hands, fingers, mouth, and thighs,
Ere she can raise the member she enjoys.
    All monarchs I hate, and the thrones they sit on,
    From the hector[60] of France to the cully[61] of Britain.

4.3 SAMUEL JOHNSON, "DRYDEN" IN *THE LIVES OF THE ENGLISH POETS*

SAMUEL JOHNSON, "DRYDEN" in *The Lives of the English Poets: and a Criticism of Their Works*. Dublin: Messrs. Whitestone, Williams, Colles, Wilson, Lynch, Jenkin, Walker, Burnet, Hallhead, Flin, Exshaw, Beatty, and White. 1779, 279. Johnson (1709–1784), besides compiling a famous dictionary, was well respected for his literary criticism and an edition of Shakespeare.

All for Love, or the World Well Lost, a tragedy founded upon the story of Antony and Cleopatra, he tells us, *is the only play which he wrote for himself*; the rest were given to the people. It is by universal consent accounted the work in which he has admitted the fewest improprieties of style or character; but it has one fault equal to many, though rather moral than critical, that, by admitting the romantick omnipotence of Love, he has recommended as laudable and worthy of imitation that conduct which, through all ages, the good have censured as vitious, and the bad despised as foolish.

Of this play the prologue and the epilogue, though written upon the common topicks of malicious and ignorant criticism, and without any particular relation to the characters or incidents of the drama, are deservedly celebrated for their elegance and spriteliness.

4.4 PIERRE MIGNARD, *PORTRAIT OF LOUISE RENEE DE KEROUALLE*

Pierre Mignard (1612–1695), *Portrait of Louise Renee de Kerouralle* (1649–1734), Duchess of Portsmouth and Aubigny: Pierre Mignard was a portrait artist famous for his many depictions of French courtiers. The Duchess, who sat for this painting on a visit to Paris in 1682, was one of Charles II's most politically powerful mistresses, though she was unpopular with the public due to her French origins and Catholic faith. The child offering exotic tokens, coral and pearls, is unidentified. National Portrait Gallery, London.

4.5 THOMAS HAWKER, *KING CHARLES II*

King Charles II, attributed to Thomas Hawker, circa 1680. Painted towards the end of the king's life, this portrait shows a rather dissolute, if gorgeously dressed Charles showing off the aristocratic male's pride—his legs. National Portrait Gallery, London.

4.6 ANTONIO VERRIO, *THE SEA TRIUMPH OF CHARLES II*

Antonio Verrio, *The Sea Triumph of Charles II*: Verrio (ca. 1639–1707) depicted Charles as a godlike figure reminiscent of Neptune, the mythical god of the sea. Three women who carry the crowns of his three kingdoms accompany Charles under Fame's banner, the text of which praises the reach of his reputation as consonant with the reach of his military might. It is likely that this image is meant to commemorate the Treaty of Westminster (1674), which brought an end to the Third Anglo-Dutch War. National Portrait Gallery, London.

Notes

1–2 From the edition of 1692. Printed in the Savoy for H. Herringman, sold by R. Bently, J. Tonson, F. Saunders, and T. Bennet. Corrected from 1696 edition.

3 Rochester was known to expose his body, as well as his wit, when inebriated.

4 In Virgil's epic poem *The Aeneid*, Dido falls in love with Aeneas, who deserts her at the command of the gods to fulfill his destiny. Unwilling to live without him, she commits suicide.

5 Goes against his character.

6 Simpletons.

7 The pit of the theatre, where the middling class of the audience was likely to sit.

8 Bullies, men seeking a fight.

9 A portion of bacon.

10 Peasants.

11 Seals.

12 Probably hippopotami.

13 The ruling dynasty of Egypt, beginning with Ptolomy in 323 BC; it would end with the Roman conquest of Cleopatra the VII in 30 BC.

14 Ptolomy XIII who succeeded to the throne at the age of ten and ruled jointly with his sister and wife, the 17-year-old Cleopatra VII.

15 With the murder of Caesar in 44 BC, Roman power split between Marc Antony and Octavian. Cleopatra aligned herself with the former, whose navy was defeated by Octavian at Actium.

16 Marcus Vipsanius Agrippa, the Roman general leading the battle at Actium.

17 Musical instruments, like tambourines.

18 Marcus Tullius Cicero, Roman philosopher, politician, and orator.

19 Antony defeated the Roman general Cassius at the Battle of Philipi.

20 Officers who attended upon magistrates and executed their sentences. Fasces were the symbols of their office, consisting of rods with an axe in the middle, its blade projecting.

21 Antony was in league with Octavian at Philippi.

22 A poisonous plant.

23 Pimp.

24 A person with dark skin from Ethiopia. A pointless enterprise.

25 In Greek mythology, the site of Zeus' defeat of the ancient race of giants who preceded the rule of the gods.

26 Vulcan was the god of fire, volcanoes, and the forge; known for his skill as a blacksmith, he was also associated with making the arms of war. Jupiter gave him Venus, the beautiful (but also unfaithful) goddess of love for his wife. He caught Venus and Mars within his nets in an act of adultery.

27 Staunch.

28 Goal.

29 A river in Cicilia, an early Roman province.

30 Sea nymphs.

31 A money-lender.

32 Contempt, disdain—in this case, for himself.

33 Waist.

34 A wooden-soled shoe, worn to protect one's feet from mud and water. Not glamorous footwear.

35 Porpoise.

36 Cornelius Gallus, a Roman poet and orator, celebrated the beauty of his mistress, the notorious actress Cytheris. Tibullus, another Roman poet, was known for his love lyrics for his mistress, Delia.

37 Under Roman law, a freed slave had considerable access to civil liberties, but commonly remained under patronage of his former master.

38 In mythology, Thessaly was noted for the number and power of its witches.

39 Test.

40 Looking for you.

41 An ancient civilization of Mesopotamia.

42 India and Meroe, an ancient city on the banks of the Nile.

43 In Greek mythology, Sisyphus was a Corinthian king who was punished by the gods for his deceitfulness by being forced to roll a huge boulder up a hill, only to watch it roll down and start over.

44 Prometheus, in Hesiod's *Theogony*, was punished by the gods for returning fire to earth. Tied to a rock, his liver is consumed every day by an eagle. Dryden makes this bird an even less attractive vulture.

45 The lighthouse.

46 In Ovid's *Fasti*, Lucrece is raped by the son of Tarquin, king of Rome and kills herself in despair. Shakespeare had published a poem based on this story, *The Rape of Lucrece*, in 1594.

47 A small dagger.

48 A merchant's representatives, salesmen.

49 Asps, small, poisonous snakes.

50 Holiday, an occasion for public spectacle and entertainment.

51 Accompaniment.

52 Type name for a poet, but also the character meant to satirize Dryden in George Villars' Second Duke of Buckingham's, comic play *The Rehearsal.*

53 An act of forgiveness from serving, as in being excused from a jury.

54 Louis XIV.

55 James, the Duke of York, later James II.

56 Fuck.

57 Most preemptory.

58 Louise de Keroualle, the Duchess of Portsmouth.

59 Nell Gwyn, Charles's mistress and a famous actress.

60 Bully.

61 Dupe.

5. *The Widdow Ranter*

THE WIDDOW RANTER OR, THE HISTORY OF BACON IN VIRGINIA.
A TRAGI-COMEDY, ACTED BY THEIR MAJESTIES' SERVANTS.[1]
APHRA BEHN. FIRST PERFORMED 20 NOVEMBER 1689 AND FIRST PUBLISHED 1689

5.1 *THE WIDDOW RANTER OR, THE HISTORY OF BACON IN VIRGINIA.* A TRAGI-COMEDY, ACTED BY THEIR MAJESTIES' SERVANTS.[2]

Aphra Behn

First Performed 20 November 1689 and First Published 1689

APHRA BEHN (1640?–1689) IS AN EXTRAORDINARY figure in literary and theatre history. A woman who made her living in ways uncharacteristic of her gender in the seventeenth century, she served as a spy for the government of Charles II and was most notably a successful poet and playwright. She also produced one of the first English texts that might be rightly called a novel, *Oroonoko, or the Royal Slave*, in 1688. She was prolific as a playwright and her most well-known play, *The Rover, Part I* (1677) has received considerable modern attention from both scholars and modern theatre professionals. *The Widdow Ranter* is Behn's last play, probably written in 1688 and performed and published posthumously in 1689. Behn's editor, Janet Todd, points out the dangers of posthumous production and print.[3] The first and only performance was not well received, perhaps for its untimely staging of a rebellion during the turbulent years around the exile of Charles II's brother James and William and Mary's invasion of England by invitation in 1688. The first printing left out and garbled material as well as including a prologue and epilogue that were probably substituted by a hasty publisher for those actually performed with the play. (We have included both printed and performed texts of these.) The editors of this volume chose this play to represent Behn not because of its performance history—it has very little compared to other plays in this volume—but because, like her well-known novel, it reveals a political consciousness that is critical to transatlantic imaginings of government and nation as they were beginning to develop in the seventeenth century. Behn's tragi-comedy attempts to imagine unifying values of governance and social order in a colonialist context in which differences of class, religion and ethnicity make a homogeneous society impossible.

The play's main character, Nathaniel Bacon, and its action are based very loosely on Bacon's Rebellion in the British colony of Virginia in 1676. A young gentleman, second son, and a talented artist (see his self portrait in the contextual materials to this play), Bacon had already run through his allotted fortune in England. In Virginia, he took leadership in reprisals against Indian attacks on the colonists, killing indiscriminately members of friendly as well as hostile tribes and acting against the policy of the colony's government headed by Sir William Berkeley. He had considerable success in taking leadership of the colony, gaining Jamestown before falling ill and dying. Governor Berkeley quickly regained power and reacted with bloody reprisals against the rebels. Behn would probably have had access to at least one printed account, but she set the action six years earlier than historical events and took Berkeley out of the picture, probably to avoid political trouble. Behn had been imprisoned several years earlier when, in her support of the reigning monarch, Charles II, she publicly attacked the Duke of Monmouth, the king's upstart, illegitimate son.[4] When Behn was writing this play, feelings over the impending ascension of the Catholic, French-sympathizing James were running high, and she may have wished to avoid anything that would look like a personal attack on a ruling governor.

It is also helpful for readers of this play to remember that Bacon's rebellion is an important chapter in the history of modern racism. Bacon's ability to forge coalition between poor British and African servants in a rebellion that went as far as to burn down Jamestown left a legacy of fear among colonial planters who began, practically and rhetorically, to drive a wedge between black and white populations. Behn's play is more closely related to the politics of England at the time of the Glorious Revolution than to the historical events of Virginia and does not, therefore, reflect either solidarity across African and British supporters of Bacon or its deadly aftermath of reinforcing modern racism. But in parsing out the racial politics of this play, it is important to remember that Behn's audience understood racial difference in ways that are not the product of this history, which had not yet happened.

The "low" comic characters of the colonists who oppose the noble Bacon reflect English contempt for their colonial counterparts who were often transported criminals seeking a better life. They also reflect the perception of collective, plebian action as a political loose cannon, likely to land the community in the kind of trouble experienced during the English Civil War. Both colonists and Indians generally divide up along class lines: the well-born English have natural authority over their plebian counterparts and the Indian King and Queen deport themselves in dignified contrast to the "savage" dancing and singing of the lesser Indians. Bacon embodies the noble qualities of a natural leader and a romantic lover, qualities that resonate with Restoration tragic heroes such as Dryden's Antony and reflect a fascination with the heroic individual who rises above the politics of the crowd.

The exception to this class bias is, of course, the Widdow Ranter. The Ranters were a radical dissenting religious group that emerged during the Civil War, along with groups such as the Diggers and the Levellers. They held unorthodox beliefs about common property and sexuality, and were satirized as monstrous over-consumers. They were vilified as having gross appetites for drinking, sex, and smoking, in particular, characteristics that take a more benign and sociable form in the Widdow. This character blends these plebian appetites with the courage and sword-wielding prowess reserved for aristocratic men. Her incorporation in the marriages that restore community and social order at the end of this play signifies a vision of community that allows for a hybridization of plebian and aristocratic identity. The fact that this hybrid is a cross-dressed woman who, strikingly, shows no sign of resuming her skirts at the end of the play, gives us matter to think on. Is Behn's image of a trans-class and transatlantic hero a woman who is also, in some sense, transgender?

TO THE MUCH HONOURED MADAM WELLDON.[5]

Madam,

Knowing Mrs. Behn in her life-time design'd to dedicate some of her works to you, you have a naturall title, and claim to this and I could not without being unjust to her memory, but fix your name to it, who have not only a wit above that of most of your sex; but a goodliness and affability extreamly charming, and engaging beyond measure, and perhaps there are few to be found like you, that are so eminent for hospitality, and a ready and generous assistance to the distress'd and indigent, which are quallities that carry much more of divinity with them, then a puritanicall outward zeal for virtue and religion.

Our author, Madam, who was so true a judge of wit, was (no doubt of it) satisfied in the patroness she had pitcht upon: if ever she had occasion for a wit and sense like yours 'tis now, to defend this (one of the last of her works) from the malice of her enemies, and the ill nature of the critticks, who have had ingratitude enough not to consider the obligations they had to her when living; but to do those gentlemen justice, 'tis not (altogether) to be imputed to their criticism, that the play had not that success which it deserv'd, and was expected by her friends; the main fault ought to lye on those who had the management of it. Had our authour been alive she would have committed it to the flames rather than have suffer'd it to have been acted with such omissions as was made, and on which the foundation of the play depended: For example, they thought fit to leave out a whole scene of the Virginian Court of Judicature, which was a lively resemblance of that country-justice; and on which depended a great part of the plot, and wherein were many unusuall and very natural jests which would at least have made some sort of people laugh: In another part of the play is omitted the appearance of the ghost of the Indian King, kill'd by Bacon[6], and tho' the like may have been represented in other plays, yet I never heard or found but that the sight was very agreeable to an audience, and very awfull: Besides the apparition of the ghost was necessary, for it was that which struck a terror in the Queen, and fright'ned her from heark'ning to the love of Bacon, believing it a horrid thing to receive the caresses and embraces of her husband's murderer: and lastly, many of the parts being false cast, and given to those whose tallants and geniuses suited not our author's intention: These, Madam, are some of the reasons that this play was unsuccessfull, and the best play that ever was writ must prove so: if it have the fate to be murder'd like this.

However, Madam, I can't but believe you will find an hour's diversion in the reading, and will meet with not only wit, but true comedy (tho' low,) by reason many of the characters are such only as our Newgate[7] afforded, being criminals transported.

This play, Madam, being left in my hands by the author to introduce to the publick, I thought my self oblig'd to say thus much in its defence, and that it was also a duty upon me to choose a patroness proper for it, and the author having pitcht upon your name to do honour to some of her works, I thought your protection, could be so useful to none, as to this, whose owning it may silence the malice of its enemies; your wit and judgment being to be submitted to in all cases; besides your natural tenderness and compassion for the unfortunate, gives you in a manner another title to it: the preference which is due to you upon so many accounts is therefore the reason of this present address, for at the worst, if this play should be so unfortunate as not to be thought worthy of your acceptance; yet it is certain, that it's worth any man's while to have the honour of subscribing himself,

Madam,
Your Most Obedient Humble
Servant,
G. J.[8]

PROLOGUE[9]

Written by Mr. Dryden.

Spoken by a woman.

Plays you will have; and to supply your store,
Our poets trade to ev'ry foreign shore:
This is the product of *Virginian* ground,
And to the port of *Covent-Garden*[10] bound.
Our cargo is, or should at least, be wit:
Bless us from you damn'd pyrates of the pit:[11]
And vizard-masks,[12] those dreadful apparitions;
She-privateers, of venomous conditions,
That clap us oft aboard with *French* commissions.[13]
You Sparks, we hope, will wish us happy trading;
For you have ventures in our vessel's lading;
And tho you touch at this or t'other nation;
Yet sure *Virginia* is your dear plantation.
Expect no polish'd scenes of love shou'd rise
From the rude growth of *Indian* colonies.
Instead of courtship, and a tedious pother,
They only tip the wink at one another;
Nay often the whole nation, pig together.
You civil *Beaus*, when you pursue the game,
With manners mince the meaning of–that same:
But ev'ry part has there its proper name.
Good Heav'ns defend me, who am yet unbroken
From living there, where such bug-words[14] are spoken:
Yet surely, Sirs, it does good stomachs show,
To talk so savour'ly[15] of what they do.

But were I bound to that broad speaking land,
What e're they said, I would not understand,
But innocently, with a ladies grace,
Wou'd learn to whisk my fan about my face.
However, to secure you, let me swear,
That no such base *Mundungus*[16] stuff is here.
We bring you of the best the soyl affords:
Buy it for once, and take it on our words.
You wou'd not think a countrey-girl the worse,
If clean and wholsome, tho her linnen's course.
Such are our scenes; and I dare boldly say,
You may laugh less at a far better play.
The story's true; the fact not long a-go;
The *hero* of our stage was *English* too:
And bate him one small frailty of rebelling,
As brave as e're was born at *Iniskelling*.[17]

PROLOGUE.[18]

Written by Mr. Dryden.

Heav'n save ye Gallants:[19] and this hopeful age,
Y' are welcome to the downfall of the stage:
The fools have labour'd long in their vocation;
And vice, (the manufacture of the nation)
O're-stocks the Town so much, and thrives so well,
That fopps and knaves grow druggs[20] and will not sell.
In vain our wares on theatres are shown,
When each has a plantation of his own.
His cause[21] ne'r fails; for whatsoe're he spends,
There's still God's plenty for himself and friends.
Shou'd men be rated by poetick rules,
Lord what a pole[22] would there be rais'd from fools!
Mean time poor wit prohibited must lye,
As if 'twere made some *French* commodity.[23]
Fools you will have, and rais'd at vast expence,
And yet as soon as seen, they give offence.
Time was, when none would cry that oaf was me,
But now you strive about your pedigree:
Bawble[24] and cap no sooner are thrown down,[25]

But there's a muss[26] of more then half the Town.
Each one will challenge a child's part at least,
A sign the family is well increas'd.
Of forreign cattle! there's no longer need,
When we're supply'd so fast with *English* breed.
Well! Flourish, Countrymen: drink swear and roar,
Let every free-born subject keep his whore;
And wandring in the wilderness about,
At end of 40 years not wear her out.
But when you see these pictures let none dare
To own beyond a limb or single share:
For where the punk[27] is common! He's a sot,[28]
Whose needs will father what the parish got.

Dramatis Personae

Men

Cavarnio, *Indian King*	*Mr. Bowman.*
Bacon, *Generall of the English*	*Mr. Williams.*
Colonel Wellman, *Deputy Governor*	*Mr. Freeman.*
Colonel Downright, *a loyall honest Count*	*Mr. Harris.*
Hazard and Friendly, *two friends known to one another many years in England*	*Mr. Alexander.*
	Mr. Powell.
Dareing and Fearless, *Lieutenant Generals to Bacon*	*Mr. Sandford.*
	Mr. Cudworth.[29]
Dullman, *a Captain*	*Mr. Bright.*[30]
Timerous, *Cornet*	*Mr. Underhill.*
Whimsey, Whiff and Boozer, *Justices of the Peace and very great cowards*	*Mr. Trefuse.*[31]
	Mr. Bowen.[32]
	Mr. Barns.[33]
Brag, *a Captain*	
Grubb, *one complain'd on by Capt. Whiff for calling his wife whore*	
Mr. Blunt, *a petitioner against Brag*	
Mr. Baker, *Parson Dunce, formerly a farrier fled from England and chaplain to the Governour*	*Mr. Baker.*
Clerk	

Boy, *To Madame Surelove*
Jefery, *Coachman to Widdow Ranter*
Jack, a sea-boy
Cavaro
Officer
Sea-Man
Highlander and Bagpiper
Indian Messenger
First Rabble

Women

Semernia, *Indian Queen belov'd by Bacon*	*Mrs. Bracegirdle.*
Madam Surelove, *belov'd by Hazard*	*Mrs. Knight.*
Mrs. Crisante, *Daughter to Col. Downright*	*Mrs. Jordan*[34].
Widdow Ranter, *in Love with Dareing*	*Mrs. Currer.*
Mrs. Flirt	*Mrs. Corey.*

Mrs. Whimsey
Mrs. Whiff
2 Maids: Jenny, *Maid to Widdow Ranter, and Nell, maid to Mrs. Flirt*
Anaria, *confidante of Indian Queen*
Maid to Madam Surelove
Singing Girl
Priests, Indians, Coachman, Soldiers, with other Attendants
Rabble, Negroes, Footmen, Women, Bailiffs

Act I. Scene I.

[*Virginia in* Bacon's *camp. A room with several tables. Enter* Hazard *in a traveling habit, and a sea-boy carrying his port-mantle.*[35]]

HAZARD. What Town's this Boy?

BOY. *James-Town,*[36] Master.

HAZARD. Take care my trunk be brought ashore tonight, and there's for your pains.

BOY. God bless you Master.

HAZARD. What do you call this house?

BOY. Mrs. *Flirt's,* Master, the best house for commendation in all *Virginia.*

HAZARD. That's well, has she any handsome ladys sirrah?

BOY. Oh! She's woundly[37] handsome her self Master, and the kindest gentlewoman – look here she comes Master –

[*Enter* Mrs. Flirt.

God bless you Mistriss, I have brought you a young gentleman here.

FLIRT. That's well, honest *Jack* – Sir, you are most heartily welcome.

HAZARD. [*Salutes her*] Madam, your servant.

FLIRT. Please you to walk into a chamber Sir.

HAZARD. By and by, Madam, but I'll repose here a while for the coolness of the air.

FLIRT. This is a publick room, Sir, but 'tis at your service.

HAZARD. Madam, you oblige me.

FLIRT. A fine-spoken person – a gentleman I'll warrant him, come *Jack*, I'll give thee a cogue[38] of brandy for old acquaintance. [*Exeunt* Landlady *and* Boy. Hazard *pulls out pen, ink and paper, and goes to write.*

[*Enter* Friendly *and* Nell.

FRIENDLY. Here *Nell*, a tankard of cool drink quickly.

NELL. You shall have it, Sir. [*Exit* Nell.

FRIENDLY. Hah! Who's that stranger? He seems to be a gentleman.

HAZARD. If I should give credit to mine eyes, that should be *Friendly*.

FRIENDLY. Sir, you seem a stranger, may I take the liberty to present my service to you?

HAZARD. If I am not mistaken Sir, you are the only man in the world whom I would soonest pledge, you'll credit me if three years absence has not made you forget *Hazard*.

FRIENDLY. *Hazard*, my friend! Come to my arms and heart.

HAZARD. This unexpected happiness o're-joys me. Who could have imagin'd to have found thee in *Virginia*? I thought thou hadst been in *Spain* with thy brother.

FRIENDLY. I was so till ten months since, when my uncle Colonel *Friendly* dying here, left me a considerable plantation; and faith I find diversions not altogether to be despis'd; the god of Love reigns here, with as much power, as in courts or popular cities: but prethee what chance, (fortunate for me) drove thee to this part of the New World?

HAZARD. Why (faith) ill company, and that common vice of the Town, gaming, soon run out my younger brother's fortune, for imagining like some of the luckier gamesters to improve my stock at the groom-porters;[39] ventur'd on and lost all – my elder brother an errant Jew, had neither friendship, nor honour enough to support me, but at last was mollified by persuasions and the hopes of being for ever rid of me, sent me hither with a small cargo to seek my fortune, –

FRIENDLY. And begin the world withall.

HAZARD. I thought this a better venture then to turn sharping[40] bully, cully in[41] prentices and country squires, with my pocket full of false dice, your high and low flats and bars,[42] or turn broker to young heirs; take up goods, to pay ten fold at the death of their fathers, and take fees on both sides;[43] or set up all night at the *groom porters* begging his honour to go a guinney the better of the lay.[44] No. *Friendly*, I had rather starve abroad then live pitty'd and dispised at home.

FRIENDLY. Thou art in the right, and art come just in the nick of time to make thy fortune – wilt thou follow my advice?

HAZARD. Thou art too honest to command any thing that I shall refuse.

FRIENDLY. You must know then, there is about a mile from *James Town* a young gentlewoman – no matter for her birth, her breeding's the best this world affords, she is marryed to one of the richest merchants here, he is old and sick, and now gone into *England* for the recovery of his health, where he'll e'en give up the ghost, he has writ her word he finds no amendment, and resolves to stay another year, the letter I accidently took up and have about me; 'tis easily counterfeited and will be of great use to us.

HAZARD. Now do I fancy I conceive thee.

FRIENDLY. Well, hear me first, you shall get another letter writ like this character,[45] which shall say, you are his kinsman, that is come to trafick[46] in this country, and 'tis his will you should be received into his house as such.

HAZARD. Well, and what will come of this?

FRIENDLY. Why thou art young and handsome; she young and desiring; t'were easy to make her love thee, and if the old gentleman chance to dye, you guess the rest, you are no fool.

HAZARD. Ay, but if he shou'd return –

FRIENDLY. If – why if she love you, that other will be but a slender bar to thy happiness; for if thou canst not marry her, thou mayst lye with her, (and gad) a younger brother may pick out a pretty livelihood here that way, as well as in *England* – or if this fail, there thou wilt find a perpetual visiter the Widdow *Ranter*, a woman bought from the ship[47] by old Col. *Ranter*, she serv'd him half a year, and then he married her, and dying in a year more, left her worth fifty thousand pounds sterling, besides plate and jewells: she's a great gallant, but assuming the humour of the country gentry, her extravagancy is very pleasant, she retains something of her primitive quality still, but is good natur'd and generous.

HAZARD. I like all this well.

FRIENDLY. But I have a further end in this matter, you must know there is in the same house a young heiress, one Colonel *Downright*'s daughter, whom I love, I think not in vain, her father indeed has an implacable hatred to me, for which reason I can but seldom visit her, and in this affair I have need of a friend in that house.

HAZARD. Me you're sure of.

FRIENDLY. And thus you'll have an opportunity to mannage both our amours: Here you will find occasion to shew your courage as well as express your love; for at this time the *Indians* by our ill management of trade, whom we have armed against our selves, very frequently make war upon us with our own weapons, tho' often coming by the worst are forced to make peace with us again, but so, as upon every turn they fall to massacring us wherever we lye exposed to them.

HAZARD. I heard the news of this in *England,* which hastens the new governour's[48] arrival here, who brings you fresh supplys.

FRIENDLY. Would he were landed, we hear he is a noble gentleman.

HAZARD. He has all the qualities of a gallant man, besides he is nobly born.

FRIENDLY. This Country wants nothing but to be people'd with a wellborn race to make it one of the best collonies in the world, but for want of a governour we are ruled by a council, some of which have been perhaps transported criminals, who having acquired great estates are now become your Honour, and Right Worshipfull, and possess all places of authority; there are amongst 'em some honest gentlemen who now begin to take upon 'em, and manage affairs as they ought to be.[49]

HAZARD. *Bacon* I think was one of the Council.

FRIENDLY. Now you have named a man indeed above the common rank, by nature generous; brave, resolv'd, and dareing; who studying the lives of the Romans and great men, that have raised themselves to the most elevated fortunes, fancies it easy for ambitious men, to aim at any pitch of glory, I've heard him often say, why cannot I conquer the universe as well as *Alexander*? Or like another *Romulus* form a new *Rome*, and make my self ador'd?

HAZARD. Why might he not? Great souls are born in common men, sometimes as well as princes.

FRIENDLY. This thirst of glory cherisht by sullen melancholly, I believe was the first motive that made him in love with the young *Indian*-Queen, fancying no *hero* ought to be without his princess. And this was the reason why he soearnestly prest for a commission, to be made general against the *Indians*, which long was promis'd him, but they fearing his ambition, still put him off, till the grievances grew so high, that the whole Country flockt to him, and beg'd he would redress them, – he took the opportunity, and led them forth to fight, and vanquishing brought the enemy to fair terms, but now instead of receiving him as a conquerour, we treat him as a traytor.

HAZARD. Then it seems all the crime this brave fellow has committed, is serving his country without authority.

FRIENDLY. 'tis so, and however I admire the man, I am resolv'd to be of the contrary party, that I may make an interest in our new governour; thus stands affairs, so that after you have seen Madam *Surelove*, I'll present you to the Council for a commission.

HAZARD. But my kinsman's character –

FRIENDLY. He was a *Lester-shire* younger brother,[50] came over hither with a small fortune, which his industry has increas'd to a thousand pound a year, and he is now Col. *John Surelove,* and one of the Council.

HAZARD. Enough.

FRIENDLY. About it then, Madam *Flirt* to direct you.

HAZARD. You are full of your madams here.

FRIENDLY. Oh! 'tis the greatest affront imaginable, to call a woman mistris, tho' but a retale brandy-munger.[51] – Adieu! – one thing more, tomorrow is our country-court, pray do not fail to be there, for the rarity of the entertainment: but I shall see you anon at *Surelove*'s where I'll salute thee as my first meeting, and as an old acquaintance in *England* – here's company, farewell. [*Exeunt* Friendly.

[*Enter* Dullman, Timerous, *and* Boozer. Hazard *sits at a table and writes.*

DULLMAN. Here *Nell* – Well Lieutenant *Boozer,* what are you for?

[*Enter* Nell.

BOOZER. I am for cooling *Nants,*[52] Major.

DULLMAN. Here *Nell*, a quart of *Nants*, and some pipes and smoak.

TIMEROUS. And do ye hear *Nell*, bid your mistress come in to joke a little with us, for adzoors I was damnable drunk last night, and am better at the petticoat than the bottle today. [*Exit* Nell.

DULLMAN. Drunk last night, and sick to day, how comes that about Mr. Justice? You use to bear your brandy well enough.

TIMEROUS. Ay your shier-brandy[53] I'll grant you, but I was drunk at Coll. *Downright*'s with your high Burgundy claret.

DULLMAN. A pox of that paltry liquor, your *English French* wine, I wonder how the gentlemen do to drink it.

TIMEROUS. Ay so do I, 'tis for want of a little *Virginia* breeding: how much more like a gentleman 'tis, to drink as we do, brave edifying punch and brandy, – But they say the young noble-men now and sparks in *England* begin to reform, and take it for their morning's, draught, get drunk by noon, and despise the lousy juice of the grape.

[*Enter* Mrs. Flirt *with* Nell.

DULLMAN. Come landlady, come, you are so taken up with Parson *Dunce*, that your old friends can't drink a dram with you, – What no smutty catch now, no jibe or joke to make the punch go down merrily, and advance trading? Nay, they say, gad forgive ye, you never miss going to church when Mr. *Dunce* preaches – but here's to you. [*Drinks*.

FLIRT. Lords, your Honours are pleas'd to be merry – but my service to your Honour [*Drinks*.

HAZARD. Honours, who the Devil have we here? – [*Aside*] *Some of the wise Council at least, I'd sooner took 'em for hoggerds*.[54]

FLIRT. Say what you please of the Doctor, but I'll swear he's a fine gentleman, he makes the prettiest sonnets, nay, and sings 'em himself to the rarest tunes.

TIMEROUS. Nay the man will serve for both soul and body, for they say he was a farrier in *England*, but breaking turn'd life-guard man, and his horse dying – he counterfeited a deputation from the bishop, and came over here a substantiall orthodox:[55] But come, where stands the cup? – Here, my service to you Major.

FLIRT. Your Honours are pleas'd – but me-thinks Doctor *Dunce* is a very edifying person, and a gentleman, and I pretend to know a gentleman, – for I my self am a gentlewoman; my father was a barronet, but undone in the late Rebellion[56] – and I am fain to keep an ordinary[57] now, heaven help me.

TIMEROUS. Good lack, why see how virtue may be belied – We heard your father was a taylor, but trusting for old *Oliver*'s funerall,[58] broke, and so came hither to hide his head, – but my service to you; what, you are never the worse?

FLIRT. Your Honours knows this is a scandalous place, for they say your Honour was but a broken excise-man,[59] who spent the King's money to buy your wife fine petticoats, and at last not worth a groat, you came over a poor servant, though now a Justice of Peace, and of the honourable Council.

TIMEROUS. Adz zoors if I knew who 'twas said so, I'd sue him for *scandalum magnatum*.[60]

DULLMAN. Hang 'em scoundrells, hang 'em, they live upon scandal, and we are scandall-proof, – they say too, that I was a tinker and running the country, robb'd a gentleman's house there, was put into *Newgate,* got a reprieve after condemnation, and was transported hither – and that you *Boozer* was a common pick-pocket, and being often flogg'd at the carts-tale[61], afterwards turn'd evidence,[62] and when the times grew honest was fain to fly.

BOOZER. Ay, ay, Major, if scandal would have broke our hearts, we had not arriv'd to the honour of being privy-councellors – but come Mrs. *Flirt*, what never a song to entertain us?

FLIRT. Yes, and a singer too newly come ashore:

TIMEROUS. Adz zoors, let's have it then:

[*Enter girl, who sings, they bear the bob*.[63]

HAZARD. Here maid, a tankard of your drink.

FLIRT. Quickly *Nell*, wait upon the gentleman;

DULLMAN. Please you Sir to taste of our liquor – my service to you; I see you are a stranger and alone, please you to come to our table? [*He rises and comes*.

FLIRT. Come Sir, pray sit down here, these are very honourable persons I assure you, – this is Major *Dullman*, major of his excellencie's own regiment, when he arrives, this is Mr. *Timerous*, Justice a Peace in *Corum*.[64] This Capt. Boozer, all of the honourable Council.

HAZARD. With your leave, Gentlemen. [*Sits*.

TIMEROUS. My service to you Sir. [*Drinks*] What have you brought over any cargo Sir, I'll be your customer.

BOOZER. [*Aside*] *Ay, and cheat him too, I'll warrant him*.

HAZARD. I was not bred to merchandizing Sir, nor do intend to follow the drudgery of trading.

DULLMAN. Men of fortune seldom travel hither Sir to see fashions.

TIMEROUS. Why Brother, it may be the gentleman has a mind to be a planter, will you hire your self to make a crop of tobacco this year?

HAZARD. I was not born to work Sir.

TIMEROUS. Not work Sir, zoors your betters have workt Sir, I have workt my self Sir, both set and stript tobacco, for all I am of the honourable Council, not work quoth a – I suppose Sir you wear your fortune upon your back Sir?

HAZARD. [*Rises*] Is it your custom here Sir to affront strangers? I shall expect satisfaction.

TIMEROUS. Why, does any body here owe you any thing?

DULLMAN. No, unless he means to be paid for drinking with us – ha, ha, ha!

HAZARD. No Sir, I have money to pay for what I drink: here's my club – my guinea. [*Flings down a guinea*] I scorn to be oblig'd to such scoundrells.

BOOZER. [*Rises in huff*] Hum – Call men of honour scoundrels.

TIMEROUS. Let him alone, let him alone Brother, how should he learn manners, he never was in *Virginia* before.

DULLMAN. He's some Covent-Garden[65] bully.

TIMEROUS. Or some broken citizen turn'd factor.[66]

HAZARD. Sir you lye, [*Flings the brandy in his face*] and you're a rascall.

TIMEROUS. Adz zoors he has spill'd all the brandy. [Timerous *runs behind the door,* Dullman *and* Boozer *strike* Hazard.

HAZARD. I understand no cudgel play, but wear a sword to right my self.[67] [*Draws, they run off.*

FLIRT. Good heavens, what quarelling in my house?

HAZARD. Do the persons of quality in this country treat strangers thus?

FLIRT. Alas Sir, 'tis a familiar way they have, Sir.

HAZARD. I'm glad I known it, – pray Madam can you inform one how I may be furnisht with a horse and a guide to Madam *Surelove*'s?

FLIRT. A most accomplisht Lady, and my very good friend you shall be immediately – [*Exeunt.*

Scene II.

[*Enter* Wellman, Downright, Dunce, Whimsey, Whiff, *and others.*]

WELLMAN. Come Mr. *Dunce*, tho' you are no Councellour, yet your counsel may be good in time of necessity, as now.

DUNCE. If I may be worthy advice, I do not look upon our danger to be so great from the *Indians*, as from young *Bacon*, whom the people have nick-nam'd *Fright-all*.

WHIMSEY. Ay, Ay that same *Bacon*, I would he were well hang'd, I am afraid that under pretence of killing all the *Indians* he means to murder us, lye with our wives, and hang up our little children, and make himself lord and king.

WHIFF. Brother *Whimsey*, not so hot, with leave of the Honourable Board,[68] my wife is of opinion, that *Bacon* came seasonably to our aid, and what he has done was for our defence, the *Indians* came down upon us, and ravisht[69] us all, men, women, and children.

WELLMAN. If these grievances were not redrest we had our reasons for it, it was not that we were insensible Capt. *Whiff* of what we suffer'd from the insolence of the *Indians*: but all knew what we must expect from *Bacon* if that by lawfull authority he had arriv'd to so great a command as General, nor would we be huft[70] out of our commissions.

DOWNRIGHT. 'Tis most certain that *Bacon* did not demand a commission out of a design of serving us, but to satisfy his ambition and his love, it being no secret that he passionately admires the *Indian Queen*, and under the pretext of a war, intends to kill the King her husband, establish himself in her heart, and on all occasions have himself a more formidable enemy, than the *Indians* are.

WHIMSEY. Nay, nay, I ever foresaw he would prove a villain.

WHIFF. Nay, and he be thereabout, my *Nancy* shall have no more to do with him.

WELLMAN. But Gentlemen, the people daily flock to him, so that his army is too considerable for us to oppose by any thing but policy.

DOWNRIGHT. We are sensible, Gentlemen, that our fortunes, our honours, and our lives are at stake, and therefore you are call'd together to consult what's to be done in this grand affair, till our governour and forces arrive from *England*; the truce he made with the *Indians* will be out tomorrow.

WHIFF. Ay, and then he intends to have another bout with the *Indians*. Let's have patience I say till he has thrum'd[71] their jackets, and then to work with your politicks as soon as you please.

DOWNRIGHT. Colonel *Wellman* has answer'd that point good Captain *Whiff*, 'tis the event of this battle we ought to dread, and if won or lost will be equally fatal for us, either from the *Indians* or from *Bacon*.

DUNCE. With the permission of the Honourable Board I think I have hit upon an expedient that may prevent this battle, your Honours shall write a letter to *Bacon*, where you shall acknowledge his services, invite him kindly home, and offer him a commission for general –

WHIFF. Just my *Nancy*'s counsell – Doctor *Dunce* has spoken like a cherubin, he shall have my voice for general, what say you brother *Whimsey*?

DOWNRIGHT. I say, he is a noble fellow, and fit for a general.

DUNCE. But conceive me right Gentlemen, as soon as he shall have render'd himself, seize him and strike off his head at the fort.

WHIFF. Hum! His head – Brother.

WHIMSEY. Ay, ay, Doctor *Dunce* speaks like a cherubin.

WELLMAN. Mr *Dunce*, your counsell in extremity I confess is not amiss, but I should be loath to deal dishonourably with any man.

DOWNRIGHT. His crimes deserve death, his life is forfeited by law, but shall never be taken by my consent by trechery: If by any stratagem we could take him a-live, and either send him for *England* to receive there his punishment, or keep him prisoner here till the Governour arrive, I should agree to't, but I question his coming in upon our invitation.

DUNCE. Leave that to me –

WHIMSEY. Come, I'll warrant him, the rogue's as stout as Hector,[72] he fears neither Heaven nor Hell.

DOWNRIGHT. He's too brave and bold to refuse our summons, and I am for sending him for *England* and leaving him to the King's mercy.

DUNCE. In that you'll find more difficulty Sir, to take him off here will be more quick and sudden: for the people worship him.

WELLMAN. I'll never yield to so ungenerous an expedient. The seizing him I am content in the extremity wherein we are, to follow. What say you Colonel *Downright*? Shall we send him a letter now while this two days' truce lasts, between him and the *Indians*?

DOWNRIGHT. I approve it.

ALL. And I, and I, and I.

DUNCE. If your Honours please to make me the messenger, I'll use some arguments of my own to prevail with him.

WELLMAN. You say well Mr. *Dunce*, and we'll dispatch you presently. [*Exeunt* Wellman, Downright *and all but* Whimsey, Whiff, & Dunce.

WHIFF. Ah Doctor, if you could but have persuaded Colonel Wellman and Colonel Downright to have hang'd him –

WHIMSEY. Why Brother *Whiff* you were for making him a general but now.

WHIFF. The councils of wise states-men Brother *Whimsey* must change as causes do, d'ye see.

DUNCE. Your Honours are in the right, and whatever those two leading councellors say, they would be glad if *Bacon* were dispatcht, but the punctillio[73] of honour is such a thing.

WHIMSEY. Honour, a pox on't, what is that honour that keeps such a bustle in the World, yet never did good as I heard of.

DUNCE. Why 'tis a foolish word only, taken up by great men, but rarely practic'd, – but if you would be great men indeed –

WHIFF. If we would Doctor, name, name the way.

DUNCE. Why, you command each of you a company, – When *Bacon* comes from the camp, as I am sure he will, (and full of this silly thing call'd honour will come unguarded too,) lay some of your men in ambush along those ditches by the *sevana*[74] about a mile from the town, and as he comes by, seize him, and hang him upon the next tree.

WHIFF. Hum – hang him! A rare plot.

WHIMSEY. Hang him – we'll do't, we'll do't Sir, – [*Aside*] *and I doubt not but to be made generall for the action* – I'll take it all upon my self.

DUNCE. If you resolve upon this, you must about it instantly – thus I shall at once serve my Country, & revenge my self on the rascall for affronting my dignity once at the councell-table, by calling me farrier. [*Exit* Doctor.

WHIFF. Do you know Brother what we are to do?

WHIMSEY. To do, yes, to hang a generall, Brother, that's all.

WHIFF. All, but is it lawfull to hang any generall?

WHIMSEY. Lawfull, yes, that 'tis lawfull to hang any generall that fights against law.

WHIFF. But in what he has done, he has serv'd the King and our Country, and preserv'd all our lives and fortunes.

WHIMSEY. That's all one, Brother, if there be but a quirk in the law offended in this case, tho' he fought like *Alexander*,[75] and preserv'd the whole world from perdition, yet if he did it against law, 'tis lawful to hang him; why what Brother, is it fit that every impudent fellow that pretends to a little honour, loyalty & courage, should serve his King and Country against the law? No, no, Brother, these things are not to be suffer'd in a civil government by law establish'd, – wherefore let's about it – [*Exeunt.*

Scene III.

[Surelove*'s house. Enter* Ranter *and* Jefrey *her coachman.*]

RANTER. Here *Jefrey,* ye drunken dog, set your coach and horses up, I'll not go till the cool of the evening, I love to ride in *fresco*.[76]

[*Enter a* Boy.

JEFREY. – [*Aside*] *Yes after hard drinking* – It shall be done, Madam.

RANTER. How now Boy, is Madam *Surelove* at home?

BOY. Yes Madam.

RANTER. Go tell her I am here, Sirrah.

BOY. Who are you pray, forsooth?

RANTER. Why you son of *baboone* don't you know me?

BOY. No Madam, I came over but in the last ship.

RANTER. What from *Newgate* or *Bridewell*?[77] From shoving the tumbler, sirrah, lifting or filing the cly?[78]

BOY. I don't understand this country-language for sooth, yet.

RANTER. You Rogue, 'tis what we transport from *England* first – go ye Dog, go tell your lady, the Widdow *Ranter* is come to dine with her – I hope I shall not find that Rogue *Dareing* here, sniveling after Mrs. Crisante. [*Exit* Boy] If I do, by the Lord, I'll lay him thick,[79] pox on him why should I love the dog, unless it be a judgment upon me.

[*Enter* Surelove *and* Crisante.

– My dear Jewel, how do'st do? – As for you Gentlewoman you are my rivall, & I am in rancor against you till you have renounc'd my *Dareing*.

CRISANTE. All the interest I have in him Madam, I resign to you.

RANTER. Ay – but your house lying so near the camp, gives me mortal fears – but prithee how thrives thy amour with honest *Friendly*?

CRISANTE. As well as an amour can, that is absolutely forbid by a father on one side, and pursu'd by a good resolution on the other.

RANTER. Hay gad I'll warrant for *Friendly*'s resolution, what, tho' his fortune be not answerable to yours, we are bound to help one another– here Boy – some pipes and a bowle of punch, you know my humour Madam, I must smoke and drink in a morning, or I am maukish[80] all day. [*Exit* Boy.

SURELOVE. But will you drink punch in a morning?

RANTER. Punch, 'tis my morning's draught, my table-drink, my treat, my regalio,[81] my every thing, ah my dear *Surelove*, if thou woud'st but refresh & chear thy heart with punch in a morning, thou wou'dst not look thus clowdy all the day. [*Enter pipes and a great bowl, she falls to smoaking.*

SURELOVE. I have reason Madam to be melancholy, I have receiv'd a letter from my husband, who gives me an account that he is worse in *England* than when he was here, so that I fear I shall see him no more, the doctors can do no good on him.

RANTER. A very good hearing. I wonder what the Devil thou hast done with him so long? An old fusty[82] weather-beaten skelleton, as dried as stock-fish,[83] and much of the hue. – Come, come, here's to the next, may he be young, Heaven, I beseech thee. [*Drinks.*

SURELOVE. You have reason to praise an old man, who dy'd and left you worth fifty thousand pound.

RANTER. Ay gad – and what's better Sweet-heart, dy'd in good time too, and left me young enough to spend this fifty thousand pound in better company – rest his soul for that too.

CRISANTE. I doubt 'twill be all laid out in *Bacon*'s mad lieutenant Generall *Dareing*.

RANTER. Faith I think I could lend it the rogue on good security.

CRISANTE. What's that, to be bound body for body?

RANTER. Rather that he should love nobody's body besides my own, but my fortune is too good to trust the rogue, my money makes me an *infidell.*

CRISANTE. You think they all love you for that:

RANTER. For that, ay what else? If it were not for that, I might sit still and sigh, and cry out, a miracle! A miracle! At sight of a man within my doors.

[*Enter* Maid.

MAID. Madam here's a young gentleman without would speak with you.

SURELOVE. With me, sure thou'rt mistaken, is it not *Friendly*?

MAID. No Madam 'tis a stranger;

RANTER. 'Tis not *Dareing* that rogue, is it?

MAID. No Madam.

RANTER. Is he handsome? Does he look like a gentleman?

MAID. He's handsome and seems a gentleman.

RANTER. Bring him in then, I hate a conversation without a fellow. [*Exit* Maid.

[*Enter* Hazard *with a letter.*

– Hah – a good handsome lad indeed:

SURELOVE. With me Sir would you speak?

HAZARD. If you are Madam *Surelove*:

SURELOVE. So I am call'd;

HAZARD. Madam I am newly arriv'd from *England*, and from your husband my kinsman bring you this – [*Gives a letter.*

RANTER. Please you to sit Sir.

HAZARD. [*Aside*] *She's extreamly handsome* – [*Sits down.*

RANTER. Come Sir will you smoke a pipe?

HAZARD. I never do Madam –

RANTER. Oh fy upon't you must learn then, we all smoke here, 'tis a part of good breeding, – well, well, what cargo, what goods have ye? Any poynts,[84] lace, rich stuffs, jewells; if you have I'll be your chafferer,[85] I live hard by, any body will direct you to the Widdow *Ranter*'s.

HAZARD. I have already heard of you, Madam.

RANTER. What you are like all the young fellows, the first thing they do when they come to a strange place, is to enquire what fortunes there are.

HAZARD. Madam I had no such ambition.

RANTER. Gad, then you're a fool, Sir, but come, my service to you; [*This while she reads the letter*] we rich widdows are the best commodity this country affords, I'll tell you that.

SURELOVE. Sir, my husband has recommended you here in a most particular manner, by which I do not only find the esteem he has for you, but the desire he has of gaining you mine, which on a double score I render you, first for his sake, next for those merits that appear in your self.

HAZARD. Madam, the endeavours of my life shall be to express my gratitude for this great bounty.

[*Enter* Maid.

MAID. Madam Mr. *Friendly*'s here.

SURELOVE. Bring him in.

HAZARD. *Friendly*, – I had a dear friend of that name, who I hear is in these parts – pray Heaven it may be he.

RANTER. How now *Charles.*

[*Enter* Friendly.

FRIENDLY. Madam your servant – Hah! [*Embracing him*] Should not I know you for my dear friend *Hazard.*

HAZARD. Or you're to blame my *Friendly*:

FRIENDLY. Prethee what calm brought thee ashore?

HAZARD. Fortune *de la garr*,[86] but prethee ask me no questions in so good company; where a minute lost from this conversation is a misfortune not to be retriev'd.

FRIENDLY. [*Softly aside*] *Do'st like her Rogue* –

HAZARD. Like her! Have I sight, or sense – why I adore her.

FRIENDLY. My *Crisante*, I heard your father would not be here to day, which made me snatch this opportunity of seeing you.

RANTER. Come, come, a pox of this whining love, it spoils good company.

FRIENDLY. You know my dear friend, these opportunities come but seldom, and therefore I must make use of 'em.

RANTER. Come, come, I'll give you a better opportunity at my house tomorrow, we are to eat a buffilo there, and I'll secure the old gentleman from coming.

FRIENDLY. Then I shall see *Crisante* once more before I go.

CRISANTE. Go – Heavens – whether my *Friendly*?

FRIENDLY. I have received a commission to go against the *Indians*, *Bacon* being sent for home.

RANTER. But will he come when sent for?

FRIENDLY. If he refuse we are to endeavour to force him.

CRISANTE. I do not think he will be forc'd, not even by *Friendly*.

FRIENDLY. And faith it goes against my conscience to lift my sword against him, for he is truly brave, and what he has done, a service to the Country, had it but been by authority.

CRISANTE. What pity 'tis there should be such false maxims in the world, that noble actions how ever great, must be criminall for want of a law to authorise 'em.

FRIENDLY. Indeed 'tis pity that when laws are faulty they should not be mended or abolish'd.

RANTER. Hark'ye *Charles*, by Heaven if you kill my *Dareing* I'll pistol you.

FRIENDLY. No, Widdow I'll spare him for your sake. [*They joyn with* Surelove.

HAZARD. Oh she is all divine, and all the breath she utters serves but to blow my flame.

[*Enter* Maid.

MAID. Madam's dinner's on the table –

SURELOVE. Please you Sir, to walk in – Come Mr. *Friendly*. [*She takes* Hazard.

RANTER. Prethee good Wench bring in the punch-bowle. [*Exeunt*.

Act II. Scene I.

[*A pavillion. Discovers the Indian* King *and* Queen *sitting in state, with guards of Indians, men and women attending: to them* Bacon *richly dress'd, attended by* Dareing, Fearless, *and other officers, he bows to the* King *and* Queen, *who rise to receive him.*]

KING. I am sorry Sir, we meet upon these terms, we who so often have embrac'd as friends.

BACON. – [*Aside*] *How charming is the Queen?* – War, Sir, is not my bus'ness, nor my pleasure: nor was I bred in arms; my Country's good has forc'd me to assume a soldier's life: and 'tis with much regret that I employ the first effects of it against my friends; yet whilst I may – whilst this cessation lasts, I beg we may exchange those friendships, Sir, we have so often paid in happier peace.

KING. For your part, Sir, you've been so noble, that I repent the fatall difference that makes us meet in arms. Yet tho' I'm young I'm sensible of injuries; and oft have heard my grandsire say – that we were monarchs once of all this spacious world; till you an unknown people landing here, distress'd and ruin'd by destructive storms, abusing all our charitable hospitality, usurp'd our right, and made your friends your slaves.

BACON. I will not justify the ingratitude of my fore-fathers, but finding here my inheritance, I am resolv'd still to maintain it so, and by my sword which first cut out my portion, defend each inch of land with my last drop of blood.

QUEEN. [*Aside*] *Ev'n his threats have charms that please the heart.*

KING. Come Sir, let this ungratefull theme alone, which is better disputed in the field.

QUEEN. Is it impossible there might be wrought an understanding betwixt my Lord and you? 'Twas to that end I first desired this truce, my self proposing to be mediator, to which my Lord *Cavarnio* shall agree, could you but condescend – I know you're noble: and I have heard you say our tender sex could never plead in vain.

BACON. Alas! I dare not trust your pleading Madam! A few soft words from such a charming mouth would make me lay the conqueror at your feet as a sacrifice for all the ills he has done you.

QUEEN. [*Aside*] *How strangely am I pleas'd to hear him talk.*

KING. *Semernia* see – the dancers do appear;
[*To* Bacon] Sir will you take your seat? [*He leads the* Queen *to a seat, they sit and talk.*

BACON. [*Aside*] *Curse on his sports that interrupted me, my very soul was hovering at my lip, ready to have discover'd all its secrets. But oh! I dread to tell her of my pain, and when I wou'd, an awfull trembling seizes me, and she can only from my dying eyes, read all the sentiments of my captive heart.* [*Sits down, the rest wait.*

[*Enter* Indians *that dance anticks; after the dance the* King *seems in discourse with* Bacon, *the* Queen *rises, and comes forth.*

QUEEN. The more I gaze upon this English stranger, the more confusion struggles in my soul, oft I have heard of love, and oft this gallant man (when peace had made him pay his idle visits) has told a thousand tales of dying maids. And ever when he spoke, my panting heart, with a prophetick fear in sighs reply'd, I shall fall such a victim to his eyes.

[*Enter an* Indian.

INDIAN. Sir here's a messenger from the English Council desires admittance to the General. [*To the* King.

BACON. With your permission Sir, he may advance. [*To the* King.

[*Re-enter* Indian *with* Dunce. *A letter.*

DUNCE. All health and happyness attend your Honour, [*Gives him a letter*] this from the honourable Council.

KING. I'll leave you till you have dispatch'd the messenger, and then expect your presence in the royal tent. [*Exeunt* King, Queen, *and* Indians.

BACON. *Lieutenant*, read the letter. [*To* Dareing.

DAREING. [*Reads*] *SIR, the necessity of what you have acted makes it pardonable, and we could wish we had done the Country, and our selves so much justice as to have given you that commission you desired – we now finde it reasonable to raise more forces, to oppose these insolences, which possibly yours may be too weak to accomplish, to which end the Council is ordered to meet this evening, and desiring you will come and take your place there, and be pleas'd to accept from us a commission to Command in Chief in this war – therefore send those soldiers under your command to their respective houses, and haste, Sir, to your affectionate friends –*

FEARLESS. Sir, I fear the hearts and pen did not agree when this was writ.

DAREING. A plague upon their shallow politicks! Do they think to play the old game twice with us?

BACON. Away, you wrong the Council, who of themselves are honourable gentlemen, but the base coward fear of some of them, puts the rest on tricks that suit not with their nature.

DUNCE. Sir, 'tis for noble ends you're sent for, and for your safety I'll engage my life.

DAREING. By Heaven and so you shall – and pay it too with all the rest of your wise-headed Council.

BACON. Your zeal is too officious now: I see no treachery, and can fear no danger.

DUNCE. Treachery! Now Heavens forbid, are we not Christians Sir, all friends and countrymen! Believe me Sir, 'tis honour calls you to increase your fame, and he who would dissuade you is your enemy.

DAREING. Go *cant*,[87] Sir to the rabble – for us – we know you.

BACON. You wrong me when you but suspect for me, let him that acts dishonourably fear. My innocence, and my good sword's my guard.

DAREING. If you resolve to go, we will attend you.

BACON. What go like an invader? No *Dareing*, the invitation's friendly, and as a friend, attended only by my menial servants, I'll wait upon the Council, that they may see that when I could command it I came an humble suppliant for their favour – you may return, and tell 'em I'll attend.

DUNCE. I kiss your Honour's hand – [*Goes out.*

DAREING. 'Sdeath will you trust the faithless Council Sir, who have so long held you in hand with promises, that curse of states-men, that unlucky vice that renders even nobility despis'd.

BACON. Perhaps the Council thought me too aspiring, and would not add wings to my ambitious flight.

DAREING. A pox of their considering caps, and now they find that you can soar alone, they send for you to nip your spreading wings. Now by my soul you shall not go alone.

BACON. Forbear, lest I suspect you for a mutineer; I am resolv'd to go.

FEARLESS. What, and send your army home? A pretty fetch.[88]

DAREING. By Heaven we'll not disband – not till we see how fairly you are dealt with: if you have a commission to be general, here we are ready to receive new orders: if not – we'll ring 'em such a thundring peal shall beat the town about their treacherous ears.

BACON. I do command you not to stir a man, till you're inform'd how I am treated by 'em: – leave me all –

[*Exeunt officers. While* Bacon *reads the letter again, to him the Indian* Queen, *with women waiting.*

QUEEN. [*Aside*] *Now while my lord's asleep in his pavilion I'll try my power with the general, for an accommodation of a peace: the very dreams of war fright my soft slumbers that us'd to be employ'd in kinder bus'ness.*

BACON. [*Aside*] *Ha! – the Queen – what happyness is this presents it self which all my industry could never gain?*

QUEEN. Sir – [*Approaching him.*

BACON. [*Aside*] *Prest with the great extreams of joy and fear I trembling stand, unable to approach her.*

QUEEN. I hope you will not think it fear in me, tho' Timerous as a dove, by Nature fram'd: nor that my lord, whose youth's unskill'd in war can either doubt his courage, or his forces, that makes me seek a reconciliation on any honourable terms of peace.

BACON. Ah Madam! If you knew how absolutely you command my fate I fear but little honour would be left me, since what so e're you ask me I should grant.

QUEEN. Indeed I would not ask your honour, Sir, that renders you too brave in my esteem. Nor can I think that you would part with that. No not to save your life.

BACON. I would do more to serve your least commands than part with triviall life.

QUEEN. Bless me! Sir, how came I by such a power?

BACON. The gods, and Nature gave it you in your creation, form'd with all the charms that ever grac'd your sex.

QUEEN. I'st possible? Am I so beautifull?

BACON. As Heaven, or angels there.

QUEEN. Supposing this, how can my beauty make you so obliging?

BACON. Beauty has still a power over great souls, and from the moment I beheld your eyes, my stubborn heart melted to compliance, and from a nature rough and turbulent, grew soft and gentle as the God of Love.

QUEEN. The God of Love! What is the God of Love?

BACON. 'Tis a resistless fire, that's kindled thus – [*Takes her by the hand and gazes on her*] at every gaze we take from fine eyes, from such bashfull looks, and such soft touches – it makes us sigh – and pant as I do now, and stops the breath when e're we speak of pain.

QUEEN. [*Aside*] *Alas, for me if this should be love!*

BACON. It makes us tremble, when we touch the fair one, and all the blood runs shiv'ring thro' the veins, the heart's surrounded with a feeble languishment, the eyes are dying, and the cheeks are pale, the tongue is faltring, and the body fainting.

QUEEN. – [*Aside*] *Then I'm undone, and all I feel is love.* – If love be catching Sir, by looks and touches, let us at distance parley – [*Aside*] *or rather let me fly, for within view, is too near –*

BACON. *Ah! She retires – displeas'd I fear with my presumptuous love.* – [*Kneels*] Oh pardon, fairest creature.

QUEEN. I'll talk no more, our words exchange our souls, and every look fades all my blooming honour, like sun beams, on unguarded roses – take all our kingdoms – make our people slaves, and let me fall beneath your conquering sword. But never let me hear you talk again or gaze upon your eyes – [*Goes out.*

BACON. She loves! By Heaven she loves! And has not art enough to hide her flame, tho' she have cruel honour to suppress it. However I'll pursue her to the banquet. [*Exit.*

Scene II.

[*The* Widdow Ranter's *hall. Enter* SureLove *fan'd by two negros, followed by* Hazard.]

SURELOVE. This Madam *Ranter* is so prodigious a treat – oh! I hate a room that smells of a great dinner, and what's worse a desert of punch and tobacco – what! Are you taking leave so soon Cousin?

HAZARD. Yes Madam, but 'tis not fit I should let you know with what regret I go, – but business will be obey'd.

SURELOVE. Some letters to dispatch to *English* ladies you have left behind – come Cousin confess.

HAZARD. I own I much admire the *English* beauties, but never yet have put their fetters on –

SURELOVE. Never in love – oh then you have pleasure to come.

HAZARD. Rather a pain when there's no hope attends it.

SURELOVE. Oh such diseases quickly cure themselves.

HAZARD. I do not wish to find it so; for even in pain I find a pleasure too.

SURELOVE. You are infected then, and came abroad for cure.

HAZARD. Rather to receive my wounds Madam.

SURELOVE. Already Sir. – Who e'er she be, she made good haste to conquer, we have few here, boast that dexterity.

HAZARD. What think you of *Crisante*, Madam?

SURELOVE. I must confess your love & your dispair are there placed right, of which I am not fond of being made a confident, since I'm assur'd she can love none but *Friendly*. [*Coldly*.

HAZARD. Let her love on, as long as life shall last, let *Friendly* take her, and the universe, so I had my next wish, – [*Sighs*] Madam it is your self that I adore, – I should not be so vain to tell you this, but that I know you've found the secret out already from my sighs.

SURELOVE. Forbear Sir, and know me for your kinsman's wife, & no more.

HAZARD. Be scornfull as you please, rail at my passion, and refuse to hear it; yet I'll love on, and hope in spite of you, my flame shall be so constant and submissive, it shall compell your heart to some return.

SURELOVE. You're very confident of your power I perceive, but if you chance to finde your self mistaken, say your opinion and your affectation were misapply'd, and not that I was cruell. [*Exit* Surelove.

HAZARD. Whate'er denials dwell upon your tongue, your eyes assure me that your heart is tender. [*Goes out.*

[*Enter the* Bag-Piper, *playing before a great bowl of punch, carryed between two negros, a* Highlander *dancing after it, the* Widdow Ranter *led by* Timerous, Crisante *by* Dullman; Mrs. Flirt *and* Friendly *all dancing after it; they place it on the table.*

DULLMAN. This is like the noble Widdow all over I'faith.

TIMEROUS. Ay, Ay, the Widdow's health in a full ladle, Major, [*Drinks*] – but a pox on't what made that young fellow here, that affronted us yesterday Major?

DULLMAN. Some damn'd sharper[89] that wou'd lay his knife aboard your Widdow *Cornet*.[90] [*While they drink about.*

TIMEROUS. Zoors if I thought so, I'd arrest him for salt and battery, lay him in prison for a swinging[91] fine and take no baile.

DULLMAN. Nay, had it not been before my Mrs. here, Mrs. *Crisante,* I had swing'd[92] him for his yesterday's affront, – ah my sweet Mistriss *Crisante* – if you did but know what a power you have over me –

CRISANTE. Oh you're a great courtier Major.

DULLMAN. Would I were any thing for your sake Madam.

RANTER. Thou art any thing, but what thou shouldst be, prethee Major leave off being an old buffoon, that is a lover turn'd to ridicule by age, consider thy self a meer rouling tun of nants, – a walking chimney, ever smoaking with nasty mundungus,[93] – and then thou hast a countenance like an old worm-eaten cheese.

DULLMAN. Well Widdow, you will joke, ha, ha, ha –

TIMEROUS. Gad', zoors she's pure company, ha, ha –

DULLMAN. No matter for my countenance – Colonel *Downright* likes my estate and is resolv'd to have it a match.

FRIENDLY. Dear Widdow, take off your damn'd Major, for if he speak another word to *Crisante*, I shall be put past all my patience, and fall foul upon him.

RANTER. S'life not for the world – Major I bar love-making within my territories, 'tis inconsistent with the punch-bowl, if you'll drink, do, if not be gone.

TIMEROUS. Nay Gad's zooks if you enter me at the punch-bowl, you enter me in politicks – well *'tis* the best drink in Christendom for a statesman. [*They drink about, the bag-pipe playing.*

RANTER. Come, now you shall see what my Highland varlet can do – [*A* Scots *dance.*

DULLMAN. So – I see let the world go which way it will, Widdow, you are resolv'd for mirth, – but come – to the conversation of the times.

RANTER. The times, why what a Devil ails the times, I see nothing in the times but a company of coxcombs that fear without a cause.

TIMEROUS. But if these fears were laid and *Bacon* were hang'd, I look upon *Virginia* to be the happiest part of the world, gads zoors, – why there's *England* – 'tis nothing to't – I was in *England* about 6 years ago, & was shew'd the Court of Aldermen, some were nodding, some saying nothing, and others very little to purpose, but how could it be otherwise, for they had neither bowl of punch, bottles of wine or tobacco before 'em to put life & soul into 'em as we have here: then for the young gentlemen – their farthest travels is to *France* or *Italy*, they never come hither.

DULLMAN. The more's the pitty by my troth. [*Drinks.*

TIMEROUS. Where they learn to swear mor-blew, mor-dee:[94]

FRIENDLY. And tell you how much bigger the *Louvre* is then *White-Hall*;[95] buy a suit a-la-mode, get a swinging cap of some *French* marquis, spend all their money and return just as they went.

DULLMAN. For the old fellows, their bus'ness is usury, extortion, and undermining young heirs.

TIMEROUS. Then for young merchants, their Exchange[96] is the tavern, their ware-house the play-house, and their bills of exchange billet-doux,[97] where to sup with their wenches at the other end of the Town, – Now judge you what a condition poor *England* is in: for my part I look upon't as a lost nation gads zoors.

DULLMAN. I have consider'd it, and have found a way to save all yet.

TIMEROUS. As how I pray.

DULLMAN. As thus, we have men here of great experience and ability – now I would have as many sent into *England* as would supply all places, and offices, both civil and military, d'e see, their young gentry should all travel hither for breeding, and to learn the misteries of state.

FRIENDLY. As for the old covetous fellows, I would have the tradesmen get in their debts, break and turn troupers.[98]

TIMEROUS. And they'd be soon weary of extortion gadz zoors;

DULLMAN. Then for the young merchants, there should be a law made, none should go beyond *Ludgate*.[99]

FRIENDLY. You have found out the only way to preserve that great kingdom. [*Drinking all this while sometimes.*

TIMEROUS. Well, gad zoors 'tis a fine thing to be a good statesman.

FRIENDLY. Ay *Cornet*,[100] which you had never been had you staid in old *England*.

DULLMAN. Why Sir we were somebody in *England*.

FRIENDLY. So I heard Major.

DULLMAN. You heard Sir, what have you heard, he's a kidnapper that says he heard any thing of me – and so my service to you – I'll sue you Sir for spoiling my marriage here, by your scandalls with Mrs. *Crisante*, but that shan't do Sir, I'll marry her for all that, & he's a rascal that denies it.

FRIENDLY. S'death you lie Sir – I do.

TIMEROUS. Gad zoors Sir lie to a privy-councellour, a major of horse, Brother, this is an affront to our dignities, draw and I'll side with you. [*They both draw on* Friendly, *the ladies run off.*

FRIENDLY. If I disdain to draw, 'tis not that I fear your base and cowardly force, but for the respect I bear you as magistrates, and so I leave you – [*Goes out.*

TIMEROUS. An errant coward gad zoors.

DULLMAN. A meer paultroon,[101] and I scorn to drink in his company. [*Exeunt, putting up their swords.*

Scene III.

[*A sevana, or large heath. Enter* Whimsey, Whiff, *and* Boozer, *with some soldiers, arm'd.*]

WHIMSEY. Stand – stand – and hear the word of command – do ye see yon cops,[102] and that ditch that runs along Major *Dullman*'s plantation.

BOOZER. We do.

WHIMSEY. Place your men there, and lye flat on your bellies, and when *Bacon* comes (if alone) seize him dy' see:

WHIFF. Observe the command now, (if alone) for we are not for bloudshed.

BOOZER. I'll warrant you for our parts. [*Exeunt all but* Whimsey *&* Whiff.

WHIMSEY. Now we have ambusht our men, let's light our pipes and sit down and take an encouraging dram of the bottle. [*Pulls out a bottle of brandy out of his pocket – they sit.*

WHIFF. Thou art a knave and hast emptyed half the bottle in thy leathern pockets, but come here's young *Fright-all*'s health.

WHIMSEY. What, wilt drink a man's health thou'rt going to hang?

WHIFF. 'Tis all one for that, we'll drink his health first, and hang him afterwards, and thou shalt pledge me de see, and tho' 'twere under the gallows.

WHIMSEY. Thou'rt a traitor for saying so, and I defy thee.

WHIFF. Nay, since we are come out like loving brothers to hang the Generall, let's not fall out among our selves, and so here's to you [*Drinks*] tho' I have no great maw[103] to this business.

WHIMSEY. Prethee Brother *Whiff*, do not be so villanous a coward, for I hate a coward.

WHIFF. Nay 'tis not that – but my *wife*, my *Nancy* dreamt to night she saw me hang'd.

WHIMSEY. 'Twas a cowardly dream, think no more on't, but as dreams are expounded by contraries, thou shalt hang the Generall.

WHIFF. Ay – but he was my friend, and I owe him at this time a hundred pounds of tobacco.

WHIMSEY. Nay, then I'm sure thoud'st hang him if he were thy brother.

WHIFF. But hark – I think I hear the neighing of horses, where shall we hide our selves, for if we stay here, we shall be mawl'd damnably. [*Exeunt both behind a bush, peeping.*

[*Enter* Bacon, Fearless *and 3 or 4 footmen.*

BACON. Let the groom lead the horses o're the *sevana*; we'll walk it on foot, 'tis not a quarter of a mile to the Town; & here the air is cool.

FEARLESS. The breazes about this time of the day begin to take wing and fan refreshment to the trees and flowers.

BACON. And at these hours how fragrant are the groves.

FEARLESS. The Country's well, were but the people so.

BACON. But come let's on – [*They pass to the entrance.*

WHIMSEY. There Boys – [*The soldiers come forth and fall on* Bacon.

BACON. Hah! Ambush – [*Draws.* Fearless *and footmen draw, the soldiers after a while fighting take* Bacon & Fearless *they having laid 3 or 4 dead.*

WHIFF. So, so, he's taken. Now we may venture out.

WHIMSEY. But are you sure he's taken?

WHIFF. Sure can't you believe your eyes, come forth, I hate a coward – oh Sir, have we caught your Mightiness?

BACON. Are you the authors of this valliant act? None but such villainous cowards dar'st have attempted it.

WHIMSEY. Stop his railing tongue.

WHIFF. No, no, let him rail, let him rail now his hands are tyed, ha, ha, why good Generall *Fright-all*, what, was nobody able d'ye think to tame the roaring lyon?

BACON. You'll be hang'd for this!

WHIMSEY. Come, come, away with him to the next tree.

BACON. What mean you Villains?

WHIFF. Only to hang your Honour a little, that's all. We'll teach you Sir, to serve your Country against law [*As they go off, Enter* Dareing *with soldiers.*

DAREING. Hah – my General betray'd – this I suspected. [*His men come in, they fall on, release* Bacon *and* Fearless *and his man, who get swords.* Whimsey*'s party put* Whimsey *and* Whiff *before 'em striking 'em as they endeavour to run on this side or that, and forcing 'em to bear-up, they are taken after some fighting.*

FEARLESS. Did not the General tell you Rogues, you'd be all hang'd?

WHIFF. Oh *Nancy, Nancy*, how prophetick are thy dreams?

BACON. Come let's on –

DAREING. S'death what mean you Sir?

BACON. As I design'd – to present my self to the Council:

DAREING. By Heavens we'll follow then to save you from their treachery, 'twas this that has befallen you that I fear'd, which made me at a distance follow you.

BACON. Follow me still, but still at such a distance as your aids may be assisting on all occasion – *Fearless* go back and bring your regiment down, and *Dareing* let your sergeant with his party guard these villains to the Council. [*Exeunt* Bacon, Dareing & Fearless.

WHIFF. A pox on your Worship's plot;

WHIMSEY. A pox on your forwardness to come out of the hedge. [*Exit officers with* Whimsey & Whiff.

Scene IV.

[*The Council-table. Enter Colonel* Wellman, *Colonel* Downright, Dullman, Timerous, *and about 7 or 8 more seat themselves.*]

WELLMAN. You heard Mr. *Dunce*'s opinion Gentlemen, concerning *Bacon*'s coming upon our invitation. He believes he will come, but I rather think, tho' he be himself undaunted, yet the persuasions of his two Lieutenant-Generalls, *Dareing* and *Fearless*, may prevent him, – Colonel, have you order'd our men to be in arms?

[*Enter a* Soldier.

DOWNRIGHT. I have, and they'll attend further order on the *sevana*:

SOLDIER. May it please your Honours, *Bacon* is on his way, he comes unattended by any but his footmen, and Colonel *Fearless*.

DOWNRIGHT. Who is this fellow?

WELLMAN. A spy I sent to watch *Bacon's* motions.

SOLDIER. But there is a company of soldiers in ambush on this side of the *sevana* to seize him as he passes by.

WELLMAN. That's by no order of the Council.

OMNES. No, no, no order;

WELLMAN. Nay, 'twere a good design if true.

TIMEROUS. Gad zoors would I had thought on't for my troup.

DOWNRIGHT. I am for no unfair dealing in any extremity.

[*Enter* Brag *in haste.*

BRAG. An't please your Honours, the saddest news – an ambush being laid for *Bacon*, they rusht out upon him, on the *sevana*, and after some fighting took him and *Fearless* –

TIMEROUS. Is this your sad news – zoors would I had had a hand in't.

BRAG. When on a sudden, *Dareing* and his party fell in upon us, turn'd the tide – kill'd our men and took Capt. *Whimsey*, and Capt. *Whiff* prisoners, the rest run away, but *Bacon* fought like a fury.

TIMEROUS. A bloudy fellow.

DOWNRIGHT. *Whimsey* and *Whiff*? They deserve death for acting without order.

TIMEROUS. I'm of the Colonel's opinion, they deserve to hang for't.

DULLMAN. Why Brother, I thought you had wisht the plot had been yours but now?

TIMEROUS. Ay, but the case is alter'd since that, good Brother.

WELLMAN. Now he's exasperated past all hopes of a reconciliation.

DULLMAN. You must make use of the statesman's refuge, wise dissimulation.

BRAG. For all this Sir, he will not believe but that you mean honourably, and no persuasions could hinder him from coming, so he has dismist all his soldiers, and is entring the town on foot.

WELLMAN. What pitty 'tis a brave man should be guilty of an ill action.

BRAG. But the noise of his danger has so won the hearts of the mobile,[104] that they increase his train as he goes, & follow him in the town like a victor.

WELLMAN. Go wait his coming. [*Exit* Brag] He grows too popular, and must be humbled.

TIMEROUS. I was ever of your mind Colonel.

WELLMAN. Ay right or wrong – but what's your counsell now?

TIMEROUS. E'en as it us'd to be, I leave it to wiser heads.

[*Enter* Brag.

BRAG. *Bacon* Sir is entring.

TIMEROUS. Gad zoors wou'd I were safe in bed.

DULLMAN. Colonel keep in your heat and treat calmly with him.

WELLMAN. I rather wish you wou'd all follow me, I'd meet him at the head of all his noisy rabble, and seize him from the rout.

DOWNRIGHT. What men of authority dispute with rake-hells?[105] 'Tis below us Sir.

TIMEROUS. To stake our lives and fortunes against their nothing.

[*Enter* Bacon, *after him the rabble with staves and clubs bringing in* Whimsey *&* Whiff *bound.*

WELLMAN. What means this insolence – What Mr. *Bacon* do you come in arms?

BACON. I'd need Sir come in arms, when men that should be honourable can have so poor designs to take my life.

WELLMAN. Thrust out his following rabble.

FIRST RABBLE. We'll not stirr till we have the General safe back again.

BACON. Let not your loves be too officious – but retire –

FIRST RABBLE. At your command we vanish – [*The rabble retire.*

BACON. I hope you'll pardon me, if in my own defence I seiz'd on these two murderers.

DOWNRIGHT. You did well Sir, 'twas by no order they acted, – stand forth and hear your sentence – in time of war we need no formall tryalls to hang knaves that act without order.

WHIFF. Oh mercy mercy Colonel – 'twas Parson *Dunce*'s plot.

DOWNRIGHT. Issue out a warrant to seize *Dunce* immediately – you shall be carry'd – to the fort to pray –

WHIMSEY. Oh good your Honour I never pray'd in all my life.

DOWNRIGHT. From thence drawn upon a sledg to the place of execution, – where you shall hang till you are dead – and then be cut down and –

WHIMSEY. Oh hold – hold – we shall never be able to endure half this. [*Kneeling.*

WELLMAN. I think th'offence needs not so great punishment, their crime Sir is but equal to your own, acting without commission.

BACON. 'Tis very well explain'd Sir, – had I been murder'd by commission then, the deed had been approv'd, and now perhaps, I am beholden to the rabble for my life: –

WELLMAN. A fine pretence to hide a popular fault, but for this once we pardon them and you.

BACON. Pardon, for what? By Heaven I scorn your pardon, I've not offended honour nor religion.

WELLMAN. You have offended both in taking arms.

BACON. Shou'd I stand by and see my Country ruin'd, my King dishonour'd, and his subjects murder'd, hear the sad cries of widdows and of orphans. You heard it lowd, but gave no pitying care to't. And till the war and massacre was brought to my own door, my flocks, and herds surpriz'd, I bore it all with patience. Is it unlawfull to defend my self against a thief that breaks into my doors?

WELLMAN. And call you this defending of your self?

BACON. I call it doing of my self that right, which upon just demand the Council did refuse me. If my ambition as you're pleas'd to call it, made me demand too much, I left my self to you.

WELLMAN. Perhaps we thought it did.

BACON. Sir you affront my birth, – I am a gentleman, and yet my thoughts were humble – I wou'd have fought under the meanest of your parasites –

TIMEROUS. There's a bob[106] for us Brother. [*To* Dullman.

BACON. But still you put me off with promises – and when compell'd to stir in my defence I call'd none to my aid, and those that came, 'twas their own wrongs that urg'd 'em.

DOWNRIGHT. 'Tis fear'd Sir, under this pretence you aim at government.

BACON. I scorn to answer to so base an accusation, the height of my ambition is, to be an honest subject.

WELLMAN. An honest rebell, Sir –

BACON. You know you wrong me, and 'tis basely urg'd – but this is trifling – here are my commissions. [*Throws down papers,* Downright *reads.*

DOWNRIGHT. – To be general of the forces against the *Indians*, and blank commissions for his friends.

WELLMAN. Tear them in peices – are we to be imposed upon? De ye come in hostile manner to compel us?

DOWNRIGHT. Be not too rough Sir, let us argue with him –

WELLMAN. I am resolved I will not.

TIMEROUS. Then we are all dead men, gudzoors! He will not give us time to say our prayers.

WELLMAN. We every day expect fresh force from *England*, till then we of our selves shall be sufficient to make defence, against a sturdy traytor.

BACON. Traytor, 'sdeath traytor – I defie ye, but that my honour's yet above my anger; I'd make you answer me that traytor dearly. [*Rises.*

WELLMAN. Hah – am I threatened – Guards secure the rebel. [*Guards seize him.*

BACON. Is this your honourable invitation? Go – triumph in your short liv'd victory, the next turn shall be mine. [*Exeunt guards with* Bacon.

[*A noise of fighting–*

[*Enter* Bacon, Wellman, *his guards beat back by the rabble,* Bacon *snatches a sword from one, and keeps back the rabble,* Timerous *gets under the table.*

DOWNRIGHT. What means this insolence!

RABBLE. We'll have our General, and knock that fellow's brains out, and hang up Colonel *Wellman*.

ALL. Ay ay, hang up *Wellman.* [*The rabble seize* Wellman, *and* Dullman, *and the rest.*

DULLMAN. Hold, hold Gentleman, I was always for the General.

RABBLE. Let's barbicu[107] this fat rogue.

BACON. Begone, and know your distance to the Council. [*The rabble let 'em go.*

WELLMAN. I'd rather perish by the meanest hand, than owe my safety poorly thus to *Bacon.* [*In rage.*

BACON. If you persist still in that mind I'll leave you, and conquering, make you happy 'gainst your will. [*Exeunt* Bacon *and* Rabble, *hollering 'a Bacon, a Bacon.'*

WELLMAN. Oh villainous cowards, who will trust his honour with sycophants so base? Let us to arms – by Heaven I will not give my body rest, till I've chastiz'd the boldness of this rebel. [*Exeunt* Wellman, Downright, *and the rest all but* Dullman.

TIMEROUS. What is the roistering Hector[108] gone Brother? [*Peeps from under the table.*

DULLMAN. Ay, ay, and the Devil go with him. [*Looking sadly.* Timerous *comes out.*

TIMEROUS. Was there ever such a Bull of *Bashan*?[109] Why what if he should come down upon us and kill us all for traytors?

DULLMAN. I rather think the Council will hang us all for cowards – ah – oh – a drum – a drum – oh – [*He goes out.*

TIMEROUS. This is the misery of being great,
We're sacrific'd to every turn of state.

Act III. Scene I.

[*The Country Court, a great table, with papers, a clerk writing. Enter a great many people of all sorts, then* Friendly, *after him* Dullman.]

FRIENDLY. How now Major; what, they say *Bacon* scar'd you all out of the Council yesterday: What say the people?

DULLMAN. Say? They curse us all, and drink young *Frightall*'s health, and swear they'll fight through fire and brimstone for him.

FRIENDLY. And to morrow will hallow[110] him to the gallows, if it were his chance to come there.

DULLMAN. 'Tis very likely: why I am forc'd to be guarded to the Court now, the rabble swore they would *De Wit*[111] me, but I shall hamper some of 'em. Wou'd the Governour were here to bear the brunt on't, for they call us the evil counsellors.

[*Enter* Hazard, *goes to* Friendly.

Here's the young rogue that drew upon us too, we have rods in piss[112] for him i'faith.

[*Enter* Timerous *with bailiffs, whispers to* Dullman, *after which to the bailiffs.*

TIMEROUS. Gadzoors that's he, do your office.

BAILIFF. We arrest you Sir, in the King's name, at the suit of the Honourable Justice *Timerous.*

HAZARD. Justice *Timerous*, who the Devil's he?

TIMEROUS. I am the man Sir, de see, for want of a better; you shall repent gads zoors your putting of tricks upon persons of my rank and quality. [*After he has spoke he runs back as afraid of him.*

HAZARD. Your rank and quality!

TIMEROUS. Ay Sir, my rank and quality; first I am one of the Honourable Council, next a Justice of Peace in *Quorum*, Cornet of a Troop of Horse de see, and Church-warden.

FRIENDLY. From whence proceeds this Mr. Justice, you said nothing of this at Madam *Ranter*'s yesterday; you saw him there, then you were good friends?

TIMEROUS. Ay, however I have carried my body swimmingly before my mistress, de see, I had rancour in my heart, gads zoors.

FRIENDLY. Why, this gentleman's a stranger, and but lately come a shore.

HAZARD. At my first landing I was in company with this fellow and two or three of his cruel brethren, where I was affronted by them, some words past and I drew –

TIMEROUS. Ay ay Sir, you shall pay for't, – why – what Sir, cannot a Civil Magistrate affront a man, but he must be drawn upon presently?

FRIENDLY. Well Sir, the gentleman shall answer your suit, and I hope you'll take my bail for him.

TIMEROUS. 'Tis enough – I know you to be a civil person.

[Timerous *and* Dullman *take their places, on a long bench placed behind the table, to them* Whimsey *and* Whiff, *they seat themselves, then* Boozer *and two or three more; who seat themselves: then enter two bearing a bowl of punch, and a great ladle or two in it; the rest of the stage being filled with people.*

WHIFF. Brothers it has been often mov'd at the Bench, that a new punch bowl shou'd be provided, and one of a larger circumference, when the Bench sits late about weighty affairs, oftentimes the bowl is emptyed before we end.

WHIMSEY. A good motion, Clerk set it down.

CLERK. Mr. Justice *Boozer* the Council has ordered you a writ of ease,[113] and dismiss your Worship from the Bench.

BOOZER. Me from the Bench, for what?

WHIMSEY. The complaint is Brother *Boozer*, for drinking too much punch in the time of hearing tryals.

WHIFF. And that you can neither write nor read, nor say the Lord's Prayer.

TIMEROUS. That your warrants are like a brewer's tally a notch on a stick;[114] if a special warrant, then a couple. Gads zoors, when his Excellency comes he will have no such justices.

BOOZER. Why Brother, tho I can't read my self, I have had *Dolton*'s Country-Justice[115] read over to me two or three times, and understand the law; this is your malice Brother *Whiff*, because my wife does not come to your ware-house to buy her commodities, – but no matter, to show I have no malice in my heart, I drink your health – I care not this, I can turn lawyer and plead at the Board.[116] [*Drinks, all pledge him and hum.*[117]

DULLMAN. Mr. Clerk, come, to the tryals on the docket.

CLERK. The first is between his Worship Justice *Whiff*, and one *Grubb*. [Clerk *reads.*

DULLMAN. Ay, that *Grubb*'s a common disturber, Brother your cause, is a good cause if well manag'd, here's to't [*Drinks.*

WHIFF. I thank you Brother *Dullman* [*Drinks*] – read my petition.

CLERK. The Petition of Captain *Thomas Whiff* sheweth, whereas *Gilbert Grubb*, calls his Worship's wife *Ann Whiff* whore, and said he would prove it; your Petitioner desires the Worshipful Bench to take it into consideration, and your Petitioner shall pray, *&c.* – here's two witnesses have made affidavit *vive voce*,[118] an't like your Worships.

DULLMAN. Call *Grubb*.

CLERK. *Gilbert Grubb*, come into the court.

GRUBB. Here.

WHIMSEY. Well, what can you say for your self Mr. *Grubb*.

GRUBB. Why an't like your Worship, my wife invited some neighbours' wives to drink a cagg[119] of cider, now your Worship's wife Madam *Whiff* being there fuddl'd, would have thrust me out of doors, and bid me go to my old whore Madam *Whimsey*, meaning your worship's wife. [*To* Whimsey.

WHIMSEY. Hah! My wife called whore, she's a jade, & I'll arrest her husband here – in an action of debts.

TIMEROUS. Gads zours she's no better than she should be I'll warrant her.

WHIFF. Look ye Brother *Whimsey*, be patient, you know the humour of my *Nancy* when she's drunk, but when she's sober, she's a civil person, and shall ask your pardon.

WHIMSEY. Let this be done and I am satisfied. And so here's to you [*Drinks.*

DULLMAN: Go on to the tryal.

GRUBB. I being very angry said indeed, I would prove her a greater whore than Madam *Whimsey*.

CLERK. An't like your worships, he confesses the words in open court.

GRUBB. Why, an't like your Worships, she has had two bastards I'll prove it.

WHIFF. Sirrah, sirrah, that was when she was a maid, not since I married her, my marrying her made her honest.

DULLMAN. Let there be an order of Court to sue him, for *scandalum magnatum*.[120]

TIMEROUS. Mr. *Clerk*, let my cause come next.

CLERK. The defendant's ready Sir. [Hazard *comes to the Board.*

TIMEROUS. Brothers of the Bench take notice, that this Hector[121] here coming into Mrs. *Flirt*'s ordinary where I was, with my Brother *Dullman* and Lieutenant *Boozer*, we gave him good counsel to fall to work, now my gentleman here was affronted at this forsooth, and makes no more to do but calls us scoundrels, and drew his sword on us, and had not I defended my self by running away, he had murdered me, and assassinated my two brothers.

WHIFF. What witness have you Brother?

TIMEROUS. Here's Mrs. *Flirt* and her maid *Nell*, – besides we may be witness for one another I hope, our words may taken.

CLERK. Mrs. *Flirt* and *Nell* are sworn. [*They stand forth.*

WHIMSEY. By the oaths that you have taken, speak nothing but the truth.

FLIRT. An't please your Worships, your Honours came to my house, where you found this young gentleman; and your Honours invited him to drink with your Honours: where after some opprobrious words given him, Justice *Dullman*, and Justice *Boozer* struck him over the head; and after that indeed the gentleman drew.

TIMEROUS. Mark that Brother he drew.

HAZARD. If I did, it was *se defendendo*.[122]

TIMEROUS. Do you hear that Brothers, he did in defiance.

HAZARD. Sir, you ought not to sit judge and accuser too.

WHIFF. The gentleman's in the right Brother, you cannot do it according to law.

TIMEROUS. Gads zoors, what new tricks, new querks?[123]

HAZARD. Gentlemen take notice, he swears in Court.

TIMEROUS. Gads zoors what's that to you Sir.

HAZARD. This is the second time of his swearing.

WHIMSEY. What do you think we are deaf Sir? Come, come proceed.

TIMEROUS. I desire he may be bound to his good behaviour, fin'd and deliver up his sword, what say you Brother? [*Jogs* Dullman *who nods.*

WHIMSEY. He's asleep, drink to him and waken him, [*Drinks*] – you have mist the cause by sleeping Brother.

DULLMAN. Justice may nod, but never sleeps Brother – you were at – deliver his sword – a good motion, let it be done. [*Drinks.*

HAZARD. No Gentlemen, I wear a sword to right my self.

TIMEROUS. That's fine i'faith, gads zoors, I have worn a sword this duzen year and never cou'd right my self.

WHIFF. Ay, 'twou'd be a fine world if men shou'd wear swords to right themselves, he that's bound to the peace shall wear no sword.

WHIMSEY. I say he that's bound to the peace ought to wear no peruke,[124] they may change 'em for black or white, and then who can know them.

HAZARD. I hope Gentlemen I may be allowed to speak for my self.

WHIFF. Ay, what can you say for your self, did you not draw your sword Sirrah?

HAZARD. I did.

TIMEROUS. 'Tis sufficient he confesses the fact, and we'll hear no more.

HAZARD. You will not hear the provocation given.

DULLMAN. 'Tis enough Sir, you drew –

WHIMSEY. Ay, ay, 'tis enough he drew – let him be fin'd.

FRIENDLY. The gentleman shou'd be heard, he's a kinsman too, to Colonel *John Surelove*.

TIMEROUS. Hum – Colonel *Surelove*'s kinsman.

WHIFF. Is he so, nay, then all the reason in the world he should be heard, Brothers.

WHIMSEY. Come, come Cornet, you shall be friends with the gentleman, this was some drunken bout I'll warrant you.

TIMEROUS. Ha, ha, ha – so it was gads zoors.

WHIFF. Come drink to the gentleman, and put it up.

TIMEROUS. Sir, my service to you, I am heartily sorry for what's past, but it was in my drink. [*Drinks.*

WHIMSEY. You hear his acknowledgements Sir, and when he is sober he never quarrels, come Sir sit down, my service to you.

HAZARD. I beg your excuse Gentlemen – I have earnest business.

DULLMAN. Let us adjourn the Court, and prepare to meet the regiments on the *sevana*. [*All go but* Friendly *and* Hazard.

HAZARD. Is this the best Court of Judicature your Country affords?

FRIENDLY . To give it its due it is not. But how does thy amour thrive?

HAZARD. As well as I can wish, in so short a time.

FRIENDLY. I see she regards thee with kind eyes, sighs and blushes.

HAZARD. Yes, and tells me I am so like a brother she had – to excuse her kind concern, – then blush so prettily, that gad I cou'd not forbear making a discovery of my heart.

FRIENDLY. Have a care of that, come upon her by slow degrees, for I know she's vertuous; – but come let's to the *sevana*, where I'll present you to the two Colonels, *Wellman* and *Downright*, the men that manage all till the arrival of the Governour.

Scene II.

[*The Sevana or heath: Enter* Wellman, Downright, Boozer, *and officers.*]

WELLMAN. Have you dispatcht the scouts, to watch the motions of the enemies? I know that *Bacon*'s violent and haughty, and will resent our vain attempts upon him; therefore we must be speedy in prevention.

DOWNRIGHT. What forces have you raised since our last order.

BOOZER. Here's a list of 'em, they came but slowly in, till we promised every one a bottle of brandy.

[*Enter* Officer *and* Dunce.

OFFICER. We have brought Mr. *Dunce* here, as your Honour commanded us after strict search we found him this morning in bed with Madam *Flirt*.

DOWNRIGHT. No matter he'll exclaim no less against the vices of the flesh, the next Sunday.

DUNCE. I hope Sir, you will not credit the malice of my enemies.

WELLMAN. No more, you are free, and what you councell'd about the ambush was both prudent and seasonable, and perhaps I now wish it had taken effect.

[*Enter* Friendly *and* Hazard.

FRIENDLY. I have brought an English gentleman to kiss your hands, Sir, and offer you his service, he is young and brave, and kinsman to Col. *Surelove*.

WELLMAN. Sir, you are welcome, and to let you see you are so, we will give you your kinsman's command, captain of a troop of horse-guards, and which I am sure will be continued to you when the Governour arrives.

HAZARD. I shall endeavour to deserve the honour, Sir.

[*Enter* Dullman, Timerous, Whimsey *and* Whiff, *all in buff, scarf and feathers.*[125]

DOWNRIGHT. So Gentlemen, I see you're in a readiness.

TIMEROUS. Readiness! What means he, I hope we are not to be drawn out to go against the enemy, Major?

DULLMAN. If we are, they shall look a new major for me.

WELLMAN. We were debating, Gentlemen, what course were best to pursue against this powerful rebel.

FRIENDLY. Why, Sir, we have forces enough, let's charge him instantly, delays are dangerous.

TIMEROUS. Why, what a damn'd fiery fellow's this?

DOWNRIGHT. But if we drive him to extremities, we fear his siding with the *Indians*.

DULLMAN. Colonel *Downright* has hit it; why should we endanger our men against a desperate termagant?[126] If he loves wounds and scars so well, let him exercise on our enemies – but if he will needs fall upon us, 'tis then time for us enough to venture our lives and fortunes.

TIMEROUS. How, we go to *Bacon*, under favour I think 'tis his duty to come to us, an you go to that gads zoors.

FRIENDLY. If he do, 'twill cost you dear, I doubt Cornet. – I find by our list, Sir, we are four thousand men.

TIMEROUS. Gads zoors, not enough for a breakfast for that insatiate *Bacon,* and his two Lieutenant Generals *Fearless* and *Daring*. [Whiff *sits on the ground with a bottle of brandy.*

WHIMSEY. A morsel, a morsel.

WELLMAN. I am for an attack, what say you Gentlemen to an attack? – What, silent all? – What say you Major?

DULLMAN. I say, Sir, I hope my courage was never in dispute. [*Speaks big*] But, Sir, I am going to marry Colonel *Downright*'s daughter here – and should I be slain in this battel 'twou'd break her heart; – besides, Sir, I should lose her fortune.

WELLMAN. I'm sure here's a captain will never flinch. [*To* Whimsey.

WHIMSEY. Who I, an't like your Honour?

WELLMAN. Ay, you.

WHIMSEY. Who I? Ha, ha, ha: why did your Honour think that I would fight?

WELLMAN. Fight, yes? Why else do you take commissions?

WHIMSEY. Commissions! O Lord, O Lord, take commissions to fight? Ha ha ha; that's a jest, if all that take commissions should fight –

WELLMAN. Why do you bear arms then?

WHIMSEY. Why for the pay; to be called Captain, noble Captain, to show, to cock[127] and look big and bluff as I do; to be bow'd to thus as we pass, to domineer, and beat our souldiers: fight quoth a, ha ha ha.

FRIENDLY. But what makes you look so simply Cornet?

TIMEROUS. Why a thing that I have quite forgot, all my accounts for *England* are to be made up, and I'm undone if they be neglected – [*Looks big*] else I wou'd not flinch for the stoutest he that wears a sword –

DOWNRIGHT. What say you Captain *Whiff*?

WHIFF. I am trying Colonel what mettle I'm made on; I think I am valiant, I suppose I have courage, but I confess 'tis a little of the *D* – breed, but a little inspiration from the bottle, and the leave of my *Nancy*, may do wonders. [Whiff *almost drunk.*

[*Enter* Seaman *in haste.*

SEAMAN. An't please your Honours, *Frightall*'s officers have seiz'd all the ships in the river, and rid now round the shore, and had by this time secur'd the sandy beach, and landed men to fire the town, but that they are high in drink aboard the ship call'd the Good Subject; the master of her sent me to let your Honours know, that a few men sent to his assistance will surprize them, and retake the ships.

WELLMAN. Now, Gentlemen, here's a brave occasion for emulation – why writ not the master?

DULLMAN. Ay, had he writ, I had soon been amongst them i'faith; but this is some plot to betray us.

SEAMAN. Keep me here, and kill me if it be not true.

DOWNRIGHT. He says well – there's a *brigantine* and a *shallop*[128] ready, I'll embark immediately.

FRIENDLY. No Sir, your presence is here more necessary, let me have the honour of this expedition.

HAZARD. I'll go your volunteer *Charles*.

WELLMAN. Who else offers to go.

WHIMSEY. A meer trick to kidnap us, by *Bacon*, – if the Captain had writ –

TIMEROUS. Ay, ay, if he had writ –

WELLMAN. I see you're all base cowards, and here cashier ye from all commands and offices.

WHIMSEY. Look ye Colonel, you may do what you please, but you lose one of the best drest officers in your whole camp, Sir –

TIMEROUS. And in me, such a head piece.

WHIFF. I'll say nothing, but let the state want me.

DULLMAN. For my part I am weary of weighty affairs. [*In this while* Wellman, Downright, Friendly *and* Hazard *talk.*

WELLMAN. Command what men you please, but expedition makes you half a conquerour. [*Exit* Friendly *and* Hazard.

[*Enter another seaman with a letter, gives it to* Downright, *he and* Wellman *read it.*

DOWNRIGHT. Look ye now Gentlemen the master has writ.

DULLMAN. Has he – he might have writ sooner, while I was in command, – if he had –

WHIMSEY. Ay Major – if he had – but let them miss us –

WELLMAN. Colonel haste with your men and reinforce the beach, while I follow with the Horse;[129] – Mr. *Dunce* pray let that proclamation be read concerning *Bacon*, to the souldiers.

DUNCE. It shall be done Sir, [*Exit* Downright *and* Wellman.

Gentlemen how simply you look now.

[*The scene opens and discovers a body of souldiers.*

TIMEROUS. – Why Mr. Parson I have a scruple of conscience upon me. I am considering whether it be lawful to kill, tho it be in war; I have a great aversion to't, and hope it proceeds from religion.

WHIFF. I remember the fit took you just so, when the *Dutch* besieged us, for you cou'd not then be perswaded to strike a stroke.

TIMEROUS. Ay, that was because they were Protestants as we are, but gads zoors had they been *Dutch* papists[130] I had maul'd them! But conscience –

WHIMSEY. I have been a Justice of Peace this six years and never had a conscience in my life.

TIMEROUS. Nor I neither, but in this damn'd thing of fighting.

DUNCE. Gentlemen I am commanded to read the declaration of the Honourable Council to you. [*To the souldiers.*

ALL. Hum hum hum –

BOOZER. Silence – silence –

DUNCE. By an order of Council dated *May* the 10*th* 1670: To all gentlemen souldiers, marchants, planters, and whom else it may concern. Whereas *Bacon*, contrary to law and equity, has to satisfie his own ambition taken up arms, with a pretence to fight the *Indians*, but indeed to molest and enslave the whole colony, and to take away their liberties and properties; this is to declare, that whoever shall bring this traytor dead or alive to the Council shall have three hundred pounds reward. *And so God save the King.* [Dunce *reads.*

ALL. A Council, a Council! Hah – [*Hollow.*

[*Enter a* Souldier *hastily.*

SOULDIER. Stand to your arms Gentlemen, stand to your arms, *Bacon* is marching this way.

DUNCE. Hah – what numbers has he?

SOULDIER. About a hundred Horse, in his march he has surpriz'd Colonel *Downright*, and taken him prisoner.

ALL. Let's fall on *Bacon* – let's fall on *Bacon* hay – [*Hollow.*

BOOZER. We'll hear him speak first – and see what he can say for himself.

ALL. Ay, ay, we'll hear *Bacon* speak – [Dunce *pleads with them.*

TIMEROUS. Well Major I have found a stratagem shall make us four the greatest men in the colony, we'll surrender our selves to *Bacon*, and say we disbanded on purpose.

DULLMAN. Good –

WHIFF. Why, I had no other design in the world in refusing to fight.

WHIMSEY. Nor I, d'e think I wou'd have excus'd it with the fear of disordering my cravat string else –

DUNCE. Why Gentlemen, he designs to fire *James* Town; murder you all, and then lye with your wives, and will you slip this opportunity of seizing him?

BOOZER. Here's a termagant rogue Neighbours – we'll hang the dog.

ALL. Ay, ay, hang *Bacon*, hang *Bacon*.

[*Enter* Bacon, *and* Fearless, *some souldiers leading in* Downright *bound;* Bacon *stands and stares a while on the regiments, who are silent all.*

BACON. Well Gentlemen – in order to your fine declaration you see I come to render my self –

DUNCE. How came he to know of our declaration?

WHIMSEY. Rogues, rogues among our selves – that inform.

BACON. What are ye silent all, – not a man lift his hand in obedience to the Council to murder this traytor, that has exposed his life so often for you? Hah what not for three hundred pound, – you see I've left my troops behind, and come all wearied with the toils of war, worn out by Summer's heats and Winter's colds, march'd tedious days and nights thro bogs and fens as dangerous as your clamors, and as faithless, – what tho 'twas to preserve you all in safety, no matter, you shou'd obey the grateful Council, and kill this honest man that has defended you?

ALL. Hum, hum hum.

WHIFF. The General speaks like a gorgon.[131]

TIMEROUS. Like a cherubim, Man.

BACON. All silent yet – where's that mighty courage that cryed so loud but now? A Council a Council, where is your resolution, cannot three hundred pound excite your valour, to seize that traytor *Bacon* who has bled for you? –

ALL. A *Bacon*, a *Bacon*, a *Bacon*. – [*Holler.*

DOWNRIGHT. Oh villanous cowards – Oh the faithless multitude!

BACON. What say you Parson – you have a forward zeal?

DUNCE. I wish my coat Sir did not hinder me, from acting as becomes my zeal and duty.

WHIMSEY. A plaguey rugged dog – that parson –

BACON. *Fearless* seize me that canting knave from out the herd, and next those honourable officers. [*Points to* Dullman, Whimsey, Whiff, *and* Timerous. Fearless *seizes them, and gives them to the souldiers, and takes the proclamation from* Dunce *and shews* Bacon, *they read it.*

DULLMAN. Seize us, Sir, you shall not need, we laid down our commissions on purpose to come over to your Honour.

WHIFF. We ever lov'd and honour'd your Honour.

TIMEROUS. [*Aside*] *So intirely, Sir – that I wish I were safe in James Town for your sake, and your Honour were hang'd.*

BACON. This fine piece is of your penning Parson – though it be countenanc'd by the Council's names – oh in gratitude – burn – burn the treacherous town – fire it immediately –

WHIMSEY. We'll obey you, Sir –

WHIFF. Ay, ay, we'll make a bonfire on't, and drink your Honour's health round about it. [*They offer to go.*

BACON. Yet hold, my revenge shall be more merciful, I ordered that all the women of rank shall be seiz'd and brought to my camp. I'll make their husbands pay their ransoms dearly; they'd rather have their hearts bleed than their purses.

FEARLESS. Dear General, let me have the seizing of Colonel *Downright*'s daughter; I would fain be plundering for a trifle call'd a maiden-head.

BACON. On pain of death treat them with all respect; assure them of the safety of their honour. Now, all that will follow me, shall find a welcome, and those that will not may depart in peace.

ALL. Hay, a General, a General, a General. [*Some soldiers go off, some go to the side of* Bacon.

[*Enter* Dareing *and souldiers with* Crisante, Surelove, Mrs. Whimsey *and* Mrs. Whiff, *and several other women*.

BACON. Successful *Dareing* welcome, what prizes have ye?

DAREING. The fairest in the world Sir, I'm not for common plunder.

DOWNRIGHT. Hah, my daughter and my kinswoman! –

BACON. 'Tis not with women Sir, nor honest men like you that I intend to combat; not their own parents shall not be more indulgent, nor better safeguard to their honours Sir: but 'tis to save the expence of blood, I seize on their most valu'd prizes.

DOWNRIGHT. But Sir, I know your wild Lieutenant General has long lov'd my *Crisante*, and perhaps, will take this time to force her to consent.

DAREING. I own I have a passion for *Crisante*, yet by my General's life – or her fair self – what now I act is on the score of war, I scorn to force the maid I do adore.

BACON. Believe me Ladies, you shall have honourable treatment here.

CRISANTE. We do not doubt it Sir, either from you or *Dareing*. If he love me – that will secure my honour, or if he do not, he's too brave to injure me.

DARING. I thank you for your just opinion of me, Madam.

CRISANTE. But Sir, 'tis for my father I must plead; to see his reverend hands in servile chains – and then perhaps if stubborn to your will, his head must fall a victim to your anger.

DOWNRIGHT. No my good pious Girl, I cannot fear ignoble usage from the General – and if thy beauty can preserve thy fame, I shall not mourn in my captivity.

BACON. I'll ne're deceive your kind opinion of me – Ladies I hope you're all of that opinion too.

SURELOVE. If seizing us Sir can advance your honour, or be of any use considerable to you, I shall be proud of such a slavery.

MRS. WHIMSEY. I hope Sir we shan't be ravish'd in your camp.

DAREING. Fie Mrs. *Whimsey*, do souldiers use to ravish?

MRS. WHIFF. Ravish – marry I fear 'em not, I'd have 'em know I scorn to be ravish'd by any man!

FEARLESS. Ay a my conscience Mrs *Whiff*, you are too good natur'd.

DAREING. Madam, I hope you'll give me leave to name love to you, and try by all submissive ways to win your heart?

CRISANTE. Do your worst Sir, I give you leave, if you assail me only with your tongue.

DAREING. That's generous and brave, and I'll requite it.

[*Enter* Souldier *in haste*.

SOULDIER. The truce being ended, Sir, the *Indians* grow so insolent as to attack us even in our camp, and have kill'd several of our men.

BACON. 'Tis time to check their boldness; *Dareing* haste draw up our men in order, to give 'em battel, I rather had expected their submission.

The Country now may see what they're to fear,
Since we that are in arms are not secure.

[*Exeunt leading the ladies*.

Act IV. Scene I.

[*A temple, with an Indian god placed upon it, priests and priestesses attending; enter* Indian King *on one side attended by Indian men, the* Queen *enters on the other side with women, all bow to the idol, and divide on each side of the stage, then the musick playing lowder, the priest and priestesses dance about the idol, with ridiculous postures and crying (as for incantations.) Thrice repeated,* Agah Yerkin, Agah Boah, Sulen Tawarapah, Sulen Tawarapah.

[*After this soft musick plays again, then they sing something fine, after which the priests lead the* King *to the altar, and the priestessess, the* Queen, *they take off little crowns from their heads, and offer them at the alter*.

KING. Invoke the god, of our Quiocto[132] to declare, what the event shall be of this our last war against the *English* General.

[*Soft musick ceases. The musick changes to confused tunes, to which the* Priest *and* Priestess *dance antickly singing between; the same incantation as before, and then dance again, and so invoke again alternately: which dance ended a voice behind the alter cries, while soft musick plays–.*

The *English* General shall be,
A captive to his enemy;
And you from all your toils be freed,
When by your hand the foe shall bleed
And ere the sun's swift course be run,
This mighty conquest, shall be won.

KING. I thank the gods for taking care of us, prepare new sacrifice against the evening, when I return a conqueror, I will my self perform the office of a priest.

QUEEN. Oh Sir, I fear you'll fall a victim first.

KING. What means *Semernia*, why are thy looks so pale?

QUEEN. Alas the oracles have double meanings, their sense is doubtful, and their words inigmas, I fear Sir I cou'd make a truer interpretation –

KING. How *Semernia*! By all thy love I charge thee as you respect my life, to let me know your thoughts.

QUEEN. Last night I dream'd a lyon fell with hunger, spight of your guards slew you, and bore you hence.

KING. This is thy sexe's fear, and no interpretation of the Oracle.

QUEEN. I cou'd convince you farther.

KING. Hast thou a secret thou canst keep from me? Thy soul a thought that I must be stranger too? This is not like the justice of *Semernia*, come unriddle me the Oracle.

QUEEN. The *English* General shall be, a captive to his enemy; he is so Sir already to my beauty, he says he languishes for love of me.

KING. Hah – the General my rival – but go on –

QUEEN. And you from all your war be freed: oh let me not explain that fatal line, for fear it mean, you shall be freed by death.

KING. What, when by my hand the foe shall bleed? – Away – – it cannot be –

QUEEN. No doubt my Lord, you'll bravely sell your life, and deal some wounds where you'll receive so many.

KING. 'Tis love *Semernia* makes thee dream, while waking I'll trust the gods, and am resolved for battle.

[*Enter an* Indian.

INDIAN. Haste, haste great Sir to arms, *Bacon* with all his forces is prepar'd, and both the armies ready to engage.

KING. Hast to my general, bid him charge em instantly, I'll bring up the supplys of stout *Teroomians*, those so well skill'd in the envenom'd arrow, [*Exit* Indian] – *Semernia* – words but poorly do express the griefs of parting lovers – 'tis with dying eyes, and a heart trembling – thus – [*Puts her hand on his heart*] they take a heavy leave, – one parting kiss, and one love pressing sigh, and then farewell – but not a long farewell; I shall return victorious to thy arms, – commend me to the gods and still remember me. [*Exit* King.

QUEEN. Alas! What pitty 'tis I saw the General, before my fate had given me to the King – but now – like those that change their gods, my faithless mind 'twixt two opinions wavers; while to the gods my monarch I commend; my wandring thoughts in pitty of the General makes that zeal cold, declin'd – ineffectual; – if for the General I implore the deities, methinks my prayers shou'd not ascend the skies since honour tells me 'tis an impious zeal.

Which way so ever my devotions move,
I am too wretched to be heard above. [*Goes in, all exeunt.*

Scene II.

[*Shows a field of tents, seen at some distance thro' the trees of a wood, drums, trumpets and the noise of battel with hollowing. The Indians are seen with battle-axes to retreat fighting from the English and all go off, when they re-enter immediately beating back the English, the* Indian King *at the head of his men, with bows and arrows;* Dareing *being at the head of the English: they fight off; the noise continues less loud as more at distance. Enter* Bacon *with his sword drawn, meets* Fearless *with his sword drawn.*]

FEARLESS. Haste, haste Sir to the entrance of the wood, *Dareing*'s engaged past hope of a retreat, ventring too far, persuing of the foe; the King in ambush with his poyson'd archers, fell on and now we're dangerously distrest.

BACON. *Dareing* is brave, but, he's withal too rash, come on and follow me to his assistance – [*Goes out. A hollowing within, the fight renews, enter the Indians beaten back by* Bacon, Dareing *and* Fearless, *they fight off, the noise of fighting continues a while, this still behind the wood.*

[*Enter Indians flying over the stage, pursu'd by the* King.

KING. Turn, turn ye fugitive Slaves, and face the enemy; oh Villains, Cowards, deaf to all command, by Heaven I had my rival in my view and aim'd at nothing but my conquering him – now like a coward I must fly with cowards, or like a desperate mad-man fall, thus singly midst the numbers. [*Follows the Indians.*

[*Enter* Bacon *inrag'd with his sword drawn,* Fearless, *and* Dareing *following him.*

BACON. – Where is the King, oh ye perfidious Slaves, how have you hid from my just revenge – search all the brakes, the furzes and the trees; and let him not escape on pain of death.

DAREING. We cannot do wonders Sir.

BACON. But you can run away –

DAREING. Yes, when we see occasion – yet – shou'd any but my General tell me so – by Heaven he shou'd find I were no starter.[133]

BACON. Forgive me, I'm mad – the King's escap'd, hid like a trembling slave in some close ditch, where he will sooner starve than fight it out.

[*Re-enter Indians running over the stage, pursued by the* King *who shoots them as they fly, some few follow him.*

KING. All's lost – the day is lost – and I'm betray'd – oh Slaves, that even wounds can't animate. [*In rage.*

BACON. The King!

KING. The General here, by all the powers betray'd by my own men.

BACON. Abandon'd as thou art I scorn to take thee basely, you shall have souldier's chance Sir for your life, since chance so luckily has brought us hither; without more aids we will dispute the day: this spot of earth bears both our armies' fates, I'll give you back the victory I have won, and thus begin a new, on equal terms.

KING. That's nobly said – the powers have heard my wish! You Sir first taught me how to use a sword, which heretofore has serv'd me with success, but now – 'tis for *Semernia* that it draws, a prize more valu'd than my kingdom, Sir –

BACON. Hah *Semernia*!

KING. Your blushes do betray your passion for her.

DAREING. 'Sdeath have we fought for this, to expose the victor to the conquer'd foe?

FEARLESS. What fight a single man – our prize already.

KING. Not so Young Man while I command a dart.

BACON. Fight him, by Heaven no reason shall disswade me, and he that interrupts me is a coward, whatever be my fate, I do command ye to let the King pass freely to his tents.

DAREING. The Devil's in the General.

FEARLESS. 'Sdeath his romantick humour will undo us. [*They fight and pause.*

KING. You fight as if you meant to outdo me this way, as you have done in generosity.

BACON. You're not behind hand with me Sir in courtesie, come here's to set us even – [*Fight again.*

KING. You bleed apace.

BACON. You've only breath'd a vein, and given me new health and vigour by it.[134] [*They fight again, wounds on both sides, the* King *staggers,* Bacon *takes him in his arms, the* King *drops his sword.*
How do you Sir?

KING. Like one – that's hovering between Heaven and Earth, I'm – mounting – somewhere – upwards – but giddy with my flight, – I know not where.

BACON. Command my surgions, – instantly – make haste; honour returns and love all bleeding's fled. [*Exit* Fearless.

KING. Oh *Semernia*, how much more truth had thy divinity[135] than the predictions of the flattering oracles. Commend me to her – I know you'll – visit – your fair captive Sir, and tell her – oh – but death prevents the rest. [*Dies.*

[*Enter* Fearless.

BACON. He's gone – and now like *Caesar* I cou'd weep over the hero I my self destroy'd.[136]

FEARLESS. I'm glad for your repose I see him there – 'twas a mad hot brain'd youth and so he dy'd.

BACON. Come bear him on your shoulders to my tent, from whence with all the solemn state we can, we will convey him to his own pavillion.

[*Enter a* Souldier.

SOULDIER. Some of our troops pursuing of the enemy even to their temples, which they made their sanctuary, finding the Queen at her devotion there with all her *Indian* ladies, I'd much ado to stop their violent rage from setting fire to the holy pile.[137]

BACON. Hang em immediately that durst attempt it, while I my self will flye to rescue her.

[*Goes out, they bear off the* King's *body, Exeunt all.*

[*Enter* Whimsey *pulling in* Whiff, *with a halter about his neck.*

WHIMSEY. Nay I'm resolv'd to keep thee here till his honour the General comes, – what to call him traytor, and run away after he had so generously given us our freedom, and listed us Cadees[138] for the next command that fell in his army; – I'm resolv'd to hang thee –

WHIFF. Wilt thou betray and peach[139] thy friend: thy friend that kept thee company all the while thou wert a prisoner – drinking at my own charge. –

WHIMSEY. No matter for that, I scorn ingratitude and therefore will hang thee – but as for thy drinking with me – I scorn to be behind hand with thee in civility and therefore here's to thee. [*Takes a bottle of brandy out of his pocket, drinks.*

WHIFF. I can't drink.

WHIMSEY. A certain sign thou would be hang'd.

WHIFF. You us'd to be at my side when a Justice, let the cause be how it wou'd.

WHIMSEY. Ay – when I was a Justice I never minded honesty, but now I'll be true to my General, and hang thee to be a great man. –

WHIFF. If I might but have a fair tryal for my life –

WHIMSEY. A fair tryal – come I'll be thy judge – and if thou can'st clear thy self by law I'll acquit thee, Sirrah, Sirrah, what can'st thou say for thy self for calling his Honour rebel? [*Sits on a drumhead.*

WHIFF. 'Twas when I was drunk an't like your Honour.

WHIMSEY. That's no plea, for if you kill a man when you are sober you must be hang'd when you are drunk, hast thou any thing else to say for thy self, why sentence may not pass upon thee?

WHIFF. I desire the benefit of the clergy.[140]

WHIMSEY. The clergy, I never knew any body that ever did benefit by em, why thou canst not read a word.

WHIFF. Transportation then –

WHIMSEY. It shall be to *England* then – but hold – Who's this?

[Dullman *creeping from a bush.*

DULLMAN. So the dangers over, I may venture out, – pox on't I would not be in this fear again, to be Lord Chief Justice of our Court.

[*Enter* Timerous *with battle ax, bow and arrows, and feathers on his head.*

Why how now Cornet – what in dreadful equipage? Your battle ax bloody, with bow and arrows?

TIMEROUS. I'm in the posture of the times Major – I cou'd not be idle where so much action was, I'm going to present my self to the General with these trophies of my victory here –

DULLMAN. Victory – what victory – did not see thee creeping out of yonder bush, where thou wert hid all the fight – stumble on a dead *Indian*, and take away his arms?

TIMEROUS. Why, didst thou see me?

DULLMAN. See thee ay – and what a fright thou wert in, till thou wert sure he was dead.

TIMEROUS. Well, well, that's all one – gads zoors if every man that pass for valiant in a battel, were to give an account how he gain'd his reputation, the world wou'd be but thinly stock'd with heroes, I'll say he was a great war captain, and that I kill'd him hand to hand, and who can disprove me?

DULLMAN. Disprove thee – why that pale face of thine, that has so much of the coward in't.

TIMEROUS. Shaw, that's with loss of blood – Hah I am overheard I doubt – who's yonder – [*Sees* Whimsey *and* Whiff] How Brother *Whiff* in a hempen cravat-string?[141]

WHIMSEY. He call'd the General traytor and was running away, and I'm resolved to peach.

DULLMAN. Hum – and one witness will stand good in law, in case of treason –

TIMEROUS. Gads zoors in case of treason he'll be hang'd if it be proved against him, were there ne're a witness at all, but he must be try'd by a Council of War, Man – come, come let's disarm him – [*They take away his arms, and pull a bottle of brandy out of his pocket.*

WHIFF. What, I hope you will not take away my brandy Gentlemen, my last comfort.

TIMEROUS. Gads zoors it's come in good time – we'll drink it off, here Major – [*Drinks,* Whiff *takes him aside.*

WHIFF. Hark ye Cornet – you are my good friend, get this matter made up before it come to the General.

TIMEROUS. But this is treason Neighbour.

WHIFF. If I hang – I'll declare upon the ladder, how you kill'd your war captain.

TIMEROUS. Come Brother *Whimsey* – we have been all friends and loving magistrates together, let's drink about, and think no more of this business.

DULLMAN. Ay, ay, if every sober man in the nation, should be call'd to account of the treason he speaks in's drink the Lord have mercy upon us all – put it up – and let us like loving brothers take an honest resolution to run away together; for this same *Frightall* minds nothing but fighting.

WHIMSEY. I'm content, provided we go all to the Council and tell them (to make our peace) we went in obedience to the proclamation to kill *Bacon*, but the traytor was so strongly guarded we could not effect it, but mum – who's here –

[*To them, enter* Ranter *and* Jenny, *as* Man *and* Footman.

RANTER. Hah, our four Reverend Justices – I hope the blockheads will not know me – Gentlemen, can you direct me to Lieutenant General *Dareing*'s tents.

WHIFF. Hum, who the Devil's this – that's he that you see coming this way, 'sdeath yonder's *Dareing* – let's slip away before he advances. [*Exeunt all but* Ranter *and* Jenny.

JENNY. I am scar'd with those dead bodies we have past over, for God's sake Madam, let me know your design in coming.

RANTER. Why? Now I'll tell thee – my damn'd mad fellow *Dareing* who has my heart and soul – loves *Crisante*, has stolen her, and carryed her away to his tents, she hates him, while I am dying for him.

JENNY. Dying Madam! I never saw you melancholy.

RANTER. Pox on't no, why should I sigh and whine, and make my self an ass, and him conceited, no, instead of snevelling I'm resolv'd –

JENNY. What Madam?

RANTER. Gad to beat the rascal, and bring off *Crisante.*

JENNY. Beat him Madam? What a woman beat a Lieutenant General.

RANTER. Hang 'em, they get a name in war, from command, not courage; how know I but I may fight, gad I have known a fellow kickt from one end of the town to t'other, believing himself a coward, at last forc'd to fight, found he could, got a reputation and bullyed all he met with, and got a name, and a great commission.

JENNY. But if he should kill you Madam?

RANTER. I'll take care to make it as comical a duel as the best of 'em, as much in love as I am, I do not intend to dy its martyr.

[*Enter* Dareing *and* Fearless.

FEARLESS. Have you seen *Crisante* since the fight?

DAREING. Yes, but she is still the same, as nice and coy as fortune, when she's courted by the wretched, yet she denys me, so obligingly she keeps my love still in its humble calm.

RANTER. Can you direct me Sir, to one *Dareing*'s tent. [*Sullenly.*

DAREING. One *Dareing* – he has another epithet to his name?

RANTER. What's that, rascal, or coward?

DAREING. Hah, which of thy stars young man, has sent thee hither, to find that certain fate they have decreed.

RANTER. I know not what my stars have decreed, but I shall be glad if they have ordain'd me to fight with *Dareing*, – by thy concern thou shou'dst be he?

DAREING. I am, prithee who art thou?

RANTER. Thy rival, tho newly arriv'd from *England*, and came to marry fair *Crisante*, whom thou hast ravish'd, for whom I hear another lady dies.

DAREING. Dies for me?

RANTER. Therefore resign her fairly – or fight me fairly –

DAREING. Come on Sir – but hold – before I kill thee, prithee inform me who this dying lady is?

RANTER. Sir I owe ye no courtesie, and therefore will do you none by telling you – come Sir for *Crisante* – draws. [*They offer to fight,* Fearless *steps in.*

FEARLESS. Hold – what mad frolick's this? – Sir you fight for one you never saw [*To* Ranter] and you for one that loves you not. [*To* Dareing.

DAREING. Perhaps she'll love him as little.

RANTER. Gad put it to the tryal, if you dare – if thou be'st generous bring me to her, and whom she does neglect shall give the other place.

DAREING. That's fair put up thy sword – I'll bring thee to her instantly. [*Exeunt.*

Scene III.

[*A tent; enter* Crisante *and* Surelove.]

CRISANTE. I'm not so much afflicted for my confinement as I am, that I cannot hear of *Friendly*.

SURELOVE. Art not persecuted with *Dareing*?

CRISANTE. Not at all, tho he tells me daily of his passions I rally[142] him, and give him neither hope nor despair, – he's here.

[*Enter* Dareing Fearless. Ranter *and* Jenny.

DAREING. Madam, the complaisance I show in bringing you my rival, will let you see how glad I am to oblige you every way.

RANTER. I hope the danger I have expos'd my self to for the honour of kissing your hand Madam, will render me something acceptable – here are my credentials – [*Gives her a letter.*

CRISANTE. – [*Reads*] Dear Creature, I have taken this habit to free you from an impertinent lover, and to secure the damn'd rogue *Dareing* to my self, receive me as sent by Colonel *Surelove* from *England* to marry you – favour me – no more – your *Ranter* – [*Aside*] *hah* Ranter? –

– Sir you have too good a character from my cousin Colonel *Surelove*, not to receive my welcome. [*Gives* Surelove *the letter.*

RANTER. Stand by General – [*Pushes away* Dareing *and looks big, and takes* Crisante *by the hand and kisses it.*

DAREING. 'Sdeath Sir there's room – enough – at first sight so kind? Oh youth – youth and Impudence, what temptations are you – to villanous woman.

CRISANTE. I confess Sir we women do not love these rough fighting fellows, they're always scaring us with one broil or other.

DAREING. Much good may do you with your tame coxcomb.

RANTER. Well Sir, then you yield the prize?

DAREING. Ay gad, were she an angel, that can prefer such a callow fop as thou before a man – take her and domineer. [*They all laugh*] – 'Sdeath am I grown ridiculous.

FEARLESS. Why hast thou not found the jest? By Heaven 'tis *Ranter*, 'tis she that loves you, carry on the humour. Faith Sir, if I were you, I would devote my self to Madam *Ranter*.

CRISANTE. Ay, she's the fittest wife for you, she'll fit your humour.

DAREING. – Gad I'd sooner marry a she bear, unless for a pennance for some horrid sin, we should be eternally challenging one another to the field, and ten to one she beats me there; or if I should escape there, she would kill me with drinking.

RANTER. – [*Aside*] *Here's a rogue* – does your Country abound with such ladies?

DAREING. The Lord forbid, half a dozen wou'd ruine the land, debauch all the men, and scandalize all the women.

FEARLESS. No matter, she's rich.

DAREING. Ay that will make her insolent.

FEARLESS. Nay she's generous too.

DAREING. Yes when she's drunk, and then she'll lavish all.

RANTER. A pox on him – how he vexes me.

DAREING. Then such a tongue – she'll rail and smoak till she choak again then six gallons of punch hardly recovers her, and never but then is she good natur'd.

RANTER. I must lay him on –

DAREING. There's not a blockhead in the Country that has not –

RANTER. – What –

DAREING. – Been drunk with her.

RANTER. I thought you had meant something else Sir. [*In huff.*

DAREING. Nay – as for that – I suppose there's no great difficulty.

RANTER. 'Sdeath Sir you lye – and you're a son of a whore. [*Draws and fences with him, and he runs back round the stage.*

DAREING. Hold – hold Virago[143] – dear Widdow hold, and give me thy hand.

RANTER. Widdow!

DAREING. 'Sdeath I knew thee by instinct Widdow tho I seem'd not to do so, in revenge for the trick you put on me in telling me a lady dy'd for me.

RANTER. Why, such an one there is, perhaps she may dwindle forty or fifty years – or so – but will never be her own woman again that's certain.

SURELOVE. This we are all ready to testifie, we know her.

CRISANTE. Upon my life 'tis true.

DAREING. Widdow I have a shrewd suspicion, that you your self may be this dying lady.

RANTER. Why so Coxcomb?

DAREING. Because you took such pains to put your self into my hands.

RANTER. Gad if your heart were but half so true as your guess, we should conclude a peace before *Bacon* and the Council will – besides this thing whines for *Friendly* and there's no hopes. [*To* Crisante.

DAREING. Give me thy hand Widdow, I am thine – and so intirely, I will never – be drunk out of thy company – *Dunce* is in my tent – prithee let's in and bind the bargain.

RANTER. Nay, faith, let's see the wars at an end first.

DAREING. Nay, prithee, take me in the humour, while thy breeches are on – for I never lik'd thee half so well in petticoats.

RANTER. Lead on General, you give me good incouragement to wear them. [*Exeunt.*

Act V. Scene I.

[*The sevana in sight of the camp; the moon rises. Enter* Friendly, Hazard *and* Boozer, *and a party of men.*]

FRIENDLY. We are now in the sight of the tents.

BOOZER. Is not this a rash attempt, Gentlemen, with so small force to set upon *Bacon*'s whole army?

HAZARD. Oh, they are drunk with victory and wine; there will be naught but revelling to night.

FRIENDLY. Would we cou'd learn in what quarter the ladies are lodg'd, for we have no other business but to release them – but hark – who comes here?

BOOZER. Some scouts, I fear, from the enemy.

[*Enter* Dullman, Timerous, Whimsey *and* Whiff, *creeping as in the dark.*

FRIENDLY. Let's shelter our selves behind yonder trees – lest we be surpriz'd.

TIMEROUS. Wou'd I were well at home – gad zoors – If e're you catch me a cadeeing[144] again, I'll be content to be set in the fore front of the battel for hawk's meat.

WHIMSEY. Thou'rt affraid of every bush.

TIMEROUS. Ay, and good reason too: gad zoors, there may be rogues hid – prithee Major, do thou advance.

DULLMAN. No, no, go on – no matter of ceremony in these cases of running away. [*They advance.*

FRIENDLY. They approach directly to us, we cannot escape them – their numbers are not great – let us advance.

[*They come up to them.*

TIMEROUS. Oh, I am annihilated.

WHIFF. Some of *Frightall*'s scouts; we are lost men. [*They push each other foremost.*

FRIENDLY. Who goes there?

WHIMSEY. Oh, they'll give us no quarter; 'twas along of you Cornet, that we ran away from our colours.

TIMEROUS. Me – 'twas the Major's ambition here – to make himself a great man with the Council again.

DULLMAN. Pox o' this ambition, it has been the ruin of many a gallant fellow.

WHIFF. If I get home again, the height of mine shall be to top tobacco;[145] would I'd some brandy.

TIMEROUS. Gads zoors, would we had, 'tis the best armour against fear – hum – I hear no body now – prithee advance a little.

WHIMSEY. What, before a horse officer?[146]

FRIENDLY. Stand on your lives –

TIMEROUS. Oh, 'tis impossible – I am dead already.

FRIENDLY. What are ye – speak – or I'll shoot?

WHIMSEY. Friends to thee – who the Devil are we friends to?

TIMEROUS. E'ne who you please, gad zoors.

FRIENDLY. Hah – gad zoors – who's there, *Timerous*?

TIMEROUS. Hum – I know no such scoundrel – [*Gets behind.*

DULLMAN. Hah – that's *Friendly*'s voice.

FRIENDLY. Right – thine's that of *Dullman* – who's with you?

DULLMAN. Only *Timerous*, *Whimsey* and *Whiff*, all valiantly running away from the arch rebel that took us prisoners.

HAZARD. Can you inform us where the ladies are lodg'd?

DULLMAN. In the hither quarter in *Dareing*'s tents; you'll know them by lanterns on every corner –

there was never better time to surprize them – for this day *Dareing*'s married, and there's nothing but dancing and drinking.

HAZARD. Married! To whom?

DULLMAN. That I ne'r inquir'd.

FRIENDLY. 'Tis to *Crisante*, Friend – and the reward of my attempt is lost. Oh, I am mad, I'll fight away my life, and my dispair shall yet do greater wonders, than even my love could animate me to. Let's part our men, and beset his tents on both sides. [Friendly *goes out with a party.*

HAZARD. Come, Gentlemen, let's on –

WHIFF. On Sir – we on Sir? –

HAZARD. Ay, you on, Sir – to redeem the ladies.

WHIFF. Oh, Sir, I am going home for money to redeem my *Nancy*.

WHIMSEY. So am I, Sir.

TIMEROUS. I thank my stars I am a batchellor – Why, what a plague is a wife?

HAZARD. Will you march forward?

DULLMAN. We have atchiev'd honour enough already, in having made our campaign here – [*Looking big.*

HAZARD. 'Sdeath, but you shall go – put them in the front, and prick them on – If they offer to turn back run them through.

TIMEROUS. Oh, horrid – [*The soldiers prick them on with their swords.*

WHIFF. Oh, *Nancy*, thy dream will yet come to pass.

HAZARD. Will you advance, Sir? [*Pricks* Whiff.

WHIFF. Why, so we do, Sir; the Devil's in these fighting fellows. [*Exeunt.*

[*An alarm at a distance.*

[*Within*] To arms, to arms, the enemy's upon us.

[*A noise of fighting, after which enters* Friendly *with his party, retreating and fighting, from* Dareing *and some souldiers,* Ranter *fighting like a fury by his side, he putting her back in vain; they fight out. Re-enter* Dareing *with* Friendly *all bloody. Several souldiers enter with flambeaux.*[147]

DAREING. Now, Sir – what injury have I ever done you, that you should use this treachery against me?

FRIENDLY. To take advantage any way in war, was never counted treachery – and had I murder'd thee, I had not paid thee half the debt I owe thee.

DAREING. You bleed too much to hold too long a parley – come to my tent, I'll take a charitable care of thee.

FRIENDLY. I scorn thy courtesie, who against all the laws of honour and of justice, hast ravish'd innocent ladies.

DAREING. Sir, your upbraiding of my honour shall never make me forfeit it, or esteem you less – Is there a lady here you have a passion for?

FRIENDLY. Yes, on a nobler score than thou darest own.

DAREING. To let you see how you're mistaken, Sir, who e're that lady be whom you affect, I will resign, and give you both your freedoms.

FRIENDLY. Why, for this courtesie, which shows thee brave, in the next fight I'll save thy life, to quit the obligation.

DAREING. I thank you, Sir – come to my tent – and when we've drest your wounds, and yielded up the ladies, I'll give you my passport for your safe conduct back, and tell your friends i'th' town we'll visit them i'th' morning.

FRIENDLY. They'll meet you on your way, Sir –

DAREING. Come, my young Souldier, now thou'st won my soul.

[*An alarm beats: enter at another passage* Boozer *with all the ladies; they pass over the stage, while* Hazard, Downright, *beating back a party of souldiers.* Dullman, Timerous, Whimsey *and* Whiff, *prickt on by their party to fight, so that they lay about them like madmen.* Bacon, Fearless *and* Dareing *come in, rescue their men, and fight out the other party, some falling dead.* Bacon, Fearless *and* Dareing *return tired, with their swords drawn.*

[*Enter souldier running.*

SOULDIER. Return, Sir, where your sword will be more useful – a party of *Indians*, taking advantage of the night, have set fire on your tents, and born away the Queen.

BACON. Hah, the Queen! By Heaven this victory shall cost them dear; come, let us fly to rescue her. [*Goes out.*

Scene II.

[Wellman*'s tent. Enter* Wellman, Brag, Grub *and officers.*]

WELLMAN. I cannot sleep my impatience is so great, to ingage this haughty enemy, before they have reposed their weary limbs – Is not yon ruddy light the morning's dawn.

BRAG. 'Tis, and please your Honour.

WELLMAN. Is there no news of *Friendly* yet, and *Hazard?*

BRAG. Not yet – 'tis thought they left the camp to night, with some design against the enemy.

WELLMAN. What men have they?

BRAG. Only *Boozer*'s party, Sir.

WELLMAN. I know they are brave, and mean to surprize me with some handsom action.

[*Enter* Friendly.

FRIENDLY. I ask a thousand pardons, Sir, for quitting the camp without your leave.

WELLMAN. Your conduct and your courage cannot err; I see thou'st been in action by thy blood.

FRIENDLY. Sir I'm ashamed to own these slender wounds, since without more my luck was to be taken, while *Hazard* did alone effect the business; the rescuing of the ladies.

WELLMAN. How got ye liberty?

FRIENDLY. By *Dareing*'s generosity, who sends you word he'll visit you this morning.

WELLMAN. We are prepared to meet him.

[*Enter* Downright, Hazard, *Ladies,* Whimsey, Whiff, Dullman, Timerous*, looking big;* Wellman *embraces* Downright.

WELLMAN. My worthy Friend how am I joyed to see you.

DOWNRIGHT. We owe our liberties to these brave youths, who can do wonders when they fight for ladies.

TIMEROUS. With our assistance, Ladies.

WHIMSEY. For my part I'll not take it as I have done, gad I find when I am damnable angry I can beat both friend and foe.

WHIFF. When I fight for my *Nancy* here – adsfish I'm a dragon.

MRS. WHIFF. Lord you need not have been so hasty.

FRIENDLY. Do not upbraid me with your eyes *Crisante*, but let these wounds assure you I endeavour'd to serve you, tho *Hazard* had the honour on't.

WELLMAN. But Ladies we'll not expose you in the camp, – a party of our men shall see you safely conducted to Madam *Surelove*'s; 'tis but a little mile from our camp.

FRIENDLY. Let me have that honour Sir.

CRISANTE. No, I conjure you let your wounds be drest, obey me if you love me, and *Hazard* shall conduct us home.

WELLMAN. He had the toyl, 'tis fit he have the recompence.

WHIFF. He the toyl, Sir, what did we stand for cyphers?

WHIMSEY. The very appearance I made in the front of the battle, aw'd the enemy.

TIMEROUS. Ay, ay, let the enemy say how I maul'd 'em – but gads zoors I scorn to brag.

WELLMAN. Since you've regain'd your honour so gloriously – I restore you to your commands, you lost by your seeming cowardise.

DULLMAN. Valour is not always in humour Sir.

WELLMAN. Come Gentlemen since they're resolv'd to engage us, let's set our men in order to receive 'em. [*Exeunt all but the four* Justices.

TIMEROUS. Our commissions again – you must be bragging, and see what comes on't; I was modest ye see and said nothing of my prowess.

WHIFF. What a Devil, does the Colonel think we are made of iron, continually to be beat on the anvil?

WHIMSEY. Look Gentlemen here's two evils – if we go we are dead men if we stay we are hang'd – and that will disorder my cravat-string – therefore the least evil is to go – and set a good face on the matter as I do – [*Goes out singing.*

Scene III.

[*A thick wood. Enter* Queen *drest like an Indian man, with a bow in her hand and quiver at her back,* Anaria *her confidant disguis'd so too, and about a duzen Indians led by* Cavaro.]

QUEEN. I tremble yet, dost think we're safe *Cavaro*.

CAVARO. Madam these woods are intricate and vast; and 'twill be difficult to find us out – or if they do, this habit will secure you from the fear of being taken.

QUEEN. Dost think if *Bacon* find us he will not know me? Alas my fears and blushes will betray me.

ANARIA. 'Tis certain Madam if we stay we perish; for all the wood's surrounded by the conqueror.

QUEEN. Alas 'tis better we shou'd perish here, than stay to expect the violence of his passion; to which my heart's too sensibly inclin'd.

ANARIA. Why do you not obey its dictates then, why do you fly the conqueror?

QUEEN. Not fly – not fly the murderer of my Lord?

ANARIA. What world, what resolution can preserve you, and what he cannot gain by soft submission, force will at last o'recome.

QUEEN. I wish there were in Nature one excuse either by force or reason to compel me: – for oh *Anaria* – I adore this General, – take from my soul a truth – till now conceal'd – at twelve years old – at the *Pauwmungian*[148] court I saw this conqueror. I saw him young and gay as new born Spring, glorious and charming as the mid-day's sun, I watch't his looks, and listned when he spoke, and thought him more than mortal.

ANARIA. He has a graceful form.

QUEEN. At last a fatal match concluded was, between my Lord and me. I gave my hand, but oh how far my heart was from consenting, the angry gods are witness.

ANARIA. 'Twas pity.

QUEEN. Twelve tedious moons I past in silent languishment; honour endeavouring to destroy my love, but all in vain, for still my pain return'd when ever I beheld my conqueror, but now when I consider him as murderer of my Lord – [*Fiercely*] I sigh and wish – some other fatal hand had given him his death – but now there's a necessity I must be brave and overcome my heart: What if I do? Ah whether shall I fly, I have no *Amazonian* fire about me, all my artillery is sighs and tears, the earth my bed, and heaven my canopy. [*Weeps.*

[*After a noise of fighting*] Hah, we are surpris'd, oh whether shall I fly? And yet methinks a certain trembling joy, spight of my soul, spight of my boasted honour, runs shivering round my heart.

[*Enter an* Indian.

INDIAN. Madam your out guards are surpriz'd by *Bacon*, who hews down all before him, and demands the Queen with such a voice and eyes so feirce and angry, he kills us with his looks.

CAVARO. Draw up your poyson'd arrows to the head,[149] and aim them at his heart, sure some will hit.

QUEEN. [*Aside*] *Cruel* Cavaro, *– wou'd 'twere fit for me to contradict thy justice.*

BACON. [*Within*] The Queen ye slaves, give me the Queen and live!

[*He enters furiously beating back some Indians,* Cavaro*'s party going to shoot, the* Queen *runs in.*

QUEEN. Hold, hold, I do command ye. [Bacon *flys on 'em as they shoot and miss him, and fights like a fury, and wounds the* Queen *in the disorder; beats them all out.*

– Hold thy commanding hand, and do not kill me, who wou'd not hurt thee to regain my kingdom – [*He snatches her in his arms she reels.*

BACON. Hah – a woman's voice, – what art thou? Oh my fears!

QUEEN. Thy hand has been too cruel to a heart – whose crime was only tender thoughts for thee.

BACON. The Queen! What is't my sacreligious hand has done?

QUEEN. The noblest office of a gallant friend, thou'st sav'd my honour and hast given me death.

BACON. Is't possible! Ye unregarding gods is't possible?

QUEEN. Now I may love you without infamy, and please my dying heart by gazing on you.

BACON. Oh I am lost – for ever lost – I find my brain turn with the wild confusion.

QUEEN. I faint – oh lay me gently on the earth.

BACON. [*Lays her down*] Who waits. – [*Turns in rage to his men*] Make of the trophies of the war a pile, and set it all on fire, that I may leap into consuming flames – while all my tents are burning round about me. [*Wildly*] Oh thou dear prize for which alone I toyl'd. [*Weeps and lyes down by her.*

[*Enter* Fearless *with his sword drawn.*

FEARLESS. Hah on the earth – how do you Sir?

BACON. What wou'dst thou?

FEARLESS. *Wellman* with all the forces he can gather attacks us even in our very camp, assist us Sir or all is lost.

BACON. Why prithee let him make the World his prize, I have no business with the trifle now; it now contains nothing that's worth my case, since my fair Queen – is dead, – and by my hand.

QUEEN. So charming and obliging is thy moan, that I cou'd wish for life to recompence it; but oh, death falls – all cold – upon my heart like mildews on the blossoms.

FEARLESS. By Heaven Sir, this love will ruin all – rise, rise and save us yet.

BACON. Leave me, what e're becomes of me – lose not thy share of glory – prithee leave me.

QUEEN. Alas, I fear, thy fate is drawing on, and I shall shortly meet thee in the clouds; till then – farewell – even death is pleasing to me, while thus – I find it in thy arms – [*Dies.*

BACON. There ends my race of glory and of life:

[*An alarm at distance–continues a while.*

BACON. Hah – Why should I idly whine away my life, since there are nobler ways to meet with death? – Up, up, and face him then – hark – there's the souldier's knell – and all the joys of life – with thee I bid farewell – [*Goes out. The Indians bear off the body of the* Queen. *The alarm continues.*

[*Enter* Downright, Wellman, *and others, swords drawn.*

WELLMAN. They fight like men possest – I did not think to have found them so prepar'd.

DOWNRIGHT. They've good intelligence – but where's the rebel?

WELLMAN. Sure he's not in the fight, oh that it were my happy chance to meet him, that while our men look on, we might dispatch the business of the war. – Come, let's fall in again now we have taken breath. [*They go out.*

[*Enter* Dareing *and* Fearless *hastily, with their swords drawn, meet* Whimsey, Whiff, *with their swords drawn, running away.*

DAREING. How now, whether away? [*In anger.*

WHIMSEY. Hah, *Dareing* here – we are pursuing of the enemy, Sir, stop us not in the pursuit of glory. [*Offers to go.*

DAREING. Stay – I have not seen you in my ranks to day.

WHIFF. Lord, does your Honour take us for starters?[150]

FEARLESS. Yes, Sirrah, and believe you are now rubbing off[151] – confess, or I'll run you through.

WHIFF. Oh mercy, Sir, mercy, we'll confess.

WHIMSEY. What will you confess – we were only going behind yon hedge to untruss a point;[152] that's all.

WHIFF. Ay, your Honours will smell out the truth if you keep us here long.

DAREING. Here, carry them prisoners to my tent. [*Exit souldier with* Whimsey *&* Whiff.

[*Enter* Ranter *without a hat; and sword drawn.* Dareing *angrily goes the other way.*

RANTER. A pox of all ill luck, how came I to lose *Dareing* in the fight? Ha – who's here? – *Dullman* and *Timerous* dead – the rogues are counterfeits – I'll see what moveables they have about them, all's lawful prize in war. [*Takes their money, watches and rings: goes out.*

TIMEROUS. What, rob the dead? – Why, what will this villanous World come to. [*Clashing of swords just as they were going to rise.*

[*Enter* Hazard *bringing in* Ranter.

HAZARD. Thou cou'dst expect no other fate young man, thy hands are yet too tender for a sword.

RANTER. Thou look'st like a good natur'd fellow, use me civilly, and *Dareing* shall ransom me.

HAZARD. Doubt not a generous treatment. [*Goes out.*

DULLMAN. So, the coast is clear, I desire to remove my quarters to some place of more safety – [*They rise and go off.*

[*Enter* Wellman *and souldiers hastily.*

WELLMAN. 'Twas this way *Bacon* fled. Five hundred pound for him who finds the rebel. [*Goes out.*

Scene IV.

[*Scene changes to a wood. Enter* Bacon *and* Fearless, *with their swords drawn, all bloody.*]

BACON. 'Tis just, ye gods! That when you took the prize for which I fought, fortune and you should all abandon me.

FEARLESS. Oh fly Sir to some place of safe retreat, for there's no mercy to be hop't if taken. What will you do, I know we are pursu'd, by Heaven I will not dye a shameful death.

BACON. Oh they'll have pitty on thy youth and bravery, but I'm above their pardon. [*A noise is heard within*] This way – this way – hay – hallow.

FEARLESS. Alas Sir we're undone – I'll see which way they take. [*Exit.*

BACON. So near! Nay then to my last shift. [*Undoes the pomel*[153] *of his sword*] Come my good poyson, like that of *Hannibal*,[154] long I have born a noble remedy for all the ills of life. [*Takes poyson*] I have too long surviv'd my Queen and glory, those two bright stars that influenc'd my life are set to all eternity. [*Lyes down.*

[*Enter* Fearless, *runs to* Bacon *and looks on his sword.*

FEARLESS. – Hah – What have ye done?

BACON. Secur'd my self from being a publick spectacle upon the common theatre of death.[155]

[*Enter* Dareing *and souldiers.*

DAREING. Victory, victory, they fly, they fly, where's the victorious General?

FEARLESS. Here – taking his last adieu.

DAREING. Dying? Then wither all the laurels on my brows, for I shall never triumph more in war, where is the wound?

FEARLESS. From his own hand by what he carried here, believing we had lost the victory.

BACON. And is the enemy put to flight my hero? [*Grasps his neck.*

DAREING. All routed horse and foot, I plac'd an ambush, and while they were pursuing you, my men fell on behind and won the day.

BACON. Thou almost makes me wish to live again, if I cou'd live now fair *Semernia*'s dead, – but oh – the baneful drug is just and kind and hastens me away – now while you are victors make a peace – with the English Council – and never let ambition – love – or interest make you forget as I have done – your duty – and allegiance – farewell – a long farewell – [*Dies embracing their necks.*

DAREING. So fell the Roman *Cassius*[156] – by mistake –

[*Enter souldiers with* Dunce, Timerous, *and* Dullman.

SOULDIER. An't please your Honour we took these men running away.

DAREING. Let 'em loose – the wars are at an end, see where the General lyes – that great soul'd man, no private body e're contain'd a nobler, and he that cou'd have conquer'd all *America*, finds only here his scanty length of earth, – go bear the body to his own pavilion. – [*Souldier goes out with the body*] Tho we are conquerers we submit to treat, and yield upon conditions, you Mr. *Dunce* shall bear our articles to the Council –

DUNCE. With joy I will obey you.

TIMEROUS. Good General let us be put in the agreement.

DARING. You come too late Gentlemen to be put into the articles, nor am I satisfy'd you're worthy of it.

DULLMAN. Why did not you Sir see us lye dead in the field.

DAREING. Yes, but I see no wound about you.

TIMEROUS. We were stun'd with being knock'd down, gads zoors a man may be kill'd with the butt end of a musquet, as soon as with the point of a sword.

[*Enter* Dunce.

DUNCE. The Council Sir wishes you health and happiness, and sends you these sign'd by their hands – [*Gives papers.*

DAREING. [*Reads*] That you shall have a general pardon for your self and friends, that you shall have all new commissions, and *Dareing* to command as general; that you shall have free leave to inter your dead general, in *James* Town, and to ratifie this – we will meet you at Madam *Surelove*'s house which stands between the armies, attended by only by our officers. The Council's noble and I'll wait upon them. [*Exit* Dunce.

Scene V.

[*A grove near Madam* Surelove*'s. Enter* Surelove *weeping,* Wellman, Crisante, *Mrs.* Flirt, Ranter *as before,* Downright, Hazard, Friendly, Boozer, Brag.]

WELLMAN. How long Madam have you heard the news of Colonel *Surelove*'s death?

SURELOVE. By a vessel last night arriv'd.

WELLMAN. You shou'd not grieve when men so old pay their debt to Nature, you are too fair not to have been reserved for some young lover's arms.

HAZARD. I dare not speak – but give me leave to hope.

SURELOVE. The way to oblige me to't, is never more to speak to me of love till I shall think it fit –

WELLMAN. Come you shan't grant it – 'tis a hopeful youth. [*Speaks to* Downright.

DOWNRIGHT. You are too much my friend to be deny'd – *Crisante* do you love *Friendly*? Nay do not blush – till you have done a fault, your loving him is none – here take her young man and with her all my fortune – when I am dead Sirrah – not a groat before – unless to buy ye baby clouts.[157]

FRIENDLY. He merits not this treasure Sir, can wish for more.

[*Enter* Dareing, Fearless, Dunce *and officers, they meet* Wellman *and* Downright *who embrace 'em.* Dullman *and* Timerous *stand.*

DAREING. Can you forgive us Sir our disobedience.

WELLMAN. Your offering peace while yet you might command it, has made such kind impressions on us, that now you may command your propositions; your pardons are all seal'd and new commissions.

DAREING. I'm not ambitious of that honour Sir, but in obedience will accept your goodness, but Sir I hear I have a young friend taken prisoner by Captain *Hazard* whom I intreat you'll render me.

HAZARD. Sir – here I resign him to you. [*Gives him* Ranter.

RANTER. Faith General you left me but scurvily in battel.

DAREING. That was to see how well you cou'd shift for your self, now I find you can bear the brunt of a campaign you are a fit wife for a souldier.

ALL. A woman – *Ranter* –

HAZARD. Faith Madam I shou'd have given you kinder quarter if I had known my happiness.

FLIRT. I have an humble petition to you Sir.

SURELOVE. In which we all joyn.

FLIRT. An't please you Sir, Mr. *Dunce* has long made love to me and on promise of marriage has – [*Simpers.*

DOWNRIGHT. What has he Mrs. *Flirt.*

FLIRT. Only been a little familiar with my person Sir –

WELLMAN. Do you hear Parson – you must marry Mrs. *Flirt.*

DUNCE. How Sir, a man of my coat Sir, marry a brandy-munger.[158]

WELLMAN. [*Aside to him*] Of your calling you mean a farrier and no parson. – She'll leave her trade – and spark it[159] above all the ladies at church, no more – take her and make her honest.

[*Enter* Whimsey *and* Whiff *stript.*

CRISANTE. Bless me, what have we here?

WHIMSEY. Why, an't like your Honours, we were taken by the enemy – hah *Dareing* here and *Fearless*?

FEARLESS. How now – Gentlemen were not you two condemn'd to be shot for running from your colours.

DOWNRIGHT. From your colours.

FEARLESS. Yes Sir, they were both listed in my regiment.

DOWNRIGHT. Then we must hang them for deserting us.

WHIMSEY. So out of the frying pan – you know where Brother –

WHIFF. Ay – he that's born to be hang'd – you know the rest, a pox of these proverbs.

WELLMAN. I know ye well – you're all rank cowards, but once more we forgive ye, your places in the Council shall be supply'd by these gentlemen of sense and honour. The Governour when he comes shall find the Country in better hands than he expects to find it.

WHIMSEY. A very fair discharge.

WHIFF. I'm glad 'tis no worse, I'll home to my *Nancy.*

DULLMAN. Have we expos'd our lives and fortunes for this?

TIMEROUS. Gads zoors I never thriv'd since I was a states-man, left planting, and fell to promising and lying, I'll to my old trade again, bask under the shade of my own tobacco, and drink my punch in peace.

WELLMAN. Come my brave youths let all our forces meet,
To make this Country happy, rich, and great;
Let scanted *Europe* see that we enjoy
Safer repose, and larger worlds than they.

EPILOGUE.[160]

Spoken by a Woman.

By this time you have lik'd, or damn'd our plot;
Which tho I know, my epilogue knows not:
For if it cou'd foretel, I shou'd not fail,
In decent wise, to thank you, or to rail.
But he who sent me here, is positive,
This farce of government is sure to thrive;
Farce is a food as proper for your lips,
As for *green-sickness*,[161] crumpt tobacco-pipes.[162]
Besides, the author's dead, and here you sit,
Like the infernal judges of the pit[163]:
Be merciful; for 'tis in you this day,
To save or damn her soul; and that's her play.
She who so well cou'd love's kind passion paint,
We piously believe, must be a saint:
Men are but bunglers, when they wou'd express
The sweets of love, the dying tenderness;[164]
But women, by their own abundance, measure,
And when they write, have deeper sense of pleasure.
Yet tho her pen did to the mark arrive,
'Twas common praise, to please you, when alive;
But of no other woman, you have read,
Except this one, to please you, now she's dead.
'Tis like the fate of bees, whose golden pains,
Themselves extinguish'd, in their hive remains.
Or in plain terms to speak, before we go,
What you young Gallants, by experience, know,
This is an orphan child; a bouncing boy,
'Tis late to lay him out, or to destroy.
Leave your dog-tricks, to lie and to forswear,
Pay *you* for nursing,[165] and we'll keep him here.

Licens'd, *Nov*. 20. 1689.
J. F.

FINIS.

EPILOGUE.

Gallants you have so long been absent hence,
That you have almost cool'd your dilligence,
For while we study or revive a play,
You like good husbands[166] in the Country stay,
There frugally wear out your summer suite,
And in frize jerkin[167] after beagles toot,[168]
Or in monntero caps[169] at field-fares shoot,
Nay some are so obdurate in their sin,
That they swear never to come up again.
But all their charge of cloathes and treat retrench,
To gloves and stockings for some Country wench.
Even they who in the summer had mishaps,
Send up to Town for physick[170] for their claps.[171]
The ladies too are as resolv'd as they,
And having debts unknown to them, they stay,
And with the gain of cheese and poultry pay.
Even in their visits, they from banquets fall,
To entertain with nuts and bottle ale.
And in discourse with secresy report

Stale-news that past a twelve-month since at court.
Those of them who are most refin'd, and gay,
Now learn the songs of the last summer's play:
While the young daughter does in private mourn,
Her loves in Town, and hopes not to return.
These Country grievances too great appear;
But cruell ladies, we have greater here;
You come not sharp as you were wont to playes;
But only on the first and second days:[172]
This made our poet, in his visits look
What new strange courses, for your time you took.
And to his great regret he found too soon,
Basset and *umbre*,[173] spent the afternoon:
So that we cannot hope to see you here
Before the little net work purse be clear.[174]
Suppose you should have luck;–
Yet sitting up so late as I am told,
You'll loose in beauty, what you win in gold:
And what each lady of another says,
Will make you new lampoons, and us new plays.

5.2 EBENEEZER COOK, *THE SOTWEED FACTOR*

London: D. Bragg, 1709.

NOTHING IS KNOWN ABOUT Ebenezer Cook except that he wrote and published this poem—from which we offer an excerpt—in London. "Sotweed" is a name for tobacco, an important export from the North American colonies to Britain, and a factor is an investor in and an importer of goods—in this case tobacco.

The Sot-weed Factor:[175] Or, a Voyage to Maryland.

A Satyr. In which is describ'd

The Laws, Government, Courts and Constitutions of the Country, and also the Buildings, Feasts, Frolicks, Entertainments and Drunken Humours of the Inhabitants of that Part of *America*. In Burlesque Verse. By Eben. Cook, Gent. Printed and Sold by *D. Bragg*, at the *Raven* in *Pater-Noster-Row*. 1708.

Condemn'd by Fate to way-ward Curse,
Of Friends unkind, and empty Purse;
Plagues worse than fill'd *Pandora's* Box,
I took my leave of *Albion's* Rocks:[176]
  With heavy Heart, concerned that I
  Was forc'd my Native Soil to fly,
  And the *Old World* must bid good-buy
But Heav'n ordain'd it should be so,
And to repine is vain we know:
Freighted with Fools from *Plymouth* sound
To *Mary-Land* our Ship was bound,
Where we arrived in dreadful Pain,
Shock'd by the Terrours of the Main;
For full three Months, our wavering Boat,
Did thro' the surley Ocean float,
And furious Storms and threat'ning Blasts,
Both tore our Sails and sprung our Masts;
Wearied, yet pleas'd we did escape
Such Ills, we anchor'd at the *Cape*;[177]
But weighing soon, we plough'd the Bay,

To Cove it[178] in *Piscato-way*,[179]
Intending there to open Store,
I put myself and Goods a-shoar:
Where soon repair'd a numerous Crew,
In Shirts and Drawers of *Scotch-cloth Blue*
With neither Stockings, Hat nor Shooe.
These *Sot-weed* Planters Crowd the Shoar,
In hue as tawny as a Moor:
Figures so strange, no God design'd,
To be a part of Humane kind:
But wanton Nature, void of Rest,
Moulded the brittle Clay in Jest.
At last a Fancy very odd
Took me, this was the Land of *Nod*;
Planted at first, when Vagrant *Cain*,
His Brother had unjustly slain;
Then Conscious of the Crime he'd done
From Vengeance dire, he hither run,
And in a hut supinely dwelt,
The first in *Furs* and *Sot-weed* dealt.
And ever since his Time, the Place,
Has harbour'd a detested Race;
Who when they cou'd not live at Home,
For refuge to these Worlds did roam;
In hopes by Flight they might prevent,
The Devil and his fell intent;
Obtain from Tripple-Tree reprieve[180],
And Heav'n and Hell alike deceive;
But e're their Manners I display,
I think it fit I open lay
My Entertainment by the way:
That Strangers well may be aware on,
What homely Diet they must fare on.
To touch that Shoar where no good Sense is found,
But Conversation's lost, and Manners drown'd.
I cros't unto the other side,
A River whose impetuous Tide,
The Savage Borders does divide;
In such a shining odd invention,
I scarce can give its due Dimention.
The *Indians* call this watry Waggon

Canoo, a Vessel none can brag on;
Cut from a *Popular-Tree* or *Pine*,
And fashion'd like a Trough for Swine:
In this most noble Fishing-Boat,
I boldly put myself afloat;
Standing erect, with Legs stretch'd wide,
We paddled to the other side:
Where being Landed safe by hap,
As *Sol* fell into *Thetis*' Lap.
A ravenous Gang bent on the stroul,
Of Wolves for Prey, began to howl;
This put me in a pannick Fright,
Least I should be devoured quite;
But as I there a musing stood,
And quite benighted in a Wood,
A Female Voice pierc'd, thro' my Ears,
Crying, *You Rogue drive home the Steirs.*
   I listen'd to th' attractive sound,
   And straight a Herd of Cattel found
   Drove by a Youth, and homeward bound;
Cheer'd with the sight, I straight thought fit,
To ask where I a Bed might get.
The surley Peasant bid me stay,
And ask'd from whom I'de run away.
Surprized at such a saucy Word,
I instantly lugg'd out my Sword;
   Swearing I was no Fugitive,
   But from *Great-Britain* did arrive,
   In hopes I better there might Thrive.
To which he mildly made reply,
I beg your Pardon, Sir, that I
Should talk to you Unmannerly;
But if you please to go with me,
To yonder House, you'll welcome be.

[The Factor accepts the hospitality of a planter and, after a dinner that he finds repellent, and drinking with the planter, spends a miserable night plagued by the noise of the planter's domesticated animals, snakes, and mosquitos. The next morning, he goes with the planter into the nearest town, where courts of justice are held.]

Steering our Barks in Trot or Pace,
We sail'd directly for a place
In *Mary-Land*, of high renown,
Known by the Name of Battle-Town.
To view the Crowds did there resort,
Which Justice made, and Law their sport,
In that sagacious County Court:
Scarce had we enter'd on the way,
Which thro' thick Woods and Marshes lay;
But *Indians* strange did soon appear,
In hot persuit of wounded Deer;
No mortal Creature can express,
His wild fantastick Air and Dress;
His painted Skin in Colours dy'd,
His sable hair in Satchel ty'd,
Shew'd Savages not free from Pride;
His tawny Thighs, and Bosom bare,
Disdain'd a useless Coat to wear,
Scorn'd Summer's Heat, and Winter's Air;
His manly shoulders such as please
Widows and Wives, were bathed in grease,
Of Cub and Bear, whose supple Oil
Prepar'd his Limbs 'gainst Heat or Toil.
Thus naked Pict in Battel fought,
Or undisguis'd his Mistress sought;
And knowing well his Ware was good,
Refus'd to screen it with a Hood;
His visage dun, and chin that ne'er
Did Raizor feel or Scissers bare,
Or knew the Ornament of Hair,
Look'd sternly Grim, surprized with Fear,
I spur'd my Horse as he drew near:
But Rhoan who better knew than I,
The little Cause I had to fly;
Seem'd by his solemn steps and pace,
Resolv'd I shou'd the Specter face,
Nor faster mov'd, tho' spur'd and lick'd,
Than *Balaam*'s Ass by Prophet kick'd.
Kekicknitop[181] the Heathen cry'd;
How is it, *Tom*, my Friend reply'd,
Judging from thence the Brute was civil,
I boldly fac'd the Courteous Devil;

And lugging out a Dram of Rum,
I gave his Tawny worship some:
Who in his language as I guess,
(My Guide informing me no less,)
Implored the Devil, me to bless.[182]

I thank'd him for his good Intent,
And forwards on my Journey went,
Discoursing as along I rode,
Whether this Race was framed by God,
Or whether some Malignant pow'r,
Contriv'd them in an evil hour,
And from his own Infernal Look,
Their Dusky form and Image took:
From hence we fell to Argument
Whence Peopled was this Continent.

[The Factor and the Planter propose various theories about the origins of the American Indians. The latter theorizes that they are Chinese in descent; the former that they are Indonesian.]

Scarce had we finish'd serious Story,
But I espy'd the Town before me,
And roaring Planters on the ground,
Drinking of Healths in Circle round:
Dismounting Steed with friendly Guide,
Our Horses to a Tree we ty'd,
And forwards pass'd among the Rout,
To chuse convenient *Quarters* out:
But being none were to be found,
We sat like others on the ground
Carousing Punch in open Air,
Till Cryer did the Court declare;
The planting Rabble being met
Their Drunken Worships likewise set;
Cryer proclaims that Noise shou'd cease
And streight the Lawyers broke the Peace:
Wrangling for Plantiff and Defendant,
I thought they ne'er wou'd make an end on't:
With nonsense, stuff and false quotations,
With brazen Lyes and Allegations;
And in the splitting of the Cause,

They used much Motions with their Paws,
As shew'd their Zeal was strongly bent,
In Blows to end the Argument.
A reverend Judge, who to the shame
Of all the Bench, cou'd write his Name;
At Petty-fogger took offence,
And wonder'd at his Impudence.
My Neighbour *Dash* with scorn replies,
And in the Face of Justice flies;
The Bench in fury streight divide,
And Scribble's take or Judge's side;
The Jury, Lawyers and their Clyents,
Contending fight like earth-born Gyants;
But Sheriff wily lay perdue,
Hoping Indictments wou'd ensue,
And when——————————
A Hat or Wig fell in the way,
He seized them for the *Queen* as stray:
The Court adjourn'd in usual manner
In Battle Blood and fractious Clamour;
I thought it proper to provide,
A Lodging for myself and Guide,
So to our Inn we march'd away,
Which at a little distance lay;
Where all things were in such Confusion,
I thought the World at its conclusion;
A Herd of Planters on the ground,
O'er-whelm'd with Punch, dead drunk, we found;
Others were fighting and contending,
Some burnt their Cloaths to save the mending.
A few whose Heads by frequent use,
Could better bare the potent Juice,
Gravely debated State Affairs.

[The Factor, after another bout of serious drinking, encounters a group of women playing cards. After another uncomfortable night, he wakes in an inn to find his clothing stolen and the horse run away. He regroups with the help of another planter and goes about the business for which he came—contracting for tobacco to sell in England.]

I then began to think with Care,
How I might sell my *British* Ware,
That with my Freight I might comply,

Did on my Charter party lie;
To this intent, with Guide before,
I tript it to the Eastern Shoar;
While riding near a Sandy Bay,
I met a *Quaker, Yea* and *Nay*;
A Pious Consientious Rogue,
As e'er woar Bonnet or a Brogue,
Who neither Swore nor kept his Word
But cheated in the Fear of God;
And when his Debts he would not pay,
By Light within he ran away.
With this sly Zealot soon I struck
A Bargain for my *English* Truck
Agreeing for ten thousand weight,
Of *Sot-weed* good and fit for freight,
Broad Oronooko bright and sound,
The growth and product of his ground;
In Cask that should contain compleat,
Five hundred of Tobacco neat.
The Contract thus betwixt us made,
Not well acquainted with the Trade,
My Goods I trusted to the Cheat,
Whose crop was then aboard the Fleet;
And going to receive my own,
I found the Bird was newly flown:
Cursing this execrable Slave,
This damn'd pretended Godly Knave;
On dire Revenge and Justice bent,
I instantly to Counsel went,
Unto an ambodexter *Quack*,[183]
Who learnedly had got the Knack
Of giving Glisters, making Pills,
Of filling Bonds, and forging Wills;
And with a stock of Impudence,
Supply'd his want of Wit and Sense;
With Looks demure, amazing People,
No wiser than a Daw in Steeple;
My Anger flushing in my Face,
I stated the preceeding Case:
And of my Money was so lavish,
That he'd have poyson'd half the Parish,
And hang'd his Father on a Tree

For such another tempting Fee;
Smiling, said he, the Cause is clear,
I'll manage him you need not fear;
   The Case is judg'd, good Sir, but look
   In *Galen*, No—in my Lord Cook,
   I vow to God I was mistook:
I'll take out a Provincial Writ,
And trounce him for his Knavish Wit;
Upon my Life we'll win the Cause,
With all the ease I cure the Yaws;[184]
Resolv'd to plague the holy Brother,
I set one Rogue to catch another;
To try the cause then fully bent,
Up to *Annapolis* I went,
A City Situate on a Plain,
Where scarce a House will keep out Rain;
The Buildings framed with Cyprus rare,
Resembles much our *Southwark* Fair:[185]
But Stranger here will scarcely meet
With Market-place, Exchange, or Street;
And if the Truth I may report,
'Tis not so large as *Tottenham Court*.
   St *Mary's* once was in repute,
   Now here the Judges try the Suit
   And Lawyers twice a year dispute.
   As oft the Bench most gravely meet,
   Some to get Drunk, and some to eat
   A swinging share of Country Treat.
But as for Justice right or wrong,
Not one amongst the numerous throng,
Knows what they mean, or has the Heart,
To give his Verdict on a Stranger's part:
Now Court being call'd by beat of Drum,
The Judges left their Punch and Rum,
When Pettifogger Docter draws,
His Paper forth, and opens Cause;
And least I shou'd the better get,
Brib'd *Quack* suppress his knavish Wit.
So Maid upon the Downy Field
Pretends a Force, and Fights to yield:
The Byast Court without delay,
Adjudg'd my Debt in Country Pay;

In Pipe staves, Corn or Flesh of Boar,[186]
Rare Cargo for the *English* Shoar;
Raging with Grief, full speed I ran
To joyn the Fleet at *Kicketan*;[187]
Embarqu'd and waiting for a Wind
I left this dreadful Curse behind.
May Canniballs transported o'er the Sea
Prey on these Slaves, as they have done on me;
May never Merchant's trading Sails explore
This Cruel, this inhospitable Shoar;
But left abandon'd by the World to starve,
May they sustain the Fate they well deserve;
May they turn Savage, or as *Indians* Wild,
From Trade, Converse and Happiness exil'd;
Recreant to Heaven, may they adore the Sun,
And into Pagan Superstitions run
For Vengence ripe——————
May Wrath Divine then lay those Regions wast
Where no Man's Faithful, nor a Woman Chast.

5.3 NATHANIEL BACON, *SELF PORTRAIT*

Sir Nathaniel Bacon, *Self Portrait*, circa 1625: Nathaniel Bacon (1585–1627) was a wealthy landowner from East Anglia and a relation of Francis Bacon (1561–1626). Courtesy National Gallery of Art, Washington, D.C.

An exceptional amateur painter, Bacon was practiced in a style that emphasized dramatic contrast between light and shade to increase realism and visual impact, prevalent in the Netherlands but not much practiced in England at the time. Depicted here as a wealthy gentleman rather than an artist, Bacon is more prominently remembered as a colonist of Virginia and the leader of Bacon's Rebellion (1674), in which a group of freeholders reacted violently to administrative corruption and relaxed attitudes towards Native American tribes occupying lands surrounding the Virginia colony.

5.4 W. VINCENT, *ANNE BRACEGIRDLE AS "THE INDIAN QUEEN"*

W. Vincent, *Anne Bracegirdle as "The Indian Queen"* (engraving). London: J. Smith. Not before 1689. Courtesy of the Folger Shakespeare Library. ART 232–569.1.

This mezzotint engraving depicts Anne Bracegirdle as Sermenia in Aphra Behn's *The Widdow Ranter*, produced in 1689. All manner of curiosities fill this frame, not the least of which is Bracegirdle's rendition of Native American royalty. Adorned with feather headdress, fan, and pearl jewelry, two black children clothed in feathers carry her train while shading her under a parasol from the Virginia sun.

Notes

1–2 From the edition of 1690 printed for James Knapton at the Crown in St. Paul's Churchyard, London. The editors also made reference to Janet Todd's edition in *The Works of Aphra Behn*. Ed. Janet Todd. Columbus, OH: Ohio State University Press, 1996, Vol. 7.

3 Todd, Vol. 7, 290.

4 Todd, Vol. 7, 287.

5 Unidentified.

6 This scene does not exist in any printed versions of the play.

7 A London prison, used to hold prisoners before they were sentenced. A guilty verdict for many crimes could be execution, but it was often transportation to a British colony where the prisoner served a period of indentured servitude before being allowed to start a new life as a free colonist. The primary destination for British transported criminals at the time of *The Widdow Ranter* was the North American colonies.

8 Janet Todd identifies G.J. as George Jenkins.

9 This is the prologue that was performed with the play in 1689 but published separately.

10 The site of the theatre, of course, but also a marketplace.

11 A reference to the practice of publishers pirating plays by copying them from the audience, or pit.

12 Masks worn by ladies, but also prostitutes at the theatres.

13 That give English men venereal diseases.

14 Rude language.

15 To talk with pleasure.

16 Smelly tobacco.

17 A reference to a battle fought in 1689 when a small group of Protestant men from Enniskillen in Northern Ireland defeated Catholic forces of James II.

18 This prologue was printed with the play, but not spoken in performance. Janet Todd identifies it as a prologue originally printed with Thomas Shadwell's *True Widow* in 1678 and speculates that the printer simply inserted it into his edition of *Widdow Ranter.*

19 A person, usually male, who makes a gay and splendid appearance. The Widdow Ranter is referred to as a gallant, denoting her masculine qualities.

20 That is, there are so many that they will not sell.

21 "Cruse" in the prologue of Shadwell's play—a small ceramic pot—it was changed to "cause" when printed with Behn's play.

22 Revenue raised by taxes.

23 Goods made in France but also a reference to venereal disease.

24 The cap and stick traditionally carried by fools, but also a child's toys.

25 Depicted on the stage.

26 A disturbance, a public battle, but also a child's game.

27 Prostitute.

28 A foolish or stupid person.

29 Not much is known about "Mr. Cudworth," beyond the fact that, like many of his fellow actors, he began his career in Dublin before playing Fearless at Drury Lane in London.

30 Unidentified, but possibly George Bright who also played Old Bellair in *The Man of Mode.*

31 An actor and dancer, Joseph Trefusis played Whimsey early in his career.

32 Unidentified.

33 Unidentified.

34 "Mrs. Jordan" was best known for her role as Crisante.

35 Traveling case.

36 The capital of the Virginia colony at the time of Bacon's Rebellion.

37 An adjective meaning very, derived from the oath, "God's wounds."

38 A dram. The word also refers to a conch shell or a small drinking cup made of wood. The exotic nature of this drinking vessel is more in keeping with the colonial setting than an ordinary tankard or cup.

39 Officer in charge of gaming.
40 Cheating.
41 Take in.
42 Fixed cards and loaded dice.
43 To give promissory notes on an inheritance and charge huge fees upon the father's death.
44 To increase the stakes.
45 Handwriting.
46 Do business.
47 Convicts and poor immigrants were auctioned off the ship as servants upon arrival.
48 Sir William Berkeley was governor during the Rebellion; he was deposed by Bacon, but regained his position by the latter's defeat. Behn puts Berkeley safely out of the way, perhaps to avoid dramatizing the deposition of a legitimate governor.
49 This passage reflects the mix of men governing the colonies peopled in considerable part by transported criminals.
50 A younger brother, under the informal rules of primogeniture, does not inherit the family estate kept intact as the inheritance of the eldest male.
51 A tavern keeper, a woman who sells beer, wine or spirits.
52 A brandy or white wine produced in the Nantes province of France.
53 Thin, clear, hence, not very strong.
54 Pig farmers.
55 The man under discussion used to shoe horses for a living, but went bankrupt and became a soldier of the Royal Body Guard. Losing that job when his horse died, he forged a document that gained him an appointment in the colony and is now "orthodox," that is, a conforming member of his society.
56 The English Civil Wars (1642–1649).
57 An inn where meals are provided at a fixed price.
58 Oliver Cromwell, whose funeral was never fully paid for. Flirt's father immigrated to avoid financial embarrassment after not being paid.
59 Tax collector and enforcer of tax laws.
60 Libel.
61 Whipping while being dragged by a cart through a public street was a common punishment for pick-pockets.
62 Gave evidence against another criminal in order to gain clemency or release.
63 The assembled group sings the chorus.
64 For the Crown.
65 The London neighborhood known for its prostitutes and their pimps.
66 Businessman.
67 The choice of weapon is indicative of class; gentlemen carry swords to defend themselves while lower class men would fight with a cudgel.
68 Members of the council.
69 Assaulted, taken prisoner.
70 Deprived.
71 Cut into pieces.
72 Hero of Homer's *Illiad*, known for his skill and bravery as a warrior. The name also could apply to a boastful, loud man or braggart.
73 Nicety.
74 Open, grassy plain.
75 Alexander the Great, at one time considered the conqueror of the known world.
76 In the open air and on horseback (like a man).
77 London prisons.
78 From being a footpad (mugger) or pickpocket.
79 Beat him up.
80 Queasy.

81 Special meal.
82 Peevish, boring.
83 Dried fish, usually cod.
84 Fasteners, used instead of buttons.
85 Agent.
86 Elsewhere *de la guarr*; fortunes of war.
87 Whine or beg.
88 Trick.
89 A swindler or cheat.
90 Live off the Widdow.
91 Large.
92 Hanged.
93 A barrel of brandy and poor quality, bad-smelling tobacco.
94 Bad English imitations of French oaths.
95 The Louvre Palace royal residence to the French monarchy until abandoned by Louis XIV in 1782; the Palace at Whitehall in London was royal residence until lost to fire in 1698. Afterwards, Whitehall Street was still the site of many government buildings.
96 The Royal Exchange in London was a center for domestic and international trade.
97 Love letters.
98 Go bankrupt and become members of a group of strolling players.
99 Western gate of the old London city wall.
100 Commissioned officer in a troop of calvary.
101 A worthless person.
102 Copse, a thicket of small trees.
103 Stomach; tolerance for this business.
104 The mob.
105 Scoundrels.
106 A blow, as from a fist; in this case, a verbal hit.
107 First use of this term in print.
108 See note 65. [[PMQ1]]
109 Psalms 22: 12–15: "strong bulls of Bashan have compassed me round." A reference to figures symbolic of cruelty and rage.
110 Follow him, with loud shouts.
111 From Johan De Witt, a Dutch statesman, first supported by but then killed by a mob in 1672.
112 Twigs soaked in urine, used for whipping.
113 Certificate of release from employment.
114 The amount owed by one party to another was recorded as a notch on a stick; the stick was then divided between the two parties.
115 Michael Dalton, *The Countrey Justice, Conteyning the practise of the Justices of the Peace . . . Gathered for the better helpe of such Justices of the Peach as have not beene conversant in the studie of the laws of this realm* (London, 1618).
116 Council Table.
117 Hum as in making unintelligible noises of assent.
118 A written affidavit; the witnesses "write" their affidavit verbally, probably because they cannot write.
119 Keg.
120 Libel.
121 See note 65.[[PMQ2]]
122 Self defense.
123 A verbal twist or trick.
124 A wig made to imitate natural hair.
125 British military dress.
126 Savage, violent person.
127 To strut and act important.

128 A brigantine is a small boat that can be rowed and maneuvered more quickly than a larger, slower vessel; a shallop is large, heavy boat, fitted with sails and often guns, but both were used to ferry between larger vessels and the shore.
129 Soldiers on horseback.
130 Catholics.
131 Greek mythical figure the sight of whom could turn men to stone.
132 Quiocos were part of a hierarchy of Indian deities whose tendency for causing harm to humans could be derailed with gifts.
133 Deserter.
134 Medical theory saw bleeding as therapeutic for a variety of ailments.
135 Ability to divine the future.
136 Julius Caesar is depicted by Plutarch as weeping as he presented with the head of his defeated enemy Pompey.
137 Stronghold.
138 A gentleman who enlists in the army without a commission in hopes of learning the military profession and being promoted.
139 Inform on.
140 An aspect of British law which in the late seventeenth century allowed offenders reduced sentences for their crimes if they could pass a literacy test.
141 That is, a noose.
142 Tease.
143 A masculine woman.
144 Being a cadet, in the army.
145 The best tobacco, coming from the top of the plant.
146 A cavalry officer.
147 Torches.
148 Possibly refers to the Pamunkey Indians of the Virginian coastal plain.
149 Put the archers using poisoned arrows at the front of the attack.
150 Deserters or runaways.
151 Running away.
152 To unfasten a garment (in order to urinate).
153 A spherical ornament at the top of the sword's hilt.
154 Hannibal, General of Carthage, killed himself rather than become captive of the conquering Romans.
155 Punishments such as hanging or drawing and quartering, as of a traitor, were highly public and popular spectacles until the end of the eighteenth century.
156 Roman senator who was a primary instigator in the plot to assassinate Julius Caesar. Mistakenly thinking that he and his brother-in-law, Brutus, had been defeated by Antony, he ordered a servant to kill him.
157 Swaddling clothes.
158 One who sells brandy.
159 She will show off, wearing fine clothes and putting on upper-class manners.
160 This is the epilogue spoken in performance, but not printed with the play.
161 A disease believed to affect adolescent, virginal girls.
162 Curved pipes. Tobacco was supposed to be medicinal.
163 Critics in the theatre, but also judges of the dead in the classical Greek mythology of the Underworld.
164 Orgasm.
165 Bringing him up, as in the case of an illegitimate child.
166 Caretakers, but also in the sense of being married.
167 A coarse, woolen garment for the upper body worn by men.
168 Hunt with hounds.
169 A hunting cap with a spherical crown and ear flaps.
170 Medicine.

171 Venereal disease.
172 The playwright was not paid until the third night of a performance.
173 Popular and fashionable card games.
174 Before they are out of money.
175 Tobacco Merchant.
176 England.
177 The Cape of Virginia.
178 Anchor.
179 Piscato Bay.
180 To escape hanging as condemned criminals.
181 Cook notes that this is an Indian expression meaning, "How are you?"
182 These *Indians* worship the Devil, and pray to him as we do to God Almighty. 'Tis suppos'd, that *America* was peopled from *Scythia* or *Tartaria*, which Borders on *China*, by reason the *Tartarians* and *Americans*, very much agree in their Manners, Arms and Government. Other persons are of Opinion, that the *Chinese* first peopled the *West-Indies*; imagining *China* and the Southern part of *America* to be contiguous. Others believe that the Phœnicians who were very skilful Mariners, first planted a Colony in the Isles of *America*, and supply'd the Persons left to inhabit there with Women and all other Necessaries; till either the Death or Shipwreck of the first Discoverers, or some other Misfortune, occasioned the loss of the Discovery, which had been purchased by the Peril of the first Adventurers [Cook's note].
183 This Fellow was an Apothecary, and turned an Attorney at Law [Cook's note].
184 A contagious disease associated with tropical countries.
185 One of the famous English markets or fairs, the sites of many cross-class entertainments as well as commerce, known for the rowdy behavior of many of its attendees.
186 There is a Law in this Country, the Plaintiff may pay his Debt in Country pay, which consists in the produce of his Plantation[Cook's note].
187 The homeward bound fleet meets here [Cook's note].

6. *The Relapse*

THE RELAPSE; OR, VIRTUE IN DANGER: BEING THE SEQUEL OF THE FOOL IN FASHION. **A COMEDY. ACTED AT THE THEATRE-ROYAL IN DRURY-LANE.**[1] **JOHN VANBRUGH. FIRST PERFORMED 29 NOVEMBER 1696 AND FIRST PUBLISHED 1697**

6.1 *THE RELAPSE; OR, VIRTUE IN DANGER: BEING THE SEQUEL OF THE FOOL IN FASHION*, A COMEDY. ACTED AT THE *THEATRE-ROYAL* IN *DRURY-LANE*.[2]

John Vanbrugh

First Performed 29 November 1696 and First Published 1697

THIS PLAY BY SIR JOHN VANBRUGH (1664–1726) was a hit at its first performance in 1696. A sequel to the actor, playwright, and theatre manager Colley Cibber's *Love's Last Shift*, *The Relapse*'s popularity out-stripped that of the original, which was rarely performed after the 1790s. Vanbrugh's sequel has an enduring stage history during the eighteenth and nineteenth centuries, although it was adapted to the more conservative moral tastes of audiences as the century drew on. Thomas Sheridan's sanitized *A Trip to Scarborough*, which largely displaced Vanbrugh's play from its debut in 1777, toned down its sexuality by renaming Worthy "Townley," making Coupler a prim old woman, and generally scaling back on the original's representations of sexual desire and behavior.

Cibber's comedy (which can be read in the online supplement) mixed the frank sexuality of earlier Restoration comedies such as *The Man of Mode* and *The Country Wife* with a sentimental morality that was gradually displacing libertine comedy and social satire. Its plot entails the reform of the aristocratic male libertine through the morally motivated trickery of his loving and virtuous wife. It features a subplot with the popular character of Sir Novelty Fashion, in the style of Sir Fopling Flutter and Sparkish in *Man of Mode* and *Country Wife* respectively, played with great hilarity by Cibber. *The Relapse* picks up the characters of Loveless, the libertine but now reformed husband, and Amanda, his wife, as they both encounter new temptations to stray from the path of monogamy. *The Relapse* also continues and expands on the character of Sir Novelty Fashion, ennobling him as Lord Foppington and embedding him in a comic subplot that takes up most of the play. Cibber played this role to even greater applause than was given to Sir Novelty, and the persona of Lord Foppington became the most widely circulated, celebrated—and mocked—public face of the Drury Lane manager who would become Poet Laureate of England.

Vanbrugh's husband and wife meet their temptations, in the form of Berinthia and Worthy, with a more complex and conflicted response than Cibber's couple. Cibber's Amanda is the perfect wife who never varies from virtuous love, even after her husband's ten years of philandering, drink, and desertion, and his Loveless's instantaneous reform is untainted by any psychologically plausible motive. *The Relapse*'s Loveless and Amanda begin where they left off in an idyll of married, monogamous love, but end seriously tried by the temptations offered by public, town life. The play repeats Cibber's pattern of illicit love followed by reform, but in the person of Amanda's would-be lover, Worthy, not her husband, Loveless. Its claims to the psychological realism of a later theatre culture have given it popular revivals in the late twentieth and twenty-first centuries, as well as a mash-up with *Love's Last Shift* in the 2005 Amy Freed play, *Restoration Comedy*.

The circumstances of its original production were vexed, to say the least, following on the equally if not more troubled production of *Love's Last Shift*. The 1690s saw the splitting of the one licensed London company into two rival theatres as the result of what was known as "the Actors' Rebellion." Greed on the part of investors in the then-sole United Company of London lead to the intolerable exploitation and ill treatment of its actors, who petitioned the Lord Chamberlain for redress and finally walked out on the manager, John Rich, succeeding, much to Rich's chagrin, in establishing their own licensed company. Rich was left without most of the more experienced and talented performers, including Thomas Betterton, the legendary actor and leader of the new company. Cibber, at that time a minor actor, stayed with Rich and presented him with *Love's Last Shift*, a play successful enough to keep the playhouse open. Rich was also able to retain John and Susanna Verbruggen, casting the former as Loveless and the latter in a secondary role, and Cibber played the fop Sir Novelty with unexpected success.

The Relapse again cast John Verbruggen as Loveless, with Susanna as Berinthia, capitalizing on the success of *Love's Last Shift* and adding sexual chemistry for an audience familiar with the Verbruggens as a loving, married couple. Cibber carried on as Sir Novelty, now Lord Foppington, but the casting of his handsome younger brother, Tom Fashion, encountered problems when Hildebrand Horden, the original choice, was killed in a tavern brawl. He was replaced by Mary Kent, who played the first Tom Fashion as a breeches part. Finally, as Vanbrugh mentions in his preface, the talented but alcoholic George Powell almost scuttled the play's performance by nearly succeeding in what was supposed to be only an attempt on Amanda's virtue. Apparently sexually excited and too drunk to remember he was acting, Powell scandalized audiences by nearly raping Jane Rogers, the actress who played Amanda, on stage.

Like many gentlemen of the Restoration period, Vanbrugh had a mixed career as businessman, military officer, and architect as well as playwright. He was, apparently unjustly, imprisoned in France for most of his twenties on a spying charge. A committed Protestant, he is famous for his membership in the Kit-Kat Club, a group of Whigs dedicated to displacing the Catholic James II with a Protestant monarchy.

THE PREFACE.

To go about to excuse half the defects this abortive brat is come into the world with, wou'd be to provoke the Town with a long useless preface, when 'tis, I doubt, sufficiently sour'd already, by a tedious play.

I do therefore (with all the humility of a repenting sinner) confess, it wants every thing–but length; and in that, I hope the severest critique will be pleas'd to acknowledge, I have not been wanting. But my modesty will sure attone for every thing, when the World shall know it is so great, I am even to this day insensible of those two shining graces in the play (which some part of the Town is pleas'd to compliment me with) Blasphemy and Bawdy.

For my part, I cannot find 'em out. If there was any obscene expressions upon the stage, here they are in the print; for I have dealt fairly, I have not sunk a syllable, that cou'd (tho' by racking of mysteries) be rang'd under that head; and yet I believe with a steady faith, there is not one woman of a real reputation in Town, but when she has read it impartially over in her closet,[3] will find it so innocent, she'll think it no affront to her prayer-book, to lay it upon the same shelf. So to them, (with all manner of deference,) I entirely refer my cause, and I'm confident they'll justify me, against those pretenders to good manners, who, at the same time, have so little respect for the ladies, they wou'd extract a bawdy jest from an ejaculation, to put 'em out of countenance. But I expect to have these well-bred persons always my enemies, since I'm sure I shall never write any thing lewd enough, to make 'em my friends.

As for the Saints (your thorough-pac'd ones I mean) with screw'd faces and wry mouths) I despair of them, for they are friends to no body. They love nothing, but their altars and themselves. They have too much zeal to have any charity: they make debauches in piety, as sinners do in wine; and are as quarrelsome in their religion, as other people are in their drink: so I hope no body will mind what they say. But if any man (with flat plod shooes, a little band, greasy hair, and a dirty face, who is wiser than I, at the expence of being forty years older) happens to be offended at a story of a cock and a bull, and a priest and a bull-dog:[4] I beg his pardon with all my heart, which I hope I shall obtain, by eating my words, and making this publick recantation. I do therefore for his satisfaction, acknowledge, I ly'd, when I said, they never quit their hold; for in that little time I have liv'd in the world, I thank God I have seen 'em forc'd to't, more than once; but next time I'll speak with more caution and truth; and only say, they have very good teeth.

If I have offended any honest gentlemen of the Town, whose friendship or good word is worth the having, I am very sorry for it; I hope they'll correct me as gently as they can, when they consider I have had no other design, in running a very great risque, than to divert (if possible) some part of their spleen,[5] in spight of their wives and their taxes.[6]

One word more about the bawdy, and I have done. I own the first night this thing was acted, some indecencies had like to have happen'd, but 'twas not my fault.

The fine gentleman of the play,[7] drinking his mistress's health in *Nants* brandy, from six in the morning, to the time he wadled on upon the stage in the evening, had toasted himself up, to such a pitch of vigor, I confess I once gave *Amanda* for gone, and I am since (with all due respect to Mrs. *Rogers*) very sorry she scap't; for I am confident a certain, (let no one take it to her self that's handsome) who highly blames the play, for the barrenness of the conclusion wou'd then have allow'd it, a very natural close.

First Prologue, Spoken by Miss Cross.

Ladies, this play in too much haste was writ,
To be o'er-charg'd with either plot or wit;
'Twas got, conceiv'd, and born in six weeks space,
And wit, you know, 's as slow in growth–as grace.
Sure it can ne'er be ripen'd to your taste,
I doubt 'twill prove, our author bred too fast.
For mark'em well, who with the muses marry,
They rarely do conceive, but they miscarry.
'Tis the hard fate of those wh' are big with rhime,
Still to be brought to bed before their time.
Of our late poets, Nature few has made,
The greatest part–are only so by trade.
Still want of something, brings the scribling fit,
For want of money, some of 'em have writ,
And others do't you see–for want of wit.
Honour, they fancy, summons 'em to write,
So out they lug in wresty[8] Nature's spight,
As some of you spruce beaux do–when you fight.
Yet let the ebb of wit be ne'r so low,
Some glimpse of it, a man may hope to shew,
Upon a theme, so ample–as a beau.
So, howsoe'r true courage may decay,
Perhaps there's not one smock-face[9] here to day,
But's bold as Caesar–to attack a play.
Nay, what's yet more, with an undaunted face,
To do the thing with more heroick grace,
'Tis six to four, y'attack the strongest place.
You are such Hotspurs,[10] in this kind of venture,
Where there's no breach, just there you needs must enter.
But be advis'd.
E'n give the hero, and the critique o'er,
For Nature sent you on another score;
She form'd her beau, for nothing but her whore.

Prologue on the Third Day, Spoken by Mrs. Verbruggen.

Apologies for plays, experience shews,
Are things almost as useless – as the beaux.
What e'er we say (like them) we neither move,
Your friendship, pity, anger, nor your love,
'Tis interest turns the globe: let us but find,
The way to please you, and you'll soon be kind:
But to expect, you'd for our sakes approve,
Is just as tho' you for their sakes shou'd love,
And that, we do confess, we think a task,
Which (tho' they may impose) we never ought to ask.

This is an Age, where all things we improve,
But most of all, the art of making love.
In former days, women were only won,
By merit, truth, and constant service done,
But lovers now are much more expert grown.
They seldom wait, t'approach, by tedious form,
They're for dispatch, for taking you by storm,
Quick are their sieges, furious are their fires,
Fierce their attacks, and boundless their desires.
Before the play's half ended, I'll engage
To shew you beaux come crowding on the stage,[11]
Who with so little pains, have always sped,
They'll undertake to look a Lady dead.
How I have shook, and trembling stood with awe,
When here, behind the scenes, I've seen 'em draw
– A comb: that dead-doing weapon to the heart,
And turn each powder'd hair into a dart.
When I have seen 'em sally on the stage,
Dress'd to the war, and ready to engage,
I've mourn'd your destiny – yet more their fate,
To think, that after victories so great,
It shou'd so often prove, their hard mishap,
To sneak into a lane – and get a clap.[12]
But hush; they're here already, I'll retire,
And leave 'em to you Ladies to admire.
They'll shew you twenty thousand airs and graces,
They'll entertain you with their soft grimaces,
Their snuff-box, aukward bows – and ugly faces.
In short, they're after all, so much your friends

That lest the play should fail, the author ends,
They have resolv'd to make you some amends.
Between each act, (perform'd by nicest rules),
They'll treat you – with an interlude of fools.
Of which, that you may have the deeper sense,
The entertainment's – at their own expence.

Dramatis Personae.

Men.

Mr. Cibber. Sir *Novelty Fashion*, newly created *Lord Foppington.*
Mrs. Kent. Young *Fashion* his brother.
Mr. Verbruggen. Loveless, husband to *Amanda.*
Mr. Powell. Worthy, a gentleman of the Town.
Mr. Bullock. Sir *Tunbelly Clumsey*, a country gentleman.
Mr. Mills. Sir *John Friendly* his neighbour.
Mr. Johnson. Coupler, a match-maker.
Mr. Simson. Bull, Chaplain to Sir *Tunbelly.*
Mr. Haynes. Serringe a surgeon.
Mr. Dogget. Lory, servant to Young *Fashion.*
Shoomaker, taylor, perriwigmaker, *&c.*

Women.

Mrs. Rogers. Amanda, wife to *Loveless.*
Mrs. Verbruggen. Berrinthia, her cousin, a young widow.
Mrs. Cross. Miss Hoyden, a great fortune,[13] daughter to Sir *Tunbelly.*
Mrs. Powell. Nurse her Gouvernant.

Act I. Scene I.

[*Enter* Loveless *reading.*]

LOVELESS. How true is that philosophy, which says,
Our heaven is seated in our minds!
Through all the roving pleasures of my youth,
(Where nights and days seem'd all consum'd in joy,
Where the false face of luxury
Display'd such charms,
As might have shaken the most holy hermit,
And made him totter at his altar;)
I never knew one moment's peace like this.
Here–in this little soft retreat,
My thoughts unbent from all the cares of life,
Content with fortune,
Eas'd from the grating duties of dependance,
From envy free, ambition under foot,

The raging flame of wild destructive lust
Reduc'd to a warm pleasing fire of lawful love,
My life glides on, and all is well within.

[*Enter* Amanda.

LOVELESS. How does the happy cause of my content, my dear *Amanda*? [*Meeting her kindly*.
You find me musing on my happy state,
And full of grateful thoughts to Heaven, and you.

AMANDA. Those grateful offerings Heaven can't receive
With more delight than I do:
Wou'd I cou'd share with it as well
The dispensations of its bliss,
That I might search its choicest favours out,
And shower 'em on your head for ever.

LOVELESS. The largest boons that Heaven thinks fit to grant,
To things it has decreed shall crawl on earth,
Are in the gift of women form'd like you,
Perhaps, when time shall be no more.
When the aspiring soul shall take its flight,
And drop this pondrous lump of clay behind it,
It may have appetites we know not of,
And pleasures as refin'd as its desires–
But till that day of knowledge shall instruct me,
The utmost blessing that my thought can reach, [*Taking her in his arms*.
Is folded in my arms, and rooted in my heart.

AMANDA. There let it grow for ever.

LOVELESS. Well said, *Amanda*–let it be for ever–
Wou'd Heaven grant that–

AMANDA. 'Twere all the Heaven I'd ask.
But we are clad in black mortality, and the dark curtain
Of eternal night, at last must drop between us.

LOVELESS. It must: that mournful separation we must see,
A bitter pill it is to all; but doubles its ungrateful taste,
When lovers are to swallow it.

AMANDA. Perhaps, that pain may only be my lot,
You possibly may be exempted from it; men find out softer
Ways to quench their fires.

LOVELESS. Can you then doubt my constancy, *Amanda*?
You'll find 'tis built upon a steady basis–
The rock of reason now supports my love,
On which it stands so fix'd,
The rudest hurricane of wild desire
Would, like the breath of a soft slumbring babe,
Pass by, and never shake it.

AMANDA. Yet still 'tis safer to avoid the storm;
The strongest vessels, if they put to sea,
May possibly be lost.
Wou'd I cou'd keep you here, in this calm port, for ever!
Forgive the weakness of a woman,
I am uneasie at your going to stay so long in Town,
I know its false insinuating pleasures;
I know the force of its delusions;
I know the strength of its attacks;
I know the weak defence of nature;
I know you are a man–and I–a wife.

LOVELESS. You know then all that needs to give you rest,
For Wife's the strongest claim that you can urge.
When you would plead your title to my heart,
On this you may depend; therefore be calm,
Banish your fears, for they are traytors to your peace;
Beware of 'em, they are insinuating busie things
That gossip to and fro, and do a world of mischief
Where they come: but you shall soon be Mistress of 'em all,
I'll aid you with such arms for their destruction,
They never shall erect their heads again.
You know the business is indispensable, that obliges
Me to go for *London*; and you have no reason, that I
Know of, to believe I'm glad of the occasion;
For my honest conscience is my witness.
I have found a due succession of such charms
In my retirement here with you;
I have never thrown one roving thought that way;
But since, against my will, I'm dragg'd once more
To that uneasie theatre of noise;
I am resolv'd to make such use on't,
As shall convince you, 'tis an old-cast mistress,

Who has been so lavish of her favours,
She's now grown bankrupt of her charms,
And has not one allurement left to move me.

AMANDA. Her bow, I do believe, is grown so weak,
Her arrows (at this distance) cannot hurt you,
But in approaching 'em, you give 'em strength;
The dart that has not far to fly,
Will put the best of armour to a dangerous trial.

LOVELESS. That trial past, and y'are at ease for ever;
When you have seen the helmet prov'd,
You'll apprehend no more, for him that wears it.
Therefore to put a lasting period to your fears,
I am resolv'd, this once, to launch into temptation,
I'll give you an essay[14] of all my virtues,
My former boon companions of the bottle
Shall fairly try what charms are left in wine:
I'll take my place amongst 'em,
They shall hem me in,
Sing praises to their God, and drink his glory:
Turn wild enthusiasts[15] for his sake,
And beasts to do him honour,
Whilst I a stubborn atheist,
Sullenly look on,
Without one reverend glass to his divinity:
That for my temperance,
Then for my constancy.–

AMANDA. Ay, there take heed.

LOVELESS. Indeed the danger's small,

AMANDA. And yet my fears are great.

LOVELESS. Why are you so timerous?

AMANDA. Because you are so bold.

LOVELESS. My courage shou'd disperse your apprehensions.

AMANDA. My apprehensions shou'd allarm your courage.

LOVELESS. Fy, Fy, *Amanda*, it is not kind thus to distrust me.

AMANDA. And yet my fears are founded on my love.

LOVELESS. Your love then, is not founded as it ought,
For if you can believe 'tis possible,
I shou'd again relapse to my past follies;
I must appear to you a thing,
Of such an undigested composition,
That but to think of me with inclination,
Wou'd be a weakness in your taste,
Your virtue scarce cou'd answer.

AMANDA. 'Twou'd be a weakness in my tongue;
My prudence cou'd not answer,
If I shou'd press you farther with my fears;
I'll therefore trouble you no longer with 'em.

LOVELESS. Nor shall they trouble you much longer,
A little time shall shew you they were groundless:
This winter[16] shall be the fiery-trial of my virtue;
Which, when it once has past,
You'll be convinc'd, 'twas of no false allay,
There all your cares will end.–

AMANDA. –Pray Heaven they may. [*Exeunt hand in hand.*

Scene II.

[*Whitehall.*[17] *Enter* Young Fashion, Lory *and* Waterman.[18]]

YOUNG FASHION. Come, pay the waterman, and take the portmantle.[19]

LORY. Faith Sir, I think the waterman had as good take the portmantle and pay himself.

YOUNG FASHION. Why shure there's something left in't!

LORY. But a solitary old wastcoat, upon honour, Sir.

YOUNG FASHION. Why, what's become of the blue coat, Sirrah?

LORY. Sir, 'twas eaten at *Gravesend*; the reckoning came to thirty shillings, and your privy purse was worth but two half-crowns.

YOUNG FASHION. 'Tis very well.

WATERMAN. Pray, Master will you please to dispatch me?

YOUNG FASHION. Ay, here, a – canst thou change me a guinea?

LORY. [*Aside*] *Good.*

WATERMAN. Change a guinea, Master! Ha, ha, your Honor's pleas'd to compliment.[20]

YOUNG FASHION. I'gad I don't know how I shall pay thee then, for I have nothing but gold about me.

LORY. [*Aside*] – *Hum, hum.*

YOUNG FASHION. What dost thou expect, Friend?

WATERMAN. Why, Master, so far against wind and tide, is richly worth half a piece.[21]

YOUNG FASHION. Why, faith, I think thou art a good conscionable fellow. I'gad, I begin to have so good an opinion of thy honesty, I care not if I leave my portmantle with thee, till I send thee thy money.

WATERMAN. Ha! God bless your Honour; I shou'd be as willing to trust you, Master, but that you are, as a man may say, a stranger to me, and these are nimble times; there are a great many sharpers[22] stirring. [*Taking up the portmantle*] Well, Master, when your Worship sends the money, your portmantle shall be forth-coming; my name's *Tugg*; my wife keeps a brandy-shop in *Drab-Alley* at *Wapping.*

YOUNG FASHION. Very well; I'll send for't to morrow. [*Exit* Waterman.

LORY. So – now, Sir, I hope you'll own your self a happy man, you have out-liv'd all your cares.

YOUNG FASHION. How so, Sir?

LORY. Why, you have nothing left to take care of.

YOUNG FASHION. Yes, Sirrah, I have my self and you to take care of still.

LORY. Sir, if you cou'd but prevail with some body else to do that for you, I fancy we might both fare the better for't.

YOUNG FASHION. Why, if thou canst tell me where to apply my self, I have at present so little money and so much humility about me, I don't know but I may follow a fool's advice.

LORY. Why then, Sir, your fool advises you to lay aside all animosity, and apply to Sir *Novelty* your elder brother.[23]

YOUNG FASHION. Damn my elder brother.

LORY. With all my heart, but get him to redeem your annuity[24] however.

YOUNG FASHION. My annuity! S'death, he's such a dog, he wou'd not give his powder puff to redeem my soul.

LORY. Look you, Sir, you must wheedle him, or you must starve.

YOUNG FASHION. Look you, Sir, I will neither wheedle him, nor starve.

LORY. Why? What will you do then?

YOUNG FASHION. I'll go into the army.

LORY. You can't take the oaths; you are a *Jacobite.*[25]

YOUNG FASHION. Thou may'st as well say I can't take orders because I'm an atheist.

LORY. Sir, I ask your pardon; I find I did not know the strength of your conscience, so well as I did the weakness of your purse.

YOUNG FASHION. Methinks, Sir, a person of your experience should have known that the strength of the conscience proceeds from the weakness of the purse.

LORY. Sir, I am very glad to find you have a conscience able to take care of us, let it proceed from what it will; but I desire you'll please to consider, that the army alone will be but a scanty maintenance for a person of your generosity, (at least. as rents now are paid[26]) I shall see you stand in damnable need of some auxiliary guineas, for your *menu plaisirs*;[27] I will therefore turn fool once more for your service, and advise you to go directly to your brother.

YOUNG FASHION. Art thou then so impregnable a blockhead, to believe he'll help me with a farthing?

LORY. Not if you treat him, *de haut en bas*,[28] as you use to do.

YOUNG FASHION. Why, how wou'dst have me treat him?

LORY. Like a trout,[29] tickle him.

YOUNG FASHION. I can't flatter. –

LORY. Can you starve?

YOUNG FASHION. Yes. –

LORY. I can't; Good by t'ye Sir – [*Going.*

YOUNG FASHION. Stay, thou wilt distract me. What wou'dst thou have me say to him?

LORY. Say nothing to him, apply your self to his favourites, speak to his periwig, his cravat, his feather, his snuff-box, and when you are well with them – desire him to lend you a thousand pounds. I'll engage you prosper.

YOUNG FASHION. S'death and Furies! Why was that coxcomb thrust into the world before me? O Fortune – Fortune – thou art a bitch by gad – [*Exeunt.*

Scene III.

[*A Dressing-room. Enter* Lord Foppington *in his night-gown.*[30]]

LORD FOPPINGTON. Page. –

[*Enter* Page.

PAGE. Sir.

LORD FOPPINGTON. Sir, pray, Sir, do me the favour to teach your tongue the title the King has thought fit to honour me with.

PAGE. I ask your Lordship's pardon, my Lord.

LORD FOPPINGTON. O, you can pronounce the word then, I thought it wou'd have choak'd you – D'ye hear?

PAGE. My Lord.

LORD FOPPINGTON. Call La Verole, I wou'd dress – [*Exit* Page.

Well, 'tis an unspeakable pleasure to be a Man of Quality – strike me dumb – my Lord – your Lordship – my Lord *Foppington – Ah c'est quelque chose de beau, que le Diable m'emporte.*[31] – Why the ladies were ready to pewk at me, whilst I had nothing but Sir Novelty to recommend me to 'em – sure whilst I was but a knight, I was a very nauseous fellow – well, 'tis ten thousand pawnd well given – stap my vitals –

[*Enter* La Verole.

LA VEROLE. Me Lord, de shoomaker, de taylor, de hosier, de semstress, de barber, be all ready, if your Lordship please to be dress.

LORD FOPPINGTON. 'Tis well, admit 'em.

LA VEROLE. Hey, Messieurs, entrez.

[*Enter* Taylor, *&c.*

LORD FOPPINGTON. So, Gentlemen, I hope you have all taken pains to shew your selves masters in your professions.

TAYLOR. I think I may presume to say, Sir, –

LA VEROLE. My Lord – you Clawn[32] you.

TAYLOR. Why, is he made a lord – my Lord, I ask your Lordship's pardon, my Lord; I hope, my Lord, your Lordship will please to own, I have brought your Lordship as accomplish'd a suit of cloaths, as ever peer of *England* trod the stage in, my Lord; will your Lordship please to try 'em now.

LORD FOPPINGTON. Ay, but let my people dispose the glasses[33] so, that I may see my self before and behind, for I love to see my self all round –

[*Whilst he puts on his cloaths, enter* Young Fashion *and* Lory.

YOUNG FASHION. Hey-day, what the Devil have we here? Sure my gentleman's grown a favourite at Court, he has got so many people at his levee.[34]

LORY. Sir, these people come in order to make him a favorite at Court, they are to establish him with the ladies.

YOUNG FASHION. Good God, to what an ebb of taste are women fallen, that it shou'd be in the power of a lace'd coat to recommend a gallant to 'em. –

LORY. Sir, taylors and perriwig makers are now become the bawds of the Nation, 'tis they debauch all the women.

YOUNG FASHION. Thou say'st true; for there's that fop now, has not by nature wherewithal to move a cook-maid, and by that time these fellows have done with him, I'gad he shall melt down a countess. –

But now for my reception, I'll engage it shall be as cold a one, as a courtier's to his friend, who comes to put him in mind of his promise.

LORD FOPPINGTON. Death and eternal tortures! Sir, I say the packet's[35] too high by a foot. [*To his taylor.*

TAYLOR. My Lord, if it had been an inch lower, it would not have held your Lordship's pocket handkerchief.

LORD FOPPINGTON. Rat my pocket handkerchief, have not I a page to carry it? You may make him a packet up to his chin a purpose for it: but I will not have mine come so near my face.

TAYLOR. 'Tis not for me to dispute your Lordship's fancy.

YOUNG FASHION. His Lordship! *Lory*, did you observe that? [*To* Lory.

LORY. Yes, Sir, I always thought 'twould end there. Now I hope you'll have a little more respect for him.

YOUNG FASHION. Respect! Damn him for a coxcomb; now has he ruin'd his estate to buy a title, that he may be a fool of the first rate: but let's accost him. –

Brother, I'm your humble servant. [*To* Lord Foppington.

LORD FOPPINGTON. O Lard *Tam*, I did not expect you in *England*; Brother, I am glad to see you. – [*Turning to his taylor*] Look you, Sir, I shall never be reconcil'd to this nauseous packet, therefore pray get me another suit with all manner of expedition, for this is my eternal aversion; Mrs. *Callicoe*, are not you of my mind?

SEMSTRESS. O, directly my Lord, it can never be too low. –

LORD FOPPINGTON. You are positively in the right on't, for the packet becomes no part of the body but the knee.

SEMSTRESS. I hope your Lordship is pleas'd with your Steenkirk.[36]

LORD FOPPINGTON. In love with it, stap my vitals. Bring your bill, you shall be paid to morrow. –

SEMSTRESS. I humbly thank your Honour – [*Exit* Semstress.

LORD FOPPINGTON. Hark thee, Shooe-maker, these shooes an't ugly, but they don't fit me.

SHOOEMAKER. My Lord, my thinks they fit you very well.

LORD FOPPINGTON. They hurt me just below the instep.

SHOOEMAKER. My Lord, they don't hurt you there. [*Feeling his foot.*

LORD FOPPINGTON. I tell thee, they pinch me execrably.

SHOOEMAKER. My Lord, if they pinch you, I'll be bound to be hang'd, that's all.

LORD FOPPINGTON. Why wilt thou undertake to perswade me I cannot feel.

SHOOEMAKER. Your Lordship may please to feel what you think fit; but that shooe does not hurt you; I think I understand my trade. –

LORD FOPPINGTON. Now by all that's great and powerful, thou art an incomprehensible coxcomb; but thou makest good shoes, and so I'll bear with thee.

SHOOEMAKER. My Lord, I have work'd for half the people of quality in Town, these twenty years, and 'twere very hard I should not know when a shooe hurts, and when it don't.

LORD FOPPINGTON. Well, prithee be gone about thy business. – [*Exit* Shooemaker] Mr. Mend-Legs, a word with you; the calves of these stockings are thicken'd a little too much.[37] They make my legs look like a chairman's.[38] – [*To the Hosier.*

MEND-LEGS. My Lord, my thinks they look mighty well.

LORD FOPPINGTON. Ay, but you are not so good a judge of these things as I am, I have study'd 'em all my life; therefore pray let the next be the thickness of a crawn-piece[39] less – [*Aside*] *If the Town takes notice my legs are fallen away, 'twill be attributed to the violence of some new intrigue.* – [*To the* Periwig-maker] Come, Mr. *Foretop*, let me see what you have done, and then the fatigue of the morning will be over.

FORETOP. My Lord, I have done what I defie any prince in *Europe* to outdo; I have made you a periwig so long, and so full of hair, it will serve you for hat and cloak in all weathers.

LORD FOPPINGTON. Then thou hast made me thy friend to eternity; come, comb it out.

YOUNG FASHION. Well, *Lory*, what do'st think on't? A very friendly reception from a brother after three years absence.

LORY. Why, Sir, it's your own fault; we seldom care for those that don't love what we love; if you would creep into his heart, you must enter into his pleasures – here have you stood ever since you came in, and have not commended any one thing that belongs to him.

YOUNG FASHION. Nor never shall, whilst they belong to a coxcomb.

LORY. Then, Sir, you must be content to pick a hungry bone.

YOUNG FASHION. No, Sir, I'll crack it, and get to the marrow before I have done.

LORD FOPPINGTON. Gad's curse; Mr. *Foretop*, you don't intend to put this upon me for a full periwig?

FORETOP. Not a full one, my Lord? I don't know what your Lordship may please to call a full one, but I have cram'd 20 ounces of hair into it.

LORD FOPPINGTON. What it may be by weight, Sir, I shall not dispute, but by tale, there are not 9 hairs of a side.

FORETOP. O Lord! O Lord! O Lord! Why, as Gad shall judge me, your Honour's side-face is reduc'd to the tip of your nose.

LORD FOPPINGTON. My side-face may be in eclipse for ought I know; but, I'm sure, my full-face is like the full-moon.

FORETOP. Heavens bless my eye-sight! – [*Rubbing his eyes*] Sure I look through the wrong end of the perspective,[40] for by my faith, an't please your Honour, the broadest place I see in your face, does not seem to me to be two inches diameter.

LORD FOPPINGTON. If it did, it would be just two inches too broad; for a periwig to a man, shou'd be like a mask to a woman, nothing shou'd be seen but his eyes –

FORETOP. My Lord, I have done; if you please to have more hair in your wig, I'll put it in.

LORD FOPPINGTON. Passitively, yes.

FORETOP. Shall I take it back now, my Lord?

LORD FOPPINGTON. Noh: I'll wear it to day, though it shew such a monstrous pair of cheeks: stap my vitals, I shall be taken for a trumpeter. [*Exit* Foretop.

YOUNG FASHION. Now your people of business are gone, Brother, I hope I may obtain a quarter of an hour's audience of you.

LORD FOPPINGTON. Faith, Tam; I must beg you'll excuse me at this time, for I must away to the House of Lards immediately; my Lady *Teaser*'s case is to come on to day, and I would not be absent for the salvation of mankind. Hey *Page*, is the coach at the door?

PAGE. Yes, my Lord.

LORD FOPPINGTON. You'll excuse me, Brother. [*Going*.

YOUNG FASHION. Shall you be back at dinner?

LORD FOPPINGTON. As Gad shall jidge me, I can't tell; for 'tis passible I may dine with some of our House at *Lackets*.[41]

YOUNG FASHION. Shall I meet you there? For I must needs talk with you.

LORD FOPPINGTON. That I'm afraid mayn't be so praper; far the lards I commonly eat with, are people of a nice conversation, and you know, *Tam*, your education has been a little at large; but if you'll stay here, you'll find a family-dinner.[42] Hey Fellow! What is there for dinner? There's beef; I suppose, my brother will eat beef. Dear *Tam*, I'm glad to see thee in *England*, stap my vitals. [*Exit with his equipage*.[43]

YOUNG FASHION. Hell and Furies, is this to be borne?

LORY. Faith, Sir, I cou'd almost have given him a knock o'th' pate my self.

YOUNG FASHION. 'Tis enough; I will now shew thee the excess of my passion by being very calm: come, *Lory*, lay your loggerhead to mine, and in cool blood let us contrive his destruction.

LORY. Here comes a head, Sir, would contrive it better than us both, if he wou'd but join in the confederacy.

[*Enter* Coupler.

YOUNG FASHION. By this light, old *Coupler* alive still! Why, how now, Match-maker, art thou here still to plague the world with matrimony? You old Bawd, how have you the impudence to be hobling out of your grave years after you are rotten.

COUPLER. When you begin to rot, Sirrah, you'll go off like a pippin,[44] one winter will send you to the Devil. What mischief brings you home again? Ha! You young lascivious rogue you; let me put my hand in your bosom, Sirrah.

YOUNG FASHION. Stand off, old *Sodom*.

COUPLER. Nay, prithee now don't be so coy.

YOUNG FASHION. Keep your hands to your self, you old Dog you, or I'll wring your nose off.

COUPLER. Hast thou then been a year in *Italy*, and brought home a fool at last? By my conscience, the young fellows of this Age profit no more by their going abroad, than they do by their going to church.[45] Sirrah, Sirrah, if you are not hang'd before you come to my years, you'll know a cock from a hen. But come, I'm still a friend to thy person, though I have a contempt of thy understanding; and therefore I wou'd willingly know thy condition, that I may see whether thou stand'st in need of my assistance, for widows swarm, my Boy, the Town's infected with 'em.

YOUNG FASHION. I stand in need of any body's assistance, that will help me to cut my elder brother's throat, without the risque of being hang'd for him.

COUPLER. I'gad, Sirrah, I cou'd help thee to do him almost as good a turn, without the danger of being burnt in the hand for't.[46]

YOUNG FASHION. Sayest thou so, old Satan? Shew me but that, and my soul is thine.

COUPLER. Pox o'thy soul, give me thy warm body, Sirrah; I shall have a substantial title to it when I tell thee my project.

YOUNG FASHION. Out with it then, dear Dad, and take possession as soon as thou wilt.

COUPLER. Say'st thou so my *Hephestion*?[47] Why, then thus lies the scene – but hold, who's that? If we are heard we are undone.

YOUNG FASHION. What have you forgot, *Lory*?

COUPLER. Who, trusty *Lory*, is it thee?

LORY. At your service, Sir.

COUPLER. Give me thy hand, Old Boy, I'gad I did not know thee again, but I remember thy honesty, though I did not thy face; I think thou had'st like to have been hang'd once or twice for thy master.

LORY. Sir, I was very near once having that honour.

COUPLER. Well, live and hope, don't be discourag'd, eat with him, and drink with him, and do what he bids thee, and it may be thy reward at last, as well as another's.

Well, Sir, you must know I have done you the kindness to make up a match for your brother. [*To* Young Fashion.

YOUNG FASHION. Sir, I am very much beholden to you, truly.

COUPLER. You may be, Sirrah, before the wedding-day yet; the lady is a great heiress; fifteen hundred pound a year, and a great bag of money; the match is concluded, the writings are drawn, and the pipkin's to be crack'd[48] in a fortnight – now you must know, Stripling, (with respect to your mother) your brother's the son of a whore.

YOUNG FASHION. Good.

COUPLER. He has given me a bond of a thousand pounds for helping him to this fortune, and has promis'd me as much more in ready money upon the day of marriage, which I understand by a friend, he ne'r designs to pay me; if therefore you will be a generous young dog, and secure me five thousand pounds, I'll be a covetous old rogue, and help you to the lady.

YOUNG FASHION. I'gad, if thou canst bring this about, I'll have thy statue cast in brass. But don't you doat,[49] you old Pandor, you, when you talk at this rate?

COUPLER. That your youthful parts shall judge of; this plump partridge that I tell you of, lives in the country, fifty miles off, with her honoured parents, in a lonely old house which no body comes near; she never goes abroad, nor sees company at home: to prevent all misfortunes, she has her breeding[50] within doors, the parson of the parish teaches her to play upon the base-viol, the clerk to sing, her nurse to dress, and her father to dance: in short, no body can give you admittance there but I, nor can I do it any other way, than by making you pass for your brother.

YOUNG FASHION. And how the Devil wilt thou do that?

COUPLER. Without the Devil's aid, I warrant thee. Thy brother's face not one of the family ever saw, the whole business has been manag'd by me, and all the letters go through my hands: the last that was writ to Sir *Tunbelly Clumsey* (for that's the old gentleman's name) was to tell him, his Lordship wou'd be down in a fortnight to consummate. Now you shall go away immediately, pretend you writ that letter only to have the romantick pleasure of surprizing your mistress; fall desperately in love, as soon as you see her; make that your plea for marrying her immediately, and when the fatigue of the wedding-night's over, you shall send me a swinging purse of gold, you Dog you.

YOUNG FASHION. I'gad, Old Dad, I'll put my hand in thy bosom now. –

COUPLER. Ah, you young hot lusty Thief, let me muzzle you – [*Kissing*] – Sirrah, let me muzzle you.

YOUNG FASHION. [*Aside*] *P'sha, the old Letcher* –

COUPLER. Well, I'll warrant thou hast not a farthing of money in thy pocket now; no, one may see it in thy face –

YOUNG FASHION. Not a souse,[51] by *Jupiter*.

COUPLER. Must I advance then – well Sirrah, be at my lodgings in half an hour, and I'll see what may be done; we'll sign and seal, and eat a pullet,[52] and when I have given thee some farther instructions, thou sha't hoyst sail and be gone. – [*Kissing*] – T'other buss[53] and so adieu.

YOUNG FASHION. U'm, p'sha.

COUPLER. Ah, you young warm Dog you, what a delicious night will the bride have on't. [*Exit* Coupler.

YOUNG FASHION. So, *Lory*. Providence, thou see'st at last, takes care of men of merit; we are in a fair way to be great people.

LORY. Ay Sir, if the Devil don't step between the cup and the lip, as he uses to do.

YOUNG FASHION. Why, faith, he has play'd me many a damn'd trick to spoil my fortune, and I'gad I'm almost afraid he's at work about it again now, but if I shou'd tell thee how, thou'dst wonder at me.

LORY. Indeed, Sir, I shou'd not.

YOUNG FASHION. How dost know?

LORY. Because, Sir, I have wondred at you so often, I can wonder at you no more.

YOUNG FASHION. No; what wou'dst thou say, if a qualm of conscience shou'd spoil my design.

LORY. I wou'd eat my words, and wonder more than ever.

YOUNG FASHION. Why faith, *Lory*, though I am a young rake-hell, and have plaid many a roguish trick; this is so full grown a cheat, I find I must take pains to come up to't, I have scruples. –

LORY. They are strong symptoms of death; if you find they increase, pray, Sir, make your will.

YOUNG FASHION. No, my conscience shan't starve me neither. But thus far I will hearken to it, before I execute this project. I'll try my brother to the bottom, I'll speak to him with the temper of a philosopher, my reasons, (though they press him home,) shall yet be cloath'd with so much modesty, not one of all the truths they urge, shall be so naked to offend his sight; if he has yet so much humanity about him, as to assist me, (though with a moderate aid) I'll drop my project at his feet, and shew him how I can – do for him, much more than what I ask, he'd do for me. This one conclusive trial of him I resolve to make. –

Succeed or no, still victory's my lot,
If I subdue his heart, 'tis well; if not,
I shall subdue my conscience to my plot. [*Exeunt.*

Act II. Scene I.

[*Enter* Loveless *and* Amanda.]

LOVELESS. How do you like these lodgings, my Dear? For my part, I am so well pleas'd with 'em, I shall hardly remove whilst we stay in Town, if you are satisfy'd.

AMANDA. I am satisfy'd with every thing that pleases you; else I had not come to Town at all.

LOVELESS. O, a little of the noise and bussle of the world, sweetens the pleasures of retreat: we shall find the charms of our retirement doubled, when we return to it.

AMANDA. That pleasing prospect will be my chiefest entertainment, whilst (much against my will) I am oblig'd to stand surrounded with these empty pleasures, which 'tis so much the fashion to be fond of.

LOVELESS. I own most of them are indeed but empty; nay, so empty, that one wou'd wonder by what magick power they act, when they induce us to be vicious for their sakes. Yet some there are we may speak kindlier of: there are delights, (of which a private life is destitute) which may divert an honest man, and be a harmless entertainment to a virtuous woman. The conversation of the Town is one; and truly (with some small allowances) the plays, I think, may be esteem'd another.

AMANDA. The plays, I must confess, have some small charms, and wou'd have more, wou'd they restrain that loose obscene encouragement to vice, which shocks, if not the virtue of some women, at least the modesty of all.

LOVELESS. But till that reformation can be made, I wou'd not leave the wholsome corn, for some intruding tares that grow amongst it. Doubtless, the moral of a well-wrought scene, is of prevailing force. – Last night there happen'd one, that mov'd me strangely.

AMANDA. Pray, what was that?

LOVELESS. Why 'twas about – but 'tis not worth repeating.

AMANDA. Yes, pray let me know it.

LOVELESS. No, I think 'tis as well let alone.

AMANDA. Nay, now you make me have a mind to know.

LOVELESS. 'Twas a foolish thing: you'd perhaps grow jealous, shou'd I tell it you, tho' without cause Heaven knows.

AMANDA. I shall begin to think I have cause, if you persist in making it a secret.

LOVELESS. I'll then convince you, you have none, by making it no longer so. Know then, I happen'd in the play to find my very character, only with the addition of a *relapse*; which struck me so, I put a suddain stop to a most harmless entertainment, which till then, diverted me between the acts. 'Twas to admire the workmanship of nature, in the face of a young lady, that sate some distance from me, she was so exquisitely handsome.

AMANDA. So exquisitely handsome!

LOVELESS. Why do you repeat my words, my Dear?

AMANDA. Because you seem'd to speak 'em with such pleasure, I thought I might oblige you with their eccho.

LOVELESS. Then you are alarm'd, *Amanda*?

AMANDA. It is my duty to be so, when you are in danger.

LOVELESS. You are too quick in apprehending for me; all will be well when you have heard me out. I do confess I gaz'd upon her; nay, eagerly I gaz'd upon her.

AMANDA. Eagerly! That's with desire.

LOVELESS. No, I desir'd her not; I view'd her with a world of admiration, but not one glance of love.

AMANDA. Take heed of trusting to such nice distinctions.

LOVELESS. I did take heed; for observing in the play, that he who seem'd to represent me there, was by an accident like this, unwarily surpriz'd into a net, in which he lay a poor intangl'd slave, and brought a train of mischiefs on his head, I snatch'd my eyes away; they pleaded hard for leave to look again, but I grew absolute, and they obey'd.

AMANDA. Were they the only things that were inquisitive? Had I been in your place, my tongue, I fancy, had been curious too; I shou'd have ask'd her name, and where she liv'd, (yet still without design) – Who was she, I pray?

LOVELESS. Indeed I cannot tell.

AMANDA. You will not tell.

LOVELESS. By all that's sacred then, I did not ask.

AMANDA. Nor do you know what company was with her?

LOVELESS. I do not.

AMANDA. Then I am calm again.

LOVELESS. Why were you disturb'd?

AMANDA. Had I then no cause?

LOVELESS. None certainly.

AMANDA. I thought I had.

LOVELESS. But you thought wrong, *Amanda*: for turn the case, and let it be your story; shou'd you come home and tell me you had seen a handsome man, shou'd I grow jealous, because you had eyes?

AMANDA. But shou'd I tell you, he were exquisitely so; that I had gaz'd on him with admiration; that I had look'd with eager eyes upon him, shou'd you not think 'twere possible I might go one step farther, and enquire his name?

LOVELESS. – [*Aside*] *She has reason on her side: I have talk'd too much: but I must turn it off another way.* – Will you then make no difference, *Amanda*, between the language of our sex and yours? There is a modesty restrains your tongues, which makes you speak by halves when you commend; but roving flattery gives a loose to ours, which makes us still speak double what we think: you shou'd not therefore in so strict a sense take what I said to her advantage.

AMANDA. Those flights of flattery, Sir, are to our faces only: when women once are out of hearing, you are as modest in your commendations as we are. But I shan't put you to the trouble of further excuses, if you please this business shall rest here. Only give me leave to wish both for your peace and mine, that you may never meet this miracle of beauty more.

LOVELESS. I am content.

[*Enter* Servant.

SERVANT. Madam, there's a young lady at the door in a chair, desires to know whether your Ladyship sees company. I think her name is *Berinthia*.

AMANDA. O dear! 'Tis a relation I have not seen these five years. Pray her to walk in. [*Exit* Servant.
Here's another beauty for you. She was young when I saw her last; but I hear she's grown extremely handsome. [*To* Loveless.

LOVELESS. Don't you be jealous now; for I shall gaze upon her too.

[*Enter* Berinthia.

LOVELESS. [*Aside*] *Ha! By Heavens the very woman!*

BERINTHIA. Dear *Amanda*, I did not expect to meet with you in Town. [*Saluting* Amanda.

AMANDA. Sweet Cousin, I'm overjoy'd to see you. [*To* Loveless] Mr. *Loveless*, here's a relation and a friend of mine, I desire you'll be better acquainted with.

LOVELESS. If my wife never desires a harder thing, Madam, her request will be easily granted. [*Saluting* Berinthia.

BERINTHIA. I think, Madam, I ought to wish you joy. [*To* Amanda.

AMANDA. Joy! Upon what?

BERINTHIA. Upon your marriage: you were a widow when I saw you last.

LOVELESS. You ought rather, Madam, to wish me joy upon that, since I am the only gainer.

BERINTHIA. If she has got so good a husband as the World reports, she has gain'd enough to expect the complements of her friends upon it.

LOVELESS. Ay, the World is so favourable to me, to allow I deserve that title, I hope 'tis so just to my wife to own I derive it from her.

BERINTHIA. Sir, it is so just to you both, to own you are (and deserve to be) the happiest pair that live in it.

LOVELESS. I'm afraid we shall lose that character, Madam, whenever you happen to change your condition.

[*Enter* Servant.

SERVANT. Sir, my Lord *Foppington* presents his humble service to you, and desires to know how you do. He but just now heard you were in Town. He's at the next door; and if it be not inconvenient, he'll come and wait upon you.

LOVELESS. Lord *Foppington*! – I know him not.

BERINTHIA. Not his dignity, perhaps, but you do his person. 'Tis Sir *Novelty*; he has bought a barony[54] in order to marry a great fortune: his patent[55] has not been past eight and forty hours, and he has already sent how do'ye's to all the Town, to make 'em acquainted with his title.

LOVELESS. Give my service to his Lordship, and let him know, I am proud of the honour he intends me. [*Exit* Servant] Sure this addition of quality, must have so improv'd this coxcomb, he can't but be very good company for a quarter of an hour.

AMANDA. Now it moves my pity more than my mirth, to see a man whom nature has made no fool, be so very industrious to pass for an ass.

LOVELESS. No, there you are wrong, *Amanda*; you shou'd never bestow your pity upon those who take pains for your contempt. Pity those whom nature abuses, but never those who abuse nature.

BERINTHIA. Besides, the Town wou'd be robb'd of one of its chief diversions, if it shou'd become a crime to laugh at a fool.

AMANDA. I could never yet perceive the Town inclin'd to part with any of its diversions, for the sake of their being crimes; but I have seen it very fond of some, I think had little else to recommend 'em.

BERINTHIA. I doubt, *Amanda*, you are grown its enemy, you speak with so much warmth against it.

AMANDA. I must confess I am not much its friend.

BERINTHIA. Then give me leave to make you mine, by not engaging in its quarrel.

AMANDA. You have many stronger claims than that, *Berinthia*, whenever you think fit to plead your title.

LOVELESS. You have done well to engage a second,[56] my Dear; for here comes one will be apt to call you to an account for your country-principles.

[*Enter* Lord Foppington.

LORD FOPPINGTON. Sir, I am your most humble servant. [*To* Loveless.

LOVELESS. I wish you joy, my Lord.

LORD FOPPINGTON. O Lard, Sir – Madam, your Ladyship's welcome to Tawn.

AMANDA. I wish your Lordship joy.

LORD FOPPINGTON. O Heavens, Madam –

LOVELESS. My Lord this young Lady is a relation of my wives.

LORD FOPPINGTON. The beautifullest race of people upon earth. [*Saluting her*] Rat me. Dear *Loveless*, I'm overjoy'd to see you have brought your family to Tawn again; I am, stap my vitals – [*Aside*] *far I design to lye with your wife.* – [*To* Amanda] Far Gad's sake, Madam, haw has your Ladyship been able to subsist thus long, under the fatigue of a country life?

AMANDA. My life has been very far from that, my Lord; it has been a very quiet one.

LORD FOPPINGTON. Why, that's the fatigue I speak of Madam: for 'tis impossible to be quiet, without thinking: Now thinking is to me, the greatest fatigue in the world.

AMANDA. Does not your Lordship love reading then?

LORD FOPPINGTON. Oh, passionately, Madam – but I never think of what I read.

BERINTHIA. Why, can your Lordship read without thinking?

LORD FOPPINGTON. O Lard – Can your Ladyship pray without devotion – Madam?

AMANDA. Well, I must own I think books the best entertainment in the world.

LORD FOPPINGTON. I am so much of your Ladyship's mind, Madam, that I have a private gallery, where I walk sometimes, is furnish'd with nothing but books and looking-glasses. Madam, I have gilded 'em, and rang'd 'em so prettily, before Gad, it is the most entertaining thing in the world to walk and look upon 'em.

AMANDA. Nay, I love a neat library too; but 'tis, I think, the inside of the book, shou'd recommend it most to us.

LORD FOPPINGTON. That I must confess I am not altogether so fand of. Far to mind the inside of a book, is to entertain one's self with the forc'd product of another man's brain. Naw I think a Man of Quality and breeding may be much better diverted with the natural sprauts of his own. But to say the truth, Madam, let a man love reading never so well, when once he comes to know this Tawn, he finds so many better ways of passing the four and twenty hours, that 'twere ten thousand pities he shou'd consume his time in that. Far example, Madam, my life: my life, Madam, is a perpetual stream of pleasure, that glides through such a variety of entertainments, I believe the wisest of our ancestors never had the least conception of any of 'em.

I rise, Madam, about ten a-clock. I don't rise sooner, because 'tis the worst thing in the world for the complexion; nat that I pretend to be a beau: but a man must endeavour to look wholesome, lest he make so nauseous a figure in the side-bax, the ladies shou'd be compell'd to turn their eyes upon the play. So at ten a-clock I say I rise. Naw if I find 'tis a good day, I resalve to take a turn in the park, and see the fine women: so huddle on my cloaths, and get dress'd by one. If it be nasty weather, I take a turn in the chocolate-hause; where, as you walk, Madam, you have the prettiest prospect in the world; you have looking-glasses all round you. – but I'm afraid I tire the company.

BERINTHIA. Not at all. Pray go on.

LORD FOPPINGTON. Why then, Ladies, from thence I go to dinner at *Lacket*'s, where you are so nicely and delicately serv'd, that, stap my vitals, they shall compose you a dish no bigger than a saucer, shall come to fifty shillings. Between eating my dinner (and washing my mouth, Ladies) I spend my time, 'till I go to the play; where, 'till nine a-clack, I entertain my self with looking upon the company; and usually dispose of one hour more in leading them aut. So there's twelve of the four and twenty pretty well over.

The other twelve, Madam, are dispos'd of in two articles: in the first four, I toast my self drunk, and in t'other eight, I sleep my self sober again. Thus, Ladies, you see my life is an eternal raund of delights.

LOVELESS. 'Tis a heavenly one, indeed.

AMANDA. But I thought, my Lord, you *Beaux*, spent a great deal of your time in intrigues:[57] you have given us no account of them yet.

LORD FOPPINGTON. – [*Aside*] *Soh; she wou'd enquire into my amours – that's jealousie – she begins to be in love with me.* – [*To Amanda*] Why, Madam – as to time for my intrigues, I usually make detachments of it from my other pleasures, according to the exigency: far your Ladyship may please to take notice, that those who intrigue with Women of Quality, have rarely occasion far above half an hour at a time: people of that rank being under those decorums, they can seldom give you a langer view than will just serve to shoot 'em flying. So that the course of my other pleasures, is not very much interrupted by my amours.

LOVELESS. But your Lordship is now become a pillar of the State, you must attend the weighty affairs of the nation.

LORD FOPPINGTON. Sir – as to weighty affairs – I leave them to weighty heads. I never intend mine shall be a burthen to my body.

LOVELESS. O but you'll find the House will expect your attendance.

LORD FOPPINGTON. Sir you'll find the House will compound for my appearance.

LOVELESS. But your friends will take it ill if you don't attend their particular causes.

LORD FOPPINGTON. Not, Sir, if I come time enough, to give 'em my particular vote.

BERINTHIA. But pray, my Lord, how do you dispose of your self on *Sundays*; for that, methinks, is a day shou'd hang wretchedly upon your hands.

LORD FOPPINGTON. Why Faith, Madam – *Sunday* – is a vile day I must confess. I intend to move for leave to bring in a bill, that players may work upon it, as well as the hackney-coaches.[58] Tho' this I must say for the government, it leaves us the churches to entertain us – but then again, they begin so abominable early, a man must rise by candle-light to get dress'd by the psalm.

BERINTHIA. Pray which church does your Lordship most oblige with your presence?

LORD FOPPINGTON. Oh, Saint *James*'s, Madam – there's much the best company.

AMANDA. Is there good preaching too?

LORD FOPPINGTON. Why Faith, Madam – I can't tell. A man must have very little to do there, that can give an account of the sermon.

BERINTHIA. You can give us an account of the ladies at least?

LORD FOPPINGTON. Or I deserve to be excommunicated. – There is my Lady *Tattle*, my Lady *Prate*, my Lady *Titter*, my Lady *Leer*, my Lady *Giggle*, and my Lady *Grin*. These sit in the front of the boxes, and all church time, are the prettiest company in the world, stap my vitals. [*To* Amanda] Mayn't we hope for the honour to see your Ladyship added to our society, Madam?

AMANDA. Alas, my Lord, I am the worst company in the world at church: I'm apt to mind the prayers, or the sermon, or –

LORD FOPPINGTON. One is indeed strangely apt at church, to mind what one should not do. But I hope, Madam, at one time or other, I shall have the honour to lead your Ladyship to your coach there. [*Aside*] *Methinks she seems strangely pleas'd with every thing I say to her. – 'Tis a vast pleasure to receive encouragement from a woman, before her husband's face – I have a good mind to pursue my conquest, and speak the thing plainly to her at once – I gad I'll do't, and that in so cavallier a manner, she shall be surpris'd at it.* – Ladies, I'll take my leave; I'm afraid I begin to grow troublesome with the length of my visit.

AMANDA. Your Lordship's too entertaining to grow troublesome any where.

LORD FOPPINGTON. – [*Aside*] *That now was as much as if she had said – pray lye with me. I'll let her see I'm quick of apprehension.* – [*To* Amanda] O Lard, Madam, I had like to have forgot a secret, I must needs tell your Ladyship. [*To* Loveless] *Ned,* you must not be so jealous now as to listen.

LOVELESS. Not I, my Lord; I am too fashionable a husband to pry into the secrets of my wife.

LORD FOPPINGTON. I am in love with you, to desperation, strike me speechless. [*To* Amanda, *squeezing her hand.*

AMANDA. Then thus I return your passion; an impudent fool! [*Giving him a box o'th' ear.*

LORD FOPPINGTON. Gads Curse, Madam, I'm a peer of the realm.

LOVELESS. Hey, what the Devil do you affront my wife, Sir, nay then – [*They draw and fight.*

AMANDA. Ah! What has my folly done? [*The women run shrieking for help*] Help, murder, help: part 'em for Heaven's sake.

LORD FOPPINGTON. Ah – quite through the body – stap my vitals. [*Falling back, and leaning upon his sword.*

[*Enter* Servants.

LOVELESS. I hope I han't kill'd the fool however – bare him up! Where's your wound? [*Running to him.*

LORD FOPPINGTON. Just through the guts.

LOVELESS. Call a surgeon there: unbutton him quickly.

LORD FOPPINGTON. Ay, pray make haste.

LOVELESS. This mischief you may thank your self for.

LORD FOPPINGTON. I may so – love's the Devil indeed, *Ned.*

[*Enter* Seringe *and* Servant.

SERVANT. Here's Mr. *Seringe,* Sir, was just going by the door.

LORD FOPPINGTON. He's the welcom'st man alive.

SERINGE. Stand by, stand by, stand by. Pray Gentlemen stand by. Lord have mercy upon us, did you never see a man run through the body before? Pray stand by.

LORD FOPPINGTON. Ah, Mr. *Seringe* – I'm a dead man.

SERINGE. A dead man and I by – I shou'd laugh to see that, I gad.

LOVELESS. Prithee don't stand prating, but look upon his wound.

SERINGE. Why, what if I won't look upon his wound this hour, Sir?

LOVELESS. Why then he'll bleed to death, Sir.

SERINGE. Why, then I'll fetch him to life again, Sir.

LOVELESS. 'Slife he's run through the guts I tell thee.

SERINGE. Wou'd he were run through the heart, I shou'd get the more credit by his cure. Now I hope you're satisfy'd? – Come, now let me come at him; now let me come at him. [*Viewing his wound*] Oons, what a gash is here? – Why, Sir, a man may drive a coach and six horses into your body.

LORD FOPPINGTON. Ho –

SERINGE. Why, what the Devil, have you run the gentleman through with a sythe – [*Aside*] *a little prick, between the skin and the ribs, that's all.*

LOVELESS. Let me see his wound.

SERINGE. Then you shall dress it, Sir, for if any body looks upon it, I won't.

LOVELESS. Why, thou art the veriest coxcomb I ever saw.

SERINGE. Sir, I am not master of my trade for nothing.

LORD FOPPINGTON. Surgeon.

SERINGE. Well, Sir.

LORD FOPPINGTON. Is there any hopes?

SERINGE. Hopes? – I can't tell. – What are you willing to give for your cure?

LORD FOPPINGTON. Five hundred paunds with pleasure.

SERINGE. Why then perhaps there may be hopes. But we must avoid farther delay. Here: help the gentleman into a chair, and carry him to my house presently, that's the properest place, – [*Aside*] *to bubble him out of his money.* – Come, a chair, a chair quickly – there, in with him. [*They put him into a chair.*

LORD FOPPINGTON. Dear *Loveless* – adieu. If I die – I forgive thee; and if I live – I hope thou wilt do as much by me. I'm very sorry you and I shou'd quarrel; but I hope here's an end on't, for if you are satisfy'd – I am.

LOVELESS. I shall hardly think it worth my prosecuting any farther, so you may be at rest, Sir.

LORD FOPPINGTON. Thou art a generous fellow, strike me dumb. – [*Aside*] *But thou hast an impertinent wife, stap my vitals.*

SERINGE. So, carry him off, carry him off, we shall have him prate himself into a fever by and by, carry him off. [*Exit* Seringe *with* Lord Foppington.

AMANDA. Now on my knees, my Dear, let me ask your pardon for my indiscretion, my own I never shall obtain.

LOVELESS. O! There's no harm done: you serv'd him well.

AMANDA. He did indeed deserve it. But I tremble to think how dear my indiscreet resentment might have cost you.

LOVELESS. O no matter, never trouble your self about that.

BERINTHIA. For Heaven's sake, what was't he did to you?

AMANDA. O nothing; he only squeez'd me kindly by the hand, and frankly offer'd me a coxcomb's heart. I know I was to blame to resent it as I did, since nothing but a quarrel cou'd ensue. But the fool so surpriz'd me with his insolence, I was not mistress of my fingers.

BERINTHIA. Now I dare swear, he thinks you had 'em at great command, they obey'd you so readily.

[*Enter* Worthy.

WORTHY. Save you, save you good People: I'm glad to find you all alive; I met a wounded peer carrying off: for Heaven's sake what was the matter?

LOVELESS. O a trifle: he wou'd have lain with my wife before my face, so she oblig'd him with a box o'th' ear, and I run him through the body: that was all.

WORTHY. *Bagatelle*[59] on all sides. But, pray Madam, how long has this noble Lord been an humble servant of yours?

AMANDA. This is the first I have heard on't. So I suppose 'tis his quality more than his love, has brought him into this adventure. He thinks his title an authentick passport to every woman's heart, below the degree of a peeress.

WORTHY. He's coxcomb enough to think any thing. But I wou'd not have you brought into trouble for him: I hope there's no danger of his life?

LOVELESS. None at all: he's fallen into the hands of a roguish surgeon, I perceive designs to frighten a little money out of him. But I saw his wound, 'tis nothing; he may go to the play to night if he pleases.

WORTHY. I am glad you have corrected him without farther mischief. And now, Sir, if these ladies have no farther service for you, you'll oblige me if you can go to the place I spoke to you of t'other day.

LOVELESS. With all my heart. – [*Aside*] *Tho' I cou'd wish, methinks, to stay and gaze a little longer on that creature. Good Gods! How beautiful she is – but what have I to do with beauty? I have already had my portion, and must not covet more.* – [*To* Worthy] Come, Sir, when you please.

WORTHY. Ladies, your servant.

AMANDA. Mr. *Loveless*, pray one word with you before you go.

LOVELESS. [*To* Worthy] I'll overtake you, Sir, [*Exit* Worthy] What wou'd my Dear?

AMANDA. Only a woman's foolish question, how do you like my couzen here?

LOVELESS. Jealous already, *Amanda*?

AMANDA. Not at all; I ask you for another reason.

LOVELESS. – [*Aside*] *Whate'er her reason be, I must not tell her true.* – [*To* Amanda] Why, I confess she's handsome. But you must not think I slight your kinswoman, if I own to you, of all the women who may claim that character, she is the last wou'd triumph in my heart.

AMANDA. I'm satisfi'd.

LOVELESS. Now tell me why you ask'd?

AMANDA. At night I will. Adieu.

LOVELESS. I'm yours. [*Kissing her. Exit* Loveless.

AMANDA. – [*Aside*] *I'm glad to find he does not like her; for I have a great mind to perswade her to come and live with me.* – [*To* Berinthia] Now dear *Berinthia*, let me enquire a little into your affairs: for I do assure you I am enough your friend, to interest my self in every thing that concerns you.

BERINTHIA. You formerly have given me such proofs on't, I shou'd be very much to blame to doubt it. I am sorry I have no secrets to trust you with, that I might convince you how entire a confidence I durst repose in you.

AMANDA. Why is it possible, that one so young and beautiful as you shou'd live and have no secrets?

BERINTHIA. What secrets do you mean?

AMANDA. Lovers.

BERINTHIA. O twenty; but not one secret one amongst 'em. Lovers in this age have too much honour to do any thing underhand; they do all above board.

AMANDA. That now methinks wou'd make me hate a man.

BERINTHIA. But the women of the Town are of another mind: for by this means a lady may (with the expence of a few coquet glances) lead twenty fools about in a string, for two or three years together. Whereas, if she shou'd allow 'em greater favours, and oblige 'em to secresie, she wou'd not keep one of 'em a fortnight.

AMANDA. There's something indeed in that to satisfie the vanity of a woman, but I can't comprehend how the men find their account in it.

BERINTHIA. Their entertainment I must confess is a riddle to me. For there's very few of them ever get farther, than a bow and an ogle. I have half a score for my share, who follow me all over the Town; and at the play, the park, and the church, do (with their eyes) say the violent'st things to me – but I never hear any more of 'em.

AMANDA. What can be the reason of that?

BERINTHIA. One reason is, they don't know how to go farther. They have had so little practice, they don't understand the trade. But besides their ignorance, you must know there is not one of my half score lovers but what follows half a score mistresses. Now their affections being divided amongst so many, are not strong enough for any one to make 'em pursue her to the purpose. Like a young puppy in a warren, they have a flirt at all, and catch none.

AMANDA. Yet they seem to have a torrent of love to dispose of.

BERINTHIA. They have so: but 'tis like the rivers of a modern philosopher[60] (whose works, tho' a woman, I have read) it sets out with a violent stream, splits in a thousand branches, and is all lost in the sands.

AMANDA. But do you think this river of love runs all its course without doing any mischief? Do you think it overflows nothing.

BERINTHIA. O yes; 'tis true it never breaks into any bodies ground that has the least fence about it; but it overflows all the commons that lye in its way. And this is the utmost atchievement of those dreadful champions in the field of love – the beaux.

AMANDA. But prithee, *Berinthia*, instruct me a little farther, for I'm so great a novice, I am almost asham'd on't. My husband's leaving me whilst I was young and fond, threw me into that depth of discontent, that ever since I have led so private and recluse a life, my ignorance is scarce conceivable. I therefore fain wou'd be instructed: not (Heaven knows) that what you call intrigues have any charms for me; my love and principles are too well fix'd. The practick part of all unlawful love is –

BERINTHIA. O 'tis abominable: but for the speculative; that we must all confess is entertaining. The conversation of all the virtuous women in the Town turns upon that and new cloaths.

AMANDA. Pray be so just then to me, to believe, 'tis with a world of innocency I wou'd enquire, whether you think those women we call Women of Reputation, do really 'scape all other men, as they do those shadows of 'em, the beaux.

BERINTHIA. O no, *Amanda*; there are a sort of men make dreadful work amongst 'em: men that may be call'd, the Beaux Antipathy, for they agree in nothing but walking upon two legs:
These have brains: the beau has none.
These are in love with their mistress: the beau with himself.
They take care of her reputation: he's industrious to destroy it.
They are decent: he's a fop.
They are sound: he's rotten.[61]
They are men: he's an ass.

AMANDA. If this be their character, I fancy we had here e'en now a pattern of 'em both.

BERINTHIA. His Lordship and Mr. *Worthy*?

AMANDA. The same.

BERINTHIA. As for the Lord, he's eminently so: and for the other, I can assure you, there's not a man in Town who has a better interest with the women, that are worth having an interest with. But 'tis all private: he's like a Back-stair Minister at Court, who, whilst the reputed favorites are sauntering in the Bed-Chamber, is ruling the roast in the Closet.

AMANDA. He answers then the opinion I had ever of him. Heavens! What a difference there is between a man like him, and that vain nauseous fop, Sir *Novelty*. [*Taking her hand*] I must acquaint you with a secret, Couzen. 'Tis not that fool alone, has talk'd to me of love. *Worthy* has been tampering too. 'Tis true, he has don't [62] in vain: not all his charms or art have power to shake me. My love, my duty, and my virtue, are such faithful guards, I need not fear my heart shou'd e'er betray me. But what I wonder at is this. I find I did not start at his proposal, as when it came from one whom I contemn'd. I therefore mention his attempt, that I may learn from you, whence it proceeds; that vice (which cannot change its nature) shou'd so far change at least its shape, as that the self-same crime propos'd from one shall seem a monster gaping at your ruine; when from another it shall look so kind, as tho' it were your friend, and never meant to harm you. Whence think you can this difference proceed? For 'tis not love, Heaven knows.

BERINTHIA. O no; I wou'd not for the world believe it were. But possibly, shou'd there a dreadful sentence pass upon you, to undergo the rage of both their passions, the pain you'd apprehend from one, might seem so trivial to the other, the danger wou'd not quite so much alarm you.

AMANDA. Fy, fy, *Berinthia*, you wou'd indeed alarm me, cou'd you incline me to a thought, that all the merit of mankind combin'd, cou'd shake that tender love I bear my husband. No! He sits triumphant in my heart, and nothing can dethrone him.

BERINTHIA. But shou'd he abdicate again, do you think you shou'd preserve the vacant throne ten tedious winters more in hopes of his return?

AMANDA. Indeed I think I shou'd. Tho' I confess, after those obligations he has to me, shou'd he abandon me once more, my heart wou'd grow extreamly urgent with me to root him thence, and cast him out for ever.

BERINTHIA. Were I that thing they call a slighted wife, somebody shou'd run the risque of being that thing they call – a husband.

AMANDA. O fy, *Berinthia*, no revenge shou'd ever be taken against a husband. But to wrong his bed is a vengeance which of all vengeance –

BERINTHIA. Is the sweetest, ha, ha, ha. Don't I talk madly?

AMANDA. Madly indeed.

BERINTHIA. Yet I'm very innocent.

AMANDA. That I dare swear you are. I know how to make allowances for your humour. You were always very entertaining company; but I find since marriage and widowhood have shewn you the world a little, you are very much improv'd.

BERINTHIA. [*Aside*] *Alack a day, there has gone more than that to improve me, if she knew all.*

AMANDA. For Heaven's sake, *Berinthia*, tell me what way I shall take to perswade you to come and live with me?

BERINTHIA. Why, one way in the world there is – and but one.

AMANDA. Pray which is that?

BERINTHIA. It is, to assure me – I shall be very welcome.

AMANDA. If that be all, you shall e'en lye here to night.

BERNITHIA. To night?

AMANDA. Yes, to night.

BERINTHIA. Why, the people where I lodge will think me mad.

AMANDA. Let 'em think what they please.

BERINTHIA. Say you so, *Amanda*? Why, then they shall think what they please: for I'm a young widow, and I care not what any body thinks. Ah, *Amanda*, it's a delicious thing to be a young widow.

AMANDA. You'll hardly make me think so.

BERINTHIA. Phu, because you are in love with your husband: but that is not every woman's case.

AMANDA. I hope 'twas yours, at least.

BERINTHIA. Mine, say ye? Now have I a great mind to tell you a lie, but I shou'd do it so awkardly, you'd find me out.

AMANDA. Then e'en speak the truth.

BERINTHIA. Shall I? – Then after all I did love him, *Amanda* – as a nun does penance.

AMANDA. Why did not you refuse to marry him then?

BERINTHIA. Because my mother wou'd have whipt me.

AMANDA. How did you live together?

BERINTHIA. Like man and wife, asunder.
He lov'd the country, I the Town.
He hawks and hounds, I coaches and equipage.
He eating and drinking, I carding and playing,
He the sound of a horn, I the squeak of a fiddle.
We were dull company at table, worse abed.
Whenever we met, we gave one another the spleen.
And never agreed but once, which was about lying alone.

AMANDA. But tell me one thing, truly and sincerely.

BERINTHIA. What's that?

AMANDA. Notwithstanding all these jars, did not his death at last – extremely trouble you?

BERINTHIA. O yes: not that my present pangs were so very violent, but the after-pains were intollerable. I was forc'd to wear a beastly widow's band a twelvemonth for't.

AMANDA. Women, I find, have different inclinations.

BERINTHIA. Women, I find, keep different company. When your husband ran away from you, if you had fallen into some of my acquaintance, 'twou'd have sav'd you many a tear. But you go and live with a grandmother, a bishop, and an old nurse; which was enough to make any woman break her heart for her husband. Pray, *Amanda*, if ever you are a widow again, keep your self so as I do.

AMANDA. Why do you then resolve you'll never marry?

BERINTHIA. O, no; I resolve I will.

AMANDA. How so?

BERINTHIA. That I never may.

AMANDA. You banter me.

BERINTHIA. Indeed I don't. But I consider I'm a woman, and form my resolutions accordingly.

AMANDA. Well, my opinion is, form what resolution you will, matrimony will be the end on't.

BERINTHIA. Faith it won't.

AMANDA. How do you know?

BERINTHIA. I'm sure on't.

AMANDA. Why, do you think 'tis impossible for you to fall in love?

BERINTHIA. No.

AMANDA. Nay, but to grow so passionately fond, that nothing but the man you love can give you rest?

BERINTHIA. Well, what then?

AMANDA. Why, then you'll marry him.

BERINTHIA. How do you know that?

AMANDA. Why, what can you do else?

BERINTHIA. Nothing – but sit and cry.

AMANDA. Psha.

BERINTHIA. Ah, poor *Amanda*; you have led a country life; but if you'll consult the widows of this Town, they'll tell you, you shou'd never take a lease of a house you can hire for a quarter's warning. [*Exeunt.*

Act III. Scene I.

[*Enter* Lord Foppington *and* Servant.]

LORD FOPPINGTON. Hey, Fellow, let the coach come to the door.

SERVANT. Will your Lordship venture so soon to expose your self to the weather?

LORD FOPPINGTON. Sir, I will venture as soon as I can, to expose my self to the ladies; tho' give me my cloak however, for in that side-box, what between the air that comes in at the door on one side, and the intolerable warmth of the masks on t'other, a man gets so many heats and colds, 'twou'd destroy the canstitution of a harse.

SERVANT. I wish your Lordship wou'd please to keep house a little longer, I'm afraid your Honour does not well consider your wound. [*Putting on his cloak.*

LORD FOPPINGTON. My wound? – I wou'd not be in eclipse another day, tho' I had as many wounds in my guts as I have had in my heart.

[*Enter* Young Fashion.

YOUNG FASHION. Brother, your servant. How do you find your self to day?

LORD FOPPINGTON. So well, that I have arder'd my coach to the door: so there's no great danger of death this baut, *Tam*.

YOUNG FASHION. I'm very glad of it.

LORD FOPPINGTON. – [*Aside*] *That I believe's a lie.* – Prithee, *Tam*, tell me one thing. Did nat your heart cut a caper up to your mauth, when you heard I was run through the bady?

YOUNG FASHION. Why do you think it shou'd?

LORD FOPPINGTON. Because I remember mine did so, when I heard my father was shat through the head.

YOUNG FASHION. It then did very ill.

LORD FOPPINGTON. Prithee, why so?

YOUNG FASHION. Because he us'd you very well.

LORD FOPPINGTON. Well? – naw strike me dumb, he starv'd me. He has let me want a thausand women, for want of a thausand pound.

YOUNG FASHION. Then he hindred you from making a great many ill bargains, for I think no woman is worth money, that will take money.

LORD FOPPINGTON. If I were a younger brother, I shou'd think so too.

YOUNG FASHION. Why, is it possible you can value a woman that's to be bought.

LORD FOPPINGTON. Prithee, why not as well as a pad-nag?[63]

YOUNG FASHION. Because a woman has a heart to dispose of; a horse has none.

LORD FOPPINGTON. Look you *Tam*, of all things that belang to a woman, I have an aversion to her heart: far when once a woman has given you her heart – you can never get rid of the rest of her body.

YOUNG FASHION. This is strange doctrine. But pray in your amours how is it with your own heart?

LORD FOPPINGTON. Why, my heart in my amours – is like my heart aut of my amours: *à la glace.*[64]

My bady *Tam* is a watch; and my heart is the pendulum to it; whilst the finger runs raund to every hour in the circle, that still beats the same time.

YOUNG FASHION. Then you are seldom much in love?

LORD FOPPINGTON. Never, stap my vitals.

YOUNG FASHION. Why then did you make all this bustle about *Amanda*?

LORD FOPPINGTON. Because she was a woman of an insolent virtue, and I thought my self prickt in honour to debauch her.

YOUNG FASHION. Very well. – [*Aside*] *Here's a rare fellow for you, to have the spending of five thousand pounds a year. But now for my business with him.* – Brother, tho' I know to talk to you of business (especially of money) is a theme not quite so entertaining to you as that of the ladies; my necessities are such, I hope you'll have patience to hear me.

LORD FOPPINGTON. The greatness of your necessities *Tam*, is the worst argument in the world for your being patiently heard. I do believe you are going to make me a very good speech, but, strike me dumb, it has the worst beginning of any speech I have heard this twelve-month.

YOUNG FASHION. I'm very sorry you think so.

LORD FOPPINGTON. I do believe thau art. But come, let's know thy affair quickly, far 'tis a new play, and I shall be so rumpled and squeez'd with pressing through the crawd, to get to my servant, the women will think I have lain all night in my cloaths.

YOUNG FASHION. Why then (that I may not be the author of so great a misfortune) my case in a word is this.

The necessary expences of my travels have so much exceeded the wretched income of my annuity,[65] that I have been forc'd to mortgage it for five hundred pounds, which is spent; so that unless you are so kind to assist me in redeeming it, I know no remedy, but to go take a purse.[66]

LORD FOPPINGTON. Why, Faith *Tam* – to give you my sense of the thing, I do think taking a purse the best remedy in the world; for if you succeed, you are reliev'd that way; if you are taken – you are reliev'd t'other.

YOUNG FASHION. I'm glad to see you are in so pleasant a humour, I hope I shall find the effects on't.

LORD FOPPINGTON. Why, do you then really think it a reasonable thing I shou'd give you five hundred paunds?

YOUNG FASHION. I do not ask it as a due, Brother, I am willing to receive it as a favour.

LORD FOPPINGTON. Thau art willing to receive it any haw, strike me speechless. But these are damn'd times to give money in, taxes are so great, repairs so exorbitant, tenants such rogues, and periwigs so dear, that the Devil take me, I am reduc'd to that extremity in my cash, I have been forc'd to retrench in that one article of sweet pawder,[67] till I have braught it dawn to five guineas a manth. Naw judge, *Tam*, whether I can spare you five hundred paunds.

YOUNG FASHION. If you can't, I must starve, that's all. – [*Aside*] *Damn him.*

LORD FOPPINGTON. All I can say is, you shou'd have been a better husband.[68]

YOUNG FASHION. Oons if you can't live upon five thousand a year, how do you think I shou'd do't upon two hundred?

LORD FOPPINGTON. Don't be in a passion, *Tam*, far passion is the most unbecoming thing in the world – to the face.

Look you, I don't love to say any thing to you to make you melancholy; but upon this occasion I must take leave to put you in mind, that a running horse[69] does require more attendance than a coach-horse. Nature has made some difference 'twixt you and I.

YOUNG FASHION. Yes, she has made you older. – [*Aside*] *Pox take her.*

LORD FOPPINGTON. That is nat all, *Tam*.

YOUNG FASHION. Why, what is there else?

LORD FOPPINGTON. – Ask the ladies. [*Looking first upon himself, then upon his brother.*

YOUNG FASHION. Why, thou essence-bottle,[70] thou musk-cat,[71] dost thou then think thou hast any advantage over me, but what Fortune has given thee?

LORD FOPPINGTON. I do – stap my vitals.

YOUNG FASHION. Now, by all that's great and powerful, thou art the Prince of Coxcombs.

LORD FOPPINGTON. Sir – I am praud of being at the head of so prevailing a party.

YOUNG FASHION. Will nothing then provoke thee? – Draw Coward.

LORD FOPPINGTON. Look you, *Tam*, you know I have always taken you for a mighty dull fellow, and here is one of the foolishest plats[72] broke out, that I have seen a long time. Your paverty makes your life so burthensome to you, you wou'd provoke me to a quarrel, in hopes either to slip through my lungs into my estate, or to get your self run through the guts, to put an end to your pain. But I will disappoint you in both your designs; far with the temper of a philasapher, and the discretion of a statesman – I will go to the play with my sword in my scabbard. [*Exit* Lord Foppington.

YOUNG FASHION. Soh, farewel Snuff-Box. And now, conscience, I defie thee. *Lory*.

[*Enter* Lory.

LORY. Sir.

YOUNG FASHION. Here's rare news, *Lory*: his Lordship has given me a pill has purg'd off all my scruples.

LORY. Then my heart's at ease again: for I have been in a lamentable fright, Sir, ever since your conscience had the impudence to intrude into your company.

YOUNG FASHION. Be at peace; it will come there no more. My brother has given it a wring by the nose, and I have kick'd it down stairs. So run away to the inn; get the horses ready quickly, and bring 'em to Old *Coupler*'s, without a moment's delay.

LORY. Then, Sir, you are going strait about the fortune?

YOUNG FASHION. I am; away. Fly, *Lory*.

LORY. The happiest day I ever saw. I'm upon the wing already. [*Exeunt several ways*.

Scene II.

[*A garden. Enter* Loveless *and* Servant.]

LOVELESS. Is my wife within?

SERVANT. No, Sir, she has been gone out this half hour.

LOVELESS. 'Tis well; leave me.

[*Solus*.

Sure Fate has yet some business to be done,
Before *Amanda*'s heart and mine must rest:
Else, why amongst those legions of her sex,
Which throng the world,
Shou'd she pick out for her companion
The only one on earth,
Whom nature has endow'd for her undoing.
Undoing was't, I said?–who shall undo her?
Is not her empire fix'd? Am I not hers?
Did she not rescue me, a grovling slave?
When chain'd and bound by that black tyrant Vice
I labour'd in his vilest drudgery,
Did she not ransome me, and set me free?
Nay more:
When by my follies sunk
To a poor tatter'd despicable beggar,
Did she not lift me up to envied fortune?
Give me her self, and all that she possest?
Without a thought of more return,
Than what a poor repenting heart might make her.
Han't she done this? And if she has,
Am I not strongly bound to love her for it?
To love her!–Why, do I not love her then?
By Earth and Heaven I do.
Nay, I have demonstration that I do:
For I wou'd sacrifice my life to serve her.
Yet hold–if laying down my life
Be demonstration of my love,
What is't I feel in favour of *Berinthia*?
For shou'd she be in danger, methinks I cou'd incline
To risque it for her service too; and yet I do not love her.
How then subsists my proof?–
–O, I have found it out.
What I wou'd do for one, is demonstration of my love; and if I'd do as much for t'other. If there is demonstration of my friendship – ay – it must be so. I find I'm very much her friend.
–Yet let me ask my self one puzzling question more.
Whence springs this mighty friendship all at once?
For our acquaintance is of later date.
Now friendship's said to be a plant of tedious

growth; its root compos'd of tender fibers, nice in their taste, cautious in spreading, check'd with the least corruption in the soil; long e'er it take, and longer still e'er it appear to do so: whilst mine is in a moment shot so high, and fix'd so fast, it seems beyond the power of storms to shake it. I doubt it thrives too fast. [*Musing*.

[*Enter* Berinthia.

– Ha, she here! – Nay, then take heed my heart, for there are dangers towards.

BERINTHIA. What makes you look so thoughtful, Sir? I hope you are not ill?

LOVELESS. I was debating, Madam, whether I was so or not; and that was it which made me look so thoughtful.

BERINTHIA. Is it then so hard a matter to decide? I thought all people had been acquainted with their own bodies, though few people know their own minds.

LOVELESS. What, if the distemper, I suspect, be in the mind?

BERINTHIA. Why, then I'll undertake to prescribe you a cure.

LOVELESS. Alas, you undertake you know not what.

BERINTHIA. So far at least then allow me to be a physician.

LOVELESS. Nay, I'll allow you so yet farther: for I have reason to believe, shou'd I put my self into your hands, you wou'd increase my distemper.

BERINTHIA. Perhaps I might have reasons from the Colledge[73] not to be too quick in your cure; but 'tis possible I might find ways to give you often ease, Sir.

LOVELESS. Were I but sure of that, I'd quickly lay my case before you.

BERINTHIA. Whither you are sure of it or no, what risque do you run in trying?

LOVELESS. O, a very great one.

BERINTHIA. How?

LOVELESS. You might betray my distemper to my wife.

BERINTHIA. And so lose all my practice.

LOVELESS. Will you then keep my secret?

BERINTHIA. I will, if it don't burst me.

LOVELESS. Swear.

BERINTHIA. I do.

LOVELESS. By what?

BERINTHIA. By Woman.

LOVELESS. That's swearing by my deity. Do it by your own, or I shan't believe you.

BERINTHIA. By Man, then.

LOVELESS. I'm satisfy'd. Now hear my symptoms,
And give me your advice. The first were these:
When 'twas my chance to see you at the play,
A randome glance you threw, at first alarm'd me,
I cou'd not turn my eyes from whence the danger came:
I gaz'd upon you, 'till you shot again,
And then my fears came on me.
My heart began to pant, my limbs to tremble,
My blood grew thin; my pulse beat quick,
My eyes grew hot and dim, and all the frame of Nature
Shook with apprehension.
'Tis true, some small recruits of resolution
My manhood brought to my assistance,
And by their help I made a stand a while,
But found at last your arrows flew so thick,
They cou'd not fail to pierce me;
So left the field,
And fled for shelter to *Amanda*'s arms.
What think you of these symptoms, pray.

BERINTHIA. Feverish every one of 'em.
But what relief pray did your wife afford you?

LOVELESS. Why, instantly she let me blood;[74]
Which for the present much asswag'd my flame.
But when I saw you, out it burst again,
And rag'd with greater fury than before.
Nay, since you now appear, 'tis so encreas'd,
That in a moment if you do not help me,
I shall, whilst you look on, consume to ashes.
[*Taking hold of her hand*.

BERINTHIA. O Lard, let me go:
'Tis the plague, and we shall all be infected. [*Breaking from him*.

LOVELESS. Then we'll dye together, my Charming Angel. [*Catching her in his arms and kissing her*.

BERINTHIA. O Ged – the Devil's in you.
Lord, let me go, here's some body coming.

[*Enter* Servant.

SERVANT. Sir, my Lady's come home, and desires to speak with you: she's in her chamber.

LOVELESS. Tell her I'm coming. [*Exit* Servant.
But before I go, one glass of nectar more to drink her health. [*To* Berinthia.

BERINTHIA. Stand off, or I shall hate you, by Heavens.

LOVELESS. In matters of love, a woman's oath is no more to be minded than a man's. [*Kissing her*.

BERINTHIA. Um –

[*Enter* Worthy.

WORTHY. Ha! What's here? My old mistress, and so close, I faith? I wou'd not spoil her sport for the universe. [*He retires.*

BERINTHIA. O Ged–now do I pray to Heaven,
[*Exit* Loveless *running.*
With all my heart and soul, that the Devil
In Hell may take me, if ever–I was better pleas'd in
My life–this man has bewitch'd me, that's certain. [*Sighing.*
Well, I am condemn'd; but thanks to Heaven I feel
My self each moment more and more prepar'd for my
Execution. Nay, to that degree, I don't perceive I have
The least fear of dying. No, I find, let the–
Executioner be but a man, and there's nothing will
Suffer with more resolution than a woman.
Well, I never had but one intrigue yet:
But I confess I long to have another.
Pray Heaven it end as the first did tho',
That we may both grow weary at a time;
For 'tis a melancholy thing for lovers to out-live one another.

[*Enter* Worthy.

WORTHY. – [*Aside*] *This discovery's a lucky one, I hope to make a happy use on't. That gentlewoman there is no fool; so I shall be able to make her understand her interest.* – [*To* Berinthia] Your servant Madam, I need not ask you how you do, you have got so good a colour.

BERINTHIA. No better than I us'd to have I suppose.

WORTHY. A little more blood in your cheeks.

BERINTHIA. The weather's hot.

WORTHY. If it were not, a woman may have a colour.

BERINTHIA. What do you mean by that?

WORTHY. Nothing.

BERINTHIA. Why do you smile then?

WORTHY. Because the weather's hot.

BERINTHIA. You'll never leave roguing, I see that.

WORTHY. You'll never leave – I see that. [*Putting his finger to his nose.*

BERINTHIA. Well, I can't imagine what you drive at. Pray tell me what you mean?

WORTHY. Do you tell me it's the same thing?

BERINTHIA. I can't.

WORTHY. Guess!

BERINTHIA. I shall guess wrong.

WORTHY. Indeed you won't.

BERINTHIA. Psha! Either tell, or let it alone.

WORTHY. Nay, rather than let it alone, I will tell. But first I must put you in mind, that after what has past 'twixt you and I, very few things ought to be secrets between us.

BERINTHIA. Why, what secrets do we hide? I know of none.

WORTHY. Yes, there are two; one I have hid from you, and t'other you wou'd hide from me. You are fond of *Loveless*, which I have discover'd; and I am fond of his wife –

BERINTHIA. Which I have discover'd.

WORTHY. Very well, now I confess your discovery to be true: what do you say to mine?

BERINTHIA. Why, I confess – I wou'd swear 'twere false, if I thought you were fool enough to believe me.

WORTHY. Now am I almost in love with you again. Nay, I don't know but I might be quite so, had I made one short campaign with *Amanda*. Therefore if you find 'twou'd tickle your vanity, to bring me down once more to your lure,[75] e'en help me quickly to dispatch her business, that I may have nothing else to do, but to apply my self to yours.

BERINTHIA. Do you then think, Sir, I am old enough to be a bawd?

WORTHY. No, But I think you are wise enough to –

BERINTHIA. To do what?

WORTHY. To hoodwink *Amanda* with a gallant, that she mayn't see who is her husband's mistress.

BERINTHIA. [*Aside*] *He has reason: the hint's a good one.*

WORTHY. Well, Madam, what think you on't?

BERINTHIA. I think you are so much a deeper politician in these affairs than I am; that I ought to have a very great regard to your advice.

WORTHY. Then give me leave to put you in mind, that the most easie, safe, and pleasant situation for your own amour, is the house in which you now are; provided you keep *Amanda* from any sort of suspicion. That the way to do that is to engage her in an intrigue of her own, making your self her confident. And the way to bring her to intrigue, is to make her jealous of her husband in a wrong place; which the more you foment, the less you'll be suspected. This is my scheme, in short; which if you follow as you shou'd do (my dear *Berinthia*) we may all four pass the winter very pleasantly.

BERINTHIA. Well, I cou'd be glad to have no body's sins to answer for but my own. But where there is a necessity –

WORTHY. Right as you say, where there is a necessity, a Christian is bound to help his neighbour. So good *Berinthia*, lose no time, but let us begin the dance as fast as we can.

BERINTHIA. Not till the fiddles are in tune, pray Sir. Your lady's strings will be very apt to fly, I can tell you that, if they are wound up too hastily. But if you'll have patience to screw 'em to their pitch by degrees, I don't doubt but she may endure to be play'd upon.

WORTHY. Ay, and will make admirable musick too, or I'm mistaken; but have you had no private closet discourse with her yet about males and females, and so forth, which may give you hopes in her constitution; for I know her morals are the Devil against us.

BERINTHIA. I have had so much discourse with her, that I believe were she once cur'd of her fondness to her husband, the fortress of her virtue wou'd not be so impregnable as she fancies.

WORTHY. What? She runs, I'll warrant you, into that common mistake of fond wives, who conclude themselves virtuous, because they can refuse a man they don't like, when they have got one they do.

BERINTHIA. True, and therefore I think 'tis a presumptuous thing in a woman, to assume the name of virtuous, till she has heartily hated her husband, and been soundly in love with somebody else. Whom, if she has withstood – then – much good may it do her.

WORTHY. Well, so much for her virtue. Now, one word of her inclinations, and every one to their post. What opinion do you find she has of me?

BERINTHIA. What you cou'd wish; she thinks you handsome and discreet.

WORTHY. Good, that's thinking half seas over. One tide more brings us into port.

BERINTHIA. Perhaps it may, tho' still remember, there's a difficult bar to pass.

WORTHY. I know there is, but I don't question I shall get well over it, by the help of such a pilot.

BERINTHIA. You may depend upon your pilot, she'll do the best she can; so weigh anchor and be gone as soon as you please.

WORTHY. I'm under sail already. Adieu. [*Exit* Worthy.

BERINTHIA. Bon Voyage.

[*Sola.*

So, here's fine work. What a business have I undertaken? I'm a very pretty gentlewoman truly; but there was no avoiding it: he'd have ruin'd me if I had refus'd him. Besides, faith, I begin to fancy there may be as much pleasure in carrying on another body's intriegue, as one's own. This at least is certain, it exercises almost all the entertaining faculties of a woman. For there's employment for hypocrisie, invention, deceit, flattery, mischief, and lying.

[*Enter* Amanda, *her* Woman *following her.*

WOMAN. If you please, Madam, only to say, whither you'll have me buy 'em or not?

AMANDA. Yes, no, go fiddle; I care not what you do. Prithee leave me.

WOMAN. I have done. [*Exit* Woman.

BERINTHIA. What in the name of *Jove*'s the matter with you?

AMANDA. The matter *Berinthia*, I'm almost mad, I'm plagu'd to death.

BERINTHIA. Who is it that plagues you?

AMANDA. Who do you think shou'd plague a wife, but her husband?

BERINTHIA. O ho, is it come to that? We shall have you wish your self a widow by and by.

AMANDA. Wou'd I were any thing but what I am; a base ungrateful man, after what I have done for him, to use me thus!

BERINTHIA. What, he has been ogling now I'll warrant you?

AMANDA. Yes, he has been ogling.

BERINTHIA. And so you are jealous? Is that all?

AMANDA. That all! Is jealousie then nothing?

BERINTHIA. It shou'd be nothing, if I were in your case.

AMANDA. Why, what wou'd you do?

BERINTHIA. I'd cure my self.

AMANDA. How?

BERINTHIA. Let blood in the fond vein: care as little for my husband, as he did for me.

AMANDA. That wou'd not stop his course.

BERINTHIA. Nor nothing else, when the wind's in the warm corner. Look you, *Amanda*, you may build castles in the air, and fume, and fret, and grow thin and lean, and pale and ugly, if you please. But I tell you, no man worth having, is true to his wife, or can be true to his wife, or ever was, or ever will be so.

AMANDA. Do you then really think he's false to me? For I did but suspect him.

BERINTHIA. Think so? I know he's so.

AMANDA. Is it possible? Pray tell me what you know?

BERINTHIA. Don't press me then to name names; for that I have sworn I won't do.

AMANDA. Well I won't; but let me know all you can without perjury.

BERINTHIA. I'll let you know enough to prevent any wise woman's dying of the pip;[76] and I hope you'll pluck up your spirits, and shew upon occasion, you can be as good a wife as the best of 'em.

AMANDA. Well, what a woman can do I'll endeavour.

BERINTHIA. O, a woman can do a great deal, if once she sets her mind to it. Therefore pray don't stand trifling any longer, and teasing your self with this and that, and your love and your virtue, and I know not what. But resolve to hold up your head, get a tiptoe, and look over 'em all; for to my certain knowledge your husband is a pickering[77] elsewhere.

AMANDA. You are sure on't?

BERINTHIA. Positively; he fell in love at the play.

AMANDA. Right, the very same; do you know the ugly thing?

BERINTHIA. Yes, I know her well enough; but she's no such an ugly thing neither.

AMANDA. Is she very handsome?

BERINTHIA. Truly I think so.

AMANDA. Hey ho.

BERINTHIA. What do you sigh for now?

AMANDA. Oh my heart.

BERINTHIA. [*Aside*] *Only the pangs of nature; she's in labour of her love; Heaven send her a quick delivery, I'm sure she has a good midwife.*

AMANDA. I'm very ill, I must go to my chamber. Dear *Berinthia*, don't leave me a moment.

BERINTHIA. No, don't fear. [*Aside*] *I'll see you safe brought to bed, I'll warrant you.* [*Exeunt* Amanda *leaning upon* Berinthia.

Scene III.

[*A Country House. Enter* Young Fashion *and* Lory.]

YOUNG FASHION. So, here's our inheritance, *Lory*, if we can but get into possession. But methinks the seat of our family looks like *Noah*'s Ark, as if the chief part on't were design'd for the fowls of the air, and the beasts of the field.

LORY. Pray, Sir, don't let your head run upon the orders of building here; get but the heiress, let the Devil take the house.

YOUNG FASHION. Get but the house, let the Devil take the heiress, I say, at least if she be as old *Coupler* describes her. But come, we have no time to squander. Knock at the door. [Lory *knocks two or three times*] What the Devil, have they got no ears in this house? Knock harder.

LORY. I gad, Sir, this will prove some Inchanted Castle; we shall have the gyant come out by and by with his club, and beat our brains out. [*Knocks again*.

YOUNG FASHION. Hush; they come.

Who is there? [*From within*.

LORY. Open the door and see: is that your country breeding?

[*Within*] Ay, but two words to a bargain: *Tummas*, is the blunderbus[78] prim'd?

YOUNG FASHION. Oons, give 'em good words, *Lory*; we shall be shot here a fortune catching.

LORY. I gad, Sir, I think y'are in the right on't. Ho, Mr. What d'ye call 'um. [Servant *appears at the window with a blunderbus*.

SERVANT. Weall, naw what's yare business?

YOUNG FASHION. Nothing, Sir, but to wait upon Sir *Tunbelly*, with your leave.

SERVANT. To weat upon Sir *Tunbelly*? Why, you'll find that's just as Sir *Tunbelly* pleases.

YOUNG FASHION. But will you do me the favour, Sir, to know whether Sir *Tunbelly* pleases or not?

SERVANT. Why, look you, do you see, with good words much may be done. *Ralph*, go thy weas, and ask Sir *Tunbelly* if he pleases to be waited upon. And do'st hear? Call to Nurse, that she may lock up Miss *Hoyden* before the geats open.

YOUNG FASHION. D'ye hear that Lory?

LORY. Ay, Sir, I'm afraid we shall find a difficult job on't. Pray Heaven that old rogue Coupler han't sent us to fetch milk out of the gunroom.[79]

YOUNG FASHION. I'll warrant thee all will go well: see, the door opens.

[*Enter* Sir Tunbelly, *with his servants arm'd, with guns, clubs, pitchforks, sythes, &c.*

LORY. O Lord, O Lord, O Lord, we are both dead men. [*Running behind his master.*

YOUNG FASHION. Take heed, Fool, thy fear will ruine us.

LORY. My fear, Sir, 'sdeath, Sir, I fear nothing. – [*Aside*] *Wou'd I were well up to the chin in a horse-pond.*

SIR TUNBELLY. Who is it here has any business with me?

YOUNG FASHION. Sir, 'tis I, if your name be Sir *Tunbelly Clumsey.*

SIR TUNBELLY. Sir, my name is Sir *Tunbelly Clumsey*, whither you have any business with me or not. So you see I am not asham'd of my name – nor my face neither.

YOUNG FASHION. Sir, you have no cause, that I know of.

SIR TUNBELLY. Sir, if you have no cause neither, I desire to know who you are; for till I know your name, I shall not ask you to come into my house; and when I know your name – 'tis six to four I don't ask you neither.

YOUNG FASHION. Sir, I hope you'll find this letter an authentick passport. [*Giving him a letter.*

SIR TUNBELLY. Cod's my life, I ask your Lordship's pardon ten thousand times. [*To his servants*] Here, run in a-doors quickly: get a Scotch coal fire in the great parlour; set all the turkey-work[80] chairs in their places; get the great brass candlesticks out, and be sure stick the sockets full of laurel,[81] run. [*Turning to* Young Fashion] My Lord, I ask your Lordship's pardon. [*To other servants*] And do you hear, run away to Nurse, bid her let Miss *Hoyden* loose again, and if it was not shifting day[82], let her put on a clean tucker[83] quick. [*Exeunt servants confusedly. To* Young Fashion] I hope your Honour will excuse the disorder of my family, we are not us'd to receive men of your Lordship's great quality every day; pray where are your coaches, and servants, my Lord?

YOUNG FASHION. Sir, that I might give you and your fair daughter a proof how impatient I am to be nearer a-kin to you, I left my equipage to follow me, and came away post,[84] with only one servant.

SIR TUNBELLY. Your Lordship does me too much honour, it was exposing your person to too much fatigue and danger, I protest it was; but my daughter shall endeavour to make you what amends she can; and tho' I say it, that shou'd not say it – *Hoyden* has charms.

YOUNG FASHION. Sir, I am not a stranger to them, tho' I am to her. Common fame has done her justice.

SIR TUNBELLY. My Lord, I am Common Fame's very grateful humble servant. My Lord – my girl's young, *Hoyden* is young, my Lord; but this I must say for her, what she wants in art, she has by nature; what she wants in experience, she has in breeding; and what's wanting in her age, is made good in her constitution. So pray, my Lord, walk in; pray my Lord, walk in.

YOUNG FASHION. Sir, I wait upon you. [*Exeunt.*

[Miss Hoyden *Sola.*

MISS HOYDEN. Sure never no body was us'd as I am. I know well enough what other girls do, for all they think to make a fool of me; it's well I have a husband a coming, or I cod, I'd marry the baker, I wou'd so. No body can knock at the gate, but presently I must be lockt up, and here's the young greyhound bitch can run loose about the house all day long she can, 'tis very well.

NURSE. Miss *Hoyden*, Miss, Miss, Miss; Miss *Hoyden*. [*Without, opening the door.*

[*Enter* Nurse.

MISS HOYDEN. Well, what do you make such a noise for, ha? What do you din a body's ears for? Can't one be at quiet for you?

NURSE. What do I din your ears for? Here's one come will din your ears for you.

MISS HOYDEN. What care I who's come; I care not a fig who comes, nor who goes, as long as I must be lock'd up like the ale-cellar.

NURSE. That, Miss, is for fear you shou'd be drank, before you are ripe.

MISS HOYDEN. O, don't you trouble your head about that; I'm as ripe as you, tho' not so mellow.

NURSE. Very well; now have I a good mind to lock you up again, and not let you see my Lord to night.

MISS HOYDEN. My Lord? Why is my husband come?

NURSE. Yes marry is he, and a goodly person too.

MISS HOYDEN. O my dear *Nurse*, forgive me this once, and I'll never misuse you again; no, if I do, you shall give me three thumps on the back, and a great pinch by the cheek. [*Hugging* Nurse.

NURSE. Ah the poor thing, see how it melts, it's as full of good nature, as an egg's full of meat.

MISS HOYDEN. But, my dear *Nurse*, don't lie now; is he come by your troth?[85]

NURSE. Yes, by my truly, is he.

MISS HOYDEN. O Lord! I'll go put on my lac'd smock,[86] tho' I'm whipt 'till the blood run down my heels for't. [*Exit running.*

NURSE. Eh – the Lord succour thee, how thou art delighted. [*Exit after her.*

[*Enter* Sir Tunbelly, *and* Young Fashion. *A* Servant *with wine.*

SIR TUNBELLY. My Lord, I am proud of the honour to see your Lordship within my doors; and I humbly crave leave to bid you welcome, in a cup of sack wine.[87]

YOUNG FASHION. Sir, to your daughter's health. [*Drinks.*

SIR TUNBELLY. Ah poor girl, she'll be scar'd out of her wits on her wedding night; for, honestly speaking, she does not know a man from a woman, but by his beard, and his britches.

YOUNG FASHION. Sir, I don't doubt but she has a virtuous education, which with the rest of her merit, makes me long to see her mine. I wish you wou'd dispence with the Canonical hour,[88] and let it be this very night.

SIR TUNBELLY. O not so soon neither; that's shooting my girl before you bid her stand.[89] No, give her fair warning, we'll sign and seal to night, if you please; and this day seven-night – let the jade look to her quarters.[90]

YOUNG FASHION. This day sennight?[91] – Why, what do you take me for a ghost, Sir? 'Slife, Sir, I'm made of flesh and blood, and bones and sinews, and can no more live a week without your daughter – [*Aside*] *than I can live a month with her.*

SIR TUNBELLY. Oh, I'll warrant you my Hero, young men are hot I know, but they don't boyl over at that rate, neither; besides, my wench's wedding gown is not come home yet.

YOUNG FASHION. O, no matter Sir, I'll take her in her shift.

– [*Aside*] *A pox of this old fellow, he'll delay the business 'till my damn'd star finds me out, and discovers me.* – [*To* Sir Tunbelly] Pray, Sir, let it be done without ceremony, 'twill save money.

SIR TUNBELLY. Money? – Save money when *Hoyden*'s to be married? Udswoons I'll give my wench a wedding-dinner, tho' I go to grass with the King of *Assyria* for't; and such a dinner it shall be, as is not to be cook'd in the poaching of an egg. Therefore, my Noble Lord, have a little patience, we'll go and look over our deeds and settlements[92] immediately; and as for your bride, tho' you may be sharp set before she's quite ready, I'll engage for my girl, she stays your stomach at last. [*Exeunt.*

Act IV. Scene I.

[*Enter* Miss Hoyden, *and* Nurse.]

NURSE. Well, *Miss*, how do you like your husband that is to be?

MISS HOYDEN. O Lord, *Nurse*, I'm so overjoy'd, I can scarce contain my self.

NURSE. O but you must have a care of being too fond, for men now a days hate a woman that loves 'em.

MISS HOYDEN. Love him? Why do you think I love him, *Nurse*? I cod I wou'd not care if he were hang'd, so I were but once married to him – no – that which pleases me, is to think what work I'll make when I get to *London*; for when I am a wife and a lady both Nurse, I cod I'll flant[93] it with the best of 'em.

NURSE. Look, look, if his Honour be not coming again to you; now if I were sure you would behave your self handsomly, and not disgrace me that have brought you up, I'd leave you alone together.

MISS HOYDEN. That's my best Nurse, do as you wou'd be done by; trust us together this once, and if I don't shew my breeding from the head to the foot of me, may I be twice married, and die a maid.

NURSE. Well, this once I'll venture you, but if you disparage me –

MISS HOYDEN. Never fear, I'll shew him my parts,[94] I'll warrant him. [*Exit* Nurse. *Sola*] These old women are so wise when they get a poor girl in their clutches but e'er it be long, I shall know what's what, as well as the best of 'em.

[*Enter* Young Fashion.

YOUNG FASHION. Your servant, Madam, I'm glad to find you alone, for I have something of importance to speak to you about.

MISS HOYDEN. Sir, (my Lord, I meant) you may speak to me about what you please, I shall give you a civil answer.

YOUNG FASHION. You give me so obliging a one, it encourages me to tell you in few words, what I think both for your interest, and mine. Your father, I suppose you know, has resolv'd to make me happy in being your husband, and I hope I may depend upon your consent, to perform what he desires.

MISS HOYDEN. Sir, I never disobey my father in any thing, but eating of green goosberries.

YOUNG FASHION. So good a daughter must needs make an admirable wife, I am therefore impatient 'till you are mine; and hope you will so far consider the violence of my love, that you won't have the cruelty to defer my happiness, so long as your father designs it.

MISS HOYDEN. Pray, my Lord, how long is that?

YOUNG FASHION. Madam, a thousand year – a whole week.

MISS HOYDEN. A week – why I shall be an old woman by that time.

YOUNG FASHION. And I an old man, which you'll find a greater misfortune than t'other.

MISS HOYDEN. Why I thought 'twas to be to morrow morning, as soon as I was up; I'm sure Nurse told me so.

YOUNG FASHION. And it shall be to morrow morning still, if you'll consent?

MISS HOYDEN. If I'll consent? Why I thought I was to obey you as my husband?

YOUNG FASHION. That's when we are married; 'till then, I am to obey you.

MISS HOYDEN. Why then if we are to take it by turns, it's the same thing; I'll obey you now, and when we are married, you shall obey me.

YOUNG FASHION. With all my heart, but I doubt we must get Nurse on our side, or we shall hardly prevail with the Chaplain.

MISS HOYDEN. No more we shan't indeed, for he loves her better than he loves his pulpit, and wou'd always be a preaching to her by his good will.

YOUNG FASHION. Why then my dear little Bedfellow, if you'll call her hither, we'll try to perswade her presently.

MISS HOYDEN. O Lord, I can tell you a way how to perswade her to any thing.

YOUNG FASHION. How's that?

MISS HOYDEN. Why tell her she's a wholsom, comely woman – and give her half a crown.

YOUNG FASHION. Nay, if that will do, she shall have half a score of 'em.

MISS HOYDEN. O Gemmini, for half that, she'd marry you her self; I'll run and call her. [*Exit* Miss Hoyden.

YOUNG FASHION. [*Solus*] So, matters go swimmingly, this is a rare girl, I faith, I shall have a fine time on't with her at *London*. I'm much mistaken, if she don't prove a *March* Hare[95] all the year round. What a scampring chase will she make on't, when she finds the whole kennel of beaux at her tail! Hey to the park, and the play, and the church, and the Devil; she'll shew 'em sport I'll warrant 'em. But no matter, she brings an estate will afford me a separate maintenance.

[*Enter* Miss Hoyden *and* Nurse.

YOUNG FASHION. How do you do, good Mistress Nurse; I desir'd your young lady would give me leave to see you, that I might thank you for your extraordinary care and conduct in her education; pray accept of this small acknowledgment for it at present, and depend upon my farther kindness, when I shall be that happy thing her husband.

NURSE. [*Aside*] *Gold by makings,* – your Honour's goodness is too great; Alas, all I can boast of is, I gave her pure good milk,[96] and so your Honour wou'd have said, an you had seen how the poor thing suckt it – eh, God's blessing on the sweet face on't, how it us'd to hang at this poor tett, and suck and squeeze, and kick and sprawl it wou'd, 'till the belly on't was so full, it wou'd drop off like a leech.

MISS HOYDEN. [*To* Nurse, *taking her angrily aside*] Pray one word with you; prithee Nurse don't stand ripping up old stories, to make one asham'd before one's love; do you think such a fine proper gentleman as he, cares for a fiddlecome tale[97] of a draggle-tail'd girl;[98] If you have a mind to make him have a good opinion of a woman; don't tell him what one did then, tell him what one can do now. [*To* Young Fashion] I hope your Honour will excuse my mismanners to whisper before you, it was only to give some orders about the family.

YOUNG FASHION. O every thing, Madam, is to give way to business; besides, good housewifry is a very commendable quality in a young lady.

MISS HOYDEN. Pray Sir, are the young ladies good house-wives at *London* Town? Do they darn their own linnen?

YOUNG FASHION. O no, they study how to spend money, not to save it.

MISS HOYDEN. I cod, I don't know but that may be better sport than t'other, ha, Nurse.

YOUNG FASHION. Well, you shall have your choice when you come there.

MISS HOYDEN. Shall I – then by my troth I'll get there as fast as I can. [*To* Nurse] His Honour desires you'll be so kind, as to let us be married to morrow.

NURSE. To morrow, my dear Madam?

YOUNG FASHION. Yes, to morrow sweet Nurse; privately; young folks you know are impatient, and Sir *Tunbelly* wou'd make us stay a week for a wedding-dinner. Now all things being sign'd, and seal'd, and agreed, I fancy there cou'd be no great harm in practising a scene or two of matrimony in private, if it were only to give us the better assurance when we come to play it in publick.

NURSE. Nay, I must confess stoln pleasures are sweet; but if you shou'd be married now, what will you do when Sir *Tunbelly* calls for you to be wedd?

MISS HOYDEN. Why then we'll be married again.

NURSE. What, twice my Child?

MISS HOYDEN. I cod, I don't care how often I'm married, not I.

YOUNG FASHION. Pray Nurse don't you be against your young lady's good, for by this means she'll have the pleasure of two wedding-days.

MISS HOYDEN. [*To* Nurse *softly*] And of two wedding-nights too, Nurse.

NURSE. Well, I'm such a tender hearted fool, I find I can refuse nothing; so you shall e'en follow your own inventions.

MISS HOYDEN. Shall I? [*Aside*] *O Lord, I cou'd leap over the moon.*

YOUNG FASHION. Dear Nurse, this goodness of yours shan't go unrewarded; but now you must imploy your power with Mr. *Bull* the Chaplain, that he may do us his friendly office too, and then we shall all be happy; do you think you can prevail with him?

NURSE. Prevail with him – or he shall never prevail with me, I can tell him that.

MISS HOYDEN. My Lord, she has had him upon the hip this seven year.

YOUNG FASHION. I'm glad to hear it; however, to strengthen your interest with him, you may let him know I have several fat livings in my gift, and that the first that falls shall be in your disposal.[99]

NURSE. Nay, then I'll make him marry more folks than one, I'll promise him.

MISS HOYDEN. Faith do Nurse, make him marry you too, I'm sure he'll do't for a fat living, for he loves eating, more than he loves his Bible; and I have often heard him say, a fat living was the best meat in the world.

NURSE. Ay, and I'll make him commend the sauce too, or I'll bring his gown to a cassock,[100] I will so.

YOUNG FASHION. Well Nurse, whilst you go and settle matters with him, then your lady and I will go take a walk in the garden.

NURSE. I'll do your Honour's business in the catching up of a garter. [*Exit* Nurse.

YOUNG FASHION. Come, Madam, dare you venture your self alone with me? [*Giving her his hand.*

MISS HOYDEN. O dear, yes, Sir, I don't think you'll do any thing to me I need be afraid on. [*Exeunt.*

Scene II

[*Enter* Amanda *and* Berinthia.]

A SONG.

I.

I smile at Love, and all its arts,
The charming Cynthia cry'd;
Take heed, for Love has piercing darts,
A wounded swain[101] *reply'd.*
Once free and blest as you are now,
I trifl'd with his charms,
I pointed at his little bow,
And sported with his arms:
'Till urg'd too far, revenge he crys,
A fatal shaft he drew,
It took its passage thro' your eyes,
And to my heart it flew.

II.
To tear it thence, I try'd in vain,
To strive, I quickly found,
Was only to encrease the pain,
And to enlarge the wound.
Ah! Much too well I fear you know
What pain I'm to endure,
Since what your eyes alone could do,
Your heart alone can cure.
And that (grant Heaven I may mistake)
I doubt is doom'd to bear
A burthen for another's sake,
Who ill rewards its care.

AMANDA. Well, now *Berinthia,* I'm at leisure to hear what 'twas you had to say to me.

BERINTHIA. What I had to say, was only to eccho the sighs and groans of a dying lover.

AMANDA. Phu, will you never learn to talk in earnest of any thing?

BERINTHIA. Why this shall be in earnest, if you please: for my part, I only tell you matter of fact, you may take it which way you like best; but if you'll follow the women of the Town, you'll take it both ways; for when a man offers himself to one of them, first she takes him in jest, and then she takes him in earnest.

AMANDA. I'm sure there's so much jest and earnest in what you say to me, I scarce know how to take it; but I think you have bewitched me, for I don't find it possible to be angry with you, say what you will.

BERINTHIA. I'm very glad to hear it, for I have no mind to quarrel with you, for more reasons than I'll brag of; but quarrel or not, smile or frown, I must tell you what I have suffer'd upon your account.

AMANDA. Upon my account?

BERINTHIA. Yes, upon yours; I have been forc'd to sit still and hear you commended for two hours together, without one compliment to my self; now don't you think a woman had a blessed time of that?

AMANDA. Alas! I shou'd have been unconcern'd at it; I never knew where the pleasure lay of being prais'd by the men; but pray who was this that commended me so?

BERINTHIA. One you have a mortal aversion to, Mr. *Worthy*; he us'd you like a text, he took you all to pieces, but spoke so learnedly upon every point, one might see the spirit of the church was in him; if you are a woman, you'd have been in an extasie to have hear'd how feelingly he handled your hair, your eyes, your nose, your mouth, your teeth, your tongue, your chin, your neck, and so forth. Thus he preach'd for an hour, but when he came to use an application, he observ'd that all these without a gallant were nothing – now consider of what has been said, and Heaven give you grace to put it in practice.

AMANDA. Alas! *Berinthia*, did I incline to a gallant[102] (which you know I do not), do you think a man so nice as he, cou'd have the least concern for such a plain unpolisht thing as I am? It is impossible!

BERINTHIA. Now have you a great mind to put me upon commending you.

AMANDA. Indeed that was not my design.

BERINTHIA. Nay, if it were, it's all one, for I won't do't, I'll leave that to your looking-glass. But to shew you I have some good nature left, I'll commend him, and may be that may do as well.

AMANDA. You have a great mind to perswade me I am in love with him.

BERINTHIA. I have a great mind to perswade you, you don't know what you are in love with.

AMANDA. I am sure I am not in love with him; nor never shall be, so let that pass; but you were saying something you wou'd commend him for.

BERINTHIA. O you'd be glad to hear a good character of him however.

AMANDA. Psha.

BERINTHIA. Psha – Well 'tis a foolish undertaking for women in these kind of matters, to pretend to deceive one another – have not I been bred a woman as well as you?

AMANDA. What then?

BERINTHIA. Why then I understand my trade so well, that when ever I am told of a man I like, I cry psha; but that I may spare you the pains of putting me a second time in mind to commend him, I'll proceed, and give you this account of him; that though 'tis possible he may have had women with as good faces as your Ladyship's (no discredit to it neither) yet you must know your cautious behaviour, with that reserve in your humour, has given him his death's wound; he mortally hates a coquett;[103] he says 'tis impossible to love where we cannot esteem; and that no woman can be esteem'd by a man who has sense, if she makes her self cheap in the eye of a fool. That pride to a woman, is as necessary as humility to a divine;[104] and that far fetch'd, and dear bought, is meat for gentlemen, as well as for ladies – In short, that every woman who has beauty, may set a price upon her self, and that by under-selling the market, they ruine the trade. This is his doctrine, how do you like it?

AMANDA. So well, that since I never intend to have a gallant for my self, if I were to recommend one to a friend, he shou'd be the man.

[*Enter* Worthy.

Bless me! He's here, pray Heaven he did not hear me.

BERINTHIA. If he did, it won't hurt your reputation; your thoughts are as safe in his heart, as in your own.

WORTHY. I venture in at an unseasonable time of night, Ladies; I hope if I'm troublesome, you'll use the same freedom in turning me out again.

AMANDA. I believe it can't be late, for Mr. *Loveless* is not come home yet, and he usually keeps good hours.

WORTHY. Madam, I'm afraid he'll transgress a little to night; for he told me about half an hour ago, he was going to sup with some company, he doubted would keep him out 'till three or four a clock in the morning, and desir'd I wou'd let my servant acquaint you with it, that you might not expect him; But my fellow's a blunder-head, so lest he shou'd make some mistake, I thought it my duty to deliver the message my self.

AMANDA. I'm very sorry he shou'd give you that trouble, Sir. But –

BERINTHIA. But since he has, will you give me leave, Madam, to keep him to play at ombre with us?

AMANDA. Cousin, you know you command my house.

WORTHY. And, Madam, you know you command me, tho' I'm a very wretched gamester. [*To* Berinthia.

BERINTHIA. O you play well enough to lose your money, and that's all the ladies require, so without any more ceremony, let us go into the next room, and call for the cards.

AMANDA. With all my heart. [*Exit* Worthy *leading* Amanda.

BERINTHIA. [*Sola*] Well, how this business will end, Heaven knows; but she seems to me to be in as fair a way – as a boy is to be a rogue, when he's put clerk to an attorney. [*Exit* Berinthia.

Scene III.

[Berinthia*'s chamber. Enter* Loveless *cautiously in the dark.*]

LOVELESS. So, thus far all's well, I'm got into her bed-chamber, and I think no body has perceiv'd me steal into the house; my wife don't expect me home 'till four a clock, so if *Berinthia* comes to bed by eleven, I shall have a chase of five hours; let me see, where shall I hide my self? Under her bed? No; we shall have her maid searching there for something or other; her closet's a better place, and I have a master key will open it; I'll e'en in there, and attack her just when she comes to her prayers, that's the most likely to prove her critical minute, for then the Devil will be there to assist me. [*He opens the closet, goes in, and shuts the door after him.*

[*Enter* Berinthia *with a candle in her hand.*

BERINTHIA. Well, sure I am the best natur'd woman in the world, I that love cards so well (there is but one thing upon earth I love better) have pretended letters to write, to give my friends – *à tate à tate*; However, I'm innocent, for picquet is the game I set 'em to; at her own peril be it, if she ventures to play with him at any other. But now what shall I do with my self? I don't know how in the world to pass my time, wou'd *Loveless* were here to badiner[105] a little; Well, he's a charming fellow, I don't wonder his wife's so fond of him; what if I shou'd sit down and think of him 'till I fall asleep, and dream of the Lord knows what? O but then if I shou'd dream we were married, I shou'd be frightned out of my wits. [*Seeing a book*] What's this book? I think I had best go read. O Splenatique![106] It's a sermon; well, I'll go into my closet, and read the *Plotting-Sisters*.[107] [*She opens the closet, sees* Loveless*, and shrieks out*] O Lord, a ghost, a ghost, a ghost, a ghost.

[*Enter* Loveless *running to her.*

LOVELESS. Peace, my Dear, it's no ghost, take it in your arms, you'll find 'tis worth a hundred of 'em.

BERINTHIA. Run in again, here's some body coming.

[*Enter her* Maid.

MAID. Lord, Madam, what's the matter?

BERINTHIA. O Heav'ns! I'm almost frighted out of my wits, I thought verily I had seen a ghost, and 'twas nothing but the white curtain, with a black hood pinn'd up against it; you may be gone again, I am the fearful'st fool. [*Exit* Maid.

[*Re-enter* Loveless.

LOVELESS. Is the coast clear?

BERINTHIA. The coast clear! I suppose you are clear, you'd never play such a trick as this else.

LOVELESS. I'm very well pleas'd with my trick thus far, and shall be so 'till I have play'd it out, if it be'nt your fault; where's my wife?

BERINTHIA. At cards.

LOVELESS. With whom?

BERINTHIA. With *Worthy*.

LOVELESS. Then we are safe enough.

BERINTHIA. Are you so? Some husbands wou'd be of another mind, if he were at cards with their wives.

LOVELESS. And they'd be in the right on't too. But I dare trust mine – besides, I know he's in love in another place, and he's not one of those who court half a dozen at a time.

BERINTHIA. Nay, the truth on't is, you'd pity him if you saw how uneasie he is at being engag'd with us, but 'twas my malice, I fancy'd he was to meet his mistress somewhere else, so did it to have the pleasure of seeing him fret.

LOVELESS. What says *Amanda* to my staying abroad so late?

BERINTHIA. Why she's as much out of humour as he, I believe they wish one another at the Devil.

LOVELESS. Then I'm afraid they'll quarrel at play, and soon throw up the cards. [*Offering to pull her into the closet*] Therefore my Dear Charming Angel, let us make a good use of our time.

BERINTHIA. Heavens, what do you mean?

LOVELESS. Pray what do you think I mean?

BERINTHIA. I don't know.

LOVELESS. I'll shew you.

BERINTHIA. You may as well tell me.

LOVELESS. No, that wou'd make you blush worse than t'other.

BERINTHIA. Why, do you intend to make me blush?

LOVELESS. Faith, I can't tell that, but if I do, it shall be in the dark. [*Pulling her.*

BERINTHIA. O Heavens! I wou'd not be in the dark with you for all the world.

LOVELESS. I'll try that. [*Puts out the candles.*

BERINTHIA. O Lord! Are you mad, what shall I do for light?

LOVELESS. You'll do as well without it.

BERINTHIA. Why, one can't find a chair to sit down?

LOVELESS. Come into the closet, Madam, there's moon-shine upon the couch.

BERINTHIA. Nay, never pull, for I will not go.

LOVELESS. Then you must be carryed. [*Carrying her.*

BERINTHIA. Help, help, I'm ravish'd, ruin'd, undone. O Lord, I shall never be able to bear it. [*Very softly.*

Scene IV.

[Sir Tunbelly*'s house. Enter Miss* Hoyden, Nurse, Young Fashion*, and* Bull.]

YOUNG FASHION. This quick dispatch of yours, Mr. *Bull*, I take so kindly, it shall give you a claim to my favour as long as I live, I do assure you.

MISS HOYDEN. And to mine too, I promise you.

BULL. I most humbly thank your Honours; and I hope, since it has been my lot, to join you in the holy bands of wedlock, you will so well cultivate the soil, which I have crav'd a blessing on, that your children may swarm about you, like bees about a honey comb.

MISS HOYDEN. I cod with all my heart, the more the merrier, I say; ha, Nurse?

[*Enter* Lory *taking his Master hastily aside.*

LORY. One word with you, for Heaven's sake.

YOUNG FASHION. What the Devil's the matter?

LORY. Sir, your fortune's ruin'd; and I don't think your life's worth a quarter of an hour's purchase: yonder's your brother arriv'd with two coaches and six horses, twenty footmen and pages, a coat worth fourscore pound, and a periwig down to his knees; so judge what will become of your lady's heart.

YOUNG FASHION. Death and Furies, 'tis impossible!

LORY. Fiends and Spectres, Sir, 'tis true.

YOUNG FASHION. Is he in the house yet?

LORY. No, they are capitulating with him at the gate; the porter tells him, he's come to run away with Miss *Hoyden*, and has cock'd the blunderbuss at him; your brother swears Gad Damme, they are a parcel of clawns, and he has a good mind to break off the match; but they have given the word for Sir *Tunbelly*, so I doubt all will come out presently. Pray Sir resolve what you'll do this moment, for I gad they'll maul you.

YOUNG FASHION. Stay a little. [*To Miss* Hoyden] My Dear, here's a troublesome business my man tells me of, but don't be frighten'd, we shall be too hard for the rogue. Here's an impudent fellow at the gate (not knowing I was come hither *incognito*) has taken my name upon him, in hopes to run away with you.

MISS HOYDEN. O the brazen fac'd varlet,[108] it's well we are married, or may be we might never a been so.

YOUNG FASHION. – [*Aside*] *I gad, like enough:* – Prithee, dear Doctor, run to Sir *Tunbelly*, and stop him from going to the gate, before I speak with him.

BULL. I fly, my good Lord – [*Exit* Bull.

NURSE. An't please your Honour, my Lady and I had best lock our selves up 'till the danger be over.

YOUNG FASHION. Ay, by all means.

MISS HOYDEN. Not so fast, I won't be lock'd up any more. I'm marry'd.

YOUNG FASHION. Yes, pray my Dear do, 'till we have seiz'd this rascal.

MISS HOYDEN. Nay, if you pray me, I'll do any thing. [*Exeunt* Miss Hoyden *and* Nurse.

YOUNG FASHION. O! Here's Sir *Tunbelly* coming. Hark you, Sirrah, things are better than you imagine; the wedding's over.

LORY. The Devil it is, Sir.

YOUNG FASHION. Not a word, all's safe: but Sir *Tunbelly* don't know it, nor must not yet; so I am resolv'd to brazen the business out, and have the pleasure of turning the impostor upon his Lordship, which I believe may easily be done.

[*Enter* Sir Tunbelly, Chaplain, *and servants arm'd.*

YOUNG FASHION. Did you ever hear, Sir, of so impudent an undertaking?

SIR TUNBELLY. Never, by the Mass, but we'll tickle him I'll warrant him.

YOUNG FASHION. They tell me, Sir, he has a great many people with him disguis'd like servants.

SIR TUNBELLY. Ay, ay, rogues, enough; but I'll soon raise the *posse* upon 'em.

YOUNG FASHION. Sir, if you'll take my advice, we'll go a shorter way to work; I find who ever this spark[109] is, he knows nothing of my being privately here; so if you pretend to receive him civilly, he'll enter without suspicion; and as soon as he is within the gate, we'll whip up the draw-bridge upon his back, let fly the blunderbuss to disperse his crew, and so commit him to gaol.

SIR TUNBELLY. I gad, your Lordship is an ingenious person, and a very great general; but shall we kill any of 'em or not?

YOUNG FASHION. No, no, fire over their heads only to fright 'em, I'll warrant the regiment scours when the Colonel's a prisoner.

SIR TUNBELLY. Then come along my Boys, and let your courage be great – for your danger is but small. [*Exeunt.*

Scene V.

[*The gate. Enter* Lord Foppington *and followers.*]

LORD FOPPINGTON. A pax of these bumkinly people, will they open the gate, or do they desire I should grow at their moat side like a willow? [*To the* Porter] Hey, Fellow – prithee do me the favour, in as few words as thou canst find to express thy self, to tell me whether thy master will admit me or not, that I may turn about my coach and be gone?

PORTER. Here's my master himself now at hand; he's of age, he'll give you his answer.

[*Enter* Sir Tunbelly, *and servants.*

SIR TUNBELLY. My most noble Lord, I crave your pardon, for making your Honour wait so long, but my orders to my servants have been to admit no body, without my knowledge; for fear of some attempt upon my daughter, the times being full of plots and roguery.

LORD FOPPINGTON. Much caution, I must confess, is a sign of great wisdom: but, stap my vitals, I have got a cold enough to destroy a porter – he, hem –

SIR TUNBELLY. I am very sorry for't, indeed, my Lord; but if your Lordship please to walk in, we'll help you to some brown sugar-candy. My Lord, I'll shew you the way.

LORD FOPPINGTON. Sir, I follow you with pleasure. [*Exeunt. As* Lord Foppingto*n's servants go to follow him in, they clap the door against* La Verole.

Nay, hold you me there, Sir. [*Servants within.*

LA VEROLE. Jernie qu'est ce que veut dire ça?[110]

SIR TUNBELLY. [*Within*] – Fire, Porter. [Porter *fires*] – Have among ye, my Masters.

LA VEROLE. Ah Je suis mort – [*The servants all run off.*

PORTER. Not one soldier left, by the Mass.

SCENE VI.

[*Changes to the Hall. Enter* Sir Tunbelly, *the* Chaplain *and servants, with* Lord Foppington disarm'd.]

SIR TUNBELLY. Come, bring him along, bring him along.

LORD FOPPINGTON. What the pax do you mean, Gentlemen, is it fair time,[111] that you are all drunk before dinner?

SIR TUNBELLY. Drunk, Sirrah? Here's an impudent rogue for you; drunk or sober, Bully, I'm a Justice of the Peace, and know how to deal with strolers.[112]

LORD FOPPINGTON. Strolers!

SIR TUNBELLY. Ay, strolers; come, give an account of your self; what's your name, where do you live? Do you pay Scott and Lott?[113] Are you a *Williamite*, or a *Jacobite*?[114] Come.

LORD FOPPINGTON. And why dost thou ask me so many impertinent questions?

SIR TUNBELLY. Because I'll make you answer 'em before I have done with you, you Rascal you.

LORD FOPPINGTON. Before Gad, all the answer I can make thee to 'em, is, that thou art a very extraordinary old fellow; stap my vitals –

SIR TUNBELLY. Nay, if you are for joking with deputy lieutenants, we'st know how to deal with you. Here, draw a warrant for him immediately.

LORD FOPPINGTON. A warrant – what the Devil is't thou would'st be at, Old Gentleman?

SIR TUNBELLY. I wou'd be at you, Sirrah, (if my hands were not ty'd as a magistrate) and with these two double fists, beat your teeth down your throat, you Dog you.

LORD FOPPINGTON. And why would'st thou spoil my face at that rate?

SIR TUNBELLY. For your design to rob me of my daughter, Villain.

LORD FOPPINGTON. Rab thee of thy daughter – now do I begin to believe I am a bed and asleep, and that all this is but a dream – If it be, 'twill be an agreeable surprise enough, to waken by and by; and instead of the impertinent company of a nasty country justice, find my self, perhaps, in the arms of a Woman of Quality. [*To* Sir Tunbelly] Prithee, Old Father, wilt thou give me leave to ask thee one question?

SIR TUNBELLY. I can't tell whether I will or not, 'till I know what it is.

LORD FOPPINGTON. Why, then it is, whether thou didst not write to my Lord *Foppington* to come down and marry thy daughter?

SIR TUNBELLY. Yes, marry did I; and my Lord *Foppington* is come down, and shall marry my daughter before she's a day older.

LORD FOPPINGTON. Now give me thy hand, dear Dad, I thought we should understand one another at last.

SIR TUNBELLY. This fellow's mad – here, bind him hand and foot. [*They bind him down.*

LORD FOPPINGTON. Nay, prithee, Knight, leave fooling, thy jest begins to grow dull.

SIR TUNBELLY. Bind him, I say, he's mad – bread and water, a dark room and a whip, may bring him to his senses again.[115]

LORD FOPPINGTON. [*Aside*] *I gad, If I don't waken quickly, by all I can see, this is like to prove one of the most impertinent dreams that ever I dreamt in my life.*

[*Enter* Miss Hoyden *and* Nurse. *Miss going up to him.*

MISS HOYDEN. Is this he that would have run away with me? Fough, how he stinks of sweets! Pray, Father, let him be dragg'd through the horse pond.

LORD FOPPINGTON. [*Aside*] *This must be my wife by her natural inclination to her husband.*

MISS HOYDEN. Pray, Father, what do you intend to do with him, hang him?

SIR TUNBELLY. That, at least, Child.

NURSE. Ay, and its e'en too good for him too.

LORD FOPPINGTON. [*Aside*] *Madam la Gouvernante, I presume; hitherto this appears to me, to be one of the most extraordinary families that ever Man of Quality match'd into.*

SIR TUNBELLY. What's become of my Lord, Daughter?

MISS HOYDEN. He's just coming, Sir.

LORD FOPPINGTON. [*Aside*] *My Lord – What does he mean by that, now?*

[*Enter* Young Fashion, *and* Lory.

Stap my vitals, *Tam*, now the dream's out. [*Seeing him.*

YOUNG FASHION. Is this the fellow, Sir, that design'd to trick me of your daughter?

SIR TUNBELLY. This is he, my Lord, how do you like him? Is not he a pretty fellow to get a fortune?

YOUNG FASHION. I find by his dress, he thought your daughter might be taken with a beau.

MISS HOYDEN. O gimmeni! Is this a beau? Let me see him again – ha! I find a beau's no such an ugly thing neither.

YOUNG FASHION. I gad, she'll be in love with him presently; I'll e'en have him sent away to gaol. [*To* Lord Foppington] Sir, tho' your undertaking shews you are a person of no extraordinary modesty, I suppose you han't confidence enough to expect much favour from me?

LORD FOPPINGTON. Strike me dumb, *Tam*. Thou art a very impudent fellow.

NURSE. Look if the varlet has not the frontery to call his Lordship plain *Thomas*.

BULL. The business is, he would feign himself mad, to avoid going to gaol.

LORD FOPPINGTON. [*Aside*] *That must be the chaplain, by his unfolding of mysteries.*

SIR TUNBELLY. Come, is the warrant writ?

CLERK. Yes, Sir.

SIR TUNBELLY. Give me the pen, I'll sign it – so, now Constable away with him.

LORD FOPPINGTON. Hold one moment – Pray, Gentlemen; my Lord *Foppington*, shall I beg one word with your Lordship?

NURSE. O ho, it's my Lord with him now; see how afflictions will humble folks.

MISS HOYDEN. Pray, my Lord, don't let him whisper too close, lest he bite your ear off.

LORD FOPPINGTON. I am not altogether so hungry, as your Ladyship is pleas'd to imagine. [*To* Young Fashion] Look you, *Tam*, I am sensible I have not been so kind to you as I ought, but I hope you'll forget what's past, and accept of the five thousand pounds I offer; thou may'st live in extream splendour with it; stap my vitals.

YOUNG FASHION. It's a much easier matter to prevent a disease than to cure it; a quarter of that sum would have secur'd your mistress; twice as much won't redeem her. [*Leaving him.*

SIR TUNBELLY. Well, what says he?

YOUNG FASHION. Only the rascal offer'd me a bribe to let him go.

SIR TUNBELLY. Ay, he shall go with a pox to him: lead on, Constable.

LORD FOPPINGTON. One word more, and I have done.

SIR TUNBELLY. Before Gad, thou art an impudent fellow, to trouble the Court at this rate, after thou art condemn'd; but speak once for all.

LORD FOPPINGTON. Why then once for all, I have at last luckily call'd to mind, that there is a gentleman of this country, who, I believe, cannot live far from this place (if he were here) would satisfie you, I am *Navelty*, Baron of *Foppington*, with five thousand pounds a year, and that fellow there, a rascal not worth a groat.

SIR TUNBELLY. Very well; now who is this honest gentleman you are so well acquainted with? [*To* Young Fashion] Come, Sir, we shall hamper him.

LORD FOPPINGTON. 'Tis Sir *John Friendly*.

SIR TUNBELLY. So; he lives within half a mile, and came down into the country but last night; this bold-fac'd fellow thought he had been at *London* still, and so quoted him; now we shall display him in his colours: I'll send for Sir *John* immediately. Here, Fellow, away presently, and desire my neighbour he'll do me the favour to step over, upon an extraordinary occasion; and in the mean while you had best secure this sharper in the *gate-house*.

CONSTABLE. An't please your Worship, he may chance to give us the slip thence: if I were worthy to advise, I think the dog-kennel's a surer place.

SIR TUNBELLY. With all my heart, any where.

LORD FOPPINGTON. Nay, for Heaven's sake, Sir, do me the favour to put me in a clean room, that I mayn't daub my cloaths.

SIR TUNBELLY. O when you have married my daughter, her estate will afford you new ones: away with him.

LORD FOPPINGTON. A dirty country justice, is a barbarous magistrate; stap my vitals. – [*Exit* Constable *with* Lord Foppington.

YOUNG FASHION. – [*Aside*] *I gad, I must prevent this knight's coming, or the house will grow soon too hot to hold me.* – [*To* Sir Tunbelly] Sir, I fancy 'tis not worth while to trouble Sir *John* upon this impertinent fellow's desire: I'll send and call the messenger back. –

SIR TUNBELLY. Nay, with all my heart; for to be sure he thought he was far enough off, or the rogue wou'd never have nam'd him.

[*Enter* Servant.

SERVANT. Sir, I met Sir *John* just lighting at the gate, he's come to wait upon you.

SIR TUNBELLY. Nay, then it happens as one cou'd wish.

YOUNG FASHION. [*Aside to* Lory] The Devil it does. Lory, you see how things are, here will be a discovery presently, and we shall have our brains beat out; for my brother will be sure to swear he don't know me; therefore run into the stable, take the two first horses you can light on, I'll slip out at the back door, and we'll away immediately.

LORY. What, and leave your lady, Sir?

YOUNG FASHION. There's no danger in that, as long as I have taken possession, I shall know how to treat with 'em well enough, if once I am out of their reach: away, I'll steal after thee. [*Exit* Lory, *his Master follows him out at one door, as* Sir John Friendly *enters at t'other.*

[*Enter* Sir John Friendly.

SIR TUNBELLY. Sir *John*, you are the welcom'st man alive, I had just sent a messenger to desire you'd step over, upon a very extraordinary occasion – we are all in arms here.

SIR JOHN. How so?

SIR TUNBELLY. Why you must know – a finical[116] sort of a tawdry fellow here (I don't know who the Devil he is, not I) hearing I suppose, that the match was concluded between my Lord *Foppington*, and my girl *Hoyden*, comes impudently to the gate, with a whole pack of rogues in liveries,[117] and wou'd have past upon me for his Lordship; but what does I? I comes up to him boldly at the head of his guards, takes him by the throat, strikes up his heels, binds him hand and foot, dispatches a warrant, and commits him prisoner to the dog-kennel.

SIR JOHN. So, but how do you know but this was my Lord? For I was told he set out from *London* the day before me, with a very fine retinue, and intended to come directly hither.

SIR TUNBELLY. Why now to shew you how many lies people raise in that damn'd Town, he came two nights ago post, with only one servant, and is now in the house with me, but you don't know the cream of the jest yet; this same rogue (that lies yonder neck and heels among the hounds) thinking you were out of the country, quotes you for his acquaintance, and said, if you were here, you'd justifie him to be Lord *Foppington*, and I know not what.

SIR JOHN. Pray will you let me see him?

SIR TUNBELLY. Ay, that you shall presently – here, fetch the prisoner. [*Exit* Servant.

SIR JOHN. I wish there be'nt some mistake in this business, where's my Lord? I know him very well.

SIR TUNBELLY. He was here just now; see for him, Doctor, tell him Sir *John* is here to wait upon him. [*Exit* Chaplain.

SIR JOHN. I hope, Sir *Tunbelly*, the young lady is not married yet.

SIR TUNBELLY. No, things won't be ready this week; but why do you say you hope she is not married?

SIR JOHN. Some foolish fancies only, perhaps I'm mistaken.

[*Re-enter* Chaplain.

BULL. Sir, his Lordship is just rid out to take the air.

SIR TUNBELLY. To take the air! Is that his *London* breeding to go take the air, when gentlemen come to visit him?

SIR JOHN. 'Tis possible he might want it, he might not be well, some sudden qualm perhaps.

[*Enter* Constable, *&c. with* Lord Foppington.

LORD FOPPINGTON. Stap my vitals, I'll have satisfaction.

SIR JOHN. [*Running to him*] My dear Lord *Foppington*.

LORD FOPPINGTON. Dear *Friendly*, thou art come in the critical minute, strike me dumb.

SIR JOHN. Why, I little thought I shou'd have found you in fetters.

LORD FOPPINGTON. Why truly the World must do me the justice to confess I do use to appear a little more degage;[118] but this old gentleman, not liking the freedom of my air, has been pleas'd to skewer down my arms like a rabbit.

SIR TUNBELLY. Is it then possible that this shou'd be the true Lord *Foppington* at last?

LORD FOPPINGTON. Why, what do you see in his face to make you doubt of it? Sir, without presuming to have any extraordinary opinion of my figure, give me leave to tell you, if you had seen as many lords as I have done, you wou'd not think it impossible a person of a worse taille[119] than mine, might be a modern Man of Quality.

SIR TUNBELLY. Unbind him, Slaves; my Lord, I'm struck dumb, I can only beg pardon by signs, but if a sacrifice will appease you, you shall have it. Here, pursue this tartar, bring him back – away, I say, a dog-oons – I'll cut off his ears, and his tail, I'll draw out all his teeth, pull his skin over his head – and – and what shall I do more?

SIR JOHN. He does indeed deserve to be made an example of.

LORD FOPPINGTON. He does deserve to be Chartre,[120] stap my vitals.

SIR TUNBELLY. May I then hope I have your Honour's pardon?

LORD FOPPINGTON. Sir, we courtiers do nothing without a bribe, that fair young lady might do miracles.

SIR TUNBELLY. *Hoyden*, come hither *Hoyden*.

LORD FOPPINGTON. *Hoyden* is her name, Sir?

SIR TUNBELLY. Yes, my Lord.

LORD FOPPINGTON. The prettiest name for a song I ever heard.

SIR TUNBELLY. My Lord – here's my girl, she's yours, she has a wholsom body, and a virtuous mind, she's a woman compleat, both in flesh and in spirit; she has a bag of mill'd crowns,[121] as scarce as they are, and fifteen hundred a year stitch'd fast to her tail, so go thy ways *Hoyden*.

LORD FOPPINGTON. Sir, I do receive her like a gentleman.

SIR TUNBELLY. Then I'm a happy man, I bless Heaven, and if your Lordship will give me leave, I will, like a good Christian at *Christmass*, be very drunk by way of thanksgiving; come, my Noble Peer, I believe dinner's ready, if your Honour pleases to follow me, I'll lead you on to the attack of a venison pasty.[122] [*Exit* Sir Tunbelly.

LORD FOPPINGTON. Sir, I wait upon you, will your Ladyship do me the favour of your little finger, Madam?

MISS HOYDEN. My Lord, I'll follow you presently, I have a little business with my Nurse.

LORD FOPPINGTON. Your Ladyship's most humble servant; come *Sir John*, the ladies have *des affaires*. [*Exeunt* Lord Foppington *and* Sir John.

MISS HOYDEN. So Nurse, we are finely brought to bed, what shall we do now?

NURSE. Ah dear Miss, we are all undone; Mr. *Bull*, you were us'd to help a woman to a remedy. [*Crying*.

BULL. A lack a day, but it's past my skill now, I can do nothing.

NURSE. Who wou'd have thought that ever your invention shou'd have been drain'd so dry.

MISS HOYDEN. Well, I have often thought old folks fools, and now I'm sure they are so; I have found a way my self to secure us all.

NURSE. Dear Lady, what's that?

MISS HOYDEN. Why, if you two will be sure to hold your tongues, and not say a word of what's past, I'll e'en marry this Lord too.

NURSE. What! two husbands, my Dear?

MISS HOYDEN. Why you have had three, good Nurse, you may hold your tongue.

NURSE. Ay, but not altogether, sweet Child.

MISS HOYDEN. Psha, if you had, you'd ne'er a thought much on't.

NURSE. O but 'tis a sin – Sweeting.

BULL. Nay that's my business to speak to, Nurse; I do confess, to take two husbands for the satisfaction of the flesh, is to commit the sin of exorbitancy, but to do it for the peace of the spirit, is no more than to be drunk by way of physick;[123] besides, to prevent a parent's wrath, is to avoid the sin of disobedience; for when the parent's angry, the child is froward. So that upon the whole matter, I do think, tho' Miss shou'd marry again, she may be sav'd.

MISS HOYDEN. I cod and I will marry again then, and so there's an end of the story.

Act V. Scene I.

[*London. Enter* Coupler, Young Fashion, *and* Lory.]

COUPLER. Well, and so *Sir John* coming in –

YOUNG FASHION. And so *Sir John* coming in, I thought it might be manners in me to go out, which I did, and getting on horseback as fast as I cou'd, rid away as if the Devil had been at the reer of me; what has happen'd since, Heav'n knows.

COUPLER. I gad Sirrah, I know as well as Heaven.

YOUNG FASHION. What do you know?

COUPLER. That you are a cuckold.

YOUNG FASHION. The Devil I am? By who?

COUPLER. By your brother.

YOUNG FASHION. My brother! Which way?

COUPLER. The old way, he has lain with your wife.

YOUNG FASHION. Hell and Furies, what dost thou mean?

COUPLER. I mean plainly, I speak no parable.

YOUNG FASHION. Plainly! Thou do'st not speak common sense, I cannot understand one word thou say'st.

COUPLER. You will do soon, Youngster. In short, you left your wife a widow, and she married again.

YOUNG FASHION. It's a lie.

COUPLER. – I cod, if I were a young fellow, I'd break your head, Sirrah.

YOUNG FASHION. Dear Dad, don't be angry, for I'm as mad as *Tom* of *Bedlam*.[124]

COUPLER. Then I had fitted you with a wife, you shou'd have kept her.

YOUNG FASHION. But is it possible the young strumpet cou'd play me such a trick?

COUPLER. A young strumpet, Sir – can play twenty tricks.

YOUNG FASHION. But prithee instruct me a little farther; whence comes thy intelligence?

COUPLER. From your brother, in this letter, there, you may read it. [Young Fashion *reads.*

> *Dear* Coupler, [*Pulling off his hat.*
>
> *I have only time to tell thee in three lines, or thereabouts, that here has been the Devil, that rascal Tam having stole the letter thou hadst formerly writ for me to bring to Sir Tunbelly, form'd a damnable design upon my mistress, and was in a fair way of success when I arriv'd. But, after having suffer'd some indignities (in which I have all daub'd my embroider'd coat), I put him to flight. I sent out a party of horse*[125] *after him, in hopes to have made him my prisoner, which if I had done, I wou'd have qualify'd him for the seraglio,*[126] *stap my vitals.*
>
> *The danger I have thus narrowly 'scapt, has made me fortifie my self against further attempts, by entring immediately into an association with the young Lady, by which we engage to stand by one another, as long as we both shall live.*
>
> *In short, the papers are seal'd, and the contract is sign'd, so the business of the lawyer is achevé, but I defer the divine part of the thing 'till I arrive at London; not being willing to consummate in any other bed but my own.*
>
> *Postscript.*
>
> *'Tis possible I may be in Tawne as soon as this letter, far I find the lady is so violently in love with me, I have determin'd to make her happy with all the dispatch that is practicable, without disardering my coach-harses.*

So, here's rare work, I saith.

LORY. I gad, Miss *Hoyden* has lay'd about her bravely.

COUPLER. I think my country girl has play'd her part as well, as if she had been born and bred in St. *James*'s Parish.[127]

YOUNG FASHION. – That rogue the chaplain.

LORY. And then that jade the nurse, Sir.

YOUNG FASHION. And then that drunken sot *Lory*, Sir, that cou'd not keep himself sober, to be a witness to the marriage.

LORY. Sir – with respect – I know very few drunken sots that do keep themselves sober.

YOUNG FASHION. Hold your prating Sirrah, or I'll break your head; dear *Coupler*, what's to be done?

COUPLER. Nothing's to be done, 'till the bride and bridegroom come to Town.

YOUNG FASHION. Bride, and bridegroom! Death and Furies, I can't bear that thou should'st call 'em so.

COUPLER. Why what shall I call 'em, dog and cat?

YOUNG FASHION. Not for the world, that sounds more like man and wife than t'other.

COUPLER. Well, if you'll hear of 'em in no language, we'll leave 'em for the nurse and the chaplain.

YOUNG FASHION. The Devil and the witch.

COUPLER. When they come to Town –

LORY. We shall have stormy weather.

COUPLER. Will you hold your tongues, Gentlemen, or not?

LORY. Mum.

COUPLER. I say when they come, we must find what stuff they are made of, whether the churchman be chiefly compos'd of the flesh, or the spirit; I presume the former – for as chaplains now go, 'tis probable he eats three pound of beef to the reading of one chapter – this gives him carnal desires, he wants money, preferment,[128] wine, a whore; therefore we must invite him to supper, give him fat capons, sack and sugar, a purse of gold, and a plump sister. Let this be done, and I'll warrant thee, my Boy, he speaks truth like an oracle.

YOUNG FASHION. Thou art a profound statesman I allow it; but how shall we gain the nurse?

COUPLER. O never fear the nurse, if once you have got the priest, for the Devil always rides the nag. Well, there's nothing more to be said of the matter at this time, that I know of; so let us go and enquire, if there's any news of our people yet, perhaps they may be come. But let me tell you one thing by the way, Sirrah, I doubt you have been an idle fellow, if thou had'st behav'd thy self as thou should'st have done, the girl wou'd never have left thee. [*Exeunt.*

Scene II.

[Berinthia*'s apartment. Enter her* Maid *passing the stage, followed by* Worthy.]

WORTHY. Hem, Mrs. *Abigal*, is your Mistress to be spoken with?

ABIGAL. By you, Sir, I believe she may.

WORTHY. Why 'tis by me I wou'd have her spoken with.

ABIGAL. I'll acquaint her, Sir. [*Exit* Abigal.

WORTHY. [*Solus*] One lift more I must perswade her to give me, and then I'm mounted. Well, a young bawd and a handsome one for my money, 'tis they do the execution; I'll never go to an old one, but when I have occasion for a witch. Lewdness looks heavenly to a woman, when an angel appears in its cause; but when a hag is advocate, she thinks it comes from the Devil. An old woman has something so terrible in her looks, that whilst she is perswading your mistress to forget she has a soul, she stares Hell and damnation full in her face.

[*Enter* Berinthia.

BERINTHIA. Well Sir, what news bring you?

WORTHY. No news, Madam, there's a woman going to cuckold her husband.

BERINTHIA. *Amanda*?

WORTHY. I hope so.

BERINTHIA. Speed her well.

WORTHY. Ay, but there must be more than a God speed, or your charity won't be worth a farthing.

BERINTHIA. Why han't I done enough already?

WORTHY. Not quite.

BERINTHIA. What's the matter?

WORTHY. The lady has a scruple still, which you must remove.

BERINTHIA. What's that?

WORTHY. Her virtue – she says.

BERINTHIA. And do you believe her?

WORTHY. No, but I believe it's what she takes for her virtue; it's some relicks of lawful love; she is not yet fully satisfy'd her husband has got another mistress, which unless I can convince her of, I have open'd the trenches in vain, for the breach must be wider, before I dare storm the town.

BERINTHIA. And so I'm to be your engineer?

WORTHY. I'm sure you know best how to manage the battery.

BERINTHIA. What think you of springing a mine? I have a thought just now come into my head, how to blow her up at once.

WORTHY. That wou'd be a thought indeed.

BERINTHIA. – Faith I'll do't, and thus the execution of it shall be: we are all invited to my Lord *Foppington*'s to night to supper, he's come to Town with his bride, and makes a ball with an entertainment of musick. Now you must know, my undoer here, *Loveless*, says he must needs meet me about some private business (I don't know what 'tis) before we go to the company. To which end, he has told his wife one lie, and I have told her another. But to make her amends, I'll go immediately, and tell her a solemn truth.

WORTHY. What's that?

BERINTHIA. Why, I'll tell her; that to my certain knowledge, her husband has a rendezvous with his mistress this afternoon; and that if she'll give me her word, she'll be satisfied with the discovery, without making any violent inquiry after the woman, I'll direct her to a place, where she shall see 'em meet.

Now, Friend, this I fancy may help you to a critical minute. For home she must go again to dress. You (with your good breeding) come to wait upon us to the ball, find her all alone, her spirit enflam'd against her husband for his treason, and her flesh in a heat from some contemplations upon the treachery, her blood on a fire, her conscience in ice, a lover to draw, and the Devil to drive – ah poor *Amanda*.

WORTHY. [*Kneeling*] Thou Angel of Light, let me fall down and adore thee?

BERINTHIA. Thou Minister of Darkness, get up again, for I hate to see the Devil at his devotions.

WORTHY. Well, my incomparable *Berinthia* – how I shall requite you –

BERINTHIA. O ne'er trouble your self about that: virtue is its own reward. There's a pleasure in doing good, which sufficiently pays it self. Adieu.

WORTHY. Farewell, thou best of women. [*Exeunt several ways.*

[*Enter* Amanda, *meeting* Berinthia.

AMANDA. Who was that went from you?

BERINTHIA. A friend of yours.

AMANDA. What does he want?

BERINTHIA. Something you might spare him, and be ne'er the poorer.

AMANDA. I can spare him nothing but my friendship; my love already's all dispos'd of. Tho', I confess, to one ungrateful to my bounty.

BERINTHIA. Why there's the mystery: you have been so bountiful, you have cloy'd him. Fond wives do by their husbands, as barren wives do by their lap-dogs; cram 'em with sweet meats 'till they spoil their stomachs.

AMANDA. Alas! Had you but seen how passionately fond he has been since our last reconciliation, you wou'd have thought it were impossible, he ever shou'd have breath'd an hour without me.

BERINTHIA. Ay, but there you thought wrong again, *Amanda*, you shou'd consider, that in matters of love, men's eyes are always bigger than their bellies. They have violent appetites, 'tis true; but they have soon din'd.

AMANDA. Well; there's nothing upon earth astonishes me more, than men's inconstancy.

BERINTHIA. Now there's nothing upon earth astonishes me less, when I consider what they and we are compos'd of. For nature has made them children, and us babies. Now, *Amanda*, how we us'd our babies, you may remember. We were mad to have 'em, as soon as we saw 'em; kist 'em to pieces, as soon as we got 'em. Then pull'd off their cloaths, saw 'em naked, and so threw 'em away.

AMANDA. But do you think all men are of this temper?

BERINTHIA. All but one.

AMANDA. Who is that?

BERINTHIA. *Worthy*.

AMANDA. Why he's weary of his wife too, you see.

BERINTHIA. Ay, that's no proof.

AMANDA. What can be a greater?

BERINTHIA. Being weary of his mistress.

AMANDA. Don't you think 'twere possible he might give you that too?

BERINTHIA. Perhaps he might, if he were my gallant; not if he were yours.

AMANDA. Why do you think he shou'd be more constant to me, than he wou'd to you? I'm sure, I'm not so handsome.

BERINTHIA. Kissing goes by favour; he likes you best.

AMANDA. Suppose he does? That's no demonstration he wou'd be constant to me.

BERINTHIA. No, that I'll grant you: But there are other reasons to expect it. For you must know after all, *Amanda*, the inconstancy we commonly see in men of brains, does not so much proceed from the uncertainty of their temper, as from the misfortunes of their love. A man sees perhaps a hundred women he likes well enough for an intrigue, and away. But possibly, through the whole course of his life, does not find above one, who is exactly what he could wish her; now her, 'tis a thousand to one, he never gets. Either she is not to be had at all, (tho' that seldom happens you'll say) or he wants those opportunities that are necessary to gain her. Either she likes some body else much better than him, or uses him like a dog, because he likes no body so well as her. Still something or other Fate claps in the way between them and the woman they are capable of being fond of: and this makes them wander about, from mistress to mistress, like a pilgrim from town to town, who every night must have a fresh lodging, and's in haste to be gone in the morning.

AMANDA. 'Tis possible there may be something in what you say; but what do you infer from it, as to the man we were talking of?

BERINTHIA. Why, I infer, that you being the woman in the world, the most to his humour, 'tis not likely he would quit you for one that is less.

AMANDA. That is not to be depended upon, for you see Mr. *Loveless* does so.

BERINTHIA. What does Mr. *Loveless* do?

AMANDA. Why? He runs after something for variety, I'm sure he does not like so well as he does me.

BERINTHIA. That's more than you know, Madam.

AMANDA. No, I'm sure on't: I am not very vain, *Berinthia*, and yet I'd lay my life, if I cou'd look into his heart, he thinks I deserve to be preferr'd to a thousand of her.

BERINTHIA. Don't be too positive in that neither; a million to one, but she has the same opinion of you. What wou'd you give to see her?

AMANDA. Hang her, dirty Trull; tho' I really believe she's so ugly, she'd cure me of my jealousie.

BERINTHIA. All the men of sense about Town, say she's handsome.

AMANDA. They are as often out in those things as any people.

BERINTHIA. Then I'll give you farther proof – All the women about Town, say, she's a fool: now I hope you're convinc'd?

AMANDA. What e're she be, I'm satisfi'd he does not like her well enough, to bestow any thing more, than a little outward gallantry upon her.

BERINTHIA. Outward gallantry? – [*Aside*] *I can't bear this.* – [*To* Amanda] Don't you think she's a woman to be fobb'd off so. Come, I'm too much your friend, to suffer you should be thus grossly impos'd upon, by a man who does not deserve the least part about you, unless he knew how to set a greater value upon it. Therefore in one word, to my certain knowledge, he is to meet her now, within a quarter of an hour, somewhere about that *Babylon* of wickedness, *White-Hall*. And if you'll give me your word, that you'll be content with seeing her mask'd in his hand, without pulling her headcloaths off, I'll step immediately to the person, from whom I have my intelligence, and send you word where abouts you may stand to see 'em meet. My friend and I'll watch 'em from another place, and dodge 'em to their private lodging: but don't you offer to follow 'em, lest you do it awkwardly, and spoil all. I'll come home to you again, as soon as I have earth'd 'em, and give you an account, in what corner of the house, the scene of their lewdness lies.

AMANDA. If you can do this, *Berinthia*; he's a villain.

BERINTHIA. I can't help that, men will be so.

AMANDA. Well! I'll follow your directions; for I shall never rest 'till I know the worst of this matter.

BERINTHIA. Pray, go immediately, and get your self ready then. Put on some of your woman's cloaths, a great scarf and a mask, and you shall presently receive orders. [*Calls within*] Here, who's there? Get me a chair quickly.

SERVANT. There are chairs at the door, Madam.

BERINTHIA. 'Tis well, I'm coming.

AMANDA. But pray, *Berinthia*, before you go, tell me how I may know this filthy thing, if she should be so forward, (as I suppose she will) to come to the rendezvous first, for methinks I would fain view her a little.

BERINTHIA. Why she's about my height; and very well shap'd.

AMANDA. I thought she had been a little crooked?

BERINTHIA. O no, she's as strait as I am. But we lose time, come away. [*Exeunt.*

Scene III.

[*Enter* Young Fashion, *meeting* Lory.]

YOUNG FASHION. Well, will the doctor come?

LORY. Sir, I sent a porter to him as you order'd me. He found him with a pipe of tobacco and a great tankard of ale, which he said he wou'd dispatch while I cou'd tell three, and be here.

YOUNG FASHION. He does not suspect 'twas I that sent for him?

LORY. Not a jot, Sir; he divines as little for himself, as he does for other folks.

YOUNG FASHION. Will he bring Nurse with him?

LORY. Yes.

YOUNG FASHION. That's well; where's *Coupler*?

LORY. He's half way up the stairs taking breath; he must play his bellows a little, before he can get to the top.

[*Enter* Coupler.

YOUNG FASHION. O here he is. Well, Old Physick, the doctor's coming.

COUPLER. Wou'd the pox had the doctor – I'm quite out of wind. [*To* Lory] Set me a chair, Sirrah, ah – [*Sits down. To* Young Fashion] Why the plague can'st not thou lodge upon the ground floor?

YOUNG FASHION. Because I love to lye as near Heaven as I can.

COUPLER. Prithee let Heaven alone; ne'er affect tending that way: thy center's downwards.

YOUNG FASHION. That's impossible. I have too much ill luck in this world, to be damn'd in the next.

COUPLER. Thou art out in thy logick. Thy major is true, but thy minor is false; for thou art the luckiest fellow in the universe.

YOUNG FASHION. Make out that.

COUPLER. I'll do't: Last night the Devil ran away with the parson of fat-goose living.[129]

YOUNG FASHION. If he had run away with the parish too, what's that to me?

COUPLER. I'll tell thee what it's to thee. This living is worth five hundred pound a year, and the presentation of it is thine, if thou can'st prove they self a lawful husband to Miss *Hoyden*.

YOUNG FASHION. Say'st thou so, my Protector? Then I Gad I shall have a brace of evidences here presently.

COUPLER. The nurse and the doctor?

YOUNG FASHION. The same: the Devil himself won't have interest enough to make 'em withstand it.

COUPLER. That we shall see presently. Here they come.

[*Enter* Nurse *and* Chaplain*: they start back, seeing* Young Fashion.

NURSE. Ah goodness, *Roger*, we are betray'd.

YOUNG FASHION. [*Laying hold on'em*] Nay, nay, ne'er flinch for the matter; for I have you safe. Come, to your tryals immediately: I have no time to give you copies of your indictment. There sits your judge.

BOTH. [*Kneeling*] Pray, Sir, have compassion on us.

NURSE. I hope, Sir, my years will move your pity, I am an aged woman.

COUPLER. That is a moving argument indeed.

BULL. I hope, Sir, my character will be consider'd; I am Heaven's ambassador.

COUPLER. [*To* Bull] Are not you a Rogue of Sanctity?

BULL. Sir, (with respect to my function) I do wear a gown.

COUPLER. Did not you marry this vigorous young fellow, to a plump young buxom wench?

NURSE. [*To* Bull] Don't confess, *Roger*, unless you are hard put to it indeed.

COUPLER. Come, out with't – now is he chewing the cud of his roguery, and grinding a lie between his teeth.

BULL. Sir – I cannot positively say – I say, Sir – positively I cannot say –

COUPLER. Come, no equivocations; no Roman[130] turns upon us. Consider thou standest upon Protestant ground, which will slip from under thee, like a *Tyburn* cart;[131] for in this Country, we have always ten hangmen for one Jesuit.[132]

BULL. [*To* Young Fashion] Pray, Sir, then will you but permit me to speak one word in private with Nurse.

YOUNG FASHION. Thou art always for doing something in private with Nurse.

COUPLER. But pray let his betters be serv'd before him for once. I would do something in private with her my self: *Lory*, take care of this Reverend Gown-man in the next room a little. Retire Priest. [*Exit* Lory *with* Bull] Now, Virgin, I must put the matter home to you a little: do you think it might not be possible to make you speak truth?

NURSE. Alas! Sir, I don't know what you mean by truth.

COUPLER. Nay, 'tis possible thou may'st be a stranger to it.

YOUNG FASHION. Come, Nurse, you and I were better friends when we saw one another last; and I still believe, you are a very good woman in the bottom. I did deceive you and your young lady, 'tis true, but I always design'd to make a very good husband to her, and to be a very good friend to you. And 'tis possible in the end, she might have found her self happier, and you richer, than ever my brother will make you.

NURSE. Brother! Why is your Worship then his Lordship's brother?

YOUNG FASHION. I am, which you should have known, if I durst have staid to have told you; but I was forc'd to take horse a little in haste you know.

NURSE. You were indeed, Sir; poor young man, how he was bound to scaure[133] for't. Now won't your Worship be angry, if I confess the truth to you; when I found you were a cheat (with respect be it spoken) I verily believ'd, Miss had got some pitiful skip-jack varlet[134] or other to her husband; or I had ne'er let her think of marrying again.

COUPLER. But where was your conscience all this while, Woman? Did not that stair in your face, with huge saucer eyes, and a great horn upon the fore-head? Did not you think you shou'd be damn'd for such a sin? Ha?

YOUNG FASHION. Well said, Divinity, pass that home upon her.

NURSE. Why, in good truly Sir, I had some fearful thoughts on't, and cou'd never be brought to consent, 'till Mr. *Bull* said it was a *Peckadilla*,[135] and he'd secure my soul, for a tythe pigg.[136]

YOUNG FASHION. There was a rogue for you.

COUPLER. And he shall thrive accordingly: he shall have a good living. Come, honest *Nurse*, I see you have butter in your compound; you can melt. Some compassion you can have of this handsome young fellow.

NURSE. I have indeed, Sir.

YOUNG FASHION. Why then I'll tell you, what you shall do for me. You know what a warm living here is fallen; and that it must be in the disposal of him, who has the disposal of *Miss*. Now if you and the Doctor will agree to prove my marriage, I'll present him to it, upon condition he makes you his bride.

NURSE. Naw the Blessing of the Lord follow your good Worship both by night and by day. Let him be fetch'd in by the ears; I'll soon bring his nose to the grind-stone.

COUPLER. – [*Aside*] *Well said old White Leather.* – Hey; bring in the prisoner there.

[*Enter* Lory *with* Bull.

COUPLER. Come, advance Holy Man: Here's your duck, does not think fit to retire with you into the chancel at this time: but she has a proposal to make to you, in the face of the congregation. Come, *Nurse*, speak for your self; you are of age.

NURSE. *Roger*, are not you a wicked man, *Roger*, to set your strength against a weak woman; and perswade her it was no sin to conceal *Miss*'s nuptials? My conscience flies in my face for it, thou Priest of *Baal*;[137] and I find by woful experience, thy absolution, is not worth an old cassock. Therefore I am resolv'd to confess the truth to the whole World, tho' I die a beggar for it. But his Worship overflows with his mercy and his bounty: he is not only pleas'd to forgive us our sins, but designs thou sha't squat thee down in *fat-goose* living, and which is more than all, has prevail'd with me to become the wife of thy bosom.

YOUNG FASHION. All this I intend for you, Doctor. What you are to do for me; I need not tell you.

BULL. Your Worship's goodness is unspeakable: yet there is one thing, seems a point of conscience: and conscience is a tender babe. If I shou'd bind my self, for the sake of this living, to marry Nurse, and maintain her afterwards, I doubt it might be look'd on as a kind of symony.[138]

COUPLER. [*Rising up*] If it were sacriledge, the living's worth it: therefore no more words, good Doctor. But with the [*Giving* Nurse *to him*] parish – here – take the parsonage house. 'Tis true, 'tis a little out of repair; some delapidations there are to be made good; the windows are broke, the wainscot is warpt, the ceilings are peel'd, and the walls are crack'd; but a little glasing, painting, whitewash and playster, will make it last thy time.

BULL. Well, Sir, if it must be so, I shan't contend: what Providence orders, I submit to.

NURSE. And so do I, with all humility.

COUPLER. Why, that now was spoke like good people: come, my Turtle Doves, let us go help this poor pidgeon to his wandring mate again; and after institution and induction,[139] you shall all go a cooing together. [*Exeunt.*

Scene IV

[*Enter* Amanda *in a scarf, &c. as just return'd, her woman following her.*]

AMANDA. Prithee what care I who has been here.

WOMAN. Madam, 'twas my Lady Bridle, and my Lady Tiptoe.

AMANDA. My Lady *Fiddle*, and my Lady *Faddle*. What do'st stand troubling me with the visits of a parcel of impertinent women; when they are well seam'd with the small pox, they won't be so fond of shewing their faces – there are more cocquets about this Town.

WOMAN. Madam, I suppose they only came to return your Ladiship's visit, according to the custom of the World.

AMANDA. Wou'd the World were on fire, and you in the middle on't. Be gone; leave me. [*Exit* Woman.

[*Sola*] At last I am convinc'd. My eyes are testimonies of his falshood.
The base, ungrateful, perjur'd villain–
Good Gods!–what slippery stuff are men compos'd of?
Sure, the account of their creation's false,
And 'twas the woman's rib that they were form'd of;
But why am I thus angry?
This poor relapse shou'd only move my scorn.
'Tis true: the roving flights of his unfinisht youth,
Had strong excuse, from the plea of nature;
Reason had thrown the reins loose on his neck,
And slipt him to unlimited desire.
If therefore he went wrong,
He had a claim to my forgiveness, and I did him right.
But since the years of manhood rein him in,
And reason, well digested into thought,
Has pointed out the course he ought to run;
If now he strays,
'Twou'd be as weak, and mean in me to pardon,
As it has been in him t'offend.
But hold:
'Tis an ill cause indeed, where nothing's to be said for't.
My beauty possibly is in the wain;
Perhaps sixteen has greater charms for him:
Yes, there's the secret: but let him know,
My quiver's not entirely empty'd yet,
I still have darts, and I can shoot 'em too;
They're not so blunt, but they can enter still,
The wants not in my power, but in my will.
Virtue's his friend, or through another's heart,
I yet cou'd find the way, to make his smart.
[*Going off she meets* Worthy.
Ha! He here? Protect me Heav'n, for this looks ominous.

WORTHY. You seem disorder'd, Madam; I hope there's no misfortune happen'd to you?

AMANDA. None that will long disorder me, I hope.

WORTHY. What e're it be disturbs you, I wou'd to Heaven 'twere in my power to bear the pain, 'till I were able to remove the cause.

AMANDA. I hope e'er long it will remove it self.
At least, I have given it warning to be gone.

WORTHY. Wou'd I durst ask, where 'tis the thorn torments you?
Forgive me, if I grow inquisitive.
'Tis only with desire to give you ease.

AMANDA. Alas! 'tis in a tender part.
It can't be drawn without a world of pain.
Yet out it must;
For it begins to fester in my heart.

WORTHY. If 'tis the sting of unrequited love, remove it instantly:
I have a balm will quickly heal the wound.

AMANDA. You'll find the undertaking difficult:
The surgeon, who already has attempted it,
Has much tormented me.

WORTHY. I'll aid him with a gentler hand.
–If you will give me leave.

AMANDA. How soft so'er the hand may be,
There still is terrour in the operation.

WORTHY. Some few preparatives wou'd make it easie,
Cou'd I perswade you to apply 'em.
Make home reflections, Madam, on your slighted love.
Weigh well, the strength and beauty of your charms:
Rouze up that spirit women ought to bear,
And slight your god; if he neglects his angel.
With arms of ice receive his cold embraces,
And keep your fire for those who come in flames.
Behold a burning lover at your feet,
His fever raging in his veins.

See how he trembles, how he pants!
See how he glows, how he consumes!
Extend the arms of mercy to his aid;
His zeal may give him title to your pity,
Altho' his merit cannot claim your love.

AMANDA. Of all my feeble sex,
Sure I must be the weakest,
Shou'd I again presume to think on love.
[*Sighing*.
–Alas! My heart has been too roughly treated.

WORTHY. 'Twill find the greater bliss, in softer usage.

AMANDA. But where's that usage to be found?

WORTHY. 'Tis here,
Within this faithful breast; which if you doubt,
I'll rip it up before your eyes;
Lay all its secrets open to your view:
And then, you'll see 'twas sound.

AMANDA. With just such honest words as these,
The worst of men deceiv'd me.

WORTHY. He therefore merits
All revenge can do; his fault is such,
The extent and stretch of vengeance cannot reach it.
O make me but your instrument of justice;
You'll find me execute it with such zeal,
As shall convince you, I abhor the crime.

AMANDA. The rigour of an executioner
Has more the face of cruelty than justice:
And he who puts the cord about the wretch's neck
Is seldom known to exceed him in his morals.

WORTHY. What proof then can I give you of my truth?

AMANDA. There is on earth, but one.

WORTHY. And is that in my power?

AMANDA. It is:
And one that wou'd so thoroughly convince me,
I shou'd be apt to rate your heart so high,
I possibly might purchas't with a part of mine.

WORTHY. Then Heav'n thou art my friend, and I am blest,
For if 'tis in my power, my will I'm sure
Will reach it. No matter what the terms may be,
When such a recompence is offer'd.
O tell me quickly what this proof must be!
What is it, will convince you of my love?

AMANDA. I shall believe you love me as you ought,
If, from this moment, you forbear to ask
Whatever is unfit for me to grant.
You pause upon it, Sir–I doubt, on such hard terms,
A woman's heart is scarcely worth the having.

WORTHY. A heart like yours, on any terms is worth it;
'twas not on that I paus'd. But I was thinking,
[*Drawing nearer to her*]
Whether some things there may not be,
Which women cannot grant without a blush,
And yet which men may take without offence.
[*Taking her hand*]
Your hand, I fancy, may be of the number:
O pardon me, if I commit a rape
Upon it, [*Kissing it eagerly*] and thus devour it with my kisses.

AMANDA. O Heavens! Let me go.

WORTHY. Never whilst I have strength to hold you here. [*Forcing her to sit down on a couch*.
My Life, my Soul, my Goddess–O forgive me!

AMANDA. O whither am I going? Help, Heaven, or I am lost.

WORTHY. Stand neuter, gods, this once I do invoke you.

AMANDA. Then save me, Virtue, and the glory's thine.

WORTHY. Nay, never strive.

AMANDA. I will; and conquer too.
My forces rally bravely to my aid, [*Breaking from him*.
And thus I gain the day.

WORTHY. Then mine as bravely double their attack, [*Seizing her again*.
And thus I wrest it from you. Nay struggle not;
For all's in vain: or death or victory;
I am determin'd.

AMANDA. And so am I. [*Rushing from him*.
Now keep your distance, or we part for ever.

WORTHY. For Heaven's sake– [*Offering again*.

AMANDA. Nay, then farewell. [*Going*.

WORTHY. O stay, and see the magick force of love:
Behold this raging lion at your feet,
Struck dead with fear, and tame as charms can make him.
What must I do to be forgiven by you?
[*Kneeling and holding by her cloaths*.

AMANDA. Repent, and never more offend.

WORTHY. Repentance for past crimes is just and easie;
But sin no more's a task too hard for mortals.

AMANDA. Yet those who hope for Heaven,
Must use their best endeavours to perform it.

WORTHY. Endeavours we may use, but flesh and blood
Are got in t'other scale; and they are pondrous things.
AMANDA. What e'er they are;
There is a weight in resolution
Sufficient for their ballance. The soul, I do confess,
Is usually so careless of its charge,
So soft, and so indulgent to desire,
It leaves the reins in the wild hand of Nature,
Who like a *Phaeton*, drives the fiery chariot,
And sets the world on flame.[140]
Yet still the soveraignty is in the mind,
When e're it pleases to exert its force.
Perhaps you may not think it worth your while,
To take such mighty pains for my esteem,
But that I leave to you.
You see the price I set upon my heart,
Perhaps 'tis dear: but spight of all your art,
You'll find on cheaper terms, we ne'er shall part. [*Exit* Amanda.
WORTHY. [*Solus*] Sure there's divinity about her;
And sh'as dispenc'd some portion on't to me.
For what but now was the wild flame of love,
Or (to dissect that specious term)
The vile, the gross desires of flesh and blood,
Is in a moment turn'd to adoration.
The coarser appetite of nature's gone,
And 'tis methinks the food of angels I require;
How long this influence may last, Heaven knows.
But in this moment of my purity,
I cou'd on her own terms, accept her heart.
Yes, lovely Woman; I can accept it.
For now 'tis doubly worth my care.
Your charms are much encreas'd, since thus adorn'd.
When truth's extorted from us, then we own
The robe of virtue is a graceful habit.
Cou'd women but our secret councils scan,
Cou'd they but reach the deep reserves of man,
They'd wear it on, that that of love might last,
For when they throw off one, we soon the other cast.
Their sympathy is such–
The fate of one, the other scarce can fly;
They live together, and together dye. [*Exit.*

Scene V.

[*Enter* Miss Hoyden *and* Nurse.]

MISS HOYDEN. But is it sure and certain, say you, he's my Lord's own brother?

NURSE. As sure, as he's your lawful husband.

MISS HOYDEN. I cod if I had known that in time, I don't know but I might have kept him: for between you and I *Nurse*, he'd have made a husband worth two of this I have. But which do you think you shou'd fancy most, Nurse?

NURSE. Why truly, in my poor fancy, Madam, your first husband is the prettier gentleman.

MISS HOYDEN. I don't like my Lord's shapes, *Nurse*.

NURSE. Why in good truly, as a body may say, he is but a slam.[141]

MISS HOYDEN. What do you think now he puts me in mind of? Don't you remember, a long, loose, shambling sort of a horse my father call'd *Washy*?

NURSE. As like as two twin brothers.

MISS HOYDEN. I cod, I have thought so a hundred times; faith I'm tir'd of him.

NURSE. Indeed, Madam, I think you had e'en as good stand to your first bargain.

MISS HOYDEN. O but, *Nurse*, we han't consider'd the main thing yet. If I leave my Lord, I must leave my Lady too; and when I rattle about the streets in my coach, they'll only say, there goes Mistress – Mistress – Mistress what? What's this man's name, I have married, Nurse?

NURSE. Squire Fashion.

MISS HOYDEN. Squire Fashion is it? – Well Squire,[142] that's better than nothing: Do you think one cou'd not get him made a Knight,[143] Nurse?

NURSE. I don't know but one might, Madam, when the King's in a good humour.

MISS HOYDEN. I cod, that wou'd do rarely. For then he'd be as good a man as my father, you know?

NURSE. Birlady,[144] and that's as good as the best of 'em.

MISS HOYDEN. So 'tis, Faith; for then I shall be my Lady, and your Ladyship at every word, and that's all I have to care for. Ha, *Nurse*, but hark you me, one thing more, and then I have done. I'm afraid, if I change my husband again, I shan't have so much money to throw about, *Nurse*?

NURSE. O, enough's as good as a feast: besides, Madam, one don't know, but as much may fall to your share with the younger brother as with the elder. For tho' these Lords have a power of wealth indeed: yet, as I have heard say, they give it all to their sluts and their trulls,[145] who joggle it about in their coaches, with a murrain[146] to 'em, whilst poor Madam, sits sighing and wishing, and knotting[147] and crying, and has not a spare half crown, to buy her a *Practice of Piety*.[148]

MISS HOYDEN. O, but for that, don't deceive your self, Nurse. For this I must [*Snapping her fingers*] say for my Lord, and a – for him. He's as free as an open house at *Christmas*. For this very morning, he told me, I shou'd have two hundred a year to buy pins. Now, Nurse, if he gives me two hundred a year to buy pins, what do you think he'll give me to buy fine petticoats?

NURSE. A, my dearest, he deceives thee faully;[149] and he's no better than a rogue for his pains. These *Londoners* have got a gibberidge with 'em, wou'd confound a gypsey. That which they call pin-money, is to buy their wives every thing in the varsal world, dawn to their very shoe-tyes. Nay, I have heard folks say, that some ladies, if they will have gallants, as they call 'um; are forc't to find them out of their pin-money too.

MISS HOYDEN. Has he serv'd me so, say ye? – Then I'll be his wife no longer, so that's fixt. Look, here he comes, with all the fine folk at's heels. I cod, Nurse, these *London* ladies will laugh 'till they crack again, to see me slip my collar, and run away from my husband. But d'ye hear? Pray take care of one thing: when the business comes to break out, be sure you get between me and my father, for you know his tricks; he'll knock me down.

NURSE. I'll mind him, ne'er fear, Madam.

[*Enter* Lord Foppington, Loveless, Worthy, Amanda, *and* Berinthia.

LORD FOPPINGTON. Ladies and Gentlemen, you are all welcome [*To* Loveless] *Loveless* – that's my wife; prithee do me the favour to salute her: and do'st hear, – [*Aside to him*] if thou hast a mind to try thy fartune, to be reveng'd of me, I won't take it ill, stap my vitals.

LOVELESS. You need not fear, Sir, I'm too fond of my own wife, to have the least inclination to yours. [*All salute* Miss Hoyden.

LORD FOPPINGTON. I'd give you a thousand paund he would make love to her, that he may see she has sense enough to prefer me to him, tho' his own wife has not. [*Aside; viewing him*] – He's a very beastly fellow in my opinion.

MISS HOYDEN. What a power of fine men there are in this *London*? He that kist me first is a goodly gentleman, I promise you: – [*Aside*] *sure those wives have a rare time on't, that live here always?*

[*Enter* Sir Tunbelly *with musitians, dancers, &c.*

SIR TUNBELLY. Come; come in, good people, come in, come tune your fiddles, tune your fiddles. Bag-pipes, make ready there. [*To the Hautboys.*[150]] Come strike up. [*Sings.*

For this is Hoyden's wedding-day,
And therefore we keep Holy-day,
And come to be merry.

Ha! There's my wench, I Faith: touch and take, I'll warrant her. Shee'll breed like a tame rabbet.

MISS HOYDEN. [*Aside*] *I cod, I think my father's gotten drunk before supper.*

SIR TUNBELLY. [*To* Loveless *and* Worthy] Gentlemen, you are welcome. [*Saluting* Amanda *and* Berinthia] Ladies by your leave. Ha – they bill like turtles.[151] Udsookers, they set my old blood a-fire; I shall cuckold some body before morning.

LORD FOPPINGTON. Sir, you being Master of the Entertainment; will you desire the company to sit? [*To* Sir Tunbelly.

SIR TUNBELLY. Oons, Sir – I'm the happiest man on this side the *Ganges*.

LORD FOPPINGTON. – [*Aside*] *This is a mighty unaccountable old fellow.* – [*To* Sir Tunbelly] I said, Sir, it would be convenient to ask the company to sit.

SIR TUNBELLY. Sit – with all my heart. Come, take your places, Ladies, take your places, Gentlemen: come sit down, sit down; a pox of ceremony, take your places. [*They sit, and the Mask*[152] *begins.*

[*Dialogue between* Cupid *and* Hymen.[153]

CUPID.

1.
Thou bane to my empire, thou spring of contest,
Thou source of all discord, thou period to rest;
Instruct me, what wretches in bondage can see,
That the aim of their life, is still pointed to thee.

HYMEN.

2.
Instruct me, thou little impertinent god,
From whence all thy subjects have taken the mode,
To grow fond of a change, to whatever it be,
And I'll tell thee why those wou'd be bound, who are free?
Chorus.
For change, w'are for change, to whatever it be,
We are neither contented, with freedom nor thee.
Constancy's an empty sound,
Heaven and Earth, and all go round,
All the works of Nature move,
And the joys of life and love
Are is variety.

CUPID.

3.
Were love the reward of a pains-taking life,
Had a husband the art to be fond of his wife,
Were virtue so plenty, a wife cou'd afford,
These very hard times, to be true to her Lord,
Some specious account, might be given of those,
Who are ty'd by the tail, to be led by the nose.

4.
But since 'tis the fate, of a man and his wife
To consume all their days in contention and strife:
Since whatever the bounty of Heaven may create her,
He's morally sure, he shall heartily hate her,
I think 'twere much wiser to ramble at large,
And the volleys of love on the herd to discharge.

HYMEN.

5.
Some colour of reason, thy council might hear,
Could a man have no more, than his wife to his share:
Or were I a monarch, so cruelly just,
To oblige a poor wife to be true to her trust;
But I have not pretended, for many years past,
By marrying of people, to make 'em grow chast.

6.
I therefore advise thee to let me go on,
Thou'lt find I'm the strength and support of thy throne;
For hadst thou but eyes, thou woud'st quickly perceive it,
How smoothly thy dart
Slips into the heart
Of a woman that's wed,
Whilst the shivering maid,
Stands trembling and wishing, but dare not receive it.

CHORUS.

For change, &c.

[*The Mask ended, enter* Young Fashion, Coupler, *and* Bull.

SIR TUNBELLY. So, very fine, very fine I faith, this is something like a wedding; now if supper were but ready, I'd say a short grace; and if I had such a bedfellow as *Hoyden* to night – I'd say as short prayers. [*Seeing* Young Fashion] How now? – What have we got here? A Ghost? Nay it must be so, for his flesh and his blood cou'd never have dar'd to appear before me. [*To him*] Ah Rogue—

LORD FOPPINGTON. Stap my vitals, *Tam* again.

SIR TUNBELLY. My Lord, will you cut his throat? Or shall I?

LORD FOPPINGTON. Leave him to me, Sir, if you please. Prithee *Tam* be so ingenuous now, as to tell me what thy business is here?

YOUNG FASHION. 'Tis with your bride.

LORD FOPPINGTON. Thau art the impudent'st fellow that nature has yet spawn'd into the warld, strike me speechless.

YOUNG FASHION. Why you know my modesty wou'd have starv'd me; I sent it a begging to you, and you wou'd not give it a groat.

LORD FOPPINGTON. And dost thau expect by an excess of assurance, to extart a maintenance fram me?

YOUNG FASHION. I do intend to extort your mistress from you, and that I hope will prove one. [*Taking* Miss Hoyden *by the hand.*

LORD FOPPINGTON. I ever thaught *Newgate* or *Bedlam* wou'd be his fartune, and naw his fate's decided. Prithee *Loveless* dost know of ever a mad doctor hard by?

YOUNG FASHION. There's one at your elbow will cure you presently. [*To* Bull] Prithee Doctor take him in hand quickly.

LORD FOPPINGTON. Shall I beg the favour of you, Sir, to pull your fingers out of my wife's hand.

YOUNG FASHION. His wife! Look you there; now I hope you are all satisfy'd he's mad?

LORD FOPPINGTON. Naw is it nat passible far me to penetrate what species of fally it is that art driving at.

SIR TUNBELLY. Here, here, here, let me beat out his brains, and that will decide all.

LORD FOPPINGTON. No, pray Sir hold, we'll destray him presently, according to law.

YOUNG FASHION. [*To* Bull] Nay, then advance Doctor; come, you are a man of conscience, answer boldly to the questions I shall ask; did not you marry me to this young lady, before ever that gentleman there saw her face?

BULL. Since the truth must out, I did.

YOUNG FASHION. Nurse, sweet Nurse, were not you a witness to it?

NURSE. Since my conscience bids me speak – I was.

YOUNG FASHION. [*To* Miss Hoyden] Madam, am not I your lawful husband?

MISS HOYDEN. Truly I can't tell, but you married me first.

YOUNG FASHION. Now I hope you are all satisfy'd?

SIR TUNBELLY. [*Offering to strike him, is held by* Loveless *and* Worthy] Oons and thunder you lie.

LORD FOPPINGTON. Pray Sir be calm, the battel is in disarder, but requires more canduct than courage to rally our forces. [*To* Bull *aside*] Pray Dactar one word with you. Look you, Sir, tho' I will not presume to calculate your notions of damnation, fram the description you give us of Hell, yet since there is at least a passibility, you may have a pitchfark thrust in your backside, methinks it shou'd not be worth your while to risque your saul in the next warld, far the sake of a beggarly yaunger brather, who is nat able to make your bady happy in this.

BULL. Alas! My Lord, I have no worldly ends, I speak the truth, Heaven knows.

LORD FOPPINGTON. Nay prithee never engage Heaven in the matter, for by all I can see, 'tis like to prove a business for the Devil.

YOUNG FASHION. Come, pray Sir, all above-board, no corrupting of evidences, if you please, this young lady is my lawful wife, and I'll justifie it in all the courts of *England*; so your Lordship (who always had a passion for variety) may go seek a new mistress if you think fit.

LORD FOPPINGTON. I am struck dumb with his impudence, and cannot passitively tell whether ever I shall speak again or not.

SIR TUNBELLY. Then let me come and examine the business a little, I'll jerk the truth out of 'em presently; here, give me my dog-whip.

YOUNG FASHION. Look you, Old Gentleman, 'tis in vain to make a noise, if you grow mutinous, I have some friends within call, have swords by their sides, above four foot long, therefore be calm, hear the evidence patiently, and when the jury have given their verdict, pass sentence according to law; here's honest *Coupler* shall be Foreman, and ask as many questions as he pleases.

COUPLER. All I have to ask is, whether Nurse persists in her evidence? The parson I dare swear will never flinch from his.

NURSE. [*To* Sir Tunbelly, *kneeling*] I hope in Heaven your Worship will pardon me, I have serv'd you long and faithfully, but in this thing I was over-reach'd; your Worship however was deceiv'd as well as I, and if the wedding dinner had been ready, you had put Madam to bed to him with your own hands.

SIR TUNBELLY. But how durst you do this, without acquainting of me?

NURSE. Alas! If your Worship had seen how the poor thing beg'd, and pray'd, and clung and twin'd about me, like ivy to an old wall, you wou'd say, I who had suckled it, and swadled it, and nurst it both wet and dry, must have had a heart of adamant to refuse it.

SIR TUNBELLY. Very well.

YOUNG FASHION. Foreman, I expect your verdict.

COUPLER. Ladies, and Gentlemen, what's your opinions?

ALL. A clear case, a clear case.

COUPLER. Then my young folks, I wish you joy.

SIR TUNBELLY. Come hither Stripling, if it be true then that thou hast marry'd my daughter, prithee tell me who thou art? [*To* Young Fashion.

YOUNG FASHION. Sir, the best of my condition is, I am your son-in-law; and the worst of it is, I am brother to that noble peer there.

SIR TUNBELLY. Art thou brother to that noble peer? – why then that noble peer, and thee, and thy wife, and the nurse, and the priest – may all go and be damn'd together. [*Exit* Sir Tunbelly.

LORD FOPPINGTON. – [*Aside*] *Now for my part, I think the wisest thing a man can do with an aking heart, is to put on a serene countenance, for a philosophical air is the most becoming thing in the world to the face of a Person of Quality; I will therefore bear my disgrace like a Great Man, and let the people see I am above an affront.* – Dear Tam, since things are thus fallen aut, prithee give me leave to wish thee jay, I do it de bon coeur, strike me dumb, you have marry'd a woman beautiful in her person, charming in her ayres, prudent in her canduct, canstant in her inclinations, and of a nice marality, split my wind-pipe. [*To* Young Fashion.

YOUNG FASHION. Your Lordship may keep up your spirits with your grimace if you please, I shall support mine with this lady, and two thousand pound a year. [*Taking* Miss Hoyden] Come, Madam.

We once again you see are man and wife,
And now perhaps the bargain's struck for life;
If I mistake, and we shou'd part again,
At least you see you may have choice of men:
Nay, shou'd the war[154] at length such havock make,
That lovers shou'd grow scarce, yet for your sake,
Kind Heaven always will preserve a beau,
[*Pointing to* Lord Foppington.
You'll find his Lordship ready to come to.

LORD FOPPINGTON. Her Ladyship shall stap my vitals if I do.

EPILOGUE.

Spoken by Lord Foppington.

Gentlemen, and Ladies,
These people have regal'd you here to day
(In my opinion) with a saucy play;
In which the author does presume to shew,
That coxcomb, *ab origine*–was beau.
Truly I think the thing of so much weight,
That if some smart chastisement ben't his fate,
God's curse it may in time destroy the State.
I hold no one its friend, I must confess,
Who would discauntenance your men of dress.
Far give me leave t'abserve, good cloaths are things,
Have ever been of great support to kings;
All treasons come from slovens, it is not
Within the reach of gentle beaux to plot.
They have no gaul, no spleen, no teeth, no stings,
Of all Gad's creatures the most harmless things.
Through all recard, no prince was ever slain,
By one who had a feather in his brain.
They're men of too refin'd an education,
To squabble with a Court–for a vile dirty Nation.
I'm very positive, you never saw
A through Republican[155] a finisht beau.
Nor truly shall you very often see
A *Jacobite* much better drest than he;
In short, through all the courts that I have been in,
Your men of mischief–still are in faule linnen.
Did ever one yet dance the Tyburn jigg,[156]
With a free air, or a well-pawder'd wigg?
Did ever highway-man yet bid you stand,
With a sweet bawdy snuff-bax in his hand;
Ar do you ever find they ask your purse
As men of breeding do?–Ladies Gad's curse,
This auther is a dagg, and 'tis not fit
You shou'd allow him ev'n one grain of wit.
To which, that his presence may ne'er be nam'd,
My humble motion is–he may de dam'd.

6.2 COLLEY CIBBER, "HENRY BRETT AND CIBBER'S PERIWIG" FROM *AN APOLOGY FOR THE LIFE OF MR. COLLEY CIBBER*

COLLEY CIBBER, *AN APOLOGY FOR the Life of Colley Cibber: with an Historical View of the Stage During his Own Time. Written by Himself.* Ed. B.R.S. Fone. Ann Arbor, MI: The University of Michigan Press, 1968, 201.

Mr. *Brett*, whom I am speaking of, had his Education, and I might say ended it, at the University of *Oxford*; for tho he was settled some time after at the *Temple*, he so little followed the Law there, that his Neglect of it, made the Law (like some of his fair and frail Admirers) very often follow *him*. As he had an uncommon Share of Social Wit, and a handsome Person, with a sanguine Bloom in his Complexion, no wonder they persuaded him, that he might have a better Chance of Fortune, by throwing such Accomplishments, into the gayer World, than by shutting them up, in a Study. The first View, that fires the Head of a young Gentleman of this modish Ambition, just broke loose, from Business, is to cut a Figure (as they call it) in a Side-box, at the Play, from whence their next Step is, to the *Green Room* behind the Scenes, sometimes their *Non ultra*. Hither, at last then, in this hopeful Quest of his Fortune, came this Gentleman-Errant, not doubting but the fickle Dame, while he was thus qualify'd to receive her, might be tempted to fall into his Lap. And though, possibly, the Charms of our Theatrical Nymphs might have their Share, in drawing him thither; yet in my Observation, the most visible Cause of his first coming, was a more sincere Passion he had conceiv'd for a fair full-bottom'd Perriwig, which I then wore in my first Play of the *Fool in Fashion*, in the Year 1695. For it is to be noted, that, the *Beaux* of those Days, were of a quite different Cast, from the modern Stamp, and had more of the Stateliness of the Peacock in their Mien, than (which now seems to be their highest Emulation) the pert Air of a Lapwing. Now whatever Contempt Philosophers may have, for a fine Perriwig; my Friend, who was not to despise the World, but to live in it, knew very well, that so material an Article of Dress, upon the Head of a Man of Sense, if it became him, could never fail of drawing to him a more partial Regard, and Benevolence, than could possibly be hop'd for, in an ill-made one. This perhaps may soften the grave Censure, which so youthful a Purchase might otherwise, have laid upon him: In a word, he made his Attack upon this Perriwig, as your young Fellows generally do upon a Lady of Pleasure; first, by a few, familiar Praises of her Person, and then, a civil Enquiry, into the Price of it. But upon his observing me a little surpriz'd at the Levity of his Question, about a Fop's Perriwig, he began to railly himself, with so much Wit, and Humour, upon the Folly of his Fondness for it, that he struck me, with an equal Desire of granting any thing, in my Power, to oblige so facetious a Customer. This singular Beginning of our Conversation, and the mutual Laughs that ensued upon it, ended in an Agreement, to finish our Bargain that Night, over a Bottle.

6.3 JEREMY COLLIER, "REMARKS ON *THE RELAPSE*"

JEREMY COLLIER, "REMARKS upon the Relapse." *A Short View of the Profaneness and Immorality of the English Stage, &c. With the Several Defences of the Same. In Answer to Mr. Congreve, Dr. Drake, &c.* London: G. Strahan, Richard Williamson, and T. Osborne, 1730. 136–51.

Collier (1650–1726) was an influential anti-theatrical polemicist whose views on the stage were informed by his position as a bishop of the Anglican Church who identified with the moral principles of a "primitive" church and refused to swear loyalty to William and Mary, the successors to the throne of the deposed James II.

"Remarks on the RELAPSE"

Jeremy Collier

The *Relapse* shall follow *Don Quixot* upon the Account of some Alliance between them. And because this *Author* swaggers so much in his *Preface*, and seems to look big upon his Performance, I shall spend a few more Thoughts than ordinary upon his *Play*, and examine it briefly in the *Fable*, the *Moral*, the *Characters*, &c. The Fable I take to be as follows.

Fashion, *a lewd, prodigal, younger Brother, is reduced to Extremity: Upon his Arrival from his Travels he meets with* Coupler, *an old sharping Match-maker; this Man puts him upon a Project of Cheating his elder Brother,* Lord Foplington, *of a rich Fortune.* Young Fashion *being refused a Sum of Money by his Brother, goes into* Coupler*'s Plot, bubbles* Sir Tunbelly *of his Daughter, and makes himself Master of a Fair Estate.*

From the Form and Constitution of the *Fable*, I observe

1. That there is a *Misnomer* in the Title. The *Play* should not have been call'd the *Relapse* or *Virtue* in *Danger. Lovelace* and *Amanda*, from whose *Characters* these Names are drawn, are Persons of inferior Consideration. *Lovelace* sinks in the middle of the *Fourth* Act, and we hear no more of him till towards the End of the *Fifth*, where he enters once more, but then 'tis as *Cato* did the Senate House, only to go out again. And as for *Amanda*, she has nothing to do but to stand a Shock of Courtship, and carry off her Virtue. This I confess is a great Task in the *Play-house*, but no main Matter in the Play.

The *Intrigue* and the *Discovery*, the great Revolution and Success, turns upon *Young Fashion*. He without Competition is the principal Person in the *Comedy*; and therefore the *Younger Brother*, or the *Fortunate Cheat*, had been much a more proper Name. Now when a *Poet* can't rig out a *Title Page*, 'tis but a bad Sign of his holding out to the *Epilogue*.

2. I observe the Moral is vicious; It points the wrong Way, and puts the *Prize* into the wrong Hand. It seems to make *Lewdness* the Reason of *Desert*, and gives *Young Fashion* a second Fortune, only for debauching away his first. A short View of his *Character* will make good this Reflection. To begin with him: He confesses himself a *Rake*, swears and blasphemes, curses and challenges his elder Brother, cheats him of his Mistress, and gets

him laid by the Heels in a Dog-Kennel. And what was the Ground of all this unnatural Quarrelling and Outrage? Why the main of it was, only because Lord *Foplington* refused to supply his Luxury, and make good his Extravagance. This *Young Fashion* after all, is the *Poet*'s Man of Merit, he provides a *Plot* and a Fortune on purpose for him. To speak freely, a lewd Character seldom wants good Luck in *Comedy*; so that whenever you see a thorough Libertine, you may almost swear he is in a rising Way, and that the *Poet* intends to make him a great Man. In short, this *Play* perverts the End of *Comedy*: Which, as Monsieur *Rapin*[157] observes, ought to regard Reformation and publick Improvement. But the *Relapser* had a more fashionable Fancy in his Head. His *Moral* holds forth this notable Instruction.

1. That all *Younger Brothers* should be careful to run out their Fortunes as fast and as ill as they can. And when they have put their Affairs in this Posture of Advantage, they may conclude themselve in the high Road to Wealth and Success. For as *Fashion* blasphemously applies it, *Providence takes Care of Men of Merit*.

2. That when a Man is press'd, his Business is not to be govern'd by Scruples, or formalize upon Conscience and Honesty. The quickest Expedients are the best; for in such Cases the Occasion justifies the Means, and a Knight of the *Post* is as good as one of the *Garter*.

[Collier goes on to critique harshly the probability of the play's plot and the morality and believability of his characters. He argues that the play violates Aristotle's unities of time, place, and action.]

Thus far I have examin'd the *Dramatick* Merits of the *Play*. And upon enquiry, it appears a Heap of Irregularities. There is neither Propriety in the *Name*, nor Contrivance in the *Plot*, nor Decorum in the *Characters*. 'Tis a thorough Contradiction to Nature, and impossible in *Time* and *Place*. Its *shining Graces*, as the Author calls them, are *Blasphemy* and *Baudy*, together with a Mixture of *Oaths* and *Cursing*. Upon the whole, the *Relapser*'s Judgment and his Morals are pretty well adjusted. The *Poet* is not much better than the *Man*. As for the *Profane* Part, 'tis hideous and superlative. But this I have consider'd elsewhere. All that I shall observe here is, that the Author was sensible of this Objection. His Defence in his *Preface* is most wretched: He pretends to know nothing of the Matter, and that 'tis *all printed*; which only proves his Confidence equal to the Rest of his Virtues. To outface Evidence in this Manner, is next to the affirming there's no such Sin as *Blasphemy*, which is the greatest Blasphemy of all. His Apology consists in railing at the *Clergy*; a certain Sign of ill Principles and ill Manners. This he does at an unusual Rate of Rudeness and Spite. He calls them the Saints with screw'd *Faces and wry Mouths*. And after a great Deal of scurrilous Abuse too gross to be mention'd, he adds; *If any Man happens to be offended at a Story of a Cock and a Bull, and a Priest and a Bull-dog, I beg his Pardon*, &c. This is brave *Bear-Garden* Language! The *Relapser* would do well to transport his Muse to *Samourgan*.[158] There it is likely he might find Leisure to lick his *Abortive Brat* into Shape; and meet with proper Business for his Temper, and Encouragement for his Talent.

6.4 JOHN SIMON, *COLLEY CIBBER*

John Simon (1675–1769) after Giuseppe Grisoni (1699–1769), *Colley Cibber from Wheatley's London*. Mezzotint engraving depicting Colley Cibber in his role as the luxuriant Lord Foppington, which he acted to great acclaim in his own play, *Love's Last Shift*, and in Vanbrugh's *The Relapse*. National Portrait Gallery, London.

As a tragic actor with a weak voice, Cibber had tried the patience of theatergoers until he was hissed off the stage. His treatment of the rakish dilettante, however, catapulted Cibber's career. Vanbrugh's revision of Sir Novelty Fashion from Cibber's *Love's Last Shift*, and Cibber's treatment of the role, impressed audiences with a balance of fashion-conscious superficiality and sinister intelligence.

Notes

1–2 This text is based on the 1697 edition printed for *Samuel Briscoe* at the corner of *Charles-street* in *Russel-street Covent-Garden*, 1697 and corrected against the second edition in 1698.

3 A small, private room, often located off a bed chamber, used for solitary activities such as reading, writing or prayer.

4 An idle story, purely for amusement.

5 Ill humour.

6 This description reflects a common stereotype of the London merchant or businessman as harried by finances (including taxes) and worried about the fidelity of his wife.

7 The actor, Powell (see headnote).

8 Restless, impatient of control.

9 A very young man, usually beardless. The term was sometimes associated with the boy-objects of homosexual desire.

10 A character from Shakespeare's *Henry IV, Part 1*, who is known for his impetuous bravery.

11 It was customary for fashionable young gentlemen—the "Beaux" in question—to pay for seats upon the stage where they posed and "performed" for the audience even as the play was being performed. While often complained of, this custom was not fully abolished until well into the eighteenth century.

12 A case of venereal disease.

13 A wealthy heiress, whose wealth would, by English law, become her husband's upon marriage.

14 A trial or testing.

15 A term used to refer to religious fanatics.

16 Fashionable and wealthy people generally spent the winter season in London and the summer months at their country estates.

17 The London street where many government agencies were located.

18 The River Thames, which bifurcates the city of London, did not at this time have enough bridges to make crossing from one bank to another easy. Hence, many boats for hire were available, manned by watermen, for convenient crossing.

19 A case for traveling.

20 Young Fashion "compliments" the waterman by implying that the latter has enough money to give change for this English gold coin worth between 20 and 21 shillings, but really, he is trying to get out of paying the fare, as the waterman well knows. After the recoinage crisis of the 1690s, when the Crown recalled British coin because of its debased value, the more frequently exchanged silver coins were scarce relative to the less frequently exchanged gold coins.

21 Half a guinea.

22 People who will try to cheat you out of your money.

23 Under the practice of primogeniture, Sir Novelty would, as elder brother, inherit the bulk of the family estate.

24 Young Fashion may have mortgaged his annuity or allowance as a younger son; his older brother could "redeem" that income with a cash repayment of the debt.

25 In order to serve the British government, it was necessary to take an oath of loyalty to the Protestant monarchy established in 1688; a Jacobite was one who supported the supplanted, Catholic Stuart monarchy. This oath would, then, be against his religion and morality.

26 Salary or revenue.

27 Small pleasures.

28 From top to bottom.

29 Young Fashion should act like a humble dependent towards his brother.

30 A loose, often rich gown worn by men over their sleeping clothes.

31 Ah, it is something beautiful, the Devil take me.

32 Clown—a rustic, country bumpkin.

33 Mirrors.

34 Reception of visitors just after rising.

35 Pocket. Lord Foppington affects an accent that turns most vowels into a long "a."

36 A neckcloth with long, laced ends.
37 The short trousers and tight-fitting, white stockings worn by upper-class men made the calf of the leg a prominent and prized feature of a man's body. If the calf were not full enough, by a certain standard of beauty, it was augmented with padding.
38 Too thick a calf denoted a plebian who did manual labor, such as the men who carried sedan chairs for transporting wealthier Londoners.
39 Crown piece, a coin.
40 Telescope.
41 A well known "ordinary" or eating establishment, established by Adam Lockett.
42 He can eat with the servants.
43 His servants and lackeys.
44 An apple.
45 The Grand Tour, a trip abroad, usually to France and Italy, was considered part of a young gentleman's education. At the same time, it was questioned for its dubious benefits and its potentially corrupting "foreign" influence on the young.
46 A punishment for theft.
47 The close male friend and confidante of Alexander the Great.
48 The marriage is to be consummated.
49 To talk foolishly.
50 Education.
51 A French coin worth only a fraction of a livre.
52 A young hen.
53 Kiss.
54 The domain of a baron, the lowest rank of British nobility. Conferring these titles was a source of much-needed revenue for the British Crown.
55 The document conferring Lord Foppington's title.
56 The representative of the principal in a duel.
57 Love affairs.
58 Coaches for hire. Lord Foppington's desire to go to plays on a Sunday goes against pervasive Christian belief that Sunday is reserved for attending church services and private dovotions.
59 A trifle, thing of no importance.
60 Philosopher and theologian Thomas Burnet's *Telluris Theoria Sacra, or Sacred Theory of the Earth* was published in English in 1690. A speculative theory of Earth's origins, Burnet's work stirred up great controversy that lasted throughout the following decade. *Sacred Theory* suggested a hollow earth was filled with water until Noah's flood, when rivers burst forth from the poles and flowed across the surface of the globe. According to Burnet, flood-water was still dispersing from the biblical event and was being slowly reabsorbed into the earth, creating mountains and other natural formations in relief as water levels declined.
61 Diseased.
62 Done it.
63 A horse with an easy gait for everyday riding.
64 Was ice.
65 His living allowance as a younger son.
66 To turn pickpocket.
67 Perfumed cosmetic powder, used on the face.
68 Caretaker of your money.
69 Race horse.
70 Perfume bottle.
71 An animal that exudes musk, like a civet cat; alternatively, a foppish man.
72 Plots.
73 The Royal College of Physicians.
74 Letting blood was a common treatment for any number of maladies in the eighteenth century. Supposedly, bleeding released excess heat and reduced fever.

75 An apparatus, usually of feathers and leather imitative of a bird, used in falconry to bring the hunting bird back to the hunter.
76 Respiratory diseases of birds; when applied to humans, it is meant humorously.
77 Engaging in lascivious behavior while hypocritically criticizing that behavior in others.
78 Shotgun.
79 To get what one wants from the wrong place.
80 Turkish tapestry work, or its imitation.
81 Put laurel (bay leaves) in the sockets of the candle holders.
82 A day when a change of clothes is scheduled.
83 A piece of lace cloth worn by women between the bodice and the neck.
84 To travel by relays of horses, usually hired for the purpose along the way.
85 By your good faith.
86 A woman's undergarment in the form of a shift worn next to the skin.
87 White wine.
88 The Church of England mandated the hours during which marriages could legally occur.
89 To give fair warning before shooting.
90 Specifically, her hindquarters.
91 A week.
92 Financial settlements.
93 Flaunt.
94 Wit, intellect, but also a pun on other "parts."
95 Referencing a traditional, English belief that the hare behaves strangely during its breeding season, mistakenly believed to be in March.
96 Hoyden's nurse was also her wet nurse. It was a common practice for gentlewomen to delegate nursing to servant or lower-class women for whom feeding and caring for children was a profession.
97 Nonsensical story.
98 Slutty girl.
99 Young Fashion pretends to be a rich landowner, like his brother, with the authority and money to bestow desireable employment on clergymen in his parish.
100 A close-fitting tunic worn over the gown by clergymen.
101 Lover.
102 A man who pays court to a woman; a ladies' man.
103 A woman who flirts, not for love, but for the gratification of sexual conquest.
104 Clergyman.
105 To banter, to chat, perhaps frivolously.
106 Likely to give one the spleen.
107 A comedy by Thomas D'Urfey, the full title of which is *The Fond Husband; or, The Plotting Sisters.*
108 A menial, low servant.
109 An overly fashionable, foppish man.
110 What does it mean?
111 The custom of fairs persisted into the eighteenth century. These were events that included markets and trading, as well as open-air entertainments such as jugglers, plays, boxing, and puppet shows. All classes participated, and alcohol consumption was generally a part of the festivities.
112 Sir Tunbelly thinks that Lord Foppington and his entourage are itinerant actors, or strollers, who moved from town to town, performing on make-shift stages. Since the strollers were not attached to a permanent theatre, or household, they were technically "rogues and vagabonds" under English law and were subject to arrest should a local magistrate, such as Sir Tunbelly, choose to draw up a warrant against them.
113 Do they pay taxes? If so, that would make them householders and not subject to arrest.
114 Do they support the Protestant King William III, who supplanted the Catholic James II in the Glorious Revolution of 1688? Or are they Jacobites, supporters of James' continued claims to the throne from his exile in France?

115 Sir Tunbelly prescribes treatments for insanity that were current in the eighteenth century.
116 Overnice, particular.
117 Liveries were uniforms worn by male servants. They were often richly decorated and showy advertisements for the wealth and status of the employer.
118 At ease.
119 Figure, shape.
120 Imprisoned.
121 Coins struck with the image of a crown made by machine with uniform, ridged edges that made them resistant to the practice of clipping, or shaving the coin's edges for silver or gold.
122 A pie of seasoned meat.
123 To drink alcohol for medicinal, not recreational purposes, therefore not a sin.
124 The subject of a popular "mad song" lyric of the seventeenth century, "Tom" is a resident of Bedlam, the Bethlam Royal Hospital for the Mad in London.
125 Soldiers sent to make the arrest.
126 To castrate Young Fashion, qualifying him to serve as a eunuch.
127 At the heart of the fashionable, sophisticated city of London.
128 Advancement to a more lucrative and prestigious office or employment.
129 The clergyman who held the living died, leaving it free to give to Bull.
130 Coupler warns Bull not to equivocate, like a Roman Catholic priest.
131 Tyburn was a place of execution. Criminals to be hanged were taken to the scaffold in a cart that was then driven out from under them after the noose was placed around their necks.
132 It was illegal to practice as a Catholic in England, and Jesuits were technically subject to arrest and severe punishment, although many wealthy and well-born Catholic families managed to persist in their faith and protect their clergy throughout the century.
133 Run, scarper for it.
134 Foolish, foppish scoundrel.
135 A minor sin.
136 Literally, a pig given to the Church as a tythe and in effect to Bull, but also the name of a country dance.
137 In I Kings 18: 21–40, the Priests of Baal confront the prophet Elijah. Nurse is implying that Bull follows the wrong god.
138 The practice of buying and selling ecclesiastical preferments.
139 After introducing Bull into his new living.
140 Phaeton, the son of Apollo the sun god, was granted the right to drive the chariot of the sun for one day; unable to control the horses, Phaeton drove too close to earth and would have destroyed it if not killed by Zeus.
141 An ugly, ill-shaped person.
142 Title applied to a country gentleman.
143 A title conferred by the King in recognition of service or the King's favor.
144 An oath, contraction of "by our lady," meaning the Virgin Mary.
145 A common prostitute.
146 Infectious disease or pestilence.
147 Tatting, or the knitting of threads into knots for fancy work, a common pastime for young gentlewomen.
148 A seventeenth-century religious work, popular in the radical protestant movements of that period.
149 Fowly.
150 Wooden, double-reed instrument approximate to an oboe.
151 Turtle doves.
152 A dramatic presentation involving song and dance. This form originated in the English courts of James I and Charles I in the seventeenth century.
153 The gods of love and marriage, respectively.
154 The Nine Years War concluded in 1697, the year of this play's first production. The War of Spanish Succession began in 1701 and continued to 1714.

155 A supporter of the Interregnum Government which displaced the British Monarchical system between 1649 and 1660.

156 Be hanged.

157 Renee Rapin (1621–1687) French literary theorist.

158 An Academy in Lithuania for the Education of Bears. Pere Aurill *Voyage en divers Etats*, &c p. 240.

Part 2
Managing Entertainment: 1700–1760

OVERVIEW

William Congreve, *The Way of the World*
Susanna Centlivre, *The Busie Body*
John Rich, *The Necromancer, or Harlequin Doctor Faustus* and John Thurmond, *Harlequin Doctor Faustus*
John Gay, *The Beggar's Opera*
Henry Fielding, *The Author's Farce*
George Lillo, *The London Merchant*
Samuel Foote, *The Minor*

WHILE THE YEAR 1700 is not as crisp a starting point for theatre history as the politically punctuated 1660, the turn of the century was the year of John Dryden's end and Millamant's beginning. As one of the great playwrights of the Restoration passed away, Congreve's sparkling female lead in *The Way of the World* launched the project of reconciling theatrical pleasures to the social ideologies of bourgeois culture. The century opened with William still on the throne (Mary had died) and a Bill of Rights now in place that formalized Lockean and politically modern conceptions of the rights-bearing individual. Whereas the Restoration began with the re-establishment of monarchy, the eighteenth century began with the renegotiation of sovereign power as something that extends to all subjects. Tracking this shift toward political modernity is a way to think through the move from the Restoration to the eighteenth century which, while much more than a reaction to the sexual candor and cynicism of the Restoration, is impossible to understand without being aware of the political resonance of libertine values in an increasingly bourgeois age.

Politically, the early eighteenth century was characterized by the Protestant compromise that first brought William and Mary to the throne in 1689. Eventually, this same demand for a Protestant line would bring the German-speaking George I (Georg Ludwig) in 1714, establishing the long-lived House of Hanover. The forced abdication of James II and the broad support for a Protestant monarch, who did not speak English is an indication of how deep anti-Catholic sentiment and paranoia ran. From William and Mary through Anne and the Hanovarian Georges, administrations supported "business-friendly" philosophies and ventures, among them, the East India Company, the slave trade, and a series of pieces of legislation known as the Enclosure Acts, which effectively destroyed the commons and privatized British land. The massive consolidation of wealth fostered by colonialism and the slave trade fed the explosion of London's population and the market for luxury goods. Liquidity in the marketplace, improved roads and turnpikes, the absence of a major plague, and modern farming techniques raised overall life expectancy, but not all benefitted equally. Gay's 1728 *The Beggar's Opera* exposed the economic savagery of modern boom-town London, as thousands of young people flocked to seek work but instead often found themselves without networks of support, food, or shelter. Press gangs conscripting sailors, a corrupt prison system, a growing list of property crimes entailing capital punishment, and government collaboration with businesses fed cynicism about the Walpole administration, which rose to power in the wake of the South Sea Bubble. The South Sea debacle was Britain's first modern stock market crash, in which South Sea share prices were driven up by insider trading and a public buying frenzy before crashing back down to below their initial price, leaving behind a trail of bankruptcies, economic depression, and a London gin-drinking epidemic. Robert Walpole became the first Lord of the Treasury and Chancellor of the Exchequer in 1721 in the wake of the crisis; a few years later, he became the first Prime Minister in 1730.

What Londoners saw on stage during this period is a mixed story of change and continuity. The diminished presence of libertine playwrights Wycherley, Etherege, Sedley, and the most frank Restoration sex comedies, such as *The Man of Mode, Love in a Wood* and *The Gentleman Dancing Master* reflects a cultural shift in taste. The repertoire began to feature plays reflecting a more bourgeois optimism about companionate marriage, sexual fidelity, the power of contract, and the harmony of capital and nation in mainstream comedies. Jeremy Collier's infamous *A Short View of the Profaneness and Immorality of the Stage* (1698) is best understood as a sign rather than as the agent of this change. Older plays such as *The Relapse, All for Love*, and *The Indian Queen* were joined by newer and more Whiggish plays such as Steele's *The Conscious Lovers*, Centlivre's *The Busie Body* and *The Wonder, A Woman Keeps a Secret*, and Farquhar's *The Beaux' Stratagem* and *The Recruiting Officer*, which valued personal autonomy, merchant-class characters, patriotism in the language of the post-1707 Great Britain, and companionate marriage. Theatrical discourse, however, was far from monotone. Playwrights such as John Gay and Henry Fielding savaged Whiggish assumptions about progress and contract culture in satiric worlds where the lives of the poor and the cruelties of the modern marketplace were on display. The ghosts of the past, including the Stuart court, the figure of the libertine, the witty

Restoration heroine, and the fop continued to walk the stage, but they were accompanied by new figures: the bourgeois tragedians, sensible couples, harlequin, hornpipe dances, ballad operas, and most of all, reformed or reforming men. It was a rich mixture of political ideologies and forms of entertainment.

Shirley Strum Kenny has called the style of comedy that became dominant after the turn of the century "humane comedy," which seems more accurate than "sentimental comedy." *The Conscious Lovers* and a few plays by Cibber and Steele can justly be called sentimental, but that term does not describe the bulk of the comedies that led at the box office. These comedies tend to appropriate elements of the witty comedies before them, but they are energetic without being cruel, mixing the likeable with the laughable and reconciling more characters into the dominant plot.[1] Compared to the ending of *The Country Wife*, in which Margery still believes she can be Horner's wife and the deception of most of the husbands continues, the ending of *The Busie Body* illustrates humane principles at work. Centlivre finds a way to reconcile both main couples, one of the two blocking guardians, and the spirit is one of good cheer, patriotism, and the triumph of British love.

Tragedy grew in new directions as well, particularly in the development of she-tragedy and the rise of bourgeois tragedy, both of which tended to feature anti-Catholic and pro-Whig themes. Nicolas Rowe, who contributed *The Fair Penitent* (1703) and *Lady Jane Grey* (1715), was the first to use the term "she-tragedy," though Southerne, Banks, and Otway had already contributed examples of the form, which focuses on the penance of a woman for her sexual sins.[2] She-tragedies created an erotic spectacle of the heroine's suffering through rape and anguish. Domestic tragedy, epitomized in Lillo's *The London Merchant*, maps mercantile class values tightly into scripts of sexuality and gender through a cautionary tale aimed at young apprentices who might sacrifice their economic duties when seduced by a more sexually experienced woman. Lillo's tragedy held the stage well into the nineteenth century and influenced the work of the German playwright and dramaturge Gotthold Ephraim Lessing and others on the continent. One could draw a line from Lillo to Henrik Ibsen to Arthur Miller, tracing the thematic and ideological force of Lillo's exposition of domestic themes. Later, the Rev. John Home's *Douglas* (1756), denounced by conservative Scottish Presbyterians, took some of the same pathetic strategies that early eighteenth-century tragedy had cultivated and deployed them in a sentimental longing for a lost Scottish line. Like Lillo's tragedy, Home's is also connected to a traditional ballad that rooted this branch of tragedy in popular and folk rather than elite experience. In Lillo's play, as in other tragedies such as Addison's *Cato* (1713) the behaviors and dispositions that signify proper masculinity and femininity do the work of regulating class identity. These tragedies unfold under the shadow of the Restoration rake and the related problem of how to make virtue, sexual continence, and bourgeois values interesting.

Celebrity culture supported the success of many plays that, while worthy on their own, became box office successes with the likes of Betterton, Cibber, Charke, Woffington, and Garrick in the cast. The expiration of the old Licensing Act in 1695 contributed to the rise of modern celebrity by making more print material available, including copies of plays, newspapers, pamphlets, and other vehicles that allowed audiences to relive, ruminate upon, and experience at a distance key theatrical events. Copperplate technologies, best illustrated in the detailed work of William Hogarth, made it possible for the general public to own images of their favorite actors. Celebrity biographies, such as Charles Gildon's *Life of Mr. Thomas Betterton* (1710), Benjamin Victor's account of Barton Booth's life, Colley Cibber's autobiographical *An Apology for the Life of Colley Cibber, with an Historical View of the Stage During His Own Time, Written by Himself* (1740) and his daughter Charlotte Charke's confessional *A Narrative of the Life of Mrs. Charlotte Charke* (1755) fed the public's appetite for intimate details, and structured performance strategies of what Julia Fawcett calls "overexpression," deliberately constructed public personae that included strategic moments self-erasure.[3] Colley Cibber's enormous Lord Foppington wig, which later appeared on the head of his cross-dressing daughter Charlotte Charke, is a material example of how performative excess could also shield the performer from the glare of new media's spotlight. The culture of theatre reviewing, which would only come into focus in the 1750s, furthered the celebration of particular performances and writers. Newspapers moved from charging theatres for brief ads at the beginning of the century to paying for access to fresh theatrical news and, eventually, the right to print the next night's cast. Stuart Sherman, building on Danny O'Quinn's work, has argued that this tightly knit "news–play nexus" forged new networks of circulation and commentary in a culture bursting with live performances and daily reporting. Like Steele's "quidnunc," the news addict, this culture produced fans, commentators, and theatregoers who inhabited networks of relations between the coffeehouse and the theatre.[4]

The availability of stage space follows a similar story of expansion, with some significant complications. After the formation of the monopoly United Company in 1682 and then the rise of Christopher Rich's management in 1693, the actor's revolt in 1694 marked the beginning of Lincoln's Inn Fields and a period of theatrical expansion, including the Queen's Theatre (later known as the King's Theatre) in 1705, the Haymarket (a project spearheaded by John Vanbrugh and John Hervey), also in 1705, and the Little Haymarket in 1720. These new spaces meant venues for more plays, which supported the development of new genres, including ballad opera, the harlequinade, various kinds of afterpieces, and alternative entr'act entertainments, such as hornpipe dances. The most notable of these new forms was the ballad opera, and chief among them Gay's oxymoronic *The Beggar's Opera*, which opened at Lincoln's Inn Fields in 1728. The form took well-known songs and gave them new lyrics, often with the original text sharpening the edge of the parody. The popular "O Jenny, O Jenny, where hast thou been," for example, a reproof sung as a duet between the "wanton" Jenny and her sister Molly, becomes Gay's "O Polly you might have toy'd and kist/By keeping men off, you keep them on," Mrs. Peachum's warning not to be chaste but rather to use sex for gain. The music itself could also surprise and unsettle, as in the contrast of the gentle "Greensleeves" and its original lyric of lost love with Macheath's closing commentary: "Since laws were made for ev'ry degree,/ To curb vice in others, as well as me,/ I wonder we han't better company,/ Upon Tyburn tree!"

The success of *The Beggar's Opera,* which was highly critical of the Robert Walpole administration, helped to precipitate the 1737 government crackdown known as the Licensing Act, which required all new plays to be scrutinized by the Lord Chamberlain. The act was built on pieces of older laws restricting or punishing players as "sturdy beggars," but the Licensing Act also took aim squarely at playwrights. The newly founded office of the Examiner of Plays would correct copies and approve an authorized version for performance; objectionable parts were struck out or entire plays turned down. Performers, writers, and theatre managers found creative strategies for evading the restrictions of the Licensing Act. Samuel Foote, after playing Iago in an illegal production of *Othello*, opened *The Diversions of a Morning, or a Dish of Chocolate* in 1747, the first of a series of skits in which he took off prominent people and other actors. The event was advertised as a concert with refreshments (hence the "dish of chocolate" or hot chocolate) at which a theatrical performance would be offered for free. Similar strategies for evading the restrictions of the Licensing Act and producing plays without an official patent or license from the state led to the rise of melodrama, which originally referred to a performance of primarily music and later morphed into the sensational and emotive genre that later gave us Rousseau's *Pygmalion*, Verdi's *La Traviata*, and Gilbert and Sullivan's parodies.

A revolution in acting styles in this period should be attributed jointly to Charles Macklin and David Garrick. Macklin transformed the role of Shylock, which had been played as a buffoonish stereotype, by studying *Antiquities of the Jews* and observing Jewish communities in London. This attention to realistic detail began a movement toward greater historical accuracy in costume and manner. The young David Garrick, after coming to London with his teacher Samuel Johnson and initially failing as a wine merchant, benefitted from Macklin's instruction and helped to move acting style further from the declamatory to a more natural style with his portrayal of Richard III. The next year, Garrick played Lear in Nahum Tate's *King Lear* with Peg Woffington's Cordelia (in this version, both live). He and Woffington then went to Dublin at the end of the London season, where they honed their skills and added more roles to their personal repertoires. By April of 1747, Garrick was managing Drury Lane, where he subsequently instituted reforms that removed patrons from the stage (on which they had previously been allowed to sit), improved the lighting, regularized box office procedures, and ushered in the modern theatrical adoration of Shakespeare. While it is difficult to know exactly what this more natural acting style looked like, both Garrick and Macklin championed it, and audience and commentators praised the revolution in style. David Garrick's "An Essay on Acting" (1744), Aaron Hill's *The Art of Acting* (1753), and James Boswell's *On The Profession of a Player* (1770) all speak to elements of this changing kinetic philosophy as well as a corresponding professionalization of the actor's art.

The audiences for eighteenth-century theatre grew and changed along with the expanding London population. The seats in the houses were priced differently, and prologues and epilogues often reflected on the class variation that these sections represented. Garrick's prologue to Arthur Murphy's *All in the Wrong* (1761) appeals to a varied audience for advice on pleasing them all:

> What shall we do your different tastes to hit?
> You relish satire (*to the pit*) you ragouts of wit—(*to the Boxes*)
> Your taste is humour and high-seasoned joke. (*First Gallery*)
> You call for hornpipe, and for hearts of oak. (*Second Gallery*)

The pit (largely populated by wits and critics), the boxes (for the wealthiest theatregoers) and galleries (the cheap and cheaper seats) stand in for different classes. While the playhouse mixed these classes, it also kept them sorted into sections. That spatial sensibility continued after Garrick abolished the footman's gallery in 1759, taking away the perquisite of free admission after the fourth act. After this practice ended, following rounds of theatre riots, it was replaced by a half-price scheme, which ensured that working class spectators filled the empty seats (usually in the galleries) after the second act. Roles for servants shifted in tone from the abused, reviled, or manipulated figures such as Foggy Nan in *The Man of Mode* and Waitwell in *The Way of the World* to the witty Lissardo of *The Wonder, a Woman Keeps a Secret* or the charming if naïve Davy in *The Bon Ton*. Such positive representations of servants, along with the growing number of good soldiers and merchants, presented a wider swath of the population in a more flattering light. The variety of identities and class experiences illustrated on stage and within the audience, along with the circulation of news, put mid-century theatres at the heart of an experience of public culture, especially in London. Theatres were a site of contest, often riot, but they were also a space in which the "imagined community" of the new Great Britain represented itself to itself.

Notes

1 Shirley S. Kenny, "Humane Comedy." *Modern Philology* 75:1 (1977), 29–43: 31.
2 For more on she-tragedy, Jean I. Marsden, *Fatal Desire: Women, Sexuality, and the English Stage, 1660–1720*. Ithaca, NY: Cornell University Press, 2006.
3 See Julia Fawcett, *Spectacular Disappearances: Celebrity and Privacy, 1696–1801*. Ann Arbor, MI: University of Michigan Pres, 2016.
4 Stuart Sherman, "'The General Entertainment of My Life': The *Tatler*, the *Spectator*, and the Quidnunc's Cure." *Eighteenth-Century Fiction* 27.3–4 (Spring-Summer 2015): 343–71.

7. *The Way of the World*

***THE WAY OF THE WORLD*. A COMEDY. AS IT IS ACTED AT THE THEATRE IN LINCOLN'S-INN-FIELDS. BY HIS MAJESTY'S SERVANTS. WILLIAM CONGREVE.[1] FIRST PERFORMED 3 MARCH 1700 AND FIRST PUBLISHED 1700**

7.1 *THE WAY OF THE WORLD*, A COMEDY, AS IT IS ACTED AT THE THEATRE IN *LINCOLN'S-INN-FIELDS*, BY HIS MAJESTY'S SERVANTS.

William Congreve[2]

First Performed 3 March 1700 and First Published1700

CONGREVE'S *THE WAY OF THE WORLD* has a complex plot that warrants a summary. Mirabell is in love with the heiress Millamant, but he has been flirting with Lady Wishfort, her aunt, to conceal his suit. Mrs. Marwood, currently having an affair with Fainall but angry that Mirabell rejected her, exposes the trick to Lady Wishfort, who in turn threatens to deprive her niece of half her inheritance if she marries him. Mirabell disguises his servant Waitwell as his uncle Sir Rowland, who comes to propose to the ever-ready Lady Wishfort. He hopes this humiliating deception will force Lady Wishfort to consent to his marriage to Millamant with her fortune. Mrs. Marwood discovers this plot as well as a past one: Mirabell had an affair with Mrs. Fainall when she was Miss Wishfort, daughter of Lady Wishfort, and Mirabell then married her off to Mr. Fainall when the couple feared she was pregnant. When Fainall receives the news of the past affair, he threatens to divorce his wife and to discredit Lady Wishfort unless he is given full control of Mrs. Fainall's property and Millamant's money is handed over to him, but both schemes fail. Mrs. Fainall denies everything and proves that her husband is having an affair with Mrs. Marwood, while Mirabell produces a deed that made him trustee of all Mrs. Fainall's property before her marriage, a measure taken to protect her against the possible revenge of Mr. Fainall. Lady Wishfort, relieved to be saved from Fainall's threat, forgives Mirabell and consents to the marriage.

The Way of the World, sometimes called the last Restoration comedy, is also the last major play of Congreve's theatrical career. It served as a rebuttal to Jeremy Collier's lengthy *A Short View of the Immorality and Profaneness of the English Stage, Together with the Sense of Antiquity upon this Argument* (1698), which charged Wycherley's *The Country Wife*, Etherege's *The Man of Mode*, Vanbrugh's *The Relapse*, and Congreve's *The Old Batchelor* with the sins of profanity, sexual indelicacy, anti-clericalism, and corrupting the public. Congreve crafted his last comedy to give audiences the pleasures of a Restoration comedy without the direct affronts of ongoing adultery, liaisons, or women who, in the words of Collier, "speak smuttily." Instead, we have a reformed (though still devious) rake, a virginal witty heiress, an older woman who is humiliated for her sexual interest, and an ending that punishes the worst offenders while uniting the couple in a legitimate and prosperous marriage arrangement.

1698 was also the year Parliament granted a divorce to the Earl of Macclesfield that allowed his remarriage, making real (though very rare) the possibility of divorce sometimes raised by comic plots.[3] At the same time, then, that William and Mary exemplified the ascendant bourgeois, companionate ideology of marriage, contract theory exerted its own pragmatic influence on marriage law. What is known as the "proviso scene" of Act IV, in which Mirabell and Millamant work out the terms of their relationship, draws on Locke's 1690 *Second Treatise of Civil Government.* Locke proposes that all people have property in themselves, and that from this point of origin, it is possible for more and less powerful parties to negotiate fairly. Locke's liberal premise that all have natural rights came into conflict, however, with the experience of women as both property and as persons. Marriage represented for most women the only contract they could make *and* the contract that brought an end to their legal identity as individuals under the principle of coverture, in which a woman's legal existence is "covered" by that of her husband.[4] The nature of Mirabell and Millamant's conditions (hers about her autonomy, his about regulating that autonomy) highlight the wife's role as natural subordinate and even property, which undercuts the sense that the two lovers are equal parties negotiating fairly.

The play was not only topical but also cast with well-known celebrities. Thomas Betterton (Fainall) and Anne Bracegirdle (Millamant) had recently headlined in Congreve's *Love for Love* as Valentine and Angellica, and in his *The Old Batchelor* as Heartwell and Araminta. Significantly, after playing such a string of couples, they are not coupled in the play; instead, Bracegirdle was matched with Jack Verbruggen (Mirabell), the rising star who had recently originated the role of Oroonoko in Southerne's adaptation of Behn's novella. Betterton, who had played many rakes, including Dorimant in *The Man of Mode*, Tom Wilding in Behn's *The City Heiress*, and Don Juan in Shadwell's *The Libertine*, was getting older, and Verbruggen was beginning to take over his former roles. Cast here as the devious and bitter husband Fainall, Betterton ceded center stage to Verbruggen's Mirabell, the reformed rake who was still a man of wit, but one with his life of infidelity behind him and marriage before him. The comically interchangeable William Bowen and John Bowman played Witwoud and Petulant, thus doubling the joke of their characters' modish ineptitude. Mrs. Bowman, who like Bracegirdle, had been a ward of the Bettertons, took the slighted but likeable Mrs. Fainall, who must manage the crowd-pleasing Act IV.i scene in which her husband plays a drunken Witwoud. Elizabeth Barry, former lover of Etherege and the now-dead Rochester, played the scheming Mrs. Marwood. The older actors, who represent the passing Restoration ethos, are uniformly cast as the foils to Mirabell and Millamant's story of wit reformed into companionate marriage.

Audire est Operæ pretium, procedere recte
Qui mæchis non vultis–

Hor. Sat. 2. l. 1.

–Metuat doti deprensa.–

Ibid.[5]

TO THE RIGHT HONOURABLE RALPH, EARL OF MONTAGUE, ETC.

My Lord,—Whether the world will arraign me of vanity or not, that I have presumed to dedicate this comedy to your lordship, I am yet in doubt; though, it may be, it is some degree of vanity even to doubt of it. One who has at any time had the honour of your lordship's conversation, cannot be supposed to think very meanly of that which he would prefer to your perusal. Yet it were to incur the imputation of too much sufficiency to pretend to such a merit as might abide the test of your lordship's censure.

Whatever value may be wanting to this play while yet it is mine, will be sufficiently made up to it when it is once become your Lordship's; and it is my security, that I cannot have overrated it more by my dedication than your Lordship will dignify it by your patronage.

That it succeeded on the stage was almost beyond my expectation; for but little of it was prepared for that general taste which seems now to be predominant in the palates of our audience. Those characters which are meant to be ridiculed in most of our comedies are of fools so gross, that in my humble opinion they should rather disturb than divert the well-natured and reflecting part of an audience; they are rather objects of charity than contempt, and instead of moving our mirth, they ought very often to excite our compassion.

This reflection moved me to design some characters which should appear ridiculous not so much through a natural folly (which is incorrigible, and therefore not proper for the stage) as through an affected wit: a wit which, at the same time that it is affected, is also false. As there is some difficulty in the formation of a character of this nature, so there is some hazard which attends the progress of its success upon the stage: for many come to a play so overcharged with criticism, that they very often let fly their censure, when through their rashness they have mistaken their aim. This I had occasion lately to observe: for this play had been acted two or three days before some of these hasty judges could find the leisure to distinguish betwixt the character of a Witwoud and a Truewit.[6]

I must beg your Lordship's pardon for this digression from the true course of this epistle; but that it may not seem altogether impertinent, I beg that I may plead the occasion of it, in part of that excuse of which I stand in need, for recommending this comedy to your protection. It is only by the countenance of your lordship, and the *few* so qualified, that such who write with care and pains can hope to be distinguished: for the prostituted name of poet promiscuously levels all that bear it.

Terence, the most correct writer in the world, had a Scipio and a Lelius,[7] if not to assist him, at least to support him in his reputation. And notwithstanding his extraordinary merit, it may be their countenance was not more than necessary.

The purity of his style, the delicacy of his turns, and the justness of his characters, were all of them beauties which the greater part of his audience were incapable of tasting. Some of the coarsest strokes of Plautus, so severely censured by Horace, were more likely to affect the multitude; such, who come with expectation to laugh out the last act of a play, and are better entertained with two or three unseasonable jests than with the artful solution of the fable.

As Terence excelled in his performances, so had he great advantages to encourage his undertakings, for he built most on the foundations of Menander: his plots were generally modelled, and his characters ready drawn to his hand. He copied Menander; and Menander had no less light in the formation of his characters from the observations of Theophrastus, of whom he was a disciple; and Theophrastus, it is known, was not only the disciple, but the immediate successor of Aristotle, the first and greatest judge of poetry.[8] These were great models to design by; and the further advantage which Terence possessed towards giving his plays the due ornaments of purity of style, and justness of manners, was not less considerable from the freedom of conversation which was permitted him with Lelius and Scipio, two of the greatest and most polite men of his age. And, indeed, the privilege of such a conversation is the only certain means of attaining to the perfection of dialogue.

If it has happened in any part of this comedy that I have gained a turn of style or expression more correct, or at least more corrigible, than in those which I have formerly written, I must, with equal pride and gratitude, ascribe it to the honour of your Lordship's admitting me into your conversation, and that of a society where everybody else was so well worthy of you, in your retirement last summer from the town: for it was immediately after, that this comedy was written. If I have failed in my performance, it is only to be regretted, where there were so many not inferior either to a Scipio or a Lelius, that there should be one wanting equal in capacity to a Terence.

If I am not mistaken, poetry is almost the only art which has not yet laid claim to your Lordship's patronage. Architecture and painting, to the great honour of our country, have flourished under your influence and protection. In the meantime, poetry, the eldest sister of all arts, and parent of most, seems to have resigned her birthright, by having neglected to pay her duty to your Lordship, and by permitting others of a later extraction to prepossess that place in your esteem, to which none can pretend a better title. Poetry, in its nature, is sacred to the good and great: the relation between them is reciprocal, and they are ever propitious to it. It is the privilege of poetry to address them, and it is their prerogative alone to give it protection.

This received maxim is a general apology for all writers who consecrate their labours to great men: but I could wish, at this time, that this address were exempted from the common pretence of all dedications; and that as I can distinguish your Lordship even among the most deserving, so this offering might become remarkable by some particular instance of respect, which should assure your Lordship that I am, with all due sense of your extreme worthiness and humanity, my Lord, your Lordship's most obedient and most obliged humble servant,

WILL. CONGREVE.

PROLOGUE, Spoken by Mr. Betterton.

Of those few fools, who with ill stars are curs'd,
Sure scribbling fools, call'd poets, fare the worst.
For they're a sort of fools which fortune makes,
And after she has made 'em fools, forsakes.
With Nature's oafs 'tis quite a diff'rent case,
For fortune favours all her idiot-race:
In her own nest the cuckow-eggs we find,[9]
O'er which she broods to hatch the changling-kind.
No portion for her own she has to spare,
So much she doats on her adopted care.
Poets are bubbles, by the Town drawn in,
Suffer'd at first some trifling stakes to win:
But what unequal hazards do they run!
Each time they write, they venture all they've won:
The 'squire that's butter'd still, is sure to be undone.
This author, heretofore, has found your favour,
But pleads no merit from his past behaviour.
To build on that might prove a vain presumption,
Should grants to poets made, admit resumption:
And in Parnassus he must lose his seat,
If that be found a forfeited estate.
He owns, with toil, he wrought the following scenes,
But if they're naught ne're spare him for his pains:
Damn him the more; have no commiseration
For dulness on mature deliberation.
He swears he'll not resent one hiss'd-off scene,
Nor, like those peevish wits, his play maintain,
Who, to assert their sense, your taste arraign.
Some plot we think he has, and some new thought;
Some humour too, no farce; but that's a fault.
Satire, he thinks, you ought not to expect,
For so reform'd a Town, who dares correct?[10]
To please, this time, has been his sole pretence,
He'll not instruct least it should give offence.
Should he by chance a knave or fool expose,
That hurts none here, sure here are none of those.
In short, our play, shall (with your leave to shew it)
Give you one instance of a passive poet.
Who to your judgments yields all resignation;
So save or damn, after your own discretion.

Personæ Dramatis.

MEN.

Fainall, in love with *Mrs.* Marwood.	Mr. *Betterton.*
Mirabell, in love with *Mrs.* Millamant.	Mr. *Verbrugen.*[11]
Witwoud, Follower[12] of *Mrs.* Millamant.	Mr. *Bowen.*
Petulant, Follower of *Mrs.* Millamant.	Mr. *Bowman.*
Sir *Willfull Witwoud*, Nephew to Lady *Wishfort.*	Mr. *Underhill.*
Waitwell, Servant to *Mirabell.*	Mr. *Bright.*

WOMEN.

Lady *Wishfort*, Enemy to *Mirabell*, for having pretended love to her.	Mrs. *Leigh.*
Mrs. *Millamant*, Niece to Lady *Wishfort*, loves *Mirabell.*	Mrs. *Bracegirdle.*[13]
Mrs. *Marwood*, Friend to *Mr.* Fainall, and likes *Mirabell.*	Mrs. *Barry.*
Mrs. *Fainall*, Daughter to Lady *Wishfort*, and Wife to *Fainall*, formerly Friend[14] to *Mirabell.*	Mrs. *Bowman.*
Foible, Woman to Lady *Wishfort.*	Mrs. *Willis.*
Mincing, Woman to Mrs. *Millamant.*	Mrs. *Prince.*
Betty, a maid.	
Peg, a maid.	
Dancers, Footmen, and Attendants.	

ACT I. SCENE I. London. A Chocolate-house.[15]

[Mirabell *and* Fainall*, rising from cards,* Betty *waiting.*]

MIRABELL. You are a fortunate man, Mr. *Fainall.*

FAINALL. Have we done?

MIRABELL. What you please. I'll play on to entertain you.

FAINALL. No, I'll give you your revenge another time, when you are not so indifferent; you are thinking of something else now, and play too negligently; the coldness of a losing gamester lessens the pleasure of the winner: I'd no more play with a man that slighted his ill fortune, than I'd make love to a woman who undervalu'd the loss of her reputation.

MIRABELL. You have a taste extremely delicate, and are for refining on your pleasures.

FAINALL. Prithee, why so reserv'd? Something has put you out of humour.

MIRABELL. Not at all: I happen to be grave to day; and you are gay; that's all.

FAINALL. Confess, *Millamant* and you quarrel'd last night, after I left you; my fair cousin has some humours that wou'd tempt the patience of a stoic. What, some coxcomb[16] came in, and was well receiv'd by her, while you were by.

MIRABELL. *Witwoud* and *Petulant*; and what was worse, her aunt, your wife's mother, my evil genius; or to sum up all in her own name, my old Lady *Wishfort* came in. –

FAINALL. O there it is then – She has a lasting passion for you, and with reason. – What, then my Wife was there?

MIRABELL. Yes, and Mrs. *Marwood* and three or four more, whom I never saw before; seeing me, they all put on their grave faces, whisper'd one another; then complain'd aloud of the vapours,[17] and after fell into a profound silence.

FAINALL. They had a mind to be rid of you.

MIRABELL. For which reason I resolv'd not to stir. At last the good old lady broke thro' her painful taciturnity, with an invective against long visits. I would not have understood her, but *Millamant* joining in the argument, I rose and with a constrain'd smile, told her I thought nothing was so easy as to know when a visit began to be troublesome; she reddened[18] and I withdrew, without expecting her reply.

FAINALL. You were to blame to resent what she spoke only in compliance with her aunt.

MIRABELL. She is more mistress of her self, than to be under the necessity of such a resignation.

FAINALL. What? Tho' half her fortune depends upon her marrying with my lady's approbation?

MIRABELL. I was then in such a humour, that I shou'd have been better pleas'd if she had been less discreet.

FAINALL. Now I remember, I wonder not they were weary of you; last night was one of their cabal-nights;[19] they have 'em three times a week, and meet by turns, at one another's apartments, where they come together like the coroner's inquest, to sit upon the murder'd reputations of the week. You and I are excluded; and it was once propos'd that all the male sex shou'd be excepted; but somebody mov'd that to avoid scandal there might be one man of the community; upon which motion *Witwoud* and *Petulant* were enroll'd members.

MIRABELL. And who may have been the foundress of this sect? My Lady *Wishfort*, I warrant, who publishes her detestation of mankind; and full of the vigor of fifty-five, declares for a friend and *ratafia*;[20] and let posterity shift for it self, she'll breed no more.

FAINALL. The discovery of your sham addresses to her, to conceal your love to her niece, has provok'd this separation. Had you dissembl'd better, things might have continu'd in the state of Nature.

MIRABELL. I did as much as man cou'd, with any reasonable conscience; I proceeded to the very last act of flattery with her, and was guilty of a song in her commendation. Nay, I got a friend to put her into a lampoon, and complement her with the imputation of an affair with a young fellow, which I carry'd so far, that I told her the malicious Town took notice that she was grown fat of a sudden; and when she lay in of a dropsie,[21] persuaded her she was reported to be in labour. The Devil's in it, if an old woman is to be flatter'd further, unless a man shou'd endeavour downright personally to debauch her; and that my virtue forbad me. But for the discovery of that amour, I am indebted to your friend, or your wife's friend Mrs. *Marwood*.

FAINALL. What should provoke her to be your enemy, without she has made you advances, which you have slighted? Women do not easily forgive omissions of that nature.

MIRABELL. She was always civil to me, till of late; I confess I am not one of those coxcombs who are apt to interpret a woman's good manners to her prejudice; and think that she who does not refuse 'em every thing, can refuse 'em nothing.

FAINALL. You are a gallant man, *Mirabell*; and though you may have cruelty enough, not to satisfy a lady's longing, you have too much generosity not to be tender of her honour. Yet you speak with an indifference which seems to be affected, and confesses you are conscious of a negligence.

MIRABELL. You pursue the argument with a distrust that seems to be unaffected, and confesses you are conscious of a concern for which the lady is more indebted to you, than your wife.

FAINALL. Fie, fie friend, if you grow censorious I must leave you; – I'll look upon the gamesters in the next room.

MIRABELL. Who are they?

FAINALL. *Petulant* and *Witwoud*. – [*To* Betty] Bring me some chocolate.[22] [*Exit* Fainall.

MIRABELL. *Betty*, what says your clock?

BETTY. Turn'd of the last canonical hour, Sir.[23] [*Exit* Betty.

MIRABELL. How pertinently the jade answers me! Ha? almost one o'clock! [*Looking on his Watch*] O, y'are come – [*Enter a* Servant] Well; is the grand affair over?[24] You have been something tedious.

SERVANT. Sir, there's such coupling at *Pancras*,[25] that they stand behind one another, as 'twere in a country dance. Ours was the last couple to lead up; and no hopes appearing of dispatch. Besides, the parson growing hoarse, we were afraid his lungs would have fail'd before it came to our turn; so we drove round to *Duke*'s *Place*; and there they were riveted in a trice.[26]

MIRABELL. So, so, you are sure they are married.

SERVANT. Married and bedded, Sir: I am witness.

MIRABELL. Have you the certificate?

SERVANT. Here it is, Sir.

MIRABELL. Has the taylor brought *Waitwell*'s clothes home, and the new liveries?

SERVANT. Yes, Sir.

MIRABELL. That's well. Do you go home again, d'ye hear, and adjourn the consummation till farther order; bid *Waitwell* shake his ears, and Dame *Partlet* rustle up her feathers,[27] and meet me at one o'clock by *Rosamond*'s Pond. That I may see her before she returns to her lady; and as you tender your ears be secret.

[*Exit* Servant. *Re-Enter* Fainall.

FAINALL. Joy of your success, *Mirabell*; you look pleas'd.

MIRABELL. Ay; I have been engag'd in a matter of some sort of mirth, which is not yet ripe for discovery. I am glad this is not a Cabal-night. I wonder, *Fainall*, that you who are married, and of consequence should be discreet, will suffer your wife to be of such a party.

FAINALL. Faith, I am not jealous. Besides, most who are engag'd are women and relations; and for the men, they are of a kind too contemptible to give scandal.

MIRABELL. I am of another opinion. The greater the coxcomb, always the more the scandal. For a woman who is not a fool, can have but one reason for associating with a man that is.

FAINALL. Are you jealous as often as you see *Witwoud* entertain'd by *Millamant*?

MIRABELL. Of her understanding I am, if not of her person.

FAINALL. You do her wrong; for to give her her due, she has wit.

MIRABELL. She has beauty enough to make any man think so; and complaisance enough not to contradict him who shall tell her so.

FAINALL. For a passionate lover, methinks you are a man somewhat too discerning in the failings of your mistress.

MIRABELL. And for a discerning man, somewhat too passionate a lover; for I like her with all her faults; nay, like her for her faults. Her follies are so natural, or so artful, that they become her; and those affectations which in another woman wou'd be odious, serve but to make her more agreeable. I'll tell thee, *Fainall*, she once us'd me with that insolence, that in revenge I took her to pieces; sifted her and separated her failings; I study'd 'em, and got 'em by rote. The catalogue was so large, that I was not without hopes one day or other to hate her heartily: to which end I so used my self to think of 'em, that at length, contrary to my design and expectation, they gave me every hour less and less disturbance; 'till in a few days it became habitual to me, to remember 'em without being displeased. They are now grown as familiar to me as my own frailties; and in all probability in a little time longer I shall like 'em as well.

FAINALL. Marry her, marry her; be half as well acquainted with her charms, as you are with her defects, and my life on't, you are your own man again.

MIRABELL. Say you so?

FAINALL. Aye, aye, I have experience: I have a wife, and so forth.

[*Enter* Messenger.

MESSENGER. Is one Squire *Witwoud* here?

BETTY. Yes; what's your business?

MESSENGER. I have a letter for him, from his brother Sir *Willfull*, which I am charg'd to deliver into his own hands.

BETTY. He's in the next room, friend – That way. [*Exit* Messenger.

MIRABELL. What, is the chief of that noble family in town, Sir *Willfull Witwoud*?

FAINALL. He is expected to day. Do you know him?

MIRABELL. I have seen him, he promises to be an extraordinary person; I think you have the honour to be related to him.

FAINALL. Yes; he is half brother to this *Witwoud* by a former wife, who was sister to my Lady *Wishfort*, my wife's mother. If you marry *Millamant*, you must call cousins too.

MIRABELL. I had rather be his relation than his acquaintance.

FAINALL. He comes to town in order to equip himself for travel.

MIRABELL. For travel! Why the man that I mean is above forty.[28]

FAINALL. No matter for that; 'tis for the honour of *England*, that all *Europe* should know we have blockheads of all ages.

MIRABELL. I wonder there is not an act of Parliament to save the credit of the nation, and prohibit the exportation of fools.

FAINALL. By no means, 'tis better as 'tis; 'tis better to trade with a little loss, than to be quite eaten up, with being overstock'd.

MIRABELL. Pray, are the follies of this knight-errant, and those of the squire his brother, any thing related?

FAINALL. Not at all; *Witwoud* grows by the knight, like a medlar grafted on a crab.[29] One will melt in your mouth, and t'other set your teeth on edge; one is all pulp, and the other all core.

MIRABELL. So one will be rotten before he be ripe, and the other will be rotten without ever being ripe at all.

FAINALL. Sir *Willfull* is an odd mixture of bashfulness and obstinacy. – But when he's drunk, he's as loving as the monster in *The Tempest*; and much after the same manner.[30] To give the t'other his due; he has something of good nature, and does not always want wit.

MIRABELL. Not always; but as often as his memory fails him, and his common place of comparisons. He is a fool with a good memory, and some few scraps of other folks wit. He is one whose conversation can never be approv'd, yet it is now and then to be endured. He has indeed one good quality; he is not exceptious; for he so passionately affects the reputation of understanding raillery that he will construe an affront into a jest, and call downright rudeness and ill language, satire and fire.

FAINALL. If you have a mind to finish his picture, you have an opportunity to do it at full length. Behold the original.

[*Enter* Witwoud.

WITWOUD. Afford me your compassion, my dears; pity me, *Fainall*, *Mirabell*, pity me.

MIRABELL. I do from my soul.

FAINALL. Why, what's the matter?

WITWOUD. No letters for me, *Betty*?

BETTY. Did not the messenger bring you one, but now Sir?

WITWOUD. Ay, but no other?

BETTY. No, Sir.

WITWOUD. That's hard, that's very hard. – A messenger, a mule, a beast of burden, he has brought me a letter from the fool my brother, as heavy as a panegyrick[31] in a funeral sermon, or a copy of commendatory verses from one poet to another. And what's worse, 'tis as sure a forerunner of the author, as an epistle dedicatory.

MIRABELL. A fool, and your brother *Witwoud*!

WITWOUD. Ay, ay, my half brother. My half brother he is, no nearer upon honour.

MIRABELL. Then 'tis possible he may be but half a fool.

WITWOUD. Good, good *Mirabell, le drôle*![32] Good, good, hang him, don't let's talk of him. – *Fainall*, how does your lady? Gad, I say any thing in the World to get this fellow out of my head. I beg pardon that I should ask a man of pleasure, and the Town, a question at once so foreign and domestick. But I talk like an old maid at a marriage, I don't know what I say. But she's the best woman in the World.

FAINALL. 'Tis well you don't know what you say, or else your commendation would go near to make me either vain or jealous.

WITWOUD. No man in town lives well with a wife but *Fainall*: your judgment, *Mirabell*?

MIRABELL. You had better step and ask his wife, if you would be credibly informed.

WITWOUD. *Mirabell*!

MIRABELL. Ay.

WITWOUD. My Dear, I ask ten thousand pardons; – Gad[33] I have forgot what I was going to say to you.

MIRABELL. I thank you heartily, heartily.

WITWOUD. No, but prithee excuse me, – my memory is such a memory.

MIRABELL. Have a care of such apologies, *Witwoud*; – for I never knew a fool but he affected to complain, either of the spleen or his memory.

FAINALL. What have you done with *Petulant*?

WITWOUD. He's reckoning his money, – my money it was, – I have no luck today.

FAINALL. You may allow him to win of you at play; – for you are sure to be too hard for him at repartee: since you monopolize the wit that is between you, the fortune must be his of course.

MIRABELL. I don't find that *Petulant* confesses the superiority of wit to be your talent, *Witwoud*.

WITWOUD. Come, come, you are malicious now, and wou'd breed debates. – *Petulant*'s my friend, and a very honest fellow, and a very pretty fellow, and has a smattering – faith and troth a pretty deal of an odd sort of a small wit: nay, I'll do him justice. I'm his friend, I won't wrong him neither. And if he had but any judgment in the World, he would not be altogether contemptible. Come come, don't detract from the merits of my friend.

FAINALL. You don't take your friend to be overnicely bred.

WITWOUD. No, no, hang him, the rogue has no manners at all, that I must own – No more breeding than a bum-baily,[34] that I grant you, – 'Tis pity faith; the fellow has fire and life.

MIRABELL. What, courage?

WITWOUD. Hum, faith I don't know as to that, – I can't say as to that. – Yes, faith, in a controversie he'll contradict any body.

MIRABELL. Tho' 'twere a man whom he fear'd, or a woman whom he lov'd.

WITWOUD. Well, well, he does not always think before he speaks; – We have all our failings; you're too hard upon him, you are faith. Let me excuse him, – I can defend most of his faults, except one or two; one he has, that's the truth on't, if he were my brother, I could not acquit him – That indeed I cou'd wish were otherwise.

MIRABELL. Ay marry, what's that, *Witwoud*?

WITWOUD. O pardon me – expose the infirmities of my friend? – No, my dear, excuse me there.

FAINALL. What I warrant he's unsincere, or 'tis some such trifle.

WITWOUD. No, no, what if he be? 'tis no matter for that, his wit will excuse that. A wit shou'd no more be sincere, than a woman constant; one argues a decay of parts, as t'other of beauty.

MIRABELL. Maybe you think him too positive?

WITWOUD. No, no, his being positive is an incentive to argument, and keeps up conversation.

FAINALL. Too illiterate.

WITWOUD. That! *That's* his happiness – His want of learning gives him the more opportunities to shew his natural parts.

MIRABELL. He wants words.

WITWOUD. Ay; but I like him for that now; for his want of words gives me the pleasure very often to explain his meaning.

FAINALL. He's impudent.

WITWOUD. No; that's not it.

MIRABELL. Vain.

WITWOUD. No.

MIRABELL. What, he speaks unseasonable truths sometimes, because he has not wit enough to invent an evasion.[35]

WITWOUD. Truths! Ha, ha, ha! No, no, since you will have it, – I mean he never speaks truth at all, – that's all. He will lie like a chambermaid, or a woman of quality's porter. Now that is a fault.

[*Enter* Coachman.

COACHMAN. Is Master *Petulant* here, mistress?

BETTY. Yes.

COACHMAN. Three gentlewomen in the coach would speak with him.

FAINALL. O brave *Petulant*, three!

BETTY. I'll tell him.

COACHMAN. You must bring two dishes of chocolate and a glass of cinnamon-water. [*Exit.*

WITWOUD. That should be for two fasting strumpets, and a bawd troubl'd with wind.[36] Now you may know what the three are.

MIRABELL. You are very free with your friend's acquaintance.

WITWOUD. Ay, ay, friendship without freedom is as dull as love without enjoyment, or wine without toasting; but to tell you a secret, these are trulls[37] that he allows coach-hire, and something more by the week, to call on him once a day at publick places.

MIRABELL. How!

WITWOUD. You shall see he won't go to 'em because there's no more company here to take notice of him – Why this is nothing to what he used to do; – Before he found out this way, I have known him call for himself –

FAINALL. Call for himself? What dost thou mean?

WITWOUD. Mean, why he wou'd slip you out of this chocolate-house, just when you had been talking to him – As soon as your back was turn'd – whip he was gone; – Then trip to his lodging, clap on a hood and scarf, and mask, slap into a hackney-coach, and drive hither to the door again in a trice; where he would send in for himself, that I mean, call for himself, wait for himself, nay and what's more, not finding himself, sometimes leave a letter for himself.

MIRABELL. I confess this is something extraordinary – I believe he waits for himself now, he is so long a coming; O I ask his pardon.

[*Enter* Petulant.

BETTY. Sir, the coach stays.

PETULANT. Well, well; I come – S'bud, a Man had as good be a profess'd midwife as a profest whoremaster, at this rate; to be knocked up and raised[38] at all hours, and in all places. Pox on 'em I won't come. – D'ye hear, tell 'em I won't come. – Let 'em snivel and cry their hearts out.

FAINALL. You are very cruel, *Petulant.*

PETULANT. All's one, let it pass – I have a humour to be cruel.

MIRABELL. I hope they are not persons of condition that you use at this rate.

PETULANT. Condition! Condition's a dry'd fig, if I am not in humour – By this hand, if they were your – a – a – your what-dee-call-'ems themselves, they must wait or rub off, if I want appetite.

MIRABELL. What-dee-call-'ems! What are they, *Witwoud*?

WITWOUD. Empresses, my dear – By your what-dee-call-'ems he means sultana queens.

PETULANT. Ay, *Roxolanas*.[39]

MIRABELL. Cry you mercy.

FAINALL. *Witwoud* says they are –

PETULANT. What does he say th' are?

WITWOUD. I; fine ladies I say.

PETULANT. Pass on, *Witwoud* – Hearkee, by this light his relations – Two co-heiresses his cousins, and an old aunt, that loves catterwauling better than a conventicle.[40]

WITWOUD. Ha, ha, ha; I had a mind to see how the rogue wou'd come off – Ha, ha, ha; Gad I can't be angry with him; if he said they were my mother and my sisters.

MIRABELL. No!

WITWOUD. No; the rogue's wit and readiness of invention charm me, dear *Petulant*.

BETTY. They are gone sir, in great anger.

PETULANT. Enough, let 'em trundle. Anger helps complexion, saves paint.

FAINALL. This continence is all dissembled; this is in order to have something to brag of the next time he makes court to *Millamant*, and swear he has abandon'd the whole sex for her sake.

MIRABELL. Have you not left off your impudent pretensions there yet? I shall cut your throat, sometime or other *Petulant*, about that business.

PETULANT. Ay, ay, let that pass – There are other throats to be cut –

MIRABELL. Meaning mine, sir?

PETULANT. Not I – I mean no body – I know nothing – But there are uncles and nephews in the World – And they may be rivals – What then? All's one for that –

MIRABELL. How! hearkee *Petulant*, come hither – Explain, or I shall call your interpreter.

PETULANT. Explain, I know nothing – Why you have an uncle, have you not, lately come to town, lodges by my Lady *Wishfort*'s?

MIRABELL. True.

PETULANT. Why that's enough – You and he are not friends; and if he shou'd marry and have a child, you may be disinherited, ha?

MIRABELL. Where hast thou stumbled upon all this truth?

PETULANT. All's one for that; why then say I know something.

MIRABELL. Come, thou art an honest fellow *Petulant*, and shalt make love to my mistress, thou sha't, faith. What hast thou heard of my uncle?

PETULANT. I, nothing I. If throats are to be cut, let swords clash; snugs the word, I shrug and am silent.

MIRABELL. O raillery, raillery. Come, I know thou art in the women's secrets – What, you're a cabalist, I know you stayed at *Millamant*'s last night, after I went. Was there any mention made of my uncle, or me? Tell me; if thou hadst but good nature equal to thy wit *Petulant*, *Tony Witwoud*, who is now thy competitor in fame, wou'd shew as dim by thee as a dead whiting's eye, by a pearl of orient; he wou'd no more be seen by thee, then *Mercury* is by the sun. Come, I'm sure thou wo't tell me.

PETULANT. If I do, will you grant me common sense then, for the future?

MIRABELL. Faith I'll do what I can for thee; and I'll pray that heav'n may grant it thee in the mean time.

PETULANT. Well, hearkee.

FAINALL. *Petulant* and you both will find *Mirabell* as warm a rival as a lover.

WITWOUD. Pshaw, pshaw, that she laughs at *Petulant* is plain. And for my part – But that it is almost a fashion to admire her, I shou'd – Hearkee – To tell you a secret, but let it go no further – Between friends, I shall never break my heart for her.

FAINALL. How!

WITWOUD. She's handsome; but she's a sort of an uncertain woman.

FAINALL. I thought you had dy'd for her.

WITWOUD. Umh – No –

FAINALL. She has wit.

WITWOUD. 'Tis what she will hardly allow any body else; – Now, demme, I shou'd hate that, if she were as handsome as *Cleopatra*. *Mirabell* is not so sure of her as he thinks for.

FAINALL. Why do you think so?

WITWOUD. We staid pretty late there last night; and heard something of an uncle to *Mirabell*, who is lately come to town, – and is between him and the best part of his estate; *Mirabell* and he are at some distance, as my Lady *Wishfort* has been told; and you know she hates *Mirabell*, worse than a quaker hates a parrot;[41] or then a fishmonger hates a hard frost. Whether this uncle has seen Mrs. *Millamant* or not, I cannot say; but there were items of such a treaty being in embrio; and if it shou'd come to life; poor *Mirabell* wou'd be in some sort unfortunately fobb'd[42] ifaith.

FAINALL. 'Tis impossible *Millamant* should hearken to it.

WITWOUD. Faith, my dear, I can't tell; she's a woman and a kind of a humorist.

MIRABELL. And this is the sum of what you cou'd collect last night.

PETULANT. The quintessence. May be *Witwoud* knows more, he stay'd longer – Besides they never mind him; they say any thing before him.

MIRABELL. I thought you had been the greatest favourite.

PETULANT. Ay, *tête à tête,* But not in publick, because I make remarks.

MIRABELL. Do you.

PETULANT. Ay, ay, pox I'm malicious, man. Now he's soft you know, they are not in awe of him – The fellow's well bred, he's what you call a – what-dee-call-'em. A fine gentleman, but he's silly withal.

MIRABELL. I thank you, I know as much as my curiosity requires. *Fainall*, are you for the *mall*?

FAINALL. Ay, I'll take a turn before dinner.

WITWOUD. Ay, we'll all walk in the park, the ladies talk'd of being there.

MIRABELL. I thought you were oblig'd to watch for your brother Sir *Willfull*'s arrival.

WITWOUD. No, no, he comes to his aunts, my Lady *Wishfort*; pox on him, I shall be troubled with him too; what shall I do with the fool?

PETULANT. Beg him for his estate; that I may beg you afterwards; and so have but one trouble with you both.

WITWOUD. O rare *Petulant*; thou art as quick as a fire in a frosty morning; thou shalt to the *mall* with us, and we'll be very severe.

PETULANT. Enough, I'm in a humour to be severe.

MIRABELL. Are you? Pray then walk by your selves, – Let not us be accessary to your putting the ladies out of countenance, with your senseless ribaldry; which you roar out aloud as often as they pass by you; and when you have made a handsome woman blush, then you think you have been severe.

PETULANT. What, what? Then let 'em either shew their innocence by not understanding what they hear, or else shew their discretion by not hearing what they would not be thought to understand.

MIRABELL. But hast not thou then sense enough to know that thou ought'st to be most asham'd thyself, when thou hast put another out of countenance.

PETULANT. Not I, by this hand – I always take blushing either for a sign of guilt, or ill breeding.

MIRABELL. I confess you ought to think so. You are in the right, that you may plead the error of your judgment in defence of your practice.

Where modesty's ill manners, 'tis but fit
That impudence and malice, pass for wit.
[*Exeunt.*

ACT II. SCENE I. St. James's Park.

[*Enter* Mrs. Fainall *and* Mrs. Marwood.]

MRS. FAINALL. Ay, ay, dear *Marwood*, if we will be happy, we must find the means in our selves, and among our selves. Men are ever in extreams; either doating or averse. While they are lovers, if they have fire and sense, their jealousies are insupportable: And when they cease to love, (we ought to think at least) they loath; they look upon us with horror and distaste; they meet us like the ghosts of what we were, and as such fly from us.

MRS. MARWOOD. True, 'tis an unhappy circumstance of life, that love shou'd ever die before us; and that the man so often shou'd out-live the lover. But say what you will, 'tis better to be left, than never to have been lov'd. To pass our youth in dull indifference, to refuse the sweets of life because they once must leave us; is as preposterous, as to wish to have been born old, because we one day must be old. For my part, my youth may wear and waste, but it shall never rust in my possession.

MRS. FAINALL. Then it seems you dissemble an aversion to mankind, only in compliance with my mother's humour.

MRS. MARWOOD. Certainly. To be free; I have no taste of those insipid dry discourses, with which our sex of force must entertain themselves, apart from men. We may affect endearments to each other, profess eternal friendships, and seem to doat like lovers; but 'tis not in our natures long to persevere. Love will resume his empire in our breasts, and every heart, or soon or late, receive and readmit him as its lawful tyrant.

MRS. FAINALL. Bless me, how have I been deceiv'd! Why you profess a libertine.

MRS. MARWOOD. You see my friendship by my freedom. Come, be as sincere, acknowledge that your sentiments agree with mine.

MRS. FAINALL. Never.

MRS. MARWOOD. You hate mankind.

MRS. FAINALL. Heartily, inveterately.

MRS. MARWOOD. Your husband.

MRS. FAINALL. Most transcendantly; ay, tho' I say it, meritoriously.

MRS. MARWOOD. Give me your hand upon it.

MRS. FAINALL. There.

MRS. MARWOOD. I join with you; what I have said, has been to try you.

MRS. FAINALL. Is it possible? Dost thou hate those vipers, men?

MRS. MARWOOD. I have done hating 'em; and am now come to despise 'em; the next thing I have to do, is eternally to forget 'em.

MRS. FAINALL. There spoke the spirit of an *Amazon*, a *Penthesilea*.[43]

MRS. MARWOOD. And yet I am thinking sometimes, to carry my aversion further.

MRS. FAINALL. How?

MRS. MARWOOD. Faith by marrying; if I cou'd but find one that lov'd me very well, and would be thoroughly sensible of ill usage; I think I shou'd do my self the violence of undergoing the ceremony.

MRS. FAINALL. You would not make him a cuckold?

MRS. MARWOOD. No; but I'd make him believe I did, and that's as bad.

MRS. FAINALL. Why, had not you as good do it?

MRS. MARWOOD. O if he shou'd ever discover it, he wou'd then know the worst; and be out of his pain; but I wou'd have him ever to continue upon the rack of fear and jealousy.

MRS. FAINALL. Ingenious mischief! Wou'd thou wert married to *Mirabell*.

MRS. MARWOOD. Wou'd I were.

MRS. FAINALL. You change colour.

MRS. MARWOOD. Because I hate him.

MRS. FAINALL. So do I; but I can hear him nam'd. But what reason have you to hate him in particular?

MRS. MARWOOD. I never lov'd him; he is, and always was insufferably proud.

MRS. FAINALL. By the reason you give for your aversion, one wou'd think it dissembl'd; for you have laid a fault to his charge, of which his enemies must acquit him.

MRS. MARWOOD. O then it seems you are one of his favourable enemies. Methinks you look a little pale, and now you flush again.

MRS. FAINALL. Do I? I think I am a little sick o' the suddain.

MRS. MARWOOD. What ails you?

MRS. FAINALL. My husband. Don't you see him? He turn'd short upon me unawares, and has almost overcome me.

[*Enter* Fainall and Mirabell.

MRS. MARWOOD. Ha, ha, ha; he comes opportunely for you.

MRS. FAINALL. For you, for he has brought *Mirabell* with him.

FAINALL. My dear.

MRS. FAINALL. My soul.

FAINALL. You don't look well to day, child.

MRS. FAINALL. Dee[44] think so?

MIRABELL. He is the only man that does, madam.

MRS. FAINALL. The only man that would tell me so at least; and the only man from whom I could hear it without mortification.

FAINALL. O my dear I am satisfy'd of your tenderness; I know you cannot resent any thing from me; especially what is an effect of my concern.

MRS. FAINALL. Mr. *Mirabell*; my mother interrupted you in a pleasant relation last night: I wou'd fain hear it out.

MIRABELL. The persons concern'd in that affair, have yet a tollerable reputation – I am afraid Mr. *Fainall* will be censorious.

MRS. FAINALL. He has a humour more prevailing than his curiosity, and will willingly dispence with the hearing of one scandalous story, to avoid giving an occasion to make another by being seen to walk with his wife. This way Mr. *Mirabell*, and I dare promise you will oblige us both. [*Exeunt* Mrs. Fainall *and* Mirabell.

FAINALL. Excellent creature! Well sure if I shou'd live to be rid of my wife, I shou'd be a miserable man.

MRS. MARWOOD. Ay!

FAINALL. For having only that one hope, the accomplishment of it, of consequence must put an end to all my hopes; and what a wretch is he who must survive his hopes! Nothing remains when that day comes, but to sit down and weep like *Alexander*, when he wanted other Worlds to conquer.

MRS. MARWOOD. Will you not follow 'em?

FAINALL. Faith, I think not.

MRS. MARWOOD. Pray let us; I have a reason.

FAINALL. You are not jealous?

MRS. MARWOOD. Of whom?

FAINALL. Of *Mirabell*.

MRS. MARWOOD. If I am, is it inconsistent with my love to you that I am tender of your honour?

FAINALL. You wou'd intimate then, as if there were a *fellow-feeling* between my wife and him.

MRS. MARWOOD. I think she does not hate him to that degree she wou'd be thought.

FAINALL. But he, I fear, is too insensible.

MRS. MARWOOD. It may be you are deceiv'd.

FAINALL. It may be so. I do now begin to apprehend it.

MRS. MARWOOD. What?

FAINALL. That I have been deceiv'd madam, and you are false.

MRS. MARWOOD. That I am false! What mean you?

FAINALL. To let you know I see through all your little arts – Come, you both love him; and both have equally dissembl'd your aversion. Your mutual jealousies of one another, have made you clash till you have both struck fire. I have seen the warm confession red'ning on your cheeks, and sparkling from your eyes.

MRS. MARWOOD. You do me wrong.

FAINALL. I do not – 'Twas for my ease to oversee and wilfully neglect the gross advances made him by my wife; that by permitting her to be engag'd, I might continue unsuspected in my pleasures, and take you oftner to my arms in full security. But cou'd you think because the nodding husband would not wake, that e'er the watchful lover slept!

MRS. MARWOOD. And wherewithal can you reproach me?

FAINALL. With infidelity, with loving of another, with love of *Mirabell*.

MRS. MARWOOD. 'Tis false. I challenge you to shew an instance that can confirm your groundless accusation. I hate him.

FAINALL. And wherefore do you hate him? He is insensible,[45] and your resentment follows his neglect. An instance? The injuries you have done him are a proof. Your interposing in his love. What cause had you to make discoveries of his pretended passion? To undeceive the credulous aunt, and be the officious obstacle of his match with *Millamant*?

MRS. MARWOOD. My obligations to my Lady urg'd me: I had profess'd a friendship to her; and could not see her easie nature so abus'd by that dissembler.

FAINALL. What, was it conscience then! profess'd a friendship! O the pious friendships of the female sex!

MRS. MARWOOD. More tender, more sincere, and more enduring, than all the vain and empty vows of men, whether professing love to us, or mutual faith to one another.

FAINALL. Ha, ha, ha; you are my wife's friend too.

MRS. MARWOOD. Shame and ingratitude! Do you reproach me? You, you upbraid me! Have I been false to her, thro' strict fidelity to you, and sacrific'd my friendship to keep my love inviolate? And have you the baseness to charge me with the guilt, unmindful of the merit! To you it shou'd be meritorious, that I have been vicious. And do you reflect that guilt upon me, which should lie buried in your bosom?

FAINALL. You misinterpret my reproof. I meant but to remind you of the slight account you once could make of strictest ties, when set in competition[46] with your love to me.

MRS. MARWOOD. 'Tis false, you urg'd it with deliberate malice – 'Twas spoke in scorn, and I never will forgive it.

FAINALL. Your guilt, not your resentment, begets your rage. If yet you lov'd, you could forgive a jealousy. But you are stung to find you are discover'd.

MRS. MARWOOD. It shall be all discover'd. You too shall be discover'd; be sure you shall. I can but be expos'd – If I do it my self I shall prevent your baseness.

FAINALL. Why, what will you do?

MRS. MARWOOD. Disclose it to your wife; own what has past between us.

FAINALL. Frenzy!

MRS. MARWOOD. By all my wrongs I'll do't – I'll publish to the World the injuries you have done me, both in my fame and fortune: With both I trusted you, you bankrupt in honour, as indigent of wealth.

FAINALL. Your fame I have preserv'd. Your fortune has been bestow'd as the prodigality of your love would have it, in pleasures which we both have shar'd. Yet had not you been false, I had e'er this repaid it – 'Tis true – Had you permitted *Mirabell* with *Millamant* to have stoll'n their marriage, my Lady had been incens'd beyond all means of reconcilement: *Millamant* had forfeited the moiety of her fortune; which then wou'd have descended to my wife; – And wherefore did I marry, but to make lawful prize of a rich widow's wealth, and squander it on love and you?

MRS. MARWOOD. Deceit and frivolous pretence.

FAINALL. Death, am I not married? What's pretence? Am I not imprison'd, fetter'd? Have I not a wife? Nay a wife that was a widow, a young widow, a handsome widow; and would be again a widow, but that I have a heart of proof, and something of a constitution to bustle thro' the ways of wedlock and this World. Will you yet be reconcil'd to truth and me?

MRS. MARWOOD. Impossible. Truth and you are inconsistent – I hate you, and shall forever.

FAINALL. For loving you?

MRS. MARWOOD. I loath the name of love after such usage; and next to the guilt with which you wou'd asperse me, I scorn you most. Farewell.

FAINALL. Nay, we must not part thus.

MRS. MARWOOD. Let me go.

FAINALL. Come, I'm sorry.

MRS. MARWOOD. I care not – Let me go – Break my hands, do – I'd leave 'em to get loose.

FAINALL. I would not hurt you for the World. Have I no other hold to keep you here?

MRS. MARWOOD. Well, I have deserv'd it all.

FAINALL. You know I love you.

MRS. MARWOOD. Poor dissembling! – O that – Well, it is not yet –

FAINALL. What? What is it not? What is it not yet? It is not yet too late –

MRS. MARWOOD. No, it is not yet too late – I have that comfort.

FAINALL. It is to love another.

MRS. MARWOOD. But not to loath, detest, abhor mankind, my self and the whole treacherous World.

FAINALL. Nay, this is extravagance – Come I ask your pardon – No tears – I was to blame, I cou'd not love you and be easie in my doubts – Pray forbear – I believe you; I'm convinc'd I've done you wrong; and any way, every way will make amends; – I'll hate my wife yet more, damn her, I'll part with her, rob her of all she's worth, and will retire somewhere, any where to another World, I'll marry thee – Be pacify'd – 'Sdeath they come, hide your face, your tears – You have a mask, wear it a moment. This way, this way, be persuaded. [*Exeunt.*

[*Enter* Mirabell *and* Mrs. Fainall.

MRS. FAINALL. They are here yet.

MIRABELL. They are turning into the other walk.

MRS. FAINALL. While I only hated my husband, I could bear to see him; but since I have despis'd him, he's too offensive.

MIRABELL. O you should hate with prudence.

MRS. FAINALL. Yes, for I have lov'd with indiscretion.

MIRABELL. You shou'd have just so much disgust for your husband, as may be sufficient to make you relish your lover.

MRS. FAINALL. You have been the cause that I have lov'd without bounds, and wou'd you set limits to that aversion, of which you have been the occasion? Why did you make me marry this man?

MIRABELL. Why do we daily commit disagreeable and dangerous actions? To save that idol, reputation. If the familiarities of our loves had produc'd that consequence, of which you were aprehensive, where could you have fix'd a father's name with credit, but on a husband? I knew *Fainall* to be a man lavish of his morals, an interested and professing friend, a false and a designing lover; yet one whose wit and outward fair behaviour, have gain'd a reputation with the Town, enough to make that woman stand excus'd, who has suffer'd herself to be won by his addresses. A better man ought not to have been sacrific'd to the occasion; a worse had not answer'd to the purpose. When you are weary of him, you know your remedy.

MRS. FAINALL. I ought to stand in some degree of credit with you, *Mirabell.*

MIRABELL. In justice to you, I have made you privy to my whole design, and put it in your power to ruin or advance my fortune.

MRS. FAINALL. Whom have you instructed to represent your pretended uncle?

MIRABELL. *Waitwell*, my servant.

MRS. FAINALL. He is an humble servant to *Foible* my mother's woman; and may win her to your interest.

MIRABELL. Care is taken for that – She is won and worn by this time. They were married this morning.

MRS. FAINALL. Who?

MIRABELL. *Waitwell* and *Foible*. I wou'd not tempt my servant to betray me by trusting him too far. If your mother, in hopes to ruin me, shou'd consent to marry my pretended uncle, he might like *Mosca* in the *Fox*, stand upon terms; so I made him sure before-hand.[47]

MRS. FAINALL. So, if my poor mother is caught in a contract, you will discover the imposture betimes; and release her by producing a certificate of her gallants former marriage.

MIRABELL. Yes, upon condition she consent to my marriage with her niece, and surrender the moiety of her fortune in her possession.

MRS. FAINALL. She talk'd last night of endeavouring at a match between *Millamant* and your uncle.

MIRABELL. That was by *Foible*'s direction, and my instructions that she might seem to carry it more privately.

MRS. FAINALL. Well, I have an opinion of your success; for I believe my Lady will do any thing to get a husband; and when she has this, which you have provided for her, I suppose she will submit to any thing to get rid of him.

MIRABELL. Yes, I think the good Lady wou'd marry any thing that resembl'd a man, tho' 'twere no more than what a butler cou'd pinch out of a napkin.

MRS. FAINALL. Female frailty! We must all come to it, if we live to be old and feel the craving of a false appetite when the true is decay'd.

MIRABELL. An old woman's appetite is deprav'd like that of a girl – 'Tis the green sickness of a second childhood; and like the faint offer of a latter spring, serves but to usher in the fall; and withers in an affected bloom.

MRS. FAINALL. Here's your mistress.

[*Enter* Mrs. Millamant, Witwoud, *and* Mincing.

MIRABELL. Here she comes I'faith full sail, with her fan spread and her streamers out, and a shoal of fools for tenders[48] – Ha, no, I cry her mercy.

MRS. FAINALL. I see but one poor empty sculler; and he tows her woman after him.

MIRABELL. You seem to be unattended, madam – You us'd to have the *beau-mond* throng after you; and a flock of gay fine perrukes[49] hovering round you.

WITWOUD. Like moths about a candle – I had like to have lost my comparison for want of breath.

MILLAMANT. O I have deny'd my self airs to day. I have walk'd as fast through the crowd. –

WITWOUD. As a favourite in disgrace; and with as few followers.

MILLAMANT. Dear Mr. *Witwoud*, truce with your similitudes. For I am as sick of 'em –

WITWOUD. As a physician of a good Air – I cannot help it madam, tho' 'tis against my self.

MILLAMANT. Yet again! *Mincing*, stand between me and his wit.

WITWOUD. Do Mrs. *Mincing*, like a skreen before a great fire. I confess I do blaze to day, I am too bright.[50]

MRS. FAINALL. But dear *Millamant*, why were you so long?

MILLAMANT. Long! Lord, have I not made violent haste? I have ask'd every living thing I met for you; I have enquir'd after you, as after a new fashion.

WITWOUD. Madam, truce with your similitudes – No, you met her husband and did not ask him for her.

MIRABELL. By your leave *Witwoud*, that were like enquiring after an old fashion, to ask a husband for his wife.

WITWOUD. Hum, a hit, a hit, a palpable hit,[51] I confess it.

MRS. FAINALL. You were dress'd before I came abroad.

MILLAMANT. Ay, that's true – O but then I had – *Mincing* what had I? Why was I so long?

MINCING. O Mem, your La'ship staid to peruse a pecquet[52] of letters.

MILLAMANT. O ay, letters – I had letters – I am persecuted with letters – I hate letters – No body knows how to write letters; and yet one has 'em, one does not know why – They serve one to pin up one's hair.

WITWOUD. Is that the way? Pray madam, do you pin up your hair with all your letters? I find I must keep copies.

MILLAMANT. Only with those in verse, Mr. *Witwoud*. I never pin up my hair with prose.[53] I fancy one's hair wou'd not curl if it were pinn'd up with prose. I think I try'd once *Mincing*.

MINCING. O Mem, I shall never forget it.

MILLAMANT. Ay, poor *Mincing* tift[54] and tift all the morning.

MINCING. 'Till I had the cremp in my fingers I'll vow mem. And all to no purpose. But when your la'ship pins it up with poetry, it sits so pleasant the next day as any thing, and is so pure and so crips.

WITWOUD. Indeed, so crips?

MINCING. You're such a critick, Mr. *Witwoud*.

MILLAMANT. *Mirabell*, Did not you take exceptions last night? O ay, and went away – Now I think on't I'm angry – No, now I think on't I'm pleas'd – For I believe I gave you some pain.

MIRABELL. Does that please you?

MILLAMANT. Infinitely; I love to give pain.

MIRABELL. You wou'd affect a cruelty which is not in your nature; your true vanity is in the power of pleasing.

MILLAMANT. O I ask your pardon for that – One's cruelty is one's power, and when one parts with one's cruelty, one parts with one's power; and when one has parted with that, I fancy one's old and ugly.

MIRABELL. Ay, ay, suffer your cruelty to ruin the object of your power, to destroy your lover – And then how vain how lost a thing you'll be! Nay, 'tis true: You are no longer handsome when you've lost your lover; your beauty dies upon the instant: For beauty is the lovers gift;

'tis he bestows your charms – Your glass is all a cheat. The ugly and the old, whom the looking-glass mortifies, yet after commendation can be flatter'd by it, and discover beauties in it: for that reflects our praises, rather than your face.

MILLAMANT. O the vanity of these men! *Fainall*, dee hear him? If they did not commend us, we were not handsome! Now you must know they could not commend one, if one was not handsome. Beauty the lover's gift – Lord, what is a lover, that it can give? Why one makes lovers as fast as one pleases, and they live as long as one pleases, and they die as soon as one pleases: And then if one pleases, one makes more.

WITWOUD. Very pretty. Why you make no more of making of lovers, madam, than of making so many card-matches.

MILLAMANT. One no more owes one's beauty to a lover, than one's wit to an eccho: They can but reflect what we look and say; vain empty things if we are silent or unseen, and want a being.

MIRABELL. Yet to those two vain empty things, you owe two of the greatest pleasures of your life.

MILLAMANT. How so?

MIRABELL. To your lover you owe the pleasure of hearing your selves prais'd; and to an eccho the pleasure of hearing your selves talk.

WITWOUD. But I know a lady that loves talking so incessantly, she won't give an eccho fair play; she has that everlasting rotation of tongue, that an eccho must wait till she dies, before it can catch her last words.

MILLAMANT. O fiction; *Fainall*, let us leave these men.

MIRABELL. [*Aside to* Mrs. Fainall] Draw off Witwoud.[55]

MRS. FAINALL. Immediately; I have a word or two for Mr. *Witwoud*.

[*Exit* Witwoud *and* Mrs. Fainall.

MIRABELL. I wou'd beg a little private audience too – You had the tyranny to deny me last night; tho' you knew I came to impart a secret to you, that concern'd my love.

MILLAMANT. You saw I was engag'd.

MIRABELL. Unkind. You had the leisure to entertain a herd of fools; things who visit you from their excessive idleness; bestowing on your easiness that time, which is the incumbrance of their lives. How can you find delight in such society? It is impossible they should admire you, they are not capable: or if they were, it shou'd be to you as a mortification; for sure to please a fool is some degree of folly.

MILLAMANT. I please my self – Besides sometimes to converse with fools, is for my health.

MIRABELL. Your health! Is there a worse disease than the conversation of fools?

MILLAMANT. Yes, the vapours; fools are physick for it, next to *assa-fœtida*.[56]

MIRABELL. You are not in a course[57] of fools?

MILLAMANT. *Mirabell*, if you persist in this offensive freedom – You'll displease me – I think I must resolve after all, not to have you – We shan't agree.

MIRABELL. Not in our physick it may be.

MILLAMANT. And yet our distemper in all likelihood will be the same; for we shall be sick of one another. I shan't endure to be reprimanded, nor instructed; 'tis so dull to act always by advice, and so tedious to be told of one's faults – I can't bear it. Well, I won't have you *Mirabell* – I'm resolv'd – I think – You may go – Ha, ha, ha. What wou'd you give, that you cou'd help loving me?

MIRABELL. I would give something that you did not know, I cou'd not help it.

MILLAMANT. Come, don't look grave then. Well, what do you say to me?

MIRABELL. I say that a man may as soon make a friend by his wit, or a fortune by his honesty, as win a woman with plain dealing and sincerity.

MILLAMANT. Sententious *Mirabell*! Prithee don't look with that violent and inflexible wise face, like *Solomon* at the dividing of the child in an old tapestry-hanging.

MIRABELL. You are merry, madam, but I wou'd perswade you for one moment to be serious.

MILLAMANT. What, with that face? No, if you keep your countenance, 'tis impossible I shou'd hold mine. Well, after all, there is something very moving in a love-sick face. Ha, ha, ha – Well I won't laugh, don't be peevish – Heigho! Now I'll be melancholly, as melancholly as a watch-light. Well *Mirabell*, if ever you will win me woo me now – Nay, if you are so tedious, fare you well; – I see they are walking away.

MIRABELL. Can you not find in the variety of your disposition one moment –

MILLAMANT. To hear you tell me that *Foible*'s married, and your plot like to speed – No.

MIRABELL. But how you came to know it –

MILLAMANT. Unless by the help of the Devil you can't imagine; unless she shou'd tell me her self. Which of the two it may have been, I will leave you to consider; and when you have done thinking of that; think of me. [*Exit*.

MIRABELL. I have something more – Gone – Think of you! To think of a whirlwind, tho' 'twere in a whirlwind, were a case of more steady contemplation; a very tranquility of mind and mansion. A fellow that lives in a windmill, has not a more whimsical dwelling than the heart of a man that is lodg'd in a woman. There is no point of the compass to which they cannot turn, and by which they are not turn'd; and by one as well as another; for motion not method is their occupation. To know this, and yet continue to be in love, is to be made wise from the dictates of reason, and yet persevere to play the fool by the force of instinct – O here come my pair of turtles – What, billing so sweetly! Is not *Valentine*'s day over with you yet? [*Enter* Waitwell *and* Foible] Sirrah, *Waitwell*, why sure you think you were married for your own recreation, and not for my conveniency.

WAITWELL. Your pardon, Sir. With submission, we have indeed been solacing in lawful delights; but still with an eye to business, Sir. I have instructed her as well as I cou'd. If she can take your directions as readily as my instructions, Sir, your affairs are in a prosperous way.

MIRABELL. Give you joy, Mrs. *Foible*.

FOIBLE. O la' Sir, I'm so asham'd – I'm afraid my Lady has been in a thousand inquietudes for me. But I protest, Sir, I made as much haste as I could.

WAITWELL. That she did indeed, Sir. It was my fault that she did not make more.

MIRABELL. That I believe.

FOIBLE. But I told my Lady as you instructed me, sir, that I had a prospect of seeing Sir *Rowland* your uncle; and that I wou'd put her Ladyship's picture in my pocket to shew him; which I'll be sure to say has made him so enamour'd of her beauty, that he burns with impatience to lie at her Ladyship's feet and worship the original.

MIRABELL. Excellent *Foible*! Matrimony has made you eloquent in love.

WAITWELL. I think she has profited, sir. I think so.

FOIBLE. You have seen madam *Millamant*, Sir?

MIRABELL. Yes.

FOIBLE. I told her sir, because I did not know that you might find an opportunity; she had so much company last night.

MIRABELL. Your diligence will merit more – In the mean time – [*Gives money*.

FOIBLE. O dear Sir, your humble servant.

WAITWELL. Spouse.

MIRABELL. Stand off Sir, not a penny – Go on and prosper, *Foible* – The lease shall be made good and the farm stock'd, if we succeed.

FOIBLE. I don't question your generosity, sir: and you need not doubt of success. If you have no more commands sir, I'll be gone; I'm sure my Lady is at her toilet, and can't dress till I come – O dear, I'm sure that [*looking out*] was Mrs. *Marwood* that went by in a mask; if she has seen me with you I'm sure she'll tell my Lady. I'll make haste home and prevent her. Your servant Sir. B'w'y *Waitwell*. [*Exit* Foible.

WAITWELL. Sir *Rowland* if you please. The jade's so pert upon her preferment she forgets her self.

MIRABELL. Come Sir, will you endeavour to forget your self – And transform into Sir *Rowland*.

WAITWELL. Why sir; it will be impossible I shou'd remember my self – Married, knighted and attended all in one day! 'Tis enough to make any man forget himself. The difficulty will be how to recover my acquaintance and familiarity with my former self; and fall from my transformation to a reformation into *Waitwell*. Nay, I shan't be quite the same *Waitwell* neither – For now I remember me, I am married, and can't be my own man again.

Ay there's the grief; that's the sad change of life;
To lose my title, and yet keep my wife.

[*Exeunt*.

ACT III. SCENE I. A room in Lady Wishfort's house.

[Lady Wishfort *at her toilet,* Peg *waiting*.]

LADY WISHFORT. Merciful, no news of *Foible* yet?

PEG. No, Madam.

LADY WISHFORT. I have no more patience – If I have not fretted my self till I am pale again, there's no veracity in me. Fetch me the red – The red, do you hear, sweet-heart? An errant ash colour, as I'm a person. Look you how this wench stirs! Why dost thou not fetch me a little red? Did'st thou not hear me, Mopus?

PEG. The red *ratifia*[58] does your Ladyship mean, or the cherry brandy?

LADY WISHFORT. *Ratifia*, fool. No fool. Not the *ratifia* fool – Grant me patience! I mean the *Spanish* paper idiot, complexion darling.[59] Paint, paint, paint, dost thou understand that, changeling, dangling thy hands like bobbins before thee. Why dost thou not stir, puppet? Thou wooden thing upon wires.

PEG. Lord, madam, your Ladyship is so impatient – I cannot come at the paint, madam; Mrs. *Foible* has lock'd it up, and carry'd the key with her.

LADY WISHFORT. A pox take you both – Fetch me the cherry-brandy then – [*Exit* Peg.

I'm as pale and as faint, I look like Mrs. Qualmsick the curate's wife, that's always breeding – Wench, come, come, wench, what art thou doing, sipping? Tasting? Save thee, dost thou not know the bottle?

[*Enter* Peg *with a Bottle and China cup.*

PEG. Madam, I was looking for a cup.

LADY WISHFORT. A cup, save thee, and what a cup hast thou brought! Dost thou take me for a *fairy*, to drink out of an *acorn*? Why didst thou not bring thy thimble? Hast thou ne'er a brass-thimble clinking in thy pocket with a bit of nutmeg? I warrant thee. Come, fill, fill. – So – again. See who that is – [*One knocks*]

Set down the bottle first. Here, here, under the table – What wou'dst thou go with the bottle in thy hand like a tapster. As I'm a person, this wench has liv'd in an inn upon the road, before she came to me, like *Maritornes* the *Asturian* in *Don Quixote*.[60] No *Foible* yet?

PEG. No madam, Mrs. *Marwood*.

LADY WISHFORT. O *Marwood*, let her come in. Come in good *Marwood*.

[*Enter* Mrs. Marwood.

MRS. MARWOOD. I'm surpriz'd to find your Ladyship in *dishabilie*[61] at this time of day.

LADY WISHFORT. Foible's a lost thing; has been abroad since morning, and never heard of since.

MRS. MARWOOD. I saw her but now, as I came mask'd through the park, in conference with *Mirabell*.

LADY WISHFORT. With *Mirabell*! You call my blood into my face, with mentioning that traytor. She durst not have the confidence. I sent her to negotiate an affair, in which if I'm detected I'm undone. If that wheadling villain has wrought upon *Foible* to detect me, I'm ruin'd. Oh my dear friend, I'm a wretch of wretches if I'm detected.

MRS. MARWOOD. O madam, you cannot suspect Mrs. *Foible*'s integrity.

LADY WISHFORT. O, he carries poyson in his tongue that wou'd corrupt integrity it self. If she has given him an opportunity, she has as good as put her integrity into his hands. Ah dear *Marwood*, what's integrity to an opportunity? – Hark! I hear her – Go you thing and send her in. [*Exit* Peg] Dear friend retire into my closet, that I may examine her with more freedom – You'll pardon me dear friend, I can make bold with you – There are books over the chimney – *Quarles* and *Pryn*, and the *Short View of the Stage*, with *Bunyan*'s Works to entertain you.[62] [*Exit* Marwood, *Enter* Foible] O *Foible*, where hast thou been? What hast thou been doing?

FOIBLE. Madam, I have seen the party.

LADY WISHFORT. But what hast thou done?

FOIBLE. Nay, 'tis your ladyship has done, and are to do; I have only promis'd. But a man so enamour'd – So transported! Well, here it is, all that is left; all that is not kiss'd away – Well, if worshipping of pictures be a sin – Poor Sir *Rowland*, I say.

LADY WISHFORT. The miniature has been counted like – But hast thou not betray'd me, *Foible*? Hast thou not detected me to that faithless *Mirabell*? – What had'st thou to do with him in the park? Answer me, has he got nothing out of thee?

FOIBLE. – [*Aside*] *So, the Devil has been before hand with me, what shall I say?* – Alas, madam, cou'd I help it, if I met that confident thing? Was I in fault? If you had heard how he us'd me, and all upon your Ladyship's account, I'm sure you wou'd not suspect my fidelity. Nay, if that had been the worst I cou'd have born: but he had a fling at your Ladyship too; and then I could not hold; but I'faith I gave him his own.

LADY WISHFORT. Me? What did the filthy fellow say?

FOIBLE. O madam; 'tis a shame to say what he said – With his taunts and his fleers, tossing up his nose. Humh (says he) what you are a hatching some plot (says he) you are so early abroad, or catering[63] (says he) ferreting for some disbanded officer I warrant – Half pay is but thin subsistance (says he) – Well, what pension does your Lady propose? Let me see (says he) what she must come down pretty deep now, she's superannuated (says he) and –

LADY WISHFORT. Ods my life, I'll have him, I'll have him murder'd. I'll have him poyson'd. Where does he eat? I'll marry a drawer to have him poyson'd in his wine. I'll send for *Robin* from *Lockets*[64] – Immediately.

FOIBLE. Poyson him? Poysoning's too good for him. Starve him madam, starve him, marry Sir *Rowland* and get him disinherited. O you would bless your self, to hear what he said.

LADY WISHFORT. A villain, superanuated!

FOIBLE. Humh (says he) I hear you are laying designs against me too (says he), and Mrs. *Millamant* is to marry my uncle; (he does not suspect a word of your Ladyship;) but (says he) I'll fit you for that, I warrant you (says he) I'll hamper you for that (says he) you and your old frippery[65] too (says he) I'll handle you –

LADY WISHFORT. Audacious villain! handle me, wou'd he durst – Frippery? Old frippery! Was there ever such a foul-mouth'd fellow? I'll be married to morrow; I'll be contracted to night.

FOIBLE. The sooner the better, madam.

LADY WISHFORT. Will Sir *Rowland* be here, say'st thou? When *Foible*?

FOIBLE. Incontinently, Madam. No new sheriff's wife expects the return of her husband after knighthood, with that impatience in which Sir *Rowland* burns for the dear hour of kissing your Ladyship's hands after dinner.

LADY WISHFORT. Frippery? Superannuated frippery! I'll frippery the villain; I'll reduce him to frippery and rags. A tatterdemallion[66] – I hope to see him hung with tatters, like a long lane pent-house, or a gibbet-thief. A slander mouth'd railer: I warrant the spendthrift prodigal's in debt as much as the million lottery, or the whole court upon a birth day. I'll spoil his credit with his taylor. Yes, he shall have my niece with her fortune, he shall.

FOIBLE. He! I hope to see him lodge in *Ludgate*[67] first, and angle into *Blackfriars*[68] for brass farthings, with an old mitten.

LADY WISHFORT. Ay dear *Foible*; thank thee for that dear *Foible*. He has put me out of all patience. I shall never recompose my features, to receive Sir *Rowland* with any economy of face. This wretch has fretted me that I am absolutely decay'd. Look *Foible*.

FOIBLE. Your Ladyship has frown'd a little too rashly, indeed madam. There are some cracks discernable in the white varnish.

LADY WISHFORT. Let me see the glass – Cracks, say'st thou? Why I am arrantly flea'd – I look like an old peel'd wall. Thou must repair me *Foible*, before Sir *Rowland* comes; or I shall never keep up to my picture.

FOIBLE. I warrant you, madam; a little art once made your picture like you; and now a little of the same art, must make you like your picture. Your picture must sit for you, madam.

LADY WISHFORT. But art thou sure Sir *Rowland* will not fail to come? Or will he not fail when he does come? Will he be importunate *Foible*, and push? For if he shou'd not be importunate – I shall never break decorums – I shall die with confusion, if I am forc'd to advance – Oh no, I can never advance – I shall swoon if he shou'd expect advances. No, I hope Sir *Rowland* is better bred, than to put a lady to the necessity of breaking her forms. I won't be too coy neither. – I won't give him despair – But a little disdain is not amiss; a little scorn is alluring.

FOIBLE. A little scorn becomes your Ladyship.

LADY WISHFORT. Yes, but tenderness becomes me best – A sort of a dyingness – You see that picture has a sort of a – Ha *Foible*? A swimminess in the eyes – Yes, I'll look so – My niece affects it; but she wants features. Is Sir *Rowland* handsome? Let my toilet be remov'd – I'll dress above. I'll receive Sir *Rowland* here. Is he handsome? Don't answer me. I won't know: I'll be surpriz'd. I'll be taken by surprize.

FOIBLE. By storm, madam. Sir *Rowland*'s a brisk man.

LADY WISHFORT. Is he! O then he'll importune, if he's a brisk man. I shall save decorums if Sir *Rowland* importunes. I have a mortal terror at the apprehension of offending against decorums. Nothing but importunity can surmount decorums. O I'm glad he's a brisk man. Let my things be remov'd, good *Foible*. [*Exit*.

[*Enter* Mrs. Fainall.

MRS. FAINALL. O *Foible*, I have been in a fright, least I shou'd come too late. That Devil *Marwood* saw you in the park with *Mirabell*, and I'm afraid will discover it to my Lady.

FOIBLE. Discover what, madam?

MRS. FAINALL. Nay, nay, put not on that strange face. I am privy to the whole design, and know that *Waitwell*, to whom thou wert this morning married, is to personate *Mirabell*'s uncle, and as such winning my Lady, to involve her in those difficulties, from which *Mirabell* only must release her, by his making his conditions to have my cousin and her fortune left to her own disposal.

FOIBLE. O dear madam, I beg your pardon. It was not my confidence in your Ladyship that was deficient; but I thought the former good correspondence between your Ladyship and Mr. *Mirabell*, might have hinder'd his communicating this secret.

MRS. FAINALL. Dear *Foible* forget that.

FOIBLE. O dear madam, Mr. *Mirabell* is such a sweet winning gentleman – But your Ladyship is the pattern of generosity. – Sweet Lady, to be so good! Mr. *Mirabell* cannot chuse but be grateful. I find your Ladyship has his heart still. Now, madam, I can safely tell your Ladyship our success, Mrs. *Marwood* had told my Lady; but I warrant I manag'd my self. I turn'd it all for the better. I told my Lady that Mr. *Mirabell* rail'd at her. I laid horrid things to his charge, I'll vow; and my Lady is so incens'd, that she'll be contracted to Sir *Rowland* to night, she says; – I warrant I work'd her up, that he may have her for asking for, as they say of a *Welch* maiden-head.

MRS. FAINALL. O rare *Foible*!

FOIBLE. Madam, I beg your Ladyship to acquaint Mr. *Mirabell* of his success. I wou'd be seen as little as possible to speak to him, – besides, I believe Madam *Marwood* watches me. – She has a month's mind;[69] but I know Mr. *Mirabell* can't abide her.

[*Enter* Footman

John – remove my Lady's toilet. Madam your servant. My Lady is so impatient, I fear she'll come for me, if I stay.

MRS. FAINALL. I'll go with you up the back stairs, lest I shou'd meet her. [*Exeunt.*

[*Enter* Mrs. Marwood.

MRS. MARWOOD. Indeed Mrs. Engine, is it thus with you? Are you become a go-between of this importance? Yes, I shall watch you. Why this wench is the *pass-par-tout*, a very master-key to every body's strong box. My friend *Fainall*, have you carried it so swimmingly? I thought there was something in it; but it seems it's over with you. Your loathing is not from a want of appetite then, but from a surfeit. Else you could never be so cool to fall from a principal to be an assistant; to procure for him! A pattern of generosity, that I confess. Well, Mr. *Fainall*, you have met with your match. – O Man, man! Woman, woman! The Devil's an ass: If I were a painter, I wou'd draw him like an idiot, a driveler, with a bib and bells. Man shou'd have his head and horns, and woman the rest of him. Poor simple fiend! Madam *Marwood* has a month's mind, but he can't abide her – 'twere better for him you had not been his confessor in that affair; without you cou'd have kept his counsel closer. I shall not prove another pattern of generosity; and stalk for him, till he takes his stand to aim at a fortune; he has not oblig'd me to that, with those excesses of himself; and now I'll have none of him. Here comes the good Lady, panting ripe; with a heart full of hope, and a head full of care, like any chymist upon the day of projection.[70]

[*Enter* Lady Wishfort.

LADY WISHFORT. O dear *Marwood* what shall I say, for this rude forgetfulness – But my dear friend is all goodness.

MRS. MARWOOD. No apologies, dear madam. I have been very well entertained.

LADY WISHFORT. As I'm a person I am in a very chaos to think I shou'd so forget my self – But I have such an olio[71] of affairs really I know not what to do – [*Calls*] – *Foible* – I expect my nephew Sir *Willfull* every moment too – Why *Foible* – He means to travel for improvement.

MRS. MARWOOD. Methinks Sir *Willfull* should rather think of marrying than travelling at his years. I hear he is turn'd of forty.

LADY WISHFORT. O he's in less danger of being spoil'd by his travels – I am against my nephews marrying too young. It will be time enough when he comes back, and has acquir'd discretion to choose for himself.

MRS. MARWOOD. Methinks Mrs. *Millamant* and he wou'd make a very fit match. He may travel afterwards. 'Tis a thing very usual with young gentlemen.

LADY WISHFORT. I promise you I have thought on't – And since 'tis your judgment, I'll think on't again. I assure you I will; I value your judgment extreamly. On my word I'll propose it.

[*Enter* Foible

Come, come *Foible* – I had forgot my nephew will be here before dinner – I must make haste.

FOIBLE. Mr. *Witwoud* and Mr. *Petulant* are come to dine with your Ladyship.

LADY WISHFORT. O dear, I can't appear till I'm dress'd. Dear *Marwood* shall I be free with you again, and beg you to entertain 'em. I'll make all imaginable haste. Dear friend excuse me. [*Exit* Lady Wishfort *and* Foible.

[*Enter* Mrs. Millamant *and* Mincing.

MILLAMANT. Sure never any thing was so unbred as that odious man – *Marwood*, your Servant.

MRS. MARWOOD. You have a colour, what's the matter?

MILLAMANT. That horrid fellow *Petulant*, has provok'd me into a Flame – I have broke my fan – *Mincing*, lend me yours; – Is not all the powder out of my hair?

MRS. MARWOOD. No. What has he done?

MILLAMANT. Nay, he has done nothing; he has only talk'd – Nay, he has said nothing neither; but he has contradicted every thing that has been said. For my part, I thought *Witwoud* and he wou'd have quarrell'd.

MINCING. I vow mem, I thought once they wou'd have fit.

MILLAMANT. Well, 'tis a lamentable thing I'll swear, that one has not the liberty of choosing one's acquaintance, as one does one's cloaths.

MRS. MARWOOD. If we had the liberty, we shou'd be as weary of one set of acquaintance, tho' never so good, as we are of one suit, tho' never so fine. A fool and a *doily* stuff[72] wou'd now and then find days of grace, and be worn for variety.

MILLAMANT. I could consent to wear 'em, if they wou'd wear alike; but fools never wear out – they are such *drap-auberry*[73] things without one cou'd give 'em to one's chambermaid after a day or two.

MRS. MARWOOD. 'Twere better so indeed. Or what think you of the play-house? A fine gay glossy fool, shou'd be given there, like a new masking habit, after the masquerade is over, and we have done with the disguise. For a fool's visit is always a disguise; and never admitted by a woman of wit, but to blind her affair with a lover of sense. If you wou'd but appear bare fac'd now, and own *Mirabell*; you might as easily put off *Petulant* and *Witwoud*, as your hood and scarf. And indeed 'tis time, for the Town has found it: the secret is grown too big for the pretence. 'Tis like Mrs. *Primly*'s great belly; she may lace it down before, but it burnishes on her hips. Indeed, *Millamant*, you can no more conceal it than my Lady *Strammel* can her face, that goodly face, which in defiance of her rhenish-wine tea, will not be comprehended in a mask.

MILLAMANT. I'll take my death, *Marwood*, you are more censorious than a decay'd beauty, or a discarded toast; *Mincing*, tell the men they may come up. My aunt is not dressing; their folly is less provoking than your mallice, the Town has found it. [*Exit* Mincing] What has it found? That *Mirabell* loves me is no more a secret, than it is a secret that you discover'd it to my aunt, or than the reason why you discover'd it is a secret.

MRS. MARWOOD. You are nettl'd.

MILLAMANT. You're mistaken. Ridiculous!

MRS. MARWOOD. Indeed my dear, you'll tear another fan if you don't mitigate those violent airs.

MILLAMANT. O silly! Ha, ha, ha. I cou'd laugh immoderately. Poor *Mirabell*! His constancy to me has quite destroy'd his complaisance for all the World beside. I swear, I never enjoin'd it him, to be so coy – If I had the vanity to think he wou'd obey me, I wou'd command him to shew more gallantry – 'Tis hardly well bred to be so particular on one hand, and so insensible on the other. But I despair to prevail, and so let him follow his own way. Ha, ha, ha. Pardon me, dear creature, I must laugh, Ha, ha, ha; tho' I grant you 'tis a little barbarous, Ha, ha, ha.

MRS. MARWOOD. What pity 'tis, so much fine raillery, and deliver'd with so significant gesture, shou'd be so unhappily directed to miscarry.

MILLAMANT. Ha? Dear creature I ask your pardon – I swear I did not mind you.

MRS. MARWOOD. Mr. *Mirabell* and you both, may think it a thing impossible, when I shall tell him, by telling you –

MILLAMANT. O dear, what? For it is the same thing, if I hear it – Ha, ha, ha.

MRS. MARWOOD. That I detest him, hate him, madam.

MILLAMANT. O madam, why so do I – And yet the creature loves me, Ha, ha, ha. How can one forbear laughing to think of it – I am a Sybil[74] if I am not amaz'd to think what he can see in me. I'll take my death, I think you are handsomer – And within a year or two as young. – If you cou'd but stay for me, I shou'd overtake you – But that cannot be – Well, that thought makes me melancholly – Now I'll be sad.

MRS. MARWOOD. Your merry note may be chang'd sooner than you think.

MILLAMANT. Dee[75] say so? Then I'm resolv'd I'll have a song to keep up my spirits.

[*Enter* Mincing.

MINCING. The gentlemen stay but to comb,[76] madam; and will wait on you.

MILLAMANT. Desire Mrs. – that is in the next Room to sing the song, I wou'd have learnt yesterday. You shall hear it madam – Not that there's any great matter in it – But 'tis agreeable to my humour.

SONG, Set by Mr. John Eccles, *and Sung by* Mrs. Hodgson.

I.

Love's but the frailty of the mind,
When 'tis not with ambition join'd;
A sickly flame, which if not fed expires;
And feeding, wastes in self-consuming fires.

II.

'Tis not to wound a wanton boy
Or am'rous youth, that gives the joy;
But 'tis the glory to have pierc'd a swain,
For whom inferiour beauties sigh'd in vain.

III.

Then I alone the conquest prize
When I insult a rival's eyes:
If there's delight in love, 'tis when I see
That heart which others bleed for, bleed for me.

[*Enter* Petulant *and* Witwoud.

MILLAMANT. Is your animosity compos'd, gentlemen?

WITWOUD. Raillery, raillery, madam, we have no animosity – We hit off a little wit now and then, but no animosity – The falling out of wits is like the falling out of lovers – We agree in the main, like treble and base. Ha, Petulant!

PETULANT. Ay in the main – But when I have a humour to contradict.

WITWOUD. Ay, when he has a humour to contradict, then I contradict too. What, I know my cue. Then we contradict one another like two battle-dores. For contradictions beget one another like *Jews*.

PETULANT. If he says black's black – If I have a humour to say 'tis blue – Let that pass – All's one for that. If I have a humour to prove it, it must be granted.

WITWOUD. Not positively must – But it may – It may.

PETULANT. Yes, it positively must, upon proof positive.

WITWOUD. Ay, upon proof positive it must; but upon proof presumptive it only may. That's a logical distinction now, madam.

MRS. MARWOOD. I perceive your debates are of importance and very learnedly handl'd.

PETULANT. Importance is one thing, and learning's another; but a debate's a debate, that I assert.

WITWOUD. Petulant's an enemy to learning; he relies altogether on his parts.

PETULANT. No, I'm no enemy to learning; it hurts not me.

MRS. MARWOOD. That's a sign indeed it's no enemy to you.

PETULANT. No, no, it's no enemy to any body, but them that have it.

MILLAMANT. Well, an illiterate man's my aversion. I wonder at the impudence of any illiterate man, to offer to make love.

WITWOUD. That I confess I wonder at too.

MILLAMANT. Ah! to marry an ignorant, that can hardly read or write.

PETULANT. Why shou'd a man be ever the further from being married tho' he can't read, any more than he is from being hang'd. The ordinary's paid for setting the *Psalm*, and the parish-priest for reading the ceremony. And for the rest which is to follow in both cases, a man may do it without book – So all's one for that.

MILLAMANT. D'ye hear the creature? Lord, here's company, I'll be gone. [*Exeunt* Millamant *and* Mincing.

WITWOUD. In the name of *Bartholomew* and his fair, what have we here?

MRS. MARWOOD. 'Tis your brother, I fancy. Don't you know him?

WITWOUD. Not I – Yes, I think it is he – I've almost forgot him; I have not seen him since the revolution.

[*Enter* Sir Willfull Witwoud *in a country riding habit, and servant to* Lady Wishfort.

SERVANT. Sir, my Lady's dressing. Here's company, if you please to walk in the mean time.

SIR WILLFULL. Dressing! What it's but morning here I warrant with you in *London*; we shou'd count it towards afternoon in our parts, down in *Shropshire* – Why then belike my aunt han't din'd yet – Ha, friend?

SERVANT. Your aunt, Sir?

SIR WILLFULL. My aunt sir, yes my aunt sir, and your Lady sir; your Lady is my aunt, sir – Why, what do'st thou not know me, friend? Why then send somebody here that does. How long hast thou liv'd with thy Lady, fellow, ha!

SERVANT. A week, sir; longer than any body in the house, except my Lady's woman.

SIR WILLFULL. Why then belike thou dost not know thy Lady, if thou see'st her, ha friend?

SERVANT. Why truly sir, I cannot safely swear to her face in a morning, before she is dress'd. 'Tis like I may give a shrew'd guess at her by this time.

SIR WILLFULL. Well prithee try what thou can'st do; if thou can'st not guess, enquire her out, do'st hear fellow? And tell her, her nephew Sir *Willfull Witwoud* is in the house.

SERVANT. I shall, sir.

SIR WILLFULL. Hold ye, hear me friend; a word with you in your ear, prithee who are these gallants?

SERVANT. Really sir, I can't tell; here come so many here, 'tis hard to know 'em all. [*Exit* Servant

SIR WILLFULL. Oons this fellow knows less than a starling; I don't think a' knows his own name.

MRS. MARWOOD. Mr. *Witwoud*, your brother is not behind hand in forgetfulness – I fancy he has forgot you too.

WITWOUD. I hope so – The Devil take him that remembers first, I say.

SIR WILLFULL. Save you gentlemen and lady.

MRS. MARWOOD. For shame Mr. *Witwoud*; why won't you speak to him? – And you, sir.

WITWOUD. Petulant speak.

PETULANT. And you, sir.

SIR WILLFULL. No offence, I hope. [*Salutes* Marwood.

MRS. MARWOOD. No sure, sir.

WITWOUD. This is a vile dog, I see that already. No offence! Ha, ha, ha, to him; to him *Petulant*, smoke him.

PETULANT. It seems as if you had come a journey, sir; hem, hem. [*Surveying him round.*

SIR WILLFULL. Very likely, Sir, that it may seem so.

PETULANT. No offence, I hope, sir.

WITWOUD. Smoke the boots, the boots; *Petulant*, the boots; ha, ha, ha.

SIR WILLFULL. May be not, sir; thereafter as 'tis meant, sir.

PETULANT. Sir, I presume upon the information of your boots.

SIR WILLFULL. Why, 'tis like you may, Sir: If you are not satisfy'd with the information of my boots, sir, if you will step to the stable, you may enquire further of my horse, sir.

PETULANT. Your Horse, Sir! Your horse is an ass, sir!

SIR WILLFULL. Do you speak by way of offence,sir?

MRS. MARWOOD.The gentleman's merry, that's all, sir – S'life, we shall have a quarrel betwixt an horse and an ass, before they find one another out. You must not take any thing amiss from your friends, sir. You are among your friends here, tho' it may be you don't know it – If I am not mistaken, you are Sir *Willfull Witwoud.*

SIR WILLFULL. Right lady; I am Sir *Willfull Witwoud*, so I write my self; no offence to any body, I hope; and nephew to the Lady *Wishfort*, of this mansion.

MRS. MARWOOD. Don't you know this gentleman, sir?

SIR WILLFULL. Hum! What sure 'tis not – Yea by'r lady, but 'tis – 'Sheart I know not whether 'tis or no – Yea but 'tis, by the Rekin.[77] Brother *Anthony*! What *Tony, ifaith!* What do'st thou not know me? By'r lady nor I thee, thou art so becravated, and beperriwig'd – 'Sheart why do'st not speak? Art thou o'er-joy'd?

WITWOUD. Odso brother, is it you? Your servant brother.

SIR WILLFULL. Your servant! Why yours, sir. Your servant again – 'Sheart, and your friend and servant to that – And a – [*Puff*] and a flap dragon for your service, Sir: And a hare's foot, and a hare's scut for your service, sir; an you be so cold and so courtly!

WITWOUD. No offence, I hope, brother.

SIR WILLFULL. 'Sheart, sir, but there is, and much offence. – A pox, is this your inns o' court breeding, not to know your friends and your relations, your elders, and your betters?

WITWOUD. Why Brother *Willfull* of *Salop*, you may be as short as a *Shrewsbury* cake, if you please. But I tell you, 'tis not modish to know relations in town. You think you're in the country, where great lubberly brothers slabber and kiss one another when they meet, like a call of serjeants – 'tis not the fashion here; 'tis not indeed, dear brother.

SIR WILLFULL. The fashion's a fool; and you're a fop, dear Brother. 'Sheart, I've suspected this – By'r Lady I conjectur'd you were a fop, since you began to change the stile of your letters, and write in a scrap of paper gilt round the edges, no broader than a *Subpœna.* I might expect this, when you left off honour'd brother; and hoping you are in good health, and so forth – To begin with a rat me, Knight, I'm so sick of a last nights debauch – O'ds heart, and then tell a familiar tale of a cock and a bull, and a whore and a bottle, and so conclude – You cou'd write news before you were out of your time, when you liv'd with honest *Pumple Nose* the attorney of *Furnival*'s Inn – You cou'd intreat to be remember'd then to your friends round the *Rekin*. We cou'd have gazettes then, and *Dawks*'s letter,[78] and the weekly bill, 'till of late days.

PETULANT. S'life, *Witwoud*, were you ever an attorney's clerk? Of the family of the *Furnivals*. Ha, ha, ha!

WITWOUD. Ay, ay, but that was for a while. Not long, not long; pshaw, I was not in my own power then. An orphan, and this fellow was my guardian; ay, ay, I was glad to consent to that man to come to *London*. He had the disposal of me then. If I had not agreed to that, I might have been bound prentice to a felt maker in *Shrewsbury*; this fellow wou'd have bound me to a maker of felts.

SIR WILLFULL. 'Sheart, and better than to be bound to a maker of fops; where, I suppose, you have serv'd your time; and now you may set up for your self.

MRS. MARWOOD.You intend to travel, sir, as I'm inform'd.

SIR WILLFULL. Belike I may madam. I may chance to sail upon the salt seas, if my mind hold.

PETULANT. And the wind serve.

SIR WILLFULL. Serve or not serve, I shant ask licence of you, sir; nor the weather-cock your companion. I direct my discourse to the lady, sir: 'tis like my aunt may have told you, madam – Yes, I have settl'd my concerns, I may say now, and am minded to see foreign parts. If and how that the peace holds, whereby that is, taxes abate.

MRS. MARWOOD. I thought you had design'd for *France* at all adventures.

SIR WILLFULL. I can't tell that; 'tis like I may, and 'tis like I may not. I am somewhat dainty in making a resolution, – because when I make it I keep it. I don't stand shill I, shall I, then; if I say't, I'll do't: But I have thoughts to tarry a small matter in town, to learn somewhat of your *Lingo* first, before I cross the seas. I'd gladly have a spice of your *French* as they say, whereby to hold discourse in foreign countries.

MRS. MARWOOD. Here is an academy in town for that use.

SIR WILLFULL. There is? 'Tis like there may.

MRS. MARWOOD. No doubt you will return very much improv'd.

WITWOUD. Yes, refin'd, like a *Dutch* skipper from a whale-fishing.

[*Enter* Lady Wishfort *and* Fainall.

LADY WISHFORT. Nephew, you are welcome.

SIR WILLFULL. Aunt, your servant.

FAINALL. Sir *Willfull*, your most faithful servant.

SIR WILLFULL. Cousin *Fainall*, give me your hand.

LADY WISHFORT. Cousin *Witwoud*, your servant; Mr. *Petulant*, your servant. – Nephew, you are welcome again. Will you drink any thing after your journey, nephew, before you eat? Dinner's almost ready.

SIR WILLFULL. I'm very well I thank you Aunt – However, I thank you for your courteous offer. 'Sheart, I was afraid you wou'd have been in the fashion too, and have remember'd to have forgot your relations. Here's your cousin *Tony*, belike, I may'nt call him brother for fear of offence.

LADY WISHFORT. O he's a rallier, nephew – My cousin's a wit. And your great wits always rally their best friends to chuse. When you have been abroad, nephew, you'll understand raillery better. [Fainall *and* Mrs. Marwood *talk a-part.*

SIR WILLFULL. Why then let him hold his tongue in the mean time; and rail when that day comes.

[*Enter* Mincing.

MINCING. Mem, I come to acquaint your La'ship that dinner is impatient.

SIR WILLFULL. Impatient? Why then belike it won't stay, 'till I pull off my boots. Sweet-heart, can you help me to a pair of slippers? – My man's with his horses, I warrant.

LADY WISHFORT. Fie, fie, nephew, you wou'd not pull off your boots here – Go down into the hall – Dinner shall stay for you – My nephew's a little unbred, you'll pardon him, madam – Gentlemen will you walk. *Marwood* –

MRS. MARWOOD. I'll follow you, madam – Before Sir *Willfull* is ready.

[*Manent* Mrs. Marwood *and* Fainall.

FAINALL. Why then *Foible*'s a bawd, an errant, rank, match-making bawd. And I it seems am a husband, a rank-husband; and my wife a very errant, rank-wife, – all in the way of the World. 'Sdeath to be an anticipated cuckold, a cuckold in embrio? Sure I was born with budding antlers like a young satyre, or a citizens child. 'Sdeath to be out-witted, to be out-jilted – out-matrimony'd, – If I had kept my speed like a stag, 'twere somewhat, – but to crawl after, with my horns like a snail, and out-strip'd by my wife – 'tis scurvy wedlock.

MRS. MARWOOD. Then shake it off, you have often wish'd for an opportunity to part; – and now you have it. But first prevent their plot, – the half of *Millamant*'s fortune is too considerable to be parted with, to a foe, to *Mirabell*.

FAINALL. Dam him, that had been mine – had you not made that fond discovery – that had been forfeited, had they been married. My wife had added lustre to my horns, by that encrease of fortune, – I cou'd have worn 'em tipt with gold, tho' my forehead had been furnish'd like a deputy-lieutenant's hall.

MRS. MARWOOD. They may prove a cap of maintenance to you still, if you can away with your wife. And she's no worse than when you had her – I dare swear she had given up her game, before she was marry'd.

FAINALL. Hum! That may be – She might throw up her cards; but I'll be hang'd if she did not put pam in her pocket.[79]

MRS. MARWOOD. You married her to keep you; and if you can contrive to have her keep you better than you expected; why should you not keep her longer than you intended?

FAINALL. The means, the means.

MRS. MARWOOD. Discover to my Lady your wife's conduct; threaten to part with her – My Lady loves her, and will come to any composition to save her reputation, take the opportunity of breaking it, just upon the discovery of this imposture. My Lady will be enraged beyond bounds, and sacrifice niece, and fortune, and all at that conjuncture. And let me alone to keep her warm; if she should flag in her part, I will not fail to prompt her.

FAINALL. Faith this has an appearance.

MRS. MARWOOD. I'm sorry I hinted to my Lady to endeavour a match between *Millamant* and Sir *Willfull*, that may be an obstacle.

FAINALL. O, for that matter leave me to manage him; I'll disable him for that. He will drink like a *Dane*: after dinner, I'll set his hand in.

MRS. MARWOOD. Well, how do you stand affected towards your Lady?

FAINALL. Why faith I'm thinking of it. – Let me see – I am married already; so that's over, – my wife has plaid the jade with me – Well, that's over too – I never lov'd her, or if I had, why that wou'd have been over too by this time – Jealous of her I cannot be, for I am certain; so there's an end of jealousie. Weary of her, I am, and shall be – No, there's no end of that; No, no, that were too much to hope. Thus far concerning my repose. Now for my reputation, – As to my own, I married not for it; so that's out of the question, – And as to my part in my wife's – Why she had parted with hers before; so bringing none to me, she can take none from me, 'tis against all rule of play, that I should lose to one, who has not wherewithal to stake.

MRS. MARWOOD. Besides you forget, marriage is honourable.

FAINALL. Hum! Faith and that's well thought on; marriage is honourable as you say; and if so, wherefore should cuckoldom be a discredit, being deriv'd from so honourable a root?

MRS. MARWOOD. Nay I know not; if the root be honourable, why not the branches?

FAINALL. So, so, why this point's clear, – Well how do we proceed?

MRS. MARWOOD. I will contrive a letter which shall be deliver'd to my Lady at the time when that rascal who is to act Sir *Rowland* is with her. It shall come as from an unknown hand – for the less I appear to know of the truth – the better I can play the incendiary. Besides I would not have *Foible* provok'd if I cou'd help it, – because you know she knows some passages – Nay I expect all will come out – But let the mine be sprung first, and then I care not if I'm discover'd.

FAINALL. If the worst come to the worst, – I'll turn my wife to grass – I have already a deed of settlement of the best part of her estate; which I wheadl'd out of her, and that you shall partake at least.[80]

MRS. MARWOOD. I hope you are convinc'd that I hate *Mirabell*. Now you'll be no more jealous.

FAINALL. Jealous no, – by this kiss – let husbands be jealous; But let the lover still believe. Or if he doubt, let it be only to endear his pleasure, and prepare the joy that follows, when he proves his mistress true; but let husband's doubts convert to endless jealousie; or if they have belief, let it corrupt to superstition, and blind credulity. I am single; and will herd no more with 'em. True, I wear the badge; but I'll disown the order. And since I take my leave of 'em, I care not if I leave 'em a common motto, to their common crest.

All husbands must, or pain, or shame, endure;
The wise too jealous are, fools too secure.

[*Exeunt.*

ACT IV. SCENE I.

[*Scene Continues. Enter* Lady Wishfort *and* Foible.

LADY WISHFORT. Is Sir *Rowland* coming say'st thou, *Foible*? And are things in order?

FOIBLE. Yes, *Madam*. I have put wax-lights in the sconces; and plac'd the foot-men in a row in the hall, in their best liveries, with the coach-man and postilion to fill up the equipage.

LADY WISHFORT. Have you pullvill'd[81] the coach-man and postilion, that they may not stink of the stable, when Sir *Rowland* comes by?

FOIBLE. Yes, *Madam*.

LADY WISHFORT. And are the dancers and the musick ready, that he may be entertain'd in all points with correspondence to his passion?

FOIBLE. All is ready, *Madam*.

LADY WISHFORT. And – well – and how do I look, *Foible*?

FOIBLE. Most killing well, *Madam*.

LADY WISHFORT. Well, and how shall I receive him? In what figure shall I give his heart the first impression? There is a great deal in the first impression. Shall I sit? – No I won't sit – I'll walk – aye I'll walk from the door upon his entrance; and then turn full upon him – No, that will be too sudden. I'll lie – aye, I'll lie down – I'll receive him in my little dressing room, there's a couch – Yes, yes, I'll give the first impression on a couch – I won't lie neither but loll and lean upon one elbow; with one foot a little dangling off, jogging in a thoughtful way – Yes – and then as soon as he appears, start, ay, start and be surpriz'd, and rise: to meet him in a pretty disorder – Yes – O, nothing is more alluring than a levee from a couch in some confusion. – It shews the foot to advantage, and furnishes with blushes, and re-composing airs beyond comparison. Hark! There's a coach.

FOIBLE. 'Tis he, *Madam*.

LADY WISHFORT. O dear, has my *nephew* made his addresses to *Millamant*? I order'd him.

FOIBLE. Sir *Willfull* is set into drinking, *Madam*, in the parlour.

LADY WISHFORT. Ods my life, I'll send him to her. Call her down, *Foible*; bring her hither. I'll send him as I go – When they are together, then come to me *Foible*, that I may not be too long alone with Sir *Rowland*. [*Exit*].

[*Enter* Mrs. Millamant, *and* Mrs. Fainall.

FOIBLE. *Madam*, I stay'd here, to tell your Ladyship that Mr. *Mirabell* has waited this half hour for an opportunity to talk with you. Tho' my Lady's orders were to leave you and Sir *Willfull* together. Shall I tell Mr. *Mirabell* that you are at leisure?

MILLAMANT. No – What would the dear man have? I am thoughtfull and would amuse my self, – bid him come another time. [*Repeating and walking about*.

There never yet was woman made,
Nor shall but to be curs'd.

That's hard!

MRS. FAINALL. You are very fond of Sir *John Suckling*[82] to day, *Millamant*, and the *Poets*.

MILLAMANT. He? Ay, and filthy verses – So I am.

FOIBLE. Sir *Willfull* is coming, *Madam*. Shall I send Mr. *Mirabell* away?

MILLAMANT. Ay, if you please *Foible*, send him away, – Or send him hither, – just as you will dear *Foible*. – I think I'll see him – Shall I? Ay, let the wretch come. [*Repeating*] *Thyrsis a youth of the inspir'd train* – Dear *Fainall*, Entertain Sir *Willfull* – Thou hast philosophy to undergo a fool, thou art married and hast patience – I would confer with my own Thoughts.

MRS. FAINALL. I am oblig'd to you, that you would make me your proxy in this affair; but I have business of my own. [*Enter* Sir Willfull] O Sir *Willfull*; you are come at the critical instant. There's your Mistress up to the ears in love and contemplation, pursue your point, now or never.

SIR WILLFULL. Yes; my Aunt would have it so, – I would gladly have been encouraged with a bottle or two, because [*This while* Millamant *walks about repeating to herself*] I'm somewhat wary at first, before I am acquainted; – But I hope after a time, I shall break my mind – that is upon further acquaintance, – So for the present cousin, I'll take my leave – If so be you'll be so kind to make my excuse, I'll return to my company –

MRS. FAINALL. O fie Sir *Willfull*! What, you must not be daunted.

SIR WILLFULL. Daunted, no, that's not it, it is not so much for that – for if so be that I set on't, I'll do't. But only for the present, 'tis sufficient till further acquaintance, that's all – your servant.

MRS. FAINALL. Nay, I'll swear you shall never lose so favourable an opportunity, if I can help it. I'll leave you together and lock the door. [*Exit.*

SIR WILLFULL. Nay, nay cozen, – I have forgot my gloves, – What d'ye do? 'Shart a'has lock'd the door indeed I think – Nay cousin *Fainall*, open the door – Pshaw, what a vixen trick is this? – Nay, now a'has seen me too – Cousin, I made bold to pass thro' as it were, – I think this door's enchanted – .

MILLAMANT. [Repeating.

I prithee spare me gentle boy,
Press me no more for that slight toy.[83]

SIR WILLFULL. Anan? Cozen, your servant.

MILLAMANT. – *That foolish trifle of a heart* – Sir *Willfull!*

SIR WILLFULL. Yes, – your servant. No offence I hope, Cozen.

MILLAMANT. [Repeating.

I swear it will not do its part,
Tho' thou do'st thine, employ'st thy power and art.

Natural, easie *Suckling*!

SIR WILLFULL. Anan? Suckling? No such suckling neither, cozen, nor stripling: I thank Heav'n, I'm no minor.

MILLAMANT. Ah rustick! Ruder than Gothick.

SIR WILLFULL. Well, well, I shall understand your lingo one of these days, cozen, in the mean while, I must answer in plain English.

MILLAMANT. Have you any business with me, Sir *Willfull*?

SIR WILLFULL. Not at present cozen, – Yes, I made bold to see, to come and know if that how you were dispos'd to fetch a walk this evening, if so be that I might not be troublesome, I wou'd have fought a walk with you.

MILLAMANT. A walk? What then?

SIR WILLFULL. Nay nothing – Only for the walks sake, that's all –

MILLAMANT. I nauseate walking; 'tis a country diversion, I loath the country and every thing that relates to it.

SIR WILLFULL. Indeed! Hah! Look ye, look ye, you do? Nay, 'tis like you may – Here are choice of pastimes here in town, as plays and the like that must be confess'd indeed. –

MILLAMANT. *Ah l'etourdie!*[84] I hate the Town too.

SIR WILLFULL. Dear heart, that's much – Hah! that you shou'd hate 'em both! Hah! 'tis like you may; there are some can't relish the Town, and others can't away with the country, – 'tis like you may be one of those, cozen.

MILLAMANT. Ha, ha, ha. Yes, 'tis like I may. – You have nothing further to say to me?

SIR WILLFULL. Not at present, cozen. – 'tis like when I have an opportunity to be more private, – I may break my mind in some measure, – I conjecture you partly guess – However that's as time shall try, – But spare to speak and spare to speed, as they say.

MILLAMANT. If it is of no great importance, Sir *Willfull*, you will oblige me to leave me: I have just now a little business. –

SIR WILLFULL. Enough, enough, cozen, yes, yes, all a case – When you're dispos'd, when you're dispos'd. Now's as well as another time; and another time as well as now. All's one for that, – yes, yes, if your concerns call you, there's no hast; it will keep cold as they say, – Cousin, your servant, I think this door's lock'd.

MILLAMANT. You may go this way Sir.

SIR WILLFULL. Your servant, then with your leave I'll return to my company. [*Exit.*

MILLAMANT. Ay, ay, ha, ha, ha.
Like Phoebus sung the no less am'rous boy.

[*Enter* Mirabell.

MIRABELL. – *Like Daphne she as lovely and as Coy.*[85] Do you lock your self up from me, to make my search more curious? Or is this pretty artifice contriv'd, to signifie that here the chase must end, and my pursuit be crown'd, for you can fly no further. –

MILLAMANT. Vanity! No – I'll fly and be follow'd to the last moment, tho' I am upon the very verge of matrimony, I expect you shou'd solicit me as much as if I were wavering at the grate of a monastery, with one foot over the threshold. I'll be solicited to the very last, nay and afterwards.

MIRABELL. What, after the last?

MILLAMANT. O, I should think I was poor and had nothing to bestow, If I were reduc'd to an inglorious ease; and free'd from the agreeable fatigues of solicitation.

MIRABELL. But do not you know, that when favours are conferr'd upon instant and tedious sollicitation, that they diminish in their value, and that both the giver loses the grace, and the receiver lessens his pleasure?

MILLAMANT. It may be in things of common application; but never sure in love. O, I hate a lover, that can dare to think, he draws a moments air, independent of the bounty of his mistress. There is not so impudent a thing in Nature, as the sawcy look of an assured man, confident of success. The pedantick arrogance of a very husband, has not so pragmatical an air. Ah! I'll never marry, unless I am first made sure of my will and pleasure.

MIRABELL. Wou'd you have 'em both before marriage? Or will you be contented with the first now, and stay for the other till after grace?

MILLAMANT. Ah don't be impertinent – my dear liberty, shall I leave thee? My faithful solitude, my darling contemplation must I bid you then adieu? ay-h adieu. – my morning thoughts, agreeable wakings, indolent slumbers, all ye *douceurs*, ye *Someils du Matin adieu*[86] – I can't do't, 'tis more than impossible – positively *Mirabell*, I'll lie a bed in a morning as long as I please.

MIRABELL. Then I'll get up in a morning as early as I please.

MILLAMANT. Ah! Idle creature, get up when you will – and d'ye hear, I won't be call'd names after I'm married; positively I won't be call'd names.

MIRABELL. Names!

MILLAMANT. Ay as wife, spouse, my dear, joy, jewel, love, sweet heart and the rest of that nauseous cant, in which men and their wives are so fulsomely familiar, – I shall never bear that, – Good *Mirabell* don't let us be familiar or fond, nor kiss before folks, like my Lady *Fadler* and Sr. *Francis*: Nor go to *Hyde-Park* together the first *Sunday* in a new chariot, to provoke eyes and whispers; And then never to be seen there together again; as if we were proud of one another the first week, and asham'd of one another for ever after. Let us never visit together, nor go to a play together, but let us be very strange and well bred: let us be as strange as if we had been married a great while; and as well bred as if we were not marry'd at all.

MIRABELL. Have you any more conditions to offer? Hither-to your demands are pretty reasonable.

MILLAMANT. Trifles, – As liberty to pay and receive visits to and from whom I please, to write and receive letters, without interrogatories or wry faces on your part. To wear what I please; and choose conversation with regard only to my own taste; to have no obligation upon me to converse with wits that I don't like, because they are your acquaintance, or to be intimate with fools, because they may be your relations. Come to dinner when I please, dine in my dressing room when I'm out of humour without giving a reason. To have my closet inviolate; to be sole empress of my tea-table, which you must never presume to approach without first asking leave. And lastly, where ever I am, you shall always knock at the door before you come in. These articles subscrib'd, if I continue to endure you a little longer, I may by degrees dwindle into a wife.

MIRABELL. Your bill of fare is something advanc'd in this latter account. Well, have I liberty to offer conditions – that when you are dwindl'd into a wife, I may not be beyond measure enlarg'd into a husband?

MILLAMANT. You have free leave; propose your utmost, speak and spare not.

MIRABELL. I thank you. *Inprimis* then,[87] I covenant that your acquaintance be general; that you admit no sworn confident, or intimate of your own sex, no she friend to skreen her affairs under your countenance and tempt you to make tryal of a mutual secresie. No decoy-duck to wheadle you a *fop* – *scrambling* to the play in a mask – then bring you home in a pretended fright, when you think you shall be found out. – And rail at me for missing the play, and disappointing the frolick which you had, to pick me up and prove my constancy.

MILLAMANT. Detestable *Inprimis*! I go to the play in a mask!

MIRABELL. *Item*, I article, that you continue to like your own face, as long as I shall. And while it passes current with me, that you endeavour not to new-coin it. To which end, together with all vizards for the day, I prohibit all masks for the night, made of oil'd-skins and I know not what – hog's-bones, hare's-gall, pig-water, and the marrow of a roasted cat. In short, I forbid all commerce with the gentlewoman in *what-de-call-it-court*. *Item*, I shut my doors against all bauds with baskets, and penny-worths of *muslin, china, furs, atlases*, &c. – *Item* when you shall be breeding. –

MILLAMANT. Ah! Name it not.

MIRABELL. Which may be presum'd, with a blessing on our endeavours –

MILLAMANT. Odious endeavours!

MIRABELL. I denounce against all strait-laceing, squeezing for a shape, 'till you mold my boy's head like a sugar-loaf; and instead of a man-child, make me the father to a crooked-billet.[88] Lastly to the dominion of the *tea-table*, I submit. – But with *proviso*, that you exceed not in your province; but restrain your self to native and simple *tea-table* drinks, as *tea, chocolate* and *coffee*. As likewise to genuine and, authoriz'd *tea-table* talk, – such as mending of fashions spoiling reputations, railing at absent friends, and so forth – but that on no account you encroach upon the men's prerogative, and presume to drink healths, or toast fellows; for prevention of which; I banish all *Foreign Forces*, all auxiliaries to the *tea-table*, as *orange-brandy*, all *anniseed*, *cinamon*, *citron* and *barbados-waters*, together with *ratifia* and the most noble spirit of *clary*, – but for *cowslip-wine*, *poppy-water* and all *dormitives*, those I allow, – these *proviso* admitted, in other things I may prove a tractable and complying husband.[89]

MILLAMANT. O horrid *provisos*! filthy strong waters! I toast fellows, odious men! I hate your odious provisos.

MIRABELL. Then we're agreed. Shall I kiss your hand upon the contract? And here comes one to be a witness to the sealing of the deed.

[*Enter* Mrs. Fainall.

MILLAMANT. *Fainall*, what shall I do? shall I have him? I think I must have him.

MRS. FAINALL. Ay, ay, take him, take him, what shou'd you do?

MILLAMANT. Well then – I'll take my death I'm in a horrid fright – *Fainall*, I shall never say it – well – I think – I'll endure you.

MRS. FAINALL. Fy, fy, have him, have him, and tell him so in plain terms. For I am sure you have a mind to him.

MILLAMANT. Are you? I think I have – and the horrid man looks as if he thought so too – Well, you ridiculous thing you, I'll have you, – I won't be kiss'd, nor I won't be thank'd – here kiss my hand tho' – so hold your tongue now, and don't say a word.

MRS. FAINALL. Mirabell, there's a necessity for your obedience; – You have neither time to talk nor stay. My mother is coming; and in my conscience if she should see you, would fall into fits, and maybe not recover time enough to return to Sir *Rowland*, who as *Foible* tells me is in a fair way to succeed. Therefore spare your ecstasies for another occasion, and slip down the back-stairs, where *Foible* waits to consult you.

MILLAMANT. Ay, go, go. In the mean time I suppose you have said something to please me.

MIRABELL. I am all obedience. [*Exit* Mirabell.

MRS. FAINALL. Yonder Sir *Willfull*'s drunk; and so noisy that my mother has been forced to leave Sir *Rowland* to appease him; but he answers her only with singing and drinking – what they have done by this time I know not. But *Petulant* and he were upon quarrelling as I came by.

MILLAMANT. Well, if *Mirabell* shou'd not make a good husband, I am a lost thing; – for I find I love him violently.

MRS. FAINALL. So it seems, when you mind not what's said to you, – if you doubt him, you had best take up with Sir *Willfull*.

MILLAMANT. How can you name that superannuated lubber, soh!

[*Enter* Witwoud *from drinking*]

MRS. FAINALL. So, is the fray made up, that you have left 'em?

WITWOUD. Left 'em? I cou'd stay no longer – I have laugh'd like ten Christnings – I am tipsy with laughing – If I had staid any longer I shou'd have burst, – I must have been let out and piec'd in the sides like an unsiz'd camlet,[90] – Yes, yes the fray is compos'd; my Lady came in like a *noli prosequi* and stop't their proceedings.[91]

MILLAMANT. What was the dispute?

WITWOUD. That's the jest, there was no dispute, they cou'd neither of 'em speak for rage; And so fell a sputt'ring at one another like two roasting apples. [*Enter* Petulant *drunk*] Now *Petulant*, all's over, all's well; Gad my head begins to whim it about – Why dost thou not speak? Thou art both as drunk and as mute as a fish.

PETULANT. Look you Mrs. *Millamant*, – If you can love me dear nymph – say it – and that's the conclusion – pass on, or pass off, – that's all.

WITWOUD. Thou hast utter'd *volumes, folios*, in less than *decimo sexto*, my Dear *Lacedemonian*.[92] Sirrah, *Petulant*, thou art an epitomizer of words.

PETULANT. *Witwoud* – You are an annihilator of sense.

WITWOUD. Thou art a retailer of phrases; and dost deal in remnants of remnants, like a maker of pincushions – thou art in truth (metaphorically speaking) a speaker of shorthand.

PETULANT. Thou art (without a figure) just one half of an ass; and *Baldwin*[93] yonder, thy half brother is the rest – A *gemini* of asses split, would make just four of you.

WITWOUD. Thou dodst bite my dear mustard-seed; kiss me for that.

PETULANT. Stand off – I'll kiss no more males, – I have kiss'd your *twin* yonder in a humour of reconciliation, till he [*hiccup*] rises upon my stomack like a radish.

MILLAMANT. Eh! filthy creature – what was the quarrel?

PETULANT. There was no quarrel – there might have been a quarrel.

WITWOUD. If there had been words enow between 'em to have express'd provocation; they had gone together by the ears like a pair of castanets.

PETULANT. You were the quarrel.

MILLAMANT. Me!

PETULANT. If I have a humour to quarrel, I can make less matters conclude premises, – if you are not handsom, what then? If I have a humour to prove it. – if I shall have my reward, say so; if not, fight for your face the next time your self – I'll go sleep.

WITWOUD. Do, rap thy self up like a *wood-louse* and dream revenge – and hear me, if thou canst learn to write by to morrow morning, pen me a challenge – I'll carry it for thee.

PETULANT. Carry your mistresses *Monkey* a *Spider*,[94] – go flea dogs, and read romances – I'll go to bed to my maid. [*Exit.*

MRS. FAINALL. He's horridly drunk – how came you all in this pickle? –

WITWOUD. A plot, a plot, to get rid of the knight, – your husband's advice; but he sneak'd off.

[*Enter* Lady Wishfort *and* Sir Willfull *drunk.*

LADY WISHFORT. Out upon't, out upon't, at years of discretion, and comport your self at this rantipole[95] rate.

SIR WILLFULL. No offence Aunt.

LADY WISHFORT. Offence? As I'm a person, I'm asham'd of you, – Fogh! how you stink of wine! D'ye think my niece will ever endure such a *borachio*![96] You're an absolute *borachio*.

SIR WILLFULL. Borachio!

LADY WISHFORT. At a time when you shou'd commence an amour and put your best foot foremost –

SIR WILLFULL. 'Sheart, an you grutch me your liquor, make a bill. Give me more drink and take my purse.

[*Sings.*

Prithee fill me the Glass
Till it laugh in my Face,
With Ale that is Potent and Mellow;
He that Whines for a Lass,
Is an Ignorant Ass,
For a Bumper has not its Fellow.

But if you wou'd have me marry my cousin, – say the word, and I'll do't – *Willfull* will do't, that's the word – *Willfull* will do't, that's my crest – my motto I have forgot.

LADY WISHFORT. My nephew's a little overtaken cousin – but 'tis with drinking your health – O' my word you are oblig'd to him.

SIR WILLFULL. In Vino Veritas Aunt, – If I drunk your health to day cousin – I am a *borachio*. But if you have a mind to be marry'd, say the word, and send for the piper, *Willfull* will do't. If not, dust it away, and let's have tother round – *Tony*, Ods heart where's *Tony* – *Tony's* an honest fellow, but he spits after a bumper, and that's a fault.

[*Sings.*

We'll drink and we'll never ha'done boys[97]
Put the glass then around with the sun, boys
Let Apollo's example invite us;
For he's drunk every night,
And that makes him so bright,
That he's able next morning to light us.

The sun's a good pimple, an honest soaker, he has a cellar at your *Antipodes*.[98] If I travel Aunt, I touch at your *Antipodes* – your *Antipodes* are a good rascally sort of topsy turvy fellows – If I had a bumper I'd stand upon my head and drink a health to 'em – a match or no match, cousin, with the hard name, – Aunt, *Willfull* will do't, if she has her maidenhead let her look to't, – if she has not, let her keep her own counsel in the mean time, and cry out at the nine months end.

MILLAMANT. Your pardon madam, I can stay no longer – Sir *Willfull* grows very powerful, Egh! how he smells! I shall be overcome if I stay. Come, cousin. [*Exeunt* Millamant *and* Mrs. Fainall.

LADY WISHFORT. Smells! He would poison a tallow-chandler and his family. Beastly creature, I know not what to do with him – Travel quoth a; Ay travel, travel, get thee gone, get thee but far enough, to the *Saracens* or the *Tartars*, or the *Turks* – for thou are not fit to live in a Christian commonwealth, thou beastly pagan.

SIR WILLFULL. Turks, no; no *Turks*, Aunt: Your *Turks* are infidels, and believe not in the grape. Your *Mahometan*, your *Mussulman* is a dry stinkard – No offence, Aunt. My map says that your *Turk* is not so honest a man as your Christian – I cannot find by the map that your *Mufti* is Orthodox – Whereby it is a plain case, that Orthodox is a hard word, Aunt, and [*hiccup*] Greek for claret.

[*Sings.*

To drink is a Christian diversion,
Unknown to the Turk and the Persian:
Let Mahometan fools
Live by heathenish rules,
And be damn'd over tea-cups and coffee.
But let British lads sing,
Crown a health to the king,
And a fig for your Sultan and Sophy.[99]

Ah *Tony*!

[*Enter* Foible, *and whispers* Lady Wishfort.

LADY WISHFORT. Sir *Rowland* impatient? Good lack! what shall I do with this beastly tumbril?[100] – Go lie down and sleep, you sot – Or as I'm a person, I'll have you bastinado'd[101] with broom-sticks. Call up the wenches. [*Exit* Foible.

SIR WILLFULL. Ahey! Wenches, where are the wenches?

LADY WISHFORT. Dear cousin *Witwou'd*, get him away, and you will bind me to you inviolably. I have an affair of moment that invades me with some precipitation – You will oblige me to all futurity.

WITWOUD. Come Knight – Pox on him. I don't know what to say to him – will you go to a cock-match?

SIR WILLFULL. With a wench, *Tony*? Is she a shake-bag sirrah? let me bite your cheek for that.

WITWOUD. Horrible! He has a breath like a *bagpipe* – ay, ay, come will you march my *Salopian*?[102]

SIR WILLFULL. Lead on little *Tony* – I'll follow thee my *Anthony*, My *Tantony*, sirrah thou sha't be my *Tantony*; and I'll be thy *pig*.[103]

–And a fig for your Sultan and Sophy.

[*Exit Singing with* Witwoud.

LADY WISHFORT. This will never do. It will never make a match. – At least before he has been abroad. [*Enter Waitwell, disguis'd as for* Sir Rowland] Dear Sir *Rowland*, I am confounded with confusion at the retrospection of my own rudeness, – I have more pardons to ask than the *Pope* distributes in the year of *Jubilee*. But I hope where there is likely to be so near an alliance, – We may unbend the severity of *Decorum* – and dispence with a little ceremony.

WAITWELL. My impatience *Madam*, is the effect of my transport; – and till I have the possession of your adoreable person, I am tantaliz'd on a rack; And do but hang *Madam*, on the tenter of expectation.

LADY WISHFORT. You have excess of gallantry Sir *Rowland*; and press things to a conclusion, with a most prevailing vehemence. – But a day or two for decency of marriage –

WAITWELL. For decency of funeral, *Madam*. The delay will break my heart – or if that should fail. I shall be poyson'd. My *nephew* will get an inkling of my designs and poison me, – and I wou'd willingly starve him before I die – I wou'd gladly go out of the world with that satisfaction. – That wou'd be some comfort to me, if I cou'd but live so long as to be reveng'd on that unnatural *viper*.

LADY WISHFORT. Is he so unnatural say you? Truely I wou'd contribute much both to the saving of your life; and the accomplishment of your revenge – Not that I respect my self; tho' he has been a perfidious wretch to me.

WAITWELL. Perfidious to you!

LADY WISHFORT. O Sir *Rowland*, the hours that he has dy'd away at my feet, the tears that he has shed, the oaths that he has sworn, the palpitations that he has felt, the trances, and the tremblings, the ardors and the ecstacies, the kneelings and the risings, the heart-heavings, and the hand-gripings, the pangs and the pathetick regards of his protesting eyes! Oh no memory can register.

WAITWELL. What, my rival! is the rebell my rival? a'dies.

LADY WISHFORT. No, don't kill him at once Sir *Rowland*, starve him gradually inch by inch.

WAITWELL. I'll do't. In three weeks he shall be bare-foot; in a month out at knees with begging an *alms*, – he shall starve upward and upward, till he has nothing living but his head, and then go out in a stink like a candle's end upon a save-all.

LADY WISHFORT. Well Sir *Rowland*, you have the way, – You are no novice in the labyrinth of love – you have the clue – But as I am a person, Sir *Rowland*, you must not attribute my yielding to any sinister appetite, or indigestion of widdow-hood; nor impute my complacency, to any lethargy of continence – I hope you do not think me prone to any iteration of nuptials. –

WAITWELL. Far be it from me –

LADY WISHFORT. If you do, I protest I must recede – or think that I have made a prostitution of decorums, but in the vehemence of compassion, and to save the life of a person of so much importance –

WAITWELL. I esteem it so –

LADY WISHFORT. Or else you wrong my condescension –

WAITWELL. I do not, I do not –

LADY WISHFORT. Indeed you do.

WAITWELL. I do not, fair shrine of vertue.

LADY WISHFORT. If you think the least scruple of carnality was an ingredient –

WAITWELL. Dear *Madam*, no. You are all *camphire* and *frankincense*,[104] all *chastity* and *odour*.

LADY WISHFORT. Or that –

[*Enter* Foible.

FOIBLE. *Madam*, the dancers are ready, and there's one with a letter, who must deliver it into your own hands.

LADY WISHFORT. Sir *Rowland*, will you give me leave? Think favourably, judge candidly and conclude you have found a person who wou'd suffer racks in honour's cause, dear Sir *Rowland*, and will wait on you incessantly. [*Exit*.

WAITWELL. Fie, fie! – What a slavery have I undergone; spouse, hast thou any *cordial* – I want *spirits*.

FOIBLE. What a washy rogue art thou, to pant thus for a quarter of an hours lying and swearing to a fine lady?

WAITWELL. O, she is the *antidote* to desire. Spouse, thou will't fare the worse for't – I shall have no appetite to iteration of nuptials – this eight and fourty hours – by this hand I'd rather be a *chairman* in the *dog-days* – than act Sir *Rowland*, till this time tomorrow.

[*Enter* Lady Wishfort *with a letter*.

LADY WISHFORT. Call in the *dancers*; – Sir *Rowland*, we'll sit if you please, and see the entertainment. [*Dance*] Now with your permission Sir *Rowland* I will peruse my letter – I wou'd open it in your presence, because I wou'd not make you uneasie. If it shou'd make you uneasie I wou'd burn it – speak if it do's – but you may see by the superscription it is like a woman's hand.

FOIBLE. [*To him*] By Heaven! Mrs. *Marwood*'s, I know it, – my heart akes – get it from her –

WAITWELL. A woman's hand? No *Madam*, that's no woman's hand, I see that already. That's some body whose throat must be cut.

LADY WISHFORT. Nay Sir *Rowland*, since you give me a proof of your passion by your jealousie, I promise you I'll make you a return, by a frank communication – you shall see it – we'll open it together – look you here.

[*Reads*.

– Madam, tho' unknown to you

Look you there, 'tis from no body that I know

– I have that honour for your character, that I think my self oblig'd to let you know you are abus'd. He who pretends to be Sir Rowland is a cheat and a rascal. –

Oh Heavens! What's this?

FOIBLE. Unfortunate, all's ruin'd.

WAITWELL. How, how, Let me see, let me see – [*Reading*] A rascal and disguis'd and subborn'd for that imposture, – O villany O villany! – by the contrivance of –

LADY WISHFORT. I shall faint, I shall die, I shall die, oh!

FOIBLE. [*To him*] Say 'tis your nephew's hand. – quickly, his plot, swear, swear it. –

WAITWELL. Here's a villain! Madam, don't you perceive it, don't you see it?

LADY WISHFORT. Too well, too well. I have seen too much.

WAITWELL. I told you at first I knew the hand – A woman's hand? The rascal writes a sort of a large hand; your *Roman* hand – I saw there was a throat to be cut presently. If he were my son as he is my nephew I'd pistoll him –

FOIBLE. O Treachery! But are you sure Sir *Rowland*, it is his writing?

WAITWELL. Sure? Am I here? Do I live? Do I love this pearl of *India*? I have twenty letters in my pocket from him, in the same character.

LADY WISHFORT. How!

FOIBLE. O what luck it is Sir *Rowland*, that you were present at this juncture! This was the business that brought Mr. *Mirabell* disguis'd to *Madam Millamant* this afternoon. I thought something was contriving, when he stole by me and would have hid his face.

LADY WISHFORT. How, how! – I heard the villain was in the house indeed, and now I remember, my *niece* went away abruptly, when Sir *Willfull* was to have made his addresses.

FOIBLE. Then, then *Madam*, Mr. *Mirabell* waited for her in her chamber, but I wou'd not tell your Lady-ship to discompose you when you were to receive Sir *Rowland*.

WAITWELL. Enough, his date is short.

FOIBLE. No, good Sir *Rowland*, don't incurr the law.

WAITWELL. Law? I care not for law. I can but die, and 'tis in a good cause – my Lady shall be satisfied of my truth and innocence, tho' it cost me my life.

LADY WISHFORT. No, dear Sir *Rowland*, don't fight, if you shou'd be kill'd I must never shew my face, or hang'd, – O consider my reputation Sir *Rowland* – No you shan't fight, – I'll go in and examine my *niece*; I'll make her confess. I conjure you Sir *Rowland* by all your love not to fight.

WAITWELL. I am charm'd *Madam*, I obey. But some proof you must let me give you; – I'll go for a black box, which contains the writings of my whole estate, and deliver that into your hands.

LADY WISHFORT. Ay dear Sir *Rowland*, that will be some comfort; bring the black-box.

WAITWELL. And may I presume to bring a contract to be sign'd this night? May I hope so far?

LADY WISHFORT. Bring what you will; but come alive, pray come alive. O this is a happy discovery.

WAITWELL. Dead or alive I'll come – and married we will be in spight of treachery; Ay and get an heir that shall defeat the last remaining glimpse of hope in my abandon'd *nephew*. Come my buxom widdow.

Ere long you shall substantial proof receive
That I'm an arrant knight–

FOIBLE. Or arrant knave. [*Exeunt.*

ACT V. SCENE I.

[*Scene Continues.* Lady Wishfort *and* Foible.]

LADY WISHFORT. Out of my house, out of my house, thou *viper*, thou *serpent*, that I have foster'd, thou bosom traitress, that I rais'd from nothing – begon, begon, begon, go, go, – that I took from washing of old gauze and weaving of dead hair,[105] with a bleak blew nose, over a chafeing-dish of starv'd embers and dining behind a traver's rag, in a shop no bigger than a bird-cage, – go, go, starve again, do, do.

FOIBLE. Dear *Madam*, I'll beg pardon on my knees.

LADY WISHFORT. Away, out, out, go set up for your self again – do, drive a trade, do, with your three penny worth of small ware, flaunting upon a packthread, under a brandy-sellers bulk, or against a dead wall by a ballad-monger. Go hang out an old *Frisoncer-gorget*, with a yard of yellow *colberteen* again;[106] do; an old gnaw'd *mask*, two rows of *pins* and a *child's fiddle*; a *glass necklace* with the beads broken, and a *quilted night-cap* with one ear. Go, go, drive a trade, – these were your *commodities* you treacherous trull, this was your *merchandize* you dealt in, when I took you into my house, plac'd you next my self and made you governante of my whole family. You have forgot this, have you? Now you have feather'd your nest.

FOIBLE. No, no, dear *Madam*. Do but hear me, have but a moment's patience – I'll confess all. Mr. *Mirabell* seduc'd me; I am not the first that he has wheadl'd with his dissembling tongue; Your Lady-ship's own wisdom has been deluded by him, then how shou'd I, a poor ignorant, defend my self? O *Madam*, If you knew but what he promis'd me; and how he assur'd me your Ladyship shou'd come to no damage – Or else the wealth of the *Indies* shou'd not have brib'd me to conspire against so good, so sweet, so kind a Lady as you have been to me.

LADY WISHFORT. No damage? What to betray me, to marry me to a cast-serving-man; to make me a receptacle, an hospital for a decay'd pimp? No damage? O thou frontless[107] impudence, more than a big-belly'd actress.

FOIBLE. Pray do but here me *Madam*, he cou'd not marry your Lady-ship, *Madam* – No indeed his marriage was to have been void in law; for he was married to me first, to secure your Lady-ship. He cou'd not have bedded your Lady-ship: for if he had consummated with your Lady-ship; he must have run the risque of the law, and been put upon his *clergy* – Yes indeed, I enquir'd of the law in that case before I wou'd meddle or make.

LADY WISHFORT. What, then I have been your property, have I? I have been convenient to you it seems, – while you were catering for *Mirabell*; I have been broaker for you? What, have you made a passive bawd of me? – this exceeds all precedent; I am brought to fine uses, to become a botcher of second hand marriages, between *Abigails* and *Andrews*![108] I'll couple you, yes, I'll baste you together, you and your *Philander*. I'll *Dukes-Place* you, as I'm a person. Your turtle is in custody already; You shall coo in the same cage, if there be constable or warrant in the parish. [*Exit.*

FOIBLE. O that ever I was born, O that I was ever married, – a bride, ay I shall be a *Bridewell*-bride.[109] Oh!

[*Enter* Mrs. Fainall.

MRS. FAINALL. Poor *Foible*, what's the matter?

FOIBLE. O *Madam*, my Lady's gone for a constable; I shall be had to a justice, and put to *Bridewell* to beat hemp, poor *Waitwell*'s gone to prison already.

MRS. FAINALL. Have a good heart *Foible*, *Mirabell*'s gone to give security for him, this is all *Marwood*'s and my husband's doing.

FOIBLE. Yes, yes; I know it *Madam*; she was in my Lady's closet, and over-heard all that you said to me before dinner. She sent the letter to my Lady, and that missing effect, Mr. *Fainall* laid this plot to arrest *Waitwell*, when he pretended to go for the papers; and in the mean time Mrs. *Marwood* declar'd all to my Lady.

MRS. FAINALL. Was there no mention made of me in the letter? – My mother does not suspect my being in the confederacy? I fancy *Marwood* has not told her, tho' she has told my husband.

FOIBLE. Yes *Madam*; but my Lady did not see that part; we stifl'd the letter before she read so far. Has that mischevious Devil told Mr. *Fainall* of your Ladyship then?

MRS. FAINALL. Ay, all's out, my affair with *Mirabell*, every thing discover'd. This is the last day of our living together, that's my comfort.

FOIBLE. Indeed *Madam*, and so 'tis a comfort if you knew all, – he has been even with your Ladyship; which I cou'd have told your long enough since, but I love to keep peace and quietness by my good will: I had rather bring friends together, than set 'em at distance. But Mrs. *Marwood* and he are nearer related than ever their parents thought for.

MRS. FAINALL. Say'st thou so *Foible*? Canst thou prove this?

FOIBLE. I can take my oath of it *Madam*, so can Mrs. *Mincing*; we have had many a fair word from *Madam Marwood*, to conceal something that pass'd in our chamber one evening when you were at *Hyde-Park*; – And we were thought to have gone a walking: But we went up unawares, – tho' we were sworn to secresie too; *Madam Marwood* took a book and swore us upon it: but it was but a book of verses and poems, – So as long as it was not a Bible-oath, we may break it with a safe conscience.

MRS. FAINALL. This discovery is the most opportune thing I cou'd wish. Now *Mincing*?

[*Enter* Mincing.

MINCING. My Lady wou'd speak with Mrs. *Foible*, *Mem*. Mr. *Mirabell* is with her, he has set your spouse at liberty Mrs. *Foible*; and wou'd have you hide your self in my Lady's closet, till my old Lady's anger is abated. O, my old Lady is in a perilous passion, at something Mr. *Fainall* has said, he swears, and my old Lady cries. There's a fearful hurricane I vow. He says *Mem*; how that he'll have my Lady's fortune made over to him, or he'll be divorced.

MRS. FAINALL. Does your Lady and *Mirabell* know that?

MINCING. Yes *Mem*, they have sent me to see if Sir *Willfull* be sober, and to bring him to them. My Lady is resolv'd to have him I think, rather than loose such a vast sum as six thousand pound. O, come Mrs. *Foible*, I hear my old Lady.

MRS. FAIN *Foible*, you must tell *Mincing*, that she must prepare to vouch when I call her.

FOIBLE. Yes, yes *Madam*.

MINCING. O yes *Mem*, I'll vouch any thing for your Lady-ship's service, be what it will.

[*Exeunt* Mincing *and* Foible, *Enter* Lady Wishfort *and* Marwood.

LADY WISHFORT. O my dear friend, how can I enumerate the benefits that I have receiv'd from your goodness? To you I owe the timely discovery of the false vows of *Mirabell*; To you the detection of the impostor Sir *Rowland*. And now you are become an intercessor with my Son-in-law, to save the honour of my house, and compound for the frailty's of my daughter. Well friend, you are enough to reconcile me to the bad World, or else I wou'd retire to desarts and solitudes; and feed harmless sheep by *groves* and *purling streams*. Dear *Marwood*, let us leave the World, and retire by our selves and be *shepherdesses*.

MRS. MARWOOD. Let us first dispatch the affair in hand, madam; we shall have leisure to think of retirement afterwards. Here is one who is concern'd in the treaty.

LADY WISHFORT. O daughter, daughter, is it possible thou shoud'st be my child, bone of my bone, and flesh of my flesh, and as I may say, another me, and yet transgress the most minute particle of severe vertue? Is it possible you should lean aside to iniquity who have been cast in the direct mold of vertue? I have not only been a mold but a pattern for you, and a model for you, after you were brought into the World.

MRS. FAINALL. I don't understand your Ladyship.

LADY WISHFORT. Not understand? Why have you not been taught? Have you not been sophisticated? Not understand? Here I am ruin'd to compound for your *caprices* and your *cuckoldomes*. I must pawn my plate, and my jewells and ruin my niece, and all little enough –

MRS. FAINALL. I am wrong'd and abus'd, and so are you. 'Tis a false accusation, as false as *Hell*, as false as your friend there, ay or your friend's friend, my false husband.

MRS. MARWOOD. My friend, Mrs. *Fainall*? Your husband my friend, what do you mean?

MRS. FAINALL. I know what I mean *Madam*, and so do you; and so shall the World at a time convenient.

MRS. MARWOOD. I am sorry to see you so passionate, madam. More temper wou'd look more like innocence. But I have done. I am sorry my zeal to serve your Ladyship and family, shou'd admit of misconstruction, or make me liable to affronts. You will pardon me, madam, If I meddle no more with an affair, in which I am not personally concern'd.

LADY WISHFORT. O dear Friend; I am so asham'd that you should meet with such returns; – you ought to ask pardon on your knees, ungratefull creature; she deserves more from you, than all your life can accomplish – O don't leave me destitute in this perplexity; – No, stick to me my good genius.

MRS. FAINALL. I tell you *Madam* you're abus'd – stick to you? ay, like a leach, to suck your best blood – she'll drop off when she's full. Madam you shan't pawn a bodkin, nor part with a brass counter in composition for me. I defie 'em all. Let 'em prove their aspersions; I know my own innocence, and dare stand by a tryall. [*Exit.*

LADY WISHFORT. Why, if she shou'd be innocent, if she shou'd be wrong'd after all, ha? I don't know what to think, – and I promise you, her education has been unexceptionable – I may say it; for I chiefly made it my own care to initiate her very infancy in the rudiments of vertue, and to impress upon her tender years, a young *odium* and *aversion* to the very sight of men, – ay friend, she wou'd ha' shriek'd, if she had but seen a man, till she was in her teens. As I'm a person 'tis true – she was never suffer'd to play with a male-child, tho' but in coats; nay her very babies were of the *feminine gender*; – O, she never look'd a man in the face but her own father, or the chaplain, and him we made a shift to put upon her for a woman, by the help of his long garments, and his sleek-face; till she was going in her fifteen.

MRS. MARWOOD. 'Twas much she shou'd be deceiv'd so long.

LADY WISHFORT. I warrant you, or she wou'd never have born to have been catechis'd by him; and have heard his long lectures, against singing and dancing, and such debaucheries; and going to filthy *plays*; and profane *musick-meetings*, where the lewd trebles squeek nothing but bawdy, and the bases roar *blasphemy*. O, she wou'd have swooned at the sight or name of an obscene play-book – and can I think after all this, that my daughter can be naught? What, a whore? And thought it excommunication to set her foot within the door of a play-house. O my dear friend, I can't believe it, no, no; as she says, let him prove it, let him prove it.

MRS. MARWOOD. Prove it *Madam*? What, and have your name prostituted in a publick court; yours and your daughter's reputation worry'd at the bar by a pack of bawling lawyers? To be ushered in with an *oyez*[110] of scandal; and have your case open'd by an old fumbling leacher in a quoif[111] like a man midwife to bring your daughter's infamy to light, to be a theme for legal punsters, and quiblers by the statute; and become a jest, against a rule of court, where there is no precedent for a jest in any record; not even in *Doomsday-Book*:[112] to discompose the gravity of the bench, and provoke naughty interrogatories, in more naughty *law Latin*; while the good judge tickl'd with the proceeding, simpers under a grey beard, and fidges off and on his cushion as if he had swallow'd *cantharides*, or sat upon *cow-itch*.[113]

LADY WISHFORT. O, 'tis very hard!

MRS. MARWOOD. And then to have my young *revellers* of the *Temple*, take notes like prentices at a *conventicle*; and after, talk it all over again in commons, or before drawers in an *eating-house*.[114]

LADY WISHFORT. Worse and worse.

MRS. MARWOOD. Nay this is nothing; if it wou'd end here, 'twere well. But it must after this be consign'd by the short-hand writers to the publick press; and from thence be transfer'd to the hands, nay into the throats and lungs of hawkers, with voices more licentious than the loud *flounder-man*'s or the *woman* that cries *grey-peas*; and this you must hear till you are stunn'd; nay you must hear nothing else for some days.

LADY WISHFORT. O, 'tis insupportable. No, no, dear friend make it up, make it up; ay, ay, I'll compound. I'll give up all, my self and my all, my *niece* and her all, – any thing, every thing for composition.

MRS. MARWOOD. Nay *Madam*, I advise nothing, I only lay before you as a friend the inconveniencies which perhaps you have overseen. Here comes Mr. *Fainall*. If he will be satisfi'd to huddle up all in silence, I shall be glad. You must think I would rather congratulate, then condole with you. [*Enter* Fainall.

LADY WISHFORT. Ay, ay, I do not doubt it, dear *Marwood*: No, no, I do not doubt it.

FAINALL. Well Madam; I have suffer'd my self to be overcome by the importunity of this lady your friend; and am content you shall enjoy your own proper estate during life; on condition you oblige your self never to marry, under such penalty as I think convenient.

LADY WISHFORT. Never to marry?

FAINALL. No more Sir *Rowlands*, – the next imposture may not be so timely detected.

MRS. MARWOOD. That condition I dare answer, my Lady will consent to, without difficulty; she has already, but too much experienc'd the perfidiousness of men. Besides Madam, when we retire to our pastoral solitude we shall bid adieu to all other thoughts.

LADY WISHFORT. Aye that's true; but in case of necessity; as of health, or some such emergency –

FAINALL. O, if you are prescrib'd marriage, you | shall be consider'd; I will only reserve to my self the power to chuse for you. If your physick be wholsome, it matters not who is your apothecary. Next, my wife shall settle on me the remainder of her fortune, not made over already; and for her maintenance depend entirely on my discretion.

LADY WISHFORT. This is most inhumanly savage; exceeding the barbarity of a *Muscovite* husband.

FAINALL. I learn'd it from his *Czarish* Majestie's retinue, in a winter evenings conference over brandy and pepper, amongst other secrets of matrimony and policy, as they are at present practis'd in the *northern* hemisphere. But this must be agreed unto, and that positively. Lastly, I will be endow'd in right of my wife, with that six thousand pound, which is the moiety of Mrs. *Millamant's* fortune in your possession: And which she has forfeited (as will appear by the last will and testament of your deceas'd husband Sir *Jonathan Wishfort*) by her disobedience in contracting her self against your consent or knowledge; and by refusing the offer'd match with Sir *Willfull Witwou'd*, which you like a careful aunt had provided for her.

LADY WISHFORT. My nephew was *non compos*, and cou'd not make his addresses.[115]

FAINALL. I come to make demands, – I'll hear no objections.

LADY WISHFORT. You will grant me time to consider.

FAINALL. Yes, while the instrument is drawing, to which you must set your hand till more sufficient deeds can be perfected, which I will take care shall be done with all possible speed. In the mean while, I will go for the said instrument, and till my return, you may balance this matter in your own discretion. [*Exit* Fainall.

LADY WISHFORT. This insolence is beyond all precedent, all parallel, must I be subject to this merciless villain?

MRS. MARWOOD. 'Tis severe indeed *Madam*, that you shou'd smart for your daughters wantonness.

LADY WISHFORT. 'Twas against my consent that she married this barbarian, but she wou'd have him, tho' her year was not out. – Ah! her first husband my Son *Languish*, would not have carry'd it thus. Well, that was my choice, this is hers; she is match'd now with a witness – I shall be mad, dear friend, is there no comfort for me? Must I live to be confiscated at this rebel-rate? – Here come two more of my *Egyptian* plagues too.

[*Enter* Millamant *and* Sir Willfull.

SIR WILLFULL. Aunt, your servant.

LADY WISHFORT. Out *caterpillar*, call not me aunt, I know thee not.

SIR WILLFULL. I confess I have been a little in disguise as they say, – 'Sheart! and I'm sorry for't. What wou'd you have? I hope I committed no offence Aunt – and if I did I am willing to make satisfaction; and what can a man say fairer? If I have broke any thing, I'll pay for't, an it cost a pound. And so let that content for what's past, and make no more words. For what's to come to pleasure you I'm willing to marry my cousin. So pray let's all be friends; she and I are agreed upon the matter, before a witness.

LADY WISHFORT. How's this dear *niece*? Have I any comfort? Can this be true?

MILLAMANT. I am content to be a sacrifice to your repose *Madam*; and to convince you that I had no hand in the plot, as you were misinform'd; I have laid my commands on *Mirabell* to come in person, and be a witness that I give my hand to this flower of *knight-hood*; and for the contract that past between *Mirabell* and me, I have oblig'd him to make a resignation of it, in your Ladyship's presence; – He is without and waits your leave for admittance.

LADY WISHFORT. Well, I'll swear I am something reviv'd at this testimony of your obedience; but I cannot admit that traytor, – I fear I cannot fortifie my self to support his appearance. He is as terrible to me as a *Gorgon*; if I see him, I fear I shall turn to stone, petrifie incessantly.

MILLAMANT. If you disoblige him he may resent your refusal and insist upon the contract still. Then 'tis the last time he will be offensive to you.

LADY WISHFORT. Are you sure it will be the last time? – if I were sure of that – shall I never see him again?

MILLAMANT. Sir *Willfull*, you and he are to travel together, are you not?

SIR WILLFULL. 'Sheart the gentleman's a civil gentleman, Aunt, let him come in; why we are sworn brothers and fellow travellers. – We are to be *Pylades* and *Orestes*, he and I[116] – he is to be my interpreter in foreign parts. He has been overseas once already; and with proviso that I marry my cousin, will cross 'em once again, only to bear me company, – 'Sheart, I'll call him in, – an I set on't once, he shall come in; and see who'll hinder him. [*Exit.*

MRS. MARWOOD. This is precious fooling, if it wou'd pass, but I'll know the bottom of it.

LADY WISHFORT. O dear *Marwood*, you are not going?

MRS. MARWOOD. Not far Madam; I'll return immediately. [*Exit.*

[*Re-enter* Sir Willfull *and* Mirabell.

SIR WILLFULL. Look up man, I'll stand by you, 'sbud an she do frown, she can't kill you; – besides – hearkee she dare not frown desperately, because her face is none of her own; 'Sheart an she shou'd her forehead wou'd wrinkle like the coat of a cream-cheese, but mum for that, fellow traveller.

MIRABELL. If a deep sense of the many injuries I have offer'd to so good a Lady, with a sincere remorse, and a hearty contrition, can but obtain the least glance of compassion I am too happy, – Ah *Madam*, there was a time – but let it be forgotten – I confess I have deservedly forfeited the high place I once held, of sighing at your feet; nay kill me not, by turning from me in disdain, – I come not to plead for favour; – Nay not for pardon, I am a suppliant only for your pity – I am going where I never shall behold you more –

SIR WILLFULL. How, fellow traveller! – You shall go by your self then.

MIRABELL. Let me be pitied first; and afterwards forgotten, – I ask no more.

SIR WILLFULL. By'r Lady a very reasonable request; and will cost you nothing, Aunt – Come, come, forgive and forget Aunt, why you must an you are a Christian.

MIRABELL. Consider *Madam*, in reality; you cou'd not receive much prejudice; it was an innocent device; tho' I confess it had a face of guiltiness, – it was at most an artifice which love contriv'd – and errors which love produces have ever been accounted *venial*. At least think it is punishment enough, that I have lost what in my heart I hold most dear, that to your cruel indignation, I have offer'd up this beauty, and with her my peace and quiet; nay all my hopes of future comfort.

SIR WILLFULL. An he does not move me, wou'd I might never be O' the Quorum[117] – an it were not as good a deed as to drink, to give her to him again, – I wou'd I might never take shipping – Aunt, if you don't forgive quickly; I shall melt, I can tell you that. My contract went no further than a little mouth-glew, and that's hardly dry; – One dolefull sigh more from my fellow traveller and 'tis dissolv'd.

LADY WISHFORT. Well *nephew*, upon your account – ah, he has a false insinuating tongue – Well Sir, I will stifle my just resentment at my *nephew*'s request. – I will endeavour what I can to forget, – but on *proviso* that you resign the contract with my *niece* immediately.

MIRABELL. It is in writing and with papers of concern; but I have sent my servant for it, and will deliver it to you, with all acknowledgments for your transcendent goodness.

LADY WISHFORT. [*Apart*] Oh, he has *witch-craft* in his eyes and tongue; – When I did not see him I cou'd have brib'd a villain to his assassination; but his appearance rakes the *embers* which have so long layn smother'd in my breast. –

[*Enter* Fainall *and* Mrs. Marwood.

FAINALL. Your date of deliberation *Madam*, is expir'd. Here is the instrument, are you prepar'd to sign?

LADY WISHFORT. If I were prepar'd; I am not impowr'd. My *niece* exerts a lawfull claim, having match'd her self by my direction to Sir *Willfull*.

FAINALL. That sham is too gross to pass on me, – tho 'tis impos'd on you, *Madam*.

MILLAMANT. Sir, I have given my consent.

MIRABELL. And Sir, I have resign'd my pretensions.

SIR WILLFULL. And Sir, I assert my right; and will maintain it in defiance of you Sir, and of your instrument. 'Sheart an you talk of an instrument Sir, I have an old *fox* by my thigh shall hack your instrument of *ram vellam* to shreds, sir.[118] It shall not be sufficient for a *mittimus*[119] or a tailor's measure; therefore withdraw your instrument Sir, or by'r Lady I shall draw mine.

LADY WISHFORT. Hold *Nephew*, hold.

MILLAMANT. Good Sir *Willfull*, respite your valour.

FAINALL. Indeed? are you provided of a guard, with your single beef-eater there? but I'm prepar'd for you; and insist upon my first proposal. You shall submit your own estate to my management, and absolutely make over my wife's to my sole use; as pursuant to the purport and tenor of this other covenant, – I suppose *Madam*, your consent is not requisite in this case; nor Mr. *Mirabell*, your resignation; nor Sir *Willfull*, your right – you may draw your *fox* if you please Sir, and make a *bear-garden*[120] flourish somewhere else; for here it will not avail. This my Lady *Wishfort* must be subscrib'd, or your darling daughter's turn'd a drift, like a leaky hulk to sink or swim, as she and the current of this lewd town can agree.

LADY WISHFORT. Is there no means, no remedy, to stop my ruin? Ungrateful wretch! dost thou not owe thy being, thy subsistance to my daughter's fortune?

FAINALL. I'll answer you when I have the rest of it in my possession.

MIRABELL. But that you wou'd not accept of a remedy from my hands – I own I have not deserv'd you shou'd owe any obligation to me; or else perhaps I cou'd advise. –

LADY WISHFORT. O what? what? to save me and my child from ruin, from want, I'll forgive all that's past; nay I'll consent to any thing to come, to be deliver'd from this tyranny.

MIRABELL. Ay madam; but that is too late, my reward is intercepted. You have dispos'd of her, who only cou'd have made me a compensation for all my services; – But be it as it may. I am resolv'd I'll serve you, you shall not be wrong'd in this *savage* manner.

LADY WISHFORT. How! dear Mr. *Mirabell*, can you be so generous at last! But it is not possible. Hearkee. I'll break my *nephew*'s match, you shall have my *niece* yet, and all her fortune; if you can but save me from this imminent danger.

MIRABELL. Will you? I take you at you word. I ask no more. I must have leave for two criminals to appear.

LADY WISHFORT. Ay, ay, anybody, anybody.

MIRABELL. *Foible* is one and a penitent.

[*Enter* Mrs. Fainall, Foible, *and* Mincing.

MRS. MARWOOD. [*To* Fainall] O my shame! These corrupt things are bought and brought hither to expose me –

[Mirabell *and* Lady Wishfort *go to* Mrs. Fainall *and* Foible.

FAINALL. If it must all come out, why let 'em know it, 'tis but *the Way of the World*. That shall not urge me to relinquish or abate one tittle of my terms, no, I will insist the more.

FOIBLE. Yes indeed *Madam*; I'll take my Bible-oath of it.

MINCING. And so will I, *Mem*.

LADY WISHFORT. O *Marwood*, *Marwood* art thou false? my friend deceive me? hast thou been a wicked accomplice with that profligate man?

MRS. MARWOOD. Have you so much ingratitude and injustice, to give credit against your friend, to the aspersions of two such mercenary trulls?

MINCING. Mercenary, *Mem*? I scorn your words. 'Tis true we found you and Mr. *Fainall* in the blew garret, by the same token, you swore us to secrecy upon *Messalinas*'s poems. Mercenary? No, if we wou'd have been mercenary, we shou'd have held our tongues; you wou'd have brib'd us sufficiently.

FAINALL. Go, you are an insignificant thing, – well, what are you the better for this? Is this Mr. *Mirabell*'s expedient? I'll be put off no longer – You thing that was a wife, shall smart for this. I will not leave thee wherewithall to hide thy shame; your body shall be naked as your reputation.

MRS. FAINALL. I despise you and defy your malice – you have aspers'd me wrongfully – I have prov'd your falsehood – Go you and your treacherous – I will not name it, but starve together – perish.

FAINALL. Not while you are worth a groat, indeed my dear. *Madam*, I'll be fool'd no longer.

LADY WISHFORT. Ah Mr. *Mirabell*, this is small comfort, the detection of this affair.

MIRABELL. O in good time – Your leave for the other offender and penitent to appear, *Madam*.

[*Enter* Waitwell *with a box of writings.*

LADY WISHFORT. O Sir *Rowland* – well rascal.

WAITWELL. What your Ladyship pleases. – I have brought the black box at last, *Madam.*

MIRABELL. Give it me. *Madam*, you remember your promise.

LADY WISHFORT. I, dear Sir!

MIRABELL. Where are the gentlemen?

WAITWELL. At hand Sir, rubbing their eyes, – just risen from sleep.

FAINALL. 'Sdeath what's this to me? I'll not wait your private concerns.

[*Enter* Petulant *and* Witwoud.

PETULANT. How now? What's the matter? Who's hand's out?

WITWOUD. Hey day! What are you all got together like players at the end of the last act?

MIRABELL. You may remember gentlemen, I once requested your hands as witnesses to a certain parchment.

WITWOUD. Ay I do, my hand I remember – *Petulant* set his mark.

MIRABELL. You wrong him, his name is fairly written as shall appear[121] – you do not remember gentlemen, any thing of what that parchment contain'd – [*Undoing the box.*

WITWOUD. No.

PETULANT. Not I. I writ. I read nothing.

MIRABELL. Very well, now you shall know – Madam, your promise.

LADY WISHFORT. Ay, ay, Sir, upon my honour.

MIRABELL. Mr. *Fainall*, it is now time that you shou'd know, that your Lady while she was at her own disposal, and before you had by your insinuations wheedled her out of a pretended settlement of the greatest part of her fortune –

FAINALL. Sir! pretended!

MIRABELL. Yes Sir. I say that this Lady while a widdow, having it seems receiv'd some cautions respecting your inconstancy and tyranny of temper, which from her own partial opinion and fondness of you, she cou'd never have suspected – she did I say by the wholesome advice of friends and of sages learned in the laws of this land, deliver this same as her act and deed to me in trust, and to the uses within mention'd. You may read if you please – [*Holding out the parchment*] tho perhaps what is inscrib'd on the back may serve your occasions.

FAINALL. Very likely sir. What's here? Damnation! [*Reads*] A deed of conveyance of the whole estate real of *Arabella Languish* widdow in trust to Edward *Mirabell.* Confusion!

MIRABELL. Even so sir, 'tis *the Way of the World*, Sir: of the widdows of the World. I suppose this deed may bear an elder date than what you have obtain'd from your lady.

FAINALL. Perfidious fiend! then thus I'll be reveng'd. – [*Offers to run at* Mrs. Fainall.

SIR WILLFULL. Hold sir, now you may make your *bear-garden* flourish somewhere else Sir.

FAINALL. *Mirabell*, you shall hear of this sir, be sure you shall. Let me pass *oaf.* [*Exit.*

MRS. FAINALL. *Madam*, you seem to stifle your resentment: You had better give it vent.

MRS. MARWOOD. Yes it shall have vent – and to your confusion, or I'll perish in the attempt. [*Exit.*

LADY WISHFORT. O daughter, daughter, 'tis plain thou hast inherited thy mother's prudence.

MRS. FAINALL. Thank Mr. *Mirabell*, a cautious friend, to whose advice all is owing.

LADY WISHFORT. Well Mr. *Mirabell*, you have kept your promise, – and I must perform mine. – First I pardon for your sake, Sir *Rowland* there and *Foible*, – The next thing is to break the matter to my *nephew* – and how to do that –

MIRABELL. For that, madam, give your self no trouble – let me have your consent – Sir *Willfull* is my friend; he has had compassion upon lovers and generously engag'd a volunteer in this action, for our service, and now designs to prosecute his travels.

SIR WILLFULL. 'Sheart aunt, I have no mind to marry. My cousin's a fine lady, and the gentleman loves her and she loves him, and they deserve one another; my resolution is to see foreign parts – I have set on't – And when I'm set on't, I must do't. And if these two gentlemen wou'd travel too, I think they may be spar'd.

PETULANT. For my part, I say little – I think things are best off or on.

WITWOUD. I Gad I understand nothing of the matter, – I'm in a maze yet, like a dog in a dancing school.

LADY WISHFORT. Well Sir, take her, and with her all the joy I can give you.

MILLAMANT. Why does not the man take me? Wou'd you have me give my self to you over again?

MIRABELL. Ay, and over and over again; for I wou'd have you as often as possibly I can. [*Kisses her hand*] Well, heav'n grant I love you not too well, that's all my fear.

SIR WILLFULL. 'Sheart you'll have him time enough to toy after you're married; or if you will toy now. Let us have a dance in the mean time, that we who are not lovers, may have some other employment, besides looking on.

MIRABELL. With all my heart dear Sir *Willfull*, what shall we do for musick?

FOIBLE. O Sir, some that were provided for Sir *Rowland*'s entertainment are yet within call.

[*A dance.*

LADY WISHFORT. As I am a person I can hold out no longer; – I have wasted my spirits so to day already; that I am ready to sink under the fatigue; and I cannot but have some fears upon me yet, that my son *Fainall* will pursue some desperate course.

MIRABELL. *Madam*, disquiet not your self on that account; to my knowledge his circumstances are such, he must of force comply. For my part I will contribute all that in me lies to a reunion, in the mean time, madam, let me [*To Mrs. Fainall*] before these witnesses, restore to you this deed of trust. It may be a means well managed to make you live easily together.

From hence let those be warned, who meant to wed;
Lest mutual falsehood stain the bridal-bed:
For each deceiver to his cost may find,
That marriage frauds, too oft are paid in kind.

[*Exeunt Omnes.*

EPILOGUE

[*Spoken by* Mrs. Bracegirdle.]

After our epilogue this crowd dismisses,
In thinking how this play'll be pull'd to pieces.
But pray consider, ere you doom its fall,
How hard a thing 'twould be, to please you all.
There are some criticks so with spleen diseas'd,
They scarcely come inclining to be pleas'd:
And sure he must have more than mortal skill,
Who pleases any one against his will.
Then, all bad poets we are sure are foes,
And how their numbers swell'd the Town well knows:
In shoals, I've mark'd 'em judging in the pit;
Tho' they're on no pretence for judgment fit
But that they have been damn'd for want of wit.
Since when, they by their own offences taught
Set up for spys on plays and finding fault.
Others there are whose malice we'd prevent;
Such, who watch plays, with scurrilous intent
To mark out who by characters are meant.
And tho' no perfect likeness they can trace;
Yet each pretends to know the copy'd face.
These with false glosses, feed their own ill-nature,
And turn to libel, what was meant a satire.
May such malicious fops this fortune find,
To think themselves alone the fools design'd:
If any are so arrogantly vain,
To think they singly can support a scene,
And furnish fool enough to entertain.
For well the learned and the judicious know,
That satire scorns to stoop so meanly low,
As any one abstracted fop to show.
For, as when painters form a matchless face,
They from each fair one catch some different grace;
And shining features in one portrait blend,
To which no single beauty must pretend:
So poets oft, do in one piece expose
Whole *belles assembles* of coquettes and beaux.

Finis.

7.2 FROM JEREMY COLLIER, *A SHORT VIEW OF THE IMMORALITY AND PROFANENESS OF THE ENGLISH STAGE*

London, 1698. London: Printed for S. Keble, et al., 2nd ed.

CONGREVE WROTE *The Way of the World* in part as an answer to Collier's mislabeled screed (it is not short). Collier draws on antitheatrical discourse from Ovid to St. Augustine to Prynne (whose *Historio-Matrix* Lady Wishfort hypocritically keeps in her closet) to make an argument that the English stage of the recent past is lewd and hostile to Christianity. His first five principle complaints, in his own words, are:

> The poets make women speak smuttily; . . . They represent their single ladies and persons of condition under these disorders of liberty; . . . They have oftentimes not so much as the poor refuge of a double meaning to fly to; . . . And which is still more extraordinary, the prologues and epilogues are sometimes scandalous to the last degree; . . . and finally, Smut is still more insufferable with respect to religion.

Collier goes on to enumerate theatrical infractions against modesty, the use of profanity, mocking the clergy, the charge of rewarding vicious characters, paganism, and closer looks at plays by Dryden, D'Urfey, and Vanbrugh, while sniping at Congreve and Wycherley. Throughout, he manifests an anxiety about representation that extends to his own text: he is reluctant to quote lest he spread the "Infection."

From Chapter 1, The Immodesty of the Stage.

In treating this Head, I hope the Reader does not expect that I should set down Chapter and Page, and give him the Citations at Length. To do this would be a very unacceptable and Foreign Employment. Indeed the Passages, many of them, are in no Condition to be handled: He that is desirous to see these Flowers let him do it in their own Soil: 'tis my business rather to kill the Root than Transplant it. But that the Poets may not complain of Injustice; I shall point to the Infection at a Distance, and refer in General to Play and Person.

Now among the Curiosities of this kind we may reckon Mrs. Pinchwife, Horner, and Lady Fidget in *The Country Wife*; Widdow Blackacre and Olivia in *The Plain Dealer*. These, tho' not all the exceptionable Characters, are the most remarkable. I'm sorry the Author should stoop his Wit thus Low, and use his Understanding so unkindly. Some People appear Coarse, and Slovenly out of Poverty: They can't well go to the Charge of Sense. They are Offensive like Beggars for want of Necessaries. But this is none of the Plain Dealer's case; He can afford his Muse a better Dress when he pleases. But then the Rule is; where the Motive is the less, the Fault is the greater. To proceed. Jacinta, Elvira, Dalinda, and Lady Plyant, in *The Mock Astrologer*, *Spanish Friar*, *Love Triumphant* and *Double*

Dealer, forget themselves extreamly: And almost all the Characters in the *Old Batchelour*, are foul and nauseous. *Love for Love*, and *The Relapse*, strike sometimes upon this Sand, and so likewise does Don Sebastian.

I don't pretend to have read the Stage Through, neither am I Particular to my Utmost. Here is quoting enough unless 'twere better: Besides, I may have occasion to mention somewhat of this kind afterwards. But from what has been hinted already, the Reader may be over furnish'd. Here is a large Collection of Debauchery; such Pieces are rarely to be met with: 'tis Sometimes painted at Length too, and appears in great Variety of Progress and Practise. It wears almost all sorts of Dresses to engage the Fancy, and fasten upon the Memory, and keep up the Charm from Languishing. Sometimes you have it in Image and Description; sometimes by way of Allusion; sometimes in Disguise; and sometimes without it. And what can be the Meaning of such a Representation, unless it be to Tincture the Audience, to extinguish Shame, and make Lewdness a Diversion? This is the natural Consequence, and therefore one would think 'twas the Intention too. Such Licentious Discourse tends to no point but to stain the Imagination, to awaken Folly, and to weaken the Defences of Virtue: It was upon the account of these Disorders that Plato banish'd Poets his Common Wealth: And one of the Fathers calls Poetry, Vinum Daemonum an intoxicating Draught, made up by the Devils Dispensatory.

I grant the Abuse of a Thing is no Argument against the use of it. However Young people particularly, should not entertain themselves with a Lewd Picture; especially when 'tis drawn by a Masterly Hand. For such a Liberty may probably raise those Passions which can neither be discharged without Trouble, nor satisfyed without a Crime: 'tis not safe for a Man to trust his Virtue too far, for fear it should give him the slip! But the danger of such an Entertainment is but part of the Objection: 'tis all Scandal and meanness into the bargain: it does in effect degrade Human Nature, sinks Reason into Appetite, and breaks down the Distinctions between Man and Beast. Goats and Monkeys if they could speak, would express their Brutality in such Language as This . . .

From Chapter 6, The Opinion of the Heathen Philosophers, Orators, and Historians, concerning the Stage.

. . . In the Theodosian Code,[122] Players are call'd Personae inhonestae; that is, to Translate it softly, Persons Maim'd, and Blemish'd in their Reputation. Their Pictures might be seen at the Play-House, but were not permitted to hang in any creditable Place of the Town, Upon this Text Gothofred tells us the Function of Players was counted scandalous by the Civil Law. L. 4. And that those who came upon the Stage to divert the people, had a mark of Infamy set upon them. Famosi sunt ex Edicto.[123]

I shall now come down to our own Constitution. And I find by 39. Eliz. cap. 4. 1. Jae. cap. 7.[124] That all Bearwards, Common Players of Enterludes, Counterfeit Egyptians &c. shall be taken, adjudged and deem'd Rogues, Vagabonds, and sturdy beggars, and shall sustain all pain and Punishment, as by this Act is in that behalf appointed. The Penalties are infamous to the last degree, and Capital too, unless they give over. 'Tis true, the first Act excepts those Players which belong to a Baron or other Personage of higher Degree, and are authorized to Play under the hand and Seal of Aimes of such Baron, or Personage. But by the later Statute this Privilege of Licensing is taken away: And all of them are expresly brought under the Penalty without Distinction.

7.3 FROM JOHN VANBRUGH, *A SHORT VINDICATION OF* THE RELAPSE *AND* THE PROVOK'D WIFE, *FROM IMMORALITY AND PROPHANENESS*

London: Printed for N. Walwyn, 1698.

VANBRUGH TAKES OBVIOUS PLEASURE in taking Collier down, turning his reply into a comic tour-de-force.

WHEN first I saw Mr. *Collier*'s Performance upon the Irregularities of the Stage (in which, amongst the rest of the Gentlemen, he's pleas'd to afford me some particular Favours), I was far from designing to trouble either my self or the Town with a Vindication; I thought his Charges against me for Immorality and Prophaneness were grounded upon so much Mistake, that every one (who had had the curiosity to see the Plays, or on this Occasion should take the trouble to read 'em) would easily discover the Root of the Invective, and that 'twas the Quarrel of his Gown, and not of his God, that made him take Arms against me . . .

The First Chapter in his Book is upon the Immodesty of the Stage; where he tells you how valuable a Qualification Modesty is in a Woman: For my part I am wholly of his mind; I think 'tis almost as valuable in a Woman as in a Clergyman; and had I the ruling of the Roost, the one shou'd neither have a Husband, nor the t'other a Benefice without it. If this Declaration won't serve to shew I'm a Friend to't, let us see what Proof this Gentleman can give of the contrary . . . I don't find him over-stock'd with Quotations in this Chapter: He's forc'd, rather than say nothing, to fall upon poor Miss *Hoyden*. He does not come to Particulars, but only mentions her with others, for an immodest Character. What kind of Immodesty he means, I can't tell: But I suppose he means Lewdness, because he generally means wrong. For my part, I know of no Bawdy she talks: If the Strength of his Imagination gives any of her Discourse that Turn, I suppose it may be owing to the Number of Bawdy Plays he has read, which have debauch'd his Taste, and made every thing seem Salt, that comes in his way.

7.4 FROM WILLIAM CONGREVE, AMENDMENTS OF *MR. COLLIER'S FALSE AND IMPERFECT CITATIONS*

London, Printed for J. Tonson, 1698

CONGREVE PRESENTS EXTENDED PROOFS of Collier's weaknesses, with quotations from four of his plays. Like Vanbrugh and Dennis, Congreve displays his wit in skewering Collier's project and defending the stage.

I Have been told by some, That they should think me very idle, if I threw away any time in taking notice ev'n of so much of Mr. *Collier*'s late Treatise of the Immorality, *&c.* of the *English* Stage, as related to my self, in respect of some Plays written by me: For that his malicious and strain'd Interpretations of my Words were so gross and palpable, that any indifferent and unprejudic'd Reader would immediately condemn him upon his own Evidence, and acquit me before I could make my Defence. On the other hand, I have been tax'd of Laziness, and too much Security in neglecting thus long to do my self a necessary Right, which might be effected with so very little Pains; since very little more is requisite in my Vindication, than to represent truly and at length, those Passages which Mr. *Collier* has shewn imperfectly, and for the most part by halves. I would rather be thought Idle than Lazy; and so the last Advice prevail'd with me.

I have no Intention to examine all the Absurdities and Falshoods in Mr. *Collier*'s Book; to use the Gentleman's own Metaphor in his Preface, *An Inventory of such a Ware-house would be a large Work*. My Detection of his Malice and Ignorance, of his Sophistry and vast Assurance, will lie within a narrow Compass, and only bear a Proportion to so much of his Book as concerns my self. Least of all, would I undertake to defend the Corruptions of the Stage; indeed if I were so inclin'd, Mr. *Collier* has given me no occasion; for the greater part of those Examples which he has produc'd, are only Demonstrations of his own Impurity, they only savour of his Utterance, and were sweet enough till tainted by his Breath.

I will not justifie any of my own Errors; I am sensible of many; and if Mr. *Collier* has by any Accident stumbled on one or two, I will freely give them up to him, *Nullum unquam ingenium placuit sine venia*. But I hope I have done nothing that can deprive me of the Benefit of my Clergy; and tho' Mr. *Collier* himself were the Ordinary, I may hope to be acquitted.

My Intention therefore, is to do little else, but to restore those Passages to their primitive Station, which have suffer'd so much in being transplanted by him: I will remove 'em from his Dunghil, and replant 'em in the Field of Nature; and when I have wash'd 'em of that Filth which they have contracted in passing thro' his very dirty hands, let their own Innocence protect them.

Mr. *Collier*, in the high Vigour of his Obscenity, first commits a Rape upon my Words, and then arraigns 'em of Immodesty; he has Barbarity enough to accuse the very Virgins that he has deflowr'd, and to make sure of their Condemnation, he has himself made 'em guilty: But he forgets that while he publishes their shame he divulges his own.

His Artifice to make Words guilty of Profaness, is of the same nature; for where the Expression is unblameable in its own clear and genuine Signification, he enters into it himself like the evil Spirit; he possesses the innocent Phrase, and makes it bellow forth his own Blasphemies; so *that* one would think the Muse was Legion.

To reprimand him a little in his own Words, if these Passages produc'd by Mr. *Collier* are obscene and profane, Why were they rak*'d* in and disturb*'d unless it were to conjure up Vice,* and revive Impurities? *Indeed Mr.* Collier *has a very untoward way with him;* his Pen has such a Libertine Stroke*, that 'tis a question whether the Practice or the Reproof be the more licentious*.

He teaches those Vices he would correct, and writes more like a Pimp than a P–. Since the business must be undertaken, why was not the Thought blanch'd, the Expression made remote, and the ill Features cast into Shadows? So far from this, which is his own Instruction in his own words, is Mr. *Collier*'s way of Proceeding, that he has blackned the Thoughts with his own *Smut*; the Expression that was remote, he has brought nearer; and lest by being brought near its native Innocence might be more visible, he has frequently varied it, he has new-molded it, and stamp'd his own Image on it; so that it at length is become Current Deformity, and fit to be paid into the Devil's Exchequer.

7.5 WILLIAM CONGREVE, "CONCERNING HUMOUR IN COMEDY"

From *Letters on Several Occasions, Written by and Between Mr. Dryden, Mr. Wycherley, Mr. ____, Mr. Congreve, and Mr. Dennis.* London: Printed for Sam Briscoe, 1696.

PRIOR TO COLLIER'S SCREED, Congreve had been carrying on a print conversation about aesthetics and theatricality with John Dennis. In this letter, he articulates the difference between humor (rising from fundamental characteristics, in the tradition of Jonsonian "humours" characters) and wit (which he links to intelligence and verbal mastery).

I have observed, that when a few things have been wittily and pleasantly spoken by any Character in a Comedy, it has been very usual for those, who make their Remarks on a Play, while it is acting, to say, Such a thing is very humorously spoken; There is a great deal of Humour in that Part. Thus the Character of the Person speaking, may be, surprisingly and pleasantly, is mistaken for a Character of Humour; which indeed is a Character of Wit: But there is a great Difference between a Comedy, wherein there are many things humorously, as they call it, which is pleasantly spoken; and one, where there are several Characters of Humour, distinguish'd by the particular and different Humours, appropriated to the several Persons represented, and which naturally arise from the different Constitutions, Complexions, and Dispositions of Men. The saying of Humorous Things, does not distinguish Characters; for every Person in a Comedy may be allow'd to speak them. From a witty Man they are expected; and even a Fool may be permitted to stumble on 'em by chance. Tho' I make a Difference betwixt Wit and Humour; yet I do not think that Humorous Characters exclude Wit: No, but the manner of Wit should be adapted to the Humour. As for Instance, A Character of a Splenetick and Peevish Humour, should have a Satyrical Wit; a Jolly and Sanguine Humour, should have a Facetious Wit: The former should speak positively; the latter, carelesly: For the former observes, and shews things as they are; the latter rather overlooks Nature, and speaks things as he would have them; and his Wit and Humour have both of them a less Alloy of Judgment than the others.

As Wit, so, its opposite, Folly, is sometimes mistaken for Humour. When a Poet brings a Character on the Stage, committing a thousand Absurdities, and talking Impertinencies, Roaring aloud, and Laughing immoderately, on every, or rather upon no occasion; this is a Character of Humour.

Is any thing more common, than to have a pretended Comedy, stuff'd with such Grotesque Figures, and Farce-Fools? Things, that either are not in Nature, or if they are, are Monsters, and Births of Mischance; and consequently as such, should be stifled, and huddled out of the way, like Sooterkins, that Mankind may not be shock'd with an appearing Possibility of the Degeneration of a God-like Species. For my part, I am as willing to Laugh, as any body, and as easily diverted with an Object truly ridiculous: but at the same time, I can never care for seeing things, that force me to entertain low Thoughts of my Nature. I don't know how it is with others, but I confess freely to you, I could never look long upon a Monkey, without very mortifying Reflections; tho' I never heard any thing to the contrary, why that Creature is not Originally of a distinct Species. As I don't think Humour exclusive of Wit, neither do I think it inconsistent with Folly; but I think the Follies should be only such, as Mens Humours may incline 'em to; and not Follies intirely abstracted from both Humour and Nature.

7.6 SAMUEL JOHNSON, *THE LIVES OF THE POETS*, "Congreve."

From *The Yale Edition of the Works of Samuel Johnson* vol. 22, Ed. John H. Middendorf. New Haven, CT and London: Yale University Press, 2010, 741–5.

JOHNSON'S *LIVES OF THE POETS* is an achievement in early biography, combining critical appraisal with biographical detail. His appreciation for Congreve is undercut by his approval of a post-Collier prudishness about the stage.

But whatever objections may be made either to his comic or tragic excellence, they are lost at once in the blaze of admiration, when it is remembered that he had produced these four plays[125] before he had passed his twenty-fifth year, before other men, even such as are some time to shine in eminence, have passed their probation of literature, or presume to hope for any other notice than such as is bestowed on diligence and inquiry. Among all the efforts of early genius, which literary history records, I doubt whether any one can be produced that more surpasses the common limits of nature than the plays of Congreve.

About this time began the long-continued controversy between Collier and the poets. In the reign of Charles I, the Puritans had raised a violent clamour against the drama, which they considered as an entertainment not lawful to Christians, an opinion held by them in common with the Church of Rome; and Prynne published "Histriomastix," a huge volume in which stage-plays were censured. The outrages and crimes of the Puritans brought afterwards their whole system of doctrine into disrepute, and from the Restoration the poets and players were left at quiet; for to have molested them would have had the appearance of tendency to puritanical malignity.

This danger, however, was worn away by time, and Collier, a fierce and implacable non-juror, knew that an attack upon the theatre would never make him suspected for a Puritan; he therefore (1698) published "A Short View of the Immorality and Profaneness of the English Stage," I believe with no other motive than religious zeal and honest indignation. He was formed for a controvertist, with sufficient learning, with diction vehement and pointed, though often vulgar and incorrect, with unconquerable pertinacity, with wit in the highest degree and sarcastic, and with all those powers exalted and invigorated by just confidence in his cause.

Thus qualified and thus incited, he walked out to battle, and assailed at once most of the living writers, from Dryden to Durfey. His onset was violent; those passages, which, while they stood single, had passed with little notice, when they were accumulated and exposed together, excited horror. The wise and the pious caught the alarm, and the nation wondered why it had so long suffered irreligion and licentiousness to be openly taught at the public charge.

Nothing now remained for the poets but to resist or fly. Dryden's conscience or his prudence, angry as he was, withheld him from the conflict. Congreve and Vanbrugh attempted answers. Congreve, a very young man, elated with success, and impatient of censure, assumed an air of confidence and security. His chief art of controversy is to retort upon his adversary his own words: he is very angry, and hoping to conquer Collier with his own weapons, allows himself in the use of every term of contumely and contempt, but he has the sword without the arm of Scanderbeg; he has his antagonist's coarseness but not his strength. Collier replied; for contest was his delight, he was not to be frighted from his purpose or his prey.

The cause of Congreve was not tenable; whatever glosses he might use for the defence or palliation of single passages, the general tenour and tendency of his plays must always be condemned. It is acknowledged, with universal conviction, that the perusal of his works will make no man better, and that their ultimate effect is to represent pleasure in alliance with vice, and to relax those obligations by which life ought to be regulated.

The stage found other advocates, and the dispute was protracted through ten years: but at last comedy grew more modest, and Collier lived to see the reformation of the theatre . . . Congreve's last play was *The Way of The World*, which, though as he hints in his dedication was written with great labour and much thought, was received with so little favour that being in a high degree offended and disgusted, Congreve resolved to commit his quiet and his fame no more to the caprices of an audience.

From this time his life ceased to be public; he lived for himself and his friends, and among his friends was able to name every man of his time whom wit and elegance had raised to reputation. It may be therefore reasonably supposed that his manners were polite, and his conversation pleasing.

He seems not to have taken much pleasure in writing, as he contributed nothing to the *Spectator*, and only one paper to the *Tatler*, though published by men with whom he might be supposed willing to associate: and though he lived many years after the publication of his "Miscellaneous Poems" he added nothing to them, but lived on in literary indolence, engaged in no controversy, contending with no rival, neither soliciting flattery by public commendations nor provoking enmity by malignant criticism; rather passing his time among the great and splendid, in the placid enjoyment of his fame and fortune.

7.7 J. ROBERTS, *MISS DE CAMP AS FOIBLE*

Miss De Camp as Foible. J. Roberts, pinxit. In *Bell's British Theatre*, London: George Cawthorn, 1797. Courtesy of the University of Tennessee Library, Hodges Special Collections.

The image shows Maria Theresa de Camp (later Kemble, after she married Charles Kemble in 1806) playing the comic role of Foible, with the inscription "so mischief has been before-hand with me." She performed many comic roles, including a breeches Macheath to John Bannister's Polly in a 1792 Haymarket production of *The Beggar's Opera*. The empire-waist dress reflects late-century styles and is a reminder that *The Way of the World* still saw occasional revivals.

Notes

1–2 From the London edition of 1700. Printed for Jacob Tonson [etc.].
3 For more on divorce in Restoration and early eighteenth-century comedies, see Paula Backscheider, "'Endless Aversion Rooted in the Soul': Divorce in the 1690–1730 Theater." *The Eighteenth Century*, 37.2 (1996): 99–135.
4 Carole Pateman, *The Sexual Contract*, Stanford, CA: Stanford UP, 1988, anatomizes the implications of seventeenth- and eighteenth-century marriage law brilliantly.
5 "You who wish trouble on adulterers in their affairs, it is worth your time to hear how badly theyfare on every side.–Caught in the act, she fears for her dowry." Horace, *Satires* II.1.
6 Witwoud is a fool in this play; Truewit is a man of intelligence and "true wit" in Jonson's *Epicoene*.
7 Patrons of Terence, one of the great Roman comic playwrights.
8 In this geneology, Congreve traces the line of Greek comic drama back to Aristotle to argue that comedy can be a culturally significant form of dramatic art when playwrights have intelligent patrons (like the Earl of Montagu) who allow them to observe true wit in high society and then support their more refined comedies with patronage.
9 Cuckoos were known for laying their eggs in other birds' nests; the "cuckoo egg" is hence a reference to a bastard child.
10 Congreve's swipe at Collier's recent and somewhat puritanical attack on the licentiousness of the stage.
11 Verbruggen had recently played Loveless in *The Relapse*.
12 Millamant is very fashionable and has "followers" in her entourage.
13 Bracegirdle promoted herself as a virginal actress. She had been Betterton's ward and acting pupil.
14 Euphemism for lover.
15 Like coffeehouses, chocolate houses were important gathering spaces, in which people (mostly men) gathered to discuss current events and drink the popular imported chocolate drinks and coffee that global trade made available. One of the most fashionable, White's, charged a penny for admission and served expensive chocolate drinks as well as food.
16 A vain man, often overly concerned with clothing.
17 A generalized complaint of stress or mild illness, usually made by women.
18 Originally, "redned."
19 A secret society or club.
20 A fortified sweet wine.
21 Edema, or the swelling of soft tissue.
22 Hot chocolate, a fashionable drink at the time.
23 The Church of England maintained that marriage had to be performed between 8 am and noon.
24 Mirabell wants to make sure that Waitwell is legally married so that he can't pursue an actual marriage with Lady Wishfort when he poses as Sir Rowland.
25 St. Pancras Church, a city church at which people could marry without a license.
26 Instantly.
27 Tell the new couple to hurry.
28 Usually, gentlemen made the "grand tour" of Europe between the ages of 16 and 20 as a capstone to their formal education.
29 A medlar is an apple-like fruit; a crab is a kind of wild apple.
30 Caliban.
31 Poem of praise.
32 The funny guy.
33 A minor oath, for "God."
34 A low-ranking bailiff or policeman.
35 He sometimes is inadvertently honest because he can't think of a lie.
36 Intestinal gas.
37 Prostitutes.
38 Called for.

39 Literally, the references to "sultana queens" and Roxolanas are to the strong female characters featured in D'Avenant's *The Seige of Rhodes*, parts I and II, and Orrery's *The Tragedy of Mustapha, Son of Solyman the Magnificent*. Both plays were popular heroic tragedies at the time, but Congreve's characters are using these names as euphemisms for prostitutes.
40 A secret religious assembly, usually of dissenters of Puritan leaning.
41 Quakers took one's word as bond, so a parrot, which can speak without meaning, was an affront to their philosophy.
42 Cheated.
43 Amazonian queen represented in Greek mythology and killed by Achilles. Sir Toby Belch calls Maria a Penthesilea in *Twelfth Night*.
44 Do ye.
45 Has no feeling for her.
46 The first edition reads "Competion."
47 A reference to Ben Jonson's *Volpone*.
48 Mirabell compares her to a great ship coming into a harbor.
49 Beau-mond: the beautiful people (literally, the beautiful world); perukes are wigs, which in this case is shorthand for fashionable young men.
50 They are joking about his "brilliance."
51 Partial quotation from *Hamlet*.
52 Packet.
53 While using twisted paper as hair curlers was a real practice, Millamant jokes about the effects of prose versus poetry on her hair.
54 To arrange her hair.
55 He instructs Mrs. Fainall to distract Witwoud.
56 A strong smelling resin compound used to treat hysteria and digestive ailments.
57 A series of treatments.
58 Spanish red wine.
59 Rouge.
60 Maritorne is a chambermaid in *Don Quixote*.
61 Not fully dressed, probably in a loose morning dress.
62 Lady Wishfort's library is decidedly and ironically Puritan.
63 Looking for a poor husband who would take Lady Wishfort.
64 Locket's was a popular tavern; Lady Wishfort proposes to marry a waiter to get him to poison Mirabell.
65 A gaudy and useless ornament.
66 A person dressed in rags. She wishes this fate on Mirabell, hoping he will wear rags from a long lane penthouse, which is a rag and scrap clothing stall in a market, and thus look like a hanged thief.
67 Debtors' prison.
68 A common place for beggars.
69 A strong inclination, as in her mind has been made up for a month.
70 The last step in an alchemist's experiment to change metal into gold.
71 Mixture.
72 Cheap wool.
73 Coarse wool.
74 A woman who can see the future, from Greek mythology.
75 Do ye.
76 Witwoud and Petulant are fixing their hair.
77 The Wrekin, or Rekin, is a hill in Shropshire that serves as a landmark.
78 A thrice-weekly newspaper.
79 The highest card (the ace) in loo, a popular game.
80 Fainall believes that he has the documents to take most of the money in a divorce.
81 From pulvillio, a kind of powdered perfume.

82 A Cavalier poet and playwright with a rakish reputation and a royalist battle record; 1609–1642. Millamant has just quoted from his "There Never Yet Was Woman Made." Later in the scene, Sir Willfull fails to recognize the poet and assumes Millamant is calling him a baby.
83 Another John Suckling poem.
84 Boredom.
85 Mirabell completes the couplet from Waller's *Phoebus and Daphne*, proving they have similar tastes and reading habits.
86 Sweet pleasures; in other words, goodbye to sleeping in in the morning.
87 Legal term for "in the first place."
88 An oddly shaped piece of firewood.
89 Mirabell forbids Millamant to serve distilled liquors and fortified wines at her ladies' tea table, but allows for milder teas and weak wines.
90 Unstiffened fabric.
91 Official notice that a lawsuit has been abandoned.
92 Decimo sexto means small book. Lacedemonians, or Spartans, were famous for their brevity.
93 The name of the ass in *Reynard the Fox,* a popular beast fable.
94 Monkeys were fashionable pets; Petulant is drunkenly riffing on "carry."
95 Rude or ill-mannered.
96 Drunkard.
97 A popular drinking song, the musical setting for which is uncertain.
98 A pimple is a good friend. Antipodes are opposite points on earth.
99 The "sophy" is the Shah of Persia.
100 Dung cart.
101 Beaten on the feet with sticks.
102 Someone from Shropshire, a rural region.
103 St. Anthony was the patron saint of swineheards, a joke that returns to his misunderstanding about "suckling."
104 Camphor, to reduce sexual urges, and frankincense, used in religious settings.
105 Wig making.
106 A neck scarf made of wool and cheap lace.
107 Shameless.
108 Standard servants' names.
109 Bridewell was the women's prison.
110 French for "hear ye," as in a courtroom.
111 The hat worn by a sergeant-at-law.
112 The survey of landholders in England, completed in 1086.
113 Cantharides (Spanish fly) and cow-itch (cowhage, an herb) would both make the judge fidget.
114 Mrs. Marwood paints a vision of young lawyers taking notes on the case and discussing it in the dining halls.
115 Non compos mentos, or not in his right mind.
116 The strong friendship between Pylades and Orestes is part of Greek mythology.
117 Of the quorum of justices of the peace necessary for a legal court session.
118 An old fox is slang for his sword; vellum is a type of paper.
119 Arrest warrant.
120 A place for bear-bating, a low and violent form of entertainment.
121 Mirabell is making the point, *contra* Wiwoud's suggestion, that Petulant is literate.
122 A fifth-century compilation of extant Roman law.
123 Infamous (or notorious) in accordance with the edict.
124 A section of Elizabethan law still in force criminalizing unlicensed performances.
125 *The Old Batchelor* (1693); *The Double Dealer* (1693); *Love for Love* (1695); and *The Mourning Bride* (1697).

---

8. *The Busie Body*

***THE BUSIE BODY*. A COMEDY. AS IT IS ACTED AT THE THEATRE-ROYAL IN DRURY-LANE. BY HER MAJESTY'S SERVANTS. WRITTEN BY MRS. SUSANNA CENTLIVRE. FIRST PERFORMED 12 MAY 1709 AND FIRST PUBLISHED 1709**

8.1 *THE BUSIE BODY*: A COMEDY. AS IT IS ACTED AT THE THEATRE-ROYAL IN *DRURY-LANE*, BY HER MAJESTY'S SERVANTS.

Susanna Centlivre

First Performed 12 May 1709 and First Published 1709

SUSANNA CENTLIVRE was one of the most popular playwrights of the eighteenth century. Even in her own moment, critics grudgingly noted that Centlivre's plays had eclipsed recent classics such as *The Way of the World*, which, by comparison, "could scarcely make its way at all."[1] She had several successful plays, including *The Gamester*, *The Bassett Table*, *The Wonder: a Woman Keeps a Secret*, and *A Bold Stroke for a Wife*, but *The Busie Body* (later titled *The Busy Body*) was her most popular, with over 325 London performances during the eighteenth century and untold numbers of regional and amateur productions. The play premiered at Drury Lane on May 12, 1709. It transferred to the Queen's Theatre later that year, after which it appeared in most of the major London houses as a crowd-pleasing comedy that held the stage into the nineteenth century. The core of the plot depends on conventional blocking father figures; Sir Francis Gripe, Miranda's guardian, hopes to marry her and "engross the whole" in twin fits of lust and greed. The witty and wise Miranda plays along as she tries to find a way to get her estate out of his hands so that she can marry her beloved George. Meanwhile, her friend Isabinda, who is in love with Charles, faces a possible forced marriage with a Spanish merchant, arranged by her greedy and controlling father Sir Jealous Traffick.

Into this somewhat formulaic set of circumstances, Centlivre releases Marplot, a principle of chaos worthy of his name. Like Restoration fops, Marplot longs for male friendship and approval, but he is fundamentally amiable, and Centlivre treats his over-powering curiosity about other people's affairs with sympathy rather than satiric bite. She may have found some source material for Marplot in Dryden's title character in *Sir Martin Mar-All* (1667), though Marplot invites gentle, good-natured laughter rather than the disdain provoked by Dryden's Sir Martin. He stumbles into scenes, accidentally exposes the lovers to the fathers, and ruins carefully laid plans. Wherever he is, Marplot creates narrative motion even as he puts the happy comic ending at risk. Isabinda's equally well-named maid Patch and Charles' man Whisper provide the cover and distractions that allow the young lovers to succeed. The appeal of Marplot as a character can be gauged by the prints of various actors in the role and Centlivre's sequel, *Marplot in Lisbon*, which never reached *The Busie Body*'s success, but which did reflect Centlivre's nationalism. Like *The Busie Body*, it compared British "liberty" to foreign (and Roman Catholic) strictures on women and used foreign settings or characters as an occasion to laud British and English virtues. Centlivre was a well-known supporter of the Whig cause and the Hanovarian succession. *The Patriot* noted in its January 12, 1715 issue that she was "Mistress of a True *British* Principle" and praised her "Noble Passion for the Protestant Succession" in her dedication of *The Wonder* to George Augustus, the eventual George II.

Centlivre had acted herself, including a breeches role as Alexander the Great in a court performance of Lee's *The Rival Queens*, during which Joseph Centlivre, the king's cook, fell in love with her; they later married. Her understanding of comic timing and practical stage principles led William Hazlitt to call her play, *The Wonder*, "one of the best of our acting plays."[2] She had a gift for writing strong, interesting parts for women that diminished the need for a strong rescuing male, a situation that did not always sit well with comic leading man Robert Wilks. Wilks nearly ruined the first production of *The Busie Body* when he threw down his script in rehearsal and pronounced his part, Sir George Airy, to be ridiculous and the play itself trash. He did the same with *The Wonder: A Woman Keeps a Secret*, but both plays went on to be two of the most successful comedies of the age. John Palmer and Snelling Powell both played Sir George, while Mrs. Palmer, Anne Oldfield, and Mary (Wilford) Bulkley all played Miranda, the part created by Frances Cross. Thomas King and Henry Woodward were especially popular Marplots, enough to have celebrity engravings of their performances in this energetic comic role. Centlivre seems to have been popular in amateur theatres and home theatricals as well; Jane Austen's family performed *The Wonder*, and Centlivre's comedies were widely produced in regional theatres. Garrick chose *The Wonder* and the part of Don Felix for his farewell to the stage in 1776. Notable revivals include Jessica Swale's 2012 production at Red Handed Theatre, London, and UT's Clarence Brown Theatre 2017 production, directed by John Sipes, which is featured on this anthology's website.

Quem tulit ad scenam ventoso Gloria curru,
Exanimat lentus Spectator, sedulus inflat.
Sic Leve, sic parvum est, animum quod laudis avarum
Subruit aut reficit–[3]

Horace, Epistles Book II, Epistle I.

TO THE RIGHT HONOURABLE JOHN Lord SOMMERS, Lord-President of Her Majesty's most Honourable Privy-Council.

May it please Your Lordship,

As it's an establish'd custom in these latter ages, for all writers, particularly the poetical, to shelter their productions under the protection of the most distinguish'd, whose approbation produces a kind of inspiration, much superior to that which the *heathenish* poets pretended to derive from their fictitious Apollo:[4] So it was my ambition to address one of my weak performances to your Lordship, who, by universal consent, are justly allow'd to be the best judge of all kinds of writing.

I was indeed at first deterr'd from my design, by a thought that it might be accounted unpardonable rudeness to obtrude a trifle of this nature to a person, whose sublime wisdom moderates that council, which at this critical juncture, over-rules the fate of all Europe. But then I was encourag'd by reflecting, that Lelius and Scipio, the two greatest men in their time, among the Romans, both for political and military virtues, in the height of their important affairs, thought the perusal and improving of *Terence*'s comedies the noblest way of unbinding their minds. I own I were guilty of the highest vanity, should I presume to put my composures in parallel with those of that celebrated dramatist. But then again, I hope that your Lordship's native goodness and generosity, in condescension to the taste of the best and fairest part of the Town, who have been pleas'd to be diverted by the following scenes, will excuse and overlook such faults as your nicer judgment might discern.

And here, my Lord, the occasion seems fair for me to engage in a panegyrick[5] upon those natural and acquired abilities, which so brightly adorn your person: But I shall resist that temptation, being conscious of the inequality of a female pen to so masculine an attempt; and having no other ambition, than to subscribe my self,

My Lord, Your Lordship's Most Humble and Most Obedient Servant, Susanna Centlivre.

PROLOGUE. [By Baker, T.]

By the Author of **Tunbridge-Walks**.

Tho' modern prophets[6] were expos'd of late,
The author cou'd not prophesie his fate;
If with such scenes an audience had been fir'd,
The poet must have really been inspir'd.
But these, alas! are melancholy days
For modern prophets, and for modern plays.
Yet since prophetick lyes please fools o'fashion,
And women are so fond of agitation;
To men of sense, I'll prophesie anew,
And tell you wond'rous things, that will prove true:
Undaunted colonels will to camps repair,
Assur'd, there'll be no skirmishes this year;
On our own terms will flow the wish'd-for peace,
All wars, except 'twixt man and wife, will cease.[7]
The grand monarch may wish his son a throne,
But hardly will advance to lose his own.
This season most things hear a smiling face;
But play'rs in summer have a dismal case,
Since your appearance only is our act of grace.

Court ladies will to Country seats be gone,
My Lord can't all the year live great in Town,
Where wanting operas, basset,[8] and a play,
They'll sigh and stitch a gown, to pass the time away.
Gay City-wives at Tunbridge will appear,
Whose husbands long have labour'd for an heir;
Where many a courtier may their wants relieve,
But by the waters only they conceive.
The Fleet-Street sempstress[9]–toast of Temple sparks,
That runs spruce neckcloths for attorney's clerks;
At Cupid's gardens will her hours regale,
Sing fair Dorinda, and drink bottl'd ale.
At all assemblies, rakes are up and down,
And gamesters, where they think they are not known.
Shou'd I denounce our author's fate to day,
To cry down prophecies, you'd damn the play:
Yet whims like these have sometimes made you laugh;
'Tis tattling all, like Isaac Bickerstaff.[10]
Since war, and places claim the bards that write,
Be kind, and bear a woman's treat to night;
Let your indulgence all her fears allay,
And none but woman-haters damn this play.

Dramatis Personæ.

Sir *George Airy*.	Mr. *Wilks*.
Sir *Francis Gripe*.	Mr. *Estcourt*.
Charles.	Mr. *Mills*.
Sir *Jealous Traffick*.	Mr. *Bullock*.
Marplot.	Mr. *Pack*.
Whisper.	Mr. *Bullock* jun.
Miranda.	Mrs. *Cross*.
Isabinda.	Mrs. *Rogers*.
Patch.	Mrs. *Saunders*.
Scentwell.	Mrs. *Mills*.

ACT I. SCENE I. *The Park.*

[*Enter* Sir George Airy *meeting* Charles.]

CHARLES. Ha! Sir *George Airy*! A birding thus early, what forbidden game rouz'd you so soon?[11] For no lawful occasion cou'd invite a person of your figure abroad at such unfashionable hours.

SIR GEORGE. There are some men, *Charles*, whom Fortune[12] has left free from inquietudes, who are diligently studious to find out ways and means to make themselves uneasie.

CHARLES. Is it possible that any thing in nature can ruffle the temper of a man, whom the four seasons of the year compliment with as many thousand pounds, nay! and a father at rest with his ancestors.

SIR GEORGE. Why there 'tis now! A man that wants money thinks none can be unhappy that has it; but my affairs are in such a whimsical posture, that it will require a calculation of my nativity to find if my gold will relieve me or not.[13]

CHARLES. Ha, ha, ha, never consult the stars about that; gold has a power beyond them; gold unlocks the midnight councils; gold out-does the wind, becalms the ship, or fills her sails; gold is omnipotent below; it makes whole armies fight, or fly; it buys even souls, and bribes the wretches to betray their Country: then what can thy business be, that gold won't serve thee in?

SIR GEORGE. Why, I'm in love.

CHARLES. In love – Ha, ha, ha, ha; in love, ha, ha, ha, with what, prithee, a *Cherubin*!

SIR GEORGE. No, with a woman.

CHARLES. A woman, good! Ha, ha, ha, and gold not help thee?

SIR GEORGE. But suppose I'm in love with two –

CHARLES. Ay, if thou'rt in love with two hundred, gold will fetch 'em, I warrant thee, boy. But who are they? Who are they? Come.

SIR GEORGE. One is a lady, whose face I never saw, but witty as an angel; the other beautiful as *Venus* –

CHARLES. And a fool –

SIR GEORGE. For ought I know, for I never spoke to her, but you can inform me; I am charm'd by the wit of one, and dye for the beauty of the other?

CHARLES. And pray, which are you in quest of now?

SIR GEORGE. I prefer the sensual pleasure, I'm for her I've seen, who is thy father's ward *Miranda*.

CHARLES. Nay then, I pity you; for the Jew my father will no more part with her, and 30,000 pound, than he wou'd with a guinea to keep me from starving.

SIR GEORGE. Now you see gold can't do every thing, *Charles*.

CHARLES. Yes, for 'tis her gold that bars my father's gate against you.

SIR GEORGE. Why, if he is this avaricious wretch, how cam'st thou by such a liberal education?

CHARLES. Not a souse[14] out of his pocket, I assure you; I had an uncle who defray'd that charge, but for some little wildnesses of youth, tho' he made me his heir, left Dad my guardian till I came to years of discretion, which I presume the old gentleman will never think I am; and now he has got the estate into his clutches, it does me no more good, than if it lay in *Prester John*'s dominions.[15]

SIR GEORGE. What, can'st thou find no stratagem to redeem it?

CHARLES. I have made many essays to no purpose; tho' want, the mistress of invention, still tempts me on, yet still the old fox is too cunning for me – I am upon my last project, which if it fails, then for my last refuge, a brown musket.[16]

SIR GEORGE. What is't, can I assist thee?

CHARLES. Not yet; when you can, I have confidence enough in you to ask it.

SIR GEORGE. I am always ready, but what do's[17] he intend to do with *Miranda*? Is she to be sold in private? Or will he put her up by way of auction, at who bids most? If so, egad, I'm for him; my gold, as you say, shall be subservient to my pleasure.

CHARLES. To deal ingeniously with you, Sir *George*, I know very little of her, or home; for since my uncle's death, and my return from travel, I have never been well with my father; he thinks my expenses too great, and I his allowance too little; he never sees me, but he quarrels; and to avoid that, I shun his house as much as possible. The report is, he intends to marry her himself.

SIR GEORGE. Can she consent to it?

CHARLES. Yes faith, so they say; but I tell you, I am wholly ignorant of the matter. *Miranda* and I are like two violent members of a contrary party, I can scarce allow her beauty, tho' all the World do's; nor she me civility, for that contempt, I fancy she plays the mother-in-law already, and sets the old gentleman on to do mischief.

SIR GEORGE. Then I've your free consent to get her.

CHARLES. Ay and my helping-hand, if occasion be.

SIR GEORGE. Pugh, yonder's a fool coming this way. Let's avoid him.

CHARLES. What, *Marplot*? no no, he's my instrument; there's a thousand conveniences in him, he'll lend me his money when he has any, run of my errands and be proud on't; in short, he'll pimp for me, lye for me, drink for me, do any thing but fight for me, and that I trust to my own arm for.

SIR GEORGE. Nay then he's to be endur'd; I never knew his qualifications before.

[*Enter* Marplot *with a patch*[18] *cross his face.*

MARPLOT. Dear *Charles*, yours, – [*Aside*] *Ha! Sir George Airy, the man in the World, I have an ambition to be known to.* – Give me thy hand, Dear Boy –

CHARLES. A good assurance! But heark ye, how came your beautiful countenance clouded in the wrong place?

MARPLOT. I must confess 'tis a little *mal-a-propos*, but no matter for that; a word with you, *Charles*; prithee, introduce me to Sir *George* – he is a man of wit, and I'd give ten guineas to –

CHARLES. When you have 'em, you mean.

MARPLOT. Ay, when I have 'em; pugh, pox, you cut the thread of my discourse – I wou'd give ten guinea's, I say, to be rank'd in his acquaintance: Well, 'tis a vast addition to a man's fortune, according to the rout of the World, to be seen in the company of leading men; for then we are all thought to be politicians, or Whigs, or Jacks, or High-flyers, or Low-flyers, or Levellers – and so forth; for you must know, we all herd in parties now.[19]

CHARLES. Then a fool for diversion is out of fashion, I find.

MARPLOT. Yes, without it be a mimicking fool, and they are darlings every where; but prithee introduce me.

CHARLES. Well, on condition you'll give us a true account how you came by that mourning nose, I will.

MARPLOT. I'll do it.

CHARLES. Sir *George*, here's a gentleman has a passionate desire to kiss your hand.

SIR GEORGE. Oh, I honour men of the sword; and I presume this gentleman is lately come from *Spain* or *Portugal* – by his scars.

MARPLOT. No really, Sir *George*, mine sprung from civil fury, happening last night into the Groom-Porters – I had a strong inclination to go ten guineas with a sort of a, sort of a – kind of a milk sop, as I thought: a pox of the dice he flung out, and my pockets being empty as *Charles* knows they sometimes are, he prov'd a surly *North-Britain*, and broke my face for my deficiency.[20]

SIR GEORGE. Ha! ha! and did not you draw?

MARPLOT. Draw, Sir, why, I did but lay my hand upon my sword to make a swift retreat, and he roar'd out. Now the deel a ma sol, Sir, gin ye touch yer steel, ise whip mine through yer wem.[21]

SIR GEORGE. Ha, ha, ha,

CHARLES. Ha, ha, ha, ha, safe was the word, so you walk'd off, I suppose.

MARPLOT. Yes, for I avoid fighting, purely to be serviceable to my friends you know –

SIR GEORGE. Your friends are much oblig'd to you, Sir, I hope you'll rank me in that number.

MARPLOT. Sir *George*, a bow from the side box, or to be seen in your chariot, binds me ever yours.

SIR GEORGE. Trifles, you may command 'em when you please.

CHARLES. Provided he may command you –

MARPLOT. Me! Why I live for no other purpose – Sir *George*, I have the honour to be caressed[22] by most of the reigning toasts of the Town, I'll tell 'em you are the finest gentleman –

SIR GEORGE. No, no, prithee let me alone to tell the ladies – my parts – can you convey a letter upon occasion, or deliver a message with an air of business, ha!

MARPLOT. With the assurance of a page and the gravity of a statesman.

SIR GEORGE. You know *Miranda*!

MARPLOT. What, my sister ward? Why, her guardian is mine, we are fellow sufferers: Ah! he is a covetous, cheating, sanctify'd curmudgeon; that Sir Francis Gripe is a damn'd old –

CHARLES. I suppose, friend, you forget that he is my father –

MARPLOT. I ask your pardon, *Charles*, but it is for your sake I hate him. Well, I say, the World is mistaken in him, his out-side piety, makes him every man's executor, and his inside cunning, makes him every heir's jaylor. Egad, *Charles*, I'm half persuaded that thou'rt some *ward* too, and never of his getting: For thou art as honest a debauchee as ever cuckolded man of quality.

SIR GEORGE. A pleasant fellow.

CHARLES. The dog is diverting sometimes, or there wou'd be no enduring his impertinence: He is pressing to be employ'd and willing to execute, but some ill fate generally attends all he undertakes, and he oftner spoils an intreague than helps it –

MARPLOT. If I miscarry 'tis none of my fault. I follow my instructions.

CHARLES. Yes, witness the merchant's wife.

MARPLOT. Pish, pox, that was an accident.

SIR GEORGE. What was it, prithee?

CHARLES. Why, you must know, I had lent a certain merchant my hunting horses, and was to have met his wife in his absence. Sending him along with my groom to make the compliment, and to deliver a letter to the lady at the same time; what does he do, but gives the husband the letter, and offers her the horses.

MARPLOT. I remember you was even with me, for you deny'd the letter to be yours, and swore I had a design upon her, which my bones paid for.

CHARLES. Come, Sir *George*, let's walk round, if you are not ingag'd, for I have sent my man upon a little earnest business, and have order'd him to bring me the answer into the park.

MARPLOT. [*Aside*] *Business, and I not know it, egad I'll watch him.*

SIR GEORGE. I must beg your pardon, *Charles*, I am to meet your father here.

CHARLES. My father!

SIR GEORGE. Aye! and about the oddest bargain perhaps you ever heard of but I'll not impart till I know the success.

MARPLOT. [*Aside*] *What can his business be with Sir* Francis*? Now wou'd I give all the World to know it; why the devil should not one know every man's concern.*

CHARLES. Prosperity to't whate'er it be, I have private affairs too; over a bottle we'll compare notes.

MARPLOT. [*Aside*] Charles *knows I love a glass as well as any man. I'll make one; shall it be to night? – Ad*[23] *I long to know their secrets.*

[*Enter* Whisper.

WHISPER. Sir, Sir, Miss *Patch* says *Isabinda*'s Spanish father has quite spoil'd the plot, and she can't meet you in the park, but he infallibly will go out this afternoon, she says; but I must step again to know the hour.

MARPLOT. [*Aside*] *What did Whisper say now? I shall go stark mad, if I'm not let into this secret.*

CHARLES. Curst misfortune, come along with me, my heart feels pleasure at her name. Sir *George*, yours; we'll meet at the old place the usual hour.

SIR GEORGE. Agreed; I think I see Sir *Francis* yonder. [*Exit.*

CHARLES. *Marplot*, you must excuse me, I am engag'd. [*Exit.*

MARPLOT. Engag'd, egad I'll engage my life, I'll know what your engagement is. [*Exit.*

MIRANDA. [*Coming out of a Chair*][24] Let the chair wait. My servant that dog'd Sir *George* said he was in the Park. [*Enter* Patch] Ha! Miss *Patch* alone, did not you tell me you had contriv'd a way to bring *Isabinda* to the park?

PATCH. Oh, Madam, your Ladyship can't imagine what a wretched disappointment we have met with. Just as I had fetch'd a suit of my cloaths for a disguise, comes my old master into his closet, which is right against her chamber door; this struck us into a terrible fright – at length I put on a grave face, and ask'd him if he was at leisure for his chocolate, in hopes to draw him out of his hole; but he snap'd my nose off, 'no, I shall be busie here this two hours'; at which my poor mistress seeing no way of escape, order'd me to wait on your Ladyship with the sad relation.

MIRANDA. Unhappy *Isabinda*! Was ever any thing so unaccountable as the humour of Sir *Jealous Traffick*.

PATCH. Oh, Madam, it's his living so long in *Spain*. He vows he'll spend half his estate, but he'll be a Parliament-man on purpose to bring in a bill for women to wear veils, and the other odious *Spanish* customs – he swears it is the height of impudence to have a woman seen bare-fac'd even at church, and scarce believes there's a true begotten child in the City.

MIRANDA. Ha, ha, ha, how the old fool torments himself! Suppose he could introduce his rigid rules – does he think we cou'd not match them in contrivance? No, no; let the tyrant man make what laws he will, if there's a woman under the government, I warrant she finds a way to break 'em: is his mind set upon the *Spaniard* for his son-in-law still?

PATCH. Ay, and he expects him by the next fleet, which drives his daughter to melancholy and despair: But, Madam, I find you retain the same gay, cheerful spirit you had, when I waited on your Ladyship. – My Lady is mighty good-humour'd too, and I have found a way to make

Sir *Jealous* believe I am wholly in his interest, when my real design is to serve her; he makes me her jailor, and I set her at liberty.

MIRANDA. I knew thy prolifick brain wou'd be of singular service to her, or I had not parted with thee to her father.

PATCH. But, Madam, the report is that you are going to marry your guardian.

MIRANDA. It is necessary such a report shou'd be, *Patch*.

PATCH. But is it true, Madam?

MIRANDA. That's not absolutely necessary.

PATCH. I thought it was only the old strain, coaxing him still for your own, and railing at all the young fellows about Town; in my mind now, you are as ill plagu'd with your guardian, Madam, as my Lady is with her father.

MIRANDA. No, I have liberty, wench, that she wants; what would she give now to be in this *dissabilee*[25] in the – open air, nay more, in pursuit of the young fellow she likes; for that's my case, I assure thee.

PATCH. As for that, Madam, she's even with you; for tho' she can't come abroad, we have a way to bring him home in spight of old *Argus*.

MIRANDA. Now *Patch*, your opinion of my choice, for here he comes – ha! my guardian with him; what can be the meaning of this? I'm sure Sir *Francis* can't know me in this dress – let's observe 'em. [*They withdraw.*

[*Enter* Sir Francis Gripe *and* Sir George Airy.

SIR FRANCIS. Verily, Sir *George*, thou wilt repent throwing away thy money so, for I tell thee sincerely, *Miranda*, my charge do's not love a young fellow, they are all vicious, and seldom make good husbands; in sober sadness she cannot abide 'em.

MIRANDA. [*Peeping*] In sober sadness you are mistaken – what can this mean?

SIR GEORGE. Look ye, Sir *Francis*, whether she can or cannot abide young fellows is not the business; will you take the fifty guineas?

SIR FRANCIS. In good truth, I will not, for I knew thy father. He was a hearty wary man, and I cannot consent that his son should squander away what he sav'd, to no purpose.

MIRANDA. [*Peeping*] Now, in the name of wonder, what bargain can he be driving about me for fifty guineas?

PATCH. I wish it had been for the first night's lodging, Madam.[26]

SIR GEORGE. Well, Sir *Francis*, since you are so conscientious for my father's sake, then permit me the favour, *gratis*.

MIRANDA. [*Peeping*] The favour! Oh my life! I believe 'tis as you said, *Patch*.

SIR FRANCIS. No verily, if thou dost not buy thy experience, thou wou'd never be wise; therefore give me a hundred and try fortune.

SIR GEORGE. The scruples arose, I find, from the scanty sum – let me see – a hundred guineas – [*Takes 'em out of a purse and chinks 'em*] Ha! they have a very pretty sound, and a very pleasing look – but then, *Miranda* – but if she should be cruel –

MIRANDA. [*Peeping*] As ten to one I shall –

SIR FRANCIS. Ay, do consider on't, he, he, he, he.

SIR GEORGE. No, I'll do't.

PATCH. Do't, what, whether you will or no, Madam?

SIR GEORGE. Come to the point, here's the gold, sum up the conditions –

[Sir Francis *pulling out a paper.*

MIRANDA. [*Peeping*] Ay for heaven's sake do, for my expectation is on the rack.

SIR FRANCIS. Well at your own peril be it.

SIR GEORGE. Aye, aye, go on.

SIR FRANCIS. Imprimis,[27] you are to be admitted into my house in order to move your suit to *Miranda*, for the space of ten minutes, without lett or molestation, provided I remain in the same room.

SIR GEORGE. But out of ear shot –

SIR FRANCIS. Well, well, I don't desire to hear what you say, ha, ha, ha, in consideration I am to have that purse and a hundred guineas.

SIR GEORGE. Take it – [*Gives him the purse.*

MIRANDA. [*Peeping*] So, 'tis well it's no worse, I'll fit you both –

SIR GEORGE. And this agreement is to be perform'd to day.

SIR FRANCIS. Aye, aye, the sooner the better, poor fool, how *Miranda* and I shall laugh at him – Well, Sir *George*, ha, ha, ha, take the last sound of your guineas, ha, ha, ha. [*Chinks 'em. Exit* Sir Francis.

MIRANDA. [*Peeping*] Sure he does not know I am *Miranda*.

SIR GEORGE. A very extraordinary bargain I have made truly, if she should be really in love with this old cuff now – psha, that's morally impossible – but then what hopes have I to succeed, I never spoke to her –

MIRANDA. [*Peeping*] Say you so? Then I am safe.

SIR GEORGE. What tho' my tongue never spoke, my eyes said a thousand things, and my hopes flatter'd me hers answer'd 'em. If I'm lucky – if not, 'tis but a hundred guineas thrown away. [Miranda *and* Patch *come forwards*.

MIRANDA. Upon what Sir *George*?

SIR GEORGE. Ha! my *Incognita* – upon a woman, Madam.

MIRANDA. They are the worst things you can deal in, and damage the soonest; your very breath destroys 'em, and I fear you'll never see your return, Sir *George*, ha, ha!

SIR GEORGE. Were they more brittle than *china*, and drop'd to pieces with a touch, every atom of her I have ventur'd at, if she is but mistress of thy wit, ballances ten times the sum – prithee let me see thy face.

MIRANDA. By no means, that may spoil your opinion of my sense –

SIR GEORGE. Rather confirm it, Madam.

PATCH. So rob the lady of your gallantry, Sir.

SIR GEORGE. No Child, a dish of chocolate in the morning never spoils my dinner; the other lady, I design a set meal; so there's no danger –

MIRANDA. Matrimony! Ha, ha, ha; what crimes have you committed against the god of love, that he should revenge 'em so severely to stamp husband upon your forehead –

SIR GEORGE. For my folly in having so often met you here, without pursuing the laws of nature, and exercising her command – but I resolve e'er we part now, to know who you are, where you live, and what kind of flesh and blood your face is; therefore unmask and don't put me to the trouble of doing it for you.

MIRANDA. My face is the same flesh and blood with my hand, Sir *George*, which if you'll be so rude to provoke.

SIR GEORGE. You'll apply it to my cheek – the ladies favours are always welcome; but I must have that cloud withdrawn. [*Taking hold of her*] Remember you are in the *park*, Child, and what a terrible thing would it be to lose this pretty white hand.

MIRANDA. And how will it found in a *chocolate-house*, that Sir *George Airy* rudely pull'd off a ladies mask, when he had given her his honour, that he never would, directly or indirectly endeavour to know her till she gave him leave.

PATCH. [*Aside*] *I wish we were safe out.*

SIR GEORGE. But if that lady thinks fit to pursue and meet me at every turn like some troubl'd spirit, shall I be blam'd if I inquire into the reality? I would have nothing dissatisfy'd in a female shape.

MIRANDA. [*Pause*] What shall I do?

SIR GEORGE. Ay, prithee consider, for thou shalt find me very much at thy service.

PATCH. Suppose, Sir, the lady shou'd be in love with you.

SIR GEORGE. Oh! I'll return the obligation in a moment.

PATCH. And marry her?

SIR GEORGE. Ha, ha, ha, that's not the way to love her, Child.

MIRANDA. If he discovers me I shall die – which way shall I escape? – let me see. [*Pauses*.

SIR GEORGE. Well, Madam –

MIRANDA. I have it – Sir *George*, 'tis fit you should allow something; if you'll excuse my face, and turn your back (if you look upon me I shall sink, even mask'd as I am) I will confess why I have engag'd you so often, who I am, and where I live.

SIR GEORGE. Well, to show you I'm a man of honour I accept the conditions. – [*Aside*] *Let me but once know those, and the face won't be long a secret to me.*

PATCH. What mean you, Madam?

MIRANDA. To get off.

SIR GEORGE. 'Tis something indecent to turn one's back upon a lady; but you command and I obey. [*Turns his back*] Come, Madam, begin –

MIRANDA. First then it was my unhappy lot to see you at *Paris* [*Draws back a little while and speaks*] at a ball upon a birth-day; your shape and air charm'd my eyes; your wit and complaisance my soul, and from that fatal night I lov'd you. [*Drawing back*] And when you left the place, grief seiz'd me so – no rest my heart, no sleep my eyes cou'd know. – Last I resolv'd a hazardous point to try, and quit the place in search of liberty. [*Exit*.

SIR GEORGE. Excellent – I hope she's handsome – well, now, Madam, to the other two things: Your name, and where you live? – I am a gentleman, and this confession will not be lost upon me. – Nay, prithee don't weep, but go on – for I find my heart melts in thy behalf – speak quickly or I shall turn about – not yet. – Poor lady, she expects I shou'd comfort her; and to do her justice, she has said enough to encourage me. [*Turns about*] Ha? gone! The devil, jilted? Why, what a tale has she invented – of *Paris*, balls, and birth-days. – Egad I'd give ten guineas to know who this gipsie is. – A curse of my folly – I deserve to lose her; what woman can forgive a man that turns his back.

The bold and resolute, in love and war,
To conquer take the right, and swiftest way;
The boldest lover soonest gains the fair,
As courage makes the rudest force obey,
Take no denial, and the dames adore ye,
Closely pursue them and they fall before ye.

ACT II. SCENE I.

[*Enter* Sir Francis Gripe, Miranda.]

SIR FRANCIS. Ha, ha, ha, ha, ha, ha, ha.

MIRANDA. Ha, ha, ha, ha, ha, ha, ha; Oh, I shall die with laughing. – The most romantick adventure: ha, ha! what does the odious young fop mean? A hundred pieces to talk an hour with me; ho, ha.

SIR FRANCIS. And I'm to be by too; there's the jest. Adod,[28] if it had been in private, I shou'd not have car'd to trust the young dog.

MIRANDA. Indeed and indeed, but you might *Gardy*[29] – now methinks there's no body handsomer than you: so neat, so clean, so good-humour'd, and so loving. –

SIR FRANCIS. Pritty rogue, pritty rogue, and so thou shalt find me, if thou do'st prefer thy *Gardy* before these caperers of the age, thou shalt outshine the Queen's box on an *opera* night; thou shalt be the envy of the ring (for I will carry thee to *Hyde-Park*) and thy equipage shall surpass, the what – d'ye call 'em, ambassadors.

MIRANDA. Nay, I'm sure the discreet part of my sex will envy me more for the inside furniture, when you are in it, than my outside equipage.

SIR FRANCIS. A cunning baggage, a faith thou art, and a wise one too; and to show thee thou hast not chose amiss, I'll this moment disinherit my son, and settle my whole estate upon thee.

MIRANDA. – [*Aside*] *There's an old rogue now.* – No, *Gardy*, I would not have your name be so black in the World – you know my father's will runs, that I am not to possess my estate, without your consent, till I'm five and twenty; you shall only abate the odd seven years, and make me mistress of my estate to day, and I'll make you master of my person to morrow.

SIR FRANCIS. Humph? That may not be safe – no *Chargy*, I'll settle it upon thee for *pin-money*[30] and that will be every bit as well, thou know'st.

MIRANDA. [*Aside*] *Unconscionable old wretch, bribe me with my own money – which way shall I get out of his hands?*

SIR FRANCIS. Well, what art thou thinking on, my girl, ha? How to banter Sir *George*?

MIRANDA. – [*Aside*] *I must not pretend to banter: he knows my tongue too well.* – No, *Gardy*, I have thought of a way will confound him more than all I cou'd say, if I shou'd talk to him seven years.

SIR FRANCIS. How's that? Oh! I'm transported, I'm ravish'd, I'm mad –

MIRANDA. – [*Aside*] *It wou'd make you mad, if you knew all.*– I'll not answer him one word, but be dumb to all he says –

SIR FRANCIS. Dumb, good; ha, ha, ha. Excellent, ha, ha, I think I have you now, Sir *George*: dumb! He'll go distracted – well, she's the wittiest rogue – ha, ha, dumb! I can but laugh, ha, ha, to think how damn'd mad he'll be when he finds he has given his money away for a dumb show. Ha, ha, ha.

MIRANDA. Nay, *Gardy*, if he did but know my thoughts of him, it wou'd make him ten times madder: ha, ha, ha.

SIR FRANCIS. Ay, so it wou'd *Chargy*, to hold him in such derision, to scorn to answer him, to be dumb: ha, ha, ha, ha.

[*Enter* Charles.

SIR FRANCIS. How now, Sirrah, who let you in?

CHARLES. My necessity, Sir.

SIR FRANCIS. Sir, your necessities are very impertinent, and ought to have sent before they entred.

CHARLES. Sir, I knew 'twas a word wou'd gain admittance nowhere.

SIR FRANCIS. Then, Sirrah, how durst you rudely thrust that upon your father, which no body else wou'd admit?

CHARLES. Sure the name of a son is a sufficient plea. I ask this lady's pardon if I have intruded.

SIR FRANCIS. Ay, Ay, ask her pardon and her blessing too, if you expect any thing from me.

MIRANDA. I believe yours, Sir *Francis*, in a purse of guineas wou'd be more material. Your son may have business with you; I'll retire.

SIR FRANCIS. I guess his business, but I'll dispatch him; I expect the knight every minute: you'll be in readiness.

MIRANDA. Certainly! [*Aside*] *My expectation is more upon the wing than yours, Old Gentleman.* [*Exit.*

SIR FRANCIS. Well, Sir!

CHARLES. Nay, it is very ill, Sir; my circumstances are, I'm sure.

SIR FRANCIS. And what's that to me, Sir: your management shou'd have made them better.

CHARLES. If you please to intrust me with the management of my estate, I shall endeavour it, Sir.

SIR FRANCIS. What, to set upon a card, and buy a Lady's favour at the price of a thousand pieces, to rig out an equipage for a wench, or by your carelessness enrich your steward to fine for sheriff, or put up for Parliament-man.

CHARLES. I hope I shou'd not spend it this way: however, I ask only for what my uncle left me; yours you may dispose of as you please, Sir.

SIR FRANCIS. That I shall, out of your reach, I assure you, Sir. Adod these young fellows think old men get estates for nothing but them to squander away, in dicing, wenching, drinking, dressing, and so forth.

CHARLES. I think I was born a gentleman, Sir; I'm sure my uncle bred me like one.

SIR FRANCIS. From which you wou'd infer, Sir, that gaming, whoring, and the pox, are requisites to a gentleman.

CHARLES. [*Aside*] *Monstrous! When I wou'd ask him only for a support, he falls into these unmannerly reproaches; I must, tho' against my will, employ invention, and by stratagem relieve my self.*

SIR FRANCIS. Sirrah, what is it you mutter, Sirrah, ha? [*Holds up his cane*] I say, you sha'n't have a groat out of my hands till I please – and may be I'll never please, and what's that to you?

CHARLES. Nay, to be robb'd, or have one's throat cut is not much –

SIR FRANCIS. What's that, Sirrah? Wou'd ye rob me, or cut my throat, ye rogue?

CHARLES. Heaven forbid, Sir, – I said no such thing.

SIR FRANCIS. Mercy on me! What a plague it is to have a son of one and twenty, who wants to elbow one out of one's life, to edge himself into the estate.

[*Enter* Marplot.

MARPLOT. – [*Aside*] *Egad he's here – I was afraid I had lost him: his secret cou'd not be with his father, his wants are publick there* – Guardian, – your servant *Charles*, I know by that sorrowful countenance of thine. The old man's fist is as close as his strong box – but I'll help thee –

SIR FRANCIS. So: here's another extravagant coxcomb, that will spend his fortune before he comes to't; but he shall pay swinging interest, and so let the fool go on – well, what do's necessity bring you too, Sir?

MARPLOT. You have hit it, Guardian – I want a hundred pound.

SIR FRANCIS. For what?

MARPLOT. Po'gh, for a hundred things, I can't for my life tell you for what.

CHARLES. Sir, I suppose I have received all the answer I am like to have.

MARPLOT. Oh, the devil, if he gets out before me, I shall lose him again.

SIR FRANCIS. Ay, Sir, and you may be marching as soon as you please – I must see a change in your temper e'er you find one in mine.

MARPLOT. Pray, Sir, dispatch me; the money, Sir, I'm in mighty haste.

SIR FRANCIS. Fool, take this and go to the cashier; I sha'n't be long plagu'd with thee. [*Gives him a Note.*

MARPLOT. Devil take the cashier, I shall certainly have *Charles* gone before I come back again. [*Runs out.*

CHARLES. Well, Sir, I take my leave – but remember, you expose an only son to all the miseries of wretched poverty, which too often lays the plan for scenes of mischief.

SIR FRANCIS. Stay, *Charles*, I have a sudden thought come into my head, may prove to thy advantage.

CHARLES. Ha, does he relent?

SIR FRANCIS. My Lady *Wrinkle*, worth forty thousand pound, sets up for a handsome young husband; she prais'd thee t'other day; tho' the match-makers can get twenty guineas for a sight of her, I can introduce thee for nothing.

CHARLES. My Lady *Wrinkle*, Sir, why she has but one eye.

SIR FRANCIS. Then she'll see but half your extravagance, Sir.

CHARLES. Condemn me to such a piece of deformity! Toothless, dirty, wry-neck'd, hunch-back'd hag.

SIR FRANCIS. Hunch-back'd! so much the better, then she has a rest for her misfortunes; for thou wilt load her swingingly. Now I warrant you think, this is no offer of a father; forty thousand pound is nothing with you.

CHARLES. Yes, Sir, I think it is too much; a young beautiful woman with half the money wou'd be more agreeable. I thank you, Sir; but you chose better for your self, I find.

SIR FRANCIS. Out of my doors, you dog; you pretend to meddle with my marriage, Sirrah.

CHARLES. Sir, I obey: but –

SIR FRANCIS. But me no buts – be gone, Sir: dare to ask me for money again – refuse forty thousand pound! Out of my doors, I say, without reply. [*Exit* Charles.

[*Enter* Servant.

SERVANT. One Sir *George Airy* enquires for you, Sir.

[*Enter* Marplot *running*.

MARPLOT. Ha? gone! Is *Charles* gone, Guardian?

SIR FRANCIS. Yes; and I desire your wise worship to walk after him.

MARPLOT. Nay, egad, I shall run, I tell you but that. Ah, pox of the cashier for detaining me so long, where the devil shall I find him now. I shall certainly lose this secret. [*Exit hastily*.

SIR FRANCIS. What is the fellow distracted? – Desire Sir *George* to walk up – now for a tryal of skill that will make me happy, and him a fool. Ha, ha, ha, in my mind he looks like an ass already.

[*Enter* Sir George.

SIR FRANCIS. Well, Sir *George*, dee ye hold in the same mind? Or wou'd you capitulate? Ha, ha, ha: look, here are the guinea's, [*Chinks them*] ha, ha, ha.

SIR GEORGE. Not if they were twice the sum, Sir *Francis*: therefore be brief, call in the lady, and take your post – [*Aside*] *if she's a woman, and not seduc'd by witchcraft to this old rogue, I'll make his heart ake; for if she has but one grain of inclination about her, I'll vary a thousand shapes, but find it.*

[*Enter* Miranda.

SIR FRANCIS. Agreed – Miranda. There Sir George, try your fortune. [*Takes out his watch*.

SIR GEORGE. So from the eastern chambers breaks the sun, dispels the clouds, and gilds the vales below. [*Salutes her*.

SIR FRANCIS. Hold, Sir, kissing was not in our agreement.

SIR GEORGE. Oh! That's by way of prologue: – prithee, old Mammon,[31] to thy post.

SIR FRANCIS. Well, young *Timon*, 'tis now 4 exactly; one hour, remember is your utmost limit, not a minute more. [*Retires to the bottom of the stage*.

SIR GEORGE. Madam, whether you will excuse or blame my love, the author of this rash proceeding depends upon your pleasure, as also the life of your admirer; your sparkling eyes speak a heart susceptible of love; your vivacity a soul too delicate to admit the embraces of decay'd mortality.

MIRANDA. [*Aside*] *Oh, that I durst speak* –

SIR GEORGE. Shake off this tyrant *guardian*'s yoke, assume your self, and dash his bold aspiring hopes; the deity of his desires is avarice; a heretick in love, and ought to be banish'd by the queen of beauty. See, Madam, a faithful servant kneels and begs to be admitted in the number of your slaves. [Miranda *gives him her hand to raise him*.

SIR FRANCIS. I wish I cou'd hear what he says now. [*Running up*] Hold, hold, hold, no palming, that's contrary to articles –

SIR GEORGE. Death, Sir, keep your distance, or I'll write another article[32] in your guts. [*Lays his hand to his sword*.

SIR FRANCIS. [*Going back*] A bloody-minded fellow! –

SIR GEORGE. Not answer me! Perhaps she thinks my address too grave: I'll be more free – can you be so unconscionable, Madam, to let me say all these fine things to you without one single compliment in return? View me well, am I not a proper handsome fellow, ha? Can you prefer that old, dry, wither'd, sapless log of sixty-five, to the vigorous, gay, sprightly love of twenty-four? With snoring only he'll awake thee, but I with ravishing delight wou'd make thy senses dance in consort with the joyful minutes – ha? not yet, sure she is dumb – thus wou'd I steal and touch thy beauteous hand, [*Takes hold of her hand*] till by degrees I reach'd thy snowy breasts, then ravish kisses thus. [*Embraces her in ecstasy*.

MIRANDA. [*Struggles and flings from him, aside*] *Oh Heavens! I shall not be able to contain my self.*

SIR FRANCIS. [*Running up with his watch in his hand*] Sure she did not speak to him – there's three quarters of the hour gone, Sir *George* – adod, I don't like those close conferences –

SIR GEORGE. More interruptions – you will have it, Sir. [*Lays his hand to his sword*.

SIR FRANCIS. [*Going back, aside*] *No, no, you shan't have her neither.*

SIR GEORGE. Dumb still – [*Aside*] *sure this old dog has enjoyn'd her silence; I'll try another way* – I must conclude, Madam, that in compliance to your guardian's humour, you refuse to answer me –

consider the injustice of his injunction. This single hour cost me a hundred pound – and wou'd you answer me, I cou'd purchase the 24 so: however, Madam, you must give me leave to make the best interpretation I can for my money, and take the indication of your silence for the secret liking of my person: therefore, Madam, I will instruct you how to keep your word inviolate to Sir *Francis*, and yet answer me to every question: as for example, when I ask any thing, to which you wou'd reply in the affirmative, gently nod your head – thus; and when in the negative thus; [*Shakes his head*] and in the doubtful a tender sigh, thus [*Sighs*.

MIRANDA. [*Aside*] *How every action charms me – but I'll fit him for signs I warrant him.*

SIR FRANCIS. [*Aside*] *Ha, ha, ha, ha, poor Sir* George*, ha, ha, ha, ha.*

SIR GEORGE. Was it by his desire that you are dumb, Madam, to all that I can say? [Miranda *nods*] Very well! She's tractable I find – and is it possible that you can love him? [Miranda *nods*] Miraculous! Pardon the bluntness of my questions, for my time is short; may I not hope to supplant him in your esteem? [Miranda *sighs*] Good! She answers me as I could wish – you'll not consent to marry him then? [Miranda *sighs*] How, doubtful in that – undone again – humph! but that may proceed from his power to keep her out of her estate till twenty five; I'll try that – come, Madam, I cannot think you hesitate in this affair out of any motive, but your fortune – let him keep it till those few years are expir'd; make me happy with your person, let him enjoy your wealth – [Miranda *holds up her hands*] Why, what sign is that now? Nay, nay, Madam, except you observe my lesson, I can't understand your meaning –

SIR FRANCIS. What a vengeance, are they talking by signs? Gad I may be fool'd here; what do you mean, Sir *George*?

SIR GEORGE. To cut your throat if you dare mutter another syllable.

SIR FRANCIS. Od! I wish he were fairly out of my house.

SIR GEORGE. Pray, Madam, will you answer me to the purpose? [Miranda *shakes her head, and points to* Sir Francis] What! Does she mean she won't answer me to the purpose, or is she afraid yon' old cuff should understand her signs? – Aye, it must be that, I perceive, Madam, you are too apprehensive of the promise you have made to follow my rules; therefore I'll suppose your mind and answer for you – first, for my self, Madam, that I am in love with you is an infallible truth. Now for you: [*Turns on her side*] "indeed, Sir, and may I believe it" [*Turns again*] – as certainly, Madam, as that 'tis day light, or that I die if you persist in silence – bless me with the musick of your voice, and raise my spirits to their proper Heaven: thus low let me intreat; e'er I'm oblig'd to quit this place, grant me some token of a favourable reception to keep my hopes alive. [*Arises hastily turns of her side*] "Rise, Sir, and since my guardian's presence will not allow me privilege of tongue, read that and rest assured you are not indifferent to me." [*Offers her a Letter*] Ha! right woman! [*She strikes it down*] But no matter I'll go on.[33]

SIR FRANCIS. Ha! what's that a letter – Ha, ha, ha, thou art baulk'd.

MIRANDA. [*Aside*] *The best assurance I ever saw –*

SIR GEORGE. Ha? a letter, Oh! let me kiss it with the same raptures that I would do the dear hand that touch'd it. [*Opens it*] Now for a quick fancy and a long *extempore* – What's here? [*Reads*] "Dear, Sir *George*, this Virgin Muse I consecrate to you, which when it has receiv'd the addition of your voice, 'twill charm me into desire of liberty to love, which you, and only you can fix." My angel! Oh you transport me! [*Kisses the letter*] And see the power of your command; the god of love has set the verse already; the flowing numbers dance into a tune, and I'm inspir'd with a voice to sing it.

MIRANDA. [*Aside*] *I'm sure thou art inspir'd with impudence enough.*

SIR GEORGE. [*Sings*.

Great love inspire him;
Say I admire him.
Give me the lover
That can discover
Secret devotion
From silent motion;
Then don't betray me,
But hence convey me.

SIR GEORGE. [*Taking hold of* Miranda] With all my heart, this moment let's retire.

SIR FRANCIS. [*Coming up hastily*] The hour is expir'd, Sir, and you must take your leave. There, my girl, there's the hundred pound which thou hast won, go, I'll be with you presently, ha, ha, ha, ha. [*Exit* Miranda.

SIR GEORGE. Ads heart, Madam, you won't leave me just in the nick, will you?

SIR FRANCIS. Ha, ha, ha, she has nick'd you, Sir *George*, I think, ha, ha, ha: have you any more hundred pounds to throw away upon courtship, ha, ha, ha.

SIR GEORGE. He, he, he, he, a curse of your fleering[34] jests – yet, however ill I succeeded, I'll venture the same wager, she does not value thee a spoonful of snuff – nay more, though you enjoyn'd her silence to me, you'll never make her speak to the purpose with your self.

SIR FRANCIS. Ha, ha, ha, did not I tell thee thou would'st repent thy money? Did not I say she hated young fellows, ha, ha, ha.

SIR GEORGE. And I'm positive she's not in love with age.

SIR FRANCIS. Ha, ha, no matter for that, ha, ha, she's not taken with your youth, nor your rhetorick to boot, ha, ha.

SIR GEORGE. Whate'er her reasons are for disliking of me, I am certain she can be taken with nothing about thee.

SIR FRANCIS. Ha, ha, ha; how he swells with envy! – Poor man, poor man – ha, ha; I must beg your pardon, Sir *George*, *Miranda* will be impatient to have her share of mirth: verily we shall laugh at thee most egregiously; ha, ha, ha.

SIR GEORGE. With all my heart, faith – I shall laugh in my turn too – for if you dare marry her old *Belzebub*, you would be cuckolded most egregiously; remember that, and tremble –

She that to age her beauteous self resigns,
Shows witty management for close designs.
Then if thou'rt grac'd with fair Miranda's bed,
Actæon's[35] horns she means, shall crown thy head. [*Exit.*

SIR FRANCIS. Ha, ha, ha; he is mad.

These fluttering fops imagine they can wind,
Turn, and decoy to love, all women-kind:
But here's a proof of wisdom in my charge,
Old men are constant, young men live at large.
The frugal hand can bills at sight defray,
When he that lavish is, has nought to pay.

[*Exit.*

SCENE II.

Changes to Sir Jealous Traffick*'s House.* [*Enter* Sir Jealous, Isabinda, Patch *following.*]

SIR JEALOUS. What, in the balcony again, notwithstanding my positive commands to the contrary! – Why don't you write a bill upon your forehead, to show passengers there's something to be let –

ISABINDA. What harm can there be in a little fresh air, Sir?

SIR JEALOUS. Is your constitution so hot, Mistriss, that it wants cooling, ha? Apply the virtuous *Spanish* rules, banish your taste, and thoughts of flesh, feed upon roots, and quench your thirst with water.

ISABINDA. That, and a close room, wou'd certainly make me die of the vapours.

SIR JEALOUS. No, Mistriss, 'tis your high-fed, lusty, rambling, rampant ladies that are troubl'd with the vapours; 'tis your Ratifia, Persico, Cynamon, Citron, and Spirit of Clary,[36] cause such swi – m – ing in the brain, that carries many a guinea full-tide to the doctor. But you are not to be bred this way; no galloping abroad, no receiving visits at home; for in our loose Country, the women are as dangerous as the men.

PATCH. So I told her, Sir; and that it was not decent to be seen in a balcony – but she threaten'd to slap my chaps, and told me, I was her servant, not her governess.

SIR JEALOUS. Did she so? But I'll make her to know, that you are her *Duenna*:[37] oh that incompar able custom of *Spain*! Why here's no depending upon old women in my Country – for they are as wanton at eighty as a girl of eighteen; and a man may as safely trust to *Asgill*'s translation,[38] as to his great grand-mother's not marrying again.

ISABINDA. Or to the *Spanish* ladies's veils, and *Duennas*, for the safeguard of their honour.

SIR JEALOUS. Dare to ridicule the cautious conduct of that wise nation, and I'll have you lock'd up this fortnight, without a peephole.

ISABINDA. – [*Aside*] *If we had but the ghostly helps in England, which they have in Spain, I might deceive you if you did,* – Sir, 'tis not the restraint, but the innate principles, secures the reputation and honour of our sex – let me tell you, Sir, confinement sharpens the invention, as want of sight strengthens the other senses, and is often more pernicious than the recreation innocent liberty allows.

SIR JEALOUS. Say you so, Mistress, who the devil taught you the art of reasoning? I assure you, they must have a greater faith than I pretend to, that can think any woman innocent who requires liberty. Therefore, *Patch*, to your charge I give her; lock her up till I come back from change: I shall have some sauntring coxcomb, with nothing but a red coat and a feather, think, by leaping into her arms, to leap into my estate – but I'll prevent them. She shall be only Signior *Babinetto*'s.

PATCH. Really, Sir, I wish you wou'd employ any body else in this affair; I lead a life like a dog with obeying your commands. Come, Madam, will you please to be lock'd up.

ISABINDA. [*Aside*] *Ay, to enjoy more freedom than he is aware of.* [*Exit with* Patch.

SIR JEALOUS. I believe this wench is very true to my interest: I am happy I met with her, if I can but keep my daughter from being blown upon till Signior *Babinetto* arrives; who shall marry her as soon as he comes, and carry her to *Spain* as soon as he has marry'd her; she has a pregnant wit, and I'd no more have her an *English* wife, than the Grand Signior's Mistress. [*Exit.*

[*Enter* Whisper.

WHISPER. So, I see Sir *Jealous* go out; where shall I find Mrs. *Patch* now.

[*Enter* Patch.

PATCH. Oh Mr. *Whisper*, my Lady saw you out at the window, and order'd me to bid you fly, and let your master know she's now alone.

WHISPER. Hush, speak softly; I go, go: But hark'e Mrs. *Patch*, shall not you and I have a little confabulation, when my master and your Lady is engag'd?

PATCH. Ay, ay, farewell. [*Goes in, and shuts the door.*

[*Re-enter* Sir Jealous Traffick *meeting* Whisper.

SIR JEALOUS. Sure whil'st I was talking with Mr. *Tradewell*, I heard my door clap. [*Seeing* Whisper] Ha! a man lurking about my house; who do you want there, Sir?

WHISPER. [*Aside*] *Want – want, a pox, Sir Jealous! What must I say now? –*

SIR JEALOUS. Ay, want; have you a letter or message for any body there? – O my conscience, this is some he-bawd[39] –

WHISPER. Letter or message, Sir!

SIR JEALOUS. Ay, letter or message, Sir.

WHISPER. No, not I, Sir.

SIR JEALOUS. Sirrah, Sirrah, I'll have you set in the stocks, if you don't tell me your business immediately.

WHISPER. Nay, Sir, my business – is no great matter of business neither; and yet 'tis business of consequence too.

SIR JEALOUS. Sirrah, don't trifle with me.

WHISPER. Trifle, Sir, have you found him, Sir?

SIR JEALOUS. Found what, you rascal.

WHISPER. Why *Trifle* is the very lap-dog my Lady lost, Sir; I fancy'd I see him run into this house. I'm glad you have him – Sir, my Lady will be over-joy'd that I have found him.

SIR JEALOUS. Who is your Lady, friend?

WHISPER. My Lady Love-puppy, Sir.

SIR JEALOUS. My Lady Love-puppy! Then prithee carry thy self to her, for I know no other whelp that belongs to her; and let me catch ye no more puppy-hunting about my doors, lest I have you prest into the service, Sirrah.

WHISPER. By no means, Sir – your humble servant. – [*Aside*] *I must watch whether he goes, or no, before I can tell my master.* [*Exit.*

SIR JEALOUS. This fellow has the officious leer of a pimp; and I half suspect a design, but I'll be upon them before they think on me, I warrant 'em. [*Exit.*

SCENE III.

Charles' Lodging. [*Enter* Charles *and* Marplot.]

CHARLES. Honest Marplot, I thank thee for this supply; I expect my lawyer with a thousand pound I have order'd him to take up, and then you shall be repaid.

MARPLOT. Pho, pho, no more of that: here comes Sir *George Airy* – [*Enter* Sir George] cursedly out of humour at his disappointment; see how he looks! Ha, ha, ha.

SIR GEORGE. Ah, *Charles*, I am so humbled in my pretensions to plots upon women, that I believe I shall never have courage enough to attempt a chamber-maid again. – I'll tell thee.

CHARLES. Ha, ha; I'll spare you the relation by telling you – impatient to know your business with my father, when I saw you enter, I slipt back into the next room, where I overheard every syllable.

SIR GEORGE. That I said – but I'll be hang'd if you heard her answer – but prithee tell me, *Charles*, is she a fool?

CHARLES. I ne'er suspected her for one; but *Marplot* can inform you better, if you'll allow him a judge.

MARPLOT. A fool! I'll justifie she has more wit than all the rest of her sex put together; why she'll rally[40] me, till I han't one word to say for my self.

CHARLES. A mighty proof of her wit truly –

MARPLOT. There must be some trick in't, Sir *George*; egad I'll find it out if it cost me the sum you paid for't.

SIR GEORGE. Do and command me –

MARPLOT. Enough, let me alone to trace a secret.

[*Enter* Whisper, *and speaks aside to his master.*

MARPLOT. [*Aside*] *The devil! Whisper here again, that fellow never speaks out; is this the same, or a new secret? Sir George, won't you ask Charles what news Whisper brings?*

SIR GEORGE. Not I, Sir; I suppose it does not relate to me.

MARPLOT. Lord, Lord, how little curiosity some people have! Now my chief pleasure lies in knowing every body's business.

SIR GEORGE. I fancy, *Charles*, thou hast some engagement upon thy hands: I have a little business too. *Marplot*, if it falls in your way to bring me any intelligence from *Miranda*, you'll find me at the thatch'd house at six –

MARPLOT. You do me much honour.

CHARLES. You guess right, Sir *George*, wish me success.

SIR GEORGE. Better than attended me. *Adieu.* [*Exit.*

CHARLES. *Marplot*, you must excuse me –

MARPLOT. Nay, nay, what need of any excuse amongst friends! I'll go with you.

CHARLES. Indeed you must not.

MARPLOT. No, then I suppose 'tis a duel, and I will go to secure ye.

CHARLES. Secure me Why you won't fight.

MARPLOT. What then! I can call people to part ye.

CHARLES. Well, but it is no duel, consequently no danger. Therefore prithee be answer'd.

MARPLOT. What is't a mistress then? – Mum – you know I can be silent upon occasion.

CHARLES. I wish you cou'd be civil too: I tell you, you neither must nor shall go with me. Farewell. [*Exit.*

MARPLOT. Why then – I must and will follow you. [*Exit.*

ACT III. SCENE I.

[*Enter* Charles.]

CHARLES. Well, here's the house, which holds the lovely prize quiet and serene; here no noisy footmen throng to tell the World, that beauty dwells within; no ceremonious visit makes the lover wait; no rival to give my heart a pang; who wou'd not scale the window at midnight without fear of the jealous father's pistol, rather than fill up the train of a coquet, where every minute he is jostled out of place. [*Knocks softly.* Mrs. *Patch*, Mrs. *Patch.*

[*Enter* Patch.

PATCH. Oh, are you come, Sir? All's safe.

CHARLES. So in, in then.

[*Enter* Marplot.

MARPLOT. There he goes: who the devil lives here? Except I can find out that, I am as far from knowing his business as ever; gad I'll watch, it may be a bawdy-house, and he may have his throat cut; if there shou'd be any mischief, I can make oath, he went in. Well, *Charles*, in spight of your endeavour to keep me out of the secret; I may save your life, for ought I know: at that corner I'll plant my self; there I shall see whoever goes in, or comes out. Gad, I love discoveries. [*Exit.*

SCENE II.

[*SCENE Draws.*[41] Charles, Isabinda, *and* Patch.]

ISABINDA. *Patch*, look out sharp; have a care of Dad.

PATCH. I warrant you. [*Exit.*

ISABINDA. Well, Sir, if I may judge your love by your courage, I ought to believe you sincere; for you venture into the lyons den when you come to see me.

CHARLES. If you'd consent whilst the furious beast is abroad, I'd free you from the reach of his paws.

ISABINDA. That wou'd be but to avoid one danger, by running into another; like the poor wretches, who fly the burning ship and meet their fate in the water. Come, come, *Charles*, I fear if I consult my reason, confinement and plenty is better than liberty and starving. I know you'd make the frolick pleasing for a little time, by saying and doing a world of tender things; but when our small substance is once exhausted, and a thousand requisits for life are wanting; love, who rarely dwells with poverty, wou'd also fail us.

CHARLES. Faith, I fancy not; methinks my heart has laid up a stock will last for life; to back which, I have taken a thousand pound upon my uncle's estate; that surely will support us, till one of our fathers relent.

ISABINDA. There's no trusting to that my friend, I doubt your father will carry his humour to the grave, and mine till he sees me settled in *Spain*.

CHARLES. And can ye then cruelly resolve to stay till that curs'd *Don* arrives, and suffer that youth, beauty, fire and wit, to be sacrific'd to the arms of a dull *Spaniard*, to be immur'd[42] and forbid the sight of any thing that's humane.

ISABINDA. No, when it comes to the extremity, and no stratagem can relieve us, thou shalt list for a soldier, and I'll carry thy knapsack after thee.

CHARLES. Bravely resolv'd; the World cannot be more savage than our parents, and fortune generally assists the bold; therefore consent now: why shou'd we put it to a future hazard? Who knows when we shall have another opportunity?

ISABINDA. Oh, you have your ladder of ropes, I suppose, and the closet window stands just where it did; and if you han't forgot to write in characters,[43] *Patch* will find a way for our assignations. Thus much of the *Spanish* contrivancemy father's severity has taught me. I thank him; tho' I hate the nation, I admire their management in these affairs.

[*Enter* Patch.

PATCH. Oh, Madam, I see my master coming up the street.

CHARLES. Oh the devil, wou'd I had my ladder now; I thought you had not expected him till night; why, why, why, why; what shall I do, Madam?

ISABINDA. Oh, for Heaven's sake! Don't go that way, you'll meet him full in the teeth: Oh unlucky moment! –

CHARLES. Adsheart,[44] can you shut me into no cupboard, ram me into no chest, ha?

PATCH. Impossible, Sir, he searches every hole in the house.

ISABINDA. Undone for ever! If he sees you, I shall never see you more.

PATCH. I have thought on't: run you to your chamber, Madam; and Sir, come you along with me, I'm certain you may easily get down from the balcony.

CHARLES. My life, *Adieu* – lead on, guide. [*Exit.*

ISABINDA. Heaven preserve him. [*Exit.*

SCENE III. SCENE changes to the street.

[*Enter* Sir Jealous, *with* Marplot *behind him.*]

SIR JEALOUS. I don't know what's the matter; but I have a strong suspicion, all is not right within; that fellow's sauntring about my door, and his tale of a puppy had the face of a lye, methought. By St. *Iago*, if I shou'd find a man in the house, I'd make mince-meat of him –

MARPLOT. [*Aside*] *Ah, poor Charles – ha? Agad he is old – I fancy I might bully him, and make Charles have an opinion of my courage.*

SIR JEALOUS. My own key shall let me in; I'll give them no warning. [*Feeling for his key.*

MARPLOT. What's that you say, Sir. [*Going up to* Sir Jealous.

SIR JEALOUS. What's that to you, Sir. [*Turns quick upon him.*

MARPLOT. Yes, 'tis to me, Sir; for the gentleman you threaten is a very honest gentleman. Look to't, for if he comes not as safe out of your house, as he went in, I have half a dozen *Mirmidons*[45] hard by shall beat it about your ears.

SIR JEALOUS. Went in; what is he in then? Ah! A combination to undo me – I'll *Mirmidon* you, ye dog you – thieves, thieves. [*Beats* Marplot, *all this while he cries thieves.*

MARPLOT. Murder, murder; I was not in your house, Sir.

[*Enter* Servant.

SERVANT. What's the matter, Sir?

SIR JEALOUS. The Matter, rascals? Have you let a man into my house; but I'll flea him alive. Follow me, I'll not leave a mousehole unsearch'd; if I find him, by St. I*ago*, I'll equip him for the *Opera*.[46] [*Exit.*

MARPLOT. A duce of his cane, there's no trusting to age – what shall I do to relieve *Charles*! Egad, I'll raise the neighbourhood – murder, murder – [Charles *drops down upon him from the balcony*] *Charles*, faith I'm glad to see thee safe out, with all my heart.

CHARLES. A pox of your bawling. How the devil came you here?

MARPLOT. Here, gad I have done you a piece of service; I told the old thunderbolt that the gentleman that was gone in was –

CHARLES. Was it you that told him, Sir? [*Laying hold of him*] Z'death, I cou'd crush thee into atoms. [*Exit* Charles.

MARPLOT. What will you choak me for my kindness? – Will my enquiring soul never leave searching into other peoples affairs, till it gets squeez'd out of my body? I dare not follow him now, for my blood, he's in such a passion – I'll to *Miranda*; if I can discover ought that may oblige Sir *George*, it may be a means to reconcile me again to *Charles*. [*Exit.*

[*Enter* Sir Jealous *and* Servants.

SIR JEALOUS. Are you sure you have search'd every where?

SERVANT. Yes, from the top of the house to the bottom.

SIR JEALOUS. Under the beds, and over the beds?

SERVANT. Yes, and in them too, but found no body, Sir.

SIR JEALOUS. Why, what cou'd this rogue mean?

[*Enter* Isabinda *and* Patch.

PATCH. [*Aside to* Isabinda] Take courage, Madam, I saw him safe out.

ISABINDA. Bless me! What's the matter, Sir?

SIR JEALOUS. You know best – pray where's the man that was here just now?

ISABINDA. What man, Sir? I saw none!

PATCH. Nor I, by the trust you repose in me; do you think I wou'd let a man come within these doors, when you were absent?

SIR JEALOUS. Ah *Patch*, she may be too cunning for thy honesty; the very scout that he had set to give warning discover'd it to me – and threaten'd me with half a dozen *Mirmidons* – but I think I maul'd the villain. These afflictions you draw upon me, Mistress!

ISABINDA. Pardon me, Sir, 'tis your own ridiculous humour draws you into these vexations, and gives every fool pretence to banter you.

SIR JEALOUS. No, 'tis your idle conduct, your coquetish flurting into the balcony – oh with what joy shall I resign thee into the arms of Don *Diego Babinetto*!

ISABINDA. [*Aside*] *And with what industry shall I avoid him!*

SIR JEALOUS. Certainly that rogue had a message from some body or other; but being baulk'd by my coming, popt that sham upon me. Come along, ye sots, let's see if we can find the dog again. *Patch*, lock her up; d'ye hear? [*Exit with* Servants.

PATCH. Yes, Sir – ay, walk till your heels ake, you'll find no body, I promise you.

ISABINDA. Who cou'd that scout be, which he talks of?

PATCH. Nay, I can't imagine, without it was *Whisper*.

ISABINDA. Well, dear *Patch*, let's employ all our thoughts how to escape this horrid Don *Diego*; my very heart sinks at his terrible name.

PATCH. Fear not, Madam, Don *Carlo* shall be the man, or I'll lose the reputation of contriving; and then what's a chambermaid good for?

ISABINDA. Say'st thou so, my girl: Then – Let Dad be jealous, multiply his cares,
While love instructs me to avoid the snares;
I'll, spight of all his Spanish caution, show
How much for love a British maid can do.
[*Exit.*

SCENE IV. Sir Francis Gripe's House.

[Sir Francis *and* Miranda *meeting.*]

MIRANDA. Well, *Gardee*, how did I perform my dumb scene?

SIR FRANCIS. To admiration – thou dear little rogue, let me buss[47] thee for it: nay, adod, I will, *Chargee*, so muzle, and tuzle, and hug thee; I will, I faith, I will. [*Hugging and kissing her.*

MIRANDA. Nay, *Gardee*, don't be so lavish; who wou'd ride post, when the journey lasts for life?

SIR FRANCIS. Ah wag, ah wag – I'll buss thee again for that.

MIRANDA. [*Aside*] *Faugh! How he stinks of tobacco! What a delicate bedfellow I shou'd have!*

SIR FRANCIS. Oh I'm transported! When, when, my dear, wilt thou convince the World of thy happy day? When shall we marry, ha?

MIRANDA. There's nothing wanting but your consent, Sir *Francis*.

SIR FRANCIS. My consent! What do's my charmer mean?

MIRANDA. Nay, 'tis only a whim: But I'll have every thing according to form – therefore when you sign an authentick paper, drawn up by an able lawyer, that I have your leave to marry, the next day makes me yours, *Gardee*.

SIR FRANCIS. Ha, ha, ha, a whim indeed! Why is it not demonstration I give my leave when I marry thee.

MIRANDA. Not for your reputation, *Gardee*; the malicious World will be apt to say, you trick'd me into marriage, and so take the merit from my choice. Now I will have the act my own, to let the idle fops see how much I prefer a man loaded with years and wisdom.

SIR FRANCIS. Humph! Prithee leave out years, *Chargee*, I'm not so old, as thou shalt find: adod, I'm young; there's a caper[48] for ye. [*Jumps.*

MIRANDA. Oh never excuse it, why I like you the better for being old – but I shall suspect you don't love me, if you refuse me this formality.

SIR FRANCIS. Not love thee, *Chargee*! Adod I do love thee better than, than, than, better than – what shall I say? Egad, better than money, I faith I do –

MIRANDA. [*Aside*] *That's false I'm sure.* [*To* Sir Francis] *To prove it do this then.*

SIR FRANCIS. Well, I will do it, *Chargee*, provided I bring a license at the same time.

MIRANDA. Ay, and a parson too, if you please; ha, ha, ha, I can't help laughing to think how all the young coxcombs about Town will be mortify'd when they hear of our marriage.

SIR FRANCIS. So they will, so they will; ha, ha, ha.

MIRANDA. Well, I fancy I shall be so happy with my *Gardee*!

SIR FRANCIS. If wearing pearls and jewels, or eating gold, as the old saying is, can make thee happy, thou shall be so, my sweetest, my lovely, my charming, my – verily I know not what to call thee.

MIRANDA. You must know, *Gardee*, that I am so eager to have this business concluded, that I have employ'd my woman's brother, who is a lawyer in the *Temple*, to settle matters just to your liking, you are to give your consent to my marriage, which is to your self, you know: but mum, you must take no notice of that. So then I will, that is, with your leave, put my writings into his hands; then to morrow we come slap upon them with a wedding that no body thought on; by which you seize me and my estate, and I suppose make a bonfire of your own act and deed.

SIR FRANCIS. Nay, but Chargee, if –

MIRANDA. Nay, Gardee, no ifs – have I refus'd three Northern lords, two British peers, and half a score knights, to have you put in your ifs? –

SIR FRANCIS. So thou hast indeed, and I will trust to thy management. Od, I'm all of a fire.

MIRANDA. 'Tis a wonder the dry stubble does not blaze.

[*Enter* Marplot.

SIR FRANCIS. How now! Who sent for you, Sir? What's the hundred pound gone already?

MARPLOT. No, Sir, I don't want money now.

SIR FRANCIS. No, that's a miracle! But there's one thing you want, I'm sure.

MARPLOT. Ay, what's that, *Guardian*?

SIR FRANCIS. Manners; what had I no servants without?

MARPLOT. None that cou'd do my business, *Guardian*, which is at present with this Lady.

MIRANDA. With me, Mr. *Marplot*! What is it, I beseech you?

SIR FRANCIS. Ay, Sir, what is it? Any thing that relates to her may be deliver'd to me.

MARPLOT. I deny that.

MIRANDA. That's more than I do, Sir.

MARPLOT. Indeed, Madam, why then to proceed: fame says, that you and my most conscionable *Guardian* here, design'd, contriv'd, plotted and agreed to chouse a very civil, honourable, honest gentleman, out of a hundred pound.

MIRANDA. That I contrived it!

MARPLOT. Ay you – you said never a word against it, so far you are guilty.

SIR FRANCIS. Pray tell that civil, honourable, honest gentleman, that if he has any more such sums to fool away, they shall be received like the last; ha, ha, ha, ha, chous'd, quotha! But hark ye, let him know at the same time, that if he dare to report I trick'd him of it, I shall recommend a lawyer to him shall shew him a trick for twice as much; d'ye hear, tell him that.

MARPLOT. So, and this is the way you use a gentleman, and my friend.

MIRANDA. Is the wretch thy friend?

MARPLOT. The wretch! Look ye, Madam, don't call names, egad I won't take it.

MIRANDA. Why you won't beat me, will you? Ha, ha.

MARPLOT. I don't know whether I will or no.

SIR FRANCIS. Sir, I shall make a servant shew you out at the window if you are sawcy.

MARPLOT. I am your most humble servant, *Guardian*; I design to go out the same way I came in. I wou'd only ask this Lady, if she do's not think in her soul Sir *George Airy* is not a fine gentleman.

MIRANDA. He dresses well.

SIR FRANCIS. Which is chiefly owing to his taylor, and *Valet de Chamber*.

MIRANDA. And if you allow that a proof of his being a fine gentleman, he is so.

MARPLOT. The judicious part of the World allow him wit, courage, gallantry and management; tho' I think he forfeited that character, when he flung away a hundred pound upon your dumb Ladyship.

SIR FRANCIS. Does that gaul him? Ha, ha, ha.

MIRANDA. So, Sir *George* remaining in deep discontent, has sent you his trusty squire, to utter his complaint: ha, ha, ha.

MARPLOT. Yes, Madam; and you, like a cruel, hard-hearted Jew, value it no more – than I wou'd your Ladyship, were I Sir *George*, you, you, you –

MIRANDA. Oh, don't call names. I know you love to be employ'd, and I'll oblige you; and you shall carry him a message from me.

MARPLOT. According as I like it: what is it?

MIRANDA. Nay, a kind one you may be sure – first tell him, I have chose this gentleman to have, and to hold, and so forth. [*Clapping her hand into* Sir Francis*'s*.

SIR FRANCIS. [*Aside*] *Oh the dear rogue, how I dote on her!*

MIRANDA. And advise his impertinence to trouble me no more, for I prefer Sir *Francis* for a husband before all the fops in the universe.

MARPLOT. Oh Lord, oh Lord! She's bewitch'd, that's certain; here's a husband for eighteen – here's a shape – here's bones ratling in a leathern bag. [*Turning* Sir Francis *about*] Here's buckram, and canvass,[49] to scrub you to repentance.

SIR FRANCIS. Sirrah, my cane shall teach you repentance presently.

MARPLOT. No faith, I have felt its twin-brother from just such a wither'd hand too lately.

MIRANDA. One thing more; advise him to keep from the garden gate on the left hand. For if he dares to saunter there, about the hour of eight, as he used to do, he shall be saluted with a pistol or a blunderbuss.

SIR FRANCIS. Oh monstrous! Why *Chargee*; did he use to come to the garden gate?

MIRANDA. The gardner describ'd just such another man that always watch'd his coming out, and fain wou'd have bribed him for his entrance – tell him he shall find a warm reception if he comes this night.

MARPLOT. Pistols and blunderbusses! Egad, a warm reception indeed; I shall take care to inform him of your kindness, and advise him to keep farther off.

MIRANDA. [*Aside*] *I hope he will understand my meaning better, than to follow your advice.*

SIR FRANCIS. Thou hast sign'd, seal'd, and ta'en possession of my heart; for ever, *Chargee*, ha, ha, ha; and for you, Mr. Sauce-box, let me have no more of your messages, if ever you design to inherit your estate, Gentleman.

MARPLOT. Why there 'tis now. Sure I shall be out of your clutches one day. – Well, *Guardian*, I say no more; but if you be not as errant a cuckold as e're drove bargain upon the exchange, or paid attendance to a court, I am the son of a whetstone; and so your humble servant. [*Exit.*

MIRANDA. Don't forget the message; ha, ha.

SIR FRANCIS. I am so provok'd! – 'Tis well he's gone.

MIRANDA. Oh mind him not, *Gardee*, but let's sign articles, and then –

SIR FRANCIS. And then – adod, I believe I am metamorphos'd; my pulse beats high, and my blood boils, methinks – [*Kissing and hugging her.*

MIRANDA. Oh fye, *Gardee*, be not so violent; consider the market lasts all the year – well, I'll in and see if the lawyer be come, you'll follow. [*Exit.*

SIR FRANCIS. Ay, to the World's end, my dear. Well, *Frank*, thou art a lucky fellow in thy old age, to have such a delicate morsel, and thirty thousand pound in love with thee; I shall be the envy of batchelors, the glory of marry'd men, and the wonder of the Town. Some guardians wou'd be glad to compound for part of the estate at dispatching an heiress, but I engross the whole: *O! Mihi præteritos referet si Jupiter Annos.*[50] [*Exit.*

SCENE V. Changes to a Tavern.

[*Discovers* Sir George *and* Charles *with wine before them, and* Whisper *waiting.*]

SIR GEORGE. Nay, prithee don't be grave, *Charles*; misfortunes will happen: ha, ha, ha, 'tis some comfort to have a companion in our sufferings.

CHARLES. I am only apprehensive for *Isabinda*, her father's humour is implacable; and how far his jealousie may transport him to her undoing, shocks my soul to think.

SIR GEORGE. But since you escap'd undiscover'd by him, his rage will quickly lash into a calm, never fear it.

CHARLES. But who knows what that unlucky dog, *Marplot*, told him; nor can I imagine what brought him thither; that fellow is ever doing mischief; and yet, to give him his due, he never designs it. This is some blundering adventure, wherein he thought to shew his friendship, as he calls it: a curse on him.

SIR GEORGE. Then you must forgive him; what said he?

CHARLES. Said! Nay, I had more mind to cut his throat, than hear his excuses.

SIR GEORGE. Where is he?

WHISPER. Sir, I saw him go into Sir *Francis Gripe*'s just now.

CHARLES. Oh! Then he is upon your business, Sir *George*; a thousand to one, but he makes some mistake there too.

SIR GEORGE. Impossible, without he huffs the lady, and makes love to Sir *Francis*.

[*Enter* Drawer.

DRAW. Mr. *Marplot* is below, Gentlemen, and desires to know if he may have leave to wait upon ye.

CHARLES. How civil the rogue is when he has done a fault!

SIR GEORGE. Ho! Desire him to walk up. Prithee, *Charles*, throw off this chagreen,[51] and be good company.

CHARLES. Nay, hang him, I'm not angry with him. *Whisper*, fetch me pen, ink and paper.

WHISPER. Yes, Sir.

[*Exit* Whisper. *Enter* Marplot.

CHARLES. Do but mark his sheepish look, Sir *George*.

MARPLOT. Dear *Charles*, don't o'erwhelm a man – already under insupportable affliction. I'm sure I always intend to serve my friends; but if my malicious stars deny the happiness, is the fault mine?

SIR GEORGE. Never mind him, Mr. *Marplot*, he is eat up with spleen. But tell me, what says *Miranda*?

MARPLOT. Says – nay, we are all undone there too.

CHARLES. I told you so; nothing prospers that he undertakes.

MARPLOT. Why can I help her having chose your father for better for worse?

CHARLES. So: there's another of fortune's strokes; I suppose I shall be edg'd out of my estate, with twins every year, let who will get 'em.

SIR GEORGE. What is the woman really possest?

MARPLOT. Yes with the spirit of contradiction, she rail'd at you most prodigiously.

SIR GEORGE. That's no ill sign.

[*Enter* Whisper, *with pen, ink and paper.*

MARPLOT. You'd say it was no good sign, if you knew all.

SIR GEORGE. Why, prithee?

MARPLOT. Hark'e, Sir *George*. Let me warn you, pursue your old haunt no more, it may be dangerous. [Charles *sits down to write.*

SIR GEORGE. My old haunt, what d'you mean?

MARPLOT. Why in short then, since you will have it, *Miranda* vows if you dare approach the garden-gate at eight a clock, as you us'd, you shall be saluted with a blunderbuss, Sir. These were her words; nay, she bid me tell you so too.

SIR GEORGE. Ha! The garden-gate at eight, as I us'd to do! There must be a meaning in this. Is there such a gate, *Charles*?

CHARLES. Yes, yes; it opens into the park, I suppose her Ladyship has made many a scamper through it.

SIR GEORGE. It must be an assignation then. Ha, my heart springs with joy, 'tis a propitious omen. My dear *Marplot*, let me embrace thee, thou art my friend, my better angel –

MARPLOT. What do you mean, Sir *George*?

SIR GEORGE. No matter what I mean. Here take a bumper to the garden-gate, ye dear rogue, you.

MARPLOT. You have reason to be transported, Sir *George*; I have sav'd your life.

SIR GEORGE. My life! Thou hast sav'd my soul, man. *Charles*, if thou do'st not pledge this health, may'st thou never taste the joys of love.

CHARLES. *Whisper*, be sure you take care how you deliver this [*gives him the Letter*] Bring me the answer to my lodgings.

WHISPER. I warrant you, Sir. [*Exit.*

MARPLOT. Whither does that letter go? – Now dare I not ask for my blood.

CHARLES. Now I'm for you.

SIR GEORGE. To the garden-gate at the hour of eight, *Charles*, along, huzza!

CHARLES. I begin to conceive you.

MARPLOT. That's more than I do, egad – to the garden-gate, huzza, [*Drinks*] but I hope you design to keep far enough off on't, Sir *George*.

SIR GEORGE. Ay, ay, never fear that; she shall see I despise her frowns, let her use her blunderbuss against the next fool, she shan't reach me with the smoak, I warrant her, ha, ha, ha.

MARPLOT. Ay, *Charles*, if you cou'd receive a disappointment thus *en cavalier*[52] one shou'd have some comfort in being beat for you.

CHARLES. The fool comprehends nothing.

SIR GEORGE. Nor wou'd I have him; prithee take him along with thee.

CHARLES. Enough: *Marplot*, you shall go home with me.

MARPLOT. I'm glad I'm well with him however. Sir *George*, yours. Egad, *Charles*, asking me to go home with him, gives me a shrewd suspicion there's more in the garden-gate, than I comprehend. Faith, I'll give him the drop, and away to *Guardian*'s, and find it out.

SIR GEORGE. I kiss both your hands – and now for the garden-gate.

Its beauty gives the assignation there,
And love too powerful grows t'admit of fear.
[*Exit.*

ACT IV. SCENE I.

[*Scene the Outside of* Sir Jealous Traffick*'s House.* Patch *peeping out of door.* *Enter* Whisper.]

WHISPER. Ha, Mrs. *Patch*, this is a lucky minute to find you so readily; my master dies with impatience.

PATCH. My Lady imagin'd so, and by her orders I have been scouting this hour in search of you, to inform you that Sir *Jealous* has invited some friends to supper with him to night, which gives an opportunity to your master to make use of his ladder of ropes: the closet window shall be open, and *Isabinda* ready to receive him; bid him come immediately.

WHISPER. Excellent, he'll not disappoint I warrant him: but hold, I have a letter here, which I'm to carry an answer of. I can't think what language the direction is.

PATCH. Pho, 'tis no language, but a character which the lovers invented to avert discovery: ha, I hear my old master coming down stairs, it is impossible you shou'd have an answer; away, and bid him come himself for that – begone we are ruin'd if you're seen, for he has doubl'd his care since the last accident.

WHISPER. I go, I go. [*Exit.*

PATCH. There, go thou into my pocket. [*Puts it besides, and it falls down*] Now I'll up the back stairs, lest I meet him. Well, a dexterous chamber-maid is the ladies best utensil, I say. [*Exit.*

[*Enter* Sir Jealous *with a Letter in his Hand.*

SIR JEALOUS. So, this is some comfort, this tells me that *Signior Don Diego Babinetto* is safely arriv'd, he shall marry my daughter the minute he comes, ha. What's here [*Takes up the letter Patch drop'd*] a letter! I don't know what to make of the superscription. I'll see what's within side, [*Opens it*] humph; 'tis *Hebrew* I think. What can this mean. There must be some trick in it; this was certainly design'd for my daughter, but I don't know that she can speak any language but her mother-tongue. No matter for that, this may be one of love's hieroglyphicks, and I fancy I saw *Patch*'s tail sweep by. That wench may be a slut, and instead of guarding my honour, betray it; I'll find it out I'm resolv'd; who's there? What answer did you bring from the gentlemen I sent you to invite?

SERVANT. That they'd all wait of you, Sir, as I told you before, but I suppose you forget, Sir.

SIR JEALOUS. Did I so, Sir, but I shan't forget to break your head, if any of 'em come, Sir.

SERVANT. Come, Sir, why did not you send me to desire their company, Sir?

SIR JEALOUS. But I send you now to desire their absence; say I have something extraordinary fallen out, which calls me abroad, contrary to expectation, and ask their pardon, and d'ye hear, send the butler to me.

SERVANT. Yes, Sir. [*Exit.*

[*Enter* Butler.

SIR JEALOUS. If this paper has a meaning I'll find it. Lay the cloth in my daughter's chamber, and bid the cook send supper thither presently.[53]

BUTLER. Yes, Sir, – [*Aside*] *hey day, what's the matter now?* [*Exit.*

SIR JEALOUS. He wants the eyes of Argus, that has a young handsome daughter in this Town, but my comfort is, I shall not be troubl'd long with her. He that pretends to rule a girl once in her teens, had better be at sea in a storm, and would be in less danger.

For let him do, or counsel all he can,
She thinks and dreams of nothing else but
man. [*Exit.*

SCENE II. Isabinda's Chamber.

[Isabinda *and* Patch.]

ISABINDA. Are you sure, no body saw you speak to *Whisper*?

PATCH. Yes, very sure Madam, but I heard Sir *Jealous* coming down stairs, so I clap'd this letter into my pocket. [*Feels for the letter.*

ISABINDA. A letter! Give it me quickly.

PATCH. Bless me! What's become on't – I'm sure I put it – [*Searching still.*

ISABINDA. Is it possible, thou could'st be so careless – Oh! I'm undone for ever if it be lost.

PATCH. I must have drop'd it upon the stairs. But why are you so much alarm'd, if the worst happens no body can read it, Madam, nor find out whom it was design'd for.

ISABINDA. If it falls into my father's hands the very figure of a letter will produce ill consequences. Run and look for it upon the stairs this moment.

PATCH. Nay, I'm sure it can be no where else. – [*As she's going out of the door meets the* Butler] How now, what do you want?

BUTLER. My Master order'd me to lay the cloth here for his supper.

ISABINDA. [*Aside*] *Ruin'd past redemption* –

PATCH. You mistake sure; what shall we do?

ISABINDA. I thought he expected company to night – Oh! Poor *Charles* – Oh! Unfortunate *Isabinda.*

BUTLER. I thought so too Madam, but I suppose he has alter'd his mind. [*Lays the cloth, and Exit.*

ISABINDA. The letter is the cause; this heedless action has undone me: fly and fasten the closet-window, which will give *Charles* notice to retire. Ha, my father, oh! Confusion.

[*Enter* Sir Jealous.

SIR JEALOUS. Hold, hold, *Patch*, whither are you going. I'll have no body stir out of the room till after supper.

PATCH. Sir, I was only going to reach your easie chair – Oh! Wretched accident!

SIR JEALOUS. I'll have no body stir out of the room. I don't want my easie chair.

ISABINDA. [*Aside*] *What will be the event of this?*

SIR JEALOUS. Hark ye daughter, do you know this hand?

ISABINDA. As I suspected – *hand* do you call it, Sir? 'Tis some school-boy's scrawl.

PATCH. [*Aside*] *Oh! Invention, thou chamber-maid's best friend, assist me.*

SIR JEALOUS. Are you sure you don't understand it?

[Patch *feels in her bosom, and shakes her coats.*

ISABINDA. Do you understand it, Sir?

SIR JEALOUS. I wish I did.

ISABINDA. – [*Aside*] *Thank Heaven you do not.* – [*To* Sir Jealous] Then I know no more of it than you do indeed, Sir.

PATCH. Oh Lord, oh Lord, what have you done, Sir? Why the paper is mine, I drop'd it out of my bosom. [*Snatching it from him.*

SIR JEALOUS. Ha! Yours, Mistress.

ISABINDA. [*Aside*] *What does she mean by owning it.*

PATCH. Yes, Sir, it is.

SIR JEALOUS. What is it? Speak.

PATCH. Why, Sir, it is a charm for the tooth-ach – I have worn it this seven year, 'twas given me by an angel for ought I know when I was raving with the pain; for no body knew from whence he came, nor whither he went. He charg'd me never to open it, lest some dire vengeance befal me, and Heaven knows what will be the event. Oh! Cruel misfortune that I should drop it, and you should open it – if you had not open'd it –

ISABINDA. [*Aside*] *Excellent wench.*

SIR JEALOUS. Pox of your charms, and whims for me, if that be all 'tis well enough; there, there, burn it, and I warrant you no vengeance will follow.

PATCH. [*Aside*] *So, all's right again thus far.*

ISABINDA. – [*Aside*] *I would not lose Patch for the World – I'll take courage a little.* – Is this usage for your daughter, Sir, must my virtue and conduct be suspected? For every trifle, you immure me like some dire offender here, and deny me all recreations which my sex enjoy, and the custom of the Country and modesty allow; yet not content with that you make my confinement more intolerable by your mistrusts and jealousies; wou'd I were dead, so I were free from this. [*Weeps.*

SIR JEALOUS. To morrow rids you of this tiresome load, – *Don Diego Babinetto* will be here, and then my care ends and his begins.

ISABINDA. [*Aside*] *Is he come then! Oh how shall I avoid this hated marriage?*

[*Enter* Servants *with supper.*

SIR JEALOUS. Come will you sit down?

ISABINDA. I can't eat, Sir.

PATCH. [*Aside*] *No, I dare swear he has given her supper enough. I wish I cou'd get into the closet –*

SIR JEALOUS. Well, if you can't eat, then give me a song whilst I do.

ISABINDA. I have such a cold I can scarce speak, Sir, much less sing. – [*Aside*] *How shall I prevent Charles coming in.*

SIR JEALOUS. I hope you have the use of your fingers, Madam. Play a tune upon your *spinnet*, whilst your woman sings me a song.

PATCH. [*Aside*] *I'm as much out of tune as my Lady, if he knew all.*

ISABINDA. [*Aside*] *I shall make excellent musick.* [*Sits down to play.*

PATCH. Really, Sir, I'm so frighted about your opening this charm, that I can't remember one song.

SIR JEALOUS. Pish, hang your charm; come, come, sing any thing.

PATCH. – [*Aside*] *Yes, I'm likely to sing truly.* – humph, humph, bless me, Sir, I cannot raise my voice, my heart pants so.

SIR JEALOUS. Why, what does you heart pant so that you can't play neither? Pray what key are you in ha?

PATCH. [*Aside*] *Ah, wou'd the key was turn'd of you once.*

SIR JEALOUS. Why don't you sing, I say!

PATCH. When Madam has put her *spinnet* in tune, Sir, humph, humph. –

ISABINDA. I cannot play, Sir, whatever ails me. [*Rising.*

SIR JEALOUS. Zounds sit down, and play me a tune, or I'll break the *spinnet* about your ears.

ISABINDA. What will become of me? [*Sits down and plays.*

SIR JEALOUS. Come, Mistress. [*To* Patch.

PATCH. Yes, Sir. [*Sings, but horribly out of tune.*[54]

SIR JEALOUS. Hey, hey, why you are a top of the house, and you are down in the cellar. What is the meaning of this? Is it on purpose to cross me, ha?

PATCH. Pray Madam, take it a little lower, I cannot reach that note – nor any note I fear.

ISABINDA. Well, begin – Oh! *Patch* we shall be discover'd.

PATCH. I sink with the apprehension, Madam, – humph, humph – [*Sings*.

[Charles *pulls open the closet door.*

CHARLES. Musick and singing

'Tis thus the bright celestial court above,
Beguiles the hours with musick and with love.

Death! Her father there, [*The women shriek*] then I must fly – [*Exit into the closet.* Sir Jealous *rises up hastily, seeing* Charles *slip back into the closet.*

SIR JEALOUS. Hell and Furies, a man in the closet!

PATCH. Ah! A ghost, a ghost – he must not enter the closet – [Isabinda *throws her self down before the closet-door as in a swoon.*

SIR JEALOUS. The devil! I'll make a ghost of him I warrant you. [*Strives to get by.*

PATCH. Oh hold, Sir, have a care, you'll tread upon my Lady – who waits there? Bring some water: oh! this comes of your opening the charm: oh, oh, oh, oh. [*Weeps aloud.*

SIR JEALOUS. I'll charm you, house-wife, here lies the charm, that conjur'd this fellow in I'm sure on't, come out you rascal, do so: Zounds take her from the door, or I'll spurn her from it, and break your neck down stairs.

ISABINDA. Oh, oh, where am I – [*Aside to* Patch] He's gone, I heard him leap down.

PATCH. Nay, then let him enter – here, here Madam, smell to this; come give me your hand; come nearer to the window, the air will do you good.

SIR JEALOUS. I wou'd she were in her grave. Where are you, Sirrah, villain, robber of my honour; I'll pull you out of your nest. [*Goes into the closet.*

PATCH. You'll be mistaken, old Gentleman, the bird is flown.

ISABINDA. I'm glad I have 'scap'd so well. I was almost dead in earnest with the fright.

[*Re-enter* Sir Jealous *out of the closet.*

SIR JEALOUS. Whoever the dog were he has escap'd out of the window, for the sash is up. But tho' he is got out of my reach, you are not: and first Mrs. *Pandor*, with your charms for tooth-ach, get out of my house, go, troop; yet hold, stay, I'll see you out of my doors my self, but I'll secure your charge e'er I go.

ISABINDA. What do you mean, Sir? Was she not a creature of your own providing?

SIR JEALOUS. She was of the Devil's providing for ought I know.

PATCH. What have I done, Sir, to merit your displeasure?

SIR JEALOUS. I don't know which of you have done it; but you shall both suffer for it, till I can discover whose guilt it is: go get in there, I'll move you from this side of the house [*Pushes* Isabinda *in at the other door, and locks it; puts the key in his pocket*] I'll keep the key my self: I'll try what ghost will get into that room. And now forsooth I'll wait on you down stairs.

PATCH. Ah, my poor Lady – down stairs, Sir, but I won't go out, Sir, till I have look'd up my cloaths.

SIR JEALOUS. If thou wer't as naked as thou wer't born, thou should'st not stay to put on a smock. Come along, I say; when your Mistress is marry'd you shall have your rags, and every thing that belongs to you; but till then – [*Exit, pulling her out.*

PATCH. Oh! Barbarous usage for nothing.

[*Re-enter at the lower door.*

SIR JEALOUS. There, go, and come no more within sight of my habitation, these three days, I charge you. [*Slaps the door after her.*

PATCH. Did ever any body see such an old monster!

[*Enter* Charles.

PATCH. Oh! Mr. *Charles* your affairs and mine are in an ill posture.

CHARLES. I am immur'd to the frowns of fortune: but what has befal'n thee?

PATCH. Sir *Jealous*, whose suspicious nature's always on the watch; nay, even whilst one eye sleeps, the other keeps sentinel: upon sight of you, flew into such a violent passion, that I cou'd find no stratagem to appease him, but in spight of all arguments, lock'd his daughter into his own apartment, and turn'd me out of doors.

CHARLES. Ha! Oh, *Isabinda.*

PATCH. And swears she shall neither see sun nor moon, till she is *Don Diego Babinetto*'s wife, who arrived last night, and is expected with impatience.

CHARLES. He dies, yes, by all the wrongs of love he shall; here will I plant my self, and thro' my breast he shall make his passage, if he enters.

ATCH. A most heroick resolution. There might be ways found out more to your advantage. Policy is often preferr'd to open force.

CHARLES. I apprehend you not.

PATCH. What think you of personating this *Spaniard*, imposing upon the father, and marrying your mistress by his own consent?

CHARLES. Say'st thou so my Angel! Oh cou'd that be done, my life to come wou'd be too short to recompence thee: but how can I do that, when I neither know what ship he came in, nor from what part of *Spain*; who recommends him, nor how attended.

PATCH. I can solve all this. He is from *Madrid*, his father's name *Don Pedro Questo Portento Babinetto*. Here's a letter of his to Sir *Jealous*, which he drop'd one day; you understand *Spanish*, and the hand may be counterfeited: you conceive me, Sir.

CHARLES. My better genius, thou hast reviv'd my drooping soul: I'll about it instantly. Come to my lodgings, and we'll concert matters. [*Exeunt* Charles *and* Patch.

SCENE III. A Garden Gate open, Scentwell waiting within.

[*Enter* Sir George Airy.]

SIR GEORGE. So, this is the gate, and most invitingly open. If there shou'd be a blunderbuss here now, what a dreadful ditty wou'd my fall make for fools; and what a jest for the wits; how my name wou'd be roar'd about streets. Well, I'll venture all.

SCENTWELL. Hist, hist, Sir *George Airy* – [*Enters.*

SIR GEORGE. A female voice. Thus far I'm safe, my dear.

SCENTWELL. No, I'm not your dear, but I'll conduct you to her. Give me your hand; you must go thro' many a dark passage and dirty step before you arrive –

SIR GEORGE. I know I must before I arrive at Paradise; therefore be quick my charming guide.

SCENTWELL. For ought you know; come, come your hand and away.

SIR GEORGE. Here, here Child, you can't be half so swift as my desires. [*Exeunt* Sir George *and* Scentwell.

SCENE IV. *The house.*

[*Enter Miranda.*]

MIRANDA. Well, let me reason a little with my mad self. Now don't I transgress all rules to venture upon a man, without the advice of the grave and wise; but then a rigid knavish guardian who wou'd have marry'd me. To whom? Even to his nauseous self, or no body: Sir *George* is what I have try'd in conversation, inquir'd into his character, am satisfied in both. Then his love; who wou'd have given a hundred pound only to have seen a woman he had not infinitely loved? So I find my liking him has furnish'd me with arguments enough of his side; and now the only doubt remains whether he will come or no.

[*Enter* Scentwell.

SCENTWELL. That's resolv'd, Madam, for here's the knight. [*Exit* Scentwell.

SIR GEORGE. And do I once more behold that lovely object, whose idea fills my mind, and forms my pleasing dreams!

MIRANDA. What beginning again in heroicks! – Sir *George*, don't you remember how little fruit your last prodigal oration produced, not one bare single word in answer.

SIR GEORGE. Ha! The voice of my *Incognita* – why did you take ten thousand ways to captivate a heart your eyes alone had vanquish'd?

MIRANDA. Prithee, no more of these flights; for our time's but short, and we must fall into business: do you think we can agree on that same terrible bugbear,[55] *matrimony*, without heartily repenting on both sides.

SIR GEORGE. It has been my wish since first my longing eyes beheld ye.

MIRANDA. And your happy ears drank in the pleasing news, I had thirty thousand pound.

SIR GEORGE. Unkind! Did I not offer you in those purchas'd minutes to run the risque of your fortune, so you wou'd but secure that lovely person to my arms.

MIRANDA. Well, if you have such love and tenderness, (since our wooing has been short) pray reserve it for our future days, to let the World see we are lovers after wedlock; 'twill be a novelty –

SIR GEORGE. Haste then, and let us tye the knot, and prove the envy'd pair –

MIRANDA. Hold! Not so fast, I have provided better than to venture on dangerous experiments headlong – my *Guardian*, trusting to my dissembled love, has given up my fortune to my own dispose; but with this *proviso*, that he tomorrow morning weds me. He is now gone to *Doctors Commons* for a license.

SIR GEORGE. Ha, a license!

MIRANDA. But I have planted emissaries that infallibly take him down to *Epsom*, under pretence that a brother usurer of his, is to make him his executor; the thing on earth he covets.

SIR GEORGE. 'Tis his known character.

MIRANDA. Now my instruments confirm him, this man is dying, and he sends me word he goes this minute; it must be to morrow e'er he can be undeceiv'd. That time is ours.

SIR GEORGE. Let us improve it then, and settle on our coming years, endless, endless happiness.

MIRANDA. I dare not stir till I hear he's on the road – then I and my writings, the most material point, are soon removed.

SIR GEORGE. I have one favour to ask; if it lies in your power, you wou'd be a friend to poor *Charles*, tho' the son of this tenacious man: he is as free from all his vices, as nature and a good education can make him; and what now I have vanity enough to hope will induce you, he is the man on earth I love.

MIRANDA. I never was his enemy, and only put it on as it help'd my designs on his father. If his uncle's estate ought to be in his possession, which I shrewdly suspect, I may do him a singular piece of service.

SIR GEORGE. You are all goodness.

[*Enter* Scentwell.

SCENTWELL. Oh, Madam, my master and Mr. *Marplot* are just coming into the house.

MIRANDA. Undone, undone! If he finds you here in this crisis, all my plots are unravell'd.

SIR GEORGE. What shall I do! Can't I get back into the garden?

SCENTWELL. Oh, no! He comes up those stairs.

MIRANDA. Here, here, here! Can you condescend to stand behind this chimney-board, Sir *George*?

SIR GEORGE. Any where, any where, dear Madam, without ceremony.

SCENTWELL. Come, come, Sir; lie close – [*They put* George *behind the chimney-board.*

[*Enter* Sir Francis *and* Marplot, Sir Francis *peeling an orange.*

SIR FRANCIS. I cou'd not go, tho' 'tis upon life and death, without taking leave of dear *Chargee*. Besides, this fellow buz'd in my ears, that thou might'st be so desperate to shoot that wild rake which haunts the garden-gate; and that wou'd bring us into trouble, dear –

MIRANDA. So, *Marplot* brought you back then: I am oblig'd to him for that, I'm sure – [*Frowning at* Marplot *aside.*

MARPLOT. By her looks she means she is not oblig'd to me. I have done some mischief now, but what I can't imagine.

SIR FRANCIS. Well, *Chargee*, I have had three messengers to come to *Epsom* to my neighbour *Squeezum*'s, who, for all his vast riches, is departing. [*Sighs.*

MARPLOT. Ay, see what all your usurers must come to.

SIR FRANCIS. Peace, ye young knave! Some forty years hence I may think on't – but, *Chargee*, I'll be with thee to morrow, before those pretty eyes are open; I will, I will, *Chargee*, I'll rouze you, I faith. – Here Mrs. *Scentwell*, lift up your Lady's chimney-board, that I may throw my peel in, and not litter her chamber.

MIRANDA. Oh my stars! What will become of us now?

SCENTWELL. Oh, pray Sir, give it me; I love it above all things in nature, indeed I do.

SIR FRANCIS. No, no, hussy; you have the green pip[56] already, I'll have no more apothecary's bills. [*Goes towards the chimney.*

MIRANDA. Hold, hold, hold, dear *Gardee*, I have a, a, a, a, a monkey shut up there; and if you open it before the man comes that is to tame it, 'tis so wild 'twill break all my china, or get away, and that wou'd break my heart; for I am fond on't to distraction, next thee, dear *Gardee*. [*In a flattering tone.*

SIR FRANCIS. Well, well, *Chargee*, I wont open it; she shall have her monkey, poor rogue; here throw this peel out of the window. [*Exit* Scentwell.

MARPLOT. A monkey, dear Madam, let me see it; I can tame a monkey as well as the best of them all. Oh how I love the little miniatures of man.

MIRANDA. Be quiet, mischief, and stand farther from the chimney – you shall not see my monkey – why sure – [*Striving with him.*

MARPLOT. For Heaven's sake, dear Madam, let me but peep, to see if it be as pretty as my Lady *Fiddle-Faddle*'s. Has it got a chain?

MIRANDA. Not yet, but I design it one shall last its life-time: nay, you shall not see it – look, *Gardee*, how he teases me!

SIR FRANCIS. [*Getting between him and the chimney*] Sirrah, Sirrah, let my *Chargee*'s monkey alone, or *Bambo* shall fly about your ears. What is there no dealing with you?

MARPLOT. Pugh, pox of the monkey! Here's a rout: I wish he may rival you.

[*Enter a* Servant.

SERVANT. Sir, they put two more horses in the coach, as you order'd, and 'tis ready at the door.

SIR FRANCIS. Well, I'm going to be executor, better for thee, jewel. B'ye *Chargee*, one buss! – I'm glad thou hast got a a monkey to divert thee a little.

MIRANDA. Thank'e, dear *Gardee*. – Nay, I'll see you to the coach.

SIR FRANCIS. That's kind, adod.

MIRANDA. Come along, impertinence. [*To* Marplot.

MARPLOT. [*Stepping back*] Egad, I will see the monkey: now [*Lifts up the board, and discovers* Sir George] Oh Lord, oh Lord! Thieves, thieves, murder!

SIR GEORGE. Dam'e, you unlucky dog! 'Tis I, which way shall I get out, shew me instantly, or I'll cut your throat.

MARPLOT. Undone, undone! At that door there. But hold, hold, break that china, and I'll bring you off. [*He runs off at the corner, and throws down some china.*

[*Re-enter* Sir Francis*,* Miranda*, and* Scentwell.

SIR FRANCIS. Mercy on me! What's the matter?

MIRANDA. Oh, you toad! What have you done?

MARPLOT. No great harm, I beg of you to forgive me: longing to see the monkey, I did but just raise up the board, and it flew over my shoulders, scratch'd all my face, broke yon' china, and whisk'd out of the window.

SIR FRANCIS. Was ever such an unlucky rogue! Sirrah, I forbid you my house. Call the servants to get the monkey again; I wou'd stay my self to look it, but that you know my earnest business.

SCENTWELL. Oh my Lady will be the best to lure it back; all them creatures love my Lady extremely.

MIRANDA. Go, go, dear *Gardee*; I hope I shall recover it.

SIR FRANCIS. B'ye, by'e, Dear'e. Ah, mischief, how you look now! B'ye, b'ye. [*Exit.*

MIRANDA. *Scentwell*, see him in the coach, and bring me word.

SCENTWELL. Yes, Madam.

MIRANDA. So, Sir, you have done your friend a signal piece of service, I suppose.

MARPLOT. Why look you, Madam! If I have committed a fault, thank your self; no man is more serviceable when I am let into a secret, nor none more unlucky at finding it out. Who cou'd divine your meaning; when you talk'd of a blunderbuss, who thought of a rendevous? And when you talk'd of a monkey, who the devil dreamt of Sir *George*?

MIRANDA. A sign you converse but little with our sex, when you can't reconcile contradictions.

[*Enter* Scentwell.

SCENTWELL. He's gone, Madam, as fast as the coach, and six can carry him.

[*Enter* Sir George.

SIR GEORGE. Then I may appear.

MARPLOT. Dear, Sir *George*, make my peace! On my soul, I did not think of you.

SIR GEORGE. I dare swear thou didst not. Madam, I beg you to forgive him.

MIRANDA. Well, Sir *George*, if he can be secret.

MARPLOT. Ods heart, Madam, I'm as secret as a priest when I'm trusted.

SIR GEORGE. Why 'tis with a priest our business is at present.

SCENTWELL. Madam, here's Mrs. *Isabinda*'s woman to wait on you.

MIRANDA. Bring her up. [*Enter* Patch] How do'e, Mrs. *Patch*, what news from your Lady?

PATCH. That's for your private ear, Madam. Sir *George*, there's a friend of yours has an urgent occasion for your assistance.

SIR GEORGE. His name.

PATCH. *Charles*.

MARPLOT. Ha! Then there is something a-foot that I know nothing of. I'll wait on you, Sir *George*.

SIR GEORGE. A third person may not be proper perhaps; as soon as I have dispatch'd my own affairs, I am at his service. I'll send my servant to tell him, I'll wait upon him in half an hour.

MIRANDA. How come you employ'd in this message, Mrs. *Patch*?

PATCH. Want of business, Madam. I am discharg'd by my master, but hope to serve my Lady still.

MIRANDA. How discharg'd! You must tell me the whole story within.

PATCH. With all my heart, Madam.

MARPLOT. [*Aside*] *Pish! Pox, I wish I were fairly out of the house. I find marriage is the end of this secret: and now I am half mad to know what Charles wants him for.*

SIR GEORGE. Madam, I'm doubly press'd, by love and friendship: this exigence admits of no delay. Shall we make *Marplot* of the party?

MIRANDA. If you'll run the hazard, Sir *George*; I believe he means well.

MARPLOT. Nay, nay, for my part, I desire to be let into nothing: I'll be gone, therefore pray don't mistrust me. [*Going.*]

SIR GEORGE. So now has he a mind to be gone to *Charles*: but not knowing what affairs he may have upon his hands at present, I'm resolv'd he sha'n't stir: No, Mr. *Marplot*, you must not leave us, we want a third person. [*Takes hold of him.*

MARPLOT. I never had more mind to be gone in my life.

MIRANDA. Come along then; if we fail in the voyage, thank your self for taking this ill starr'd gentleman on board.

SIR GEORGE. That vessel ne'er can unsuccessful prove,
Whose freight is beauty, and whose pilot love.

ACT V. SCENE I.

[*Enter* Miranda, Patch, *and* Scentwell.]

MIRANDA. Well, *Patch*, I have done a strange bold thing! My fate is determin'd, and expectation is no more. Now to avoid the impertinence and roguery of an old man, I have thrown my self into the extravagance of a young one; if he shou'd despise, slight or use me ill, there's no remedy from a husband, but the grave; and that's a terrible sanctuary to one of my age and constitution.

PATCH. O fear not, Madam, you'll find your account in Sir *George Airy*; it is impossible a man of sense shou'd use a woman ill, indued with beauty, wit and fortune. It must be the lady's fault, if she does not wear the unfashionable name of wife easie, when nothing but complaisance and good humour is requisite on either side to make them happy.

MIRANDA. I long till I am out of this house, lest any accident shou'd bring my *Guardian* back. *Scentwell*, put my best jewels into the little casket, slip them into thy pocket, and let us march off to Sir. *Jealous*'.

SCENTWELL. It shall be done, Madam. [*Exit.* Scentwell.

PATCH. Sir *George* will be impatient, Madam; if their plot succeeds, we shall be well receiv'd; if not, he will be able to protect us. Besides, I long to know how my young Lady fares.

MIRANDA. Farewell, old *Mammon*, and thy detested walls; 'twill be no more sweet Sir *Francis*. I shall be compell'd to the odious task of dissembling no longer to get my own, and coax him with the wheedling names of my *Precious*, my *Dear*, Dear *Gardee*. Oh Heavens!

[*Enter* Sir Francis *behind.*

SIR FRANCIS. Ah, my sweet *Chargee*, don't be frighted. [*She starts*] But thy poor *Gardee* has been abused, cheated, fool'd, betray'd, but no body knows by whom.

MIRANDA. [*Aside*] *Undone! Past redemption.*

SIR FRANCIS. What won't you speak to me, *Chargee*!

MIRANDA. I'm so surpriz'd with joy to see you, I know not what to say.

SIR FRANCIS. Poor, dear girl! But do'e know that my son, or some such rogue, to rob or murder me, or both, contriv'd this journey? For upon the road I met my neighbour *Squeezum* well, and coming to Town.

MIRANDA. Good lack, good lack! What tricks are there in this World!

[*Enter* Scentwell, *with a diamond necklace in her hand; not seeing* Sir Francis.

SCENTWELL. Madam, be pleas'd to tye this necklace on; for I can't get it into the – [*Seeing* Sir Francis.

MIRANDA. The wench is a fool, I think! Cou'd you not have carry'd it to be mended, without putting it in the box?

SIR FRANCIS. What's the matter?

MIRANDA. Only dear'e, I bid her, I bid her – your ill usage has put every thing out of my head. But won't you go, *Gardee*, and find out these fellows, and have them punish'd! and, and –

SIR FRANCIS. Where shou'd I look them, Child? No I'll sit me down contented with my safety, nor stir out of my own doors, till I go with thee to a parson.

MIRANDA. [*Aside*] *If he goes into his closet I am ruin'd. Oh! Bless me in this fright, I had forgot Mrs. Patch.*

PATCH. Ay, Madam, and I stay for your speedy answer.

MIRANDA. [*Aside*] *I must get him out of the house. Now assist me fortune.*

SIR FRANCIS. Mrs. *Patch*, I profess I did not see you, how dost thou do, Mrs. *Patch*; well don't you repent leaving my *Chargee*?

PATCH. Yes, every body must love her – but I came now – [*Aside to* Miranda] Madam, what did I come for, my invention is at the last ebb.

SIR FRANCIS. Nay, never whisper, tell me.

MIRANDA. She came, dear *Gardee,* to invite me to her Lady's wedding, and you shall go with me *Gardee*, 'tis to be done this moment to a *Spanish* merchant; old Sir *Jealous* keeps on his humour, the first minute he sees her, the next he marries her.

SIR FRANCIS. Ha, ha, ha, I'd go if I thought the sight of matrimony wou'd tempt *Chargee* to perform her promise: there was a smile, there was a consenting look with those pretty twinklers, worth a million. Ods precious, I am happier than the great *Mogul*, the Emperour of *China*, or all the potentates[57] that are not in wars. Speak, confirm it, make me leap out of my skin.

MIRANDA. When one has resolv'd, 'tis in vain to stand shall I, shall I; if ever I marry, positively this is my wedding day.

SIR FRANCIS. Oh! Happy, happy man – verily I will beget a son, the first night shall disinherit that dog, *Charles*. I have estate enough to purchase a barony, and be the immortalizing the whole family of the Gripes.

MIRANDA. Come then *Gardee*, give me thy hand, let's to this house of *Hymen*. My choice is fix'd, let good or ill betide.

SIR FRANCIS. The joyful bridegroom, I.

MIRANDA. And I the happy bride. [*Exeunt* Miranda, Sir Francis, *and* Patch.

[*Enter* Sir Jealous *meeting a* Servant.

SERVANT. Sir, here's a couple of gentlemen enquire for you; one of 'em calls himself *Señior Diego Babinetto*.

SIR JEALOUS. Ha! *Señior Babinetto*! Admit 'em instantly – joyful minute; I'll have my daughter marry'd to night.

[*Enter* Charles *in Spanish habit, with* Sir George *drest like a merchant*.

SIR JEALOUS. *Señior, beso las manos vuestra merced es muy bienvenido en esta tierra.*

CHARLES. *Señior*, soy muy humilde, y muy obligado cryado de vuestra merced: mi padre embia a vuestra merced, los mas profondos de sus respetos; y a commissionado este mercadel Ingles, de concluyr un negocio, que me haze el mas dichoso hombre del mundo, haziendo me sit yerno.[58]

SIR JEALOUS. I am glad on't, for I find I have lost much of my *Spanish*. Sir, I am your most humble servant. *Señior Don Diego Babinetto* has inform'd me that you are commission'd by *Señior Don Pedro*, &c. his worthy father.

SIR GEORGE. To see an affair of marriage consummated between a daughter of yours, and *Señior Diego Babinetto* his son here. True, Sir, such a trust is repos'd in me as that letter will inform you. – [*Aside*] *I hope 'twill pass upon him.* [*Gives him a letter.*

SIR JEALOUS. Ay, 'tis his hand. [*Seems to read.*

SIR GEORGE. [*Aside to* Charles] Good – you have counterfeited to a nicety, *Charles*.

CHARLES. If the whole plot succeeds as well, I'm happy.

SIR JEALOUS. Sir I find by this, that you are a man of honour and probity; I think, Sir, he calls you *Meanwell*.

SIR GEORGE. *Meanwell* is my name, Sir.

SIR JEALOUS. A very good name, and very significant.

CHARLES. [*Aside*] *Yes, faith if he knew all.*

SIR JEALOUS. For to mean-well is to be honest, and to be honest is the virtue of a friend, and a friend is the delight and support of human society.

SIR GEORGE. You shall find that I'll discharge the part of a friend in what I have undertaken, Sir *Jealous*.

CHARLES. [*Aside*] *But little does he think to whom.*

SIR GEORGE. Therefore, Sir, I must intreat the presence of your fair daughter, and the assistance of your chaplain; for Señior Don Pedro strictly enjoyn'd me to see the marriage rites perform'd as soon as we should arrive, to avoid the accidental overtures of Venus.

SIR JEALOUS. Overtures of *Venus*!

SIR GEORGE. Ay, Sir, that is, those little hawking females that traverse the park, and the playhouse to put off their damag'd ware – they fasten upon foreigners like leeches, and watch their arrival as carefully, as the *Kentish* men[59] do a ship-wreck. I warrant you they have heard of him already.

SIR JEALOUS. Nay, I know this Town swarms with them.

SIR GEORGE. Ay, and then you know the *Spaniards* are naturally amorous, but very constant, the first face fixes 'em, and it may be dangerous to let him ramble e'er he is tied.

CHARLES. [*Aside*] *Well hinted*.

SIR JEALOUS. Pat to my purpose – well, Sir, there is but one thing more, and they shall be married instantly.

CHARLES. [*Aside*] *Pray Heaven, that one thing more don't spoil all*.

SIR JEALOUS. Don Pedro writ me word in his last but one, that he design'd the sum of five thousand crowns by way of joynture for my daughter; and that it shou'd be paid into my hand upon the day of marriage.

CHARLES. [*Aside*] *Oh! The devil*.

SIR JEALOUS. In order to lodge it in some of our funds, in case she should become a widow, and return for *England*.

SIR GEORGE. [*Aside*] *Pox on't, this is an unlucky turn. What shall I say?*

SIR JEALOUS. And he does not mention one word of it in this letter.

CHARLES. [*Aside*] *I don't know how he should*.

SIR GEORGE. Humph! True, Sir *Jealous*, he told me such a thing, but, but, but, but – he, he, he, he – he did not imagine that you would insist upon the very day, for, for, for, for money you know is dangerous returning by sea, an, an, an, an –

CHARLES. [*Aside to* Sir George] Zounds, say we have brought it in commodities.

SIR GEORGE. And so Sir, he has sent it in merchandize, *tobacco, sugars, spices, limons*, and so forth, which shall be turn'd into money with all expedition: in the mean time, Sir, if you please to accept of my bond for performance.[60]

SIR JEALOUS. It is enough, Sir, I am so pleas'd with the countenance of *Señior Diego*, and the harmony of your name, that I'll take your word, and will fetch my daughter this moment. Within there [*Enter* Servant] desire Mr. *Tackum* my neighbour's chaplain to walk hither.

SERVANT. Yes, Sir. [*Exit*.

SIR JEALOUS. Gentlemen, I'll return in an instant. [*Exit*.

CHARLES. Wondrous well. Let me embrace thee.

SIR GEORGE. Egad that 5000 *l*. had like to have ruin'd the plot.

CHARLES. But that's over! And if Fortune throws no more rubs in our way.

SIR GEORGE. Thou'lt carry the prize – but hist, here he comes.

[*Enter* Sir Jealous, *dragging in* Isabinda.

SIR JEALOUS. Come along, you stubborn baggage you, come along.

ISABINDA. Oh hear me, Sir! Hear me but speak one word, do not destroy my everlasting peace; my soul abhors this *Spaniard* you have chose, nor can I wed him without being curst.

SIR JEALOUS. How's that!

ISABINDA. Let this posture move your tender nature. [*Kneels*] For ever will I hang upon these knees; nor loose my hands till you cut off my hold, if you refuse to hear me, Sir.

CHARLES. [*Aside*] *Oh! That I cou'd discover my self to her*.

SIR GEORGE. [*Aside*] *Have a care what you do. You had better trust to his obstinacy*.

SIR JEALOUS. Did you ever see such a perverse slut: off I say. Mr. *Meanwell* pray help me a little.

SIR GEORGE. Rise, Madam, and do not disoblige your father, who has provided a husband worthy of you, one that will love you equal with his soul, and one that you will love, when once you know him.

ISABINDA. Oh! Never, never. Cou'd I suspect that falshood in my heart, I wou'd this moment tear it from my breast, and streight present him with the treacherous part.

CHARLES. [*Aside*] *Oh! My charming faithful dear*.

SIR JEALOUS. Falshood! Why, who the devil are you in love with? Ha! Don't provoke me, for by St. *Iago* I shall beat you, housewife.

CHARLES. [*Aside*] *Heaven forbid; for I shall infallibly discover my self if he should*.

SIR GEORGE. Have patience, Madam! And look at him: why will you prepossess your self against a man that is master of all the charms you would desire in a husband?

SIR JEALOUS. Ay, look at him, *Isabinda, Señior pase vind adelante.*[61]

CHARLES. My heart bleeds to see her grieve, whom I imagin'd would with joy receive me. *Señiora obligue me vuestra merced de sumano.*[62]

SIR JEALOUS. [*Pulling up her head*] Hold up your head, hold up your head, housewife, and look at him: is there a properer, handsomer, better shap'd fellow in *England*, ye jade you. Ha! See, see the obstinate baggage shuts her eyes; by St. *Iago*, I have a good mind to beat 'em out. [*Pushes her down.*

ISABINDA. Do then, Sir, kill me, kill me instantly. 'Tis much the kinder action of the two, for 'twill be worse than death to wed him.

SIR GEORGE. Sir *Jealous*, you are too passionate. Give me leave, I'll try by gentle words to work her to your purpose.

SIR JEALOUS. I pray do, Mr. *Meanwell*, I pray do; she'll break my heart. [*Weeps*] There is in that, jewels of the value of 3000 *l.* which were her mother's; and a paper wherein I have settled one half of my estate upon her now, and the whole when I dye. But provided she marries this gentleman, else by St. *Iago*, I'll turn her out of doors to beg or starve. Tell her this, Mr. *Meanwell*, pray do. [*Walks off.*

SIR GEORGE. Ha! This is beyond expectation – trust to me, Sir, I'll lay the dangerous consequence of disobeying you at this juncture before her, I warrant you.

CHARLES. [*Aside*] *A sudden joy runs thro' my heart like a propitious omen.*

SIR GEORGE. Come, Madam, do not blindly cast your life away just in the moment you would wish to save it.

ISABINDA. Pray cease your trouble, Sir, I have no wish but sudden death to free me from this hated *Spaniard*. If you are his friend inform him what I say; my heart is given to another youth, whom I love with the same strength of passion that I hate this *Diego*; with whom, if I am forc'd to wed, my own hand shall cut the Gordian knot.

SIR GEORGE. Suppose this *Spaniard* which you strive to shun should be the very man to whom you'd flye?

ISABINDA. Ha!

SIR GEORGE. Would you not blame your rash result, and curse those eyes that would not look on *Charles*.

ISABINDA. On *Charles*! Oh you have inspir'd new life, and collected every wandring sense. Where is he? Oh! Let me flye into his arms. [*Rises.*

SIR GEORGE. Hold, hold, hold, 'Zdeath, Madam, you'll ruin all, your father believes him to be *Señior Babinetto*. Compose your self a little, pray Madam. [*He runs to* Sir Jealous.

CHARLES. [*Aside*] *Her eyes declare she knows me.*

SIR GEORGE. She begins to hear reason, Sir, the fear of being turn'd out of doors has done it. [*Runs back to* Isabinda.

ISABINDA. 'Tis he, oh! My ravish'd soul.

SIR GEORGE. Take heed, Madam, you don't betray your self. Seem with reluctance to consent, or you are undone, [*Runs to* Sir Jealous] speak gently to her, Sir, I'm sure she'll yield, I see it in her face.

SIR JEALOUS. Well, *Isabinda*, can you refuse to bless a father, whose only care is to make you happy, as Mr. *Meanwell* has inform'd you. Come, wipe thy eyes; nay, prithee do, or thou wilt break thy father's heart; see thou bring'st the tears in mine to think of thy undutiful carriage to me. [*Weeps.*

ISABINDA. Oh! Do not weep, Sir, your tears are like a ponyard[63] to my soul; do with me what you please, I am all obedience.

SIR JEALOUS. Ha! Then thou art my child again.

SIR GEORGE. 'Tis done, and now friend the day's thy own.

CHARLES. The happiest of my life, if nothing intervene.

SIR JEALOUS. And wilt thou love him?

ISABINDA. I will endeavour it, Sir.

[*Enter* Servant

SERVANT. Sir, here is Mr. *Tackum*.

SIR JEALOUS. Show him into the parlour – *Señior tome vind sueipora; cete momento les junta les manos.*[64] [*Gives her to* Charles.

CHARLES. Oh! Transport – *Señior yo la recibo como se deve un tesoro tan grande.*[65] Oh! my joy, my life, my soul. [*They embrace.*

ISABINDA. My faithful everlasting comfort.

SIR JEALOUS. Now, Mr. *Meanwell* let's to the parson,

Who, by his art will join this pair for life,
Make me the happiest Father, her the happiest Wife. [*Exit.*

SCENE II. Changes to the street before Sir Jealous's door.

[*Enter* Marplot, Solus.]

MARPLOT. I have hunted all over the Town for *Charles*, but can't find him; and by *Whisper*'s scouting at the end of the street, I suspect he must be in this house again. I'm inform'd too that he has borrow'd a *Spanish* habit out of the *playhouse*; what can it mean? [*Enter a* Servant *of* Sir Jealous*'s to him, out of the house*] Hark'e, Sir, do you belong to this house?

SERVANT. Yes, Sir.

MARPLOT. Pray can you tell if there be a gentleman in it in *Spanish* habit?

SERVANT. There is a *Spanish* gentleman within, that is just a going to marry my young Lady, Sir.

MARPLOT. Are you sure he is a *Spanish* gentleman?

SERVANT. I'm sure he speaks no *English*, that I hear of.

MARPLOT. Then that can't be him I want; for 'tis an *English* gentleman, tho' I suppose he may be dress'd like a *Spaniard*, that I enquire after.

SERVANT. – [*Aside*] *Ha! Who knows but this may be an impostor? I'll inform my master; for if he shou'd be impos'd upon, he'll beat us all round.* – Pray, come in, Sir, and see if this be the person you enquire for.

SCENE III. Changes to the inside of the house.

[*Enter* Marplot.]

MARPLOT. So, this was a good contrivance: if this be *Charles*, now will he wonder how I found him out.

[*Enter* Servant *and* Jealous.

SIR JEALOUS. What is your earnest business, blockhead, that you must speak with me before the ceremony's past? Ha! Who's this?

SERVANT. Why this gentleman, Sir, wants another gentleman in *Spanish* habit, he says.

SIR JEALOUS. In *Spanish* habit! 'Tis some friend of Seignior *Don Diego*'s, I warrant. Sir, I suppose you wou'd speak with Seignior *Babinetto* –

MARPLOT. Hy-day! What the devil does he say now! – Sir, I don't understand you.

SIR JEALOUS. Don't you understand *Spanish*, Sir?

MARPLOT. Not I indeed, Sir.

SIR JEALOUS. I thought you had known Seignior *Babinetto*.

MARPLOT. Not I, upon my word, Sir.

SIR JEALOUS. What then you'd speak with his friend, the *English* merchant, Mr. *Meanwell*.

MARPLOT. Neither, Sir; not I.

SIR JEALOUS. Why who are you then, Sir? And what do you want? [*In an angry tone*.

MARPLOT. Nay, nothing at all, not I, Sir. Pox on him! I wish I were out, he begins to exalt his voice, I shall be beaten again.

SIR JEALOUS. Nothing at all, Sir! Why then what business have you in my house? Ha?

SERVANT. You said you wanted a gentleman in *Spanish* habit.

MARPLOT. Why ay, but his name is neither *Babinetto* nor *Meanwell*.

SIR JEALOUS. What is his name then, Sirrah, ha? Now I look at you again, I believe you are the rogue threaten'd me with half a dozen *Mirmidons* – speak, Sir, who is it you look for? Or, or –

MARPLOT. A terrible old dog! – Why, Sir, only an honest young fellow of my acquaintance – I thought that here might be a ball, and that he might have been here in a masquerade; 'tis *Charles*, Sir *Francis Gripe*'s son, because I know he us'd to come hither sometimes.

SIR JEALOUS. Did he so? – Not that I know of, I'm sure. Pray Heaven that this be *Don Diego* – If I shou'd be trick'd now – Ha! My heart misgives me plaguily – within there! Stop the marriage – run, Sirrah, call all my servants! I'll be satisfy'd that this is Seignior *Pedro*'s son e're he has my daughter.

MARPLOT. Ha, Sir *George*, what have I done now?

[*Enter* Sir George *with a drawn sword between the scenes.*

SIR GEORGE. Ha! *Marplot*, here – oh the unlucky dog – what's the matter, Sir *Jealous*?

SIR JEALOUS. Nay, I don't know the matter, Mr. *Meanwell*.

MARPLOT. Upon my soul, Sir *George* – [*Going up to* Sir George.

SIR JEALOUS. Nay then, I'm betray'd, ruin'd, undone: thieves, traytors, rogues! [*Offers to go in*] Stop the marriage, I say –

SIR GEORGE. I say, go on Mr. *Tackum* – Nay, no ent'ring here, I guard this passage, old gentleman; the act and deed were both your own, and I'll see 'em sign'd, or die for't.

[*Enter* Servants.

SIR JEALOUS. A pox on the act and deed! – Fall on, knock him down.

SIR GEORGE. Ay, come on, scoundrils! I'll prick your jackets for you.

SIR JEALOUS. Zounds, Sirrah, I'll be reveng'd on you. [*Beats Marplot*]

SIR GEORGE. Ay, there your vengeance is due; ha, ha.

MARPLOT. Why, what do you beat me for? I ha'nt marry'd your daughter.

SIR JEALOUS. Rascals! Why don't you knock him down?

SERVANT. We are afraid of his sword, Sir; if you'll take that from him, we'll knock him down presently.

[*Enter* Charles *and* Isabinda.

SIR JEALOUS. Seize her then.

CHARLES. Rascals, retire; she's my wife, touch her if you dare, I'll make dogs meat of you.

SIR JEALOUS. Ah! Downright *English*: – oh, oh, oh, oh!

[*Enter* Sir Francis Gripe, Miranda, Patch, Scentwell, *and* Whisper.

SIR FRANCIS. Into the house of joy we enter without knocking: ha! I think 'tis the house of sorrow, Sir *Jealous*.

SIR JEALOUS. Oh Sir *Francis*! Are you come? What was this your contrivance, to abuse, trick, and chouse me of my child!

SIR FRANCIS. My contrivance! What do you mean?

SIR JEALOUS. No, you don't know your son there in *Spanish* habit.

SIR FRANCIS. How! My son in *Spanish* habit. Sirrah, you'll come to be hang'd; get out of my sight, ye dog! Get out of my sight.

SIR JEALOUS. Get out of your sight, Sir! Get out with your bags; let's see what you'll give him now to maintain my daughter on.

SIR FRANCIS. Give him! He shall be never the better for a penny of mine – and you might have look'd after your daughter better, Sir *Jealous*. Trick'd, quotha! Egad, I think you design'd to trick me: but look ye, gentlemen, I believe I shall trick you both. This lady is my wife, do you see? And my estate shall descend only to the heirs of her body.

SIR GEORGE. Lawfully begotten by me – I shall be extremely oblig'd to you, Sir *Francis*.

SIR FRANCIS. Ha, ha, ha, ha, poor Sir *George*! You see your project was of no use. Does not your hundred pound stick in your stomach? Ha, ha, ha.

SIR GEORGE. No faith, Sir *Francis*, this lady has given me a cordial for that. [*Takes her by the hand*.

SIR FRANCIS. Hold, Sir, you have nothing to say to this lady.

SIR GEORGE. Nor you nothing to do with my wife, Sir.

SIR FRANCIS. Wife, Sir!

MIRANDA. Ay really, *Guardian*, 'tis even so. I hope you'll forgive my first offence.

SIR FRANCIS. What have you chous'd me out of my consent, and your writings then, mistress, ha?

MIRANDA. Out of nothing but my own, *Guardian*.

SIR JEALOUS. Ha, ha, ha, 'tis some comfort at least to see you are over-reach'd as well as my self. Will you settle your estate upon your son now?

SIR FRANCIS. He shall starve first.

MIRANDA. That I have taken care to prevent. There, Sir, is the writings of your uncle's *estate*, which has been your due these three years. [*Gives* Charles *the papers*.

CHARLES. I shall study to deserve this favour.

SIR FRANCIS. What have you robb'd me too, Mistress! Egad I'll make you restore 'em. – Huswife, I will so.

SIR JEALOUS. Take care I don't make you pay the arrears, Sir. 'Tis well it's no worse, since 'tis no better. Come, young man, seeing thou hast out-witted me, take her, and bless you both.

CHARLES. I hope, Sir, you'll bestow your blessing too, 'tis all I'll ask. [*Kneels*.

SIR FRANCIS. Confound you all! [*Exit*.

MARPLOT. Mercy upon us! How he looks!

SIR GEORGE. Ha, ha, ne'er mind his curses, *Charles*; thou'lt thrive not one jot the worse for 'em. Since this gentleman is reconcil'd, we are all made happy.

SIR JEALOUS. I always lov'd precaution, and took care to avoid dangers. But when a thing was past, I ever had philosophy to be easie.

CHARLES. Which is the true sign of a great soul: I lov'd your daughter, and she me, and you shall have no reason to repent her choice.

ISABINDA. You will not blame me, Sir, for loving my own Country best.

MARPLOT. So here's every body happy, I find, but poor *Pilgarlick*. I wonder what satisfaction I shall have, for being cuff'd, kick'd, and beaten in your service.

SIR JEALOUS. I have been a little too familiar with you, as things are fallen out; but since there's no help for't, you must forgive me.

MARPLOT. Egad I think so – but provided that you be not so familiar for the future.

SIR GEORGE. Thou hast been an unlucky rogue.

MARPLOT. But very honest.

CHARLES. That I'll vouch for; and freely forgive thee.

SIR GEORGE. And I'll do you one piece of service more, *Marplot*, I'll take care that Sir *Francis* make you master of your estate.

MARPLOT. That will make me as happy as any of you.

PATCH. Your humble servant begs leave to remind you, Madam.

ISABINDA. Sir, I hope you'll give me leave to take *Patch* into favour again.

SIR JEALOUS. Nay, let your husband look to that, I have done with my care.

CHARLES. Her own liberty shall always oblige me. Here's no body but honest *Whisper* and Mrs. *Scentwell* to be provided for now. It shall be left to their choice to marry, or keep their services.

WHISPER. Nay then, I'll stick to my Master.

SCENTWELL. Coxcomb! And I prefer my Lady before a footman.

SIR JEALOUS. Hark, I hear musick, the fidlers smell a wedding. What say you, young fellows, will ye have a dance?

SIR GEORGE. With all my heart; call 'em in.

A DANCE.

SIR JEALOUS. Now let us in and refresh our selves with a chearful glass, in which we'll bury all animosities: and

By my example let all parents move,
And never strive to cross their children's love;
But still submit that care to providence above.

EPILOGUE.

Spoken by Mr. Pack.

In me you see one busie-body more;
Tho' you may have enough of one before.
With epilogues, the busie-body's way,
We strive to help; but sometimes mar a play.
At this mad sessions,[66] half condemn'd e'er try'd,
Some, in three days, have been turn'd off, and dy'd.
In spight of parties, their attempts are vain,
For like false prophets, they ne'er rise again.
Too late, when cast, your favour one beseeches,
And epilogues prove execution speeches.
Yet sure I spy no busie-bodies here;
And one may pass, since they do ev'ry where.
Sowr criticks, time and breath, and censures waste,
And baulk your pleasure to refine your taste.
One busie don ill-tim'd high tenets preaches,
Another yearly shows himself in speeches.
Some snivling cits,[67] wou'd have a peace for spight,
To starve those warriours who so bravely fight.
Still of a foe upon his knees affraid;
Whose well-bang'd troops want money, heart, and bread.
Old Beaux,[68] who none not ev'n themselves can please,
Are busie still; for nothing–but to teize,
The young; so busie to engage a heart,
The mischief done, are busie most to part.
Ungrateful wretches, who still cross one's will,
When they more kindly might be busie still!
One to a husband, who ne'er dreamt of horns,[69]
Shows how dear spouse, with friend his brows adorns.
Th' officious tell-tale fool, (he shou'd repent it)

Parts three kind souls that liv'd at peace
contented.
Some with law quirks set houses by the ears;
With physick one what he wou'd heal impairs.
Like that dark mob'd up fry, that neighb'ring
curse,
Who to remove love's pain, bestow a worse.
Since then this meddling tribe infest the age,
Bear one a while, expos'd upon the stage.
Let none but busie-bodies vent their spight!
And with good humour, pleasure crown the
night!

8.2 SUSANNA CENTLIVRE, *EPISTLE XL*

To Mr. Farquhar upon his Comedy *A Trip to the Jubilee*. In Abel Boyer, *Letters of Wit, Politicks, and Morality*, London: Printed for J. Hartley, 1701.

CENTLIVRE OFTEN FOREGROUNDED her sex when she talked about herself as a writer, a strategy that Aphra Behn also used. Her self-representations regularly used stereotypes about female weakness (of mind or body) only to overcome them. Here, she praises her friend and fellow comic playwright George Farquhar and refers to their post-Collier controversy circumstances. Both understood the constraints involved in writing comedy without *double entendres* or sexual candor.

Sir,
Amongst the many friends your Wit has made,
Permit my humble Tribute may be paid;
My Female Genius is too weakly fraught
With learned Expressions to adorn my Thought.
My Muse too blushed, when she this Task began,
To think that she must Compliment a Man.
She paused a while—at last she bid me say,
She liked the Man, and I admired the Play.
For since the learned *Collier* first essayed
To teach religion to the Rhiming Trade,
The *Comick* Muse in *Tragick* posture fit,
And seemed to mourn the Downfall of her State;
Her eldest sons she often did implore,
That they her ancient Credit would restore.
Strait they essayed, but quickly to their cost
They found that all their industry was lost.
For since the *Double Entendre* was forbid,
They could not get a Clap for what they did.
As last *Thalia* called her youngest Son,
The graceful and the best beloved one:
My Son, said she, I have observed Thee well,
Thou doest already all my Sons excel;
Thy Spring does promise a large harvest Crop,
And Thou alone must keep my Glory up.
Go, something Write, my Son, that may atone

Thy Brethren's Faults, and make thy virtues known.
I'll teach Thee Language in a pleasant stile:
Which, without Smut, can make an Audience smile.
Let fall no word that may offend the Fair;
Observe Decorums, dress the Thoughts with Air;
Go – lay the Plot, which Vertue shall adorn;
Thus spoke the Muse; and thus didst Thou perform.
Thy *Constant Couple* does our Fame redeem,
And shews our Sex can love, when yours esteem.
And *Wild-Air's* Character does plainly shew,
A man of sence may dress and be a Beau.
In *Vizor* many may their Picture fine;
A pious Out-side, but a poisonous Mind.
Religious Hypocrites thou'st open laid,
Those holy Cheats by which our Isle is swayed
Oh may'st thou live! and *Dryden*'s Place supply,
So long till thy best Friends shall bid thee die;
Could I from bounteous Heaven one wish obtain,
I'd make thy person lasting as thy Fame.

8.3 CHARLES GILDON, *A COMPARISON BETWEEN THE TWO STAGES* London, 1702.

GILDON'S ACCOUNT OF THE STAGE includes jokes at the expense of actors and playwrights. Even in that cheeky context, the insulting remarks aimed at female playwrights as a group are notable for the way they single out women. This belittling of women writers illustrates the environment in which Centlivre had to work. The *Comparison* is a dialogue between Ramble, Sullen, and Chagrin the Critic, who wax cynical and catty about the stage.

R: Proceed to the next.

S: *The Lost Lover*, or, *The Jealous Husband.*

R: I never heard of that.

S: Oh this is a Lady's!

C: How's that? – *Audetq; Viris contendere virgo*?

R: See how *Critick* starts at the naming a Lady.

C: What occasion had you to name a Lady in the confounded Work you're about?

S: Here's a Play of hers.

C: The Devil there is: I wonder in my Heart we are so lost to all Sense and Reason: What a Pox have the Women to do with the Muses? I grant you the Poets call the Nine Muses by the Names of Women, but why so? Not because the Sex had anything to do with Poetry, but because in the Sex they're much fitter for prostitution.

R: Abusive, now you're abusive Mr. *Critick*.

C: Sir I tell you we are abused: I hate these Petticoat-Authors; 'tis false Grammer, there's no Feminine for the Latin word, it is entirely of the Masculine Gender, and the Language won't bear such a thing as a She-Author.

S: Come, come, you forget yourself; you know it was a Lady carried the Prize of Poetry in *France* the other Day; and I assure you, if the Account were fairly stated, there have been in *England* some of that Sex who have done admirably.

C: I'll hear no more on it: Come Sir, drink about.

R: To the Fair Author of the *Fatal Friendship.*

C: Ay, come; away with it, anything that the Glass may go round. So – now I'll make an end of my Nap.

S: And we'll go on. Observe, *Love's a Fest.*

R: What's that?

S: This is a *French* Author's, but his Thefts are from the *Italian*; It's good for little, so we'll pass it over. Here's another, *Amintas.*

R: What a Plague's that? A *Pastoral* I warrant; well, what became of it?

S: Oh Damned Damned! *Ibrahim.*

R: That's a Woman's again, I remember it; so ho! Mr. *Critick.*

C: For Charity's sake let me alone: I desire to have nothing to do with not them in this affair: Let them scribble on, till they can serve all the Pastrycooks.

8.4 SUSANNA CENTLIVRE, DEDICATION TO *THE PLATONICK LADY*

London: printed for James Knapton at the Crown in St. Paul's Church-Yard, and Egbert Sanger, at the Post-House at the Middle-Temple-Gate in Fleetstreet, Feb. 1707.

CENTLIVRE PUBLISHED *THE PLATONICK LADY* anonymously, which makes this account of the way that audiences and readers judged women writers more poignant and powerful.

To all the Generous Encouragers of Female Ingenuity, this Play is Humbly Dedicated.

Gentlemen and Ladies,

My Muse chose to make this Universal Address, hoping, among the numerous Crowd, to find some Souls Great enough to protect her against the Carping Malice of the Vulgar World; who think it a proof of their Sense, to dislike every thing that is writ by Women. I was the more induc'd to this General Application, from the Usage I have met on all sides.

A Play secretly introduc'd to the House, whilst the Author remains unknown, is approv'd by every Body: The Actors cry it up, and are in expectation of a great Run; the Bookseller of a Second Edition, and the Scribler of a Sixth Night: But if by chance the Plot's discover'd, and the Brat found Fatherless, immediately it flags in the Opinion of those that extoll'd it before, and the Bookseller falls in his Price, with the Reason only, *It is a Woman's*. Thus they alter their Judgment, by the Esteem they have for the Author, tho' the Play is still the same. They ne'er reflect, that we have had some Male-Productions of this kind, void of Plot and Wit, and full as insipid as ever a Woman's of us all.

I can't forbear inserting a Story which my Bookseller, that printed my *Gamester*, told me, of a Spark that had seen my *Gamester* three or four times, and lik'd it extremely: Having bought one of the Books, ask'd who the Author was; and being told, a Woman, threw down the Book, and put up his Money, saying, he had spent too much after it already, and was sure if the Town had known that, it wou'd never have run ten days. No doubt this was a Wit in his own Eyes. It is such as these that rob us of that which inspires the Poet, Praise. And it is such as these made him that Printed my Comedy call'd, *Love's Contrivance*; or, *Medicin Malgre lui*, put two Letters of a wrong Name to it; which tho' it was the height of Injustice to me, yet his imposing on the Town turn'd to account with him; and thus passing for a Man's, it has been play'd at least a hundred times.

And why this Wrath against the Women's Works? Perhaps you'll answer, because they meddle with things out of their Sphere: But I say, no; for since the Poet is born, why not a Woman as well as a Man? Not that I wou'd derogate from those great Men who have a Genius, and Learning to improve that Genius: I only object against those ill-natur'd Criticks, who wanting both, think they have a sufficient claim to Sense, by railing at what they don't understand. Some have arm'd themselves with resolution not to like the Play they paid to see; and if in spite of Spleen they have been pleas'd against their Will, have maliciously reported it was none of mine, but given me by some Gentleman: Nay, even my own Sex, which shou'd assert our Prerogative against such Detractors, are often backward to encourage a Female Pen.

Wou'd these profest Enemies but consider what Examples we have had of Women that excell'd in all Arts; in Musick, Painting, Poetry; also in War: Nay, to our immortal Praise, what Empresses and Queens have fill'd the World? What cannot *England* boast from Women? The mighty *Romans* felt the Power of *Boadicea*'s Arm; *Eliza* made *Spain* tremble; but *ANN*, greatest of the Three, has shook the Man that aim'd at Universal Sway. After naming this Miracle, the Glory of our Sex, sure none will spitefully cavil at the following Scenes, purely because a Woman writ 'em. This I dare venture to say in their behalf, there is a Plot and Story in them, I hope will entertain the Reader; which is the utmost Ambition of,

Gentlemen and Ladies,

Your most obedient humble Servant,

8.5 JOHN MOTTLEY, *A COMPLEAT LIST OF ALL THE ENGLISH DRAMATIC POETS*

Appended to Thomas Whincop's *Scanderbeg*. London: Printed for W. Reeve, 1747.

MOTTLEY'S THEATRICAL HISTORY, like Giles Jacob's before him and John Genest's after, provides valuable insight into the responses and reactions to various plays, though the popularity of some stories may not be an index of their truth so much as their appeal. Robert Wilks probably did object to the part of George Airy, and he had the celebrity standing as the reigning leading man of the early eighteenth-century stage to risk such behavior in the rehearsal room.

The Busy Body, a Comedy, acted at the Theatre-Royal in *Drury-lane*, in the Year 1708, with very great Applause. This Play, when it was first offered to the Players, was received very cooly, and it was with great Difficulty that the Author could prevail upon them to think of acting it, which was not till very late in the Season. At the Rehearsal of it, *Mr. Wilks* had so mean an Opinion of his Part, [of Sir *George Airy*] that one Morning in a Passion he threw it off the Stage into the Pit, and swore that no body would bear to sit to hear such Stuff; which shews how excellently the Actors commonly judge before hand. The poor frighted Poetess begg'd him with Tears to take it up again, which he did mutteringly; and about the latter End of *April* the Play was acted, for the first Time. There had been scarce any thing mentioned of it in the Town before it came out, and those who had heard of it, were told it was a silly thing wrote by a Woman, that the Players had no Opinion of it, and on the very first Day there was a very poor House, scarce Charges. Under these Circumstances it cannot be supposed the Play appeared to much Advantage, the Audience only came there for want of another Place to go to, but without any Expectation of being much diverted; they were yawning at the Beginning of it, but were agreeably surprised, more and more every Act, till at last the House rung with as much Applause as was possible to be given by so thin an Audience. The next Day there was a better House, and the third crowded for the Benefit of the Author, and so it continued until the thirteenth. The next Year, a strong Proof of this Play having greatly pleased, was, upon the Company's dividing, and one Part of them going to the *Haymarket*, that it was acted at both Houses together for six Nights running in Opposition to one another; *Pack*, who did it first, playing the Part of *Marplot* at *Drury-lane*, and *Dogget* the same Part in the *Hay-market*.

8.6 *MORNING CHRONICLE AND LONDON ADVERTISER* REVIEW

Wednesday, October 16, 1776, "Theatrical Intelligence."

THIS REVIEW OF A 1776 PRODUCTION of *The Busy Body* illustrates the difficulties that actors faced even after some of Garrick's reforms of the playhouse. Woodward's very popular rendition of Marplot did not save the actor from having fruit thrown at him by a rowdy audience member.

Mrs. Barry being suddenly taken ill yesterday morning, the comedy of *The Busy Body* was substituted for the tragedy of *Douglas* last night at Covent-Garden Theatre—and allowing for the short notice which the performers had to prepare for the representation, we must do them the justice to say they acquitted themselves extremely well. Mr. Quick's Sir Francis Grip would be still more characteristic, if he was a small degree less alert, and did not so frequently exhibit the vigour of youth, a circumstance which as much destroys the poet's figure of the old man, as some certain tokens of real antiquity in a certain actress (whom a recollection of the pleasure she has often afforded on the stage in early life, ought to save from too particular remark), did that of the young Lady. Woodward, as usual, was still the giddy, sprightly, unthinking Marplot—he play'd the character last night admirably, and was speaking his occasional Epilogue as admirably, when a brute from the gallery threw an apple at him, on which, after bowing to the audience, he cut short the matter, and retired behind the scenes.—We applaud Mr. Woodward highly for this well-timed mark of indignation; it shewed a proper feeling for the dignity and decency of the Theatre; and we heartily wish, whenever so savage and indefensible a custom as that of pelting the Performers is practiced, the Prompter would [b]ring down the curtain. Such a custom would soon teach the riotous part of our audiences the difference between a play-house and a bear-garden.

Notes

1 *Biographia Dramatica: Or, a Companion to the Playhouse*, vol.1, 99.
2 *The Collected Works of William Hazlitt*. Ed. A. R. Waller and Arnold Glover. London: J. M. Dent, 1903.
3 "The man whom Glory carries to the stage in her windy car, the listless spectator leaves spiritless, the eager one exultant; so light, so small is what casts down or upbuilds a soul that craves for praise." *Horace: Satires, Epistles, and Ars Poetica*. Trans. H. Rushton Fairclough, Loeb Classical Library, Cambridge, MA: Harvard University Press, 1926; 1978, pp. 411–13. Congreve also used this epigram before *The Old Batchelor*. The next line is "Farewell the comic stage," as Horace proceeds to explain why comedy is deceptively hard to do well.
4 By the 1768 edition, the use of italics for Apollo, Europe, Scipio, Lelius, Romans, and dramatist had all been removed.
5 A poem of praise.
6 A group of millenarian Camisards, known as the French Prophets, came to London in 1706 prophesying the second coming and the fall of the Pope; they quickly grew into a small movement of a few hundred. They were Protestant charismatic Huguenots fleeing persecution in France.
7 Great Britain was in the midst of the War of Spanish Succession.
8 A fashionable card game, one of the London pleasures the ladies miss in the summer.
9 Seamstress.
10 Journalistic persona used by both Jonathan Swift and Sir Richard Steele.
11 Charles is joking that George is out hunting birds (women) early.
12 "Fortune" is capitalized in the 1768 text, even after other capitalization has been modernized, a choice that emphasized its metaphysical or mystical connotations.
13 Horoscope.
14 From the French "sous," a small coin.
15 Prester "Presbyter Johannes" John was the legendary Christian king of the eastern church (Ethiopia, India, Central Asia), a figure of distant Christian dominion.
16 If he fails, he will go into the army.
17 Does.
18 Bandage.
19 Rout means fashion; Whigs, etc. are all political parties and factions.
20 Marplot goes to a grubby gambling club, makes a bet with someone he thinks is a weakling, can't pay, and is beaten up by his mark, who is actually a strong Scotsman.
21 "Now the devil, oh my soul, Sir, if you touch your sword again I'll whip mine through your guts."
22 Originally, carest.
23 Probably "Gad," a mild oath, though the 1759 edition corrects it to "And."
24 Miranda is coming in from a sedan chair, a box-like carriage for one person, usually carried by two porters who hoisted it on poles.
25 Informal dress.
26 Patch jokes about a room for their wedding night.
27 In the first place.
28 A mild oath, like "gosh."
29 "Gardy" is a pet name for "guardian." "Chargee" is likewise his baby-talk version of charge, or the ward of a guardian.
30 An agreed-upon allowance for a married woman, who otherwise had no claim to what became her husband's money.
31 Greed personified.
32 Contract; Sir George is threatening Sir Francis with a swordfight.
33 It would have been inappropriate for Miranda to write or to receive a letter from Sir George, so in this spirit of his improvisational routine, he pretends she has written to him.
34 A mocking grin.
35 Hunter in greek mythology who sees Diana bathing and is turned into a stag. The reference is a double entrendre for cuckholding.

36 Kinds of alcohol women kept as "medicinal waters."
37 A female chaperone.
38 John Asgill argued that Christians who believe in translation (going directly to heaven) need not die. The book left him in disgrace.
39 A pimp.
40 Tease.
41 "Drawing" or drawing off involved pulling two flats apart to reveal a new scene further upstage.
42 Buried.
43 Secret code.
44 A mild oath, from "God's Heart."
45 Paid thugs or hitmen.
46 Castrate him.
47 Kiss.
48 A dancing jump.
49 Rough fabrics; a reference to his skin.
50 Oh, if only Jupiter would restore to me those bygone years! (Virgil, *The Aeneid,* book 7).
51 Chagrin.
52 With style.
53 Sir Jealous is going to make her eat in her room.
54 Possible song?
55 Boogyman or ghost.
56 Greensickness, a form of pica, which leads to cravings for non-edible substances. Young unmarried women were thought to be especially succeptible.
57 Foreign rulers, especially tyrants.
58 Sir Jealous: Sir, I kiss your hands. Your grace is very welcome in this land.
Charles: Sir, I am the humble and dedicated servant of Your Grace: my father sends to Your Grace his deepest respects, and has commissioned this English merchant to resolve a business matter, which makes me the most fortunate man in the world and your son-in-law. *My thanks to Greg Kaplan for these translations.*
59 The coast of Kent, to the south of England, was the site of many shipwrecks in an age of increased sea traffic and piracy.
60 A certified receipt of delivery of goods (George does not actually have the money).
61 Sir, please come forward.
62 Madam, please oblige me with the favour of your hand.
63 Small dagger.
64 This moment their hands are joined. [NB: "sueipora" is not conventional Spanish.]
65 Sir, I receive her as befits a great treasure.
66 Sessions of a court of law.
67 Short for "citizens," which implies a professional as distinct from noble or gentle identity.
68 Aging rake figures, associated with the libertinism of the Restoration. They would now be approaching their fifties and sixties.
69 The cuckhold's horns, a trope based on the idea that everyone but the husband knows about the affair.

9. *The Necromancer* and *Harlequin Doctor Faustus*

***THE NECROMANCER, OR HARLEQUIN DOCTOR FAUSTUS.* JOHN RICH. FIRST PERFORMED 20 DECEMBER 1723 AND FIRST PUBLISHED 1723, AND *HARLEQUIN DOCTOR FAUSTUS* WITH *THE NECROMANCER.* JOHN THURMOND. FIRST PERFORMED 26 NOVEMBER 1723 AND FIRST PUBLISHED 1723**

9.1 JOHN RICH, *THE NECROMANCER OR HARLEQUIN DOCTOR FAUSTUS* First Performed 20 December 1723 and First Published 1723

JOHN THURMOND, *HARLEQUIN DOCTOR FAUSTUS* First Performed 26 November 1723 and First Published 1723

THE HARLEQUIN FAUSTUS MANIA OF 1723 transformed the British stage and made the trickster Harlequin at once the most familiar and the most despised of figures in theatre. The commercial success of harlequinades has been explained demographically as the size of theatres and the audiences they could hold ballooned in the 1720s, then expanded even more at the end of the night as footmen, apprentices, and workers who could not afford full price crowded in for the afterpiece.[1] The competition between Drury Lane (managed by Cibber) and Lincoln's Inn Fields (managed by John Rich) heated up in a series of harlequinades featuring the Faustus narrative. On December 20, 1723, partly in response to Drury Lane's *Harlequin Dr. Faustus* the previous month, Rich staged the first performance of *The Necromancer, or Harlequin Dr. Faustus* at Lincoln's Inn Fields, along with Addison's ghost story farce *The Drummer*, for an evening of supernatural entertainment. The Haymarket jumped on the harlequin Faustus bandwagon with Mountfort's version *The Life and Death of Doctor Faustus, Made into a Farce, with the Humours of Harlequin and Scaramouche*, on January 31, 1724. All three ran concurrently through the season, though Rich's production of *The Necromancer*, featuring himself as Harlequin, was the greatest success. The *London Journal* December 28 reported "'Tis said, they had not less than 260 £ in the House." While usual receipts for Lincoln's Inn Fields ranged from just over £30 to £85, receipts were between £140 and £170 most of the nights *The Necromancer* played. It was still bringing in £135 a night in May of the season, and it carried many other plays that season.

These nominally secular pantomimes were a mélange of medieval morality plays, aspects of the Faust legends from the *Faustbuch* (in particular, its comic elements), Marlowe's largely unperformed *Dr. Faustus*, last judgment scenes, Roman mythology, and the physical materials of harlequinade. They mixed a strong dose of allegorical and biblical judgment into their entertaining *lazzi*, the short scenes populated by stock characters from the Italian *commedia del'arte* tradition. The result was the most commercially successful theatrical event in London before *The Beggar's Opera*. There is little doubt that much of the success rested in the appeal of spectacle. The flying dragon featured in most of these plays, the cutting off and regrowing of legs, Harlequin's blood pact with the devil, the talking animals (Owl, Ass, Goat, Cat, and/or Hog), Harlequin's tricks on others517

, and the visions presented to him all made use of stage machinery, engines, flies, cloud machines, and other special effects adapted from the continental operatic stage.

That these print texts seek to reproduce a mostly unspoken evening of entertainment is fascinating for several reasons. These are not so much scripts as accounts of the action and spectacle. John O'Brien argues that the fantasy content of these narratively compressed entertainments engaged cultural anxieties about race, nationality, ritual, technology, and mass culture itself. Rich dedicates more than half of his text to a note about the stories of Faust, focusing on the particular legend that Faust was presumed to be a sorcerer who had made a deal with the devil to acquire a handwriting font that allowed him to sell cheap copies of the Bible. Faust then goes to Germany to teach printing, hastening the arrival of the age of print in which Britons now lived. The Faustus harlequinades are also at the intersection of ancient and pre-reformation mysticism and modern theatrical and scientific technologies. As Al Coppola has demonstrated, *The Necromancer* in particular was conjuring up "the single most influential scientific discovery of the period: Newtonian attraction."[2] Rich's version minimizes the Dr. Faustus story and depends instead on spectacular puppetry and stagecraft, in which books, people, food, money, and other objects are drawn to Harlequin Faustus. By comparison, *Harlequin Dr. Faustus* stays closer to the Faust legend, with echoes of Marlowe's *The Tragical History of Dr. Faustus*, which had a mere single performance at the Red Bull in 1662 and another two at Dorset Gardens in 1675. *The British Stage, or, The Exploits of Harlequin, a Farce* (excerpted in the online supplement) foregrounds absurdity by opening with a conversation between the Dragon, the Windmill, the Owl, and the Ass. Faust may have come to the English stage as tragedy, but it only really succeeded on stage in the eighteenth century as farce.

The two texts below, *A Dramatick Entertainment, Call'd the Necromancer: or, Harlequin, Doctor Faustus*, based on Rich's production, and *An Exact Description of the Two Fam'd Entertainments Of Harlequin Doctor Faustus; With the Grand Masque of the Heathen Deities, And the Necromancer, or, Harlequin Doctor Faustus*, based on a combination of Thurmond's and Rich's productions, include some overlap in the Necromancer account, but they are nonetheless distinct texts. They reflect the original capitalization and punctuation as they are designed primarily for reading rather than as acting copy.

A
Dramatick
Entertainment,
Call'd the

NECROMANCER:
OR,
Harlequin, Doctor Faustus.

As Perform'd at the

THEATRE ROYAL
In Lincoln's-Inn-Fields

The Third Edition

To which is Prefix'd
A short Account of Doctor Faustus; and how
He came to be reputed a Magician.

London:
Printed, and Sold by T. Wood, at the Theatre
Royal in Lincoln's-Inn-Fields. 1724

[Price Six Pence]

A Short ACCOUNT Of Doctor Faustus, &c.

If Dr. Faustus was ambitious of being thought a Necromancer, it was no very hard Matter, at the Time in which he liv'd to obtain such a Character; and Tradition has been very faithful in supporting that Honour to him, which Ignorance and Credulity were, at first, so forward to give into.

He was born in Germany, about the Beginning of the 14th Century, a Period of Dullness and Barbarism. Monkery and Imposition prevail'd much stronger than, perhaps, they ever will again: And Knowledge was in so few hands that an uncommon Share of Learning, or uncommon Qualifications, were sufficient to make a Man be thought a Conjurer.

Add to this, That Faustus took his Studies at Cracovia, a Place in Germany, where, as we are told, the Art of Magick was formerly profess'd, and taught in publick Schools. He turn'd his occult Qualities to the best Account he could; and as the Age was easy to swallow the Belief of his Supernatural Power, he stroll'd about from Place to Place, both to propagate his Reputation, and enhance his Profit.

What particular Artifices he was Master of are but very darkly handed down to us; and some Circumstances, that are related, are so absurd, that they will scarce bear a second Telling.

'Tis certain, Superstition look'd upon him as a Person in League with Infernal Spirits, and acting a thousand strange Things by their Assistance.[3] Lonicerus, in his Zeal, calls a most unclean Beast, and a Sink of many Devils, that he had a Familiar always attending him in the Shape of a Dog. That his Inchantments and Diabolical Practices had like to have drawn a Prosecution upon him, and that he very narrowly escaped being seiz'd at Wittenberg. The same Author has given us an Account of his Death, as remarkable as any thing else that is recorded of him. The Night before he died, his Landlord taking Notice that he appear'd very melancholy, was importunate to know the Occasion: But Faustus waving a direct Answer, bade his Landlord not to be frighten'd that Night, whatever Noise he heard, or however the House should be shaken. When the Morning came, Faustus was found dead in his Apartment, with his Neck twisted round.

Wierus,[4] in the Account which he gives of Faustus, relates his putting a Trick upon a Chaplain, in a Story which proves rather his waggish and unlucky Disposition, than any Confederacy with the Devil. And Camerarius[5] likewise, who recounts an Action of him, in which, if it was true, some Magical Deception must have been used: Yet gives his story such a Turn, that he owns the Thing ridiculous, tho' diabolical. Both of them, however, seem to espouse the receiv'd Opinion of his being a Magician: And the latter of them relates the Manner of his Death, as if he thought that he was strangled by the Devil, upon the Expiration of his Contract.

Another Author[6] gives us yet greater Reason to suspect, that Faustus not only profess'd Magick, but grew presumptious upon the Opinion of his extraordinary Power. For, at

Venice, he gave out that he would fly thro' the Air, and accordingly put his Promise into Execution. But the Devil, or his Skill, so failed him in his pretended Flight, that he was dash'd violently against the Ground, and almost bruis'd to Death with his Fall.

Thus far, all the Writers (at least, all that I have met with) who strike in with the Superstition of his being a Magician: But a later Writer,[7] (in a Tract printed at Wittemberg, in 1683) has examin'd what Credit is to be given to these Relations: And whether there ever was such a Sorcerer, as Faustus is pretended to have been. I must confess, I have not been able to meet with this Piece; so cannot tell to what Cause he imputes the Tradition of Faustus being reputed a Conjurer.

But this Author is not the only Person who had a Suspicion of the Fable: And therefore I shall subjoin here a probable Narrative, how Faustus came into such Vogue and Reputation at that time of Day.

About the middle of the 14th Century, Laurence Coster, at Mentz in Germany, invented the Rudiments of Printing; which was at first in Gothick Characters, and resembling the Hand-Writings used at that Time. As soon as he had improv'd his Art to some Degree of Perfection, John Faustus, who work'd under him, (and who is probably the same who has since obtained the Title of Doctor Faustus) took the opportunity of the Christmas-Vigils, stole all his Master's Types and other Implements, and made off with them. In a few Years, Faustus, with these Materials, printed off an Edition of the Bible upon Parchment, and carried it with him to Paris.

As this new Invention had yet got no Air in that Country, it was a Surprize to find Faustus proffer his Books to Sale at a Price ten times lower than they had ever paid for Manuscripts. As the Impression too so nearly resembled the Hand-Writing then in Use; and as, upon comparison, they found every Copy so exactly the same, not a Stop differing, nor a Letter more in one Page than another, they grew astonish'd to see such a Number of Bibles all transcrib'd, as they thought, by one Hand: A labour that would have requir'd more Time to accomplish, than the Life of a Patriarch.

The Consequence of this was, that they wisely suspected, Faustus must have dealt with the Devil, and hereupon accus'd him of Magick. He apprehending the Danger of such a Profession, fled from Paris, return'd to Germany and there undertook to teach the Art of Printing.

Whoever is desirous of reading this Part of his Story more at large, may find it in the *Annales Typographici, &c.* publish'd about four Years ago, by Mr. Mattaire.

The Theatres having reviv'd the Memory of Faustus, by drawing him into their Grotesques; I thought some Curiosity might be excited of knowing who he was: And that therefore this short Account might be acceptable, prefix'd to an Entertainment, which takes its Name from Him.

Dramatis Personae.

Infernal Spirit	Mr. Leveridge.
Helen	Mrs. Chambers.
A Good Spirit	
A Bad Spirit	
Leander	Mr. LaGuerre.
Hero	Mrs. Chambers.
Charon	Mr. Leveridge.

The Necromancer: Or, Harlequin, Doctor Faustus.

Scene I

A Study. The Doctor *discover'd reading at a Table.*

A Good *and* Bad Spirit *appear.*

Good Spirit.
O Faustus! thy good Genius warns,
Break off in time; pursue no more
An Art, that will thy Soul ensnare.

Bad Spirit.
Faustus, go on: That Fear is vain:
Let they great Heart aspire to trace
Dark Nature to her secret Springs,
Till Knowledge make thee deem'd a God.

[Good *and* Bad Spirit *disappear:* The Doctor *uses Magical Motions, and an Infernal Spirit rises.*

Infernal Spirit.
Behold! Thy pow'rful Charms prevail,
And draw me from the Deeps below,
To listen to thy great Command.
On easy Terms the King of Night
Is pleas'd thy might Wand t'obey,
And offers to divide his Pow'r.
Sign thy Consent his Sway to own,

[*Shews a Paper.*

Ten thousand Demons stand prepar'd,
Thro' Seas, thro' Air, thro' raging Fires,
To start, and execute thy Will.

Good Spirit.
[*Within*] O Faustus! fear the dread Event.
Infernal Spirit.
Think, what Renown, what Treasures wait thee;
Each glitt'ring Vein, that Earth infolds,
Shall spread its ripen'd Ores for thee.

Good Spirit.
[*Within*] Think, Vengeance is offended Heav'n's!

Infernal Spirit.
Heav'n envies not poor Mortal's Bliss.
Thy Spirit is dull:–Our Art shall chear thee,
And chase this unavailing Gloom.

INCANTATION.

Arise! ye subtle Forms, that sport
Around the Throne of sable Night:
Whose Pleasures in her silent Court,
Are unprophan'd with baleful Light.

Arise! the Schreech-Owl's Voice proclaims,
Darkness is her awful Noon:
The Stars keep back their glimm'ring Flames,
And Veils of Clouds shut in the Moon.
Arise! ye subtle, &c.

Infernal Spirit.
Still art thou sad?—awake to Joy:

[*Strikes the Table, and it appears cover'd with Gold, Crowns, Sceptres, &c.*

See!—Wealth unbounded courts thy Hand.
Is it despis'd?—Then other Charms,
With full Delight, shall feast thy Sense.

[*Waves his Wand.*

Helen, appear; in Bloom and Grace
Lovely, as when they Beauties shone,
And fir'd the amorous Prince of Troy.

[*The spirit of* Helen *rises.*

Helen.
Why am I drawn from blissful Shades,
Where happy Pairs the circling Hours
In never-fading Transports wear,
And find Delights with Time renew?
Say, what deserving Youth to bless,
Is Helen call'd to Earth again?
Shew me the dear inchanting Form,
Where Truth and Constancy reside,
And I embrace the noble Flame.

Cupid! God of pleasing Anguish,
Teach th'enamour'd Swain to languish,
Teach him fierce Desires to know.
Heroes would be lost in Story,
Did not Love inspire their Glory,
Love does all that's great below.

[The Doctor *preparing to address* Helen *with Fondness, the* Infernal Spirit *interposes.*

Infernal Spirit.
Hold:—and the Terms of Pleasure know;
This Contract sign, thy Faith to bind,

[*Offers the Paper.*

Then revel in Delight at large,
And give a loose to Joy.

[The Doctor *gazing at* Helen, *signs the Paper, and gives it to the* Infernal Spirit*: After which attempting to approach* Helen, *the Phantom of* Envy *interferes.* The Doctor *starts, and turns in Surprize to the* Infernal Spirit, *who sinks laughing, as having deceiv'd him.* The Doctor *retires discontented, and the Scene closes.*

Scene ii

The Doctor's *School of Magick.*

Several Scholars seated on each Side of the Stage, to see the Power of his Art. The Doctor *waves his Wand, and the Spirits of* Hero *and* Leander *rise.*

Leander.
Enough have our disastrous Loves
Felt the Severities of Fate:
Drench'd in the Salt and Swelling Surge,
We found one common Grave.—And now,
If what the Poets sing be true,
In flow'ry Fields, the Seats assign'd
For happy Souls, shall we enjoy
A long Eternity of Bliss.

Hero.
Grant me, ye Pow'rs, where e'er my Lot is plac'd,
To have my lov'd Leander there,
And I no other Bliss require.

Leander.
O charming Hero! Times to come
Shall celebrate thy Name:
And lovers dwell upon the Praise
Of thy unequall'd Constancy

While on ten thousand Charms I gaze,
With Love's Fires my Bosom burns:

But ah! so bright thy Virtues blaze,
Love to Adoration turns.

While on ten thousand Charms I gaze,
With Love's Fires my Bosom burns:

Hero.
O my Soul's Joy! To hold thee thus,
Repays for all my Sorrows past:
Crown'd with this Pleasure, I forgive
The raging Wind and dashing Stream,
And welcome Death, that brings me back to thee.
Blest in thy Arms, the gloomy Vales,
Where shuddering Ghosts with Horror glide;
Gay as Elysium seem to smile,
And all is Paradise around.

Cease, injurious Maids, to blame
A fondness which you ne'er have known:

Feel but once the Lover's Flame,
The Fault will soon become your own.

Cease, injurious Maids, to blame
A Fondness which you ne'er have known:

[Charon *rises to them.*

Charon.
What mean this whining, pining Pair,
Must I for you detain my Fare?
Or do your Wisdoms think my Wherry,
Should wait your Time to cross the Ferry?

Leander.
Charon, thy rigorous Humour rule.

Charon.
And stand to hear a Love-sick Fool,
Talk o'er the Cant of flames,—and Darts,—
And Streaming Eyes, and bleeding hearts?
Give o'er this Stuff.—Why, what the Devil!
Won't drowning cure this amorous Evil?
I thought, when once Men's Heads were laid,
Their Passion with their Lives had fled:
But find, tho' Flesh and Blood no more,
The Whims i'th' Brain maintain their power.

Hero.
Oh! could thy savage Nature measure
The Joys of Love, th'inchanting Pleasure.

Charon.
No Doubt, ye Women may discover
Pleasures in a substantial Lover;
But what great Transports can you boast;
To find from One, that is, at most,
But a thin, unperforming Ghost?
Away; for, on the distant Shore,
Pluto expects my Cargo o'er:
The crowded Boat but waits for you;
Come, join with its fantastic Crew.

Ghosts of ev'ry Occupation,
Ev'ry Rank, and ev'ry Nation,
Some with Crimes all fould and spotted,
Some to happy Fates allotted,
Press the Stygian to pass.
Here a Soldier roars like Thunder,
Prates of Wenches, Wine, and Plunder:
Statesmen here the Times accusing;
Poets Sense for Rhymes abusing;
Lawyers chatt'ring,
Courtiers flatt'ring,
Bullies ranting,
Zealots canting,
Knaves and Fools of ev'ry Class!

[*At the End of the Air,* Hero, Leander, *and* Charon *vanish.*

Scene iii

[Doctor *waves his Wand, and the Scene is converted to a Wood; a monstrous* Dragon *appears, and from each Claw drops a* Dæmon, *representing divers Grotesque Figures; several Female Spirits rise in Character to each Figure, and join in Antick Dance. As they are performing, a Clock strikes, the* Doctor *is seiz'd, hurried away by Spirits, and devour'd by the Monster, which immediately take Flight; and while it is disappearing, Spirits vanish, and other* Dæmons *rejoice in the following Words:*

Now Triumph Hell, and Fiends be gay,
The Sorc'rer is become our Prey.

[*At the end of the Chorus the Curtain falls.*

FINIS.

An Exact
DESCRIPTION
Of the Two Fam'd
ENTERTAINMENTS

Of
Harlequin Doctor Faustus;
With the
Grand MASQUE of the Heathen Deities.
And the
NECROMANCER,
OR
Harlequin Doctor Faustus.

As now Perform'd, in Grotesque Characters,
At both Theatres
Containing
The particular Tricks, Incidents, Songs, Dances,
Alterations, and Additions, throughout both
Performances.
Regularly adjusted into distinct Scenes.
With the Names of the Persons of both Dramas.

London,
Printed for T. Payne, at the Crown, near
Stationers-Hall, (Price Six-pence)

The Preface.

The Entertainment of Doctor Faustus has at both Houses met with such prodigious Success, that it's grown the Subject of almost all Companies, both in Town and Country; and indeed 'tis a Diversion so very uncommon and surprising, that the Representation of it must certainly be a Satisfaction to every one that is not eaten up with Spleen and Ill-nature. Few, I believe, in, or near, London, but by Experience can and will join with me in my Assertion; and there are scarce any in the Country, especially young People, who have had but a bare mention of it, that do not long as much for the Sight of the Doctor, as a French Head, or a new Suit of Cloaths.

'Tis for their Sakes chiefly I have collected the following Scenes, that they may have the Pleasure of seeing, in Print at least, the wonderful Tricks and powerful Art of the so much talk'd of Faustus, as perform'd at both Theatres.

A further Preface I think needless, and therefore shall directly proceed to the Business, which wants no Harangue in its Favour, and can best speak for itself.

Harlequin Dr. Faustus, with the Grand Masque of the Heathen Deities

As Perform'd at the Theatre Royal in Drury-Lane

Dramatis Personæ

Doctor Faustus	Mr. Shaw.
Mephostophilus	Mr. Thurmond.
Scaramouch, student	Mr. Topham, sen.
Punch, student	Br. Boval.
Pierot, student	Mr. Topham, jun.
Helen	Mrs. Younger.
The Usurer	Mr. Norris.
The Bawd	Mr. Harper.
The Courtezan	Mrs. Tenoe.
The Salesman	Mr. Pinkethman.
His Wife	Mrs. Willis, sen.
Landlady	Mr. Harper.
Time	Mr. Rainton.
Death	Mr. Ray.
Six Countrymen	
Two Countrywomen	

The Heathen Deities

Flora	Mrs. Bullock.
Iris	Mrs. Tenoe.
Mars	Mr. Thurmond.
Bacchus	Mr. Boval.
Ceres	Mrs. Younger.
Mercury	Mr. Shaw.
Diana	Mrs. Booth.

Scene i.

The Doctor*'s Study*

The Doctor *enters, reading the Contract, with the greatest Inquietude; but, at length, after several Pauses, and Shews of Anxiety, he signs it with Blood drawn from his Finger by a Pin which he finds on the Ground.*

Lightning and Thunder immediately succeed, and Mephostophilus, *a Dæmon, flies down upon a Dragon, which throws from its Mouth and Nostrils Flames of Fire. He alights, receives the Contract from the* Doctor, *and another Dæmon arises, takes it from him, and sinks with it. The* Doctor *earnestly endeavours to get clear of the Fiend but he soon stops his Flight, and by a caressing Behaviour, quickly dissipates the gloomy consternation that he painfully labour'd under; and now the* Doctor, *fill'd with unusual Gladness by every Action, shews his rising Joy.*

The Dæmon then gives him into his Hand the End of his Black Wand; and the Doctor, *as they both turn round, receives from thence a White One, by which he has the Gift and Power of Enchantment. No sooner has he attain'd the Conjuring Faculty, but* Mephostophilus *leaves him, and two* Countrymen *and their Wives enter, in order to have their Fortunes told. After giving the* Doctor *Money, they let him know their Business; he examines their Hands, and carefully observes each Feature of their several Faces; then makes a Circle, and, upon waving his Wand, the Books that were rang'd on the Shelves disappear; and in their room are seen the Portraitures of an Officer, a Judge, a Woman of Fashion, and another in a Riding-Hood, as Representatives of their future Fortune. They, with the utmost Satisfaction, gaze on the Figures; and, having sufficiently fill'd their Eyes with the delightful Objects, join in a Dance proper to their Characters with all imaginable Joy and Transport; and then go off, expressing, in the most obsequious Manner, their Thanks to the* Doctor, *who, having an Inclination to the Women, immediately follows 'em.*

Scene ii.

The Outside of the Doctor's *House.*

Enter the two Countrymen *and their Wives Arm in Arm. They perceiving that the* Doctor *still continues behind 'em, endeavor to get rid of him, and accordingly take their Leaves, and are marching off; but the* Doctor, *not willing to part so, lays hold of the Women, and is carrying 'em away with him: The Husbands, enrag'd at such Usage, and uneasy for their Wives, interpose in their Behalfs, and strive to rescue 'em from the* Doctor; *upon which the* Doctor *makes Use of his Wand; it lightens and thunders, and several Devils appear, who so terrify the two* Country-men, *that they take to their Heels, and make towards the Porch of the Door, in order to escape safe, and shun such frightful Appearances. They no sooner enter the Porch, but it turns in with them, and in their stead, at the same Instant, a Table runs out nicely equip'd with an Entertainment.*

The Doctor *and the Women sit down to the Banquet, and* Mephostophilus *makes the fourth Person; but the Women, being shock'd at the Appearance of so disagreeable a Personage, discover their Uneasiness by several ways; at which the* Doctor *waves his Wand, and the Dæmon directly loses his frightful Shape, and appears a gay accomplish'd Shepherd. The Women seem delighted at the pleasing Transformation; and* Mephostophilus, *to add to their Satisfaction, entertains them with a suitable Dance, then makes his Obeisance, and sinks.*

The Women still regale themselves; and after a short time looking about, they perceive their Husbands gaping and staring at 'em out of the Windows of the House, (which by this time they had got the Way to) and finding themselves threaten'd by 'em for keeping the Doctor *Company, they acquaint him with it: On which the* Doctor *at once conjures a large Pair of Horns upon each of their Foreheads;*[8] *which so distract the poor Fellows, that tho' fasten'd to the Windows by the said Incumbrance, they express by all possible Means their Rage and Enmity against the* Doctor; *notwithstanding which, their Wives go off with the* Doctor, *making the greatest Scoff and Ridicule of their Husbands comical Fortunes: The* Doctor *at his* Exit *beckons the Table, which obeys the Summons, and follows him.*

Scene iii.

The Street.

Enter Scaramouch, Punch, *and* Pierot, *as Students. After a Dance proper to their different Characters, they knock at the* Doctor's *Door; a Dæmon Servant opens it, and conducts 'em in.*

Scene iv.

A Room in the Doctor's *House.*

A Table is discover'd set out with Bottles and Glasses. The Doctor *enters alone; and having dance a little Time, is accosted by the three Students, that just before were admitted by the Servant. The* Doctor *returns their Compliments in a very obliging Manner; and, after several courteous Addresses on all sides, begs 'em to refresh themselves with a Glass of Wine; accordingly they sit down at the Table, which (whilst they are drinking) upon the* Doctor's *waving hiss Wand, rises by degrees, and forms a stately Canopy, under which is discover'd the Spirit of* Helen,[9] *who gets up and dances; and on her return to her Seat, the Canopy gradually falls, and is a Table again. The Students, after great Astonishment and Wonder at the* Doctor's *Mastery of Art, return to their Wine; and whilst each of them drinks his Glass, a Pair of Ass's Ears sprout up on their Heads, without any further visible Means than the Wave of the* Doctor's *Wand. Each of them are pleased at the ridiculous Figure of the other, not perceiving themselves to be in the same Condition; and pointing and laughing at each other, they go out with the* Doctor.

Scene v.

The Street.

An Usurer crosses with a Bag of Money, and knocks at the Doctor's *Door; the Servant comes to it, and in a very obliging Manner introduces him.*

Scene vi.

A Room in the Doctor's *House.*

The Usurer with his Bag is brought in by the Servant to the Doctor, *who is sitting at a Table writing, and perusing several Papers. Upon his delivery of the Bag, the* Doctor *offers his Note; but he entirely contemns the Proposal, and gives him to understand that nothing but his Right Leg shall purchase it; the* Doctor *endeavours to dissuade him from that Demand, and lets him know his Head or Arms are at his Service; but nothing can prevail with the Usurer to desist from his Resolution of having his Right Leg; upon which the* Doctor *no longer argues with him, but lays it on the Table, and suffers him with a Knife to cut it off; which as soon as he has done, he laughs at the* Doctor, *and with the utmost Joy walks away with his Purchase.*

The Doctor *immediately, with his Wand, makes Application to his familiar* Mephostophilus, *who directly answers his Call; and sensible of his Wants, causes several Legs of different Colours, Forms, and Sizes, to appear; the* Doctor *makes his Choice of one, which is a Woman's; and in an instant it quits the rest, and fixes to his Stump. The* Doctor *no sooner has it, but he leaps upon the Table, and having admir'd and shewn his Satisfaction for his new Leg, in transport tries its Use and Power by a brisk Dance.*

He has scarce done, when an old Bawd enters with a gay Girl of Pleasure; the Doctor *runs and embraces* The Bawd *for her Civility, and then addresses the young one in order to carry her off; but the old Lady steps between, and informs him, that nothing is to be done without Money; the* Doctor *therefore takes the Bag, which he had of the Usurer, from off the Table, and presents it to the Matron, who seems extreamly well satisfied, and returns him Thanks: The* Doctor *and his new Mistress join in a Dance, and by turns Madam Governess makes one: That Diversion being over, the* Doctor *is going to retire with his Lady, but* The Bawd *again interposes, and insists upon more Money; upon which the* Doctor *hangs his Hat upon a Peg in the Room, and then gives her Instructions to hold her Apron under it; which she no sooner does, but vast Quantities of Silver from thence fall into it; whilst she is thus busied, the* Doctor *takes his Opportunity, and goes off with the Girl.* The Bawd *soon after, imagining that she has enough, walks to the Front of the Stage, expressing a perfect Rapture for her lucky Booty; but going again to bless her Eyes with the agreeable Sight, she finds, instead of all those Heaps of Wealth, an empty Apron, and her Riches flown. After shewing the greatest Signs of Wonder and Astonishment, she pursues 'em with all the Fury and Indignation of a disappointed, couzen'd Woman.*

Scene vii.

A Chamber in the Doctor*'s House*

Enter Faustus with his own Leg in Statu quo *before it was cut off, followed by three Students, they have all four put off their Scholastick Habits, and appear now in the Grotesque Characters of* Harlequin, Scaramouch, Punch, *and* Pierot. [10]

The Students, who at their first coming, saw such extraordinary Instances of the Doctor*'s great Power, having remain'd in his House 'till now, and being privy to the many comical Tricks and Whims ever since transacted by the* Doctor, *resolve, upon his Invitation, to continue with him, and be Partakers in his future Adventures: In pursuance of which, they have divested themselves of their Gowns and Caps, and appear dress'd as abovemention'd; in which Characters they continue throughout the Remainder of the Entertainment. The* Doctor *signifies to his Guests the Intent of his next Enterprize, and thereupon they follow him out.*

Scene viii.

A Salesman*'s Shop.*

Enter the Doctor *and the three Students. They apply to the Master, who is behind the Counter, for Cloaths; try several Sorts, and ask the Price of others; they seem not pleased with the Goods, and whilst they are letting the Man know it, four Red Cloaks, that hang up in the Shop, upon the* Doctor*'s waving his Wand, fly down on their respective Shoulders. The Master enrag'd at the Deceit, is very earnest and pressing for Payment; and the* Doctor *in the midst of his*

Importunity turns him into an old Woman. The Man's Wife by this time is allarm'd, and comes into the Shop; and surprised to see a Woman behind the Counter, and her Husband not in the Shop, falls foul on him in a very outrageous Manner, 'till by tearing off his Headcloths she perceives it to be her own Lord and Master. He informs his Wife of what had happen'd; she then likewise applies to 'em for the Money. The Doctor *and his Companions jump upon the Counter; from whence arise four Spirits, in the Forms of a Goat, a Cat, an Owl, and a Hog, and fly up with 'em; at the same time all the Goods in the Shop disappear at once. The Shopkeeper and his Wife, terrified at these strange Transactions, run out in all the Confusion imaginable.*

Scene ix.

The Street. A Tavern Sign hanging out.

Four Country Fellows, with Whips in their Hands enter, and form an awkward Dance. The Doctor *and his three Companions join 'em, and dance with 'em; which ended, the* Doctor *proposes to go into the Tavern, which they all gladly comply with; and so he leads 'em all thither.*

Scene x.

A Room in the Tavern.

The Doctor, *his three Companions, and the four Country Fellows, enter. They place themselves at the Table, and join in very humourous Behaviour; during which the* Doctor *and his Companions put Tricks on the Country Fellows, pick their pockets, &c. The* Countrymen *endeavor to take their Turns in Drinking, but never can make any Liquor come out of the Flask; tho' the* Doctor *and his Friends fill plentifully from the same: Upon which they lay hold of a Bowl of Punch, which stands upon the Table; but there again they find themselves deceiv'd; for upon their Attempt to secure it, the Liquor vanishes, and they are Masters only of an empty Bowl. The* Doctor *helps each of his three Companions to a Fowl and a Flask of Wine; and they immediately go off with the same: Upon which, the* Doctor, *having secur'd one of each for himself, jumps upon the Table, which flies up with him, and hangs in the Air. The* Countrymen *make strong Application to the* Doctor *that they may partake with him: He then offers a Flask; which upon the Touch goes off like a Pistol. They, enrag'd to the last degree, mount the Chairs, and from thence strike at him with their Whips. The* Doctor *drops through the Table (which is still hanging in the Air) in the Form of a Bear; in which Shape he attacks the* Landlady; *who, surpriz'd at the Uproar, was just before enter'd with her Husband; and so makes his Escape. The* Countrymen, *almost dead with Fear, tumble from their Chairs, on which they stood, quite through the Windows.*

Scene xi.

The Street.

Enter a Constable and a great Mob, headed by the Salesman *and Landlord of the Tavern, and knock at a Justice's Door. The* Doctor *watches their Motions; and turning himself into a Countryman joins 'em, and goes in along with 'em.*

Scene xii.

The Justice's Hall.

The Mob, &c. enter; and desire the Justice, who sits at the Table, to grant his Warrant for the apprehending of the Doctor *and his Companions, and the Justice complies. All this while the* Doctor *(in his Countryman's Dress) seems to be very assiduous in the Business, and taking the Warrant to peruse, tears it in several Pieces. Upon which the Mob lay hold of him; but the* Doctor, *leaving his Countryman's Cloaths in their Hands, gives 'em the Slip, and flies up through the Ceiling. They all, struck with Dread and Wonder at the Trick he has play'd 'em, look simply at each other, and so walk off.*

Scene xiii.

The Street.

The Doctor *and his three Companions enter, and sit down upon the Ground to rest themselves after the Fatigue of the Day. They being hungry, the* Doctor *strikes the Ground with his Wand, and from thence, in an Instant, turns out a Repast with Plates, Knives, Forks, &c. They having eat heartily, he again makes Use of his Wand, and it all at once disappears. A Porter then crosses with a Hamper of Wine, the* Doctor *makes a Motion to one of the Flasks, and it comes directly into his Hand. Whilst they are drinking, a Fellow goes by with a Basket of Oranges; and as he stands to give a Customer Change, several of 'em trundle from the Basket along the Ground to the* Doctor, *upon his giving 'em a Beckon. When they have thus refresh'd themselves, he strikes the Ground again, upon which the Banquet disappears. No sooner is this done, but they find the Mob is still in Pursuit of 'em; they therefore make the best of their Way off, and the Populace, with the strictest Watch, cross the Street in order to lay hold of 'em.*

Scene xiv.

A Yard belonging to a Farm-House. Part of the House and a large Thatcht Barn adjacent, in Prospect. A Mastiff-Dog chain'd in his Kennel in the Yard.

Two Fellows appear Threshing in the Barn; the Doctor *and his Companions enter, and, making up to it, beg that they'll give 'em Refuge and Protection. The great Dog in his Kennell falls a Barking, and the Threshers in a huffing Boisterous Manner entirely refuse it; which so enrages the* Doctor, *that he turns 'em both into Whisps of Straw, and then makes 'em, as such, jump out of the Barn. The* Doctor *and his Companions immediately enter, and make fast the Doors; the Mob, keeping close at their Heels, perceive where they are shelter'd, and force their Way into the Barn. Upon which the* Doctor *and his Companions get up to the Top of it, and from thence throw themselves down the Chimney of the House; but the* Doctor, *as he quits the Barn-Top, waves his Wand, and sets it all on Fire; it burns some time very fiercely, and the Top at last falling in, the Mob, in the utmost Dread, scour away.*

Scene xv.

The Doctor*'s Study.*

The Doctor *enters in the greatest Consternation, expecting now the dreadful Effect of his hellish Agreement, while the Musick plays a Tune of Horror; which over, the Clock strikes One, (the suppos'd Hour that terminated the* Doctor*'s Life) and* Time, *properly habited with his Scythe and Hour-Glass, accosts the* Doctor, *and sings to him the following Words:*

> *Mortal, thy dreadful Hour is come,*
> *Thy Days are past, the Glass is run.*

That finish'd, Death *enters opposite to* Time, *and in the subsequent Song gives him to know his Doom:*

> *Tremble, while Death now strikes the Blow,*
> *Let thy Black Soul prepare to go*
> *To everlasting Flames below.*

Before he concludes the last Line, he strikes the Doctor *with his Dart, at which he drops down dead.* [Time *and* Death *Exeunt.*]

Then two Fiends enter, in Lightning and Thunder, and laying hold of the Doctor, *turn him on his Head, and so sink downwards with him, through Flames, that from below blaze up in a dreadful Manner; other Dæmons, at the same Time, as he is going down, tear him Limb from Limb, and, with his mangled Pieces, fly rejoicing upwards.*

Scene xvi.

A Poetical Heaven. The Prospect terminating in plain Clouds.

Several Gods and Goddesses are discover'd rang'd on each Side, expressing the utmost Satisfaction at the Doctor's *Fall, because he, by his Magick Art, was deem'd to have an Influence on the Sun, Moon, and Season of the Year.*

First, Flora, *Goddess of Flowers, and* Iris, *Attendant on* Juno, *come forward, and join in a Dance.*

Next, Mars, *the God of War, approaches, and dances a Pyrrhic. He is succeeded by* Bacchus, *God of Wine, and* Ceres, *Goddess of Harvest, who dance together.*

Then Mercury, *Messanger to* Jupiter, *appears, and performs a Dance compos'd of several attitudes belonging to the Character.*

This Dance ended, the Cloud that finishes the Prospect flies up, and discovers a further View of a glorious transcendent Cœlum.

Diana *standing in a fix'd Posture on an Altitude form'd by Clouds, the Moon transparent over her Head in an Azure Sky, tinctur'd with little Stars, she descends to a Symphony of Flutes; and having deliver'd her Bow and Quiver to two attending Deities, she dances. At the Conclusion of which, the other Deities, both Gods and Goddesses, join her in a* Choral *Dance, which finishes the Entertainment.*

The NECROMANCER; OR Harlequin Doctor Faustus.

As Perform'd at the Theatre Royal In Lincoln's-Inn-Fields.

Dramatis Personæ

Doctor Faustus.	Mr. Rich.
Infernal Spirit.	Mr. Leveridge.
Five Furies.	Mr. Dupre.
	Mr. Nevelon, sen.
	Mr. Nevelon, jun.
	Mr. Lanyon.
	Mr. Newhouse.
The Shade of Helen.	Mrs. Chambers.
The Doctor's Man.	Mr. Spiller.
Two Men in the	Mr. Nevelon, sen.
Fifth Scene.	Mr. Nevelon, jun.
The Miller.	Mr. Nevelon, sen.
His Wife.	Mrs. Rogier.
His Man.	Mr. Nevelon, jun.
Leander.	Mr. La Guerre.
Hero.	Mrs. Chambers.
Charon.	Mr. Leveridge.
Harlequin Man	Mr. Dupre.
And Woman.	Mrs. Rogier.
Punch Ditto.	Mr. Nevelon, sen. Mrs. Wall.
Scaramouch Ditto.	Mr. Lanyon, Mrs. Ogden.
Mezzetin Ditto.	Mr. Nevelon, jun. Mrs. Cross.

The Necromancer, &c

Scene I.

The Doctor*'s Study.*

The Doctor *is discover'd at a Table, on which are several Papers, which he with Earnestness peruses, 'till interrupted by a Letter which drops from the Top of the Ceiling into his Hand; in surprise he quits the Table, opens it, and walking to the Front of the Stage, reads it by a Candle; which being held by him on the contrary Side, makes the Direction, viz. To* Doctor Faustus, *visible to the Audience.*

After a short Pause he returns to the Table, and writes an Answer; which he brings forward, as before, and by the Superscription, it appears to be wrote To the Impostor Faustus. *He comes back to the Table, and having seal'd it, he gives it a Toss, and it flies up on the contrary Side to that where the other came down.*

The Doctor *then sits down at the Table to read. A* Good and Bad Spirit *appear.*

Good Spirit.
O Faustus! thy good Genius warns,
Break off in time; pursue no more
An Art, that will thy Soul ensnare.

Bad Spirit.
Faustus, go on: That Fear is vain:
Let they great Heart aspire to trace
Dark Nature to her secret Springs,
Till Knowledge make thee deem'd a God.

[*The* Good *and* Bad Spirit *then disappear. The* Doctor *by Motions invokes his Familiar, and an* Infernal Spirit *rises and sings.*

Infernal Spirit.
Behold! Thy pow'rful Charms prevail,
And draw me from the Deeps below,
To listen to thy great Command.
On easy Terms the King of Night
Is pleas'd thy might Wand t'obey,
And offers to divide his Pow'r.
Sign thy Consent his Sway to own,

[*Shews a Paper.*

Ten thousand Demons stand prepar'd,
Thro' Seas, thro' Air, thro' raging Fires,
To start, and execute thy Will.

Good Spirit.
[*Within*] O Faustus! fear the dread Event.

Infernal Spirit.
Think, what Renown, what Treasures wait thee;
Each glitt'ring Vein, that Earth infolds,
Shall spread its ripen'd Ores for thee.

Good Spirit.
[*Within*] Think, Vengeance is offended Heav'n's!

Infernal Spirit.
Heav'n envies not poor Mortal's Bliss.
Thy Spirit is dull:—Our Art shall chear thee,
And chase this unavailing Gloom.

INCANTATION.

Arise! ye subtle Forms, that sport
Around the Throne of sable Night:
Whose Pleasures in her silent Court,
Are unprophan'd with baleful Light.

Arise! the Schreech-Owl's Voice proclaims,
Darkness is her awful Noon:
The Stars keep back their glimm'ring
Flames,
And Veils of Clouds shut in the Moon.
Arise! ye subtle, &c.

[*Here the* Five Furies *rise and dance, and then vanish.*

Infernal Spirit.
Still art thou sad?—awake to Joy:

[*Strikes the Table, and it appears cover'd with Gold, Crowns, Sceptres, &c.*

See!—Wealth unbounded courts thy Hand.
Is it despis'd?—Then other Charms,
With full Delight, shall feast thy Sense.

[*Waves his Wand.*

Helen, appear; in Bloom and Grace
Lovely, as when they Beauties shone,
And fir'd the amorous Prince of Troy.

[*The spirit of* Helen *rises.*

Helen.

Why am I drawn from blissful Shades,
Where happy Pairs the circling Hours
In never-fading Transports wear,
And find Delights with Time renew?
Say, what deserving Youth to bless,
Is Helen call'd to Earth again?
Shew me the dear inchanting Form,
Where Truth and Constancy reside,
And I embrace the noble Flame.

Cupid! God of pleasing Anguish,
Teach th'enamour'd Swain to languish,
Teach him fierce Desires to know.
Heroes would be lost in Story,
Did not Love inspire their Glory,
Love does all that's great below.

[The Doctor *preparing to address* Helen *with Fondness, the* Infernal Spirit *interposes.*

Infernal Spirit.

Hold:—and the Terms of Pleasure know;
This Contract sign, thy Faith to bind,

[*Offers the Paper.*

Then revel in Delight at large,
And give a loose to Joy.

[The Doctor *gazing at* Helen, *signs the Paper, and gives it to the* Infernal Spirit*: After which attempting to approach* Helen, *the Phantom of* Envy *interferes.* The Doctor *starts, and turns in Surprize to the* Infernal Spirit, *who sinks laughing, as having deceiv'd him.* The Doctor *retires discontented, and makes Experiment of his new-purchas'd Art, by touching with his Wand a particular Book on one of the Shelves; it immediately obeys his Summons, and comes to him. He seems pleas'd at his Success, and the Scene closes.*

Scene ii.

A Country Prospect.

Four Couple of Men and Women dress'd like Haymakers, with Rakes, Forks, &c. cross Arm in Arm. The Doctor *coming along in Pursuit of Pleasure, sees 'em, and follows 'em.*

Scene iii.

A Farm-House, &c.

The Men *and* Women *are discover'd on the Ground a Merry-making; (behind 'em one sits milking a Cow, and others are busied in loading a Cart;) the* Doctor *enters, and after having look'd slily at 'em a little time, he waves his Wand, and Musick is heard. The People, surpriz'd and wond'ring from whence it came, start up and join in a Country-Dance: During which the* Doctor *still views 'em, and with several little Fooleries, keeps Time with 'em. Just as they have done, he takes hold of one of the* Men's *Hands, (who is going to lead 'em round in a Line one after another,) and fixing the Person still, who is at the other End, he runs round with 'em, till they are all bundled up together: Then, after peeping roguishly at 'em in that Posture, he waves his Wand, and in that Manner they dance off, and he makes his Exit.*

Scene iv.

The Doctor's *Study.*

The two Girls *enter, introduc'd by the* Servant*; the* Doctor *waits on 'em immediately, and after saluting and toying with 'em, leads 'em to the upper End of the Study. He strikes his Wand against the lower Part of the Wainscot, and on the Touch there comes out a Table ready furnish'd* *with an Entertainment, and a Chair of each side. They all three sit down and regale themselves; and after a little time the* Servant *brings in, by his Master's Permission,* Two Men *to have their Fortunes told. The* Doctor *complements the Girls, leaves 'em at the Table, and comes forward to the* Two Men. *After looking stedfastly in their Faces, and perusing their respective Hands, he by Signs, gives 'em to understand that they will be hang'd. They are very uneasy at that Fate, and importune him to examine again: Accordingly he is persuaded; and complying with their Request, gives 'em the same Account as before. They seem very much disgusted, but however take out Money, as if they were going to satisfy the* Doctor *for his Trouble. He puts out his Hand in order to receive it, on which they re-put it in their Pockets, and go off laughing and overjoy'd with the Thoughts of cheating the* Doctor; *but he soon puts a Stop to their Mirth, by the Wave of his Wand, and in an Instant brings 'em back on their Hands, making 'em in that Posture dance a Minuet round the Room; that finish'd, he permits 'em to go off. The* Doctor *then returns to the Table, and taking each of the* Women *under his Arm, conducts 'em into another Room.*

No sooner is the Doctor's *Back turn'd, but his man, longing to partake of the Repast, makes towards the Table, and after several times looking carefully about to see if he's observ'd, and finding no Body near, he joyfully falls to: Having sufficiently indulg'd himself with eating, he takes up a Bottle and Glass in order to drink; whilst he is pulling out the Cork, the* Doctor *comes in unseen, waves his Wand, and retires. The* Man *then fills himself a Glass, and, with the utmost Shew of Pleasure goes to take it off, when, to his unspeakable Terror and Surprize, the Bottle flies out of his Hand, and the Wine vanishes in a Flash of Fire. He immediately falls a roaring, and runs out in the greatest Dread and Perplexity.*

Scene vi.

A Mill.

The Miller's Wife *comes down the Stairs from the Mill, and dances; in the Interim her* Husband *enters, and in a very angry Manner is for driving her up again; she endeavours to persuade him from it; but he persisting; she in a very obsequious Manner leaves him, and is going up; he mollified at Behaviour, calls her back, is reconcil'd, and dances with her.*

She then goes up, and he is accosted by the Doctor; *who wanting an Opportunity to get rid of him, in order to come at his* Wife, *entreats him to carry a Letter for him to a House a little distant; but the* Miller *entirely declines it. After the* Doctor *has made use of several Arguments to no purpose, whilst the* Miller *is directing him to the House, he trips him up, and runs up the Stairs to his* Wife, *who is looking out of a little Window.*

The Miller *recovering himself, gets up, and looks about for the* Doctor; *at last he sees him making Love to his* Wife *at the Window; and in the utmost Rage makes up after him.*

Upon this the Doctor *gets up to the Top of the Mill; the* Miller *pursues him, and courses him round it several times; at last the* Doctor *slips away, and runs down the Stairs: The* Miller, *after searching for him above to no purpose, looks down, perceives him, and makes after him: The* Doctor *finding the* Miller *at his Heels, catches hold of one of the Sails of the Windmill, and climbs to the Top, where he makes several Mockeries at the* Miller; *who enrag'd at that and his former ill Treatment, follows him up the Sail, and endeavours to come up at him: The* Doctor *by his Art immediately sets the Mill a going; and the poor* Miller, *fix'd to the Sail, keeps continually turning round; during which, the* Doctor *makes his Escape with his* Wife.

The Miller's Man *entering with a Sack of Corn on his Back, seeing his Master in that whimsical Posture, puts down his Burden, and goes to his assistance: After some difficulty he gets him loose, brings him to the Front of the Stage, and by several Applications brings him to himself.*

That is scarce done, when a Person, in a frightful out-of-the-way Dress enters, and dances; they soon perceive 'tis the Doctor, *and, drawing their Knives, resolve to dispatch him: Accordingly they seize him, and cut off his Arms; he, regardless, continues dancing; they then take off his Head; and finding him still alive, resolve to make a sure end of him by ripping up his Belly; which is no sooner completed, but out jumps the* Doctor *whole and entire; they affrighted to the last degree run away. The* Miller's Wife *comes down at the Instant, and goes off with the* Doctor; *who at his Exit touches the Sack of Corn with his Wand, and it follows him out.*

Immediately the Doctor *appears above in the Air, seated in an open Chariot drawn by the* Miller *and his* Man; *with the* Wife *by his Side, and the Sack behind him; he whips 'em along, and drives a-cross.*

Scene vii.

The Outside of the Doctor*'s House.*

Two Scholars *cross, knock at the Door, and are conducted in by the* Man.

Scene viii.

The Doctor*'s Study.*

Several Scholars, *(come with the Design of seeing the Power of* Doctor*'s Art) are discover'd; and the* Man *introduces to them the other two just admitted. The* Doctor *enters, and after a great many compliments on all Sides, orders Chairs, &c. As soon as they are seated, he waves his Wand, and the Spirits of* Hero *and* Leander[11] *rise, and sing.*

Leander.

Enough have our disastrous Loves
Felt the Severities of Fate:
Drench'd in the Salt and Swelling Surge,
We found one common Grave.—And now,
If what the Poets sing be true,
In flow'ry Fields, the Seats assign'd
For happy Souls, shall we enjoy
A long Eternity of Bliss.

Hero.

Grant me, ye Pow'rs, where e'er my Lot is plac'd,
To have my lov'd Leander there,
And I no other Bliss require.

Leander.

O charming Hero! Times to come
Shall celebrate thy Name:
And lovers dwell upon the Praise
Of thy unequall'd Constancy

While on ten thousand Charms I gaze,
With Love's Fires my Bosom burns:

But ah! so bright thy Virtues blaze,
Love to Adoration turns.

While on ten thousand Charms I gaze,
With Love's Fires my Bosom burns:

Hero.
O my Soul's Joy! To hold thee thus,
Repays for all my Sorrows past:
Crown'd with this Pleasure, I forgive
The raging Wind and dashing Stream,
And welcome Death, that brings me back to
thee.
Blest in thy Arms, the gloomy Vales,
Where shuddering Ghosts with Horror glide;
Gay as Elysium seem to smile,
And all is Paradise around.

Cease, injurious Maids, to blame
A fondness which you ne'er have known:

Feel but once the Lover's Flame,
The Fault will soon become your own.

Cease, injurious Maids, to blame
A Fondness which you ne'er have known:

[Charon, Ferry-man of Hell*, rises to 'em, and sings.*

Charon.
What mean this whining, pining Pair,
Must I for you detain my Fare?
Or do your Wisdoms think my Wherry,
Should wait your Time to cross the Ferry?

Leander.
Charon, thy rigorous Humour rule.

Charon.
And stand to hear a Love-sick Fool,
Talk o'er the Cant of flames,—and Darts,—
And Streaming Eyes, and bleeding hearts?
Give o'er this Stuff.—Why, what the Devil!
Won't drowning cure this amorous Evil?
I thought, when once Men's Heads were laid,
Their Passion with their Lives had fled:
But find, tho' Flesh and Blood no more,
The Whims i'th' Brain maintain their power.

Hero.
Oh! could thy savage Nature measure
The Joys of Love, th'inchanting Pleasure.

Charon.
No Doubt, ye Women may discover
Pleasures in a substantial Lover;
But what great Transports can you boast;
To find from One, that is, at most,
But a thin, unperforming Ghost?
Away; for, on the distant Shore,
Pluto expects my Cargo o'er:
The crowded Boat but waits for you;
Come, join with its fantastic Crew.

Ghosts of ev'ry Occupation,
Ev'ry Rank, and ev'ry Nation,
Some with Crimes all fould and spotted,
Some to happy Fates allotted,
Press the Stygian to pass.
Here a Soldier roars like Thunder,
Prates of Wenches, Wine, and Plunder:
Statesmen here the Times accusing;
Poets Sense for Rhymes abusing;
Lawyers chatt'ring,
Courtiers flatt'ring,
Bullies ranting,
Zealots canting,
Knaves and Fools of ev'ry Class!

[*At the End of the Song,* Hero, Leander, *and* Charon *vanish.*

The Doctor *waves his Wand, and the Scene changes to a Wood; a monstrous* Dragon *appears, and descends about half way down the Stage, and from each Claw drops a* Dæmon, *representing divers Grotesque Figures, viz.* Harlequin, Punch, Scaramouch, *and* Mezzetin. *Four Female Spirits rise in Character to each Figure, and join in Antick Dance; as they are performing, a Clock strikes;* the Doctor *is seiz'd by Spirits, and thrown into the Dragon's Mouth, which opens and shuts several times, 'till he has swallow'd* the Doctor *down, belching out Flames of Fire, and roaring in a horrible Manner. The* Dragon *rises slowly; the four* Dæmons *that drop from his Claws, take hold of 'em again, and rise with it; the Spirits vanish; and other* Dæmons *rejoice in the following Words:*

Now Triumph Hell, and Fiends be gay,
The Sorc'rer is become our Prey.

[*At the end of the Chorus, the Curtain falls.*

FINIS.

9.2 *HARLEQUIN & PUNCH KICK APOLLO OUT*

Harlequin & Punch Kick Apollo Out, printed by Gerard van der Gucht, 1735–1744. © Trustees of The British Museum.

In this satire of popular entertainments, Apollo, holding a volume of Horace, is kicked from a stage by Punch, while Harlequin, wearing a black mask, pursues him, brandishing his signature slap-stick and waving a scroll that reads "Harlequin Horace." The verse below reads "Shakespear, Rowe, Johnson, now are quite undone/These are thy Tryumphs, thy Exploits O Lun!" "Lun" was harlequin John Rich's stage name. George Stephens suggests that the print would have been originally published about 1729 when the satire "Harlequin Horace" (see BM Satires 1834) first appeared. Stephens notes that the style of the print suggests it was engraved some years after 1729, but before its earliest recorded appearance in 1759 as an illustration to "An Epistle from Theophilus Cibber, to David Garrick, Esq.: with Dissertations on Theatrical Subjects" which is dated "MDCCLIX" on the title-page.

Notes

1. See John O'Brien, *Harlequin Britain: Pantomime and Entertainment,* 1690–1760. Baltimore, MD and London: The Johns Hopkins University Press, 2004, and Harry William Pedicord, *The Theatrical Public in the Time of Garrick*. Carbondale, IL: Southern Illinois Univerity Press, 1966.
2. Al Coppola, "Harlequin Newton: John Rich's *The Necromancer* and the Public Science of the 1720s." In *"The Stage's Glory:" John Rich, 1692–1761*, ed. Berta Joncus and Jeremy Barlow. Newark, DE: University of Delaware Press, 2011, 334–355; 339.
3. In his *Theatrum Historicum*, translated from the German by Andreas Hondorff.
4. *De Præstigiis Dæmonem.*
5. *Opera Subcisisa: Centuria Prima.*
6. *Joh. Manlius in Collectaneir suis.*
7. *Johannes Georg. Neumannus in Dissertat. De Fausto Præstigiatore.*
8. Cuckolds are traditionally figured wearing horns.
9. In Greek mythology, Helen was reputed to be the most beautiful woman on earth.
10. The three students, Scaramouche, Punchinello and Pierrot, are all standard *zanni* or clown characters from the *commedia dell'arte*. With the exception of Pierrot, who usually was unmasked, each would have a distinctive mask and costume. Harlequin, recognized by his checkered costume, black mask and clapper, became the focal point of English pantomime and thus the emergence of the harlequinade genre.
11. Like *The Tragedy of Dr. Faustus*, the story of Hero and Leander was the subject of Christopher Marlowe's most famous poem. Hero, the priestess of Aphrodite, lived in a tower at Sestos on the European side of the Hellespont. Her lover Leander lived on the opposite shore at Abydos and, guided by a light in her window, would swim across the straight to be with her. Their affair ended when a storm blew out Hero's lamp and Leander was washed out to sea. In dejection at the sight of his corpse, Hero flung herself from the tower.

---

10. *The Beggar's Opera*

THE BEGGAR'S OPERA. AS IT IS ACTED AT THE THEATRE ROYAL IN LINCOLN'S-INN-FIELDS.[1] JOHN GAY. FIRST PERFORMED 29 JANUARY 1728 AND FIRST PUBLISHED 1728

10.1 *THE BEGGAR'S OPERA*. AS IT IS ACTED AT THE THEATRE ROYAL IN LINCOLN'S-INN-FIELDS.[2]

John Gay

First Performed 29 January 1728 and First Published 1728

IT IS SAFE TO SAY THAT *The Beggar's Opera*, the play that "made Gay rich and Rich gay," was the biggest theatrical phenomenon of the eighteenth century. Jonathan Swift first suggested the idea of a "Newgate pastoral" in a 1716 letter to Alexander Pope. While others such as Thomas D'Urfey, who wrote ten of the 68 songs used in *The Beggar's Opera*, had reworked extant songs and their lyrics, Gay's ballad opera realized the potential of the genre with its heady theatrical brew of musical, poetic, and narrative inversion. It tells the story of a gang of highwaymen managed by the Peachums and led by the charismatic and handsome Macheath. Peachum conspires with the jailer Lockit to turn in the highwaymen who fail to earn (steal) enough as criminals and the two split the reward, so that they continually profit from all aspects of the corrupt system. Gay drew on the exploits of the real-life "thief-taker" Jonathan Wild and escape artist Jack Shepphard for the characters of Peachum and Macheath. Wild ran a criminal gang and collected the lost-property rewards for the goods that he and his gang had stolen, then blackmailed those who might expose him. The burglar and jail-breaker Jack Shepphard, a sometime member of Wild's gang who was eventually betrayed by them, became a folk hero of sorts for his many escapes from capture and prison. In the play, the prison guard Lockit's daughter Lucy and Peachum's daughter Polly are both in love with the rakish and faithless Macheath, who is captured in a seduction set-up by a group of prostitutes. Macheath asks to be hanged when throngs of women appear at the jail in Act 3 and identify him as the father of their infants.

Beginning with its title, *The Beggar's Opera* uses a saturnalian "world-turned-upside-down" structure in its themes, its generic conventions, and its setting. Thwarted musical and social expectations, especially about domesticity in Peachum's house and in Polly's hopes, continue the process of disorienting the audience in proto-Brechtian fashion. The complicity between the underworld and the legitimate business worlds is more than a *leitmotif*. As Michael Denning notes, "the moral problem of the play becomes a political one. For the gang is not just a party, a conspiracy, a set of evil individuals; it is a new system, the mercantile commercial capitalism."[3] The ironic use of keywords such as honor, conscience, and industriousness keep the satiric finger pointed at the new global capitalism, in which ill-gotten profits, including those from the slave trade (which left few parts of the British economy untouched) were deemed legitimate business. References to the "great man" target Robert Walpole. While reading *The Beggar's Opera* to decode the political scandal can, as Stuart Sherman has suggested, lead us to miss the power of Gay's analogy between crime and legitimate business backed by the government, Walpole's administration and influence lurk around most corners.

The play begins "meta-generically" as well as metatheatrically, substituting the rehearsal-frame talk between the Player and the Beggar for the operatic recitative, and only then opening into Pepusch's custom-crafted overture, an aural signal that an opera was to begin. These layers of disruptive referentiality deepen as audiences discover a setting that is not the exotic and lavish world of operas such as *Artaxerxes* and *King Arthur*, but Peachum's house of rogues and highwaymen. The music came from familiar ballads, many of which are included in Allan Ramsay's *The Gentle Shepherd* (1725), rather than from the Italianate strains of art song. As Macheath and Polly, both Thomas Walker and Lavinia Fenton sang in a relatively untrained and "natural" style that pleased audiences and aurally distinguished ballad opera from its Italianate sources. This style may also have encouraged early fans to identify the actors with their roles and refer to them as "Macheath" and "Polly" in reviews and descriptions of the events, a crystalizing moment in the history of celebrity. Fenton, a working-class actress who had played Cherry in Farquhar's *The Beaux' Stratagem*, became the Duchess of Bolton after the Duke fell in love with her on the stage, took her as his lover, then married her in 1751. Their theatrically mediated relationship is immortalized in Hogarth's oil painting of Act 5, in which a kneeling Fenton as Polly directs her gaze past Peachum and toward the Duke of Bolton, represented in the side box *qua* jury.

The popularity of *The Beggar's Opera* is hard to overestimate, as is its influence. Gay's 1729 sequel, *Polly*, set in the West Indies amid slaving planters, included a cross-dressed Polly, a Macheath who passes as a black man, and Native American characters. Though *Polly* was suppressed by the Walpole administration and so could never achieve the popular success of *The Beggar's Opera*, it did emphasize the carnivalesque play with class and gender roles that made the original tick and that inspired so many cross-dressed performances, including Charlotte Charke as Macheath. The play ushered in a host of other ballad operas; by 1765, 81 of the 189 playing nights in the London theatres were devoted to musical mainpieces.[4] *The Beggar's Opera* enjoyed a very successful revival in 1920 at the Lyric, Hammersmith, and, exactly 200 years after its Lincoln's Inn Field's premiere, Kurt Weill and Bertolt Brecht reinvented it as *Die Dreigroschenoper* (*The Threepenny Opera*). *The Threepenny Opera* retained Gay's biting social commentary about political corruption, social justice, and economic inequality and transposed it to Weimar Germany. Weill's jazz-age music featured poor Berliners who sing "feed us and then we'll behave," and the cruel Macheath's "Mack the Knife" ("Die Moritat"), a haunting clash of tunefulness, rape, and murder that was captured by Lyle Lovett's 1994 recording but largely lost in the oblivious Bobby Darin 1959 rendition. Brecht's own theory of the alienation effect comes from an account of the Peking Opera, bringing his powerful concept full circle around the globe and back through another adaptation of opera that dates back to the eighteenth century.

—*Nos hæc novimus esse nihil.*[5]

Dramatis Personæ.

MEN.

Peachum.	Mr. *Hippesley.*
Lockit.	Mr. *Hall.*
Macheath.	Mr. *Walker.*
Filch.	Mr. *Clark.*
Jemmy Twitcher. A member of Macheath's gang.	Mr. H. *Bullock.*
Crook-finger'd Jack. A member of Macheath's gang.	Mr. *Houghton.*
Wat Dreary. A member of Macheath's gang.	Mr. *Smith.*
Robin of Bagshot. A member of Macheath's gang.	Mr. *Lacy.*
Nimming Ned. A member of Macheath's gang.	Mr. *Pit.*
Harry Padington. A member of Macheath's gang.	Mr. *Eaton.*
Ben Budge. A member of Macheath's gang.	Mr. *Morgan.*
Beggar.	Mr. *Chapman.*
Player.	Mr. *Milward.*
Drawer.	
Servant.	
Jailor.	
Constables, Turnkey, &c.	

WOMEN.

Mrs. Peachum.	Mrs. *Martin.*
Polly Peachum.	Miss *Fenton.*
Lucy Lockit.	Mrs. *Egleton.*
Diana Trapes.	Mrs. *Martin.*
Mrs. Coaxer. A woman of the town.	Mrs. *Holiday.*
Dolly Trull. A woman of the town.	Mrs. *Lacy.*
Mrs. Vixen. A woman of the town.	Mrs. *Rice.*
Betty Doxy. A woman of the town.	Mrs. *Rogers.*
Jenny Diver. A woman of the town.	Mrs. *Clarke.*
Mrs. Slammekin. A woman of the town.	Mrs. *Morgan.*
Suky Tawdry. A woman of the town.	Mrs. *Palin.*
Molly Brazen. A woman of the town.	Mrs. *Sallee.*

INTRODUCTION.

[Beggar. Player.]

BEGGAR. If poverty be a title to poetry, I am sure no-body can dispute mine. I own myself of the company of beggars; and I make one at their weekly festivals at St. *Giles*'s.[6] I have a small yearly salary for my catches, and am welcome to a dinner there whenever I please, which is more than most poets can say.

PLAYER. As we live by the muses, 'tis but gratitude in us to encourage poetical merit where-ever we find it. The muses, contrary to all other ladies, pay no distinction to dress, and never partially mistake the pertness of embroidery for wit, nor the modesty of want for dulness. Be the author who he will, we push his play as far as it will go. So (though you are in want) I wish you success heartily.

BEGGAR. This piece I own was originally writ for the celebrating the marriage of *James Chanter* and *Moll Lay*, two most excellent ballad-singers.[7] I have introduc'd the similes that are in all your celebrated *operas*: the *swallow*, the *moth*, the *bee*, the *ship*, the *flower*, &c. Besides, I have a prison scene which the ladies always reckon charmingly pathetick. As to the parts, I have observ'd such a nice impartiality to our two ladies, that it is impossible for either of them to take offence. I hope I may be forgiven, that I have not made my opera throughout unnatural, like those in vogue; for I have no recitative: excepting this, as I have consented to have neither prologue nor epilogue, it must be allow'd an opera in all its forms. The piece indeed hath been heretofore frequently represented by ourselves in our great room at St. *Giles*'s, so that I cannot too often acknowledge your charity in bringing it now on the stage.

PLAYER. But I see 'tis time for us to withdraw; the actors are preparing to begin. Play away the overture. [*Exeunt.*

ACT I.

ACT I. SCENE I.
Peachum's house.

[Peachum *sitting at a table with a large book of accounts before him.*

AIR I. An old Woman cloathed in Gray, &c.

PEACHUM. *Through all the employments of life*
Each neighbour abuses his brother;
Whore and rogue they call husband and wife:
All professions be-rogue one another.
The priest calls the lawyer a cheat,
The lawyer be-knaves the divine;
And the statesman, because he's so great,
Thinks his trade as honest as mine.

PEACHUM. A lawyer is an honest employment, so is mine. Like me too he acts in a double capacity, both against rogues and for 'em; for 'tis but fitting that we should protect and encourage cheats, since we live by them.

ACT I. SCENE II.

[Peachum, Filch.

FILCH. Sir, Black *Moll* hath sent word her tryal comes on in the afternoon, and she hopes you will order matters so as to bring her off.

PEACHUM. Why, she may plead her belly at worst; to my knowledge she hath taken care of that security. But as the wench is very active and industrious, you may satisfy her that I'll soften the evidence.[8]

FILCH. *Tom Gagg*, Sir, is found guilty.

PEACHUM. A lazy dog! When I took him the time before, I told him what he would come to if he did not mend his hand. This is death without reprieve. I may venture to book him. [*Writes*] "For *Tom Gagg*, forty pounds." Let *Betty Sly* know that I'll save her from transportation, for I can get more by her staying in *England*.[9]

FILCH. *Betty* hath brought more goods into our lock to-year[10] than any five of the gang; and in truth, 'tis a pity to lose so good a customer.

PEACHUM. If none of the gang take her off, she may, in the common course of business, live a twelve-month longer.[11] I love to let women scape. A good sportsman always lets the hen partridges fly, because the breed of the game depends upon them. Besides, here the law allows us no reward; there is nothing to be got by the death of women – except our wives.

FILCH. Without dispute, she is a fine woman! 'Twas to her I was oblig'd for my education, and (to say a bold word) she hath train'd up more young fellows to the business than the gaming-table.

PEACHUM. Truly, *Filch*, thy observation is right. We and the surgeons are more beholden to women than all the professions besides.[12]

AIR II. The bonny grey-ey'd Morn &c.

FILCH. *'Tis woman that seduces all mankind,*
By her we first were taught the wheedling arts:
Her very eyes can cheat; when most she's kind,
She tricks us of our money with our hearts.
For her, like wolves by night we roam for prey,
And practise ev'ry fraud to bribe her charms;
For suits of love, like law, are won by pay,
And beauty must be fee'd into our arms.

PEACHUM. But make haste to Newgate,[13] boy, and let my friends know what I intend; for I love to make them easy one way or other.

FILCH. When a gentleman is long kept in suspence, penitence may break his spirit ever after. Besides, certainty gives a man a good air upon his tryal, and makes him risque another without fear or scruple. But I'll away, for 'tis a pleasure to be the messenger of comfort to friends in affliction.

ACT I. SCENE III.

PEACHUM. But 'tis now high time to look about me for a decent execution against next Sessions.[14] I hate a lazy rogue, by whom one can get nothing 'till he is hang'd. A Register of the Gang, [*Reading*] Crook-finger'd *Jack*. A year and a half in the service; let me see how much the stock owes to his industry: one, two, three, four, five gold watches, and seven silver ones. A mighty clean-handed fellow! Sixteen snuff boxes, five of them of true gold. Six dozen of handkerchiefs, four silver-hilted swords, half a dozen of shirts, three tye-perriwigs, and a piece of broad cloth. Considering these are only the fruits of his leisure hours, I don't know a prettier fellow, for no man alive hath a more engaging presence of mind upon the road. *Wat Dreary*, alias *Brown Will*, an irregular dog, who hath an underhand way of disposing of his goods. I'll try him only for a Sessions or two longer upon his good behaviour. *Harry Padington*, a poor petty-larceny rascal, without the least genius; that fellow, though he were to live these six months, will never come to the gallows with any credit. Slippery *Sam*; he goes off the next Sessions, for the villain hath the impudence to have views of following his trade as a taylor, which he calls an honest employment. *Mat* of the *Mint*; listed not above a month ago, a promising sturdy fellow, and diligent in his way; somewhat too bold and hasty, and may raise good contributions on the publick, if he does not cut himself short by murder. *Tom Tipple*, a guzzling soaking sot, who is always too drunk to stand himself, or to make others stand. A cart is absolutely necessary for him. *Robin* of *Bagshot*, alias *Gorgon*, alias *Bluff Bob*, alias *Carbuncle*, alias *Bob Booty*.[15]

ACT I. SCENE IV.

[Peachum, Mrs. Peachum.

MRS. PEACHUM. What of *Bob Booty*, husband? I hope nothing bad hath betided him. You know, my dear, he's a favourite customer of mine. 'Twas he made me a present of this ring.

PEACHUM. I have set his name down in the black-list,[16] that's all, my dear; he spends his life among women, and as soon as his money is gone, one or other of the ladies will hang him for the reward, and there's forty pound lost to us for-ever.

MRS. PEACHUM. You know, my dear, I never meddle in matters of death; I always leave those affairs to you. Women indeed are bitter bad Judges in these cases, for they are so partial to the brave that they think every man handsome who is going to the camp or the gallows.[17]

AIR III. Cold and Raw, &c.

MRS. PEACHUM. *If any wench Venus's girdle wear,*
Though she be never so ugly;
Lillys and roses will quickly appear,
And her face look wond'rous smuggly.
Beneath the left ear so fit but a cord,
(A rope so charming a zone is!)
The youth in his cart hath the air of a Lord,
And we cry, there dies an Adonis!

MRS. PEACHUM. But really, husband, you should not be too hard-hearted, for you never had a finer, braver set of men than at present. We have not had a murder among them, all these seven months. And truly, my dear, that is a great blessing.

PEACHUM. What a dickens is the woman always a whimp'ring about murder for? No gentleman is ever look'd upon the worse for killing a man in his own defence; and if business cannot be carried on without it, what would you have a gentleman do?

MRS. PEACHUM. If I am in the wrong, my dear, you must excuse me, for no-body can help the frailty of an over-scrupulous conscience.

PEACHUM. Murder is as fashionable a crime as a man can be guilty of. How many fine gentlemen have we in *Newgate* every year, purely upon that article! If they have where withal to persuade the jury to bring it in manslaughter, what are they the worse for it? So, my dear, have done upon this subject. Was Captain *Macheath*[18] here this morning, for the bank-notes he left with you last week?

MRS. PEACHUM. Yes, my dear; and though the bank hath stopt payment, he was so cheerful and so agreeable! Sure there is not a finer gentleman upon the road than the captain! If he comes from *Bagshot* at any reasonable hour he hath promis'd to make one this evening with *Polly* and me, and *Bob Booty*, at a party of quadrille. Pray, my dear, is the captain rich?

PEACHUM. The captain keeps too good company ever to grow rich. *Mary-bone* and the chocolate-houses[19] are his undoing. The man that proposes to get money by play should have the education of a fine gentleman, and be train'd up to it from his youth.

MRS. PEACHUM. Really, I am sorry upon *Polly*'s account the captain hath not more discretion. What business hath he to keep company with lords and gentlemen? He should leave them to prey upon one another.

PEACHUM. Upon *Polly*'s account! What, a plague, does the woman mean? – Upon *Polly*'s account!

MRS. PEACHUM. Captain *Macheath* is very fond of the girl.

PEACHUM. And what then?

MRS. PEACHUM. If I have any skill in the ways of women, I am sure *Polly* thinks him a very pretty man.

PEACHUM. And what then? You would not be so mad to have the wench marry him! Gamesters and highwaymen are generally very good to their whores, but they are very devils to their wives.

MRS. PEACHUM. But if *Polly* should be in love, how should we help her, or how can she help herself? Poor girl, I am in the utmost concern about her.

AIR IV. Why is your faithful Slave disdain'd? &c.

MRS. PEACHUM. *If love the virgin's heart invade,*
How, like a moth, the simple maid
Still plays about the flame!
If soon she be not made a wife,
Her honour's sing'd, and then for life,
She's – what I dare not name.

PEACHUM. Look ye, wife. A handsome wench in our way of business is as profitable as at the bar of a *Temple* coffee-house,[20] who looks upon it as her livelihood to grant every liberty but one. You see I would indulge the girl as far as prudently we can. In any thing, but marriage![21] After that, my dear, how shall we be safe? Are we not then in her husband's power? For a husband hath the absolute power over all a wife's secrets but her own. If the girl had the discretion of a court lady, who can have a dozen young fellows at her ear without complying with one, I should not matter it; but *Polly* is tinder, and a spark will at once set her on a flame. Married! If the wench does not know her own profit, sure she knows her own pleasure better than to make herself a property! My daughter to me should be, like a court lady to a minister of state, a key to the whole gang.[22] Married! If the affair is not already done, I'll terrify her from it, by the example of our neighbours.

MRS. PEACHUM. May-hap, my dear, you may injure the girl. She loves to imitate the fine ladies, and she may only allow the captain liberties in the view of interest.

PEACHUM. But 'tis your duty, my dear, to warn the girl against her ruin, and to instruct her how to make the most of her beauty. I'll go to her this moment, and sift her. In the mean time, wife, rip out the coronets and marks of these dozen of cambric handkerchiefs, for I can dispose of them this afternoon to a chap in the city.[23]

ACT I. SCENE V.

MRS. PEACHUM. Never was a man more out of the way in an argument than my husband! Why must our *Polly*, forsooth, differ from her sex, and love only her husband? And why must *Polly*'s marriage, contrary to all observation, make her the less followed by other men? All men are thieves in love, and like a woman the better for being another's property.

AIR V. Of all the simple Things we do, &c.

MRS. PEACHUM. *A maid is like the golden oar,*[24]
Which hath guineas intrinsical in't,
Whose worth is never known, before
It is try'd and imprest in the mint.
A wife's like a guinea in gold,
Stampt with the name of her spouse;
Now here, now there; is bought, or is sold;
And is current in every house.

ACT I. SCENE VI.

[Mrs. Peachum, Filch.

MRS. PEACHUM. Come hither *Filch*. I am as fond of this child, as though my mind misgave me he were my own. He hath as fine a hand at picking a pocket as a woman, and is as nimble finger'd as a juggler. If an unlucky session does not cut the rope of thy life, I pronounce, boy, thou wilt be a great man in history. Where was your post last night, my boy?

FILCH. I ply'd at the opera, Madam; and considering 'twas neither dark nor rainy, so that there was no great hurry in getting chairs and coaches, made a tolerable hand on't. These seven handkerchiefs, Madam.

MRS. PEACHUM. Colour'd ones, I see. They are of sure sale from our ware-house at *Redriff* among the seamen.

FILCH. And this snuff-box.

MRS. PEACHUM. Set in gold! A pretty encouragement this to a young beginner.

FILCH. I had a fair tug at a charming gold Watch. Pox take the Taylors for making the Fobs so deep and narrow! It stuck by the way, and I was forc'd to make my Escape under a Coach. Really, Madam, I fear I shall be cut off in the Flower of my Youth, so that every now and then (since I was pumpt[25]) I have thoughts of taking up and going to Sea.

MRS. PEACHUM. You should go to *Hockley in the Hole*, and to *Marybone*, child, to learn valour. These are the schools that have bred so many brave men. I thought, boy, by this time, thou hadst lost fear as well as shame. Poor lad! How little does he know as yet of the *Old-Baily*![26] For the first fact I'll insure thee from being hang'd; and going to sea, *Filch*, will come time enough upon a sentence of transportation. But now, since you have nothing better to do, ev'n go to your book, and learn your catechism; for really a man makes but an ill figure in the ordinary's paper, who cannot give a satisfactory answer to his questions.[27] But, hark you, my lad. Don't tell me a lye; for you know I hate a lyar. Do you know of any thing that hath past between Captain *Macheath* and our *Polly*?

FILCH. I beg you, Madam, don't ask me; for I must either tell a lye to you or to Miss *Polly*; for I promis'd her I would not tell.

MRS. PEACHUM. But when the honour of our family is concern'd –

FILCH. I shall lead a sad life with Miss *Polly*, if ever she come to know that I told you. Besides, I would not willingly forfeit my own honour by betraying any body.

MRS. PEACHUM. Yonder comes my husband and *Polly*. Come, *Filch*, you shall go with me into my own room, and tell me the whole story. I'll give thee a most delicious glass of a cordial that I keep for my own drinking.

ACT I. SCENE VII.

[Peachum, Polly.

POLLY. I know as well as any of the fine Ladies how to make the most of my self and of my man too. A woman knows how to be mercenary, though she hath never been in a court or at an assembly. We have it in our natures, Papa. If I allow Captain *Macheath* some trifling liberties, I have this watch and other visible marks of his favour to show for it. A girl who cannot grant some things, and refuse what is most material, will make but a poor hand of her beauty, and soon be thrown upon the common.

AIR VI. What shall I do to show how much I love her, &c.

POLLY. *Virgins are like the fair flower in its lustre,*
Which in the garden enamels the ground;
Near it the bees in play flutter and cluster,
And gaudy butterflies frolick around.
But, when once pluck'd, 'tis no longer alluring,
To Covent-Garden 'tis sent, (as yet sweet,)
There fades, and shrinks, and grows past all enduring,
Rots, stinks, and dies, and is trod under feet.

PEACHUM. You know, *Polly*, I am not against your toying and trifling with a customer in the way of business, or to get out a secret, or so. But if I find out that you have play'd the fool and are married, you jade you, I'll cut your throat, hussy. Now you know my mind.

ACT I. SCENE VIII.

[Peachum, Polly, Mrs. Peachum.

AIR VII. Oh London is a fine Town.

MRS. PEACHUM. [*In a very great passion*] *Our Polly is a sad slut! Nor heeds what we taught her.*
I wonder any man alive will ever rear a daughter!
For she must have both hoods and gowns, and hoops to swell her pride,
With scarfs and stays, and gloves and lace; and she will have men beside;
And when she's drest with care and cost, all-tempting, fine and gay,
As men should serve a cowcumber[28]*, she flings herself away.*
Our Polly is a sad slut, &c.

MRS. PEACHUM. You baggage! You hussy! You inconsiderate jade! Had you been hang'd, it would not have vex'd me, for that might have been your misfortune; but to do such a mad thing by choice! The wench is married, husband.

PEACHUM. Married! The Captain is a bold man, and will risque any thing for money; to be sure he believes her a fortune. Do you think your mother and I should have liv'd comfortably so long together, if ever we had been married? Baggage!

MRS. PEACHUM. I knew she was always a proud slut; and now the wench hath play'd the fool and married, because forsooth she would do like the gentry. Can you support the expence of a husband, hussy, in gaming, drinking and whoring? Have you money enough to carry on the daily quarrels of man and wife about who shall squander most? There are not many husbands and wives, who can bear the charges of plaguing one another in a handsome way. If you must be married, could you introduce no-body into our family but a highwayman? Why, thou foolish jade, thou wilt be as ill-us'd, and as much neglected, as if thou hadst married a Lord!

PEACHUM. Let not your anger, my dear, break through the rules of decency, for the Captain looks upon himself in the military capacity, as a gentleman by his profession. Besides what he hath already, I know he is in a fair way of getting, or of dying; and both these ways, let me tell you, are most excellent chances for a wife. Tell me hussy, are you ruin'd[29] or no?

MRS. PEACHUM. With *Polly*'s fortune, she might very well have gone off to a person of distinction. Yes, that you might, you pouting slut!

PEACHUM. What, is the wench dumb? Speak, or I'll make you plead by squeezing out an answer from you. Are you really bound wife to him, or are you only upon liking? [*Pinches her.*

POLLY. Oh! [*Screaming.*

MRS. PEACHUM. How the mother is to be pitied who hath handsome daughters! Locks, bolts, bars, and lectures of morality are nothing to them: They break through them all. They have as much pleasure in cheating a father and mother, as in cheating at cards.

PEACHUM. Why, *Polly*, I shall soon know if you are married, by *Macheath*'s keeping from our house.

AIR VIII. Grim King of the Ghosts, &c.

POLLY. *Can love be controul'd by advice?*
Will cupid our mothers obey?
Though my heart were as frozen as ice,
At his flame 'twould have melted away.
When he kist me so closely he prest,
'Twas so sweet that I must have comply'd:
So I thought it both safest and best
To marry, for fear you should chide.

MRS. PEACHUM. Then all the hopes of our family are gone for ever and ever!

PEACHUM. And *Macheath* may hang his father and mother-in-law, in hope to get into their daughter's fortune.[30]

POLLY. I did not marry him (as 'tis the fashion) cooly and deliberately for honour or money. But, I love him.

MRS. PEACHUM. Love him! Worse and worse! I thought the girl had been better bred. Oh husband, husband! Her folly makes me mad! My head swims! I'm distracted! I can't support myself – Oh! [*Faints.*

PEACHUM. See, wench, to what a condition you have reduc'd your poor mother! A glass of cordial, this instant. How the poor woman takes it to heart!

[*Polly goes out, and returns with it.*

Ah, hussy, now this is the only comfort your mother has left!

POLLY. Give her another glass, Sir; my mama drinks double the quantity whenever she is out of order. This, you see, fetches her.

MRS. PEACHUM. The girl shows such a readiness, and so much concern, that I could almost find in my heart to forgive her.

AIR. IX. O Jenny, O Jenny, where hast thou been.

MRS. PEACHUM. *O Polly, you might have toy'd and kist.*
By keeping men off, you keep them on.

POLLY. *But he so teaz'd me,*
And he so pleas'd me,
What I did, you must have done.

MRS. PEACHUM. Not with a highwayman. – You sorry slut!

PEACHUM. A word with you, wife. 'Tis no new thing for a wench to take man without consent of parents. You know 'tis the frailty of woman, my dear.

MRS. PEACHUM. Yes, indeed, the sex is frail. But the first time a woman is frail, she should be somewhat nice methinks, for then or never is the time to make her fortune. After that, she hath nothing to do but to guard herself from being found out, and she may do what she pleases.

PEACHUM. Make your self a little easy; I have a thought shall soon set all matters again to rights. Why so melancholy, *Polly*? Since what is done cannot be undone, we must all endeavour to make the best of it.

MRS. PEACHUM. Well, *Polly*; as far as one woman can forgive another, I forgive thee. – Your father is too fond of you, hussy.

POLLY. Then all my sorrows are at an end.

MRS. PEACHUM. A mighty likely speech in troth, for a wench who is just married!

AIR X. Thomas, I cannot &c.

POLLY. *I, like a ship in storms, was tost;*
Yet afraid to put in to land;
For seiz'd in the port the vessel's lost,
Whose treasure is contreband.
The waves are laid,
My duty's paid.
O joy beyond expression!
Thus, safe a-shore,
I ask no more,
My all is in my possession.

PEACHUM. I hear customers in t'other room; Go, talk with 'em, *Polly*; but come to us again, as soon as they are gone. – But, heark ye, Child, if 'tis the gentleman who was here yesterday about the repeating-watch;[31] say, you believe we can't get intelligence of it, till to-morrow. For I lent it to *Suky Straddle*, to make a figure with it to-night at a tavern in *Drury-Lane*. If t'other gentleman calls for the silver-hilted sword; you know beetle-brow'd *Jemmy* hath it on, and he doth not come from *Tunbridge* till *Tuesday* night; so that it cannot be had till then.

ACT I. SCENE IX.

[Peachum, Mrs. Peachum.

PEACHUM. Dear wife, be a little pacified. Don't let your passion run away with your senses. *Polly*, I grant you, hath done a rash thing.

MRS. PEACHUM. If she had had only an intrigue with the fellow, why the very best families have excus'd and huddled up a frailty of that sort. 'Tis marriage, husband, that makes it a blemish.

PEACHUM. But money, wife, is the true Fuller's Earth for reputations, there is not a spot or a stain but what it can take out. A rich rogue now-a-days is fit company for any gentleman; and the world, my dear, hath not such a contempt for roguery as you imagine. I tell you, wife, I can make this match turn to our advantage.

MRS. PEACHUM. I am very sensible, husband, that Captain *Macheath* is worth money, but I am in doubt whether he hath not two or three wives already, and then if he should dye in a Session or two, *Polly*'s dower would come into dispute.

PEACHUM. That, indeed, is a point which ought to be consider'd.

AIR XI. A Soldier and a Sailor.

PEACHUM. *A fox may steal your hens, Sir,*
A whore your health and pence, Sir,
Your daughter rob your chest, Sir,
Your wife may steal your rest, Sir,
A thief your goods and plate.
But this is all but picking;
With rest, pence, chest and chicken,
It ever was decreed, Sir,
If lawyer's hand is fee'd, Sir,
He steals your whole estate.

PEACHUM. The lawyers are bitter enemies to those in our way. They don't care that any body should get a clandestine livelihood but themselves.

ACT I. SCENE X.

[Mrs. Peachum, Peachum, Polly.

POLLY. 'Twas only Nimming *Ned*. He brought in a damask window-curtain, a hoop-petticoat, a pair of silver candlesticks, a perriwig, and one silk stocking, from the fire that happen'd last night.

PEACHUM. There is not a fellow that is cleverer in his way, and saves more goods out of the fire than *Ned*. But now, *Polly*, to your affair; for matters must not be left as they are. You are married then, it seems?

POLLY. Yes, Sir.

PEACHUM. And how do you propose to live, child?

POLLY. Like other women, Sir, upon the industry of my husband.

MRS. PEACHUM. What is, the wench turn'd fool? A highwayman's wife, like a soldier's, hath as little of his pay, as of his company.

PEACHUM. And had not you the common views of a gentlewoman in your marriage, *Polly*?

POLLY. I don't know what you mean, Sir.

PEACHUM. Of a jointure, and of being a widow.[32]

POLLY. But I love him, Sir: how then could I have thoughts of parting with him?

PEACHUM. Parting with him! Why, that is the whole scheme and intention of all marriage articles. The comfortable estate of widow-hood, is the only hope that keeps up a wife's spirits. Where is the woman who would scruple to be a wife, if she had it in her power to be a widow whenever she pleas'd? If you have any views of this sort, *Polly*, I shall think the match not so very unreasonable.

POLLY. How I dread to hear your advice! Yet I must beg you to explain yourself.

PEACHUM. Secure what he hath got, have him peach'd the next Sessions, and then at once you are made a rich widow.

POLLY. What, murder the man I love! The blood runs cold at my heart with the very thought of it.

PEACHUM. Fye, *Polly*! What hath murder to do in the affair? Since the thing sooner or later must happen, I dare say, the Captain himself would like that we should get the reward for his death sooner than a stranger. Why, *Polly*, the Captain knows, that as 'tis his employment to rob, so 'tis ours to take robbers; every man in his business. So that there is no malice in the case.

MRS. PEACHUM. Ay, husband, now you have nick'd the matter. To have him peach'd is the only thing could ever make me forgive her.

AIR XII. Now ponder well, ye Parents dear.

POLLY. *Oh, ponder well! Be not severe;*
So save a wretched wife!
For on the rope that hangs my dear
Depends poor Polly's life.

MRS. PEACHUM. But your duty to your parents, hussy, obliges you to hang him. What would many a wife give for such an opportunity!

POLLY. What is a jointure, what is widow-hood to me? I know my heart. I cannot survive him.

AIR XIII. Le printemps rappelle aux armes.

POLLY. *The turtle thus with plaintive crying,*
Her lover dying,
The turtle thus with plaintive crying,
Laments her dove.
Down she drops quite spent with sighing,
Pair'd in death, as pair'd in love.

POLLY. Thus, Sir, it will happen to your poor *Polly*.

MRS. PEACHUM. What, is the fool in love in earnest then? I hate thee for being particular: Why, wench, thou art a shame to thy very sex.

POLLY. But hear me, mother. – If you ever lov'd –

MRS. PEACHUM. Those cursed play-books she reads have been her ruin. One word more, hussy, and I shall knock your brains out, if you have any.

PEACHUM. Keep out of the way, *Polly*, for fear of mischief, and consider of what is propos'd to you.

MRS. PEACHUM. Away, hussy. Hang your husband, and be dutiful.

ACT I. SCENE XI.

[Mrs. Peachum, Peachum. Polly *listening*.

MRS. PEACHUM. The thing, husband, must and shall be done. For the sake of intelligence we must take other measures, and have him peach'd the next session without her consent. If she will not know her duty, we know ours.

PEACHUM. But really, my dear, it grieves one's heart to take off a great man. When I consider his personal bravery, his fine stratagem, how much we have already got by him, and how much more we may get, methinks I can't find in my heart to have a hand in his death. I wish you could have made *Polly* undertake it.

MRS. PEACHUM. But in a case of necessity – our own lives are in danger.

PEACHUM. Then, indeed, we must comply with the customs of the world, and make gratitude give way to interest. – He shall be taken off.

MRS. PEACHUM. I'll undertake to manage *Polly*.

PEACHUM. And I'll prepare matters for the *Old-Baily*.

ACT I. SCENE XII.

POLLY. Now I'm a wretch, indeed. – Methinks I see him already in the cart,[33] sweeter and more lovely than the nosegay in his hand! – I hear the crowd extolling his resolution and intrepidity! – What vollies of sighs are sent from the windows of *Holborn*, that so comely a youth should be brought to disgrace! – I see him at the tree! The whole circle are in tears! – Even butchers weep! – *Jack Ketch* himself hesitates to perform his duty, and would be glad to lose his fee, by a reprieve. What then will become of *Polly*! – As yet I may inform him of their design, and aid him in his escape. – It shall be so. – But then he flies, absents himself, and I bar my self from his dear dear conversation! That too will distract me. – If he keep out of the way, my papa and mama may in time relent, and we may be happy. – If he stays, he is hang'd, and then he is lost for ever! – He intended to lye conceal'd in my room, 'till the dusk of the evening: If they are abroad, I'll this instant let him out, lest some accident should prevent him. [*Exit, and returns.*

ACT I. SCENE XIII.

[Polly, Macheath.

AIR XIV. Pretty Parrot, say–

MACHEATH. *Pretty Polly, say,*
When I was away,
Did your fancy never stray
To some newer lover?

POLLY. *Without disguise,*
Heaving sighs,
Doating eyes,
My constant heart discover.
Fondly let me loll!

MACHEATH. O pretty, pretty Poll.

POLLY. And are you as fond as ever, my dear?

MACHEATH. Suspect my honour, my courage, suspect any thing but my love. – May my pistols miss fire, and my mare slip her shoulder while I am pursu'd, if I ever forsake thee!

POLLY. Nay, my dear, I have no reason to doubt you, for I find in the romance you lent me, none of the great heroes were ever false in love.

AIR XV. Pray, Fair One, be kind–

MACHEATH. *My heart was so free,*
It rov'd like the bee,
'Till Polly my passion requited;
I sipt each flower,
I chang'd ev'ry hour,
But here ev'ry flower is united.

POLLY. Were you sentenc'd to transportation, sure, my dear, you could not leave me behind you – could you?

MACHEATH. Is there any power, any force that could tear me from thee? You might sooner tear a pension out of the hands of a courtier, a fee from a lawyer, a pretty woman from a looking-glass, or any woman from *quadrille*. – But to tear me from thee is impossible!

AIR XVI. Over the Hills and far away.

MACHEATH. *Were I laid on Greenland's coast,*
And in my arms embrac'd my lass;
Warm amidst eternal frost,
Too soon the half year's night would pass.

POLLY. *Were I sold on Indian soil,*
Soon as the burning day was clos'd,
I could mock the sultry toil,
When on my charmer's breast repos'd.

MACHEATH. *And I would love you all the day,*

POLLY. *Every night would kiss and play,*

MACHEATH. *If with me you'd fondly stray*

POLLY. *Over the hills and far away.*

POLLY. Yes, I would go with thee. But oh! – How shall I speak it? I must be torn from thee. We must part.

MACHEATH. How! Part!

POLLY. We must, we must. – My papa and mama are set against thy life. They now, even now are in search after thee. They are preparing evidence against thee. Thy life depends upon a moment.

AIR XVII. Gin thou wert mine awn thing–

POLLY. *O what pain it is to part!*
Can I leave thee, can I leave thee?
O what pain it is to part!
Can thy Polly ever leave thee?
But lest death my love should thwart,
And bring thee to the fatal cart,

Thus I tear thee from my bleeding heart!
Fly hence, and let me leave thee.

POLLY. One kiss and then – one kiss – begone – farewell.

MACHEATH. My hand, my heart, my dear, is so rivited to thine, that I cannot unloose my hold.

POLLY. But my papa may intercept thee, and then I should lose the very glimmering of hope. A few weeks, perhaps, may reconcile us all. Shall thy *Polly* hear from thee?

MACHEATH. Must I then go?

POLLY. And will not absence change your love?

MACHEATH. If you doubt it, let me stay – and be hang'd.

POLLY. O how I fear! How I tremble! – Go – but when safety will give you leave, you will be sure to see me again; for 'till then *Polly* is wretched.

AIR XVIII. O the Broom, &c.

MACHEATH. *The Miser thus a Shilling sees,*

[*Parting, and looking back at each other with fondness; he at one door, she at the other.*

MACHEATH. *Which he's oblig'd to pay,*
With sighs resigns it by degrees,
And fears 'tis gone for aye.

POLLY. *The boy, thus, when his sparrow's flown,*
The bird in silence eyes;
But soon as out of sight 'tis gone,
Whines, whimpers, sobs and cries.

ACT II.

ACT II. SCENE I. A tavern near Newgate.

[Jemmy Twitcher, Crook-finger'd Jack, Wat Dreary, Robin of Bagshot, Nimming Ned, Henry Paddington, Matt of the Mint, Ben Budge, *and the rest of the gang, at the table, with wine, brandy and tobacco.*

BEN. But pr'ythee, *Matt*, what is become of thy brother *Tom*? I have not seen him since my return from transportation.

MATT. Poor brother *Tom* had an accident this time twelve-month, and so clever a made fellow he was, that I could not save him from those fleaing rascals the surgeons; and now, poor man, he is among the otamys at *Surgeon's Hall*.[34]

BEN. So it seems, his time was come.

JEMMY. But the present time is ours, and no body alive hath more. Why are the laws levell'd at us? Are we more dishonest than the rest of mankind? What we win, gentlemen, is our own by the law of arms, and the right of conquest.

JACK. Where shall we find such another set of practical philosophers, who to a man are above the fear of death?

WAT. Sound men, and true!

ROBIN. Of try'd courage, and indefatigable industry!

NED. Who is there here that would not dye for his friend?

HARRY. Who is there here that would betray him for his interest?

MATT. Show me a gang of courtiers that can say as much.

BEN. We are for a just partition of the world, for every man hath a right to enjoy life.

MATT. We retrench the superfluities of mankind. The world is avaritious, and I hate avarice. A covetous fellow, like a Jack-daw, steals what he was never made to enjoy, for the sake of hiding it. These are the robbers of mankind, for money was made for the free-hearted and generous, and where is the injury of taking from another, what he hath not the heart to make use of?

JEMMY. Our several stations for the day are fixt. Good luck attend us all. Fill the glasses.

AIR XIV. Fill ev'ry Glass, &c.[35]

MATT. *Fill ev'ry glass, for wine inspires us,*
And fires us
With courage, love and joy.
Women and wine should life employ.
Is there ought else on earth desirous?

CHORUS. *Fill ev'ry glass, &c.*

ACT II. SCENE II.

[*To them enter* Macheath.

MACHEATH. Gentlemen, well met. My heart hath been with you this hour; but an unexpected affair hath detain'd me. No ceremony, I beg you.

MATT. We were just breaking up to go upon duty. Am I to have the honour of taking the air with you, sir, this evening upon the heath? I drink a dram now and then with the stage-coachmen in the way of friendship and intelligence; and I know that about this time there will be passengers upon the western road, who are worth speaking with.

MACHEATH. I was to have been of that party – but –

MATT. But what, Sir?

MACHEATH. Is there any man who suspects my courage?

MATT. We have all been witnesses of it.

MACHEATH. My honour and truth to the gang?

MATT. I'll be answerable for it.

MACHEATH. In the division of our booty, have I ever shown the least marks of avarice or injustice?

MATT. By these questions something seems to have ruffled you. Are any of us suspected?

MACHEATH. I have a fixt confidence, gentlemen, in you all, as men of honour, and as such I value and respect you. *Peachum* is a man that is useful to us.

MATT. Is he about to play us any foul play? I'll shoot him through the head.

MACHEATH. I beg you, gentlemen, act with conduct and discretion. A pistol is your last resort.

MATT. He knows nothing of this meeting.

MACHEATH. Business cannot go on without him. He is a man who knows the world, and is a necessary againt to us. We have had a slight difference, and till it is accommodated I shall be oblig'd to keep out of his way. Any private dispute of mine shall be of no ill consequence to my friends. You must continue to act under his direction, for the moment we break loose from him, our gang is ruin'd.

MATT. As a bawd to a whore, I grant you, he is to us of great convenience.

MACHEATH. Make him believe I have quitted the gang, which I can never do but with life. At our private quarters I will continue to meet you. A week or so will probably reconcile us.

MATT. Your instructions shall be observ'd. 'Tis now high time for us to repair to our several duties; so till the evening at our quarters in *Moor-fields* we bid you farewell.

MACHEATH. I shall wish my self with you. Success attend you. [*Sits down melancholy at the Table.*

AIR XX. March in Rinaldo, with Drums and Trumpets.

MATT. *Let us take the road.*
Hark! I hear the sound of coaches!
The hour of attack approaches,
To your arms, brave boys, and load.
See the ball I hold!
Let the chymists toil like asses,
Our fire their fire surpasses,
And turns all our lead to gold.[36]

[*The gang, rang'd in the front of the stage, load their pistols, and stick them under their girdles; then go off singing the first part in chorus.*

ACT II. SCENE III.

[Macheath, Drawer.

MACHEATH. What a fool is a fond wench! *Polly* is most confoundedly bit. – I love the sex. And a man who loves money, might as well be contented with one guinea, as I with one woman. The town perhaps hath been as much oblig'd to me, for recruiting it with free-hearted ladies, as to any recruiting officer in the army. If it were not for us and the other gentlemen of the sword, *Drury-Lane* would be uninhabited.[37]

AIR XXI. Would you have a Young Virgin, &c.

MACHEATH. *If the heart of a man is depress with cares,*
The mist is dispell'd when a woman appears;
Like the notes of a fiddle, she sweetly, sweetly
Raises the spirits, and charms our ears,
Roses and lillies her cheeks disclose,
But her ripe lips are more sweet than those.
Press her,
Caress her
With blisses,
Her kisses
Dissolve us in pleasure, and soft repose.

MACHEATH. I must have women. There is nothing unbends the mind like them. Money is not so strong a cordial for the time. Drawer. –

[*Enter* Drawer.

MACHEATH. Is the porter gone for all the ladies, according to my directions?

DRAWER. I expect him back every minute. But you know, Sir, you sent him as far as *Hockley in the Hole*, for three of the ladies, for one in *Vinegar*

Yard, and for the rest of them somewhere about *Lewkner's Lane*.[38] Sure some of them are below, for I hear the bar bell. As they come I will show them up. Coming, coming.

ACT II. SCENE IV.

[Macheath, Mrs. Coaxer, Dolly Trull, Mrs. Vixen, Betty Doxy, Jenny Diver, Mrs. Slammekin, Suky Tawdry, *and* Molly Brazen.

MACHEATH. Dear Mrs. *Coaxer*, you are welcome. You look charmingly to-day. I hope you don't want the repairs of quality, and lay on paint. – *Dolly Trull*! Kiss me, you slut; are you as amorous as ever, hussy? You are always so taken up with stealing hearts, that you don't allow your self time to steal any thing else. – Ah *Dolly*, thou wilt ever be a coquette! – Mrs. *Vixen*, I'm yours, I always lov'd a woman of wit and spirit; they make charming mistresses, but plaguy wives. – *Betty Doxy*! Come hither, hussy. Do you drink as hard as ever? You had better stick to good wholesome beer; for in troth, *Betty*, strong-waters will in time ruin your constitution. You should leave those to your betters. – What! And my pretty *Jenny Diver* too! As prim and demure as ever! There is not any prude, though ever so high bred, hath a more sanctify'd look, with a more mischievous heart. Ah! Thou art a dear artful hypocrite. – Mrs. *Slammekin*! As careless and genteel as ever! All you fine ladies, who know your own beauty, affect an undress.[39] – But see, here's *Suky Tawdry* come to contradict what I was saying. Every thing she gets one way she lays out upon her back. Why, *Suky*, you must keep at least a dozen tally-men. *Molly Brazen*! [*She kisses him*] That's well done. I love a free-hearted wench. Thou hast a most agreeable assurance, girl, and art as willing as a turtle. – But hark! I hear musick. The harper is at the door. *If musick be the food of love, play on*. E'er you seat your selves, ladies, what think you of a dance? Come in.

[*Enter* Harper.

MACHEATH. Play the *French* tune, that Mrs. *Slammekin* was so fond of.

[*A dance a la ronde in the French manner; near the end of it this song and chorus.*

AIR XXII. Cotillon.

MACHEATH. *Youth's the season made for joys,*
Love is then our duty,
She alone who that employs,
Well deserves her beauty.
Let's be gay,
While we may,
Beauty's a flower, despis'd in decay.

LADIES. *Youth's the season &c.*

MACHEATH. *Let us drink and sport to-day,*
Ours is not to-morrow.
Love with youth flies swift away,
Age is nought but sorrow.
Dance and sing,
Time's on the wing,
Life never knows the return of spring.

LADIES. *Let us drink &c.*

MACHEATH. Now, pray ladies, take your places. Here fellow, [*Pays the* Harper] bid the Drawer bring us more wine.

[*Exit* Harper.

MACHEATH. If any of the ladies chuse ginn, I hope they will be so free to call for it.

JENNY. You look as if you meant me. Wine is strong enough for me. Indeed, Sir, I never drink strong-waters, but when I have the cholic.

MACHEATH. Just the excuse of the fine ladies! Why, a lady of quality is never without the cholic. I hope, Mrs. *Coaxer*, you have had good success of late in your visits among the mercers.

COAXER. We have so many interlopers – Yet with industry, one may still have a little picking. I carried a silver flower'd lutestring, and a piece of black padesoy to Mr. *Peachum*'s lock but last week.

VIXEN. There's *Molly Brazen* hath the ogle of a rattle-snake. She rivetted a linnen-draper's eye so fast upon her, that he was nick'd of three pieces of cambric before he could look off.

MOLLY. Oh dear Madam! – But sure nothing can come up to your handling of laces! And then you have such a sweet deluding tongue! To cheat a man is nothing; but the woman must have fine parts indeed who cheats a woman!

VIXEN. Lace, Madam, lyes in a small Compass, and is of easy Conveyance. But you are apt, Madam, to think too well of your Friends.

COAXER. If any woman hath more art than another, to be sure, 'tis *Jenny Diver*. Though her fellow be never so agreeable, she can pick his pocket as cooly, as if money were her only pleasure. Now that is a command of the passions uncommon in a woman!

JENNY. I never go to the tavern with a man, but in the view of business. I have other hours, and other sort of men for my pleasure. But had I your address, Madam –

MACHEATH. Have done with your compliments, ladies; and drink about: You are not so fond of me, *Jenny*, as you use to be.

JENNY. 'Tis not convenient, Sir, to show my fondness among so many rivals. 'Tis your own choice, and not the warmth of my inclination that will determine you.

AIR XXIII. All in a misty Morning, &c.

JENNY. *Before the barn-door crowing,*
The cock by hens attended,
His eyes around him throwing,
Stands for a while suspended.
Then one he singles from the crew,
And cheers the happy hen;
With how do you do, and how do you do,
And how do you do again.

MACHEATH. Ah *Jenny*! Thou art a dear slut.

DOLLY. Pray, Madam, were you ever in keeping?[40]

SUKY. I hope, Madam, I ha'nt been so long upon the town, but I have met with some good fortune as well as my neighbours.

DOLLY. Pardon me, Madam, I meant no harm by the question; 'twas only in the way of conversation.

SUKY. Indeed, Madam, if I had not been a fool, I might have liv'd very handsomely with my last friend. But upon his missing five guineas, he turn'd me off. Now I never suspected he had counted them.

SLAMMEKIN. Who do you look upon, Madam, as your best sort of keepers?

DOLLY. That, Madam, is thereafter as they be.

SLAMMEKIN. I, Madam, was once kept by a *Jew*; and bating their religion, to women they are a good sort of people.

SUKY. Now for my part, I own I like an old fellow: for we always make them pay for what they can't do.

VIXEN. A spruce prentice, let me tell you, ladies, is no ill thing, they bleed freely. I have sent at least two or three dozen of them in my time to the plantations.[41]

JENNY. But to be sure, Sir, with so much good fortune as you have had upon the road, you must be grown immensely rich.

MACHEATH. The road, indeed, hath done me justice, but the gaming-table hath been my ruin.

AIR XXIV. When once I lay with another Man's Wife, &c.

JENNY. *The gamesters and lawyers are jugglers alike,*
If they meddle your all is in danger.
Like gypsies, if once they can finger a souse,
Your pockets they pick, and they pilfer your house,
And give your estate to a stranger.

JENNY. These are the tools of a man of honour. Cards and dice are only fit for cowardly cheats, who prey upon their friends. [*She takes up his Pistol.* Tawdry *takes up the other.*

SUKY. This, Sir, is fitter for your hand. Besides your loss of money, 'tis a loss to the ladies. Gaming takes you off from women. How fond could I be of you! But before Company, 'tis ill bred.

MACHEATH. Wanton hussies!

JENNY. I must and will have a kiss to give my wine a zest. [*They take him about the neck, and make signs to* Peachum *and* Constables, *who rush in upon him.*

ACT II. SCENE V.

[*To them,* Peachum *and* Constables.

PEACHUM. I seize you, Sir, as my prisoner.

MACHEATH. Was this well done, *Jenny*? – Women are decoy ducks; who can trust them! Beasts, jades, jilts, harpies, furies, whores!

PEACHUM. Your case, Mr. *Macheath*, is not particular. The greatest heroes have been ruin'd by women. But, to do them justice, I must own they are a pretty sort of creatures, if we could trust them. You must now, sir, take your leave of the ladies, and if they have a mind to make you a visit, they will be sure to find you at home. The gentleman, ladies, lodges in *Newgate*. Constables, wait upon the Captain to his lodgings.

AIR XXV. When first I laid Siege to my Chloris, &c.

MACHEATH. *At the tree I shall suffer with pleasure,*
At the tree I shall suffer with pleasure,
Let me go where I will,
In all kinds of ill,
I shall find no such Furies as these are.

PEACHUM. Ladies, I'll take care the reckoning shall be discharg'd.[42]

[*Exit* Macheath, *guarded with* Peachum *and* Constables.

ACT II. SCENE VI.

[*The women remain.*

VIXEN. Look ye, Mrs. *Jenny*, though Mr. *Peachum* may have made a private bargain with you and *Suky Tawdry* for betraying the Captain, as we were all assisting, we ought all to share alike.

COAXER. I think Mr. *Peachum*, after so long an acquaintance, might have trusted me as well as *Jenny Diver*.

SLAMMEKIN. I am sure at least three men of his hanging, and in a year's time too, (if he did me justice) should be set down to my account.

DOLLY. Mrs. *Slammekin*, that is not fair. For you know one of them was taken in bed with me.

JENNY. As far as a bowl of punch or a treat, I believe Mrs. *Suky* will join with me. – As for any thing else, ladies, you cannot in conscience expect it.

SLAMMEKIN. Dear Madam –

DOLLY. I would not for the world –

SLAMMEKIN. 'Tis impossible for me –

DOLLY. As I hope to be sav'd, Madam –

SLAMMEKIN. Nay, then I must stay here all night –

DOLLY. Since you command me.

[*Exeunt with great Ceremony.*

ACT II. SCENE VII. Newgate

[Lockit, Turnkeys, Macheath, Constables.

LOCKIT. Noble Captain, you are welcome. You have not been a lodger of mine this year and half. You know the custom, Sir. Garnish, Captain, garnish.[43] Hand me down those fetters there.

MACHEATH. Those, Mr. *Lockit*, seem to be the heaviest of the whole sett. With your leave, I should like the further pair better.

LOCKIT. Look ye, Captain, we know what is fittest for our prisoners. When a gentleman uses me with civility, I always do the best I can to please him. – Hand them down I say. – We have them of all prices, from one guinea to ten, and 'tis fitting every gentleman should please himself.

MACHEATH. I understand you, Sir. [*Gives Money*] The fees here are so many, and so exorbitant, that few fortunes can bear the expence of getting off handsomly, or of dying like a gentleman.

LOCKIT. Those, I see, will fit the Captain better. – Take down the further pair. Do but examine them, Sir. – Never was better work. – How genteely they are made! – They will sit as easy as a glove, and the nicest man in *England* might not be asham'd to wear them. [*He puts on the Chains*] If I had the best gentleman in the land in my custody I could not equip him more handsomly. And so, Sir – I now leave you to your private meditations.

ACT II. SCENE VIII.

[Macheath.

AIR XXVI. Courtiers, Courtiers think it no harm, &c.

MACHEATH. *Man may escape from rope and gun;*
Nay, some have out-liv'd the doctor's pill;
Who takes a woman must be undone,
That basilisk is sure to kill.
The fly that sips treacle is lost in the sweets,
So he that tastes woman, woman, woman,
He that tastes woman, ruin meets.

MACHEATH. To what a woful plight have I brought my self! Here must I (all day long, 'till I am hang'd) be confin'd to hear the reproaches of a wench who lays her ruin at my door. – I am in the custody of her father, and to be sure, if he knows of the matter, shall have a fine time on't betwixt this and my execution. – But I promis'd the wench marriage. – What signifies a promise to a woman? Does not man in marriage itself promise a hundred things that he never means to perform? Do all we can, women will believe us; for they look upon a promise as an excuse for following their own inclinations. – But here comes *Lucy*, and I cannot get from her – wou'd I were deaf!

ACT II. SCENE IX.

[Macheath, Lucy.

LUCY. You base man you, – how can you look me in the face after what hath past between us? – See here, perfidious wretch, how I am forc'd to bear about the load of infamy you have laid upon me – O *Macheath*! Thou hast robb'd me of my quiet – to see thee tortur'd would give me pleasure.

AIR XXVII. A lovely Lass to a Friar came, &c.

LUCY. *Thus when a good huswife sees a rat*
In her trap in the morning taken,
With pleasure her heart goes pit a pat,
In revenge for her loss of bacon.
Then she throws him
To the dog or cat,
To be worried, crush'd and shaken.

MACHEATH. Have you no bowels, no tenderness, my dear *Lucy*, to see a husband in these circumstances?

LUCY. A husband!

MACHEATH. In ev'ry respect but the form, and that, my dear, may be said over us at any time. – Friends should not insist upon ceremonies. From a man of honour, his word is as good as his bond.

LUCY. 'Tis the pleasure of all you fine men to insult the women you have ruin'd.

AIR XXVIII. 'Twas when the Sea was roaring, &c.

LUCY. *How cruel are the traytors,*
Who lye and swear in jest,
To cheat unguarded creatures
Of virtue, fame, and rest!
Whoever steals a shilling,
Through shame the guilt conceals:
In love the perjur'd villain
With boasts the theft reveals.

MACHEATH. The very first opportunity, my dear, (have but patience) you shall be my wife in whatever manner you please.

LUCY. Insinuating monster! And so you think I know nothing of the affair of Miss *Polly Peachum*. – I could tear thy eyes out!

MACHEATH. Sure *Lucy*, you can't be such a fool as to be jealous of *Polly*!

LUCY. Are you not married to her, you brute, you?

MACHEATH. Married! Very good. The wench gives it out only to vex thee, and to ruin me in thy good opinion. 'Tis true, I go to the house; I chat with the girl, I kiss her, I say a thousand things to her (as all gentlemen do) that mean nothing, to divert my self; and now the silly jade hath set it about that I am married to her, to let me know what she would be at. Indeed, my dear *Lucy*, these violent passions may be of ill consequence to a woman in your condition.

LUCY. Come, come, Captain, for all your assurance, you know that Miss *Polly* hath put it out of your power to do me the justice you promis'd me.

MACHEATH. A jealous woman believes ev'ry thing her passion suggests. To convince you of my sincerity, if we can find the ordinary, I shall have no scruples of making you my wife; and I know the consequence of having two at a time.

LUCY. That you are only to be hang'd, and so get rid of them both.

MACHEATH. I am ready, my dear *Lucy*, to give you satisfaction – if you think there is any in marriage. – What can a man of honour say more?

LUCY. So then it seems, you are not married to Miss *Polly*.

MACHEATH. You know, *Lucy*, the girl is prodigiously conceited. No man can say a civil thing to her, but (like other fine ladies) her vanity makes her think he's her own for ever and ever.

AIR XXIX. The Sun had loos'd his weary Teams, &c.

MACHEATH. *The first time at the looking-glass*
The mother sets her daughter,
The image strikes the smiling lass
With self-love ever after.
Each time she looks, she, fonder grown,
Thinks ev'ry charm grows stronger.
But alas, vain maid, all eyes but your own
Can see you are not younger.

MACHEATH. When women consider their own beauties, they are all alike unreasonable in their demands; for they expect their lovers should like them as long as they like themselves.

LUCY. Yonder is my father – perhaps this way we may light upon the ordinary, who shall try if you will be as good as your word. – For I long to be made an honest woman.

ACT II. SCENE X.

[Peachum, Lockit *with an account-book.*

LOCKIT. In this last affair, brother *Peachum*, we are agreed. You have consented to go halves in *Macheath*.

PEACHUM. We shall never fall out about an execution. – But as to that article, pray how stands our last year's account?

LOCKIT. If you will run your eye over it, you'll find 'tis fair and clearly stated.

PEACHUM. This long arrear of the government is very hard upon us! Can it be expected that we should hang our acquaintance for nothing, when our betters will hardly save theirs without being paid for it. Unless the people in employment pay better, I promise them for the future, I shall let other rogues live besides their own.

LOCKIT. Perhaps, brother, they are afraid these matters may be carried too far. We are treated too by them with contempt, as if our profession were not reputable.

PEACHUM. In one respect indeed, our employment may be reckon'd dishonest, because, like great statesmen, we encourage those who betray their friends.

LOCKIT. Such language, brother, any where else, might turn to your prejudice. Learn to be more guarded, I beg you.

AIR. XXX. How happy are we, &c.

LOCKIT. *When you censure the age,*
Be cautious and sage,
Lest the courtiers offended should be:
If you mention vice or bribe,
'Tis so pat to all the tribe;
Each crys–That was levell'd at me.

PEACHUM. Here's poor *Ned Clincher*'s name, I see. Sure, brother *Lockit*, there was a little unfair proceeding in *Ned*'s case: for he told me in the condemn'd hold, that for value receiv'd, you had promis'd him a session or two longer without molestation.

LOCKIT. Mr. *Peachum*, – This is the first time my honour was ever call'd in question.

PEACHUM. Business is at an end – if once we act dishonourably.

LOCKIT. Who accuses me?

PEACHUM. You are warm, brother.

LOCKIT. He that attacks my honour, attacks my livelyhood. – And this usage – Sir – is not to be born.

PEACHUM. Since you provoke me to speak – I must tell you too, that Mrs. *Coaxer* charges you with defrauding her of her information-money, for the apprehending of curl-pated *Hugh*. Indeed, indeed, brother, we must punctually pay our spies, or we shall have no information.

LOCKIT. Is this language to me, Sirrah – who have sav'd you from the gallows, Sirrah! [*Collaring each other.*

PEACHUM. If I am hang'd, it shall be for ridding the world of an arrant rascal.

LOCKIT. This hand shall do the office of the halter you deserve, and throttle you – you dog! –

PEACHUM. Brother, brother, – We are both in the wrong – We shall be both losers in the dispute – for you know we have it in our power to hang each other. You should not be so passionate.

LOCKIT. Nor you so provoking.

PEACHUM. 'Tis our mutual interest; 'tis for the interest of the world we should agree. If I said any thing, brother, to the prejudice of your character, I ask pardon.

LOCKIT. Brother *Peachum* – I can forgive as well as resent. – Give me your hand. Suspicion does not become a friend.

PEACHUM. I only meant to give you occasion to justifie yourself: But I must now step home, for I expect the gentleman about this snuff-box, that *Filch* nimm'd two nights ago in the park. I appointed him at this hour.

ACT II. SCENE XI.

[Lockit, Lucy.

LOCKIT. Whence come you, hussy?

LUCY. My tears might answer that question.

LOCKIT. You have then been whimpering and fondling, like a spaniel, over the fellow that hath abus'd you.

LUCY. One can't help love; one can't cure it. 'Tis not in my power to obey you, and hate him.

LOCKIT. Learn to bear your husband's death like a reasonable woman. 'Tis not the fashion, now-a-days, so much as to affect sorrow upon these occasions. No woman would ever marry, if she had not the chance of mortality for a release. Act like a woman of spirit, hussy, and thank your father for what he is doing.

AIR XXXI. Of a noble Race was Shenkin.

LUCY. *Is then his fate decreed, Sir?*
Such a man can I think of quitting?
When first we met, so moves me yet,
O see how my heart is splitting!

LOCKIT. Look ye, *Lucy* – There is no saving him. – So, I think, you must ev'n do like other widows – Buy your self weeds, and be cheerful.

AIR XXXII.[44]

LOCKIT. *You'll think e'er many days ensue*
This sentence not severe;
I hang your husband, child, 'tis true,
But with him hang your care.
Twang dang dillo dee.

LOCKIT. Like a good wife, go moan over your dying husband. That, child, is your duty – Consider, girl, you can't have the man and the money too – so make yourself as easy as you can, by getting all you can from him.

ACT II. SCENE XII.

[Lucy, Macheath.

LUCY. Though the ordinary was out of the way to-day, I hope, my dear, you will, upon the first opportunity, quiet my scruples – Oh Sir! –

My father's hard heart is not to be soften'd, and I am in the utmost despair.

MACHEATH. But if I could raise a small sum – would not twenty guineas, think you, move him? – Of all the arguments in the way of business, the perquisite is the most prevailing. – Your father's perquisites for the escape of prisoners must amount to a considerable sum in the year. Money well tim'd, and properly apply'd, will do any thing.

AIR XXXIII. London Ladies.

MACHEATH. *If you at an office solicit your due,*
And would not have matters neglected;
You must quicken the clerk with the perquisite too,
To do what his duty directed.
Or would you the frowns of a lady prevent,
She too has this palpable failing,
The perquisite softens her into consent;
That reason with all is prevailing.

LUCY. What love or money can do shall be done for all my comfort depends upon your safety.

ACT II. SCENE XIII.

[Lucy, Macheath, Polly.

POLLY. Where is my dear husband? – Was a rope ever intended for this neck! – O let me throw my arms about it, and throttle thee with love! – Why dost thou turn away from me? – 'Tis thy *Polly* – 'Tis thy wife.

MACHEATH. Was ever such an unfortunate rascal as I am!

LUCY. Was there ever such another villain!

POLLY. O *Macheath*! Was it for this we parted? Taken! Imprison'd! Try'd! Hang'd! – Cruel reflection! I'll stay with thee 'till death – no force shall tear thy dear wife from thee now. – What means my love? – Not one kind word! Not one kind look! Think what thy *Polly* suffers to see thee in this condition.

AIR XXXIV. All in the Downs, &c.

POLLY. *Thus when the swallow, seeking prey,*
Within the sash is closely pent,
His consort, with bemoaning lay,
Without sits pining for th' event.
Her chatt'ring lovers all around her skim;
She heeds them not (poor bird!) her soul's with him.

MACHEATH. – [*Aside*] *I must disown her.* – The wench is distracted.

LUCY. Am I then bilk'd of my virtue? Can I have no reparation? Sure men were born to lye, and women to believe them! O villain! Villain!

POLLY. Am I not thy wife? – Thy neglect of me, thy aversion to me too severely proves it. – Look on me. – Tell me, am I not thy wife?

LUCY. Perfidious wretch!

POLLY. Barbarous husband!

LUCY. Hadst thou been hang'd five months ago, I had been happy.

POLLY. And I too – If you had been kind to me 'till death, it would not have vex'd me – And that's no very unreasonable request, (though from a wife) to a man who hath not above seven or eight days to live.

LUCY. Art thou then married to another? Hast thou two wives, monster?

MACHEATH. If women's tongues can cease for an answer – hear me.

LUCY. I won't. – Flesh and blood can't bear my usage.

POLLY. Shall I not claim my own? Justice bids me speak.

AIR XXXV. Have you heard of a frolicksome Ditty, &c.

MACHEATH. *How happy could I be with either,*
Were t'other dear charmer away!
But while you thus teaze me together,
To neither a word will I say;
But tol de rol, &c.

POLLY. Sure, my dear, there ought to be some preference shown to a wife! At least she may claim the appearance of it. He must be distracted with his misfortunes, or he could not use me thus!

LUCY. O villain, villain! Thou hast deceiv'd me – I could even inform against thee with pleasure. Not a prude wishes more heartily to have facts against her intimate acquaintance, than I now wish to have facts against thee. I would have her satisfaction, and they should all out.

AIR XXXVI. Irish Trot.

POLLY. *I'm bubbled.*

LUCY. –*I'm bubbled.*

POLLY. *Oh how I am troubled!*

LUCY. *Bambouzled, and bit!*

POLLY. –*My distresses are doubled.*

LUCY. *When you come to the tree, should the hangman refuse,*
These fingers, with pleasure, could fasten the noose.

POLLY. *I'm bubbled, &c.*

MACHEATH. Be pacified, my dear *Lucy* – This is all a fetch of *Polly*'s, to make me desperate with you in case I get off. If I am hang'd, she would fain have the credit of being thought my widow – Really, *Polly*, this is no time for a dispute of this sort; for whenever you are talking of marriage, I am thinking of hanging.

POLLY. And hast thou the heart to persist in disowning me?

MACHEATH. And hast thou the heart to persist in persuading me that I am married? Why, *Polly*, dost thou seek to aggravate my misfortunes?

LUCY. Really, Miss *Peachum*, you but expose yourself. Besides, 'tis barbarous in you to worry a gentleman in his circumstances.

AIR XXXVII.

POLLY. *Cease your funning;*
Force or cunning
Never shall my heart trapan[45]
All these sallies
Are but malice
To seduce my constant man.
'Tis most certain,
By their flirting
Women oft' have envy shown;
Pleas'd, to ruin
Others wooing;
Never happy in their own!

POLLY. Decency, Madam, methinks might teach you to behave yourself with some reserve with the husband, while his wife is present.

MACHEATH. But seriously, *Polly*, this is carrying the joke a little too far.

LUCY. If you are determin'd, Madam, to raise a disturbance in the prison, I shall be oblig'd to send for the Turnkey to show you the door, I am sorry, Madam, you force me to be so ill-bred.

POLLY. Give me leave to tell you, Madam; These forward airs don't become you in the least, Madam. And my duty, Madam, obliges me to stay with my husband, Madam.

AIR XXXVIII. Good-morrow, Gossip Joan.

LUCY. *Why how now, Madam Flirt?*
If you thus must chatter;
And are for flinging dirt,
Let's try who best can spatter;
Madam Flirt!

POLLY. *Why how now, saucy jade;*
Sure the wench is tipsy!
How can you see me made [*To him.*
The scoff of such a gipsy?
Saucy jade! [*To her.*

ACT II. SCENE XIV.

[Lucy, Macheath, Polly, Peachum.

PEACHUM. Where's my wench? Ah hussy! Hussy! – Come you home, you slut; and when your fellow is hang'd, hang yourself, to make your family some amends.

POLLY. Dear, dear Father, do not tear me from him – I must speak; I have more to say to him – Oh! Twist thy fetters about me, that he may not haul me from thee!

PEACHUM. Sure all women are alike! If ever they commit the folly, they are sure to commit another by exposing themselves – Away – Not a word more – You are my prisoner now, hussy.

AIR XXXIX. Irish Howl.

POLLY. *No power on Earth can e'er divide,*
The knot that sacred love hath ty'd.
When parents draw against our mind,
The true-love's knot they faster bind.
Oh, oh ray, oh Amborah–oh, oh, &c.

[*Holding* Macheath, Peachum *pulling her.*

ACT II. SCENE XV.

[Lucy, Macheath.

MACHEATH. I am naturally compassionate, wife; so that I could not use the wench as she deserv'd; which made you at first suspect there was something in what she said.

LUCY. Indeed, my dear, I was strangely puzzled.

MACHEATH. If that had been the case, her father would never have brought me into this circumstance – No, *Lucy*, – I had rather dye than be false to thee.

LUCY. How happy am I, if you say this from your heart! For I love thee so, that I could sooner bear to see thee hang'd than in the arms of another.

MACHEATH. But couldst thou bear to see me hang'd?

LUCY. O *Macheath*, I can never live to see that day.

MACHEATH. You see, *Lucy*; in the account of love you are in my debt, and you must now be convinc'd, that I rather chuse to die than be another's. – Make me, if possible, love thee more, and let me owe my life to thee – If you refuse to assist me, *Peachum* and your father will immediately put me beyond all means of escape.

LUCY. My father, I know, hath been drinking hard with the prisoners: and I fancy he is now taking his nap in his own room – If I can procure the keys, shall I go off with thee, my dear?

MACHEATH. If we are together, 'twill be impossible to lye conceal'd. As soon as the search begins to be a little cool, I will send to thee – 'Till then my heart is thy prisoner.

LUCY. Come then, my dear husband – owe thy life to me – and though you love me not – be grateful – But that *Polly* runs in my head strangely.

MACHEATH. A moment of time may make us unhappy for-ever.

AIR. XL. The Lass of Patie's Mill, &c.

LUCY. *I like the fox shall grieve,*
Whose mate hath left her side,
Whom hounds, from morn to eve,
Chase o'er the country wide.
Where can my lover hide?
Where cheat the weary pack?
If love be not his guide,
He never will come back!

ACT III.

ACT III. SCENE I. Newgate

[Lockit, Lucy.

LOCKIT. To be sure, wench, you must have been aiding and abetting to help him to this escape.

LUCY. Sir, here hath been *Peachum* and his daughter *Polly*, and to be sure they know the ways of *Newgate* as well as if they had been born and bred in the place all their lives. Why must all your suspicion light upon me?

LOCKIT. *Lucy*, *Lucy*, I will have none of these shuffling answers.

LUCY. Well then – If I know any thing of him I wish I may be burnt!

LOCKIT. Keep your temper, *Lucy*, or I shall pronounce you guilty.

LUCY. Keep yours, Sir, – I do wish I may be burnt. I do – And what can I say more to convince you?

LOCKIT. Did he tip handsomely? – How much did he come down with? Come hussy, don't cheat your father; and I shall not be angry with you – Perhaps you have made a better bargain with him than I could have done – How much, my good girl?

LUCY. You know, Sir, I am fond of him, and would have given money to have kept him with me.

LOCKIT. Ah *Lucy*! Thy education might have put thee more upon thy guard; for a girl in the bar of an ale-house is always besieg'd.

LUCY. Dear Sir, mention not my education – for 'twas to that I owe my ruin.

AIR XLI. If Love's a sweet Passion, &c.

LUCY. *When young at the bar you first taught me to score,*
And bid me be free of my lips, and no more;
I was kiss'd by the parson, the squire, and the sot.
When the guest was departed, the kiss was forgot.
But his kiss was so sweet, and so closely he prest,
That I languish'd and pin'd 'till I granted the rest.

LUCY. If you can forgive me, Sir, I will make a fair confession, for to be sure he hath been a most barbarous villain to me.

LOCKIT. And so you have let him escape, hussy – Have you?

LUCY. When a woman loves, a kind look, a tender word can persuade her to any thing – And I could ask no other bribe.

LOCKIT. Thou wilt always be a vulgar slut, *Lucy* – If you would not be look'd upon as a fool, you should never do any thing but upon the foot of interest. Those that act otherwise are their own bubbles.

LUCY. But Love, Sir, is a misfortune that may happen to the most discreet woman, and in love we are all fools alike. – Notwithstanding all he swore, I am now fully convinc'd that *Polly Peachum* is actually his wife. – Did I let him escape, (fool that I was!) to go to her? – *Polly* ill wheedle herself into his money, and then *Peachum* will hang him, and cheat us both.

LOCKIT. So I am to be ruin'd, because, forsooth, you must be in love! – A very pretty excuse!

LUCY. I could murder that impudent happy strumpet: – I gave him his life, and that creature enjoys the sweets of it. – Ungrateful *Macheath*!

AIR XLII. South-Sea Ballad.[46]

LUCY. *My love is all madness and folly,*
Alone I lye,
Toss, tumble, and cry,
What a happy creature is Polly!
Was e'er such a wretch as I!
With rage I redden like scarlet,
That my dear inconstant varlet,
Stark blind to my charms,
Is lost in the arms
Of that jilt, that inveigling harlot!
Stark blind to my charms,
Is lost in the arms
Of that jilt, that inveigling harlot!
This, this my resentment alarms.

LOCKIT. And so, after all this mischief, I must stay here to be entertain'd with your catterwauling, Mistress Puss! – Out of my sight, wanton strumpet! You shall fast and mortify yourself into reason, with now and then a little handsome discipline to bring you to your senses. – Go.

ACT III. SCENE II.

LOCKIT. *Peachum* then intends to outwit me in this affair; but I'll be even with him. – The dog is leaky in his liquor, so I'll ply him that way, get the secret from him, and turn this affair to my own advantage. – Lions, wolves, and vultures don't live together in herds, droves or flocks. – Of all animals of prey, man is the only sociable one. Every one of us preys upon his neighbour, and yet we herd together.[47] – *Peachum* is my companion, my friend – According to the custom of the world, indeed, he may quote thousands of precedents for cheating me – And shall not I make use of the privilege of friendship to make him a return?

AIR XLIII. Packington's Pound.

LOCKIT. *Thus gamesters united in friendship are found,*
Though they know that their industry all is a cheat;
They flock to their prey at the dice-box's sound,
And join to promote one another's deceit.
But if by mishap
They fail of a chap,
To keep in their hands, they each other entrap.
Like pikes, lank with hunger, who miss of their ends,
They bite their companions, and prey on their friends.

LOCKIT. Now, *Peachum*, you and I, like honest tradesmen, are to have a fair tryal which of us two can over-reach the other.– *Lucy*.–

[*Enter* Lucy.

LOCKIT. Are there any of *Peachum*'s people now in the house?

LUCY. *Filch*, Sir, is drinking a quartern of strong-waters in the next room with black *Molly*.

LOCKIT. Bid him come to me.

ACT III. SCENE III.

[Lockit, Filch.

LOCKIT. Why, boy, thou lookest as if thou wert half starv'd; like a shotten[48] herring.

FILCH. One had need have the constitution of a horse to go through the business. – Since the favourite child-getter was disabled by a mishap, I have pick'd up a little money by helping the ladies to a pregnancy against their being call'd down to sentence. – But if a man cannot get an honest livelyhood any easier way, I am sure, 'tis what I can't undertake for another session.

LOCKIT. Truly, if that great man should tip off, 'twould be an irreparable loss. The vigor and prowess of a knight errant never sav'd half the ladies in distress that he hath done. – But, boy, can'st thou tell me where thy master is to be found?

FILCH. At his lock, Sir, at the *Crooked Billet*.

LOCKIT. Very well. – I have nothing more with you.

[*Ex*. Filch.

LOCKIT. I'll go to him there, for I have many important affairs to settle with him; and in the way of those transactions, I'll artfully get into his secret. – So that *Macheath* shall not remain a day longer out of my clutches.

ACT III. SCENE IV. A gaming-house.

[Macheath *in a fine tarnish'd coat,* Ben Budge, Matt of the Mint.

MACHEATH. I am sorry, gentlemen, the road was so barren of money. When my friends are in difficulties, I am always glad that my fortune can be serviceable to them. [*Gives them money*] You see, gentlemen, I am not a meer court friend, who professes every thing and will do nothing.

AIR XLIV. Lillibullero.

MACHEATH. *The modes of the court so common are grown,*
That a true friend can hardly be met;
Friendship for interest is but a loan,
Which they let out for what they can get.
'Tis true, you find
Some friends so kind,
Who will give you good counsel themselves to defend.
In sorrowful ditty,
They promise, they pity,
But shift you for money, from friend to friend.

MACHEATH. But we, gentlemen, have still honour enough to break through the corruptions of the world. – And while I can serve you, you may command me.

BEN. It grieves my heart that so generous a man should be involv'd in such difficulties, as oblige him to live with such ill company, and herd with gamesters.

MATT. See the partiality of mankind! – One man may steal a horse, better than another look over a hedge – Of all mechanics, of all servile handy-crafts-men, a gamester is the vilest. But yet, as many of the quality are of the profession, he is admitted amongst the politest company. I wonder we are not more respected.

MACHEATH. There will be deep play[49] to-night at *Marybone*, and consequently money may be pick'd up upon the road. Meet me there, and I'll give you the hint who is worth setting.

MATT. The fellow with a brown coat with a narrow gold binding, I am told, is never without money.

MACHEATH. What do you mean, *Matt*? – Sure you will not think of meddling with him! – He's a good honest kind of a fellow, and one of us.

BEN. To be sure, Sir, we will put our selves under your direction.

MACHEATH. Have an eye upon the money-lenders. – A *Rouleau,*[50] or two, would prove a pretty sort of an expedition. I hate extortion.

MATT. Those *Rouleaus* are very pretty things. – I hate your bank bills. – There is such a hazard in putting them off.

MACHEATH. There is a certain man of distinction, who in his time hath nick'd me out of a great deal of the ready. He is in my cash, *Ben*; – I'll point him out to you this evening, and you shall draw upon him for the debt. – The company are met; I hear the dice box in the other room. So, gentlemen, your servant. You'll meet me at *Marybone*.

ACT III. SCENE V. Peachum's LOCKIT. A Table with Wine, Brandy, Pipes and Tobacco.

[Peachum, Lockit.

LOCKIT. The coronation account, brother *Peachum*, is of so intricate a nature, that I believe it will never be settled.

PEACHUM. It consists indeed of a great variety of articles. – It was worth to our people, in fees of different kinds, above ten instalments. – This is part of the account, brother, that lies open before us.

LOCKIT. A lady's tail of rich brocade – that, I see, is dispos'd of.

PEACHUM. To Mrs. *Diana Trapes*, the tally-woman, and she will make a good hand on't in shoes and slippers, to trick out young ladies, upon their going into keeping. –

LOCKIT. But I don't see any article of the jewels.

PEACHUM. Those are so well known, that they must be sent abroad – You'll find them enter'd under the article of exportation. – As for the snuff-boxes, watches, swords, &c. – I thought it best to enter them under their several heads.

LOCKIT. Seven and twenty women's pockets compleat; with the several things therein contain'd; all seal'd, number'd, and enter'd.

PEACHUM. But, brother, it is impossible for us now to enter upon this affair. – We should have the whole day before us. – Besides, the account of the last half year's plate is in a book by it self, which lies at the other office.

LOCKIT. Bring us then more liquor. – To-day shall be for pleasure – To-morrow for business. – Ah brother, those daughters of ours are two slippery hussies – Keep a watchful eye upon *Polly*, and *Macheath* in a day or two shall be our own again.

AIR XLV. Down in the North Country, &c.

LOCKIT. *What gudgeons*[51] *are we men!*
Ev'ry woman's easy prey.
Though we have felt the hook, again
We bite and they betray.
The bird that hath been trapt,
When he hears his calling mate,
To her he flies, again he's clapt
Within the wiry grate.

PEACHUM. But what signifies catching the bird, if your daughter *Lucy* will set open the door of the cage?

LOCKIT. If men were answerable for the follies and frailties of their wives and daughters, no friends could keep a good correspondence together for two days. – This is unkind of you, brother; for among good friends, what they say or do goes for nothing.

[*Enter a* Servant.

SERVANT. Sir, here's Mrs. *Diana Trapes* wants to speak with you.

PEACHUM. Shall we admit her, brother *Lockit*?

LOCKIT. By all means – She's a good customer, and a fine-spoken woman – And a woman who drinks and talks so freely, will enliven the conversation.

PEACHUM. Desire her to walk in.

[*Exit* Servant.

ACT III. SCENE VI.

[Peachum, Lockit, Mrs. Trapes.

PEACHUM. Dear Mrs. *Dye*, your servant – One may know by your kiss, that your ginn is excellent.

TRAPES. I was always very curious in my liquors.

LOCKIT. There is no perfum'd breath like it – I have been long acquainted with the flavour of those lips – han't I, Mrs. *Dye*?

TRAPES. Fill it up. – I take as large draughts of liquor, as I did of love. – I hate a flincher in either.

AIR XLVI. A Shepherd kept Sheep, &c.

TRAPES. *In the days of my youth I could bill like a dove, fa, la, la, &c.*
Like a sparrow at all times was ready for love, fa, la, la, &c.
The life of all mortals in kissing should pass,
Lip to lip while we're young–then the lip to the glass, fa, &c.

TRAPES. But now, Mr. *Peachum*, to our business. – If you have blacks of any kind, brought in of late; mantoes – velvet scarfs – petticoats – let it be what it will – I am your chap – for all my ladies are very fond of mourning.

PEACHUM. Why, look ye, Mrs. *Dye* – you deal so hard with us, that we can afford to give the gentlemen, who venture their lives for the goods, little or nothing.

TRAPES. The hard times oblige me to go very near in my dealing. – To be sure, of late years I have been a great sufferer by the Parliament. – Three thousand pounds would hardly make me amends. – The Act for destroying the Mint,[52] was a severe cut upon our business – 'Till then, if a customer stept out of the way – we knew where to have her – No doubt you know Mrs. *Coaxer* – there's a wench now ('till to-day) with a good suit of cloaths of mine upon her back, and I could never set eyes upon her for three months together. – Since the Act too against Imprisonment for small Sums,[53] my loss there too hath been very considerable, and it must be so, when a lady can borrow a handsome petticoat, or a clean gown, and I not have the least hank upon her! And, o' my conscience, now-a-days most ladies take a delight in cheating, when they can do it with safety.

PEACHUM. Madam, you had a handsome gold watch of us t'other day for seven guineas. – Considering we must have our profit – To a gentleman upon the road, a gold watch will be scarce worth the taking.

TRAPES. Consider, Mr. *Peachum*, that watch was remarkable, and not of a very safe sale. – If you have any black velvet scarfs – they are a handsome winterwear; and take with most gentlemen who deal with my customers. – 'Tis I that put the ladies upon a good foot. 'Tis not youth or beauty that fixes their price. The gentlemen always pay according to their dress, from half a crown to two guineas; and yet those hussies make nothing of bilking of me. – Then too, allowing for accidents. – I have eleven fine customers now down under the surgeon's hands, – what with fees and other expences, there are great goings-out, and no comings-in, and not a farthing to pay for at least a month's cloathing. – We run great risques – great risques indeed.

PEACHUM. As I remember, you said something just now of Mrs. *Coaxer*.

TRAPES. Yes, Sir. – To be sure I stript her of a suit of my own cloaths about two hours ago; and have left her as she should be, in her shift, with a lover of hers at my house. She call'd him up stairs, as he was going to *Marybone* in a hackney coach. – And I hope, for her own sake and mine, she will perswade the Captain to redeem her, for the Captain is very generous to the ladies.

LOCKIT. What Captain?

TRAPES. He thought I did not know him – An intimate acquaintance of yours, Mr. *Peachum* – Only Captain *Macheath* – as fine as a lord.

PEACHUM. To-morrow, dear Mrs. *Dye*, you shall set your own price upon any of the goods you like – We have at least half a dozen velvet scarfs, and all at your service. Will you give me leave to make you a present of this suit of night-cloaths for your own wearing? – But are you sure it is Captain *Macheath*?

TRAPES. Though he thinks I have forgot him; no body knows him better. I have taken a great deal of the Captain's money in my time at second-hand, for he always lov'd to have his ladies well drest.

PEACHUM. Mr. *Lockit* and I have a little business with the Captain; – You understand me – and we will satisfye you for Mrs. *Coaxer*'s debt.

LOCKIT. Depend upon it – we will deal like men of honour.

TRAPES. I don't enquire after your affairs – so whatever happens, I wash my hands on't. – It hath always been my maxim, that one friend should assist another – But if you please – I'll take one of the scarfs home with me. 'Tis always good to have something in hand.

ACT III. SCENE VII. Newgate.

LUCY. Jealousy, rage, love and fear are at once tearing me to pieces. How I am weather-beaten and shatter'd with distresses!

AIR XLVII. One Evening, having lost my Way, &c.

LUCY. *I'm like a skiff on the ocean tost,*
Now high, now low, with each billow born,
With her rudder broke, and her anchor lost,
Deserted and all forlorn.
While thus I lye rolling and tossing all night,
That Polly lyes sporting on seas of delight!
Revenge, revenge, revenge,
Shall appease my restless sprite.

LUCY. I have the rats-bane ready. – I run no risque; for I can lay her death upon the ginn, and so many dye of that naturally that I shall never be call'd in question.[54] – But say, I were to be hang'd – I never could be hang'd for any thing that would give me greater comfort, than the poysoning that slut.

[*Enter* Filch.

FILCH. Madam, here's our Miss *Polly* come to wait upon you.

LUCY. Show her in.

ACT III. SCENE VIII.

[Lucy, Polly.

LUCY. Dear Madam, your servant. – I hope you will pardon my passion, when I was so happy to see you last. – I was so over-run with the spleen, that I was perfectly out of my self. And really when one hath the spleen, every thing is to be excus'd by a friend.

AIR XLVIII. Now Roger, I'll tell thee, because thou'rt my Son.

LUCY. *When a wife's in her pout,*
(As she's sometimes, no doubt;)
The good husband as meek as a lamb,
Her vapours to still,
First grants her her will,
And the quieting draught is a dram.
Poor man! And the quieting draught is a dram.

LUCY. – I wish all our quarrels might have so comfortable a reconciliation.

POLLY. I have no excuse for my own behaviour, Madam, but my misfortunes. – And really, Madam, I suffer too upon your account.

LUCY. But, Miss *Polly* – in the way of friendship, will you give me leave to propose a glass of cordial to you?

POLLY. Strong-waters are apt to give me the head-ache – I hope, Madam, you will excuse me.

LUCY. Not the greatest lady in the land could have better in her closet, for her own private drinking. – You seem mighty low in spirits, my dear.

POLLY. I am sorry, Madam, my health will not allow me to accept of your offer. – I should not have left you in the rude manner I did when we met last, Madam, had not my papa haul'd me away so unexpectedly – I was indeed somewhat provok'd, and perhaps might use some expressions that were disrespectful. – But really, Madam, the

Captain treated me with so much contempt and cruelty, that I deserv'd your pity, rather than your resentment.

LUCY. But since his escape, no doubt all matters are made up again. – Ah *Polly*! *Polly*! 'Tis I am the unhappy wife; and he loves you as if you were only his mistress.

POLLY. Sure, Madam, you cannot think me so happy as to be the object of your jealousy. – A man is always afraid of a woman who loves him too well – so that I must expect to be neglected and avoided.

LUCY. Then our cases, my dear *Polly*, are exactly alike. Both of us indeed have been too fond.

AIR XLIX. O Bessy Bell.

POLLY. *A curse attends that woman's love,*
Who always would be pleasing.
LUCY. *The pertness of the billing dove,*
Like tickling, is but teazing.
POLLY. *What then in love can woman do?*
LUCY. *If we grow fond they shun us.*
POLLY. *And when we fly them, they pursue.*
LUCY. *But leave us when they've won us.*

LUCY. Love is so very whimsical in both sexes, that it is impossible to be lasting. – But my heart is particular, and contradicts my own observation.

POLLY. But really, Mistress *Lucy*, by his last behaviour; I think I ought to envy you. – When I was forc'd from him, he did not shew the least tenderness. – But perhaps, he hath a heart not capable of it.

AIR L. Would Fate to me Belinda give –

POLLY. *Among the men, coquets we find,*
Who court by turns all woman-kind;
And we grant all their hearts desir'd,
When they are flatter'd, and admir'd.

POLLY. The coquets of both sexes are self-lovers, and that is a love no other whatever can dispossess. I fear, my dear *Lucy*, our husband is one of those.

LUCY. Away with these melancholy reflections, – indeed, my dear *Polly*, we are both of us a cup too low. – Let me prevail upon you, to accept of my offer.

AIR LI. Come, sweet Lass, &c.

LUCY. *Come, sweet lass,*
Let's banish sorrow
'Till to-morrow;
Come, sweet lass,
Let's take a chirping glass.
Wine can clear
The vapours of despair;
And make us light as air;
Then drink, and banish care.

LUCY. I can't bear, child, to see you in such low spirits. – And I must persuade you to what I know will do you good. – [*Aside*] *I shall now soon be even with the hypocritical strumpet.*

ACT III. SCENE IX.

[Polly.

POLLY. All this wheedling of *Lucy* cannot be for nothing. – At this time too! when I know she hates me! – The dissembling of a woman is always the fore-runner of mischief. – By pouring strong-waters down my throat, she thinks to pump some secrets out of me. – I'll be upon my guard, and won't taste a drop of her liquor, I'm resolv'd.

ACT III. SCENE X.

[Lucy, *with strong-waters.* Polly.

LUCY. Come, Miss *Polly*.

POLLY. Indeed, child, you have given yourself trouble to no purpose. – You must, my dear, excuse me.

LUCY. Really, Miss *Polly*, you are so squeamishly affected about taking a cup of strong-waters as a lady before company. I vow, *Polly*, I shall take it monstrously ill if you refuse me. – Brandy and men (though women love them never so well) are always taken by us with some reluctance – unless 'tis in private.

POLLY. I protest, Madam, it goes against me. – What do I see! *Macheath* again in custody! – Now every glimm'ring of happiness is lost. [*Drops the glass of liquor on the ground.*

LUCY. [*Aside*] *Since things are thus, I'm glad the wench hath escap'd: for by this event, 'tis plain, she was not happy enough to deserve to be poison'd.*

ACT III. SCENE XI.

[Lockit, Macheath, Peachum, Lucy, Polly.

LOCKIT. Set your heart to rest, Captain. – You have neither the chance of love or money for another escape, – for you are order'd to be call'd down upon your tryal immediately.

PEACHUM. Away, hussies! – This is not a time for a man to be hamper'd with his wives. – You see, the gentleman is in chains already.

LUCY. O husband, husband, my heart long'd to see thee; but to see thee thus distracts me!

POLLY. Will not my dear husband look upon his *Polly*? Why hadst thou not flown to me for protection? With me thou hadst been safe.

AIR LII. The last time I went o'er the Moor.

POLLY. *Hither, dear husband, turn your eyes.*

LUCY. *Bestow one glance to cheer me.*

POLLY. *Think with that look, thy Polly dyes.*

LUCY. *O shun me not – but hear me.*

POLLY. *'Tis Polly sues.*

LUCY. – *'Tis Lucy speaks.*

POLLY. *Is thus true love requited?*

LUCY. *My heart is bursting.*

POLLY. – *Mine too breaks.*

LUCY. *Must I?*

POLLY. – *Must I be slighted?*

MACHEATH. What would you have me say, ladies? – You see, this affair will soon be at an end, without my disobliging either of you.

PEACHUM. But the settling this point, Captain, might prevent a law-suit between your two widows.

AIR LIII. Tom Tinker 's my true Love.

MACHEATH. *Which way shall I turn me?–How can I decide?*
Wives, the day of our death, are as fond as a bride.
One wife is too much for most husbands to hear,
But two at a time there's no mortal can bear.
This way, and that way, and which way I will,
What would comfort the one, t'other wife would take ill.

POLLY. But if his own misfortunes have made him insensible to mine – A father sure will be more compassionate. – Dear, dear Sir, sink the material evidence, and bring him off at his tryal – *Polly* upon her knees begs it of you.

AIR LIV. I am a poor Shepherd undone.

POLLY. *When my hero in court appears,*
And stands arraign'd for his life;
Then think of poor Polly's tears;
For ah! Poor Polly's his wife.
Like the sailor he holds up his hand,
Distrest on the dashing wave.
To die a dry death at land,
Is as bad as a watry grave.
And alas, poor Polly!
Alack, and well-a-day!
Before I was in love,
Oh! Every month was May.

LUCY. If *Peachum*'s heart is harden'd; sure you, Sir, will have more compassion on a daughter. – I know the evidence is in your power. – How then can you be a tyrant to me? [*Kneeling*.

AIR LV. Ianthe the lovely, &c.

LUCY. *When he holds up his hand arraign'd for his life,*
O think of your daughter, and think I'm his wife!
What are cannons, or bombs, or clashing of swords?
For death is more certain by witnesses words.
Then nail up their lips; that dread thunder allay;
And each month of my life will hereafter be May.

LOCKIT. *Macheath*'s time is come, *Lucy*. – We know our own affairs, therefore let us have no more whimpering or whining.

Air LVI. A Cobler there was, &c.

LOCKIT. *Our selves, like the great, to secure a retreat,*
When matters require it, must give up our gang
And good reason why,
Or, instead of the fry,
Ev'n Peachum and I,
Like poor petty rascals, might hang, hang;
Like poor petty rascals, might hang.

PEACHUM. Set your heart at rest, *Polly*. – Your husband is to dye to-day. – Therefore, if you are not already provided, 'tis high time to look about for another. There's comfort for you you slut.

LOCKIT. We are ready, Sir, to conduct you to the *Old Baily*.

AIR LVII. Bonny Dundee.

MACHEATH. *The charge is prepar'd; the lawyers are met,*
The judges all rang'd (a terrible show!)
I go, undismay'd.–For death is a debt,
A debt on demand.–So, take what I owe.
Then farewell, my love–dear charmers, adieu.

Contended I die–'tis the better for you.
Here ends all dispute the rest of our lives.
For this way at once I please all my wives.

MACHEATH. Now, gentlemen, I am ready to attend you.

ACT III. SCENE XII.

[Lucy, Polly, Filch.

POLLY. Follow them, *Filch*, to the court. And when the tryal is over, bring me a particular account of his behaviour, and of every thing that happen'd. – You'll find me here with Miss *Lucy*.

[*Ex.* Filch.

POLLY. But why is all this musick?

LUCY. The prisoners, whose tryals are put off till next session, are diverting themselves.

POLLY. Sure there is nothing so charming as musick! I'm fond of it to distraction! – But alas! – Now, all mirth seems an insult upon my affliction. – Let us retire, my dear *Lucy*, and indulge our sorrows. – The noisy crew, you see, are coming upon us.

[*Exeunt. A Dance of Prisoners in Chains, &c.*

ACT III. SCENE XIII.
The condemn'd hold.

[Macheath, *in a melancholy posture.*

AIR LVIII. Happy Groves.

MACHEATH. *O cruel, cruel, cruel case!*
Must I suffer this disgrace?

AIR LIX. Of all the Girls that are so smart.

MACHEATH. *Of all the friends in time of grief,*
When threatning death looks grimmer,
Not one so sure can bring relief,
As this best friend, a brimmer. [*Drinks.*

AIR LX. Britons strike home.

MACHEATH. *Since I must swing,–I scorn, I scorn to wince or whine.* [*Rises.*

AIR LXI. Chevy Chase.

MACHEATH. *But now again my spirits sink;*
I'll raise them high with wine. [*Drinks a glass of wine.*

AIR LXII. To old Sir Simon the King.

MACHEATH. *But valour the stronger grows,*
The stronger liquor we're drinking.
And how can we feel our woes,
When we've lost the trouble of thinking? [*Drinks.*

AIR LXIII. Joy to great Cæsar.

MACHEATH. *If thus – a man can die*
Much bolder with brandy. [*Pours out a bumper of brandy.*

AIR LXIV. There was an old Woman.

MACHEATH. *So I drink off this bumper.– And now I can stand the test.*
And my comrades shall see, that I die as brave as the best. [*Drinks.*

AIR LXV. Did you ever hear of a gallant Sailor.

MACHEATH. *But can I leave my pretty hussies,*
Without one tear, or tender sigh?

AIR LXVI. Why are mine Eyes still flowing.

MACHEATH. *Their eyes, their lips, their busses*
Recall my love.–Ah must I die!

AIR LXVII. Green Sleeves.

MACHEATH. *Since laws were made for ev'ry degree,*
To curb vice in others, as well as me,
I wonder we han't better company,
Upon Tyburn tree!
But gold from law can take out the sting;
And if rich men like us were to swing,
'Twou'd thin the land, such numbers to string
Upon Tyburn tree!

JAILOR. Some friends of yours, Captain, desire to be admitted. – I leave you together.

ACT III. SCENE XIV.

[Macheath, Ben Budge, Matt of the Mint.

MACHEATH. For my having broke prison, you see, gentlemen, I am order'd immediate execution. – The sheriffs officers, I believe, are now at the door. – That *Jemmy Twitcher* should peach me, I own surpriz'd me! – 'Tis a plain proof that the world is all alike, and that even our gang can no more trust one another than other people. Therefore, I beg you, gentlemen, look well to yourselves, for in all probability you may live some months longer.

MATT. We are heartily sorry, Captain, for your misfortune. – But 'tis what we must all come to.

MACHEATH. *Peachum* and *Lockit*, you know, are infamous scoundrels. Their lives are as much in your power, as yours are in theirs. – Remember your dying friend! – 'Tis my last request. – Bring those villains to the gallows before you, and I am satisfied.

MATT. We'll do't.

JAILOR. Miss *Polly* and Miss *Lucy* intreat a word with you.

MACHEATH. Gentlemen, adieu.

ACT III. SCENE XV.

[Lucy, Macheath, Polly.

MACHEATH. My dear *Lucy* – My dear *Polly* – Whatsoever hath past between us is now at an end. – If you are fond of marrying again, the best advice I can give you, is to ship yourselves off for the *West-Indies*, where you'll have a fair chance of getting a husband a-piece; or by good luck, two or three, as you like best.

POLLY. How can I support this sight!

LUCY. There is nothing moves one so much as a great man in distress.

AIR LXVIII. All you that must take a Leap, &c.

LUCY. *Would I might be hang'd!*

POLLY. – *And I would so too!*

LUCY. *To be hang'd with you.*

POLLY. – *My Dear, with you.*

MACHEATH. *O leave me to thought! I fear! I doubt! I tremble! I droop!–See, my courage is out.* [*Turns up the empty bottle.*

POLLY. *No token of love?*

MACHEATH. – *See, my courage is out.* [*Turns up the empty pot.*

LUCY. *No token of love?*

POLLY. – *Adieu.*

LUCY. – *Farewell.*

MACHEATH. *But hark! I hear the toll of the bell.*

CHORUS. *Tol de rol lol, &c.*

JAILOR. Four women more, Captain, with a child a-piece! See, here they come.

[*Enter women and children.*

MACHEATH. What – four wives more! – This is too much. – Here – tell the sheriff's officers I am ready. [*Exit* Macheath *guarded.*

ACT III. SCENE XVI.

[*To them, enter* Player *and* Beggar.

PLAYER. But, honest friend, I hope you don't intend that *Macheath* shall be really executed.

BEGGAR. Most certainly, sir. – To make the piece perfect, I was for doing strict poetical justice. – *Macheath* is to be hang'd; and for the other personages of the drama, the audience must have suppos'd they were all either hang'd or transported.

PLAYER. Why then, friend, this is a down-right deep tragedy. The catastrophe is manifestly wrong, for an opera must end happily.

BEGGAR. Your objection, sir, is very just; and is easily remov'd. For you must allow, that in this kind of drama, 'tis no matter how absurdly things are brought about. – So – you rabble there – run and cry a reprieve – let the prisoner be brought back to his wives in triumph.

PLAYER. All this we must do, to comply with the taste of the town.

BEGGAR. Through the whole piece you may observe such a similitude of manners in high and low life, that it is difficult to determine whether (in the fashionable vices) the fine gentlemen imitate the gentlemen of the road, or the gentlemen of the road the fine gentlemen. – Had the play remain'd, as I at first intended, it would have carried a most excellent moral. 'Twould have shown that the lower sort of people have their vices in a degree as well as the rich: And that they are punish'd for them.

ACT III. SCENE XVII.

[*To them,* Macheath *with rabble, &c.*

MACHEATH. So, it seems, I am not left to my choice, but must have a wife at last. – Look ye, my dears, we will have no controversie now. Let us give this day to mirth, and I am sure she who thinks herself my wife will testifie her joy by a dance.

ALL. Come, a dance – a dance.

MACHEATH. Ladies, I hope you will give me leave to present a partner to each of you. And (if I may without offence) for this time, I take *Polly* for mine. – And for life, you slut, – for we were really marry'd. – As for the rest. – [*To* Polly] But at present keep your own secret.

[*A dance.*

AIR LXIX. Lumps of Pudding, &c.

MACHEATH. *Thus I stand like the Turk, with his doxies around;*
From all sides their glances his passion confound;
For black, brown, and fair, his inconstancy burns,
And the different beauties subdue him by turns:
Each calls forth her charms, to provoke his desires:
Though willing to all; with but one he retires.
But think of this maxim, and put off your sorrow,
The wretch of to-day, may be happy to-morrow.

CHORUS. *But think of this maxim, &c.*

FINIS.

10.2 SONGS FROM *WIT AND MIRTH*

***Wit and Mirth: Or Pills to Purge Melancholy: Being A Collection of the Best Merry Ballads and Songs, Old and New.* 6 vols. The fourth edition, for J. Tonson, London: Printed by W. Pearson, 1719.**

THESE ARE A FEW of the popular songs from *The Beggar's Opera* with their original lyrics. Some work by contrast ("Lumps of Pudding") and others by a close parody that shifts the discussion more subtly ("The Willoughby Whim.")

From *Lumps of Pudding*
(basis for Air LXIX, "Thus I stand like a Turk")

WHEN I was in the low Country,
When I was in the low Country,
What slices of Pudding and pieces of Bread,
My Mother gave me when I was in need.

My Mother she kill'd a good fat Hog,
She made such Puddings would choak a Dog;
And I shall ne'er forget 'till I dee,
What lumps of Pudding my Mother gave me.

She hung them up upon a Pin,
The Fat run out and the Maggots crept in;
If you won't believe me you may go and see,
What lumps, *&c.*

The Willoughby WHIM (basis for Air IX, "Oh Polly, you might have toy'd and kist")

A Scotch Song
In a DIALOGUE *between two Sisters.*

Molly. OH *Jenny*, *Jenny*, where hast thou been?
Father and Mother are seeking for thee,
You have been ranting, playing the Wanton,
Keeping of *Jockey* Company.

Jenny. Oh *Molly*, I've been to hear Mill clack,
And grind Grist for the Family,
Full as it went I've brought home my Sack,
For the Miller has tooken his Toll of me.

Molly. You hang your Smickets abroad to bleach,
When that was done, where could you be?
Jenny. I slipt down in the quickset Hedge,
And *Jockey* the Loon fell after me.

Molly. My Father you told you'd go to Kirk,
When Prayers were done, where could you be?
Jenny. Taking a Kiss of the Parson and Clerk,
And of other young Laddys some two or three.

Molly. Oh *Jenny*, *Jenny*, what wilt thou do,
If Belly should swell, where wilt thou be?
Jenny. Look to your self for *Jockey* is true,
And whilst Clapper goes will take care of me.

"Would ye have a young Virgin," (basis for Air XXI, "If the heart of a man is deprest with cares"

Would ye have a young Virgin of fifteen Years,
You must tickle her Fancy with sweets and dears,
Ever toying, and playing, and sweetly, sweetly,
Sing a Love Sonnet, and charm her Ears:
Wittily, prettily talk her down,
Chase her, and praise her, if fair or brown,
        Sooth her, and smooth her
        And teaze her, and please her,
And touch but her Smicket, and all's your own.

Do ye fancy a Widow well known in a Man?
With a front of Assurance come boldly on,
Let her rest not an Hour, but briskly, briskly,
Put her in mind how her Time steals on;
Rattle and prattle although she frown,
Rowse her, and towse her from Morn to Noon,
Shew her some Hour y'are able to grapple,
Then get but her Writings, and all's your own.

Do ye fancy a Punk of a Humour free,
That's kept by a Fumbler of Quality,
You must rail at her Keeper, and tell her, tell her
        Pleasure's best Charm is Variety,
Swear her much fairer than all the Town,
Try her, and ply her when Cully's gone,
        Dog her, and jog her,
        And meet her, and treat her,
And kiss with two Guinea's, and all's your own.

10.3 HENRY CAREY, "POLLY PEACHUM"

In *Poems on Several Occasions*, 3rd ed., London: E. Say, 1729: 151–4.

CAREY'S POEM is nicely meta-media about *The Beggar's Opera*'s success and comments on the internal operatic struggles trumped by the popularity of Gay's ballad opera, the ready availability of prints (mezzotints) for enthusiastic fans, and the theatrical politics of celebrity.

Polly Peachum

Of all the Toasts, that the *Britain* boasts;
The Gim, the Gent, the Jolly,
The Brown, the Fair, the Debonair,
There's none cried up like POLLY;
She's fir'd the Town, has quite cut down
The Opera of *Rolli*:
Go were you will, the Subject still,
Is pretty, pretty, POLLY.
There's Madam *Faustina*, Catso!
And eke Madame *Catsoni*;
Likewise *Signior Senesino*,
Are *tutti Addandonni*
Ha, ha, ha, ha; *Do, re, mi, fa*,
Are now but Farce and Folly,
We're ravished all with Toll, loll, loll,
And pretty! pretty POLLY.
The Sons of *Bayes*, in Lyric lays,
Sound forth her Fame in Print O!
And, as we pass, in Frame and Glass,
We see her *Mezz-tint-O*!
In *Ivy-Lane*, the City Strain,
Is now no more on DOLLY;
And all the Brights, at *Man's* and *White's*
Of nothing talk, but POLLY.
Ah! *Johnny Gay*! thy lucky Play,
Has made the Criticks grin, a;
They cry 'tis slat, 'tis this, 'tis that,
But let them Laugh that win, a:
I swear *Parbleu*, 'tis nais and new
I'll Nature is but Folly;
That lent a stitch to rent of RICH,
And set up Madam POLLY.
AH Tuneful Fair! Beware! Beware!
Nor Toy with Star and Garter;
Fine Clothes may hide a foul Inside
And you may catch a Tartar:
If powdered Fop, blow up your Shop,
'Twill make you Melancholy;
Then left to rot, you'll die forgot,
Alas! Alas! poor POLLY.

10.4 JAMES BOSWELL, *LONDON JOURNAL*, 1762–1763

Ed. Gordon Turnbull. New York: Penguin, 2010, pp. 225–6.

BOSWELL WAS INTERESTED in the character Macheath as well as the actors who played Macheath, especially West Digges, whom Boswell regarded as a model of modern manliness. His journals record his reactions to London life and his struggles to establish a sense of independent identity as a young man in his twenties. On this particular day, Boswell flirted with the Scottish Miss Rutherford, passed himself off as a Scotch highlander named MacDonald with a Miss Watts, and then partially reconstructed Act II, scene iv of *The Beggar's Opera* with two prostitutes.

"I then sallied forth to the Piazzas in rich flow of animal spirits, and burning with fierce desire. I met two very pretty little Girls, who asked me to take them with me. 'My Dear Girls' said I—'I am a poor fellow. I can give you no money. But if you chuse to have a glass of wine and my company, and let us be gay & obliging to each other, without money, I am your Man.' They agreed with great good humour. So back to the Shakespear I went. 'Waiter' said I, 'I have got here a couple of human beings, I don't know how they'll do.' I'll look, your honour (cried he) & with inimitable effrontery stared them in the face, & then cried they'll do very well. What said I, are they good fellow-creatures? bring them up, then. We were shown into a good room & had a bottle of Sherry before us in a minute. I surveyed my Seraglio & found them both good subjects for amorous play. I toyed with them, & drank about & sung 'Youth's the season' and thought myself Captain Macheath: and then I solaced my existence with them, one after the other, according to their Seniority. I was quite *raised*, as the phrase is. Thought I was in a London Tavern, the Shakespear's head, enjoying high debauchery, and after my sober winter. I parted with my Ladies politely & came home in a glow of spirits." Thursday 19 May, 1763.

10.5 EXCERPT FROM THE *ST. JAMES CHRONICLE OR THE BRITISH EVENING POST*

October 13, 1781–October 16, 1781, Issue 3217.

THIS EXCERPT ILLUSTRATES the importance of the natural singing style attributed to Lavinia Fenton, who originated the role of Polly. Critics distinguished this style both from operatic singing and, later, the professional training of a singer such as Elizabeth Linley, who would become Mrs. Richard Brinsley Sheridan.

(Drury-Lane.)

Last Night Miss Wheeler, of the Theatre-Royal at Bath, made her first Appearance in the Part of Polly in the Beggar's Opera. Her Figure is small but pleasing; her Manner a little too restrained to be elegant; and her Style of Singing, like that of the Scholars of Linley, correct, but too dolorous and melancholy. She has many Advantages over her Rival (Miss Harper) at the other House, but has not so fine a Voice.

10.6 JAMES BOSWELL, *THE LIFE OF JOHNSON*, 1791

Ed. David Womersley. New York: Penguin, 2008: 457–8 and 815–16.

BOSWELL, THE FIRST MODERN BIOGRAPHER, went far beyond recording the words of Samuel Johnson to crafting a persona, a narrative experience of a biographical subject, which would define the genre for years. Here, he and Johnson discuss the matter of the deleterious effects of *The Beggar's Opera* as a celebration of criminal characters, weighed against the pleasures of the ballad opera.

The Beggar's Opera, and the common question, whether it was pernicious in its effects, having been introduced; Johnson. 'As to this matter, which has been very much contested, I myself am of opinion, that more influence has been ascribed to *The Beggar's Opera*, than it in reality ever had; for I do not believe that any man was ever made a rogue by being present at its representation. At the same time I do not deny that it may have some influence, by making the character of a rogue familiar, and in some degree pleasing.' Then collecting himself as it were, to give a heavy stroke: 'There is in it such a *labefactation* of all principles, as may be injurious to morality.'

While he pronounced this response, we sat in a comical sort of restraint, smothering a laugh, which we were afraid might burst out. In his *Life of Gay*, he has been still more decisive as to the inefficiency of *The Beggar's Opera* in corrupting society. But I have ever thought somewhat differently; for, indeed, not only are the gaiety and heroism of a highwayman very captivating to a youthful imagination, but the arguments for adventurous depredation are so plausible, the allusions so lively, and the contrasts with the ordinary and more painful modes of acquiring property are so artfully displayed, that it requires a cool and strong judgement to resist so imposing an aggregate; yet, I own, I should be very sorry to have *The Beggar's Opera* suppressed; for there is in it so much of real London life, so much brilliant wit, and such a variety of airs, which, from early association of ideas, engage, soothe, and enliven the mind, that no performance which the theatre exhibits, delights me more.

The late '*worthy*' Duke of Queensberry, as Thomson, in his *Seasons*, justly characterises him, told me, that when Gay first shewed him *The Beggar's Opera*, his Grace's observation was, 'This is a very odd thing, Gay; I am satisfied that it is either a very good thing, or a very bad thing.' It proved the former, beyond the warmest expectations of the authour or his friends. Mr. Cambridge, however, shewed us to-day, that there was good reason enough to doubt concerning its success. He was told by Quin, that during the first night of its appearance it was long in a very dubious state; that there was a disposition to damn it, and that it was saved by the song,

'Oh ponder well! be not severe!'

the audience being much affected by the innocent looks of Polly, when she came to those two lines, which exhibit at once a painful and ridiculous image,

'For on the rope that hangs my Dear,
Depends poor Polly's life.'

Quin himself has so bad an opinion of it, that he refused the part of Captain Macheath, and gave it to Walker, who acquired great celebrity by his grave yet animated performance of it.

★ ★ ★

Some time after this, upon his making a remark which escaped my attention, Mrs. Williams and Mrs. Hall were both together striving to answer him. He grew angry, and called out loudly, 'Nay, when you both speak at once, it is intolerable.' But checking himself, and softening, he said, 'This one may say, though you *are* ladies.' Then he brightened into gay humour, and addressed them in the words of one of the songs in *The Beggar's Opera*:

'But two at a time there's no mortal can bear.'

'What, Sir, (said I,) are you going to turn Captain Macheath?' There was something as pleasantly ludicrous in this scene as can be imagined. The contrast between Macheath, Polly, and Lucy–and Dr. Samuel Johnson, blind, peevish Mrs. Williams, and lean, lank, preaching Mrs. Hall, was exquisite.

10.7 PORTRAIT OF *M. WALKER IN THE CHARACTER OF CAP'N MACHEATH*

Portrait of *M. Walker in the Character of Cap'n Macheath*. Engraving by Faber, after Elly's portrait. Portraits W 177 no. 1. Courtesy the Lewis Walpole Library, Yale University.

Walker originated the role of Macheath after James Quin turned it down. After starting his career at Drury Lane, he began performing in summer fairs and then defected to Lincoln's Inn Fields in 1721. Other key roles include both Worthy and Kite in *The Recruiting Officer*, Aimwell in *The Beaux' Stratagem*, and the title role in *Oroonoko*. Audiences identified Walker as Macheath and his celebrity was tied to this role, as was that of his co-star Lavinia Fenton as Polly. This print is also an example of the fan culture around *The Beggar's Opera*, which created a market for likenesses, ballads, and prints that referenced the play. The inscription beneath reads:

If Wit can please, or Gallantry engage,
Macheath may boast he justly charms ye Age.
A second Dorimant, like him in Fame,
The Fops Example, & the Ladies Flame

The Fair in Troops attend his sprightly Call,
Nor longer doat upon an Eunuch's Squall;
Well pleas'd they blush, & own behind ye Fan;
His Voice, his Looks, his Actions speak a Man.

10.8 *HARLEQUIN SHEPPARD*

HARLEQUIN, SHEPPARD.

Anon. *Harlequin Sheppard* in John Thurmond, *Harlequin Sheppard. A night scene in grotesque characters: as it is perform'd at the Theatre-Royal in Drury-Lane*. London: printed and sold by J. Roberts and A. Dodd, 1724. Courtesy of the British Library.

The image illustrates folk hero Jack Sheppard, a model for Macheath, as he attempts to escape from Newgate. Sheppard was a thief and escape artist of legendary talent. Jonathan Wild (the model for Peachum) tried unsuccessfully to recruit him to his gang, and Defoe marveled at his exploits in his *The History of the Remarkable Life of John Sheppard* (London: 1724), as did multiple ballads, a farce, an entry in *The Newgate Calendar*, and, in the nineteenth century, a novel and melodrama. Thurmond's *Harlequin Sheppard* appeared only two weeks after Sheppard was hanged; it was yet another, a testament to his popularity and the rapid mediation of current events on the stage.

10.9 WILLIAM HOGARTH, PLATE 3, *A HARLOT'S PROGRESS*

Plate 3 of William Hogarth, *A Harlot's Progress*, 1731/1732. Courtesy the Lewis Walpole Library, Yale University.

In this plate, Moll, who has now gone from being a kept courtesan to being a regular prostitute, faces an investigation by Justice Gonson as part of a general crackdown on prostitution after 1730. Moll has a print of Captain Macheath on the wall, probably the popular image of Walker as Macheath printed above. The general disarray, the gentleman's pocket watch she holds, the bottles of medicine, kinky props on the wall, and the tankards from beer gardens suggest the underworld existence of *The Beggar's Opera* into which Moll has now fallen.

10.10 *PERFORMED AT A LITTLE THEATRE WITH GREAT APPLAUSE*

Performed at a little theatre with great applause, Thomas Cornell, publisher, 16 July 1786. Courtesy of the Lewis Walpole Library, Yale University.

Mrs. Edwards plays Macheath to Mrs. Webb's Lucy in this 1786 print. The tombstone in the foreground records their roles with, at the bottom, "here lies Gay," a probable reference to his tombstone, which stated "Life is a jest, and all things show it; I thought so once, and now I know it."

Notes

1–2 The text for this edition is based on the 1728 printing: London: Printed for John Watts.

3 Denning, "Beggars and Thieves: the Ideology of the Gang." *Literature and History*, 8: 41–55.

4 Mark S. Auburn, review of "The Dramatic Cobbler: The Life and Works of Isaac Bickerstaff," *Modern Philology* (Feb. 1974): 338.

5 We know these to be nothing. Marcus Valerius Martialis, from his *Books of Epigrams*.

6 At the time, a crime-ridden area, as featured in Hogarth's "Gin Lane."

7 Ballad singers worked the streets and often collaborated with pick-pockets, which makes this rehearsal frame conversation more ironic in its sense of propriety.

8 Pregnant women could not be hanged, and Peachum suggests that he knows Moll has already gotten pregnant for that reason. He also plans to "soften" the evidence against her because she is a good thief, an inversion of the idea of an "industrious" worker.

9 Transportation was a sentence that compelled criminals to become colonists, to serve in penal colonies in Georgia, or sometimes to be sold into indenture in North America. After the American Revolution, Great Britain had to seek new penal colonies for transported felons, which led to the founding of Australia.

10 To their warehouse this year.

11 If someone in the gang doesn't inform on her for the reward, she might live another year.

12 The joke is that women bring in business for doctors (through venereal disease) and for the gang (by corrupting young men), so both professions should be grateful to them.

13 The main London prison.

14 Criminal trials held eight times a year in the Old Bailey.

15 The nick-names in this last list were also used for Sir Robert Walpole, the first Prime Minister of Great Britain.

16 The list of those to be executed, later adapted during the cold war to mean the list of those who would be barred from work because of their political associations.

17 Going into the army or about to be executed.

18 He borrows the military title, and his name means "son of the heath," a common place for burglaries.

19 Both places known for gambling.

20 Near the Inns of Court, where lawyers train.

21 The obvious reversal of social mores here is their concern that she would marry; they are very comfortable with her having sex with Macheath.

22 Here, as with many of the references to the court, the suggestion is about corruption in the Walpole administration.

23 Peachum promises to question (sift) Polly then instructs his wife to take out the identifying marks in expensive stolen handkerchiefs so he can resell them.

24 Ore.

25 Being held under a water pump, a common punishment for pickpockets.

26 The Old Bailey, where criminal trials were held.

27 The Ordinary is the Newgate chaplain who tested the literacy of felons pleading "benefit of the clergy," a loophole that allowed criminals to escape if they proved they could read, usually Psalm 51, hence Mrs. Peachum sends him to learn his "catechism."

28 Cucumber.

29 Gay inverts the usual meaning of ruined, to have had sex before marriage, with Peachum's fear that she *is* married, a strategy he will use for other keywords such as work, honest, and great.

30 They fear he will inform against them.

31 A watch that struck the most recent hour and quarter hour when one pressed its lever.

32 Legal arrangements and circumstances where Polly would get Macheath's money; otherwise, under the law of coverture, wives could not hold property themselves.

33 The cart that carried criminals from Newgate through the neighborhood of Holborn to Tyburn, the site of most hangings in London.

34 Autopsies, from "to cut into." The dead bodies of criminals could be used as cadavers for medical students.

35 In the 1735 edition, the numbering of the airs is sequential; some earlier editions restart the numbering at the act.

36 A joke about alchemy; the highwaymen turn lead into gold by shooting and stealing.

37 Macheath suggests that actresses are cast-off mistresses.

38 Site of brothels near Drury Lane.

39 Informal dress.

40 A kept mistress, which would be a higher form of prostitution than streetwalking.

41 Young apprentices who can be made to steal, as in *The London Merchant*, and are sentenced to transportation in the colonies when they are caught.

42 He will pay the bill.

43 New prisoners had to pay "garnishes," or fees to the guards and senior prisoners.

44 This air is unnamed in early editions.

45 Entrapped.

46 The South Sea Bubble of 1720 was a company stock crash that rendered thousands of small investors' holdings worthless while government figures and company founders were protected by insider trading.

47 Lockit is paraphrasing Rochester's "A Satire Against Reason and Mankind."

48 A fish that has recently ejected its spawn.

49 Heavy betting.

50 A roll of coins.

51 An easily fooled person.

52 After 1722 debtors could no longer use the Mint as a sanctuary from arrest.

53 In 1725, Parliament passed a law against imprisoning people for small amounts of debt.

54 A gin craze hit London in the 1720s, much of it cheaply made and poisonous.

11. *The Author's Farce; and The Pleasures of the Town*

THE AUTHOR'S FARCE AND THE PLEASURES OF THE TOWN.
AS ACTED AT THE THEATRE IN THE HAY-MARKET.[1] HENRY FIELDING.
FIRST PERFORMED 30 MARCH 1730 AND FIRST PUBLISHED 1730

11.1 *THE AUTHOR'S FARCE*; AND THE PLEASURES OF THE TOWN. AS ACTED AT THE THEATRE IN THE HAY-MARKET.[2]

Henry Fielding

First Performed 30 March 1730 and First Published 1730

FIELDING'S FIRST BIG THEATRICAL HIT was *The Author's Farce*, which opened on March 30, 1730, at the Haymarket on Suffolk Street when Fielding was barely 23. His first play, *Love in Several Masques*, had appeared at Drury Lane on February 16, 1728, where it languished in the shadow of the season's unprecedented hit, *The Beggar's Opera*, which had opened 17 days earlier. After this experience, Fielding was well aware of the vicissitudes of popular taste and the explosion of the entertainment industry. In Fielding's farce, Luckless, the penniless playwright, is reduced to negotiating with his landlady when he in fact loves her daughter. Luckless cannot get a play accepted for the stage, and so he eventually (in Act III) turns it into a puppet show to make money. As he explains, "Who would not then rather eat by his nonsense than starve by his wit?" Puppet characters (played by the human actors from the first two acts) include Mrs. Novel, Signior Opera, Dr. Orator, Monsieur Pantomime, Sir Farcical Comic, Punch, Joan, and a host of others who satirize the public appetite for entertainment and novelty in a media-rich age, with Luckless serving as master of ceremonies.

By the time Henry Fielding brought *The Author's Farce* to the Haymarket stage, alternative entertainments in the form of harlequinades, operas, ballad operas, puppet shows, and dance had been growing for over ten years. Colley Cibber's *Venus and Adonis* (1715), John Rich's *The Necromancer, or Harlequin Doctor Faustus* (1723), John Gay's *The Beggar's Opera* (1728), and Samuel Johnson's *Hurlothrumbo* (1729) each provided examples of the genre-bending entertainments that Fielding satirized in *The Author's Farce*, even as these transgressive pieces informed his theatrical experimentation. His *Tom Thumb, or The Tragedy of Tragedies* (also 1730) and *The Grub Street Opera* (1731) likewise used the entertainment strategies they mocked. Like *The Beggar's Opera*, penned by his fellow Scriblerian, Gay, *The Author's Farce* also trafficked in sub-rosa political critique. Fielding borrowed many of Gay's successful techniques, including ballad opera, the meta-theatrical placement of characters who comment on the action, and intensely satirical dialogue. Fielding's *The Author's Farce* would cement the Haymarket's reputation as an opposition (Tory) playhouse, a connection he proudly announced on the title page of the play, written by "Scriblerius Secundus," the fictional son of the fictional Martinus Scriblerus, the persona created by the Scriblerians (who included Swift, Pope, Arbuthnot, Parnell, and Gay).

Like the first version of Pope's *The Dunciad* (1728), *The Author's Farce* skewers the excesses and absurdities of the new literary and theatrical marketplace. Both Pope and Fielding would revise their satires to attack Colley Cibber, best known as the clownish fop of the late Restoration stage turned poet laureate, and later, his son Theophilus. Colley Cibber's laureateship was widely understood to be a partial reward for his fidelity to the

Whigs and Hanover, and both Pope and Fielding read this as a sign of corrupt times. Fielding uses Gay's more obviously political critique of the Walpole administration in *The Beggar's Opera* to undergird his own references to the wealth and corruption associated with modern authorship, resulting in a politicized, satiric aesthetics. Unrealistic or fantastic elements (most obviously, the puppets) share the stage with the realistic and representational struggles of Luckless the playwright. Fielding sustains an ironic distance on his characters through a combination of emblematic names (Opera, Novel, Pantomime), broad farce, and generic parody to produce a Brechtian alienation effect long before Brecht in his satire on popular culture and entertainment media.

Fielding's later work, in particular, *The Historical Register for the year 1736*, would precipitate the 1737 Licensing Act, through which the Walpole administration attempted to shut down critiques of the administration by restricting the number of licensed theatres and insisting that all plays go through review in the Lord Chamberlain's office before they could be performed. *The Beggar's Opera* had long been a thorn in Walpole's side, and he used his influence to shut down Gay's sequel, *Polly*. Fielding took shots at Walpole in *Tom Thumb* (1730) and *Pasquin* (1736), while the anonymous *A Vision of the Golden Rump* (1737), with its sweeping critique of the current parliament, brought the situation to crisis. By comparison, *The Author's Farce* is politically tame, but it comes out of the Little Haymarket, Fielding's theatre, which had been an incubator for alternative and edgy plays. Technically, the play first banned under the 1737 act was *Gustavus Vasa*, by Henry Brook. Walpole thought Brook's hero was intended to insult him, though largely because Brook's earlier Tory play *The Earl of Essex* had already raised hackles.

Fielding revised his play for the 1733–34 season, with a new character, Marplay, Junior, aimed at Theophilus Cibber, and a good deal of other new material. As Charles B. Woods notes, the revision touches nearly every page, though "the new material fails to mesh perfectly with the old," and the revival in 1734 was "cooly received."[3] This later version of *The Author's Farce* is the basis for the version that appears in Fielding's *Works*, 1755. The text in this anthology is based on the 1730 edition, with occasional notes to variants of interest. For a more comprehensive scholarly edition of the differences, students may consult Woods' edition of the play (University of Nebraska, 1966) or compare the original texts, available as pdfs through *Eighteenth-Century Collections Online*.

—*Quis iniquæ Tam patiens urbis, tam ferreus, ut teneat se?*[4]

Juv. Sat. 1.

PROLOGUE

Spoken by Mr. JONES.

Too long the tragick muse hath aw'd the stage,
And frightned wives and children with her rage.
Too long Drawcansir roars, Parthenope weeps,[5]
While ev'ry lady cries, and critick sleeps.
With ghosts, rapes, murders, tender hearts they wound,
Or else, like thunder, terrifie with sound.
When the skill'd actress to her weeping eyes,
With artful sigh, the handkerchief applies,
How griev'd each sympathizing nymph appears?
And box and gallery both melt in tears.
Or, when in armour of Corinthian brass,[6]
Heroick actor stares you in the face,
And cries aloud with emphasis that's fit, on
Liberty, freedom, liberty and Briton;
While frowning, gaping for applause he stands,
What generous Briton can refuse his hands?
Like the tame animals design'd for show,
You have your cues to clap, as they to bowe?
Taught to commend, your judgments have no share;
By chance you guess aright, by chance you err.

But handkerchiefs and Britain laid aside,
To-night we mean to laugh, and not to chide.
In days of yore, when fools were held in fashion,
Tho' now, alas! All banish'd from the nation,
A merry jester had reform'd his Lord,
Who wou'd have scorn'd the sterner stoick's word.

Bred in Democritus his laughing schools,
Our author flies sad Heraclitus' rules:
No tears, no terror plead in his behalf;
The aim of farce is but to make you laugh.
Beneath the tragick or the comick name,
Farces and puppet-shows ne'er miss of fame.
Since then, in borrow'd dress, they've pleased the town;
Condemn them not, appearing in their own.

Smiles we expect, from the good-natur'd few;
As ye are done by, ye malicious, do;
And kindly laugh at him, who laughs at you.

Persons in the Farce.

Luckless, the Author, and Master of the Show	Mr. Mullart.
Witmore, his Friend	Mr. Lacy.
Marplay, A Comedian	Mr. Reynolds.
Sparkish, A Comedian	Mr. Stopler.
Bookweight, a Bookseller	Mr. Jones.
Scarecrow, A Scribler	Mr. Marshal.
Dash, A Scribler	Mr. Hallam.
Quibble, A Scribler	Mr. Dove.
Blotpage, A Scribler	Mr. Wells, Jun.
Index[7]	
Jack, Servant to Luckless	Mr. Achurch.
Jack-Pudding	Mr. Reynolds.
Bantomite	Mr. Marshal.
Messenger	
Mrs. Moneywood, the Author's Landlady	Mrs. Mullart.
Harriot, her Daughter	Miss Palms.

Persons in the Puppet-Show.

Player	Mr. Dove.
Constable	Mr. Wells.
Murder-text, a Presbyterian Parson	Mr. Hallam.
Goddess of Nonsense	Mrs. Mullart.
Charon	Mr. Ayres.
Curry, a Bookseller	Mr. Dove.
A Poet	Mr. W. Hallam.
Signior Opera	Mr. Stopler.
Don Tragedio	Mr. Marshal.
Sir Farcical Comick	Mr. Davenport.
Dr. Orator	Mr. Jones.
Monsieur Pantomime	Mr. Knott.
Mrs. Novel	Mrs. Martin.
Robgrave, the Sexton	Mr. Harris.
Saylor	Mr. Achurch.
Somebody	Mr. Harris, Jun.
Nobody	Mr. Wells, Jun.
Punch	Mr. Reynolds.
Joan	Mr. Hicks.
Lady Kingcall	Miss Clarke.
Mrs. Cheat'em	Mrs. Wind.
Mrs. Glass-ring	Mrs. Blunt.

ACT I.

ACT I. SCENE I. Luckless's room in Mrs. Moneywood's house.

[*Enter* Mrs. Moneywood, Harriot, *and* Luckless]

MRS. MONEYWOOD. Never tell me, Mr. *Luckless*, of your play, and your play – I say, I must be paid. I would no more depend on a benefit-night of an un-acted play, than I wou'd on a benefit-ticket in an un-drawn lottery. – Cou'd I have guess'd that I had a poet in my house! Cou'd I have look'd for a poet under lac'd cloaths!

LUCKLESS. Why not, since you may often find poverty under them?

MRS. MONEYWOOD. Do you make a jest of my misfortune, Sir?

LUCKLESS. Rather, my misfortune. – I am sure I have a better title to poverty than you. – You wallow in wealth, and I know not where to dine.

MRS. MONEYWOOD. Never fear that; you'll never want a dinner 'till you have dined at all the eating-houses round. – No one shuts their doors against you, the first time – and I think you are so kind, never to trouble them a second.

LUCKLESS. No – and if you will give me leave to walk out of your doors, the de'el take me if ever I come into them again.

MRS. MONEYWOOD. Whenever you please, Sir; leaving your moveables behind.

LUCKLESS. All but my books, dear Madam, they will be of no service to you.

MRS. MONEYWOOD. When they are sold, Sir; and that's more than your other effects wou'd; for I believe you may carry away every thing else in your pockets – if you have any.

HARRIOT. Nay, Mamma, it is barbarous to insult him.

MRS. MONEYWOOD. No doubt you'll take his part. – Pray, get about your business. – I suppose he intends to pay me, by ruining you. Get you in – and if ever I see you together again, I'll turn you out of doors; remember that.

ACT I. SCENE II.

[*Enter* Luckless, *and* Mrs. Moneywood.

LUCKLESS. Discharge all your ill-nature on me, Madam, but spare poor Miss *Harriot*.

MRS. MONEYWOOD. Oh! then it is plain. – I have suspected your familiarity a great while. You are a base man. Is it not enough to stay three months in my house without paying me a farthing, but you must ruin my child?

LUCKLESS. I love her as I love my soul. – Had I the world, I'd give it her all –

MRS. MONEYWOOD. But as you happen to have nothing in the world, I desire you would have nothing to say to her. – I suppose you wou'd have settled all your castles in the air. – Oh! I wish you had lodg'd in one of them, instead of my house. Well, I am resolv'd, when you are gone away (which I heartily hope will be very soon) I'll hang over my door in great red letters, *No Lodgings for Poets*. – Sure, never was such a guest as you have been. – My floor is all spoil'd with ink – my windows with verses, and my door has been almost beat down with duns.[8]

LUCKLESS. Wou'd your house had been beaten down, and every thing, but my dear *Harriot*, crush'd under it. Must I be your scolding-stock every morning? And because my pocket is empty, must my head be fill'd with noise and impertinence? Naturalists say, that all creatures, even the most venomous, are of some use in the creation – but I'm sure a scolding old woman is of none; – unless she serves in this world, as the Devil will in the other, to torment us. And if our torment were to lie in noise, I defy the Devil to invent a worse.

MRS. MONEYWOOD. Sir, Sir –

LUCKLESS. Madam, Madam! I will attack you at your own weapon. – I'll pay you in your own coin. –

MRS. MONEYWOOD. I wish you wou'd pay me in any coin, Sir.

LUCKLESS. Pay you! – that word is always uppermost in your mouth, as Gelt[9] is in a Dutchman's. – Look you, Madam, I'll do as much as a reasonable woman can require; I'll shew you all I have, – and give you all I have too, if you please to receive it. [*Turns his pockets inside out.*

MRS. MONEYWOOD. I will not be us'd in this manner. No, Sir, I will be paid, if there be any such thing as law.

LUCKLESS. By what law you will put money into my pocket, I don't know; for I never heard of any one who got money by the law, but the lawyers. I have told you already, Madam, and I tell you again, that the first money I get shall be yours; and I have great expectations from my play. In the mean time, your staying here can be of no service, and you may possibly drive some fine thoughts out of my head. I must write a love scene, and your daughter wou'd be properer company on that occasion, than you.

MRS. MONEYWOOD. You wou'd act a love scene, I believe, but I shall prevent you; for I intend to dispose of my self, before my daughter.

LUCKLESS. Dispose of your self! To whom? To the tallow-chandler! You will never have any thing to do with matrimony, 'till *Hymen* turns his torch into a tallow-candle;[10] then you may be of as much use to him, as a fine lady's eyes to *Cupid*, and may serve to light young people to bed together.

MRS. MONEYWOOD. You are a vile slanderer. I am not so old, nor so fat, nor so ugly, as you wou'd make me. And 'tis very well known, that I have had very good offers since my last dear husband died, if I wou'd have accepted them; – I might have had an attorney of *New-Inn* – or Mr. *Fillpot* the excise-man – Yes, I had my choice of two parsons, or a doctor of physick – and yet I slighted them all; yes I slighted them for you. –

LUCKLESS. For me!

MRS. MONEYWOOD. Yes, you have seen too visible marks of my passion – too visible for my reputation.

LUCKLESS. I have heard very loud tokens of your passion; but I rather took it for the passion of anger, than of love.

MRS. MONEYWOOD. Oh! It arose from love! – Do but be kind, and I'll forgive thee all.[11]

LUCKLESS. Death! Madam, stand off. – If I must be plagu'd with you, I had rather you shou'd afflict my eyes than my touch; at a distance, you offend but one sense; but nearer, you offend them all – and I wou'd sooner lose them all, than undergo you.

MRS. MONEYWOOD. You shall repent this, Sir, remember that – you shall repent it. – I'll shew you the revenge of an injur'd woman.

LUCKLESS. I shall never repent any thing that rids me of you, Madam, I assure you. [*Exit.*

ACT I. SCENE III.

[*Enter* Luckless, Harriot.

HARRIOT. My dear *Harry*, I have been waiting an opportunity to return to you.

LUCKLESS. My dear *Harriot* – come to my arms, and let me lay my aching, sick head on thy tender bosom.

HARRIOT. What's the matter, my dear?

LUCKLESS. I am sick of the most abominable distemper.

HARRIOT. Heaven forbid! What is it?

LUCKLESS. Poverty, my love – and your mother is a most excellent nurse.

HARRIOT. What shall I do for you? My money is all gone, and so are my cloaths; which, when my mother finds out, I shall have as much need of a surgeon, as you can have now of a doctor.

LUCKLESS. No, I wou'd sooner starve, or beg, or steal, or die, than one hair of my dear *Harriot* shou'd be hurt. I am armed against her utmost rage; but for you I fear; for such a spirit as your mother, no *Amazon* ever possess'd before. So, if my present design succeeds, we will leave her together –

HARRIOT. But if it shou'd fail –

LUCKLESS. Say, then, my *Harriot*, wou'd my charmer fly
To the cold climes beneath the polar sky?
Or, arm'd with love; cou'd she endure to sweat,
Beneath the sultry, dry *Equator*'s heat?
Thirst, hunger, labour, hardship, could she prove,
From conversation of the world remove,
And only know the joys of constant love?

HARRIOT. Oh! More than this, my *Luckless*, would I do:
All places are a heaven, when with you:
Let me repose but on that faithful breast,
Give me thy love–the world may take the rest.[12]

LUCKLESS. My dear *Harriot*! By heav'n, thy lips are sweeter than the honey, and thy temper is yet sweeter than them.

HARRIOT. [*Sighs.*

LUCKLESS. Why do you sigh, my sweet?

HARRIOT. I only wish I were assured of the sincerity of your love.

AIR, *Butter'd Pease.*

LUCKLESS. *Does my dearest Harriot ask*
What for love I wou'd pursue;
Wou'd you, charmer, know what task
I wou'd undertake for you?

Ask the bold ambitious, what
He for honours wou'd achieve;
Or the gay voluptuous, that
Which he'd not for pleasures give.

Ask the miser what he'd do
To amass excessive gain;
Or the saint, what he'd pursue,
His wish'd heav'n to attain.

These I wou'd attempt, and more;
For oh! my Harriot is to me,
All ambition, pleasure store,
Or what heav'n it self can be.

HARRIOT. *Wou'd my dearest Luckless know,*
What his constant Harriot can,
Her tender love and faith to show,
For her dear, her only man?

Ask the vain coquet, what she
For men's adoration wou'd;
Or from censure to be free,
Ask the vile censorious prude.

In a coach and six to ride,
What the mercenary jade;
Or the widow, to be bride
To a brisk, broad-shoulder'd blade.

All these I wou'd attempt for thee,
Cou'd I but thy passion fix';
Thy tongue my sole commander be,
And thy arms my coach and six.

LUCKLESS. It is unkind in you to doubt it. – I wish it was in my power to give you greater proofs – but I will give you the greatest in my power – which is, to marry you this instant.

HARRIOT. Then I am easy: But it is better to delay that 'till our circumstances alter – for, remember what you have your self said in the song you taught me:

Wou'd you the charming queen of love,
Invite with you to dwell;
No want your poverty shou'd prove,
No state your riches tell.

Both her, and happiness to hold,
A middle state must please;
They shun the house that shines with gold,
And that which shines with grease.

MRS. MONEYWOOD. [*Within*] Harriot! Harriot!

HARRIOT. Hear the dreadful summons; Adieu, my dear. I will take the first opportunity of seeing you again.

LUCKLESS. Adieu to my pretty charmer! – Go thy ways, for the first of thy sex. What fool wou'd dangle after, and make himself a slave to the insolent pride of a mistress, when he may find another with as much good-nature as he wou'd wish?

ACT I. SCENE IV.

[Luckless, Jack.

LUCKLESS. So! What news bring you!

JACK. An't please your honour, I have been at my Lord's, and his Lordship thanks you for the favour you have offered of reading your play to him; but he has such a prodigious deal of business, he begs to be excus'd. – I have been with Mr. *Keyber*[13] too; he made me no answer at all. – Mr. *Bookweight* will be here immediately.

LUCKLESS. *Jack*!

JACK. Sir.

LUCKLESS. Fetch my hat hither.

JACK. It is here, Sir.

LUCKLESS. Carry it to the pawn-brokers. And, in your way home, call at the cook's-shop – make haste. So, one way or other I find, my head must always provide for my belly.

ACT I. SCENE V.

[Luckless, Witmore.

LUCKLESS. I am surprized, – dear *Witmore*!

WITMORE. Dear *Harry*!

LUCKLESS. This is kind, indeed; but I do not more wonder at finding a man in this age, who can be a friend to adversity, than that fortune should be so much my friend, as to direct you to me; for she is a lady I have not been much indebted to lately.

WITMORE. She who told me, I assure you, is one you have been indebted to a long while.

LUCKLESS. Whom do you mean?

WITMORE. One who complains of your unkindness in not visiting her – Mrs. *Lovewood*.

LUCKLESS. Dost thou visit there still, then?

WITMORE. I throw an idle hour away there sometimes – when I am in an ill humour, I go there and rail, where I am sure to feed it with all the scandal in town – No news-writer is more diligent in procuring intelligence – no bawd in looking after girls with an uncrack'd maidenhead, than she in searching out women with crack'd reputations.[14]

LUCKLESS. The much more infamous office of the two.

WITMORE. Thou art still a favourer of the women, I find.

LUCKLESS. Ay, the women and the muses – the high roads to beggary.

WITMORE. What, art thou not cured of scribling yet?

LUCKLESS. No, scribling is as impossible to cure as the gout.

WITMORE. And as sure a sign of poverty as the gout of riches. S'death! In an age of learning and true politeness, where a man might succeed by his merit, it wou'd be an encouragement. – But now, when party and prejudice carry all before them, when learning is decried, wit not understood, when the theatres are puppet-shows, and the comedians ballad-singers: When fools lead the town, wou'd a man think to thrive by his wit? – If you must write, write nonsense, write operas, write entertainments, write *Hurlo-thrumbo's*[15] – Set up an *oratory* and preach nonsense; and you may meet with encouragement enough. If you wou'd receive applause, deserve to receive sentence at the *Old-Baily*: And if you wou'd ride in your coach, deserve to ride in a cart.[16]

LUCKLESS. You are warm, my friend.

WITMORE. It is because I am your friend. I cannot bear to hear the man I love ridiculed by fools and idiots – To see a fellow, who had he been born a *Chinese*, had been some low mechanick, toss up his empty noddle with a scornful disdain of what he has not understood; and women abusing what they have neither seen nor read, from an unreasonable prejudice to an honest fellow, whom they have not known. If thou wilt write against all these reasons, get a patron, be pimp to some worthless man of quality, write panegyricks[17] on him, flatter him with as many virtues as he has vices – and don't pretend to stand thy self against a tide of prejudice and ill-nature, which would have over-whelm'd a *Plato* or a *Socrates*.

LUCKLESS. I own thy advice is friendly, and I fear too much truth is on your side – but what wou'd you advise me to do?

WITMORE. Thou art a vigorous young fellow – and there are rich widows in town.

LUCKLESS. But I am already engaged.

WITMORE. Why don't you marry then – for I suppose you are not so mad, to have any engagement with a poor mistress.

LUCKLESS. Even so, faith, and so heartily that I wou'd not change her for the widow of a *Croesus*.[18]

WITMORE. Now thou art undone, indeed. Matrimony clenches ruin beyond retrieval. What unfortunate stars wert thou born under! Was it not enough to follow those nine ragged jades the Muses, but you must fasten on some Earth-born mistress as poor as them?[19]

LUCKLESS. Fie *Witmore*, thou art grown a churl.[20]

WITMORE. While thou wert happy, I cou'd bear these flights; while thy rooms were furnished, and thy cloaths whole, I cou'd bear thee. – But for a man to preach up love and the Muses in a garret, it wou'd not make me more sick to hear honesty talked of at court, conscience at *Westminster*, politeness at the University – Nay, I had rather hear women disputing on the mathematicks – [21]

ACT I. SCENE VI.

[Luckless, Witmore, Bookweight.

LUCKLESS. Mr. *Bookweight*, your very humble servant.

BOOKWEIGHT. I was told, Sir, you had particular business with me.

LUCKLESS. Yes, Mr. *Bookweight*, I have something to put into your hands. I have a play for you, Mr. *Bookweight*.

BOOKWEIGHT. Is it accepted, Sir?[22]

LUCKLESS. Not yet.

BOOKWEIGHT. Oh! Sir! When it is, it will be then time enough to talk about it. A play, like a bill, is of no value before it is accepted, nor indeed when it is, very often. This too is a plentiful year of plays – and they are like nuts: In a plentiful year they are commonly very bad.

LUCKLESS. But suppose it were accepted (as you term it) what wou'd you give me for it? (Not that I want money, Sir –)

BOOKWEIGHT. No, Sir, certainly – But before I can make any answer I must read it – I cannot offer any thing for what I do not know the value of.

WITMORE. That I imagine granted by the players' approbation: For they are, you know, very great judges.

BOOKWEIGHT. Yes, Sir, that they are, indeed – That they must be allowed to be, as being men of great learning: But a play which will do for them, will not always do for us. – There are your acting plays, and your reading plays.

WITMORE. I do not understand that distinction.

BOOKWEIGHT. Why, Sir, your acting play is entirely supported by the merit of the actor, without any regard to the author at all: – In this case, it signifies very little whether there be any sense in it or no. Now your reading play is of a different stamp, and must have wit and meaning in it – These latter I call your substantive, as being able to support themselves. The former are your adjective, as what require the buffoonry and gestures of an actor to be joined to them, to shew their signification.

LUCKLESS. Very learnedly defin'd, truly, Mr. *Bookweight.*

BOOKWEIGHT. I hope I have not had so much learning go through my hands without leaving some in my head.

LUCKLESS. Well: But, Mr. *Bookweight,* I hope you will advance something –

BOOKWEIGHT. Why, had you a great reputation I might venture: But, truly, for young beginners it is a very great hazard: For, indeed, the reputation of the author carries the greatest sway in these affairs. The town have been so fond of some authors, that they have run them up to infallibility, and wou'd have applauded them even against their senses.

WITMORE. And who but a mad-man would write in such an age?

LUCKLESS. S'death! *Witmore*! 'Tis cruel to insult my misfortunes.

WITMORE. I wou'd cure them – and that is not to be done by lenitives.[23]

BOOKWEIGHT. I am of that gentleman's opinion: I do think writing the silliest thing a man can undertake.

LUCKLESS. 'Tis Strange you shou'd say so, who live by it.

BOOKWEIGHT. Live by it! Ah! If you had lost as much by writers as I have done, you wou'd be of my opinion.

LUCKLESS. But we are losing time – Will you advance fifty guineas on my play?

BOOKWEIGHT. No – nor fifty shillings, I assure you.

LUCKLESS. S'death! Sir; do you beat me down at this rate?

BOOKWEIGHT. Sir, I wou'd not give you fifty farthings – Fifty guineas, indeed! Your name is well worth that.

LUCKLESS. Jack. –

[Jack *enters.*

Take this worthy gentleman and kick him down stairs.

BOOKWEIGHT. Sir, I shall make you repent this –

JACK. Come, Sir, will you please to brush – [24]

BOOKWEIGHT. Help – Murder – I'll have the law of you, Sir.

LUCKLESS. Ha, ha, ha. –

ACT I. SCENE VII.

[Luckless, Witmore, Mrs. Moneywood.

MRS. MONEYWOOD. What noise is this? It is a very fine thing truly, Mr. *Luckless*, that you will make these uproars in my house. –

LUCKLESS. If you dislike it, it is in your power to drown a much greater. Do you but speak, Madam, and I am sure no one will be heard but your self.

MRS. MONEYWOOD. Very well, indeed! Fine reflections on my character! – Sir, Sir, all the neighbours know that I have been as quiet a woman as any in the parish. I had no noises in my house till you came. We were the family of love – But you have been a nuisance to the whole neighbourhood – While you had money my doors were thundered at every morning at four and five, and since you have had none, my walls have echoed nothing but your noise and your poetry – [25] Then there's the rascal your man – but I'll pay the dog – I'll scour him – [*To* Wit] Sir, I am glad you are a witness to his abuses of me –

WITMORE. I am a witness indeed, Madam, how unjustly he has abus'd you.

LUCKLESS. [Jack *whispers*] *Witmore*, you'll excuse me a moment.

ACT I. SCENE VIII.

[Mrs. Moneywood, Witmore.

MRS. MONEYWOOD. Yes, Sir; and Sir, a man that has never shewn one the colour of his money.

WITMORE. Very hard, truly – How much may he be in your debt, pray? Because he has order'd me to pay you.

MRS. MONEYWOOD. Ah! Sir, I wish he had.

WITMORE. I am serious, I assure you.

MRS. MONEYWOOD. I am very glad to hear it, Sir. Here is the bill as we settled it this very morning. I always thought indeed Mr. *Luckless* had a good deal of honesty in his principles – any man may be unfortunate: but I knew when he had money I shou'd have it – I never was in any fear for my money, for my part.

WITMORE. There, Madam, is your money on the table. Please to write a receipt only.

MRS. MONEYWOOD. Sir, I give you a great many thanks. There, Sir, is the receipt – Well, if Mr. *Luckless* was but a little soberer – I shou'd like him for a lodger exceedingly: for I must say I think him a very pleasant good-natur'd man.

ACT I. SCENE IX.

[Luckless *returns.*

LUCKLESS. Those are words I never heard out of that mouth before.

MRS. MONEYWOOD. Ha, ha, ha! You are pleas'd to be merry.

LUCKLESS. Why *Witmore,* thou hast the faculty opposite to that of a witch – and can'st lay a tempest. I shou'd have as soon imagin'd one man cou'd have stopt a cannon ball in its full force, as her tongue, and I believe she may be heard as far – Were she to roar forth a summons to a town, it wou'd have more effect on the governor than a volley of artillery.

MRS. MONEYWOOD. Ha, ha, ha!

WITMORE. *Luckless,* good morrow – I will see you again soon. –

LUCKLESS. *Witmore,* I am yours.

ACT I. SCENE X.

[Luckless*,* Mrs. Moneywood.

MRS. MONEYWOOD. Well, Mr. *Luckless,* you are a comical man, to give one such a character to a stranger.

LUCKLESS. The company is gone, Madam; and now, like true man and wife, we may fall to abusing one another as fast as we please.

MRS. MONEYWOOD. Abuse me as you will, so you pay me, Sir.

LUCKLESS. S'Death! Madam, I will pay you.

MRS. MONEYWOOD. Nay, Sir, I do not ask it before it is due – I don't question your payment at all: If you were to stay in my house this quarter of a year, as I hope you will, I shou'd not ask you for a farthing.

LUCKLESS. Tol, lol, lol. – But I shall have her begin with her passion immediately; and I had rather feel the highest effects of her rage, than the lightest of her love.

MRS. MONEYWOOD. But why did you chuse to surprize me with my money? Why did you not tell me you'd pay me?

LUCKLESS. Why have I not told you!

MRS. MONEYWOOD. Yes, you told me of a play and stuff: But you never told me you wou'd order a gentleman to pay me. Well, you have comical ways with you: but you have honesty in the bottom, and I'm sure the gentleman himself will own I gave you that character.

LUCKLESS. Oh! – I smell you now – You see, Madam, I am better than my word to you; did he pay it you in gold or silver?

MRS. MONEYWOOD. All pure gold.

LUCKLESS. I have a vast deal of silver within; will you do me the favour of taking it in silver? That may be of use to you in the shop too.[26]

MRS. MONEYWOOD. Any thing to oblige you, Sir!

LUCKLESS. *Jack,* bring out the great bag number *one*. Please to tell the money, Madam, on that table.

MRS. MONEYWOOD. [*Tells the money*] It's easily told – Heaven knows there's not so much on't.

[*Enter* Jack. *When* Jack *enters,* Luckless *gets between* Mrs. Moneywood *and the table.*

JACK. Sir, the bag is so heavy, I cannot bring it in.

LUCKLESS. Why then, come and help to thrust a heavier bag[27] out.

MRS. MONEYWOOD. What do you mean, Sir?

LUCKLESS. Only to pay you in my bedchamber.

MRS. MONEYWOOD. Villain, dog, I'll swear a robbery and have you hang'd: Rogues, villains!

LUCKLESS. [*Shuts the Door*] Be as noisy as you please. – *Jack,* call a coach, and d'ye hear, get up behind it and attend me.

—The End of the First Act.—

ACT II.

ACT II. SCENE I. A tavern.

[Luckless, Marplay, Sparkish.[28]

LUCKLESS. [*Reads.*

Then hence my sorrows, hence my ev'ry fear;
No matter where, so we are bless'd together.
With thee, the barren rocks, where not one step
Of human race lies printed in the snow,
Look lovely as the smiling infant spring.

MARPLAY. [*Yawning*] Will you please to read that again, Sir?

LUCKLESS. [*Reads again.*

MARPLAY. Then hence my sorrow – Horror is a much better word, in my opinion – And then in the second line – will you please to read it again.

LUCKLESS. No matter where, so we are bless'd together.

MARPLAY. In my opinion it wou'd be better so:

No matter where, so somewhere we're together.
Where is the question, somewhere is the answer – Read on, Sir.

LUCKLESS. [*Reads on*] With thee, &c.

MARPLAY. I cou'd alter those lines to a much better idea.

With thee, the barren blocks, – [*Aside*] *that is trees.*
Where not a bit
Of human face is painted on the bark,
Look green as *Covent-Garden* in the spring.[29]

LUCKLESS. Green as Covent-Garden!

MARPLAY. Yes, Covent-Garden Market: where they sell greens.

LUCKLESS. Monstrous! Sir, I must ask your pardon, I cannot consent to such an alteration. It is downright nonsense.

MARPLAY. [*Rising from the table*] Sir, it will not do – and so I wou'd not have you think any more of it.

SPARKISH. No, no, no. It will not do.

LUCKLESS. What faults do you find?

MARPLAY. Sir, there is nothing in it that pleases me, so I am sure there is nothing in it that will please the town.

SPARKISH. There is nothing in it that will please the town.

LUCKLESS. Methinks you shou'd find some particular fault.

MARPLAY. Truly, Sir, it is so full of faults – that the eye of my judgment is so distracted with the variety of objects that it cannot fix on any.

SPARKISH. No, no, no – cannot fix on any.

MARPLAY. In short, there is not one good thing in it from the beginning to the end.

LUCKLESS. Some who have read it think otherwise.

MARPLAY. Let them think as they please – I'm sure we are the best judges.

SPARKISH. Yes, yes, we are the best judges.

LUCKLESS. Cou'd you convince me of any fault, I wou'd amend it: but you argue in plays as the Pope does in religion, or the *Aristotleists* in philosophy; you maintain your hypothesis by an *ipse dicit.*[30]

MARPLAY. I don't understand your hard words, Sir; but I think it is very hard if a man who has been so long in a trade as I have, shou'd not understand the value of his merchandize: shou'd not know what goods will best please the town. – Come – *Sparkish*, will you go to *Toms*!

LUCKLESS. Fare ye well, Gentlemen: may another play do you more service.

ACT II. SCENE II.

[Marplay, Sparkish.

MARPLAY. Ha, ha, ha!

SPARKISH. What dost think of the play?

MARPLAY. It may be a very good one, for ought I know; but I know the author has no interest.

SPARKISH. Give me interest, and rat the play. –

MARPLAY. Rather rat the play which has no interest. Interest sways as much in the theatre as at court. – And you know it is not always the companion of merit in either.

SPARKISH. But pray, Mr. *Marplay*, what was the reason of that extraordinary demand of yours upon the office?

MARPLAY. Truly, Sir, it was for the good of the office. – Some of it was given to puffs, to cry up our new plays – And one half guinea to Mr. *Scribler* for a panegyrical essay in the news-paper, with some other such services. But have you seen my new entertainment practised, *Cuckolds all a Row*?

SPARKISH. No.

MARPLAY. I will affirm this, that it is the best thing that has ever appear'd on the stage – I don't know whether I shall not lay the pit and boxes together,[31] at half a guinea a seat.

SPARKISH. I wou'd not advise that: for the town grumbles at our raising the prices as we have done.

MARPLAY. Rat the town. – Let them grumble, I'm sure they will not stay away – For their hisses – they have no more effect on me than musick wou'd have on an owl – or the curses of an undone client on an attorney – I have been us'd to them; and any man who loves hissing may have his three shillings worth at me whenever he pleases.[32]

ACT II. SCENE III. A room in Mr. Bookweight's house.

[Dash, Blotpage, Quibble, *writing at several tables.*

DASH. Pox on't, I'm as dull as an ox, tho' I have not a bit of one within me. – I have not din'd these two days, and yet my head is as heavy as any alderman's or lord's. I carry about me symbols of all the elements; my head is as heavy as water, my pockets are light as air, my appetite is as hot as fire, and my coat is as dirty as earth.

BLOTPAGE. Lend me your *Bysshe*,[33] Mr. *Dash*, I want a rhyme[34] for wind. –

DASH. Why there! Blind, and kind, and behind, and find, and mind – It is one of the easiest terminations imaginable; I have had it four times in a page.

BLOTPAGE. Devil take the first inventor of rhyming I say. Your business is much easier, Mr. *Dash*. Well, of all the places in my master's gift – I shou'd most like to be Clerk of the Ghosts and Murders. You have nothing to do but to put a set of terrible words together in the title page.

DASH. The business is easy enough, but it is at a very low ebb now. No, Mr. *Quibble* there, as Clerk of the Libels, wou'd have the best place, were it not that few men ever sat in his chair long without standing on an odd sort of a stool in the street, to be gap'd at an hour or two by the mob.

QUIBBLE. We act on different principles, Mr. *Dash*; 'tis your business to promise more than you perform, and mine to promise less.

BLOTPAGE. Pshaw! Thy business is to perform nothing at all.

DASH. It becomes an author to be diffusive in his title page. A title page is to a book, what a fine neck is to a woman – Therefore ought to be the most regarded, as it is the part which is view'd before the purchase.

AIR, Ye Commons and Peers.

BLOTPAGE. *How unhappy's the fate*
To live by one's pate,
And be forc'd to write hackney for bread?
An author's a joke,
To all manner of folk,
Where-ever he pops up his head, his head,
Where-ever he pops up his head.

Tho' he mount on that hack,
Old Pegasus' back,
And of Helicon[35] *drink till he burst,*
Yet a curse of those streams,
Poetical dreams,
They never can quench one's thirst, &c.

Ah! How shou'd he fly
On fancy so high,
When his limbs are in durance and hold?
Or how shou'd he charm,
With genius so warm,
When his poor naked body's a old, &c.

ACT II. SCENE IV.

[*To them,* Bookweight.

BOOKWEIGHT. Fie upon it gentlemen! What, not at your pens? Do you consider, Mr. *Quibble*, that it is above a fortnight since your letter from a friend in the country was publish'd. – Is it not high time for an answer to come out – at this rate, before your answer is printed your letter will be forgot – I love to keep a controversy up warm – I have had authors who have writ a pamphlet in the morning, answered it in the afternoon, and compromised the matter at night.

QUIBBLE. Sir, I will be as expeditious as possible.

BOOKWEIGHT. Well, Mr. *Dash*, have you done that murder yet?

DASH. Yes, Sir, the murder is done – I am only about a few moral reflections to place before it.

BOOKWEIGHT. Very well – then let me have the ghost finish'd by this day sevennight.

DASH. What sort of a ghost wou'd you have, Sir? The last was a pale one.

BOOKWEIGHT. Then let this be a bloody one. – Mr. *Blotpage*, what have your lucubrations produc'd? –

[*Reads*] Poetical advice to a certain – from a certain – on a certain – from a certain – Very good! I will say, Mr. *Blotpage* writes as good a dash as any man in *Europe*.[36]

ACT II. SCENE V.

[*Enter,* Index.

BOOKWEIGHT. So, Mr. *Index*, what news with you?

INDEX. I have brought my bill, Sir.

BOOKWEIGHT. What's here? – For adapting the motto of *Risum teneatis Amici* to a dozen pamphlets – at six pence *per* each – six shillings. For *Omnia vincit amor & nos cedamus Amori* – six pence. For *Difficile est Satyram non scribere* – six pence. Hum, hum, hum – ah – a sum total, for thirty six *Latin* mottos, *eighteen shillings; ditto English* seven, *one shilling* and *nine pence; ditto Greek* four, *one shilling*. Why, friend, are your *Latin* mottos dearer than your *Greek*?[37]

INDEX. Yes marry are they, Sir: for as no body now understands *Greek*, so I may use any sentence in that language, to whatsoever purpose I please.

BOOKWEIGHT. You shall have your money immediately: and pray remember that I must have two *Latin* sedition mottos, and one *Greek* moral motto, for pamphlets, by to-morrow morning.

QUIBBLE. I want two *Latin* sentences Sir, one for page the fourth, in the praise of virtue; and the other for page the tenth, in the praise of beauty.[38]

BOOKWEIGHT. Let me have those too.

INDEX. Sir, I shall take care to provide them.

ACT II. SCENE VI.

[Bookweight, Dash, Blotpage, Quibble, Scarecrow.

SCARECROW. Sir, I have brought you a libel against the ministry.

BOOKWEIGHT. Sir, I shall not take any thing against them – [*Aside*] *for I have two in the press already*.

SCARECROW. Then, Sir, I have another in defence of them.

BOOKWEIGHT. Sir, I never take any thing in defence of power.

SCARECROW. I have a translation of *Virgil's Æneid*, with notes on it.

BOOKWEIGHT. That, Sir, is what I do not care to venture on – you may try by subscription, if you please: but I wou'd not advise you: for that bubble is almost down: People begin to be afraid of authors, since they have writ and acted like stock-jobbers. So to oblige a young beginner, I don't care if I print it at my own expence.

SCARECROW. But pray, Sir, at whose expence shall I eat?

BOOKWEIGHT. That's an empty question.

SCARECROW. It comes from an empty stomach, I'm sure.

BOOKWEIGHT. From an empty head, I'm afraid. Are there not a thousand ways for a man to get his bread by?

SCARECROW. I wish you wou'd put me into one.

BOOKWEIGHT. Why then, Sir, I wou'd advise you to come and take your seat at my tables. Here will be every thing that is necessary provided for you. I am as great a friend to learning as the *Dutch* are to Trade. – No one can want bread with me, who will earn it. Besides, a translator will be of use to me: for my last is in *Newgate* for shoplifting. The rogue had gotten a trick of translating out of the shops as well as out of the languages.

SCARECROW. I prefer any thing to starving.

BOOKWEIGHT. Then, Sir, if you please to throw by your hat, which you will have no more use for, and take up your pen.

SCARECROW. But, Sir, I am afraid I am not qualified for a translator.

BOOKWEIGHT. How, not qualified!

SCARECROW. No, Sir: I understand no language but my own.

BOOKWEIGHT. What, and translate *Virgil*?

SCARECROW. Alas, Sir, I translated him out of *Dryden*.

BOOKWEIGHT. Not qualified! – If I was an Emperor thou should'st be my Prime Minister. Thou art as well vers'd in thy trade, as if thou had'st labour'd in my garret these ten years. – Let me tell you, friend, you will have more occasion for invention than learning here: you will be sometimes obliged to translate books out of all languages (especially *French*) which were never printed in any language whatsoever.

SCARECROW. Your trade abounds in mysteries.

BOOKWEIGHT. The study of bookselling is as difficult as the law, – and there are as many tricks in the one as the other. Sometimes we give a foreign name to our own labour – and sometimes we put our own names to the labour of others. Then as the lawyers have *John-a-Nokes* and *Tom-a-Stiles*, so we have Messieurs *Moore* near St. *Paul*'s, and *Smith* near the *Royal Exchange*.[39]

ACT II. SCENE VII.

[*To them,* Luckless.

LUCKLESS. Mr. *Bookweight*, your servant. Who can form to himself an idea more amiable than of a man at the head of so many patriots working for the benefit of their country?

BOOKWEIGHT. Truly, Sir, I believe it is an idea more agreeable to you – than that of a gentleman in the *Crown-Office* paying thirty or forty guineas for abusing an honest tradesman.

LUCKLESS. Pshaw, that was only jocosely done, and a man who lives by wit, must not be angry at a jest; besides, the law has been your enemy – and you wou'd not fly to an enemy for succour.

BOOKWEIGHT. Sir, I will use my enemy as I wou'd my friend, for my own ends: But pray, Sir, what has brought you hither? If you have a mind to compromise the matter, I had rather have a little of your money, than that the lawyers shou'd have a great deal.

LUCKLESS. Hast thou dealt in paper so long, and talk of money to a modern author? You might as well have talk'd *Latin* or *Greek* to him. I have brought you paper, Sir.

BOOKWEIGHT. That is not bringing me money, I own – but it shall not be taking away money, Sir, for I will have nothing to do with your paper or you either.

LUCKLESS. Why pr'ythee, man, I have not brought you a play – nor a sermon.

BOOKWEIGHT. Have you brought me an opera?

LUCKLESS. You may call it an opera if you will, but I call it a puppet-show.

BOOKWEIGHT. A puppet-show!

LUCKLESS. Ay, a puppet-show, and is to be play'd this night in the *Haymarket* play-house.

BOOKWEIGHT. A puppet-show in a play-house!

LUCKLESS. What have been all the play-houses a long time but puppet-shows?

BOOKWEIGHT. Why, I don't know but it may succeed; at least, I had rather venture on a thing of that nature, than a regular play – so if you please to come in, if I can make a bargain with you I will – Gentlemen, you may go to dinner.

ACT II. SCENE VIII. The street.

[*Enter* Jack-Pudding, Drummer *and* Mob. *The drum ceasing.*

JACK. This is to give notice to all gentlemen, ladies and others – that at the play-house opposite to the opera in the *Haymarket*, this evening will be perform'd the whole puppet-show call'd *The Pleasures of the Town*; in which will be shewn the whole Court of Dulness, with abundance of singing and dancing, and several other entertainments – also the comical and diverting humours of Some-body, and No-body: *Punch* and his Wife *Joan*, to be perform'd by living figures – some of them six foot high – beginning exactly at seven a clock. God save the King. [*Drum beats.*

ACT II. SCENE IX.

[Witmore *with a paper,* Luckless *meeting.*

WITMORE. Oh! *Luckless*, I am overjoy'd at meeting you – here, take this paper, and you will be discourag'd from writing, I warrant you.

LUCKLESS. What is it? – Oh! One of my play-bills.

WITMORE. One of thy play-bills!

LUCKLESS. Even so, Sir! – I have taken the advice you gave me this morning.

WITMORE. Explain.

LUCKLESS. Why, I had some time since given this puppet-show of mine to be rehearsed, and the actors were all perfect in their parts; but we happen'd to dissent about some particulars, and I had a design to have given it over; 'till having my play refus'd by *Marplay* and *Sparkish*, I sent for the managers of the house in a passion, join'd issue with them, and this very evening it is to be acted.

WITMORE. Well – I wish you success. –

LUCKLESS. Where are you going?

WITMORE. Any where but to hear you damn'd, which I must, if I were to go to your puppet-show – I tell you the town is prejudic'd against you, and they will damn you, whether you deserve it or no. – If they shou'd laugh till they burst – the moment they knew you were the author – they wou'd change their faces, and swear they never laugh'd at all.

LUCKLESS. Pshaw, I can't believe thee.

WITMORE. 'Sdeath! I have heard sense run down, and seen idiotism, downright idiotism triumph so often, that I cou'd almost think of wit and folly as Mr. *Hobbes* does of moral good and evil, that there are no such things.

LUCKLESS. Well, indulge me in this trial – and I assure thee if it be successless it shall be the last.

WITMORE. On that condition I will – but shou'd the torrent run against you, I shall be a fashionable friend, and hiss with the rest.

LUCKLESS. No, a man who cou'd do so unfashionable and so generous a thing, as Mr. *Witmore* did this morning. –

WITMORE. In return, will you grant me a favour?

LUCKLESS. Do you doubt it?

WITMORE. Never mention it to me more – I will now to the pit. –

LUCKLESS. And I behind the scenes.

ACT II. SCENE X. Mrs. Moneywood's.

[Mrs. Moneywood, *and* Harriot.[40]

HARRIOT. It is very hard, Madam, that you will not suffer me at least to indulge my self in grief; that it is not enough to tear me from the man I love, but I must have my ears eternally curst with hearing him abused –

MRS. MONEYWOOD. Oh monstrous! Love a puppet-show fellow!

HARRIOT. His misfortunes may lessen him in the eye of the world: But they shall never lessen him in mine. Nay, I love him for them.

MRS. MONEYWOOD. You have not a drop of my blood in you. Love a man for his misfortune! – Hussy, to be poor and unfortunate are crimes – Riches are the only recommendations to people of sense of both sexes, and a coach and six is one of the *cardinal virtues*.[41]

HARRIOT. I despise it, and the fool who was born to it. No, give me the man, who, thrown naked upon the world, like my dear *Luckless*, can make his way through it by his merit and virtuous industry.

MRS. MONEYWOOD. Virtuous industry! A very virtuous, industrious gentleman, truly. He hath robbed me of a few guineas to-day or so – but he is a very virtuous man no doubt.

HARRIOT. He hath only borrowed what you know he will repay: – You know he is honest.

MRS. MONEYWOOD. I am no more satisfied of his honesty than you can be of his love.

HARRIOT. Which I am sure he hath given me sufficient proofs of.

MRS. MONEYWOOD. Proofs! Oh the villain! Hath he given you proofs of love?

HARRIOT. All that a modest woman can require.

MRS. MONEYWOOD. If he hath given you all a modest woman can require, I am afraid he has given you more than a modest woman should take: Because he hath been so good a lodger, I suppose I shall have some more of the family to keep: It is probable I may live to see half a dozen grandsons of mine in *Grub-street*.

[*Enter* Jack.

So, rascal, what's become of your master?

JACK. Oh, Madam! I am frightned out of my wits.

MRS. MONEYWOOD and HARRIOT. What's the matter?

JACK. There's the strangest sort of man below enquiring after my master, that ever was seen.

MRS. MONEYWOOD. What, I suppose a sort of bailiff?

JACK. Oh! Madam, I fancy it is the man in the moon, or some monster – there are five hundred people at the door looking at him – he is dressed up in nothing but ruffles and cabbage nets.

MRS. MONEYWOOD. This is either some trick of his to catch me, or some trick of a bailiff to catch him – However, I'll go sift out the bottom of it. Come, shew me where he is.

HARRIOT. Heav'ns protect my dear *Luckless*.

—The End of the Second Act.—

ACT III.

The Pleasures of the Town.

ACT III. SCENE I. The play-house.

[*Enter* Luckless *as Master of the Show, and* Player.

LUCKLESS. It's very surprising, that after I have been at all this expence and trouble to set up my things in your house, you should desire me to recant; and now too, when the spectators are all assembled, and will either have the show or their money.

PLAYER. It is beneath the dignity of the stage.

LUCKLESS. That may be, so is all farce, and yet you see a farce brings more company to a house than the best Play that ever was writ – For this age would allow *Tom Durfey* a better poet than

Congreve or *Wycherly*; who would not then rather eat by his nonsense, than starve by his wit – The lodgings of wits have long been in the air, and air must be their food now-a-days.

PLAYER. I am not the first indeed that has disgrac'd the stage.

LUCKLESS. And I heartily wish you may be the last, and that my puppet-show may expell farce and opera, as they have done tragedy and comedy.[42]

PLAYER. But hark you friend, how came you to call this performance of yours a puppet-show?

LUCKLESS. You must know, Sir, that it was originally design'd to be play'd by real puppets, till a friend of mine observing the success of some things in town, advis'd me to bring it on the stage. I had offer'd it to the old house, but they say nothing but your fine sense, such plays as *Cæsar* in *Egypt*, will go down there.[43]

PLAYER. But what is the design or plot? For I could make neither head nor tail of it, for my part.

LUCKLESS. Why Sir, the Goddess of *Nonsense* is to fall in love with the ghost of Signior *Opera*.[44]

PLAYER. Fall in love with a ghost, ha, ha, ha!

LUCKLESS. Ay Sir – You must know that the scene is laid on the other side of the river *Styx*, so all the people of the play are ghosts.

PLAYER. This marrying of ghosts is a new doctrine, friend.[45]

LUCKLESS. So much the likelier to please – Tho' I can't say but I took the hint of this thing from the old house, who observing that every one could not see the real coronation brought a representation of it upon their stage – So Sir, since every one has not time or opportunity to visit all the diversions of the town, I have brought most of them together in one – But come, it is time to begin. I think we will have an overture, tho' ours be not a regular opera.

PLAYER. By all means an overture.

LUCKLESS. If you please, Sir, you shall sit down by me. Play away.

LUCKLESS. Gentlemen, the first thing I present you with is *Punchinello*.

[*The curtain drawn discovers* Punch *in a great chair.* Punch *sings.*

AIR I, Whilst the Town's brimfull of Folly.

PUNCH. *Whilst the town's brimfull of farces,*
Flocking whilst we see her asses
Thick as grapes upon a bunch,
Criticks, whilst you smile on madness,
And more stupid, solemn sadness;
Sure you will not frown on Punch.

LUCKLESS. The next is *Punch*'s wife *Joan*.

[*Enter* Joan.

JOAN. What can ail my husband? He is continually humming tunes, tho' his voice be only fit to warble at *Hogg's Norton*, where the pigs would accompany it with organs. I was in hopes death would have stopp'd his mouth at last – But he keeps his old harmonious humour even in the Shades.[46]

PUNCH. Be not angry, dear *Joan*; *Orpheus* obtain'd his wife from the Shades, by charming *Pluto* with his musick.

JOAN. Sirrah, Sirrah, should *Pluto* hear you sing you could expect no less punishment than *Tantalus* has, – Nay the waters would be brought above your mouth, to stop it.

PUNCH. Truly, Madam, I don't wish the same success *Orpheus* met with; could I gain my own liberty – the Devil might have you with all my heart.

AIR II, The First of August.

PUNCH. *Joan, Joan, Joan, has a thundring tongue,*
And Joan, Joan, Joan, is a bold one.
How happy is he,
Who from wedlock is free:
For who'd have a wife to scold one?

JOAN. *Punch, Punch, Punch, pr'ythee think of your hunch,*
Pr'ythee look at your great strutting belly:
Sirrah, if you dare
War with me declare,
I will beat your fat gutts to a jelly.

[*Here they dance.*

AIR III, Bobbing Joan.

PUNCH. *Joan, you are the plague of my life,*
A rope would be welcomer than such a wife.

JOAN. *Punch, your merits had you but shar'd,*
Your neck had been longer by half a yard:

PUNCH. *Ugly witch,*

JOAN. *Son of a bitch,*

BOTH. *Would you were hang'd or drown'd in a ditch.*

[*Here they dance again.*

PUNCH. *Since we hate, like people in vogue,*[47]
Let us call not bitch and rogue:

Gentler titles let us use,
Hate each other, but not abuse.

JOAN. *Pretty dear!*

PUNCH. *Ah! Ma chere!*

BOTH. *Joy of my life and only care.*

[*Dance and exeunt.*

LUCKLESS. Gentlemen, the next is *Charon* and a Poet; they are disputing about an affair pretty common with poets – Going off without paying.

[*Enter* Charon *and a* Poet.

CHARON. Never tell me Sir, I expect my fare – I wonder what trade these authors drive in the other world: I would with as good a will see a soldier aboard my boat. A tatter'd red-coat, and a tatter'd black one have bilk'd me so often, that I am resolv'd never to take either of them up again – unless I am paid before-hand.[48]

POET. What a wretched thing it is to be poor – My body lay a fortnight in the other world before it was buried. – And this fellow has kept my spirit a month, sunning himself on the other side the river, because my pockets were empty – Wilt thou be so kind as to shew me the way to the Court of *Nonsense*.

CHARON. Ha, ha, ha! The Court of *Nonsense*! Why pray Sir, what have you to do there? These rags look more like the dress of one of *Apollo*'s people, than of *Nonsense*'s.

POET. Why fellow, didst thou never carry rags to *Nonsense*?

CHARON. Truly Sir, I cannot say but I have, but it is a long time ago, I assure you; if you are really bound thither, I'll set your name down in my pocket-book, and I don't question your honour's payment – *Nonsense* is the best deity to me in the Shades – Look at that account, Sir.

POET. [*Reads*] Spirits imported for the Goddess of *Nonsense*, since *October*, in the year – Five people of great quality – Seven ordinary courtiers – Nineteen attorneys – Eleven counsellors – Twenty six Justices of the Peace; and one hundred Presbiterian parsons – These courtiers and people of quality pay swingingly, I suppose.

CHARON. Not always; I have wafted over many a spirit in a lac'd coat, who has been forc'd to leave it with me.

LUCKLESS. Gentlemen, the next is one of *Charon*'s men with a prisoner.

[*Enter* Saylor *and a* Sexton.

CHARON. How now?

SAYLOR. We have caught the rogue at last – This is Mr. *Robgrave* the Sexton, who has plundered so many spirits.

CHARON. Are you come at last, Sir? What have you to say for your self – ha! What's become of all the jewels and other valuable things you have stolen? Where are they, Sirrah, ha!

ROBGRAVE. Alack-a-day, I am an unfortunate poor rogue; the church-wardens and clerks have had them all, I had only a small reward for stealing them.

CHARON. Then you shall have another reward here, Sir. Carry him before Justice *Minos*[49] immediately – Away with him. [*Exit* Saylor *and* Sexton.

POET. Who knows whether this rogue has not robb'd me too. – I forgot to look in upon my body before I came away.

CHARON. Had you any thing of value buried with you?

POET. Things of inestimable value; six folio's of my own works.

LUCKLESS. Most poets of this age will have their works buried with them.

[*Enter* Saylor.

SAYLOR. There is a great number of passengers arriv'd from *England*, all bound to the Court of *Nonsense*.[50]

CHARON. Some plague I suppose, or a fresh cargo of physicians come to town from the Universities – Or perhaps a war broke out.

SAYLOR. No, no! These are all authors, and a war never sends any of them hither.

LUCKLESS. Now, Gentlemen, I shall produce such a sett of figures as I may defy all *Europe*, except our own play-houses, to equal – Come, put away.

[*Enter* Don Tragedio, Sir Farcical Comick, Dr. Orator, Signior Opera, Monsieur Pantomine, *and* Mrs. Novell.

POET. Ha! *Don Tragedio*, your most obedient servant. Sir *Farcical* – Dr. *Orator*, I am heartily glad to see you – Dear *Signior Opera* – *Monsieur Pantomine* – Mrs. *Novell* in the Shades too! What lucky distemper can have sent so much good company hither?

DON TRAGEDIO. A tragedy occasioned me to die;
That perishing the first day, so did I.

SIR FARCICAL COMICK. An entertainment sent me out of the world. – My life went out in a hiss – Stap my breath.[51]

AIR IV, Silvia, my Dearest.

SIGNIOR OPERA. *Claps universal,*[52]
Applauses resounding;
Hisses confounding
Attending my song:
My senses drowned,
And I fell down dead;
Whilst I was singing, ding, dang, dong.

POET. Well *Monsieur Pantomine*, how came you by your fate?

MONSIEUR PANTOMIME. [*Makes signs to his neck.*[53]

POET. Broke his neck: Alas poor gentleman! – And you Madam *Novel*?

MRS. NOVEL. Mine was a hard case indeed.

AIR V, 'twas when the Seas were roaring.

MRS. NOVEL. *Oh! Pity all a maiden,*
Condemn'd hard fates to prove;
I rather would have laid-in,
Then thus have dy'd for love!
'Twas hard t' encounter death a,
Before the bridal bed;
Ah! Would I had kept my breath a,
And lost my maiden-head.

POET. Poor lady!

LUCKLESS. 'Twas a hard fate indeed, in this age.

CHARON. Well, my masters, I wish you well. I must take leave of you. If you follow that path you'll arrive at the Court of *Nonsense*. [*Exit* Charon.

POET. Gentlemen, if you please I'll shew you the way. [*Exeunt.*

LUCKLESS. The next, gentlemen, is a Blackamore lady, who comes to present you with a saraband and castanets.[54]

[*A Dance.*

LUCKLESS. Now, gentlemen and ladies, I shall produce a Bookseller who is the prime minister of *Nonsense*, and the Poet.

[*Enter* Bookseller *and* Poet.

POET. 'Tis strange, 'tis wondrous strange!

CURRY. And yet 'tis true – Did you observe her eyes?

POET. Her ears rather, for there she took the infection. She saw the *Signior*'s visage in his voice.

CURRY. Did you not mark, how she melted when he sung?

POET. I saw her like another *Dido* – I saw her heart rise up to her eyes, and drop down again to her ears.[55]

CURRY. That a woman of so much sense as the Goddess of *Nonsense*, should be taken thus at first sight! I have serv'd her faithfully these thirty years as a bookseller in the upper world, and never knew her guilty of one folly before.

POET. Nay certainly, Mr. *Curry*, you know as much of her, as any man.

CURRY. I think I ought, I am sure I have made as large oblations to her, as all *Warwick-Lane* and *Pater-Noster-Row*.[56]

POET. But is she, this night, to be married to *Signior Opera*?

CURRY. This is to be the bridal night – Well, this will be the strangest thing that has happened in the Shades, since the rape of *Proserpine*[57] – But now I think on't, what news bring you from the other world?

POET. Why affairs go much in the same road there as when you were alive, authors starve and booksellers grow fat, *Grub-Street* harbours as many pirates as ever *Algiers* did – They have more theatres than are at *Paris*, and just as much wit as there is at *Amsterdam*; they have ransack'd all *Italy* for singers, and all *France* for dancers.[58]

CURRY. And all Hell for conjurers.[59]

POET. My Lord-Mayor has shorten'd the time of *Bartholomew* Fair in *Smithfield*, and so they are resolv'd to keep it all the year round at the other end of the town.[60]

CURRY. I find matters go swimmingly; but I fancy I am wanted; if you please, Sir, I will shew you the way.

POET. Sir, I follow you. [*Exeunt.*

[*Enter* Joan, Lady King-call, Mrs. Glass-ring, *and* Mrs. Cheat-em.[61]

JOAN. I ask leave.

ALL. With you, Madam.

JOAN. Clubs, and the King of Hearts.

MRS. GLASS-RING. Sure never was any thing so provoking as this; you always put me out of a great game. [*They play.*

LADY KINGCALL. There's your King, Madam; you have call'd very luckily this time. – *Spadille*, there's *Basto*;[62] we have won our game.

JOAN. I say nothing.

LADY KINGCALL. I'll play it.

MRS. GLASS-RING. Then you have lost it; there is the best diamond.

JOAN. Was ever such play seen? I wou'd not play with Lady *King-call* for farthings.

LADY KINGCALL. I have seen your Ladyship make greater mistakes.

JOAN. I wish you'd name when, Madam.

LADY KINGCALL. I have not so good a memory, Madam.

JOAN. I am sorry for it, Madam, for you seem to want one; it might be of use to you.

LADY KINGCALL. I wish you had a better, Madam, it might be of use to others.

JOAN. What do you mean, Madam?

LADY KINGCALL. I mean, that you owe me a guinea.

JOAN. I believe, Madam, you forget you owe me two.

LADY KINGCALL. Madam, I deny it.

JOAN. And I deny yours.

MRS. GLASS-RING. and MRS. CHEAT'EM. Oh fye, ladies!

LADY KINGCALL. It's happy for your enemies, that your Ladyship's character is so well known.

JOAN. It would become any body to say so, better than you. – I never stole china.

LADY KINGCALL. You are an impudent sow.

JOAN. You are an old ugly sow, and I'll make you know it. [*They fight.*

[*Enter* Punch.

PUNCH. Have I caught you, Madam? I'll put an end to your *Quadrille*, I am resolv'd. – Get you home, strumpet. And you are the fine ladies who bring her to this. – I'll drive all of you. [*Kicks them out, and over-turns the table.*

LUCKLESS. Very uncivilly done, truly, Master *Punch.*

PUNCH. Uncivilly! Why, Sir, since this game of *Quadrille* has been in fashion, she has never look'd after my family; she does nothing but eat, drink, sleep, dress, and play at *Quadrille.*[63]

AIR VI, To you Fair Ladies.

PUNCH. *To all you husbands, and you wives,*
This Punchinello sings;
For reformation of your lives,
This good advice he brings;
That if you would avoid all ill,
You shou'd leave off the dear Quadrille.

No tyrant on the earth, his slaves
With greater terrour awes;
With force more absolute behaves,
Nor gives severer laws;
Unequal tho' his taxes fall,
They're with a smile receiv'd by all.

How many beauties, rich in charms,
Are subject to his will!
The bride, when in the bridegroom's arms,
Still thinks on dear Quadrille:
Her spouse her body may enroll,
Quadrille is master of her soul.

The China people (sailors say)
When they have lost their pence,
Their family and selves will play;
Heav'n keep that custom hence![64]
For beauties of the first degree,
May so be slaves to some Marquis.

[*Exit* Punch.

LUCKLESS. Gentlemen, the next figures are *Somebody* and *No-body,*[65] who come to present you with a dance.

[*Enter* Some-body, *and* No-body. *They dance.*

AIR VII, Black Joke.

SOMEBODY.
Of all the men in London town,
Or knaves, or fools, in coat, or gown
The representative am I:

NOBODY.
Go thro' the world, and you will find,
In all the classes of human-kind,
Many a jolly no-body.

For him, a no-body, sure we may call,
Who during his life does nothing at all,
But eat, and snore,
And drink, and roar,
From whore to the tavern, from tavern to whore,
With a lac'd coat, and that is all.

LUCKLESS. Gentlemen, this is the end of the first interlude. Now, gentlemen, I shall present you with the most glorious scene that has ever appear'd on the stage; it is *The Court of Nonsense.* Play away, soft musick, and draw up the curtain.

[*The curtain drawn up to soft musick, discovers the* Goddess of Nonsense *on a throne; the* Orator, *in a tub;* Tragedio, *&c. attending.*[66]

GODDESS OF NONSENSE. Let all my votaries prepare
To celebrate this joyful day.

LUCKLESS. Gentlemen, observe what a lover of *Recitativo*[67] *Nonsense* is.

GODDESS OF NONSENSE. Monsieur *Pantomine*! You are welcome.

MONSIEUR PANTOMIME. [*Cuts a Caper.*[68]

GODDESS OF NONSENSE. Alas, poor gentleman! He is modest; you may speak; no words offend, that have no wit in them.

LUCKLESS. Why, Madam *Nonsense*, don't you know that Monsieur *Pantomine* is dumb? – And yet, let me tell you, he has been of great service to you, – he is the only one of your votaries that sets people asleep without talking. But here's *Don Tragedio* will make noise enough.

DON TRAGEDIO. Yes, *Tragedio* is indeed my name,
Long since recorded in the rolls of fame,
At *Lincolns-Inn*, and eke at *Drury-Lane*.
Let everlasting thunder sound my praise,
And forked light'ning in my scutcheon blaze;
To *Shakespear, Johnson, Dryden, Lee*, or *Rowe*,
I not a line, no, not a thought, do owe.
Me, for my novelty, let all adore,
For, as I wrote, none ever wrote before.

GODDESS OF NONSENSE. Thou art doubly welcome, welcome.

DON TRAGEDIO. That welcome, yes, that welcome is my due,
Two tragedies I wrote, and wrote for you;
And, had not hisses, hisses me dismay'd,
By this, I'd writ two-score, two-score, by jay'd.

LUCKLESS. By jay'd! Ay, that's another excellence of the Don's; he does not only glean up all the bad words of other authors, but makes new bad words of his own.[69]

SIR FARCICAL COMICK. Nay, i'gad, I have made new words, and spoil'd old ones too, if you talk of that; I have made foreigners break *English*, and Englishmen break *Latin*. – I have as great a confusion of languages in my play, as was at the building of *Babel*.

LUCKLESS. And so much the more extraordinary, because the author understands no language at all.

SIR FARCICAL COMICK. No language at all! – Stap my vitals.[70]

LUCKLESS. But, Sir *Farcical*, I hear you had once an intention to introduce a set of marrow-bones and cleavers upon the stage.

SIR FARCICAL COMICK. 'Tis true: And I did produce one bone, but it stuck so confoundedly in the stomach of the audience, that I was obliged to drop the project.

GODDESS OF NONSENSE. Dr. *Orator*, I have heard of you.

DR. ORATOR. Ay, and you might have heard me too, I bawl'd loud enough, I'm sure.

LUCKLESS. She might have heard you – But if she had understood your advertisements, I will believe *Nonsense* to have more understanding than *Apollo*.

DR. ORATOR. Have understood me, Sir! What has understanding to do? My hearers would be diverted, and they are so, – which could not be, if understanding were necessary, – because very few of them have any.

GODDESS OF NONSENSE. You've all deserv'd my hearty thanks, – but here my treasure I bestow. [*Gestures to* Signior Opera.

AIR VIII, Lillibolera.

SIGNIOR OPERA. *Let the foolish philosopher strive in his cell,*
By wisdom, or virtue, to merit true praise;
The soldier in hardship and danger still dwell,
That glory and honour may crown his last days;
The patriot sweat,
To be thought great;
Or beauty all day at the looking-glass toil;
That popular voices
May ring their applauses,
While a breath is the only reward of their coil.

But would you a wise man to action incite,
Be riches propos'd the reward of his pain,
In riches is center'd all humane delight;
No joy is on Earth, but what gold can obtain.
If women, wine,
Or grandeur fine,
Be most your delight, all these riches can;
Would you have men to flatter?
To be rich is the matter;
When you cry he is rich, you cry a great man.[71]

GODDESS OF NONSENSE. [*Repeating in an Ecstacy*] When you cry he is rich, you cry a great man. Bravissimo! I long to be your wife.

MRS. NOVEL. If all my romances ever pleas'd the ear of my Goddess – if I ever found favour in her sight – oh, do not rob me thus!

GODDESS OF NONSENSE. What means my daughter?

MRS. NOVEL. Alas, he is my husband! And I never knew any one instance of a husband here, who would take the same wife again.

CURRY. But tho' he were your husband in the other world, death solves that tie, and he is at liberty now to take another.

AIR IX, Whilst I gaze on Cloe trembling.

MRS. NOVEL. *May all maids from me take warning,*
How a lover's arms they fly:
Lest the first kind offer scorning,
They, without a second, die.

How unhappy is my passion!
How tormenting is my pain!
If you thwart my inclination,
Let me die for love again.

CURRY. Again! What, did you die for love of your husband?

MRS. NOVEL. He knows he ought to have been so. – He swore he would be so. – Yes, he knows I dy'd for love, for I dy'd in child-bed.[72]

DR. ORATOR. Why, Madam, did you not tell me all the road hither, that you was a virgin?

AIR X, Highland Laddy.

SIGNIOR OPERA. *I was told, in my life,*
Death, for ever,
Did dissever
Men from ev'ry mortal strife,
And that greatest plague, a wife.

For had the priests possest men,
That to Tartarus
Wives came after us,
Their Devil wou'd be a jest then,
And our Devil a wife.

GODDESS OF NONSENSE. Avaunt, polluted wretch! Begone; think not I'll take pollution to my arms. No, no, – no, no, – no, no, no.

SIGNIOR OPERA. Well, since I can't have a Goddess, I'll e'en prove a man of honour. – I was always in love with thee, my angel.

MRS. NOVEL. Now I am happy, verily.

SIGNIOR OPERA. My long-lost dear!

MRS. NOVEL. My new-found bud!

AIR XI, Dusty Millar.

SIGNIOR OPERA. *Will my charming creature*
Once again receive me?
Tho' I prov'd a traytor,
Will she still believe me?
I will well repay thee,
For past faults of roving,
Nor shall any day be
Without proofs of loving.

On that tender lilly breast
Whilest I lie panting,
Both together blest,
Both with transports fainting.
Sure no human hearts
Were ever so delighted!
Death, which others parts,
Hath our souls united.

AIR XII, Over the Hills and far away.[73]

SIGNIOR OPERA. *Were I laid on Scotland's coast,*
And in my arms embrac'd my dear,
Let Scrubado[74] *do its most,*
I would know no grief or fear.

MRS. NOVEL. *Were we cast on Ireland's soil,*
There confin'd in bogs to dwell,
For thee potatoes I would boil,
No Irish spouse shou'd feast so well.

SIGNIOR OPERA. *And tho' we scrubb'd it all the day,*

MRS. NOVEL. *We'd kiss, and hug the night away;*

SIGNIOR OPERA. *Scotch and Irish both shou'd say,*

BOTH. *Oh, how blest! How blest are they!*

DR. ORATOR. Since my Goddess is disengag'd from one lover, may the humblest, yet not the least diligent of her servants, hope she wou'd smile on him?

LUCKLESS. Master *Orator*, you had best try to charm the Goddess with an oration.

DR. ORATOR. The History of a Fiddle and a Fiddlestick is going to be held forth. A fiddle is a statesman: why? Because it's hollow. A fiddlestick is a drunkard: why? Because it loves ros'ning.

LUCKLESS. Gentlemen, observe how he ballances his hands; his left hand is the fiddle, and his right hand is the fiddlestick.

DR. ORATOR. A fiddle is like a beau's-nose, because the bridge is often down;[75] a fiddlestick is like a mountebank, because it plays upon a crowd. – A fiddle is like a stockjobber's tongue, because it sounds different notes; and a fiddlestick is like a stockjobber's wig, because it has a great deal of horsehair in it.

LUCKLESS. And your Oration is like your self; because it has a great deal of nonsense in it.

GODDESS OF NONSENSE. In vain you try to charm my ears, unless by musick.

DR. ORATOR. Have at you then.

LUCKLESS. Gentlemen, observe how the doctor sings in his tub – here are no wires – all alive, alive, ho!

DR. ORATOR. Chimes of the times, to the tune of *Moll Pately*.

AIR XIII, Moll Pately.

DR. ORATOR. *All men are birds by nature, Sir,*[76]
Tho' they have not wings to fly;
On Earth a soldier's a creature, Sir,
Much resembling a kite in the sky;
The physician is a fowl, Sir,
Whom most men call an owl, Sir,
Who by his hooting,
Hooting, hooting,
Hooting, hooting,
Hooting, hooting,
Tells us that death is nigh.

The usurer is a swallow, Sir,
That can swallow gold by the jorum;[77]
A woodcock is Squire Shallow, Sir;
And a goose is oft of the quorum:
The gamester is a rook, Sir;
The lawyer, with his Coke, Sir,
Is but a raven,
Croaking, croaking,
Croaking, croaking,
Croaking, croaking,
After the ready Rhinorum.[78]

Young virgins are scarce as rails, Sir;
Plenty as batts the night-walkers go;
Soft Italians are nightingales, Sir,
And a cock-sparrow mimicks a beau:

Like birds men are to be caught, Sir,
Like birds men are to be bought, Sir:
Men of a side,
Like birds of a feather,
Will flock together,
Will flock together,
Both sexes like birds will–too.

GODDESS OF NONSENSE. 'Tis all in vain.

DON TRAGEDIO. Is Nonsense of me then forgetful grown,
And must the Signior be prefer'd alone?
Is it for this, for this, ye Gods! That I
Have in one scene made some folks laugh, some cry?
For this does my low blust'ring language creep,
At once to wake you, and to make you sleep?

SIR FARCICAL COMICK. And so all my puns, and quibbles, and conundrums are quite forgetten, stap my vitals; but surely your Goddess-ship will remember a certain thing call'd *a Pastoral.*

DR. ORATOR. More chimes of the times, to the tune of *Rogues, Rogues, Rogues.*

AIR XIV, There was a jovial Beggar.

DR. ORATOR. *The stone that all things turns at will*
To gold, the chymist craves;
But gold, without the chymist's skill,
Turns all men into knaves.
For a cheating they will go, &c.

The merchant wou'd the courtier cheat,
When on his goods he lays
Too high a price–but faith he's bit,
For a courtier never pays.
For a cheating they will go, &c.

The lawyer, with a face demure,
Hangs him who steals your pelf;[79]
Because the good man can endure
No robber but himself.
For a cheating, &c.

Betwixt the quack and highwayman
What difference can there be?
Tho' this with pistol, that with pen,
Both kill you for a fee.
For a cheating, &c.

The husband cheats his loving wife,
And to a mistress goes,
While she at home, to ease her life,
Carouses with the beaus.
For a cheating, &c.

The tenant doth the steward nick,
(So low this art we find,)
The steward doth his lordship trick,
My Lord tricks all mankind.
For a cheating, &c.

One sect there are to whose fair lot
No cheating arts do fall,
And those are parsons call'd, God wot;
And so I cheat you all.
For a cheating, &c.

[*Enter* Charon.

CHARON. An't please your Majesty, there is an odd sort of a man o' t'other side the water says he's recommended to you by some people of quality. – Agad I don't care to take him aboard, not I, – he says his name his *Hurloborumbo – rumbo – Hurloborumbolo*,[80] I think he calls himself, he looks like one of *Apollo*'s people in my opinion, he seems to me mad enough to be a real poet.

GODDESS OF NONSENSE. Take him aboard.

CHARON. I had forgot to tell your ladyship, I hear rare news, they say you are to be declared Goddess of Wit.

CURRY. That's no news, Mr. *Charon.*

CHARON. Well, I'll take *Hurloborumbo* aboard. [*Exit* Charon.

DR. ORATOR. I must win the Goddess before he arrives, or else I shall lose her for ever. – A rap at the times.

AIR XV, When I was a Dame of Honour.

DR. ORATOR. *Come all who've heard my cushion beat,*
Confess me as full of dulness
As any egg is full of meat,
Or full moon is of fullness;
Let the justice and his clerk both own,
Than theirs my dulness greater;
And tell how I've harangu'd the town,
When I was a bold orator.

The lawyer wrangling at the bar,
While the reverend bench is dozing,
The scribler in a pamphlet war,
Or Grubstreet bard composing;
The trudging quack in scarlet cloak,
Or coffee-house politick prater;
Can none come up to what I have spoke,
When I was a bold orator.

The well-bred courtier telling lies,
Or levée hunter believing;
The vain coquet that rolls her eyes,
More empty fops deceiving;
The parson of dissenting gang,
Or flattering dedicator,
Could none of them like me harangue,
When I was a bold orator.

[*Enter* Punch.

PUNCH. You, you, you.

LUCKLESS. What's the matter, *Punch*?

PUNCH. Who is that?

LUCKLESS. That's an orator, Master *Punch.*

PUNCH. An orator – What's that?

LUCKLESS. Why an orator is, is agad I can't tell what; he is a man that no body dares dispute with.

PUNCH. Say you so, I'll be with him presently. – Bring out my tub there – I'll dispute with you, I'll warrant – I am a *Muggletonian.*[81]

DR. ORATOR. I am not.

PUNCH. Then you are not of my opinion.

DR. ORATOR. Sirrah, I know that you and your whole tribe would be the death of me; but I am resolved to proceed to confute you as I have done hitherto, and as long as I have breath you shall hear me, and I hope I have breath enough to blow you all out of the world.

PUNCH. If noise will.

DR. ORATOR. Sir, I –

PUNCH. Hear me, Sir.

GODDESS OF NONSENSE. Hear him – hear him – hear him.

AIR XVI, Hey Barnaby, take it for Warning.

PUNCH. *No tricks shall save your bacon,*
Orator, Orator, you are mistaken;
Punch will not be thus confuted,
Bring forth your reasons or you are nonsuited,
Heigh ho.
No tricks shall save your bacon,
Orator, Orator, you are mistaken.

DR. ORATOR. Instead of reasons advancing,
Let the dispute be concluded by dancing. Ti, to. [*They dance.*

GODDESS OF NONSENSE. 'Tis all in vain: A virgin I will live; and oh great Signior pr'ythee take this chaplet,[82] and still wear it for my sake.

DON TRAGEDIO. And does great Nonsense then at length determine
To give the chaplet to that singing vermin?

GODDESS OF NONSENSE. I do.

DON TRAGEDIO. Then *Opera* come on, and let us try,
Whether shall wear the chaplet, you or I.[83]

AIR XVII, Be kind and love.

MRS. NOVEL. *Oh, spare to take his precious life away;*
So sweet a voice must sure your passion lay:
Oh hear his gentle murmurs first, and then,
If you can kill him, I will cry amen.

DON TRAGEDIO. Since but a song you ask, a song I'll hear;
But tell him, that last song, is his last prayer.

AIR XVIII.

SIGNIOR OPERA. *Barbarous cruel man,*
I'll sing thus while I'm dying, I'm dying like a swan,

I'm dying like a swan,
A swan,
A swan,
With my face all pale and wan.
More fierce art thou than Pyrates,
Than Pyrates,
Whom the syrens musick charms,
Alarms,
Disarms;
More fierce than men on the high roads,
On the high–roads,
On the high–roads.
More fierce than men on the high roads,
Whom Polly Peachum warms.
The Devil
Was made civil,
By Orpheus tuneful charms;[84]
And can,
He gentler prove than man?

DON TRAGEDIO. I cannot do it – [*Sheaths his sword*]
Methinks I feel my flesh congeal'd to bone,
And know not when I'm flesh and blood or stone.

MONSIEUR PANTOMIME. [*Runs several times round the stage*]

GODDESS OF NONSENSE. Alas, what means Monsieur Pantomine?

CURRY. By his pointing to his head, I suppose he would have the chaplet.

GODDESS OF NONSENSE. Pretty youth!

MRS. NOVEL. Oh, my dear, how shall I express the trouble of my soul?

SIGNIOR OPERA. If there be sympathy in love, I'm sure I felt it – for I was in a damnable fright too.

MRS. NOVEL. Give me a buss[85] then.

AIR XIX, Under the Greenwood Tree.

GODDESS OF NONSENSE. *In vain a thousand heroes and kings,*
Should court me to their arms,
In vain should give me a thousand fine things,
For thee I'd reserve my charms:
On that dear breast, intranc'd in joys,
Oh, let me ever be.

SIGNIOR OPERA. *Oh, how I will kiss thee,*
How I'll embliss thee,
When thou art a-bed with me.

GODDESS OF NONSENSE. [*Repeats*] *Oh, how I will kiss thee, &c.*

SIR FARCICAL COMICK. Since nothing but a song will do, I will have my song too.

LUCKLESS. Gentlemen, pray observe and take notice how Sir *Farcical*'s song sets *Nonsense* asleep.

AIR XX, Hunt the Squirrel.

SIR FARCICAL COMICK. *Can my Goddess then forget*
Paraphonalia,
Paraphonalia?[86]
Can she the crown on another head set,
Than of her Paraphonalia?
If that had not done too,
Remember my bone too,
My bone, my bone, my bone:
Sure my Goddess never can
Forget my marrowbone.

CURRY. *Nonsense* is asleep.

DON TRAGEDIO. Oh, ye immortal powers!

SIR FARCICAL COMICK. If any thing can wake her 'tis a dance.

OMNES. A dance – a dance – a dance.

[*Enter* Charon.

LUCKLESS. How now, *Charon*? You are not to enter yet.

CHARON. To enter, Sir! Alack-a-day! We are all undone: here is a constable, and Mr. *Murder-text* the Presbyterian parson, coming in.

[*Enter* Murder-text *and* Constable.

CONSTABLE. Are you the master of the puppet-show?

LUCKLESS. Yes, Sir.

CONSTABLE. Then you must along with me, Sir; I have a warrant for you, Sir.

LUCKLESS. For what?

MURDER-TEXT. For abusing *Nonsense*, Sirrah.[87]

CONSTABLE. People of quality are not to have their diversions libel'd at this rate.

MURDER-TEXT. No, Sirrah; nor the saints are not be abus'd neither.

LUCKLESS. Of what do you accuse me, gentlemen?

MURDER-TEXT. Verily I smell a great deal of a – bomination and prophaness – a smell of brimstone offendeth my nostrils, a puppet-show is t he Devil's-house, and I will burn it – shall you abuse *Nonsense*, when the whole town supports it?[88]

LUCKLESS. Pox on't, had this fellow staid a few moments longer – till the dance had been over, I had been easy. Hark you, Mr. *Constable*, shall I only beg your patience for one dance, and then I'll wait on you?

MURDER-TEXT. Sirrah, don't try to corrupt the magistrate with thy bribes – here shall be no dancing – verily it is a prophane mystery, and hath in it a superfluity of abomination.

MRS. NOVEL. What does this fellow of a constable mean by interrupting our play?

AIR XXI, Fair Dorinda.[89]

MRS. NOVEL. *Oh Mr. Constable,*
Drunken rascal,
Would I had thee at the rose.
May'st thou be beaten,
Hang'd up and eaten,
May'st thou be eaten, eaten,
Eaten, eaten,
Eaten by the carrion crows.
The filth that lies in common shores,
May it ever lie in thy nose,
May it ever
Lie in thy nose,
Oh may it lie in thy nose.

LUCKLESS. Mollifie yourself, Madam.

MURDER-TEXT. – [*Aside*] *Verily that is a pretty creature, it were a piece of charity to take her to my self for a handmaid –*

CONSTABLE. Very pretty, very pretty truly – If magistrates are to be abus'd at this rate – the Devil may be a constable for me – Harkee, Madam, do you know who we are?

MRS. NOVEL. A rogue, Sir.

CONSTABLE. Madam, I'm a constable by day, and a Justice of Peace by night.

MRS. NOVEL. That is a buzzard by day, and an owl by night.

AIR XXII, New-market.

CONSTABLE. *Why, Madam, do you give such words as these*
To a constable and Justice of Peace?
I fancy you'll better know how to speak,
By that time you've been in Bridewell a week;
Have beaten good hemp, and been
Whipt at a post;
I hope you'll repent, when some skin
You have lost.
But if this makes you tremble, I'll not be severe;
Come down a good guinea, and you shall be clear.

MRS. NOVEL. Oh, Mr. *Murder-text*, you, I am sure, are the commander in this enterprise. If you will prevent the rest of our show, let me beg you will permit the dance.

AIR XXIII, Charming Betty.

MRS. NOVEL. *Gentle preacher,*
Non-con teacher,[90]
Pr'ythee let us take a dance;
Leave your canting,
Zealous ranting,
Come and shake a merry haunch;
Motions firing,
Sounds inspiring,
We are led to softer joys;
Where in trances,
Each soul dances,
Musick then seems only noise.

MURDER-TEXT. Verily, I am conquer'd – Pity prevaileth over severity, and the flesh hath subdued the spirit – I feel a motion in me, and whether it be of grace or no I am not certain – Pretty maid, I cannot be deaf any longer to your prayers. I will abide the performing a dance, and will my self, being thereto mov'd by an inward working, accompany you therein, taking for my partner that reverend gentleman.

LUCKLESS. Then strike up.

[*Enter* Witmore,Mrs. Moneywood, Harriot *and* Bantomite.

HARRIOT. My dear Harry!

WITMORE. Long live his Majesty of Bantam.

MRS. MONEYWOOD. Heaven preserve him.

BANTOMITE. Your gracious father, Sir, greets you well.

LUCKLESS. What, in the Devil's name, is the meaning of this?

BANTOMITE. I find he is intirely ignorant of his father.

WITMORE. Ay, Sir, it is very common in this country for a man not to know his father.

LUCKLESS. What do you mean?

BANTOMITE. His features are much alter'd.

LUCKLESS. Sir, I shall alter your features, if you proceed.

BANTOMITE. Give me leave to explain my self. I was your tutor in your earliest years, sent by your father, his present Majesty *Francis* IV. King of *Bantam*, to shew you the world. We arriv'd at *London*, when one day among other frolicks our ship's crew shooting the bridge, the boat overset, and of all our company, I and your royal self were only sav'd by swimming into *Billingsgate*; but tho' I sav'd my life, I lost for some time my senses, and you, as I then fear'd, for ever. When I recover'd, after a long fruitless search for my royal master, I set sail for *Bantam*, but was driven by the winds on far distant coasts, and wander'd several years, till at last I arriv'd once more at *Bantam*, – Guess how I was receiv'd – The King order'd me to be imprison'd for life: At last, some lucky chance brought thither a merchant, who offer'd this jewel as a present to the King of *Bantam*.[91]

LUCKLESS. Ha! It is the same which was tied upon my arm, which by good luck I preserv'd from every other accident, till want of money forc'd me to pawn it.

BANTOMITE. The merchant being strictly examin'd, said he had it of a pawn-broker, upon which I was immediately dispatch'd to *England*, and the merchant kept close prisoner till my return, then to be punish'd with death, or rewarded with the government of an island.

LUCKLESS. Know then, that at that time when you lost your senses, I also lost mine. I was taken up half dead by a waterman, and convey'd to his wife, who sold oysters, by whose assistance I recover'd. But the waters of the *Thames*, like those of *Lethe*, had caus'd an entire oblivion of my former fortune – But now it breaks in like light upon me, and I begin to recollect it all. Is not your name *Gonsalvo*?

BANTOMITE. It is.

LUCKLESS. Oh, my *Gonsalvo*! [*Embrace.*

BANTOMITE. Oh, my dearest Lord! [*Embrace.*

LUCKLESS. But say by what lucky accident you discover'd me.

BANTOMITE. I did intend to have advertis'd you in the *Evening Post*, with a reward; but being directed by the merchant to the pawn-broker, I was accidentally there enquiring after you, when your boy brought your nab. (Oh, sad remembrance, that the son of a King should pawn a hat!) The woman told me, that was the boy that pawn'd the jewel, and of him I learnt where you lodg'd.

LUCKLESS. Prodigious Fortune! [*A post-horn without.*

[*Enter* Messenger.

MESSENGER. An express is arriv'd from *Bantam* with the news of his Majesty's death.

BANTOMITE. Then, Sir, you are King. Long live *Henry* I. King of *Bantam*.

OMNES. Long live *Henry* I. King of *Bantam*.

LUCKLESS. *Witmore*, I now may repay your generosity.

WITMORE. Fortune has repaid me, I am sure more than she ow'd, by conferring this blessing on you.

LUCKLESS. My friend – But here I am indebted to the golden Goddess, for having given me an opportunity to aggrandize the mistress of my soul, and set her on the throne of *Bantam*; so once more repeat your acclamations, long live *Henry* and *Harriot*, King and Queen of *Bantam*.

OMNES. Huzza!

AIR XXIV, Gently touch the warbling Lire.

HARRIOT. *Let others fondly court a throne,*
All my joy's in you alone;
Let me find a crown in you,
Let me find a sceptre too,
Equal in the court or grove,
I am blest, do you but love.

LUCKLESS. *Were I not with you to live,*
Bantam would no pleasure give.
Happier in some forest I
Could upon that bosom lie.
I would guard you from all harms
While you slept within my arms.

HARRIOT. *Would an Alexander rise,*
Him I'd view with scornful eyes.

LUCKLESS. *Would Helen with thy charms compare,*
Her I'd think not half so fair:
Dearest shalt thou ever be,
HARRIOT. *Thou alone shalt reign in me.*

CONSTABLE. I hope your Majesty will pardon a poor ignorant constable: I did not know your worship, I assure you.

LUCKLESS. Pardon you – Ay more – You shall be chief constable of *Bantam*, – You, Mr. *Murdertext* shall be my chaplain; you, Sir, my orator; you my poet-laureat; you my bookseller; you *Don Tragedio*, Sir *Farcical* and *Signior Opera*, shall entertain the city of *Bantam* with your performances. Mrs. *Novel*, you shall be a romance writer; and to shew my generosity, *Marplay* and *Sparkish* shall superintend my theatres – All proper servants for the King of *Bantam*.

MRS. MONEYWOOD. I always thought he had something more than ordinary in him.

LUCKLESS. This gentlewoman is the Queen's mother.

MRS. MONEYWOOD. For want of a better, gentlemen.

AIR XXV, Oh ponder well.

MRS. MONEYWOOD. *Alack how alter'd is my fate!*
What changes have I seen!

For I, who lodgings let of late,
Am now again a Queen.

PUNCH. *And I, who in this puppet-show*
Have played Punchenello,
Will now let all the audience know
I am no common fellow.

PUNCH. If his Majesty of *Bantam* will give me leave, I can make a discovery which will be to his satisfaction. You have chose for a wife, *Henrietta*, Princess of *Old Brentford*.

OMNES. How!

PUNCH. When the King of *Old Brentford* was expell'd by the King of the *New*, the Queen flew away with her little daughter, then about two years old, and was never heard of since. But I sufficiently recollect the phiz of my mother, and thus I ask her blessing.

MRS. MONEYWOOD. Oh, my son!

HARRIOT. Oh, my brother!

PUNCH. Oh, my sister!

MRS. MONEYWOOD. I am sorry, in this pickle, to remember who I am. But alas! Too true is all you've said: Tho' I have been reduced to let lodgings, I was the Queen of *Brentford*, and this, tho' a player, is a King's son.

[*Enter* Joan.

JOAN. Then I am a King's daughter, for this gentleman is my husband.

MRS. MONEYWOOD. My daughter!

HARRIOT. *and* LUCKLESS. My sister!

PUNCH. My wife!

LUCKLESS. Strike up, kettle-drums and trumpets – Punch, I will restore you into your kingdom at the expence of my own. I will send an express to Bantam for my army.

PUNCH. Brother, I thank you – And now, if you please, we will celebrate these happy discoveries with a dance.[92]

A DANCE.

LUCKLESS. *Taught by my fate, let never bard despair,*
Tho' long he drudge, and feed on Grub-street air:
Since him (at last) 'tis possible to see
As happy and as great a King as me.

EPILOGUE.[93]

1 Poet	*Mr. Jones.*
2 Poet	*Mr. Dove.*
3 Poet	*Mr. Marshall.*
4 Poet	*Mr. Wells jun.*
Player	*Miss Palms.*
Cat[94]	*Mrs. Martin.*
Author	*Mr. Mullert.*

Four ***Poets*** *sitting at a Table.*

---

1 POET. *Brethren*, we are assembled here, to write
An epilogue, which must be spoke to-night.

2 POET. Let the first lines be to the pit address'd.

3 POET. If criticks too were mention'd, it were best;
With fulsome flattery, let them be cramm'd,
But if they damn the play –

1 POET. – Let them be damn'd.

2 POET. Supposing therefore, brother, we shou'd lay
Some very great encomiums on the play?[95]

3 POET. It cannot be amiss –

1 POET. – Now mount the boxes,
Abuse the beaus, and compliment the doxies.[96]

4 POET. Abuse the beaus! – But how?

1 POET. – Oh! never mind.
In ev'ry modern epilogue, you'll find
Enough, which we may borrow of that kind.

3 POET. What will the name of imitation soften?

1 POET. Oh! Sir, you cannot say good things too often;
And sure those thoughts which in another shine,
Become not duller, by becoming mine.

3 POET. I'm satisfy'd.
1 POET. – The audience is already
Divided into critick, beau, and lady;
Nor box, nor pit, nor gallery, can shew
One, who's not lady, critick, or a beau.
3 POET. It must be very difficult to please
Fancies so odd, so opposite as these.
1 POET. The task is not so difficult, as put;
There's one thing pleases all.
2 POET. – What is that?
1 POET. – Smut.
For as a whore is lik'd, for being tawdry,
So is an epilogue for –
3 POET. [*In a passion*] – I order you,
On pain of my departure, not to chatter,
One word so very sav'ry of the creature;
For, by my pen, might I Parnassus[97] share,
I'd not, to gain it all, offend the fair.
1 POET. You are too nice – for say whate'er we can,
Their modesty is safe behind a fan.
4 POET. Well, let us now begin.
3 POET. – But we omit
An epilogue's chief decoration, wit.
1 POET. It hath been so; but that stale custom's broken;
Tho' dull to read, 'twill please you when 'tis spoken.

[*Enter the* Author.

AUTHOR. Fie, gentlemen, the audience now hath staid
This half hour for the epilogue –
ALL POETS. – 'Tis not made.
AUTHOR. How! – Then I value not your aid of that,
I'll have the epilogue spoken by a cat.
Puss, puss, puss, puss, puss, puss, puss.

[*Enter* Cat.

1 POET. – I'm in a rage
When cats come on, poets shou'd leave the stage.

[*Exeunt* Poets.

CAT. Mew, mew.
AUTHOR. – Poor puss, come hither pretty rogue,
Who knows but you may come to be in vogue?
Some ladies like a cat, and some a dog.

[*Enter a* Player.

PLAYER. Cats! cats! cats! cats! Fie, Mr. Luckless, what
Can you be doing with that filthy cat?
[*Exit* Cat.
AUTHOR. Oh! Curst misfortune – what can I be doing?
This Devil's coming in has prov'd my ruin.
She's driv'n the cat and epilogue away.
PLAYER. Sure you are mad, and know not what you say.
AUTHOR. Mad you may call me, Madam; but you'll own,
I hope, I am not madder than the town.
PLAYER. A cat to speak an epilogue –
AUTHOR. – Speak! – no,
Only to act the epilogue in dumb-show.
PLAYER. Dumb-show!
AUTHOR. – Why, pray, is that so strange a comedy?
And have you not seen Perseus and Andromeda?[98]
Where you may find strange incidents intended,
And regular intrigues begun and ended,
Tho' not a word doth from an actor fall;
As 'tis polite to speak in murmurs small,
Sure, 'tis politer, not to speak at all.
PLAYER. But who is this? –

[*Enter* Cat *as a woman.*

AUTHOR. – I know her not –
CAT. – I that
Am now a woman, lately was a cat.
[*Turns to the audience.*
Gallants, you seem to think this transformation
As strange as was the rabit's procreation;
That 'tis as odd a cat shou'd take the habit
Of breeding us, as we shou'd breed a rabit.
I'll warrant eating one of them wou'd be
As easy to a beau, as – kissing me.

I wou'd not for the world that thing should catch us,
Cries scar'd Sir Plume – Fore-gad, my Lord, she'd scratch us.
Yet let not that deter you from your sport,
You'll find my nails are par'd exceeding short.
But – Ha! – What murmurs thro' the benches roam!
The husbands cry – we've cat enough at home.
This transformation can be strange to no man,
There's a great likeness 'twixt a cat and woman.

Chang'd by her lover's earnest prayers, we're told,

A cat was, to a beauteous maid of old.
Cou'd modern husbands thus the Gods prevail on;
Oh gemini! What wife wou'd have no tail on.
Puss wou'd be seen where madam lately sat,
And ev'ry Lady Townly be a cat.

Say, all of you, whose honey-moon is over,
What wou'd you give such changes to discover;
And waking in the morn, instead of bride,
To find poor pussy purring by your side.
Say, gentle husbands, which of you wou'd curse,
And cry, my wife is alter'd for the worse?

Shou'd to our sex the Gods like justice show,
And at our pray'rs transform our husbands too,
Many a lord, who now his fellows scorns,
Wou'd then exceed a cat by nothing – but his horns.
So plenty then wou'd be those foes to rats,
Henly[99] might prove that all mankind are cats.

FINIS.

11.2 EXCERPT FROM *THE LICENSING ACT OF 1737*

Reprinted in J. Raithby (Ed.): *Statutes at large*, vol. 5. London: Eyre & Strahan, 1811, pp. 266 – 8.

FIELDING'S *A HISTORICAL REGISTER FOR THE YEAR 1736*, which appeared in April of 1737, was one of the plays that precipitated the Licensing Act of 1737. In this rehearsal play, designed "to ridicule the vicious and foolish customs of the age" and "to expose the reigning follies in such a manner that men shall laugh themselves out of them before they feel that they are touched," Fielding strung together episodes of politicians, aristocrats, and wealthy citizens all behaving badly. Already nettled by *The Beggar's Opera*, the anonymous *A Vision of the Golden Rump*, and Henry Brook's Tory play *The Earl of Essex*, Walpole put his foot down in June of 1737, banning Brook's *Gustavus Vasa* and demanding that all plays be subject to the approval of the Lord Chamberlain and that they only be performed in licensed theatres. The subsequent act was not fully revoked until 1968.

An act to explain and amend so much of an act made in the twelfth year of the reign of Queen Anne, entitled, An act for reducing the laws relating to rogues, vagabonds, sturdy beggars and vagrants into one Act of Parliament; and for the more effectual punishing such rogues, vagabonds, sturdy beggars and vagrants, and sending them whither they ought to be sent, as relates to the common players of interludes. . . . it was enacted that all persons pretending themselves to be patent gatherers or collectors for prisons, gaols or hospitals, and wandering abroad for that purpose, all fencers, bearwards, common players of interludes and other persons therein named and expressed, shall be deemed rogues and vagabonds. And whereas some doubts have arisen concerning so much of the said Act as relates to common players of interludes; now for explaining and amending the same, be it declared and enacted by the King's most excellent Majesty, by and with the advice and consent of the Lords Spiritual and Temporal, and Commons, in this present Parliament assembled, and by the authority of the same, that from and after the twenty-fourth day of June, one thousand, seven hundred and thirty seven, every person who shall, for hire, gain, or reward, act, represent or perform, or cause to be acted, represented or performed any interlude, tragedy, comedy, opera, play, farce or other entertainment of the stage, or any part or parts therein, in case such person shall not have any legal settlement in the place where the same shall be acted, represented, or performed without authority by virtue of letters patent from His Majesty, his heirs, successors or predecessors, or without licence from the Lord Chamberlain of His Majesty's household for the time being, shall be deemed to be a rogue and a vagabond within the intent and meaning of the said recited Act, and shall be liable and subject to all such penalties and punishments, and by such methods of conviction as are inflicted on or appointed by the said Act for the punishment of rogues and vagabonds who shall be found wandering, begging and misordering themselves, within the intent and meaning of the said recited Act II. And be it further enacted by the authority aforesaid that if any person having or not having a legal settlement as aforesaid shall, without such authority or licence as aforesaid, act, represent or perform, or cause to be acted, represented or performed for hire, gain, or reward any interlude, tragedy, comedy, opera, play-farce, or other entertainment of the stage, or any part or parts therein, every such person shall for every such offence suffer any of the pains or penalties inflicted by the said recited Act III. And be it further enacted by the authority aforesaid, that from and after the said twenty-fourth day of June, one thousand, seven hundred and thirty seven, no person shall for hire, gain, or reward, act, perform, represent, or cause to be acted, performed or represented any new interlude, tragedy, comedy, opera, play, farce, or other entertainment of the stage, or any part of parts therein; or any new act, scene or other part added to any old interlude, tragedy, comedy, opera, play, farce or other entertainment of the stage, or any new prologue or epilogue, unless a true copy thereof be sent to the Lord Chamberlain of the King's household for the time being, fourteen days at least before the acting, representing or performing thereof, together with an account of the playhouse or other place where the same shall be and the time when the same is intended to be first acted, represented or performed, signed by the master or manager, or one of the masters or managers of such playhouse or place, or company of actors therein. . . . every person so offending shall for every such offence forfeit the sum of fifty pounds and every grant, licence, and authority (in any case there be any such) by or under which the said master or masters or manager or managers set up, formed or continued such playhouse, or such company of actors, shall cease, determine and become absolutely void to all intents and purposes whatsoever.

11.3 JOSEPH ADDISON, "THE PUPPET SHOW"

Jonathan Swift, *Miscellanies in prose and verse, with the following Additions*, Dublin, 1721

THE PRINTER INDICATES that Joseph Addison, of *Spectator* fame, wrote "The Puppet Show," a comic overview of the state of puppets in the theatre.

OF Trivial Things I sing surprizing Scenes,
Crowds void of Thought, and Nations in Machines.
A *Race Diminutive*; whose Frames were built
Free from the Sacrilege of antient Guilt;
Who from a better new PROMETHEUS came;
Nor boast the Plunder of Celestial Flame.

There, where facetious *Andrew* rises high,
And draws the Peopled Street beneath his Eye,
With witty Jests the gaping Crowd derides,
Distorts their Muscles, and fatigues their Sides.
All Sons of Mirth, the Gay, the Curious come,
Enter the *Booth*, and fill the spacious Room.
Not undistinguish'd are the Honours there;
But different Seats their different Prices bear.
At length, when now the *Curtain* mounts on high,
The narrow Scenes are open'd to the Eye;
Where Wire-Partitions twinkle to the Sight,
That cut the Vision, and divide the Light.
Ingenious Artifice! of sure Deceit,
Since naked Prospects would betray the Cheat.
And now the *squeaking Tribe* proceeding roams
O'er painted Mansions, and illustrious Domes.
Within this humble Cell, this narrow Wall,

Assemblies, Battels, Conquests, Triumphs, All
That Human Minds can Act, or Pride survey,
On their low *Stage*, the *Little Nation* play.

But One above the rest distinouwguish'd stalks;
A *Hero*, who in hoarser Accents talks.
Large is the Buckle that his Vest controuls;
His Mimic Eye with living Motion lies.
Huge, manly, tall, he frights the *Pygmy-Court*,
Who fly and wonder at his *Giant-Port*.
Audacious *Hero* He; who much relies
On his unequal Arm, and haughty Size.
Of these Superior Gifts and Talents proud,
He mocks and rallies all the *Lesser Crowd:*
Scatters his Satire round, and oft provokes
The Crowd to Laughter by facetious Jokes.
E'en when some *serious Action* is display'd,
And solemn Pomps in long Procession made,
He uncontroulable, of Humour rude,
Must with unseasonable Mirth intrude:
Scornful he grins upon their *Tragic Rage*,
And disconcerts the *Fable* of the *Stage*.
Sometimes the graceless Wight with saucy Air,
Makes rude Approaches to the *painted Fair*.
The *Nymph* retires, he scorns to be withstood,
And forces Kisses on th' *unwilling Wood*.
Not so his Fellows of inferior Parts,
They please the Theatre with *various* Arts,
Lascivious Sport, in circling Turns advance,
And tire their little Limbs in active Dance.
Sometimes the *Wooden People* you behold,
Attir'd in rich Array of figur'd Gold:
Rows of dissembled Jewels blaze around,
And Robes of *Tyrian* Purple stain the Ground.
For when their Tribes in Pageantry display
The Mimic Grandeur of some *Solemn Day*,
The painted *Nymphs* proceed a comely Train,
In Order just, and brighten all the Plain.
Nobles of Stature small attract the Eyes,
And last the *Commons* of an humbler Size.
The pleas'd Spectator, as these Scenes he views,
The *Pygmy-Nation* in his Mind renews:

He fancies now the *Cranes* Invasions cease;
Their warlike Souls are soften'd by a Peace,
And now secure in guiltless Sports they play,
Laugh down the *Sun*, and dance away the Day.
. . .

Now sing we, whence the *Puppet-Actors* came,
What hidden Power supplies the hollow Frame;
What cunning Agent o'er the Scenes presides,
And all the secret Operation glides.
The *Turner* shapes the useless Log with Care,
And forces it a Human Form to wear:
With the sharp Steel he works the *Wooden Race*,
And lends the Timber an adopted *Face*.
Tenacious Wires the *Legs and Feet* unite,
And Arms connected keep the *Shoulders* right.
Adapted Organs to fit Organs join,
And Joints with Joints, and Limbs with Limbs combine.
Then adds he active Wheels and Springs unseen,
By which he artful turns the small Machine,
That moves at Pleasure by the secret Wires;
And last his Voice the senseless Trunk inspires.

From such a Union of Inventions came,
And to Perfection grew the Puppet Frame;
The Workman's Mark its Origin reveal,
And own the Traces of the forming Steel.
Hence are its Dance, its Motions, and its Tone,
Its squeaking Voice, and Accents not its own.

11.4 WILLIAM HOGARTH, *A JUST VIEW OF THE BRITISH STAGE*

William Hogarth, *A Just View of the British Stage*. 1724. Image courtesy The Lewis Walpole Library, Yale University.

Hogarth's satire illustrates the sense of a fallen theatre and the rise of popular puppet and harlequinade entertainment that Fielding's Luckless laments. The print shows the three managers of the theatres seated around a table, each operating a puppet. To the left Robert Wilks, dangling Punch, says "Poor R-ch Faith I pitty him." Colley Cibber, in the middle with a harlequin puppet, looks up to the right at a hanged fiddler pleading "Assist ye Sacred Nine." Barton Booth on the right lowers a puppet of Jack Hall into a privy, saying "Ha this will do G-d D-me." Tragedy's head is hidden by the notice of "Harlequin Dr Faustus," and Comedy is obscured by the bill for "Harlequin Shepherd." Ben Johnson's ghost rises on the left, looking down in dismay on the broken statue of a Roman soldier. The text below announces: "This print represents the rehearsing a new farce that will include ye two famous entertainments Dr Faustus & Harlequin Shepherd to wch will be added Scaramouch Jack Hall the Chimney-Sweeper's escape from Newgate through ye privy, with ye comical humours of Ben Johnson's Ghost, Concluding wth the Hay-Dance perform'd in ye air by ye figures A, B, C, assisted by Ropes from ye Muses. Note, there are no conjurors concern'd in it as ye ignorant imagine. – The Bricks, rubbish &c. will be real, but the excrements upon Jack Hall will be made of chew'd gingerbread to prevent offence. Vivat Rex. price six pence."

11.5 *THE PLAYER'S LAST REFUGE*

The PLAYER'S LAST REFUGE: Or the STROLLERS in DISTRESS.

The Player's Last Refuge: Or, the Strollers in Distress, Copperplate, Louis Philippe Boitard, Published by Bispham Dickinson, 1735. Image courtesy of the Lewis Walpole Library, Yale University.

This graphic satire focuses on Sir John Barnard's bill of December 1735 to limit the number of playhouses, prior to the Licensing Act of 1737. The actors are identified by numbers: (1) Hannibal (Theophilus Cibber) sits dejectedly and is attended by (2) Harlequin, who emerges from a hole in the ground to offer him a mask and pistols while (3) Poverty and Despair support him on either side. (4) Sophonisba (possibly Mrs. Bullock) stands to the left holding a flask of gin. (5) Hob stands in his well, which has become a grave for Pistol (Cibber's most famous role), whose corpse (6) is being carried by Falstaff (perhaps Benjamin Griffin), Hamlet, Harlequin and Orpheus. They are followed by (7) John Hippisley and Henry Fielding, who lead the mourners with a sign proclaiming "Pistol's no more." In the background, (8) Sir John Barnard impersonates a military general brandishing his sword overthrowing a sausage-seller's brazier and trampling on Punch. The lantern of Lee and Harper's theatrical booth with a jumble of props occupies the foreground. (BM Satires 1838)

Notes

1–2 The text for this edition is based on *The Author's Farce; and The Pleasures of the Town*. As Acted at the Theatre in the Hay-Market. Written by Scriblerus Secundus. London: for J. Roberts, 1730.

3 Woods, "Introduction" *The Author's Farce (Original Version)*, Lincoln, NE: University of Nebraska Press, 1966.

4 Latin, from Juvenal's *Satires* 1.30 – 31: "Who can be so tolerant of this city, so iron of soul, as to contain himself?" This question appears right after the statement, "it is hard not to write satire" (1.30).

5 Fielding is referencing characters from George Villiers, the 2nd Duke of Buckingham's play *The Rehearsal*, which mocked heroic drama.

6 A sought-after metal from Corinth.

7 "Index" and "Messenger" both appear in the text, but no version of the play lists them as characters or identifies an actor in the parts.

8 Debt-collectors.

9 Money; the Dutch were stereotyped as greedy.

10 A tallow-chandler makes candles out of rendered animal fat, a greasy and unattractive profession; Hymen is the mythological god of marriage.

11 In the 1755 version, Moneywood adds:

> If thou can'st not pay me in money. Let me have it in love. If I break through the modesty of my sex let my passion excuse it. I know the world will call it an impudent action; but if you will let me reserve all I have to myself, I will make myself yours for ever.

12 No air is listed for this exchange.

13 Another of Fielding's stabs at Colley Cibber, now poet laureate. Fielding satirically attributed his *Shamela* to "Conny Keyber" on the title page.

14 Witmore's joke turns on the comparison of madams looking for virgins with "uncrack'd maidenheads" to work as prostitutes with Mrs. Lovewood's search for gossip about other women's sexual follies, hence their "crack'd reputations."

15 *Hurlothrumbo; or, the Super-Natural* (1729) was a rhymed nonsense play with much dancing and music, written by the dancing master Samuel Johnson (not to be confused with Dr. Samuel Johnson, lexicographer). The play ran on alternate nights at the Haymarket with *The Author's Farce*.

16 Witmore's point is that writers, in order to be recognized these days, must write trash.

17 Poems of excessive praise.

18 An extremely wealthy king of ancient Lydia, which is now Turkey.

19 He laments that not only is Luckless a poet (follower of the Muses) but he has also fallen in love with a poor girl.

20 An impolite or mean person.

21 This and the following scene were substantially altered in the 1755 edition. These alterations also change the numbering of the scenes.

22 Accepted for performance in a theatre, often a necessary condition for play publication.

23 Laxatives.

24 To leave hastily; to "scram."

25 The 1755 text goes into more detail about Luckless' visitors.

26 Having silver would indicate inherited family property, but because silver could be easily stolen, it also suggests burgled wealth. The final joke is that Luckless is bluffing and, like the "china" scene in *The Country Wife*, plans to give Mrs. Moneywood the "silver" in the bedroom.

27 Mrs. Moneywood.

28 This scene was significantly altered by Fielding in the 1755 edition.

29 Covent Garden was a bustling urban market and theatrical district.

30 Literally, "he himself has said it"; a dogmatic assertion that something is true.

31 To price them at the same rate.

32 In addition to talking about how much actors love applause, Marplay includes the following line in the 1755 edition: "The art of writing, boy, is the art of stealing old plays, by changing the name of the play, and new ones, by changing the name of the author."

33 Edward Bysshe's *The Art of English Poetry* (1708) included a rhyming dictionary as an appendix.

34 Spelled "rhime" in the 1730 and 1755 texts.

35 The river in Macedonia in which the Bacchic women who killed Orpheus washed their hands of his blood.

36 The 1755 text includes more dialogue about plagiarism as theft.

37 The joke here is that Index is being paid by the item for adding very familiar Latin and Greek mottoes to Bookweight's publications, with the full knowledge that most people can't read them. They are, in order, "Can you help laughing, friends?" (Horace), "Love conquers all things, so we too shall yield to love" (Virgil), and "it is difficult not to write satire" (Juvenal).

38 The 1755 text says "liberty and property."

39 John-a-Nokes and Tom-a-Stiles are set names for familiar legal opponents, much as we might use the name "John Doe." That "nokes" is slang for idiot and "stiles" is slang for a ditch or open sewer makes their names comical. The booksellers listed are, by Fielding's suggestion, printers of libel who disguise their sources.

40 In the 1755 edition, this scene is between Harriot and Luckless.

41 The cardinal virtues were prudence, temperance, fortitude, and justice.

42 Luckless refers to the popularity of puppet shows at fairs, booths, and some theatres, as well as the puppet components of popular harlequinades like *The Necromancer* and *The Sultan*, which depended on puppets for special effects and stunts.

43 The literal reference is to Handel's *Giulio Cesare In Egitto* (see the online supplement) but the broader comparison of puppet shows to opera as well as farce implies that "true" English theatre is being driven off the stage by foreign entertainments.

44 Having Nonsense fall in love with Signior Opera mimicks the "fall" of the theatergoing public for opera as a false or unpatriotic form of theatre, with the additional joke that many of the most popular Italian male singers, like Farinelli, were castrati and thus sexually suspect. That the Player finds it strange to have characters who are ghosts is a case of comic misdirection.

45 This joke plays on mild cultural anxieties about supernatural and sacred representations on the stage, thus lumping together scenes of ghosts in the underworld with the representations of the coronation.

46 The underworld, the mythological land of the dead.

47 Punch suggests that fashionable couples also hate each other, and that like them, he and Joan should use fancier, "gentler" language to mask their disdain.

48 The red coat is a soldier; the tattered black coat represents writers. The ferryman of the River Styx in classical mythology, to whom the dead must pay their fare for their passage to the netherworld, is saying that soldiers and writers show up broke and fail to pay him.

49 Minos fed his children to the Minotaur.

50 The suggestion is that there are so many bad writers in England that they are now filling up the afterworld, where they continue to pursue nonsense.

51 "Stap my breath" is a reference to the comedian Colley Cibber's tag line "stap my vitals" in *The Relapse*.

52 A slight double entendre here as "clap" is also slang for venereal disease.

53 Pantomimes of the day featured Harlequin, who had to be an adroit dancer and acrobat, as many of the scenes, or *lazzi*, that composed pantomimes involved extraordinary falls, acrobatics, fake hangings, and aerial rigging, any of which could have led to a broken neck.

54 A black dancer to dance a Spanish dance with castanets.

55 Dido, queen of Carthage, killed herself with sword and threw herself on a funeral pyre so as not to dishonor her first husband.

56 These were busy and often wet streets. Bookseller refers to his "oblations" or ritual cleansing but compares them to the humiliating and familiar situation of being splashed with muddy water by a passing carriage.

57 Prosperine (also Persephone), the daughter of Zeus and Demeter (goddess of agriculture) was kidnapped and taken by Hades/Pluto to the underworld where, because she ate six pomegranate seeds, could only return six months of the year (spring and summer) to Earth to be with her mother. Lewis Theobald wrote and staged a musical pantomime called *The Rape of Prosperine* in 1727 at the rival theatre Lincoln's Inn Fields.

58 A list of cultural stereotypes.

59 A reference to the Harlequin Dr. Faustus pantomimes.

60 Bartholomew Fair was a site for tightrope walking ("rope dancing"), puppet shows, and other entertainments considered low, which, Poet ruefully jokes, are now available all year in the west end theatres.

61 Calling the King in the fashionable card game quadrille was part of making an alliance with another player to win tricks; the other terms suggest they are betting and cheating in this game.

62 The ace of spades and the ace of clubs.

63 Punch complains that his wife Joan has been swept up in fashionable card games and neglected the home, a sign that she is mindlessly following trends.

64 Punch suggests that the Chinese are inveterate gamblers who will sell themselves and their family in card games.

65 Somebody and Nobody were common comic figures adapted to the puppet stage; Somebody generally featured a huge "body" with very small limbs, while Nobody had almost no actual "body," and consisted primarily of a head, legs, and arms.

66 Orators, often unlicensed preachers or working-class figures, used empty barrels (tubs) as makeshift pulpits, a connection Swift also used in his satire on religion, *The Tale of a Tub.*

67 A song sung in more speech-like rhythms, often found in opera.

68 The non-speaking pantomime is a Harlequin figure, popularized by John Rich, also known as "Lun," manager and actor at Lincoln's Inn Fields and later Covent Garden. Rich was a remarkable dancer and used the physicality, mask, and muteness of Harlequin to compensate for his own poor voice and unprepossessing face.

69 "By Jay'd" is an invention of Don Tragedio, indicating that his style of tragedy draws on bad writing and catchphrases.

70 Sir Farcical's repetition of Cibber's catchphrase is meant to skewer the actor as part of the fall of intelligent theatre.

71 John Rich was, in addition to being the most famous Harlequin of the age, the manager of the rival Lincoln's Inn Fields theatre. The epithet "great man," also used in *The Beggar's Opera,* refers to the politically adept Robert Walpole, the first Prime Minister of Britain.

72 She died giving birth, which makes Orator's subsequent line and her embrace of Opera both satirical reflections on the novel's capacity for sensationalism.

73 Their duet echoes the most famous duet from *The Beggar's Opera*, in which Polly and Macheath sing a similar song to the same tune.

74 The itch, with venereal implications.

75 The first of his analogies refers to syphilis, which would destroy the cartilage in the beau's nose, hence "the bridge." The others are meant to satirize the orator grasping for analogies.

76 After the fashion of Aristophanes' *The Birds* and other beast fables, the song compares species of birds to categories of people.

77 Large drinking vessel.

78 Slang for money, from the expression "the ready Rhino."

79 Ill-gotten money.

80 See note 15.

81 An egalitarian Protestant sect that eschewed preaching for discussion. It was founded by two tailors who broke away from the Ranter movement.

82 A wreath, worn around the neck, with liturgical associations.

83 Tragedio has just challenged Opera to a duel, which Opera concedes in his song.

84 Opera references both ballad opera in Polly Peachum, a main character in *The Beggar's Opera*, and regular opera in *Orpheus and Euridice.*

85 Kiss.
86 Paraphernalia referred to the property that married women and widows could legally possess.
87 The double joke is that the writing is so bad it's an insult to nonsense, and that Luckless has sexually assaulted Nonsense.
88 Murder-text functions as a government censor but uses the language of Puritan reformers and other religious critics of theatre.
89 This popular song also appears in *The Beaux' Stratagem* and is referenced in the prologue to *The Busy Body*.
90 Non-conformist teacher, one of the non-Anglican Protestant denominations.
91 Bantam probably comes from the Javanese port "Banten," alternately under EIC and Dutch control. It serves as a name for a strange place, as in Behn's short story, *The Court of the King of Bantam*. Spectator 545 has a letter to the King of Bantam.
92 The ludicrous discovery that Luckless is actually the King of Bantam and Mrs. Moneywood, mother of Harriot and now Punch, the former Queen of Brentford makes all the couples (Punch and Joan, Luckless and Harriot) royals.
93 Fielding uses an additional play within a play as his epilogue. "Author" is not listed but does appear in the dialogue. Mullert would have played this role in keeping with the other reprised performances of the epilogue.
94 The cat satirizes both harlequinades, which featured animal transformations through costuming effects, and the use of actual animals on stage to attract audiences.
95 They plot to praise the play excessively.
96 Prostitutes.
97 A mountain in Delphi, Greece, and mythological home of the muses.
98 *Perseus and Andromeda* was a pantomime that played at Rich's Lincoln's Inn Fields. It was full of songs, evil spirits dancing, and thus an example of the sensationalistic and spectacular theatre Fielding decried.
99 John Henley, known as "Orator Henley" was an eccentric dissenting minister who squeaked out a living writing for Edmund Curl, the notorious publisher, and later giving dramatic sermons on Sunday mornings and lectures on a wide range of topics on weekday evenings, often tending towards the fantastic and unbelievable.

---

12. *The London Merchant*

THE LONDON MERCHANT: OR, THE HISTORY OF GEORGE BARNWELL.
AS IT IS ACTED AT THE THEATRE-ROYAL IN DRURY-LANE.
BY HIS MAJESTY'S SERVANTS.[1] GEORGE LILLO.
FIRST PERFORMED 22 JUNE 1731 AND FIRST PUBLISHED 1731

12.1 *THE LONDON MERCHANT: OR, THE HISTORY OF GEORGE BARNWELL.* AS IT IS ACTED AT THE THEATRE-ROYAL IN *DRURY-LANE*. BY HIS MAJESTY'S SERVANTS.[2]

George Lillo

First Performed 22 June 1731 and First Published 1731

CAUTIONARY TALES HAVE A LONG HISTORY on the stage, but *The London Merchant* made a stir as what Theophilus Cibber called "almost a new species of tragedy," with an innovative use of a "low" hero, unapologetically Protestant and mercantile values, and a psychologically dense account of young Barnwell's downfall. The didactic tragedy tells the story of George Barnwell, an apprentice who is seduced by a female con artist, Millwood. She preys on his youthful innocence and persuades him to betray his master, steal, and even eventually murder his uncle. Lillo drew his source material from "The Ballad of George Barnwell," a ballad that had been around since at least the mid-seventeenth century. Lillo also evinces familiarity with Elizabethan domestic tragedies such as *Arden of Faversham* (which he adapted) as well as with masques, ballad operas, and contemporary tragedies.[3] The hallmark of *The London Merchant*, though, was that it brought tragic pathos to domestic scenes of everyday (as opposed to elite) life. His young, vulnerable Barnwell embodies virtue undermined by passion, while Millwood the temptress becomes a complex, tragic figure, who reflects negatively on Restoration wit yet offers a disturbing anatomy of the structural injustice of gender roles in the period. The result moves past its own moralizing to stage the conflict of passions and values with startling intensity and depth.

The play was an unanticipated success from an almost unknown author during the late-summer off season of 1731. Viewers had 17 chances to see it in that short window, which meant three author benefit nights for Lillo and a glimpse of its future trajectory. It became a stock repertoire piece for all the houses by the time Garrick retired in 1776. It appeared in eight authorized editions from 1731 to 1739, with piracies as well as more legitimate editions to follow. Its popular origins and morality tale structure made it a fitting if heavy-handed choice for traditional Christmas, Easter, and Lord Mayor's Day performances. These would have been holidays for apprentices when they could attend the theatre. During the 1730s, *The London Merchant* replaced Ravenscroft's bawdy 1681 *The London Cuckolds* as the traditional holiday fare. Motivation to stage *The London Merchant* as instruction for young apprentices seems to have buoyed its 179 performances from 1731–1776.[4] It remained a Christmas season play until 1819. Theophilus Cibber described Lillo's play as "a more instructive, moral, and cautionary drama, than many pieces that had usually been exhibited on those days with little but farce and ribaldry to recommend them."[5] The direct substitution of Lillo's for Ravenscroft's play make the shift in taste and ideology clear: even the titles redefine the figure of the merchant from a "cit," for citizen likely to be cuckolded, to a pillar of the community. This merchant's sexual and financial continence are of a piece.

The London Merchant owes a great tonal debt to conduct literature, including the advisory strains of periodicals such as *The Spectator* and manuals such as Samuel Richardson's *The Apprentice's Vade Mecum* (1734), which post-dates the play but partakes in the same cultural turn away from the sexually forthright and Tory-leaning theatre of the Restoration and toward a more bourgeois set of values in both comedy and tragedy. As apprentices swarmed to the city for work in boom industries such as textiles, construction, and retail shops, novels such as *Pamela* and plays like *The London Merchant* provided pedagogies of feeling and sentiment that could hail these young subjects into the bourgeois social order. The relationship between Trueman and Thorowgood models an idealized tutorial dynamic between an apprentice and master. The interlocking Protestant and mercantile values present the structure of feeling that Max Weber would later dub the "iron cage" of Protestant virtue, through which work itself becomes the remnant of Puritan devotion, and capitalist ideology becomes the new religion.

The play was translated into French and German during the eighteenth century and enjoyed a wide print circulation. The popularity of the play waned slightly after 1776, though Lawrence M. Price surmises that it remained alive in provincial theatres and with strolling players.[6] Lillo's domestic tragedy led the way for later continental playwrights such as Lessing, who further explored similar themes. A revival in 1797 featured Sarah Siddons as Millwood and her brother Charles Kemble as Barnwell. More recently, a 2012 revival by the Storm Theatre in New York garnered glowing reviews and proved that the unapologetically didactic play could be compelling to modern audiences.

Learn to be wise from others' harm,
And you shall do full well.
Old ballad of the lady's fall.

To *Sir* John Eyles, *Bar.* Member of Parliament for, and Alderman of the City of *London*, and Sub-Governor of the *South-Sea* Company.[7]

SIR,

If tragick poetry be, as Mr. *Dryden* has some where said, the most excellent and most useful kind of writing, the more extensively useful the moral of any tragedy is, the more excellent that piece must be of its kind.[8]

I hope I shall not be thought to insinuate that this, to which I have presumed to prefix your name, is such; that depends on its fitness to answer the end of tragedy, the exciting of the passions, in order to the correcting such of them as are criminal, either in their nature, or through their excess. Whether the following scenes do this in any tolerable degree, is, with the deference that becomes one who wou'd not be thought vain, submitted to your candid and impartial judgment.

What I wou'd infer is this, I think, evident truth; that tragedy is so far from losing its dignity, by being accommodated to the circumstances of the generality of mankind, that it is more truly august in proportion to the extent of its influence, and the numbers that are properly affected by it. As it is more truly great to be the instrument of good to many, who stand in need of our assistance, than to a very small part of that number.

If Princes, &c. were alone liable to misfortunes, arising from vice, or weakness in themselves, or others, there wou'd be good reason for confining the characters in tragedy to those of superior rank; but, since the contrary is evident, nothing can be more reasonable than to proportion the remedy to the disease.

I am far from denying that tragedies, founded on any instructive and extraordinary events in history, or a well-invented fable, where the persons introduced are of the highest rank, are without their use, even to the bulk of the audience. The strong contract between a *Tamerlane* and a *Bajazet*, may have its weight with an unsteady people, and contribute to the fixing of them in the interest of a prince of the character of the former, when, thro' their own levity, or the arts of designing men, they are render'd factious and uneasy, tho' they have the highest reason to be satisfied. The sentiments and example of a *Cato*, may inspire his spectators with a just sense of the value of liberty, when they see that honest patriots prefer death to an obligation from a tyrant, who wou'd sacrifice the constitution of his country, and the liberties of mankind, to his ambition or revenge. I have attempted, indeed, to enlarge the province of the graver kind of poetry, and should be glad to see it carried on by some abler hand. Plays, founded on moral tales in private life, may be of admirable use, by carrying conviction to the mind, with such irresistable force, as to engage all the faculties and powers of the soul in the cause of virtue, by stifling vice in its first principles. They who imagine this to be too much to be attributed to tragedy, must be strangers to the energy of that noble species of poetry. *Shakespear*, who has given such amazing proofs of his genius, in that as well as in comedy, in his *Hamlet*, has the following lines.

> *Had he the motive and the cause for passion*
> *That I have; he wou'd drown the stage with tears*
> *And cleave the general ear with horrid speech;*
> *Make mad the guilty, and appall the free,*
> *Confound the ignorant, and amaze indeed*
> *The very faculty of eyes and ears.*

And farther, in the same speech,

> *I've heard that guilty creatures at a play,*
> *Have, by the very cunning of the scene,*
> *Been so struck to the soul, that presently*
> *They have proclaim'd their malefactions.*

Prodigious! yet strictly just. But I shan't take up your valuable time with my remarks; only give me leave just to observe, that he seems so firmly persuaded of the power of a well wrote piece to produce the effect here ascribed to it, as to make *Hamlet* venture his soul on the event, and rather trust that, than a messenger from the other world, tho' it assumed, as he expresses it, his noble father's form, and assured him, that it was his spirit. I'll have grounds more relative, says Hamlet.

> *– The play's the thing,*
> *Wherein I'll catch the conscience of the king.*

Such plays are the best answers to them who deny the lawfulness of the stage.

Considering the novelty of this attempt, I thought it would be expected from me to say something in its excuse; and I was unwilling to lose the opportunity of saying something of the usefulness of tragedy in general, and what may be reasonably expected from the farther improvement of this excellent kind of poetry.

Sir, I hope you will not think I have said too much of an art, a mean specimen of which I am ambitious enough to recommend to your favour and protection. A mind, conscious of superior worth, as much despises flattery, as it is above it. Had I found in my self an inclination to so contemptible a vice, I should not have chose Sir John Eyles for my patron. And indeed the best writ panegyrick, tho' strictly true, must place you in a light, much inferior to that in which you have long been fix'd, by the love and esteem of your fellow citizens; whose choice of you for one of their representatives in parliament, has sufficiently declared their sense of your merit. Nor hath the knowledge of your worth been confined to the City.[9] The proprietors in the *South-Sea* company, in which are included numbers of persons; as considerable for their rank, fortune, and understanding, as any in the kingdom, gave the greatest proof of their confidence, in your capacity and probity, when they chose you sub-governor of their company, at a time when their affairs were in the utmost confusion, and their properties in the greatest danger.[10] Nor is the court insensible of your importance. I shall not therefore attempt your character, nor pretend to add any thing to a reputation so well established.

Whatever others may think of a dedication, wherein there is so much said of other things, and so little of the person to whom it is address'd, I have reason to believe that you will the more easily pardon it on that very account.

I am, SIR,

Your most obedient humble servant,

George Lillo.

PROLOGUE.

Spoke by Mr. Cibber, Jun.

The Tragick Muse, sublime, delights to show
Princes distrest, and scenes of royal woe;
In awful pomp, majestick, to relate
The fall of nations, or some heroe's fate:
That scepter'd chiefs may by example know
The strange vicissitude of things below:
What dangers on security attend;
How pride and cruelty in ruin end:
Hence providence supream to know; and own
Humanity adds glory to a throne.
In ev'ry former age, and foreign tongue,
With native grandure thus the goddess sung.
Upon our stage indeed, with wish'd success,
You've sometimes seen her in a humbler dress;
Great only in distress. When she complains
In Southern's, Rowe's, or Otway's moving strains,[11]
The brilliant drops, that fall from each bright eye,
The absent pomp, with brighter gems, supply.
Forgive us then, if we attempt to show,
In artless strains, a tale of private woe.
A London prentice ruin'd is our theme,
Drawn from the fam'd old song, that bears his name.
We hope your taste is not so high to scorn
A moral tale, esteem'd e'er you were born;[12]
Which for a century of rolling years,
Has fill'd a thousand-thousand eyes with tears.
If thoughtless youth to warn, and shame the age
From vice destructive, well becomes the stage;
If this example innocence secure,
Prevent our guilt, or by reflection cure;
If Millwood's dreadful guilt, and sad despair,
Commend the virtue of the good and fair,
Tho' art be wanting, and our numbers fail,
Indulge th' attempt in justice to the tale.

Dramatis Personæ.

Thorowgood,	Mr. Bridgwater.
Barnwell, Uncle to George,	Mr. Roberts.
George Barnwell,	Mr. Cibber, Jun.
Trueman,	Mr. W. Mills.
Blunt,	Mr. R. Wetherilt.
Maria,	Mrs. Cibber.
Millwood,	Mrs. Butler.
Lucy,	Mrs. Charke.
Officers with their attendants, keeper, and footmen	

SCENE London, and an adjacent village.

ACT I

ACT I. SCENE I.
A room in Thorowgood's house.

[Thorowgood *and* Trueman.

TRUEMAN. Sir, the packet from *Genoa* is arriv'd. [*Gives letters.*

THOROWGOOD. Heav'n be praised, the storm that threaten'd our royal mistress, pure religion, liberty, and laws, is for a time diverted; the haughty and revengeful *Spaniard*, disappointed of the loan on which he depended from *Genoa*, must now attend the slow return of wealth from his new world, to supply his empty coffers, e'er he can execute his purpos'd invasion of our happy island;[13] by which means time is gain'd to make such preparations on our part, as may, heav'n concurring, prevent his malice, or turn the meditated mischief on himself.

TRUEMAN. He must be insensible indeed, who is not affected when the safety of his country is concern'd. – Sir, may I know by what means – if I am too bold –

THOROWGOOD. Your curiosity is laudable; and I gratify it with the greater pleasure, because from thence you may learn, how honest merchants, as such, may sometimes contribute to the safety of their country, as they do at all times to its happiness; that if hereafter you should be tempted to any action that has the appearance of vice or meanness in it, upon reflecting on the dignity of our profession, you may with honest scorn reject whatever is unworthy of it.

TRUEMAN. Shou'd *Barnwell*, or I, who have the benefit of your example, by our ill conduct bring any imputation on that honourable name, we must be left without excuse.

THOROWGOOD. You complement, young man. – [Trueman *bows respectfully*] Nay, I'm not offended. As the name of merchant never degrades the gentleman, so by no means does it exclude him; only take heed not to purchase the character of complaisance at the expence of your sincerity. – But to answer your question, – The Bank of *Genoa* had agreed, at excessive interest and on good security, to advance the King of *Spain* a sum of money sufficient to equip his vast armado, – of which our peerless *Elizabeth* (more than in name the mother of her people) being well informed, sent *Walsingham*, her wise and faithful secretary, to consult the merchants of this loyal city, who all agreed to direct their several agents to influence, if possible, the *Genoese* to break their contract with the *Spanish* court. 'Tis done, the state and bank of *Genoa*, having maturely weigh'd and rightly judged of their true interest, prefer the friendship of the merchants of *London*, to that of a monarch, who proudly stiles himself King of both *Indies*.

TRUEMAN. Happy success of prudent councils. What an expence of blood and treasure is here saved? – Excellent Queen! O how unlike to former princes, who made the danger of foreign enemies a pretense to oppress their subjects, by taxes great and grievous to be born.

THOROWGOOD. Not so our gracious Queen, whose richest exchequer is her people's love, as their happiness her greatest glory.

TRUEMAN. On these terms to defend us, is to make our protection a benefit worthy her who confers it, and well worth our acceptance.

TRUEMAN. Sir, have you any commands for me at this time?

THOROWGOOD. Only to look carefully over the files to see whether there are any trades-mens bills unpaid; and if there are, to send and discharge 'em. We must not let artificers lose their time, so useful to the publick and their families, in unnecessary attendance.

ACT I. SCENE II.

[Thorowgood *and* Maria.

THOROWGOOD. Well, *Maria*, have you given orders for the entertainment? I would have it in some measure worthy the guests. Let there be plenty, and of the best; that the courtiers, tho' they should deny us citizens politeness, may at least commend our hospitality.

MARIA. Sir, I have endeavoured not to wrong your well-known generosity by an ill-tim'd parsimony.

THOROWGOOD. Nay, 'twas a needless caution, I have no cause to doubt your prudence.

MARIA. Sir! I find my self unfit for conversation at present; I should but increase the number of the company, without adding to their satisfaction.

THOROWGOOD. Nay, my child, this melancholy must not be indulged.

MARIA. Company will but increase it. I wish you would dispense with my absence; solitude best suits my present temper.

THOROWGOOD. You are not insensible that it is chiefly on your account these noble lords do me the honour so frequently to grace my board; shou'd you be absent, the disappointment may make them repent their condescension, and think their labour lost.

MARIA. He that shall think his time or honour lost in visiting you, can set no real value on your daughter's company, whose only merit is that she is yours. The man of quality, who chuses to converse with a gentleman and merchant of your worth and character, may confer honour by so doing, but he loses none.

THOROWGOOD. Come, come, *Maria*, I need not tell you that a young gentleman may prefer your conversation to mine, yet intend me no disrespect at all; for tho' he may lose no honour in my company, 'tis very natural for him to expect more pleasure in yours. I remember the time, when the company of the greatest and wisest man in the kingdom would have been insipid and tiresome to me, if it had deprived me of an opportunity of enjoying your mother's.

MARIA. Yours no doubt was as agreeable to her; for generous minds know no pleasure in society but where 'tis mutual.

THOROWGOOD. Thou know'st I have no heir, no child but thee; the fruits of many years successful industry must all be thine, now it would give me pleasure great as my love, to see on whom you would bestow it. I am daily solicited by men of the greatest rank and merit for leave to address you, but I have hitherto declin'd it, in hopes that by observation I shou'd learn which way your inclination tends; for as I know love to be essential to happiness in the marriage state, I had rather my approbation should confirm your choice, than direct it.

MARIA. What can I say? How shall I answer, as I ought, this tenderness, so uncommon, even in the best of parents: but you are without example; yet had you been less indulgent, I had been most wretched. That I look on the crowd of courtiers, that visit here, with equal esteem, but equal indifference, you have observed, and I must needs confess; yet had you asserted your authority, and insisted on a parent's right to be obey'd, I had submitted, and to my duty sacrificed my peace.

THOROWGOOD. From your perfect obedience in every other instance, I fear'd as much; and therefore wou'd leave you without a byass[14] in an affair wherein your happiness is so immediately concern'd.

MARIA. Whether from a want of that just ambition that wou'd become your daughter, or from some other cause I know not; but, I find high birth and titles don't recommend the man, who owns them, to my affections.

THOROWGOOD. I wou'd not that they shou'd, unless his merit recommends him more. A noble birth and fortune, tho' they make not a bad man good, yet they are a real advantage to a worthy one, and place his virtues in the fairest light.

MARIA. I cannot answer for my inclinations, but they shall ever be submitted to your wisdom and authority; and as you will not compel me to marry where I cannot love, so love shall never make me act contrary to my duty. Sir, have I your permission to retire.

THOROWGOOD. I'll see you to your chamber.

ACT I. SCENE III.
A room in Millwood's house.

[Millwood. Lucy *waiting*.

MILLWOOD. How do I look to day, *Lucy?*

LUCY. O, killingly, Madam! – A little more red, and you'll be irresistible! – But why this more than ordinary care of your dress and complexion? What new conquest are you aiming at?[15]

MILLWOOD. A conquest wou'd be new indeed!

LUCY. Not to you, who make 'em every day, – but to me. – Well! 'tis what I'm never to expect, – unfortunate as I am: – But your wit and beauty –

MILLWOOD. First made me a wretch, and still continue me so. – Men, however generous or sincere to one another, are all selfish hypocrites in their affairs with us. We are no otherwise esteemed or regarded by them, but as we contribute to their satisfaction.

LUCY. You are certainly, Madam, on the wrong side in this argument: is not the expence all theirs? And I am sure it is our own fault if we hav'n't our share of the pleasure.

MILLWOOD. We are but slaves to men.

LUCY. Nay, 'tis they that are slaves most certainly; for we lay them under contribution.

MILLWOOD. Slaves have no property; no, not even in themselves. – All is the victors.[16]

LUCY. You are strangely arbitrary in your principles, Madam.

MILLWOOD. I would have my conquests compleat, like those of the *Spaniards* in the New World; who first plunder'd the natives of all the wealth they had, and then condemn'd the wretches to the mines for life, to work for more.

LUCY. Well, I shall never approve of your scheme of government: I should think it much more politick, as well as just, to find my subjects an easier imployment.

MILLWOOD. It's a general maxim among the knowing part of mankind, that a woman without virtue, like a man without honour or honesty, is capable of any action, tho' never so vile: And yet what pains will they not take, what arts not use, to seduce us from our innocence, and make us contemptible and wicked, even in their own opinions? Then is it not just, the villains, to their cost, should find us so. – But guilt makes them suspicious, and keeps them on their guard; therefore we can take advantage only of the young and innocent part of the sex, who having never injured women, apprehend no injury from them.

LUCY. Ay, they must be young indeed.

MILLWOOD. Such a one, I think, I have found. – As I've passed thro' the city, I have often observ'd him receiving and paying considerable sums of money; from thence I conclude he is employ'd in affairs of consequence.

LUCY. Is he handsome?

MILLWOOD. Ay, ay, the stripling is well made.

LUCY. About –

MILLWOOD. Eighteen –

LUCY. Innocent, handsome, and about eighteen. – You'll be vastly happy. – Why, if you manage well, you may keep him to your self these two or three years.

MILLWOOD. If I manage well, I shall have done with him much sooner, having long had a design on him; and meeting him yesterday, I made a full stop, and gazing wishfully on his face, ask'd him his name: he blush'd, and bowing very low, answer'd, *George Barnwell*. I beg'd his pardon for the freedom I had taken, and told him, that he was the person I had long wish'd to see, and to whom I had an affair of importance to communicate, at a proper time and place. He named a tavern; I talk'd of honour and reputation, and invited him to my house: he swallow'd the bait, promis'd to come, and this is the time I expect him. [*Knocking at the door*] Some body knocks, – d'ye hear; I am at home to no body to day, but him. –

ACT I. SCENE IV.

[Millwood.

MILLWOOD. Less affairs must give way to those of more consequence; and I am strangely mistaken if this does not prove of great importance to me and him too, before I have done with him. – Now, after what manner shall I receive him? Let me consider – what manner of person am I to receive? – He is young, innocent, and bashful; therefore I must take care not to shock him at first. – But then, if I have any skill in phisiognomy, he is amorous, and, with a little assistance, will soon get the better of his modesty. – I'll trust to nature, who does wonders in these matters. – If to seem what one is not, in order to be the better liked for what one really is; if to speak one thing, and mean the direct contrary, be art in a woman, I know nothing of nature.

ACT I. SCENE V.

[*To her,* Barnwell *bowing very low,* Lucy *at a distance.*

MILLWOOD. Sir! The surprize and joy! –

BARNWELL. Madam. –

MILLWOOD. This is such a favour, – [*Advancing.*

BARNWELL. Pardon me, Madam, –

MILLWOOD. So unhop'd for, – [*Still advances.* Barnwell *salutes her, and retires in confusion.*

MILLWOOD. To see you here. – Excuse the confusion. –

BARNWELL. I fear I am too bold. –

MILLWOOD. Alas, Sir! All my apprehensions proceed from my fears of your thinking me so. – Please, Sir, to sit. – I am as much at a loss how to receive this honour as I ought, as I am surpriz'd at your goodness in confering it.

BARNWELL. I thought you had expected me – I promis'd to come.

MILLWOOD. That is the more surprizing; few men are such religious observers of their word.

BARNWELL. All, who are honest, are.

MILLWOOD. To one another: – But we silly women are seldom thought of consequence enough to gain a place in your remembrance. [*Laying her hand on his, as by accident.*

BARNWELL. [*Aside*] *Her disorder is so great, she don't perceive she has laid her hand on mine. – Heaven! How she trembles! – What can this mean!*

MILLWOOD. The interest I have in all that relates to you, (the reason of which you shall know hereafter) excites my curiosity; and, were I sure you would pardon my presumption, I should desire to know your real sentiments on a very particular affair.

BARNWELL. Madam, you may command my poor thoughts on any subject; – I have none that I would conceal.

MILLWOOD. You'll think me bold.

BARNWELL. No, indeed.

MILLWOOD. What then are your thoughts of love?

BARNWELL. If you mean the love of women, I have not thought of it all. – My youth and circumstances make such thoughts improper in me yet: But if you mean the general love we owe to mankind, I think no one has more of it in his temper than my self. – I don't know that person in the world whose happiness I don't wish, and wouldn't promote, were it in my power. – In an especial manner I love my Uncle, and my Master, but, above all, my friend.

MILLWOOD. You have a friend then, whom you love?

BARNWELL. As he does me, sincerely.

MILLWOOD. He is, no doubt, often bless'd with your company and conversation.

BARNWELL. We live in one house together, and both serve the same worthy merchant.

MILLWOOD. Happy, happy youth! – Who e'er thou art, I envy thee, and so must all, who see and know this youth. – What have I lost, by being form'd a woman! – I hate my sex, my self. – Had I been a man, I might, perhaps, have been as happy in your friendship, as he who now enjoys it: – But as it is, – Oh! –

BARNWELL. – [*Aside*] *I never observ'd women before, or this is sure the most beautiful of her sex.* – You seem disorder'd, Madam! May I know the cause?

MILLWOOD. Do not ask me, – I can never speak it, whatever is the cause; – I wish for things impossible: – I wou'd be a servant, bound to the same master as you are, to live in one house with you.

BARNWELL. –[*Aside*] *How strange, and yet how kind, her words and actions are! And the effect they have on me is as strange. – I feel desires I never knew before;* – I must be gone, while I have power to go. Madam, I humbly take my leave. –

MILLWOOD. You will not sure leave me so soon!

BARNWELL. Indeed I must.

MILLWOOD. You cannot be so cruel! – I have prepar'd a poor supper, at which I promis'd my self your company.

BARNWELL. I am sorry I must refuse the honour that you design'd me; – But my duty to my master calls me hence. – I never yet neglected his service: He is so gentle, and so good a master, that should I wrong him, tho' he might forgive me, I never should forgive my self.

MILLWOOD. Am I refus'd, by the first man, the second favour I ever stoop'd to ask? – Go then thou proud hard-hearted youth. – But know, you are the only man that cou'd be found, who would let me sue twice for greater favours.

BARNWELL. What shall I do! – How shall I go or stay!

MILLWOOD. Yet do not, do not, leave me. – I wish my sex's pride wou'd meet your scorn: – But when I look upon you, – when I behold those eyes, – Oh! Spare my tongue, and let my blushes speak. – This flood of tears to that will force their way, and declare – what woman's modesty should hide.

BARNWELL. Oh, Heavens! She loves me, worthless as I am; her looks, her words, her flowing tears confess it: – And can I leave her then? – Oh, never, – never. – Madam, dry up those tears. – You shall command me always; – I will stay here for ever, if you'd have me.

LUCY. [*Aside*] *So! She has wheedled him out of his virtue of obedience already, and will strip him of all the rest, one after another, 'till she has left him as few as her Ladyship, or my self.*

MILLWOOD. Now you are kind, indeed; but I mean not to detain you always: I would have you shake off all slavish obedience to your master; – but you may serve him still.

LUCY. [*Aside*] *Serve him still! – Aye, or he'll have no opportunity of fingering his cash, and then he'll not serve your end, I'll be sworn.*

ACT I. SCENE VI.

[*To them*. Blunt.

BLUNT. Madam, supper's on the table.

MILLWOOD. Come, Sir, you'll excuse all defects. – My thoughts were too much employ'd on my guest to observe the entertainment.

ACT I. SCENE VII.

[Lucy *and* Blunt.

BLUNT. What is all this preparation, this elegant supper, variety of wines, and musick, for the entertainment of that young fellow!

LUCY. So it seems.

BLUNT. What is our mistress turn'd fool at last! She's in love with him, I suppose.

LUCY. I suppose not, – but she designs to make him in love with her, if she can.

BLUNT. What will she get by that? He seems under age, and can't be suppos'd to have much money.

LUCY. But his master has; and that's the same thing, as she'll manage it.

BLUNT. I don't like this fooling with a handsome young fellow; while she's endeavouring to ensnare him, she may be caught her self.

LUCY. Nay, were she like me, that would certainly be the consequence; – for, I confess, there is something in youth and innocence that moves me mightily.

BLUNT. Yes, so does the smoothness and plumpness of a partridge move a mighty desire in the hawk to be the destruction of it.

LUCY. Why, birds are their prey, as men are ours; though, as you observ'd, we are sometimes caught our selves: – But that I dare say will never be the case with our mistress.

BLUNT. I wish it may prove so; for you know we all depend upon her: should she trifle away her time with a young fellow, that there's nothing to be got by, we must all starve.

LUCY. There's no danger of that, for I am sure she has no view in this affair, but interest.

BLUNT. Well, and what hopes are there of success in that?

LUCY. The most promising that can be. – 'Tis true, the youth has his scruples; but she'll soon teach him to answer them, by stifling his conscience. – O, the lad is in a hopeful way, depend upon't.

ACT I. SCENE VIII.

[Barnwell *and* Millwood *at an entertainment.*

BARNWELL. What can I answer! – All that I know is, that you are fair, and I am miserable.

MILLWOOD. We are both so, and yet the fault is in our selves.

BARNWELL. To ease our present anguish, by plunging into guilt, is to buy a moment's pleasure with an age of pain.

MILLWOOD. I should have thought the joys of love as lasting as they are great: If ours prove otherwise, 'tis your inconstancy must make them so.

BARNWELL. The law of Heaven will not be revers'd; and that requires us to govern our passions.

MILLWOOD. To give us sense of beauty and desires, and yet forbid us to taste and be happy, is cruelty to nature. – Have we passions only to torment us!

BARNWELL. To hear you talk, – tho' in the cause of vice, – to gaze upon your beauty, – press your hand, – and see your snow-white bosom heave and fall, – enflames my wishes; – my pulse beats high, – my senses all are in a hurry, and I am on the rack of wild desire; – yet for a moment's guilty pleasure, shall I lose my innocence, my peace of mind, and hopes of solid happiness?

MILLWOOD. Chimeras all, –
–Come on with me and prove,
No joy's like woman kind, nor Heav'n like love.

BARNWELL. *I wou'd not,–yet I must on.–*
Reluctant thus, the merchant quits his ease,
And trusts to rocks, and sands, and stormy seas;
In hopes some unknown golden coast to find,
Commits himself, tho' doubtful, to the wind,
Longs much for joys to come, yet mourns those left behind.

ACT II

ACT II. SCENE I.
A room in Thorowgood's house.

[Barnwell.

BARNWELL. How strange are all things round me? Like some thief, who treads forbidden ground, fearful I enter each apartment of this well known house. To guilty love, as if that was too little, already have I added breach of trust. – A thief! – Can I know my self that wretched thing, and look my honest friend and injured master in the face? – Tho' hypocrisy may a while conceal my guilt, at length it will be known, and publick shame and ruin must ensue. In the mean time, what must be my life? Ever to speak a language foreign to my heart; hourly to add to the number of my crimes in order to conceal 'em. – Sure such was the condition of the grand apostate, when first he lost his purity; like me disconsolate he wander'd, and while yet in Heaven, bore all his future hell about him.

ACT II. SCENE II.

[Barnwell *and* Trueman.

TRUEMAN. *Barnwell*! O how I rejoice to see you safe! So will our master and his gentle daughter, who during your absence often inquir'd after you.

BARNWELL. [*Aside*] *Wou'd he were gone, his officious love will pry into the secrets of my soul.*

TRUEMAN. Unless you knew the pain the whole family has felt on your account, you can't conceive how much you are belov'd; but why thus cold and silent? When my heart is full of joy for your return, why do you turn away? Why thus avoid me? What have I done? How am I alter'd since you saw me last? Or rather what have you done? And why are you thus changed? For I am still the same.

BARNWELL. [*Aside*] *What have I done indeed?*

TRUEMAN. Not speak nor look upon me.

BARNWELL. [*Aside*] *By my face he will discover all I wou'd conceal; methinks already I begin to hate him.*

TRUEMAN. I cannot bear this usage from a friend, one whom till now I ever found so loving, whom yet I love, tho' this unkindness strikes at the root of friendship, and might destroy it in any breast but mine.

BARNWELL. I am not well [*Turning to him*] Sleep has been a stranger to these eyes since you beheld them last.

TRUEMAN. Heavy they look indeed, and swoln with tears; – now they o'erflow; – rightly did my sympathizing heart forebode last night when thou wast absent, something fatal to our peace.

BARNWELL. Your friendship ingages you too far. My troubles, whate'er they are, are mine alone, you have no interest in them, nor ought your concern for me give you a moment's pain.

TRUEMAN. You speak as if you knew of friendship nothing but the name. Before I saw your grief I felt it. Since we parted last I have slept no more than you, but pensive in my chamber sat alone, and spent the tedious night in wishes for your safety and return; e'en now, tho' ignorant of the cause, your sorrow wounds me to the heart.

BARNWELL. 'Twill not be always thus, friendship and all engagements cease, as circumstances and occasions vary; and since you once may hate me, perhaps it might be better for us both that now you lov'd me less.

TRUEMAN. Sure I but dream! Without a cause would *Barnwell* use me thus, ungenerous and ungrateful youth farewell, – I shall endeavour to follow your advice, – [*Going*] Yet stay, perhaps I am too rash, and angry when the cause demands compassion. Some unforeseen calamity may have befaln him too great to bear.

BARNWELL. What part am I reduc'd to act; – 'tis vile and base to move his temper thus, the best of friends and men.

TRUEMAN. I am to blame, prithee forgive me *Barnwell.* – Try to compose your ruffled mind, and let me know the cause that thus transports you from your self; my friendly counsel may restore your peace.

BARNWELL. All that is possible for man to do for man, your generous friendship may effect; but here even that's in vain.

TRUEMAN. Something dreadful is labouring in your breast. O give it vent and let me share your grief, 'twill ease your pain shou'd it admit no cure; and make it lighter by the part I bear.

BARNWELL. Vain supposition! My woes increase by being observ'd, shou'd the cause be known they wou'd exceed all bounds.

TRUEMAN. So well I know thy honest heart, guilt cannot harbour there.

BARNWELL. [*Aside*] *O torture insupportable!*

TRUEMAN. Then why am I excluded, have I a thought I would conceal from you?

BARNWELL. If still you urge me on this hated subject, I'll never enter more beneath this roof, nor see your face again.

TRUEMAN. 'Tis strange, – but I have done, say but you hate me not.

BARNWELL. Hate you! – I am not that monster yet.

TRUEMAN. Shall our friendship still continue?

BARNWELL. It's a blessing I never was worthy of, yet now must stand on terms; and but upon conditions can confirm it.

TRUEMAN. What are they?

BARNWELL. Never hereafter, tho' you shou'd wonder at my conduct, desire to know more than I am willing to reveal.

TRUEMAN. 'Tis hard, but upon any conditions I must be your friend.

BARNWELL. Then, as much as one lost to himself can be another's, I am yours. [*Embracing.*

TRUEMAN. Be ever so, and may Heav'n restore your peace.

BARNWELL. Will yesterday return? – We have heard the glorious sun, that till then incessant roll'd, once stopp'd his rapid course, and once went back: the dead have risen; and parched rocks pour'd forth a liquid stream to quench a peoples thirst; the sea divided, and form'd walls of water, while a whole nation pass'd in safety thro' its sandy bosom; hungry lions have refus'd their prey; and men unhurt have walk'd amidst consuming flames; but never yet did time once past, return.

TRUEMAN. Tho' the continued chain of time has never once been broke, nor ever will, but uninterrupted must keep on its course, till lost in eternity it ends there where it first begun; yet as Heav'n can repair whatever evils time can bring upon us, he who trusts Heaven ought never to despair. But business requires our attendance; business the youth's best preservative from ill, as idleness his worst of snares. Will you go with me?

BARNWELL. I'll take a little time to reflect on what has past, and follow you.

ACT II. SCENE III.

BARNWELL. I might have trusted *Trueman* to have applied to my uncle to have repaired the wrong I have done my master; but what of *Millwood*? Must I expose her too? Ungenerous and base! Then Heav'n requires it not. – But Heaven requires that I forsake her. What! Never see her more! Does Heaven require that, – I hope I may see her, and Heav'n not be offended. Presumptuous hope, – dearly already have I prov'd my frailty; should I once more tempt Heav'n, I may be left to fall never to rise again. Yet shall I leave her, for ever leave her, and not let her know the cause? She who loves me with such a boundless passion; can cruelty be duty? I judge of what she then must feel, by what I now indure. The love of life and fear of shame, oppos'd by inclination strong as death or shame, like wind and tide in raging conflict met, when neither can prevail, keep me in doubt. – How then can I determine?

ACT II. SCENE IV.

[Thorowgood *and* Barnwell.

THOROWGOOD. Without a cause assign'd, or notice given, to absent your self last night was a fault, young man, and I came to chide you for it, but hope I am prevented; that modest blush, the confusion so visible in your face, speak grief and shame: when we have offended Heaven, it requires no more; and shall man, who needs himself to be forgiven, be harder to appease: if my pardon or love be of moment to your peace, look up secure of both.

BARNWELL. – [*Aside*] *This goodness has o'er come me.* – O Sir! you know not the nature and extent of my offence; and I shou'd abuse your mistaken bounty to receive 'em. Tho' I had rather die than speak my shame; tho' racks could not have forced the guilty secret from my breast, your kindness has.

THOROWGOOD. Enough, enough, whate'er it be, this concern shews you're convinc'd, and I am satisfied. How painful is the sense of guilt to an ingenuous mind; – some youthful folly, which it were prudent not to enquire into. – When we consider the frail condition of humanity, it may raise our pity, not our wonder, that youth should go astray; when reason, weak at the best when oppos'd to inclination, scarce form'd, and wholly unassisted by experience, faintly contends, or willingly becomes the slave of sense. The state of youth is much to be deplored; and the more so because they see it not; they being then to danger most expos'd, when they are least prepar'd for their defence.

BARNWELL. It will be known, and you recall your pardon and abhor me.

THOROWGOOD. I never will; so Heav'n confirm to me the pardon of my offences. Yet be upon your guard in this gay thoughtless season of your life; now, when the sense of pleasure's quick, and passion high, the voluptuous appetites raging and fierce demand the strongest curb; take heed of a relapse: when vice becomes habitual, the very power of leaving it is lost.

BARNWELL. Hear me then on my knees confess.

THOROWGOOD. I will not hear a syllable more upon this subject; it were not mercy, but cruelty, to hear what must give you such torment to reveal.

BARNWELL. This generosity amazes and distracts me.

THOROWGOOD. This remorse makes thee dearer to me than if thou hadst never offended; whatever is your fault, of this I'm certain, 'twas harder for you to offend than me to pardon.

ACT II. SCENE V.

[Barnwell.

BARNWELL. Villain, villain, villain! Basely to wrong so excellent a man: shou'd I again return to folly – detested thought; – but what of *Millwood* then? – Why, I renounce her, – I give her up; – the struggle's over, and virtue has prevail'd. Reason may convince, but gratitude compels. This unlook'd for generosity has sav'd me from destruction. [*Going.*

ACT II. SCENE VI.

[*Enter a* footman.

FOOTMAN. Sir, two ladies, from your uncle in the country, desire to see you.BARNWELL. – [*Aside*] *Who shou'd they be?* – Tell them I'll wait upon 'em.

ACT II. SCENE VII.

[Barnwell.

BARNWELL. Methinks I dread to see 'em. – Guilt, what a coward hast thou made me? – Now every thing alarms me.

ACT II. SCENE VIII.
Another room in Thorowgood's house.

[Millwood *and* Lucy, *and to them goes a* Footman.

FOOTMAN. Ladies, he'll wait upon you immediately.

MILLWOOD. 'Tis very well. – I thank you.

ACT II. SCENE IX.

[Barnwell, Millwood, *and* Lucy.

BARNWELL. Confusion! *Millwood.*

MILLWOOD. That angry look tells me that here I'm an unwelcome guest; I fear'd as much, – the unhappy are so every where.

BARNWELL. Will nothing but my utter ruin content you?

MILLWOOD. Unkind and cruel! Lost my self, your happiness is now my only care.

BARNWELL. How did you gain admission?

MILLWOOD. Saying we were desir'd by your uncle to visit and deliver a message to you, we were receiv'd by the family without suspicion, and with much respect directed here.

BARNWELL. Why did you come at all?

MILLWOOD. I never shall trouble you more, I'm come to take my leave for ever. Such is the malice of my fate. I go hopeless, despairing ever to return. This hour is all I have left me. One short hour is all I have to bestow on love and you, for whom I thought the longest life too short.

BARNWELL. Then we are met to part for ever?

MILLWOOD. It must be so; – yet think not that time or absence ever shall put a period to my grief, or make me love you less; tho' I must leave you, yet condemn me not.

BARNWELL. Condemn you? No, I approve your resolution, and rejoice to hear it; 'tis just, – 'tis necessary, – I have well weigh'd, and found it so.

LUCY. [*Aside*] *I'm afraid the young man has more sense than she thought he had.*

BARNWELL. Before you came I had determin'd never to see you more.

MILLWOOD. [*Aside*] *Confusion!*

LUCY. [*Aside*] *Ay! we are all out; this is a turn so unexpected, that I shall make nothing of my part, they must e'en play the scene betwixt them-selves.*

MILLWOOD. 'Twas some relief to think, tho' absent, you would love me still; but to find, tho' fortune had been kind, that you, more cruel and inconstant, had resolv'd to cast me off. – This, as I never cou'd expect, I have not learnt to bear.

BARNWELL. I am sorry to hear you blame in me, a resolution that so well becomes us both.

MILLWOOD. I have reason for what I do, but you have none.

BARNWELL. Can we want a reason for parting, who have so many to wish we never had met.

MILLWOOD. Look on me *Barnwell*, am I deform'd or old, that satiety so soon succeeds enjoyment? Nay, look again, am I not she whom yesterday you thought the fairest and the kindest of her sex? Whose hand, trembling with extacy, you prest and moulded thus, while on my eyes you gazed with such delight, as if desire increas'd by being fed.

BARNWELL. No more, let me repent my former follies, if possible, without remembring what they were.

MILLWOOD. Why?

BARNWELL. Such is my frailty that 'tis dangerous.

MILLWOOD. Where is the danger, since we are to part?

BARNWELL. The thought of that already is too painful.

MILLWOOD. If it be painful to part, then I may hope at least you do not hate me?

BARNWELL. No, – no, – I never said I did, – O my heart! –

MILLWOOD. Perhaps you pity me?

BARNWELL. I do, – I do, – indeed, I do.

MILLWOOD. You'll think upon me?

BARNWELL. Doubt it not while I can think at all.

MILLWOOD. You may judge an embrace at parting too great a favour, though it would be the last? [*He draws back*] A look shall then suffice, – farewell for ever.

ACT II. SCENE X.

[Barnwell.

BARNWELL. If to resolve to suffer be to conquer, I have conquer'd. Painful victory!

ACT II. SCENE XI.

[Barnwell, Millwood *and* Lucy.

MILLWOOD. One thing I had forgot, – I never must return to my own house again. This I thought proper to let you know, lest your mind should change, and you shou'd seek in vain to find me there. Forgive me this second intrusion; I only came to give you this caution, and that perhaps was needless.

BARNWELL. I hope it was, yet it is kind, and I must thank you for it.

MILLWOOD. [*To* Lucy] My friend, your arm. Now I am gone for ever. [*Going.*

BARNWELL. One thing more; – sure there's no danger in my knowing where you go? If you think otherwise? –

MILLWOOD. Alas! [*Weeping.*

LUCY. – [*Aside*] *We are right I find, that's my cue.* – Ah; dear sir, she's going she knows not whether; but go she must.

BARNWELL. Humanity obliges me to wish you well; why will you thus expose your self to needless troubles?

LUCY. Nay, there's no help for it: she must quit the town immediately, and the kingdom as soon as possible; it was no small matter you may be sure, that could make her resolve to leave you.

MILLWOOD. No more, my friend; since he for whose dear sake alone I suffer, and am content to suffer, is kind and pities me. Wheree'er I wander through wiles and deserts, benighted and forlorn, that thought shall give me comfort.

BARNWELL. For my sake! O tell me how; which way am I so curs'd as to bring such ruin on thee?

MILLWOOD. No matter, I am contented with my lot.

BARNWELL. Leave me not in this incertainty.[17]

MILLWOOD. I have said too much.

BARNWELL. How, how am I the cause of your undoing?

MILLWOOD. 'Twill but increase your troubles.

BARNWELL. My troubles can't be greater than they are.

LUCY. Well, well, sir, if she won't satisfy you, I will.

BARNWELL. I am bound to you beyond expression.

MILLWOOD. Remember, sir, that I desir'd you not to hear it.

BARNWELL. Begin, and ease my racking expectation.

LUCY. Why you must know, my lady here was an only child; but her parents dying while she was young, left her and her fortune, (no inconsiderable one, I assure you) to the care of a gentleman, who has a good estate of his own.

MILLWOOD. Ay, ay, the barbarous man is rich enough; – but what are riches when compared to love?

LUCY. For a while he perform'd the office of a faithful guardian, settled her in a house, hir'd her servants; – but you have seen in what manner she liv'd, so I need say no more of that.

MILLWOOD. How I shall live hereafter, Heaven knows.

LUCY. All things went on as one cou'd wish, till, some time ago, his wife dying, he fell violently in love with his charge, and wou'd fain have marry'd her: now the man is neither old nor ugly, but a good personable sort of a man, but I don't know how it was she cou'd never endure him; in short, her ill usage so provok'd him, that he brought in an account of his executorship, wherein he makes her debtor to him. –

MILLWOOD. A trifle in it self, but more than enough to ruin me, whom, by this unjust account, he had stripp'd of all before.

LUCY. Now she having neither money, nor friend, except me, who am as unfortunate as her self, he compell'd her to pass his account, and give bond for the sum he demanded; but still provided handsomely for her, and continued his courtship, till being inform'd by his spies (truly I suspect some in her own family) that you were entertain'd at her house, and stay'd with her all night, he came this morning raving, and storming like a madman, talks no more of marriage; so there's no hopes of making up matters that way, but vows her ruin, unless she'll allow him the same favour that he supposes she granted you.[18]

BARNWELL. Must she be ruin'd, or find her refuge in another's arms?

MILLWOOD. He gave me but an hour to resolve in, that's happily spent with you; – and now I go. –

BARNWELL. To be expos'd to all the rigours of the various seasons; the summer's parching heat, and winter's cold, unhous'd to wander friendless thro' the unhospitable world, in misery and want; attended with fear and danger, and pursu'd by malice and revenge, woud'st thou endure all this for me, and can I do nothing, nothing to prevent it?

LUCY. 'Tis really a pity, there can be no way found out.

BARNWELL. O where are all my resolutions now; like early vapours, or the morning dew, chas'd by the sun's warm beams they're vanish'd and lost, as tho' they had never been.

LUCY. Now I advis'd her, sir, to comply with the gentleman, that wou'd not only put an end to her troubles, but make her fortune at once.

BARNWELL. Tormenting fiend, away. – I had rather perish, nay, see her perish, than have her sav'd by him; I will my self prevent her ruin, tho' with my own. A moment's patience, I'll return immediately. –

ACT II. SCENE XII.

[Millwood *and* Lucy.

LUCY. 'Twas well you came, or, by what I can perceive, you had lost him.

MILLWOOD. That, I must confess, was a danger I did not foresee; I was only afraid he should have come without money. You know a house of entertainment, like mine, is not kept with nothing.

LUCY. That's very true; but then you shou'd be reasonable in your demands; 'tis pity to discourage a young man.

ACT II. SCENE XIII.

[Barnwell, Millwood, *and* Lucy.

BARNWELL. What am I about to do! – Now you, who boast your reason all-sufficient, suppose your selves in my condition, and determine for me; whether it's right to let her suffer for my faults, or, by this small addition to my guilt, prevent the ill effects of what is past.

LUCY. These young sinners think every thing in the ways of wickedness so strange, – but I cou'd tell him that this is nothing but what's very common; for one vice as naturally begets another, as a father a son: – But he'll find out that himself, if he lives long enough.

BARNWELL. Here take this, and with it purchase your deliverance; return to your house, and live in peace and safety.

MILLWOOD. So I may hope to see you there again.

BARNWELL. Answer me not, – but fly, – lest in the agonies of my remorse, I take again what is not mine to give, and abandon thee to want and misery.

MILLWOOD. Say but you'll come. –

BARNWELL. You are my fate, my heaven, or my hell; only leave me now, dispose of me hereafter as you please.

ACT II. SCENE XIV.

BARNWELL. What have I done. – Were my resolutions founded on reason, and sincerely made, – why then has Heaven suffer'd me to fall? I sought not the occasion; and, if my heart deceives me not, compassion and generosity were my motives. – Is virtue inconsistent with it self, or are vice and virtue only empty names? Or do they depend on accidents, beyond our power to produce, or to prevent, – wherein we have no part, and yet must be determin'd by the event? – But why should I attempt to reason? All is confusion, horror, and remorse; – I find I am lost, cast down from all my late erected hopes, and plung'd again in guilt, yet scarce know how or why –

Such undistinguish'd horrors make my brain,
Like hell, the seat of darkness, and of pain.

ACT III

ACT III. SCENE I.

[Thorowgood *and* Trueman.

THOROWGOOD. Methinks I wou'd not have you only learn the method of merchandize, and practise it hereafter, merely as a means of getting wealth. – 'Twill be well worth your pains to study it as a science. – See how it is founded in reason, and the nature of things. – How it has promoted humanity, as it has opened and yet keeps up an intercourse between nations, far remote from one another in situation, customs and religion; promoting arts, industry, peace and plenty; by mutual benefits diffusing mutual love from pole to pole.

TRUEMAN. Something of this I have consider'd, and hope, by your assistance, to extend my thoughts much farther. – I have observ'd those countries, where trade is promoted and encouraged, do not make discoveries to destroy, but to improve mankind, – by love and friendship, to tame the fierce, and polish the most savage, – to teach them the advantages of honest traffick, – by taking from them, with their own consent, their useless superfluities, and giving them, in return, what, from their ignorance in manual arts, their situation, or some other accident they stand in need of.

THOROWGOOD. 'Tis justly observ'd: – The populous east, luxuriant, abounds with glittering gems, bright pearls, aromatick spices, and health-restoring drugs: The late found western world[19] glows with unnumber'd veins of gold and silver ore. – On every climate, and on every country, Heaven has bestowed some good peculiar to it self. – It is the industrious merchant's business to collect the various blessings of each soil and climate, and, with the product of the whole, to enrich his native country. – Well! I have examin'd your accounts: they are not only just, as I have always found them, but regularly kept, and fairly enter'd. – I commend your diligence. Method in business is the surest guide. He who neglects it, frequently stumbles, and always wanders perplex'd, uncertain, and in danger. Are *Barnwell*'s accounts ready for my inspection; he does not use to be the last on these occasions.

TRUEMAN. Upon receiving your orders he retir'd, I thought in some confusion. – If you please, I'll go and hasten him. – I hope he hasn't been guilty of any neglect.

THOROWGOOD. I'm now going to the *Exchange*;[20] let him know, at my return, I expect to find him ready.

ACT III. SCENE II.

[Maria *with a book sits and reads.*

MARIA. How forcible is truth? The weakest mind, inspir'd with love of that, – fix'd and collected in it self, – with indifference beholds – the united force of earth and hell opposing: such souls are rais'd above the sense of pain, or so supported, that they regard it not. The martyr cheaply purchases his heaven. – Small are his sufferings, great is his reward; – not so the wretch, who combats love with duty; when the mind, weaken'd and dissolved by the soft passion, feeble and hopeless opposes its own desires. –

What is an hour, a day, a year of pain, to a whole life of tortures, such as these?

ACT III. SCENE III.

[Trueman *and* Maria.

TRUEMAN. O, *Barnwell*! – O, my friend, how art thou fallen?

MARIA. Ha! *Barnwell*! What of him? Speak, say what of *Barnwell*.

TRUEMAN. 'Tis not to be conceal'd. – I've news to tell of him that will afflict your generous father, your self, and all who knew him.

MARIA. Defend us Heaven!

TRUEMAN. I cannot speak it. – See there. [*Gives a letter.*

MARIA. [*Reads*] Trueman, I know my absence will surprize my honour'd master, and your self; and the more, when you shall understand that the reason of my withdrawing, is my having embezzled part of the cash with which I was entrusted. After this, 'tis needless to inform you that I intend never to return again: though this might have been known, by examining my accounts; yet, to prevent that unnecessary trouble, and to cut off all fruitless expectations of my return, I have left this from the lost,

[George Barnwell.

TRUEMAN. Lost indeed! Yet how he shou'd be guilty of what he there charges himself withal, raises my wonder equal to my grief. – Never had youth a higher sense of virtue – justly he thought, and as he thought he practised; never was life more regular than his; an understanding uncommon at his years; an open, generous, manliness of temper; his manners easy, unaffected and engaging.

MARIA. This and much more you might have said with truth. – He was the delight of every eye, and joy of every heart that knew him.

TRUEMAN. Since such he was, and was my friend, can I support his loss? – See the fairest and happiest maid this wealthy city boasts, kindly condescends to weep for thy unhappy fate, poor ruin'd *Barnwell*!

MARIA. *Trueman*, do you think a soul so delicate as his, so sensible of shame, can e'er submit to live a slave to vice?

TRUEMAN. Never, never. So well I know him, I'm sure this act of his, so contrary to his nature, must have been caused by some unavoidable necessity.

MARIA. Is there no means yet to preserve him?

TRUEMAN. O! That there were. – But few men recover reputation lost. – A merchant never. – Nor wou'd he, I fear, though I shou'd find him, ever be brought to look his injur'd master in the face.

MARIA. I fear as much, – and therefore wou'd never have my father know it.

TRUEMAN. That's impossible.

MARIA. What's the sum?

TRUEMAN. 'Tis considerable. – I've mark'd it here, to show it, with the letter, to your father, at his return.

MARIA. If I shou'd supply the money, cou'd you so dispose of that, and the account, as to conceal this unhappy mismanagement from my father.

TRUEMAN. Nothing more easy: – but can you intend it? Will you save a helpless wretch from ruin? Oh! 'Twere an act worthy such exalted virtue, as *Maria*'s. – Sure Heaven, in mercy to my friend, inspired the generous thought.

MARIA. Doubt not but I wou'd purchase so great a happiness at a much dearer price. – But how shall he be found?

TRUEMAN. Trust to my diligence for that. – In the mean time, I'll conceal his absence from your father, or find such excuses for it, that the real cause shall never be suspected.

MARIA. In attempting to save from shame, one whom we hope may yet return to virtue, to Heaven, and you, the judges of this action, I appeal, whether I have done any thing misbecoming my sex and character.

TRUEMAN. Earth must approve the deed, and Heaven, I doubt not, will reward it.

MARIA. If Heaven succeed it, I am well rewarded. A virgin's fame is sullied by suspicion's slightest breath; and therefore as this must be a secret from my father, and the world, for *Barnwell*'s sake; for mine let it be so to him.

ACT III. SCENE IV.
Millwood's house.

[Lucy *and* Blunt.

LUCY. Well! what do you think of *Millwood*'s conduct now!

BLUNT. I own it is surprizing: – I don't know which to admire most, her feign'd, or his real passion; tho' I have sometimes been afraid that her avarice wou'd discover her: – But his youth and want of experience make it the easier to impose on him.

LUCY. No, it is his love. To do him justice, notwithstanding his youth, he don't want understanding; but you men are much easier imposed on, in these affairs, than your vanity will allow you to believe. – Let me see the wisest of you all, as much in love with me, as *Barnwell* is with *Millwood*, and I'll engage to make as great a fool of him.

BLUNT. And all circumstances consider'd, to make as much money of him too.

LUCY. I can't answer for that. Her artifice in making him rob his master at first, and the various stratagems, by which she has obliged him to continue in that course, astonish even me, who know her so well. –

BLUNT. But then you are to consider that the money was his master's.

LUCY. There was the difficulty of it. – Had it been his own, it had been nothing. – Were the world his, she might have it for a smile: – but these golden days are done; – he's ruin'd, and *Millwood*'s hopes of farther profits there, are at an end.

BLUNT. That's no more than we all expected.

LUCY. Being call'd, by his master, to make up his accounts, he was forc'd to quit his house and service, and wisely flies to *Millwood* for relief and entertainment.

BLUNT. I have not heard of this before! How did she receive him?

LUCY. As you wou'd expect. – She wonder'd what he meant, was astonish'd at his impudence, – and, with an air of modesty peculiar to her self, swore so heartily, that she never saw him before, – that she put me out of countenance.

BLUNT. That's much indeed! But how did *Barnwell* behave?

LUCY. He griev'd, and, at length, enrag'd at this barbarous treatment, was preparing to be gone; and, making toward the door, show'd a bag of money, which he had stol'n from his master, – the last he's ever like to have from thence.

BLUNT. But then *Millwood*?

LUCY. Aye, she, with her usual address, return'd to her old arts of lying, swearing, and dissembling. – Hung on his neck, and wept, and swore 'twas meant in jest; till the easy fool, melted into tears, threw the money into her lap, and swore he had rather die, than think her false.

BLUNT. Strange infatuation!

LUCY. But what follow'd was stranger still. As doubts and fears, follow'd by reconcilement, ever increase love, where the passion is sincere; so in him it caus'd so wild a transport of excessive fondness, such joy, such grief, such pleasure, and such anguish, that nature in him seem'd sinking with the weight, and the charm'd soul dispos'd to quit his breast for hers, – just then, when every passion with lawless anarchy prevail'd, – and reason was in the raging tempest lost; – the cruel artful *Millwood* prevail'd upon the wretched youth to promise what I tremble but to think on.

BLUNT. I am amaz'd! What can it be?

LUCY. You will be more so, to hear it is to attempt the life of his nearest relation, and best benefactor. –

BLUNT. His uncle, whom we have often heard him speak of, as a gentleman of a large estate and fair character in the country, where he lives.

LUCY. The same. – She was no sooner possess'd of the last dear purchase of his ruin, but her avarice, insatiate as the grave, demands this horrid sacrifice – *Barnwell*'s near relation, and unsuspected virtue must give too easy means to seize the good man's treasure; whose blood must seal the dreadful secret, and prevent the terrors of her guilty fears.

BLUNT. Is it possible she cou'd perswade him to do an act like that! He is, by nature, honest, grateful, compassionate, and generous: and though his love, and her artful persuasions, have wrought him to practise what he most abhors; yet we all can witness for him, with what reluctance he has still comply'd! So many tears he shed o'er each offence, as might, if possible, sanctify theft, and make a merit of a crime.

LUCY. 'Tis true, at the naming the murder of his uncle, he started into rage; and, breaking from her arms, where she till then had held him, with well dissembled love and false endearments, call'd her, cruel monster, devil, and told her she was born for his destruction. – She thought it not for her purpose to meet his rage with rage, but affected a most passionate fit of grief; – rail'd at her fate, and curs'd her wayward stars, – that still her wants shou'd force her to press him to act such deeds, as she must needs abhor, as well as he; but told him necessity had no law, and love no bounds; that therefore he never truly lov'd, but meant, in her necessity, to forsake her; – then kneel'd and swore, that since, by his refusal, he had given her cause to doubt his love, she never wou'd see him more; unless, to prove it true, he robb'd his uncle to supply her wants, and murder'd him, to keep it from discovery.

BLUNT. I am astonish'd! What said he?

LUCY. Speechless he stood; but in his face you might have read, that various passions tore his very soul. Oft he, in anguish, threw his eyes towards Heaven, and then as often bent their beams on her; then wept and groan'd, and beat his breast; at length, with horror, not to be express'd, he cry'd, thou cursed fair! Have I not given dreadful proofs of love! What drew me from my youthful innocence, to stain my then unspotted soul, but love? What caus'd me to rob my gentle master, but cursed love? What makes me now a fugitive from his service, loath'd by my self, and scorn'd by all the world, but love? What fills my eyes with tears, my soul with torture, never felt on this side death before? Why love, love, love. And why, above all, do I resolve, (for, tearing his hair, he cry'd I do resolve) to kill my uncle.

BLUNT. Was she not mov'd? It makes me weep to hear the sad relation.

LUCY. Yes, with joy, that she had gain'd her point. – She gave him no time to cool, but urg'd him to attempt it instantly. He's now gone; if he performs it, and escapes, there's more money for her; if not, he'll ne'er return, and then she's fairly rid of him.

BLUNT. 'Tis time the world was rid of such a monster. –

LUCY. If we don't do our endeavours to prevent this murder, we are as bad as she.

BLUNT. I'm afraid it is too late.

LUCY. Perhaps not. – Her barbarity to *Barnwell* makes me hate her. – We've run too great a length with her already. – I did not think her or my self so wicked, as I find, upon reflection, we are.

BLUNT. 'Tis true, we have all been too much so. – But there is something so horrid in murder, – that all other crimes seem nothing when compared to that. – I wou'd not be involv'd in the guilt of that for all the world.

LUCY. Nor I, Heaven knows; – therefore let us clear our selves, by doing all that is in our power to prevent it. I have just thought of a way, that, to me, seems probable. – Will you join with me to detect this curs'd design?

BLUNT. With all my heart. – How else shall I clear my self? He who knows of a murder intended to be committed, and does not discover it, in the eye of the law, and reason, is a murderer.

LUCY. Let us lose no time; – I'll acquaint you with the particulars as we go.

ACT III. SCENE V.
A walk at some distance from a country seat.

BARNWELL. A dismal gloom obscures the face of day; either the sun has slip'd behind a cloud, or journeys down the west of Heaven, with more than common speed, to avoid the sight of what I'm doom'd to act. Since I set forth on this accursed design, where'er I tread, methinks, the solid earth trembles beneath my feet. – Yonder limpid stream, whose hoary fall has made a natural cascade, as I pass'd by, in doleful accents seem'd to murmur, murder. The earth, the air, and water, seem concern'd; but that's not strange, the world is punish'd, and nature feels the shock, when providence permits a good man's fall! – Just Heaven! Then what shou'd I be! For him that was my father's only brother, and since his death has been to me a father, who took me up an infant, and an orphan; rear'd me with tenderest care, and still indulged me with most paternal fondness; – yet here I stand avow'd his destin'd murderer: – I stiffen with horror at my own impiety; – 'tis yet unperform'd. – What if I quit my bloody purpose, and fly the place! [*Going, then stops*] – But whether, O whether, shall I fly! – My master's once friendly doors are ever shut against me; and without money *Millwood* will never see me more, and life is not to be endured without her: – She's got such firm possession of my heart, and governs there with such despotick sway; – Aye, there's the cause of all my sin and sorrow: – 'Tis more than love; 'tis the fever of the soul, and madness of desire. – In vain does nature, reason, conscience, all oppose it; the impetuous passion bears down all before it, and drives me on to lust, to theft, and murder. – Oh conscience! feeble guide to virtue, who only shows us when we go astray, but wants the power to stop us in our course. – Ha! in yonder shady walk I see my uncle. – He's alone. – Now for my disguise. – [*Plucks out a vizor.*[21]] This is his hour of private meditation. Thus daily he prepares his soul for Heaven, – whilst I – But what have I to do with Heaven! – Ha! No struggles, conscience. –

> Hence! Hence remorse, and ev'ry thought that's good;
> The storm that lust began, must end in blood.

[*Puts on the vizor, and draws a pistol.*

ACT III. SCENE VI.
A close walk in a wood.

UNCLE. If I was superstitious, I shou'd fear some danger lurk'd unseen, or death were nigh: – a heavy melancholy clouds my spirits; my imagination is fill'd with gashly[22] forms of dreary graves, and bodies chang'd by death, – when the pale lengthen'd visage attracts each weeping eye, – and fills the musing soul, at once, with grief and horror, pity and aversion. – I will indulge the thought. The wise man prepares himself for death, by making it familiar to his mind. – When strong reflections hold the mirror near, – and the living in the dead behold their future selves, how does each inordinate passion and desire cease or sicken at the view? – The mind scarce moves; – the blood, curdling, and chill'd, creeps slowly thro' the veins, – fix'd, still, and motionless, like the solemn object of our thoughts. – We are almost at present – what we must be hereafter, 'till curiosity awakes the soul, and sets it on inquiry. –

ACT III. SCENE VII.

[Uncle, George Barnwell *at a distance.*

UNCLE. O Death, thou strange mysterious power, – seen every day, yet never understood – but by the incommunicative dead, what art thou? – The extensive mind of man, that with a thought circles the earth's vast globe, – sinks to the centre, or ascends above the stars; that world's exotick finds, or thinks it finds, – thy thick clouds attempts to pass in vain, lost and bewilder'd in the horrid gloom, – defeated she returns more doubtful than before; of nothing certain, but of labour lost. [*During this speech,* Barnwell *sometimes presents the pistol, and draws it back again*]

BARNWELL. Oh, 'tis impossible! [Barnwell *drops the pistol, at which his Uncle starts, and draws his sword.*

UNCLE. A man so near me, arm'd and masqu'd!

BARNWELL. Nay, then there's no retreat. [*Plucks a poniard from his bosom, and stabs him.*

UNCLE. Oh! I am slain! All gracious Heaven regard the prayer of thy dying servant. Bless, with thy choicest blessings, my dearest nephew; forgive my murderer, and take my fleeting soul to endless mercy. [Barnwell *throws off his mask, runs to him, and, kneeling by him, raises and chases him*]

BARNWELL. Expiring Saint! Oh, murder'd, martyr'd uncle! Lift up your dying eyes, and view your nephew in your murderer. – O do not look so tenderly upon me. – Let indignation lighten from your eyes, and blast me e're you die. – By Heaven, he weeps in pity of my woes. – Tears, – tears, for blood. – The murder'd, in the agonies of death, weeps for his murderer. – O, speak your pious purpose, – pronounce my pardon then, – and take me with you. – He wou'd, but cannot. – O why, with such fond affection do you press my murdering hand! – What! will you kiss me! [*Kisses him.* Uncle *groans and dies.*

BARNWELL. He's gone for ever, – and oh! I follow. – [*Swoons away upon his* Uncle*'s dead body*] Do I still live to press the suffering bosom of the earth? – Do I still breathe, and taint with my infectious breathe the wholesome air! – Let Heaven, from its high throne, in justice or in mercy, now look down on that dear murder'd saint, and me the murderer. – And, if his vengeance spares, – let pity strike and end my wretched being. – Murder the worst of crimes, and parricide the worst of murders, and this the worst of parricides. *Cain,* who stands on record from the birth of time, and must to its last final period, as accurs'd, slew a brother, favour'd above him. – Detested *Nero,* by another's hand, dispatch'd a mother, that he fear'd and hated. – But I, with my own hand, have murder'd a brother, mother, father, and a friend; most loving and belov'd. – This execrable act of mine's without a parallel. – O may it ever stand alone, – the last of murders, as it is the worst. –

The rich man thus, in torment and despair,
Prefer'd his vain, but charitable prayer.
The fool, his own soul lost, wou'd fain be wise
For others good; but Heaven his suit denies.
By laws and means well known we stand or fall,
And one eternal rule remains for all.

ACT IV

ACT IV. SCENE I.

[Maria.

MARIA. How falsly do they judge who censure or applaud, as we're afflicted or rewarded here. I know I am unhappy, yet cannot charge my self with any crime, more than the common frailties of our kind, that shou'd provoke just Heaven to mark me out for sufferings so uncommon and severe. Falsly to accuse our selves, Heaven must abhor, then it is just and right that innocence should suffer; for Heaven must be just in all its ways. – Perhaps by that they are kept from moral evils, much worse than penal, or more improv'd in virtue: or may not the lesser ills that they sustain, be the means of greater good to others? Might all the joyless days and sleepless nights that I have past, but purchase peace for thee –

Thou dear, dear cause of all my grief and pain,
Small were the loss, and infinite the gain:
Tho' to the grave in secret love I pine,
So life, and fame, and happiness were thine.

ACT IV. SCENE II.

[Trueman *and* Maria.

MARIA. What news of *Barnwell*?

TRUEMAN. None. – I have sought him with the greatest diligence, but all in vain.

MARIA. Doth my father yet suspect the cause of his absenting himself?

TRUEMAN. All appear'd so just and fair to him, it is not possible he ever shou'd; but his absence will no longer be conceal'd. Your father's wise; and though he seems to hearken to the friendly excuses, I wou'd make for *Barnwell*; yet, I am afraid, he regards 'em only as such, without suffering them to influence his judgment.

MARIA. How does the unhappy youth defeat all our designs to serve him, yet I can never repent what we have done. Shou'd he return, 'twill make his reconciliation with my father easier, and preserve him from future reproach from a malicious unforgiving world.

ACT IV. SCENE III.

[Thorowgood *and* Lucy, *to* Maria *and* Trueman.

THOROWGOOD. This woman here has given me a sad, (and bating some circumstances) too probable account of *Barnwell*'s defection.

LUCY. I am sorry, Sir, that my frank confession of my former unhappy course of life shou'd cause you to suspect my truth on this occasion.

THOROWGOOD. It is not that; your confession has in it all the appearance of truth. [*To them*] Among many other particulars, she informs me that *Barnwell* has been influenc'd to break his trust, and wrong me, at several times, of considerable sums of money; now, as I know this to be false, I wou'd fain doubt the whole of her relation, – too dreadful – to be willingly believ'd.

MARIA. Sir, your pardon; I find my self on a sudden so indispos'd, that I must retire. – [*Aside*] *Providence opposes all attempts to save him. – Poor ruin'd Barnwell! – wretched lost* Maria*! –*

ACT IV. SCENE IV.

[Thorowgood, Trueman *and* Lucy.

THOROWGOOD. How am I distress'd on every side? Pity for that unhappy youth, fear for the life of a much valued friend – and then my child – the only joy and hope of my declining life. Her melancholy increases hourly, and gives me painful apprehensions of her loss. – O *Trueman*! this person informs me, that your friend, at the instigation of an impious woman, is gone to rob and murder his venerable uncle.

TRUEMAN. O execrable deed, I am blasted with the horror of the thought.

LUCY. This delay may ruin all.

THOROWGOOD. What to do or think I know not; that he ever wrong'd me, I know is false, – the rest may be so too, there's all my hope.

TRUEMAN. Trust not to that, rather suppose all true than lose a moment's time; even now the horrid deed may be a doing; – dreadful imagination; – or it may be done, and we are vainly debating on the means to prevent what is already past.

THOROWGOOD. This earnestness convinces me that he knows more than he has yet discover'd. What ho! Without there! Who waits?

ACT IV. SCENE V.

[*A* servant.

THOROWGOOD. Order the groom to saddle the swiftest horse, and prepare himself to set out with speed. – An affair of life and death demands his diligence.

ACT IV. SCENE VI.

[Thorowgood, Trueman *and* Lucy.

THOROWGOOD. For you, whose behaviour on this occasion I have no time to commend as it deserves, I must engage your farther assistance. – Return and observe this *Millwood* till I come. I have your directions, and will follow you as soon as possible.

ACT IV. SCENE VII.

[Thorowgood *and* Trueman.

THOROWGOOD. *Trueman*, you I am sure wou'd not be idle on this occasion.

ACT IV. SCENE VIII.

TRUEMAN. He only who is a friend can judge of my distress.

ACT IV. SCENE IX.
Millwood's house.

MILLWOOD. I wish I knew the event of his design; – the attempt without success would ruin him. – Well! what have I to apprehend from that? I fear too much. The mischief being only intended, his friends, in pity of his youth, turn all their rage on me. I should have thought of that before. – Suppose the deed done, then, and then only I shall be secure; or what if he returns without attempting it at all?

ACT IV. SCENE X.

[Millwood, *and* Barnwell *bloody*.

MILLWOOD. But he is here, and I have done him wrong; his bloody hands show he has done the deed, but show he wants the prudence to conceal it.

BARNWELL. Where shall I hide me? Whether shall I fly to avoid the swift unerring hand of justice?

MILLWOOD. Dismiss those fears; tho' thousands had pursu'd you to the door, yet being enter'd here you are safe as innocence; I have such a cavern, by art so cunningly contriv'd, that the piercing eyes of jealousy and revenge may search in vain, nor find the entrance to the safe retreat, there will I hide you if any danger's near.[23]

BARNWELL. O hide me from my self if it be possible; for while I bear my conscience in my bosom, tho' I were hid where man's eye never saw, nor light e'er dawn'd, 'twere all in vain. For that inmate, – that impartial judge, will try, convict, and sentence me for murder; and execute me with never ending torments. Behold these hands all crimson'd o'er with my dear uncle's blood! Here's a sight to make a statue start with horror, or turn a living man into a statue.

MILLWOOD. Ridiculous! Then it seems you are afraid of your own shadow; or what's less than a shadow, your conscience.

BARNWELL. Tho' to man unknown I did the accursed act, what can we hide from Heav'ns omniscient eye?

MILLWOOD. No more of this stuff; – what advantage have you made of his death? Or what advantage may yet be made of it? – Did you secure the keys of his treasure, – those no doubt were about him? – What gold, what jewels, or what else of value have you brought me?

BARNWELL. Think you I added sacrilege to murder? Oh! Had you seen him as his life flowed from him in a crimson flood, and heard him praying for me by the double name of nephew and of murderer; alas, alas! he knew not then that his nephew was his murderer; how wou'd you have wish'd as I did, tho' you had a thousand years of life to come, to have given them all to have lengthen'd his one hour. But being dead, I fled the sight of what my hands had done, nor cou'd I to have gain'd the empire of the world, have violated by theft his sacred corps.

MILLWOOD. Whining preposterous canting villain, to murder your uncle, rob him of life, nature's first, last, dear prerogative, after which there's no injury, then fear to take what he no longer wanted; and bring to me your penury and guilt. Do you think I'll hazard my reputation; nay my life to entertain you?

BARNWELL. Oh! – *Millwood*! – This from thee; – but I have done, – if you hate me, if you wish me dead; then are you happy, – for Oh! 'tis sure my grief will quickly end me.

MILLWOOD. In his madness he will discover all, and involve me in his ruin; – we are on a precipice from whence there's no retreat for both, – then to preserve my self. – [*Pauses*] There is no other way, – 'tis dreadful, – but reflection comes too late when danger's pressing, – and there's no room for choice. – It must be done. [*Stamps*.

ACT IV. SCENE XI.

[*Enter a* servant.

MILLWOOD. Fetch me an officer and seize this villain, he has confess'd himself a murderer, shou'd I let him escape, I justly might be thought as bad as he.

ACT IV. SCENE XII.

[Millwood *and* Barnwell.

BARNWELL. O *Millwood*! Sure thou dost not, cannot mean it. Stop the messenger, upon my knees I beg you, call him back. 'Tis fit I die indeed, but not by you. I will this instant deliver my self into the hands of justice, indeed I will, for death is all I wish. But thy ingratitude so tears my wounded soul, 'tis worse ten thousand times than death with torture.

MILLWOOD. Call it what you will, I am willing to live; and live secure; which nothing but your death can warrant.

BARNWELL. If there be a pitch of wickedness that seats the author beyond the reach of vengeance, you must be secure. But what remains for me, but a dismal dungeon, hard-galling fetters, an awful tryal, and ignominious death, justly to fall unpitied and abhorr'd? – After death to be suspended between Heaven and Earth, a dreadful spectacle, the warning and horror of a gaping crowd. This I cou'd bear, nay wish not to avoid, had it but come from any hand but thine. –

ACT IV. SCENE XIII.

[Millwood, Barnwell, Blunt, Officer *and attendants*.

MILLWOOD. Heaven defend me! Conceal a murderer! Here, Sir, take this youth into your custody, I accuse him of murder; and will appear to make good my charge.

[*They seize him*.

BARNWELL. To whom, of what, or how shall I complain; I'll not accuse her, the hand of Heav'n is in it, and this the punishment of lust and parricide; yet Heav'n that justly cuts me off, still suffers her to live, perhaps to punish others; tremendous mercy! So fiends are curs'd with immortality, to be the executioners of Heaven. –

Be warn'd ye youths, who see my sad despair,
Avoid lewd women, false as they are fair,
By reason guided, honest joys pursue,
The fair to honour, and to virtue true,
Just to her self, will ne'er be false to you.
By my example learn to shun my fate,
(How wretched is the man who's wise too late?)
E'er innocence, and fame, and life be lost,
Here purchase wisdom, cheaply, at my cost.[24]

ACT IV. SCENE XIV.

[Millwood *and* Blunt.

MILLWOOD. Where's *Lucy*, why is she absent at such a time?

BLUNT. Wou'd I had been so too, thou Devil!

MILLWOOD. Insolent! This to me?

BLUNT. The worst that we know of the devil is, that he first seduces to sin, and then betrays to punishment.

ACT IV. SCENE XV.

MILLWOOD. They disapprove of my conduct, – and mean to take this opportunity to set up for themselves. – My ruin is resolv'd, – I see my danger, but scorn both it and them. – I was not born to fall by such weak instruments. – [*Going*.

ACT IV. SCENE XVI.

[Thorowgood *and* Millwood.

THOROWGOOD. Where is this scandal of her own sex, and curse of ours?

MILLWOOD. What means this insolence? Who do you seek?

THOROWGOOD. *Millwood*.

MILLWOOD. Well, you have found her then. – I am *Millwood*. –

THOROWGOOD. Then you are the most impious wretch that e'er the sun beheld.

MILLWOOD. From your appearance I shou'd have expected wisdom and moderation, but your manners bely your aspect. – What is your business here? I know you not.

THOROWGOOD. Hereafter you may know me better; I am *Barnwell*'s master.

MILLWOOD. Then you are master to a villain; which, I think, is not much to your credit.

THOROWGOOD. Had he been as much above thy arts, as my credit is superior to thy malice, I need not blush to own him.

MILLWOOD. My arts; – I don't understand you, Sir! If he has done amiss, what's that to me? Was he my servant, or yours? – You shou'd have taught him better.

THOROWGOOD. Why shou'd I wonder to find such uncommon impudence in one arriv'd to such a height of wickedness. – When innocence is banish'd, modesty soon follows. Know, sorceress, I'm not ignorant of any of your arts, by which you first deceiv'd the unwary youth: I know how, step by step, you've led him on, (reluctant and unwilling) from crime to crime, to this last horrid act, which you contriv'd, and, by your curs'd wiles, even forced him to commit, and then betray'd him.

MILLWOOD. [*Aside*] *Ha! Lucy has got the advantage of me, and accused me first, unless I can turn the accusation, and fix it upon her and Blunt, I am lost.*

THOROWGOOD. Had I known your cruel design sooner, it had been prevented. To see you punish'd as the law directs, is all that now remains. – Poor satisfaction, – for he, innocent as he is, compared to you, must suffer too. But Heaven, who knows our frame, and graciously distinguishes between frailty and presumption, will make a difference, tho' man cannot, who sees not the heart, but only judges by the outward action. –

MILLWOOD. I find, Sir, we are both unhappy in our servants. I was surpriz'd at such ill treatment, from a gentleman of your appearance, without cause, and therefore too hastily return'd it; for which I ask your pardon. I now perceive you have been so far impos'd on, as to think me engaged in a former correspondence with your servant, and, some way or other, accessary to his undoing.

THOROWGOOD. I charge you as the cause, the sole cause of all his guilt, and all his suffering, of all he now endures, and must endure, till a violent and shameful death shall put a dreadful period to his life and miseries together.

MILLWOOD. 'Tis very strange; but who's secure from scandal and detraction? – So far from contributing to his ruin, I never spoke to him till since that fatal accident, which I lament as much as you: 'tis true, I have a servant, on whose account he has of late frequented my house; if she has abus'd my good opinion of her, am I to blame? Hasn't *Barnwell* done the same by you?

THOROWGOOD. I hear you; pray go on.

MILLWOOD. I have been inform'd he had a violent passion for her, and she for him; but I always thought it innocent; I know her poor, and given to expensive pleasures. Now who can tell but she may have influenced the amorous youth to commit this murder, to supply her extravagancies, it must be so. – I now recollect a thousand circumstances that confirm it: I'll have her and a man servant, that I suspect as an accomplice, secured immediately. I hope, Sir, you will lay aside your ill-grounded suspicions of me, and join to punish the real contrivers of this bloody deed. [*Offers to go.*

THOROWGOOD. Madam, you pass not this way: I see your design, but shall protect them from your malice.

MILLWOOD. I hope you will not use your influence, and the credit of your name, to skreen such guilty wretches. Consider, Sir! The wickedness of perswading a thoughtless youth to such a crime.

THOROWGOOD. I do, – and of betraying him when it was done.

MILLWOOD. That which you call betraying him, may convince you of my innocence. She who loves him, tho' she contriv'd the murder, would never have deliver'd him into the hands of justice, as I (struck with the horror of his crimes) have done. –

THOROWGOOD. How shou'd an unexperienc'd youth escape her snares; the powerful magick of her wit and form, might betray the wisest to simple dotage, and fire the blood that age had froze long since. Even I, that with just prejudice came prepared, had, by her artful story, been deceiv'd, but that my strong conviction of her guilt makes even a doubt impossible. Those whom subtilly you wou'd accuse, you know are your accusers; and what proves unanswerably, their innocence, and your guilt; they accus'd you before the deed was done, and did all that was in their power to have prevented it.

MILLWOOD. Sir, you are very hard to be convinc'd; but I have such a proof, which, when produced, will silence all objections.

ACT IV. SCENE XVII.

[Thorowgood, Lucy, Trueman, Blunt, Officers, *&c.*

LUCY. Gentlemen, pray place your selves, some on one side of that door, and some on the other; watch her entrance, and act as your prudence shall direct you. – This way – [*To* Thorowgood] and note her behaviour; I have observ'd her, she's driven to the last extremity, and is forming some desperate resolution. – I guess at her design. –

ACT IV. SCENE XVIII.

[*To them,* Millwood *with a pistol,* – Trueman *secures her.*

TRUEMAN. Here thy power of doing mischief ends; deceitful, cruel, bloody woman!

MILLWOOD. Fool, hypocrite, villain. – Man! thou can'st not call me that.

TRUEMAN. To call thee woman, were to wrong the sex, thou devil!

MILLWOOD. That imaginary being is an emblem of thy cursed sex collected. A mirror, wherein each particular man may see his own likeness, and that of all mankind.

TRUEMAN. Think not by aggravating the fault of others to extenuate thy own, of which the abuse of such uncommon perfections of mind and body is not the least.

MILLWOOD. If such I had, well may I curse your barbarous sex, who robb'd me of 'em, e'er I knew their worth, then left me, too late, to count their value by their loss. Another and another spoiler came, and all my gain was poverty and reproach. My soul disdain'd, and yet disdains dependance and contempt. Riches, no matter by what means obtain'd, I saw secur'd the worst of men from both; I found it therefore necessary to be rich; and, to that end, I summon'd all my arts. You call 'em wicked, be it so, they were such as my conversation with your sex had furnish'd me withal.

THOROWGOOD. Sure none but the worst of men convers'd with thee.

MILLWOOD. Men of all degrees and all professions I have known, yet found no difference, but in their several capacities; all were alike wicked to the utmost of their power. In pride, contention, avarice, cruelty, and revenge, the reverend priesthood were my unerring guides. From suburb-magistrates, who live by ruin'd reputations, as the unhospitable natives of *Cornwall* do by ship-wrecks, I learn'd, that to charge my innocent neighbours with my crimes, was to merit their protection; for to skreen the guilty, is the less scandalous, when many are suspected, and detraction, like darkness and death, blackens all objects, and levels all distinction. Such are your venal magistrates, who favour none but such as, by their office, they are sworn to punish: With them not to be guilty, is the worst of crimes; and large fees privately paid, is every needful virtue.

THOROWGOOD. Your practice has sufficiently discover'd your contempt of laws, both human and Divine; no wonder then that you shou'd hate the officers of both.

MILLWOOD. I hate you all. I know you, and expect no mercy; nay, I ask for none; I have done nothing that I am sorry for; I follow'd my inclinations, and that the best of you does every day. All actions are alike natural and indifferent to man and beast, who devour, or are devour'd, as they meet with others weaker or stronger than themselves.

THOROWGOOD. What pity it is, a mind so comprehensive, daring and inquisitive, shou'd be a stranger to religion's sweet, but powerful charms.

MILLWOOD. I am not fool enough to be an atheist, tho' I have known enough of men's hypocrisy to make a thousand simple women so. Whatever religion is in it self, as practis'd by mankind, it has caus'd the evils, you say, it was design'd to cure. War, plague, and famine, has not destroy'd so many of the human race, as this pretended piety has done; and with such barbarous cruelty, as if the only way to honour Heaven, were to turn the present world into Hell.

THOROWGOOD. Truth is truth, tho' from an enemy, and spoke in malice. You bloody, blind, and superstitious bigots, how will you answer this?

MILLWOOD. What are your laws, of which you make your boast, but the fool's wisdom, and the coward's valour; the instrument and skreen of all your villanies, by which you punish in others what you act your selves, or wou'd have acted, had you been in their circumstances. The judge who condemns the poor man for being a thief, had been a thief himself had he been poor. Thus you go on deceiving, and being deceiv'd, harrassing, plaguing, and destroying one another; but women are your universal prey.

Women, by whom you are, the source of joy,
With cruel arts you labour to destroy:
A thousand ways our ruin you pursue,
Yet blame in us those arts, first taught by you.

O may, from hence, each violated maid,
By flatt'ring, faithless, barb'rous man betray'd;
When robb'd of innocence, and virgin fame,
From your destruction raise a nobler name;
To right their sex's wrongs devote their mind,
And future Millwoods prove to plague mankind.

ACT V

ACT V. SCENE I.
A room in a prison.

[Thorowgood, Blunt *and* Lucy.

THOROWGOOD. I have recommended to *Barnwell* a reverend divine, whose judgment and integrity I am well acquainted with; nor has *Millwood* been neglected, but she, unhappy woman, still obstinate, refuses his assistance.

LUCY. This pious charity to the afflicted well becomes your character; yet pardon me, Sir, if I wonder you were not at their trial.

THOROWGOOD. I knew it was impossible to save him, and I and my family bear so great a part in his distress, that to have been present wou'd have aggravated our sorrows without relieving his.

BLUNT. It was mournful indeed. *Barnwell*'s youth and modest deportment, as he past, drew tears from every eye: when placed at the bar, and arraigned before the reverend judges, with many tears and interrupting sobs he confess'd and aggravated his offences, without accusing, or once reflecting on *Millwood*, the shameless author of his ruin; who dauntless and unconcern'd stood by his side, viewing with visible pride and contempt the vast assembly, who all with sympathizing sorrow wept for the wretched youth. *Millwood* when called upon to answer, loudly insisted upon her innocence, and made an artful and a bold defence; but finding all in vain, the impartial jury and the learned bench concurring to find her guilty, how did she curse her self, poor *Barnwell*, us, her judges, all mankind; but what cou'd that avail? She was condemn'd, and is this day to suffer with him.

THOROWGOOD. The time draws on, I am going to visit *Barnwell*, as you are *Millwood*.

LUCY. We have not wrong'd her, yet I dread this interview. She's proud, impatient, wrathful, and unforgiving. To be the branded instruments of vengeance, to suffer in her shame, and sympathize with her in all she suffers, is the tribute we must pay for our former ill spent lives, and long confederacy with her in wickedness.

THOROWGOOD. Happy for you it ended when it did. What you have done against *Millwood* I know proceeded from a just abhorrence of her crimes, free from interest, malice, or revenge. Proselytes to virtue shou'd be encourag'd. Pursue your proposed reformation, and know me hereafter for your friend.

LUCY. This is a blessing as unhop'd for as unmerited, but Heaven that snatched us from impending ruin, sure intends you as its instrument to secure us from apostacy.

THOROWGOOD. With gratitude to impute your deliverance to Heaven is just. Many, less virtuously dispos'd than *Barnwell* was, have never fallen in the manner he has done, – may not such owe their safety rather to providence than to themselves. With pity and compassion let us judge him. Great were his faults, but strong was the temptation. Let his ruin learn us diffidence, humanity and circumspection; – for we, – who wonder at his fate, – perhaps had we like him, been tryed, – like him, we had fallen too.

ACT V. SCENE II.
A dungeon, a table and lamp.

[Thorowgood, Barnwell *reading*.

THOROWGOOD. See there the bitter fruits of passion's detested reign, and sensual appetite indulg'd. Severe reflections, penitence and tears.

BARNWELL. My honoured injured master, whose goodness has covered me a thousand times with shame, forgive this last unwilling disrespect, – indeed I saw you not.

THOROWGOOD. 'Tis well, I hope you were better imploy'd in viewing of your self; – your journey's long, your time for preparation almost spent. – I sent a reverend divine to teach you to improve it, and shou'd be glad to hear of his success.

BARNWELL. The word of truth, which he recommended for my constant companion in this my sad retirement, has at length remov'd the doubts I labour'd under. From thence I've learn'd the infinite extent of heavenly mercy; that my offences, tho' great, are not unpardonable; and that 'tis not my interest only, but my duty to believe and to rejoice in that hope, – So shall Heaven receive the glory, and future penitents the profit of my example.

THOROWGOOD. Go on. – How happy am I who live to see this?

BARNWELL. 'Tis wonderful, – that words shou'd charm despair, speak peace and pardon to a murderer's conscience; – but truth and mercy flow in every sentence, attended with force and energy divine. How shall I describe my present state of mind? I hope in doubt, – and trembling I rejoice. – I feel my grief increase, even as my fears give way. – Joy and gratitude now supply more tears, than the horror and anguish of despair before.

THOROWGOOD. These are the genuine signs of true repentance, the only preparatory, certain way to everlasting peace. – O the joy it gives to see a soul form'd and prepar'd for Heaven! – For this the faithful minister devotes himself to meditation, abstinence and prayer, shunning the vain delights of sensual joys, and daily dies that others may live for ever. – For this he turns the sacred volumes o'er, and spends his life in painful search of truth. – The love of riches and the lust of power, he looks on with just contempt and detestation; who only counts for wealth the souls he wins; and whose highest ambition is to serve mankind. – If the reward of all his pains be to preserve one soul from wandering, or turn one from the error of his ways, how does he then rejoice, and own his little labours over paid.

BARNWELL. What do I owe for all your generous kindness? But tho' I cannot, Heaven can and will reward you.

THOROWGOOD. To see thee thus, is joy too great for words. Farewell, – Heaven strengthen thee. – Farewell.

BARNWELL. O! Sir, there's something I cou'd say, if my sad swelling heart would give me leave.

THOROWGOOD. Give it vent a while, and try.

BARNWELL. I had a friend, – 'tis true I am unworthy, yet methinks your generous example might perswade; – cou'd I not see him once before I go from whence there's no return.

THOROWGOOD. He's coming, – and as much thy friend as ever; – [*Aside*] *but I'll not anticipate his sorrow, – too soon he'll see the sad effect of his contagious ruin. This torrent of domestick misery bears too hard upon me, – I must retire to indulge a weakness I find impossible to overcome.* – Much lov'd – and much lamented youth – Farewell – Heaven strengthen thee – Eternally farewell.

BARNWELL. The best of masters and of men – Farewell – while I live let me not want your prayers.

THOROWGOOD. Thou shalt not; – thy peace being made with Heaven, death's already vanquish'd; – bear a little longer the pains that attend this transitory life, and cease from pain for ever.

ACT V. SCENE III.

BARNWELL. I find a power within that bears my soul above the fears of death, and, spight of[25] conscious shame and guilt, gives me a taste of pleasure more than mortal.

ACT V. SCENE IV.

[Trueman *and* Keeper.

KEEPER. Sir, there's the prisoner.

ACT V. SCENE V.

[Barnwell *and* Trueman.

BARNWELL. *Trueman*, – My friend, whom I so wisht to see, yet now he's here I dare not look upon him. [*Weeps.*

TRUEMAN. O *Barnwell*! *Barnwell*!

BARNWELL. Mercy! Mercy! Gracious Heaven! For death, but not for this, was I prepared.

TRUEMAN. What have I suffer'd since I saw you last? – What pain has absence given me? – But oh! to see thee thus!

BARNWELL. I know it is dreadful! I felt the anguish of thy generous soul, – but I was born to murder all who love me. [*Both weep.*

TRUEMAN. I came not to reproach you; – I thought to bring you comfort, – but I'm deceiv'd, for I have none to give; – I came to share thy sorrow, but cannot bear my own.

BARNWELL. My sense of guilt indeed you cannot know, – 'tis what the good and innocent, like you, can ne'er conceive; – but other griefs at present I have none, but what I feel for you. –

In your sorrow I read you love me still, – but yet methinks 'tis strange – when I consider what I am.

TRUEMAN. No more of that, – I can remember nothing but thy virtues, – thy honest, tender friendship, our former happy state and present misery. – O had you trusted me when first the fair seducer tempted you, all might have been prevented.

BARNWELL. Alas, thou know'st not what a wretch I've been! Breach of friendship was my first and least offence. – So far was I lost to goodness, – so devoted to the author of my ruin, – that had she insisted on my murdering thee, – I think, – I shou'd have done it.

TRUEMAN. Prithee aggravate thy faults no more.

BARNWELL. I think I shou'd! – Thus good and generous as you are, I shou'd have murder'd you!

TRUEMAN. We have not yet embrac'd, and may be interrupted. Come to my arms.

BARNWELL. Never, never will I taste such joys on earth; never will I so sooth my just remorse. Are those honest arms, and faithful bosom, fit to embrace and to support a murderer. – These iron fetters only shall clasp, and flinty pavement bear me, – [*Throwing himself on the ground,*] even these too good for such a bloody monster.

TRUEMAN. Shall fortune sever those whom friendship join'd! – Thy miseries cannot lay thee so low, but love will find thee. [*Lies down by him*] Upon this rugged couch then let us lie, for well it suits our most deplorable condition. – Here will we offer to stern calamity, – this earth the altar, and our selves the sacrifice. – Our mutual groans shall eccho to each other thro' the dreary vault. – Our sighs shall number the moments as they pass, – and mingling tears communicate such anguish, as words were never made to express.

BARNWELL. Then be it so. – Since you propose an intercourse of woe, pour all your griefs into my breast, – and in exchange take mine. [*Embracing*] Where's now the anguish that you promis'd? – You've taken mine, and make me no return. – Sure peace and comfort dwell within these arms, and sorrow can't approach me while I'm here! – This too is the work of Heaven, who, having before spoke peace and pardon to me, now sends thee to confirm it. – O take, take some of the joy that overflows my breast!

TRUEMAN. I do, I do. Almighty power, how have you made us capable to bear, at once, the extreams of pleasure and of pain?

ACT V. SCENE VI.

[*To them,* Keeper.

KEEPER. Sir.

TRUEMAN. I come.

ACT V. SCENE VII.

[Barnwell *and* Trueman.

BARNWELL. Must you leave me! – Death would soon have parted us for ever.

TRUEMAN. O, my *Barnwell,* there's yet another task behind: – again your heart must bleed for others woes.

BARNWELL. To meet and part with you, I thought was all I had to do on Earth! What is there more for me to do or suffer?

TRUEMAN. I dread to tell thee, yet it must be known. – *Maria.*

BARNWELL. Our master's fair and virtuous daughter!

TRUEMAN. The same.

BARNWELL. No misfortune, I hope, has reach'd that lovely maid! Preserve her, Heaven, from every ill, to show mankind that goodness is your care.

TRUEMAN. Thy, thy misfortunes, my unhappy friend, have reach'd her. Whatever you and I have felt, and more, if more be possible, she feels for you.

BARNWELL. – [*Aside*] *I know he doth abhor a lie, and would not trifle with his dying friend.* – This is, indeed, the bitterness of death!

TRUEMAN. You must remember, for we all observ'd it, for some time past, a heavy melancholy weigh'd her down. – Disconsolate she seem'd, and pin'd and languish'd from a cause unknown; – till hearing of your dreadful fate, – the long stifled flame blaz'd out. – She wept, she wrang her hands, and tore her hair, and, in the transport of her grief, discover'd her own lost state, whilst she lamented yours.

BARNWELL. Will all the pain I feel restore thy ease, lovely unhappy maid? [*Weeping*] Why didn't you let me die and never know it?

TRUEMAN. It was impossible; – she makes no secret of her passion for you, and is determin'd to see you e'er you die; – she waits for me to introduce her. –

ACT V. SCENE VIII.

[Barnwell.

BARNWELL. Vain busy thoughts be still! – What avails it to think on what I might have been, – I now am, – what I've made my self.

ACT V. SCENE IX.

[*Enter* Trueman *and* Maria.

TRUEMAN. Madam, reluctant I lead you to this dismal scene: This is the seat of misery and guilt. – Here awful[26] justice reserves her publick victims. – This is the entrance to shameful death. –

MARIA. To this sad place then no improper guest, the abandon'd lost *Maria* brings despair, and see the subject and the cause of all this world of woe. – Silent and motionless he stands, as if his soul had quitted her abode, – and the lifeless form alone was left behind; – yet that so perfect, that beauty and death, – ever at enmity, – now seem united there.

BARNWELL. I groan, but murmur not. – Just Heaven, I am your own; do with me what you please.

MARIA. Why are your streaming eyes still fix'd below? – As tho' thoud'st give the greedy Earth thy sorrows, and rob me of my due. – Were happiness within your power, you should bestow it where you pleas'd; – but in your misery I must and will partake.

BARNWELL. Oh! Say not so, but fly, abhor, and leave me to my fate. – Consider what you are: – How vast your fortune, and how bright your fame: – Have pity on your youth, your beauty, and unequalled virtue, – for which so many noble peers have sigh'd in vain. Bless with your charms some honourable Lord. – Adorn with your beauty; and, by your example, improve the *English* court, that justly claims such merit; so shall I quickly be to you as though I had never been. –

MARIA. When I forget you, I must be so indeed. – Reason, choice, virtue, all forbid it. – Let women, like *Millwood*, if there be more such women, smile in prosperity, and in adversity forsake. Be it the pride of virtue to repair, or to partake, the ruin such have made.

TRUEMAN. Lovely, ill-fated maid! – Was there ever such generous distress before? – How must this pierce his grateful heart, and aggravate his woes?

BARNWELL. E'er I knew guilt or shame, when fortune smil'd, and when my youthful hopes were at the highest; if then to have rais'd my thoughts to you, had been presumption in me, never to have been pardon'd, – think how much beneath your self you condescend to regard me now.

MARIA. Let her blush who, professing love, invades the freedom of your sex's choice, and meanly sues in hopes of a return. – Your inevitable fate hath render'd hope impossible as vain. – Then why shou'd I fear to avow a passion so just and so disinterested?

TRUEMAN. If any shou'd take occasion, from *Millwood*'s crimes, to libel the best and fairest part of the creation, here let them see their error. – The most distant hopes of such a tender passion, from so bright a maid, might add to the happiness of the most happy, and make the greatest proud. – Yet here 'tis lavish'd in vain: – Tho' by the rich present, the generous donor is undone, – he, on whom it is bestow'd, receives no benefit.

BARNWELL. So the aromatick spices of the east, which all the living covet and esteem, are, with unavailing kindness, wasted on the dead.

MARIA. Yes, fruitless is my love, and unavailing all my sighs and tears. – Can they save thee from approaching death? – From such a death? – O terrible idea! – What is her misery and distress, who sees the first last object of her love, for whom alone she'd live, – for whom she'd die a thousand, thousand deaths, if it were possible, – expiring in her arms? – Yet she is happy, when compar'd to me. – Were millions of worlds mine, I'd gladly give them in exchange for her condition. – The most consummate woe is light to mine. The last of curses to other miserable maids, is all I ask; and that's deny'd me.

TRUEMAN. Time and reflection cure all ills.

MARIA. All but this; – his dreadful catastrophe virtue her self abhors. – To give a holiday to suburb slaves, and passing entertain the savage herd, who, elbowing each other for a sight, pursue and press upon him like his fate.[27] – A mind with piety and resolution arm'd, may smile on death. – But publick ignominy, – everlasting shame, – shame the death of souls, – to die a thousand times, and yet survive even death it self, in never dying infamy, is this to be endured? – Can I, who live in him, and must, each hour of my devoted life, feel all these woes renew'd, – can I endure this! –

TRUEMAN. Grief has impair'd her spirits; she pants, as in the agonies of death. –

BARNWELL. Preserve her, Heaven, and restore her peace, – nor let her death be added to my crimes, – [*Bell tolls*] I am summon'd to my fate.

ACT V. SCENE X.

[*To them.* Keeper.

KEEPER. The officers attend you, Sir. – Mrs. *Millwood* is already summon'd.

BARNWELL. Tell 'em I'm ready. – And now, my friend, farewell, [*Embracing*] Support and comfort the best you can this mourning fair. – No more. – Forget not to pray for me, – [*Turning to* Maria] would you, bright excellence, permit me the honour of a chaste embrace, – the last happiness this world cou'd give were mine, [*She enclines towards him; they embrace*] Exalted goodness! – O turn your eyes from earth, and me, to Heaven, – where virtue, like yours, is ever heard. – Pray for the peace of my departing soul. – Early my race of wickedness began, and soon has reach'd the summet: – E'er nature has finish'd her work, and stamp'd me man, – just at the time that others begin to stray, – my course is finish'd; tho' short my span of life, and few my days; yet count my crimes for years, and I have liv'd whole ages. – Justice and mercy are in Heaven the same: its utmost severity is mercy to the whole, – thereby to cure man's folly and presumption, which else wou'd render even infinite mercy vain and ineffectual. – Thus justice, in compassion to mankind, cuts off a wretch like me, by one such example to secure thousands from future ruin.

If any youth, like you, – in future times,
Shall mourn my fate, – tho' he abhor my crimes;
Or tender maid, like you, – my tale shall hear,
And to my sorrows give a pitying tear:
To each such melting eye, and throbbing heart,
Would gracious heaven this benefit impart,
Never to know my guilt, – nor feel my pain,
Then must you own, you ought not to complain;
Since you nor weep, – nor shall I die in vain.

ACT V. SCENE XI.

[Trueman*,* Blunt*, and* Lucy.

LUCY. Heart-breaking sight. – O wretched, wretched *Millwood.*

TRUEMAN. You came from her then: – How is she disposed to meet her fate?

BLUNT. Who can describe unalterable woe?

LUCY. She goes to death encompassed with horror, loathing life, and yet afraid to die; no tongue can tell her anguish and despair.

TRUEMAN. Heaven be better to her than her fears; may she prove a warning to others, a monument of mercy in her self.

LUCY. O sorrow, insupportable! Break, break my heart.

TRUEMAN. In vain.

With bleeding hearts, and weeping eyes we show
A human gen'rous sense of others woe;
Unless we make what drew their ruin on,
And by avoiding that, prevent our own.

FINIS.

EPILOGUE

Written by Colley Cibber, Esq; and spoke by Mrs. Cibber.[28]

Since fate has robb'd me of the hapless youth,
For whom my heart had hoarded up its truth;
By all the laws of love and honour, now,
I'm free again to chuse, – and one of you.
But soft, – with caution first I'll round me peep;
Maids, in my case, shou'd look, before they leap:
Here's, choice enough, of various sorts, and hue,
The cit, the wit, the rake cock'd up in cue,[29]
The fair spruce mercer, and the tawney Jew.
Suppose I search the sober gallery; – No,
There's none but prentices, – and cuckolds all a row;
And these, I doubt, are those that make 'em so.

[*Pointing to the boxes.*

'Tis very well, enjoy the jest: – but you,
Fine powder'd sparks; – nay, I'm told 'tis true,
Your happy spouses – can make cuckolds too.
'Twixt you and them, the diff'rence this perhaps,
The cit's asham'd whene'er his duck he traps;
But you, when madam's tripping, let her fall,
Cock up your hats, and take no shame at all.
What if some favour'd poet I cou'd meet?
Whose love wou'd lay his laurels at my feet.
No, – painted passion real love abhors, –
His flame wou'd prove the suit of creditors.
Not to detain you then with longer pause,
In short, my heart to this conclusion draws,
I yield it to the hand, that's loudest in applause.

12.2 EXCERPT FROM "THE BALLAD OF GEORGE BARNWELL"

Anon. London: Printed by and for W. O. and A. M. and sold by the Booksellers of Pye-corner and London Bridge, *circa* 1693–4.

THE BALLAD OF GEORGE BARNWELL" dates back to at least 1651. The long didactic story warns young men about "harlots" who might seduce them away from work and into a life of crime. The complete ballad is available in the online supplement. This text was taken from the UC Santa Barbara English Broadside Ballad Archive.

From The First Part

All youths of fair England
That dwell both far and near,
Regard my story that I tell,
And to my song give ear.

A London lad I was,
A merchant's prentice bound;
My name is George Barnwell, that did spend
My master many pound.

Take heed of harlots then,
And their enticing trains,
For by that means I have been brought
To hang alive in chains.

As I upon a day
Was walking through the street,
About my master's business,
A wanton I did meet.

"Good Barnwell," then quoth she,
"Do thou to Shoreditch come,
And ask for mistress Millwood's house,
Next door unto the Gun.

She took me by the hand,
And, with a modest grace,
"Welcome, sweet Barnwell," then quoth she, "Unto this homely place.

"And since I have thee found
As good as thy word to be,
A homely supper, ere we part,
Thou shalt take here with me."

"Oh, pardon me," quoth I,
"Fair mistress, I you pray,
For why, out of my master's house
So long I dare not stay."

"Alas, good sir," she said,
"Are you so strictly tied,
You may not with your dearest friend
One hour or two abide?"

Then from my master straight
I ran in secret sort,
And unto Sarah Millwood there
My case I did report.

But how she used this youth
In this his care and woe,

And all a strumpet's wily ways,
The second part may show.

From The Second Part

"Young Barnwell comes to thee,
Sweet Sarah, my delight;
I am undone, unless thou stand
My faithful friend this night."

With that she knit her brows,
And, looking all aquoy,
Quoth she, "What should I have to do
With any 'prentice boy?

"For without money, George,
A man is but a beast;
But bringing money thou shalt be
Always my welcome guest."

And so carousing both
Their pleasures to content,
George Barnwell had in little time
His money wholly spent.

There died this gallant quean,
Such was her greatest gains;
For murder in Polonia
Was Barnwell hang'd in chains.

Lo! Here's the end of youth
That after harlots haunt,
Who in the spoil of other men
About the streets do flaunt.

12.3 *THE LONDON EVENING POST* NOTICE

October 28, 1731–October 30, 1731; Issue 611.

THIS BRIEF ARTICLE makes note of the fact that the royal family attended a production of *The London Merchant.*

Their Majesties the King and Queen, his Royal Highness the Prince of Wales, his Royal Highness Prince William, the Princess Royal, the Princess Emilia, the Princess Caroline, and the two youngest Princesses, with a great Concourse of Nobility, were on Thursday Night last at the Theatre Royal in Drury-Lane, to see the *London Merchant*, or the *True Tragical History* of *George Barnwell*; with the farce of the *Devil to Pay*.

On Thursday a great Number of the Beds that were brought from Hampton-Court Palace were carry'd to Richmond and Kew, and there put up for their Majesties and the Royal Family and their Attendants.

Mr. Lambert, the Confectioner, who hath prepared most of the Deserts for the Nobility who have hitherto entertained the Duke of Lorrain, is going, with several of his Servants, down to the Seat of Sir Robert Walpole in Norfolk, to prepare a most magnificent one there for the Entertainment of that Prince.

12.4 THEOPHILUS CIBBER, *THE LIVES OF THE POETS OF GREAT BRITAIN AND IRELAND*

Robert Shiells, London: R. Griffiths, 1753, Vol. 5, 338–40.

CIBBER'S *LIVES* PROVIDES significant information about playwrights of the period, though as the title suggests, the work was a compendium of extant sources and ultimately compiled by Robert Shiells.

Mr. George Lillo, was by profession a jeweler. He was born in London, on the 4th of Feb. 1693. He lived, as we are informed, near Moorgate, in the same neighbourhood where he received his birth, and where he was always esteemed as a person of unblemished character. 'Tis said, he was educated in the principles of the Dissenters: be that as it will, his morals, brought no disgrace on any sect or party. Indeed his principal attachment was to the muses.

His first piece, brought on the stage, was a Ballad Opera, called *Sylvia; or, the Country Burial*; performed at the Theatre Royal in Lincoln's-Inn Fields, but with no extraordinary success, in the year 1730. The year following he brought his play, called *The London Merchant; or, The True Story of George Barnwell,* to Mr. Cibber junior (then manager of the summer company, at the Theatre Royal in Drury-Lane) who originally played the part of Barnwell.—The author was not then known. As this was almost a new species of tragedy, wrote on a very uncommon subject, he rather chose it should take its fate in the summer, than run the more hazardous fate of encountering the winter criticks. The old ballad of George Barnwell (on which the story was founded) was on this occasion reprinted, and many thousands sold in one day. Many gaily-disposed spirits brought the ballad with them to the play, intending to make their pleasant remarks (as some afterwards owned) and ludicrous comparisons between the antient ditty and the modern drama. But the play was very carefully got up, and universally allowed to be well performed. The piece was thought to be well conducted and the subject well managed, and the diction proper and natural; never low, and very rarely swelling above the characters that spoke. Mr. Pope, among other persons, distinguished by their rank, or particular publick merit, had the curiosity to attend the performance, and commended the actors, and the author; and remarked, if the latter had erred through the whole play, it was only in a few places, where he had unawares led himself into a poetical luxuriancy, affecting to be too elevated for the simplicity of the subject. But the play, in general, spoke so much to the heart, that the gay persons before mentioned confessed, they were drawn in to drop their ballads, and pull out their handkerchiefs. It met with uncommon success; for it was acted above twenty times in the summer season to great audiences; was frequently bespoke by some eminent merchants and citizens, who much approved its moral tendency: and, in the winter following, was acted often to crowded houses: And all the royal family, at several different times, honoured it with their appearance. It gained reputation, and brought money to the poet, the managers, and the performers. Mr. Cibber, jun. not only gave the author his usual profits of his third day &c but procured him a benefit-night in the winter season, which turned out greatly to his advantage; so that he had four benefit-nights in all for that piece; by the profits whereof, and his copy-money, he gained several hundred pounds. It continued a stock play in Drury-Lane Theatre till Mr. Cibber left that house, and went to the Theatre in Convent-Garden. It was often acted in the Christmas and Easter holidays, and judged a proper entertainment for the apprentices, &c. as being a more instructive, moral, and cautionary drama, than many pieces that had been usually exhibited in those days, with little but farce and ribaldry to recommend them.

12.5 *GAZETTEER AND LONDON DAILY ADVERTISER*

Feb. 2, 1764, Issue 10: 882.

THERE HAS BEEN LATELY PUBLISHED at Paris a poetical performance, under the title of *a Letter from Barnwell in Prison to his Friend Trueman*. The hint of this piece was taken from the English play of *George Barnwell, or The London Merchant*. M. Dorat, the author of the French poem, was so affected by reading that tragedy, that he conceived a design of adapting it to the theatre of Paris; but as he forsaw many difficulties in the accomplishment of his purpose, he contented himself with forming a poetical letter, wherein the hero of the tragedy, the unhappy Barnwell, relates his birth and the progress of his unfortunate amour with Millwood, her seducing charms, the dangerous arts she employed in directing his weakness to the perpetration of the greatest of crimes, almost a parricide, his resistance, his struggles, the accomplishment of the deed, and the dreadful consequences of it.

12.6 LADY MARY WORTLEY MONTAGU, *THE LETTERS AND WORKS OF LADY MARY WORTLEY MONTAGU*

Introduction, Ed. James Archibald Stuart-Wortley-Mackenzie, Lord Wharncliffe. London: Richard Bentley, 1837, p. 89.

LADY MARY WORTLEY MONTAGU (1689–1762) is best known for her letters from Turkey, where her husband served as ambassador. She also lobbied for the adoption of the smallpox vaccine in Britain. Her reflections on life are an important window into the experience of elite British women in an age of empire.

From the books Lady Mary Wortley died possessed of, which were but few, she appears to have been particularly fond of that ancient English drama lately revived among us; for she had several volumes of differently sized and wretchedly printed plays bound up together, such as the Duke of Roxburgh would have bought at any price; the works of Shirley, Ford, Marston, Heywood, Webster, and the rest, as far back as *Gammer Gurton's Needle*, and coming down to the trash of Durfey. But Lillo's domestic tragedies were what she most admired; for "My lady used to declare," said the old servant so often quoted, "that whoever did not cry at George Barnwell must deserve to be hanged." And she passed the same sentence on people who could see unmoved the fine scene between Dorax and Sebastian in Dryden, who was also one of her favourite authors.

12.7 CHARLES DICKENS, FROM *GREAT EXPECTATIONS*

Charles Dickens, *Great Expectations,* (1861), Ed. Charlotte Mitchell. London: Penguin, 1996.

IN DICKENS' MOST FAMOUS *bildungsroman*, the first installments of which appeared in 1860 in *All the Year Round*, Pip identifies with Barnwell, though he is a reader of the play rather than a spectator of a production. The continued influence of the play, which shapes the novel, as Sarah Gates has argued, reached well into the nineteenth century.

When Barnwell began to go wrong, I declare that I felt positively apologetic, Pumblechook's indignant stare so taxed me with it. Wopsle, too, took pains to present me in the worst light. At once ferocious and maudlin, I was made to murder my uncle with no extenuating circumstances whatever; Millwood put me down in argument, on every occasion; it became sheer monomania in my master's daughter to care a button for me; and all I can say for my gasping and procrastinating conduct on the fatal morning, is, that it was worthy of the general feebleness of my character. Even after I was happily hanged and Wopsle had closed the book, Pumblechook sat staring at me, and shaking his head, and saying, "Take warning, boy, take warning!" as if it were a well-known fact that I contemplated murdering a near relation, provided I could only induce one to have the weakness to become my benefactor. . . With my head full of George Barnwell, I was at first disposed to believe that *I* must have had some hand in the attack upon my sister, or at all events that as her near relation, popularly known to be under obligations to her, I was a more legitimate object of suspicion than anyone else. (117; 120)

12.8 KEN JAWOROWSKIJAN, REVIEW, *THE LONDON MERCHANT*, 2012

New York Times, January 17, 2012

THE LONG TITLE OF THE PLAY: "The London Merchant, or the History of George Barnwell." The short review: excellent.

That's a simple way to sum up this co-production by the Storm Theater and the Blackfriars Repertory Theater. But there's no one word to convey the pleasure of discovering an exciting work when you'd been dreading a musty old relic.

"The London Merchant," written by George Lillo and first performed in 1731, was a hit in the eighteenth century and has mostly vanished since. The tragedy centers on the title character, a young apprentice who falls under the spell of the scheming prostitute Millwood. She soon manipulates Barnwell into embezzling his employer's money, then leads him to contemplate graver crimes.

Considered groundbreaking because of a plot that focused on working-class characters, this morality tale remains deliciously tense and dark; Lillo surely read his Shakespeare, for there are faint echoes of "Macbeth" and "Hamlet." There's also some fine poetry, and just a bit of stuffiness that betrays the script's age, as does an occasional, and forgivable, didacticism.

As Barnwell, Patrick Woodall has an exceptional presence, particularly in soliloquy. Jessica Myhr, as Millwood, is captivating and coldly wicked. As Millwood's servants, Michelle Kafel and Spencer Aste supply the welcome humor (with the clever Mr. Aste doubling as Barnwell's uncle), while Joe Danbusky, Harlan Work and Megan Stern shine in supporting roles. All of the cast, directed on a clean, spare thrust stage by Peter Dobbins, exploit the underlying emotions to full effect, and Michael Abrams's lighting heightens the foreboding mood.

There are so many surprises in the 2 hours and 10 minutes of "The London Merchant" that you may have to remind yourself that yes, you are in a basement that houses the Theater of the Church of Notre Dame, a space far off the radar of most audiences. That's not a snobbish statement, but rather an acknowledgment that, in New York, out-of-the-way places can produce some first-rate theater.

12.9 *THE LONDON MERCHANT OR THE HISTORY OF GEORGE BARNWELL*, REPRESENTED FROM THE MOST PARTICULAR MOVING INCIDENTS IN THAT PLAY

The London Merchant or the History of George Barnwell, represented from the most particular moving incidents in that play. London: Sold by . . . B. Dickinson . . . and J. Wyatt, [1731]. Courtesy of the Folger Shakespeare Library. ART File L729 no.1.

This print tells the story of *The London Merchant* in eight frames, beginning with Millwood's initial seduction of Barnwell. The text below each image quotes or paraphrases from Lillo's play.

12.10 WILLIAM HOGARTH, *INDUSTRY AND IDLENESS* PLATE 1

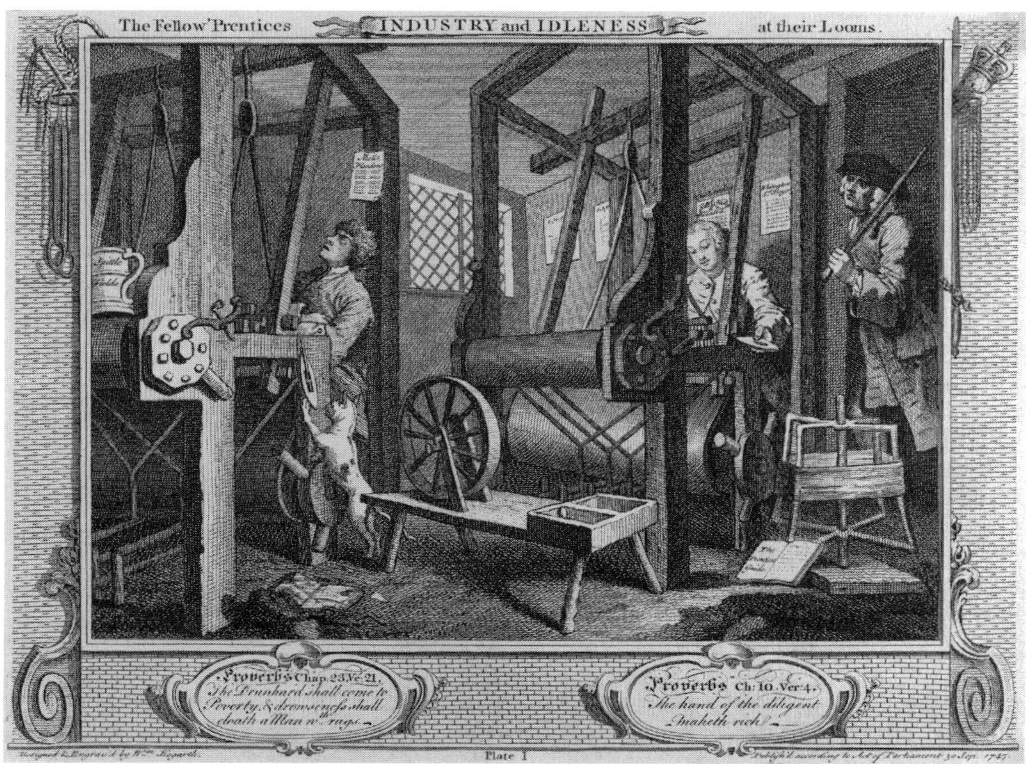

William Hogarth, *Industry and Idleness,* plate 1. London: 1747. Courtesy of the Lewis Walpole Library, Yale University.

Hogarth's many "progresses," or sequences of images of a character's rise or, more often, fall, are didactic narratives that give us a window on the visual dimensions of social life. Hogarth's richly detailed prints embed references to continental art and heraldry in scenes of urban life. The remaining plates of *Industry and Idleness* are available on the online supplement of the anthology website. This first plate shows the two apprentices at their looms. One is hard at work and destined for management, with a copy of *The London Apprentice* and *Whitington, Lord Mayor* (a reference to the famous medieval London merchant, also the subject of the popular play *Whitington,* who rose to be Lord Mayor four times, as well as Sheriff and a member of Parliament) tacked on the wall behind him. The other dozes at his loom, beneath a page from *Moll Flanders,* with a souvenir beer mug from Spittlefields pleasure garden before him and a cat in heat clawing at his machine.

Notes

1–2 This text is based on the 1731 edition: London: printed for J. Gray.

3 See Charles McBurney, "What George Lillo Read: A Speculation," *Huntington Library Quarterly*, 29.3 (May 1966): 275–86.

4 See Emmett L. Avery, "The Popularity of *The Mourning Bride* in the London Theatres in the Eighteenth Century," *Research Studies of the State College of Washington*, IX (1941): 115–116.

5 Cibber, *The Lives of the Poets of Great Britain and Ireland* (London, 1753), V, 340.

6 "*George Barnwell* Abroad," *Comparative Literature*, II (1950), 145, quoted in William H. McBurney's introduction to *The London Merchant*. Lincoln, NE: University of Nebraska Press, 1965.

7 Made a baronet by George I, Eyles served in Parliament, was elected Lord Mayor of London in 1727, and exemplified a Whiggish friendliness to business interests.

8 While Lillo explicitly references Dryden and aesthetic debates about the nature and function of dramatic tragedy, it implicitly replies to Collier's accusations of immorality on the stage.

9 The east London business district.

10 The disastrous South Sea Bubble, a stock crash brought about by widespread speculation, led to a collapse of the value of the stock in 1720. Eyles was brought in in January of 1721 to reorganize the company.

11 References to modern tragedies such as Southerne's *Oroonoko* (online), Rowe's *The Fair Penitent*, and Otway's *Venice Preserv'd* (online).

12 A reference to "The Ballad of George Barnwell," excerpted below and available in its entirety online.

13 The Spanish Armada, defeated by the English in 1588, is in Lillo's plot subverted at a prior moment by merchants. The reference is also used to damn the Spanish for their colonial exploits and slave trading, even though, by 1730, Great Britain was heavily involved in the slave trade.

14 Bias.

15 The image is an echo of Lady Wishfort preparing herself in *The Way of the World*, as does her later "after what manner shall I receive him?"

16 Millwood reiterates the Lockean model of ownership along with the more Hobbsean justification of slavery through "just war," a view Locke also supported.

17 Uncertainty.

18 The story Lucy tells is that Millwood's guardian insists that she mortgage her future assets to pay him for expenses he incurred in her care as a punishment for not marrying him, and now threatens to ruin her financially if she will not have sex with him, as she has with Barnwell.

19 The Americas.

20 The Royal Exchange, the center of commerce in the City of London.

21 A mask.

22 Ghastly.

23 The reference to *Macbeth*, a staple of the repertoire, would have been strong, especially with actresses such as Jane Bullock playing Lady Macbeth during the early runs of *The London Merchant*.

24 A reference to, though not a quotation of, the popular *Ballad of George Barnwell*.

25 In spite of.

26 Awe-inspiring.

27 Public hangings served as a kind of grisly entertainment. See plate 11 of *Industry and Idleness*.

28 Susanna Maria Cibber, wife of Theophilus Cibber.

29 Hair that is done up in a pigtail.

13. *The Minor*

THE MINOR. **A COMEDY. WRITTEN BY MR. FOOTE. AS IT IS NOW ACTING AT THE NEW THEATRE IN THE HAY-MARKET. BY AUTHORITY FROM THE LORD CHAMBERLAIN.[1] FIRST PERFORMED 28 JANUARY 1760 AND FIRST PUBLISHED 1760**

13.1 *THE MINOR*, A COMEDY. WRITTEN BY MR. FOOTE. AS IT IS NOW ACTING AT THE NEW THEATRE IN THE HAY-MARKET. BY AUTHORITY FROM THE LORD CHAMBERLAIN.[2]

Samuel Foote

First Performed 28 January 1760 and First Published 1760

SAMUEL FOOTE, KNOWN AS the "English Aristophanes," was a remarkable mimic. Samuel Johnson once said that fear of broken bones kept Foote from making fun of him on stage. Many of his most popular pieces ran on the pleasures of watching Foote take off well-known personalities of the age, often in drag, such as the Duchess of Kingston (as "Lady Kitty Crocodile" in *A Trip to Calais*), and singer Elizabeth Linley (as "Little Linney" in *The Maid of Bath*). In *The Minor*, Foote caricatures Mother Douglas, a well-known Covent Garden madam, as "Mother Cole"; Langford the well-known auctioneer as "Smirk"; and most famously, the Rev. George Whitefield, through the character of Shift imitating "Dr. Squintum." *The Minor* started at the Crow Street Theatre in Dublin on January 8, 1760 as a two-act comedy, but it was not a great success. Samuel Foote then expanded his concept to three acts, added a brief rehearsal frame, and brought it out at The Haymarket in London on June 28, 1760, where Foote had a summer license. It was an instant if controversial hit. Tate Wilkinson commented that he "found the crowds so great that it was difficult to get in," even though the play was running every Monday, Wednesday, and Friday. *The Minor* is in many respects an unremarkable mini-comedy, in which the young Sir George's profligacy, tested by his father in disguise, is reformed by his own innate sensibility when he shows kindness to his disinherited cousin Lucy. Lucy has taken refuge with Methodists, who are planning to prostitute her as one of Mrs. Cole's girls. The blocking father figures (Sir William Wealthy and Mr. Richard Wealthy) both put aside their titled and merchant-class differences once they realize that the two cousins and families will be brought together in an advantageous marriage, achieved without parental bullying. Foote's mocking representation of a living clergyman, the very popular Methodist Whitefield, was unprecedented, however, and audiences poured out to see the play. In the popular conversation, the play came to be "about" Methodism.

Other parodies and attacks on the Methodists followed Foote's. *An Additional Scene to the Comedy of The Minor* appeared in 1761 followed by the more substantial and cynical *The Methodist: A Comedy, being A Continuation of the Plan of the Minor, Written by Mr. Foote; As it was intended to have been acted at the Theatre-Royal in Covent Garden, but for obvious Reasons suppressed* (1761). Whitefield was also satirized in Charles Johnstone's *Chrysal: of the Adventures of a Guinea* (1760–65) and by George Stevens' *Lecture on Heads*, a traveling show of impressions based on a series of papier-mâché heads, first performed in 1764; the final "head" was of a Methodist minister. Foote, ever topical, roused anxieties about the reasonableness, the motives and the followers of Methodism as the popular movement gained numbers and visibility. Enthusiasm, a term that comes from the Greek for "to be possessed by a god," had negative connotations in the eighteenth century and was used to damn the Methodists as irrational and even dangerous in their affective excesses. Part of the scorn heaped upon Methodism came from post-Licensing Act strictures on where actors could perform, which shut down some regional and unlicensed theatres that were later rented by Methodists as meeting houses. Others objected to the anti-theatrical statements of Methodist ministers, especially Whitefield, who were themselves quite charismatic and theatrical in their delivery. Garrick claimed that he would give £100 if he could say "Oh" like Whitefield, and Benjamin Franklin estimated that 30,000 people at once could hear the dulcet-toned Whitefield (Belden 83). The issue was perhaps closer to home to friends of theatre manager John Rich, the most famous harlequin of the age, after his wife Priscilla left the stage and converted to Methodism. The Anglican community, not always friendly to Methodism, weighed in as well. The Archbishop of Canterbury, Thomas Secker, who was otherwise horrified by Methodist enthusiasm, tried to have Foote's play stopped, but the Duke of Devonshire, serving as the Lord Chamberlain, resisted, and only let him correct a few passages, some of which the Lord Chamberlain then restored (Belden 91). Hogarth mentions Secker in *Enthusiasm Delineat'd*, his draft of *Credulity, Superstition, and Fanaticism*, suggesting that by trying to stop the play, Secker had become a Methodist collaborator.

The print argument over whether *The Minor* was heresy or healthy corrective satire raged in newspapers and pamphlets, some of which are excerpted below. *The Minor* managed to stay in the repertoire, though it was published without Foote's infamous epilogue; even Frances Burney's careful, eponymous heroine Evelina comments that she enjoys the play. Excerpts from *The Minor* were included in the newspapers as well as jest and comedy books such as Charles Lamb and Thomas Hood's *The Laughing Philosopher* (1825). It also earned a place in the second volume of *Bell's British Theatre*. Richard Brinsley Sheridan's debt to Foote appears in his adaptation of the character Little Transfer as Little Premium in *The School For Scandal*, which also borrows from the plot when a disguised Sir Oliver returns to observe Charles Surface's youthful follies, only to discover that Charles, like Sir George Wealthy, is actually a man of sensibility and worthy of his inheritance.

Tantum Religio potuit Suadere Malorum.[3]

Persons in the Introduction.

In the COMEDY.

Foote	Mr. Foote.
Smart	Mr. Smith.
Canker	Mr. Misdale.
Pearse	
Sir William Wealthy	Mr. Badely.
Richard Wealthy	Mr. Hyde.
Sir George Wealthy	Mr. Shaw.
Shift	Mr. Foote.
Loader	Mr. Davis.
Dick	Mr. Westen.
Transfer	Mr. Blaky.
Mrs. Cole	Mr. Foote.
Lucy	Miss Burden.

TO HIS GRACE WILLIAM Duke of DEVONSHIRE, Lord Chamberlain of his Majesty's Household.

My Lord,

The Minor, who is indebted for his appearance on the stage, to your grace's indulgence, begs leave to desire your grace's further protection, at his entering into the world.

Though the allegiance due from the whole dramatic people to your grace's station, might place this address in the light of a natural tribute; yet, my lord, I should not have taken that liberty with the duke of Devonshire, if I could not, at the same time, plead some little utility in the design of my piece; and add, that the public approbation has stamped a value on the execution.

The law, which threw the stage under the absolute government of a lord chamberlain, could not fail to fill the minds of all the objects of that power, with very gloomy apprehensions; they found themselves (through their own licentiousness, it must be confess'd) in a more precarious dependent state, than any other of his majesty's subjects. But when their direction was lodged in the hands of a nobleman, whose ancestors had so successfully struggled for national liberty, they ceased to fear for their own. It was not from a patron of the liberal arts, they were to expect an oppressor; it was not from the friend of freedom, and of man, they were to dread partial monopolies, or the establishment of petty tyrannies.

Their warmest wishes are accomplished; none of their rights have been invaded, except, what without the first poetic authority, I should not venture to call a right, the Jus Nocendi.[4]

Your tenderness, my lord, for all the followers of the Muses, has been in no instance more conspicuous, than in your late favour to me, the meanest of their train; your grace has thrown open (for those who are deny'd admittance into the palaces of Parnassus) a cottage on its borders, where the unhappy migrants may be, if not magnificently, at least, hospitably entertained.

I shall detain your grace no longer, than just to eccho the public voice, that, for the honour, progress, and perfection of letters, your grace may long continue their candid CENSOR, who have always been their generous protector.

I have the honor, my lord, to be, with the greatest respect, and gratitude.

Your grace's most dutiful, Most oblig'd, And obedient servant,

SAMUEL FOOTE.

Ellestree, July 8, 1760.

INTRODUCTION.

[*Enter* Canker *and* Smart.

SMART. But are you sure he has leave?

CANKER. Certain.

SMART. I'm damn'd glad on't. For now we shall have a laugh, either with him or at him, it does not signify which.

CANKER. Not a farthing.

SMART. D'you know his scheme?

CANKER. Not I. But is not the door of the little theatre open?

SMART. Yes. Who is that fellow that seems to stand sentry there?

CANKER. By his tatter'd garb, and meagre visage, he must be one of the troop.

SMART. I'll call him. Holo, Mr. –

[*Enter* Pearse.

SMART. What, is there any thing going on over the way?

PEARSE. A rehearsal.

SMART. Of what?

PEARSE. A new piece.

SMART. Foote's?

PEARSE. Yes.

CANKER. Is he there?

PEARSE. He is.

SMART. Zounds, let's go and see what he is about.

CANKER. With all my heart.

SMART. Come along then.

[*Exeunt. Enter* Foote *and an* Actor.

FOOTE. Sir, this will never do, you must get rid of your high notes, and country cant. Oh, 'tis the true strolling – [5]

[*Enter* Smart *and* Canker.

SMART. Ha, ha, ha, what, hard at it, my boy! – Here's your old friend Canker and I come for a peep. Well, and hey, what is your plan?

FOOTE. Plan?

SMART. Ay, what are your characters? Give us your groupe; how is your cloth fill'd?[6]

FOOTE. Characters!

SMART. Ay. – Come, come, communicate. What, man, we will lend thee a lift. I have a damn'd fine original for thee, an aunt of my own, just come from the north, with the true Newcastle bur in her throat;[7] and a nose and a chin. – I am afraid she is not well enough known: But I have a remedy for that. I'll bring her the first night of your piece, place her in a conspicuous station, and whisper the secret to the whole house. That will be damn'd fine, won't it?

FOOTE. Oh, delicious!

SMART. But don't name me. For if she smokes me for the author, I shall be dash'd out of her codicil in a hurry.

FOOTE. Oh, never fear me. But I shou'd think your uncle Tom a better character.

SMART. What, the politician?

FOOTE. Ay; that every day, after dinner, as soon as the cloth is remov'd, fights the battle of Minden, batters the French with cherry-stones, and pursues 'em to the banks of the Rhine, in a stream of spilt port.

SMART. Oh, damn it, he'll do.

FOOTE. Or what say you to your father-in-law, Sir Timothy? Who, tho' as broken-winded as a Hounslow post horse, is eternally chaunting Venetian ballads. Kata tore cara higlia.[8]

SMART. Admirable! by heavens! – Have you got 'em?

FOOTE. No.

SMART. Then in with 'em, my boy.

FOOTE. Not one.

SMART. Pr'ythee why not?

FOOTE. Why look'ee, Smart, tho' you are, in the language of the world, my friend, yet there is one thing you, I am sure, love better than any body.

SMART. What's that?

FOOTE. Mischief.

SMART. No, pr'ythee –

FOOTE. How now, am I sure that you, who so readily give up your relations, may not have some design upon me.

SMART. I don't understand you.

FOOTE. Why, as soon as my characters begin to circulate a little successfully, my mouth is stopp'd in a minute, by the clamour of your relations, – Oh, damme, – 'tis a shame, – it should not be, – people of distinction brought upon the stage. – And so out of compliment to your cousins I am to be beggar'd, for treating the public with the follies of your family, at your own request.[9]

SMART. How can you think I wou'd be such a dog. What the devil, then, are we to have nothing personal? Give us the actors however.

FOOTE. Oh, that's stale. Besides, I think they have, of all men, the best right to complain.

SMART. How so?

FOOTE. Because, by rendering them ridiculous in their profession, you, at the same time, injure their pockets. Now, as to the other gentry, they have providentially something besides their understanding to rely on; and the only injury they can receive is, that the whole town is then diverted, with what before, was only the amusement of private parties.

CANKER. Give us then a national portrait: a Scotchman or an Irishman.[10]

FOOTE. If you mean merely the dialect of the two countries, I can't think it either a subject of satyr or humour; it is an accidental unhappiness, for which a man is no more accountable, than the colour of his hair. Now affectation I take to be the true comic object. If, indeed, a north Briton, struck with a scheme of reformation, should advance from the banks of the Tweed, to teach the English the true pronunciation of their own language, he would, I think, merit your laughter: nor would a Dublin mechanic, who, from heading the Liberty boys in a skirmish on Ormond Quay, should think he had a right to prescribe military laws to the first commander in Europe, be a less ridiculous object.

SMART. Are there such?

FOOTE. If you mean that the blunders of a few peasants, or the partial principles of a single scoundrel, are to stand as characteristical marks of a whole country; your pride may produce a laugh, but, believe me, it is at the expence of your understanding.

CANKER. Heyday, what a system is here! Laws for laughing! And pray, sage Sir, instruct us when we may laugh with propriety.

FOOTE. At an old beau, a superannuated beauty, a military coward, a stuttering orator, or a gouty dancer. In short, whoever affects to be what he is not, or strives to be what he cannot, is an object worthy the poet's pen, and your mirth.

SMART. Psha, I don't know what you mean by your is nots, and cannots – damn'd abstruse jargon. Ha, Canker.

CANKER. Well, but if you will not give us persons, let us have things. Treat us with a modern amour, or a state intrigue, or a –

FOOTE. And so amuse the public ear, at the expence of private peace. You must excuse me.

CANKER. And so, with these principles, you expect to thrive on this spot?

SMART. No, no, it won't do. I tell thee the plain roast and boil'd of the theatres will never do at this table. We must have high season'd ragoûts, and rich sauces.[11]

FOOTE. Why, perhaps, by way of dessert, I may produce something that may hit your palate.

SMART. Your bill of fare?

FOOTE. What think you of one of those itinerant field orators, who tho' at declar'd enmity with common sense, have the address to poison the principles, and, at the same time, pick the pockets, of half our industrious fellow subjects.

CANKER. Have a care. Dangerous ground. Ludere cum sacris,[12] you know.

FOOTE. Now I look upon it in a different manner. I consider these gentlemen in the light of public performers, like myself; and whether we exhibit at Tottenham-Court, or the Haymarket, our purpose is the same, and the place is immaterial.[13]

CANKER. Why, indeed if it be considered –

FOOTE. Nay, more, I must beg leave to assert, that ridicule is the only antidote against this pernicious poison. This is a madness that argument can never cure: and, should a little wholsome severity be apply'd, persecution would be the immediate cry: where then can we have recourse, but to the comic muse; perhaps, the archness and severity of her smile, may redress an evil, that the laws cannot reach, or reason reclaim.

CANKER. Why, if it does not cure those already distemper'd, it may be a means to stop the infection.

SMART. But how is your scheme conducted?

FOOTE. Of that you may judge. We are just going upon a repetition of the piece. I should be glad to have your opinion.

SMART. We will give it you.

FOOTE. One indulgence: As you are Englishmen, I think, I need not beg, that as from necessity most of my performers are new, you will allow for their inexperience, and encourage their timidity.

SMART. But reasonable.

FOOTE. Come then, prompter begin.

PEARSE. Lord, sir, we are all at a stand.

FOOTE. What's the matter.

PEARSE. Mrs. O-Shochnesy has return'd the part of the bawd; she says she is a gentlewoman, and it would be a reflection on her family to do any such thing.[14]

FOOTE. Indeed!

PEARSE. If it had been only a whore, says she, I should not have minded it; because no lady need be asham'd of doing that.

FOOTE. Well, there is no help for it; but these gentlemen must not be disappointed. Well, I'll do the character myself.

ACT I.

[Sir William Wealthy, *and* Mr. Richard Wealthy.

SIR WILLIAM. Come, come, brother, I know the world. People, who have their attention eternally fix'd upon one object, can't help being a little narrow in their notions.

R. WEALTHY. A sagacious remark that, and highly probable, that we merchants, who maintain a constant correspondence with the four quarters of the world, should know less of it than you fashionable fellows, whose whole experience is bounded by Westminster bridge.

SIR WILLIAM. Nay, brother, as a proof that I am not blind to the benefit of travelling, George, you know, has been in Germany these four years.

R. WEALTHY. Where he is well grounded in gaming and gluttony; France has furnish'd him with fawning and flattery; Italy equip'd him with capriols and cantatas: and thus accomplish'd, my young gentleman is return'd with a cargo of whores, cooks, valets de chambre, and fiddlesticks, a most valuable member of the British commonwealth.

SIR WILLIAM. You dislike then my system of education.

R. WEALTHY. Most sincerely.

SIR WILLIAM. The whole?

R. WEALTHY. Every particular.

SIR WILLIAM. The early part, I should imagine, might merit your approbation.

R. WEALTHY. Least of all. What, I suppose, because he has run the gauntlet thro' a public school; where, at sixteen, he had practis'd more vices than he would otherwise have heard of at sixty.

SIR WILLIAM. Ha, ha, prejudice!

R. WEALTHY. Then, indeed, you remov'd him to the university; where, lest his morals should be mended, and his understanding improv'd, you fairly set him free from the restraint of the one, and the drudgery of the other, by the priviledg'd distinction of a silk gown and velvet cap.

SIR WILLIAM. And all these evils, you think, a city-education would have prevented?

R. WEALTHY. Doubtless. – Proverbs, proverbs, brother William, convey wholesome instruction. Idleness is the root of all evil. Regular hours, constant employment, and good example, can't fail to form the mind.

SIR WILLIAM. Why truly, brother, had you stuck to your old civic vices, hypocrisy, couzenage,[15] and avarice, I don't know, whether I might not have committed George to your care; but, you cockneys now beat us suburbians at our own weapons. What, old boy, times are chang'd since the date of thy intendures; when the sleek, crop-ear'd prentice us'd to dangle after his mistress, with the great gilt Bible under his arm, to St. Bride's, on a Sunday; bring home the text, repeat the divisions of the discourse, dine at twelve, and regale, upon a gaudy day, with buns and beer at Islington, or Mile-End.[16]

R. WEALTHY. Wonderfully facetious!

SIR WILLIAM. Our modern lads are of a different metal. They have their gaming clubs in the garden, their little lodgings, the snug depositories of their rusty swords, and occasional bag-wigs; their horses for the turf; ay, and their commissions of bankruptcy too, before they are well out of their time.

R. WEALTHY. Infamous aspersion!

SIR WILLIAM. But the last meeting at Newmarket lord Lofty receiv'd, at the hazard table, the identical note from the individual taylor, to whom he had paid it but the day before, for a new set of liveries.

R. WEALTHY. Invention!

SIR WILLIAM. These are anecdotes you will never meet with in your weekly travels from Cateaton-street to your boarded box in Clapham, brother.[17]

R. WEALTHY. And yet that boarded box, as your prodigal spendthrift proceeds, will soon be the only seat of the family.

SIR WILLIAM. May be not. Who knows what a reformation our project may produce!

R. WEALTHY. I do. None at all.

SIR WILLIAM. Why so?

R. WEALTHY. Because your means are ill-proportion'd to their end. Were he my son, I would serve him –

SIR WILLIAM. As you have done your daughter. Discard him. But consider, I have but one.

R. WEALTHY. That would weigh nothing with me: for, was Charlotte to set up a will of her own, and reject the man of my choice, she must expect to share the fate of her sister. I consider families as a smaller kind of kingdoms, and would have disobedience in the one as severely punished, as rebellion in the other. Both cut off from their respective societies.

SIR WILLIAM. Poor Lucy! But surely you begin to relent. Mayn't I intercede?

R. WEALTHY. Lookee, brother, you know my mind. I will be absolute. If I meddle with the management of your son, it is at your own request; but if directly or indirectly you interfere with my banishment of that wilful, headstrong, disobedient hussy, all ties between us are broke; and I shall no more regard you as a brother, than I do her as a child.

SIR WILLIAM. I have done. But to return. You think there is probability in my plan?

R. WEALTHY. I shall attend the issue.

SIR WILLIAM. You will lend your aid, however?

R. WEALTHY. We shall see how you go on.

[*Enter* Servant.

SERVANT. A letter, sir.

SIR WILLIAM. Oh, from Capias, my attorney. Who brought it?

SERVANT. The person is without sir.

SIR WILLIAM. Bid him wait. [*Reads. Exit* Servant.

SIR WILLIAM. *Worthy Sir,*

> *The bearer is the person I promis'd to procure. I thought it was proper for you to examine him viva voce.*[18] *So if you administer a few interrogatories, you will find, by cross questioning him, whether he is a competent person to prosecute the cause you wot of. I wish you a speedy issue: and as there can be no default in your judgment, am of opinion it should be carried into immediate execution. I am,*
>
> *Worthy Sir, &C.* TIMOTHY CAPIAS.
>
> *P.S. The party's name is Samuel Shift. He is an admirable mime, or mimic, and most delectable company; as we experience every Tuesday night at our club, the Magpye and Horse-shoe, Fetter-lane.*

SIR WILLIAM. Very methodical indeed, Mr. Capias. John.

[*Enter* Servant.

Bid the person, who brought this letter, walk in. [*Exit* Servant] Have you any curiosity, brother?

R. WEALTHY. Not a jot. I must to the Change. In the evening you may find me in my counting-house, or at Jonathan's. [*Exit* R. Wealthy]

SIR WILLIAM. You shall hear from me.

[*Enter* Shift, *and* Servant.

Shut the door, John, and remember, I am not at home. [*Exit* Servant] You came from Mr. Capias?

SHIFT. I did sir.

SIR WILLIAM. Your name, I think, is Shift.

SHIFT. It is sir.

SIR WILLIAM. Did Mr. Capias drop any hint of my bus'ness with you?

SHIFT. None. He only said, with his spectacles on his nose, and his hand upon his chin, Sir William Wealthy is a respectable personage, and my client; he wants to retain you in a certain affair, and will open the case, and give you your brief himself: if you adhere to his instructions, and carry your cause, he is generous, and will discharge your bill without taxation.

SIR WILLIAM. Ha, ha, my friend Capias to a hair.[19] Well sir, this is no bad specimen of your abilities. But see that the door is fast. Now sir, you are to –

SHIFT. A moment's pause, if you please. You must know, Sir William, I am a prodigious admirer of forms. Now Mr. Capias tells me, that it is always the rule, to administer a retaining fee before you enter upon the merits.

SIR WILLIAM. Oh, sir, I beg your pardon.

SHIFT. Not that I question'd your generosity; but forms you know –

SIR WILLIAM. No apology, I beg. But as we are to have a closer connection, it may not be amiss, by way of introduction, to understand one another a little. Pray sir, where was you born?

SHIFT. At my father's.

SIR WILLIAM. Hum. – And what was he?

SHIFT. A gentleman.

SIR WILLIAM. What was you bred?

SHIFT. A gentleman.

SIR WILLIAM. How do you live?

SHIFT. Like a gentleman.

SIR WILLIAM. Cou'd nothing induce you to unbosom yourself.

SHIFT. Looke'e Sir William, there is a kind of something in your countenance, a certain openness and generosity, a *je ne sçai quoi* in your manner, that I will unlock: You shall see me all.

SIR WILLIAM. You will oblige me.

SHIFT. You must know then, that Fortune, which frequently delights to raise the noblest structures from the simplest foundations; who from a taylor made a pope, from a gin-shop an empress, and many a prime minister, from nothing at all, thought fit to raise me to my present height, from the humble employment of Light your Honour, – A link boy.

SIR WILLIAM. A pleasant fellow. – Who were your parents.

SHIFT. I was produced, sir, by a left-handed marriage,[20] in the language of the news papers, between an illustrious lamp-lighter, and an eminent itinerant cat and dog butcher. – Cat's meat, and dog's meat. – I dare say, you have heard my mother, sir. But as to this happy pair, I owe little besides my being; I shall drop them where they dropt me, in the street.

SIR WILLIAM. Proceed.

SHIFT. My first knowledge of the world I owe to a school, which has produced many a great man; the avenues of the play-house: There sir, leaning on my extinguish'd link, I learn'd dexterity from pick-pockets, connivance from constables, politics and fashions from footmen, and the art of making and breaking a promise, from their masters.[21] Here, sirrah, light me across the kennel. – I hope your honour will remember poor Jack, – You ragged rascal, I have no halfpence – I'll pay you the next time I see you. – But, lack-a-day, sir, that time I saw as seldom as his tradesmen.

SIR WILLIAM. Very well.

SHIFT. To these accomplishments from without the theatre, I must add one that I obtain'd within.

SIR WILLIAM. How did you gain admittance there?

SHIFT. My merit, sir, that, like my link, threw a radiance round me. – A detachment from the head quarters here, took possession in the summer, of a country corporation, where I did the honours of the barn, by sweeping the stage, and clipping the candles. There my skill and address was so conspicuous, that it procur'd me the same office the ensuing winter, at Drury-Lane, where I acquir'd intrepidity; the crown of all my virtues.

SIR WILLIAM. How did you obtain that?

SHIFT. By my post. For I think, sir, he that dares stand the shot of the gallery in lighting, snuffing, and sweeping, the first night of a new play, may bid defiance to the pillory, with all its customary compliments.

SIR WILLIAM. Some truth in that.

SHIFT. But an unlucky crab-apple, apply'd to my right eye, by a patriot gingerbread baker from the Borough, who would not suffer three dancers from Switzerland, because he hated the French, forced me to a precipitate retreat.[22]

SIR WILLIAM. Poor devil.

SHIFT. Broglio and Contades have done the same.[23] But as it happen'd, like a tennis-ball, I rose higher from the rebound.

SIR WILLIAM. How so?

SHIFT. My misfortune, sir, mov'd the compassion of one of our performers, a whimsical man, he took me into his service. To him I owe what, I believe, will make me useful to you.

SIR WILLIAM. Explain.

SHIFT. Why, sir my master was remarkably happy in an art, which however disesteemed at present, is, by Tully, reckon'd amonst the perfections of an orator; Mimickry.

SIR WILLIAM. Why you are deeply read, Mr. Shift.

SHIFT. A smattering. – But as I was saying, sir, nothing came amiss to my master. Bypeds, or quadrupeds; rationals, or animals; from the clamours of the bar, to the cackles of the barn door; from the soporific twang of the tabernacle at Tottenham-Court, to the melodious bray of their long-ear'd brethren[24] in Bunhill Fields; all were objects of his imitation, and my attention. In a word, sir, for two whole years, under this professor, I study'd and starv'd, impoverish'd my body, and pamper'd my mind, till thinking myself pretty near equal to my master, I made him one of his own bows, and set up for myself.

SIR WILLIAM. You have been successful, I hope.

SHIFT. Pretty well. I can't complain. My art, sir, is a pass-par-tout.[25] I seldom want employment. Let's see how stand my engagements. [*Pulls out a pocket-book*] Hum, – hum, – Oh, Wednesday at Mr. Gammut's near Hanover-square; there, there, I shall make a meal upon the Mingotti, for her ladyship is in the opera interest: but, however, I shall revenge her cause upon her rival, Mattei. Sunday evening at Lady Sustinuto's concert. Thursday I dine upon the actors, with ten templers, at the Mitre in Fleet-Street. Friday I am to give the amorous parly of two intriguing cats in a gutter, with the disturbing of a hen-roost, at Mr. Deputy Sugarsops, near the Monument. So, sir, you see my hands are full. In short, Sir William, there is not a buck or a turtle devoured within the bills of mortality, but there, I may, if I please, stick a napkin under my chin.

SIR WILLIAM. I'm afraid, Mr. Shift, I must break in a little upon your engagements; but you shall be no loser by the bargain.

SHIFT. Command me.

SIR WILLIAM. You can be secret as well as serviceable.

SHIFT. Mute as a mackrel.

SIR WILLIAM. Come hither then. If you betray me to my son.

SHIFT. Scalp me.

SIR WILLIAM. Enough. – You must know then, the hopes of our family are, Mr. Shift, center'd in one boy.

SHIFT. And, I warrant he is a hopeful one.

SIR WILLIAM. No interruption I beg. George has been abroad these four years, and from his late behaviour, I have reason to believe, that had a certain event happened, which I am afraid he wished, – my death. –

SHIFT. Yes; that's natural enough.

SIR WILLIAM. Nay, pray, – there wou'd soon be an end to an ancient and honourable family.

SHIFT. Very melancholy indeed. But families, like besoms, will wear to the stumps, and finally fret out, as you say.

SIR WILLIAM. Pry'thee peace, for five minutes.

SHIFT. I am tongue-ty'd.

SIR WILLIAM. Now I have projected a scheme to prevent this calamity.

SHIFT. Ay, I should be glad to hear that.

SIR WILLIAM. I am going to tell it you.

SHIFT. Proceed.

SIR WILLIAM. George, as I have contriv'd it, shall experience all the misery of real ruin, without running the least risque.

SHIFT. Ay, that will be a coup de maître.[26]

SIR WILLIAM. I have prevail'd upon his uncle, a wealthy citizen.

SHIFT. I don't like a city plot.

SIR WILLIAM. I tell thee it is my own.

SHIFT. I beg pardon.

SIR WILLIAM. My brother, I say, some time since, wrote him a circumstantial account of my death; upon which, he is returned, in full expectation of succeeding to my estate.

SHIFT. Immediately?

SIR WILLIAM. No; when at age. In about three months.

SHIFT. I understand you.

SIR WILLIAM. Now, sir, guessing into what hands my heedless boy would naturally fall on his return, I have, in a feign'd character, associated myself with a set of rascals, who will spread every bait that can flatter folly, inflame extravagance, allure inexperience, or catch credulity. And when by their means, he thinks himself reduc'd to the last extremity; lost even to the most distant hope –

SHIFT. What then?

SIR WILLIAM. Then will I step in like his guardian-angel, and snatch him from perdition. If, mortify'd by misery, he becomes conscious of his errors, I have sav'd my son; but if, on the other hand, gratitude can't bind, nor ruin reclaim him, I will cast him out, as an alien to my blood, and trust for the support of my name and family to a remoter branch.

SHIFT. Bravely resolv'd. But what part am I to sustain in this drama?

SIR WILLIAM. Why George, you are to know, is already stript of what money he could command, by two sharpers:[27] but as I never trust them out of my sight, they can't deceive me.

SHIFT. Out of your sight!

SIR WILLIAM. Why, I tell thee, I am one of the knot: an adept in their science, can slip, shuffle, cog, or cut with the best of 'em.

SHIFT. How do you escape your son's notice?

SIR WILLIAM. His firm persuasion of my death, with the extravagance of my disguise. – Why, I wou'd engage to elude your penetration, when I am beau'd out for the baron. But of that by and by. He has recourse, after his ill success, to the cent. per cent. gentry, the usurers, for a farther supply.

SHIFT. Natural enough.

SIR WILLIAM. Pray do you know, – I forget his name, – a wrinkled old fellow, in a thread-bare coat? He sits every morning from twelve till two, in the left corner of Lloyd's coffee-house; and every evening, from five till eight, under the clock, at the Temple-exchange.

SHIFT. What, little Transfer the broker?

SIR WILLIAM. The same. Do you know him?

SHIFT. Know him! Ay, rot him. It was but last Easter Tuesday, he had me turn'd out at a feast, in Leather-seller's Hall, for singing Room for Cuckolds, like a parrot; and vow'd it meant a reflection upon the whole body corporate.[28]

SIR WILLIAM. You have reason to remember him.

SHIFT. Yes, yes. I recommended a minor to him myself, for the loan only of fifty pounds; and wou'd you believe it, as I hope to be sav'd, we din'd, supp'd, and wetted five and thirty guineas upon tick, in meetings at the Cross-keys, in order to settle the terms; and after all, the scoundrel would not lend us a stiver.[29]

SIR WILLIAM. Cou'd you personate him?

SHIFT. Him! Oh, you shall see me shift into his shamble in a minute: and, with a wither'd face, a bit of a purple nose, a cautionary stammer, and a sleek silver head, I would undertake to deceive even his banker. But to speak the truth, I have a friend that can do this inimitably well. Have not you something of more consequence for me?

SIR WILLIAM. I have. Cou'd not you, master Shift, assume another shape? You have attended auctions.

SHIFT. Auctions! a constant puff. Deep in the mystery; a professed connoisseur, from a niger to a nautilus, from the Apollo Belvidere to a butterfly.[30]

SIR WILLIAM. One of these insinuating, oily orators, I will get you to personate: for we must have the plate and jewels in our possession, or they will soon fall into other hands.

SHIFT. I will do it.

SIR WILLIAM. Within I'll give you farther instructions.

SHIFT. I'll follow you.

SIR WILLIAM. [*Going, returns*] You will want materials.

SHIFT. Oh, my dress I can be furnished with in five minutes. [*Exit* Sir William] A whimsical old blade, this. I shall laugh if his scheme miscarries.[31] I have a strange mind to lend it a lift – never had a greater – Pho, a damn'd unnatural connection this of mine! – What have I to do with fathers and guardians! A parcel of preaching, prudent, careful curmudgeonly – dead to pleasures themselves, and the blasters of it in others – Mere dogs in a manger – No, no, I'll veer, tack about, open my budget to the boy, and join in a counter plot. But hold, hold, friend Stephen, see first how the land lies. Who knows whether this Germaniz'd genius has parts to comprehend, or spirit to reward thy merit. There's danger in that, ay, marry is there. 'Egad, before I shift the helm, I'll first examine the coast; and then if there be but a bold shore and a good bottom, have a care, old Square Toes, you will meet with your match.

[*Exit. Enter* Sir George*,* Loader*, and* Servant.

SIR GEORGE. Let the martin pannels for the vis a vis be carried to Long Acre, and the pye-balls sent to Hall's to be bitted[32] – You will give me leave to be in your debt till the evening, Mr. Loader. I have but just enough left to discharge the baron; and we must, you know, be punctual with him, for the credit of the country.

LOADER. Fire him, a snub-nos'd son of a bitch. Levant me,[33] but he got enough last night to purchase a principality amongst his countrymen, the High-dutchians and Hussarians.

SIR GEORGE. You had your share, Mr. Loader.

LOADER. Who, I! Lurch me at four, but I was mark'd to the top of your tick, by the baron, my dear. What, I am no cinque and quarter man. Come shall we have a dip in the history of the Four Kings, this morning?[34]

SIR GEORGE. Rather too early. Besides, it is the rule abroad, never to engage a-fresh, till our old scores are discharg'd.[35]

LOADER. Capot me,[36] but those lads abroad are pretty fellows, let 'em say what they will. Here, sir, they will vowel you, from father to son, to the twentieth generation. They wou'd as soon now-a-days, pay a tradesman's bill, as a play debt. All sense of honour is gone, not a stiver stirring. They cou'd as soon raise the dead as two pounds two; nick me, but I have a great mind to tie up, and ruin the rascals – What, has Transfer been here this morning?

[*Enter* Dick.

SIR GEORGE. Any body here this morning, Dick?

DICK. No body, your honour.

LOADER. Repique[37] the rascal. He promis'd to be here before me.

DICK. I beg your honour's pardon. Mrs. Cole,[38] from the Piazza, was here, between seven and eight.

SIR GEORGE. An early hour for a lady of her calling.

DICK. Mercy on me! The poor gentlewoman is mortally altered since we us'd to lodge there, in our jaunts from Oxford; wrapt up in flannels; all over the rheumatise.[39]

LOADER. Ay, ay, old Moll is at her last stake.

DICK. She bad me say, she just stopt in her way to the tabernacle;[40] after the exhortation, she says, she'll call again.

SIR GEORGE. Exhortation! Oh, I recollect. Well, whilst they only make proselytes from that profession, they are heartily welcome to them. She does not mean to make me a convert?

DICK. I believe she has some such design upon me; for she offer'd me a book of hymns, a shilling, and a dram,[41] to go along with her.

SIR GEORGE. No bad scheme, Dick. Thou hast a fine, sober, psalm-singing countenance; and when thou hast been some time in their trammels,[42] may'st make as able a teacher as the best of 'em.

DICK. Laud, sir, I want learning.

SIR GEORGE. Oh, the spirit, the spirit will supply all that Dick, never fear.

[*Enter* Sir William, *as a German baron.*

My dear baron, what news from the Haymarket? What says the Florenza?[43] Does she yield? Shall I be happy? Say yes, and command my fortune.

SIR WILLIAM. I was never did see so fine a woman since I was leave Hamburgh; dere was all de colour, all red and white, dat was quite natural; point d'artifice. Then she was dance and sing – I vow to heaven, I was never see de like.[44]

SIR GEORGE. But how did she receive my embassy? What hopes?

SIR WILLIAM. Why dere was monsieur le chevalier, when I first enter, dree or four damn'd queer people; ah, ah, drought I, by gad I guess your business. Dere was one fat big woman's, dat I know long time: le valet de chambre was tell me dat she came from a grand merchand; by your leave, stick to your shop; or, if you must have de pretty girl, dere is de play-hous, dat do very well for you; but for de opera, pardoner, by gar dat is meat for your master.

SIR GEORGE. Insolent mechanic! – but she despis'd him.

SIR WILLIAM. Ah, may foy,[45] he is damn'd rich, has beaucoup de guineas; but after de fat woman was go, I was tell the signora, madam, der is one certain chevalier of dis country, who has travell'd, see de word, bien fait, well made, beaucoup d'Esprit, a great deal of monies, who beg, by gar, to have de honour to throw himself at your feet.

SIR GEORGE. Well, well, baron.

SIR WILLIAM. She aska your name; as soon as I tell her, aha, by gar, dans an instant, she melt like de lomp of sugar: she run to her bureau, and, in de minute, return wid de paper.

SIR GEORGE. Give it me. [*Reads*] *Les preliminaires d'une traité entre le chevalier Wealthy, and la signora Diamenti.* A bagatelle, a trifle: She shall have it.

LOADER. Harkee, knight, what is all that there outlandish stuff?

SIR GEORGE. Read, read. The eloquence of angels, my dear baron.

LOADER. Slam me, but the man's mad! I don't understand their Gibberish – What is it in English?

SIR GEORGE. The preliminaries of a subsidiary treaty, between Sir G. Wealthy, and Signora Florence; That the said signora will resign the possession of her person to the said Sir George, on the payment of three hundred guineas monthly, for equipage, table, domestics, dress, dogs, and diamonds; her debts to be duly discharged, and a note advanced of five hundred, by way of entrance.

LOADER. Zounds, what a cormorant![46] She must be devilish handsome.

SIR GEORGE. I am told so.

LOADER. Told so! Why did you never see her?

SIR GEORGE. No; and possibly never may, but from my box at the opera.

LOADER. Hey-day. Why what the devil –

SIR GEORGE. Ha, ha, you stare, I don't wonder at it. This is an elegant refinement, unknown to the gross voluptuaries of this part of the world. This is, Mr. Loader, what may be called a debt to your dignity: for an opera girl is as essential a piece of equipage for a man of fashion, as his coach.[47]

LOADER. The devil.

SIR GEORGE. 'Tis for the vulgar only to enjoy what they possess: the distinction of ranks and conditions are, to have hounds, and never hunt; cooks, and dine in taverns; houses, you never inhabit; and mistresses, you never enjoy –

LOADER. And debts you never pay. Egad, I am not surpriz'd at it; if this be your trade, no wonder that you want money for necessaries, when you give such a damn'd deal for nothing at all.

[*Enter* Servant.

SERVANT. Mrs. Cole, to wait upon your honour.

SIR GEORGE. My dear baron, run, dispatch my affair, conclude my treaty, and thank her for the very reasonable conditions.

SIR WILLIAM. I shall.

SIR GEORGE. Mr. Loader, shall I trouble you to introduce the lady. She is, I think, your acquaintance.

LOADER. Who, old Moll! Ay, ay, she's your market woman. I wou'd not give six-pence for your signoras. One armful of good, wholesome British beauty, is worth a ship-load of their trapsing, tawdry trollops. But hark'ee, baron, how much for the table? Why she must have a devilish large family, or a monstrous stomach.

SIR WILLIAM. Ay, ay, dere is her maden la complaisante to walk in de park, and to go to de play; two broders, deux valets, dree Spanish lap-dogs, and de monkey.

LOADER. Strip me, if I would set five shillings against the whole gang. May my partner renounce, with the game in his hand, if I were you, knight, if I would not – [*Exit* Servant.

SIR GEORGE. But the lady waits. [*Ex.* Load. A strange fellow this. What a whimsical jargon he talks. Not an idea abstracted from play. To say truth, I am sincerely sick of my acquaintance: But, however, I have the first people in the kingdom to keep me in countenance. Death and the dice level all distinctions.

[*Enter* Mrs. Cole, *supported by* Loader *and* Dick.[48]]

MRS. COLE. Gently, gently, good Mr. Loader.

LOADER. Come along, old Moll. Why, you jade, you look as rosy this morning, I must have a smack at your muns. Here, taste her, she is as good as old hock to get you a stomach.

MRS. COLE. Fye, Mr. Loader, I thought you had forgot me.

LOADER. I forget you! I would as soon forget what is trumps.

MRS. COLE. Softly, softly, young man. There, there, mighty well. And how does your honour do? I han't seen your honour, I can't tell the – Oh, mercy on me, there's a twinge –

SIR GEORGE. What is the matter, Mrs. Cole!

MRS. COLE. My old disorder, the rheumatise; I ha'n't been able to get a wink of – Oh law, what, you have been in town these two days?

SIR GEORGE. Since Wednesday.

MRS. COLE. And never once call'd upon old Cole. No, no, I am worn out, thrown by and forgotten, like a tatter'd garment, as Mr. Squintum says.[49] Oh, he is a dear man! But for him I had been a lost sheep; never known the comforts of the new birth; no, – There's your old friend, Kitty Carrot, at home still. What, shall we see you this evening! I have kept the green room for you ever since I heard you were in town.

LOADER. What, shall we take a snap at old Moll's. Hey, beldam, have you a good batch of Burgundy abroach?

MRS. COLE. Bright as a ruby; and for flavour! You know the colonel – He and Jenny Cummins drank three flasks, hand to fist, last night.

LOADER. What, and bilk thee of thy share?

MRS. COLE. Ah, don't mention it, Mr. Loader. No, that's all over with me. The time has been, when I could have earn'd thirty shillings a day by own dry drinking, and the next morning was neither sick nor sorry: But now, O laud, a thimbleful turns me topsy turvey.

LOADER. Poor old girl!

MRS. COLE. Ay, I have done with these idle vanities; my thoughts are fix'd upon a better place. What, I suppose, Mr. Loader, you will be for your old friend the black-ey'd girl, from Rosemary-Lane. Ha, ha. Well, 'tis a merry little tit. A thousand pities she's such a reprobate! – But she'll mend; her time is not come: all shall have their call, as Mr. Squintum says, sooner or later; regeneration is not the work of a day. No, no, no. – Oh!

SIR GEORGE. Not worse, I hope.

MRS. COLE. Rack, rack, gnaw, gnaw, never easy, a bed or up, all's one. Pray, honest friend, have you any clary, or mint water in the house?

DICK. A case of French drams.

MRS. COLE. Heaven defend me! I would not touch a dram for the world.[50]

SIR GEORGE. They are but cordials, Mrs. Cole. Fetch 'em, you blockhead. [*Ex.* Dick.

MRS. COLE. Ay, I am a going; a wasting and a wasting, Sir George. What will become of the house when I am gone, heaven knows. – No. – When people are mist, then they are mourn'd. Sixteen years have I liv'd in the garden, comfortably and creditably; and, tho' I say it, could have got bail any hour of the day: Reputable tradesmen, Sir George, neighbours Mr. Loader knows; no knock me down doings in my house. A set of regular, sedate, sober customers. No rioters. Sixteen did I say – Ay, eighteen years I have paid scot and lot[51] in the parish of St. Paul's, and during the whole time, no body have said, Mrs. Cole, why do you so? Unless twice that I was before Sir Thomas De Val, and three times in the round-house.

SIR GEORGE. Nay, don't weep, Mrs. Cole.

LOADER. May I lose deal, with an honour at bottom, if old Moll does not bring tears into my eyes.

MRS. COLE. However, it is a comfort after all, to think one has past thro' the world with credit and character. Ay, a good name, as Mr. Squintum says, is better than a gallipot[52] of ointment.

[*Enter* Dick, *with a dram.*

LOADER. Come, haste, Dick, haste; sorrow is dry. Here, Moll, shall I fill thee a bumper?[53]

MRS. COLE. Hold, hold, Mr. Loader. Heaven help you. I could as soon swallow the Thames. Only a sip, to keep the gout out of my stomach.

LOADER. Why then, here's to thee. – Levant me, but it is supernaculum. – Speak when you have enough.

MRS. COLE. I won't trouble you for the glass; my hands do so tremble and shake, I shall but spill the good creature.

LOADER. Well pull'd. But now to business. Pr'ythee, Moll, did not I see a tight young wench, in a linnen gown, knock at your door this morning?

MRS. COLE. Ay; A young thing from the country.

LOADER. Could we not get a peep at her this evening?

MRS. COLE. Impossible! She is engaged to Sir Timothy Totter. I have taken earnest[54] for her these three months.

LOADER. Pho, what signifies such a fellow as that. Tip him an old trader, and give her to the knight.

MRS. COLE. Tip him an old trader! – Mercy on us, where do you expect to go when you dye, Mr. Loader?

LOADER. Crop me, but this Squintum has turn'd her brains.

SIR GEORGE. Nay, Mr. Loader, I think the gentleman has wrought a most happy reformation.

MRS. COLE. Oh, it was a wonderful work. There had I been tossing in a sea of sin, without rudder or compass. And had not the good gentleman piloted me into the harbour of grace, I must have struck against the rocks of reprobation, and have been quite swallow'd up in the whirlpool of despair. He was the precious instrument of my spiritual sprinkling. – But however, Sir George, if your mind be set upon a young country thing, to-morrow night I believe I can furnish you.[55]

LOADER. As how?

MRS. COLE. I have advertis'd this morning, in the register-office, for servants under seventeen; and ten to one but I light on something that will do.

LOADER. Pillory me, but it has a face.

MRS. COLE. Truly, consistently with my conscience, I wou'd do any thing for your honour.

SIR GEORGE. Right, Mrs. Cole, never lose sight of that monitor. But pray, how long has this heavenly change been wrought in you?

MRS. COLE. Ever since my last visitation of the gout. Upon my first fit, seven years ago, I began to have my doubts, and my waverings; but I was lost in a labyrinth, and no body to shew me the road. One time, I thought of dying a Roman, which is truly a comfortable communion enough for one of us: but it wou'd not do.

SIR GEORGE. Why not?

MRS. COLE. I went one summer over to Boulogne to repent; and, wou'd you believe it, the barefooted, bald-pate beggars, would not give me absolution, without I quitted my business! – Did you ever hear of such a set of scabby – Besides, I could not bear their barbarity. Wou'd you believe it, Mr. Loader, they lock up for their lives, in a nunnery, the prettiest, sweetest, tender, young things! – Oh, six of them, for a season, wou'd finish my business here, and then I shou'd have nothing to do, but to think of hereafter.

LOADER. Brand me, what a country!

SIR GEORGE. Oh, scandalous!

MRS. COLE. O no, it would not do. So, in my last illness, I was wish'd to Mr. Squintum, who stepp'd in with his saving grace, got me with the new birth, and I became, as you see, regenerate, and another creature.

[*Enter* Dick.

DICK. Mr. Transfer, sir, has sent to know if your honour be at home.

SIR GEORGE. Mrs. Cole, I am mortify'd to part with you. But bus'ness, you know –

MRS. COLE. True, Sir George. Mr. Loader, your arm – Gently, oh, oh!

SIR GEORGE. Wou'd you take another thimbleful, Mrs. Cole?

MRS. COLE. Not a drop – I shall see you this evening.

SIR GEORGE. Depend upon me.

MRS. COLE. To-morrow I hope to suit you – We are to have, at the tabernacle, an occasional hymn, with a thanksgiving sermon for my recovery. After which, I shall call at the register-office, and see what goods my advertisement has brought in.

SIR GEORGE. Extremely obliged to you, Mrs. Cole.

MRS. COLE. Or if that shou'd not do, I have a tid bit at home, will suit your stomach. Never brush'd by a beard. Well, heaven bless you – Softly, have a care, Mr. Loader – Richard, you may as well give me the bottle into the chair, for fear I should be taken ill on the road. Gently – so, so. [*Exit* Mrs. Cole *and* Loader.

SIR GEORGE. Dick, shew Mr. Transfer in – Ha, ha, what a hodge podge! How the jade has jumbled together the carnal and the spiritual; With what ease she reconciles her new birth to her old calling! – No wonder these preachers have plenty of proselytes, whilst they have the address, so comfortably to blend the hitherto jarring interests of the two worlds.

[*Enter* Loader.

LOADER. Well, knight, I have hous'd her; but they want you within, sir.

SIR GEORGE. I'll go to them immediately.

ACT II.

[*Enter* Dick, *introducing* Transfer.

DICK. My master will come to you presently.

[*Enter* Sir George.

SIR GEORGE. Mr. Transfer, your servant.

TRANSFER. Your Honour's very humble. I thought to have found Mr. Loader here.

SIR GEORGE. He will return immediately. Well, Mr. Transfer – but take a chair – you have had a long walk. Mr. Loader, I presume, open'd to you the urgency of my bus'ness.

TRANSFER. Ay, ay, the general cry, money, money! I don't know, for my part, where all the money is flown to. Formerly a note, with a tolerable endorsement, was as current as cash. If your uncle Richard now would join in this security –

SIR GEORGE. Impossible.

TRANSFER. Ay, like enough. I wish you were of age.

SIR GEORGE. So do I. But as that will be consider'd in the premium –

TRANSFER. True, true – I see you understand bus'ness – And what sum does your Honour lack at present?

SIR GEORGE. Lack! – How much have you brought?

TRANSFER. Who, I? – Dear me, None.

SIR GEORGE. Zounds, none!

TRANSFER. Lack-a-day, none to be had, I think. All the morning have I been upon the hunt. There, Ephraim Barbones, the tallow-chandler, in Thames-street, us'd to be a never-failing chap; not a guinea to be got there. Then I totter'd away to Nebuchadnezzar Zebulon, in the Old Jewry, but it happen'd to the Saturday; and they never touch on the Sabbath, you know.[56]

SIR GEORGE. Why what the devil can I do?

TRANSFER. Good me, I did not know your honour had been so press'd.

SIR GEORGE. My Honour prest! Yes, my Honour is not only prest, but ruin'd, unless I can raise money to redeem it. That blockhead Loader, to depend upon this old doating –

TRANSFER. Well, well, now I declare, I am quite sorry to see your Honour in such a taking.

SIR GEORGE. Damn your sorrow.

TRANSFER. But come, don't be cast down: Tho' money is not to be had, money's worth may, and that's the same thing.

SIR GEORGE. How, dear Transfer?

TRANSFER. Why I have, at my warehouse in the city, ten casks of whale-blubber, a large cargo of Dantzick dowlass, with a curious sortment of Birmingham hafts, and Whitney blankets for exportation.[57]

SIR GEORGE. Hey!

TRANSFER. And stay, stay, then again, at my country-house, the bottom of Gray's-Inn-Lane, there's a hundred tun of fine old hay, only damag'd a little last winter, for want of thatching; with forty load of flint stones.

SIR GEORGE. Well.

TRANSFER. Your Honour may have all these for a reasonable profit, and convert them into cash.

SIR GEORGE. Blubber and blankets! Why, you old rascal, do you banter me?

TRANSFER. Who I! O law, marry heaven forbid.

SIR GEORGE. Get out of my – you stuttering scoundrel.

TRANSFER. If your honour would but hear me. –

SIR GEORGE. Troop, I say, unless you have a mind to go a shorter way than you came. [*Exit* Transfer] And yet there is something so uncommonly ridiculous in his proposal, that were my mind more at ease. [*Enter* Loader] So, sir, you have recommended me to a fine fellow.

LOADER. What's the matter?

SIR GEORGE. He can't supply me with a shilling! And wants, besides, to make me a dealer in dowlass.

LOADER. Ay, and a very good commodity too. People that are upon ways and means, must not be nice, knight. A pretty piece of work you have made here. Thrown up the cards, with the game in your hands.

SIR GEORGE. Why, prythee, of what use wou'd his –

LOADER. Use! of every use. Procure you the spankers,[58] my boy. I have a broker, that in a twinkling, shall take off your bargain.

SIR GEORGE. Indeed.

LOADER. Indeed! Ay, indeed. You sit down to hazard, and not know the chances! I'll call him back. – Holo, Transfer. – A pretty, little, busy, bustling – You may travel miles, before you will meet with his match. If there is one pound in the city, he will get it. He creeps, like a ferret, into their bags, and makes the yellow boys bolt again.[59]

[*Enter* Transfer.

Come hither, little Transfer; what, man, our Minor was a little too hasty; He did not understand trap; knows nothing of the game, my dear.

TRANSFER. What I said, was to serve Sir George; as he seem'd –

LOADER. I told him so; Well, well, we will take thy commodities, were they as many more. But try, pr'ythee, if thou coud'st not procure us some of the ready, for present spending.

TRANSFER. Let me consider.

LOADER. Ay, do, come: shuffle thy brains; never fear the baronet. To let a lord of lands want shiners; 'tis a shame.

TRANSFER. I do recollect, in this quarter of the town, an old friend, that us'd to do things in this way.

LOADER. Who?

TRANSFER. Statute, the scrivener.

LOADER. Slam me, but he has nick'd the chance.

TRANSFER. A hard man, master Loader.

SIR GEORGE. No matter.

TRANSFER. His demands are exorbitant.

SIR GEORGE. That is no fault of ours.

LOADER. Well said, knight.

TRANSFER. But to save time, I had better mention his terms.

LOADER. Unnecessary.

TRANSFER. Five per cent. legal interest.

SIR GEORGE. He shall have it.

TRANSFER. Ten, the præmium.

SIR GEORGE. No more words.

TRANSFER. Then, as you are not of age, five more for ensuring your life.

LOADER. We will give it.

TRANSFER. As for what he will demand for the risque –

SIR GEORGE. He shall be satisfy'd.

TRANSFER. You pay the attorney.

SIR GEORGE. Amply, amply. Loader, dispatch him.

LOADER. There, there, little Transfer; now every thing is settled. All terms shall be comply'd with, reasonable or unreasonable. What, our principal is a man of honour. [*Ex.* Transfer] Hey, my knight, this is doing business. This Pinch is a sure card.

[*Re-enter* Transfer.

TRANSFER. I had forgot one thing. I am not the principal; you pay the brokerage.

LOADER. Ay, ay; and a handsome present into the bargain, never fear.

TRANSFER. Enough, enough.

LOADER. Hark'ee, Transfer, we'll take the Birmingham hafts and Whitney wares.

TRANSFER. They shall be forth coming. – You would not have the hay, with the flints!

LOADER. Every pebble of 'em. The magistrates of the Borough, baronet, are infirm and gouty. He shall deal them as new pavement. [*Exit* Transfer.

LOADER. So, that's settled. I believe, knight, I can lend you a helping hand as to the last article. I know some traders that will tick: fellows with finery. Not commodities of such clumsey conveyance as old Transfer's.

SIR GEORGE. You are obliging.

LOADER. I'll do it boy. And get you, into the bargain, a bonny auctioneer, that shall dispose of 'em all in a crack. [*Exeunt.* Loader]

[*Enter* Dick.

DICK. Your uncle, sir, has been waiting some time.

SIR GEORGE. He comes in a lucky hour. Shew him in. [*Exit* Dick.

SIR GEORGE. Now for a lecture. My situation sha'n't sink my spirits however. Here comes the musty trader, running over with remonstrances. I must banter the cit.

[*Enter* Richard Wealthy.

R. WEALTHY. So, sir, what, I suppose, this is a spice of your foreign breeding, to let your uncle kick his heels in your hall, whilst your present chamber is crowded with pimps, bawds, and gamesters.

SIR GEORGE. Oh, a proof of my respect, dear nuncle. Would it have been decent now, nuncle, to have introduc'd you into such company?

R. WEALTHY. Wonderfully considerate! Well, young man, and what do you think will be the end of all this! Here, I have received by the last mail, a quire of your draughts[60] from abroad. I see you were determin'd our neighbours should taste of your magnificence.

SIR GEORGE. Yes, I think I did some credit to my country.

R. WEALTHY. And how are all these to be paid?

SIR GEORGE. That I submit to you, dear nuncle.

R. WEALTHY. From me! – Not a souse to keep you from the Counter.

SIR GEORGE. Why then let the scoundrels stay. It is their duty. I have other demands, debts of honour, which must be discharg'd.

R. WEALTHY. Here's a diabolical distinction! Here's a prostitution of words! – Honour! 'Sdeath, that a rascal, who has pick'd your pocket, shall have his crime gilded with the most sacred distinction, and his plunder punctually paid, whilst the industrious mechanic, who ministers to your very wants, shall have his debt delay'd, and his demand treated as insolent.

SIR GEORGE. Oh, a truce to this threadbare trumpery, dear nuncle. I confess my folly. But make yourself easy; you won't be troubled with many more of my visits.

R. WEALTHY. I own I was weak enough to design a short expostulation with you; but as we in the city know the true value of time, I shall take care not to squander away any more of it upon you.

SIR GEORGE. A prudent resolution.

R. WEALTHY. One commission, however, I can't dispense with myself from executing. – It was agreed between your father and me, that as he had but one son and I one daughter –

SIR GEORGE. Your gettings should be added to the estate, and my cousin Margery and I squat down together in the comfortable state of matrimony.

R. WEALTHY. Puppy! Such was our intention. Now his last will claims this contract.

SIR GEORGE. Dispatch, dear nuncle.

R. WEALTHY. Why then, in a word, see me here demand the execution.

SIR GEORGE. What d'you mean? For me to marry Margery?

R. WEALTHY. I do.

SIR GEORGE. What, moi-me?

R. WEALTHY. You, you. – Your answer, ay, or no?

SIR GEORGE. Why then concisely and briefly, without evasion, equivocation, or farther circumlocution, – No.

R. WEALTHY. I am glad of it.

SIR GEORGE. So am I.

R. WEALTHY. But pray, if it would not be too great a favour, what objections can you have to my daughter? Not that I want to remove 'em, but merely out of curiosity. What objections?

SIR GEORGE. None. I neither know her, nor have seen her; enquired after her, or ever intend it.

R. WEALTHY. What, perhaps, I am the stumbling block.

SIR GEORGE. You have hit it.

R. WEALTHY. Ay, now we come to the point. Well, and pray –

SIR GEORGE. Why it is not so much a dislike to your person, tho' that is exceptionable enough, but your profession, dear nuncle, is an insuperable obstacle.

R. WEALTHY. Good lack! And what harm has that done, pray?

SIR GEORGE. Done! So stain'd, polluted, and tainted the whole mass of your blood, thrown such a blot on your 'scutcheon,[61] as ten regular successions can hardly efface.

R. WEALTHY. The duce.

SIR GEORGE. And could you now, consistently with your duty as a faithful guardian, recommend my union with the daughter of a trader?

R. WEALTHY. Why, indeed, I ask pardon; I am afraid I did not weigh this matter as maturely as I ought.

SIR GEORGE. Oh, a horrid, barbarous scheme?

R. WEALTHY. But then I thought her having the honour to partake of the same flesh and blood with yourself, might prove in some measure, a kind of Fuller's-earth, to scoure out the dirty spots, contracted by commerce.

SIR GEORGE. Impossible!

R. WEALTHY. Besides, here it has been the practice even of peers.

SIR GEORGE. Don't mention the unnatural intercourse! Thank heav'n, Mr. Richard Wealthy, my education has been in another country; where I have been too well instructed in the value of nobility, to think of intermixing it with the offspring of a Bourgois. Why, what apology cou'd I make to my children, for giving them such a mother?

R. WEALTHY. I did not think of that. Then I must despair, I am afraid.

SIR GEORGE. I can afford but little hopes. Tho', upon recollection – Is the grissette pretty?

R. WEALTHY. A parent may be partial. She is thought so.

SIR GEORGE. Ah la jolie petite Bourgoise; Poor girl, I sincerely pitty her. And I suppose, to procure her emersion from the mercantile mud, no consideration wou'd be spar'd.

R. WEALTHY. Why, to be sure, for such an honour, one wou'd strain a point.

SIR GEORGE. Why then, not totally to destroy your hopes, I do recollect an edict in favour of Britany; that when a man of distinction engages in commerce, his nobility is suffer'd to sleep.

R. WEALTHY. Indeed!

SIR GEORGE. And upon his quitting the contagious connexion, he is permitted to resume his rank.

R. WEALTHY. That's fortunate.

SIR GEORGE. So, nuncle Richard, if you will sell out of the stocks, shut up your counting-house, and quit St. Mary Ax for Grosvenor-square –

R. WEALTHY. What then?

SIR GEORGE. Why, when your rank has had time to rouse itself, for I think your nobility, nuncle, has had a pretty long nap, if the girl's person is pleasing, and the purchase money is adequate to the honour, I may in time, be prevail'd upon to restore her to the right of her family.[62]

R. WEALTHY. Amazing condescension!

SIR GEORGE. Good-nature is my foible. But, upon my soul, I wou'd not have gone so far for any body else.

R. WEALTHY. I can contain no longer. Hear me, spend-thrift, prodigal, do you know, that in ten days your whole revenue won't purchase you a feather to adorn your empty head.

SIR GEORGE. Hey day, what's the matter now?

R. WEALTHY. And that you derive every acre of your boasted patrimony, from your great uncle, a soap-boiler!

SIR GEORGE. Infamous aspersion!

R. WEALTHY. It was his bags, the fruits of his honest industry, that preserv'd your lazy, beggarly nobility. His wealth repair'd your tottering hall, from the ruins of which, even the rats had run.

SIR GEORGE. Better our name had perish'd! insupportable! soap-boiler, uncle!

R. WEALTHY. Traduce a trader, in a country of commerce! It is treason against the community. And, for your punishment, I wou'd have you restor'd to the sordid condition from whence we drew you. And like your predecessors, the Picts,[63] stript, painted, and fed upon hips, haws, and black-berries.

SIR GEORGE. A truce, dear haberdasher.

R. WEALTHY. One pleasure I have, that to this goal you are upon the gallop; but have a care, the sword hangs but by a thread. When next we meet, know me for the master of your fate. [*Exit.*

SIR GEORGE. Insolent mechanic! But that his Bourgois blood would have soil'd my sword –

[*Enter* Baron *and* Loader.

SIR WILLIAM. What is de matter?

SIR GEORGE. A fellow here, upon the credit of a little affinity, has dar'd to upbraid me with being sprung from a soap-boiler.

SIR WILLIAM. Vat, you from the boiler of soap!

SIR GEORGE. Me.

SIR WILLIAM. Aha, begar, dat is anoder ting – And harka you, mister monsieur, ha – how dare a you have d'affontry –

SIR GEORGE. How!

SIR WILLIAM. De impertinence to sit down, play wid me?

SIR GEORGE. What is this?

SIR WILLIAM. A beggarly Bourgois vis a vis, a baron of twenty descents.

LOADER. But baron –

SIR WILLIAM. Bygar, I am almost asham'd to win of such a low, dirty – Give me my monies, and let a me never see your face.

LOADER. Why, but baron, you mistake this thing, I know the old buck this fellow prates about.

SIR WILLIAM. May be.

LOADER. Pigeon me, as true a gentleman as the grand signor. He was, indeed, a good-natur'd obliging, friendly fellow; and being a great judge of soap, tar, and train oil, he us'd to have it home to his house, and sell it to his acquaintance for ready money, to serve them.

SIR WILLIAM. Was dat all!

LOADER. Upon my honour.

SIR WILLIAM. Oh, dat, dat is anoder ting. Bygar I was afraid he was negotiant.

LOADER. Nothing like it.

[*Enter* Dick.

DICK. A gentleman, to enquire for Mr. Loader.

LOADER. I come – A pretty son of a bitch, this baron! pimps for the man, picks his pocket, and then wants to kick him out of company, because his uncle was an oil-man. [*Exit.*

SIR WILLIAM. I beg pardon, chevalier, I was mistake.

SIR GEORGE. Oh, don't mention it; had the flam been fact, your behaviour was natural enough.

[*Enter* Loader.

LOADER. Mr. Smirk, the auctioneer.

SIR GEORGE. Shew him in, by all means. [*Exit* Load.

SIR WILLIAM. You have affair.

SIR GEORGE. If you'll walk into the next room, they will be finished in five minutes.

[*Enter* Loader, *with* Shift, *as* Smirk.

LOADER. Here, master Smirk, this is the gentleman. Harkee, knight, did not I tell you, old Moll was your mark. Here she has brought you a pretty piece of man's meat already; as sweet as a nosegay, and as ripe as a cherry, you rogue. Dispatch him, mean time we'll manage the girl.

[*Exit* Loader.

SMIRK. You are the principal.

SIR GEORGE. Even so. I have, Mr. Smirk, some things of a considerable value, which I want to dispose of immediately.

SMIRK. You have.

SIR GEORGE. Could you assist me?

SMIRK. Doubtless.

SIR GEORGE. But directly?

SMIRK. We have an auction at twelve. I'll add your cargo to the catalogue.

SIR GEORGE. Can that be done?

SMIRK. Every day's practice: it is for the credit of the sale. Last week, amongst the valuable effects of a gentleman, going abroad, I sold a choice collection of china, with a curious service of plate; though the real party was never master of two Delft dishes, and a dozen of pewter, in all his life.

SIR GEORGE. Very artificial. But this must be conceal'd.

SMIRK. Bury'd here. Oh, many an aigrette and solitaire[64] have I sold, to discharge a lady's play-debt. But then we must know the parties; otherwise it might be knock'd down to the husband himself. Ha, ha – Hey ho!

SIR GEORGE. True, upon my word, your profession requires parts.

SMIRK. No body's more. Did you ever hear, Sir George, what first brought me into the business?

SIR GEORGE. Never.

SMIRK. Quite an accident, as I may say. You must have known my predecessor, Mr. Prig, the greatest man in the world, in his way, ay, or that ever was, or ever will be, quite a jewel of a man, he would touch you up a lot; there was no resisting him. He would force you to bid, whether you would or no. I shall never see his equal.

SIR GEORGE. You are modest, Mr. Smirk.

SMIRK. No, no, but his shadow. Far be it from me, to vie with that great man. But as I was saying, my predecessor, Mr. Prig, was to have a sale as it might be on a Saturday. On Friday at noon, I shall never forget the day, he was suddenly seiz'd with a violent cholic. He sent for me to his bed-side, squeez'd me by the hand; dear Smirk, said he, what an accident! You know what is to-morrow; the greatest shew this season; prints, pictures, bronzes, butterflies, medals, and minionettes; all the world will be there; lady Dy Toss, Mrs. Nankyn, the dutchess of Dupe, and every body at all: You see my state, it will be impossible for me to mount. What can I do? It was not for me, you know, to advise that great man.

SIR GEORGE. No, no.

SMIRK. At last, looking wishfully at me, Smirk, says he, d'you love me? – Mr. Prig, can you doubt it? – I'll put it to the test, says he; supply my place to-morrow. – I, eager to shew my love, rashly and rapidly replied, I will.

SIR GEORGE. That was bold.

SMIRK. Absolute madness. But I had gone too far to recede. Then the point was, to prepare for the aweful occasion. The first want that occurr'd to me, was a wig; but this was too material an article, to depend on my own judgement. I resolv'd to consult my friends. I told them the affair – you hear, gentlemen, what has happen'd; Mr. Prig, one of the greatest men, in his way, the world ever saw, or ever will, quite a jewel of a man, taken with a violent fit of the cholic; to-morrow, the greatest shew this season; prints, pictures, bronzes, butterflies, medals, and minionettes; every body in the world to be there; lady Dy Toss, Mrs. Nankyn, dutchess of Dupe, and all mankind; it being impossible he should mount, I have consented to sell – They star'd – It is true, gentlemen. Now I should be glad to have your opinions as to a wig. They were divided: some recommended a tye, others a bag; one mentioned a bob, but was soon overrul'd. Now, for my part, I own, I rather inclin'd to the bag; but, to avoid the imputation of rashness, I resolv'd to take Mrs. Smirk's judgment, my wife, a dear good woman, fine in figure, high in taste, a superior genius, and knows old china like a Nabob.

SIR GEORGE. What was her decision?

SMIRK. I told her the case – My dear, you know what has happen'd. My good friend, Mr. Prig, the greatest man in the world, in his way, that ever was, or ever will be, quite a jewel of a man, a violent fit of the cholic – the greatest shew this season, to-morrow, pictures and every thing in the world; all the world will be there: now, as it is impossible he should, I mount in his stead. You know the importance of a wig; I have ask'd my friends – some recommend a tye, others a bag – what is your opinion? Why, to deal freely, Mr. Smirk, says she, a tye for your round, regular, smiling face would be rather too formal, and a bag too boyish, deficient in dignity for the solemn occasion; were I worthy to advise, you should wear a something between both. I'll be hang'd, if you don't mean a major. I jumpt at the hint, and a major it was.

SIR GEORGE. So, that was fixt.

SMIRK. Finally. But next day, when I came to mount the rostrum, then was the trial. My limbs shook, and my tongue trembled. The first lot was a chamber-utensil, in Chelsea china, of the pea-green pattern. It occasioned a great laugh; but I got thro' it. Her Grace, indeed, gave me great encouragement. I overheard her whisper to lady Dy, Upon my word, Mr. Smirk does it very well. Very well, indeed, Mr. Smirk, addressing herself to me. I made an acknowledging bow to her Grace, as in duty bound. But one flower flounc'd involuntarily from me, that day, as I may say. I remember, Dr. Trifle call'd it enthusiastic, and pronounc'd it a presage of my future greatness.

SIR GEORGE. What was that?

SMIRK. Why, sir, the lot was a Guido;[65] a single figure, a marvellous fine performance; well preserv'd, and highly finished. It stuck at five and forty; I, charm'd with the picture, and piqu'd at the people, A going for five and forty, no body more than five and forty? – Pray, ladies and gentlemen, look at this piece, quite flesh and blood, and only wants a touch from the torch of Prometheus, to start from the canvass and fall a bidding. A general plaudit ensu'd, I bow'd, and in three minutes knock'd it down at sixty-three, ten.

SIR GEORGE. That was a stroke at least equal to your master.

SMIRK. O dear me! You did not know the great man, alike in every thing. He had as much to say upon a ribbon as a Raphael. His manner too was inimitably fine. I remember, they took him off at the play-house, some time ago; pleasant, but wrong. Public characters shou'd not be sported with – They are sacred – But we lose time.

SIR GEORGE. Oh, in the lobby, on the table, you will find the particulars.

SMIRK. We shall see you. There will be a world of company. I shall please you. But the great nicety of our art is the eye. Mark how mine skims round the room. Some bidders are shy, and only advance with a nod; but I nail them. One, two, three, four, five. You will be surpris'd – Ha, ha, ha, – heigh ho.

[*Exit.*

ACT III.

[*Enter* Sir George *and* Loader.

SIR GEORGE. A most infernal run. Let's see. [*Pulls out a card*] Loader a thousand, the Baron two, Tally – Enough to beggar a banker. Every shilling of Transfer's supply exhausted! Nor will even the sale of my moveables prove sufficient to discharge my debts. Death and the devil! In what a complication of calamities has a few days plung'd me! And no resource!

LOADER. Knight, here's old Moll come to wait on you; she has brought the tid bit I spoke of. Shall I bid her send her in?

SIR GEORGE. Pray do.

[*Exit* Loader. *Enter* Mrs. Cole *and* Lucy.

MRS. COLE. Come along Lucy. You bashful baggage. I thought I had silenc'd your scruples. Don't you remember what Mr. Squintum said? A woman's not worth saving, that won't be guilty of a swinging sin;[66] for then they have matter to repent upon. Here, your honour, I leave her to your management. She is young, tender and timid; does not know what is for her own good: but your honour will soon teach her. I wou'd willingly stay, but I must not lose the lecture. [*Exit.*

SIR GEORGE. Upon my credit a fine figure. Awkard – Can't produce her publicly as mine; but she will do for private amusement – Will you be seated miss? – Dumb! Quite a picture! She too wants a touch of the Promethean torch – Will you be so kind, Ma'am, to walk from your frame and take a chair? – Come, pr'ythee, why so coy? Nay, I am not very adroit in the custom of this country. I suppose I must conduct you – Come, miss.

LUCY. O, sir.

SIR GEORGE. Child.

LUCY. If you have humanity, spare me.

SIR GEORGE. In tears! What can this mean? Artifice. A project to raise the price, I suppose. Lookee, my dear, you may save this piece of pathetic for another occasion. It won't do with me: I am no novice – So, child, a truce to your tragedy, I beg.

LUCY. Indeed you wrong me, sir; indeed you do.

SIR GEORGE. Wrong you! How came you here, and for what purpose?

LUCY. A shameful one. I know it all, and yet believe me, sir, I am innocent.

SIR GEORGE. Oh, I don't question that. Your pious patroness is a proof of your innocence.

LUCY. What can I say to gain your credit? And yet, sir, strong as appearances are against me, by all that's holy, you see me here, a poor distrest, involuntary victim.

SIR GEORGE. Her style's above the common class; her tears are real. – Rise, child. – How the poor creature trembles!

LUCY. Say then I am safe.

SIR GEORGE. Fear nothing.

LUCY. May heaven reward you. I cannot.

SIR GEORGE. Pr'ythee, child, collect yourself, and help to unravel this mystery. You came hither willingly. There was no force?

LUCY. None.

SIR GEORGE. You know Mrs. Cole?

LUCY. Too well.

SIR GEORGE. How came you then to trust her!

LUCY. Mine, sir, is a tedious, melancholy tale.

SIR GEORGE. And artless too?

LUCY. As innocence.

SIR GEORGE. Give it me.

LUCY. It will tire you.

SIR GEORGE. Not if it be true. Be just, and you will find me generous.

LUCY. On that, sir, I rely'd in venturing hither.

SIR GEORGE. You did me justice. Trust me with all your story. If you deserve, depend on my protection.

LUCY. Some months ago, sir, I was consider'd as the joint heiress of a respectable, wealthy merchant; dear to my friends, happy in my prospects, and my father's favourite.

SIR GEORGE. His name.

LUCY. There you must pardon me. Unkind and cruel tho' he has been to me, let me discharge the duty of a daughter, suffer in silence, nor bring reproach on him who gave me being.

SIR GEORGE. I applaud your piety.

LUCY. At this happy period, my father judging an addition of wealth must bring an increase of happiness, resolv'd to unite me with a man, sordid in his mind, brutal in his manners, and riches his only recommendation. My refusal of this ill-suited match, tho' mildly given, enflam'd my father's temper, naturally choleric, alienated his affections, and banish'd me his house, distrest and destitute.

SIR GEORGE. Wou'd no friend receive you?

LUCY. Alas, how few are friends to the unfortunate! Besides, I knew, sir, such a step wou'd be consider'd by my father, as an appeal from his justice. I therefore retir'd to a remote corner of the town, trusting, as my only advocate, to the tender calls of nature, in his cool, reflecting hours.

SIR GEORGE. How came you to know this woman?

LUCY. Accident plac'd me in a house, the mistress of which profess'd the same principles with my infamous conductress. There, as enthusiasm is the child of melancholy, I caught the infection. A constant attendance on their assemblies procur'd me the acquaintance of this woman, whose extraordinary zeal and devotion first drew my attention and confidence. I trusted her with my story, and in return, receiv'd the warmest invitation to take the protection of her house. This I unfortunately accepted.

SIR GEORGE. Unfortunately indeed!

LUCY. By the decency of appearances, I was some time imposed upon. But an accident, which you will excuse my repeating, reveal'd all the horror of my situation. I will not trouble you with a recital of all the arts us'd to seduce me: Happily they hitherto have fail'd. But this morning I was acquainted with my destiny; and no other election left me, but immediate compliance, or a jail. In this desperate condition, you cannot wonder, sir, at my choosing rather to rely on the generosity of a gentleman, than the humanity of a creature, insensible to pity, and void of every virtue.

SIR GEORGE. The event shall justify your choice. You have my faith and honour for your security. For tho' I can't boast of my own goodness, yet I have an honest feeling for afflicted virtue; and, however unfashionable, a spirit that dares afford it protection. Give me your hand. As soon as I have dispatch'd some pressing business here, I will lodge you in an asylum, sacred to the distresses of your sex; where indigent beauty is guarded from temptations, and deluded innocence rescu'd from infamy.

[*Exeunt* Sir George *and* Lucy. *Enter* Shift.

SHIFT. Zooks, I have toil'd like a horse; quite tir'd, by Jupiter. And what shall I get for my pains? The old fellow here, talks of making me easy for life. Easy! And what does he mean by easy? He'll make me an excise-man, I suppose, a gauger of beer barrels. No, that will never do. This lad here is no fool. Foppish, indeed. He does not want parts, no, nor principles neither. I overheard his scene with the girl. I think I may trust him. I have a great mind to venture it. It is a shame to have him dup'd by this old don. It must not be. I'll in, and unfold, – Ha – Egad I have a thought too, which, if my heir apparent can execute, I shall still lye conceal'd, and, perhaps, be rewarded on both sides.

I have it, – 'tis engender'd, piping hot.
And now, Sir Knight, I'll match you with a plot.

[*Exit. Enter* Sir William *and* Richard Wealthy.

R. WEALTHY. Well, I suppose, by this time, you are satisfied what a scoundrel you have brought into the world, and are ready to finish your foolery.

SIR WILLIAM. Get to the catastrophe, good brother.

R. WEALTHY. Let us have it over then.

SIR WILLIAM. I have already alarm'd all his tradesmen. I suppose we shall soon have them here, with a legion of bayliffs and constables. – Oh, you have my will about you.

R. WEALTHY. Yes, yes.

SIR WILLIAM. It is almost time to produce it, or read him the clause that relates to his rejecting your daughter. That will do his business. But they come. I must return to my character.

[*Enter* Shift.

SHIFT. Sir, sir, we are all in the wrong box; our scheme is blown up; your son has detected Loader and Tally, and is playing the very devil within.

SIR WILLIAM. Oh, the bunglers?

SHIFT. Now for it, youngster.

[*Enter* Sir George, *driving in* Loader *and another.*

SIR GEORGE. Rascals, robbers, that like the locust, mark the road you have taken, by the ruin and desolation you leave behind you.

LOADER. Sir George.

SIR GEORGE. And can youth, however cautious, be guarded against such deep-laid complicated villany? Where are the rest of your diabolical crew? Your auctioneer, usurer, and – O sir, are you here! – I am glad you have not escap'd us however.

SIR WILLIAM. What de devil is de matter!

SIR GEORGE. Your birth, which I believe an imposition, preserves you however, from the discipline those rogues have receiv'd. A baron, a nobleman, a sharper! Oh shame! It is enough to banish all confidence from the world. On whose faith can we rely, when those, whose honour is held as sacred as an oath, unmindful of their dignity, descend to rival pick-pockets in their infamous arts. What are these [*Pulls out dice*] pretty implements, the fruits of your leisure hours. They are dexterously done. You have a fine mechanical turn. – Dick, secure the door.

[Mrs. Cole, *speaking as entering.*

MRS. COLE. Here I am, at last. Well, and how is your honour, and the little gentlewoman. – Bless me, what is the matter here?

SIR GEORGE. I am, Madam, treating your friends with a cold collation, and, you are opportunely come for your share. The little gentlewoman is safe, and in much better hands than you design'd her. Abominable hypocrite! Who, tottering under the load of irreverent age, and infamous diseases, inflexibly proceeds in the practice of every vice, impiously prostituting the most sacred institutions, to the most infernal purposes.

MRS. COLE. I hope your Honour –

SIR GEORGE. Take her away. As you have been singular in your penitence, you ought to be distinguish'd in your pennance. Which, I promise you, shall be most publickly and plentifully bestowed.

[*Exit.* Cole. *Enter* Dick.

DICK. The constables, sir.

SIR GEORGE. Let them come in, that I may consign these gentlemen to their care. [*To* Sir Will] Your letters of nobility you will produce in a court of justice. Tho', if I read you right, you are one of those indigent, itinerant nobles, of your own creation, which our reputation for hospitality draws hither in shoals, to the shame of our understanding, the impairing of our fortunes, and when you are trusted, the betraying of our designs. Officers, do your duty.

SIR WILLIAM. Why, don't you know me!

SIR GEORGE. Just as I guess'd. An impostor. He has recover'd the free use of his tongue already.

SIR WILLIAM. Nay, but George.

SIR GEORGE. Insolent familiarity! Away with him.

SIR WILLIAM. Hold, hold, a moment. Brother Richard, set this matter to rights.

R. WEALTHY. Don't you know him?

SIR GEORGE. Know him! The very question is an affront.

R. WEALTHY. Nay, I don't wonder at it. 'Tis your father, you fool.

SIR GEORGE. My father! Impossible!

SIR WILLIAM. That may be, but 'tis true.

SIR GEORGE. My father alive! Thus let me greet the blessing.

SIR WILLIAM. Alive! Ay, and I believe I sha'n't be in a hurry to dye again.

SIR GEORGE. But, dear sir, the report of your death – and this disguise – to what –

SIR WILLIAM. Don't ask any questions. Your uncle will tell you all. For my part I am sick of the scheme.

R. WEALTHY. I told you what would come of your politicks.

SIR WILLIAM. You did so. But if it had not been for those clumsey scoundrels, the plot was as good a plot – O George, such discoveries I have to make. Within I'll unravel the whole.

SIR GEORGE. Perhaps, sir, I may match 'em.

SHIFT. Sir. [*Pulls him by the sleeve.*

SIR GEORGE. Never fear. It is impossible, gentlemen, to determine your fate, till this matter is more fully explain'd. Till when, keep 'em in safe custody. – Do you know them, sir?

SIR WILLIAM. Yes, but that's more than they did me. I can cancel your debts there, and, I believe, prevail on those gentlemen to refund too. – But you have been a sad profligate young dog, George.

SIR GEORGE. I can't boast of my goodness, sir, but I think I could produce you a proof, that I am not so totally destitute of –

SIR WILLIAM. Ay? Why then pr'ythee do.

SIR GEORGE. I have, sir, this day, resisted a temptation, that greater pretenders to morality might have yielded to. But I will trust myself no longer, and must crave your interposition and protection.

SIR WILLIAM. To what?

SIR GEORGE. I will attend you with the explanation in an instant. [*Exit.*

SIR WILLIAM. Pr'ythee, Shift, what does he mean.

SHIFT. I believe I can guess.

SIR WILLIAM. Let us have it.

SHIFT. I suppose the affair I overheard just now, a prodigious fine elegant girl faith; that, discarded by her family, for refusing to marry her grandfather, fell into the hands of the venerable lady you saw, who being the kind caterer for your son's amusements, brought her hither for a purpose obvious enough. But the young gentleman, touch'd with her story, truth and tears, was converted from the spoiler of her honour, to the protector of her innocence.

SIR WILLIAM. Look'e there, brother, did not I tell you that George was not so bad at the bottom!

R. WEALTHY. This does indeed attone for half the – But they are here.

[*Enter* Sir George *and* Lucy.

SIR GEORGE. Fear nothing, madam, you may safely rely on the –

LUCY. My father!

R. WEALTHY. Lucy!

LUCY. O, sir, can you forgive your poor distrest unhappy girl? You scarce can guess how hardly I've been us'd, since my banishment from your paternal roof. Want, pining want, anguish and shame, have been my constant partners.

SIR WILLIAM. Brother!

SIR GEORGE. Sir!

LUCY. Father!

R. WEALTHY. Rise, child, 'tis I must ask of thee forgiveness. Can'st thou forget the woes I've made thee suffer? Come to my arms once more thou darling of my age. – What mischief had my rashness nearly completed. Nephew, I scarce can thank you as I ought, but –

SIR GEORGE. I am richly paid, in being the happy instrument – Yet, might I urge a wish –

R. WEALTHY. Name it.

SIR GEORGE. That you would forgive my follies of to-day; and, as I have been providentially the occasional guardian of your daughter's honour, that you would bestow on me that right for life.

R. WEALTHY. That must depend on Lucy; her will, not mine, shall now direct her choice – What says your father?

SIR WILLIAM. Me! Oh, I'll shew you in an instant. Give me your hands. There, children, now you are join'd, and the devil take him that wishes to part you.

SIR GEORGE. I thank you for us both.

R. WEALTHY. Happiness attend you.

SIR WILLIAM. Now, brother, I hope, you will allow me to be a good plotter. All this was brought to bear by my means.

SHIFT. With my assistance, I hope, you'll own, sir.

SIR WILLIAM. That's true, honest Shift, and thou shalt be richly rewarded; nay, George shall be your friend too. This Shift is an ingenious fellow, let me tell you, son.

SIR GEORGE. I am no stranger to his abilities, sir. But, if you please, we will retire. The various struggles of this fair sufferer require the soothing softness of a sister's love. And now, sir, I hope your fears for me are over; for had I not this motive to restrain my follies; yet I now know the town too well to be ever its bubble, and will take care to preserve, at least,

Some more estate, and principles, and wit,
Than brokers, bawds, and gamesters shall think fit.

[*Shift, addressing himself to* Sir George.

SHIFT. And what becomes of your poor servant Shift?
Your father talks of lending me a lift–
A great man's promise, when his turn is serv'd!
Capons on promises, would soon be starv'd:
No, on myself alone, I'll now rely:
'Gad I've a thriving traffic in my eye–[67]
Near the mad mansions of Moorfields I'll bawl;
Friends, fathers, mothers, sisters, sons and all,
Shut up your shops, and listen to my call.
With labor, toil, all second means dispense,
And live a rent-charge upon providence.
Prick up your ears; a story now I'll tell,
Which once a widow, and her child befell,
I knew the mother, and her daughter well;
Poor, it is true, they were; but never wanted,
For whatsoe'er they ask'd, was always granted:
One fatal day, the matron's truth was try'd,
She wanted meat and drink, and fairly cry'd.

[Child.

Mother, you cry!

[Mother.

Oh, child, I've got no bread.

[Child.

What matters that? Why providence an't dead!
With reason good, this truth the child might say,
For there came in at noon, that very day,
Bread, greens, potatoes, and a leg of mutton,
A better sure, a table ne'er was put on:[68]

Ay, that might be, ye cry, with those poor
souls;
But we ne'er had a rasher for the coals.

And d'ye deserve it? How d'ye spend your
days:
In pastimes, prodigality, and plays!
Let's go see Foote! ah, Foote's a precious limb!
Old-nick will soon a football make of him![69]
For foremost rows in side-boxes you shove,
Think you to meet with side-boxes above?
Where giggling girls, and powder'd fops may
sit,
No, you will all be cram'd into the pit,
And crowd the house for Satan's benefit.
Oh, what you snivel; well, do so no more,
Drop, to attone, your money at the door,
And, if I please, – I'll give it to the poor.[70]

13.2 *THE LONDON CHRONICLE* 1760 OCTOBER 21–23, ISSUE 597.

THE FOLLOWING REVIEW lambasts Foote's "impious" and "obscene" play. Quoting Voltaire, degrading Foote's work as "low" and "puerile," and even supplying original verse, the reviewer demonstrates great disdain for Foote's work. Later on the same page there is an advertisement stating that Foote has written a rejoinder to this negative response, which is on sale now. This information has also been provided below.

> "Il n'étoit point le Poëte des honnêtes gens. Ses pieces, goutées pendant quelques Representations par le people, étoient dedaignées par tous les gens de bon gout, & ressembloient à tant ce pieces que j'ai vû en France attirir la foule et revolter les lecteurs."
>
> *Lettres de Voltaire sur les Anglois.*

THE above remarks of the learned Voltaire on Shadwell's plays, may justly be apply'd to a late publish'd Farce, called the *Minor*, a piece as impious as obscene; in which several texts of sacred Scriptures, and articles of the Church of England, are ridiculed in a most scandalous manner.—Besides, the nicknaming and abusing a Minister of that Church, merely for the natural defects of his eyes, is something so low and puerile, that I am surpriz'd how any one of common understanding can read it, without despising the Author. I remember to have seen a School-Boy well whipp'd for calling another (who had an odd cast of the eyes) *Squintum*, and I think Mr. F**te deserves a double lashing for the same offence. I have endeavoured, in what follows, to have one stroke at him myself.

In fulsome language, and with impious wit,
    To ridicule the Scripture's sacred page
A comedy the D-v-l lately writ,
    And sent it as a present to the stage.
But lest it should offend the people's nose,
    So strong it smell'd of sulphur, smoak, and
To write it o'er afresh old Satan chose [foot,
    His undivided (not his cloven) FOOTE.

Your's, &c. ANTI-MINOR.
Bristol, Oct. 18, 1760.

13.3 SAMUEL FOOTE, *THE DIVERSIONS OF A MORNING*

Reprinted in Tate Wilkinson, *The Wandering Patentee; or, a history of the Yorkshire theatres, from 1770 to the present time.* York: Wilson, Spence, & Mawman, 1795: 244–5.

FOOTE'S *DIVERSIONS* WERE DRAWN from his earlier *A Dish of Chocolate* and *A Cup of Tea* sketches and depended primarily on parodies of other actors. *Diversions* includes a mock acting lesson, with the footnote that "the scene between Puzzle and Bounce was meant as mimicry of Macklin's teaching [Spranger] Barry Othello." This excerpt ends with the two howling like dogs.

Now for the deportment of the hands.—You can't but have observed how often they embarrass the actor, gentlemen: Sometimes here, sometimes there, in short, eternally in the say.—[*The players exercise*]—First—Invocation, 'Tendens ad sidera palmas.'—Distinction; the pointed finger.—Now, anger; the clinch'd fist for rage.—Total relaxation, dilapidation, &c. for sorrow.—Very well!—Now for a general disposition. Erect your heads; clench your fists; throw your heads upon your left shoulders; start, and to the left about.—Exceedingly well! A fine expression of anger!—Now your grief; drop your heads; strike your breasts; dilate your jaws, and to the right about.—Very well! Drop your jaw a little lower.—[*One of the players extends his mouth very wide*]—Zounds! I must raise that man's salary to stop his mouth.—Now, for an application of these rules to a particular part.—Advance, Bounce; take a turn or two;—there's a well-formed figure, fall of shoulders, and fine features. He shall treat you with a rant in Othello; you will there judge of his powers. Begin at 'Othello's occupation gone.' Now catch at me, as if you would tear the very strings and all. Keep your voice low—loudness is no mark of passion.—Mind your attitude.

Boun. Villain—

Puz. Very well!

Boun. Be sure you prove my love a whore—

Puz. Admirable!

Boun. Be sure on't—

Puz. Bravo!

Boun. Give me the occular proof—

Puz. Lay your emphasis a little stronger upon occ—occ—occ—

Boun. Occ—occ—occular proof—

Puz. That's right!

Boun. Or by the worth of my eternal soul, Thou had'st better been born a dog—

Puz. Grind dog—a d—o—o—g, Iag—

Boun. A do-og, Iago, than answer my wak'd wrath.

Puz. Charming!—Now quick—[*Speaking all the time.*

Boun. Make me see it, or at least so prove it, That the probation bears no hinge or loop, To hang a doubt on;—or wo—

Puz. A little more terror upon woe—wo-o-e, like a mastiff in a tanner's yard—w-o-o-e—

[*They answer each other—w-o-o-o-e, &c.*

13.4 HENRY OVERTON AND AMEDÉ VAN LOO, *THE REVEREND GEORGE WHITEFIELD*

Henry Overton (printmaker) and Amedé Van Loo, *The Reverend George Whitefield*, London: circa 1750. Courtesy the Lewis Walpole Library, Yale University.

This image shows Whitefield's squint as a wall-eye of sorts and includes the doggerel lines that mock the different directions of his eyes as a sign of a division in his focus between the inward and outward man. This low-church concept was widely mocked as the origin of hypocrisy, as in Centlivre's *A Bold Stroke for a Wife*, in which prudish Quakers prove to be sexually lascivious:

Two men there are the Inward & the Out
Whom Satan to insnare still roveth about
But whilest great Whitefield with his Eyes on crook
Forever watchful on th'Inward man doth look

From that goodly Pattern take the hint
With Eyes out cast on th'Outward man I squint
Thus safely we guard both your Body and Soul
And keep you from falling into the Pit hole.

13.5 WILLIAM HOGARTH, *CREDULITY, SUPERSTITION, AND FANATICISM*

William Hogarth, *Credulity, Superstition, and Fanaticism*. London: Wm. Hogarth, March 15, 1762. Courtesy the Lewis Walpole Library, Yale University.

Hogarth's remarkable print is a monument to anti-Methodist sentiment and its complicated relationship to theatricality. It allegedly shows the inside of Whitefield's London Tabernacle and the overwhelmed enthusiasts within. The parson, with harlequin's costume beneath his robes, does a religious puppet show for the congregants (a reference to both basic populist tastes and to the evasion of the Licensing Act, of which Foote accused Methodism), with angels, demons, and ghosts from famous plays. Mary Toth, who allegedly gave birth to rabbits, is in the foreground, though in the original, "Enthusiasm Delineat'd" Mother Douglas, the model for Foote's Mrs. Cole, occupied the space. The glowing images of Christ in the initial draft have here been replaced with images of Fanny Phantom, the alleged "Methodist" ghost who scratched on the walls of a Methodist's residence. Hogarth's equation of Methodism with both superstition and sexual excess reflects elements of Foote's satire.

13.6 *FOOTE AS MRS. COLE*

The MINOR.

Dodd delin.

W. Walker sc.

Mr. FOOTE as Mrs. COLE.

My thoughts are fix'd upon a better place.
What. I suppose Mr. Loader, you will be
for your old Friend the black-ey'd Girl, &c.
Act I.

J. Dodd, pinxit, *Mr. Foote as Mrs. Cole*. Image courtesy of The University Library, University of Illinois at Champaign-Urbana.

This engraving of Foote appeared in several editions of the afterpiece and in various collections, including *The New English Theatre vol. 11, 1777*. The inscription below reads "My thoughts are fix'd upon a better place. What, I suppose Mr. Loader you will be for your old friend the black ey'd girl, &c.," in order to emphasize the mingling of Mrs. Cole's religious and sexual vocabularies.

Notes

1–2 Text is based on the 1760 edition. London: J. Coote, G. Kearsly, T. Davies, *1760*.
3 "To such heights are evil men driven by religion." Lucretius, *De Rerum Natura*.
4 Respect yourself, or a matter of self-respect.
5 Strollers were unlicensed players, often from the provinces, hence Foote's complaints about accent and style.
6 What is your cast list?
7 A northern England accent.
8 Sir Timothy has a bad voice and sings in broken Italian, something approximating "sing, my beautiful lily."
9 Foote suggests he faces libel damages for impersonating Smart's family, even though Smart suggested the impersonations.
10 Standard stereotypes on the stage. Foote goes on to denounce cheap jokes at the expense of minority and disempowered groups.
11 Smart is saying that Foote must do new, unfamiliar imitations to please the audience.
12 Mocking sacred things.
13 Tottenham Court was the site of Whitefield's church, while the Haymarket was a theatre.
14 His actress has refused to play the part of Mrs. Cole.
15 Cheating.
16 Sir William mocks the mercantile virtues his brother favors by associating them with a nostalgia for Puritan culture.
17 He makes fun of the simplicity of his brother's house and its humble address in this familial struggle between mercantile and aristocratic values.
18 Orally, rather than in writing.
19 A reference to Foote's abilities as a mimic.
20 Technically, an irregular marriage between someone of high birth and a commoner or poor person, jokingly used by Foote as a euphemism for illegitimacy.
21 Shift, who was a link boy, someone who offered to light the way through the streets for travelers, claims to have "street smarts."
22 An audience member threw fruit at him.
23 Both French military commanders who were forced to retreat at the Battle of Minden.
24 Slang for preachers.
25 All-purpose.
26 Master-stroke.
27 Crooks.
28 The leather-sellers guild run him out because they think he is calling them cuckholds.
29 A small coin.
30 A list of interests from natural science (in which he includes black people) to high aesthetics, meant to illustrate the range of his expertise. The Apollo Belvedere was a marble statue of Apollo from antiquity.
31 Miscarries; goes wrong.
32 George is giving instructions to deliver panels for a fancy two-person carriage and to fit his spotted (pye-ball) horses with bits.
33 To sneak out without paying a debt.
34 A series of gambling terms.
35 George is declining to bet more until he has settled his last debts.
36 Taking all the tricks of a hand of cards.
37 To give a bonus score.
38 Mother Cole was a well known madam in Covent Garden.
39 Someone with rheumatism.
40 George Whitefield's Methodist house of worship.
41 A shot of alcohol.

42 Traps.
43 A prostitute from Florence. His request is a reference to Harris's List, a published catalogue of available "higher quality" prostitutes.
44 Sir William impersonates the baron, who has been serving as a pimp and here brags on the beauty of his prostitutes.
45 I swear.
46 Greedy person.
47 George is paying for the rumor that he sleeps with signora Florence to create a reputation at the opera.
48 See the image in the following context section.
49 Squintum was a nickname for the Rev. George Whitefield, who has a wall eye. Her subsequent speeches mix the language of evangelical conversation with her ongoing trade, prostitution. The joke is that the prostitutes can repent and be saved later but can work in the meantime.
50 Mrs. Cole protests that she doesn't drink alcohol when that seems to be what she is hoping to get. Cordials are medicinal alcohols.
51 City taxes.
52 Small fancy container.
53 A good sized glass.
54 Pre-payments.
55 She uses a series of seafaring images, much like a Whitefield sermon, to talk about the journey of the soul, and then shift abruptly back to the language of pimping.
56 An anti-semitic joke; Transfer complains that he can't find a Jewish money-lender to lend George more money.
57 Thick cloth, knife handles, and "Witney" blankets, an early blanket factory.
58 The good stuff (slang).
59 Makes the money flow.
60 A stack of your bills.
61 A stain on your reputation.
62 Sir George's classism is especially ridiculous because he is talking about his own cousin.
63 Ancient Britons.
64 Fancy hair ornaments and jeweled rings.
65 Probably Guido Reni (1575–1642), Italian painter whose religious and mythological works were very popular with eighteenth-century collectors.
66 A big sin; the reference is to hanging.
67 This line, a reference to the Rev. George Whitefield's wall-eye, marks the moment in which Foote as Shift begins to impersonate Whitefield.
68 Probably a reference to an evangelical story of miraculous provision.
69 A partial quote from a Whitefield sermon, in which he suggested the devil ("Old Nick") will make a football out of Foote.
70 Foote suggests that Whitefield gathered large sums for the poor but kept them for himself.

Part 3
Entertainment in the Age of Revolutions: 1760–1800

OVERVIEW

THE PERIOD FOLLOWING THE SEVEN YEARS' WAR should have been one of national consolidation and imperial dominance. The defeat of the French seemed to consolidate British dominance over Atlantic trade and lay the groundwork for territorial empire in South Asia. Instead it became an era of imperial fragmentation and national crisis. As part of an ill-advised plan to pay off the debts incurred during the Seven Years' War by taxing the American colonies, the British government set into motion the first successful act of decolonization in the Atlantic World. Because the narrative of the American Revolution is so familiar it is difficult to fully appreciate how confusing these events were to Britons at the time. Most Britons viewed the residents of the 13 colonies as brethren, and the colonists' resistance to British colonial policy was carried out on terms largely derived from British political theory. When rebellion came it called into question the very foundations of British cultural and social identity. The Ministry's failure to comprehend the difficulty in reconquering the colonies after they had declared independence may well have been a refusal to recognize a historical bifurcation in

Britishness itself. Actions taken in the name of Liberty by British settlers in North America forced those living in the British Isles to differentiate themselves from people they commonly understood in familial terms. Overconfidence in a military solution to the American crisis in retrospect looks like an attempt to avoid a true reckoning with the new global world after the Peace of Paris in 1763. Britain's own imperial holdings were now strangely double: governing the territorial empire in North America and the mercantile empire in India required radically different economic and political strategies. The loss of the 13 colonies sent shock waves through the British economy that were partially alleviated by the injection of capital from India, but the decades-long struggle to regulate the East India Company, which reached its period of most intensity during the 1780s, indicates that this recalibration was itself destabilizing. If the 1770s were about American decolonization and the 1780s were about reorienting the empire to face the East, then the 1790s turned attention towards political divisions within the nation itself. The French Revolution resuscitated unresolved anxieties associated with the American war and suddenly the government was fighting battles against radical factions at home and against Revolutionary France in Europe. And yet this 30-year period, marked by almost constant war and a sense of social insecurity, was a crucible for many of the most salient changes in what by now was a full-fledged entertainment industry.

Theatre history has been slow to recognize these developments and many of the most important playwrights of the period are only recently receiving the attention they deserve. Perhaps because the string of plays from *The Rivals* through *The Duenna* and *The School for Scandal* to *The Critic* essentially moves from masterpiece to masterpiece, consideration of the 1770s has revolved around Richard Brinsley Sheridan's remarkable transit across the London stage. Much ink has been spilled on a supposed turn from sentimental to laughing comedy first heralded by Oliver Goldsmith, but this simple substitution no longer seems convincing even with regard to Sheridan.[1] A case could be made for similar explosions of high caliber work in the 1780s and 1790s: Hannah Cowley and Elizabeth Inchbald, in comedy after comedy, offered complex ripostes to Sheridan's cultural dominance by combining laughter and sentiment in increasingly subtle fashion. In many ways, five-act comedy reaches its full elaboration in the work of Sheridan, Cowley and Inchbald, but the most significant aspects of late eighteenth-century theatrical culture are to be found beyond the work of these specific playwrights. Rather, we have to turn to transformations in the playhouses themselves, to remarkable innovations in design and spectacle, to the increasing prevalence of musical entertainment, to new forms of celebrity and finally, to the ever increasing integration of print and performance media to gain some sense of the theatrical world that played host to the productions selected in this section.

When Garrick staged *The Jubilee* in 1769, Drury Lane Theatre held an audience of approximately 2,360 patrons. Garrick's slight afterpiece turned the rain-soaked fiasco in Stratford-upon-Avon into a source of consistent receipts, easily recouping his losses from the failed Jubilee celebration. But the play is also a harbinger of many things to come. Bardolatry was a going concern in the final 30 years of the century, but *The Jubilee's* reliance on ethnic mimicry, its obsession with class mobility, its blatant nationalism, the exploitation and immediate publication of songs from the play and above all its remarkable procession of favorite characters from Shakespeare all point to increasingly spectacular, musical expressions of ethnocentric and nationalist sentiment in the theatres of London. By the time John Philip Kemble opened the refurbished Covent Garden Theatre in September 1809 and sparked 67 days of rioting—known now as the Old Price War[2]—London audiences had become accustomed to large, cavernous playhouses designed to maximize capacity. Huge spectacular productions, leavened by musical interludes, were becoming increasingly the norm. Across the last third of the eighteenth century, both patent theatres were remodeled, both patent theatres burned down and both were re-built to accommodate more and more seats in the pit, in the galleries and in the stalls. Theatre went from being a fairly intimate experience to a form of mass entertainment. This expansion had an immediate impact on acting style, on the repertoire, on design and on the forms of affiliation felt between audience members. Bigger houses meant highly stylized gestures and a performance pattern that tended to move increasingly from point to point. The dialogue in five-act tragedy and comedy needed to be supplemented by music and visual spectacle so that key scenes registered in the back seats and stalls. Designers, led by Philippe Jacques De Loutherbourg, developed extraordinary visual effects and the scenographic experience became a draw in itself. This emphasis on spectacle had always been the case in pantomime, but Garrick and especially Kemble started bringing new scenographic techniques to bear on productions of Shakespeare and other plays from the stock repertoire. And finally, the new houses generated new forms of observational and conversational sociability. Playhouses were still fully lit throughout this period so audiences enjoyed the spectacle of fashionable life regardless of what was on the playbill.

The repertory itself also went through significant transformations. In the wake of Garrick's simultaneous restoration of some Shakespearean scripts and his re-writing of others, celebrity in this period was never very distant from Shakespeare. With the partial exception of Frances Abington, the most important players—Sarah Siddons, John Philip Kemble and Dorothy (Dora) Jordan—owned specific Shakespearean roles and used them to articulate a specifically English national culture. The Siddons phenomena—audience members were frequently described in emotional paroxysms during her performances of Lady Macbeth, Katherine of Aragon and non-Shakespearean roles such as Lady Randolph and Belvedira—lasted for a remarkably long time and her powers of declamation and statuesque presence generated highly expressive forms of tragedy. Her brother's impact was in many ways the opposite. Kemble's learned productions often strove for one intense effect—usually hammered home by the elimination of comic subplots and the insertion of tableaux and processions. Neither of these players excelled in comedy and thus this part of the repertoire fell to Abington and Jordan. Both women were very much associated with fashionable society or the Ton and their celebrity was entwined with stylistic innovation outside the playhouse.

Despite the prominence of celebrity actors–such as Siddons, Kemble and Jordan—associated with Shakespeare, perhaps too much attention has been placed on Garrick's legacy of coupling virtuoso acting with the Bard's plays in these years. As Robert D. Hume has argued, John Rich's cultivation of spectacle, dance and musical entertainment earlier in the century arguably had a more vivid afterlife than any mode of theatrical entertainment in the late eighteenth century.[3] Comic opera, harlequinade and all manner of musical interludes and afterpieces became the driving force of receipts in both the patent houses and the illegitimate venues outside the borough of Westminster. Sadler's Wells, Astley's Royal Amphitheatre and a host of smaller companies emerged in this period and their blend of music, dance, pantomime, hippodrama and spectacle was both inviting in its own right and deeply influential on the managerial practice of Thomas Harris, Richard Brinsley Sheridan, George Colman and Kemble. By the early nineteenth century even Kemble was supplementing Shakespeare and plays such as Addison's *Cato* with equestrian productions of *Bluebeard*, pantomimes foregrounding the antics of Grimaldi, and musical afterpieces by John O'Keefe and Charles Dibdin.[4] At least part of the impetus behind these productions was to co-opt the attractions of competitors; with new forms of leisure being commodified every day towards the century's end, the entertainment marketplace became more and more saturated. But there is also evidence that the social unrest of the 1790s, with its incipient demand for the performance of patriotism, fostered hybrid musical genres. As Gillian Russell has argued, the theatre of the 1790s was a wartime theatre; managers and audiences alike were finely attuned to nationalist sentiment in the playhouse and to events on the continent.[5] The theatre became a site where military and naval characters were celebrated. The outpouring of musical plays celebrating Nelson's victory at the Nile is one notable example, but even a cursory review of the newspapers indicates how frequently productions were interrupted or framed by calls for and performances of "Rule Britannia" and "Britons Strike Home."

The performance of patriotism was a crucial issue among players and audiences alike, but so too was dissent. Many of the most successful and important plays of the 1770s and early 1780s directly satirized the failure of the North government to retain the American colonies. Indeed Sheridan's entire career can be understood in terms of political commentary.[6] Likewise, the 1790s saw similar forms of dissent in the playhouse. Despite government censorship, scripts by Inchbald and Holcroft still managed to engage with the policies of the Pitt government. And audiences, most notably under the influence of radicals such as John Thelwall, fundamentally politicized the reception of even "loyal" scripts such as *Venice Preserv'd*. Audience intervention could readily challenge government regulation of theatrical culture.[7]

Considering the market for novelty and the tendency of audiences to construct topical meaning, it is not surprising that so much of the theatre in the period addressed colonial and national issues. Throughout this period both patent houses staged a wide variety of plays representing zones of colonial contact and imperial desire. In quite fascinating ways, London audiences were being shown the world, and their place in it, on a regular basis on the boards of Drury Lane and Covent Garden. The increasing integration of colonial and metropolitan economies meant that there was a market for ethnographic display and demonstrations of imperial efficacy. Foreign locales and peoples were often a pre-text for lavish design and costume, but many plays explicitly took up the challenge of transmitting knowledge about these distant societies. Many of the most successful plays of the period, Samuel Foote's *The Nabob*, Cumberland's *The West Indian* and Sheridan's *The School for Scandal*, come immediately to mind, satirized with varying degrees of intensity the class mobility made possible by the influx of colonial money.

This interest in cultural difference and social mobility was also played out in relation to long-standing forms of ethnic difference within the British Isles. Michael Ragussis has identified a significant proliferation of "multi-ethnic spectacles"—plays staging interactions between ethnic types—in both patent houses.[8] Many of the performance protocols associated with specific ethnic types were refined and consolidated in this period. Individual actors carried out deeply significant cultural work by implicitly challenging or reinforcing stereotypes: for example, John Moody established one form of stage Irishness in Garrick's *The Jubilee* only to implicitly critique it in his performance of Major O'Flaherty in *The West Indian*. Likewise John Quick moved beyond Charles Macklin's famous representations of Jewishness by enacting a different form of anti-Semitism in the character of Isaac Mendoza in Sheridan's *The Duenna*, only to reprise and critique the role in the masquerade scene of Hannah Cowley's *The Belle's Stratagem*. Plays such as *The Padlock* and *Inkle and Yarico* also pushed the use of blackface beyond its prior deployment in *Othello* and *Oroonoko* towards demeaning forms of racist comedy.

The self-conscious engagement with the theatrical repertoire by players and playwrights alike gives some sense of the deeply immersive world of Georgian theatre. Theatre professionals clearly expected and relied upon audience knowledge not only of prior productions, but also of performance protocols. Many of the most important developments in acting were based on an implicit and assumed departure from received practice. When Sarah Siddons first appeared as Lady Randolph in Home's *Douglas*, much of the thrill for the audience lay in recognizing how and when she modified the points pioneered by Mary Barry. Actors' modes of performative differentiation were often aimed solely at carving out a different stage persona. But often these changes were tied to complex forms of social critique. This strategy is perhaps most visible in the work of Hannah Cowley. As Sheridan's most formidable competitor in the 1770s and 1780s, Cowley's plays often consciously rehearse scenarios from Sheridan's scripts to argue for a different vision of sociability. Cowley's plays explored the changing laws around marriage and the shifting norms around women's behavior. These themes were also directly addressed by Inchbald's comedies but her concerns often strayed into the realm of politics proper.[9] As Gillian Russell has argued, a complex debate about women's place in the public sphere was repeatedly engaged by activating the audience's knowledge of the repertoire.[10]

That knowledge was by our standards extraordinary. Audiences were deeply informed not only about the plays, but also about the lives of the managers, the players and musical performers. That knowledge was gained in part from the sheer repetition that marked play-going during this period and in part from the convergence of theatrical culture with print media. When the *Morning Chronicle*, the *Morning Post*, and other papers gained the right to print parliamentary debate in the late 1760s, London saw a veritable explosion in newspaper culture. As papers became more numerous and expanded to a full four pages, "Theatrical Intelligence" remained the only form of cultural information published on a daily basis in the London press. Throughout the middle of the century the relationship between theatrical management and the booksellers behind daily newspapers had become a synergistic cultural force. Each relied on the other for revenue and for subject matter: papers advertised plays and reported on theatrical scandal, whereas plays frequently represented the world of ephemeral print culture and brought the news into the playhouse. This tight feedback loop of re-mediation meant that it became increasingly difficult to separate the nightly experience at the theatre from the daily experience of reading the news. This shift is visible in the "Contexts" of this third section of the anthology. By the early 1770s one can always find a wide array of reviews of new plays, and some newspapers, such as the *Morning Chronicle*, begin to develop a specific critical language for talking about the theatre.

The convergence of theatre and the press radically changed the culture of celebrity. Garrick had already shown the possibilities for the daily press to keep performance "alive" in spite of its inherent transience, but his involvement with the press was hardly singular. The great celebrities who followed Garrick's example all recognized the importance of managing the mediation of their fame not only in print, but also in visual representations. As Shearer West has shown, the proliferation of engravings of players in representative roles had a significant impact on audience expectations and on the articulation of a specifically English theatrical culture.[11] And there is an argument to be made for a similar transformation in the behavior of audiences. If we look closely at theatrical reporting in this period we can see audiences performing with the knowledge that their interventions will be re-mediated in the newspapers. With this knowledge in hand the theatres became a place where political praxis could be engaged with an eye to its widespread dissemination. The media convergence of theatre and newspapers became particularly important during the Revolutionary wars with France. As John Barrell has argued, within the government controlled precincts of the theatre both radical and loyalist constituencies had their say with the full knowledge that performative debates would be transmitted in the print public sphere.[12] Despite the censorship inherent to the Licensing Act of 1737, managers, playwrights, players and audiences devised ways of instantiating publics and counter-publics in the theatres. These complex practices often led to productions that were genuinely difficult to locate politically. Sheridan's *Pizarro*, which was in many ways the culmination of much of the theatrical experimentation of the eighteenth century, was widely celebrated for its loyalism even though equally if not more convincing arguments can be made for Sheridan's criticism of the Ministry. This undecidability eventually found its way into audience behavior, perhaps nowhere more famously than in the Old Price War. The politics of those protesting the rise in prices and the proliferation of private boxes in Covent Garden looked backward to a Burkean fantasy of loyalty to King and Constitution, but expressed through tactics derived from radical popular convention. In quite tangible ways, the complex interplay between performance and print allowed these convergent media to increasingly capture the dynamic forces of everyday life.

This permeability between drama and life would seem to set the stage for the birth of nineteenth-century realism, but it is important to recognize the degree to which late eighteenth-century theatre clung to performative artifice. Theatrical culture in the 1790s tended to approach the real via the emergent genres of the Gothic and melodrama. Highly expressive productions such as *The Castle Spectre* and *The Iron Chest* seemed to catch the social insecurity of the age by conspicuously displacing anxiety onto gloomy castles and psychologically extreme states. We can point to a similar indirect strategy in harlequinade. The rise of the great clowns Delpini and Grimaldi is inseparable from the way that their transformation tricks engaged with the incipient forces of commodity capitalism. Grimaldi's transformation of a post-chaise into a wheelbarrow engaged with mounting anxieties about class mobility, and his remarkable animation and subsequent dismemberment of the "Vegetable Man" in *Harlequin Asmodeus* explored the affective cost of wartime in a way that was beyond spoken drama. What Grimaldi did with things on stage was both magically funny and dead serious. Perhaps this mixture of the grave and the ridiculous is the challenge posed by the plays and the dramaturgical innovations of the latter eighteenth century: comprehending the transit from the trivial to the blindingly serious requires that we think about the importance of minor forms, of sudden shifts in performative register, of seemingly meretricious forms of display. In other words, the gravity that we tend to bring to the analysis of contemporary culture serves us well in this historically distant manifestation of the entertainment industry.

Notes

1 See Lisa A. Freeman, *Character's Theater: Genre and Identity on the Eighteenth-Century English Stage*. Philadelphia, PA: University of Pennsylvania Press, 2002, for a thorough discussion of this issue.

2 See Marc Baer, *Theatre and Disorder in Late Georgian London*. Oxford: Clarendon Press, 1992.

3 Robert D. Hume, "John Rich as Manager and Entrepreneur," in Berta Joncus and Jeremy Barlow, *The Stage's Glory: John Rich 1692–1761* (29–60). Newark, DE: University of Delaware Press, 2011.

4 Jane Moody, *Illegitimate Theatre in London, 1770–1840*. Cambridge: Cambridge University Press, remains the definitive account of these developments.

5 Gillian Russell, *The Theatres of War: Performance, Politics, and Society, 1793–1815*. Oxford University Press, 1995.

6 See Daniel O'Quinn, *Entertaining Crisis in the Atlantic Imperium, 1770–1800*. Baltimore, MD: The Johns Hopkins University Press, 2011 and David Francis Taylor, *Theatres of Opposition: Empire, Revolution and Richard Brinsley Sheridan*. Oxford: Oxford University Press, 2012.

7 See John Barrell, *Imagining the King's Death: Figurative Treason, Fantasies of Regicide*, Oxford: Oxford University Press, 2000, 554–70 and Daniel O'Quinn, "Insurgent Allegories: Staging *Venice Preserv'd*, *The Rivals* and *Speculation* in 1795," *Literature Compass*, 1 (2004): 1–30.

8 Michael Ragussis, *Theatrical Nation: Jews and Other Outlandish Englishmen in Georgian England*. Philadelphia, PA: University of Pennsylvannia Press, 2010, 24 and 43–5.

9 See Misty G. Anderson, *Female Playwrights and Eighteenth-Century Comedy: Negotiating Marriage on the London Stage*. New York: Palgrave, 2002, 139–200.

10 Gillian Russell, *Women, Sociability and Theatre in Georgian London*. Cambridge: Cambridge University Press, 2010.

11 Shearer West, *The Image of the Actor: Verbal and Visual Representation in the Age of Garrick and Kemble*. New York: St. Martin's Press, 1991.

12 See John Barrell, "An Entire Change of Performances," *Lumen*, 17 (1998): 14–15, and his *Imagining the King's Death: Figurative Treason, Fantasies of Regicide, 1793–1796*. Oxford: Oxford University Press, 2000, 554–70.

---

14. *The Jubilee, in Honour of Shakespeare. A Musical Entertainment*

THE JUBILEE, IN HONOUR OF SHAKESPEARE. A MUSICAL ENTERTAINMENT. DAVID GARRICK. FIRST PERFORMED 14 OCTOBER 1769 AND FIRST PUBLISHED 1773

14.1 *THE JUBILEE, IN HONOUR OF SHAKESPEARE. A MUSICAL ENTERTAINMENT*[1]

David Garrick

First Performed 14 October 1769 and First Published 1773

DAVID GARRICK (1717–79) casts an extraordinarily long shadow on eighteenth-century theatre history. After a revelatory debut season as an actor at Goodman's Fields in 1741/42, Garrick was a fixture at Drury Lane Theatre until his retirement in 1776. A remarkably versatile player, he redefined many of the primary roles in the repertory by moving away from the declamatory style of his forebears. Garrick's unsettling performances as Hamlet, Richard III, Bayes, Abel Drugger, Coriolanus and others electrified the town and became part of many tourists' itineraries. Audiences from near and far recorded his idiosyncratic movements and delivery to the point where he is perhaps the most documented performer of any age. His impact on the theatrical world was made even more pervasive when he became manager of Drury Lane in 1747. In this role he fostered the careers of a host of playwrights and players. But his managerial legacy is perhaps most strongly felt in three related areas. He was a gifted manipulator of the press and perhaps more than any other manager cemented the tight relationship between the nocturnal performances at the theatre and the diurnal world of newspapers. Under Garrick's management the theatre's presence in the news vastly accelerated to the point where some scholars now consider them co-extensive media. He was also a highly active author of prologues and epilogues to plays and a productive playwright in his own right. Many of his plays are adaptations and it is in this area that we can gain some sense of his third major contribution. Even though Garrick wrote numerous adaptations of Shakespeare's plays and thus was part of the widespread corruption of the original texts, his veneration for Shakespeare was instrumental to his canonization as England's national poet.[2] Shakespeare was revered well before Garrick came onto the scene, but as we have seen elsewhere in this anthology, the Shakespearean corpus was often at odds with neo-classical literary theory. In all aspects of his career, Garrick altered how his audiences experienced these plays and changed how they thought about their author. In some cases, as in *Hamlet*, he utterly changed the performance protocols for the play by presenting a very different Hamlet than his predecessors. In some cases, he made steps towards restoring a more accurate playing text. These interventions were matched by somewhat more dubious strategies of self-promotion. Throughout his career he commissioned artwork that aligned himself with the Bard. In 1769 he conceived of and executed the Shakespeare Jubilee in Stratford-upon-Avon that used the talent and resources of Drury Lane Theatre to celebrate Shakespeare's life and achievement.[3] Given Garrick's talents with the press, and his numerous enemies, *The Jubilee* was the subject of much anticipation and newspaper coverage both positive and negative. The three-day event involved the construction of a temporary building, a complex pageant, the composition and performance of an ode to Shakespeare's genius, and a host of commercial tie-ins. When rain turned everything into a fiasco, the press was there to ensure that Garrick was the object of public ridicule.

Garrick, however, snatched victory from the jaws of defeat by quickly penning a musical entertainment entitled *The Jubilee* that was first performed in October of 1769. The play went on to become one of the most popular and frequently performed scripts of the century. Receipts for the play easily covered Drury Lane's losses at the rained-out Jubilee. Salvaging key components of the celebration in Stratford-upon-Avon—most notably the dedicatory ode and the elaborate pageant—Garrick spared no expense in making *The Jubilee* one of the most entertaining spectacles of the age. The songs, first penned for the celebration, were augmented and became part of popular culture. The Dedicatory Ode eventually became a detachable entity and was performed repeatedly as a separate set-piece for Garrick himself—it further cemented the relationship between the player, manager, and Bard. The pageant warrants serious consideration in its own right not only because it gives a glimpse into how audiences understood the Shakespearean corpus, but also because it shows the very scenographic limits of Drury Lane itself. Garrick's enemies loathed the play but it remains an important indicator of the degree to which Garrick was willing to use "low means" to secure and promulgate the cause of "high culture" for nationalist ends. Because of the importance of this play to so many aspects of theatrical culture at mid century, we have provided extensive contextual materials. Accounts and images of the Shakespeare Jubilee are followed by reviews of *The Jubilee* and by a large sample of spin-offs in commercial print culture. These range from treatises attacking Garrick, printed panegyric to Shakespeare (hoping to cash in on the rage for the Bard), collections of song lyrics from the play and printed versions of the Dedicatory Ode. The sheer number and range of these materials gives some sense of the degree to which a theatrical production could permeate everyday culture, and readers are invited to access many of these in the online supplement to this volume.

Dramatis Personæ[4]

Ralph, a Country Clown	Mr. King
Gentlemen	Mr. Wheeler
	Mr. Hurst
Irishman	Mr. Moody
Ballad Singer	Mr. Vernon
Showmen	Mr. Hartry
	Mr. Messink
Ostler	Mr. Parsons
Cook	Mr. Ackman
Cook's Boy	Master Cape
Two Country Ladies	Mrs. Baddeley
	Miss Radley
Goody Benson	Mrs. Bradshaw
Margery Jarvis	Mrs. Love
Female Ballad Singer	Mr. Dibdin
Passengers, Waiters, Pedlars, and Mob	

Scene—Stratford upon Avon.

Time—the Morning.

I.i

Goody Benson's *house.* Goody Benson *discovered sitting in a straw chair; a bottle beside her, and a cushion under her.*

MARGERY. [*Without*] Goody Benson? Goody Benson? What! a'n't you up yet?

GOODY. Who's there?

MARGERY. 'Tis I Margery Jarvis. Will you let me in, neighbour?

GOODY. Ay, and thank you too, Margery. [*Lets her in.*

MARGERY. What! you're up too I see.

GOODY. Up! Why I hav'n't been in bed ever since this racket began, but have been striving to take a nap in my chair. Well, and what news, neighbour?

MARGERY. News! This Jubilee will be the ruin of us all.—The murrain on 'em for making such a noise in our town.—Our Ralph says as how he thinks the Papithes has gotten among 'em.

[*Enter* Ralph.

RALPH. In troth do I, neighbour.

MARGERY. Lord! Ralph, why would you frighten once so?—Why then you don't sleep no more than we?

RALPH. Sleep! Why is this a town for the rest?—I shou'dn't like to wake, and find my self a hundred miles off.—We shall be eaten up alive; there are a hundred taylors in town. Why, the taylors and barbers alone are enough to breed a famine among us.

GOODY & MARGERY. O Lud! O Lud!

RALPH. Why, I thought there was something going forward, when they cou'dn't let Shakespeare's image alone there in the church[5], but painted him all over, to make un look like a popish saint. And then they have brought down great cannon guns, and as much powder as will kill all the fowl in Christendom. We sha'n't have so much as a hen or chicken left; and when they've should all them, they'll shoot us too I believe. [*Weeps.*

GOODY & MARGERY. Mercy on us!

MARGERY. But, Ralph, what is that round house there in the meadow for?

RALPH. For! Why, to be sure, to drive us, poor souls! all into it, like a flock of sheep. Why, there's little Dolly Dobson says, she'll take her bible oath, she seed as good as fifty couple of devils at work together in Farmer Hodging's cow-house and barn; and if they once get loose about this town, not all our parson's preaching will drive 'em out again; and if they stay, they'll ravish! ravish! ay that they will, man, woman, and child!

GOODY & MARGERY. Lord save us!

GOODY. Harky' Ralph; when will this ravishment begin?

AIR

When I were young, tho' now am old,
The men were kind and true;
But now they're grown so false and bold!
What can a woman do?
Now what can a woman do?
For men are truly
So unruly
I tremble at seventy-two!

When I were fair, tho' now so so,
No hearts were given to rove,
Our pulses beat nor fast nor slow,
But all was faith and love;
Now what can a woman do?
For men are truly
So unruly
I tremble at seventy-two!

MARGERY. Ay, ay, dame; 'tis the men's delight to make us, poor women! tremble.—And yet, Ralph, there is some good to be gotten among these fine gentry; for I could have letten my little room for a matter of two guineas; ecod! an' I would too, if they had gi'n me t'other guinea.

RALPH. More shame for you, dame, more shame for you; ecod! if they get any thing among us, they shou'd pay well for it.

GOODY. Very true, Ralph.—But ha' you seen the Steward, as they call him, that's come down?

RALPH. Yes, yes, I ha' seen him, with his mulberry box on his breast, and his white rod in his hond, speaking his oration among the gentle-folks. Why, he's not much bigger than I am, but a good deal plumper: but let un alone; he knows what he's about. He has brought down the pipers along wi' him; but ecod! let who will dance, he'll make *us* pay the piper:—he has gotten a good long head of his own.

[*Cannon fire.*

ALL. O Lud! O Lud! What's that?

RALPH. [*Recovering from his fright*] Don't be frightened dame: I'll go and see what's the matter: don't be frightened dame, don't be frightened.

[*Exeunt different ways.*

I.ii

—An inn-yard; in it a post-chaise; balconies fronting. Enter Serenaders, *with dominos and guitars.*

SERENADE

Let Beauty with the sun arise,
To Shakespeare tribute pay;
With heavenly smiles and speaking eyes
Give lustre to the day.
Each smile she gives protects his name;
What face shall dare to frown?
Not Envy's self can blast the fame
Which beauty deigns to crown. [*Exeunt all but one.*

IRISH MAN. [*Lets down the window of the post-chaise.* Arrah! what the devil's the matter with you there, to keep such a noise and a racket with your marks and coloured surplices?

SERENADER. O Sir! this is part of the Jubilee.

IRISH MAN. Well, and I dare say you think it mighty entertaining. I did not come down to the Jubilee 'til past twelve o'clock last night; and I wandered for more than an hour to look for a lodging, and a bit of something to eat; but the devil a tooth-full of either one or t'other could I get: so last I was obliged to take up my lodging in the first floor of this post-chaise, at half a crown a head; and they have crammed a bed-fellow with me into the bargain; so that not being able to lie down upright in my bed, I could not get one wink of sleep 'til you were pleased to waken me with your damned scraping and nonsense.—But pray, Sir, will you be after telling me what this Jubilee is?

SERENADER. Sir, if you will please to come out, I will do my self the honour of informing you.

IRISH MAN. Faith, that I will and thank you too, if you will be so kind as to open my chamber-door. [Serenader *opens the chaise-door*] But stay a little, my dear, 'til I shut the door upon my bed-fellow, for fear he should chance to snatch cold.—Upon my soul! I was obliged to make a night-cap of my wig, that the hair might keep me a little warm.—Well, Sir.

SERENADER. Sir, at a Jubilee you must expect odes without poetry, music without harmony, dinners without victuals, and lodging without beds.

IRISH MAN. Oh ho! To be sure you did not take that from what's said of old Kilkenny; where there's wit without joke, fire without smoke, air without fog, land without bog, men without heads,—"lodging without beds,"—Oh no! that's the Jubilee rig.—*Ecce Signum*![6] Puddings without eggs, rabbits without legs.

SERENADER. How, Sir! Rabbits without legs?

IRISH MAN. Ay, Sir, Welch ones.

VOICE [*Within*] Ho! this fame is entitled and called, the Warwickshire lad.

SERENADER. Now, Sir, we shall rouze you.

[*Enter* Ballad Singers.

SONG

Ye Warwickshire lads and ye lasses,
See what at our Jubilee passes;
Come revel away, rejoice and be glad,
For the lad of all lads was a Warwickshire lad,[7]
Warwickshire lad,
All be glad,
For the lad of all lads was a Warwickshire lad.

Be proud of the charms of your country,
Where Nature has lavish'd her bounty,
Where so much she's given, that some may be spar'd,
For the bard of all bards was a Warwickshire bard.
Warwickshire bard,
Never pair'd
For the bard of all bards was a Warwickshire bard.

Each shire has its different pleasures,
Each shire has its different treasures,
But to rare Warwickshire all shires must submit,
For the wit of all wits was a Warwickshire wit.
Warwickshire wit,
How he writ!
For the wit of all wits was a Warwickshire wit,

Old Ben, Thomas Otway, John Dryden,
And a half a score more, we take pride in;
Of famous Will Congreve we boast too the skill,
But the Will of all Wills was a Warwickshire Will,
Warwickshire Will,
Matchless still,
But the Will of all Wills, was a Warwickshire Will.

Our Shakespeare compar'd is to no man,
Nor French man, nor Grecian, nor Roman,
Their swans are all geese to the Avon's sweet swan,
And the man of all men was a Warwickshire man,
Warwickshire man,
Avon's swan,
And the man of all men was a Warwickshire man.

As ven'son is very inviting,
To steal it our bard took delight in,
To make his friends merry he was never lag,
And the wag of all wags was a Warwickshire wag,
Warwickshire wag,
Ever brag,
And the wag of all wags was a Warwickshire wag.

There never was such a creature,
Of all she was worth he robb'd Nature,
He took all her smiles, and he took all her grief,
And the thief of all thieves was a Warwickshire thief,
Warwickshire thief,
He's the chief,
And the thief of all thieves was a Warwickshire thief.

SERENADER. Well, Sir, I hope you like our thief. Your servant.

[*Exeunt* Serenader & Ballad Singers.

IRISH MAN. By my soul I believe you are all thieves.

Jubilee thief,
It's my belief,
The worst of all thieves is a Jubilee thief. [*Exit.*

I.iii

—*The hall. Bells ring;* Waiters *passing in great confusion.*

1ST GUEST. Waiter! bring the hot rolls and butter to the Julius Cæsar.

WAITER. Coming up, Sir.

2D GUEST. [*At a balcony*] Waiter! Waiter! will you, or will you not, bring the refreshment I ordered an hour ago?

WAITER. Coming up, Sir.

2D GUEST. Coming, Sir! You're always coming.—The lady and I shall be starved. Harky' Waiter, bring half a dozen more jellies. [*Goes in.*

WAITER. Here, Tom! Tom! bring half a dozen more jellies to that little fribbling gentleman and the tall lady, in Love's Labour Lost. And harky' Dick, do you make haste with half a dozen of claret to the gentlemen in the Merry Wives[8]; they have been up all night you know; we must not disoblige good customers. [*Bells ring*] Hey, William! Why don't you run up to the Moon? Do you hear what a ringing they keep?—I find I must go myself. [*Exit.*

[*Enter a* Guest.

3D GUEST. Here, Waiter! Where's the Boot-catcher gone to?—I cannot get any thing to eat here, nor my boots, to go any where else. [*Sees* Boot-catcher, *and drags him in*] Here, you rascal! Where's my boots?

BOOT-CATCHER. Lord, your honour! All the boots lie yonder in a heap, and first come why first served.

3D GUEST. Mine are a new pair, you rascal, and never wore before; they were made on purpose for the Jubilee; I would not lose them for all your Shakespeares and your Jubilees: Damn your Jubilees. [*Exit.*

BOOT-CATCHER. [*Solus*] Lord, meester, you need not make such haste, for all the new boots have been gone this heef hour. [*Exit.*

[*Enter* Waiter *with a breakfast.*

WAITER. Sir, I shall be with you in one minute.

[*Enter a* Guest.

4TH GUEST. Here, Waiter! By the Lord I shall be starved; where's my breakfast?

WAITER. Here, your honour.

4TH GUEST. Bring it this way. [*Exit.*

[*Enter another* Guest.

5TH GUEST. Where are you going to with that, sirrah!

WAITER. To that gentleman's room, Sir; he has waited this hour for it.

5TH GUEST. You lie, you dog; it is my breakfast: He's a book-customer, and I'm ready money. [*Takes it off.*

[*Exeunt both. Enter two people with a piece of beef.*

1ST PERSON. Come along, Tom, I have got it. [*Exeunt.*

[*Enter* Cook.

COOK. Hollo! Bring that back; 'tis for my Lord's servants.—Ay, ay, they are at it: Hunger has no manners. Here, boy, run to the butcher's, bid him kill all he has, fat and lean—D'ye hear?—Bid him kill away, or by the Lord I must run away. [*Exit.*

[*Bells ring:* Waiters *passing in great confusion.*

WAITER. Ho! Tom! William! Send my master up stairs; there are all the actor people quarelling in the Catherine and Petruchio.[9] [*Exit.*

[*Enter* Irish man.

IRISH MAN. Harky' Sir, it's a family business, and ought to be settled by themselves; so let 'em fight it out, and when they're tired, they'll stop. Arrah! Fighting's the only right way to settle a dispute. Old Ireland for that. [*Exit.*

I.iv

—*The inn-yard.*

IRISH MAN. [*Solus*] O there's nothing like a Jubilee! Such noise and confusion! By my soul, if they go on this way for a hand-full of weeks, they'll equal Corke's own self.—By the Lord I believe their Shakespeare was a mad-man, for he has turned all their heads: I never saw such doings about St. Patrick, but by God I know which was the better sort of a man. O 'tis he could handle a cudgel with e'er a fellow that ever put leg in a brogue.

[*Enter a* Pedlar *with his box.*

PEDLAR. Here are all sorts of ladles, spoons, nutmeg-graters, snuff-boxes, and many curious things, all made out of the mulberry tree.[10]

IRISH MAN. Why then, let me have a bit of the sincere, real thing, to carry over to my foolish relations.—And let me see that ribband you've got there, for I promised to bring my sister Joany something handsome.

PEDLAR. There, Sir's a ribband for you; not a colour in the world but what's on it; it was made to represent Shakespeare, Sir, (as the little gentleman from London says) in the variety of his genius. Read, Sir, but the fine verse that's on it: "Each scene of many-colour'd life he drew." And, I'm sure, Sir, you cannot refuse me the trifle of two shillings for it.

IRISH. Well, let's have it, though by my soul it's a little too dear. Now give us that piece of mulberry.

PEDLAR. Here, your honour.

[*Enter another* Pedlar.

2D PEDLAR. Don't buy of him, your honour; he ha'n't a bit of the true mulberry; all his ladles are made out of old chairs and joint stools: I bought the whole tree, and see here, your honour, here's my affidavy of it.

1ST PEDLAR. Ay, you dog, but it's gone long ago, and you've sold as much since, as would make a tree large enough to hang all your lousy generation on. He has got a little money, your honour, and thinks nobody has a right to cheat gentle-folks but himself. Do, your honour, (Heaven bless you!) buy of me.

2D PEDLAR. Buy of me, your honour,—buy of me.

IRISH MAN. Harky' you two mulberry radicals, clear the Yard of yourselves, and let me see you both out of my sight this moment, or I'll make the mulberry juice fly about your sconces. What! are you going to chatter again? [*Beats them off: in the struggle a bit of the wood falls*] A couple of rascals! To think to impose on a gentleman that has travelled all the foreign countries born at home and abroad. [*Takes up the bit*] The chance of war directly: First break their heads, then seize on the booty. They may talk just what they please of their mulberry bushes, but commend me to a bit of old Shillela. Oh there's nothing can come up to it!

[*Enter a man beating a drum: mob following.*

SPOKESMAN. This is to give notice, that the wonderful and suprizing porcupine-man, and several other wild birds and beasts, are to be seen at the Amphi-Theatre, at so small a price as a shilling. [*Beats off.*

IRISH MAN. O! that booby of a fellow will never make a fortune at the Jubilee, to ask a shilling to see strange sights, when one sees so many strange creatures every day for nothing. But who have we here?

[*Enter* Trumpeter, Horse-rider, *and* Woman.

SPOKESMAN. This is to give notice, that the wonderful and surprising Mr. Sampson is just going to mount four horses at once, with a leg upon every horse: Also, the most wonderful feats of horsemanship by the notorious Mrs. Sampson.

[*Exeunt* Trumpeter, *&c.*

IRISH MAN. By the stick of St. Patrick this is a comical way of riding upon one's feet; but I believe that it's the way many a good gentleman travels from Ireland, ay and from Scotland too. [*Enter* Waiter] Harky' Waiter, come here. Can't you come near you gander-faced gag you? There's two turteens for yourself.

WAITER. Your honour need not fear me, I'll do it.

IRISH MAN. What do you say?

WAITER. Your honour may depend upon me; I'll take care of you, upon my honour. [*Exit.*

IRISH MAN. [*Solus*] O!—Well, there's nothing to be done here, and I find, without a little bribery and corruption. As I hope to return safe to Ireland, I believe I snatched cold by going to bed in the post-chaise. So, now I'll go and have a sup in a snug corner, and steal a nap for nothing into the bargain. [*Exit.*

II.i

Scene—the Rotunda.[11] *Several discovered; one of whom speaks:*

Peace to this meeting,
Joy and fair time, health and good wishes!
Now, worthy friends, the cause why we are
met
Is in celebration of the day that gave
Immortal Shakespeare to this favour'd Isle,
The most replenished sweet work of Nature,
Which from the prime creation e'er she
frame'd.
O thou divinest Nature! how thyself thou
blazon'st
In this thy son! form'd in thy prodigality,
To hold thy mirror up, and give the time
Its very form and pressure!—When he
speaks
Each aged ear plays truant at his tales,
And younger hearers are quite ravished,
So voluble is his discourse.—Gentle
As Zephyr blowing underneath the vi'let,
Not waging its sweet head; yet as rough
(His noble blood enchas'd) as the rude wind.
That by the top doth take the mountain pine,
And make him stoop to th'vale. 'Tis
wonderful,
That an invisible instinct shou'd frame him
To royalty, unlearn'd; honour, untaught;
Civility, not seen in others; knowledge,
That wildly grows in him, but yields a crop
As if it had been sown. What a piece of
work!
How noble in faculty! infinite in reason!
A combination and a form indeed.
Where ev'ry God did seem to set his seal.

Heav'n has him now; yet let our idolatrous
fancy
Still sanctify his reliques; and this day
Stand aye distinguished in the kalendar
To the last syllable of recorded time.
For, if we take him but for all in all,
We ne'er shall look upon his like again.

SONG, *by a person bearing a bottle and goblet.*

Behold this fair goblet, 'twas carv'd from the tree
Which, O my sweet Shakespeare! was planted by thee.
As a relique I kiss it, and bow at thy shrine:
What comes from thy hands must be ever divine.
All shall yield to the mulberry tree,
Bend to thee
Blest mulberry;
Matchless was he
Who planted thee,

And thou like him immortal shall be.
Ye trees of the forest so rampant and high,
Who spread round your branches, whose heads sweep the sky,
Ye curious exotics whom Taste has brought here,
To root out the natives at prices so dear;
All shall yield, &c.

The oak is held royal in Britain's great boast,
Preserv'd once our king, and will always our coast,
Of ships made of fir we have thousands that fight,
But one, only one, like our Shakespeare can write.
All shall yield, &c.

Let Venus delight in her gay myrtle bowers,
Pomona in fruit trees, and Flora in flowers:
The garden of Shakespeare all fancies will suit,
With the sweetest of flowers and the fairest of fruit.
All shall yield, &c.

With learning and knowledge the well letter'd birch,
Supplies law and physic, and grace for the church:
But law and the gospel in Shakespeare we find,
And he gives the best physic for body and mind.
All shall yield, &c.

The fame of the patron gives fame to the tree;
From him and his merits this takes its degree:
Give Phœbus and Bacchus their laurel and vine,
The tree of our Shakespeare is still more divine.
All shall yield, &c.

As the genius of Shakespeare, out-shining the day,
More rapture than wine to the heart can convey:
So the tree which he planted by making his own,
Has the laurel and bays and the vine all in one.
All shall yield, &c.

Then take each a relique of this hallow'd tree,
From Folly and Fashion a charm let it be.
Fill to the planter the cup to the brim:
To honour your country do honour to him.
All shall yield to the mulberry tree,
Bend to thee,
Blest mulberry;
Matchless was he
Who planted thee,
And thou like him immortal shall be.

[*Exeunt* Omnes.

II.ii

—A street; on one side the house wherein Shakespeare *was born.*

CHORUS, by a full band of performers.

This is the day, a holiday! a holiday!
Drive Spleen and Rancour far away:
This is the day, a holiday! a holiday!
Drive Care and Sorrow away.
There [pointing to the house] *Nature nurs'd her darling boy,*
From whom all care and sorrow fly.
Whose harp the Muses strung;
From heart to heart let joy rebound;
Now, now, we tread enchanted ground,
Here Shakespeare walk'd and sung.

[*The Order of the Pageant exhibited in honour of* Shakespeare[12]

1. Sixteen attendants with Tambours.
2. Two attendants bearing the inscriptions *Veluti in Speculo*[13] and *Totus mundus agit histrionem.*[14]
3. A band of music.
4. *As You Like It.* Touchstone and Audrey; Orlando and Rosalind; Jaques, Adam and Forresters.
5. *Tempest.* Prospero, Ferdinando, and Miranda; Ariel, Caliban and drunken sailors.
6. *Merchant of Venice.* Bassanio, Portia; the caskets on a bier richly ornamented; Shylock the Jew with his knife and bond, Senators, &c.
7. *Twelfth Night.* Sir Andrew Aque-Cheek, Sir Toby Belch, Malvolio, Oliva, and attendants.
8. *Midsummer Night's Dream.* Bottom with an ass's head, a number of children representing fairies; Oberon the fairy king and Titania his queen seated in an elegant carriage; Robin Good-fellow, Pease Blossom, Cobweb, &c.
9. *Merry Wives of Windsor.* Justice Shallow, Slender, Sir Hugh Evans, Dr. Caius, Jack Rugby, Host of the Garter, Ancient Pistol; Sir John Falstaff, between Mrs. Ford and Mrs. Page; Bardolph, Nym, &c.
10. *Much-a-do about Nothing.* Benedict and Beatrice; Pedro, Leonato and Masqueraders.

11. *The Comic Muse*, (Mrs. Abingdon)[15] seated on a magnificent car, drawn by Satyrs, and attended by the different characters of the ancient comedy.
12. A band of martial music.
13. *Richard III*. King Richard giving directions to Tyrrell, with respect to the murder of the two young princes, who follow, led by the Queen Dowager, their mother. Yeomen of the guards, &c.
14. *Cymbeline*. Bellarius, Guiderius, Arviragus, Imogen, Posthumus, and attendants.
15. *Hamlet*. The ghost beckoning to Hamlet, who is led by his mother; Ophelia in the mad scene; the two grave diggers.
16. *Othello*. The Duke conversing with Brabantio; Othello leading Desdemona; Iago, Roderigo, officers, &c.
17. *Romeo and Juliet*. Peter and the nurse, the friar, Romeo and Juliet, servants, &c.
18. *Henry VIII*. Lord Chamberlain, the King, leaning on Cardinal Wolsey; Anna Bullen, Archbishop Cranmer, guards, &c.
19. *King Lear*. Edgar in the storm scenes, Lear between Kent and Cordelia; heralds and attendents.
20. *Macbeth*. Macbeth and his lady in the dagger scene. Hecate and the witches with the burning cauldron.
21. *Julius Caesar*. Lictors, tribunes, &c. Caesar and the soothsayer followed by Brutus and Cassius.
22. *Anthony and Cleopatra*. Egyptian slaves, Anthony and Cleopatra, black eunuchs, &c.
23. *Apollo* with his lyre (Mr. Vernon).
24. *The Tragic Muse* (Mrs. Barry)[16] on a triumphal car, surrounded by Calliope, Clio, Erato, Euterpe, Polyhymnia, Terpsichore, and Urania.[17]
25. The figure of Shakespeare from his monument in Westminster Abbey, with emblematical ornaments, and a numerous train of attendants, which closed the procession.

II.iii

—*The meadow. Two* Country Girls *discovered.*

1ST GIRL. What a pretty song, Sue, is the "Warwickshire lad"! O I could be singing it for ever!

2ND GIRL. Ay, and you promised me the ballad of it. But, pr'ythee, what's this fame Jubelo, that makes all this confounded racket in our town?

1ST GIRL. Why doat you know what a Jubelo is?

2ND GIRL. Not I indeed. What is it?

1ST GIRL. Why I'll tell you: A Jubelo is—it is—it is—a Jubelo. You have seen the Pageant, and that's some of it; the rest is to be, by-and-by, at the great round house yonder, that they call the Oratunda.

2ND GIRL. Well, well, I understand you; but pray who is this Shakspur that they are making all this fuss about?

1ST GIRL. Sure you have seen his tomb in the church.

2ND GIRL. Lord! Was that his? But why is he that has been dead a great while, to have finer doings for him than there is on our Mayor's day? Answer me this, was Shakspur a greater man than the Mayor of Stratford?

1ST GIRL. Yes, for he was a great Poet.

2ND GIRL. O!—He made ballads then; such as the Babes in the Wood, and the Dragon of Wantly, and Robinhood?

1ST GIRL. No, you fool, he made plays; but how should you know any-thing about plays, who have been only a dairy-maid all your life-time, milking of cows, churning of butter, and pressing of cheese?

2ND GIRL. Nay, Kate, you need not mock me. Have not I seen shows and actors? Yes I have. I have seen Punch and his wife, with the Devil and Doctor Faustus, that I have; and Fair Robinson, with the whole court of the King of Prussia; and—[18]

1ST GIRL. Ah, you poor simpleton: They were all wooden actors; but when I lived servant with the rich butter-maker at Birmingham, and with Mr. Alderman Shuttle the weaver at Coventry, I saw plays with men and women actors, all alive; and there I saw this Shakspur plays, and they were the finest that ever were seen; I am sure I have cried at them, ay, and laughed at them, twenty and twenty time.—And so as the player-folks have got a good deal of money by his plays, they have gratitude enough to make this Jubelo in honour of him.

SONG

The pride of all Nature was sweet Willy O;
The first of all swains
That gladden'd the plains;
None ever was like to the sweet Willy O.

He sung it so rarely (the sweet Willy O)
He melted each maid;
So skilful he play'd,
No shepherd e'er pip'd like the sweet Willy O,

He would be a soldier (the sweet Willy O);
When arm'd in the field
With sword and with shield
The laurel was won by the sweet Willy O.

All Nature obey'd him (the sweet Willy O);
Where-ever he came,
What-e'er had a name,
When-ever he sung, follow'd sweet Willy O.

He charm'd all when living (the sweet Willy O);
And when Willy di'd
'Twas Nature that sigh'd,
To part with her all in her sweet Willy O.

2ND GIRL. Ah! poor fellow!—But let us go to the Oratunda, for there's the sweetest music you ever heard.

1ST GIRL. With all my heart. And your talking of it puts me in mind of what the fine little gentleman there from Lon'on (that's the heat of 'em all) said: "This same Shakspur," says he, "could look into any one's breast, and tell what they were thinking of, with the greatest ease;" and I'm sure it's well he's not alive now, else what naughty tales might he tell of some folks!

SONG

Let us sing it and dance it,
Rejoice it and prance it,
That no man has now such an art.
What would come of us all,
Both the great ones and small,
Did he live now to peep in each heart?
Tho' sins I have none,
I'm glad he is gone;
No maid could live near such a mon.

[*Exeunt. Enter* Irish man.

IRISH MAN. Och ho! Stay my dear creatures. Do you know what you are running from? By my soul, a bit of old Ireland. What! Are you gone? Fait' if I had time I would go and speak a little love to dem. Indeed I had never an intrigue since I left Chester, and that's almost a week now, and for an Irish man to be so long without one is a big burning shame. Och, 'tis a business we are all famous for, especially when we get among the Bugs. But upon my soul, I have had a fine sleep now, that I have. Och! I like a little nod now and then; and I think a nap of nine hours is as good as half a night's sleep at any time. [*Going.*

[*Enter* Cook's Boy.

BOY. By your leave, Sir, by your leave.

IRISH MAN. Fait' honey, I've no leave to sell; but where are you going in such a confounded hurry?

BOY. Pray don't stop me: I am going to the Rotunda.

IRISH MAN. So am I, as soon as I have seen the Pageant go by. Fait' they boddered my head about it all the way I came, and they said it would be ten times finer than the Fringes in Dublin.

BOY. If you stay for that you'll wait long enough; it's all dickey, it's all in my eye; the Pagans ha' been gone this half hour. By your leave. [*Exit.*

IRISH MAN. [*Solus*] Tender and turf! The Pageant gone by? And tho' I were asleep I had never a dream about it to wake me. Upon my soul when I go home to Ireland again, they will be after making a laugh at me, for not seeing it.—What a poor unfortunate creature I am! Here have I come three hundred miles to see a Jubilee; fell fast asleep when I should have been awake,—was broad awake when I should have been fast asleep—have go nothing at all, and paid double for that too; so I'll go to the 'Tunda, and hear what's to be seen then. [*Exit.*

II.iv

—The Rotunda. Vocal and instrumental performers, spectators, &c.

ROUNDELAY

Sisters of the tuneful strain!
Attend your parent's jocund train;
'Tis Fancy calls you, follow me,
To celebrate the Jubilee.

On Avon's banks, where Shakespeare's bust
Points out and guards his sleeping dust,
The sons of scenic mirth agree
To celebrate this Jubilee.

Come, daughters come, and bring with you
Th'ærial sprite and fairy crew,
And the Sister-Graces three,
To celebrate our Jubilee.

Hang around the scuptur'd tomb
The 'broider'd vest, the nodding plume,
And the mask of comic glee,
To celebrate our Jubilee.

From Birnam-wood and Bosworth field
Bring the standard, bring the shield,
With drums, and marital symphony,
To celebrate our Jubilee.

In mournful numbers now relate
Poor Desdemona's hapless fate,
With frantic deeds of jealousy,
To celebrate our Jubilee.

Nor be Windsor's Wives forgot,
With their harmless, merry plot,
(The whit'ning mead and haunted tree,)
To celebrate our Jubilee.

Now in jocund strains recite
The humours of the braggart knight,
Fat knight and ancient Pistol, be!
To celebrate our Jubilee.

But see, in crowds the gay, the fair,
To the splendid scene repair,
A scene as fine as fine can be,
To celebrate the Jubilee.

ODE

To what blest Genius of the Isle
Shall Gratitude her tribute pay,
Decree the festive day,
Erect the statue, and devote the pile?
Do not your sympathetic hearts accord
To own the "bosom's lord?"
'Tis he! 'Tis he! that demi-god
Who Avon's flow'ry margin trod,
While sportive Fancy round him flew,
Where nature led him by the hand,
Instructed him in all she knew,
And gave him absolute command.
'Tis he! 'Tis he!
"The god of our idolatry!"
To him the song, the edifice we raise,
He merits all our wonder, all our praise!
Yet ere impatient joy break forth
In sounds that lift the soul from earth,
And to spell-bound minds impart
Some faint idea of his magic art,
Let awful silence still the air!
From the dark cloud the hidden light
Bursts ten-fold bright!
Prepare! prepare! prepare!
Now swell the choral song!
Roll the full tide of harmony along!
Let Rapture sweep the trembling strings!
And Fame, expanding all her wings,
With all her trumpet-tongues proclaim
The lov'd, rever'd, immortal name!
Shakespeare, Shakespeare, Shakespeare.
Let th'inchanting sound
From Avon's shores rebound;
Thro' the air
Let it bear
The precious freight to envious nations
round.

CHORUS

Swell the choral song!
Roll the full tide of harmony along!
Let Rapture sweep the trembling strings!
And Fame, expanding all her wings,
With all her trumpet-tongues proclaim
The lov'd, rever'd, immortal name!
Shakespeare, Shakespeare, Shakespeare.

AIR I

Sweetest Bard that ever sung,
Nature's glory, Fancy's child;
Never sure did witching tongue
Warble forth such wood-notes wild!
Come each Muse and Sister-Grace,
Loves and Pleasures hither come,
Well you know this happy place,
Avon's banks were once your home.
Bring the laurel, bring the flow'rs,
Songs of triumph to him raise:
He united all your pow'rs,
All uniting, sing his praise!
Tho' Philip's fam'd, unconquer'd son,
Had ev'ry blood-stain'd laurel won,
He sighs that his creative word
(Like that which rules the skies,)
Could not bid other nations rise,
To glut his yet unsated sword:
But when our Shakespeare's matchless pen,
Like Alexander's sword, had done with men,
He heav'd no sigh, he made no mean;
Not limited to human kind,
He fir'd his wonder-teeming mind,
Rais'd other worlds and beings of his own!

AIR II

When Nature, smiling, hail'd his birth,
To him unbounded power was giv'n;
The Whirlwind's wing, to sweep the sky,
"The frenzy-rolling eye,
To glance from Heav'n to Earth,
From Earth to Heav'n!"
O from his Muse of Fire
Could but one spark be caught,
Then might these humble strains aspire
To tell the wonders he has wrought!
To tell, how sitting on his magic throne,
Unaided, and alone,

In dreadful state, the subject Passions round him wait;
Who, tho' unchain'd, and raging there,
He checks, inflames, or turns their mad career;
With that superior skill
Which winds the fiery steed at will,
He gives the awful word,
And they all foaming, trembling, own him for their lord.
With these, his slave, he can controul,
Or charm the soul,
So realiz'd are all his golden dreams,
Of terror, pity, love, and grief,
Tho' conscious that the vision only seems,
The woe-struck mind finds no relief:
Ingratitude would drop the tear,
Cold-blooded Age take fire,
To see the thankless children of old Lear
Spurn at their king and fire.
With his our reason too grows wild!
When Nature had disjoin'd,
The Poet's pow'r combin'd,
Madness and age, ingratitude and child.
Ye guilty, lawless tribe,
Escap'd from punishment, by art, or bribe,
At Shakespeare's bar appear;
No bribing, shuffl'ing there;
His Genius, like a rushing flood,
Cannot be withstood;
Out [bursts] *the penitential tear,*
The look appall'd the crime reveals;
The marble hearted moniter feels,
Whose hand is stain'd with blood.

SEMI-CHORUS

When Law is weak, and Justice fails,
The Poet holds the sword and scales.

AIR III

Though crimes from death and torture fly,
The twister Muse, their flight pursues;
Guilty mortals more than die!
They live indeed, but live to feel
The scourge and wheel,
"On the torture of the mind they lie.
Should harras'd Nature sink to rest,
The Poet wakes the scorpion in the breast.
Guilty mortals more than die!
When our Magician, more inspir'd,
By charms and spells and incantations fir'd,
Exerts his most tremendous pow'r,
The Thunder growls, the Heav'ns lour;
And to his darken'd throne repair,
The dæmons of the deep, and spirits of the air!
But soon these horrors pass away;
Thro' storms and night breaks forth the day:
He smiles, they vanish into air;
The buskin'd warriors disappear;
Mute the trumpets, mute the drums;
The scene is chang'd—Thalia comes,
Leading the nymph Eurosyne,
Goddess of joy and liberty!
She and her sisters hand in hand,
Link'd to a num'rous frolic band,
With roses and with myrtle crown'd,
O'er the green velvet lightly bound,
Circling the monarch of th'inchanted land.

AIR IV

Wild, frantic with pleasure,
They trip it in measure,
To bring him their treasure,
The treasure of joy.
How gay is the measure,
How sweet is the pleasure,
How great is the treasure,
The treasure of joy.
Like roses fresh blowing,
Their dimpled cheeks glowing,
His mind is o'er-flowing
A treasure of joy.
His rapture perceiving,
They smile while they're giving,
He smiles at receiving
A treasure of joy.
With kindling cheeks and sparkling eyes,
Surrounded thus, the Bard in transport lies;
The little Loves, like bees,
Clust'ring, and climbing up his knees,
His brows, with roses bind;
While Fancy, Wit, and Humour spread
Their wings, and hover round his head,
Impregnating his mind,
Which teaming soon, as soon brought forth,
Not a tiny, spurious birth,
But out of a mountain came,
A mountain of delight;
Laughter roar'd out to see the sight,
And Falstaff was his name.
With sword and shield he puffing strides;
The joyous revel rout
Receive him with a shout,
And modest Nature holds her sides:
No single pow'r the deed had done,

But great and small;
Wit, Fancy, Humour, Whim, and Jest,
The huge, misshapen heap imprest;
And lo—Sir John!
A compound of 'em all,
A comic world in one.

AIR V

A world where all pleasures abound,
So fruitful the Earth,
So quick to bring forth,
And the world too is wicked and round.
As the well teeming Earth,
With rivers and show'rs:
Will smiling bring forth
Her fruits and her flow'rs:
So Falstaff will never decline;
Still fruitful and gay,
He moistens his clay,
And his rain and his river are wine.
Of the world he has all but its care;
No load but of flesh will he bear;
He laughs off his pack,
Takes a cup of old sack,
And away with all sorrow and care.
Like the rich rainbow's various dies,
Whose circle sweeps o'er earth and skies,
The heav'n-born Muse appears:
Now in the brightest colours gay,
Now quench'd in show'rs, she fades away,
Now blends her smiles and tears.
Sweet swan of Avon, ever may thy stream
Of tuneful numbers be the darling theme;
Not Thames himself, who in his silver course,
Triumphant rolls along,
Britannia's riches and her force,
Shall more harmonious flow in song!
O had those Bards who charm the list'ning shore
Of Cam and Isis, tun'd their classic lays,
And from their full and precious store,
Vouchsaf'd to fairy-haunted Avon praise!
Nor Greek, nor Roman streams would flow along,
More sweetly clear, or more sublimely strong,
Nor thus a shepherd's feeble notes reveal,
At once the weakest numbers and the warmest zeal.

AIR VI

Thou soft flowing Avon, by thy silver stream,
Of things more than mortal sweet Shakespeare would dream.
The fairies by moon-light dance round his green bed,
For hallow'd the turf is which pillow'd his head.
The love-stricken maiden, the soft-sighing swain,
Here rove without danger and sigh without pain,
The sweet bud of beauty no blight here shall dread,
For hollow'd the turf is which pillow'd his head.
Here youth shall be fam'd for their love and their truth,
And chearful old age feel the spirit of youth,
For the raptures of Fancy here Poets shall tread,
For hallow'd the turf is that pillow'd his head.
Flow on, silver Avon, in song ever flow,
Be the swans on thy bosom still whiter than snow;
Ever full be thy stream, like his fame may it spread,
And the turf ever hallow'd which pillow'd his head,
Tho' Bards with envy-aching eyes,
Behold a towering eagle rise,
And would his sight retard;
Yet to each Shakespeare's genius bows,
Each weaves a garland for his brows,
To crown th'heav'n-distinguish'd Bard.
Nature had form'd him on the noblest plan,
And to the genius join'd the feeling man.
What tho' with more than mortal art,
Like Neptune he directs the storm,
Lets loose like winds the passions of the heart,
To wreck the human form;
Tho' fro his mind rush forth the dæmons to destroy,
His heart ne'er knew but love, and gentleness, and joy.

AIR VII

More gentle than the southern gale,
Which softly fans the blossom'd vale,
And gathers on its balmy wing,
The fragrant treasures of the spring,
Breathing delight on all it meets,
"And giving, as it steals the sweets."
Look down, blest spirit, from above,
With all thy wonted gentleness and love;
When all the wonders of thy pen,
By heav'n inspir'd,
To virtue fir'd
The charm'd, astonish'd sons of men!
With no reproach, even now, thou view'st thy work,
To nature sacred as to truth,
Where no alluring mischiefs lurk,
To taint the mind of youth.
Can British gratitude delay,
To him the Glory of this Isle,

To give the festive day,
The song, the statue, and devoted pile?
To him the first of Poets, best of Men?
"We ne'er shall look upon his like again."

DUET

Shall the hero laurels gain
For ravag'd fields, and thousands slain?
And shall his brows no laurels bind,
Who charms to virtue human-kind?

CHORUS

We will his brows with laurel bind,
Who charms to virtue human-kind:
Raise the pile, the statue raise,
Sing immortal Shakespeare's praise!
The song will cease, the stone decay,
But his name,
And undiminish'd fame,
Shall never, never pass away.

Curtain drops.

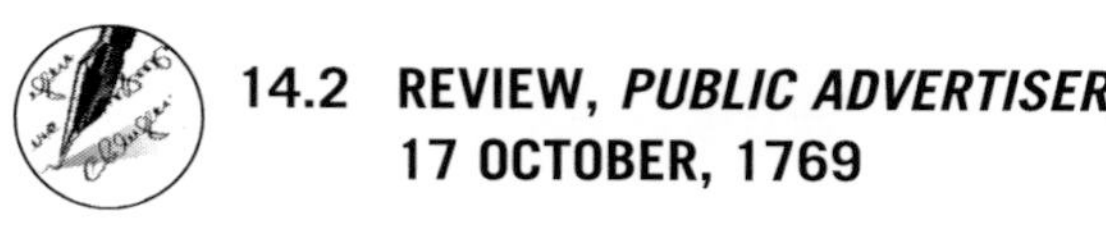

14.2 REVIEW, *PUBLIC ADVERTISER*, 17 OCTOBER, 1769

An Account of the New Entertainment call'd The Jubilee, *as it is now performing at the Theatre Royal in Drury Lane.*

THE FIRST SCENE IS SUPPOSED to begin before five in the morning of the Jubilee at Stratford. It exhibits the characters and sentiments of two old women and a young fellow of the town, with all the prejudices and suspicions of ignorance about the Jubilee. They are frightened by the discharge of cannon, and are thoroughly persuaded that there is some plot. They separate in great fear, and Ralph, the country fellow, promises to inform them of what passes. This character was excellently acted by Mr. King.

Second scene presents some houses at Stratford, and a post-chaise without horses. There is a serenade to the ladies: it wakes an Irish man in the post-chaise, who gives an account of his distresses. They are interrupted by Ballad Singers. The scene finishes with the song and chorus of Warwickshire, and the remarks of the Irishman upon it. The hero of this little piece is the Irishman, who came from Dublin on purpose for the Jubilee, and is admirably performed by Mr. Moody.

Third scene is the inn yard of the White Lyon at Stratford, and a very lively representation of the confusion, and the different characters which came to the Jubilee. There was great variety and vivacity in this scene, and Mr. Moody still appears the first figure, and adds life to the whole. Some company who had sat up all night, and were in liquor, come from the house into the yard, surrounded by various characters, and sing the Mulberry-Tree. Messrs. Vernon, Bannister, and Dibdin, give great spirit and humour to the song. They are all dispersed with the ringing of bells, the noise of drums and fifes, firing of cannon, and the cry of the pageant.

Fourth scene represents the high street of Stratford, which is decorated with flags and streamers, a multitude of people are represented at a distance, and constables appear from top to bottom, and keep the crowd off. After the ringing of bells, &c. the pageant begins to appear. It is preceded by nine men dancers with tambours, the three Graces and seven Muses, who dance all the way, and give an idea of the greatest festivity; then follow to a most sprightly air by the drums and fifes, attended with the ringing of bells, the comic characters of Shakespeare, representing some striking scenes in the several plays: each play is attended by a rich banner, on which the name of the play is in gold or silver letters. It would take up too much room to describe the different scenes, and their effects upon the audience. Mr. King was the general of the comic troop, as Mr. Holland was of the tragic. Mr. Garrick marched under the command of General King in the character of Benedict, with Miss Pope in that of Beatrice. The fairies, with their king and queen, were in a very light, brilliant, airy chariot. This part of the procession was let by Thalia, the Comic Muse, in an emblematic carriage, drawn by satyrs and cupids. The little boys wore great masks after the antique, and played their gambols round the chariot, while

Venus and her son walked before it. Then came a band of singers clothed in a uniform of green and white, like Arcadian shepherds, and sung a chorus to usher in the statue of Shakespeare. It was supposed by the laughing deities, Momus, Comus, Mercury, &c. &c. &c. attended by Apollo, the Graces, and seven of the Muses, with their different ensigns. Then the tragic troop came on to a most solemn march. It was headed by Mr. Holland, in the character of Richard the Third; his giving the ring to Deighton, and his looks at the children who came after with the queen dowager, had a most striking effect upon the audience. I must pass over the rest of the tragedies with their decorations. Macbeth and his wife followed by the witches huddled together and pointing at them, and the cauldron which was drawn by demons chained to it, gave a strong picture of the horror of the play. The Tragic Muse, who closed this part of the pageant, was ushered upon the stage by Pallas, and she was followed by a demon, with a flaming sword and a torch, representing terror and revenge. The Car of Melpomene was drawn by other demons, representing envy, despair, madness, and jealousy, attended by the furies, in the car: at her feet lay grief and pity: and it was followed by Mars, representing rage and war, with his sword drawn, spiriting up his followers, who closed the pageant. Mrs. Barry's excellent expression and different attitudes exhibited Melpomene in all her tragic glory.

The fifth scene was another new representation of the town of Stratford: in this two country girls, the one affected, the other quite simple, talked about the Jubilee and Shakespeare, and sung two Ballads; and after they had raised themselves up to a pitch of mirth and spirits, they *exeunt* dancing and singing. The Irishman, who is fuddled and was asleep while the pageant passed by, calls out to the girls, and pursues them: they are gone, and he resolves to find them out. After the pageant, he is told, by a little boy, that the pageant is over: he is astonish'd, sums up his misfortunes, and resolves to return to Kilkenny, as wise and as instructed as other travellers as to their own country.

The last scene exhibits several characters of Shakespeare in transparency, with the statue of Shakespeare crowned by the Tragic and Comic Muse, which ends by a general rejoicing of all the characters, with dances, songs, and chorusses.

14.3 GARRICK'S *ODE TO SHAKESPEARE*

David Garrick, *An ode upon dedicating a building, and erecting a statue, to Shakespeare, at Stratford upon Avon* (London: T. Becket, and P.A. De Hondt, 1769.)

GARRICK'S "ODE", first delivered in Stratford and then incorporated into *The Jubilee*, became a regularly performed interlude in its own right.

Advertisement

Could some gentleman of approved ability have been prevailed upon to do justice to the subject of the following ode, the present apology would have been unnecessary;—but as it was requisite to produce something of this kind upon the occasion, and the lot having unluckily fallen on the person perhaps the least qualified to succeed in the attempt, it is hoped the candour of the public will esteem the performance rather as an act of duty, than vanity in the author.

As some news-paper writers have illiberally endeavoured to shake the poetic character of our immortal bard (too deeply indeed rooted in the heart to be affected by them) it is recommended to those who are not sufficiently established in their dramatic faith, to peruse a work lately published, called, *An Essay of the Writings and Genius of Shakespeare*, by which they will with much satisfaction be convinced, that *England* may justly boast the honour of producing the greatest dramatic poet in the world.

To strengthen and justify the general admiration of this astonishing genius, it has been thought proper to subjoin to the ode some undeniable testimonies (both in prose and verse) of his unequalled original talents.

It shall be found, that *speaking* that part of the ode, which has usually been conveyed in recitative, produces a better effect, the author flatters himself he may lay claim to some little merit on that account: as to the ode itself, he presents it to the public as an object of their good nature,—to his friends as an exercise of their partiality,—to his enemies, as a lucky opportunity of venting their wit, humour, criticism, spleen, or whatever else they please, should they think it worthy of their notice.

Ode

To what blest genius of the isle,
Shall Gratitude her tribute pay,
Decree the festive day,
Erect the statue, and devote the pile?

Do not your sympathetic hearts accord,
To own the "bosom's lord?"
'Tis he! 'tis he!—that demi-god!
Who Avon's flow'ry margin trod,
While sportive *Fancy* round him flew,
Where *Nature* led him by the hand,
Instructed him in all she knew,
And gave him absolute command!
'Tis he! 'tis he!
"The god of our idolatry!"

To him the song, the Edifice we raise,
He merits all our wonder, all our praise!
Yet ere impatient joy break forth,
In sounds that lift the soul from earth;
And to our spell-bound minds impart
Some faint idea of his magic art;
Let awful silence still the air!
From the dark cloud, the hidden light
Bursts tenfold bright!
Prepare! prepare! prepare!
Now swell the choral song,
Roll the full tide of harmony along;
Let Rapture sweep the trembling strings,
And Fame expanding all her wings,
With all her trumpet-tongues proclaim,
The lov'd, rever'd, immortal name!
Shakespeare! Shakespeare! Shakespeare!
Let th'inchanting sound,
From Avon's shores rebound;
Thro' the air,
Let it bear,
The precious freight the envious nations round!

CHORUS

Swell the choral song,
Roll the tide of harmony along,
Let Rapture sweep the strings,
Fame expand her wings,
With her trumpet-tongues proclaim,
The lov'd, rever'd, immortal name!
Shakespeare! Shakespeare! Shakespeare!

AIR [Mr. Baddely]

Sweetest bard that ever sung,
Nature's glory, *Fancy*'s child;
Never sure aid witching tongue,
Warble forth such wood-notes wild!

Come each *Muse*, and sister *Grace*,
Loves and *Pleasures* hither come;
Well you know this happy place,
Avon's banks were once your home.

Bring the laurel, bring the flow'rs,
Songs of triumph to him raise;
He united all your pow'rs,
All uniting, sung his praise!

Tho' *Philip*'s fam'd unconquer'd son,
Had ev'ry blood-stain'd laurel won;
He sigh'd—that his creative word,
(Like that which rules the skies,)
Could not bid other nations rise,
To glut his yet unsated sword:

But when our Shakespeare's matchless pen,
Like *Alexander*'s sword, had done with men;
He heav'd no sigh, he made no moan,
Not limited to human kind,
He fir'd his wonder-teeming mind,
Rais'd other worlds, and beings of his own!

AIR [Mr. Vernon]

When *Nature*, smiling, hail'd his birth,
To him unbounded pow'r was given;
The whirlwind's wing to sweep the sky,
"The frenzy-rowling eye,
To glance from heav'n to earth,
From earth to heav'n!"
O from his muse of fire
Could but one spark be caught,
Then might these humble strains aspire
To tell the wonders he has wrought.
To tell,—how sitting on his magic throne,
Unaided and alone,
In dreadful state,
The subject passions round him wait;
Who tho' unchain'd, and raging there,
He checks, inflames, or turns their mad career;
With that superior skill,
Which winds the fiery steed at will,
He gives the aweful word—
And they, all foaming, trembling, own him for their Lord.

With these, his slaves, he can controul,
Or charm the soul;
So realiz'd are all his golden dreams,

Of terror, pity, love, and grief,
Tho' conscious that the vision only seems,
The woe-struck mind finds no relief:
Ingratitude would drop the tear,
Cold-blooded age take fire,
To see the thankless children of old *Lear*,
Spurn at their king, and fire!
With *his* our reason too grows wild!
What nature had disjoin'd,
The poet's pow'r combin'd,
Madness and *age*, *ingratitude* and *child*.

Ye guilty, lawless tribe,
Escap'd from punishment, by art or bribe,
At *Shakespeare*'s bar appear!
No bribing, shuffling there—
His genius, like a rushing flood,
Cannot be withstood,
Out bursts the penitential tear!
The look appall'd, the crime reveals,
The marble-hearted monster feels,
Whose hand is stain'd with blood.

SEMI-CHORUS

When law is weak, and justice fails,
The poet holds the sword and scales.

AIR [Champness]

Though crimes from death and torture fly,
The swifter muse,
Their flight pursues,
Guilty morals more than die!
They live indeed, but live to feel
The scourge and wheel,
"On the torture of the mind they lie:"
Should harrass'd nature sink to rest,
The Poet wakes the scorpion in the breast,
Guilty mortals more than die!

When our *Magician*, more inspir'd,
By charms, and spells, and incantations fir'd,
Exerts his most tremendous pow'r;
The thunder growls, the heavens low'r,
And to his darken'd throne repair,
The *Demons* of the deep, and *Spirit* of the air!

But soon these horrors pass away,
Thro' storms and night breaks forth the day:
He smiles,—they vanish into air!
The buskin'd warriors disappear!
Mute the trumpets, mute the drums,
The scene is chang'd—*Thalia* comes,
Leading the nymph *Euphrosyne*,
Goddess of joy and liberty!
She and her sisters, hand in hand,
Link'd to a num'rous frolick band,
With roses and with myrtle crown'd
O'er the green velvet lightly bound,
Circling the Monarch of th'inchanted
land!

AIR [Miss Radley]

Wild, frantick with pleasure,
They trip it in measure,
To bring him their treasure,
The treasure of joy.

How gay is the measure,
How sweet is the pleasure,
How great is the treasure,
The treasure of joy.

Like roses fresh blowing,
Their dimpled-cheeks glowing,
His mind is o'erflowing;
A treasure of joy!

His rapture perceiving,
They smile while they're giving,
He smiles at receiving,
A treasure of joy.

With kindling cheeks, and sparking eyes,
Surrounded thus, the Bard in transport
dies;
The little *Loves*, like bees,
Clust'ring and climbing up his knees,
His brows with roses bind;
While *Fancy*, *Wit*, and *Humour* spread
Their wings, and hover round his head,
Impregnating his mind.
Which teeming soon, as soon brought
forth,
Not a tiny spurious birth,
But out a mountain came,
A mountain of delight!
Laughter roar'd out to see the sight,
And Falstaff was his name!
With sword and shield he, puffing, strides;
The joyous revel-rout
Receive him with a shout,
And modest *Nature* holds her sides:
No single pow'r the deed had done,
But great and small,
Wit, *Fancy*, *Humour*, *Whim*, and *Jest*,
The huge, misshapen heap impress'd;
And lo—Sir John!
A compound of 'em all,
A comic world in one.

AIR [Mr. Vernon]

A world where all pleasures abound,
So fruitful the earth,
So quick to bring forth,
And the world too is wicked and round.

As the well-teeming earth,
With rivers and show'rs,
Will smiling bring forth
Her fruits and her flow'rs;
So *Falstaff* will never decline;
Still fruitful and gay,
He moistens his clay,
And his rain and his rivers are wine;
Of the world he has all, but its care;
No load, but of flesh, will he bear;
He laughs off his pack,
Takes a cup of old sack,
And away with all sorrow and care.
Like the rich rainbow's various dyes,
Whose circle sweeps o'er earth and skies,
The heav'n-born muse appears;
Now in the brightest colours gay,
Now quench'd in show'rs, she fades away,
Now blends her smiles and tears.
Sweet *Swan of Avon!* ever may thy stream
Of tuneful numbers be the daring theme;
Not *Thames* himself, who in his silver course
Triumphant rolls along,
Britannia's riches and her force,
Shall more harmonious flow in song.

O had those bards, who charm the list'ning
shore
Of Cam and Isis, tun'd their classic lays,
And from their full and precious store,
Vouchsaf'd to fairy-haunted *Avon* praise!
(Like that kind bounteous hand*,
Which lately gave the ravish'd eyes
Of Stratford swains
A rich command,
Of widen'd river, lengthen'd plains,
And opening skies)
Nor *Greek*, nor *Roman* streams would flow
along,
More sweetly clear, or more sublimely strong,
Nor thus a shepherd's feeble notes reveal,
At once the weakest numbers, and the
warmest zeal.

*The D— of D—, with the concurrence of Mr. B—y, most generously ordered a great [. . .] of trees to be cut down, to open the river *Avon* for the Jubilee.

AIR

Thou soft-flowing *Avon*, by thy silver stream,
Of things more than mortal, sweet Shakespear
would dream,
The fairies by moonlight dance round his
green bed,
For hallow'd the turf is which pillow'd his
head.

The love-stricken maiden, the soft-sighing
swain,
Here rove without danger, and sigh without
pain,
The sweet bud of beauty, no blight shall here
dread,
For hallow'd the turf is which pillow'd his
head.

Here youth shall be fam'd, for their love, and
their truth,
And cheerful old age, feel the spirit of youth;
For the raptures of fancy here poets shall tread,
For hallow'd the turf is that pillow'd his head.

Flow on, silver *Avon*, in song ever flow,
Be the swans on thy bosom still whiter than
snow,
Ever full be thy stream, like his fame may it
spread,
And the turf ever hallow'd which pillow'd his
head.

Tho' bards with envy-aching eyes,
Behold a tow'ring eagle rise,
And would his flight retard;
Yet each to *Shakespeare*'s genius bows,
Each weaves a garland for his brows,
To crown th'heaven-distinguish'd Bard.
Nature had form'd him on her noblest plan,
And to the genius join'd the feeling man.
What tho' with more than mortal art,
Like *Neptune* he directs the storm,
Lets loose like winds the passions of the
heart,
To wreck the human form;
Tho' from his mind rush forth, the demons to
destroy,
His heart ne'er knew but love, and gentleness,
and joy.

AIR [Mr. Baddely]

More gentle than the southern gale,
Which softly fans the blossom'd vale,
And gathers on its balmy wing,

The fragrant treasures of the spring,
Breathing delight on all it meets,
"And giving, as it steals, the sweets."

Look down blest Spirit from above,
With all thy wonted gentleness and love;
And as the wonders of thy pen,
By heav'n inspir'd,
To virtue fir'd,
The charm'd astonish'd, sons of men!
With no reproach, even now, thou view'st thy work,
To nature sacred as to truth,
Where no alluring mischiefs lurk,
To taint the mind of youth.
Still to thy native spot thy smiles extend,
And as thou gav'st it fame, that fame defend;
And may no sacrilegious hand
Near *Avon*'s banks be found,
To dare to parcel out the land,
And limit Shakespear's hallow'd ground.
For ages free, still be it unconfin'd,
As broad, and general, as thy boundless mind.

Can *British* gratitude delay,
To him the glory of this isle,
To give the festive day
The song, the statue, and devoted pile?
To him the first of poets, best of men?
"We ne'er shall look upon his like again!"

DUETT

Shall the hero laurels gain,
For ravag'd fields, and thousands slain?
And shall his brows no laurels bind,
Who charms to virtue humankind?

CHORUS

We will,—brows with laurel bind,
Who charms to virtue human kind:
Raise the pile, the statue raise,
Sing immortal *Shakespeare*'s praise!
The song will cease, the stone decay,
But his Name,
And indiminish'd fame,
Shall never, never pass away.

14.4 *MR. GARRICK DELIVERING HIS ODE AT DRURY LANE THEATRE*

Anonymous. *Mr. Garrick delivering his Ode at Drury Lane Theatre*. Courtesy of the Folger Shakespeare Library. ART file G241 no. 106.

14.5 BENJAMIN VAN DER GUCHT, *MR. GARRICK AS STEWARD OF THE STRATFORD JUBILEE, SEPTEMBER 1769*

Benjamin Van der Gucht, *Mr. Garrick as Steward of the Stratford Jubilee, September 1769*. Engraving. Courtesy of the Folger Shakespeare Library. ART 242301 [6884].

14.6 *THE PRINCIPAL CHARACTERS IN THE PROCESSION OF THE PAGEANT EXHIBITED IN THE JUBILEE AT DRURY LANE THEATRE*

Anonymous. *The Principal Characters in the Procession of the Pageant Exhibited in the Jubilee at Drury Lane Theatre*. Engraving. Courtesy of the Folger Shakespeare Library. ART File G241.3 no. 5.

Notes

1 The copy text is *The Jubilee, In Honour of Shakespeare. A Musical Entertainment. As performed at the Theatre in Waterford. With Additions.* Waterford: Printed by Esther Crawley and Son, at Euclid's Head, in Peter's Street, 1773. Because this version is based on a later provincial performance, the Procession of Shakespearean Characters in Act 2 has been derived from the opening night review in the *Middlesex Journal or Chronicle of Liberty,* 14–17 October 1769.

2 See Michael Dobson, *The Making of the National Poet: Shakespeare, Adaptation and Authorship, 1660–1769.* Oxford: Clarendon Press, 1995.

3 See Christian Deelman, *The Great Shakespeare Jubilee.* New York: Viking, 1964 for a painstaking account of the lead-up to the event and a day-by-day description of the soggy mess that ensued.

4 The cast list, from *Lloyd's Evening Post,* October 13–16, 1769, has been altered to match the first performance.

5 Shakespeare's memorial bust is on the wall of the sanctuary in Holy Trinity Church in Stratford-upon-Avon.

6 *Ecce Signum!*: Behold the Sign!

7 Stratford-upon-Avon is in Warwickshire therefore Shakespeare is a Warwickshire lad.

8 Love's Labour Lost and Merry Wives refer to Shakespearean themed rooms at the Inn.

9 The Inn's rooms have been given Shakespearean names, but *Catherine and Petruchio* was also the title of Garrick's 1754 re-working of *The Taming of the Shrew.*

10 The Jubilee involved a ceremonial planting of a mulberry tree and thus many of the souvenirs were fashioned from mulberry wood.

11 A special Rotunda was constructed to house the festivities.

12 As reported in the *Middlesex Journal or Chronicle of Liberty*, 14–17 October 1769. "The Characters of each play were proceeded by persons properly habited, bearing streamers of various colours, on which were elegantly inscribed on a scroll, the name of the performance." The copy text records the pageant differently, but this is likely because it refers to a later provincial production of the play (see Contexts).

13 After the Latin *Veluti in Speculum*: As in a mirror.

14 *Totus mundus agit histrionem*: All the World's a Stage.

15 Fanny Abingdon was the foremost comic actress of the age and thus is cast as Thalia, the Comic Muse.

16 Mrs. Barry was Drury Lane's leading tragic actress and thus suited to play Melpomene, the Tragic Muse.

17 The Muses of epic poetry, history, love poetry, flutes and lyric poetry, sacred poetry, dance and astronomy respectively. Thalia (comedy) and Melpomene (tragedy) are of course given pride of place.

18 She is referring to common puppet shows.

15. ***The West Indian***

THE WEST INDIAN. A COMEDY.[1] RICHARD CUMBERLAND. FIRST PERFORMED 19 JANUARY 1771 AND FIRST PUBLISHED 1771

15.1 *THE WEST INDIAN: A COMEDY*[2]

Richard Cumberland

First Performed 19 January 1771 and First Published 1771

RICHARD CUMBERLAND (1731/32-1811) was very much a Cambridge man, born, raised and educated at Trinity College. A respected man of letters, his various efforts in prose, verse, and drama met with great success throughout his long life. Both his connections and his success meant that he travelled among the foremost literary figures of his generation. And yet contemporary notices and reminiscences are usually qualified, if not directly negative. He struggled to affiliate himself with Johnson and his circle; he seems to have been more tolerated than accepted. Garrick was happy to benefit from Cumberland's theatrical success, but tended to keep him at a distance. Sheridan was extremely impatient with much of his work and ridiculed him as a bore and a plagiarist. It was widely acknowledged that Cumberland borrowed liberally from others; Sheridan immortalized that quality in his caricature of Cumberland as Sir Fretful Plagiary in *The Critic*. If the republic of letters treated him with some level of disdain, the public did not. His plays, from *The Brothers* of 1769 to his final play, *The Wheel of Fortune* (1795) were among the most successful of his generation. The first run of *The West Indian* went for 28 nights and he sold the copyright to the play for £150. It was rapidly disseminated around the English-speaking world and became a mainstay on both sides of the Atlantic. The play's immense popularity in America is intriguing. Its portrait of the West Indian planter had multiple political valences. It is worth considering that the play was equally acclaimed in Boston and Richmond. At moments when British fortunes in America were at their lowest point, George III commanded performances of *The West Indian* as expressions of loyalism and the British nation's intense interest in maintaining control of the Caribbean.

It is perhaps inevitable that a play so manifestly about the relationship between colony and metropole would capture the public imagination in the latter third of the eighteenth century. But Cumberland himself pointed to a different reason for the play's success:

> I perceive that I had fallen upon a time when great eccentricity of character was pretty nearly gone by, but still I fancy there was an opening for some originality, and an opportunity for showing at least my good-will to mankind, if I introduced the characters of persons who had been usually exhibited on the stage, as the butt for ridicule and abuse, and endeavoured to present them in such lights as might tend to reconcile the world to them, and them to the world.
>
> (Cumberland, *Memoirs*, 141–2)

Cumberland's two greatest plays are *The West Indian* and *The Jew*. The former obviously features the introduction of a West Indian planter onto the London stage, but it also marks a sea change in the representation of Irish subjects. Likewise, *The Jew* (1794), which surpassed *The West Indian* in popularity, transformed the representation of Jews in European theatre and had a significant impact on the anti-Semitism of British society. *The West Indian* is a vital example of what Michael Ragussis has called a multi-ethnic spectacle.[3] Throughout the latter half of the eighteenth century audiences were drawn to plays featuring a wide array of ethnically defined characters. The differential relation between these characters allowed playwrights to explore emerging notions of ethnic and national identity at a historical moment when these categories were very much in flux. Thus the way that Irish, Jewish or various colonial characters travel through these plays necessarily activated a host of anxieties regarding the make-up of British society. One of the most interesting aspects of these kinds of plays is the way that class becomes the site of most intense scrutiny. In this play London is the backdrop for the encounter between two ethnic others—the eponymous planter Belcour and the wonderful Irish character Major O'Flaherty—and representatives from all classes of English society. On the English side of the equation we have the aristocratic widow Lady Rusport, the valorized merchant Stockwell, the beleaguered military family, the Dudleys, and a pair of criminal working class con artists. After a host of intricately plotted transactions the play eventually shames both the aristocratic and working class characters. A remarkable covenant between merchant, planter and the military family emerges as a moral core for a new imperial world. As a fantasy of what British domination of the world might look like after the Seven Years' War, *The West Indian* is perhaps unparalleled.

Significantly, this fantasy is secured by the activities of Belcour and O'Flaherty. The impulsive Belcour, who is initially defined by a climatological theory of ethnic difference—his impulsiveness is a result of his torrid homeland—brings all of the characters together. And it is the taming of Belcour that allows Stockwell to emerge as the epitome of good judgment and moral rectitude. O'Flaherty is even more interesting. First played by John Moody, the Drury Lane actor who specialized in ethnic performance, O'Flaherty's role took the energy of the stage Irishman and re-directed it to effect moral change at the level of the plot. In a way, his violence, like Belcour's sexual licentiousness, is necessary for the articulation of middle class equanimity. In this regard, both Belcour and O'Flaherty are interesting because they work like constitutive outsides for English society—ethnic others that are necessary for English identity to cohere. The fact that they are so explicitly connected to colonial locales indicates the degree to which English identity at this moment presupposed economic and social exploitation. It is perhaps no surprise that George III called for this play above all others when the prized colonies were all but gone.

PROLOGUE

Spoken by Mr. Reddish.

Critics, hark forward! noble game and new;
A fine West Indian[4] started full in view:
Hot as the soil, the clime, which gave him birth.
You'll run him on a burning scent to earth;
Yet don't devour him in his hiding place;
Bag him, he'll serve you for another chace;
For sure that country has no feeble claim,
Which swells your commerce, and supports your fame.
And in this humble sketch, we hope you'll find,
Some emanations of a noble mind;
Some little touches, which, tho' void of art,
May find perhaps their way into the heart.
Another hero[5] your excuse implores,
Sent by your sister kingdom to your shores;
Doom'd by Religion's too severe command.
To fight for bread against his native land:
A brave, unthinking, animated rogue,
With here and there a touch upon the brogue;
Laugh, but despise him not, for on his lip
His errors lie; his heart can never trip.
Others there are—but may we not prevail
To let the gentry tell their own plain tale?
Shall they come in? They'll please you, if they can;
If not, condemn the bard—but spare the *Man*.
For speak, think, act, or write in angry times,
A wish to please is made the worst of crimes;
Dire slander now with black envenom'd dart,
Stands ever arm'd to stab you to the heart.

Rouse, Britons, rouse, for honour of your isle,
Your old good humour; and be seen to smile.
You say we write not like our fathers—true,
Nor were our fathers half so strict as you,
Damn'd not each error of the poet's pen,
But judging man, remember'd they were men.
Aw'd into silence by the times abuse.
Sleeps many a wise, and many a witty muse;
We that for mere experiment come out,
Are but the light arm'd rangers on the scout:

High on Parnassus' lofty summit stands
The immortal camp; there lie the chosen bands!
But give fair quarter to us puny elves,
The giants then will sally forth themselves;
With wit's sharp weapons vindicate the age,
And drive ev'n *Arthur's* magic from the *Stage*.[6]

Dramatis Personae.

Men.

Stockwell	Mr. Aickin
Belcour	Mr. King
Captain Dudley	Mr. Packer
Charles Dudley	Mr. Cautherly
Major O'Flaherty	Mr. Moody[7]
Stukely	Mr. J. Aickin
Fulmer	Mr. Baddely
Varland	Mr. Parsons
Servant to Stockwell	Mr. Wheeler

Women.

Lady Rusport	Mrs. Hopkins
Charlotte Rusport	Mrs. Abington[8]
Louisa, daughter to Dudley	Mrs. Baddely
Mrs. Fulmer	Mrs. Egerton
Lucy	Mrs. Love
Housekeeper belonging to Stockwell	Mrs. Bradshaw

Clerks belonging to Stockwell, Servant, Sailors, Negroes,[9] &c.

SCENE, LONDON

I.i

A merchant's compting house. In an inner room, set off by glass doors, are discovered several clerks employed at their desks. A writing table in the front room. Stockwell *is discovered reading a letter;* Stukely *comes gently out of the back room, and observes him some time before he speaks.*

STUKELY. He seems disordered: something in that letter; and I'm afraid of an unpleasant sort. He has many ventures of great account at sea; a ship richly freighted for Barcelona; another for Lisbon; and others expected from Cadiz of still greater value. Besides these, I know he has many deep concerns in foreign bottoms, and underwritings to a vast amount.[10] I'll accost him. Sir! Mr. Stockwell!

STOCKWELL. Stukely!—Well, have you ship'd the cloths?

STUKELY. I have, Sir; here's the bill of lading, and copy of the invoice: the assortments are all compared: Mr. Traffick will give you the policy upon 'Change.[11]

STOCKWELL. 'Tis very well; lay these papers by; and no more of business for a while. Shut the door Stukely; I have had long proof of your friendship and fidelity to me; a matter of most intimate concern lies on my mind, and 'twill be a sensible relief to unbosom myself to you; I have just now been informed of the arrival of the young West Indian, I have so long been expecting; you know who I mean.

STUKELY. Yes, Sir; Mr. Belcour, the young gentleman, who inherited old Belcour's great estates in Jamaica.

STOCKWELL. Hush, not so loud; come a little nearer this way. This Belcour is now in London; part of his baggage is already arrived; and I expect him every minute. Is it to be wonder'd at, if his coming throws me into some agitation, when I tell you, Stukely, he is my son?

STUKELY. Your son!

STOCKWELL. Yes, Sir, my only son; early in life I accompanied his grandfather to Jamaica as his clerk; he had an only daughter, somewhat older than myself; the mother of this gentleman; it was my chance (call it good or ill) to engage her affections: and, as the inferiority of my condition made it hopeless to expect her father's consent, her fondness provided an expedient, and we were privately married; the issue of that concealed engagement is, as I have told you, this Belcour.[12]

STUKELY. That event, surely, discovered your connexion.

STOCKWELL. You shall hear. Not many days after our marriage old Belcour set out for England, and, during his abode here, my wife was, with great secresy, delivered of this son. Fruitful in expedients to disguise her situation, without parting from her infant, she contrived to have it laid and received at her door as a foundling. After some time her father returned, having left me here; in one of those favourable moments that decide the fortunes of prosperous men, this child was introduced; from that instant, he treated him as his own, gave him his name, and brought him up in his family.

STUKELY. And did you never reveal this secret, either to old Belcour, or your son?

STOCKWELL. Never.

STUKELY. Therein you surprise me; a merchant of your eminence, and a member of the British parliament, might surely aspire, without offence, to the daughter of a planter. In this case too, natural affection would prompt to a discovery.

STOCKWELL. Your remark is obvious; nor could I have persisted in this painful silence, but in obedience to the dying injunctions of a beloved wife. The letter, you found me reading, conveyed those injunctions to me; it was dictated in her last illness, and almost in the article of death; (you'll spare me the recital of it) she there conjures me, in terms as solemn, as they are affecting, never to reveal the secret of our marriage, or withdraw my son, while her father surviv'd.

STUKELY. But on what motives did your unhappy lady found these injunctions?

STOCKWELL. Principally, I believe, from apprehension on my account, lest old Belcour, on whom at her decease I wholly depended, should withdraw his protection: in part from consideration of his repose, as well knowing the discovery would deeply affect his spirit, which was haughty, vehement, and unforgiving: and lastly, in regard to the interest of her infant, whom he had warmly adopted; and for whom, in case of a discovery, every thing was to be dreaded from his resentment. And, indeed though the alteration in my condition might have justified me in discovering myself, yet I always thought my son safer in trusting to the caprice than to the justice of his grand-father. My judgment has not suffered by the event; old Belcour is dead, and has bequeathed his whole estate to him we are speaking of.

STUKELY. Now then you are no longer bound to secresy.

STOCKWELL. True: but before I publickly reveal myself, I could wish to make some experiment of my son's disposition; this can only be done by letting his spirit take its course without restraint; by these means, I think I shall discover much more of his real character under the title of his merchant, than I should under that of his father.

I.ii

[*A* Sailor *enters, ushering in several black* Servants, *carrying portmanteaus, trunks, &c.*

SAILOR. Save your honour! is your name Stockwell pray?

STOCKWELL. It is.

SAILOR. Part of my master Belcour's baggage an't please you; there's another cargo not far a-stern of us; and the cockswain has got charge of the dumb creatures.

STOCKWELL. Pr'ythee, friend, what dumb creatures do you speak of; has Mr. Belcour brought over a collection of wild beasts?

SAILOR. No, Lord love him; no, not he: let me see; there's two green monkies, a pair of grey parrots, a Jamaica sow and pigs, and a Mangrove dog; that's all.

STOCKWELL. Is that all?

SAILOR. Yes, your honour; yes, that's all; bless his heart; a'might have brought over the whole island if he would; a didn't leave a dry eye in it.

STOCKWELL. Indeed! Stukely, shew 'em where to bestow their baggage. Follow that gentleman.

SAILOR. Come, bear a hand, my lads, bear a hand.

[*Exit with* Stukely *and* Servants.

STOCKWELL. If the principal tallies with his purveyors, he must be a singular spectacle in this place: he has a friend, however, in this sea-faring fellow; 'tis no bad prognostic of a man's heart, when his ship-mates give him a good word. [*Exit.*

I.iii

[*Scene changes to a drawing room, a* Servant *discovered setting the chairs by, &c. A* Woman Servant[13] *enters to him.*

HOUSEKEEPER. Why, what a fuss does our good master put himself in about this West Indian: see what a bill of fare I've been forced to draw out: seven and nine I'll assure you, and only a family dinner as he calls it: why if my Lord Mayor was expected, there couldn't be a greater to-do about him.

SERVANT. I wish to my heart you had but seen the loads of trunks, boxes, and portmanteaus he has sent hither. An ambassador's baggage, with all the smuggled goods of his family, does not exceed it.

HOUSEKEEPER. A fine pickle he'll put the house into: had he been master's own son, and a Christian Englishman, there cou'd not be more rout than there is about this Creolian,[14] as they call 'em.

SERVANT. No matter for that; he's very rich, and that's sufficient. They say he has rum and sugar enough belonging to him[15] to make all the water in the Thames into punch. But I see my master's coming.

[*Exeunt.*

I.iv

[Stockwell *enters, followed by a* Servant.

STOCKWELL. Where is Mr. Belcour? Who brought this note from him?

SERVANT. A waiter from the London Tavern, Sir; he says the young gentleman is just drest, and will be with you directly.

STOCKWELL. Shew him in when he arrives.

SERVANT. I shall, Sir.—[*Aside*] *I'll have a peep at him first, however; I've a great mind to see this outlandish spark. The sailor fellow says he'll make rare doings amongst us.*

STOCKWELL. You need not wait; leave me. [*Exit* Servant] Let me see [*Reads*] "*Sir, I write to you under the hands of the hair-dresser; as soon as I have made myself decent, and slipped on some fresh cloaths, I will have the honour of paying you my devoirs. Yours, Belcour.*" He writes at his ease; for he's unconscious to whom his letter is addressed; but what a palpitation does it throw my heart into; a father's heart! 'Tis an affecting interview; when my eyes meet a son, whom yet they never saw, where shall I find constancy to support it? Should he resemble his mother, I am overthrown. All the letters I have had from him, (for I industriously drew him into a correspondence with me) bespeak him of quick and ready understanding. All the reports I ever received, give me favourable impressions of his character; wild, perhaps, as the manner of his country is, but, I trust, not frantic or unprincipled.

I.v

[Servant *enters*.

SERVANT. Sir, the foreign gentleman is come.

[*Another* Servant.

SERVANT. Mr. Belcour.

[Belcour *enters*.

STOCKWELL. Mr. Belcour, I'm rejoiced to see you; you're welcome to England.

BELCOUR. I thank you heartily, good Mr. Stockwell; you and I have long conversed at a distance; now we are met, and the pleasure this meeting gives me, amply compensates for the perils I have run through in accomplishing it.

STOCKWELL. What perils, Mr. Belcour? I could not have thought you would have made a bad passage at this time o'year.

BELCOUR. Nor did we: courier like, we came posting to your shores, upon the pinions of the swiftest gales that ever blew; 'tis upon English ground all my difficulties have arisen; 'tis the passage from the river-side I complain of.

STACK. Ay, indeed! What obstructions can you have met between this and the river-side?

BELCOUR. Innumerable! Your town's as full of defiles as the Island of Corsica;[16] and, I believe, they are as obstinately defended: so much hurry, bustle, and confusion, on your quays; so many sugar-casks, porter-butts, and common councilmen, in your streets, that, unless a man marched with artillery in his front, 'tis more than the labour of a Hercules can effect to make any tolerable way through your town.[17]

STOCKWELL. I am sorry you have been so incommoded.

BELCOUR. Why, faith, 'twas all my own fault; accustomed to a land of slaves, and out of patience with the whole tribe of custom-house extortioners, boat-men, tide-waiters and water-bailiffs, that beset me on all sides, worse than a swarm of musquetoes, I proceeded a little too roughly to brush them away with my rattan; the sturdy rogues took this in dudgeon, and beginning to rebel, the mob chose different sides, and a furious scuffle ensued; in the course of which, my person and apparel suffered so much, that I was obliged to step into the first tavern to refit, before I could make my approaches in any decent trim.

STOCKWELL.—[*Aside*] *All without is as I wish; dear Nature add the rest, and I am happy.*— [*To him*] Well, Mr. Belcour, 'tis a rough sample you have had of my countrymen's spirit; but, I trust, you'll not think the worse of them for it.

BELCOUR. Not at all, not at all; I like 'em the better; was I only a visitor, I might, perhaps, wish them a little more tractable; but, as a fellow subject, and a sharer in their freedom, I applaud their spirit, though I feel the effects of it in every bone of my skin.

STOCKWELL. That's well; I like that well.—[*Aside*] *How gladly I could fall upon his neck, and own myself his father!*

BELCOUR. Well, Mr. Stockwell, for the first time in my life, here am I in England; at the fountain-head of pleasure, in the land of beauty, of arts, and elegancies. My happy stars have given me a good estate, and the conspiring winds have blown me hither to spend it.

STOCKWELL. To use it, not to waste it, I should hope; to treat it, Mr. Belcour, not as a vassal, over whom you have a wanton and a despotic power, but as a subject, which you are bound to govern with a temperate and retrained authority.

BELCOUR. True, Sir; most truly said; mine's a commission, not a right: I am the offspring of distress, and every child of sorrow is my brother; while I have hands to hold, therefore, I will hold them open to mankind: but, Sir, my passions are my masters; they take me where they will; and oftentimes they leave to reason and to virtue nothing but my wishes and my sighs.

STOCKWELL. Come, come, the man who can accuse corrects himself.

BELCOUR. Ah! that's an office I am weary of: I wish a friend would take it up: I would to Heaven you had leisure for the employ; but, did you drive a trade to the four corners of the world, you would not find the talk so toilsome as to keep me free from faults.

STOCKWELL. Well, I am not discouraged: this candour tells me I should not have the fault of self-conceit to combat; that, at least, is not amongst the number.

BELCOUR. No; if I knew that man on earth who thought more humbly of me than I do of myself, I would take up his opinion, and forego my own.

STOCKWELL. And, was I to chuse a pupil, it should be one of your complexion: so if you'll come along with me, we'll agree upon your admission, and enter on a course of lectures directly.

BELCOUR. With all my heart.

[*Exeunt.*

I.vi

Scene changes to a room in Lady Rusport*'s house.* Lady Rusport *and* Charlotte.

LADY RUSPORT. Miss Rusport, I desire to hear no more of Captain Dudley and his destitute family: not a shilling of mine shall ever cross the hands of any of them: because my sister chose to marry a beggar, am I bound to support him and his posterity?

CHARLOTTE. I think you are.

LADY RUSPORT. You think I am; and pray where do you find the law that tells you so?

CHARLOTTE. I am not proficient enough to quote chapter and verse; but I take charity to be a main clause in the great statute of Christianity.

LADY RUSPORT. I say charity, indeed! And pray, Miss, are you sure that it is charity, pure charity, which moves you to plead for Captain Dudley? Amongst all your pity, do you find no spice of a certain anti-spiritual passion, called love? Don't mistake yourself; you are no saint, child, believe me; and, I am apt to think the distresses of old Dudley, and of his daughter into the bargain, would never break your heart, if there was not a certain young fellow of two and twenty in the case; who, by the happy recommendation of a good person, and the brilliant appointments of an ensigncy, will, if I am not mistaken, cozen you out of a fortune of twice twenty thousand pounds, as soon as ever you are of age to bestow it upon him.

CHARLOTTE. A nephew of your ladyship's can never want any other recommendation with me; and, if my partiality for Charles Dudley is acquitted by the rest of the world, I hope Lady Rusport will not condemn me for it.

LADY RUSPORT. I condemn you! I thank Heaven, Miss Rusport, I am no ways responsible for your conduct; nor is it any concern of mine how you dispose of yourself; you are not my daughter, and, when I married your father, poor Sir Stephen Rusport, I found you a forward spoiled Miss of fourteen, far above being instructed by me.

CHARLOTTE. Perhaps your ladyship calls this instruction.

LADY RUSPORT. You're strangely pert; but 'tis no wonder: your mother, I'm told was a fine lady; and according to the modern stile of education you was brought up. It was not so in my young days; there was then some decorum in the world, some subordination, as the great Locke expresses it.[18] Oh! 'Twas an edifying sight, to see the regular deportment observed in our family: no giggling, no gossiping was going on there; my good father, Sir Oliver Roundhead,[19] never was seen to laugh himself, nor ever allowed it in his children.

CHARLOTTE. Ay; those were happy times, indeed.

LADY RUSPORT. But, in this forward age, we have coquets in the egg-shell,[20] and philosophers in the cradle; girls of fifteen that lead the fashion in new caps and new opinions, that have their sentiments and their sensations, and the idle fops[21] encourage 'em in it: O' my conscience, I wonder what it is the men can see in such babies.

CHARLOTTE. True, Madam; but all men do not overlook the maturer beauties of your ladyship's age; witness your admirer Major Dennis O'Flaherty; there's an example of some discernment; I declare to you, when your Ladyship is by, the major takes no more notice of me than if I was part of the furniture of your chamber.

LADY RUSPORT. The Major, child, has travelled through various kingdoms and climates, and has more enlarged notions of female merit than falls to the lot of an English home-bred lover; in most other countries, no woman on your side forty would ever be named in a polite circle.

CHARLOTTE. Right, Madam; I've been told that in Vienna they have coquets upon crutches, and Venuses in their grand climacteric; a lover there celebrates the wrinkles not the dimples, in his mistress's face. The major, I think, has served in the imperial army.[22]

LADY RUSPORT. Are you piqu'd, my young madam? Had my sister, Louisa, yielded to the addresses of one of Major O'Flaherty's person and appearance, she would have had some excuse: but to run away, as she did, at the age of sixteen too, with a man of old Dudley's sort—

CHARLOTTE. Was, in my opinion, the most venial trespass that ever girl of sixteen committed; of a noble family, an engaging person, strict honour, and sound understanding, what accomplishment was there wanting in Captain Dudley, but that which the prodigality of his ancestors had deprived him of?

LADY RUSPORT. They left him as much as he deserves; hasn't the old man captain's half pay? And is not the son an ensign?[23]

CHARLOTTE. An ensign! Alas, poor Charles! Would to Heaven he knew what my heart feels and suffers for his sake.

[Servant *enters*.

SERVANT. Ensign Dudley to wait upon your ladyship.

LADY RUSPORT. Who! Dudley! What can have brought him to town?

CHARLOTTE. Dear Madam, 'tis Charles Dudley, 'tis your nephew.

LADY RUSPORT. Nephew! I renounce him as my nephew; Sir Oliver renounced him as his grandson: wasn't he son of the eldest daughter, and only male descendant of Sir Oliver; and didn't he cut him off with a shilling? Didn't the poor dear good man leave his whole fortune to me, except a small annuity to my maiden sister, who spoiled her constitution with nursing him?[24] And, depend upon it, not a penny of that fortune shall ever be disposed of otherwise than according to the will of the donor. [Charles Dudley *enters*] So young man, whence come you? What brings you to town?

CHARLES. Is there is any offence in my coming to town, your ladyship is in some degree responsible for it, for part of my errand was to pay my duty here.

LADY RUSPORT. I hope you have some better excuse than all this.

CHARLES. 'Tis true, Madam, I have other motives; but, if I consider my trouble repaid by the pleasure I now enjoy, I should hope my aunt would not think my company the less welcome for the value I set upon her's.

LADY RUSPORT. Coxcomb! And where is your father, child; and your sister? Are they in town too?

CHARLES. They are.

LADY RUSPORT. Ridiculous! I don't know what people do in London, who have no money to spend in it.

CHARLOTTE. Dear Madam, speak more kindly to your nephew; how can you oppress a youth of his sensibility?

LADY RUSPORT. Miss Rusport, I insist upon your retiring to your apartment; when I want your advice I'll send to you. [*Exit* Charlotte] So you have put on a red coat too, as well as your father; 'tis plain what value you set upon the good advice Sir Oliver used to give you; how often has he caution'd you against the army?

CHARLES. Had it pleased my grandfather to enable me to have obeyed his caution, I would have done it; but you well know how destitute I am; and 'tis not to be wonder'd at if I prefer the service of my king to that of any other master.

LADY RUSPORT. Well, well, take your own course; 'tis no concern of mine: you never consulted me.

CHARLES. I frequently wrote to your ladyship, but could obtain no answer; and, since my grandfather's death, this is the first opportunity I have had of waiting upon you.

LADY RUSPORT. I must desire you not to mention the death of that dear good man in my hearing, my spirits cannot support it.

CHARLES. I shall obey you: permit me to say, that, as that event has richly supplied you with the materials of bounty, the distresses of my family can furnish you with objects of it.

LADY RUSPORT. The distresses of your family, child, are quite out of the question at present; had Sir Oliver been pleased to consider them, I should have been well content; but he has absolutely taken no notice of you in his will, and that to me must and shall be a law. Tell your father and your sister I totally disapprove of their coming up to town.

CHARLES. Must I tell my father that before your ladyship knows the motive that brought him hither? Allur'd by the offer of exchanging for a commission on full pay, the veteran, after thirty years service, prepares to encounter the fatal heats of Senegambia;[25] but wants a small supply to equip him for the expedition.

[Servant *enters*.

SERVANT. Major O'Flaherty to wait on your ladyship.

[Major *enters*.

O'FLAHERTY. Spare your speeches, young man; don't you think her ladyship can take my word for that? I hope, Madam, 'tis evidence enough of my being present, when I've the honour of telling you so myself.

LADY RUSPORT. Major O'Flaherty, I am rejoiced to see you. Nephew Dudley, you perceive I'm engaged.

CHARLES. I shall not intrude upon your ladyship's more agreeable engagements. I presume I have my answer.

LADY RUSPORT. Your answer, child! What answer can you possibly expect; or how can your romantic father suppose that I am to abet him in all his idle and extravagant undertakings? Come, Major, let me shew you the way into my dressing-room; and let us leave this young adventurer to his meditation. [*Exit.*

O'FLAHERTY. I follow you, my lady. Young gentleman, your obedient! Upon my conscience, as fine a young fellow as I wou'd wish to clap my eyes on: he might have answer'd my salute, however—well, let it pass; Fortune, perhaps, frowns upon the poor lad; she's a damn'd slippery lady, and very apt to jilt us poor fellows, that wear cockades in our hats. Fare-thee-well, honey, whoever thou art. [*Exit.*

CHARLES. So much for the virtues of a puritan; out upon it, her heart is flint; yet that woman, that aunt of mine, without one worthy particle in her composition, wou'd, I dare be sworn, as soon set her foot in a pest-house, as in a play-house.[26] [*Going.*

[Miss Rusport *enters to him.*

CHARLOTTE. Stop, stay a little, Charles, whither are you going in such haste?

CHARLES. Madam; Miss Rusport; what are your commands?

CHARLOTTE. Why so reserved? We had used to answer to no other names than those of Charles and Charlotte.

CHARLES. What ails you? You've been weeping.

CHARLOTTE. No, no; or if I have—your eyes are full too; but I have a thousand things to say to you: before you go, tell me, I conjure you, where you are to be found; here, give me your direction; write it upon the back of this visiting-ticket[27]—Have you a pencil?

CHARLES. I have: but why shou'd you desire to find us out? 'Tis a poor little inconvenient place; my sister has no apartment fit to receive you in.

[Servant *enters.*

SERVANT. Madam, my lady desires your company directly.

CHARLOTTE. I am coming—well, have you wrote it? Give it me. O Charles! either you do not, or you will not understand me.

[*Exeunt severally.*

II.i

A Room, Fulmer*'s House.* Fulmer *and* Mrs. Fulmer.

MRS. FULMER. Why how you sit, musing and mopeing, sighing and desponding! I'm ashamed of you, Mr. Fulmer: is this the country you described to me, a second Eldorado, rivers of gold and rocks of diamonds? You found me in a pretty snug retir'd way of life at Bologne, out of the noise and bustle of the world, and wholly at my ease; you, indeed, was upon the wing, with a fiery persecution at your back: but, like a true son of Loyola,[28] you had then a thousand ingenious devices to repair your fortune; and this, your native country was to be the scene of your performances: fool that I was, to be inveigled into it by you: but, thank Heaven, our partnership is revocable; I am not your wedded wife, praised be my stars! for what have we got, whom have we gull'd but ourselves; which of all your trains has taken fire; even this poor expedient of your bookseller's shop seems abandoned;[29] for if a chance customer drops in, who is there, pray, to help him to what he wants?

FULMER. Patty, you know it is not upon slight grounds that I despair; there had us'd to be a livelihood to be pick'd up in this country, both for the honest and dishonest; I have tried each walk, and am likely to starve at last: there is not a point to which the wit and faculty of man can turn, that I have not set mine to; but in vain, I am beat through every quarter of the compass.

MRS. FULMER. Ah! common efforts all: strike me a master-stroke, Mr. Fulmer, if you wish to make any figure in this country.

FULMER. But where, how, and what? I have blustered for prerogative; I have bellowed for freedom; I have offered to serve my country; I have engaged to betray it; a master-stroke, truly; why, I have talked treason, writ treason, and if a man can't live by that he can live by nothing. Here I set up as a bookseller; why men left off reading; and if I was to turn butcher, I believe o'my conscience they'd leave off eating.[30]

[Capt. Dudley *crosses the stage.*

MRS. FULMER. Why there now's your lodger, old Captain Dudley, as he calls himself; there's no flint without fire; something might be struck out of him, if you'd the wit to find the way.

FULMER. Hang him, an old dry skin'd curmudgeon; you may as well think to get truth out of a courier, or candour out of a critic: I can make nothing of him; besides, he's poor, and therefore not for our purpose.

MRS. FULMER. The more fool he! Wou'd any man be poor that had such a prodigy in his possession?

FULMER. His daughter, you mean; she is indeed uncommonly beautiful.

MRS. FULMER. Beautiful! Why she need only be seen to have the first men in the kingdom at her feet. Egad, I wish I had the leasing of her beauty; what would some of our young Nabobs[31] give—?

FULMER. Hush; here comes the captain; good girl, leave us to ourselves, and let me try what I can make of him.

MRS. FULMER. Captain, truly; i'faith I'd have a regiment, had I such a daughter, before I was three months older.[32] [*Exit.*

II.ii

[Captain Dudley *enters to him.*

FULMER. Captain Dudley, good morning to you.

DUDLEY. Mr. Fulmer, I have borrow'd a book from your shop; 'tis the sixth volume of my deceased friend Tristram: he is a flattering writer to us poor soldiers; and the divine story of Le Fevre, which makes part of this book, in my opinion of it, does honour not to its author only, but to human nature.[33]

FULMER. He is an author I keep in the way of trade, but one I never relish'd: he is much too loose and profligate for my taste.

DUDLEY. That's being too severe: I hold him to be a moralist in the noblest sense; he plays indeed with the fancy, and sometimes perhaps too wantonly; but while he thus designedly masks his main attack, he comes at once upon the heart; refines, amends it, softens it; beats down each selfish barrier from about it; and opens every sluice of pity and benevolence.

FULMER. We of the Catholic persuasion are not much bound to him.—Well, Sir, I shall not oppose your opinion; a favourite author is like a favourite mistress; and there you know, Captain, no man likes to have his taste arraigned.

DUDLEY. Upon my word, Sir, I don't know what a man likes in that case; 'tis an experiment I never made.

FULMER. Sir!—Are you serious?

DUDLEY. 'Tis of little consequence whether you think so.

FULMER.—[*Aside*] *What a formal old prig it is!*—[*To him*] I apprehend you, Sir; you speak with caution; you are married?

DUDLEY. I have been.

FULMER. And this young lady, which accompanies you—

DUDLEY. Passes for my daughter.

FULMER.—[*Aside*] *Passes for his daughter! humph*—[*To him*] She is exceedingly beautiful, finely accomplish'd, of a most enchanting shape and air.

DUDLEY. You are much too partial; she has the greatest defect a woman can have.

FULMER. How so, pray?

DUDLEY. She has no fortune.

FULMER. Rather say that you have none; and that's a sore defect in one of your years, Captain Dudley: you've serv'd, no doubt?

DUDLEY. [*Aside*] *Familiar coxcomb! But I'll humour him.*

FULMER. [*Aside*] *A close old fox! But I'll unkennel him.*

DUDLEY. Above thirty years I've been in the service, Mr. Fulmer.

FULMER. I guess'd as much; I laid it at no less: why 'tis a wearisome time; 'tis an apprenticeship to a profession, fit only for a patriarch. But preferment must be closely follow'd: you never could have been so far behind-hand in the chace, unless you had palpably mistaken your way. You'll pardon me, but I begin to perceive you have lived in the world, not with it.

DUDLEY. It may be so; and you, perhaps, can give me better council. I'm now soliciting a favour; an exchange to a company on full pay; nothing more; and yet I meet a thousand bars to that; tho', without boasting, I should think the certificate of services, which I sent in, might have purchased that indulgence to me.

FULMER. Who thinks or cares about 'em? Certificate of services, indeed! Send in a certificate of your fair daughter; carry her in your hand with you.

DUDLEY. What! Who! My daughter! Carry my daughter, well, and what then?

FULMER. Why, then your fortune's made, that's all.

DUDLEY. I understand you: and this you call knowledge of the world? Despicable knowledge; but, sirrah, I will have you know—[*Threatening him.*

FULMER. Help! Who's within? Wou'd you strike me, Sir; wou'd you lift up your hand against a man in his own house?

DUDLEY. In a church, if he dare insult the poverty of a man of honour.

FULMER. Have a care what you do; remember there is such a thing in law as an assault and battery; ay, and such trifling forms as warrants and indictments.

DUDLEY. Go, Sir; you are too mean[34] for my resentment: 'tis that, and not the law, protects you. Hence!

FULMER. [*Aside*] *An old, absurd, incorrigible blockhead! I'll be reveng'd of him.* [*Exit.*

II.iii

[Young Dudley *enters to him.*

CHARLES. What is the matter, Sir? Sure I heard an out-cry as I enter'd the house.

DUDLEY. Not unlikely; our landlord and his wife are for ever wrangling.—Did you find your Aunt Rusport at home?

CHARLES. I did.

DUDLEY. And what was your reception?

CHARLES. Cold as our poverty, and her pride, could make it.

DUDLEY. You told her the pressing occasion I had for a small supply to equip me for this exchange; has she granted me the relief I asked?

CHARLES. Alas! Sir, she has peremptorily refused it.

DUDLEY. That's hard; that's hard, indeed! My petition was for a small sum; she has refused it, you say: well, be it so; I must not complain. Did you see the broker about the insurance on my life?

CHARLES. There again I am the messenger of ill news; I can raise no money, so fatal is the climate: alas! that ever my father shou'd be sent to perish in such a place!

II.iv

[Miss Dudley *enters hastily.*

DUDLEY. Louisa, what's the matter? You seem frighted.

LOUISA. I am, indeed: coming from Miss Rusport's, I met a young gentleman in the streets, who has beset me in the strangest manner.

CHARLES. Insufferable! Was he rude to you?

LOUISA. I cannot say he was absolutely rude to me, but he was very importunate to speak to me, and once or twice attempted to lift up my hat: he follow'd me to the corner of the street, and there I gave him the slip.

DUDLEY. You must walk no more in the streets, child, without me, or your brother.

LOUISA. O Charles! Miss Rusport desires to see you directly; Lady Rusport is gone out, and she has something particular to say to you.

CHARLES. Have you any commands for me, Sir?

DUDLEY. None, my dear; by all means wait upon Miss Rusport. Come, Louisa, I shall desire you to go up to your chamber, and compose yourself.

[*Exeunt.*

II.v

[Belcour *enters, after peeping in at the door.*

BELCOUR. Not a soul, as I'm alive. Why, what an odd sort of a house is this! Confound the little jilt, she has fairly given me the slip. A plague upon this London, I shall have no luck in it: such a crowd, and such a hurry, and such a number of shops, and one so like the other, that whether the wench turn'd into this house or the next, or whether she went up stairs or down stairs, (for there's a world above and a world below, it seems) I declare, I know no more than if I was in the Blue Mountains.[35] In the name of all the devils at once, why did she run away? If every handsome girl I meet in this town is to lead me such a wild-goose chace, I had better have stay'd in the torrid zone: I shall be wasted to the size of a sugar cane: what shall I do? Give the chace up? Hang it, that's cowardly: shall I, a true-born son of Phoebus, suffer this little nimble-footed Daphne to escape me?—"Forbid it honour, and forbid it love."[36] Hush! hush! here she comes! Oh! the devil! What tawdry thing have we got here?

[Mrs. Fulmer *enters to him.*

MRS. FULMER. Your humble servant, Sir.

BELCOUR. Your humble servant, Madam.

MRS. FULMER. A fine summer's day, Sir.

BELCOUR. Yes, Ma'am, and so cool, that if the calendar didn't call it July, I shou'd swear it was January.

MRS. FULMER. Sir!

BELCOUR. Madam!

MRS. FULMER. Do you wish to speak to Mr. Fulmer, Sir?

BELCOUR. Mr. Fulmer, Madam? I havn't the honour of knowing such a person.

MRS. FULMER. No, I'll be sworn, have you not; thou art much too pretty a fellow, and too much of a gentleman, to be an author thyself, or to have any thing to say to those that are so. 'Tis the Captain, I suppose, you are waiting for.

BELCOUR. I rather suspect it is the Captain's wife.

MRS. FULMER. The Captain has no wife, Sir.

BELCOUR. No wife? I'm heartily sorry for it; for then she's his mistress; and that I take to be the more desperate case of the two: pray, Madam, wasn't there a lady just now turn'd into your house? 'Twas with her I wish'd to speak.

MRS. FULMER. What sort of a lady, pray?

BELCOUR. One of the loveliest sort my eyes ever beheld; young, tall, fresh, fair; in short, a goddess.

MRS. FULMER. Nay, but dear, dear Sir, now I'm sure you flatter; for 'twas me you followed into the shop-door this minute.

BELCOUR. You! No, no, take my word for it, it was not you, Madam.

MRS. FULMER. But what is it you laugh at?

BELCOUR. Upon my soul, I ask your pardon; but it was not you, believe me; be assur'd it wasn't.

MRS. FULMER. Well, Sir, I shall not contend for the honour of being notic'd by you; I hope you think you woudn't have been the first man that notic'd me in the streets;[37] however, this I'm positive of, that no living woman but myself has enter'd these doors this morning.

BELCOUR. Why then I'm mistaken in the house, that's all; for 'tis not humanly possible I can be so far out in the lady. [*Going.*

MRS. FULMER.—[*Aside*] *Coxcomb! But hold—a thought occurs; as sure as can be he has seen Miss Dudley.*—[*To him*] A word with you, young gentleman; come back.

BELCOUR. Well, what's your pleasure?

MRS. FULMER. You seem greatly captivated with this young lady; are you apt to fall in love thus at first sight?

BELCOUR. Oh, yes: 'tis the only way I can ever fall in love; any man may tumble into a pit by surprize, none but a fool would walk into one by choice.

MRS. FULMER. You are a hasty lover it seems; have you spirit to be a generous one? They that will please the eye mustn't spare the purse.

BELCOUR. Try me; put me to the proof; bring me to an interview with the dear girl that has thus captivated me, and see whether I have spirit to be grateful.

MRS. FULMER. But how, pray, am I to know the girl you have set your heart on?

BELCOUR. By an undescribable grace, that accompanies every look and action that falls from her: there can be but one such woman in the world, and nobody can mistake that one.

MRS. FULMER. Well, if I should stumble upon this angel in my walks, where am I to find you? What's your name?

BELCOUR. Upon my soul, I can't tell you my name.

MRS. FULMER. Not tell me! Why so?

BELCOUR. Because I don't know what it is myself; as yet I have no name.

MRS. FULMER. No name!

BELCOUR. None; a friend, indeed, lent me his; but he forbad me to use it on any unworthy occasion.

MRS. FULMER. But where is your place of abode?

BELCOUR. I have none; I never slept a night in England in my life.

MRS FULMER. Hey-day!

II.vi

[Fulmer *enters.*

FULMER. A fine case, truly, in a free country; a pretty pass things are come to, if a man is to be assaulted in his own house.

MRS. FULMER. Who has assaulted you, my dear?

FULMER. Who! why this Captain Drawcansir,[38] this old Dudley, my lodger; but I'll unlodge him; I'll unharbour him, I warrant.

MRS. FULMER. Hush! hush! hold your tongue man; pocket the affront, and be quiet; I've a scheme on foot will pay you a hundred beatings. Why you surprize me, Mr. Fulmer; Captain Dudley assault you! Impossible.

FULMER. Nay, I can't call it an absolute assault; but he threatened me.

MRS. FULMER. Oh, was that all? I thought how it would turn out—a likely thing, truly, for a person of his obliging compassionate turn: no, no, poor Captain Dudley, he has sorrows and distresses enough of his own to employ his spirits, without setting them against other people. Make it up as fast as you can: watch this gentleman out; follow him wherever he goes; and bring me word who and what he is; be sure you don't lose sight of him; I've other business in hand. [*Exit.*

BELCOUR. Pray, Sir, what sorrows and distresses have befallen this old gentleman you speak of?

FULMER. Poverty, disappointment, and all the distresses attendant thereupon: sorrow enough of all conscience; I soon found how it was with him by his way of living, low enough of all reason; but what I overheard this morning put it out of all doubt.

BELCOUR. What did you overhear this morning?

FULMER. Why, it seems he wants to join his regiment, and has been beating the town over to raise a little money for that purpose upon his pay; but the climate, I find, where he is going, is so unhealthy, that nobody can be found to lend him any.[39]

BELCOUR. Why then your town is a damn'd good-for-nothing town: and I wish I had never come into it.

FULMER. That's what I say, Sir; the hard-heartedness of some folks is unaccountable. There's an old Lady Rusport, a near relation of this gentleman's; she lives hard by here, opposite to Stockwell's, the great merchant; he sent to her a begging, but to no purpose; though she is as rich as a Jew, she would not furnish him with a farthing.

BELCOUR. Is the Captain at home?

FULMER. He is upstairs, Sir.

BELCOUR. Will you take the trouble to desire him to step hither? I want to speak to him.

FULMER. I'll send him to you directly. I don't know what to make of this young man; but, if I live, I will find him out, or know the reason why. [*Exit.*

BELCOUR. I've lost the girl it seems; that's clear; she was the first object of my pursuit; but the case of this poor officer touches me; and, after all, there may be as much true delight in rescuing a fellow creature from distress, as there would be in putting one into it—But let me see; it's a point that must be managed with some delicacy—Apropos! there's pen and ink—I've struck upon a method that will do [*Writes*]. Ay, ay, this is the very thing; 'twas devilish lucky I happen'd to have these bills about me. There, there, fare you well; I'm glad to be rid of you; you stood a chance of being worse applied, I can tell you. [*Encloses and seals the paper.*

II.vii

[Fulmer *brings in* Dudley.

FULMER. That's the gentleman, Sir.—[*Aside*] *I shall make bold, however, to lend an ear.*

DUDLEY. Have you any commands for me, Sir?

BELCOUR. Your name is Dudley, Sir—?

DUDLEY. It is.

BELCOUR. You command a company, I think, Captain Dudley?

DUDLEY. I did: I am now upon half-pay.

BELCOUR. You've served some time?

DUDLEY. A pretty many years; long enough to see some people of more merit, and better interest than myself, made general officers.

BELCOUR. Their merit I may have some doubt of; their interest I can readily give credit to; there is little promotion to be look'd for in your profession, I believe, without friends, Captain?

DUDLEY. I believe so too: have you any other business with me, may I ask?

BELCOUR. Your patience for a moment. I was informed you was about to join your regiment in distant quarters abroad.

DUDLEY. I have been soliciting an exchange to a company on full-pay, quarter'd at James's Fort,[40] in Senegambia; but, I'm afraid, I must drop the undertaking.

BELCOUR. Why so, pray?

DUDLEY. Why so, Sir? 'Tis a home question for a perfect stranger to put; there is something very particular in all this.

BELCOUR. If it is not impertinent Sir, allow me to ask you what reason you have for despairing of success.

DUDLEY. Why really, Sir, mine is an obvious reason for a soldier to have—Want of money; simply that.

BELCOUR. May I beg to know the sum you have occasion for?

DUDLEY. Truly, Sir, I cannot exactly tell you on a sudden; nor is it, I suppose, of any great consequence to you to be informed; but I should guess, in the gross, that two hundred pounds would serve.

BELCOUR. And do you find a difficulty in raising that sum upon your pay? 'Tis done every day.

DUDLEY. The nature of the climate makes it difficult: I can get no one to insure my life.

BELCOUR. Oh! that's a circumstance may make for you, as well as against: in short, Captain Dudley, it so happens, that I can command the sum of two hundred pounds: seek no farther; I'll accomodate you with it upon easy terms.

DUDLEY. Sir! do I understand you rightly?—I beg your pardon; but am I to believe that you are in earnest?

BELCOUR. What is your surprize? Is it an uncommon thing for a gentleman to speak truth? Or is it incredible that one fellow creature should assist another?

DUDLEY. I ask your pardon—May I beg to know to whom? Do you propose this in the way of business?

BELCOUR. Entirely: I have no other business on earth.

DUDLEY. Indeed! you are not a broker, I'm persuaded.

BELCOUR. I am not.

DUDLEY. Nor an army agent I think?

BELCOUR. I hope you will not think the worse of me for being neither; in short, Sir, if you will peruse this paper, it will explain to you who I am, and upon what terms I act; while you read it, I will step home, and fetch the money; and we will conclude the bargain without loss of time. In the meanwhile, good day to you. [*Exit hastily.*

DUDLEY. Humph! there's something very odd in all this—let me see what we've got here—This paper is to tell me who he is, and what are his terms: in the name of wonder, why has he sealed it! Hey-day! what's here? Two banknotes, of a hundred each! I can't comprehend what this means. Hold; here's a writing; perhaps that will show me. "*Accept this trifle; pursue your fortune, and prosper.*" Am I in a dream? Is this a reality?

II.viii

[*Enter* Major O'Flaherty.

O'FLAHERTY. Save you, my dear! Is it you now that are Captain Dudley, I would ask?—Whuh! What's the hurry the man's in? If 'tis the lad that run out of the shop you wou'd overtake, you might as well stay where you are; by my soul he's as nimble as a Croat,[41] you are a full hour's march in his rear—Ay, faith, you may as well turn back, and give over the pursuit; well, Captain Dudley, if that's your name, there's a letter for you. Read, man; read it; and I'll have a word with you after you've done.

DUDLEY. More miracles on foot! So, so, from Lady Rusport.

O'FLAHERTY. You're right; it's from her ladyship.

DUDLEY. Well, Sir, I have cast my eye over it; 'tis short and peremptory; are you acquainted with the contents?

O'FLAHERTY. Not at all, my dear, not at all.

DUDLEY. Have you any message from Lady Rusport?

O'FLAHERTY. Not a syllable, honey; only, when you've digested the letter, I've a little bit of a message to deliver you from myself.

DUDLEY. And may I beg to know who yourself is?

O'FLAHERTY. Dennis O'Flaherty, at your service; a poor major of grenadiers; nothing better.[42]

DUDLEY. So much for your name and title, Sir; now be so good to favour me with your message.

O'FLAHERTY. Why then, Captain, I must tell you I have promised Lady Rusport you shall do whatever it is she bids you to do in that letter there.

DUDLEY. Ay, indeed; have you undertaken so much, Major, without knowing either what she commands, or what I can perform?

O'FLAHERTY. That's your concern, my dear, not mine; I must keep my word, you know.

DUDLEY. Or else, I suppose, you and I must measure swords.

O'FLAHERTY. Upon my soul, you've hit it.

DUDLEY. That wou'd hardly answer to either of us; you and I have, probably, had enough of fighting in our time before now.

O'FLAHERTY. Faith and troth, Master Dudley, you may say that; 'tis thirty years, come the time, that I have follow'd the trade, and in a pretty many countries.—Let me see—In the war before last I serv'd in the Irish brigade, d'ye see; there, after bringing off the French monarch, I left his service, with a British bullet in my body, and this ribband in my button-hole. Last war I follow'd the fortunes of the German eagle, in the corps of grenadiers; there I had my belly-full of fighting, and a plentiful scarcity of every thing else. After six and twenty engagements, great and small, I went off, with this gash on my skull, and a kiss of the Empress Queen's sweet hand, (Heaven bless it!) for my pains.[43] Since the peace, my dear, I took a little turn with the Confederates there in Poland—but such another set of madcaps!—by the lord Harry, I never knew what it was they were scuffling about.[44]

DUDLEY. Well, Major, I won't add another action to the list; you shall keep your promise with Lady Rusport; she requires me to leave London; I shall go in a few days, and you may take what credit you please from my compliance.

O'FLAHERTY. Give me your hand, my dear boy! this will make her my own; when that's the case, we shall be brothers, you know, and we'll share her fortune between us.

DUDLEY. Not so, Major; the man who marries Lady Rusport will have a fair title to her whole fortune without division. But, I hope, your expectations of prevailing are founded upon good reasons.

O'FLAHERTY. Upon the best grounds in the world; first, I think she will comply, because she is a woman; secondly, I am persuaded she won't hold out long, because she's a widow; and thirdly, I make sure of her, because I've married five wives, (*en militaire*,[45] Captain) and never failed yet; and, for what I know, they're all alive and merry at this very hour.

DUDLEY. Well, Sir, go on and prosper; if you can inspire Lady Rusport with half your charity, I shall think you deserve all her fortune; at present, I must beg your excuse: good morning to you. [*Exit.*

O'FLAHERTY. A good sensible man, and very much of a soldier; I did not care if I was better acquainted with him: but 'tis an awkward kind of country for that; the English, I observe, are close friends, but distant acquaintance. I suspect the old lady has not been over-generous to poor Dudley; I shall give her a little touch about that: upon my soul, I know but one excuse a person can have for giving nothing, and that is, like myself, having nothing to give. [*Exit.*

II.ix

Scene changes to Lady Rusport*'s house. A dressing-room.* Miss Rusport *and* Lucy.

CHARLOTTE. Well, Lucy, you've dislodg'd the old lady at last; but methought you was a tedious time about it.

LUCY. A tedious time, indeed; I think they who have least to spare, contrive to throw the most away; I thought I shou'd never have got her out of the house.

CHARLOTTE. Why, she's as deliberate in canvassing every article of her dress, as an ambassador would be in settling the preliminaries of a treaty.

LUCY. There was a new hood and handkerchief, that had come express from Holborn Hill[46] on the occasion, that took as much time in adjusting—

CHARLOTTE. As they did in making, and she was as vain of them as an old maid of a young lover.

LUCY. Or a young lover of himself. Then, Madam, this being a visit of great ceremony to a person of distinction, at the west end of the town, the old state chariot was dragg'd forth on the occasion, with strict charges to dress out the box with the leopard-skin hammer-cloth.[47]

CHARLOTTE. Yes, and to hang the false tails on the miserable stumps of the old crawling cattle. Well, well, pray Heaven the crazy affair don't break down again with her! at least till she gets to her journey's end.—But where's Charles Dudley? Run down, dear girl, and be ready to let him in; I think he's as long in coming as she was in going.

LUCY. Why, indeed, Madam, you seem the more alert of the two, I must say. [*Exit.*

CHARLOTTE. Now the deuce take the girl for putting that notion into my head: I'm sadly afraid Dudley does not like me; so much encouragement as I have given him to declare himself, I never cou'd get a word from him on the subject! This may be very honourable, but upon my life it's very provoking. By the way, I wonder how I look today: Oh! shockingly! hideously pale! like a witch! this is the old lady's glass and she has left some of her wrinkles on it. How frightfully have I put on my cap! all awry! and my hair dress'd so unbecomingly! altogether, I'm a most complete fright.

II.x

[Charles Dudley *comes in unobserved.*

CHARLES. That I deny.

CHARLOTTE. Ah!

CHARLES. Quarelling with your glass, cousin? Make it up; make it up and be friends; it cannot compliment you more than by reflecting you as you are.

CHARLOTTE. Well, I vow, my dear Charles, that is delightfully said, and deserves my very best curtesy: your flattery, like a rich jewel, has a value not only from its superior lustre, but from its extraordinary scarceness: I verily think this is the only civil speech you ever directed to my person in your life.

CHARLES. And I ought to ask pardon of your good sense for having done it now.

CHARLOTTE. Nay, now you relapse again: don't you know, if you keep well with a woman on the great score of beauty, she'll never quarrel with you on the trifling article of good sense? But any thing serves to fill up a dull yawning hour with an insipid cousin; you have brighter moments, and warmer spirits, for the dear girl of your heart.

CHARLES. Oh! fie upon you, fie upon you.

CHARLOTTE. You blush, and the reason is apparent; you are a novice at hypocrisy; but no practice can make a visit of ceremony pass for a visit of choice: love is ever before its time; friendship is apt to lag a little after it: pray, Charles, did you make any extraordinary haste hither?

CHARLES. By your question, I see you acquit me of the impertinence of being in love.

CHARLOTTE. But why impertinence? Why the impertinence of being in love? You have one language for me, Charles, and another for the woman of your affection.

CHARLES. You are mistaken; the woman of my affection shall never hear any other language from me than what I use to you.

CHARLOTTE. I am afraid then you'll never make yourself understood by her.

CHARLES. It is not fit I shou'd; there is no need of love to make me miserable; 'tis wretchedness enough to be a beggar.

CHARLOTTE. A beggar, do you call yourself! O Charles, Charles, rich in every merit and accomplishment, whom may you not aspire to? And why think you so unworthily of our sex, as to conclude there is not one to be found with sense to discern your virtue and generosity to reward it?

CHARLES. You distress me; I must beg to hear no more.

CHARLOTTE. Well, I can be silent.—[*Aside*] *Thus does he always serve me, whenever I am about to disclose myself to him.*

CHARLES. Why do you not banish me and my misfortunes for ever from your thoughts?

CHARLOTTE. Ay, wherefore do I not, since you never allowed me a place in yours? But go, Sir, I have no right to stay you; go where your heart directs you; go to the happy, the distinguished fair one.

CHARLES. Now, by all that's good, you do me wrong: there is no such fair one for me to go to, nor have I an acquaintance among the sex, yourself excepted, which answers to that description.

CHARLOTTE. Indeed!

CHARLES. In very truth: there then let us drop the subject. May you be happy, though I never can!

CHARLOTTE. O Charles! give me your hand; if I have offended you, I ask you pardon: you have been long acquainted with my temper, and know how to bear with its infirmities.

CHARLES. Thus, my dear Charlotte, let us seal our reconciliation [*Kissing her hand*]. Bear with thy infirmities! By Heaven, I know not any one failing in thy whole composition, except that of too great a partiality for an undeserving man.

CHARLOTTE. And you are now taking the very course to augment that failing. A thought strikes me: I have a commission that you must absolutely execute for me; I have immediate occasion for the sum of two hundred pounds; you know my fortune is shut up till I am of age; take this paltry box, (it contains my ear-rings, and some other baubles I have no use for) carry it to our opposite neighbour, Mr. Stockwell, (I don't know where else to apply) leave it as a deposit in his hands; and beg him to accommodate me with the sum.

CHARLES. Dear Charlotte, what are you about to do? How can you possibly want two hundred pounds?

CHARLOTTE. How can I possibly do without it, you mean? Doesn't every lady want two hundred pounds? Perhaps I have lost it at play; perhaps I mean to win as much to it; perhaps I want it for two hundred different uses.

CHARLES. Pooh! pooh! all this is nothing; don't I know you never play?

CHARLOTTE. You mistake; I have a spirit to set not only this trifle, but my whole fortune, upon a stake; therefore make no wry faces, but do as I bid you: you will find Mr. Stockwell a very honourable gentleman.

[Lucy *enters in haste.*

LUCY. Dear Madam, as I live, here comes the old lady in a hackney-coach.[48]

CHARLOTTE. The old chariot has given her a second tumble: away with you; you know your way out without meeting her; take the box, and do as I desire you.

CHARLES. I must not dispute your orders. Farewell! [*Exeunt* Charles *and* Charlotte.

II.xi

[Lady Rusport *enters, leaning on* Major O'Flaherty*'s arm.*

O'FLAHERTY. Rest yourself upon my arm; never spare it; 'tis strong enough: it has stood harder service than you can put it to.

LUCY. Mercy upon me, what is the matter; I am frighten'd out of my wits: has your ladyship had an accident?

LADY RUSPORT. O Lucy; the most untoward one in nature; I know not how I shall repair it.

O'FLAHERTY. Never go about to repair it, my lady; ev'n build a new one; 'twas but a crazy piece of business at best.

LUCY. Bless me, is the old chariot broke down with you again?

LADY RUSPORT. Broke, child? I don't know what might have been broke, if, by great good fortune, this obliging gentleman had not been at hand to assist me.

LUCY. Dear Madam, let me run and fetch you a cup of the cordial drops.

LADY RUSPORT. Do, Lucy. Alas! Sir, ever since I lost my husband, my poor nerves have been shook to pieces: there hangs his beloved picture; that precious relick, and a plentiful jointure,[49] is all that remains to console me for the best of men.

O'FLAHERTY. Let me see; i'faith a comely personage; by his fur cloak I suppose he was in the Russian service; and by the gold chain round his neck, I should guess he had been honoured with the order of St. Catherine.[50]

LADY RUSPORT. No, no; he meddled with no St. Catherines: that's the habit he wore in his mayoralty; Sir Stephen was Lord-Mayor of London: but he is gone, and has left me a poor, weak, solitary widow behind him.

O'FLAHERTY. By all means, then, take a strong, able, hearty man to repair his loss: if such a plain fellow as one Dennis O'Flaherty can please you, I think I may venture to say, without any disparagement to the gentleman in the furgown there—

LADY RUSPORT. What are you going to say? Don't shock my ears with any comparisons, I desire.

O'FLAHERTY. Not I, by my soul; I don't believe there's any comparison in the case.

LADY RUSPORT. [*To* Lucy] Oh, are you come? Give me the drops; I'm all in a flutter.

O'FLAHERTY. Hark'e, sweetheart, what are those same drops? Have you any more left in the bottle? I didn't care if I took a little sip of them myself.

LUCY. Oh, Sir, they are call'd the cordial restorative elixir, or the nervous golden drops; they are only for ladies' cases.

O'FLAHERTY. Yes, yes, my dear, there are gentlemen as well as ladies that stand in need of those same golden drops; they'd suit my case to a tittle.

LADY RUSPORT. Well, Major, did you give old Dudley my letter, and will the silly man do as I bid him, and be gone?

O'FLAHERTY. You are obey'd; he's on his march.

LADY RUSPORT. That's well; you have manag'd this matter to perfection; I didn't think he wou'd have been so easily prevail'd upon.

O'FLAHERTY. At the first word; no difficulty in life; 'twas the very thing he was determin'd to do, before I came; I never met a more obliging gentleman.

LADY RUSPORT. Well, 'tis no matter; so I am but rid of him, and his distresses: wou'd you believe it, Major O'Flaherty, it was but this morning he sent a begging to me for money to fit him out upon some wild-goose expedition to the coast of Africa, I know not where.

O'FLAHERTY. Well, you sent him what he wanted.

LADY RUSPORT. I sent him what he deserved, a flat refusal.

O'FLAHERTY. You refused him!

LADY RUSPORT. Most undoubtedly.

O'FLAHERTY. You sent him nothing!

LADY RUSPORT. Not a shilling.

O'FLAHERTY. Good morning to you—Your servant [*Going*.

LADY RUSPORT. Hey-day!—[*Aside*] *What ails the man?*—[*To him*] Where are you going?

O'FLAHERTY. Out of your house, before the roof falls on my head—to poor Dudley, to share the little modicum that thirty years' hard service has left me; I wish it was more for his sake.

LADY RUSPORT. Very well, Sir; take your course; I shan't attempt to stop you; I shall survive it; it will not break my heart if I never see you more.

O'FLAHERTY. Break your heart! No, o' my conscience will it not.—You preach, and you pray, and you turn up your eyes, and all the while you're as hard-hearted as a hyena—A hyena, truly! By my soul there isn't in the whole creation so savage an animal as a human creature without pity. [*Exit*.

LADY RUSPORT. A hyena, truly! Where did the fellow blunder upon that word? Now the deuce take him for using it, and the Macaronies for inventing it.[51]

[*Exeunt*.

III.i

A room in Stockwell*'s house*. Stockwell *and* Belcour.

STOCKWELL. Gratify me so far, however, Mr. Belcour, as to see Miss Rusport; carry her the sum she wants, and return the poor girl her box of diamonds, which Dudley left in my hands; you know what to say on the occasion better than I do; that part of your commission I leave to your own discretion, and you may season it with what gallantry you think fit.

BELCOUR. You cou'd not have pitch'd upon a greater bungler at gallantry than myself, if you had rummag'd every company in the city, and the whole court of aldermen into the bargain: part of your errand, however, I will do; but whether it shall be with an ill grace or a good one depends upon the caprice of a moment, the humour of the lady, the mode of our meeting, and a thousand undefinable small circumstances that nevertheless determine us upon all the great occasions of life.

STOCKWELL. I persuade myself you will find Miss Rusport an ingenious, worthy, animated girl.

BELCOUR. Why I like her the better, as a woman; but name her not to me as a wife! No, if ever I marry, it must be a staid, sober, considerate damsel, with blood in her veins as cold as a turtle's; quick of scent as a vulture when danger's in the wind; wary and sharp-fighted as a hawk when treachery is on foot: with such a companion at my elbow, forever whispering in my ear—have a care of this man, he's a cheat; don't go near that woman, she's a jilt; over head there's a scaffold, under foot there's a well: Oh! Sir, such a woman might lead me up and down this great city without difficulty or danger; but with a girl of Miss Rusport's complexion, heaven and earth. Sir! we shou'd be dup'd, undone, and distracted, in a fortnight.

STOCKWELL. Ha! ha! ha! Why you are become wond'rous circumspect of a sudden, pupil; and if you can find such a prudent damsel as you describe, you have my consent—only beware how you chuse; discretion is not the reigning quality amongst the fine ladies of the present time; and I think in Miss Rusport's particular I have given you no bad counsel.

BELCOUR. Well, well, if you'll fetch me the jewels, I believe I can undertake to carry them to her; but as for the money, I'll have nothing to do with that; Dudley would be your fittest ambassador on that occasion; and, if I mistake not, the most agreeable to the lady.

STOCKWELL. Why, indeed, from what I know of the matter, it may not improbably be destined to find its way into his pockets. [*Exit.*

BELCOUR. Then, depend upon it, these are not the only trinkets she means to dedicate to Captain Dudley. As for me, Stockwell indeed wants me to marry; but, till I can get this bewitching girl, this incognita,[52] out of my head, I can never think of any other woman. [Servant *enters, and delivers a letter*] Hey-day! Where can I have pick'd up a correspondent already? 'Tis a most execrable manuscript—Let me see—Martha Fulmer—Who is Martha Fulmer? Pshaw! I won't be at the trouble of decyphering her damn'd pot-hooks.[53] Hold, hold, hold; what have we got here? "*Dear Sir, I've discover'd the lady you was so much smitten with, and can procure you an interview with her; if you can be as generous to a pretty girl as you was to a paltry old captain,* (how did she find that out?) *you need not despair: come to me immediately; the lady is now in my house, and expects you. Yours,* Martha Fulmer." O thou dear, lovely, and enchanting paper, which I was about to tear into a thousand scraps, devoutly I entreat thy pardon: I have slighted thy contents, which are delicious; slander'd thy characters, which are divine; and all the attonement I can make is implicitly to obey thy mandates.

[Stockwell *returns.*

STOCKWELL. Mr. Belcour, here are the jewels; this letter encloses bills for the money;[54] and, if you will deliver it to Miss Rusport, you'll have no farther trouble on that score.

BELCOUR. Ah, Sir! the letter which I've been reading disqualifies me for delivering the letter which you have been writing: I have other game on foot; the loveliest girl my eyes ever feasted upon is started in view, and the world cannot now divert me from pursuing her.[55]

STOCKWELL. Hey-day! What has turned you thus on a sudden?

BELCOUR. A woman: one that can turn, and overturn me and my tottering resolutions every way she will. Oh, Sir, if this is folly in me, you must rail at Nature: you must chide the sun, that was vertical at my birth, and would not wink upon my nakedness, but swaddled me in the broadest, hottest glare of his meridian beams.

STOCKWELL. Mere rhapsody; mere childish rhapsody; the libertine's familiar plea—Nature made us, 'tis true, but we are the responsible creators of our own faults and follies.

BELCOUR. Sir!

STOCKWELL. Slave of every face you meet, some hussey has inveigled you, some handsome profligate, (the town is full of them;) and, when once fairly bankrupt in constitution, as well as fortune, nature no longer serves as your excuse for being vicious; necessity, perhaps, will stand your friend, and you'll reform.

BELCOUR. You are severe.

STOCKWELL. It fits me to be so—it well becomes a father—I would say a friend—[*Aside*] *How strangely I forget myself—How difficult it is to counterfeit indifference, and put a mask upon the heart—I've struck him hard; he reddens.*

BELCOUR. How could you tempt me so? Had you not inadvertently dropped the name of father, I fear our friendship, short as it has been, would scarce have held me—But even your mistake I reverence—Give me your hand—'tis over.

STOCKWELL. Generous young man—let me embrace you.—How shall I hide my tears? I have been to blame; because I bore you the affection of a father, I rashly took up the authority of one. I ask your pardon—pursue your course; I have no right to stop it—What would you have me do with these things?

BELCOUR. This, if I might advise; carry the money to Miss Rusport immediately; never let generosity wait for its materials; that part of the business presses. Give me the jewels; I'll find an opportunity of delivering them into her hands; and your visit may pave the way for my reception. [*Exit.*

STOCKWELL. Be it so: good morning to you. Farewel advice! Away goes he upon the wing for pleasure. What various passions he awakens in me! He pains, yet pleases me; affrights, offends, yet grows upon my heart. His very failings set him off—for ever trespassing, for ever atoning, I almost think he would not be so perfect, were he free from fault: I must dissemble longer; and yet how painful the experiment!—Even now he's gone upon some wild adventure; and who can tell what mischief may befall him! O Nature, what it is to be a father! Just such a thoughtless headlong thing was I when I beguiled his mother into love. [*Exit.*

III.ii

Scene changes to Fulmer*'s House.* Fulmer *and his* Wife.

FULMER. I tell you, Patty, you are a fool to think of bringing him and Miss Dudley together; 'twill ruin every thing, and blow your whole scheme up to the moon at once.

MRS. FULMER. Why, sure, Mr. Fulmer, I may be allowed to rear a chicken of my own hatching, as they say. Who first sprung the thought but I, pray? Who first contrived the plot? Who proposed the letter, but I, I?

FULMER. And who dogg'd the gentleman home? Who found out his name, fortune, connection; that he was a West-Indian, fresh landed, and full of cash; a gull to our heart's content; a hot brain'd headlong spark, that would run into our trap, like a wheat-ear[56] under a turf?

MRS. FULMER. Hark! he's come; disappear, march; and leave the field open to my machinations. [*Exit* Fulmer.

III.iii

[Belcour *enters to her.*

BELCOUR. O, thou dear minister to my happiness, let me embrace thee! Why thou art my polar star,[57] my propitious constellation, by which I navigate my impatient bark into the port of pleasure and delight.

MRS. FULMER. Oh, you men are sly creatures! Do you remember now, you cruel, what you said to me this morning?

BELCOUR. All a jest, a frolick; never think on't; bury it forever in oblivion; thou! why thou art all over nectar and ambrosia, powder of pearl and odour of roses; thou hast the youth of Hebe, the beauty of Venus, and the pen of Sappho;[58] but in the name of all that's lovely, where's the lady? I expected to find her with you.

MRS. FULMER. No doubt you did, and these raptures were designed for her; but where have you loitered? the lady's gone, you are too late, girls of her sort are not to be kept waiting like negro slaves in your sugar plantations.

BELCOUR. Gone! whither is she gone? tell me that I may follow her.

MRS. FULMER. Hold, hold, not so fast young gentleman, this is a case of some delicacy; shou'd Captain Dudley know that I introduced you to his daughter, he is a man of such scrupulous honour—

BELCOUR. What do you tell me! is she daughter to the old gentleman I met here this morning?

MRS. FULMER. The same; him you was so generous to.

BELCOUR. There's an end of the matter then at once; it shall never be said of me, that I took advantage of the father's necessities to trepan[59] the daughter. [*Going.*

MRS. FULMER. [*Aside*] So, *so, I've made a wrong cast, he's one of your conscientious sinners I find; but I won't lose him thus—Ha! ha! ha!*

BELCOUR. What is it you laugh at?

MRS. FULMER. Your absolute inexperience: have you lived so very little time in this country, as not to know that between young people of equal ages, the term of sister often is a cover for that of mistress? This young lady is, in that sense of the word, sister to young Dudley, and consequently daughter to my old lodger.

BELCOUR. Indeed! are you serious?

MRS. FULMER. Can you doubt it? I must have been pretty well assur'd of that before I invited you hither.

BELCOUR. That's true; she cannot be a woman of honour, and Dudley is an unconscionable young rogue to think of keeping one fine girl in pay, by raising contributions on another; he shall therefore give her up; she is a dear, bewitching, mischievous, little devil; and he shall positively give her up.

MRS. FULMER. Ay, now the freak has taken you again;[60] I say give her up; there's one way, indeed, and certain of success.

BELCOUR. What's that?

MRS. FULMER. Out-bid him, never dream of out-blustring him; buy out his lease of possession, and leave her to manage his ejectment.

BELCOUR. Is she so venal? Never fear me then; when beauty is the purchase, I shan't think much of the price.

MRS. FULMER. All things, then, will be made easy enough; let me see; some little genteel present to begin with: what have you got about you? Ay, search; I can bestow it to advantage, there's no time to be lost.

BELCOUR. Hang it, confound it; a plague upon't, say I! I hav'n't a guinea left in my pocket; I parted from my whole stock here this morning, and have forgot to supply myself since.

MRS. FULMER. Mighty well; let it pass then; there's an end; think no more of the lady, that's all.

BELCOUR. Distraction! think no more of her? let me only step home and provide myself, I'll be back with you in an instant.

MRS. FULMER. Pooh, pooh! that's a wretched shift: have you nothing of value about you? Money's a coarse slovenly vehicle, fit only to bribe electors in a borough; there are more graceful ways of purchasing a lady's favours; rings, trinkets, jewels!

BELCOUR. Jewels! Gadso, I protest I had forgot: I have a case of jewels; but they won't do, I must not part from them; no, no, they are appropriated; they are none of my own.

MRS. FULMER. Let me see, let me see! Ay, now, this were something-like: pretty creatures, how they sparkle! these wou'd ensure success.

BELCOUR. Indeed!

MRS. FULMER. These wou'd make her your own for ever.

BELCOUR. Then the deuce take 'em for belonging to another person; I cou'd find in my heart to give 'em the girl, and swear I've lost them.

MRS. FULMER. Ay, do, say they were stolen out of your pocket.

BELCOUR. No, hang it, that's dishonourable; here, give me the paltry things, I'll write you an order on my merchant for double their value.

MRS. FULMER. An order! No; order for me no orders upon merchants, with their value received, and three days grace; their noting, protesting, and endorsing, and all their counting-house formalities;[61] I'll have nothing to do with them; leave your diamonds with me, and give your order for the value of them to the owner; the money would be as good as the trinkets, I warrant you.

BELCOUR. Hey! how! I never thought of that; but a breach of trust; 'tis impossible; I never can consent, therefore, give me the jewels back again.

MRS. FULMER. Take 'em; I am now to tell you the lady is in this house.

BELCOUR. In this house?

MRS. FULMER. Yes, Sir, in this very house; but what of that? You have got what you like better; your toys, your trinkets; go, go: Oh! you're a man of a notable spirit, are you not?

BELCOUR. Provoking creature! Bring me to the sight of the dear girl, and dispose of me as you think fit.

MRS. FULMER. And of the diamonds too?

BELCOUR. Damn 'em, I wou'd there was not such a bauble in nature! But come, come, dispatch; if I had the throne of Dehli[62] I should give it to her.

MRS. FULMER. Swear to me then that you will keep within bounds, remember she passes for the sister of young Dudley. Oh! if you come to your flights, and your rhapsodies, she'll be off in an instant.

BELCOUR. Never fear me.

MRS. FULMER. You must expect to hear her talk of her father, as she calls him, and her brother, and your bounty to her family.

BELCOUR. Ay, ay, never mind what she talks of, only bring her.

MRS. FULMER. You'll be prepar'd upon that head?

BELCOUR. I shall be prepar'd, never fear; away with you.

MRS. FULMER. But hold, I had forgot: not a word of the diamonds; leave that matter to my management.

BELCOUR. Hell and vexation! Get out of the room, or I shall run distracted. [*Exit* Mrs. Fulmer] Of a certain, Belcour, thou art born to be the fool of woman: sure no man sins with so much repentance, or repents with so little amendment, as I do. I cannot give away another person's property, honour forbids me; and I positively cannot give up the girl; love, passion, constitution, every thing protests against that. How shall I decide? I cannot bring myself to break a trust, and I am not at present in the humour to baulk my inclinations. Is there no middle way? Let me consider—There is, there is: my good genius has presented me with one; apt, obvious, honourable: the girl shall not go without her baubles, I'll not go without the girl, Miss Rusport shan't lose her diamonds, I'll save Dudley from destruction, and every party shall be a gainer by the project.

III.iv

Mrs. Fulmer *introducing* Miss Dudley.

MRS. FULMER. Miss Dudley, this is the worthy gentleman you wish to see; this is Mr. Belcour.

LOUISA. [*Aside*] *As I live, the very man that beset me in the streets.*

BELCOUR. [*Aside*] *An angel, by this light! Oh I am gone past all retrieving!*

LOUISA. Mrs. Fulmer, Sir, informs me you are the gentleman from whom my father has received such civilities.

BELCOUR. Oh! never name 'em.

LOUISA. Pardon me, Mr. Belcour, they must be both named and remember'd; and if my father was here—

BELCOUR. I am much better pleased with his representative.

LOUISA. That title is my brother's, Sir; I have no claim to it.

BELCOUR. I believe it.

LOUISA. But as neither he nor my father were fortunate enough to be at home, I cou'd not resist the opportunity—

BELCOUR. Nor I neither, by my soul, Madam: let us improve it, therefore. I am in love with you to distraction; I was charmed at the first glance; I attempted to accost you; you fled; I follow'd; but was defeated of an interview; at length I have obtain'd one, and seize the opportunity of casting my person and my fortune at your feet.

LOUISA. You astonish me! Are you in your senses, or do you make a jest of my misfortunes? Do you ground pretences on your generosity, or do you make a practice of this folly with every woman you meet?

BELCOUR. Upon my life, no: as you are the handsomest woman I ever met, so you are the first to whom I ever made the like professions: as for my generosity, Madam, I must refer you on that score to this good lady, who I believe has something to offer in my behalf.

LOUISA. Don't build upon that, Sir; I must have better proofs of your generosity, than the mere divestment of a little superfluous dross, before I can credit the sincerity of professions so abruptly deliver'd. [*Exit hastily.*

BELCOUR. Oh! ye gods and goddesses, how her anger animates her beauty! [*Going out.*

MRS. FULMER. Stay, Sir; if you stir a step after her, I renounce your interest for ever: why you'll ruin every thing.

BELCOUR. Well, I must have her, cost what it will: I see she understands her own value tho'; a little superfluous dross, truly! She must have better proofs of my generosity.

MRS. FULMER. 'Tis exactly as I told you; your money she calls dross; she's too proud to stain her fingers with your coin; bait your hook well with jewels; try that experiment, and she's your own.

BELCOUR. Take 'em; let 'em go; lay 'em at her feet; I must get out of the scrape as I can; my propensity is irresistible: there! you have 'em; they are yours; they are hers; but remember they are a trust; I commit them to her keeping till I can buy 'em off with something she shall think more valuable; now tell me when shall I meet her?

MRS. FULMER. How can I tell that? Don't you see what an alarm you have put her into? Oh! you're a rare one! But go your ways for this while; leave her to my management, and come to me at seven this evening; but remember not to bring empty pockets with you—Ha! ha! ha! [*Exeunt severally.*

III.v

Lady Rusport*'s house.* Miss Rusport *enters, followed by a* Servant.

CHARLOTTE. Desire Mr. Stockwell to walk in.

[*Exit* Servant. Stockwell *enters.*

STOCKWELL. Madam, your most obedient servant: I am honoured with your commands, by Captain Dudley; and have brought the money with me as you directed: I understand the sum you have occasion for is two hundred pounds.

CHARLOTTE. It is, Sir; I am quite confounded at your taking this trouble upon yourself, Mr. Stockwell.

STOCKWELL. There is a banknote, Madam, to the amount: your jewels are in safe hands, and will be delivered to you directly. If I had been happy in being better known to you, I should have hoped you would not have thought it necessary to place a deposit in iny hands for so trifling a sum as you have now required me to supply you with.

CHARLOTTE. The bawbles I sent you may very well be spared; and, as they are the only security in my present situation I can give you, I could wish you would retain them in your hands: when I am of age, (which, if I live a few months, I shall be) I will replace your favour, with thanks.

STOCKWELL. It is obvious, Miss Rusport, that your charms will suffer no impeachment by the absence of these superficial ornaments; but they should be seen in the suite of a woman of fashion, not as creditors to whom you are indebted for your appearance, but as subservient attendants, which help to make up your equipage.

CHARLOTTE. Mr. Stockwell is determined not to wrong the confidence I reposed in his politeness.

STOCKWELL. I have only to request, Madam, that you will allow Mr. Belcour, a young gentleman, in whose happiness I particularly interest myself, to have the honour of delivering you the box of jewels.

CHARLOTTE. Most gladly; any friend of yours cannot fail of being welcome here.

STOCKWELL. I flatter myself you will not find him totally undeserving your good opinion; an education, not of the strictest kind, and strong animal spirits, are apt sometimes to betray him into youthful irregularities; but an high principle of honour, and an uncommon benevolence, in the eye of candor, will, I hope, atone for any faults, by which these good qualities are not impaired.

CHARLOTTE. I dare say Mr. Belcour's behaviour wants no apology: we've no right to be over strict in canvassing the morals of a common acquaintance.

STOCKWELL. I wish it may be my happiness to see Mr. Belcour in the list, not of your common, but particular acquaintance, of your friends, Miss Rusport—I dare not be more explicit.

CHARLOTTE. Nor need you, Mr. Stockwell: I shall be studious to deserve his friendship; and, though I have long since unaterably placed my affections on another, I trust, I have not left myself insensible to the merits of Mr. Belcour; and hope that neither you nor he will, for that reason, think me less worthy your good opinion and regards.

STOCKWELL. Miss Rusport, I sincerely wish you happy: I have no doubt you have placed your affection on a deserving man; and I have no right to combat your choice. [*Exit.*

CHARLOTTE. How honourable is that behaviour! Now, if Charles was here, I should be happy. The old lady is so fond of her new Irish acquaintance, that I have the whole house at my disposal. [*Exit* Charlotte.

III.vi

[Belcour *enters, preceded by a* Servant.

SERVANT. I ask your honour's pardon; I thought my young lady was here: who shall I inform her wou'd speak to her?

BELCOUR. Belcour is my name, Sir; and pray beg your lady to put herself in no hurry on my account; for I'd sooner see the devil than see her face. [*Exit* Servant] In the name of all that's mischievous, why did Stockwell drive me hither in such haste? A pretty figure, truly, I shall make: an ambassador without credentials.[63] Blockhead that I was to charge myself with her diamonds; officious, meddling puppy! Now they are irretrievably gone: that suspicious jade Fulmer wouldn't part even with a sight of them, tho' I would have ransom'd 'em at twice their value. Now must I trust to my poor wits to bring me off: a lamentable dependance. Fortune be my helper! Here comes the girl—If she is noble minded, as she is said to be, she will forgive me; if not, 'tis a lost cause; for I have not thought of one word in my excuse.

III.vii

[Charlotte *enters.*

CHARLOTTE. Mr. Belcour, I'm proud to see you: your friend, Mr. Stockwell, prepared me to expect this honour; and I am happy in the oppotunity of being known to you.

BELCOUR. [*Aside*] *A fine girl, by my soul! Now what a cursed hang-dog*[64] *do I look like!*

CHARLOTTE. You are newly arrived in this country, Sir?

BELCOUR. Just landed, Madam; just set a-shore, with a large cargo of Muscavado sugars,[65] rum-puncheons, mahogany-slabs, wet sweet-meats, and green paroquets.

CHARLOTTE. May I ask you how you like London, Sir?

BELCOUR. To admiration: I think the town and the town's-folk are exacty suited; 'tis a great, rich, overgrown, noisy, tumultuous place: the whole morning is a bustle to get money, and the whole afternoon is a hurry to spend it.

CHARLOTTE. Are these all the observations you have made?

BELCOUR. No, Madam; I have observed the women are very captivating, and the men very soon caught.

CHARLOTTE. Ay, indeed! Whence do you draw that conclusion?

BELCOUR. From infallible guides; the first remark I collect from what I now see, the second from what I now feel.

CHARLOTTE. Oh, the deuce take you! but to wave this subject; I believe, Sir, this was a visit of business, not compliment; was it not?

BELCOUR. Ay;—[*Aside*] *now comes on my execution.*

CHARLOTTE. You have some foolish trinkets of mine, Mr, Belcour; havn't you?

BELCOUR. No, in truth;—[*Aside*] *they are gone in search of a trinket, still more foolish than themselves.*

CHARLOTTE. Some diamonds I mean, Sir; Mr. Stockwell inform'd me you was charg'd with 'em.

BELCOUR. Oh, yes, Madam; but I have the most treacherous memory in life—Here they are! Pray put them up; they're all right; you need not examine 'em. [*Gives a box.*

CHARLOTTE. Hey-dey! right, Sir! Why these are not my diamonds; these are quite different; and, as it should seem, of much greater value.

BELCOUR. Upon my life I'm glad on't; for then I hope you value 'em more than your own.

CHARLOTTE. As a purchaser I should, but not as an owner; you mistake; these belong to somebody else.

BELCOUR. 'Tis yours, I'm afraid, that belong to somebody else.

CHARLOTTE. What is it you mean? I must insist upon your taking 'em back again.

BELCOUR. Pray, Madam, don't do that; I shall infallibly lose them; I have the worst luck with diamonds of any man living.

CHARLOTTE. That you might well say, was you to give me these in the place of mine; but pray, Sir, what is the reason of all this? Why have you changed the jewels? And where have you disposed of mine?

BELCOUR. Miss Rusport, I cannot invent a lie for my life; and, if it was to save it, I coudn't tell one: I am an idle, dissipated, unthinking fellow, not worth your notice; in short, I am a West-Indian;[66] and you must try me according to the charter of my colony, not by a jury of English spinsters: truth is, I've given away your jewels: caught with a pair of sparkling eyes, whose lustre blinded theirs, I served your property as I shou'd my own, and lavish'd it away; let me not totally despair of your forgiveness: I frequently do wrong, but never with impunity; if your displeasure is added to my own, my punishment will be too severe. When I parted from the jewels, I had not the honour of knowing their owner.

CHARLOTTE. Mr. Belcour, your sincerity charms me; I enter at once into your character, and I make all the allowances for it you can desire. I take your jewels for the present, because I know there is no other way of reconciling you to yourself; but, if I give way to your spirit in one point, you must yield to mine in another: remember I will not keep more than the value of my own jewels: there is no need to be pillaged by more than one woman at a time, Sir.

BELCOUR. Now, may every blessing that can crown your virtues, and reward your beauty, be shower'd upon you; may you meet admiration without envy, love without jealousy, and old age without malady! may the man of your heart be ever constant, and you never meet a less penitent, or less grateful offender than myself!

[Servant *enters and delivers a letter.*

CHARLOTTE. Does your letter require such haste?

SERVANT. I was bade to give it into your own hands, Madam.

CHARLOTTE. From Charles Dudley, I see—have I your permission? Good Heaven, what do I read Mr. Belcour, you are concern'd in this—

"Dear Charlotte, in the midst of our distress, Providence has cast a benefactor in our way, after the most unexpected manner: a young West-Indian, rich, and, with a warmth of heart peculiar to his climate, has rescued my father from his troubles, satisfied his wants, and enabled him to accomplish his exchange: when I relate to you the manner in which this was done, you will be charm'd; I can only now add, that it was by chance we found out that his name is Belcour, and that he is a friend of Mr. Stockwell's. I lose not a moment's time, in making you acquainted with this fortunate event, for reasons which delicacy obliges me to suppress; but, perhaps, if you have not received the money on your jewels, you will not think it necessary now to do it. I have the honour to be, Dear Madam, most faithfully yours, Charles Dudley." Is this your doing, Sir? Never was generosity so worthily exerted.

BELCOUR. Or so greatly overpaid.

CHARLOTTE. After what you have now done for this noble, but indigent family, let me not scruple to unfold the whole situation of my heart to you. Know then, Sir, (and don't think the worse of me for the frankness of my declaration) that such is my attachment to the son of that worthy officer, whom you relieved, that the moment I am of age, and in possession of my fortune, I shou'd hold myself the happiest of women to share it with young Dudley.

BELCOUR. Say you so, Madam! then let me perish if I don't love and reverence you above all woman kind; and, if such is your generous resolution, never wait till you're of age; life is too short, pleasure too fugitive; the soul grows narrower every hour; I'll equip you for your escape; I'll convey you to the man of your heart, and away with you then to the first hospitable parson that will take you in.

CHARLOTTE. O blessed be the torrid zone for ever, whose rapid vegetation quickens nature into such benignity! These latitudes are made for politics and philosophy; friendship has no root in this soil. But, had I spirit to accept your offer, which is not improbable, woud'nt it be a mortifying thing, for a fond girl to find herself mistaken, and sent back to her home, like a vagrant; and such, for what I know, might be my case.

BELCOUR. Then he ought to be proscribed the society of mankind forever—[*Aside*] *Ay, ay, 'tis the sham sister that makes him thus indifferent; 'twill be a meritorious office to take that girl out of the way.*

III.viii

[Servant *enters.*

SERVANT. Miss Dudley to wait on you, Madam.

BELCOUR. Who?

SERVANT. Miss Dudley.

CHARLOTTE. What's the matter, Mr. Belcour? Are you frighted at the name of a pretty girl? 'Tis the sister of him we were speaking of—pray admit her.

BELCOUR. The sister! So, so; he has imposed on her too—this is an extraordinary visit, truly. Upon my soul, the assurance of some folks is not to be accounted for.

CHARLOTTE. I insist upon your not running away; you'll be charm'd with Louisa Dudley.

BELCOUR. Oh, yes, I am charmed with her.

CHARLOTTE. You've seen her then, have you?

BELCOUR. Yes, yes, I've seen her.

CHARLOTTE. Well, isn't she a delightful girl?

BELCOUR. Very delightful.

CHARLOTTE. Why, you answer as if you was in a court of justice: O'my conscience! I believe you are caught; I've a notion she has trick'd you out of your heart.

BELCOUR. I believe she has, and you out of your jewels; for, to tell you the truth, she's the very person I gave 'em to.

CHARLOTTE. You gave her my jewels! Louisa Dudley my jewels? Admirable! inimitable! Oh, the sly little jade! but hush, here she comes; I don't know how I shall keep my countenance. [Louisa *enters*] My dear, I'm rejoiced to see you; how d'ye do? I beg leave to introduce Mr. Belcour, a very worthy friend of mine; I believe, Louisa, you have seen him before.

LOUISA. I have met the gentleman.

CHARLOTTE. You have met the gentleman: well, Sir, and you have met the lady; in short, you have met each other; why then don't you speak to each other? How you both stand! tongue-tied, and fix'd as statues—Ha, ha, ha! Why you'll fall asleep by-and-by.

LOUISA. Fye upon you; fye upon you; is this fair?

BELCOUR. [*Aside*] *Upon my soul, I never look'd so like a fool in my life; the assurance of that girl puts me quite down.*

CHARLOTTE. Sir—Mr. Belcour—Was it your pleasure to advance any thing? Not a syllable. Come, Louisa, women's wit, they say, is never at a loss—Nor you neither? Speechless both—Why you was merry enough before this lady came in.

LOUISA. I am sorry I have been any interruption to your happiness, Sir.

BELCOUR. Madam.

CHARLOTTE. Madam! Is that all you can say? But come, my dear girl, I won't teaze you: apropos! I must shew you what a fine present this dumb[67] gentleman has made me: are not these handsome diamonds?

LOUISA. Yes, indeed, they seem very fine; but I am no judge of these things.

CHARLOTTE. Oh, you wicked little hypocrite, you are no judge of these things, Louisa; you have no diamonds, not you.

LOUISA. You know I havn't, Miss Rusport: you know those things are infinitely above my reach.

CHARLOTTE. Ha! ha! ha!

BELCOUR. [*Aside*] *She does tell a lie with an admirable countenance, that's true enough.*

LOUISA. What ails you, Charlotte? What impertinence have I been guilty of that you should find it necessary to humble me at such a rate? If you are happy, long may you be so; but, surely, it can be no addition to it to make me miserable.

CHARLOTTE. So serious! there must be some mystery in this—Mr. Belcour, will you leave us together? You see I treat you with all the familiarity of an old acquaintance already.

BELCOUR. Oh, by all means; pray, command me. Miss Rusport, I'm your most obedient! By your condescension in accepting those poor trifles, I am under eternal obligations to you—To you, Miss Dudley, I shall not offer a word on that subject: you despise finery; you have a soul above it; I adore your spirit; I was rather unprepared for meeting you here; but I shall hope for an opportunity of making myself better known to you. [*Exit.*

III.ix

Charlotte *and* Louisa.

CHARLOTTE. Louisa Dudley, you surprize me; I never saw you act thus before: can't you bear a little innocent raillery before the man of your heart?

LOUISA. The man of my heart, Madam? Be assured I never was so visionary to aspire to any man whom Miss Rusport honours with her choice.

CHARLOTTE. My choice, my dear! Why we are playing at cross purposes; how enter'd it into your head that Mr. Belcour was the man of my choice?

LOUISA. Why, didn't he present you with those diamonds?

CHARLOTTE. Well; perhaps he did—and pray, Louisa, have you no diamonds?

LOUISA. I, diamonds truly! Who should give me diamonds?

CHARLOTTE. Who, but this very gentleman: apropos! here comes your brother—

III.x

[Charles *enters.*

CHARLOTTE. [*Continuing*] I insist upon referring our dispute to him: your sister and I, Charles, have a quarrel; Belcour, the hero of your letter, has just left us—some how or other, Louisa's bright eyes have caught him; and the poor fellow's fallen desperately in love with her—(don't interrupt me, hussey)—Well, that's excusable enough, you'll say; but the jet of the story is, that this hair-brain'd spark, who does nothing like other people, has given her the very identical jewels, which you pledged for me to Mr. Stockwell; and will you believe that this little demure slut[68] made up a face, and squeezed out three or four hypocritical tears, because I rallied her about it?

CHARLES. I'm all astonishment! Louisa, tell me without reserve, has Mr. Belcour given you any diamonds?

LOUISA. None, upon my honour.

CHARLES. Has he made any professions to you?

LOUISA. He has; but altogether in a stile so whimsical and capricious, that the best which can be said of them is to tell you that they seem'd more the result of good spirits than good manners.

CHARLOTTE. Ay, ay, now the murder's out; he's in love with her, and she has no very great dislike to him; trust to my observation, Charles, for that: as to the diamonds, there's some mistake about them, and you must clear it up: three minutes' conversation with him will put every thing in a right train; go, go, Charles, 'tis a brother's business; about it instantly; ten to one you'll find him over the way at Mr. Stockwell's.

CHARLES. I confess I'm impatient to have the case clear'd up; I'll take your advice, and find him out: good bye to you.

CHARLOTTE. Your servant; my life upon it you'll find Belcour a man of honour. Come, Louisa, let us adjourn to my dressing-room; I've a little private business to transact with you, before the old lady comes up to tea, and interrupts us. [*Exeunt.*

IV.i

Fulmer*'s house.* Fulmer *and* Mrs. Fulmer.

FULMER. Patty, wasn't Mr. Belcour with you?

MRS. FULMER. He was, and is now shut up in my chamber, in high expedation of an interview with Miss Dudley; she's at present with her brother, and 'twas with some difficulty I persuaded my hot-headed spark to wait till he has left her.

FULMER. Well, child, and what then?

MRS. FULMER. Why then, Mr. Fulmer, I think it will be time for you and me to steal a march, and be gone.

FULMER. So this is all the fruit of your ingenious project; a shameful overthrow, or a sudden flight.

MRS. FULMER. Why, my project was a mere impromptu, and can at worst but quicken our departure a few days; you know we had fairly outliv'd our credit here, and a trip to Boulogne is no ways unseasonable. Nay, never droop, man—Hark! hark! here's enough to bear charges [*Shewing a purse.*

FULMER. Let me see, let me see: this weighs well; this is of the right sort: why your West-Indian bled freely.

MRS. FULMER. But that's not all: look here! Here are the sparklers! [*Shewing the jewels*] Now what d'ye think of my performances? Heh! a foolish scheme, isn't it—a silly woman—?

FULMER. Thou art a Judith, a Joan of Arc,[69] and I'll march under thy banners, girl, to the world's end: come, let's begone; I've little to regret; my creditors may share the old books amongst them; they'll have occasion for philosophy to support their loss; they'll find enough upon my shelves: the world is my library; I read mankind—Now, Patty, lead the way.

MRS. FULMER. Adieu, Belcour!

[*Exeunt.*

IV.ii

[*Enter* Charles Dudley *and* Louisa.

CHARLES. Well, Louisa, I confess the force of what you say: I accept Miss Rusport's bounty; and, when you see my generous Charlotte, tell her—but have a care, there is a selfishness even in gratitude, when it is too profuse; to be over-thankful for any one favour is in effect to lay out for another; the best return I cou'd make my benefactress wou'd be never to see her more.

LOUISA. I understand you.

CHARLES. We that are poor, Louisa, shou'd be cautious; for this reason, I wou'd guard you against Belcour; at least till I can unravel the mystery of Miss Rusport's diamonds; I was disappointed of finding him at Mr. Stockwell's, and am now going in search of him again: he may intend honourably; but, I confess to you, I am stagger'd; think no more of him, therefore, for the present: of this be sure, while I have life, and you have honour, I will protect you, or perish in your defence. [*Exit.*

LOUISA. Think of him no more! Well, I'll obey; but if a wand'ring uninvited thought should creep by chance into my bosom, must I not give the harmless wretch a shelter? Oh! yes; the great artificer of the human heart knows every thread he wove into its fabric, nor puts his work to harder uses than it was made to bear: my wishes then, my guiltless ones, I mean, are free; how fast they spring within me at that sentence! Down, down, ye busy creatures! Whither wou'd you carry me? Ah! there is one amongst you, a forward, new intruder, that, in the likeness of an offending, generous man, grows into favour with my heart. Fye, fye upon it! Belcour pursues, insults me; yet, such is the fatality[70] of my condition, that what shou'd rouse resentment, only calls up love.

IV.iii

[Belcour *enters to her.*

BELCOUR. Alone, by all that's happy!

LOUISA. Ah!

BELCOUR. Oh! shriek not, start not, stir not, loveliest creature! but let me kneel, and gaze upon your beauties.

LOUISA. Sir! Mr. Belcour, rise! What is it you do?

BELCOUR. See, I obey you; mould me as you will, behold, your ready servant! New to your country, ignorant of your manners, habits, and desires, I put myself into your hands for instruction; make me only such as you can like yourself, and I shall be happy.

LOUISA. I must not hear this, Mr. Belcour; go; he that parted from me but this minute, now return, I tremble for the consequence.

BELCOUR. Fear nothing; let him come: I love you. Madam; he'll find it hard to make me unsay that.

LOUISA. You terrify me; your impetuous temper frightens me; you know my situation; it is not generous to pursue me thus.

BELCOUR. True; I do know your situation, your real one, Miss Dudley, and am resolv'd to snatch you from it; 'twill be a meritorious act; the old Captain shall rejoice; Miss Rusport shall be made happy; and even he, even your beloved brother, with whose resentment you threaten me, shall in the end applaud and thank me: come, thou'rt a dear enchanting girl, and I'm determin'd not to live a minute longer without thee.

LOUISA. Hold, are you mad? I see you are a bold, assuming man, and know not where to stop.

BELCOUR. Who that beholds such beauty can? By Heaven, you put my blood into a flame. Provoking girl! is it within the stretch of my fortune to content you? What is it you can further ask that I am not ready to grant?

LOUISA. Yes, with the same facility that you bestow'd upon me Miss Rusport's diamonds. For shame! for shame! was that a manly story?

BELCOUR. So! so! these devilish diamonds meet me every where—Let me perish if I mean't you any harm: Oh! I cou'd tear my tongue out for saying a word about the matter.

LOUISA. Go to her then, and contradict it; till that is done, my reputation is at stake.

BELCOUR.—[*Aside*] *Her reputation! Now she has got upon that, she'll go on for ever.*—[*To her*] What is there I will not do for your sake? I will go to Miss Rusport.

LOUISA. Do so; restore her own jewels to her, which I suppose you kept back for the purpose of presenting others to her of a greater value; but for the future, Mr. Belcour, when you wou'd do a galant action to that lady, don't let it be at my expence.

BELCOUR.—[*Aside*] *I see where she points: she is willing enough to give up Miss Rusport's diamonds, now she finds she shall be a gainer by the exchange. Be it so! 'Tis what I wish'd.*—[*To her*]—Well, Madam, I will return Miss Rusport her own jewels, and you shall have others of tenfold their value.

LOUISA. No, Sir, you err most widely; it is my good opinion, not my vanity, which you must bribe.

BELCOUR.—[*Aside*] *Why, what the devil wou'd she have now?*—[*To her*]—Miss Dudley, it is my wish to obey and please you, but I have some apprehension that we mistake each other.

LOUISA. I think we do: tell me, then, in few words, what it is you aim at.

BELCOUR. In few words, then, and in plain honesty, I must tell you, so entirely am I captivated with you, that had you but been such as it would have become me to have call'd my wife, I had been happy in knowing you by that name; as it is, you are welcome to partake my fortune, give me in return your person, give me pleasure, give me love; free, disencumber'd, antimatrimonial love.

LOUISA. Stand off, and let me never see you more.

BELCOUR. Hold, hold, thou dear, tormenting, tantalizing girl! Upon my knees I swear you shall not stir till you've consented to my bliss.

LOUISA. Unhand me, Sir: O Charles! protect me, rescue me, redress me. [*Exit.*

IV.iv

[Charles Dudley *enters.*

CHARLES. How's this! Rise, villain, and defend yourself.

BELCOUR. Villain!

CHARLES. The man who wrongs that lady is a villain—Draw!

BELCOUR. Never fear me, young gentleman; brand me for a coward, if I baulk you.

CHARLES. Yet hold! Let me not be too hasty: your name I think, is Belcour.

BELCOUR. Well, Sir.

CHARLES. How is it, Mr. Belcour, you have done this mean, unmanly wrong; beneath the mask of generosity to give this fatal stab to our domestic peace? You might have had my thanks, my blessing; take my defiance now. 'Tis Dudley speaks to you, the brother, the protector of that injur'd lady.

BELCOUR. The brother? Give yourself a truer title.

CHARLES. What is't you mean?

BELCOUR. Come, come, I know both her and you: I found you. Sir, (but how or why I know not) in the good graces of Miss Rusport—(yes, colour at the name!) I gave you no disturbance there, never broke in upon you in that rich and plenteous quarter; but, when I cou'd have blasted all your projects with a word, spar'd you, in foolish pity spar'd you, nor rouz'd her from the fond credulity in which your artifice had lull'd her.

CHARLES. No, Sir, nor boasted to her of the splendid present you had made my poor Louisa;

the diamonds, Mr. Belcour; how was that? What can you plead to that arraignment?

BELCOUR. You question me too late; the name of Belcour and of villain never met before: had you enquir'd of me before you utter'd that rash word, you might have sav'd yourself or me a mortal error: now, Sir, I neither give nor take an explanation; so, come on! [*They fight.*

IV.v

[*Enter* Louisa, *and afterwards* O'Flaherty.

LOUISA. Hold, hold, for Heaven's sake hold! Charles! Mr. Belcour! Help! Sir, Sir, make haste, they'll murder one another.

O'FLAHERTY. Hell and confusion! What's all this uproar for? Can't you leave off cutting one another's throats, and mind what the poor girl says to you? You've done a notable thing, hav'n't you both, to put her into such a flurry? I think, o' my conscience, she's the most frighted of the three.

CHARLES. Dear Louisa, recollect yourself; why did you interfere? 'Tis in your cause.

BELCOUR. Now cou'd I kill him for caressing her.

O'FLAHERTY. O Sir, your most obedient! You are the gentleman I had the honour of meeting here before; you was then running off at full speed like a Calmuc,[71] now you are tilting and driving like a Bedlamite with this lad here, that seems as mad as yourself:[72] 'tis pity but your country had a little more employment for you both.

BELCOUR. Mr. Dudley, when you've recover 'd the lady, you know where I am to be found. [*Exit.*

O'FLAHERTY. Well then, can't you stay where you are, and that will save the trouble of looking after you? Yon volatile fellow thinks to give a man the meeting by getting out of his way: by my soul 'tis a round-about method that of his. But I think he call'd you Dudley: Hark'e, young man, are you son of my friend the old Captain?

CHARLES. I am. Help me to convey this lady to her chamber, and I shall be more at leisure to answer your questions.

O'FLAHERTY. Ay will I: come along, pretty one; if you've had wrong done you, young man, you need look no further for a second; Dennis O'Flaherty's your man for that: but never draw your sword before a woman, Dudley; damn it, never while you live draw your sword before a woman.

[*Exeunt.*

IV.vi

Lady Rusport'*s house.* Lady Rusport *and* Servant.

SERVANT. An elderly gentleman, who says his name is Varland, desires leave to wait on your ladyship.

LADY RUSPORT. Shew him in; the very man I wish to see: Varland, he was Sir Oliver's sollicitor, and privy to all his affairs; he brings some good tidings, some fresh mortgage, or another bond come to light; they start up everyday. [Varland *enters*] Mr. Varland, I'm glad to see you; you're heartily welcome, honest Mr. Varland; you and I havn't met since our late irreparable loss: how have you passed your time this age?

VARLAND. Truly, my lady, ill enough: I thought I must have followed good Sir Oliver.

LADY RUSPORT. Alack-a-day, poor man! Well, Mr. Varland, you find me here overwhelmed with trouble and fatigue; torn to pieces with a multiplicity of affairs; a great fortune poured upon me unsought for and unexpected: 'twas my good father's will and pleasure it should be so, and I must submit.

VARLAND. Your ladyship inherits under a will made in the year forty-five,[73] immediately after Captain Dudley's marriage with your sister.

LADY RUSPORT. I do so, Mr. Varland; I do so.

VARLAND. I well remember it; I engrossed every syllable; but I am surprized to find your ladyship set so little store by this vast accession.

LADY RUSPORT. Why you know, Mr. Varland, I am a moderate woman; I had enough before; a small matter satisfies me; and Sir Stephen Rusport (Heaven be his portion!) took care I shouldn't want that.

VARLAND. Very true; very true, he did so; and I am overjoyed at finding your ladyship in this disposition; for, truth to say, I was not without apprehension the news I have to communicate would have been of some prejudice to your ladyship's tranquility.

LADY RUSPORT. News, Sir! What news have you for me?

VARLAND. Nay, nothing to alarm you; a trifle, in your present way of thinking: I have a will of Sir Oliver's you have never seen.

LADY RUSPORT. A will! Impossible! How came you by it, pray?

VARLAND. I drew it up, at his command, in his last illness: it will save you a world of trouble: it gives his whole estate from you to his grandson, Charles Dudley.

LADY RUSPORT. To Dudley? His estate to Charles Dudley? I can't support it! I shall faint! You've killed me, you vile man! I never shall survive it!

VARLAND. Look'e there now: I protest, I thought you would have rejoiced at being clear of the incumbrance.

LADY RUSPORT. 'Tis false; 'tis all a forgery, concerted between you and Dudley; why else did I never hear of it before?

VARLAND. Have patience, my lady, and I'll tell you: By Sir Oliver's direction, I was to deliver this will into no hands but his grandson Dudley's: the young gentleman happen'd to be then in Scotland; I was dispatch'd thither in search of him: the hurry and fatigue of my journey brought on a fever by the way, which confined me in extreme danger for several days; upon my recovery, I pursued my journey, found young Dudley had left Scotland in the interim, and am now directed hither; where, as soon I can find him, doubtless, I shall discharge my conscience, and fulfil my commission.

LADY RUSPORT. Dudley then, as yet, knows nothing of this will?

VARLAND. Nothing; that secret rests with me.

LADY RUSPORT.—[*Aside*] *A thought occurs: by this fellow's talking of his conscience, I should guess it was upon sale.*—[*To him*] Come, Mr. Varland, if 'tis as you say, I must submit. I was somewhat flurried at first, and forgot myself; I ask your pardon: this is no place to talk of business; step with me into my room; we will there compare the will, and resolve accordingly—[*Aside*] *Oh! would your fever had you, and I had your paper.*

[*Exeunt.*

IV.vii

Miss Rusport, Charles, *and* O'Flaherty.

CHARLOTTE. So, so! My lady and her lawyer have retired to close confabulation: now, Major, if you are the generous man I take you for, grant me one favour.

O'FLAHERTY. Faith will I, and not think much of my generosity neither; for, though it may not be in my power to do the favour you ask, look you, it can never be in my heart to refuse it.

CHARLES. [*Aside*] *Cou'd this man's tongue do justice to his thoughts, how eloquent would he be!*

CHARLOTTE. Plant yourself then in that room: keep guard, for a few moments, upon the enemy's motions, in the chamber beyond; and, if they should attempt a sally, stop their march a moment, till your friend here can make good his retreat down the back-stairs.

O'FLAHERTY. A word to the wise! I'm an old campaigner; make the best use of your time; and trust me for tying the old cat up to the picket.

CHARLOTTE. Hush! hush! not so loud.

CHARLES. 'Tis the office of a centinel, Major, you have undertaken, rather than that of a field-officer.

O'FLAHERTY. 'Tis the office of a friend, my dear boy; and, therefore, no disgrace to a general. [*Exit.*

IV.viii

Charles *and* Charlotte.

CHARLOTTE. Well, Charles, will you commit yourself to me for a few minutes?

CHARLES. Most readily; and let me, before one goes by, tender you the only payment I can ever make for your abundant generosity.

CHARLOTTE. Hold, hold! so vile a thing as money must not come between us. What shall I say! O Charles! O Dudley! What difficulties have you thrown upon me! Familiarly as we have lived, I shrink not at what I'm doing; and, anxiously as I have sought this opportunity, my fears almost persuade me to abandon it.

CHARLES. You alarm me!

CHARLOTTE. Your looks and actions have been so distant, and at this moment are so deterring, that, was it not for the hope that delicacy, and not disgust, inspires this conduct in you, I should sink with shame and apprehension; but time presses; and I must speak; and plainly too—Was you now in possession of your grandfather's estate, as justly you ought to be; and, was you inclined to seek a companion for life, should you, or should you not, in that case, honour your unworthy Charlotte with your choice?

CHARLES. My unworthy Charlotte! So judge me Heaven, there is not a circumstance on earth so valuable as your happiness, so dear to me as your person; but to bring poverty, disgrace, reproach from friends, ridicule from all the world, upon a generous benefactress; thievishly to steal into an open, unreserved, ingenuous heart, O Charlotte! dear, unhappy girl, it is not to be done.

CHARLOTTE. Nay, now you rate too highly the poor advantages fortune alone has given me over you: how otherwise could we bring our merits to any balance? Come, my dear Charles, I have enough; make that enough still more, by sharing it with me; sole heiress of my father's fortune, a short time will put it in my disposal; in the mean while you will be sent to join your regiment; let us prevent a separation, by setting out this very night for that happy country where marriage still is free:[74] carry me this moment to Belcour's lodgings.

CHARLES. Belcour's?—[*Aside*] *The name is ominous; there's murder in it: bloody inexorable honour!*

CHARLOTTE. D'ye pause? Put me into his hands, while you provide the means for our escape: he is the most generous, the most honourable of men.

CHARLES. Honourable! most honourable!

CHARLOTTE. Can you doubt it? Do you demur? Have you forgot your letter? Why, Belcour 'twas that prompted me to this proposal, that promised to supply the means, that nobly offer'd his unask'd assistance—

[O'Flaherty *enters hastily.*

O'FLAHERTY. Run, run, for holy St. Antony's sake, to horse and away![75] The conference is broke up, and the old lady advances upon a full piedmontese trot, within pistol-shot of your encampment.

CHARLOTTE. Here, here, down the back-stairs! O, Charles, remember me!

CHARLES. Farewell! Now, now I feel myself a coward. [*Exit.*

CHARLOTTE. What does he mean?

O'FLAHERTY. Ask no questions, but be gone: she has cooled the lad's courage, and wonders he feels like a coward. There's a damn'd deal of mischief brewing between this hyena and her lawyer: egad I'll step behind this screen and listen: a good soldier must sometimes fight in ambush as well as open field [*Retires.*

IV.xi

[*Enter* Lady Rusport *and* Varland.

LADY RUSPORT. Sure I heard somebody. Hark! No; only the servants going down the back stairs. Well, Mr. Varland, I think then we are agreed: you'll take my money; and your conscience no longer stands in your way.

VARLAND. Your father was my benefactor; his will ought to be sacred; but, if I commit it to the flames, how will he be the wiser? Dudley, 'tis true, has done me no harm; but five thousand pounds will do me much good; so, in short, Madam, I take your offer; I will confer with my clerk, who witnessed the will; and to-morrow morning put it into your hands, upon condition you put five thousand good pounds into mine.

LADY RUSPORT. 'Tis a bargain: I'll be ready for you: farewell. [*Exit.*

VARLAND. Let me consider—Five thousand pounds prompt payment for destroying this scrap of paper, not worth five farthings; 'tis a fortune easily earn'd; yes; and 'tis another man's fortune easily thrown away: 'tis a good round sum to be paid down at once for a bribe; but 'tis a damn'd rogue's trick in me to take it.

O'FLAHERTY. [*Aside*] *So, so! this fellow speaks truth to himself, tho' he lies to other people—but hush!*

VARLAND. 'Tis breaking the trust of my benefactor; that's a foul crime; but he's dead, and can never reproach me with it; and 'tis robbing young Dudley of his lawful patrimony; that's a hard case; but he's alive, and knows nothing of the matter.

O'FLAHERTY. [*Aside*] *These lawyers are so used to bring off the rogueries of others, that they are never without an excuse for their own.*

VARLAND. Were I assured now that Dudley would give me half the money for producing this will, that Lady Rusport does for concealing it, I wou'd deal with him, and be an honest man at half price; I wish every gentleman of my profession cou'd lay his hand on his heart and say the same thing.

O'FLAHERTY. A bargain, old gentleman! Nay, never start, nor stare, you wasn't afraid of your own conscience, never be afraid of me.

VARLAND. Of you, Sir; who are you, pray?

O'FLAHERTY. I'll tell you who I am; you seem to wish to be honest, but want the heart to set about it; now I am the very man in the world to make you so; for, if you do not give me up that paper this very instant, by the soul of me, fellow, I will not leave one whole bone in your skin that shan't be broken.

VARLAND. What right have you, pray, to take this paper from me?

O'FLAHERTY. What right have you, pray, to, keep it from young Dudley? I don't know what it contains, but I am apt to think it will be safer in my hands than in yours; therefore give it me without more words, and save yourself a beating: do now; you had best.

VARLAND. Well, Sir, I may as well make a grace of necessity. There! I have acquitted my conscience, at the expence of five thousand pounds.

O'FLAHERTY. Five thousand pounds! Mercy upon me! When there are such temptations in the law, can we wonder if some of the corps are a disgrace to it?

VARLAND. Well, you have got the paper; if you are an honest man, give it to Charles Dudley.

O'FLAHERTY. An honest man! look at me friend, I am a soldier, this is not the livery of a knave; I am an Irishman, honey; mine is not the country of dishonour. Now, sirrah, be gone; if you enter these doors, or give Lady Rusport the least item of what has passed, I will cut off both your ears, and rob the pillory of its due.

VARLAND. I wish I was once fairly out of his sight.

[*Exeunt.*

IV.x

A room in Stockwell's *house.*

STOCKWELL. I must disclose myself to Belcour; this noble instance of his generosity, which old Dudley has been relating, allies me to him at once; concealment becomes too painful; I shall be proud to own him for my son—But see, he's here.

[Belcour *enters, and throws himself upon a sopha.*

BELCOUR. O my curst tropical constitution! wou'd to Heaven I had been dropt upon the snows of Lapland,[76] and never felt the blessed influence of the sun, so I had never burnt with these inflammatory passions!

STOCKWELL. So so, you seem disorder'd, Mr. Belcour.

BELCOUR. Disorder'd, Sir! why did I ever quit the soil in which I grew; what evil planet drew me from that warm sunny region, where naked nature walks without disguise, into this cold contriving artificial country?

STOCKWELL. Come, Sir, you've met a rascal; what o'that? General conclusions are illiberal.

BELCOUR. No, Sir, I've met reflection by the way; I've come from folly, noise, and fury, and met a silent monitor—Well, well, a villain! 'Twas not to be pardon'd—pray never mind me, Sir.

STOCKWELL. Alas! my heart bleeds for him.

BELCOUR. And yet, I might have heard him: now, plague upon that blundering Irishman for coming in as he did; the hurry of the deed might palliate the event: deliberate execution has less to plead—Mr. Stockwell, I am bad company to you.

STOCKWELL. Oh, Sir; make no excuse. I think you have not found me forward to pry into the secrets of your pleasures and pursuits; 'tis not my disposition; but there are times when want of curiosity wou'd be want of friendship.

BELCOUR. Ah, Sir, mine is a case wherein you and I shall never think alike; the punctilious rules,[77] by which I am bound, are not to be found in your ledgers, nor will pass current in the compting-house of a trader.

STOCKWELL. 'Tis very well, Sir; if you think I can render you any service, it may be worth your trial to confide in me; if not, your secret is safer in your own bosom.

BELCOUR. That sentiment demands my confidence: pray, sit down by me. You must know, I have an affair of honour on my hands with young Dudley; and, tho' I put up with no man's insult, yet I wish to take away no man's life.

STOCKWELL. I know the young man, and am appris'd of your generosity to his father; what can have bred a quarrel between you?

BELCOUR. A foolish passion on my side, and a haughty provocation on his. There is a girl, Mr. Stockwell, whom I have unfortunately seen, of most uncommon beauty; she has withall an air of so much natural modesty, that had I not had good assurance of her being an attainable wanton, I declare I shou'd as soon have thought of attempting the chastity of Diana.[78]

[Servant *enters.*

STOCKWELL. Hey-day, do you interrupt us?

SERVANT. Sir, there's an Irish gentleman will take no denial; he says he must see Mr. Belcour directly, upon business of the last consequence.

BELCOUR. Admit him; 'tis the Irish officer that parted us, and brings me young Dudley's challenge; I should have made a long story of it, and he'll tell you in three words.

[O'Flaherty *enters.*

O'FLAHERTY. Save you, my dear; and you, Sir! I have a little bit of a word in private for you.

BELCOUR. Pray deliver your commands; this gentleman is my intimate friend.

O'FLAHERTY. Why then, Ensign Dudley will be glad to measure swords with you, yonder, at the London Tavern, in Bishopsgate-Street,[79] at nine o'clock—you know the place.

BELCOUR. I do; and shall observe the appointment.

O'FLAHERTY. [*To* Stockwell] Will you be of the party, Sir? We shall want a fourth hand.

STOCKWELL. Savage as the custom is, I close with your proposal; and tho' I am not fully inform'd of the occasion of your quarrel, I shall rely on Mr. Belcour's honour for the justice of it; and willingly stake my life in his defence.

O'FLAHERTY. Sir, you're a gentleman of honour, and I shall be glad of being better known to you—But hark'ee, Belcour, I had like to have forgot part of my errand: there is the money you gave old Dudley; you may tell it over faith; 'tis a receipt in full; now the lad can put you to death with a safe conscience, and when he has done that job for you, let it be a warning how you attempt the sister of a man of honour.

BELCOUR. The sister?

O'FLAHERTY. Ay, the sister; 'tis English, is it not? Or Irish; 'tis all one; you understand me, his sister, or Louisa Dudley, that's her name I think, call her which you will: by St. Patrick,[80] 'tis a foolish piece of a business, Belcour, to go about to take away a poor girl's virtue from her, when there are so many to be met in this town, who have dispos'd of theirs to your hands. [*Exit.*

STOCKWELL. Why I am thunderstruck! what is it you have done, and what is the shocking business in which I have engaged? If I understood him right, 'tis the sister of young Dudley you've been attempting: you talk'd to me of a profest wanton; the girl he speaks of has beauty enough indeed to inflame your desires, but she has honour, innocence and simplicity to awe the most licentious passion; if you have done that, Mr. Belcour, I renounce you, I abandon you, I forswear all fellowship or friendship with you for ever.

BELCOUR. Have patience for a moment; we do indeed speak of the same person, but she is not innocent; she is not young Dudley's sister.

STOCKWELL. Astonishing! who told you this?

BELCOUR. The woman where she lodges; the person who put me on the pursuit and contriv'd our meetings.

STOCKWELL. What woman? What person?

BELCOUR. Fulmer her name is: I warrant you I did not proceed without good grounds.

STOCKWELL. Fulmer, Fulmer? Who waits? [*a* Servant *enters*] send Mr. Stukely hither directly; I begin to see my way into this dark transaction; Mr. Belcour, Mr. Belcour, you are no match for the cunning and contrivances of this intriguing town. [Stukely *enters*] Pr'ythee, Stukely, what is the name of the woman and her husband, who were stopt upon suspicion of selling stolen diamonds at our next-door neighbour's, the jeweller?

STUKELY. Fulmer.

STOCKWELL. So!

BELCOUR. Can you procure me a sight of those diamonds?

STUKELY. They are now in my hand; I was desir'd to show them to Mr. Stockwell.

STOCKWELL. Give 'em to me; what do I see? As I live, the very diamonds Miss Rusport sent hither, and which I intrusted to you to return.

BELCOUR. Yes, but I betray'd that trust, and gave 'em Mrs. Fulmer to present to Miss Dudley.

STOCKWELL. With a view no doubt to bribe her to compliance?

BELCOUR. I own it.

STOCKWELL. For shame, for shame; and 'twas this woman's intelligence you relied upon for Miss Dudley's character?

BELCOUR. I thought she knew her; by Heaven, I wou'd have died sooner than have insulted a woman of virtue, or a man of honour.

STOCKWELL. I think you wou'd, but mark the danger of licentious courses; you are betray'd, robb'd, abus'd, and, but for this providential discovery, in a fair way of being sent out of the world with all your follies on your head—Dear Stukely, go to my neighbour, tell him I have an owner for the jewels, and beg him to carry the people under custody to the London Tavern, and wait for me there. [*Exit* Stukely] I fear the law does not provide a punishment to reach the villainy of these people; but how in the name of wonder cou'd you take any thing on the word of such an informer?

BELCOUR. Because I had not liv'd long enough in your country to know how few informers' words are to be taken: persuaded however as I was of Miss Dudley's guilt, I must own to you I was stagger'd with the appearance of such innocence, especially when I saw her admitted into Miss Rusport's company.

STOCKWELL. Good Heaven! did you meet her at Miss Rusport's, and cou'd you doubt her being a woman of reputation?[81]

BELCOUR. By you perhaps such a mistake cou'd not have been made; but in a perfect stranger, I hope it is venial: I did not know what artifices young Dudley might have us'd to conceal her character; I did not know what disgrace attended the detection of it.

STOCKWELL. I see it was a trap laid for you, which you have narrowly escap'd; you address'd a woman of honour with all the loose incense of a profane admirer, and you have drawn upon you the resentment of a man of honour who thinks himself bound to protect her: well, Sir, you must atone for this mistake.

BELCOUR. To the lady the most penitent submission I can make is justly due, but in the execution of an act of justice it never shall be said my soul was swayed by the least particle of fear: I have received a challenge from her brother; now, tho' I wou'd give my fortune, almost my life itself, to purchase her happiness, yet I cannot abate her one scruple of my honour; I have been branded with the name of villain.

STOCKWELL. Ay, Sir, you mistook her character and he mistook yours; error begets error.

BELCOUR. Villain, Mr. Stockwell, is a harsh word.

STOCKWELL. It is a harsh word, and should be unsaid.

BELCOUR. Come, come, it shall be unsaid.

STOCKWELL. Or else what follows? why the sword is drawn, and to heal the wrongs you have done to the reputation of the sister, you make an honourable amends by murdering the brother.

BELCOUR. Murdering!

STOCKWELL. 'Tis thus religion writes and speaks the word; in the vocabulary of modern honour there is no such term[82]—But come, I don't despair of satisfying the one without alarming the other; that done, I have a discovery to unfold that you will then I hope be fitted to receive.

[*Exeunt.*

V.i

The London Tavern.[83] O'Flaherty, Stockwell, Charles, *and* Belcour.

O'FLAHERTY. Gentlemen, well met! you understand each other's minds, and as I see you have brought nothing but your swords, you may set to without any further ceremony.

STOCKWELL. You will not find us backward in any worthy cause; but before we proceed any further, I would ask this young gentleman, whether he has any explanation to require of Mr. Belcour.

CHARLES. Of Mr. Belcour none; his actions speak for themselves: but to you, Sir, I would fain propose one question.

STOCKWELL. Name it.

CHARLES. How is it, Mr. Stockwell, that I meet a man of your character on this ground?

STOCKWELL. I will answer you directly, and my answer shall not displease you. I come hither in defence of the reputation of Miss Dudley, to redress the injuries of an innocent young lady.

O'FLAHERTY. By my soul the man knows he's to fight, only he mistakes which side he's to be of.

STOCKWELL. You are about to draw your sword to refute a charge against your sister's honour; you would do well, if there were no better means within reach; but the proofs of her innocence are lodg'd in our bosoms, and if we fall, you destroy the evidence that most effectually can clear her fame.

CHARLES. How's that, Sir?

STOCKWELL. This gentleman could best explain it to you, but you have given him an undeserv'd name that seals his lips against you: I am not under the same inhibition, and if your anger can keep cool for a few minutes, I desire I may call in two witnesses, who will solve all difficulties at once. Here, waiter! bring those people in that are without.

O'FLAHERTY. Out upon it, what need is there for so much talking about the matter; can't you settle your differences first, and dispute about 'em afterwards?

[Fulmer *and* Mrs. Fulmer *brought in by* Constable.

CHARLES. Fulmer and his wife in custody?

STOCKWELL. Yes, Sir, these are your honest landlord and landlady, now in custody for defrauding this gentleman of certain diamonds intended to have been presented to your sister. Be so good, Mrs. Fulmer, to inform the company why you so grossly scandalized the reputation of an innocent lady, by persuading Mr. Belcour that Miss Dudley was not the sister, but the mistress, of this gentleman.

MRS. FULMER. Sir, I don't know what right you have to question me, and I shall not answer till I see occasion.

STOCKWELL. Had you been as silent heretofore, Madam, it would have saved you some trouble; but we don't want[84] your confession. This letter, which you wrote to Mr. Belcour, will explain your design; and these diamonds, which of right belong to Miss Rusport, will confirm your guilt: the law, Mrs. Fulmer, will make you speak, tho' I can't. Constable, take charge of your prisoners.

FULMER. Hold a moment: Mr. Stockwell, you are a gentleman that knows the world, and a member of parliament; we shall not attempt to impose upon you; we know we are open to the law, and we know the utmost it can do against us.[85] Mr. Belcour has been ill used to be sure, and so has Miss Dudley; and, for my own part, I always condemn'd the plot as a very foolish plot, but it was a child of Mrs. Fulmer's brain, and she would not be put out of conceit with it.

MRS. FULMER. You are a very foolish man, Mr. Fulmer, so prythee hold your tongue.

FULMER. Therefore, as I was saying, if you send her to Bridewell,[86] it won't be amiss; and if you give her a little wholesome discipline, she may be the better for that too: but for me, Mr. Stockwell, who am a man of letters, I must beseech you, Sir, not to bring any disgrace upon my profession.

STOCKWELL. 'Tis you, Mr. Fulmer, not I, that disgrace your profession, therefore begone, nor expect that I will betray the interests of mankind so far as to shew favour to such incendiaries. Take 'em away; I blush to think such wretches should have the power to set two honest men at variance. [*Exeunt* Fulmer, *&c.*

CHARLES. Mr. Belcour, we have mistaken each other; let us exchange forgiveness. I am convinced you intended no affront to my sister, and ask your pardon for the expression I was betrayed into.

BELCOUR. 'Tis enough, Sir; the error began on my side, and was Miss Dudley here, I would be the first to atone.

STOCKWELL. Let us all adjourn to my house, and conclude the evening like friends: you will find a little entertainment ready for you; and, if I am not mistaken, Miss Dudley and her father will make part of our company. Come, Major, do you consent?

O'FLAHERTY. Most readily, Mr, Stockwell; a quarrel well made up, is better than a victory hardly earned. Give me your hand, Belcour; o' my conscience you are too honest for the country you live in. [*To* Charles] And now, my dear lad, since peace is concluded on all sides, I have a discovery to make to you, which you must find out for yourself, for deuce take me if I rightly comprehend it, only that your Aunt Rusport is in a conspiracy against you, and a vile rogue of a lawyer, whose name I forget, at the bottom of it.

CHARLES. What conspiracy? Dear Major, recollect yourself.

O'FLAHERTY. By my soul, I've no faculty at recollecting myself; but I've a paper somewhere about me, that will tell you more of the matter than I can. When I get to the merchant's, I will endeavour to find it.

CHARLES. Well, it must be in your own way; but I confess you have thoroughly rous'd my curiosity.

[*Exeunt.*

V.ii

Stockwell*'s house.* Capt. Dudley, Louisa, *and* Stukely.

DUDLEY. And are those wretches, Fulmer and his wife, in safe custody?

STUKELY. They are in good hands, I accompanied them to the Tavern, where your son was to be, and then went in search of you. You may be sure Mr. Stockwell will enforce the law against them as far as it will go.

DUDLEY. What mischief might their cursed machinations have produced, but for this timely discovery!

LOUISA. Still I am terrified; I tremble with apprehension lest Mr. Belcour's impetuosity and Charles's spirit shou'd not wait for an explanation, but drive them both to extremes, before the mistake can be unravell'd.

STUKELY. Mr. Stockwell is with them, Madam, and you have nothing to fear; you cannot suppose he wou'd ask you hither for any other purpose, but to celebrate their reconciliation and to receive Mr. Belcour's attonement.

DUDLEY. No, no, Louisa, Mr. Stockwell's honour and discretion guard us against all danger or offence; he well knows we will endure no imputation on the honour of our family, and he certainly has invited us to receive satisfaction on that score in an amicable way.

LOUISA. Wou'd to Heaven they were return'd!

STUKELY. You may expect them every minute; and see Madam, agreeable to your wish, they are here. [*Exit.*

V.iii

[Charles *enters, and afterwards* Stockwell, *and* O'Flaherty.

LOUISA. O Charles, O brother, how cou'd you serve me so, how cou'd you tell me you was going to Lady Rusport's and then set out with a design of fighting Mr. Belcour? But where is he; where is your antagonist?

STOCKWELL. Captain, I am proud to see you, and you Miss Dudley, do me particular honour: we have been adjusting, Sir, a very extraordinary and dangerous mistake, which I take for granted my friend Stukely has explain'd to you.

DUDLEY. He has; I have too good an opinion of Mr. Belcour to believe he cou'd be guilty of a design'd affront to an innocent girl, and I am much too well acquainted with your character to suppose you cou'd abet him in such design; I have no doubt therefore all things will be set to rights in very few words when we have the pleasure of seeing Mr. Belcour.

STOCKWELL. He has only stept into the compting-house and will wait upon you directly: You will not be over strict, Madam, in weighing Mr. Belcour's conduct to the minutest scruple; his manners, passions and opinions are not as yet assimilated to this climate; he comes amongst you a new character, an inhabitant of a new world and both hospitality as well as pity recommend him to our indulgence.

V.iv

[Belcour *enters, bows to* Miss Dudley.

BELCOUR. I am happy and asham'd to see you; no man in his senses wou'd offend you; I forfeited mine and err'd against the light of the sun, when I overlook'd your virtues; but your beauty was predominant and hid them from my sight; I now perceive I was the dupe of a most improbable report, and humbly entreat your pardon.

LOUISA. Think no more of it; 'twas a mistake.

BELCOUR. My life has been compos'd of little else; 'twas founded in mystery and has continued in error: I was once given to hope, Mr. Stockwell, that you was to have deliver'd me from these difficulties, but either I do not deserve your confidence, or I was deceiv'd in my expectations.

STOCKWELL. When this lady has confirm'd your pardon, I shall hold you deserving of my confidence.

LOUISA. That was granted the moment it was ask'd.

BELCOUR. To prove my title to his confidence honour me so far with yours as to allow me a few minutes' conversation in private with you. [*She turns to her father.*

DUDLEY. By all means, Louisa; come, Mr. Stockwell, let us go into another room.

CHARLES. And now, Major O'Flaherty, I claim your promise of a sight of the paper, that is to unravel this conspiracy of my Aunt Rusport's: I think I have waited with great patience.

O'FLAHERTY. I have been endeavouring to call to mind what it was I overheard; I've got the paper and will give you the best account I can of the whole transaction.

[*Exeunt.*

V.v

Belcour *and* Louisa.

BELCOUR. Miss Dudley, I have solicited this audience to repeat to you my penitence and confusion: how shall I atone? What reparation can I make to you and virtue?

LOUISA. To me there's nothing due, nor any thing demanded of you but your more favourable opinion for the future, if you should chance to think of me: upon the part of virtue I'm not empower'd to speak, but if hereafter, as you range thro' life, you shou'd surprize her in the person of some wretched female, poor as myself and not so well protected, enforce not your advantage, complete not your licentious triumph, but raise her, rescue her from shame and sorrow, and reconcile her to herself again.

BELCOUR. I will, I will; by bearing your idea ever present in my thoughts, virtue shall keep an advocate within me; but tell me, loveliest, when you pardon the offence, can you, all perfect as you are, approve of the offender? As I now cease to view you in that false light I lately did, can you, and in the fulness of your bounty will you, cease also to reflect upon the libertine addresses I have paid you, and look upon me as your reform'd, your rational admirer?

LOUISA. Are sudden reformations apt to last; and how can I be sure the first fair face you meet will not ensnare affections so unsteady, and that I shall not lose you lightly as I gain'd you?

BELCOUR. Because tho' you conquer'd me by surprize, I have no inclination to rebel; because since the first moment that I saw you, every instant has improv'd you in my eyes, because by principle as well as passion I am unalterably yours, in short there are ten thousand causes for my love to you, would to Heaven I could plant one in your soft bosom that might move you to return it!

LOUISA. Nay, Mr. Belcour.—

BELCOUR. I know I am not worthy your regard; I know I'm tainted with a thousand faults, sick of a thousand follies, but there's a healing virtue in your eyes that makes recovery certain; I cannot be a villain in your arms.

LOUISA. That you can never be; whomever you shall honour with your choice, my life upon't that woman will be happy; it is not from suspicion that I hesitate, it is from honour; 'tis the severity of my condition, it is the world that never will interpret fairly in our case.

BELCOUR. Oh, what am I, and who in this wide world concerns himself for such a nameless, such a friendless thing as I am? I see, Miss Dudley, I've not yet obtain'd your pardon.

LOUISA. Nay, that you are in full possession of.

BELCOUR. Oh, seal it with your hand then, loveliest of women, confirm it with your heart; make me honourably happy, and crown your penitent not with your pardon only, but your love.

LOUISA. My love!—

BELCOUR. By Heav'n my soul is conquer'd with your virtues more than my eyes are ravish'd with your beauty: Oh, may this soft, this sensitive alarm be happy, be auspicious! Doubt not, deliberate not, delay not: If happiness be the end of life, why do we slip a moment?

V.vi

[O'Flaherty *enters, and afterwards* Dudley *and* Charles *with* Stockwell.

O'FLAHERTY. Joy, joy, joy! sing, dance, leap, laugh for joy! Ha' done making love and fall down on your knees to every saint in the calendar, for they're all on your side and honest St. Patrick at the head of them.

CHARLES. O Louisa, such an event! by the luckiest chance in life we have discover'd a will of my grandfather's made in his last illness, by which he cuts off my Aunt Rusport with a small annuity, and leaves me heir to his whole estate, with a fortune of fifteen thousand pounds to yourself.[87]

LOUISA. What is it you tell me? [*To her father*] O Sir, instruct me to support this unexpected turn of fortune.

DUDLEY. Name not fortune; 'tis the work of providence, 'tis the justice of Heaven that wou'd not suffer innocence to be oppress'd, nor your base aunt to prosper in her cruelty and cunning.

[*A* Servant *whispers* Belcour, *and he goes out.*

O'FLAHERTY. You shall pardon me, Capt. Dudley, but you must not overlook St. Patrick neither, for by my soul if he had not put it into my head to slip behind the screen when your righteous aunt and the lawyer were plotting together, I don't see how you wou'd ever have come at the paper there, that Master Stockwell is reading.

DUDLEY. True my good friend, you are the father of this discovery, but how did you contrive to get this will from the lawyer?

O'FLAHERTY. By force, my dear, the only way of getting any thing from a lawyer's clutches.

STOCKWELL. Well, Major, when he brings his action of assault and battery against you, the least Dudley can do is to defend you with the weapons you have put into his hands.[88]

CHARLES. That I am bound to do, and after the happiness I shall have in sheltering a father's age from the vicissitudes of life, my next delight will be in offering you an asylum in the bosom of your country.

O'FLAHERTY. And upon my soul, my dear, 'tis high time I was there, for 'tis now thirty long years since I sat foot in my native country, and by the power of St. Patrick I swear I think it's worth all the rest of the world put together.

DUDLEY. Ay, Major, much about that time have I been beating the round of service, and 'twere well for us both to give over; we have stood many a tough gale and abundance of hard blows, but Charles shall lay us up in a little private, but safe, harbour, where we'll rest from our labours, and peacefully wind up the remainder of our days.

O'FLAHERTY. Agreed, and you may take it as a proof of my esteem, young man, that Major O'Flaherty accepts a favour at your hands, for by Heaven I'd sooner starve, than say I thank you to the man I despise: but I believe you are an honest lad, and I'm glad you've trounc'd the old cat, for on my conscience I believe I must otherwise have married her myself to have let you in for a share of her fortune.

STOCKWELL. Hey-day, what's become of Belcour?

LOUISA. One of your servants call'd him out just now and seemingly on some earnest occasion.

STOCKWELL. I hope, Miss Dudley, he has aton'd to you as a gentleman ought.

LOUISA. Mr. Belcour, Sir, will always do what a gentleman ought, and in my case I fear only you will think he has done too much.

STOCKWELL. What has he done; and what can be too much?—[*Aside*] *Pray Heaven, it may be as I wish!*

DUDLEY. Let us hear it, child.

LOUISA. With confusion for my own unworthiness, I confess to you he has offer'd me—

STOCKWELL. Himself.

LOUISA. 'Tis true.

STOCKWELL.—[*Aside*] *Then I am happy; all my doubts, my cares are over, and I may own him for my son.*—[*To* Dudley] Why these are joyful tidings: come, my good friend, assist me in disposing your lovely daughter to accept this returning prodigal; he is no unprincipled, no harden'd libertine; his love for you and virtue is the same.

DUDLEY. 'Twere vile ingratitude in me to doubt his merit—What says my child?

O'FLAHERTY. Begging your pardon now, 'tis a frivolous sort of a question, that of yours; for you may see plainly enough by the young lady's looks, that she says a great deal, though she speaks never a word.

CHARLES. Well, sister, I believe the major has fairly interpreted the state of your heart.

LOUISA. I own it; and what must that heart be, which love, honour and beneficence like Mr. Belcour's can make no impression on?

STOCKWELL. I thank you: what happiness has this hour brought to pass!

O'FLAHERTY. Why don't we all sit down to supper then and make a night on't.

STOCKWELL. Hold, here comes Belcour.

V.vii

[Belcour *introducing* Miss Rusport.

BELCOUR. Mr. Dudley, here is a fair refugee, who properly comes under your protection; she is equipt for Scotland, but your good fortune, which I have related to her, seems inclin'd to save you both the journey[89]—Nay, Madam, never go back; you are amongst friends.

CHARLES. Charlotte!

CHARLOTTE. The same; that fond officious girl, that haunts you every where; that persecuting spirit—

CHARLES. Say rather, that protecting angel; such you have been to me.

CHARLOTTE. O Charles, you have an honest, but proud heart.

CHARLES. Nay, chide me not, dear Charlotte.

BELCOUR. Seal up her lips then; she is an adorable girl; her arms are open to you; and love and happiness are ready to receive you.

CHARLES. Thus then I claim my dear, my destin'd wife. [*Embracing her.*

V.viii

[Lady Rusport *enters.*

LADY RUSPORT. Hey-day! mighty fine! wife truly! mighty well! kissing, embracing—did ever any thing equal this? Why you shameless hussey!—But I won't condescend to waste a word upon you.—You, Sir, you, Mr. Stockwell, you fine, sanctified, fair-dealing man of conscience, is this the principle you trade upon? Is this your neighbourly system, to keep a house of reception for run-away daughters, and young beggarly fortune-hunters?

O'FLAHERTY. Be advis'd now, and don't put yourself in such a passion; we were all very happy till you came.

LADY RUSPORT. Stand away, Sir; hav'nt l a reason to be in a passion?

O'FLAHERTY. Indeed, honey, and you have, if you knew all.

LADY RUSPORT. [*To* Charlotte] Come, Madam, I have found out your haunts; dispose yourself to return home with me: [*To* Charles] young man, let me never see you within my doors again: Mr. Stockwell, I shall report your behaviour, depend on it.

STOCKWELL. Hold, Madam, I cannot consent to lose Miss Rusport's company this evening, and I am persuaded you won't insist upon it; 'tis an unmotherly action to interrupt your daughter's happiness in this manner, believe me it is.

LADY RUSPORT. Her happiness truly; upon my word! and I suppose it's an unmotherly action to interrupt her ruin; for what but ruin must it be to marry a beggar? [*To* Captain Dudley] I think my sister had a proof of that, Sir, when she made choice of you.

DUDLEY. Don't be too lavish of your spirits, Lady Rusport.

O'FLAHERTY. By my soul you'll have occasion for a sip of the cordial elixir by and bye.

STOCKWELL. It don't appear to me, Madam, that Mr. Dudley can be call'd a beggar.

LADY RUSPORT. But it appears to me, Mr. Stockwell; I am apt to think a pair of colours[90] cannot furnish settlement quite sufficient for the heiress of Sir Stephen Rusport.

CHARLOTTE. But a good estate in aid of a commission may do something.

LADY RUSPORT. A good estate, truly! where shou'd he get a good estate pray?

STOCKWELL. Why suppose now a worthy old gentleman on his death-bed should have taken it in mind to leave him one—

LADY RUSPORT. Hah! what's that you say?

O'FLAHERTY. O ho! you begin to smell a plot, do you?

STOCKWELL. Suppose there should be a paper in the world that runs thus—"*I do hereby give and bequeath all my estates, real and personal, to Charles Dudley, son of my late daughter Louisa, &c. &c. &c.*"

LADY RUSPORT. Why I am thunder-struck! by what contrivance, what villany did you get possession of that paper?

STOCKWELL. There was no villany, Madam, in getting possession of it; the crime was in concealing it, none in bringing it to light.

LADY RUSPORT. Oh, that cursed lawyer, Varland!

O'FLAHERTY. You may say that, faith, he is a cursed lawyer, and a cursed piece of work I had to get the paper from him; your ladyship now was to have paid him five thousand pounds for it, I forc'd him to give it me of his own accord for nothing at all, at all.

LADY RUSPORT. Is it you that have done this? Am I foil'd by your blundering contrivances, after all?

O'FLAHERTY. 'Twas a blunder, faith, but as natural a one as if I'd made it o' purpose.

CHARLES. Come, let us not oppress the fallen; do right even now, and you shall have no cause to complain.

LADY RUSPORT. Am I become an object of your pity then? Insufferable! confusion light amongst you! marry and be wretched: let me never see you more. [*Exit.*

CHARLOTTE. She is outrageous; I suffer for her, and blush to see her thus exposed.

CHARLES. Come, Charlotte, don't let this angry woman disturb our happiness: we will save her in spite of herself; your sister's memory shall not be stained by the discredit of his second choice.

CHARLOTTE. I trust implicitly to your discretion, and am in all things yours.

BELCOUR. Now, lovely but obdurate, does not this example soften?

LOUISA. What can you ask for more? Accept my hand, accept my willing heart.

BELCOUR. O bliss inutterable! brother, father, friend, and you the author of this general joy—

O'FLAHERTY. Blessing of St. Patrick upon us all! 'Tis a night of wonderful and surprising ups and downs: I wish we were all fairly set down to supper, and there was an end on't.

STOCKWELL. Hold for a moment! I have yet one word to interpose—Entitled by my friendship to a voice in your disposal, I have approv'd your match; there yet remains a father's consent to be obtain'd.

BELCOUR. Have I a father?

STOCKWELL. You have a father: did not I tell you I had a discovery to make? Compose yourself: you have a father, who observes, who knows, who loves you.

BELCOUR. Keep me no longer in suspence; my heart is soften'd for the affecting discovery, and nature fits me to receive his blessing.

STOCKWELL. I am your father.

BELCOUR. My father? Do I live?

STOCKWELL. I am your father.

BELCOUR. It is too much; my happiness o'erpowers me; to gain a friend and find a father is too much; I blush to think how little I deserve you. [*They embrace.*

DUDLEY. See, children, how many new relations spring from this night's unforeseen events, to endear us to each other.

O'FLAHERTY. O my conscience, I think we shall be all related by and bye.

STOCKWELL. How happily has this evening concluded, and yet how threatning was its approach! let us repair to the supper room, where I will unfold to you every circumstance of my mysterious story. Yes, Belcour, I have watch'd you with a patient, but enquiring eye, and I have discover'd thro' the veil of some irregularities, a heart beaming with benevolence, an animated nature, fallible indeed, but not incorrigible; and your election of this excellent young lady makes me glory in acknowledging you to be my son.

BELCOUR. I thank you, and in my turn glory in the father I have gained: sensibly imprest with gratitude for such extraordinary dispensations, I beseech you, amiable Louisa, for the time to come, whenever you perceive me deviating into error or offence, bring only to my mind the Providence of this night, and I will turn to reason and obey.

[*Exeunt.*

EPILOGUE

Written by D. G. Esq.[91]
Spoken by Mrs. Abington.[92]

N.B. The lines in italics are to be spoken in a catechise[93] tone.

Confess, good folks, has not Miss Rusport shewn,
Strange whims for seventeen hundred seventy-one?
What, pawn her jewels!—There's a precious plan!
To extricate from want a brave old man;
And fall in love with poverty and honour;
A girl of fortune, fashion!—Fie upon her.
But do not think we females of the stage,
So dead to the refinements of the age,
That we agree with our old fashion'd poet:
I am point blank against him, and I'll shew it:
And that my tongue may more politely run,
Make me a lady—Lady Blabington.[94]
Now, with a rank and title to be free,
I'll make a catechism—and you shall see.
What is the *veritable Beaume de Vie*:
As I change place, I stand for that, or this,
My Lady questions first—then answers Miss.

[*She speaks as my Lady.*

"Come, tell me, Child, what were our modes and dress,
"In these strange times of that old fright Queen Bess?"[95]—
And now for Miss—

[*She changes place, and speaks for* Miss.

When Bess was England's queen,
Ladies were dismal beings, seldom seen;
They rose betimes, and breakfasted as soon
On beef and beer, then studied Greek till noon;
Unpainted cheeks with blush of health did glow,
Beruff'd and fardingald from top to toe,[96]
Nor necks, nor ancles would they ever shew.
Learnt Greek!—[*Laughs*]—Our outside head takes half a day;
Have we much time to dress the *inside*, pray?
No heads dress'd *à la Greque*; the ancients quote,
There may be learning in papillote:[97]
Cards are our classicks; and I, Lady B,
In learning will not yield to any she,
Of the late founded female university.
But now for Lady Blab,

[*Speaks as my Lady.*

"Tell me, Miss Nancy,
"What sports and what employments did they fancy?"

[*Speaks as Miss.*

The vulgar creatures seldom left their houses.
But taught their children, work'd, and lov'd their spouses;
The use of cards at Christmas only knew,
They play'd for little, and their games were few,
One-and-thirty, Put, All fours, and Lantera Loo;[98]
They bore a race of mortals stout and boney,
And never heard the name of Macaroni.—

[*Speaks as my Lady.*

"Oh brava, brava! that's my pretty dear—
"Now let a modern, modish fair appear;
"No more of these old dowdy maids and wives,
"Tell how superior beings pass their lives."—

[*Speaks as Miss.*

Till noon they sleep, from noon till night they dress.

From night till morn they game it more or less.
Next night the same sweet course of joy run o'er.
Then the night after as the night before,
And the night after that, encore, encore!—

[*She comes forward.*

Thus with' our cards we *shuffle* off all sorrow,
To morrow, and to-morrow, and to-morrow![99]
We *deal apace*, from youth unto our prime.
To the last moment of our *tabby*-time;
And all our yesterdays, from rout and drum.
Have lighted fools with empty pockets home.
Thus do our lives with rapture roll away,
Not with the nonsense of our author's play;
This is true life—true spirit—give it praise;
Don't snarl and sigh for good Queen Bess's days:
For all you look so sour, and bend the brow,
You all rejoice with me, you're living now.

15.2 OLIVER GOLDSMITH. "A DESCRIPTION OF THE MANNERS AND CUSTOMS OF THE NATIVE IRISH. IN A LETTER FROM AN ENGLISH GENTLEMAN." *THE WEEKLY MAGAZINE*, NO. 1 29 DEC. 1759.

DEAR JACK,

While our travellers are busied in studying the manners, the soil, and produce of distant countries, there are several which are at our very doors possessed of peculiarities hitherto unknown, and yet are quite neglected; like conquerors who have been too eagerly employed in foreign conquests, we leave our native dominions without notice or regard.

Perhaps our conquered kingdom of Ireland is as strong an instance of this as any that may be found, since whether we regard its natural history, or the manners of its original inhabitants, we may in both find matter for speculation and curiosity. Many wonders in the former are still left undescribed, as the mountain of Case Corin[100] in the western division of the kingdom, and several peculiarities of the latter have been injuriously or injudiciously represented.

The present inhabitants may be divided into two sorts, the Protestants and the Papists; the Protestants are almost all originally from England, and have adopted the manners of their mother-country, though at the same time it must be acknowledged that they have superinduced over the rough English character a degree of ceremony and politeness which may sufficiently serve to distinguish the two nations.

The English for instance are rough, prudently generous, and sincere, the Irish protestants are on the contrary affable, foolishly prodigal, hospitable, and often not to be depended upon. This difference from their ancestors they have acquired by long conversation with the original natives, who carry all these faults to a vicious extreme. The original Irish are therefore, frequently found fawning, insincere, and fond of pleasure, prodigality makes them poor, and poverty makes them vicious, such are their faults, but they have national virtues to recompense these defects. They are valiant, sensible, polite, and generally beautiful. Their women have exquisite complexions, through their features are a little broad somewhat approaching that turn of visage which we are told of the Tartars, from whom they pretend to be originally descended.

Whatever beauty they may have in their faces their persons are not equally irreprehensible, for the women are generally too tall for beauty, and are found to have thick legs. But then though there are no where men more lascivious than these, perhaps no country upon earth produces women more modest, we frequently find Irish men turn fortune hunters, but a fortune hunting Irish woman, even in her own country is one of the scarcest of characters.

It must be owned indeed, that no climate in the world is more apt to fan desire than that. The weather is almost always as our spring, and it is scarce known that the water is frozen sufficiently to bear a man's weight. So that if Venus were to fix a temple in any part of the world it might be here in the land of Honeys and Joys. Fanned by luxuriant airs what shepherd refuses to sing, or what nymph disdains to hear.

From hence their manners, their language, and all their poetry is turned to love. On this subject their language otherwise barren is excessively copious, and for one term of endearment in ours, they have ten in theirs.

The manners of the original inhabitants, which they to this day preserve unvaried, are entirely different from those of the English, and partake somewhat of the ancient Scythian, and modern Spanish customs, as described by travellers and historians, for from these two nations the country was at different periods inhabited. Their burials, pattons, and cakes, their houses, furniture and dress, all partake somewhat of these two different nations, and sufficiently mark the original from whence they sprung.

But in order to give you a more minute description of the inhabitants, I shall present you with one month's adventures in the country, where I was invited from Dublin by a Gentleman who had a handsome country seat upon the western shore. I set out on horseback attended only with one servant, and he an English man, being resolved to observe the manners of the inhabitants more minutely than they had been examined before.

When I had got about forty miles from the capital, I found the country begin to wear a different appearance from what it before appeared to me in. The neat inclosures, the warm and well built houses, the fine cultivated grounds, were no more to be seen, the prospect now changed into, here and there a gentleman's seat, grounds ill cultivated, though seemingly capable of cultivation, little irregular fences made of turf, and topped with brush wood, cut from some neighbouring shrub, and the peasants houses wearing all the appearance of indigence and misery. You will not be surprized, sir, as you know me, that I had curiosity enough to enter one of those mansions, which seemed by its appearance to be the habitation of despair: ordering my servant therefore to walk his horses to a neighbouring inn, I alighted and walked into the peasant's hovel. The first sight that struck me was a cow, tied by the horns at one end of the cottage, and a fire of turf without any chimney in the midst. By this sat the mistress of the house, and her daughter knitting stockings, the first seemed about fifty, her eyes bleared with smoak, the daughter about fifteen, as beautiful as an angel. To say the truth, I was surprized to the last degree to see so much beauty where I expected nothing but objects of compassion. For only conceive an hut the walls of which were about four feet high, and made of clay, thatched only with rushes, dirt, and straw, with a door which I was obliged to stoop to enter, conceive this I say, and how could it be expected to find the goddess of beauty lodged so meanly.

In every thing however I was greatly disappointed, for though nothing seemed more wretched than their situation, both seemed alert and lively, and quite insensible of their uncomfortable way of living. They both desired I might be seated upon a straw truss placed by the fire side, probably designed for the husband against his return. The daughter who could speak a little English was excessively chearful and no way surprized at the appearance of a stranger, for by her mother's directions she invited me to supper.

Though I could not imagine where they could procure any thing fit to be eaten, yet in order to see life I complied with their request; for had I refused, it would have been looked upon by the Irish as the highest affront, and the most unpardonable piece of ill breeding. The daughter and I therefore, immediately entered into conversation till the husband's return, who was by trade a labourer, by which occupation he earned four pence a day without meat and drink, but then as he had two sons and they put their profits into one stock, the daughter assured me they all contrived to live pretty comfortably.

The father and his two sons soon returned, and all instead of surprize testified the sincerest satisfaction at the arrival of their new guest, informing me at the same time that nothing was more common than for great folks to lodge a night in their house, when the neighbouring inn could hold no more. The pot was therefore put down with potatoes, and the whole family were busily employed in providing supper; all but the father who it seems is ever exempted from domestic occupations. Supper was soon upon the table, which consisted of nothing more than potatoes and milk, for the rest of the family, but for the father and me, we were honoured each with a wooden knife, and a print of butter.

We accordingly fell to, and as I had a good appetite, I assure you I never made a more comfortable meal. In order however to do things genteely I offered my landlord half a crown when supper was over for my entertainment, but this he refused with the utmost indignation, telling me at the same time that he scorned to keep an inn, and was resolved never to be such a disgrace to his family. It was with the utmost entreaties therefore, that I was permitted to send to the neighbouring alehouse for a shilling's worth of beer, which the daughter ran and fetched in a moment. The circulation of the beer soon threw us all into top spirits, I could not behold without the utmost satisfaction the faces of my fellow creatures which were but a little before wrinkled with fatigue and labour, expanding gradually into smiles, and forgetting those miseries which I had before foolishly deemed insupportable. My landlord offered to tell me the story of Kaul Kroodareg[101], but continues he it will be nothing in English, but in Irish it is finer than fine itself. I declined his offer, pretending to have heard it before, for I had a greater inclination to have some conversation (such Jack is the frailty of us mortals) with the daughter. I therefore attempted to prelude my discourse by a kiss, but guess my surprise, when a favour which the English girls think nothing of bestowing, was denied me. I was therefore obliged in spite of me to let the conversation take a general turn, and answer the news of the day, which was asked me by every one of the family. To these questions I answered to the best of my power, but I found they looked upon my answers as no way satisfactory, they wanted something *strange*, and I had only *news*, to tell them. "Lord my dear Soul, says my landlord. Taking Quebec, burning the French fleet, ruining what d'ye call him, Tierconneldrago,[102] what signifies all that, where is the wonder there, we have been told here that the king of Prussia, took the whole French army, and fifty pieces of cannon prisoners of war, there is something in such news as that; between ourselves my dear soul, I hate the double hearted French, for they have always deceived the Irish, but for all that my dear I love King James in my heart, and God knows I have a good right for my father lost a very good estate by him." With such discourse it began to grow late, and I thought it time to go to my inn; and to this my host objected, for says he, we shall have some clean straw, and you may lie by the fire side, as for us here, we all lie together, my wife, my daughter, and I at the head of the bed, and Laughlin, and Thady, and our dog at the feet. I thanked him for his offer, and went to my inn where the servant had secured me the best and perhaps the only feather-bed in the house.

Before I left that part of the country, I went to see a wake or funeral, which is entirely peculiar to these people. As soon as a person dies he is immediately carried out into the best apartment, and the bed on which he died is burned at the door. The body is wrapped in linnen all but the face, and thus laid upon the door of the house, which on this occasion is taken off the hinges, and claped under their large square table. Beer, pipes, and tobacco are immediately procured, and all the neighbours are invited to sit up the ensuing night, with the corpse, which they call waking it.

Upon this occasion all the old men and women who are generally fond of beer and tobacco, and all the young ones of both sexes, who are equally fond of diversion assemble at the house of the deceased, in order to howl, to romp, and to tell stories. If the deceased was of any substance there is always employed on this occasion a man whose only employment is story telling, and a woman whose only business is to bear a chorus in every howl. At night fall the plays begin, the young folks no way terrified at the scene of death before them, toy and play tricks and have twenty pastimes suited to the occasion, the old ones smoak, guzzle, and upon the appearance of every stranger, howl in the most dismal manner, to a particular tune which you may have seen set to music. This custom of rejoicing instead of sorrow upon the death of a relation, is still preserved among the Tartars, and I fancy from them it is that the native Irish have taken it. When they have thus watched one night for they never keep the body two, it is next day carried upon men's shoulders to the churchyard, and the women continue howling all the way.

Their cakes are also another peculiarity unknown among the English. Upon certain festivals a large cake is procured made of flower, sugar, spices, &c. and placed upon a pole adorned with ribbons and garlands of flowers. Round this the men and women dance in pairs, and that woman that holds out the longest wins the cake, and divides it as she thinks proper. Of all entertainments perhaps this it the most rational, for here they may be literally said to dance for their bread.

Their patrons also I have seen in no other Popish country in Europe; this is a term perhaps you do not understand, almost every fountain in this country is under the patronage of some saint, where the people once a year meet to shew their strength and best cloaths, drink muddy ale, dance with their mistresses, get drunk, and beat each other with cudgels most unmercifully, these religious meetings are never known to pass without blood shed and battery, and their priests often put themselves at the head of the opposite parties, and gain more renown by cudgel-playing than by piety.

But while I thus describe the lower sort of people, you must not suppose but that the gentry have as much politeness, good-nature, and humanity as those of any country whatsoever; easy in their manners, excessively fond of the English, hospitable in their houses, and fond of shew. In short I spent a month in a part of the kingdom where I expected to meet nothing but savages in as good company, which as good cheer, and as hearty reception as I ever remember to have seen. They sit however too long at their meals, I have sometimes staid at the table where we dined for several hours, until the servant came to inform us that supper was served in the next room. They still drink too much which is a certain sign they have not yet arrived at true politeness, since every country is more drunken in proportion as it is barbarous.

I am, &c.

15.3 WILLIAM DICKINSON (AFTER JOHN HAMILTON MORTIMER), *MR. PARSONS AND MR. MOODY IN THE CHARACTERS OF VARLAND AND MAJOR O'FLAHERTY*

William Dickinson (after John Hamilton Mortimer), *Mr. Parsons and Mr. Moody in the Characters of Varland and Major O'Flaherty*, in the *West Indian*, mezzotint, 1776. Trustees of the British Museum.

15.4 *THE MIDDLE TEMPLE MACARONI. IN SHORT I AM A WEST INDIAN!*

Anonymous, *The Middle Temple Macaroni. In short I am a West Indian!* from *The Macaroni Scavoir Vivre and Theatrical Magazine*, July 1773, 511, etching. Trustees of the British Museum.

Notes

1–2 The copytext is Richard Cumberland, *The West Indian: A Comedy* as it is performed at the Theatre Royal in Drury Lane. London: W. Griffin, 1771.

3 See Michael Ragussis, *Theatrical Nation: Jews and Other Outlandish Englishmen in Georgian Britain*. Philadelphia, PA: University of Pennsylvania Press, 2010.

4 Referring to both Belcour and the play itself.

5 Major O'Flaherty.

6 David Garrick and Thomas Arne's spectacular adaptation of Henry Purcell's semi-opera *King Arthur; or, The British Worthy* (libretto by John Dryden, 1691) had been Drury Lane's principle main-piece since December 20, 1770. It ran for 17 performances before being pushed aside by *The West Indian* on January 19, 1771. Cumberland's play ran for 28 nights in its first season.

7 The Irish actor John Moody pioneered a number of modes of ethnic performance in the Georgian period. In this highly acclaimed performance, and in his previous role in David Garrick's *The Jubilee*, he set many of the parameters for the stage Irishman—honest, impetuous, quick with his fists. He was also responsible for many of the first blackface/West Indian dialect roles on the London stage. Having founded a successful theatre company in Kingston, Jamaica in the wake of the Jacobite rebellion he was the original Kingston in David Garrick's *High Life Below Stairs* and he provided Mungo's dialect for Charles Dibdin's *The Padlock*. All of these aspects of Moody's career, including his Jacobite exile, would have been intelligible to the audience.

8 Fanny Abington's presence in this play was one of the reasons for its success. She was at the height of her celebrity and the play and epilogue make much of her fashionable personage.

9 There are no African characters in the play, nor are any invoked in the stage directions, but it appears that players in black-face accompanied Belcour on stage.

10 *bottoms:* the usage is unclear. Stukely may be referring either to the bottoms of other ships or the bottom lines of other transactions.

11 *'Change*: The Stock Exchange.

12 Stockwell and Belcour's mother were not married in a church, thus it was a private marriage with no legal standing.

13 i.e. the Housekeeper.

14 *Creolian*: The Housekeeper's mispronunciation of Creole.

15 Cane sugar and rum were the principle exports of Jamaica.

16 "A narrow way or passage along which troops can march only by files." (OED)

17 In classical mythology, Hercules was forced to perform a series of super-human labours to confirm his god-like status.

18 John Locke, the English philosopher. Lady Rusport is referring to his *Some Thoughts Concerning Education* (1693).

19 The name Roundhead, after the slang term for Oliver Cromwell's army, connotes a Puritan past and raises the spectre of the English Civil Wars. Charlotte picks this up in the ensuing speech.

20 *coquets*: for coquettes, or flirtatious, vain young women.

21 *fops*: usually applied to an effeminate fashionable man who pretends to wit, wisdom or accomplishments. Fops were regularly satirized on the stage during this period.

22 Charlotte is likely referring to the widely read *Letters of the Right Honourable Lady Mary Wortley Montagu: Written During Her Travels in Europe, Asia, and Africa* (1763) whose detailed account of Viennese society marveled that older women were considered highly desirable. Major O'Flaherty has served in the Habsburg Imperial Army (likely during the Seven Years' War) and thus Charlotte implies that his views on sexual relations are less narrow than the typical untraveled Englishman.

23 Charles Dudley is an ensign, the lowest rank for an officer in the British Army, and is awaiting a more lucrative commission. Captain Dudley is on half-pay, or a reduced allowance, because he is not in actual service. Both men require the intervention of someone with political clout or an actual payment to move up the ranks and return to active duty.

24 Lady Rusport's remarks on nursing partly reflect eighteenth-century medical opinion on breast-feeding, and partly underscore her lack of maternal sentiment.

25 *Senegambia*: British Senegambia was a crown colony roughly equivalent to modern day Senegal. During this period the British and the French were expanding their colonial interests in western

Africa and specifically between the Senegal and Gambia Rivers because these waterways gave access to ivory, ebony, and slaves from the interior. Such a post was considered a dangerous commission, and thus it was likely one of the few that Captain Dudley could procure. That he is having difficulty raising the funds is a further sign of the family's poverty.

26 In a further joke on her puritanism, Charles decries both her lack of charity and her anti-theatricality. Puritans had closed the theatres during the interregnum.

27 Visiting tickets or cards were left to signify that someone had come to the house. It is unclear whether the ticket has been left or whether it is one of Lady Rusport's that has not yet been used. They were often quite elaborate engravings and operated much like a form of social currency in the world of fashion, hence Charles's ensuing remark.

28 *son of Loyola*: Jesuit, here implying scheming and duplicity.

29 A book-seller not only sold books but also printed books, pamphlets, newspapers and broadsides. Fulmer's particular sector of the book trade is satirized throughout.

30 Fulmer is primarily a political hack, willing to print and publish for any and all causes. The play comes in the wake of John Wilkes's activism for parliamentary and journalistic reform; and Fulmer's remarks on prerogative and freedom indicate that he printed indiscriminately material for and against the Wilkite cause in the hopes of making money.

31 *Nabobs*: a slang term for someone who made his fortune in the East India Company and has returned to England with conspicuous wealth. At this moment, Nabobs and West Indian planters were frequently seen as social climbers unsettling the hierarchical claims of landed property, thus Fulmer's remark foreshadows Belcour's desire.

32 Mrs. Fulmer bluntly declares that she would use Louisa Dudley's beauty to procure commissions for her brother and father.

33 Dudley borrows Laurence Sterne's *The Life and Opinions of Tristam Shandy, Gentleman* (1759–67). The story of Lieutenant Le Fever and his son in Volume 6 mirrors the Dudleys' predicaments. After the Lieutenant dies Uncle Toby proposes that Le Fever's son (also a soldier) become Tristam's governor, and thus it is a story of sentimental rescue that endorses military life.

34 *mean*: low.

35 *Blue Mountains*: a mountain range in Jamaica.

36 The story of Phoebus Apollo's attempted rape of the nymph Daphne is most famously rendered in Ovid's *Metamorphoses*. In response to her cries for help Daphne was transformed into a laurel tree and Apollo's designs were foiled. Because he could not possess her in human form, Apollo claimed her as his tree and henceforth the laurel became a symbol of honour.

37 This seems to imply that Mrs. Fulmer has been a prostitute.

38 A character from Buckingham's *The Rehearsal* (1671) who kills every one of his combatants "sparing neither friend nor foe."

39 In climate-based theories of human difference, it was believed that the constitution of European bodies would be compromised by the climate in torrid zones where most colonial activity took place.

40 St. James's Fort was a fortified trading post on James Island in the Gambia River. It had been under British rule since 1702 and was a key centre for the slave trade.

41 In this case, Croat has a specifically military usage in keeping with O'Flaherty's mercenary work for the Habsburg Empire: a member of various light cavalry regiments composed (originally or primarily) of Croatians. (*OED*)

42 O'Flaherty outranks Dudley.

43 The Irish brigade was a brigade in the French army originally composed of five exiled Jacobite regiments. The brigade existed from 1690 until 1792 but O'Flaherty indicates that he served the French Crown in the War of the Austrian Succession (1740–48). Whether he fought in the Jacobite rising of 1745 is unclear, but units of the Irish brigade fought at Falkirk and Culloden. It appears that he shifted sides to fight for Empress Maria Teresa of Austria in the Seven Years' War (1754–63) as a grenadier. What remains constant is that O'Flaherty fought against the British on the Continent and thus would have served against Dudley in this period. He is also consistently aligned with Catholic powers and therefore may himself be an Irish Catholic.

44 A soldier of fortune, O'Flaherty appears to have fought for the Bar Confederation—a coalition of Polish nobles—against the Russian Empire from 1768 to the present moment of the play.

45 *Marriage à la militaire*: a type of marriage service outside of the boundaries of civil or church law in which the two partners would jump over a sword. Such marriages were not binding and thus O'Flaherty has numerous wives.
46 *Holborn*: an area of central London.
47 *hammer*-cloth: decorative cloth covering the driver's seat.
48 *hackney coach*: a hired carriage or taxi.
49 *jointure*: the holding of property to the joint use of a husband and wife for life or in tail, as a provision for the latter, in the event of her widowhood. (*OED*)
50 The Order of St. Catherine was indeed an award of Imperial Russia dating back to Peter the Great, but it was reserved for prominent women.
51 *Macaronies*: a club of young Englishmen who affected continental fashions and manners. Hyena here has the connotation of cruel or treacherous.
52 *incognita*: unknown woman, but here it may have the connotation of a woman intentionally hiding her identity as at a masquerade.
53 Slang for bad hand-writing.
54 *Bills for the money*: paper money was still a novelty and Stockwell is specifically indicating that the money is in paper currency.
55 The hunting metaphors re-engage the Apollo/Daphne trope from II.v.
56 *wheat-ear*: a small sparrow-like bird.
57 *polar star*: sailors navigate by the North Star.
58 *Hebe, Venus, Sappho*: Hebe, cupbearer to the gods (hence the reference to nectar and ambrosia) had the power to give eternal youth; Venus was the goddess of love; Sappho was the great female poet of Lesbos.
59 *trepan*: to entrap, ensnare or beguile. (*OED*)
60 *freak*: A sudden causeless change or turn of the mind. (*OED*)
61 Mrs. Fulmer's remarks reflect a broad distrust in the practice of private credit in the early 1770s. The practice of extending credit in exchange for paper bills prompted a collapse of numerous banks in 1772. That these remarks come from a fraud artist is telling.
62 *throne of Delhi*: also known as the Peacock Throne: a famous jeweled throne located in the Red Fort at Delhi. A symbol of the power of the Mughal Empire, it was appropriated by Nadir Shah in 1739 but disappeared when he was assassinated in 1747. The throne was likely dismantled and many of its huge diamonds ended up in Persian or British hands.
63 It was customary for ambassadors to a foreign court to carry letters of credential from the Crown.
64 *hang-dog*: A despicable or degraded fellow fit only to hang a dog, or to be hanged like a dog.
65 *muscavado sugars*: "raw or unrefined sugar obtained from the juice of the sugar cane by evaporating it and draining off the molasses" (*OED*).
66 This declaration is the caption for a print titled "The Middle Temple Macaroni" from *The Macaroni Scavoir Vivre and Theatrical Magazine* for July 1773. See Contexts.
67 *dumb*: i.e. mute.
68 Here *slut* means a bold or impudent girl without the serious imputation of bad qualities.
69 *a Judith, a Joan of Arc*: in the Bible, Judith was renowned for infiltrating the enemy camp and assassinating Holofernes; Joan of Arc was a famous French military leader who was ultimately beatified for her victories over the English in the Hundred Years' War.
70 *the fatality of my condition*: my destined condition or destiny.
71 A Mongolian people from the north west of the Caspian Sea known for their horsemanship.
72 Bedlam was London's asylum for the mentally ill, thus a bedlamite was a madman.
73 It is hard to discern the significance of this reference to 1745. It may be that Sir Stephen Rusport's revised will, like much of the Wilkite activism also referred to in the play, is meant to cancel the memory of the Jacobite rebellion. At the least, placing the will in that year makes it a suspect document, and thus worthy of sober replacement.
74 Charlotte is proposing that she and Charles go to Scotland where the marriage laws were considerably more lax than in England. In this case, getting married in Scotland would obviate the need for Lady Rusport's consent.
75 St. Anthony of Padua is the patron saint of lost and stolen articles, entirely fitting for the transaction between Lady Rusport and Varland.

76 *Lapland*: Scandanavia.
77 Belcour refers to the rules of honour that regulate duels.
78 Diana was goddess of the hunt and one of the three maiden goddesses who swore never to marry.
79 The immense London Tavern had only recently been completed in 1768. It was one of the most famous drinking and eating establishments in London. Because of the large size of the dining room and ballroom it was an important site for assemblies. Famously, it was where 3000*l.* was raised in support of the Wilkite cause in 1769.
80 The patron saint of Ireland.
81 Women of reputation would never accept a visit from a woman whose reputation was compromised.
82 Stockwell's condemnation of dueling as murder would have been seen as progressive quality of his class identity at the time: a sure sign of his variance from aristocratic codes of honour. Proscriptions against dueling were a key part of how middling merchants set themselves as morally superior to the aristocracy.
83 The Pillar Room in the London Tavern was decorated with Corinthian columns and other neo-classical ornaments. We know from Stockwell's remarks later in the scene that the meeting occurs in an interior space and it is likely that the scene painter would have rendered this famous room with sufficient detail to be recognized.
84 *want*: need.
85 Fraud and theft were punishable by death.
86 The disorderly poor were incarcerated at Bridewell Prison so Fulmer is simultaneously acting as witness against his wife and arguing for a mild sentence. In the 1770s Bridewell was also severely criticized for further corrupting, rather than reforming, its prisoners, so Fulmer's remark may have been interpreted as a way of abetting unlawful activity.
87 The terms of the will make Louisa independently wealthy.
88 Stockwell indicates that Charles should pay for O'Flaherty's lawyers.
89 Belcour has intercepted Charlotte, who was on her way to Scotland to elope with Charles without Lady Rusport's consent to marry.
90 Buying a *pair of colours* was military slang for buying into the lowest rank of the army. The phrase is also synonymous with the rank of ensign.
91 David Garrick.
92 Fanny Abington was the most celebrated comic actress of the period and a harbinger of all that was fashionable.
93 *catechise*: obsolete form for "catechism".
94 Abington just played Miss Rusport and will here take on the role of the aristocratic woman "Lady Blabington" in a faux dialogue regarding fashion, femininity and learning. See Gillian Russell's extended reading of this epilogue and Abington's personae in *Women, Sociability and Theatre in Georgian London* (130–32).
95 *Queen Bess*: Elizabeth I.
96 i.e women wore ruffs and farthingales.
97 *in papillote:* in parchment, from the cooking term *en papillote.*
98 *One-and-thirty, Put, All fours, Lantera Loo*: all seventeenth-century card games.
99 *Macbeth*, V.v.19–23:

To-morrow, and to-morrow, and to-morrow,
Creeps in this petty pace from day to day,
To the last syllable of recorded time;
And all our yesterdays have lighted fools
The way to dusty death.

100 Present day Keshkorren mountain in County Sligo
101 In his essay "A Flemish Tradition" in the Bee, Goldsmith identifies the story of Kaul Dereg as a traditional Irish tale."
102 The taking of Quebec, the destruction the French fleet at Quiberon Bay and the victory at Ticonderoga were crucial events in the annus mirabilis of the 1759 in the Seven Years' War .

---

16. *She Stoops to Conquer*

***SHE STOOPS TO CONQUER, OR THE MISTAKES OF A NIGHT*[1]. OLIVER GOLDSMITH. FIRST PERFORMED 15 MARCH 1773 AND FIRST PUBLISHED 1773**

16.1 *SHE STOOPS TO CONQUER, OR THE MISTAKES OF A NIGHT*

Oliver Goldsmith

First Performed 15 March 1773 and First Published 1773

THE IRISH WRITER OLIVER GOLDSMITH (1728?–1774) has the distinction of writing masterpieces in four quintessentially eighteenth-century genres. After establishing himself in the topsy-turvy world of Grub Street, Goldsmith published a complex epistolary fiction modeled on Montesquieu's *Lettres Persanes* entitled *The Citizen of the World* (1760–64). Writing from the perspective of the Chinese traveller Lien Chi Altangi, Goldsmith ironically commented on the economic, political, and cultural transformations besetting British mercantile society at mid century. Written at roughly the same time but not appearing until 1766, Goldsmith's novel *The Vicar of Wakefield* consolidated his literary reputation. It remains among the most important novels of the century. Whatever success Goldsmith had achieved in the world of poetry with *The Traveller* (1764) was eclipsed by the publication of *The Deserted Village* in 1770. One of the most admired poems of his age, Goldsmith's trenchant critique of enclosure simultaneously politicized both the pastoral and the elegy. And finally, on March 15, 1773, Goldsmith's second play, *She Stoops to Conquer* triumphed on the boards of Covent Garden. It has been in almost continuous production ever since.

Much of the early discussion of the play revolved around Goldsmith's claim that he was attempting to rescue the "laughing comedy" of Farquhar and Vanbrugh from the blight of "sentimental comedy" that he believed monopolized the London theatres. This view was presented in Goldsmith's "An Essay on the Theatre; or, A Comparison Between Sentimental and Laughing Comedy," but like many manifestos the distinction has proved to be far more complex or elusive than its author would suggest. The play often juxtaposes sentimental tropes and scenarios with the kind of ludicrous or bawdy material more commonly associated with Restoration and post-Restoration theatre. This juxtaposition is made possible by the play's intense interest in class masquerade and its anxiety regarding class mobility. Goldsmith's great conceit here was to quickly establish the nervousness of Charles Marlow, the son of a wealthy Londoner, around aristocratic women. His predilection for working-class women activates all the titular "mistakes of the night" because his intended, Kate Hardcastle, will have to "stoop to conquer"—i.e. pretend to be common. This famous phrase hearkens back to its use in Aphra Behn's *The Rover* (1677), but here the notion of "stooping" becomes almost synonymous with performance itself. As Charles Marlow and George Hastings make their way to the country seat of Mr. Hardcastle, Kate's step-brother Tony Lumpkin fools the two Town gentlemen into believing that the Hardcastle estate is an inn. Thus all the landed gentry in the play perform as commoners to enable the marriage of Kate and Charles. Goldsmith took full advantage of this meta-theatrical device to satirize the Town and Country alike.

As representatives of the Town, Charles and George are ridiculed because they cannot recognize the affluence of Hardcastle estate. As representatives of landed power, the Hardcastles are forced to enact their own humiliation to ensure the marriage of alliance that will sustain their fortune. That enactment is extraordinary because Charles and George mistakenly perform their superiority in a direct and bawdy fashion. In the process, Goldsmith dissects the necessary collusion between the landed aristocracy and the merchant class. And he does so by forcing the primary characters to either embody or interact with working class subjectivity.

Like many other plays of the early 1770s (Samuel Foote's *The Nabob* comes most forcefully to mind) the spectacle of class impersonation necessarily activated anxieties about fraud and social performance more generally. The credit crisis of 1772, which almost brought down the British banking system, was generated largely by the fact that bonds and credit notes were grounded on little more than reputation—on the performance of class privilege. For the first audiences of *She Stoops to Conquer* the close relationship between class impersonation, economic instability and social crisis would have made the comedy extremely timely. For later audiences, the ongoing anxiety around class and gender performance would be continually re-engaged by the play's cascade of misrecognitions and tricks. In many ways, Tony Lumpkin operates as Goldsmith's surrogate: he is the trickster who controls the space of performance and thus the social parameters within which actions are understood. But he also makes the audience complicit with his theatricality. Part of the play's enduring appeal lies in the way it allows the audience to ridicule and manipulate the characters for their own entertainment. If by this time audiences had developed moral resistance to the sexual innuendo and social leveling, then the play effectively re-purposes masquerade to legitimate suspect practices as necessary for the maintenance of the status quo. In *She Stoops to Conquer*, sexual and class norms are maintained by their contravention. Because audiences can have their cake and eat it too, it is not surprising that they have been so satisfied with Goldsmith's artful comedy.

To Samuel Johnson, L.L.D.

Dear Sir,

By inscribing this slight performance to you, I do not mean so much to compliment you as myself. It may do me some honour to inform the public, that I have lived many years in intimacy with you. It may serve the interests of mankind also to inform them, that the greatest wit may be found in a character, without impairing the most unaffected piety.

I have, particularly, reason to thank you for your partiality to this performance. The undertaking a comedy, not merely sentimental, was very dangerous; and Mr. Colman, who saw this piece in its various stages, always thought it so. However, I ventured to trust it to the public; and, though it was necessarily delayed till late in the season, I have every reason to be grateful.

I am, dear Sir,
Your most sincere friend
And admirer,
Oliver Goldsmith.

PROLOGUE

By David Garrick, Esq.

[*Enter* Mr. Woodward,[2] *dressed in black, and holding a handkerchief to his eyes.*

Excuse me, Sirs, I pray—I can't yet speak—
I'm crying now—and have been all the week!
'Tis not alone this mourning suit, good masters;
I've that within[3]—for which there are no plaisters!
Pray, wou'd you know the reason why I'm crying?
The Comic Muse, long sick, is now a-dying!
And if she goes, my tears will never stop;
For as a player, I can't squeeze out one drop:
I am undone, that's all—shall lose my bread—
I'd rather, but that's nothing—lose my head.
When the sweet maid is laid upon the bier,
Shuter[4] and I shall be chief mourners here.
To her a mawkish drab of spurious breed,
Who deals in sentimentals,[5] will succeed!
Poor Ned and I are dead to all intents,
We can as soon speak Greek as sentiments!

Both nervous grown, to keep our spirits up,
We now and then take down a hearty cup.
What shall we do? If Comedy forsake us,
They'll turn us out, and no one else will take us![6]
But why can't I be moral?—Let me try—
My heart thus pressing—fix'd my face and eye—
With a sententious look, that nothing means,
(Faces are blocks[7] in sentimental scenes)
Thus I begin—All is not gold that glitters,[8]
Pleasure seems sweet, but proves a glass of bitters.
When Ignorance enters, Folly is at hand:
Learning is better far than house and land.
Let not your virtue trip; who trips may stumble,
And virtue is not virtue, if she tumble.
I give it up—morals won't do for me;
To make you laugh, I must play tragedy.
One hope remains—hearing the maid was ill,
A doctor comes this night to shew his skill.
To cheer her heart, and give your muscles motion,
He, in five draughts prepar'd, presents a potion:
A kind of magic charm—for be assur'd,
If you will swallow it, the maid is cur'd:
But desp'rate the doctor,[9] and her case is,
If you reject the dose, and make wry faces!
This truth he boasts, will boast it while he lives,
No pois'nous drugs are mix'd in what he gives;
Should he succeed, you'll give him his degree;
If not, within he will receive no fee!
The college you, must his pretensions back,
Pronounce him regular, or dub him quack.

Dramatis Personæ

Men

Sir Charles Marlow	Mr. Gardener
Young Marlow (his Son)	Mr. Lee Lewes[10]
Hardcastle	Mr. Shuter
Hastings	Mr. Dubellamy
Tony Lumpkin	Mr. Quick [11]
Diggory[12]	Mr. Saunders

Women

Mrs. Hardcastle	Mrs. Green
Miss Hardcastle	Mrs. Bulkeley
Miss Neville	Mrs. Kniveton
Maid	Miss Williams
Landlord, Servants, etc., etc.	

I.i

[*Scene—A chamber in an old-fashioned house. Enter* Mrs. Hardcastle *and* Mr. Hardcastle.]

MRS. HARDCASTLE. I vow, Mr. Hardcastle, you're very particular. Is there a creature in the whole country, but ourselves, that does not take a trip to town now and then, to rub off the rust a little? There's the two Miss Hoggs, and our neighbour Mrs. Grigsby, go to take a month's polishing every winter.

HARDCASTLE. Ay, and bring back vanity and affectation to last them the whole year. I wonder why London cannot keep its own fools at home. In my time, the follies of the town crept slowly among us, but now they travel faster than a stage-coach. Its fopperies come down, not only as inside passengers, but in the very basket.[13]

MRS. HARDCASTLE. Ay, *your* times were fine times indeed; you have been telling us of *them* for many a long year. Here we live in an old rumbling[14] mansion, that looks for all the world like an inn, but that we never see company. Our best visitors are old Mrs. Oddfish, the curate's wife, and little Cripplegate, the lame dancing-master; and all our entertainment your old stories of Prince Eugene and the Duke of Marlborough.[15] I hate such old-fashioned trumpery.

HARDCASTLE. And I love it. I love everything that's old: old friends, old times, old manners, old books, old wine; and I believe, Dorothy [*Taking her hand*], you'll own I have been pretty fond of an old wife.

MRS. HARDCASTLE. Lord, Mr. Hardcastle, you're for ever at your Dorothy's and your old wife's. You may be a Darby but I'll be no Joan,[16] I promise you. I'm not so old as you'd make me, by more than one good year. Add twenty to twenty, and make money of that.

HARDCASTLE. Let me see; twenty added to twenty makes just fifty and seven.

MRS. HARDCASTLE. It's false, Mr. Hardcastle; I was but twenty when I was brought to bed of Tony, that I had by Mr. Lumpkin, my first husband; and he's not come to years of discretion[17] yet.

HARDCASTLE. Nor ever will, I dare answer for him. Ay, you have taught *him* finely.

MRS. HARDCASTLE. No matter. Tony Lumpkin has a good fortune. My son is not to live by his learning. I don't think a boy wants much learning to spend fifteen hundred a year.

HARDCASTLE. Learning, quotha! a mere composition of tricks and mischief.

MRS. HARDCASTLE. Humour, my dear; nothing but humour. Come, Mr. Hardcastle, you must allow the boy a little humour.

HARDCASTLE. I'd sooner allow him a horse-pond.[18] If burning the footmen's shoes, frighting the maids, and worrying the kittens be humour, he has it. It was but yesterday he fastened my wig to the back of my chair, and when I went to make a bow, I popt my bald head in Mrs. Frizzle's face.

MRS. HARDCASTLE. And am I to blame? The poor boy was always too sickly to do any good. A school would be his death. When he comes to be a little stronger, who knows what a year or two's Latin may do for him?

HARDCASTLE. Latin for him! A cat and fiddle. No, no; the alehouse and the stable are the only schools he'll ever go to.

MRS. HARDCASTLE. Well, we must not snub the poor boy now, for I believe we shan't have him long among us. Any body that looks in his face may see that he's consumptive.

HARDCASTLE. Ay, if growing too fat be one of the symptoms.

MRS. HARDCASTLE. He coughs sometimes.

HARDCASTLE. Yes, when his liquor goes the wrong way.

MRS. HARDCASTLE. I'm actually afraid of his lungs.

HARDCASTLE. And truly so am I; for he sometimes whoops like a speaking trumpet—[Tony *hallooing behind the scenes*]—O there he goes—a very consumptive figure, truly.

[*Enter* Tony, *crossing the stage.*

MRS. HARDCASTLE. Tony, where are you going, my charmer? Won't you give papa and I a little of your company, lovee?

TONY. I'm in haste, mother, I cannot stay.

MRS. HARDCASTLE. You shan't venture out this raw evening, my dear; you look most shockingly.

TONY. I can't stay, I tell you. The Three Pigeons expects me down every moment. There's some fun going forward.

HARDCASTLE. Ay; the alehouse, the old place; I thought so.

MRS. HARDCASTLE. A low, paltry set of fellows.

TONY. Not so low, neither. There's Dick Muggins the exciseman, Jack Slang the horse doctor, little Aminadab that grinds the music-box, and Tom Twist that spins the pewter platter.

MRS. HARDCASTLE. Pray, my dear, disappoint them for one night at least.

TONY. As for disappointing *them*, I should not so much mind; but I can't abide to disappoint *myself.*

MRS. HARDCASTLE. [*Detaining him*] You shan't go.

TONY. I will, I tell you.

MRS. HARDCASTLE. I say you shan't.

TONY. We'll see which is strongest, you or I.

[*Exit, hauling her out.*

HARDCASTLE. [*Solus*] Ay, there goes a pair that only spoil each other. But is not the whole age in a combination to drive sense and discretion out of doors? There's my pretty darling Kate; the fashions of the times have almost infected her too. By living a year or two in town, she's as fond of gauze, and French frippery, as the best of them.

[*Enter* Miss Hardcastle.

HARDCASTLE. Blessings on my pretty innocence! drest out as usual, my Kate. Goodness! what a quantity of superfluous silk hast thou got about thee, girl! I could never teach the fools of this age, that the indigent world could be cloathed out of the trimmings of the vain.

MISS HARDCASTLE. You know our agreement, Sir. You allow me the morning to receive and pay visits, and to dress in my own manner; and in the evening I put on my housewife's dress to please you.

HARDCASTLE. Well, remember, I insist on the terms of our agreement; and, by the bye, I believe I shall have occasion to try your obedience this very evening.

MISS HARDCASTLE. I protest, Sir, I don't comprehend your meaning.

HARDCASTLE. Then to be plain with you, Kate, I expect the young gentleman I have chosen to be your husband from town this very day. I have his father's letter, in which he informs me his son is set out, and that he intends to follow himself shortly after.

MISS HARDCASTLE. Indeed! I wish I had known something of this before. Bless me, how shall I behave? It's a thousand to one I shan't like him; our meeting will be so formal, and so like a thing of business, that I shall find no room for friendship or esteem.

HARDCASTLE. Depend upon it, child, I'll never controul your choice; but Mr. Marlow, whom I have pitched upon, is the son of my old friend, Sir Charles Marlow, of whom you have heard me talk so often. The young gentleman has been bred a scholar, and is designed for an employment in the service of his country. I am told he's a man of excellent understanding.

MISS HARDCASTLE. Is he?

HARDCASTLE. Very generous.

MISS HARDCASTLE. I believe I shall like him.

HARDCASTLE. Young and brave.

MISS HARDCASTLE. I'm sure I shall like him.

HARDCASTLE. And very handsome.

MISS HARDCASTLE. My dear Papa, say no more [*Kissing his hand*], he's mine; I'll have him.

HARDCASTLE. And, to crown all, Kate, he's one of the most bashful and reserved young fellows in all the world.

MISS HARDCASTLE. Eh! you have frozen me to death again. That word reserved has undone all the rest of his accomplishments. A reserved lover, it is said, always makes a suspicious husband.

HARDCASTLE. On the contrary, modesty seldom resides in a breast that is not enriched with nobler virtues. It was the very feature in his character that first struck me.

MISS HARDCASTLE. He must have more striking features to catch me, I promise you. However, if he be so young, so handsome, and so every thing as you mention, I believe he'll do still. I think I'll have him.

HARDCASTLE. Ay, Kate, but there is still an obstacle. It's more than an even wager he may not have *you*.

MISS HARDCASTLE. My dear Papa, why will you mortify one so?—Well, if he refuses, instead of breaking my heart at his indifference, I'll only break my glass for its flattery, set my cap to some newer fashion, and look out for some less difficult admirer.

HARDCASTLE. Bravely resolved! In the mean time I'll go prepare the servants for his reception; as we seldom see company, they want as much training as a company of recruits, the first day's muster. [*Exit.*

MISS HARDCASTLE. [*Alone*] Lud, this news of Papa's puts me all in a flutter. Young, handsome; these he put last; but I put them foremost. Sensible,[19] good-natured; I like all that. But then reserved and sheepish, that's much against him. Yet can't he be cured of his timidity, by being taught to be proud of his wife? Yes, and can't I—But I vow I'm disposing of the husband before I have secured the lover.

[*Enter* Miss Neville.

MISS HARDCASTLE. I'm glad you're come, Neville, my dear. Tell me, Constance, how do I look this evening? Is there any thing whimsical about me? Is it one of my well looking days, child? Am I in face today?

MISS NEVILLE. Perfectly, my dear. Yet now I look again bless me!—sure no accident has happened among the canary birds or the gold fishes. Has your brother or the cat been meddling? Or has the last novel been too moving?

MISS HARDCASTLE. No; nothing of all this. I have been threatened—I can scarce get it out—I have been threatened with a lover.

MISS NEVILLE. And his name—

MISS HARDCASTLE. Is Marlow.

MISS NEVILLE. Indeed!

MISS HARDCASTLE. The son of Sir Charles Marlow.

MISS NEVILLE. As I live, the most intimate friend of Mr. Hastings, *my* admirer. They are never asunder. I believe you must have seen him when we lived in town.

MISS HARDCASTLE. Never.

MISS NEVILLE. He's a very singular character, I assure you. Among women of reputation and virtue he is the modestest man alive; but his acquaintances give him a very different character among creatures of another stamp: you understand me.

MISS HARDCASTLE. An odd character, indeed. I shall never be able to manage him. What shall I do? Pshaw, think no more of him, but trust to occurrences for success. But how goes on your own affair, my dear, has my mother been courting you for my brother Tony, as usual?

MISS NEVILLE. I have just come from one of our agreeable *tête-à-têtes*. She has been saying a hundred tender things, and setting off her pretty monster as the very pink of perfection.

MISS HARDCASTLE. And her partiality is such, that she actually thinks him so. A fortune like yours is no small temptation. Besides, as she has the sole management of it, I'm not surprised to see her unwilling to let it go out of the family.

MISS NEVILLE. A fortune like mine, which chiefly consists in jewels, is no such mighty temptation. But at any rate, if my dear Hastings be but constant, I make no doubt to be too hard for her at last. However, I let her suppose that I am in love with her son, and she never once dreams that my affections are fixed upon another.

MISS HARDCASTLE. My good brother holds out stoutly. I could almost love him for hating you so.

MISS NEVILLE. It is a good-natured creature at bottom, and I'm sure would wish to see me married to any body but himself. But my aunt's bell rings for our afternoon's walk round the improvements. Allons![20] Courage is necessary, as our affairs are critical.

MISS HARDCASTLE. Would it were bed-time, and all were well.

[*Exeunt.*

I.ii

[*An Alehouse Room. Several shabby fellows with punch and tobacco.* Tony *at the head of the table, a little higher than the rest, a mallet in his hand.*]

OMNES. Hurrea, hurrea, hurrea. Bravo.

FIRST FELLOW. Now, gentlemen, silence for a song. The 'squire is going to knock himself down for a song.

OMNES. Ay, a song, a song!

TONY. Then I'll sing you, gentlemen, a song I made upon this alehouse, the Three Pigeons.

SONG.

Let school-masters puzzle their brain,
With grammar, and nonsense, and learning;
Good liquor, I stoutly maintain,
Gives genus[21] *a better discerning.*
Let them brag of their heathenish gods,
Their Lethes, their Styxes, and Stygians,[22]
Their Quis, and their Quœs, and their Quods,[23]
They're all but a parcel of Pigeons.
Toroddle, toroddle, toroll.

When Methodist preachers come down,
A-preaching that drinking is sinful,
I'll wager the rascals a crown,
They always preach best with a skinful.
But when you come down with your pence,
For a slice of their scurvy religion,
I'll leave it to all men of sense,
But you my good friend are the pigeon.
Toroddle, toroddle, toroll.

Then come, put the jorum about,
And let us be merry and clever,
Our hearts and our liquors are stout,
Here's the Three Jolly Pigeons for ever.
Let some cry up woodcock or hare,
Your bustards, your ducks, and your widgeons;
But of all the gay birds in the air,
Here's a health to the Three Jolly Pigeons.
Toroddle, toroddle, toroll.

OMNES. Bravo, bravo!

FIRST FELLOW. The 'squire has got spunk in him.

SECOND FELLOW. I loves to hear him sing, bekeays he never gives us nothing that's *low.*

THIRD FELLOW. O damn any thing that's *low*, I cannot bear it.

FOURTH FELLOW. The genteel thing is the genteel thing any time. If so be that a gentleman bees in a concatenation accordingly.

THIRD FELLOW. I like the maxum[24] of it, Master Muggins. What, tho' I am obligated to dance a bear, a man may be a gentleman for all that. May this be my poison, if my bear ever dances but to the very genteelest of tunes; *Water Parted,*[25] or the minuet in *Ariadne.*[26]

SECOND FELLOW. What a pity it is the 'Squire is not come to his own. It would be well for all the publicans within ten miles round of him.

TONY. Ecod[27] and so it would, Master Slang. I'd then shew what it was to keep choice of company.

SECOND FELLOW. O he takes after his own father for that. To be sure old 'Squire Lumpkin was the finest gentleman I ever set my eyes on. For winding the streight horn, or beating a thicket for a hare, or a wench, he never had his fellow. It was a saying in the place, that he kept the best horses, dogs, and girls in the whole county.

TONY. Ecod, and when I'm of age I'll be no bastard, I promise you. I have been thinking of Bett Bouncer and the miller's grey mare to begin with. But come, my boys, drink about and be merry, for you pay no reckoning. Well, Stingo, what's the matter?

[*Enter* Landlord.

LANDLORD. There be two gentlemen in a post-chaise at the door. They have lost their way upo' the forest; and they are talking something about Mr. Hardcastle.

TONY. As sure as can be, one of them must be the gentleman that's coming down to court my sister. Do they seem to be Londoners?

LANDLORD. I believe they may. They look woundily[28] like Frenchmen.

TONY. Then desire them to step this way, and I'll set them right in a twinkling. [*Exit* Landlord] Gentlemen, as they mayn't be good enough company for you, step down for a moment, and I'll be with you in the squeezing of a lemon. [*Exeunt mob.* Tony *Solus*] Father-in-law has been calling me whelp, and hound, this half-year. Now if I pleased, I could be so revenged upon the old grumbletonian. But then I'm afraid—afraid of what? I shall soon be worth fifteen hundred a year, and let him frighten me out of *that* if he can.

[*Enter* Landlord, *conducting* Marlow *and* Hastings.

MARLOW. What a tedious uncomfortable day have we had of it! We were told it was but forty miles across the country, and we have come above threescore.

HASTINGS. And all, Marlow, from that unaccountable reserve of yours, that would not let us inquire more frequently on the way.

MARLOW. I own, Hastings, I am unwilling to lay myself under an obligation to every one I meet; and often stand the chance of an unmannerly answer.

HASTINGS. At present, however, we are not likely to receive any answer.

TONY. No offence, gentlemen. But I'm told you have been inquiring for one Mr. Hardcastle, in these parts. Do you know what part of the country you are in?

HASTINGS. Not in the least, Sir, but should thank you for information.

TONY. Nor the way you came?

HASTINGS. No, Sir; but if you can inform us—

TONY. Why, gentlemen, if you know neither the road you are going, nor where you are, nor the road you came, the first thing I have to inform you is, that you have lost your way.

MARLOW. We wanted no ghost[29] to tell us that.

TONY. Pray, gentlemen, may I be so bold as to ask the place from whence you came?

MARLOW. That's not necessary towards directing us where we are to go.

TONY. No offence; but question for question is all fair, you know. Pray, gentlemen, is not this same Hardcastle: a cross-grain'd, old-fashion'd, whimsical fellow, with an ugly face, a daughter, and a pretty son?

HASTINGS. We have not seen the gentleman; but he has the family you mention.

TONY. The daughter, a tall, trapesing,[30] trolloping, talkative maypole—the son, a pretty, well-bred, agreeable youth, that everybody is fond of?

MARLOW. Our information differs in this. The daughter is said to be well-bred, and beautiful; the son an awkward booby, reared up and spoiled at his mother's apron-string.

TONY. He-he-hem!—Then, gentlemen, all I have to tell you is, that you won't reach Mr. Hardcastle's house this night, I believe.

HASTINGS. Unfortunate!

TONY. It's a damn'd long, dark, boggy, dirty, dangerous way. Stingo, tell the gentlemen the way to Mr. Hardcastle's; [*Winking upon the* Landlord] Mr. Hardcastle's, of Quagmire Marsh, you understand me.

LANDLORD. Master Hardcastle's! Lock-a-daisy, my masters, you're come a deadly deal wrong! When you came to the bottom of the hill, you should have cross'd down Squash Lane.

MARLOW. Cross down Squash Lane!

LANDLORD. Then you were to keep straight forward, till you came to four roads.

MARLOW. Come to where four roads meet!

TONY. Ay; but you must be sure to take only one of them.

MARLOW. O, Sir, you're facetious.

TONY. Then keeping to the right, you are to go sideways, till you come upon Crack-skull Common: there you must look sharp for the track of the wheel, and go forward till you come to Farmer Murrain's barn.[31] Coming to the farmer's barn, you are to turn to the right, and then to the left, and then to the right about again, till you find out the old mill—

MARLOW. Zounds, man! we could as soon find out the longitude![32]

HASTINGS. What's to be done, Marlow?

MARLOW. This house promises but a poor reception; though perhaps the landlord can accommodate us.

LANDLORD. Alack! master, we have but one spare bed in the whole house.

TONY. And to my knowledge, that's taken up by three lodgers already. [*After a pause, in which the rest seem disconcerted*] I have hit it. Don't you think, Stingo, our landlady could accommodate the gentlemen by the fire-side, with—three chairs and a bolster?

HASTINGS. I hate sleeping by the fire-side.

MARLOW. And I detest your three chairs and a bolster.

TONY. You do, do you?—then, let me see—what—if you go on a mile further, to the Buck's Head; the old Buck's Head on the hill, one of the best inns in the whole county?

HASTINGS. O ho! so we have escaped an adventure for this night, however.

LANDLORD. [*Apart to* Tony] Sure, you ben't sending them to your father's as an inn, be you?

TONY. Mum, you fool you. Let *them* find that out. [*To them*] You have only to keep on straight forward, till you come to a large old house by the road-side. You'll see a pair of large horns over the door. That's the sign. Drive up the yard, and call stoutly about you.

HASTINGS. Sir, we are obliged to you. The servants can't miss the way?

TONY. No, no: but I tell you, though, the landlord is rich, and going to leave off business; so he wants to be thought a gentleman, saving your presence, he! he! he! He'll be for giving you his company, and ecod if you mind him, he'll persuade you that his mother was an alderman, and his aunt a justice of the peace.

LANDLORD. A troublesome old blade, to be sure; but a keeps as good wines and beds as any in the whole country.

MARLOW. Well, if he supplies us with these, we shall want no further connexion. We are to turn to the right, did you say?

TONY. No, no; straight forward. I'll just step myself, and shew you a piece of the way. [*To the* Landlord] Mum.

LANDLORD. Ah, bless your heart, for a sweet, pleasant—damn'd mischievous son of a whore.

[*Exeunt.*

II.i

[*An old-fashioned house. enter* Hardcastle, *followed by three or four awkward* Servants.]

HARDCASTLE. Well, I hope you're perfect in the table exercise I have been teaching you these three days. You all know your posts and your places, and can shew that you have been used to good company, without ever stirring from home.

OMNES. Ay, ay.

HARDCASTLE. When company comes you are not to pop out and stare, and then run in again, like frighted rabbits in a warren.

OMNES. No, no.

HARDCASTLE. You, Diggory, whom I have taken from the barn, are to make a shew at the side-table; and you, Roger, whom I have advanced from the plow, are to place yourself behind *my* chair. But you're not to stand so, with your hands in your pockets. Take your hands from your pockets, Roger; and from your head, you blockhead you. See how Diggory carries his hands. They're a little too stiff, indeed, but that's no great matter.

DIGGORY. Ay, mind how I hold them. I learned to hold my hands this way when I was upon drill for the militia. And so being upon drill—

HARDCASTLE. You must not be so talkative, Diggory. You must be all attention to the guests. You must hear us talk, and not think of talking; you must see us drink, and not think of drinking; you must see us eat, and not think of eating.

DIGGORY. By the laws, your worship, that's parfectly unpossible. Whenever Diggory sees yeating going forward, ecod he's always wishing for a mouthful himself.

HARDCASTLE. Blockhead! Is not a belly full in the kitchen as good as a belly full in the parlour? Stay your stomach with that reflection.

DIGGORY. Ecod, I thank your worship, I'll make a shift to stay my stomach with a slice of cold beef in the pantry.

HARDCASTLE. Diggory, you are too talkative. Then, if I happen to say a good thing, or tell a good story at table, you must not all burst out a-laughing, as if you made part of the company.

DIGGORY. Then, ecod, your worship must not tell the story of Ould Grouse in the gun-room. I can't help laughing at that—he! he! he!—for the soul of me. We have laughed at that these twenty years—ha! ha! ha!

HARDCASTLE. Ha! ha! ha! The story is a good one. Well, honest Diggory, you may laugh at that—but still remember to be attentive. Suppose one of the company should call for a glass of wine, how will you behave? A glass of wine, Sir, if you please [*To* Diggory]—Eh, why don't you move?

DIGGORY. Ecod, your worship, I never have courage till I see the eatables and drinkables brought upo' the table, and then I'm as bauld as a lion.

HARDCASTLE. What, will nobody move?

FIRST SERVANT. I'm not to leave this pleace.

SECOND SERVANT. I'm sure it's no pleace of mine.

THIRD SERVANT. Nor mine for sartain.

DIGGORY. Wauns,[33] and I'm sure it canna be mine.

HARDCASTLE. You numskulls! and so while, like your betters, you are quarrelling for places, the guests must be starved. O you dunces! I find I must begin all over again.—But don't I hear a coach drive into the yard? To your posts, you blockheads. I'll go in the mean time and give my old friend's son a hearty reception at the gate. [*Exit* Hardcastle.

DIGGORY. By the elevens,[34] my pleace is gone quite out of my head.

ROGER. I know that my pleace is to be every where.

FIRST SERVANT. Where the devil is mine?

SECOND SERVANT. My pleace is to be no where at all; and so Ize go about my business.

[*Exeunt* Servants, *running about as if frighted, different ways. Enter* Servant *with candles, showing in* Marlow *and* Hastings.

SERVANT. Welcome, gentlemen, very welcome! This way.

HASTINGS. After the disappointments of the day, welcome once more, Charles, to the comforts of a clean room and a good fire. Upon my word, a very well-looking house; antique, but creditable.

MARLOW. The usual fate of a large mansion. Having first ruined the master by good housekeeping, it at last comes to levy contributions as an inn.

HASTINGS. As you say, we passengers are to be taxed to pay all these fineries. I have often seen a good sideboard, or a marble chimney-piece, tho' not actually put in the bill, enflame a reckoning confoundedly.

MARLOW. Travellers, George, must pay in all places; the only difference is, that in good inns, you pay dearly for luxuries; in bad inns you are fleeced and starved.

HASTINGS. You have lived very much among them. In truth, I have been often surprised, that you who have seen so much of the world, with your natural good sense, and your many opportunities, could never yet acquire a requisite share of assurance.

MARLOW. The Englishman's malady. But tell me, George, where could I have learned that assurance you talk of? My life has been chiefly spent in a college, or an inn,[35] in seclusion from that lovely part of the creation that chiefly teach men confidence. I don't know that I was ever familiarly acquainted with a single modest woman—except my mother—But among females of another class, you know—

HASTINGS. Ay, among them you are impudent enough of all conscience.

MARLOW. They are of *us*, you know.

HASTINGS. But in the company of women of reputation, I never saw such an idiot, such a trembler; you look for all the world as if you wanted an opportunity of stealing out of the room.

MARLOW. Why, man, that's because I *do* want to steal out of the room. Faith, I have often formed a resolution to break the ice, and rattle away at any rate. But I don't know how, a single glance from a pair of fine eyes has totally overset my resolution. An impudent fellow may counterfeit modesty, but I'll be hanged if a modest man can ever counterfeit impudence.

HASTINGS. If you could but say half the fine things to them, that I have heard you lavish upon the barmaid of an inn, or even a college bedmaker—

MARLOW. Why, George, I can't say fine things to them; they freeze, they petrify me. They may talk of a comet, or a burning mountain, or some such bagatelle. But to me, a modest woman, drest out in all her finery, is the most tremendous object of the whole creation.

HASTINGS. Ha! ha! ha! at this rate, man, how can you ever expect to marry!

MARLOW. Never, unless, as among kings and princes, my bride were to be courted by proxy. If, indeed, like an Eastern bridegroom, one were to be introduced to a wife he never saw before, it might be endured. But to go through all the terrors of a formal courtship, together with the episode of aunts, grandmothers, and cousins, and at last to blurt out the broad staring question of, "Madam, will you marry me?" No, no, that's a strain much above me, I assure you.

HASTINGS. I pity you. But how do you intend behaving to the lady you are come down to visit at the request of your father?

MARLOW. As I behave to all other ladies. Bow very low, answer yes, or no, to all her demands—But for the rest, I don't think I shall venture to look in her face, till I see my father's again.

HASTINGS. I'm surprized that one who is so warm a friend can be so cool a lover.

MARLOW. To be explicit, my dear Hastings, my chief inducement down was to be instrumental in forwarding your happiness, not my own. Miss Neville loves you, the family don't know you; as my friend you are sure of a reception, and let honour do the rest.

HASTINGS. My dear Marlow! But I'll suppress the emotion. Were I a wretch, meanly seeking to carry off a fortune, you should be the last man in the world I would apply to for assistance. But Miss Neville's person is all I ask, and that is mine, both from her deceased father's consent, and her own inclination.

MARLOW. Happy man! You have talents and art to captivate any woman. I'm doom'd to adore the sex, and yet to converse with the only part of it I despise. This stammer in my address, and this aukward prepossessing visage of mine, can never permit me to soar above the reach of a milliner's 'prentice, or one of the duchesses of Drury-Lane.[36] Pshaw! this fellow here to interrupt us.

[*Enter* Hardcastle.

HARDCASTLE. Gentlemen, once more you are heartily welcome. Which is Mr. Marlow? Sir, you are heartily welcome. It's not my way, you see, to receive my friends with my back to the fire. I like to give them a hearty reception in the old stile at my gate. I like to see their horses and trunks taken care of.

MARLOW.—[*Aside*] *He has got our names from the servants already.*—[*To him*] We approve your caution and hospitality, Sir. [*To* Hastings] I have been thinking, George, of changing our travelling dresses in the morning. I am grown confoundedly ashamed of mine.

HARDCASTLE. I beg, Mr. Marlow, you'll use no ceremony in this house.

HASTINGS. I fancy, Charles, you're right: the first blow is half the battle. I intend opening the campaign with the white and gold.

HARDCASTLE. Mr. Marlow—Mr. Hastings—gentlemen—pray be under no constraint in this house. This is Liberty-Hall, gentlemen. You may do just as you please here.

MARLOW. Yet, George, if we open the campaign too fiercely at first, we may want ammunition before it is over. I think to reserve the embroidery to secure a retreat.

HARDCASTLE. Your talking of a retreat, Mr. Marlow, puts me in mind of the Duke of Marlborough, when we went to besiege Denain.[37] He first summoned the garrison—

MARLOW. Don't you think the *ventre d'or* waistcoat[38] will do with the plain brown?

HARDCASTLE. He first summoned the garrison, which might consist of about five thousand men—

HASTINGS. I think not: brown and yellow mix but very poorly.

HARDCASTLE. I say, gentlemen, as I was telling you, he summoned the garrison, which might consist of about five thousand men—

MARLOW. The girls like finery.

HARDCASTLE. Which might consist of about five thousand men, well appointed with stores, ammunition, and other implements of war. Now, says the Duke of Marlborough to George Brooks,[39] that stood next to him—you must have heard of George Brooks—"I'll pawn my dukedom," says he, "but I take that garrison without spilling a drop of blood." So—

MARLOW. What, my good friend, if you gave us a glass of punch in the mean time, it would help us to carry on the siege with vigour.

HARDCASTLE. Punch, Sir!—[*Aside*] *This is the most unaccountable kind of modesty I ever met with.*

MARLOW. Yes, Sir, punch. A glass of warm punch after our journey, will be comfortable. This is Liberty-Hall, you know.

HARDCASTLE. Here's a cup, Sir.

MARLOW. [*Aside*] *So this fellow, in his Liberty-Hall, will only let us have just what he pleases.*

HARDCASTLE. [*Taking the cup*] I hope you'll find it to your mind. I have prepared it with my own hands, and I believe you'll own the ingredients are tolerable. Will you be so good as to pledge me, Sir? Here, Mr. Marlow, here is to our better acquaintance. [*Drinks.*

MARLOW.—[*Aside*] *A very impudent fellow this! but he's a character, and I'll humour him a little.*—[*To* Hardcastle] Sir, my service to you. [*Drinks.*

HASTINGS. [*Aside*] *I see this fellow wants to give us his company, and forgets that he's an innkeeper before he has learned to be a gentleman.*

MARLOW. From the excellence of your cup, my old friend, I suppose you have a good deal of business in this part of the country. Warm work, now and then, at elections, I suppose.

HARDCASTLE. No, Sir, I have long given that work over. Since our betters have hit upon the expedient of electing each other, there is no business *for us that sell ale.*[40]

HASTINGS. So, then you have no turn for politics, I find.

HARDCASTLE. Not in the least. There was a time, indeed, I fretted myself about the mistakes of government, like other people; but finding myself every day growing more angry, and the government growing no better, I left it to mend itself. Since that, I no more trouble my head about Hyder Ally, or Ally Cawn, than about Ally Croaker.[41] Sir, my service to you.

HASTINGS. So that with eating above stairs, and drinking below, with receiving your friends within, and amusing them without, you lead a good pleasant bustling life of it.

HARDCASTLE. I do stir about a great deal, that's certain. Half the differences of the parish are adjusted in this very parlour.

MARLOW. [*After drinking*] And you have an argument in your cup, old gentleman, better than any in Westminster-Hall.

HARDCASTLE. Ay, young gentleman, that, and a little philosophy.

MARLOW. [*Aside*] *Well, this is the first time I ever heard of an innkeeper's philosophy.*

HASTINGS. So then, like an experienced general, you attack them on every quarter. If you find their reason manageable, you attack it with your philosophy; if you find they have no reason, you attack them with this. Here's your health, my philosopher. [*Drinks.*

HARDCASTLE. Good, very good, thank you; ha! ha! Your generalship puts me in mind of Prince Eugene, when he fought the Turks at the battle of Belgrade.[42] You shall hear.

MARLOW. Instead of the battle of Belgrade, I believe it's almost time to talk about supper. What has your philosophy got in the house for supper!

HARDCASTLE. For supper, Sir!—[*Aside*] *Was ever such a request to a man in his own house!*

MARLOW. Yes, Sir, supper, Sir; I begin to feel an appetite. I shall make devilish work to-night in the larder, I promise you.

HARDCASTLE.—[*Aside*] *Such a brazen dog sure never my eyes beheld.*—[*To him*] Why, really, Sir, as for supper, I can't well tell. My Dorothy and the cook-maid settle these things between them. I leave these kind of things entirely to them.

MARLOW. You do, do you?

HARDCASTLE. Entirely. By-the-bye, I believe they are in actual consultation upon what's for supper this moment in the kitchen.

MARLOW. Then I beg they'll admit *me* as one of their privy-council.[43] It's a way I have got. When I travel I always choose to regulate my own supper. Let the cook be called. No offence I hope, Sir?

HARDCASTLE. O no, Sir, none in the least; yet I don't know how; our Bridget, the cook-maid, is not very communicative upon these occasions. Should we send for her, she might scold us all out of the house.

HASTINGS. Let's see your list of the larder then. I ask it as a favour. I always match my appetite to my bill of fare.

MARLOW. [*To* Hardcastle*, who looks at them with surprise*] Sir, he's very right, and it's my way too.

HARDCASTLE. Sir, you have a right to command here. Here, Roger, bring us the bill of fare for to-night's supper: I believe it's drawn out. Your manner Mr. Hastings, puts me in mind of my uncle, Colonel Wallop. It was a saying of his, that no man was sure of his supper till he had eaten it.

HASTINGS. [*Aside*] *All upon the high ropes!*[44] *his uncle a colonel! we shall soon hear of his mother being a justice of the peace. But let's hear the bill of fare.*

MARLOW. [*Perusing*] What's here? For the first course; for the second course; for the dessert. The devil, Sir, do you think we have brought down the whole Joiners' Company, or the corporation of Bedford,[45] to eat up such a supper? Two or three little things, clean and comfortable, will do.

HASTINGS. But let's hear it.

MARLOW. [*Reading*] For the first course at the top, a pig, and prune sauce.

HASTINGS. Damn your pig, I say.

MARLOW. And damn your prune sauce, say I.

HARDCASTLE. And yet, gentlemen, to men that are hungry, pig, with prune sauce, is very good eating.

MARLOW. At the bottom, a calve's tongue and brains.

HASTINGS. Let your brains be knock'd out, my good Sir; I don't like them.

MARLOW. Or you may clap them on a plate by themselves. I do.

HARDCASTLE.—[*Aside*] *Their impudence confounds me.*—[*To them*] Gentlemen, you are my guests, make what alterations you please. Is there anything else you wish to retrench or alter, gentlemen?

MARLOW. Item. A pork pie, a boiled rabbit and sausages, a florentine,[46] a shaking pudding,[47] and a dish of tiff—taff—taffety cream![48]

HASTINGS. Confound your made dishes;[49] I shall be as much at a loss in this house as at a green and yellow dinner at the French Ambassador's table.[50] I'm for plain eating.

HARDCASTLE. I'm sorry, gentlemen, that I have nothing you like, but if there be anything you have a particular fancy to—

MARLOW. Why, really, Sir, your bill of fare is so exquisite, that any one part of it is full as good as another. Send us what you please. So much for supper. And now to see that our beds are air'd, and properly taken care of.

HARDCASTLE. I entreat you'll leave all that to me. You shall not stir a step.

MARLOW. Leave that to you! I protest, Sir, you must excuse me, I always look to these things myself.

HARDCASTLE. I must insist, Sir, you'll make yourself easy on that head.

MARLOW. You see I'm resolved on it.—[*Aside*] *A very troublesome fellow this, as I ever met with.*

HARDCASTLE. Well, Sir, I'm resolved at least to attend you.—[*Aside*] *This may be modern modesty, but I never saw anything look so like old-fashioned impudence.* [*Exeunt* Marlow *and* Hardcastle.

HASTINGS. [*Solus*] So I find this fellow's civilities begin to grow troublesome. But who can be angry at those assiduities which are meant to please him? Ha! what do I see? Miss Neville, by all that's happy!

[*Enter* Miss Neville.

MISS NEVILLE. My dear Hastings! To what unexpected good fortune, to what accident, am I to ascribe this happy meeting?

HASTINGS. Rather let me ask the same question, as I could never have hoped to meet my dearest Constance at an inn.

MISS NEVILLE. An inn! sure you mistake! my aunt, my guardian, lives here. What could induce you to think this house an inn?

HASTINGS. My friend Mr. Marlow, with whom I came down, and I, have been sent here as to an inn, I assure you. A young fellow, whom we accidentally met at a house hard by, directed us hither.

MISS NEVILLE. Certainly it must be one of my hopeful cousin's tricks, of whom you have heard me talk so often, ha! ha! ha! ha!

HASTINGS. He whom your aunt intends for you? He of whom I have such just apprehensions?

MISS NEVILLE. You have nothing to fear from him, I assure you. You'd adore him if you knew how heartily he despises me. My aunt knows it too, and has undertaken to court me for him, and actually begins to think she has made a conquest.

HASTINGS. Thou dear dissembler! You must know, my Constance, I have just seized this happy opportunity of my friend's visit here to get admittance into the family. The horses that carried us down are now fatigued with their journey, but they'll soon be refreshed; and then, if my dearest girl will trust in her faithful Hastings, we shall soon be landed in France, where even among slaves the laws of marriage are respected.[51]

MISS NEVILLE. I have often told you, that though ready to obey you, I yet should leave my little fortune behind with reluctance. The greatest part of it was left me by my uncle, the India director, and chiefly consists in jewels.[52] I have been for some time persuading my aunt to let me wear them. I fancy I'm very near succeeding. The instant they are put into my possession, you shall find me ready to make them and myself yours.

HASTINGS. Perish the baubles! Your person is all I desire. In the meantime, my friend Marlow must not be let into his mistake. I know the strange reserve of his temper is such, that if abruptly informed of it, he would instantly quit the house before our plan was ripe for execution.

MISS NEVILLE. But how shall we keep him in the deception? Miss Hardcastle is just returned from walking; what if we still continue to deceive him?—This, this way—[*They confer.*

[*Enter* Marlow.

MARLOW. The assiduities of these good people teize me beyond bearing. My host seems to think it ill manners to leave me alone, and so he claps not only himself but his old-fashioned wife on my back. They talk of coming to sup with us too; and then, I suppose, we are to run the gauntlet thro' all the rest of the family.—What have we got here?

HASTINGS. My dear Charles! Let me congratulate you!—The most fortunate accident!—Who do you think has just alighted?

MARLOW. Cannot guess.

HASTINGS. Our mistresses, boy, Miss Hardcastle and Miss Neville. Give me leave to introduce Miss Constance Neville to your acquaintance. Happening to dine in the neighbourhood, they called on their return to take fresh horses here. Miss Hardcastle has just stepped into the next room, and will be back in an instant. Wasn't it lucky? eh!

MARLOW. [*Aside*] *I have been mortified enough of all conscience, and here comes something to complete my embarrassment.*

HASTINGS. Well! but wasn't it the most fortunate thing in the world?

MARLOW. Oh! yes. Very fortunate—a most joyful encounter—But our dresses, George, you know are in disorder—What if we should postpone the happiness 'till to-morrow?—To-morrow at her own house—It will be every bit as convenient—And rather more respectful—To-morrow let it be. [*Offering to go.*

MISS NEVILLE. By no means, Sir. Your ceremony will displease her. The disorder of your dress will show the ardour of your impatience. Besides, she knows you are in the house, and will permit you to see her.

MARLOW. O! the devil! how shall I support it? Hem! hem! Hastings, you must not go. You are to assist me, you know. I shall be confoundedly ridiculous. Yet, hang it! I'll take courage. Hem!

HASTINGS. Pshaw, man! it's but the first plunge, and all's over. She's but a woman, you know.

MARLOW. And of all women, she that I dread most to encounter!

[*Enter* Miss Hardcastle, *as returned from walking, a bonnet, &c.*

HASTINGS. [*Introducing them*] Miss Hardcastle, Mr. Marlow, I'm proud of bringing two persons of such merit together, that only want to know, to esteem each other.

MISS HARDCASTLE. [*Aside*] *Now, for meeting my modest gentleman with a demure face, and quite in his own manner.* [*After a pause, in which he appears very uneasy and disconcerted*] *I'm glad of your safe arrival, Sir. I'm told you had some accidents by the way.*

MARLOW. Only a few, Madam. Yes, we had some. Yes, Madam, a good many accidents, but should be sorry—Madam—or rather glad of any accidents,—that are so agreeably concluded. Hem!

HASTINGS. [*To him*] You never spoke better in your whole life. Keep it up, and I'll insure you the victory.

MISS HARDCASTLE. I'm afraid you flatter, Sir. You that have seen so much of the finest company can find little entertainment in an obscure corner of the country.

MARLOW. [*Gathering courage*] I have lived, indeed, in the world, Madam; but I have kept very little company. I have been but an observer upon life, Madam, while others were enjoying it.

MISS NEVILLE. But that, I am told, is the way to enjoy it at last.

HASTINGS. [*To him*] Cicero[53] never spoke better. Once more, and you are confirmed in assurance forever.

MARLOW. [*To him*] Hem! stand by me, then, and when I'm down, throw in a word or two to set me up again.

MISS HARDCASTLE. An observer, like you, upon life were, I fear, disagreeably employed, since you must have had much more to censure than to approve.

MARLOW. Pardon me, Madam. I was always willing to be amused. The folly of most people is rather an object of mirth than uneasiness.

HASTINGS. [*To him*] Bravo, bravo. Never spoke so well in your whole life. Well, Miss Hardcastle, I see that you and Mr. Marlow are going to be very good company. I believe our being here will but embarrass the interview.

MARLOW. Not in the least, Mr. Hastings. We like your company of all things. [*To him*] Zounds! George, sure you won't go? How can you leave us?

HASTINGS. Our presence will but spoil conversation, so we'll retire to the next room. [*To him*] You don't consider, man, that we are to manage a little *tête-à-tête* of our own. [*Exeunt.*

MISS HARDCASTLE. [*After a pause*] But you have not been wholly an observer, I presume, Sir: the ladies, I should hope, have employed some part of your addresses.

MARLOW. [*Relapsing into timidity*] Pardon me, Madam, I—I—I—as yet have studied—only—to—deserve them.

MISS HARDCASTLE. And that, some say, is the very worst way to obtain them.

MARLOW. Perhaps so, Madam. But I love to converse only with the more grave and sensible part of the sex.—But I'm afraid I grow tire-some.

MISS HARDCASTLE. Not at all, Sir; there is nothing I like so much as grave conversation myself; I could hear it forever. Indeed, I have often been surprised how a man of *sentiment* could ever admire those light airy pleasures, where nothing reaches the heart.

MARLOW. It's—a disease—of the mind, Madam. In the variety of tastes there must be some who, wanting a relish—for—um—a—um.

MISS HARDCASTLE. I understand you, Sir. There must be some who, wanting a relish for refined pleasures, pretend to despise what they are incapable of tasting.

MARLOW. My meaning, Madam, but infinitely better expressed. And I can't help observing—a—

MISS HARDCASTLE.—[*Aside*] *Who could ever suppose this fellow impudent upon some occasions!*—[*To him*] You were going to observe, Sir—

MARLOW. I was observing, Madam—I protest, Madam, I forget what I was going to observe.

MISS HARDCASTLE.—[*Aside*] *I vow and so do I.*—[*To him*] You were observing, Sir, that in this age of hypocrisy—something about hypocrisy, Sir.

MARLOW. Yes, Madam. In this age of hypocrisy there are few who upon strict inquiry do not—a—a—a—

MISS HARDCASTLE. I understand you perfectly, Sir.

MARLOW. [*Aside*] *Egad! and that's more than I do myself.*

MISS HARDCASTLE. You mean that in this hypocritical age there are few that do not condemn in public what they practise in private, and think they pay every debt to virtue when they praise it.

MARLOW. True, Madam; those who have most virtue in their mouths, have least of it in their bosoms. But I'm sure I tire you, Madam.

MISS HARDCASTLE. Not in the least, Sir; there's something so agreeable and spirited in your manner, such life and force—pray, Sir, go on.

MARLOW. Yes, Madam. I was saying—that there are some occasions, when a total want of courage, Madam, destroys all the—and puts us—upon a—a—a—

MISS HARDCASTLE. I agree with you entirely; a want of courage upon some occasions assumes the appearance of ignorance, and betrays us when we most want to excel. I beg you'll proceed.

MARLOW. Yes, Madam. Morally speaking, Madam—But I see Miss Neville expecting us in the next room. I would not intrude for the world.

MISS HARDCASTLE. I protest, Sir, I never was more agreeably entertained in all my life. Pray go on.

MARLOW. Yes, Madam, I was—But she beckons us to join her. Madam, shall I do myself the honour to attend you?

MISS HARDCASTLE. Well then, I'll follow.

MARLOW. [*Aside*] *This pretty smooth dialogue has done for me.* [*Exit.*

MISS HARDCASTLE. [*Sola*] Ha! ha! ha! Was there ever such a sober, sentimental interview? I'm certain he scarce look'd in my face the whole time. Yet the fellow, but for his unaccountable bashfulness, is pretty well too. He has good sense, but then so buried in his fears, that it fatigues one more than ignorance. If I could teach him a little confidence, it would be doing somebody that I know of a piece of service. But who is that somebody?—That, faith, is a question I can scarce answer. [*Exit.*

[*Enter* Tony *and* Miss Neville, *followed by* Mrs. Hardcastle *and* Hastings.

TONY. What do you follow me for, Cousin Con? I wonder you're not ashamed to be so very engaging.

MISS NEVILLE. I hope, cousin, one may speak to one's own relations, and not be to blame.

TONY. Ay, but I know what sort of a relation you want to make me, though; but it won't do. I tell you, Cousin Con, it won't do; so I beg you'll keep your distance, I want no nearer relationship.

[*She follows, coquetting him to the back scene.*

MRS. HARDCASTLE. Well! I vow, Mr. Hastings, you are very entertaining. There's nothing in the world I love to talk of so much as London, and the fashions, though I was never there myself.

HASTINGS. Never there! You amaze me! From your air and manner, I concluded you had been bred all your life either at Ranelagh, St. James's, or Tower Wharf.[54]

MRS. HARDCASTLE. O! Sir, you're only pleased to say so. We country persons can have no manner at all. I'm in love with the town, and that serves to raise me above some of our neighbouring rustics; but who can have a manner, that has never seen the Pantheon, the Grotto Gardens, the Borough, and such places where the nobility chiefly resort?[55] All I can do is to enjoy London at second-hand. I take care to know every *tête-à-tête* from the Scandalous Magazine, and have all the fashions, as they come out, in a letter from the two Miss Rickets of Crooked-Lane.[56] Pray how do you like this head,[57] Mr. Hastings?

HASTINGS. Extremely elegant and *degagée*, upon my word, Madam. Your *friseur* is a Frenchman, I suppose?[58]

MRS. HARDCASTLE. I protest I dressed it myself from a print in the *Ladies' Memorandum Book*[59] for the last year.

HASTINGS. Indeed. Such a head in a side-box at the playhouse would draw as many gazers as my Lady May'ress at a city ball.[60]

MRS. HARDCASTLE. I vow, since inoculation began, there is no such thing to be seen as a plain woman,[61] so one must dress a little particular, or one may escape in the crowd.

HASTINGS. [*Bowing*] But that can never be your case, Madam, in any dress.

MRS. HARDCASTLE. Yet, what signifies *my* dressing when I have such a piece of antiquity by my side as Mr. Hardcastle: all I can say will never argue down a single button from his cloaths. I have often wanted him to throw off his great flaxen wig, and where he was bald, to plaister it over like my Lord Pately, with powder.

HASTINGS. You are right, Madam; for, as among the ladies there are none ugly, so among the men there are none old.

MRS. HARDCASTLE. But what do you think his answer was? Why, with his usual Gothic vivacity, he said I only wanted him to throw off his wig to convert it into a *tête* for my own wearing.

HASTINGS. Intolerable! At your age you may wear what you please, and it must become you.

MRS. HARDCASTLE. Pray, Mr. Hastings, what do you take to be the most fashionable age about town?

HASTINGS. Some time ago, forty was all the mode; but I'm told the ladies intend to bring up fifty for the ensuing winter.

MRS. HARDCASTLE. Seriously. Then I shall be too young for the fashion.

HASTINGS. No lady begins now to put on jewels 'till she's past forty. For instance, Miss there, in a polite circle, would be considered as a child, as a mere maker of samplers.

MRS. HARDCASTLE. And yet Mrs. Niece thinks herself as much a woman, and is as fond of jewels, as the oldest of us all.

HASTINGS. Your niece, is she? And that young gentleman, a brother of yours, I should presume?

MRS. HARDCASTLE. My son, Sir. They are contracted to each other. Observe their little sports. They fall in and out ten times a day, as if they were man and wife already. [*To them*] Well, Tony, child, what soft things are you saying to your cousin Constance this evening?

TONY. I have been saying no soft things; but that it's very hard to be followed about so. Ecod! I've not a place in the house now that's left to myself but the stable.

MRS. HARDCASTLE. Never mind him, Con, my dear. He's in another story behind your back.

MISS NEVILLE. There's something generous in my cousin's manner. He falls out before faces to be forgiven in private.

TONY. That's a damned confounded crack.[62]

MRS. HARDCASTLE. Ah! he's a sly one. Don't you think they're like each other about the mouth, Mr. Hastings? The Blenkinsop mouth to a T. They're of a size too. Back to back, my pretties, that Mr. Hastings may see you. Come, Tony.

TONY. [*Measuring*] You had as good not make me, I tell you.

MISS NEVILLE. O lud! he has almost cracked my head.

MRS. HARDCASTLE. O, the monster! For shame, Tony. You a man, and behave so!

TONY. If I'm a man, let me have my fortin.[63] Ecod! I'll not be made a fool of no longer.

MRS. HARDCASTLE. Is this, ungrateful boy, all that I'm to get for the pains I have taken in your education? I that have rock'd you in your cradle, and fed that pretty mouth with a spoon! Did not I work that waistcoat to make you genteel? Did not I prescribe for you every day, and weep while the receipt was operating?

TONY. Ecod! you had reason to weep, for you have been dosing me ever since I was born. I have gone through every receipt in the *Complete Housewife*[64] ten times over; and you have thoughts of coursing me through *Quincy*[65] next spring. But, ecod! I tell you, I'll not be made a fool of no longer.

MRS. HARDCASTLE. Wasn't it all for your good, viper? Wasn't it all for your good?

TONY. I wish you'd let me and my good alone, then. Snubbing this way when I'm in spirits. If I'm to have any good, let it come of itself; not to keep dinging it, dinging it into one so.

MRS. HARDCASTLE. That's false; I never see you when you're in spirits. No, Tony, you then go to the alehouse or kennel. I'm never to be delighted with your agreeable, wild notes, unfeeling monster!

TONY. Ecod! Mamma, your own notes are the wildest of the two.

MRS. HARDCASTLE. Was ever the like? But I see he wants to break my heart; I see he does.

HASTINGS. Dear Madam, permit me to lecture the young gentleman a little. I'm certain I can persuade him to his duty.

MRS. HARDCASTLE. Well! I must retire. Come, Constance, my love. You see, Mr. Hastings, the wretchedness of my situation: was ever poor woman so plagued with a dear, sweet, pretty, provoking, undutiful boy?

[*Exeunt* Mrs. Hardcastle *and* Miss Neville.

TONY. [*Singing*] "There was a young man riding by, and fain would have his will. Rang do didlo dee."—Don't mind her. Let her cry. It's the comfort of her heart. I have seen her and sister cry over a book for an hour together, and they said they liked the book the better the more it made them cry.

HASTINGS. Then you're no friend to the ladies, I find, my pretty young gentleman?

TONY. That's as I find 'um.

HASTINGS. Not to her of your mother's chusing, I dare answer? And yet she appears to me a pretty well-tempered girl.

TONY. That's because you don't know her as well as I. Ecod! I know every inch about her; and there's not a more bitter cantanckerous toad in all Christendom.

HASTINGS. [*Aside*] *Pretty encouragement this for a lover!*

TONY. I have seen her since the height of that. She has as many tricks as a hare in a thicket, or a colt the first day's breaking.

HASTINGS. To me she appears sensible and silent!

TONY. Ay, before company. But when she's with her play-mates she's as loud as a hog in a gate.

HASTINGS. But there is a meek modesty about her that charms me.

TONY. Yes, but curb her never so little, she kicks up, and you're flung in a ditch.

HASTINGS. Well, but you must allow her a little beauty.—Yes, you must allow her some beauty.

TONY. Bandbox![66] She's all a made-up thing, mun. Ah! could you but see Bett Bouncer of these parts, you might then talk of beauty. Ecod! she has two eyes as black as sloes, and cheeks as broad and red as a pulpit cushion. She'd make two of she.

HASTINGS. Well, what say you to a friend that would take this bitter bargain off your hands?

TONY. Anon?[67]

HASTINGS. Would you thank him that would take Miss Neville and leave you to happiness and your dear Betsy?

TONY. Ay; but where is there such a friend, for who would take *her*?

HASTINGS. I am he. If you but assist me, I'll engage to whip her off to France, and you shall never hear more of her.

TONY. Assist you! Ecod! I will, to the last drop of my blood. I'll clap a pair of horses to your chaise that shall trundle you off in a twinkling, and may beget you a part of her fortin beside, in jewels, that you little dream of.

HASTINGS. My dear Squire, this looks like a lad of spirit.

TONY. Come along then, and you shall see more of my spirit before you have done with me. [*Singing*:]

> "We are the boys
> That fears no noise
> Where the thundering cannons roar."

[*Exeunt*.

III.i

[*Enter* Hardcastle *solus*.]

HARDCASTLE. What could my old friend Sir Charles mean by recommending his son as the modestest young man in town? To me he appears the most impudent piece of brass that ever spoke with a tongue. He has taken possession of the easy chair by the fire-side already. He took off his boots in the parlour, and desired me to see them taken care of. I'm desirous to know how his impudence affects my daughter.—She will certainly be shocked at it.

[*Enter* Miss Hardcastle, *plainly dress'd*.

HARDCASTLE. Well, my Kate, I see you have changed your dress, as I bid you; and yet, I believe, there was no great occasion.

MISS HARDCASTLE. I find such a pleasure, Sir, in obeying your commands, that I take care to observe them without ever debating their propriety.

HARDCASTLE. And yet, Kate, I sometimes give you some cause, particularly when I recommended my *modest* gentleman to you as a lover to-day.

MISS HARDCASTLE. You taught me to expect something extraordinary, and I find the original exceeds the description.

HARDCASTLE. I was never so surprized in my life! He has quite confounded all my faculties!

MISS HARDCASTLE. I never saw anything like it: and a man of the world too!

HARDCASTLE. Ay, he learned it all abroad,—what a fool was I, to think a young man could learn modesty by travelling. He might as soon learn wit at a masquerade.

MISS HARDCASTLE. It seems all natural to him.

HARDCASTLE. A good deal assisted by bad company and a French dancing-master.

MISS HARDCASTLE. Sure you mistake, Papa! A French dancing-master could never have taught him that timid look,—that awkward address,—that bashful manner—

HARDCASTLE. Whose look? Whose manner, child?

MISS HARDCASTLE. Mr. Marlow's: his *mauvaise honte*,[68] his timidity, struck me at the first sight.

HARDCASTLE. Then your first sight deceived you; for I think him one of the most brazen first sights that ever astonished my senses.

MISS HARDCASTLE. Sure, Sir, you rally! I never saw any one so modest.

HARDCASTLE. And can you be serious? I never saw such a bouncing, swaggering puppy since I was born. Bully Dawson[68] was but a fool to him.

MISS HARDCASTLE. Surprising! He met me with a respectful bow, a stammering voice, and a look fixed on the ground.

HARDCASTLE. He met me with a loud voice, a lordly air, and a familiarity that made my blood freeze again.

MISS HARDCASTLE. He treated me with diffidence and respect; censured the manners of the age; admired the prudence of girls that never laughed; tired me with apologies for being tiresome; then left the room with a bow, and "Madam, I would not for the world detain you."

HARDCASTLE. He spoke to me as if he knew me all his life before. Asked twenty questions, and never waited for an answer. Interrupted my best remarks with some silly pun, and when I was in my best story of the Duke of Marlborough and Prince Eugene, he asked if I had not a good hand at making punch. Yes, Kate, he ask'd your father if he was a maker of punch!

MISS HARDCASTLE. One of us must certainly be mistaken.

HARDCASTLE. If he be what he has shewn himself, I'm determined he shall never have my consent.

MISS HARDCASTLE. And if he be the sullen thing I take him, he shall never have mine.

HARDCASTLE. In one thing then we are agreed—to reject him.

MISS HARDCASTLE. Yes. But upon conditions. For if you should find him less impudent, and I more presuming—if you find him more respectful, and I more importunate—I don't know—the fellow is well enough for a man—Certainly, we don't meet many such at a horse-race in the country.

HARDCASTLE. If we should find him so—But that's impossible. The first appearance has done my business. I'm seldom deceived in that.

MISS HARDCASTLE. And yet there may be many good qualities under that first appearance.

HARDCASTLE. Ay, when a girl finds a fellow's outside to her taste, she then sets about guessing the rest of his furniture. With her, a smooth face stands for good sense, and a genteel figure for every virtue.

MISS HARDCASTLE. I hope, Sir, a conversation begun with a compliment to my good sense won't end with a sneer at my understanding?

HARDCASTLE. Pardon me, Kate. But if young Mr. Brazen can find the art of reconciling contradictions, he may please us both, perhaps.

MISS HARDCASTLE. And as one of us must be mistaken, what if we go to make further discoveries?

HARDCASTLE. Agreed. But depend on't I'm in the right.

MISS HARDCASTLE. And depend on't I'm not much in the wrong.

[*Exeunt. Enter* Tony, *running in with a casket.*

TONY. Ecod! I have got them. Here they are. My Cousin Con's necklaces, bobs[70] and all. My mother shan't cheat the poor souls out of their fortune neither. O! my genus, is that you?

[*Enter* Hastings.

HASTINGS. My dear friend, how have you managed with your mother? I hope you have amused her with pretending love for your cousin, and that you are willing to be reconciled at last? Our horses will be refreshed in a short time, and we shall soon be ready to set off.

TONY. And here's something to bear your charges by the way [*Giving the casket*], your sweetheart's jewels. Keep them and hang those, I say, that would rob you of one of them.

HASTINGS. But how have you procured them from your mother?

TONY. Ask me no questions, and I'll tell you no fibs. I procured them by the rule of thumb. If I had not a key to every drawer in mother's bureau, how could I go to the alehouse so often as I do? An honest man may rob himself of his own at any time.

HASTINGS. Thousands do it every day. But to be plain with you; Miss Neville is endeavouring to procure them from her aunt this very instant. If she succeeds, it will be the most delicate way at least of obtaining them.

TONY. Well, keep them, till you know how it will be. But I know how it will be well enough; she'd as soon part with the only sound tooth in her head.

HASTINGS. But I dread the effects of her resentment, when she finds she has lost them.

TONY. Never you mind her resentment, leave *me* to manage that. I don't value her resentment the bounce of a cracker.[71] Zounds! here they are. Morrice![72] Prance! [*Exit* Hastings.

[*Enter* Mrs. Hardcastle, *and* Miss Neville.

MRS. HARDCASTLE. Indeed, Constance, you amaze me. Such a girl as you want jewels? It will be time enough for jewels, my dear, twenty years hence, when your beauty begins to want repairs.

MISS NEVILLE. But what will repair beauty at forty, will certainly improve it at twenty, Madam.

MRS. HARDCASTLE. Yours, my dear, can admit of none. That natural blush is beyond a thousand ornaments. Besides, child, jewels are quite out at present. Don't you see half the ladies of our acquaintance, my Lady Kill-day-light, and Mrs. Crump, and the rest of them, carry their jewels to town, and bring nothing but paste and marcasites[73] back.

MISS NEVILLE. But who knows, Madam, but somebody that shall be nameless would like me best with all my little finery about me?

MRS. HARDCASTLE. Consult your glass, my dear, and then see, if with such a pair of eyes, you want any better sparklers. What do you think, Tony, my dear? Does your Cousin Con want any jewels in your eyes to set off her beauty?

TONY. That's as thereafter may be.

MISS NEVILLE. My dear aunt, if you knew how it would oblige me.

MRS. HARDCASTLE. A parcel of old-fashioned rose and table-cut things.[74] They would make you look like the court of King Solomon at a puppet-shew.[75] Besides, I believe I can't readily come at them. They may be missing, for aught I know to the contrary.

TONY. [*Apart to* Mrs. Hardcastle] Then why don't you tell her so at once, as she's so longing for them? Tell her they're lost. It's the only way to quiet her. Say they're lost, and call me to bear witness.

MRS. HARDCASTLE. [*Apart to* Tony] You know, my dear, I'm only keeping them for you. So if I say they're gone, you'll bear me witness, will you? He! he! he!

TONY. Never fear me. Ecod! I'll say I saw them taken out with my own eyes.

MISS NEVILLE. I desire them but for a day, Madam. Just to be permitted to shew them as relicks, and then they may be lock'd up again.

MRS. HARDCASTLE. To be plain with you, my dear Constance, if I could find them, you should have them. They're missing, I assure you. Lost, for aught I know; but we must have patience wherever they are.

MISS NEVILLE. I'll not believe it; this is but a shallow pretence to deny me. I know they're too valuable to be so slightly kept, and as you are to answer for the loss—

MRS. HARDCASTLE. Don't be alarmed, Constance. If they be lost, I must restore an equivalent. But my son knows they are missing, and not to be found.

TONY. That I can bear witness to. They are missing, and not to be found; I'll take my oath on't.

MRS. HARDCASTLE. You must learn resignation, my dear; for tho' we lose our fortune, yet we should not lose our patience. See me, how calm I am.

MISS NEVILLE. Ay, people are generally calm at the misfortunes of others.

MRS. HARDCASTLE. Now, I wonder a girl of your good sense should waste a thought upon such trumpery. We shall soon find them; and, in the meantime, you shall make use of my garnets till your jewels be found.

MISS NEVILLE. I detest garnets.

MRS. HARDCASTLE. The most becoming things in the world to set off a clear complexion. You have often seen how well they look upon me. You *shall* have them. [*Exit.*

MISS NEVILLE. I dislike them of all things. You shan't stir.—Was ever any thing so provoking, to mislay my own jewels, and force me to wear her trumpery.

TONY. Don't be a fool. If she gives you the garnets, take what you can get. The jewels are your own already. I have stolen them out of her bureau, and she does not know it. Fly to your spark, he'll tell you more of the matter. Leave me to manage *her.*

MISS NEVILLE. My dear cousin!

TONY. Vanish. She's here, and has missed them already. [*Exit* Miss Neville] Zounds! how she fidgets and spits about like a Catherine wheel.[76]

[*Enter* Mrs. Hardcastle.

MRS. HARDCASTLE. Confusion! thieves! robbers! we are cheated, plundered, broke open, undone.

TONY. What's the matter, what's the matter, Mamma? I hope nothing has happened to any of the good family!

MRS. HARDCASTLE. We are robbed. My bureau has been broken open, the jewels taken out, and I'm undone.

TONY. Oh! is that all? Ha! ha! ha! by the laws, I never saw it better acted in my life. Ecod, I thought you was ruin'd in earnest, ha! ha! ha!

MRS. HARDCASTLE. Why, boy, I *am* ruined in earnest. My bureau has been broke open, and all taken away.

TONY. Stick to that: ha! ha! ha! stick to that. I'll bear witness, you know; call me to bear witness.

MRS. HARDCASTLE. I tell you, Tony, by all that's precious, the jewels are gone, and I shall be ruin'd for ever.

TONY. Sure I know they're gone, and I am to say so.

MRS. HARDCASTLE. My dearest Tony, but hear me. They're gone, I say.

TONY. By the laws, Mamma, you make me for to laugh, ha! ha! I know who took them well enough, ha! ha! ha!

MRS. HARDCASTLE. Was there ever such a blockhead, that can't tell the difference between jest and earnest? I tell you I'm not in jest, booby!

TONY. That's right, that's right; you must be in a bitter passion, and then nobody will suspect either of us. I'll bear witness that they are gone.

MRS. HARDCASTLE. Was there ever such a cross-grain'd brute, that won't hear me? Can you bear witness that you're no better than a fool? Was ever poor woman so beset with fools on one hand, and thieves on the other?

TONY. I can bear witness to that.

MRS. HARDCASTLE. Bear witness again, you blockhead, you, and I'll turn you out of the room directly. My poor niece, what will become of *her*? Do you laugh, you unfeeling brute, as if you enjoy'd my distress?

TONY. I can bear witness to that.

MRS. HARDCASTLE. Do you insult me, monster? I'll teach you to vex your mother, I will.

TONY. I can bear witness to that.

[*He runs off, she follows him. Enter* Miss Hardcastle *and* Maid.

MISS HARDCASTLE. What an unaccountable creature is that brother of mine, to send them to the house as an inn, ha! ha! I don't wonder at his impudence.

MAID. But what is more Madam, the young gentleman, as you passed by in your present dress, ask'd me if you were the barmaid? He mistook you for the barmaid, Madam.

MISS HARDCASTLE. Did he? Then as I live I'm resolved to keep up the delusion. Tell me, Pimple, how do you like my present dress? Don't you think I look something like Cherry in the *Beaux' Stratagem*?[77]

MAID. It's the dress, Madam, that every lady wears in the country, but when she visits or receives company.

MISS HARDCASTLE. And are you sure he does not remember my face or person?

MAID. Certain of it.

MISS HARDCASTLE. I vow I thought so; for though we spoke for some time together, yet his fears were such, that he never once looked up during the interview. Indeed, if he had, my bonnet would have kept him from seeing me.

MAID. But what do you hope from keeping him in his mistake?

MISS HARDCASTLE. In the first place, I shall be *seen*, and that is no small advantage to a girl who brings her face to market. Then I shall perhaps make an acquaintance, and that's no small victory gained over one who never addresses any but the wildest of her sex. But my chief aim is to take my gentleman off his guard, and, like an invisible champion of romance, examine the giant's force before I offer to combat.

MAID. But are you sure you can act your part, and disguise your voice so that he may mistake that, as he has already mistaken your person?

MISS HARDCASTLE. Never fear me. I think I have got the true bar cant.—Did your honour call?—Attend the Lion there—Pipes and tobacco for the Angel.—The Lamb has been outrageous this half hour.[78]

MAID. It will do, Madam. But he's here. [*Exit* Maid.

[*Enter* Marlow.

MARLOW. What a bawling in every part of the house; I have scarce a moment's repose. If I go to the best room, there I find my host and his story. If I fly to the gallery, there we have my hostess with her curtsey down to the ground. I have at last got a moment to myself, and now for recollection. [*Walks and muses.*

MISS HARDCASTLE. Did you call, Sir? Did your honour call?

MARLOW. [*Musing*] As for Miss Hardcastle, she's too grave and sentimental for me.

MISS HARDCASTLE. Did your honour call? [*She still places herself before him, he turning away.*

MARLOW. No, child. [*Musing*] Besides, from the glimpse I had of her, I think she squints.

MISS HARDCASTLE. I'm sure, Sir, I heard the bell ring.

MARLOW. No, no. [*Musing*] I have pleased my father, however, by coming down, and I'll to-morrow please myself by returning. [*Taking out his tablets and perusing.*

MISS HARDCASTLE. Perhaps the other gentleman called, Sir?

MARLOW. I tell you, no.

MISS HARDCASTLE. I should be glad to know, Sir. We have such a parcel of servants.

MARLOW. No, no, I tell you. [*Looks full in her face*] Yes, child, I think I did call. I wanted—I wanted—I vow, child, you are vastly handsome.

MISS HARDCASTLE. O la, Sir, you'll make one asham'd.

MARLOW. Never saw a more sprightly, malicious eye. Yes, yes, my dear, I did call. Have you got any of your—a—what d' ye call it in the house?

MISS HARDCASTLE. No, Sir; we have been out of that these ten days.

MARLOW. One may call in this house, I find, to very little purpose. Suppose I should call for a taste, just by way of trial, of the nectar of your lips; perhaps I might be disappointed in that too.

MISS HARDCASTLE. Nectar! nectar! That's a liquor there's no call for in these parts. French, I suppose. We keep no French wines here, Sir.

MARLOW. Of true English growth, I assure you.

MISS HARDCASTLE. Then it's odd I should not know it. We brew all sorts of wines in this house, and I have lived here these eighteen years.

MARLOW. Eighteen years! Why, one would think, child, you kept the bar before you were born. How old are you?

MISS HARDCASTLE. O! Sir, I must not tell my age. They say women and music should never be dated.

MARLOW. To guess at this distance, you can't be much above forty. [*Approaching*] Yet nearer I don't think so much. [*Approaching*] By coming closer to some women, they look younger still; but when we come very close indeed—[*Attempting to kiss her.*

MISS HARDCASTLE. Pray, Sir, keep your distance. One would think you wanted to know one's age as they do horses, by mark of mouth.

MARLOW. I protest, child, you use me extremely ill. If you keep me at this distance, how is it possible you and I can ever be acquainted?

MISS HARDCASTLE. And who wants to be acquainted with you? I want no such acquaintance, not I. I'm sure you did not treat Miss Hardcastle, that was here awhile ago, in this obstropalous manner.[79] I'll warrant me, before her you look'd dash'd, and kept bowing to the ground, and talk'd, for all the world, as if you was before a justice of the peace.

MARLOW.—[*Aside*] *Egad, she has hit it, sure enough!*—[*To her*] In awe of her, child? Ha! ha! ha! A mere aukward squinting thing; no, no. I find you don't know me. I laugh'd and rallied her a little; but I was unwilling to be too severe. No, I could not be too severe, *curse me*!

MISS HARDCASTLE. O! then, Sir, you are a favourite, I find, among the ladies?

MARLOW. Yes, my dear, a great favourite. And yet, hang me, I don't see what they find in me to follow. At the Ladies' Club[80] in town, I'm called their agreeable Rattle. Rattle, child, is not my real name, but one I'm known by. My name is Solomons; [*Offering to salute her*] Mr. Solomons, my dear, at your service.

MISS HARDCASTLE. Hold, Sir; you were introducing me to your club, not to yourself. And you're so great a favourite there, you say?

MARLOW. Yes, my dear. There's Mrs. Mantrap, Lady Betty Blackleg,[81] the Countess of Sligo, Mrs. Langhorns, old Miss Biddy Buckskin,[82] and your humble servant, keep up the spirit of the place.

MISS HARDCASTLE. Then it's a very merry place, I suppose.

MARLOW. Yes, as merry as cards, supper, wine, and old women can make us.

MISS HARDCASTLE. And their agreeable Rattle, ha! ha! ha!

MARLOW. [*Aside*] *Egad! I don't quite like this chit. She looks knowing, methinks. You laugh, child?*

MISS HARDCASTLE. I can't but laugh to think what time they all have for minding their work[83] or their family.

MARLOW.—[*Aside*] *All's well; she don't laugh at me.*—[*To her*] Do *you* ever work, child?

MISS HARDCASTLE. Ay, sure. There's not a screen or a quilt in the whole house but what can bear witness to that.

MARLOW. Odso! then you must shew me your embroidery. I embroider and draw patterns myself a little. [*Seizing her hand*] If you want a judge of your work, you must apply to me.

MISS HARDCASTLE. [*Struggling*] Ay, but the colours do not look well by candle light. You shall see all in the morning.

MARLOW. And why not now, my angel? Such beauty fires beyond the power of resistance.—Pshaw! the father here! my old luck: I never nick'd seven that I did not throw ames ace three times following.[84] [*Exit* Marlow.

[*Enter* Hardcastle, *who stands in surprise.*

HARDCASTLE. So, Madam. So I find *this* is your *modest* lover. This is your humble admirer that kept his eyes fixed on the ground, and only ador'd at humble distance. Kate, Kate, art thou not asham'd to deceive your father so?

MISS HARDCASTLE. Never trust me, dear Papa, but he's still the modest man I first took him for; you'll be convinced of it as well as I.

HARDCASTLE. By the hand of my body, I believe his impudence is infectious! Didn't I see him seize your hand? Didn't I see him hawl you about like a milk-maid? And now you talk of his respect and his modesty, forsooth!

MISS HARDCASTLE. But if I shortly convince you of his modesty, that he has only the faults that will pass off with time, and the virtues that will improve with age, I hope you'll forgive him.

HARDCASTLE. The girl would actually make one run mad! I tell you I'll not be convinced. I am convinced. He has scarcely been three hours in the house, and he has already encroached on all my prerogatives. You may like his impudence, and call it modesty. But my son-in-law, Madam, must have very different qualifications.

MISS HARDCASTLE. Sir, I ask but this night to convince you.

HARDCASTLE. You shall not have half the time, for I have thoughts of turning him out this very hour.

MISS HARDCASTLE. Give me that hour then, and I hope to satisfy you.

HARDCASTLE. Well, an hour let it be then. But I'll have no trifling with your father. All fair and open, do you mind me?

MISS HARDCASTLE. I hope, Sir, you have ever found that I considered your commands as my pride; for your kindness is such, that my duty as yet has been inclination.

[*Exeunt.*

IV.i

[*Enter* Hastings *and* Miss Neville.]

HASTINGS. You surprise me! Sir Charles Marlow expected here this night? Where have you had your information?

MISS NEVILLE. You may depend upon it. I just saw his letter to Mr. Hardcastle, in which he tells him he intends setting out a few hours after his son.

HASTINGS. Then, my Constance, all must be completed before he arrives. He knows me; and should he find me here, would discover my name, and perhaps my designs, to the rest of the family.

MISS NEVILLE. The jewels, I hope, are safe.

HASTINGS. Yes, yes. I have sent them to Marlow, who keeps the keys of our baggage. In the meantime, I'll go to prepare matters for our elopement. I have had the Squire's promise of a fresh pair of horses; and, if I should not see him again, will write him further directions. [*Exit.*

MISS NEVILLE. Well! success attend you. In the meantime I'll go and amuse my aunt with the old pretence of a violent passion for my cousin. [*Exit.*

[*Enter* Marlow, *followed by a* Servant.

MARLOW. I wonder what Hastings could mean by sending me so valuable a thing as a casket to keep for him, when he knows the only place I have is the seat of a post-coach at an inn-door. Have you deposited the casket with the landlady, as I ordered you? Have you put it into her own hands?

SERVANT. Yes, your honour.

MARLOW. She said she'd keep it safe, did she?

SERVANT. Yes, she said she'd keep it safe enough; she ask'd me how I came by it, and she said she had a great mind to make me give an account of myself. [*Exit* Servant.

MARLOW. Ha! ha! ha! they're safe, however. What an unaccountable set of beings have we got amongst! This little bar-maid though runs in my head most strangely, and drives out the absurdities of all the rest of the family. She's mine, she must be mine, or I'm greatly mistaken.

[*Enter* Hastings.

HASTINGS. Bless me! I quite forgot to tell her that I intended to prepare at the bottom of the garden. Marlow here, and in spirits too!

MARLOW. Give me joy, George! Crown me, shadow me with laurels! Well, George, after all, we modest fellows don't want for success among the women.

HASTINGS. Some women, you mean. But what success has your honour's modesty been crowned with now, that it grows so insolent upon us?

MARLOW. Didn't you see the tempting, brisk, lovely, little thing that runs about the house with a bunch of keys to its girdle?

HASTINGS. Well, and what then?

MARLOW. She's mine, you rogue you. Such fire, such motion, such eyes, such lips; but,—egad! she would not let me kiss them though.

HASTINGS. But are you sure, so very sure of her?

MARLOW. Why, man, she talk'd of shewing me her work above-stairs, and I am to improve the pattern.

HASTINGS. But how can *you*, Charles, go about to rob a woman of her honour?

MARLOW. Pshaw! pshaw! We all know the honour of the barmaid of an inn. I don't intend to *rob* her, take my word for it, there's nothing in this house I shan't honestly *pay* for.

HASTINGS. I believe the girl has virtue.

MARLOW. And if she has, I should be the last man in the world that would attempt to corrupt it.

HASTINGS. You have taken care, I hope, of the casket I sent you to lock up? It's in safety?

MARLOW. Yes, yes. It's safe enough. I have taken care of it. But how could you think the seat of a post-coach at an inn-door a place of safety? Ah! numskull! I have taken better precautions for you than you did for yourself.—I have—HASTINGS. What!

MARLOW. I have sent it to the landlady to keep for you.

HASTINGS. To the landlady!

MARLOW. The landlady.

HASTINGS. You did.

MARLOW. I did. She's to be answerable for its forth-coming, you know.

HASTINGS. Yes, she'll bring it forth with a witness.

MARLOW. Wasn't I right? I believe you'll allow that I acted prudently upon this occasion.

HASTINGS. [*Aside*] *He must not see my uneasiness.*

MARLOW. You seem a little disconcerted though, methinks. Sure nothing has happened?

HASTINGS. No, nothing. Never was in better spirits in all my life. And so you left it with the landlady, who, no doubt, very readily undertook the charge?

MARLOW. Rather too readily. For she not only kept the casket, but, thro' her great precaution, was going to keep the messenger too. Ha! ha! ha!

HASTINGS. He! he! he! they're safe, however?

MARLOW. As a guinea in a miser's purse.

HASTINGS.—[*Aside*] *So now all hopes of fortune are at an end, and we must set off without it.*—[*To him*] Well, Charles, I'll leave you to your meditations on the pretty bar-maid, and, he! he! he! may you be as successful for yourself as you have been for me! [*Exit.*

MARLOW. Thank ye, George! I ask no more. Ha! ha! ha!

[*Enter* Hardcastle.

HARDCASTLE. I no longer know my own house. It's turned all topsy-turvy. His servants have got drunk already. I'll bear it no longer, and yet, from my respect for his father, I'll be calm. [*To him*] Mr. Marlow, your servant. [*Bowing low*] I'm your very-humble servant.

MARLOW. Sir, your humble servant.—[*Aside*] *What's to be the wonder now?*

HARDCASTLE. I believe, Sir, you must be sensible, Sir, that no man alive ought to be more welcome than your father's son, Sir. I hope you think so?

MARLOW. I do from my soul, Sir. I don't want much intreaty. I generally make my father's son welcome wherever he goes.

HARDCASTLE. I believe you do, from my soul, Sir. But tho' I say nothing to your own conduct, that of your servants is insufferable. Their manner of drinking is setting a very bad example in this house, I assure you.

MARLOW. I protest, my very good Sir, that's no fault of mine. If they don't drink as they ought, *they* are to blame. I ordered them not to spare the cellar. I did, I assure you. [*To the side-scene*] Here, let one of my servants come up. [*To him*] My positive directions were, that as I did not drink myself, they should make up for my deficiencies below.

HARDCASTLE. Then they had your orders for what they do! I'm satisfied!

MARLOW. They had, I assure you. You shall hear from one of themselves.

[*Enter* Servant, *drunk.*

MARLOW. You, Jeremy! Come forward, sirrah! What were my orders? Were you not told to drink freely, and call for what you thought fit, for the good of the house?

HARDCASTLE. [*Aside*] *I begin to lose my patience.*

JEREMY. Please your honour, liberty and Fleet-Street for ever![85] Tho' I'm but a servant, I'm as good as another man. I'll drink for no man before supper, Sir, damme! Good liquor will sit upon a good supper, but a good supper will not sit upon—hiccup—upon my conscience, Sir.

MARLOW. You see, my old friend, the fellow is as drunk as he can possibly be. I don't know what you'd have more, unless you'd have the poor devil soused in a beer-barrel.

HARDCASTLE.—[*Aside*] *Zounds! He'll drive me distracted if I contain myself any longer.*—[*To him*] Mr. Marlow. Sir; I have submitted to your insolence for more than four hours, and I see no likelihood of its coming to an end. I'm now resolved to be master here, Sir, and I desire that you and your drunken pack may leave my house directly.

MARLOW. Leave your house!—Sure you jest, my good friend? What, when I'm doing what I can to please you.

HARDCASTLE. I tell you, Sir, you don't please me; so I desire you'll leave my house.

MARLOW. Sure you cannot be serious? At this time o' night, and such a night. You only mean to banter me?

HARDCASTLE. I tell you, Sir, I'm serious; and, now that my passions are rouzed, I say this house is mine, Sir, this house is mine, and I command you to leave it directly.

MARLOW. Ha! ha! ha! a puddle in a storm. [*In a serious tone*] I shan't stir a step, I assure you. This, your house, fellow! It's my house. This is my house. Mine, while I chuse to stay. What right have you to bid me leave this house, Sir? I never met with such impudence, curse me, never in my whole life before.

HARDCASTLE. Nor I, confound me if I ever did. To come to my house, to call for what he likes, to turn me out of my own chair, to insult the family, to order his servants to get drunk, and then to tell me, "This house is mine, Sir." By all that's impudent it makes me laugh. Ha! ha! ha! [*Banteringly*] Pray, Sir, as you take the house, what think you of taking the rest of the furniture? There's a pair of silver candlesticks, and there's a fire-screen, and here's a pair of brazen-nosed bellows, perhaps you may take a fancy to them?

MARLOW. Bring me your bill, Sir, bring me your bill, and let's make no more words about it.

HARDCASTLE. There are a set of prints, too. What think you of the *Rake's Progress* for your own apartment?[86]

MARLOW. Bring me your bill, I say; and I'll leave you and your infernal house directly.

HARDCASTLE. Then there's a mahogany table that you may see your own face in.

MARLOW. My bill, I say.

HARDCASTLE. I had forgot the great chair for your own particular slumbers, after a hearty meal.

MARLOW. Zounds! bring me my bill, I say, and let's hear no more on't.

HARDCASTLE. Young man, young man, from your father's letter to me, I was taught to expect a well-bred modest man as a visitor here, but now I find him no better than a coxcomb[87] and a bully; but he will be down here presently, and shall hear more of it. [*Exit.*

MARLOW. How's this? Sure I have not mistaken the house! Everything looks like an inn. The servants cry, "Coming"; the attendance is awkward; the barmaid, too, to attend us. But she's here, and will further inform me. Whither so fast, child? A word with you.

[*Enter* Miss Hardcastle.

MISS HARDCASTLE. Let it be short, then. I'm in a hurry.—[*Aside*] *I believe he begins to find out his mistake, but it's too soon quite to undeceive him.*

MARLOW. Pray, child, answer me one question. What are you, and what may your business in this house be?

MISS HARDCASTLE. A relation of the family, Sir.

MARLOW. What, a poor relation?

MISS HARDCASTLE. Yes, Sir. A poor relation, appointed to keep the keys, and to see that the guests want nothing in my power to give them.

MARLOW. That is, you act as the bar-maid of this inn.

MISS HARDCASTLE. Inn! O law—What brought that in your head? One of the best families in the county keep an inn Ha! ha! ha! old Mr. Hardcastle's house an inn!

MARLOW. Mr. Hardcastle's house! Is this Mr. Hardcastle's house, child?

MISS HARDCASTLE. Ay, sure! Whose else should it be?

MARLOW. So then, all's out, and I have been damnably imposed on. O, confound my stupid head, I shall be laugh'd at over the whole town. I shall be stuck up in caricatura in all the print-shops. The *Dullissimo Maccaroni*.[88] To mistake this house of all others for an inn, and my father's old friend for an inn-keeper! What a swaggering puppy must he take me for! What a silly puppy do I find myself! There again, may I be hanged, my dear, but I mistook you for the barmaid.

MISS HARDCASTLE. Dear me! dear me! I'm sure there's nothing in my *behaviour* to put me on a level with one of that stamp.

MARLOW. Nothing, my dear, nothing. But I was in for a list of blunders, and could not help making you a subscriber. My stupidity saw everything the wrong way. I mistook your assiduity for assurance, and your simplicity for allurement. But it's over—This house I no more shew *my* face in.

MISS HARDCASTLE. I hope, Sir, I have done nothing to disoblige you. I'm sure I should be sorry to affront any gentleman who has been so polite, and said so many civil things to me. I'm sure I should be sorry [*Pretending to cry*] if he left the family on my account. I'm sure I should be sorry people said anything amiss, since I have no fortune but my character.

MARLOW.—[*Aside*] *By Heaven, she weeps. This is the first mark of tenderness I ever had from a modest woman, and it touches me.*—[*To her*] Excuse me, my lovely girl, you are the only part of the family I leave with reluctance. But to be plain with you, the difference of our birth, fortune and education, make an honourable connection impossible; and I can never harbour a thought of seducing simplicity that trusted in my honour, or bringing ruin upon one, whose only fault was being too lovely.

MISS HARDCASTLE.—[*Aside*] *Generous man! I now begin to admire him.*—[*To him*] But I am sure my family is as good as Miss Hardcastle's, and though I'm poor, that's no great misfortune to a contented mind, and until this moment, I never thought that it was bad to want fortune.

MARLOW. And why now, my pretty simplicity?

MISS HARDCASTLE. Because it puts me at a distance from one, that if I had a thousand pound I would give it all to.

MARLOW.—[*Aside*] *This simplicity bewitches me, so that if I stay I'm undone. I must make one bold effort, and leave her.*—[*To her*] Your partiality in my favour, my dear, touches me most sensibly, and were I to live for myself alone, I could easily fix my choice. But I owe too much to the opinion of the world, too much to the authority of a father, so that—I can scarcely speak it—it affects me. Farewell. [*Exit.*

MISS HARDCASTLE. I never knew half his merit till now. He shall not go, if I have power or art to detain him. I'll still preserve the character in which I stoop'd to conquer, but will undeceive my papa, who perhaps may laugh him out of his resolution. [*Exit.*

[*Enter* Tony, Miss Neville.

TONY. Ay, you may steal for yourselves the next time. I have done my duty. She has got the jewels again, that's a sure thing; but she believes it was all a mistake of the servants.

MISS NEVILLE. But, my dear cousin, sure you won't forsake us in this distress? If she in the least suspects that I am going off, I shall certainly be locked up, or sent to my Aunt Pedigree's, which is ten times worse.

TONY. To be sure, aunts of all kinds are damn'd bad things. But what can I do? I have got you a pair of horses that will fly like Whistlejacket;[89] and I'm sure you can't say but I have courted you nicely before her face. Here she comes, we must court a bit or two more, for fear she should suspect us. [*They retire and seem to fondle.*

[*Enter* Mrs. Hardcastle.

MRS. HARDCASTLE. Well, I was greatly fluttered, to be sure. But my son tells me it was all a mistake of the servants. I shan't be easy, however, till they are fairly married, and then let her keep her own fortune. But what do I see! Fondling together, as I'm alive. I never saw Tony so sprightly before. Ah! have I caught you, my pretty doves! What, billing, exchanging stolen glances, and broken murmurs. Ah!

TONY. As for murmurs, mother, we grumble a little now and then, to be sure. But there's no love lost between us.

MRS. HARDCASTLE. A mere sprinkling, Tony, upon the flame, only to make it burn brighter.

MISS NEVILLE. Cousin Tony promises to give us more of his company at home. Indeed, he shan't leave us any more. It won't leave us, Cousin Tony, will it?

TONY. O! it's a pretty creature. No, I'd sooner leave my horse in a pound, than leave you when you smile upon one so. Your laugh makes you so becoming.

MISS NEVILLE. Agreeable cousin! Who can help admiring that natural humour, that pleasant, broad, red, thoughtless, [*Patting his cheek*] ah! it's a bold face.

MRS. HARDCASTLE. Pretty innocence!

TONY. I'm sure I always lov'd Cousin Con's hazel eyes, and her pretty long fingers, that she twists this way and that over the haspicholls,[90] like a parcel of bobbins.[91]

MRS. HARDCASTLE. Ah, he would charm the bird from the tree. I was never so happy before. My boy takes after his father, poor Mr. Lumpkin, exactly. The jewels, my dear Con, shall be yours incontinently. You shall have them. Isn't he a sweet boy, my dear? You shall be married to-morrow, and we'll put off the rest of his education, like Dr. Drowsy's sermons, to a fitter opportunity.

[*Enter* Diggory.

DIGGORY. Where's the Squire? I have got a letter for your worship.

TONY. Give it to my mamma. She reads all my letters first.

DIGGORY. I had orders to deliver it into your own hands.

TONY. Who does it come from?

DIGGORY. Your worship mun[92] ask that o' the letter itself.

TONY. I could wish to know tho' [*Turning the letter and gazing on it*].

MISS NEVILLE.—[*Aside*] *Undone! undone! A letter to him from Hastings. I know the hand. If my aunt sees it, we are ruined for ever. I'll keep her employ'd a little if I can.*—[*To* Mrs. Hardcastle] But I have not told you, Madam, of my cousin's smart answer just now to Mr. Marlow. We so laugh'd.—You must know, Madam—this way a little, for he must not hear us. [*They confer.*

TONY. [*Still gazing*] A damn'd cramp piece of penmanship, as ever I saw in my life. I can read your print hand very well. But here there are such handles, and shanks, and dashes, that one can scarce tell the head from the tail. "To Anthony Lumpkin, Esquire." It's very odd, I can read the outside of my letters, where my own name is, well enough. But when I come to open it, it's all—buzz. That's hard, very hard; for the inside of the letter is always the cream of the correspondence.

MRS. HARDCASTLE. Ha! ha! ha! Very well, very well. And so my son was too hard for the philosopher.

MISS NEVILLE. Yes, Madam; but you must hear the rest, Madam. A little more this way, or he may hear us. You'll hear how he puzzled him again.

MRS. HARDCASTLE. He seems strangely puzzled now himself, methinks.

TONY. [*Still gazing*] A damn'd up and down hand, as if it was disguised in liquor. [*Reading*] *Dear Sir*, ay, that's that. Then there's an *M*, and a *T*, and an *S*, but whether the next be an *izzard*,[93] or an *R*, confound me, I cannot tell.

MRS. HARDCASTLE. What's that, my dear? Can I give you any assistance?

MISS NEVILLE. Pray, Aunt, let me read it. Nobody reads a cramp hand better than I [*Twitching the letter from her*]. Do you know who it is from?

TONY. Can't tell, except from Dick Ginger, the feeder.[94]

MISS NEVILLE. Ay, so it is. [*Pretending to read*] *Dear Squire, hoping that you're in health, as I am at this present. The gentleman of the Shake-bag club*[95] *has cut the gentlemen of goose-green quite out of feather. The odds—um—odd battle—long fighting—um—* Here, here, it's all about cocks and fighting; it's of no consequence, here, put it up, put it up. [*Thrusting the crumpled letter upon him.*

TONY. But I tell you, Miss, it's of all the consequence in the world. I would not lose the rest of it for a guinea. [*Giving* Mrs. Hardcastle *the letter*] Here, mother, do you make it out. Of no consequence!

MRS. HARDCASTLE. How's this? [*Reads*] *Dear Squire, I'm now waiting for Miss Neville, with a post-chaise and pair, at the bottom of the garden, but I find my horses yet unable to perform the journey. I expect you'll assist us with a pair of fresh horses, as you promised. Dispatch is necessary, as the hag (ay, the hag) your mother, will otherwise suspect us. Yours, Hastings.* Grant me patience. I shall run distracted! My rage chokes me.

MISS NEVILLE. I hope, Madam, you'll suspend your resentment for a few moments, and not impute to me any impertinence, or sinister design, that belongs to another.

MRS. HARDCASTLE. [*Curtseying very low*] Fine spoken, Madam, you are most miraculously polite and engaging, and quite the very pink of curtesy and circumspection, Madam. [*Changing her tone*] And you, you great ill-fashioned oaf, with scarce sense enough to keep your mouth shut. Were you too join'd against me? But I'll defeat all your plots in a moment. As for you, Madam, since you have got a pair of fresh horses ready, it would be cruel to disappoint them. So, if you please, instead of running away with your spark, prepare, this very moment to run off with *me*. Your old Aunt Pedigree will keep you secure, I'll warrant me. You too, Sir, may mount your horse, and guard us upon the way. Here, Thomas, Roger, Diggory! I'll shew you, that I wish you better than you do yourselves. [*Exit.*

MISS NEVILLE. So now I'm completely ruined.

TONY. Ay, that's a sure thing.

MISS NEVILLE. What better could be expected from being connected with such a stupid fool, and after all the nods and signs I made him.

TONY. By the laws, Miss, it was your own cleverness, and not my stupidity, that did your business. You were so nice and so busy with your Shake-bags and Goose-greens, that I thought you could never be making believe.

[*Enter* Hastings.

HASTINGS. So, Sir, I find by my servant, that you have shewn my letter, and betray'd us. Was this well done, young gentleman?

TONY. Here's another. Ask Miss, there, who betray'd you. Ecod, it was her doing, not mine.

[*Enter* Marlow.

MARLOW. So I have been finely used here among you. Rendered contemptible, driven into ill-manners, despised, insulted, laugh'd at.

TONY. Here's another. We shall have old Bedlam broke loose presently.

MISS NEVILLE. And there, Sir, is the gentleman to whom we all owe every obligation.

MARLOW. What can I say to him, a mere boy, an ideot, whose ignorance and age are a protection?

HASTINGS. A poor contemptible booby, that would but disgrace correction.

MISS NEVILLE. Yet with cunning and malice enough to make himself merry with all our embarrassments.

HASTINGS. An insensible cub.

MARLOW. Replete with tricks and mischief.

TONY. Baw! damme, but I'll fight you both, one after the other—with baskets.[96]

MARLOW. As for him, he's below resentment. But your conduct, Mr. Hastings, requires an explanation. You knew of my mistakes, yet would not undeceive me.

HASTINGS. Tortured as I am with my own disappointments, is this a time for explanations? It is not friendly, Mr. Marlow.

MARLOW. But, Sir—

MISS NEVILLE. Mr. Marlow, we never kept on your mistake, till it was too late to undeceive you. Be pacified.

[*Enter* Servant.

SERVANT. My mistress desires you'll get ready immediately, Madam. The horses are putting to. Your hat and things are in the next room. We are to go thirty miles before morning. [*Exit* Servant.

MISS NEVILLE. Well, well: I'll come presently.

MARLOW. [*To* Hastings] Was it well done, Sir, to assist in rendering me ridiculous? To hang me out for the scorn of all my acquaintance? Depend upon it, Sir, I shall expect an explanation.

HASTINGS. Was it well done, Sir, if you're upon that subject, to deliver what I entrusted to yourself, to the care of another, Sir?

MISS NEVILLE. Mr. Hastings! Mr. Marlow! Why will you increase my distress by this groundless dispute? I implore, I intreat you—

[*Enter* Servant.

SERVANT. Your cloak, Madam. My mistress is impatient. [*Exit* Servant.

MISS NEVILLE. I come. Pray be pacified. If I leave you thus, I shall die with apprehension.

[*Enter* Servant.

SERVANT. Your fan, muff, and gloves, Madam. The horses are waiting.

MISS NEVILLE. O, Mr. Marlow, if you knew what a scene of constraint and ill-nature lies before me, I'm sure it would convert your resentment into pity.

MARLOW. I'm so distracted with a variety of passions, that I don't know what I do. Forgive me, Madam. George, forgive me. You know my hasty temper, and should not exasperate it.

HASTINGS. The torture of my situation is my only excuse.

MISS NEVILLE. Well, my dear Hastings, if you have that esteem for me that I think, that I am sure you have, your constancy for three years will but encrease the happiness of our future connection. If—

MRS. HARDCASTLE. [*Within*] Miss Neville. Constance, why, Constance, I say.

MISS NEVILLE. I'm coming. Well, constancy, remember, constancy is the word. [*Exit.*

HASTINGS. My heart! How can I support this? To be so near happiness, and such happiness!

MARLOW. [*To* Tony] You see now, young gentleman, the effects of your folly. What might be amusement to you is here disappointment, and even distress.

TONY. [*From a reverie*] Ecod! I have hit it. It's here. Your hands. Yours and yours, my poor Sulky. My boots there, ho! Meet me two hours hence at the bottom of the garden; and if you don't find Tony Lumpkin a more good-natur'd fellow than you thought for, I'll give you leave to take my best horse, and Bet Bouncer into the bargain. Come along. My boots, ho! [*Exeunt.*

V.i

[*Scene continues. Enter* Hastings *and* Servant.]

HASTINGS. You saw the Old Lady and Miss Neville drive off, you say?

SERVANT. Yes, your honour. They went off in a post-coach, and the young 'Squire went on horseback. They're thirty miles off by this time.

HASTINGS. Then all my hopes are over.

SERVANT. Yes, Sir. Old Sir Charles is arrived. He and the Old Gentleman of the house have been laughing at Mr. Marlow's mistake this half hour. They are coming this way.

HASTINGS. Then I must not be seen. So now to my fruitless appointment at the bottom of the garden. This is about the time. [*Exeunt.*

[*Enter* Sir Charles *and* Hardcastle.

HARDCASTLE. Ha! ha! ha! The peremptory tone in which he sent forth his sublime commands!

SIR CHARLES. And the reserve with which I suppose he treated all your advances.

HARDCASTLE. And yet he might have seen something in me above a common inn-keeper, too.

SIR CHARLES. Yes, Dick, but he mistook you for an uncommon innkeeper; ha! ha! ha!

HARDCASTLE. Well, I'm in too good spirits to think of any thing but joy. Yes, my dear friend, this union of our families will make our personal friendships hereditary, and tho' my daughter's fortune is but small—

SIR CHARLES. Why, Dick, will you talk of fortune to *me*? My son is possessed of more than a competence already, and can want nothing but a good and virtuous girl to share his happiness, and encrease it. If they like each other, as they say they do—

HARDCASTLE. *If*, man! I tell you they *do* like each other. My daughter as good as told me so.

SIR CHARLES. But girls are apt to flatter themselves, you know.

HARDCASTLE. I saw him grasp her hand in the warmest manner myself; and here he comes to put you out of your *ifs*, I warrant him.

[*Enter* Marlow.

MARLOW. I come, Sir, once more, to ask pardon for my strange conduct. I can scarce reflect on my insolence without confusion.

HARDCASTLE. Tut, boy, trifle. You take it too gravely. An hour or two's laughing with my daughter will set it all to rights again. She'll never like you the worse for it.

MARLOW. Sir, I shall be always proud of her approbation.

HARDCASTLE. Approbation is but a cold word, Mr. Marlow; if I am not deceived, you have something more than approbation thereabouts. You take me?

MARLOW. Really, Sir, I have not that happiness.

HARDCASTLE. Come, boy, I'm an old fellow, and know what's what, as well as you that are younger. I know what has passed between you; but mum.

MARLOW. Sure, Sir, nothing has passed between us but the most profound respect on my side, and the most distant reserve on hers. You don't think, Sir, that my impudence has been passed upon all the rest of the family?

HARDCASTLE. Impudence! No, I don't say that—Not quite impudence—Though girls like to be play'd with, and rumpled a little, too, sometimes. But she has told no tales, I assure you.

MARLOW. I never gave her the slightest cause.

HARDCASTLE. Well, well, I like modesty in its place well enough. But this is over-acting, young gentleman. You *may* be open. Your father and I will like you the better for it.

MARLOW. May I die, Sir, if I ever—

HARDCASTLE. I tell you, she don't dislike you; and as I'm sure you like her—

MARLOW. Dear Sir—I protest, Sir—

HARDCASTLE. I see no reason why you should not be joined as fast as the parson can tie you.

MARLOW. But hear me, Sir—

HARDCASTLE. Your father approves the match, I admire it, every moment's delay will be doing mischief, so—

MARLOW. But why won't you hear me? By all that's just and true, I never gave Miss Hardcastle the slightest mark of my attachment, or even the most distant hint to suspect me of affection. We had but one interview, and that was formal, modest, and uninteresting.

HARDCASTLE. [*Aside*] *This fellow's formal modest impudence is beyond bearing.*

SIR CHARLES. And you never grasp'd her hand or made any protestations?

MARLOW. As Heaven is my witness, I came down in obedience to your commands. I saw the lady without emotion, and parted without reluctance. I hope you'll exact no farther proofs of my duty, nor prevent me from leaving a house in which I suffer so many mortifications. [*Exit.*

SIR CHARLES. I'm astonish'd at the air of sincerity with which he parted.

HARDCASTLE. And I'm astonish'd at the deliberate intrepidity of his assurance.

SIR CHARLES. I dare pledge my life and honour upon his truth.

HARDCASTLE. Here comes my daughter, and I would stake my happiness upon her veracity.

[*Enter* Miss Hardcastle.HARDCASTLE. Kate, come hither, child. Answer us sincerely and without reserve: has Mr. Marlow made you any professions of love and affection?

MISS HARDCASTLE. The question is very abrupt, Sir! But since you require unreserved sincerity, I think he has.

HARDCASTLE. [*To* Sir Charles] You see.

SIR CHARLES. And pray, Madam, have you and my son had more than one interview?

MISS HARDCASTLE. Yes, Sir, several.

HARDCASTLE. [*To* Sir Charles] You see.

SIR CHARLES. But did he profess any attachment?

MISS HARDCASTLE. A lasting one.

SIR CHARLES. Did he talk of love?

MISS HARDCASTLE. Much, Sir.

SIR CHARLES. Amazing! And all this formally?

MISS HARDCASTLE. Formally.

HARDCASTLE. Now, my friend, I hope you are satisfied.

SIR CHARLES. And how did he behave, Madam?

MISS HARDCASTLE. As most profest admirers do: said some civil things of my face, talked much of his want of merit and the greatness of mine, mentioned his heart, gave a short tragedy speech, and ended with pretended rapture.

SIR CHARLES. Now I'm perfectly convinced, indeed. I know his conversation among women to be modest and submissive. This forward canting ranting manner by no means describes him, and I am confident he never sate for the picture.

MISS HARDCASTLE. Then what, Sir, if I should convince you to your face of my sincerity? If you and my papa, in about half an hour, will place yourselves behind that screen, you shall hear him declare his passion to me in person.

SIR CHARLES. Agreed. And if I find him what you describe, all my happiness in him must have an end. [*Exit.*

MISS HARDCASTLE. And if you don't find him what I describe—I fear my happiness must never have a beginning. [*Exeunt.*

V.ii

[*Scene changes to the back of the garden. Enter* Hastings.]

HASTINGS. What an idiot am I, to wait here for a fellow who probably takes a delight in mortifying me. He never intended to be punctual, and I'll wait no longer. What do I see? It is he! and perhaps with news of my Constance.

[*Enter* Tony, *booted and spattered.*

HASTINGS. My honest 'squire! I now find you a man of your word. This looks like friendship.

TONY. Ay, I'm your friend, and the best friend you have in the world, if you knew but all. This riding by night, by the bye, is cursedly tiresome. It has shook me worse than the basket of a stage-coach.

HASTINGS. But how? Where did you leave your fellow-travellers? Are they in safety? Are they housed?

TONY. Five and twenty miles in two hours and a half is no such bad driving. The poor beasts have smoaked for it:[97] Rabbet me,[98] but I'd rather ride forty miles after a fox than ten with such *varment*.[99]

HASTINGS. Well, but where have you left the ladies? I die with impatience.

TONY. Left them! Why where should I leave them, but where I found them?

HASTINGS. This is a riddle.

TONY. Riddle me this then. What's that goes round the house, and round the house, and never touches the house?

HASTINGS. I'm still astray.

TONY. Why, that's it, mon. I have led them astray. By jingo, there's not a pond or a slough within five miles of the place but they can tell the taste of.

HASTINGS. Ha! ha! ha! I understand; you took them in a round, while they supposed themselves going forward. And so you have at last brought them home again.

TONY. You shall hear. I first took them down Feather-bed-Lane, where we stuck fast in the mud. I then rattled them crack over the stones of Up-and-Down Hill. I then introduc'd them to the gibbet on Heavy-tree Heath; and from that, with a circumbendibus,[100] I fairly lodged them in the horse-pond at the bottom of the garden.

HASTINGS. But no accident, I hope?

TONY. No, no. Only mother is confoundedly frightened. She thinks herself forty miles off. She's sick of the journey, and the cattle can scarce crawl. So if your horses be ready, you may whip off with cousin, and I'll be bound that no soul here can budge a foot to follow you.

HASTINGS. My dear friend, how can I be grateful?

TONY. Ay, now it's "dear friend", "noble 'squire". Just now, it was all "ideot, cub, and run me through the guts." Damn *your* way of fighting, I say. After we take a knock in this part of the country, we kiss and be friends. But if you had run me through the guts, then I should be dead, and you might go kiss the hangman.

HASTINGS. The rebuke is just. But I must hasten to relieve Miss Neville; if you keep the old lady employed, I promise to take care of the young one. [*Exit* Hastings.

TONY. Never fear me. Here she comes. Vanish! She's got from the pond, and draggled up to the waist like a mermaid.

[*Enter* Mrs Hardcastle.

MRS. HARDCASTLE. Oh, Tony, I'm killed! Shook! Battered to death. I shall never survive it. That last jolt that laid us against the quickset hedge has done my business.

TONY. Alack, Mama, it was all your own fault. You would be for running away by night, without knowing one inch of the way.

MRS. HARDCASTLE. I wish we were at home again. I never met so many accidents in so short a journey. Drenched in the mud, overturned in a ditch, stuck fast in a slough, jolted to a jelly, and at last to lose our way. Whereabouts do you think we are, Tony?

TONY. By my guess we should come upon Crack-skull Common, about forty miles from home.

MRS. HARDCASTLE. O lud! O lud! The most notorious spot in all the country. We only want a robbery to make a complete night on't.

TONY. Don't be afraid, Mama, don't be afraid. Two of the five that kept here are hanged, and the other three may not find us. Don't be afraid. Is that a man that's galloping behind us? No; it's only a tree. Don't be afraid.

MRS. HARDCASTLE. The fright will certainly kill me.

TONY. Do you see anything like a black hat moving behind the thicket?

MRS. HARDCASTLE. O death!

TONY. No, it's only a cow. Don't be afraid, Mama; don't be afraid.

MRS. HARDCASTLE. As I'm alive, Tony, I see a man coming towards us. Ah! I'm sure on't. If he perceives us we are undone.

TONY. [*Aside*] *Father-in-law, by all that's unlucky, come to take one of his night walks. [To her] Ah! it's a highwayman with pistols as long as my arm. A damn'd ill-looking fellow.*

MRS. HARDCASTLE. Good Heaven defend us! He approaches.

TONY. Do you hide yourself in that thicket, and leave me to manage him. If there be any danger, I'll cough, and cry hem. When I cough, be sure to keep close. [Mrs. Hardcastle *hides behind a tree in the back scene.*

[*Enter* Hardcastle.

HARDCASTLE. I'm mistaken, or I heard voices of people in want of help. Oh, Tony! is that you? I did not expect you so soon back. Are your mother and her charge in safety?

TONY. Very safe, Sir, at my Aunt Pedigree's. Hem.

MRS. HARDCASTLE. [*From behind*] Ah death! I find there's danger.

HARDCASTLE. Forty miles in three hours; sure that's too much, my youngster.

TONY. Stout horses and willing minds make short journeys, as they say. Hem.

MRS. HARDCASTLE. [*From behind*] Sure he'll do the dear boy no harm.

HARDCASTLE. But I heard a voice here; I should be glad to know from whence it came.

TONY. It was I, Sir, talking to myself, Sir. I was saying that forty miles in four hours was very good going. Hem. As to be sure it was. Hem. I have got a sort of cold by being out in the air. We'll go in, if you please. Hem.

HARDCASTLE. But if you talk'd to yourself, you did not answer yourself. I am certain I heard two voices, and am resolved [*Raising his voice*] to find the other out.

MRS. HARDCASTLE. [*From behind*] Oh! he's coming to find me out. Oh!

TONY. What need you go, Sir, if I tell you? Hem. [*Detaining him*] I'll lay down my life for the truth—hem—I'll tell you all, Sir.

HARDCASTLE. I tell you, I will not be detained. I insist on seeing. It's in vain to expect I'll believe you.

MRS. HARDCASTLE. [*Running forward from behind*] O lud! he'll murder my poor boy, my darling! here, good gentleman, whet your rage upon me. Take my money, my life, but spare that young gentleman, spare my child, if you have any mercy.

HARDCASTLE. My wife, as I'm a Christian. From whence can she come, or what does she mean?

MRS. HARDCASTLE. [*Kneeling*] Take compassion on us, good Mr. Highwayman. Take our money, our watches, all we have, but spare our lives. We will never bring you to justice; indeed we won't, good Mr. Highwayman.

HARDCASTLE. I believe the woman's out of her senses. What, Dorothy, don't you know *me*?

MRS. HARDCASTLE. Mr. Hardcastle, as I'm alive! My fears blinded me. But who, my dear, could have expected to meet you here, in this frightful place, so far from home? What has brought you to follow us?

HARDCASTLE. Sure, Dorothy, you have not lost your wits? So far from home, when you are within forty yards of your own door! [*To him*] This is one of your old tricks, you graceless rogue, you. [*To her*] Don't you know the gate and the mulberry-tree; and don't you remember the horse-pond, my dear?

MRS. HARDCASTLE. Yes, I shall remember the horse-pond as long as I live; I have caught my death in it. [*To* Tony] And is it to you, you graceless varlet, I owe all this? I'll teach you to abuse your mother, I will.

TONY. Ecod, mother, all the parish says you have spoil'd me, and so you may take the fruits on't.

MRS. HARDCASTLE. I'll spoil you, I will. [*Follows him off the stage. Exit.*

HARDCASTLE. There's morality, however, in his reply. [*Exit.*

[*Enter* Hastings *and* Miss Neville.

HASTINGS. My dear Constance, why will you deliberate thus? If we delay a moment, all is lost for ever. Pluck up a little resolution, and we shall soon be out of the reach of her malignity.

MISS NEVILLE. I find it impossible. My spirits are so sunk with the agitations I have suffered, that I am unable to face any new danger. Two or three years' patience will at last crown us with happiness.

HASTINGS. Such a tedious delay is worse than inconstancy. Let us fly, my charmer. Let us date our happiness from this very moment. Perish fortune! Love and content will encrease what we possess beyond a monarch's revenue. Let me prevail!

MISS NEVILLE. No, Mr. Hastings; no. Prudence once more comes to my relief, and I will obey its dictates. In the moment of passion, fortune may be despised, but it ever produces a lasting repentance. I'm resolved to apply to Mr. Hardcastle's compassion and justice for redress.

HASTINGS. But tho' he had the will, he has not the power to relieve you.

MISS NEVILLE. But he has influence, and upon that I am resolved to rely.

HASTINGS. I have no hopes. But since you persist, I must reluctantly obey you. [*Exeunt.*

V.iii

Enter Sir Charles *and* Miss Hardcastle.

SIR CHARLES. What a situation am I in! If what you say appears, I shall then find a guilty son. If what he says be true, I shall then lose one that, of all others, I most wish'd for a daughter.

MISS HARDCASTLE. I am proud of your approbation; and to shew I merit it, if you place yourselves as I directed, you shall hear his explicit declaration. But he comes.

SIR CHARLES. I'll to your father, and keep him to the appointment. [*Exit* Sir Charles.

[*Enter* Marlow.

MARLOW. Tho' prepar'd for setting out, I come once more to take leave, nor did I, till this moment, know the pain I feel in the separation.

MISS HARDCASTLE. [*In her own natural manner*] I believe these sufferings cannot be very great, Sir, which you can so easily remove. A day or two longer perhaps, might lessen your uneasiness, by shewing the little value of what you now think proper to regret.

MARLOW.—[*Aside*] *This girl every moment improves upon me.*—[*To her*] It must not be, Madam. I have already trifled too long with my heart. My very pride begins to submit to my passion. The disparity of education and fortune, the anger of a parent, and the contempt of my equals, begin to lose their weight; and nothing can restore me to myself but this painful effort of resolution.

MISS HARDCASTLE. Then go, Sir. I'll urge nothing more to detain you. Tho' my family be as good as hers you came down to visit, and my education, I hope, not inferior, what are these advantages without equal affluence? I must remain contented with the slight approbation of imputed merit; I must have only the mockery of your addresses, while all your serious aims are fix'd on fortune.

[*Enter* Hardcastle *and* Sir Charles, *from behind.*

SIR CHARLES. Here, behind this screen.

HARDCASTLE. Ay, ay, make no noise. I'll engage my Kate covers him with confusion at last.

MARLOW. By heavens, Madam! fortune was ever my smallest consideration. Your beauty at first caught my eye; for who could see that without emotion? But every moment that I converse with you steals in some new grace, heightens the picture, and gives it stronger expression. What at first seem'd rustic plainness, now appears refin'd simplicity. What seem'd forward assurance, now strikes me as the result of courageous innocence and conscious virtue.

SIR CHARLES. What can it mean? He amazes me!

HARDCASTLE. I told you how it would be. Hush!

MARLOW. I am now determined to stay, Madam, and I have too good an opinion of my father's discernment, when he sees you, to doubt his approbation.

MISS HARDCASTLE. No, Mr. Marlow, I will not, cannot detain you. Do you think I could suffer a connexion in which there is the smallest room for repentance? Do you think I would take the mean advantage of a transient passion, to load you with confusion? Do you think I could ever relish that happiness which was acquired by lessening yours?

MARLOW. By all that's good, I can have no happiness but what's in your power to grant me! Nor shall I ever feel repentance but in not having seen your merits before. I will stay, even contrary to your wishes; and tho' you should persist to shun me, I will make my respectful assiduities atone for the levity of my past conduct.

MISS HARDCASTLE. Sir, I must entreat you'll desist. As our acquaintance began, so let it end, in indifference. I might have given an hour or two to levity; but seriously, Mr. Marlow, do you think I could ever submit to a connexion where *I* must appear mercenary, and *you* imprudent? Do you think I could ever catch at the confident addresses of a secure admirer?

MARLOW. [*Kneeling*] Does this look like security? Does this look like confidence? No, Madam, every moment that shews me your merit, only serves to encrease my diffidence and confusion. Here let me continue—

SIR CHARLES. I can hold it no longer. Charles, Charles, how hast thou deceived me! Is this your indifference, your uninteresting conversation?

HARDCASTLE. Your cold contempt; your formal interview! What have you to say now?

MARLOW. That I'm all amazement! What can it mean?

HARDCASTLE. It means that you can say and unsay things at pleasure; that you can address a lady in private, and deny it in public; that you have one story for us, and another for my daughter.

MARLOW. Daughter!—This lady your daughter?

HARDCASTLE. Yes, Sir, my only daughter, My Kate. Whose else should she be?

MARLOW. Oh, the devil!

MISS HARDCASTLE. Yes, Sir, that very identical tall squinting lady you were pleased to take me for [*Curtseying*]. She that you addressed as the mild, modest, sentimental man of gravity, and the bold, forward, agreeable Rattle of the Ladies' Club. Ha! ha! ha!

MARLOW. Zounds! there's no bearing this; it's worse than death!

MISS HARDCASTLE. In which of your characters, Sir, will you give us leave to address you? As the faultering gentleman, with looks on the ground, that speaks just to be heard, and hates hypocrisy;

or the loud, confident creature, that keeps it up with Mrs. Mantrap, and old Miss Biddy Buckskin, till three in the morning;—Ha! ha! ha!

MARLOW. O, curse on my noisy head. I never attempted to be impudent yet, that I was not taken down! I must be gone.

HARDCASTLE. By the hand of my body, but you shall not. I see it was all a mistake, and I am rejoiced to find it. You shall not, Sir, I tell you. I know she'll forgive you. Won't you forgive him, Kate? We'll all forgive you. Take courage, man.

[*They retire, she tormenting him, to the back scene. Enter* Mrs. Hardcastle, Tony.

MRS. HARDCASTLE. So, so, they're gone off. Let them go, I care not.

HARDCASTLE. Who gone?

MRS. HARDCASTLE. My dutiful niece and her gentleman, Mr. Hastings, from Town. He who came down with our modest visitor here.

SIR CHARLES. Who, my honest George Hastings? As worthy a fellow as lives, and the girl could not have made a more prudent choice.

HARDCASTLE. Then, by the hand of my body, I'm proud of the connexion.

MRS. HARDCASTLE. Well, if he has taken away the lady, he has not taken her fortune; that remains in this family to console us for her loss.

HARDCASTLE. Sure Dorothy you would not be so mercenary?

MRS. HARDCASTLE. Ay, that's my affair, not yours. But you know if your son, when of age, refuses to marry his cousin, her whole fortune is then at her own disposal.

HARDCASTLE. Ay, but he's not of age, and she has not thought proper to wait for his refusal.

[*Enter* Hastings *and* Miss Neville.

MRS. HARDCASTLE. [*Aside*] *What, returned so soon! I begin not to like it.*

HASTINGS. [*To* Hardcastle] For my late attempt to fly off with your niece, let my present confusion be my punishment. We are now come back, to appeal from your justice to your humanity. By her father's consent, I first paid her my addresses, and our passions were first founded in duty.

MISS NEVILLE. Since his death, I have been obliged to stoop to dissimulation to avoid oppression. In an hour of levity, I was ready to give up my fortune to secure my choice. But I'm now recovered from the delusion, and hope from your tenderness what is denied me from a nearer connexion.

MRS. HARDCASTLE. Pshaw, pshaw, this is all but the whining end of a modern novel.

HARDCASTLE. Be it what it will, I'm glad they're come back to reclaim their due. Come hither, Tony, boy. Do you refuse this lady's hand whom I now offer you?

TONY. What signifies my refusing? You know I can't refuse her till I'm of age, father.

HARDCASTLE. While I thought concealing your age, boy, was likely to conduce to your improvement, I concurred with your mother's desire to keep it secret. But since I find she turns it to a wrong use, I must now declare, you have been of age these three months.

TONY. Of age! Am I of age, Father?

HARDCASTLE. Above three months.

TONY. Then you'll see the first use I'll make of my liberty. [*Taking* Miss Neville's *hand*] Witness all men by these presents, that I, Anthony Lumpkin, Esquire, of BLANK place,[101] refuse you, Constantia Neville, spinster, of no place at all, for my true and lawful wife. So Constance Neville may marry whom she pleases, and Tony Lumpkin is his own man again.

SIR CHARLES. O brave 'squire!

HASTINGS. My worthy friend!

MRS. HARDCASTLE. My undutiful offspring!

MARLOW. Joy, my dear George, I give you joy sincerely. And could I prevail upon my little tyrant here to be less arbitrary, I should be the happiest man alive, if you would return me the favour.

HASTINGS. [*To* Miss Hardcastle] Come, Madam, you are now driven to the very last scene of all your contrivances. I know you like him, I'm sure he loves you, and you must and shall have him.

HARDCASTLE. [*Joining their hands*] And I say so too. And, Mr. Marlow, if she makes as good a wife as she has a daughter, I don't believe you'll ever repent your bargain. So now to supper. To-morrow we shall gather all the poor of the parish about us, and the Mistakes of the Night shall be crowned with a merry morning. So, boy, take her; and as you have been mistaken in the mistress, my wish is, that you may never be mistaken in the wife.

[*Exeunt Omnes.*

Epilogue[102]

Spoken by Mrs. Bulkley in the character of Miss Hardcastle[103]

Well, having stoop'd to conquer with success,
And gain'd a husband without aid from dress,
Still, as a bar-maid, I could wish it too,
As I have conquer'd him to conquer you:
And let me say, for all your resolution,
That pretty bar-maids have done execution.
Our life is a play, compos'd to please,
"We have our exits and our entrances."[104]
The first act shews the simple country maid,
Harmless and young, of ev'ry thing afraid;
Blushes when hir'd, and with unmeaning action,
"I hopes as how to give you satisfaction."
Her second act displays a livelier scene,—
Th'unblushing bar-maid of a country inn
Who whisks about the house, at market caters,
Talks loud, coquets[105] the guests, and scolds the waiters.
Next the scene shifts to town, and there she soars,
The chop-house toast of ogling connoissieurs.
On 'squires and cits she there displays her arts,
And on the gridiron broils her lovers' hearts—
And as she smiles, her triumphs to compleat,
Even common councilmen forget to eat.
The fourth act shews her wedded to the 'squire,
And Madam now begins to hold it higher;
Pretends to taste, at operas cries caro!
And quits her Nancy Dawson,[106] for Che Faró,[107]
Doats upon dancing, and in all her pride,
Swims round the room, the Heinel of Cheapside;[108]
Ogles and leers with artificial skill,
Till having lost in age the power to kill,
She sits all night at cards, and ogles at spadille.[109]
Such, thro' our lives, the eventful history—
The fifth and last act still remains for me.
The bar-maid now for your protection prays,
Turns female barrister, and pleads for Bayes.[110]

Epilogue[111]

To be spoken in the character of Tony Lumpkin

By J. Cradock, Esq.[112]

Well—now all's ended—and my comrades gone,
Pray what becomes of mother's only son?
A hopeful blade!—in town I'll fix my station,
And try to make a bluster in the nation.
As for my cousin Neville, I renounce her,
Off—in a crack—I'll carry big Bett Bouncer.
Why should not I in the great world appear?
I soon shall have a thousand pounds a year;
No matter what a man may here inherit,
In London—'gad, they've some regard to spirit.
I see the horses prancing up the streets,
And big Bett Bouncer bobs to all she meets;
Then hoikes to jiggs and pastimes ev'ry night—
Not to the plays—they say it a'n't polite;
To Sadler's-Wells perhaps, or operas go,
And once by chance, to the roratorio.[113]
Thus here and there, for ever up and down,
We'll set the fashions too, to half the town;
And then at auctions—money ne'er regard,
Buy pictures like the great, ten pounds a yard;
Zounds, we shall make these London gentry say,
We know what's damn'd genteel, as well as they.

16.2 WILLIAM WOODFALL'S REVIEW OF *SHE STOOPS TO CONQUER*

Monthly Review, March[e] 1773, xlviii, 309–14.

A WRITER SO MUCH, and so justly, in favour with the public, as the author of this play, is entitled to more than mere candor for his imperfections. When, therefore, we meet with any thing to disapprove in his compositions, it is really with some degree of concern, and we are under a difficulty in discharging our duty to the public.

Comedy has been defined by all theatrical critics, from Aristotle down to the correspondents of a news-paper. We do not, however, remember a definition exactly in the following terms: comedy is a dramatic representation of the prevailing manners of people not in very high or very low life. It must therefore vary, as those manners vary; and be wholly regulated by them. Hence the difference between Plautus and Menander; (as Menander is represented by Terence) and between all those original writers, who at different periods of time have written immediately from the manners passing in review before them. Few of our English writers of comedy have aimed at being originals. Some exception may be made in favour of Vanbrugh, Congreve, and Farquhar; the great merit of whose comedies is, that they represent the manners of the times. Sir Richard Steel Mr. Cibber, &c. did little more than translate; they were happy, however, in the choice of their plays, and in accommodating them to the customs which it was the business of the stage to regulate or correct.—Our customs and manners have undergone a gradual alteration. A general correspondence arising from trade, and the progress of the arts, has brought the nation, as it were, together, and worn off those prepossessions and habits which made every little neighbourhood a separate community, and marked every community with its peculiar character. The business of comedy is therefore changed; and a man who would now exhibit a Lady Bountiful, a Lord Foppington, or an Abel Drugger, would be considered as copying from history or from old comedies. Such characters do not now exist; at least not in the general walks of men. Some of our late writers have therefore very judiciously had recourse to what is called *Sentimental Comedy*, as better suited to the principles and manners of the age. A general politeness has given a sameness to our external appearances; and great degrees of knowledge are every where diffused. An author, therefore, has not that variety of character, and that simplicity and ignorance to describe, which were the capital ingredients in the old comedy. Modern writers may indeed have carried the matter too far, and perhaps kept their eyes too much on French models. They may have neglected some remains of English oddities which are still left, and would have very much enlivened their writings. They have erred however only in the execution: they are right in their general principle. The business of old comedy, and that of the present, are as different as the people they represent; and persons who have renounced the manners and religion of their fathers, and who would laugh at that wit which was their terror or delight, are affected and influenced by what is called sentiment. Some of our late plays might be mentioned, on this occasion, with great honour.

But Dr. Goldsmith does not seem to have been of this opinion. Having read more about even his own countrymen[114] than he had ever seen of them, and recollecting that the comedies he had perused were very different from those which now prevailed, he imagined the Comic Muse had fled the land. He determined to call her back, and employ her first in introducing the *Good-natured Man*, and afterwards the present comedy.

The fable of *She Stoops to Conquer* is a series of blunders, which the Author calls the *Mistakes of a Night*; but they are such mistakes as never were made, and, we believe, never could have been committed.

Two young men are going to the seat of a country gentleman, as lovers. They call at an alehouse, where the hopeful heir of the family which they intend to visit is drinking with his pot-companions. It comes into the head of this *genius* to put a trick on the travellers, to say, they were yet a great way from the place they were bound to, and to send them to his father's house as to an inn. Almost all the incidents at this pretended inn; the discovery of the young 'squire's plot to one of the gentlemen, and his readiness as well as that of his mistress to continue the deception of it for their own purposes; Miss Hardcastle's taking a walk at night, when his house was full of company, and himself in the highest bustle about them; Mrs. Hardcastle's thinking she was forty miles from home when at the bottom of her own garden; and Tony's[115] being of age when it was convenient he should be so;—these and several other circumstances are the most improbable, and lugged in, the most violently, of any things we ever remember to have either read or seen.

Some modern wits have endeavoured to render this kind of offence venial. They have said, that it is of no consequence; and that it is immaterial how the incidents are introduced, provided they are pleasing.

To support this strange opinion, they refer to several of our plays, in which the finest circumstances have been *forced in* against probability. We could give instances, in moral life, where the happiest consequences have attended a falsehood; and yet lying is a crime; and a man would be laughed at, if not detested, who would plead, from any accidental advantage, against the general principles of truth. All the general principles of nature are sacred; and we offend against them, in all cases, at our peril. When the temptation is great, and the advantages such as could not be obtained in any other way, we pardon the offender, and perhaps applaud the offence; but still we retain our attachment to the principles of nature. Hence the *virtuous lie* of Tasso; and hence the applauded licences of some fine writers. This, however, does not excuse a man who gives into a *habit* of immorality, or an author who writes a *series* of improbabilities.

In this light we are obliged to consider Dr. Goldsmith's play, as most of its incidents are offences against nature and probability. We are sorry for it, because he certainly has a great share of the *vis comica*; and when he has thrust his people into a situation, he makes them talk very *funnily*. His merit is in that sort of dialogue which lies on a level with the most common understandings; and in that low mischief and mirth which we laugh at, while we are ready to despise ourselves for so doing. This is the reason why the reader must peruse the present comedy without pleasure, while the representation of it may make him laugh.

We apprehend the following dialogue to be the best in the whole play, and the most proper to select as a specimen, where we cannot bestow our commendation . . .

The whole of this conversation is very laughable on the stage: so is the interview between Marlow and Miss Hardcastle; and the droll distress of Mrs. Hardcastle, when she thinks herself on Crackskull Common, forty miles from home. Shuter, Quick, and indeed all the performers, top their parts in these scenes, and make the house, the upper regions especially, very merry. We wish, however, that the ingenious author could employ his talents, so as to divert the galleries, without offending others who have a right to his attention. This he might do, by taking some story of a distant date, when the manners were generally such as he chuses to represent. He would then find characters and circumstances to his hand; and his language and dialogue would have all their effect: we should put ourselves back in imagination, and have the same kind of pleasure which is now given us by the best of our old comedies.

16.3 OLIVER GOLDSMITH, "AN ESSAY ON THE THEATRE; OR, A COMPARISON BETWEEN SENTIMENTAL AND LAUGHING COMEDY."

The Westminster Magazine, January 1773, pp. 398–402.

THE THEATRE, LIKE ALL OTHER AMUSEMENTS, has its fashions and its prejudices; and when satiated with its excellence, mankind begin to mistake change for improvement. For some years tragedy was the reigning entertainment; but of late it has entirely given way to comedy, and our best efforts are now exerted in these lighter kinds of composition. The pompous train, the swelling phrase, and the unnatural rant, are displaced for that natural portrait of human folly and frailty, of which all are judges, because all have sat for the picture.

But as in describing nature it is presented with a double face, either of mirth or sadness, our modern writers find themselves at a loss which chiefly to copy from; and it is now debated, whether the exhibition of human distress is likely to afford the mind more entertainment than that of human absurdity?

Comedy is defined by Aristotle to be a picture of the frailties of the lower part of mankind, to distinguish it from tragedy, which is an exhibition of the misfortunes of the great. When comedy, therefore, ascends to produce the characters of princes or generals upon the stage, it is out of its walk, since low life and middle life are entirely its object. The principal question, therefore, is, whether, in describing low or middle life, an exhibition of its follies be not preferable to a detail of its calamities? Or, in other words, which deserves the preference,—the weeping sentimental comedy so much in fashion at present, or the laughing, and even low comedy, which seems to have been last exhibited by Vanbrugh and Cibber?

If we apply to authorities, all the great masters in the dramatic art have but one opinion. Their rule is, that as tragedy displays the calamities of the great, so comedy should excite our laughter by ridiculously exhibiting the follies of the lower part of mankind. Boileau, one of the best modern critics, asserts, that comedy will not admit of tragic distress:

> "Le comique, ennemi des soupirs et des pleurs, N'admet point dans ses vers de tragiques douleurs."

Nor is this rule without the strongest foundation in nature, as the distresses of the mean by no means affect us so strongly as the calamities of the great. When tragedy exhibits to us some great man fallen from his height, and struggling with want and adversity, we feel his situation in the same manner as we suppose he himself must feel, and our pity is increased in proportion to the height from which he fell. On the contrary, we do not so strongly sympathize with one born in humbler circumstances, and encountering accidental distress: so that while we melt for Belisarius, we scarcely give halfpence to the beggar who accosts us in the street. The one has our pity; the other our contempt. Distress, therefore, is the proper object of tragedy, since the great excite our pity by their fall; but not equally so of comedy, since the actors employed in it are originally so mean, that they sink but little by their fall.

Since the first origin of the stage, tragedy and comedy have run in distinct channels, and never till of late encroached upon the provinces of each other. Terence, who seems to have made the nearest approaches, always judiciously stops short before he comes to the downright pathetic; and yet he is even reproached by Cæsar for wanting the vis comica. All the other comic writers of antiquity aim only at rendering folly or vice ridiculous, but never exalt their characters into buskined pomp, or make what Voltaire humorously calls a tradesman's tragedy.

Yet notwithstanding this weight of authority, and the universal practice of former ages, a new species of dramatic composition has been introduced, under the name of sentimental comedy, in which the virtues of private life are exhibited, rather than the vices exposed; and the distresses rather than the faults of mankind make our interest in the piece. These comedies have had of late great success, perhaps from their novelty, and also from their flattering every man in his favourite foible. In these plays almost all the characters are good, and exceedingly generous; they are lavish enough of their tin money on the stage; and though they want humour, have abundance of sentiment and feeling. If they happen to have faults or foibles, the spectator is taught, not only to pardon, but to applaud them, in consideration of the goodness of their hearts; so that folly, instead of being ridiculed, is commended, and the comedy aims at touching our passions without the power of being truly pathetic. In this manner we are likely to lose one great source of entertainment on the stage; for while the comic poet is invading the province of the tragic muse, he leaves her lovely sister quite neglected. Of this, however, he is no way solicitous, as he measures his fame by his profits.

But it will be said, that the theatre is formed to amuse mankind, and that it matters little, if this end be answered, by what means it is obtained. If mankind find delight in weeping at comedy, it would be cruel to abridge them in that or any other innocent pleasure. If those pieces are denied the name of comedies, yet call them by any other name and, if they are delightful, they are good. Their success, it will be said, is a mark of their merit, and it is only abridging our happiness to deny us an inlet to amusement.

These objections, however, are rather specious than solid. It is true, that amusement is a great object of the theatre, and it will be allowed that these sentimental pieces do often amuse us; but the question is, whether the true comedy would not amuse us more? The question is, whether a character supported throughout a piece, with its ridicule still attending, would not give us more delight than this species of bastard tragedy, which only is applauded because it is new?

A friend of mine, who was sitting unmoved at one of these sentimental pieces, was asked how he could be so indifferent? "Why, truly," says he, "as the hero is but a tradesman, it is indifferent to me whether he be turned out of his counting-house on Fish-street Hill, since he will still have enough left to open shop in St. Giles's."

The other objection is as ill-grounded; for though we should give these pieces another name, it will not mend their efficacy. It will continue a kind of mulish production, with all the defects of its opposite parents, and marked with sterility. If we are permitted to make comedy weep, we have an equal right to make tragedy laugh, and to set down in blank verse the jests and repartees of all the attendants in a funeral procession.

But there is one argument in favour of sentimental comedy, which will keep it on the stage, in spite of all that can be said against it. It is, of all others, the most easily written. Those abilities that can hammer out a novel, are fully sufficient for the production of a sentimental comedy. It is only sufficient to raise the characters a little; to deck out the hero with a riband, or give the heroine a title; then to put an insipid dialogue, without character or humour, into their mouths, give them mighty good hearts, very fine clothes, furnish a new set of scenes, make a pathetic scene or two, with a sprinkling of tender melancholy conversation through the whole, and there is no doubt but all the ladies will cry, and all the gentlemen applaud.

Humour at present seems to be departing from the stage, and it will soon happen that our comic players will have nothing left for it but a fine coat and a song. It depends upon the audience whether they will actually drive those poor merry creatures from the stage, or sit at a play as gloomy as at the tabernacle. It is not easy to recover an art when once lost; and it will be but a just punishment, that when, by our being too fastidious, we have banished humour from the stage, we should ourselves be deprived of the art of laughing.

16.4 *PORTRAIT OF MR SHUTER AND MRS GREEN AS MR AND MRS HARDCASTLE AND MR QUICK AS TONY LUMPKIN*

Mr. Shuter, Mr. Quick & Mrs. Green in the Characters of Hardcastle, Tony Lumpkin & Mrs. Hardcastle in *She Stoops to Conquer*, mezzotint, 1775. Trustees of the British Museum.

Notes

1 The copy text is Oliver Goldsmith, She Stoops to Conquer: or, The Mistakes of a Night. As it is acted at the Theatre Royal in Covent-Garden. London: F. Newberry, 1773.
2 Henry Woodward had refused the role of Tony Lumpkin opening the door for John Quick's triumph. See note 10.
3 *Hamlet*, 1.ii.77, 85.
4 Edward Shuter, the comic actor who played Mr. Hardcastle.
5 *sentimentals*: sentimental comedies. The Prologue goes on to parody their excessive moralizing.
6 Buckingham, *The Rehearsal* (1671), II.iv.67–68.
7 *blocks*: the wooden heads used for holding wigs.
8 *The Merchant of Venice*, II.vii.69.
9 *a doctor*: Goldsmith used the title of Doctor from 1763 onward.
10 This was Charles Lee Lewes's first important role. It was originally intended for another actor, Smith, who withdrew.
11 John Quick (1748–1831) owed much of his early celebrity to this role.
12 Diggory's character is not listed in the 1773 Newberry text.
13 *basket*: the baggage carrier at the back of a stagecoach was also used for external seating.
14 *rumbling*: rambling.
15 Prince Eugene of Savoy and the Duke of Marlborough were famed military leaders from the War of Spanish Succession (1701–14).
16 Darby and Joan were the names given to a devoted elderly couple content to live in quiet retirement. The song *The Joys of Love never forgot*, published in *The Gentleman's Magazine*, goes as follows: "Old Darby, with Joan by his side,/You've often regarded with wonder:/He's dropsical, she is sore-eyed,/Yet they're never happy asunder."
17 *years of discretion*: Giles Jacob's *A New-Law Dictionary* (1729) handles this issue as follows: "A Man . . . at Fourteen, which is his *age of Discretion,* may consent to Marriage, and chuse his Guardian; . . . A Women . . . at Twelve . . . may consent to Marriage; at Fourteen she is at Years of Discretion, and may chuse a Guardian" (4)
18 *Horse-pond*: a pond for watering horses.
19 *sensible*: imbued with sensibility or feeling.
20 *Allons*: Let's go, from the French "Allons y".
21 Tony's mispronunciation of "genius".
22 Rivers and waters of the Greek underworld. Here signifying learning.
23 *Quis . . . Quœs . . . Quods*: nominative forms of Latin relative pronouns. As in the previous line, these tags are deployed to signify learning.
24 *maxum*: for "maxim".
25 An aria from Thomas Arne's opera seria *Artaxerxes* (1762).
26 The minuet is part of the overture to Georg Friedrich Handel's *Arianna in Creta* (1734).
27 Archaic form of "Egad".
28 *woundily*: excessively.
29 *Hamlet* i.v.125–26.
30 *traipsing*: going about in a slovenly manner (*OED*).
31 *murrain*: "any virulent infectious disease of cattle or other livestock" (*OED*)
32 One of the most sought after scientific discoveries of the eighteenth-century was a convenient method for determining the longitude at sea. Parliament offered a £20,000 reward in 1713 but it wasn't until 1765 that John Harrison claimed the prize and not until 1773 that the prize was granted.
33 *Wauns*: "God's wounds", used as an oath. (*OED*)
34 "*by the elevens"*: by lunchtime.
35 Inn here means one of the Inns of Court where barristers practiced the law.
36 *Duchesses of Drury Lane*: prostitutes who worked in the district of Drury Lane Theatre.
37 Hardcastle's version of this famous battle from the War of Spanish Succession is conspicuously wrong. The French defeated the English at Denain, France in 1712 and Lord Marlborough had nothing

to do with the action. The Allied forces of England, Netherlands and Prussia were led by Lord Albemarle.

38 *ventre d'or*: gold-fronted.

39 Duke of Marlborough. . .George Brooks: Again the story spins out of control.

40 *for us that sell ale*: referring to the practice of buying votes with free drinks.

41 Hyder Ali was Sultan of Mysore from 1761–82. He fought a number of wars against the East India Company forces throughout his reign. Ali Khan was subahadar of Bengal. Ally Croker was a character from a popular Irish ballad.

42 Prince Eugene of Savoy was the general in charge of the Habsburg siege on Belgrade in 1717. The Austrians razed the city and forced the Ottoman Empire to accept new territorial limits in the Treaty of Passarowitz (1718).

43 *privy-council*: a body of advisors appointed by a monarch or head of state.

44 All upon the high ropes: on his high horse.

45 The Joiners' Company was a guild of woodworkers. The corporation of Bedford could refer to either the city council or a group of merchants from Bedford.

46 *florentine*: a meat pie.

47 *shaking pudding*: a blancmange or a jelly.

48 *taffety cream*: A dish of cream and eggs that took on the sheen of taffeta silk.

49 *made dishes*: overly prepared dishes, usually associated with foreign excess.

50 *green and yellow dinner*: This may be frogs' legs and salad. See *Notes and Queries* 42.1 (1995): 70.

51 The 1772 Royal Marriage Act prohibited relations of the King from marrying without his approval. The Act came in response to George III's brother, William Henry, Duke of Gloucester's proposed marriage to Lady Waldegrave. According to *PRIOR'S Life of Goldsmith*:

> The Duke of Gloucester, for whom, in consequence of the Royal Marriage Act, some public sympathy existed, was present the first night of representation; whether from previous intimation of a passage in the play does not appear. But when Hastings uttered the speech, 'we shall soon be landed in France, where even among slaves the laws of marriage are respected,' it was instantly applied to his Royal Highness by the audience, and several rounds of applause testified their feeling for his situation.
>
> (vol. ii. p. 394)

52 *India Director*: Director of the East India Company.

53 The great Roman orator.

54 A rather mixed list of venues. Ranelagh was a fashionable assembly room with gardens that served tea and ices; men and women of fashion promenaded in St. James's Park; Tower Wharf was decidedly the province of the lower orders.

55 Again a very mixed list. The Pantheon was a site of elite leisure in the 1760s, but because it was a commercial enterprise it also had a somewhat scandalous reputation; Grotto Gardens was a meeting place for "the vulgar classes"; and the Borough, in Southwark, was by the time of the play inhabited by wealthy merchants and tradesmen.

56 *The Town and Country Magazine*, an extremely popular monthly, featured articles designated *Tête-à-Têtes* that reported on scandalous affairs. They were accompanied by engravings of the heads of the people in question. For an example see the Contexts for *The School for Scandal.*

57 Women's hairstyles at this time often incorporated elaborate internal frames and external ornamentation. They were the subject of much ridicule.

58 *friseur*: hairdresser.

59 *Ladies Memorandum Book*: a magazine of women's fashions that first appeared in January 1773.

60 *city ball*: the ball thrown by the Lady Mayor to celebrate Lord Mayor's Day.

61 The practice of inoculation for small-pox commenced in 1721 in England.

62 *crack*: a lie (obsolete by the 1770s).

63 *fortin*: fortune.

64 Found in most eighteenth-century households, the *Complete Housewife* was a popular compendium of recipes and medicines.

65 Similarly, Dr. John Quincy's *Compleat English Dispensary*, first published in 1718 and frequently re-printed, was a popular source for medical treatments.
66 *Bandbox*: a neat yet fragile or flimsy structure.
67 *Anon?*: say that again?
68 *mauvaise honte*: excessive bashfulness.
69 Bully Dawson was a famed gambler in the time of Charles II, but his name signified any kind of a swaggering fool.
70 *bobs*: ornamental pendant or ear-drops. (*OED*)
71 *Bounce of a cracker*: bang of a firework.
72 *Morrice*: Move! From Morris-dance.
73 *marcasite*: a piece of polished steel or similar metal cut as a gem.
74 *Rose and table-cut things*: styles for cutting less valuable stones. Diamonds or emeralds would be given a brilliant-cut to accentuate their fire.
75 Biblical tales such as the Queen of Sheba's visit to King Solomon (1 Kings 10.1–13) were popular subjects for puppet shows at fairs and markets.
76 *Catherine wheel*: a type of circular firework that set off rockets as it rotated.
77 Cherry was the daughter of the landlord in Farquhar's *The Beaux' Stratagem* (1707) who falls in love with Archer.
78 Lion, Angel, Lamb all designate rooms in the Inn.
79 *obstropalous*: a ridiculous variant of obstreperous—i.e. loud and unruly.
80 The allusion here was to an actual club (the "Albemarle Street") recently established, of which ladies as well as gentlemen were privileged to be members, and the introduction of Miss Biddy Buckskin was resented by Horace Walpole and others belonging to the club as an attack on their friend and fellow-member, Miss Lloyd. Goldsmith, in the manuscript of the comedy, and on the early nights of its performance, used Miss Lloyd's name, Rachael, but altered it in the printed copies. See the *Letters of Walpole and Lady Ossory*, vol. i., p. 60.
81 *blackleg*: a swindler, here used to attack female gamesters.
82 *Biddy*: in the Larpent text "Biddy" was "Rachel" for Rachel Lloyd, a leading figure at the Albemarle Club.
83 *work*: handiwork, i.e. embroidery or sewing.
84 A dicing metaphor. Marlow never throws the winning score but he then throws the losing score three times.
85 *Liberty and Fleet Street*: a decidedly Wilkite utterance. During the height of John Wilkes's agitation for parliamentary reform in the 1760s, his supporters generated numerous slogans that linked British liberty to the freedom of the press. Fleet Street was the home of London's newspapers.
86 *A Rake's Progress* refers to William Hogarth's series of eight paintings of 1732–33 that chart the decline and fall of the spendthrift Tom Rakewell from gentility to madness. Hogarth's satire on luxury, prostitution and gambling was widely circulated as engravings from 1735 onward.
87 *Coxcomb*: a fool.
88 *Dullissimo Maccaroni*: The printmaker Mary Darly (1756–59) published the first guide to caricature drawing *A Book of Caricaturas* in (1762). Between 1771 and 1773, she and her husband Matthew Darly published six sets of "macaroni" prints, each of which contained 24 caricatures of types from all aspects of London life satirized as "macaronis"—single figures on a blank ground whose affectations were humourously lampooned. Their shop became known as "The Macaroni Print Shop." Marlow is imagining himself satirized as the "Stupid Macaroni."
89 *Whistlejacket*: One of England's most famous racehorses, owned by the Marquess of Rockingham. The horse was the subject of George Stubbs's 1762 painting of the same name, one of the most innovative equestrian portraits of the eighteenth century, which was widely reproduced as an engraving.
90 *haspicholls*: corruption of harpsichord.
91 spindles used in lacemaking
92 *mun*: must.
93 *izzard*: an obsolete word for the letter z.

94 *feeder*: a trainer of fighting cocks.
95 *Shake-bag club*: cock-fighting club.
96 *Baskets*: referring to swords with basket-hilts.
97 The horses are steaming from the effort of galloping.
98 *Rabbet me*: mild expletive—i.e. drat me.
99 *varment*: troublesome person.
100 Fake Latin for a circuitous route.
101 The place name is variable depending on the performance.
102 Goldsmith wrote two other Epilogues to this Comedy, neither of which however appear to have been spoken.
103 In the fourth volume of *A Collection of Prologues and Epilogues*, 4 vols., i2mo, 1779, there is a characteristic full-length portrait of Mrs. Bulkley in the dress she wore when she spoke this epilogue.
104 *As You Like It*, II.vii. The ensuing lines are a parody of Jacques's speech.
105 *coquets*: flirts with or compliments.
106 *Nancy Dawson*: a popular song named after a famous hornpipe dancer.
107 *Che Faró seza Euridice* is a famous aria from Glück's opera *Orfeo ed Euridice* (1764)
108 Madame Heinel was a favourite dancer in London, when this Epilogue was spoken.
109 *Spadille*: the ace of spades and the first trump in the fashionable game of Ombre.
110 Bayes was the playwright in Buckingham's *The Rehearsal* (1672); here it stands in for "poet" or "playwright" more generally.
111 This second epilogue, also by Goldsmith, was not ready in time for the first production.
112 Joseph Cradock (1742–1826) was a close associate of both David Garrick and Goldsmith. He was a conspicuous participant in the Jubilee at Stratford. He was among the last survivors of Goldsmith's circle.
113 Sadler's Wells was a popular pleasure garden offering musical entertainments. The King's Theatre presented opera regularly during the fall and winter seasons. Roratorio appears to be a corruption of oratorio, the kind of narrative musical work sung by soloists and a chorus, but without scenery or action, that was perfected by Handel. Roratorio may be a joke on the practice of audiences singing along to performances of Handel's work.
114 [original note] All the subjects of the British government are countrymen.
115 The booby-heir, before-mentioned. [original note]

---

17. *The School for Scandal*

***THE SCHOOL FOR SCANDAL*. A COMEDY BY RICHARD BRINSLEY SHERIDAN. FIRST PERFORMED 8 MAY 1777 AND FIRST PUBLISHED: SEE NOTE [1]**

17.1 *THE SCHOOL FOR SCANDAL*: A COMEDY

Richard Brinsley Sheridan

First Performed 8 May 1777 [1]

AS PLAYWRIGHT, MANAGER AND WHIG POLITICIAN, Richard Brinsley Sheridan (1751-1816) was what we would now call an "operator." The extraordinarily talented son of Thomas Sheridan—a notable actor, manager, and educator in his own right—and Frances Sheridan—a successful playwright and novelist—was born in Dublin but was largely raised in England. He first came to public notice for his participation in a pair of duels with Captain Charles Matthews, who had impugned his fiancé, the singer Elizabeth Linley, in the daily press. The first duel was a bit of a fiasco; the second nearly cost Sheridan his life. But both events made him the subject of precisely the kind of scandalous journalism and gossip later satirized in *The School for Scandal.* Sheridan's reaction to leering publicity was remarkable. He quickly transformed the story into one of the most celebrated comedies of the age and thus addressed the question of scandalous celebrity head on. In a pattern that would be repeated throughout his career, his first play, *The Rivals* (1775), had a rough first night and then became a standard of the repertory. It inaugurated one of the most dominant theatrical reigns of the century. A string of hits that extended from *The Rivals* to *The Duenna* (1776), *The School for Scandal* (1777), and finally *The Critic* (1778) made Sheridan the most celebrated playwright in London. Shortly after David Garrick's retirement in 1776, Sheridan became the manager and bought the controlling interest in Drury Lane Theatre. In many ways he drove the theatre into the ground, but he effectively controlled dramatic entertainment for the last quarter of the century. After *The Critic*, arguably his most complex satire, Sheridan temporarily retired from playwriting. His comedies were constantly performed, but he would return to writing plays one last time with the hugely successful melodramatic tragedy *Pizarro* (1799). This final play was the culmination of much of the dramaturgical experimentation of the eighteenth century and it set the stage for much of the serious drama of the nineteenth century.

The gap between *The Critic* and *Pizarro* was not a period of inactivity. If anything Sheridan was even more in the public eye because he entered Parliament in 1780 as part of the Whig opposition to Lord North's Tory government. A protégé of the Marquis of Rockingham, a close associate of Charles James Fox and Edmund Burke, he quickly became one of the most important Whigs in Parliament. He played a vocal role in Rockingham and Fox's resistance to the American War; he was a prominent player in the impeachment of Warren Hastings; and he was one of the most powerful critics of Pitt's government throughout the 1780s and 1790s, especially when proposed legislation impinged on Irish affairs or on attempts to curtail political resistance to the government. He was widely regarded as the greatest orator of his age. Although his political career technically came after the composition of his most celebrated comedies, his political education is crucial to understanding Sheridan's work. All of Sheridan's canonical work was written and staged during the American War. He strongly opposed North's bellicose policies and each of the plays can be understood as an oblique critique of the war effort at different stages of its prosecution. But more significantly, at the same time that Sheridan was writing these plays he was employed by the Marquis of Rockingham, the leader of the Whig opposition, to destroy the *Morning Post*, the only London newspaper loyal to the North Ministry. Inserting and suppressing paragraphs in papers favorable to the opposition and undermining stories in the *Morning Post* itself, Sheridan had first hand experience with manipulating the news and public opinion. These skills would serve him well in composing *The School for Scandal* and *The Critic*, two plays that explicitly address the power of the daily press, and in managing Drury Lane itself. Under his management, entertainment was always in dialogue with the highly mediated social and political world of his audience.

In *The School for Scandal*, reputation, character, and social standing exist in a precarious market for public opinion and gossip. One of Sheridan's great recognitions is that social value is determined by the market demand for scandalous information. At one level, Sheridan was merely taking the popularity of the *tête-à-têtes* in *The Town and Country Magazine* to their most disturbing conclusion—namely, that character is a fiction necessary to sate our desire for its assassination. Such a radical critique of the moral fabric of the upper ranks was both hilarious and upsetting. After all, those charged with "re-conquering" the American colonies and leading the nation through what was quickly becoming a global war were men such as Joseph and Charles Surface. It is here that we can see the play in relation to broader Enlightenment thematics. The advent of the scientific method is a crucial presupposition of most enlightened thought. Propositions are made and tested against observable evidence. In an era of religious and political skepticism this premise could easily take on moral implications and thus become a blueprint for comedy. *The School for Scandal* is essentially a moral experiment: Sir Oliver Surface hides his identity and stages a series of tests to assess the worthiness of his nephews. That the younger nephew is found to be the most appropriate heir should not go unnoticed. In contrast to the laws and conventions of the *Ancien Regime*—i.e. against the prerogative of established authority—a social experiment has found a more worthy basis on which to base cultural and social continuity.

Looking at the play as a moral experiment is also helpful for understanding its two most famous scenes. The picture auction and the screen scene quickly became iconic, and it is important to recognize that they both turn on observation. In the former scene, Sir Oliver impersonates Mr. Premium to test Charles's loyalty, but what emerges is an enquiry into what kind of history is useful for life in the present. Charles can part with some relatives because their aristocratic and military histories are obsolete; he cannot part with the picture of Sir Oliver not only because he likes him, but because Sir Oliver's ties to the emerging empire in India point to a future that can sustain Britain *after* American decolonization. Likewise, the screen scene, for all its physical hilarity, allows for a direct engagement with the transition from one set of social and sexual norms to another. Sheridan made this experiment even more trenchant by his casting decisions. Frances Abington, the original Lady Teazle, was the subject of much leering scandal in *The Town and Country* itself; John Palmer, whose hypocrisy and philandering were widely known, was the first Joseph Surface; Thomas King's representation of Sir Peter Teazle was partly imbued by his reputation as an honorable man. When the screen falls we see the rejection of Joseph's embodiment of veiled libertinism, the celebration of Charles' benevolence and a crucial recalibration of the Teazle marriage from one always threatening to revert to models of mere alliance typical of the early part of the century to one of conjugal love and restraint associated with the emerging middling orders.

A Portrait

Addressed to Mrs. Crewe[2] with the Comedy of the School for Scandal by R.B. Sheridan Esq.

Tell me, Ye prim Adepts in Scandal's School
Who rail by Precept, and detract by Rule,
Lives there no Characters so tried—so known—
So deck'd with Grace and so unlike your own
That even *you* assist her Fame to raise,
Approve by Envy, and by Silence praise?

Attend! a model shall attract your view
Daughters of Calumny!—I summon You:—
You shall decide if this a *Portrait* prove,
Or fond Creation of the Muse and Love.

Attend—Ye Virgin Criticks shrewd and sage
Ye Matron Censors of this childish Age
Whose peering Eye & wrinkled Front declare
A fix'd Antipathy to *Young* and *Fair:*
By cunning cautious or by Nature cold
In maiden Malice virulently bold—

Attend—Ye skill'd to coin the precious Tale,
Creating Proof—where Innuendos fail!
Whose practic'd Mem'ries—cruely exact—
Omit no Circumstances—except the Fact!

Attend!—All ye who boast—or Old or Young—
The living Libel of a sland'rous Tongue!

So shall my Theme as far contrasted be
As Saints by Fiends—or Hymns by Calumny

Come, gentle *Amoret*[3] (—'neath that Name
In Worthier Verse is sung thy Beauty's Fame)
Come—but for *thee* whom seeks the Muse? & while
Celestial Blushes check thy conscious Smile,
With timid Grace, and hesitating Eye—
The perfect Model which I boast—supply!
Vain Muse! could'st Thou the humblest sketch create
Of *Her*—or slightest Charm could'st imitate,
Could thy blest Strain, in kindred Colours trace
The faintest Wonder of her Form, or Face—
Poets would study the immortal Line.
And *Reynolds*[4] own *his* Art subdued by *thine!*
That Art!—which well might Added Lustre give
To Nature's best!—and Heav'n's superlative!
On *Granby's* Cheek might bid new Glories rise
Or point a purer Beam from *Devon's* Eyes![5]

Hard is the Task to shape that Beauty's Praise
Whose Judgement scorns the Homage Flatt'ry pays!
But praising *Amoret* we cannot err,
No Tongue oe'rvalues Heav'n—nor flatters *Her!*
Yet *she*—by Fate's Perversness!—She alone
Would doubt our Truth—nor deem such Praise her own!

Adorning Fashion—unadorn'd by Dress—
Simple from Taste—and not from Carelessness—
Discreet in Gesture, in Deportment mild,
Not stiff with Prudence, nor uncouthly wild—
No State has Amoret!—no studied Mien!
She frowns no *Goddess!*—and She *moves* no *Queen!*
The softer Charm that in her manner lies
Is fram'd to captivate, yet not surprize;
It justly suits the Expression of her Face,
'Tis less than Dignity—and more than Grace!

On her pure Cheeks the native Hue is such
That form'd by Heav'n to be admired so much
The hand Divine, with a less partial Care,
Might well have fix'd a fainter Crimson there

And bad[e] the gentle Inmate of her Breast,
Inshrined Modesty!—supply the rest.
But who the Peril of her Lips shall paint?
Strip them of smiles—still, still, all Words were faint!
But moving Love himself appears to teach
Their *Action* tho' denied to rule her *speech!*
And Thou—who *sees't* her speak—and dost not *hear*
Mourn not her distant Accents 'scape thine Ear,
Viewing those Lips—thou still may'st make pretence
To judge of what she says—and swear 'tis sense;
Cloath'd with such Grace, with such Expression fraught,
They moove in meaning and they pause in Thought!
But dost thou further watch, with charm'd surprize,
The mild Irresolution of her Eyes?
Curious to mark how frequent they repose
In brief Eclipse, and momentary close?
Ah!—seest Thou not?—an ambush'd Cupid there
Too tim'rous of his Charge!—with jealous care
Veils, & unveils those Beams of heav'nly Light,
Too full—to fatal else for mortal sight!
Nor Yet—such pleasing vengeance fond to meet
In pard'ning Dimples hope a safe retreat,
What tho' her peacefull Breast should ne'er allow
Subduing Frowns to arm her alter'd Brow—
By Love! I swear—and by his gentler Wiles!
More fatal still—the mercy of her Smiles!

Thus lovely!—thus adorn'd! possessing all
Of bright, or Fair—that can to Woman fall,
The height of Vanity might well be thought
Prerogative in her, and Nature's Fault
—Yet gentle *Amoret*—in mind supreme
As well as Charms—rejects the vainer Theme,
And half mistrustfull of her Beauty's Store,
She barbs with Wit—those Darts too keen before.

Read in all knowledge—that her Sex shou'd reach,
Tho *Greville* or the *Muse* shoud deign to teach;
Fond to improve—nor tim'rous to discern
How far it is a Woman's Grace to learn;
In *Millar's* Dialect she wou'd not prove
Apollo's *Priestess*—but Apollo's Love.

Grac'd by those Signs—which Truth delights to own
The timid Blush—and mild submitted Tone—
Whate'er she says—tho' Sense appear throughout
Displays the tender Hue of female Doubt
Deck'd with that Charm, how lovely Wit appears!
How gracefull *Science* when that Robe she wears!

Such too her Talents, and her Bent of Mind
As speak a sprightly Heart by Thought refin'd:
A Taste for *Mirth*—by Contemplation school'd
A Turn for Ridicule by Candour rul'd;
A Scorn of Folly—which she tries to hide,
An Awe of Talent—which she owns with Pride.

Peace idle Muse! no more thy strain prolong,
But Yield a Theme, thy warmest praises wrong:
Just to her merit tho' thou can'st not raise
Thy feeble Verse—behold the acknowledg'd Praise
Has spread Conviction thro' the envious Train,
And cast a fatal Gloom o'er Scandal's Reign!
And Lo! each pallid Hag with blister'd Tongue,
Mutters Assent to all thy Zeal has sung
Owns all the Colours just—the Out-line true,
Thee my Inspirer—and my *Model—Crewe!*

PROLOGUE

Spoken by Mr. King. Written by D. Garrick—Esq.

A School for Scandal! tell me, I beseech you,
Needs there a School, this modish Art to teach you?
No need of Lessons now, the knowing think—
We might as well be taught to eat and drink.
Caus'd by a dearth of Scandal, should the vapours
Distress our fair ones—let 'em read the papers.—
Their pow'rful mixtures, such disorders hit;
Crave what they will, there's *quantum sufficit.*[6]

Lord! cries my Lady Wormwood,[7] (who loves Tattle
And puts much salt & pepper in her prattle)

"Just ris'n at Noon, all night at cards when the threshing,
Strong Tea and Scandal—Bless me! how refreshing!
Give me the papers, Lisp—how bold, & free! [*sips*]
Last Night Lord *L*—[*sips*] was caught with Lady *D*
For Aching heads, what charming Sal volatile! [*sips*]
If Mrs. *B*— will still continue flirting,
We hope she'll *draw*—or we'll undraw the Curtain."
Fine Satire poz![8]—in public all abuse it,
But by ourselves [*sips*] our praise we can't refuse it.
Now Lisp read *you*—there, at that Dash and Star—[9]
Yes Ma'am.—"A certain Lord had best beware,
Who lives not Twenty miles from Grosv'nor Square,[10]
For should he Lady *W*— find willing,
Wormwood is bitter"—"Oh! that's me, the Villain!
Throw it behind the fire, and never more
Let that vile paper, come within the door."
Thus at our Friends we laugh, who feel the dart,
To reach our feelings, we our selves must smart.
Is our Young Bard so young, to think that he,
Can stop the full spring tide of Calumny?
Knows he the world so little, and its Trade?
Alas! the Devil is sooner rais'd, than laid:
So Strong, so Swift, the monster there's no gagging,
Cut Scandal's head off—Still the tongue is wagging.
Proud of your Smiles, once lavishly bestow'd,
Again your young Don Quixote,[11] takes the road:
To shew his Gratitude, he draws his pen,
And Seeks this Hydra,[12] Scandal, in its Den.
For your Applause all perils he would through
He'll fight—that's *write*—A Cavaliero true,
'Till every drop of blood—that's *Ink*—is spilt for you.

Dramatis Personæ

Men

Sir Peter Teazle	Mr. King
Sir Oliver Surface	Mr. Yates
Joseph Surface	Mr. Palmer
Charles Surface	Mr. Smith
Crabtree	Mr. Parsons
Sir Benjamin Backbite	Mr. Dodd
Rowley	Mr. Aiekin
Trip	Mr. La Mash
Moses	Mr. Baddeley
Snake	Mr. Packer
Careless	Mr. Farren
and other Companions to Charles, Servants, &c.	

Women

Lady Teazle	Mrs. Abington
Maria	Miss P. Hopkins
Lady Sneerwell	Miss Sherry
Mrs. Candour	Miss Pope

I.i

[Lady Sneerwell *at the dressing Table*—Snake *drinking Chocolate*—]

LADY SNEERWELL. The paragraphs[13] you say, Mr. Snake, were all inserted?

SNAKE. They were Madam, and as I copied them myself in a feign'd hand, there can be no suspicion whence they came.

LADY SNEERWELL. Did you circulate the reports of Lady *Brittle*'s Intrigue with Captain *Boastall*?

SNAKE. That is in as fine a train as your Ladyship could wish, in the common course of things, I think it must reach Mrs. *Clackit*'s ears, within four and twenty hours and then you know the business is as good as done.

LADY SNEERWELL. Why truly Mrs. *Clackit* has a very pretty talent, and a great deal of industry.

SNAKE. True Madam, and has been tolerably successfull in her day:—to my knowledge, she has been the cause of six matches[14] being broken off, and three sons being disinherited, of four forc'd elopements, as many close confinements,[15] nine separate maintenances,[16] and two divorces;[17]—nay I have more than once trac'd her causing a *tête-à-tête* in the *Town and Country Magazine*,[18] when the parties perhaps had never seen each other's faces before in the course of their lives.

LADY SNEERWELL. She certainly has talents, but her manner is gross.

SNAKE. 'Tis very true,—she generally designs well, has a free tongue, and a bold invention, but her colouring is too dark, and her out line often extravagant, she wants that *delicacy* of *hint*, and *mellowness* of *sneer*, which distinguish your Ladyship's scandal.

LADY SNEERWELL. Ah, you are partial Snake.

SNAKE. Not in the least.—Every body allows that Lady *Sneerwell* can do more with a *word*, or a *look*, than many can do with the most labour'd detail, even when they happen to have a little truth on their side to support it.

LADY SNEERWELL. Yes, my dear Snake, and I am no hypocrite to deny the satisfaction I reap from the success of my efforts. Wounded my self, in the early part of my life by the envenom'd tongue of slander, I confess I have since known no pleasure equal to the reducing others, to the level of my own injur'd reputation.

SNAKE. Nothing can be more natural;—but Lady Sneerwell, there is one affair in which you have lately employ'd me, wherein I confess I am at a loss to guess your motives.

LADY SNEERWELL. I conceive you mean with respect to my neighbour, Sir Peter Teazle and his family?

SNAKE. I do; here are two young men to whom Sir Peter has acted as a kind of guardian since their father's death, the elder possessing the most amiable character,[19] and universally wellspoken of, the youngest the most dissipated and extravagant young fellow in the kingdom, without friends, or character—the former an avow'd admirer of your Ladyship, and apparently your favourite; the latter, attach'd to Maria, Sir Peter's ward, and confessedly belov'd by her; now on the face of these circumstances, it is utterly unaccountable to me, why you, the widow of a city knight[20] with a good jointure,[21] should not close with[22] the passion of a man of such character & expectation as Mr. *Surface*, and more so, why you should be so uncommonly earnest to destroy the mutual attachment subsisting between his brother *Charles* & *Maria*.

LADY SNEERWELL. Then at once to unravel this mystery, I must inform you, that love has no share whatever in the intercourse between Mr. *Surface*, and me.

SNAKE. No!

LADY SNEERWELL. His real attachment is to *Maria*, or her fortune, but finding in his brother, a favour'd rival, he has been oblig'd to mask his pretensions, & profit by my assistance.

SNAKE. Yet still I am more puzzled why you should interest your self in his success?

LADY SNEERWELL. Heav'ns, how dull you are!—Cannot you surmise the weakness, which I hitherto thro' shame have conceal'd even from *you*—Must I confess that *Charles*, that libertine, that extravagant, that bankrupt in fortune and reputation, that he it is for whom I am thus anxious, and malicious, and to gain whom I would sacrifice every thing?

SNAKE. Now indeed your conduct appears consistent; but how came you & Mr. *Surface* so confidential?[23]

LADY SNEERWELL. For our mutual interest; I have found him out a long time since. I know him to be artful, selfish, and malicious, in short, a sentimental knave.

SNAKE. Yet, Sir Peter vows he has not his equal in England—and above all, he praises him, as a man of sentiment.[24]

LADY SNEERWELL. True, and with the assistance of his sentiments and hypocrisy, he has brought him entirely into his interest with regard to *Maria*.

[*Enter* Servant.

SERVANT. Mr. Surface.

LADY SNEERWELL. Show him up. [*Exit* Servant] He generally calls about this time, I don't wonder at people's giving him to me for a lover.

[*Enter* Surface.

SURFACE. My dear Lady Sneerwell how do you do to day? Mr. Snake your most obedient.

LADY SNEERWELL. Snake has just been arraigning me on our mutual attachment, but I have inform'd him of our real views; you know how useful he has been to us, and believe me the confidence is not ill plac'd.

SURFACE. Madam it is impossible for me to suspect a man of Mr. *Snake*'s sensibility[25] and discernment.

LADY SNEERWELL. Well, well, no compliments now;—but tell me when you saw your mistress *Maria*, or what is more material to me, your brother?

SURFACE. I have not seen either since I left you; but I can inform you that they never meet; some of your stories have taken a good effect on Maria.

LADY SNEERWELL. Ah, my dear Snake the merit of this belongs to you; but do your brother's distresses increase?

SURFACE. Every hour;—I am told he has had another execution in his house yesterday; in short, his dissipation and extravagance exceeds any thing I ever heard of.

LADY SNEERWELL. Poor Charles!

SURFACE. True Madam;—notwithstanding his vices, one can't help feeling for him.—Aye, poor Charles! I'm sure I wish it was in my power to be of any essential service to him.—For the man who does not share in the distress of a brother, even tho' merited by his own misconduct, deserves—

LADY SNEERWELL. O Lud! you are going to be moral, and forget that you are among friends.

SURFACE. Egad, that's true.—I'll keep that sentiment 'till I see Sir Peter; however it is certainly a charity to rescue Maria from such a libertine; who if he is to be reclaim'd, can be so only by a person of your Ladyship's superior accomplishments, and understanding.

SNAKE. I believe Lady Sneerwell here's company coming, I'll go and copy the letter I mentioned to you.—Mr. Surface your most obedient. [*Exit* Snake.

SURFACE. Sir your very devoted.—Lady Sneerwell, I am very sorry you have put any further confidence in that fellow.

LADY SNEERWELL. Why so?

SURFACE. I have lately detected him in frequent conference with old *Rowley*, who was formerly my father's steward, and has never, you know, been a friend of mine.

LADY SNEERWELL. And do you think he would betray us?

SURFACE. Nothing more likely: take my word for't Lady Sneerwell, that fellow hasn't virtue enough to be faithful even to his own villainy—hah! Maria.

[*Enter* Maria.

LADY SNEERWELL. Maria, my dear how do you do?—What's the matter?

MARIA. O there is that disagreeable lover[26] of mine Sir *Benjamin Backbite*, has just call'd at my guardian's, with his odious uncle *Crabtree*—so I slipt out, and run hither to avoid them.

LADY SNEERWELL. Is that all?

SURFACE. If my brother *Charles* had been of the party Ma'am perhaps you would not have been so much alarm'd!

LADY SNEERWELL. Nay, now you are severe, for I dare swear the truth of the matter is, Maria heard *you* were here;—but by dear, what has Sir Benjamin done, that you should avoid him so[?]

MARIA. Oh he has done nothing—but 'tis for what he has said, his conversation is a perpetual libel on all his acquaintance.

SURFACE. Aye, and the worst of it is, there is no advantage in not knowing him; for he'll abuse a stranger just as soon as his best friend—and his uncle's as bad.

LADY SNEERWELL. Nay but we should make allowance, Sir Benjamin is a wit and a poet.

MARIA. For my part I own Madam, wit loses its respect with me, when I see it in company with malice.—What do you think, Mr. Surface?

SURFACE. Certainly Madam, to smile at the jest which plants a thorn in another's breast, is to become a principal in the mischief.

LADY SNEERWELL. Pshaw!—there's no possibility of being witty without a little ill nature, the malice of a good thing is the barb that makes it stick—what's your opinion Mr. Surface?

SURFACE. To be sure, Madam, that conversation, where the spirit of raillery is suppress'd, will ever appear tedious & insipid.

MARIA. Well, I'll not debate how far scandal may be allowable, but in a man I am sure it is always contemptible;—we have pride, envy, rivalship, and a thousand motives to depreciate each other, but the male slanderer, must have the cowardice of a woman before he can traduce one.

[*Enter* Servant.

SERVANT. Madam, Mrs. Candour is below, and if your Ladyship's at leisure, will leave her carriage.

LADY SNEERWELL. Beg her to walk in—Now Maria, however here is a character to your taste, for tho' Mrs. Candour is a little talkative, every body allows her to be the best natur'd, and best sort of woman.

MARIA. Yes, with a very gross affectation of good nature and benevolence, she does more mischief than the direct malice of Old Crabtree.

SURFACE. 'Efaith 'tis very true Lady Sneerwell; whenever I hear the current running against the character of my friends, I never think them in such danger, as when Candour undertakes their defences.

LADY SNEERWELL. Hush, here she is.

[*Enter* Mrs. Candour.

MRS. CANDOUR. My dear Lady Sneerwell, how have you been this century? Mr. Surface, what news do you hear? Tho' indeed it is no matter, for I think one hears nothing else but scandal.

SURFACE. Just so indeed Madam.

MRS. CANDOUR. Ah Maria Child! What is the whole affair off between you and Charles?—His extravagance I presume—The Town[27] talks of nothing else.

MARIA. I am very sorry Ma'am, the Town has so little to do.

MRS. CANDOUR. True, true, child, but there is not stopping people's tongues. I own I was hurt to hear it, as indeed I was to learn from the same quarter, that your guardian Sir Peter and Lady Teazle have not agreed lately, so well as could be wish'd.

MARIA. 'Tis strangely impertinent for people to busy themselves so.

MRS. CANDOUR. Very true child, but what's to be done? People will talk, there's no preventing it.—Why it was but yesterday, I was told that Miss Gadabout had elop'd with Sir Fillegree Flirt—But Lord! there's no minding what one hears—tho' to be sure, I had this from very good authority.

MARIA. Such reports are highly scandalous.

MRS. CANDOUR. So they are child—shameful, shameful!—But the world is so censorious, no character escapes—Lord now who would have suspected your friend Miss Prim of an indiscretion,—yet such is the ill nature of people, that they say her uncle stopt her last week, just as she was stepping into the York Diligénce[28] with her dancing master.

MARIA. I'll answer for't there are no grounds for the report.

MRS. CANDOUR. Oh, no foundation in the world I dare swear, no more probably, than for the story circulated last month of Mrs. Festino's affair with Colonel Cassino; tho' to be sure that matter was never rightly clear'd up.

SURFACE. The licence of invention some people take is monstrous indeed.

MARIA. 'Tis so—But in my opinion, those who report such things are equally culpable.

MRS. CANDOUR. To be sure they are; tale bearers are as bad as the tale makers.—'Tis an old observation, and a very true one;—but what's to be done as I said before, how will you prevent people from talking?—To day Mrs. Clackit assur'd me Mr. & Mrs. Honeymoon were at last become mere man and wife like the rest of their acquaintances[29]—she likewise hinted that a certain widow in the next street had got rid of her dropsy and recover'd her shape in a most surprizing manner;[30]—and at the same time Miss Tattle who was by affirm'd that Lord Buffalo had discovered his lady at a house of no extraordinary fame.[31]—And that Sir Harry Bouquet, and Tom Saunter, were to measure swords on a similar provocation.—But Lord, do you think I would report these things? No, no, tale bearers as I said before, are just as bad as tale makers.

SURFACE. Ah, Mrs. Candour—if every body had your forbearance and good nature—

MRS. CANDOUR. I confess Mr. Surface I cannot bear to hear people attack'd behind their backs, and when ugly circumstances come out against one's acquaintance I own I always love to think the best—By the bye I hope it is not true;—that your brother is absolutely ruin'd?

SURFACE. I am afraid his circumstances are very bad indeed Ma'am.

MRS. CANDOUR. Ah! I heard so—But you must tell him to keep up his spirits—every body almost is in the same way, Lord Spindle, Sir Thomas Splint, Captain Quinze and Mr. Nickit[32]—all up[33] I hear within this week! So if Charles is undone he'll find half his acquaintances ruin'd too—and that you know is a consolation.

SURFACE. Doubtless Ma'am, a very great one.

[*Enter* Servant.

SERVANT. Mr. Crabtree, and Sir Benjamin Backbite. [*Exit* Servant.

LADY SNEERWELL. So Maria, you see your lover pursues you. Positively, you shan't escape.

[*Enter* Crabtree, *&* Sir Benjamin Backbite.

CRABTREE. Lady Sneerwell, I kiss your hands. Mrs. Candour I don't believe you are acquainted with my nephew Sir Benjamin Backbite—Egad Ma'am he has a pretty wit, and is a pretty poet too; isn't he Lady Sneerwell?

SIR BENJAMIN. O fye, Uncle—

CRABTREE. Nay egad it's true—I'll back him at a rhebus or a charade[34] against the best rhymer in the kingdom—has your Ladyship heard the Epigram he wrote last week on Lady Frizle's feather catching fire—Do Benjamin repeat it—or the charade you made last night extempore at Mrs. Drowzie's conversationé[35]—come now, your *first* is the name of a fish, your *second* a great naval commander and—

SIR BENJAMIN. Uncle—now—prithee—

CRABTREE. E'faith Ma'am—'twould surprize you to hear how ready he is at these things.

LADY SNEERWELL. I wonder Sir Benjamin, you never publish any thing.

SIR BENJAMIN. To say truth Ma'am 'tis very vulgar to print, and as my little productions are mostly satires & lampoons on particular people, I find they circulate more by giving copies in confidence to the friends of the parties—however I have some love elegies which when favour'd with this lady's smiles, I mean to give to the publick.

CRABTREE. 'Fore Heav'n, Ma'am they'll immortalize you—you'll be handed down to posterity like Petrarch's Laura, or Waller's Sacharissa.[36]

SIR BENJAMIN. Yes, Madam, I think you will like them, when you shall see them on a beautiful quarto page, where a neat rivulet of text shall murmur thro' a meadow of margin.[37]—'Fore Gad they will be the most elegant things of their kind.

CRABTREE. But Ladies, that's true—have you heard the news?

MRS. CANDOUR. What Sir, do you mean the report of—

CRABTREE. No Ma'am, that's not it.—Miss Nicely is going to be married to her own footman.

MRS. CANDOUR. Impossible!

CRABTREE. Ask Sir Benjamin—

SIR BENJAMIN. 'Tis very true Ma'am—every thing is fix'd, and the wedding livery bespoke.[38]

CRABTREE. Yes, and they *do* say, there were pressing reasons for't.

LADY SNEERWELL. Why I *have* heard something of this before.

MRS. CANDOUR. It can't be—and I wonder anyone should believe such a story of so prudent a lady as Miss Nicely.

SIR BENJAMIN. O Lud, Ma'am! That's the very reason 'twas believ'd at once—she has always been so *cautious* & so *reserv'd*, that every body was sure there was some reason for it at bottom.

MRS. CANDOUR. Why to be sure, a tale of scandal is as fatal to the credit of a prudent lady of her stamp, as a fever is generally to those of the strongest constitutions; but there is a sort of puny, sickly reputation that is always ailing, yet will out live the robuster characters of a hundred prudes.

SIR BENJAMIN. True Madam, there are valetudinarians in reputation as well as constitution, who being conscious of their weak part, avoid the least breath of air, and supply their want of stamina by care & circumspection.

MRS. CANDOUR. Well but this may be all a mistake, you know Sir Benjamin very trifling circumstances often give rise to the most injurious tales.

CRABTREE. That they do I'll be sworn Ma'am—did you ever hear how Miss Piper came to lose her lover and her character last summer at Tunbridge?—Sir Benjamin you remember it.[39]

SIR BENJAMIN. O to be sure the most whimsical circumstance—

LADY SNEERWELL. How was it pray?

CRABTREE. Why one evening at Mrs. Ponto's assembly the conversation happen'd to turn on the difficulty of breeding Nova Scotia sheep in this country—says a young lady in company, 'I have known instances of it, for Miss Lætitia Piper, a first cousin of mine, had a Nova Scotia sheep that produc'd her twins'—{osq}what' cries the old Dowager Lady Dundizzy (who you know is as deaf as a post) 'has Miss Piper had twins?' This mistake, as you may imagine, threw the whole company into a fit of laughing;—however 'twas the next morning every where reported, and in a few days believ'd by the whole Town, that miss Letitia Piper had actually been brought to bed of a fine boy and a girl—and in less than a week there were people who could name the father, and the farm-house where the babies were put out to nurse![40]

LADY SNEERWELL. Strange indeed!

CRABTREE. Matter of fact I assure you.—O Lud Mr. Surface, pray is it true, that your uncle Sir Oliver is coming home?

SURFACE. Not that I know of indeed Sir.

CRABTREE. He has been in the East Indies[41] a long time, you can scarcely remember him I believe. Sad comfort whenever he returns to hear how your brother has gone on.

SURFACE. Charles has been imprudent Sir, to be sure, but I hope no busy people have already prejudiced Sir Oliver against him,—he may reform.

SIR BENJAMIN. To be sure he may—for my part I never believ'd him to be so utterly void of principle, as people say—and tho' he has lost all his friends, I am told nobody is better spoken of by the Jews.[42]

CRABTREE. That's true egad Nephew; if the Old Jewry[43] were a ward I believe Charles would be an alderman; no man more popular there, 'fore Gad. I hear he pays as many annuities, as the Irish Tontine,[44] and that whenever he's sick, they have prayers for the recovery of his health in the synagogue.

SIR BENJAMIN. Yet no man lives in greater splendor;—they tell me, when he entertains his friends, he can sit down to dinner with a dozen of his own securities,[45] have a score of tradesmen waiting in the anti-chamber, and an officer behind every guest's chair.

SURFACE. This may be entertainment to you gentlemen, but you pay very little regard to the feelings of a brother.

MARIA. Their malice is intolerable—Lady Sneerwell I must wish you a good morning—I'm not very well. [*Exit* Maria.

MRS. CANDOUR. Oh dear, she changes colour very much!

LADY SNEERWELL. Do Mrs. Candour follow her—she may want assistance.

MRS. CANDOUR. That I will with all my soul Ma'am—poor dear girl! Who knows what her situation may be! [*Exit* Mrs. Candour.

LADY SNEERWELL. 'Twas nothing but that she could not bear to hear Charles reflected on notwithstanding their difference.

SIR BENJAMIN. The young lady's penchant is obvious.

CRABTREE. But Benjamin, you mustn't give up the pursuit for that, follow her, and put her into good humour—repeat her some of your own verses.—Come, I'll assist you.

SIR BENJAMIN. [*Going*] Mr. Surface, I did not mean to hurt you, but depend upon't, your brother is utterly undone.

CRABTREE. [*Going*] O Lud, aye! Undone as ever man was,—can't raise a guinea.

SIR BENJAMIN. [*Going*] And every thing sold, I'm told, that was moveable.

CRABTREE. [*Going*] I have seen one that was at his house—not a thing left, but some empty bottles, that were overlook'd, and the family pictures, which I believe are fram'd in the wainscot.

SIR BENJAMIN. [*Going*] And I am very sorry to hear also some bad stories against him.

CRABTREE. [*Going*] O, he has done many mean things that's certain.

SIR BENJAMIN. [*Going*] But however, as he's your brother—

CRABTREE. We'll tell you all, another opportunity.

[*Exeunt* Crabtree & Sir Benjamin.

LADY SNEERWELL. Ha! ha! ha! 'Tis very hard for them to leave a subject they have not quite run down.

SURFACE. And I believe the abuse was no more acceptable to your Ladyship than to Maria.

LADY SNEERWELL. I doubt her affections are farther engaged than we imagin'd; but the family are to be here this evening, so you may as well dine where you are, and we shall have an opportunity of observing farther;—in the mean time, I'll go and plot mischief, and you shall study sentiments.

[*Exeunt.*

I.ii

[Sir Peter's *house. Enter* Sir Peter.]

SIR PETER. When an old batchelor takes a young wife, what is he to expect!—'Tis now six months since Lady Teazle made me the happiest of men,—and I have been the miserablest dog ever since that ever committed wedlock! We tift a little going to Church, and came to a quarrel before the bells were done ringing—I was more than once nearly choak'd with gall, during the honey moon; and had lost all comfort in life, before my friends had done wishing me joy!—Yet I chose with caution—a girl bred wholy in the country, who never knew luxury beyond one silk gown—nor dissipation above the annual gala of a race ball—Yet now she plays her part in all the extravagant fopperies of the fashion and the Town with as ready a grace, as if she had never seen a bush nor a grass plat out of Grosvenor Square!—I am sneer'd at by my old acquaintance—paragraph'd in the newspapers. She dissipates my fortune, and contradicts all my humours, yet the worst of it is, I doubt[46] I love her, or I should never bear all this—however I'll never be weak enough to own it.

[*Enter* Rowley.

ROWLEY. Oh, Sir Peter your servant, how is it with you Sir?

SIR PETER. Very bad Master Rowley, very bad;—I meet with nothing but crosses, and vexations.

ROWLEY. What can have happen'd to trouble you since yesterday?

SIR PETER. A good question to a married man.

ROWLEY. Nay I'm sure your lady Sir Peter can't be the cause of your uneasiness.

SIR PETER. Why, has any one told you she was dead?

ROWLEY. Come, come, Sir Peter, you love her notwithstanding your tempers don't exactly agree.

SIR PETER. But the fault is entirely hers, Master Rowley—I am myself the sweetest temper'd man alive, and hate a teizing temper—and so I tell her a hundred times a day.

ROWLEY. Indeed!—

SIR PETER. Aye, and what is very extraordinary, in all our disputes she is always in the wrong! But Lady Sneerwell, and the set she meets at her house encourage the perverseness of her disposition—then to compleat my vexations, Maria, my ward—whom I ought to have the power of a father over, is determin'd to turn rebel too, and absolutely refuses the man whom I have long resolv'd on for her husband;—meaning I suppose to bestow herself on his profligate brother.

ROWLEY. You know Sir Peter, I have always taken the liberty to differ with you, on the subject of these two young gentlemen.—I only wish you may not be deceiv'd, in your opinion of the elder; for Charles my life on't, he will retrieve his errors yet; their worthy father, once my honour'd master, was at his years nearly as wild a spark—yet when he died, he did not leave a more benevolent heart to lament his loss.

SIR PETER. You are wrong Master Rowley—on their father's death you know I acted as a kind of guardian to them both, 'till their uncle Sir Oliver's eastern liberality gave them an early independence; of course no person could have more opportunities of judging of their hearts, and I was never mistaken in my life; Joseph is indeed a model for the young men of the age. He is a man of sentiment, and acts up to the sentiments he professes, but for the other, take my word for't if he had any grains of virtue, by descent, he has dissipated them with the rest of his inheritance;—ah my old friend Sir Oliver, will be deeply mortified when he finds how part of his bounty has been misapplied.

ROWLEY. I am sorry to find you so violent against the young man, because this may be the most critical period of his fortune;—I came hither with news that will surprize you.

SIR PETER. What; let me hear.

ROWLEY. Sir Oliver *is* arriv'd, and at this moment in Town.

SIR PETER. How! You astonish me! I thought you did not expect him this month.

ROWLEY. I did not; but his passage has been remarkably quick.

SIR PETER. 'Egad I shall rejoice to see my old friend,—'tis sixteen years since we met—we have had many a day together; but does he still enjoin us not to inform his nephew[s] of his arrival?

ROWLEY. Most strictly—he means before it is known to make some trial of their dispositions.

SIR PETER. Ah, there needs no art to discover their merits—however he shall have his way—But pray does he know I am married?

ROWLEY. Yes, and will soon wish you joy.

SIR PETER. What as we drink health to a friend in a consumption. Ah! Oliver will laugh at me—we us'd to rail at matrimony together—but he has been steady to his text[47]—well he must be at my house tho'. I'll instantly give orders for his reception—But Master Rowley don't drop a word that Lady Teazle and I ever disagree.

ROWLEY. By no means.

SIR PETER. For I should never be able to stand Noll's jokes;[48] so I'd have him think, (Lord forgive me) that we are a very happy couple.

ROWLEY. I understand you—but then you must be very careful not to differ while he's in the house with you.

SIR PETER. 'Egad, and so we must—and that's impossible—ah! Master Rowley—when an old batchelor marries a young wife—he deserves—no, the crime carries the punishment along with it.

[*Exeunt.*

II.i

[Sir Peter*'s house. Enter* Sir Peter *&* Lady Teazle.]

SIR PETER. Lady Teazle, Lady Teazle, I'll not bear it.

LADY TEAZLE. Sir Peter, Sir Peter, you may bear it or not as you please, but I ought to have my own way in every thing, and what's more I will too—what! Tho' I was educated in the country, I know very well that women of fashion in London are accountable to no body after they are married.

SIR PETER. Very well Ma'am, very well,—so a husband is to have no influence, no authority?

LADY TEAZLE. Authority! No to be sure—if you wanted authority over me, you should have adopted me, and not married me, I am sure you were old enough.

SIR PETER. Old enough!—Aye there it is—well, well Lady Teazle tho' my life may be made unhappy by your temper—I'll not be ruin'd by your extravagance.

LADY TEAZLE. My extravagance!—I'm sure I'm not more extravagant than a woman of fashion ought to be.

SIR PETER. No, no, Madam, you shall throw away no more sums on such unmeaning luxury—'Slife to spend as much to furnish your dressing room with flowers in winter, as would suffice to turn the Pantheon[49] into a green house, and give a fête-champêtre[50] at Christmas!

LADY TEAZLE. Lord Sir Peter, am I to blame, because flowers are dear in cold weather? You should find fault with the climate, and not with me—for my part, I am sure I wish it was spring all the year round, and that roses grew under one's feet.

SIR PETER. Oons! Madam, if you had been born to this, I shouldn't wonder at your talking thus.—But you forget what your situation was when I married you.

LADY TEAZLE. No, no, I don't—'twas a very disagreeable one, or I should never have married *you*.

SIR PETER. Yes, yes, Madam, you were then in somewhat an humbler stile—the daughter of a plain country squire, recollect Lady Teazle, when I saw you first, sitting at your tambour,[51] in a pretty figur'd linnen gown with a bunch of keys by your side, your hair comb'd smooth over a roll, and your apartment hung round with fruits in worsted of your own working![52]

LADY TEAZLE. O yes, I remember very well, and a curious life I led!—My daily occupation to inspect the dairy, superintend the poultry, make extracts from the family receipt book, and comb my Aunt Deborah's lap-dog.

SIR PETER. Yes, yes, Ma'am, 'twas so indeed.

LADY TEAZLE. And then you know my evening amusements to draw patterns for ruffles, which I had not the materials to make, to play Pope Joan[53] with the curate, to read a novel to my aunt, or be stuck down to an old spinnet,[54] to strum my father to sleep after a fox chace.

SIR PETER. I am glad you have so good a memory, —yes Madam these were the recreations I took you from.—But now you must have your coach, vis-à-vis,[55] and three powder'd footmen before your chair—and in summer, a pair of white cats to draw you to Kensington Gardens.[56]—No recollection I suppose when you were content to ride double behind the butler on a dock'd coach horse.

LADY TEAZLE. No—I swear I never did that—I deny the butler, and the coach horse.

SIR PETER. This Madam was your situation—and what have I not done for you?—I have made you a woman of fashion, of fortune, of rank; in short, I have made you my wife.

LADY TEAZLE. Well then, and there is but one thing more, you can make me, to add to the obligation—and that is—

SIR PETER. My widow I suppose?

LADY TEAZLE. Hem, hem!—

SIR PETER. Thank you Madam,—but don't flatter your self, for tho' your ill conduct may disturb my peace it shall never break my heart I promise you; however I am equally oblig'd to you for the hint.

LADY TEAZLE. Then why will you endeavour to make yourself so disagreeable to me, & thwart me in every little elegant expence?

SIR PETER. 'Slife Madam, I say had you any of these elegant expences when you married me?

LADY TEAZLE. Lud! Sir Peter, would you have me be out of the fashion?

SIR PETER. The fashion indeed! What had you to do with the fashion before you married me?

LADY TEAZLE. For my part, I should think you would like to have your wife thought a woman of taste.

SIR PETER. Aye, there again—taste!—Zounds Madam, you had no taste, when you married *me*!

LADY TEAZLE. That's very true indeed Sir Peter, and *after* having married you, I am sure I should never pretend to taste again! But now Sir Peter, if we have finish'd our daily tangle, I presume I may go to my engagement at Lady Sneerwell's.

SIR PETER. Aye—there's another precious circumstance! A charming set of acquaintance, you have made there.

LADY TEAZLE. Nay, Sir Peter, they are people of rank & fortune, and remarkably tenacious of reputation.

SIR PETER. Yes, 'egad they are tenacious of reputation with a vengeance, for they don't chuse any body should have a character but themselves! Such a crew! Ah! Many a wretch has rid on a hurdle, who has done less mischief, than those utterers of forg'ed tales, coiners of scandal,—and clippers of reputation.[57]

LADY TEAZLE. What, would you restrain the freedom of speech?

SIR PETER. O! They have made you just as bad as any one of the society.

LADY TEAZLE. Why I believe I do bear a part with a tolerable grace; but I vow I have no malice against the people I abuse, when I say an ill natur'd thing 'tis out of pure good humour—and I take it for granted they deal exactly in the same manner with me; but Sir Peter you know you promis'd to come to Lady Sneerwell's too.

SIR PETER. Well, well, I'll call in, just to look after my own character.

LADY TEAZLE. Then indeed you must haste after me, or you'll be too late—so good by to ye. [*Exit* Lady Teazle.

SIR PETER. So, I have gain'd much by my intended expostulations; yet with what a charming air, she contradicts every thing I say! And how pleasingly she shows her contempt of my authority! Well tho' I can't make her love me, there is a great satisfaction in quarrelling with her, and I think she never appears to such advantage, as when she's doing every thing in her power to plague me. [*Exit.*

II.ii

[Lady Sneerwell*'s House.* Lady Sneerwell, Mrs. Candour, Crabtree, Sir Benjamin, *&* Surface.]

LADY SNEERWELL. Nay, positively we will hear it.

SURFACE. Yes, yes, the epigram by all means.

SIR BENJAMIN. Plague on't Uncle—'tis mere nonsense!

CRABTREE. No, no, 'fore Gad very clever for an extempore.

SIR BENJAMIN. But ladies, you should be acquainted with the circumstance,—you must know that one day last week, as Lady Betty Curricle[58] was taking the dust in Hyde Park,[59] in a sort of a duodecimo phaeton,[60] she desir'd me to write some verses on her ponies, upon which I took out my pocket book and in one moment produc'd the following.

"Sure never were seen, two such beautiful ponies!
Other horses are clowns, & these—maccaronies![61]
Nay, to give 'em this title, I'm sure isn't wrong,
—Their legs are so slim, & their tails are so long."[62]

CRABTREE. There ladies—done in the smack of a whip, & on horseback too!

SURFACE. A very Phœbus[63] mounted—indeed Sir Benjamin.

SIR BENJAMIN. O dear Sir—trifles—trifles—

[*Enter* Lady Teazle, *&* Maria.

MRS. CANDOUR. I must have a copy—

LADY SNEERWELL. Lady Teazle—I hope we shall see Sir Peter.

LADY TEAZLE. I believe he'll wait on your Ladyship presently.

LADY SNEERWELL. Maria my love—you look grave—come you shall sit down to cards with Mr. Surface.

MARIA. I take very little pleasure in cards—however I'll do as your Ladyship pleases.

LADY TEAZLE. [*Aside*][64] *I am surpriz'd Mr. Surface should sit down with* her.—*I thought he would have embrac'd this opportunity of speaking to me before Sir Peter came.*

MRS. CANDOUR. Now I'll die but you are so scandalous, I'll forswear your society.

LADY TEAZLE. What's the matter Mrs. Candour?

MRS. CANDOUR. They'll not allow our friend, Miss Vermilion to be handsome.

LADY SNEERWELL. O surely, she's a pretty woman.

CRABTREE. I am very glad you think so Ma'am.

MRS. CANDOUR. She has a charming fresh colour.

LADY TEAZLE. Yes, when it is fresh put on.

MRS. CANDOUR. O fie! I'll swear her colour is natural. I have seen it come and go.

LADY TEAZLE. I dare swear you have Ma'am—it goes of a night and comes again in the morning.

MRS. CANDOUR. Ha! ha! ha! How I hate to hear you talk so! But surely now her sister *is*, or *was*, very handsome.

CRABTREE. Who? Mrs. Evergreen,—O Lord, she's six and fifty if she's an hour.

MRS. CANDOUR. Now positively you wrong her, fifty two, or fifty three is the utmost—and I don't think she looks more—

SIR BENJAMIN. Ah, there is no judging by her looks, unless one could see her face.

LADY SNEERWELL. Well, well, if Mrs. Evergreen *does* take some pains to repair the ravages of time, you must allow she effects it with great ingenuity—and surely that's better than the careless manner in which the Widow Ocre caulks her wrinkles.

SIR BENJAMIN. Nay, now Lady Sneerwell you are severe upon the widow, come, come, it is not that she paints so ill[65]—but when she has finish'd her face, she joins it on so badly to her neck, that she looks like a mended statue, in which the connoisseur sees at once that the head's modern tho' the trunk's an antique!

CRABTREE. Ha! ha! ha!—Well said Nephew.

MRS. CANDOUR. Ha! ha! ha! Well you make me laugh, but I vow I hate you for't,—what do you think of Miss Simper?

SIR BENJAMIN. Why, she has very pretty teeth.

LADY TEAZLE. Yes, and on that account, when she is neither speaking nor laughing (which very seldom happens) she never absolutely shuts her mouth, but leaves it always on a jar as it were.

MRS. CANDOUR. How can you be so ill natur'd?

LADY TEAZLE. Nay I allow even that's better than the pains Mrs. Prim takes to conceal her losses in front—she draws her mouth 'till it positively resembles the aperture of a poor's-box,[66] and all her words appear to slide out edgeways.

LADY SNEERWELL. Very well Lady Teazle, I see you can be a little severe.

LADY TEAZLE. In defense of a friend it is but justice;—but here comes Sir Peter to spoil our pleasantry.

[*Enter* Sir Peter.

SIR PETER. Ladies your most obedient—[*Aside*] *Mercy on me, here is the whole set! A character dead at every word I suppose.*

MRS. CANDOUR. I am rejoic'd you are come Sir Peter! They have been *so* censorious—They will allow good qualities to no body—Not even good nature to our friend Mrs. Pursy.

LADY TEAZLE. What the fat dowager, who was at Mrs. Codille's last night.

MRS. CANDOUR. Nay her bulk is her misfortune; and when she takes such pains to get rid of it, you ought not to reflect on her.

LADY SNEERWELL. That's very true indeed.

LADY TEAZLE. Yes, I know she almost lives on acids,[67] and small whey, laces herself by pullies, and often in the hottest noon of summer, you may see her on a little squat poney, with her hair platted up behind like a drummer's, and puffing round the Ring[68] on a full trot.

MRS. CANDOUR. I thank you Lady Teazle for defending her.

SIR PETER. Yes, a good defence, truly.

MRS. CANDOUR. But Sir Benjamin is as censorious as Miss Sallow.

CRABTREE. Yes, and she is a curious being to pretend to be censorious; an aukward gauky without any one good point under heaven.

MRS. CANDOUR. Positively you shall not be so very severe, Miss Sallow is a relation of mine by marriage, and as for her person great allowance is to be made, for let me tell you a woman labours under many disadvantages who trys to pass for a girl at six and thirty.

LADY SNEERWELL. Tho' surely she is handsome still, and for the weakness in her eyes, considering how much she reads by candle light, it is not to be wonder'd at.

MRS. CANDOUR. True, and then as to her manner, upon my word I think it is particularly graceful, considering she never had the least education;—for you know her mother was a Welsh milliner, and her father a sugar-baker at Bristol.

SIR BENJAMIN. Ah, you are both of you too good natur'd.

SIR PETER. [*Aside*] *Yes, dam'd good natur'd! This their own relation! Mercy on me!*

SIR BENJAMIN. And Mrs. Candour is of so moral a turn, she can sit for an hour, to hear Lady Stucco talk sentiment.

LADY TEAZLE. Nay, I vow Lady Stucco is very well with the dessert after dinner; for she's just like the French fruit one cracks for mottos, made up of paint & proverb.[69]

MRS. CANDOUR. Well, I never will join in ridiculing a friend; and so I constantly tell my cousin Ogle, and you all know what pretensions she has to be critical in beauty.

CRABTREE. O to be sure, the has herself the oddest countenance that ever was seen; 'tis a collection of features from all the different countries of the globe.

SIR BENJAMIN. So she has indeed.—An Irish front!

CRABTREE. Caledonian locks!

SIR BENJAMIN. Dutch nose!

CRABTREE. Austrian lip!

SIR BENJAMIN. Complexion of a Spaniard!

CRABTREE. And teeth à la Chinoíse![70]

SIR BENJAMIN. In short her face resembles a table doité[71] at Spa[72] where no two guests are of a nation.

CRABTREE. Or a congress at the close of a general war—wherein all the members even to her eyes appear to have a different interest, and her nose and chin are the only parties likely to join issue.[73]

MRS. CANDOUR. Ha! ha! ha!

SIR PETER. [*Aside*] *Mercy on my life! A person they dine with twice a week!*

MRS. CANDOUR. Nay, but I vow, you shall not carry the laugh off so—for give me leave to say that Mrs. Ogle—

SIR PETER. Madam, Madam, I beg your pardon—there's no stopping these good gentlemen's tongues; but when I tell *you* Mrs. Candour, that the lady they are abusing is a particular friend of mine—I hope you'll not take her part.

LADY SNEERWELL. Well said Sir Peter! But you are a cruel creature; too phlegmatic yourself for a jest, and too peevish to allow wit on others.

SIR PETER. Ah, Madam, true wit is more nearly allied to good nature, than your Ladyship is aware of.

LADY TEAZLE. True Sir Peter, I believe they are so near akin that they can never be united.[74]

SIR BENJAMIN. Or rather Madam, suppose them man and wife, because one so seldom sees them together.

LADY TEAZLE. But Sir Peter is such an enemy to scandal, I believe he would have it put down by parliament.

SIR PETER. 'Fore Heaven Madam, if they were to consider the sporting with reputation, of as much importance as poaching on manors,[75] and pass "*An Act for the Preservation of Fame.*" I believe there are many would thank them for the bill.

LADY SNEERWELL. O Lud! Sir Peter, would you deprive us of our privileges?

SIR PETER. Aye Madam, and then no person should be permitted to kill characters, or run down reputations, but qualified old maids, and disappointed widows.

LADY SNEERWELL. Go you monster!

MRS. CANDOUR. But sure you would not be quite so severe on those who only report what they hear.

SIR PETER. Yes Madam, I would have law-merchant[76] for them too—and in all cases of slander currency, whenever the drawer of the lie was not to be found, the injur'd party should have a right to come on any of the endorsers.[77]

CRABTREE. Well, for my part I believe there never was a scandalous tale without some foundation.

LADY SNEERWELL. Come ladies, shall we sit down to cards in the next room.

[*Enter* Servant *& whispers* Sir Peter.

SIR PETER. I'll be with them directly—I'll get away unperceiv'd.

LADY SNEERWELL. Sir Peter, you are not leaving us?

SIR PETER. Your Ladyship must excuse me, I'm call'd away by particular business—but I leave my character behind me. [*Exit* Sir Peter.

SIR BENJAMIN. Well certainly Lady Teazle that lord of yours is a strange being; I could tell you some stories of him would make you laugh heartily, if he wasn't your husband.

LADY TEAZLE. O pray don't mind that.—Come do let's hear them.

[*They join the rest of the company all talking as they are going into the next room.*

SURFACE. [*Rising with* Maria] Maria, I see you have no satisfaction in this society.

MARIA. How is it possible I should; if to raise malicious smiles at the infirmities, and misfortunes of those who have never injur'd us, be the province of wit or humour, Heaven grant me a double portion of dulness.

SURFACE. Yet they appear more ill natur'd than they are; they have no malice at heart.

MARIA. Then is there conduct still more contemptible; for in my opinion, nothing could excuse the intemperence of their tongues, but a natural, and ungovernable bitterness of mind.

SURFACE. But can you Maria feel thus for others, and be unkind to me alone; is hope to be denied the tenderest passion?

MARIA. Why will you distress me, by renewing this subject?

SURFACE. Ah Maria, you would not treat me thus, and oppose your guardian Sir Peter's will—but that I see that profligate *Charles* is still a favour'd rival.

MARIA. Ungenerously urg'd; but whatever my sentiments of that unfortunate young man are—be assured I shall not feel more bound to give him up, because his distresses have lost him the regard even of a brother.

[Lady Teazle *returns.*

SURFACE. Nay but Maria, do not leave me with a frown—by all that's honest I swear—[*Aside*]

Gad's life here's Lady Teazle—[*To* Maria] you must not—no you shall not—for tho' I have the greatest regard for Lady Teazle—

MARIA. Lady Teazle!

SURFACE. Yet were Sir Peter to suspect—

LADY TEAZLE. [*Coming forward*] What's this pray?—Do you take her for me? Child you are wanted in the next room. [*Exit* Maria] What's all this pray?

SURFACE. Oh the most unlucky circumstances in nature; Maria has somehow suspected the tender concern which I have for your happiness, and threat'ned to acquaint Sir Peter with her suspicions, and I was just endeavouring to reason with her, when you came.

LADY TEAZLE. Indeed!—But you seem'd to adopt a very tender method of reasoning—do you usually argue on your knees?[78]

SURFACE. O she's a child—and I thought a little bombast—but Lady Teazle, when are you to give me your judgement on my library as you promis'd?

LADY TEAZLE. No, no.—I begin to think it would be imprudent; and you know I admit you as a lover no further than *fashion* requires.

SURFACE. True—a mere platonic Ciscesbeo,[79] what every London wife is *entitled* to.

LADY TEAZLE. Certainly one must not be out of the fashion, however I have so much of my country prejudices left—that tho' Sir Peter's ill humour may vex me ever so, it never shall provoke me to—

SURFACE.—The only revenge in your power; well I applaud your moderation.

LADY TEAZLE. Go, you are an insinuating wretch—but we shall be miss'd—let us join the company.

SURFACE. But we had best not return together.

LADY TEAZLE. Well don't stay—for Maria shan't come to hear any more of your *reasoning* I promise you. [*Exit* Lady Teazle.

SURFACE. A curious dilemma truly my politics[80] have run me into! I wanted at first only to ingratiate my self with Lady Teazle that she might not be my enemy with Maria—and I have I don't know how, become her serious lover—sincerely I begin to wish I had never made such a point of gaining so *very good* a character; for it has led me into so many curs'd rogueries, that I doubt I shall be expos'd at last! [*Exit.*

II.iii

[Sir Peter*'s. Enter* Sir Oliver *&* Rowley.]

SIR OLIVER. Ha! ha! ha! And so my old friend is married hey! . . . A young wife out of the country! Ha! ha! ha! That he should have stood bluff to old batchelor for so long, and sink into a husband at last!

ROWLEY. But you must not rally him on the subject Sir Oliver, 'tis a tender point I assure you; tho' he has been married only seven months.

SIR OLIVER. Then he has been just a year on the stool of repentance![81] Poor Peter! But you say he has entirely given up Charles? Never sees him hey?

ROWLEY. His prejudice against him is astonishing.—And I am sure greatly encreas'd, by a jealousy of him with Lady Teazle, which he has been industriously led into, by a scandalous society in the neighbourhood, who have contributed not a little to Charles' ill name, whereas the truth is I believe, if the lady is partial to either of them, his brother is the favourite.

SIR OLIVER. Aye—I know there are a set of malicious prating prudent gossips, both male and female, who murder characters to kill time, and will rob a young fellow of his good name, before he has years to know the value of it, but I am not to be prejudiced against my nephew by such, I promise you; no, no;—if Charles has done nothing false or mean, I shall compound for his extravagance.[82]

ROWLEY. Then my life on't you will reclaim him.—Ah Sir, it gives me new life to find that *your* heart is not turn'd against him;—and that the son of my good old master has one friend however left.

SIR OLIVER. What, shall I forget Master Rowley, when I was at his years my self?—Egad my brother and I were neither of us very *prudent* youths—and yet I believe you have not seen many better men than your old master was.

ROWLEY. Sir, 'tis this reflection gives me assurance that Charles may yet be a credit to his family; but here comes Sir Peter—

SIR OLIVER. 'Egad so he does—Mercy on me! He's greatly alter'd, and seems to have a settled married look!—One may read husband in his face at this distance!

[*Enter* Sir Peter.

SIR PETER. Hah! Sir Oliver my old friend. Welcome to England a thousand times.

SIR OLIVER. Thank you, thank you Sir Peter—and 'efaith I am as glad to find you well—believe me—

SIR PETER. Ah! 'Tis a long time since we met,—sixteen years I doubt Sir Oliver! And many a cross accident[83] in the time.

SIR OLIVER. Aye, I have had my share—but what I find you are married hey, my old boy!—Well, well—it can't be help'd,—and so I wish you joy with all my heart.

SIR PETER. Thank you, thank you Sir Oliver—yes I have enter'd into the happy state.—But we'll not talk of that now.

SIR OLIVER. True, true, Sir Peter,—old friends should not begin on grievances at first meeting—no, no, no.

ROWLEY. [*To* Sir Oliver] Take care pray Sir.

SIR OLIVER. Well, so one of my nephews I find, is a wild rogue hey?

SIR PETER. Wild!—Ah my old friend, I grieve for your disappointment there—he's a lost young man indeed; however his brother will make you amends;—*Joseph* is indeed what a youth should be—every body in the world speaks well of him.

SIR OLIVER. I am sorry to hear it—he has too good a character to be an honest fellow.—Every body speaks well of him! Psha! Then he has bow'd as low to knaves and fools, as to the honest dignity of genius or virtue.

SIR PETER. What Sir Oliver, do you blame him for not making enemies?

SIR OLIVER. Yes, if he has merit enough to deserve them.

SIR PETER. Well, well, you'll be convinc'd, when you know him. 'Tis edification to hear him converse—he professes the noblest sentiments.

SIR OLIVER. Ah! Plague of his sentiments.—If he salutes me with a scrap of morality in his mouth, I shall be sick directly; but however don't mistake me Sir Peter, I don't mean to defend Charles' errors—but before I form my judgement of either of them, I intend to make a trial of their hearts—and my friend Rowley and I have plann'd something for the purpose.

ROWLEY. And Sir Peter shall own, he has been for once mistaken.

SIR PETER. O my life on Joseph's honour!

SIR OLIVER. Well, come, give us a bottle of good wine, and we'll drink the lads' health and tell you our scheme.

SIR PETER. Allons then!

SIR OLIVER. And don't Sir Peter be so severe against your old friend's son—Odds my life! I am not sorry that he has run out of the course a little; for my part I hate to see prudence clinging to the green succours of youth—'tis like ivy round a sapling, and spoils the growth of the tree.

III.i

[Sir Peter Teazle's. Sir Peter, Sir Oliver, & Rowley.]

SIR PETER. Well, then—we will see this fellow first, and have our wine afterwards;—but how is this Master Rowley? I don't see the jet[84] of your scheme?

ROWLEY. Why Sir, this Mr. Stanley whom I was speaking of, is nearly related to them, by their mother; he was once a merchant in Dublin, but has been ruin'd by a series of undeserv'd misfortunes. He has applied by letter since his confinement[85] both to Mr. Surface, and Charles —from the former he has received nothing but evasive promises of future service, while Charles has done all that his extravagance has left him power to do, and he is at this time endeavouring to revise a sum of money—part of which, in the midst of his own distresses, I know he intends for the service of poor Stanley.

SIR OLIVER. Ah! He is my brother's son!

SIR PETER. Well, but how is Sir Oliver personally to—

ROWLEY. Why, Sir, I will inform Charles and his brother, that Stanley has obtained permission to apply in person to his friends,[86] and as they have neither of them ever seen him, let Sir Oliver assume his character, and he will have a fair opportunity of judging at least of the benevolence of their dispositions, and believe me Sir, you will find in the youngest brother, one who in the midst of folly and dissipation—has still, as our immortal bard expresses it,—"a tear for pity and a hand open as day for melting charity."[87]

SIR PETER. Pshaw! What signifies his having an open hand or purse either, when he has nothing left to give!—Well—well—make the tryal if you please; but where is the fellow whom you brought for Sir Oliver to examine relative to Charles' affairs[?]

ROWLEY. Below waiting his commands, and no one can give him better intelligence;—this Sir Oliver, is a friendly Jew, who to do him justice, has done every thing in his power to bring your nephew to a proper sense of his extravagance.

SIR PETER. Pray let us have him in.

ROWLEY. Desire Mr. Moses to walk up stairs.

SIR PETER. But why should you suppose he will speak the truth[?]

ROWLEY. O I have convinc'd him that he has no chance of recovering certain sums advanc'd to Charles, but thro' the bounty of Sir Oliver, who he knows is arriv'd; so that you may depend on his fidelity to his interest; I have also another evidence in my power, one Snake—whom I have detected in a matter little short of forgery,[88] and shall shortly produce to remove some of *your* prejudices Sir Peter, relative to Charles and Lady Teazle.

SIR PETER. I have heard too much on that subject.

ROWLEY. Here comes the honest Israelite. [*Enter* Moses] This is Sir Oliver.

SIR OLIVER. Sir I understand you have lately had great dealings with my nephew Charles.

MOSES. Yes Sir Oliver—I have done all I could for him, but he was ruined before he came to me for assistance.

SIR OLIVER. That was unlucky truly—for you have had no opportunity of shewing your talents.

MOSES. None at all—I hadn't the pleasure of knowing his distresses—till he was some thousand worse than nothing.

SIR OLIVER. Unfortunate indeed! But I suppose you have done all in your power for him honest Moses?

MOSES. Yes he knows that—this very evening I was to have brought him a gentleman from the city who doesn't know him, and will I believe advance him some money.

SIR PETER. What one Charles has never had money from before?

MOSES. Yes; Mr. Premium of Crutched Fryars[89]—formerly a broker.

SIR PETER. Egad, Sir Oliver a thought strikes me—Charles you say doesn't know Mr. Premium?

MOSES. Not at all—

SIR PETER. Now then Sir Oliver, you may have a better opportunity of satisfying yourself than by an old romancing tale of a poor relation;—go with my friend Moses and represent[90] Mr. *Premium*, and then I'll answer for't, you will see your nephew in all his glory.

SIR OLIVER. Egad I like this idea better than the other, and I may visit *Joseph* afterwards, as old *Stanley*.

SIR PETER. True, so you may.

ROWLEY. Well, this taking Charles rather at a disadvantage to be sure—how ever Moses—you understand Sir Peter and will be faithful—

MOSES. You may depend on me,—this is near the time I was to have gone.

SIR OLIVER. I'll accompany you as soon as you please Moses; but hold I have forgot one thing—how the plague shall I be able to pass for a Jew?

MOSES. There's no need—the principal is Christian.

SIR OLIVER. Is he?—I'm sorry to hear it—but then again, an't I rather too smartly dressed to look like a money lender?

SIR PETER. Not at all; 'twould not be out of character, if you went in your own carriage—would it Moses?

MOSES. Not in the least—

SIR OLIVER. Well, but how must I talk? There's certainly some cant of usury, and mode of treating, that I ought to know.

SIR PETER. O there's not much to learn—the great point as I take it, is to be exorbitant enough in your demands, hey Moses?

MOSES. Yes, that's a very great point.

SIR OLIVER. I'll answer for't I'll not be wanting in that, I'll ask him eight or ten per cent on the loan at least.

MOSES. If you ask him no more than that, you'll be discovered immediately.

SIR OLIVER. Hey! What the plague! How much then?

MOSES. That depends upon the circumstances, if he appears not very anxious for the supply you should require only forty or fifty per cent, but if you find him in great distress, and want the monies very bad—you may ask double.

SIR PETER. A good honest trade you're learning Sir Oliver.

SIR OLIVER. Truly I think so,—and not unprofitable.

MOSES. Then you know—you hav'nt the monies yourself, but are forc'd to borrow them for him of a friend.

SIR OLIVER. Oh I borrow it of a friend do I?

MOSES. Yes, and your friend is an unconscionable dog, but you can't help it—

SIR OLIVER. My friend is an unconscionable dog is he?

MOSES. Yes, and he himself hasn't the moneys by him—but is forc'd to sell stock at a great loss.

SIR OLIVER. He is forc'd to sell stock is he, at a great loss is he, well that's very kind of him.

SIR PETER. 'Efaith! Sir Oliver, Mr. Premium I mean, you'll soon be master of the trade—but Moses—wouldn't you have him run out a little against the Annuity Bill?[91] That would be in character I should think.

MOSES. Very much?

ROWLEY. And lament that a young man now must be at years of discretion, before he is suffered to ruin himself.

MOSES. Aye, a great pity!

SIR PETER. And abuse the public for allowing merit to an Act, whose only object is to snatch misfortune and imprudence, from the rapacious relief of usury! And give the minor a chance of inheriting his estate, without being undone by coming into possession.

SIR OLIVER. So, so—Moses, shall give me further instructions as we go together.

SIR PETER. You will not have much time, for your nephew lives hard by.

SIR OLIVER. O never fear—my tutor appears so able, that tho' Charles liv'd in the next street, it must be my own fault, if I am not a compleat rogue before I turn the corner.

[*Exeunt* Sir Oliver & Moses.

SIR PETER. So now I think Sir Oliver will be convinc'd;—you are partial Rowley and would have prepared Charles for the other plot.

ROWLEY. No upon my word Sir Peter.

SIR PETER. Well go bring me this Snake, and I'll hear what he has to say presently—I see Maria, and want to speak with her. [*Exit* Rowley] I should be glad to be convinced, my suspicions of Lady Teazle and Charles were unjust—I have never yet open'd my mind on this subject to my friend *Joseph*, I'm determined I will do it; *he* will give me his opinion sincerely. [*Enter* Maria] So child—has Mr. Surface return'd with you?

MARIA. No Sir—he was engag'd.

SIR PETER. Well, Maria—do you not reflect the more you converse with that amiable young man—what return his partiality for you deserves?

MARIA. Indeed Sir Peter—your frequent importunity on this subject distresses me extremely, you compel me to declare that I know no man, who has ever paid me a particular attention whom I would not prefer to Mr. Surface.

SIR PETER. Soh! Here's perverseness! No—no—Maria—'tis Charles only whom you would prefer—'tis evident his vices and follies have won your heart.

MARIA. This is unkind Sir—you know I have obey'd you, in neither seeing nor corresponding with him, I have heard enough to convince me that he is unworthy my regard; yet I cannot think it culpable—if while my understanding severely condemns his vices—my heart suggests some pity for his distresses.

SIR PETER. Well, well, pity him as much as you please but give your heart and hand to a worthier object.

MARIA. Never to his brother.

SIR PETER. Go—perverse—and obstinate! But take care Madam, you have never yet known what the authority of a guardian is—don't compel me to inform you of it.

MARIA. I can only say you shall not have just reason—'tis true, by my father's will, I am for a short period, bound to regard you as his substitute, but must cease to think you so, when you would compel me to be miserable. [*Exit* Maria.

SIR PETER. Was even man so cross'd as I am! Every thing conspiring to fret me!—I had not been involv'd in matrimony a fortnight before her father—a hale and hearty man died,—on purpose I believe—for the pleasure of plaguing me with the care of his daughter! But here comes my helpmate, she appears in great good humour—how happy I should be if I could teize her into loving me tho' but a little.

[*Enter* Lady Teazle.

LADY TEAZLE. Lud! Sir Peter, I hope you hav'nt been quarrelling with Maria—it isn't using me well to be ill humour'd when I am not bye.

SIR PETER. Ah! Lady Teazle, you might have the power to make me good humour'd at all times.

LADY TEAZLE. I am sure I wish I had—for I want you to be in charming sweet temper at this moment—do be good humour'd now, and let me have two hundred pounds will you?

SIR PETER. Two hundred pounds! What an't I to be in a good humour without paying for it—but speak to me thus—and 'efaith there's nothing I could refuse you—you shall have it; but seal me a bond for the repayment—

LADY TEAZLE. O no—there my note of hand will do as well.[92]

SIR PETER. [*Kissing her hand*] And you shall no longer reproach me, with not giving you an independent settlement,[93] I mean shortly to surprise you—but shall we always live thus hey?

LADY TEAZLE. If you please—I'm sure I don't care how soon we leave off quarrelling, provided you'll own, *you* were tir'd first.

SIR PETER. Well—then, let our future contest be, who shall be most obliging.

LADY TEAZLE. I assure you Sir Peter, good nature becomes you; you look now as you did before we were married! When you us'd to walk with me under the elms, and tell me stories of what a gallant you were in your youth, and chuck me under the chin you would, and ask me if I thought I could love an old fellow, who would deny me nothing—didn't you?

SIR PETER. Yes—yes—and you were as kind and attentive.

LADY TEAZLE. Aye and so I was—and would always take your part when my acquaintance used to to abuse you, and turn you into ridicule.

SIR PETER. Indeed!

LADY TEAZLE. Aye and when my cousin Sophy has call'd you a stiff peevish old batchelor, and laugh'd at me, for thinking of marrying one, who might be my father—I have always defended you—and said I didn't think you so ugly by any means, and that I dar'd say you'd make a very good sort of a husband.

SIR PETER. And you prophesied right—and we shall certainly now be the happiest couple!

LADY TEAZLE. And never differ again!

SIR PETER. No, never! Tho' at the same time indeed my dear Lady Teazle—you must watch your temper very narrowly, for in all our little quarrels—my dear, if you recollect, my love, you always began first.

LADY TEAZLE. I beg your pardon my dear Sir Peter, indeed you always gave the provocation.

SIR PETER. Now see my angel, take care, *contradicting* isn't the way to keep friends.

LADY TEAZLE. Then don't *you* begin it, my love.

SIR PETER. There now—you—you are going on, you don't perceive my life, that you are just doing the very thing which you know always makes me angry.

LADY TEAZLE. Nay you know if you will be angry without any reason—

SIR PETER. There now you want to quarrel again.

LADY TEAZLE. No I am sure, I don't—but if you will be so peevish—

SIR PETER. There now, who begins first?

LADY TEAZLE. Why you to be sure, I said nothing; —but there's no bearing your temper.

SIR PETER. No, no. Madam, the fault's in your own temper.

LADY TEAZLE. Aye you are just what my cousin Sophy said you would be.

SIR PETER. Your cousin Sophy is a forward impertinent gypsey.

LADY TEAZLE. You are a great bear I'm sure to abuse my relations—

SIR PETER. Now may all the plagues of marriage be doubled on me if ever I try to be friends with you any more!

LADY TEAZLE. So much the better.

SIR PETER. No—no—Madam; 'tis evident—you never car'd a pin for me, and I was a madman to marry you, a pert rural coquet, that had refused half the honest squires in the neighbourhood.

LADY TEAZLE. And I am sure I was a fool to marry you—an old dangling batchelor, who was single at fifty only because he never could meet with anyone who would have him.

SIR PETER. Aye—aye—Madam, but you were pleased enough to listen to me—*you* never had such an offer before.

LADY TEAZLE. No! Didn't I refuse Sir Twivy Tarrier who every body said would have been a better match—for his estate is just as good as yours—and he has broke his neck since we have been married.

SIR PETER. I have done with you Madam—you are an unfeeling ungrateful—but there's an end of every thing. I believe you capable of any thing that's bad—yes Madam—I now believe the reports relative to you and Charles Madam—yes Madam, you and Charles, are not without grounds—

LADY TEAZLE. Take care Sir Peter—you had better not insinuate any such thing!—I'll not be suspected *without cause* I promise you.

SIR PETER. Very—well, Madam, very well. A separate maintenance as soon as you please—yes Madam, or a divorce—I'll make an example of myself, for the benefit of all old batchelors—let us separate Madam—

LADY TEAZLE. Agreed—agreed—and now my dear Sir Peter, we are of a mind once more—we may now be the *happiest couple!* and *never differ again!* You know; ha! ha! well you are going to be in a passion I see, and I shall only interrupt you—so bye, bye— [*Exit.*

SIR PETER. Plagues and tortures! Can't I make her angry neither? O I am the miserablest fellow! But I'll not bear her presuming to keep her temper—No, she may break my heart, but she shan't keep her temper. [*Exit.*

III.ii

[Charles' *house. Enter* Trip, Moses, *and* Sir Oliver.]

TRIP. Here Master Moses—if you'll stay a moment —I'll try whether—what's the gentleman's name?

SIR OLIVER. [*Aside*] *Mr. Moses—what is my name?*

MOSES. Mr. Premium—

TRIP. Premium, very well. [*Exit* Trip *taking snuff.*

SIR OLIVER. To judge by the servants—one wouldn't believe the Master was ruined—But what—sure this was my brother's house?

MOSES. Yes Sir, Mr. Charles bought it of Mr. Joseph,[94] with the furniture, pictures, etc. just as the old gentleman left it—Sir Peter thought it a great piece of extravagance in him—

SIR OLIVER. In my mind the other's economy in *selling* it to him was more reprehensible by half.

[*Re-enter* Trip.

TRIP. My Master says you must wait gentlemen, he has company, and can't speak with you yet.

SIR OLIVER. If he knew *who* it was wanted to see him, perhaps he woudn't have sent such a message.

TRIP. Yes—yes—Sir he knows *you* are here, I didn't forget little Premium—no, no, no—

SIR OLIVER. Very well—and I pray, Sir, what may be your name?

TRIP. Trip Sir—my name is Trip, at your service.

SIR OLIVER. Well then Mr. Trip—you have a pleasant sort of a place here I guess.

TRIP. Why yes—here are three, or four of us pass our time agreeably enough—but then our wages are some times a little in arrear—and not very great either—But fifty pounds a year and find our own bags and bouquets.[95]

SIR OLIVER. [*Aside*][96] *Bags and bouquets! Halters, and Bastinadoes!*

TRIP. But apropos Moses—have you been able to get me that little bill discounted?

SIR OLIVER. Wants to raise money too!—Mercy on me! Has his distresses, I warrant, like a lord,—and affects creditors and duns—

MOSES. 'Twas not to be done indeed Mr. Trip—[*Gives the note.*

TRIP. Good lack—you surprize me—my friend *Brush* has endors'd it,[97] and I thought when I put his mark on the back of a bill 'twas as good as cash—

MOSES. No 'twoudn't do—

TRIP. A small sum—but twenty pounds—harkee Moses do you think you couldn't get it me by way of annuity?

SIR OLIVER. An annuity, ha! ha! ha! A footman raise money by annuity, well done luxury egad!

MOSES. But you must ensure your place.

TRIP. O with all my heart—I'll ensure my place and my life too if you please—

SIR OLIVER. It's more than I would your neck.

TRIP. But then, Moses, it must be done before this d—d register[98] takes place—one wouldn't like to have one's name made public you know.

MOSES. No certainly, but is there nothing you could deposit.

TRIP. Why nothing capital of my master's wardrobe has dropp'd lately—But I could give you a mortgage on some of his winter cloaths, with equity of redemption before November; or you shall have the reversion of the French velvet—or a post obit on the blue and silver—these I should think Moses, with a few pair of point ruffles as a collateral security—hey! my little fellow?[99]

MOSES. Well, well.

[*Bell rings.*

TRIP. Gad I heard the bell—I believe, gentlemen I can now introduce you—don't forget the annuity little Moses; this way gentlemen, ensure my place! You know—

SIR OLIVER. If the man be a shadow of his master—this is the temple of dissipation indeed!

[*Exeunt.*

III.iii

[Charles, Careless, *etc. etc. at a table with wine, etc.*]

HARLES. 'Fore Heaven 'tis true—there's the great degeneracy of the age—many of our acquaintance have taste, spirit, and politeness—but plague on't they won't drink.

CARELESS. It is so indeed Charles—they give into all the substantial luxuries of the table—and abstain from nothing but wine and wit—

CHARLES. O certainly society suffers by it intolerably—for now instead of the social spirit of raillery that us'd to mantle over a glass of bright Burgundy, their conversation is become just like the spa water they drink, which has all the pertness and flatulence of champaigne without its spirit or flavour.

1ST GENTLEMAN. But what are *they* to do—who love play[100] better than wine?

CARELESS. True—there's Harry diets himself for gaming and is now under a hazard regimen.[101]

CHARLES. Then he'll have the worst of it—what you wouldn't train a horse for the course, by keeping him from corn! For my part 'egad I am now never so successful, as when I am a little merry—let me throw on a bottle of champaigne and I never lose—at least I never feel my losses, which is exactly the same thing.

2ND GENTLEMAN. Aye that I believe.

CHARLES. And then what man can pretend to be a believer in love; who is an abjuror of wine?—'Tis the test by which the lover knows his own heart—fill a dozen bumpers to a dozen beauties, and she that floats at top, is the maid that has bewitch'd you.

CARELESS. Now then Charles be honest and give us your real favourite—

CHARLES. Why I have withheld her only in compassion to you—if I toast her, you must give a round of her peers[102]—which is impossible on Earth.

CARLESS. O then we'll find some canoniz'd vestals or heathen goddesses that will do I warrant.

CHARLES. Here then bumpers, you rogues—bumpers! Maria—Maria—

[*All drink.*

1ST GENTLEMAN. Maria who?

CHARLES. I damn the surname! 'Tis too formal to be registered in love's callender—but now Sir Toby Bumper beware—we must have beauty superlative.

CARELESS. Nay never study Sir Toby, we'll stand to the toast tho' your mistress should want an eye—and you know, you have a song will excuse you.

SIR TOBY. Egad so I have—and I'll give him the song instead of the lady.

Song & Chorus.

1 *Here's to the Maiden of Bashfull fifteen*
Here's to the Widow of Fifty;
Here's to the flaunting, Extravagant Quean,
And Here's to the House Wife that's thrifty.

Chorus
Let the Toast pass—
Drink to the lass—
I'll warrant she'll prove an excuse for the glass!

2^{d} *Here's to the charmer, whose Dimples we Prize!*
Now to the Maid who has none Sir;
Here's to the girl with a pair of blue Eyes,
—And Here's to the Nymph with but one Sir!

Chorus
Let the Toast pass &c

3^{d} *Here's to the Maid with a Bosom of Snow,*
Now to her *that's as brown as a berry:*
Here's to the Wife with a face full of Woe,
And now for the Damsel that's Merry!

Chorus
Let the Toast pass &c

4th *For let 'em be clumsy or let 'em be Slim*
Young or Antient, I care not a Feather:
So fill a Pint Bumper Quite up to the Brim
—And let us E'en Toast 'em together!

Chorus
Let the Toast pass &c

ALL. Bravo. Bravo!

[*Enter* Trip *and whispers* Charles.

CHARLES. Gentlemen you must excuse me a little—Careless take the chair will you?

CARELESS. Nay prithee Charles—what now—this is one of your peerless beauties I suppose has dropt in by chance.

CHARLES. No—faith—to tell you the truth, 'tis a Jew, and a broker, who are come by appointment.

CARELESS. Damn it let's have the Jew in—

1ST GENTLEMAN. Aye, and the broker too by all means.

2ND GENTLEMAN. Yes, yes, the Jew, and the broker.

CHARLES. Egad with all my heart—Trip bid the gentlemen walk in—tho' there's one of them a stranger I can tell you—

CARELESS. Charles, let us give them some generous Burgundy—and perhaps they'll grow conscientious.

CHARLES. O hang 'em: wine does but draw forth a man's natural qualities, and to make *them* drink, would only be to whet their knavery.

[*Enter* Trip, Sir Oliver & Moses.

CHARLES. So honest Moses, walk in—walk in pray Mr. Premium that's the gentleman's name isn't it Moses?

MOSES. Yes Sir—

CHARLES. Set chairs Trip—sit down Mr. Premium —glasses Trip—Sit down Moses—Come Mr. Premium I'll give you a sentiment[103]—here's "success to usury"—Moses, fill the gentleman a bumper.

MOSES. Success to usury.

CARELESS. Bright Moses—usury is prudence and industry and deserves to succeed.

SIR OLIVER. Then here's all the success it deserves.

CARELESS. No, no—that won't do Mr. Premium, you have demur'd to the toast, and must drink it in a pint bumper.

1ST GENTLEMAN. A pint bumper at least.

MOSES. Pray Sir consider Mr. Premium's a gentleman.

CARELESS. And therefore loves good wine.

2ND GENTLEMAN. Give Moses a quart glass—this is mutiny, and a high contempt of the chair.

CARELESS. Here—now for't—I'll see justice done to the last drop of my bottle.

SIR OLIVER. Nay—pray gentlemen—I did not expect this usage.

CHARLES. No—hang it—Careless—you shan't: Mr. Premium's a stranger.

SIR OLIVER. [*Aside*] *Odd—I wish I was well out of this company*.

CARELESS. Plague on 'em then—if they won't drink—we'll not sit down with 'em; come Harry, the dice are in the next room; Charles you'll join us—when you have finish'd your business with these gentlemen—

CHARLES. I will. I will. [*Exeunt*] Careless!

CARELESS. Well—

CHARLES. Perhaps I may want *you*.

CARELESS. O—you know I am always ready—word, note—or bond 'tis all the same to me. [*Exit*.

MOSES. Sir—this is Mr. Premium, a gentleman of the strictest honour and secrecy—and always performs what he undertakes—Mr. Premium this is—

CHARLES. Pshaw have done!—Sir, my friend Moses is a very honest fellow, but a little slow at expression, he'll be an hour giving us our titles—Mr. Premium—the plain state of the matter is this—I am an extravagant young fellow; who wants money to borrow. You I take to be a prudent old fellow, who have got money to lend—I am blockhead enough to give fifty per cent, sooner than not have it, and you I presume are rogue enough to take a hundred if could get it.—Now Sir, you see we are acquainted at once, and may proceed to business without farther ceremony.

SIR OLIVER. Exceeding frank upon my word—I see Sir, you are not a man of many compliments.[104]

CHARLES. O no—Sir—plain dealing in business I always think best.

SIR OLIVER. Sir—I like you the better for't—however you are mistaken in one thing—I have no money to lend. But I believe I could procure some of a friend; but then he's an unconscionable dog isn't he Moses? And must sell stock to accommodate you—mustn't he Moses?

MOSES. Yes indeed!—You know I always speak the truth, and scorn to tell a lie—

CHARLES. Right! People that expect truth generally do—but these are trifles Mr. Premium—what—I know money isn't to be bought without paying for't.

SIR OLIVER. Well but what security could you give me—you have no land I suppose.

CHARLES. Not a mole-hill—nor a twig but what's in beau pots at the window.

SIR OLIVER. Nor any stock I presume.

CHARLES. Nothing but live stock—and that's only a few pointers and ponies. But pray Mr. Premium are you acquainted at all with any of my connections—[105]

SIR OLIVER. Why to say truth I am—

CHARLES. Then you must know that I have a devilish rich uncle in the East Indies—Sir *Oliver Surface*—from whom I have the greatest expectations.

SIR OLIVER. That you have a wealthy uncle I have heard—but how your expectations will turn out is more I believe than you can tell.

CHARLES. O no—there can be no doubt—they tell me I'm a prodigious favourite—and that he talks of leaving me every thing.

SIR OLIVER. Indeed: this is the first I've heard on't.

CHARLES. Yes, yes—'tis just so—Moses—know 'tis true—don't you Moses?

MOSES. O yes—I'll swear to't—

SIR OLIVER. [*Aside*][106] *Egad they'll persuade me presently I'm at Bengal.*

CHARLES. Now I propose Mr. Premium if it's agreeable to you to grant you a post obit[107] on Sir Oliver's life, tho' at the same time the old fellow has been so liberal to me that I give you my word, I should be very sorry to hear any thing had happen'd to him.

SIR OLIVER. Not more than *I* should I assure you; but the bond you mention happens to be just the worst security you could offer me—for I might live to a hundred and never recover the principal.[108]

CHARLES. O yes you would—the moment Sir Oliver dies you know you'd come on me for the money.

SIR OLIVER. Then I believe I should be the most unwelcome dun you ever had in your life.

CHARLES. What I suppose you are afraid now that Sir Oliver is too good a life.[109]

SIR OLIVER. No indeed I am not—tho' I have heard he is as hale and healthy as any man of his years in Christendom.

CHARLES. There again, you are misinformed—no, no, the climate has hurt him considerably—Poor Uncle Oliver—yes, he breaks apace I'm told, and so much alter'd lately that his nearest relations don't know him—

SIR OLIVER. No!—ha! ha! ha! so much altered lately that his relations don't know him, ha! ha! ha! that's droll egad—ha! ha! ha!

CHARLES. Ha! ha! You're glad to hear that little Premium.

SIR OLIVER. No—no,—I'm not.

CHARLES. Yes, yes, you are—ha! ha! ha!—you know that mends your chance.

SIR OLIVER. But I'm told Sir Oliver is coming over—nay some say he is actually arrived.

CHARLES. Pshaw! Sure I must know better than you whether he's come or not—no, no, rely on't—he is at this moment at Calcutta, isn't he Moses?

MOSES. O yes certainly.

SIR OLIVER. Very true as you say—you must know better than I; tho' I have it from pretty good authority—haven't I Moses?

MOSES. Yes—most undoubted.

SIR OLIVER. But Sir—as I understand you want a few hundreds immediately—is there nothing you would dispose of?

CHARLES. How do you mean?

SIR OLIVER. For instance now—I have heard—that your father left behind him a great quantity of massy old plate—[110]

CHARLES. O Lud that's gone, long ago—Moses can tell you how better than I can—

SIR OLIVER.—[*Aside*] *Good lack! All the family race cups and corporation bowls!*[111]—[*To him*] Then it was also suppos'd that his library was one of the most valuable and compleat—

CHARLES. Yes—yes so it was—vastly too much for a private gentleman—for my part I was always of a communicative disposition, so I thought it a shame to keep so much knowledge to myself—

SIR OLIVER. Mercy on me! Learning that had run in the family like an heir loom! Pray what are become of the books?

CHARLES. You must enquire of the auctioneer, Master Premium, for I don't believe even Moses can direct you there.

MOSES. I never meddle with books.

SIR OLIVER. So—so—nothing of the family property left I suppose.

CHARLES. Not much indeed, unless you have a mind to the family pictures—I have got a room full of ancestors above—and if you have a taste for old paintings egad, you shall have 'em for a bargain.

SIR OLIVER. Hey! and the devil! Sure you wouldn't sell your forefathers—would you?

CHARLES. Every man of 'em to the best bidder—

SIR OLIVER. What your great uncles and aunts?

CHARLES. Aye, and my great grand fathers and grand others too.

SIR OLIVER.—[*Aside*] *Now I give him up*—[*To him*] What the plague! have you now bowels for your kindred?—Odds life—do you take me for Shylock in the play, that you would raise money of me, on you own flesh and blood?[112]

CHARLES. Nay, my little broker—don't be angry—what need *you* care, if you have your money's worth.

SIR OLIVER. Well—I'll be the purchaser—I think I can dispose of the family.—[*Aside*] *Oh I'll never forgive him this—never!*

[*Enter* Careless.

CARELESS. Come Charles—what keeps you?

CHARLES. I can't come yet a 'faith! We are going to have a sale above—here's little Premium will buy all my ancestors.

CARELESS. Oh burn your ancestors—

CHARLES. No, he may do that afterwards if he pleases: stay Careless we want you, egad you shall be auctioneer. So come along with us—

CARELESS. Oh, have with you, if that's the case—I can handle a hammer, as well as a dice box.

SIR OLIVER. [*Asides*] *Oh the profligates!*

CHARLES. Come Moses—you shall be appraiser if we want one. Gad's life little Premium, you don't seem to like the business.

SIR OLIVER. Oh yes I do vastly—ha, ha, yes, yes, I think it, a rare joke, to sell one's family by auction, ha! ha!—[*Aside*] *Oh the prodigal!*

CHARLES. To be sure! When a man, wants money, where the plague should he get assistance—if he can't make free with his own relations.

[*Exeunt.*

IV.i

[*Picture room at* Charles*'s. Enter* Charles, Sir Oliver, Moses *&* Careless.]

CHARLES. Walk in gentlemen, pray walk in!—Here they are, the family of the Surfaces up to the [C]onquest.[113]

SIR OLIVER. And in my opinion a goodly collection.

CHARLES. Aye, aye, these are done in true spirit of portrait painting—no volunteer grace,[114] or expression—not like the works of your modern Raphael,[115] who gives you the strongest resemblance yet contrives to make your own portrait independent of you—so that you may sink the original and not hurt the picture—no, no, the merit of these is the inveterate likeness—all stiff and aukward as the originals, and like nothing in human nature beside!

SIR OLIVER. Ah! We shall never see such figures of men again—

CHARLES. I hope not: well you see Master Premium what a domestic character I am—here I sit of an evening surrounded by my family—But come get to your pulpit Mr. Auctioneer—here's an old gouty chair of my grand father's—will answer the purpose—

CARELESS. Aye—aye—this will do—but Charles I have ne'er a hammer—and what's an auctioneer without his hammer?

CHARLES. Egad that's true—what parchment have we here? [*Takes down a roll*] "*Richard Heir to Thomas*"[116]—our genealogy in full! Here Careless you shall have no common bit of mahogany—here's the family tree for you, you rogue—this shall be your hammer, and now you may knock down my ancestors with their own pedigree.

SIR OLIVER. What an unnatural rogue! An ex post facto parricide![117]

CARELESS. Yes, yes, here's a list of your generation indeed.—Faith Charles—this is the most convenient thing you could have found for the business, for 'twill serve not only as a hammer, but a catalogue into the bargain—but come begin—agoing—agoing—agoing!

CHARLES. Bravo! Careless—well here's my great uncle Sir Richard Raviline[118]—a marvellous good general in his day I assure you—He served in all the Duke of Marlborough's wars,[119]—and got that cut over his eye at the Battle of Malplachet;[120] what say you Mr. Premium—look at him—there's a hero, for you! Not cut out of his feathers, as your modern clipt captains are[121]—but enveloped in wig and regimentals as a general should be—what do you bid?

MOSES. Mr. Premium would have you speak.—

CHARLES. Why then he shall have him for ten pounds and I am sure that's not dear for a staff officer.

SIR OLIVER.—[*Aside*][122] *Heaven deliver me!*—[*To him*] His famous Uncle Richard for ten pounds! Very well Sir—I take him at that.

CHARLES. Careless knock down my Uncle Richard—Here now is a maiden sister of his, my great aunt Deborah done by Kneller,[123] thought to be in his best manner and a very formidable likeness—There she is you see!—A shepherdess feeding her flock—you shall have her for five pounds ten—the sheep are worth the money.

SIR OLIVER.—[*Aside*] *Ah! Poor Deborah—a woman who set such a value on herself!*—[*To him*] Five pounds ten! She's mine.

CHARLES. Knock down my Aunt Deborah! Here now are two that were a sort of cousins of theirs—you see Moses these pictures were done some time ago—when beaus wore wigs, and the ladies wore their own hair.

SIR OLIVER. Yes truly head dresses appear to have been a little lower in those days.

CHARLES. Well take that couple for the same.

MOSES. Tis good bargain.

CHARLES. Careless!—This now is a grandfather of my mother's, a learned judge, well known on the western circuit.[124]—What do you rate him at Moses?

MOSES. Four guineas.

CHARLES. Four guineas! Gad's life, you don't bid me the price of his wig! Mr. Premium—*you* have more respect for the Woolsack[125]—do let us knock his Lordship down at fifteen.

SIR OLIVER. By all means—

CARELESS. Gone.

CHARLES. And there are two brothers of his William and Walter Blunt Esquires both members of parliament and noted speakers, and what's very extraordinary, I believe this is the first time they were over bought and sold.

SIR OLIVER. That's very extraordinary indeed! I'll take them at your own price for the honour of parliament.

CARELESS. Well said little Premium—I'll knock 'em down at forty.

CHARLES. Here's a jolly fellow—I don't know what relation—but he was Mayor of Manchester, take him at eight pounds.

SIR OLIVER. No, no—six will do for the mayor.

CHARLES. Come make it guineas and I'll throw you the two aldermen there into the bargain.

SIR OLIVER. They're mine.

CHARLES. Careless—knock down the mayor and aldermen—but plague on't we shall be all day—retailing in this manner. Do let us deal wholesale—what say you little Premium—give me three hundred pounds, for the rest of the family in the lump.

CARELESS. Aye—aye—that will be the best way.

SIR OLIVER. Well, well, any thing to accommodate you, they are mine. But there is one portrait, which you have always passed over—

CARELESS. What that ill looking little fellow over the settee.

SIR OLIVER. Yes Sir, I mean that, tho' I don't think him so ill looking a little fellow by any means.

CHARLES. What that? Oh that's my Uncle Oliver; —'twas done before he went to India—

CARELESS. Your Uncle Oliver! Gad! Then you'll never be friends Charles, that now to me is as stern a looking rogue as ever I saw—an unforgiving eye, and a damn'd disinheriting countenance! An inveterate knave depend on't,—don't you think so little Premium?

SIR OLIVER. Upon my soul Sir, I do not. I think it as honest a looking face as any in the room—dead or alive; but I suppose your Uncle Oliver goes with the rest of the lumber.

CHARLES. No hang it, I'll not part with poor Noll—the old fellow, has been very good to me, and egad I'll keep his picture, while I've a room to put it in—

SIR OLIVER.—[*Aside*] *The rogue's my nephew after all!*—[*To* Charles] But Sir, I have somehow taken a fancy to that picture.

CHARLES. I'm sorry for't, for you certainly will not have it—Oon's! haven't you got enough of 'em?

SIR OLIVER.—[*Aside*] *I forgive him every thing.*—[*To* Charles] But Sir when I take a whim in my head I don't value money—I'll give as much for that as for all the rest—

CHARLES. Don't teize me, Master Broker, I tell you, I'll not part with it—And there's an end on't—

SIR OLIVER.—[*Aside*] *How like his father the dog is!—Well, well, I have done.*—[*Aside*] *I did not perceive it before but I think I never saw such a resemblance*—[*To* Charles] Well Sir—Here is a draught for your sum—

CHARLES. Why, 'tis for eight hundred pounds.

SIR OLIVER. You will not let Oliver go?

CHARLES. L—ds! No, I tell you once more.

SIR OLIVER. Then never mind the difference; we'll ballance another time, but give me your hand on the bargain—you are an honest fellow Charles—

I beg pardon Sir for being so free,—come Moses,—

CHARLES. Egad this is a whimsical old fellow—but hearkee—Premium, you'll prepare lodgings for these gentlemen.[126]

SIR OLIVER. Yes, yes, I'll send for them in a day or two—

CHARLES. But hold—do now—send a genteel conveyance for them, for I assure you they were most of them used to ride in their own carriages.

SIR OLIVER. I will, I will, for all but—Oliver—

CHARLES. Aye all, but the little honest nabob.[127]

SIR OLIVER. You're fixed on that—

CHARLES. Peremptorily!

SIR OLIVER. A dear extravagant rogue—good day come Moses,—[*Aside*] *[L]et me hear now who dares call him profligate!*

[*Exeunt* Sir Oliver *&* Moses.

CARELESS. Why, this is the oddest genius—of the sort I ever saw.

CHARLES. Egad he's the Prince of Brokers I think, I wonder how the devil, Moses got acquainted with so honest a fellow—hah! Here's Rowley, do Careless;—say I'll join the company in a moment—

CARELESS. I will, but don't you let that old blockhead persuade you to squander any of that money on old musty debts, or any such nonsense, for tradesmen, Charles, are the most exorbitant fellows!

CHARLES. Very true, and paying them is only encouraging them.

CARELESS. Nothing else.

CHARLES. Aye—Aye—never fear—[*Exit* Careless] So—this was an odd old fellow indeed! Let me see, two thirds of this is mine by right;[128] five hundred and thirty pounds 'fore Heaven, I find one's ancestors are more valuable relations than I took 'em for!—Ladies and gentlemen, your most obedient and very grateful humble servant—[*Enter* Rowley]—Hah! Old Rowley, egad you are just come in time, to take leave of your old acquaintance—

ROWLEY. Yes I heard they were going—but I wonder you can have such spirits under so many distresses—

CHARLES. Why there's the point,—my distresses are so many that I can't afford to part with my spirits, but I shall be rich and splenetic all in good time; however I suppose you are surprized that I am not more sorrowful at parting with so many near relations, to be sure 'tis very affecting—But rot 'em you see they never move a muscle, so why should I.

ROWLEY. There's no making you serious a moment.

CHARLES. Yes faith: I am so now—here my honest Rowley. Here get me this chang'd—and take a hundred pounds of it immediately to Old Stanley.

ROWLEY. A hundred pounds—consider only—

CHARLES. Gad's life don't talk about it, poor Stanley's wants are pressing—and if you don't make fast we shall have some one call that has a better right to the money.

ROWLEY. Ah! There's the point—I never will cease dunning you with the old proverb—

CHARLES. "Be *just* before *you're generous*" hey!—Why so I would if I could—but justice is an old lame hobbling beldam—and I can't get her to keep pace with generosity for the soul of me.

ROWLEY. Yet Charles, believe me—one hour's reflection—

CHARLES. Aye—Aye—it's all very true—but hearkee Rowley while I have, by heaven I'll give—so damn your œconemy—and now for hazard. . . [*Exit.*

IV.ii

[*The parlour. Enter* Sir Oliver *and* Moses.]

MOSES. Well Sir, I think as Sir Peter said you have seen Mr. Charles in high glory. 'Tis great pity he's so extravagant.

SIR OLIVER. True, but he wouldn't sell my picture.

MOSES. And loves wine and women so much.

SIR OLIVER. But he wouldn't sell my picture!

MOSES. And game so deep—[129]

SIR OLIVER. But he wouldn't sell my picture—O here's Rowley.

[*Enter* Rowley.

ROWLEY. So—Sir Oliver—I find you have made a purchase.

SIR OLIVER. Yes—yes—Our young rake has parted with his ancestors like old tapestry.

ROWLEY. And here has he commission'd me to redeliver you part of the purchase money—I mean tho' in your necessitous character of Old *Stanley*.

MOSES. Ah, there is the pity of all; he is so damn'd charitable!

ROWLEY. And I left a hosier and two taylors in the hall—who I'm sure won't be paid, and this hundred would satisfy 'em—

SIR OLIVER. Well, well—I'll pay his debts—and his benevolence too; but now I am no more a broker, and you shall introduce me to the elder brother as Old Stanley.

ROWLEY. Not yet a while; Sir Peter I know means to call there about this time.

[*Enter* Trip.

TRIP. O gentlemen I beg pardon for not shewing you out, this way. Moses a word.

[*Exeunt* Trip & Moses.

SIR OLIVER. There's a fellow for you—would you believe it; that puppy intercepted the Jew, on our coming and wanted to raise money before he got to his master.

ROWLEY. Indeed!

SIR OLIVER. Yes—they are now planning an annuity business—ah! Master Rowley in my days, servants were content with the follies of their masters, when they were worn a little thread bare—but now they have their vices, like their birth-day cloaths with the gloss on!

[*Exeunt.*

IV.iii[130]

[*A library.* Surface *and* Servant.]

SURFACE. No letter from Lady Teazle?

SERVANT. No Sir—

SURFACE. I am surpris'd she hasn't sent if she is prevented from coming—Sir Peter certainly does not suspect me—yet I wish I may not lose the heiress thro' the scrape I have drawn myself in with the wife; however Charles's impudence and bad character are great points in my favour.

[*Knocking.*

SERVANT. Sir I believe that must be Lady Teazle.

SURFACE. Hold see—whether it is or not before you go to the door—I have a particular message for you, if it should be my brother—

SERVANT. 'Tis her Ladyship Sir, she always leaves her chair at the milliner's in the next street.

SURFACE. Stay, stay—draw that screen before the window—that will do—my opposite neighbour is a maiden lady of so curious a temper—[Servant *draws the screen & exit*] I have a difficult hand to play in this affair—Lady Teazle has lately suspected my views on Maria—but she must by no means be let into that secret, at least not 'till I have her more in my power—

[*Enter* Lady Teazle.

LADY TEAZLE. What sentiment in soliloquy! Have you been very impatient now? O Lud! don't pretend to look grave, I vow I couldn't come before.

SURFACE. O Madam punctuality is a species of constancy, a very unfashionable quality in a lady!

LADY TEAZLE. Upon my word you ought to pity me, do you know that Sir Peter is grown so ill tempered to me of late—and so jealous of *Charles* too that's the best of the story isn't it!

SURFACE. [*Aside*] *I am glad my scandalous friends keep that up.*

LADY TEAZLE. I am sure I wish he would let Maria marry him, and then perhaps he would be convinced—don't you Mr. Surface?

SURFACE.—[*Aside*] *Indeed I do not.*—[*To her*] O certainly I do, for then my dear Lady Teazle would also be convinced, how wrong her suspicions were of my having any design on the silly girl—

LADY TEAZLE. Well, well I'm inclin'd to believe you, but isn't it provoking to have the most ill natur'd things said to one! And there's my friend Lady Sneerwell has circulated I don't know how many scandalous tales of me! And all without any foundation too—that's what vexes me.

SURFACE. Aye Madam to be sure that *is* the provoking circumstance—without foundation!—Yes—yes—there's the mortification indeed—for when a scandalous story is believ'd against one—there certainly is no comfort like the consciousness of having deserv'd it—

LADY TEAZLE. No to be sure—then I'd forgive their malice—but to attack me who am really so innocent—and who never say an ill natur'd thing of any body—that is of any friend—and then Sir Peter too—to have him so peevish, and so suspicious—when I know the integrity of my own heart—indeed 'tis monstrous.

SURFACE. But my dear Lady Teazle 'tis your own fault if you suffer it—when a husband entertains a groundless suspicion of his wife, and withdraws his confidence from her—the original compact is broke and she owes it to the honour of her sex to endeavour to outwit him.

LADY TEAZLE. Indeed! So that if he suspects me without cause, it follows that the best way of curing his jealousy is to give him reason for't.

SURFACE. Undoubtedly—for your husband shou'd never be deceiv'd in you, and in that case it becomes *you* to be paid in compliment to *his* discernment.

LADY TEAZLE. To be sure, what you say is very reasonable; and when the consciousness of my own innocence—

SURFACE. Ah: my dear Madam there is the great mistake 'tis this very conscious innocence that is of the greatest prejudice to you—what is it makes you negligent of forms, and careless of the world's opinion? Why the *consciousness of your* innocence. What makes you thoughtless in your conduct, and apt to run into a thousand little imprudences?—Why the consciousness of your innocence—what makes you impatient of Sir Peter's temper and outrageous at his suspicions? Why the *consciousness* of your own innocence!

LADY TEAZLE. 'Tis very true.

SURFACE. Now my dear Lady Teazle if you would but once make a trifling faux pas—you can't conceive how cautious you would grow—and how ready to humour and agree with your husband.

LADY TEAZLE. Do you think so!

SURFACE. O I am sure on't, and then you would find all scandal would cease at once, for in short your character at present is like a person in a plethora,[131] absolutely dying of too much health!

LADY TEAZLE. So—so—then I perceive your prescription is that I must sin in my own defence—and part with my virtue to preserve my reputation.

SURFACE. Exactly so upon my credit Ma'am—

LADY TEAZLE. Well certainly this is the oddest doctrine—and the newest receipt for avoiding calumny—

SURFACE. An infallable one believe me—*prudence* like *experience* must be paid for—

LADY TEAZLE. Why if my understanding were once convinc'd—

SURFACE. O certainly Madam your understanding *should* be convinc'd—yes—yes—heaven forbid I should persuade you to do any thing you *thought* wrong—no—no—I have too much honour to desire it—

LADY TEAZLE. Don't you think we may as well leave honor out of the argument?

SURFACE. Ah, the ill effects of your country education I see still remain with you.

LADY TEAZLE. I doubt they do indeed—and I will fairly own to you that if I could be perswaded to do wrong, it would be by Sir Peter's ill usage, sooner than your honorable logic after all—

SURFACE. Then by this hand which he is unworthy of—[*Enter* Servant] 'Sdeath you blockhead—what do you want—

SERVANT. I beg pardon Sir, but I thought you wouldn't chuse Sir Peter to come up without announcing him—

SURFACE. Sir Peter—oon's the devil!

LADY TEAZLE. Sir Peter! O Lud! I'm ruin'd! I'm ruin'd—

SERVANT. Sir twasn't I let him in—

LADY TEAZLE. O I'm undone—what will become of me, now Mr. Logic? O mercy he's on the stairs—I'll get behind here—and if ever I am so imprudent again—[*Goes behind the screen*]

SURFACE. Give me that book—

[*Sits down*—Servant *pretends to adjust his hair. Enter* Sir Peter.

SIR PETER. Aye, ever improving himself!—Mr. Surface, Mr. Surface!

SURFACE. Oh my dear Sir Peter—I beg your pardon . . . [*Gaping and throws away the book*] I have been dozing over a stupid book; well—I am much oblig'd to you for this call—you haven't been here I believe since I fitted up this room—books you know are the only things I am a coxcomb in.

SIR PETER. 'Tis very neat indeed—well—well that's proper—and you make even your screen a source of knowledge—hung I perceive with maps—

SURFACE. O yes I find great use in that screen—

SIR PETER. I dare say you must—certainly—when you want to find any thing in a hurry—

SURFACE. [*Aside*] *Aye, or to hide any thing in a hurry either*—

SIR PETER. Well I have a little private business.

SURFACE. [*To* Servant] You needn't stay—

SERVANT. No Sir— [*Exit.*

SURFACE. Here's a chair Sir Peter—I beg—

SIR PETER. Well—now we are alone, there is a subject my dear friend on which I wish to unburthen my mind to you—a point of the greatest moment to my peace: in short my good friend Lady Teazle's conduct of late has made me extreamly unhappy.

SURFACE. Indeed! I am very sorry to hear it—

SIR PETER. Yes 'tis but too plain, she has not the least regard for me! But what's worse I have pretty good authority to suspect that she must have form'd an attachment to another.

SURFACE. You astonish me!

SIR PETER. Yes—and between ourselves—I think I have discover'd the person.

SURFACE. How! You alarm me exceedingly!

SIR PETER. Ah! My dear friend I knew you would sympathize with me!

SURFACE. Yes—believe me Sir Peter—such a discovery would hurt me just as much as it would you—

SIR PETER. I am convinc'd of it—ah!—It is a happiness to have a friend whom one can trust even with one's family secrets! But have you no guess who I mean?

SURFACE. I haven't the most distant idea—it can't be Sir Benjamin Backbite—

SIR PETER. O no—what say you to Charles?

SURFACE. My brother! Impossible!

SIR PETER. Ah! My dear friend—the goodness of your own heart misleads you—you judge of others by yourself—

SURFACE. Certainly Sir Peter—the heart that is conscious of its own integrity is ever slow to credit another's treachery—

SIR PETER. True but your brother has no sentiment—you never hear him talk so—

SURFACE. Yet I can't but think that Lady Teazle herself has too much principle—

SIR PETER. Aye, but what's her principle—against the flattery of a handsome—lively young fellow?

SURFACE. That's very true—

SIR PETER. And then you know the difference of our ages makes it very improbable that she should have a great affection for me—and if she were to be frail, and I were to make it public—why the Town would only laugh at me, the foolish old batchelor who had married a girl—

SURFACE. That's true—to be sure they *would* laugh—

SIR PETER. Laugh!—aye—and make ballads—and paragraphs—and the devil knows what of me—

SURFACE. No—you must never make it public—

SIR PETER. But then again that the nephew of my old friend Sir Oliver should be the person to attempt such a wrong—hurts me more nearly—

SURFACE. Aye there's the point; when ingratitude barbs the dart of injury—the wound has double danger in it—

SIR PETER. Aye, I that was in a manner left his guardian—in whose house he had been so often entertain'd—who never in my life denied him my advice—

SURFACE. O 'tis not to be credited—there *may* be a man capable of such baseness to be sure, but for my part 'till you can give me positive proofs—I can not but doubt it.—However if this should be proved on him—he is no longer a brother of mine! I disclaim kindred with him—for the man who can break thro' the laws of hospitality—and attempt the wife—of his friend deserves to be branded as the pest of society—

SIR PETER. What a difference there is between you! What noble sentiments!

SURFACE. Yet I cannot suspect Lady Teazle's honor—

SIR PETER. I am sure I wish to think well of her—and to remove all ground of quarrel between us, she has lately reproach'd me more than once—with having made no settlement on her—and in our last quarrel she almost hinted that she should not break her heart if I was dead—now as we seem to differ in our ideas of expence I have resolv'd she shall be her own mistress in that respect for the future—and if I *were* to die she shall find that I have not been inattentive to her interest while living—here my friend are the draughts of two deeds, which I wish to have your opinion on by one, she will enjoy eight hundred a year independent while I live—and by the other bulk of my fortune after my death—

SURFACE. This conduct Sir Peter is indeed truly generous!—[*Aside*] *I wish it may not corrupt my pupil*—

SIR PETER. Yes I am determin'd she shall have no cause to complain tho' I would not have her as acquainted with the latter instance of my affection yet awhile—

SURFACE. [*Aside*] *Nor I if I could help it*—

SIR PETER. And now my dear friend if you please we will talk over the situation of your hopes with *Maria*—

SURFACE. [*Softly*] No—no—Sir Peter—another time if you please.

SIR PETER. I am sensibly chagrin'd at the little progress you seem to make in her affection—

SURFACE. [*Softly*] I beg you will not mention it—what are my disappointments when your happiness is in debate!—[*Aside*] *'Sdeath—I should be ruin'd every way*—

SIR PETER. And tho' you are so averse to my acquainting Lady Teazle with your passion—I am sure she's not your enemy in the affair—

SURFACE. Pray Sir Peter now oblige me—I am really too much affected by the subject we have been speaking on to bestow a thought on my own concerns—The man who is entrusted with his friends distresses can never—well Sir?

[*Enter* Servant.

SERVANT. Your brother Sir is speaking to a gentleman in the street and says he knows you are within—

SURFACE. 'Sdeath! Blockhead—I'm not within—I'm out for the day—

SIR PETER. Stay—hold—a thought has struck me—you shall be at home—

SURFACE. Well, well, let him up—[*Exit* Servant] He'll interrupt Sir Peter—however—

SIR PETER. Now my good friend, oblige me I intreat you—before Charles comes—let me conceal myself somewhere, then do you tax him on the point we have been talking on—and his answers may satisfy me at once—

SURFACE. O fie Sir Peter—would you have me join in so mean a trick—to trapan[132] my brother to—

SIR PETER. Nay, you tell me, you are *sure* he is innocent—if so you do him the greatest service in giving him an opportunity to clear himself—and you will set my heart at rest—Come you shall not refuse me; [*Going to the screen*] here behind this screen will be—hey! What the devil! There seems to be *one* listner here already, I'll swear I saw a petticoat—

SURFACE. Ha! ha! ha! Well, this is rediculous enough—I'll tell you Sir Peter, tho' I hold a man of intrigue to be a most despicable character—yet you know it doesn't follow that one is to be an absolute Joseph[133] either—hearkee! 'Tis one little French milliner, a silly rogue that plagues me—and having some character—on your coming she ran behind the screen—

SIR PETER. Ah! You rogue! But egad, she has overheard all I have been saying of my wife—

SURFACE. O 'twill never go any further—you may depend on't.

SIR PETER. No!—Then—'efaith let her hear it out—here's a closet will do as well—

SURFACE. Well—go in then—

SIR PETER. Sly rogue!—Sly rogue!—[*Goes into the closet.*

SURFACE. A very narrow escape indeed! And a curious situation I'm in—to part man and wife in this manner—

LADY TEAZLE. [*Peeping from the screen*] Couldn't I steal off?

SURFACE. Keep close my angel—

SIR PETER. [*Peeping out*] Joseph, tax him home!

SURFACE. Back! my dear friend—

LADY TEAZLE. [*Peeping*] Couldn't you lock Sir Peter in?

SURFACE. Be still my life—

SIR PETER. [*Peeping*] You're sure the little milliner won't blab?

SURFACE. In, in, my good Sir Peter—fore Gad—I wish I had a key to the door—

[*Enter* Charles.

CHARLES. Hollo! Brother—what has been the matter? Your fellow wouldn't let me up at first—what have you had a Jew or a wench with you?

SURFACE. Neither Brother I assure you—

CHARLES. But what has made Sir Peter steal off—I though he had been with you—

SURFACE. He was, Brother;—but hearing *you* were coming he did not chuse to stay—

CHARLES. What was the old gentleman afraid I wanted to borrow money of him—

SURFACE. No Sir—but I am sorry to find Charles, that you have lately given that worthy man grounds for great uneasiness—

CHARLES. Yes, they tell me I do that to a great many worthy men—but how so pray?

SURFACE. To be plain with you Brother—he thinks you are endeavouring to gain Lady Teazle's affections from him.

CHARLES. Who I—O Lud! Not I upon my word, ha! ha! ha! So the old fellow has found out that he has got a young wife has he? Or what's worse has her Ladyship discover'd that she has an old husband?

SURFACE. This is no subject to jest on Brother—He who can laugh—

CHARLES. True, true, as you were going to say—then seriously I never had the least idea of what you charge me with upon my honour—

SURFACE. [*Aloud*] Well, it will give Sir Peter great satisfaction to hear this—

CHARLES. To be sure I once thought, the lady seem'd to have taken a fancy to me but upon my soul I never gave her the least encouragement—besides you know my attachment to Maria—

SURFACE. But sure Brother even if Lady Teazle had betray'd the fondest partiality for you—

CHARLES. Why—lookee Joseph—I hope I shall never deliberately do a dishonorable action—but if a pretty woman were purposely to throw herself in my way—and that pretty woman, married to a man old enough to be her father—

SURFACE. Well?

CHARLES.—Why I believe I should be oblig'd to borrow a little of your morality that's all—but Brother—do you know now that you surprize me exceedingly by naming *me* with Lady Teazle—for faith I always understood *you* were her favorite—

SURFACE. O for shame Charles—this retort is foolish—

CHARLES. Nay I swear I have seen you exchange such significant glances—

SURFACE. Nay, nay, Sir this is no jest—

CHARLES. Egad—I'm serious—don't you remember—one day when I call'd here—

SURFACE. Nay prithee Charles—

CHARLES. And found you together—

SURFACE. Zounds—Sir I insist—

CHARLES. And another time when your servant—

SURFACE. Brother—Brother a word with you—[*Aside*] *Gad I must stop him*—

CHARLES. Inform'd me I say that—

SURFACE. Hush!—I beg your pardon—but Sir Peter has overheard all we have been saying—I knew you would clear yourself or I should not have consented—

CHARLES. How Sir Peter!—Where is he—?

SURFACE. Softly—there—[*Points to the closet*]

CHARLES. Oh! 'fore Heaven, I'll have him out—Sir Peter come forth—

SURFACE. No, no—

CHARLES. I say Sir Peter—come into court—[*Pulls in* Sir Peter] what—my old guardian—what turn inquisitor and take evidence incog—

SIR PETER. Give me your hand Charles—I believe I have suspected you wrongfully—but you mustn't be angry with Joseph—'twas my plan—

CHARLES. Indeed!

SIR PETER. But I acquit you—I promise you, I don't think near so ill, of you as I did—what I have heard has given me great satisfaction—

CHARLES. Egad then 'twas lucky you didn't hear any more—[*Half aside*] *wasn't it Joseph?*

SIR PETER. Ah! You would have retorted on him—

CHARLES. Aye, aye, that was a joke.

SIR PETER. Yes, yes, I know his honor too well—

CHARLES. But you might as well have suspected him as me in this matter, for all that,—[*Half aside*] *mightn't he Joseph?*

SIR PETER. Well, well, I believe you—

SURFACE. [*Aside*] *Would they were both out of the room!*

[*Enter* Servant *who whispers* Surface.

SIR PETER. And in future perhaps we may not be such strangers.

SURFACE. Lady Sneerwell!—Stop her by all means—[*Exit* Servant] Gentlemen—I beg pardon—I must wait on you down stairs—Here's a person come on particular business—

CHARLES. Well you can see him in another room. Sir Peter and I haven't met a long time, and I have something to say to him.

SURFACE. [*Aside*] *They must not be left together—I'll send Lady Sneerwell away and return directly. Sir Peter not a word of the French milliner.* [*Exit* Surface.

SIR PETER. O not for the world! Ah Charles if you associated more with your brother one might indeed hope for your reformation. He is a man of sentiment, well, there is nothing in the world so noble as a man of sentiment!

CHARLES. Pshaw! He is too moral by half, and so apprehensive of his good name, as he calls it, that I suppose he would as soon let a priest into his house as a girl—

SIR PETER. No, no,—come—come—you wrong him. No—no—Joseph is no rake but he is not such a saint in that respect either.—[*Aside*] *I have a great mind to tell him—we should have a laugh!*

CHARLES. Oh hang him,—he's a very anchorite—a young hermit—

SIR PETER. Hearkee, you must not abuse him, he may chance to hear of it again I promise you—

CHARLES. Why you won't tell him—

SIR PETER. No; but—this way—egad! I'll tell him!—Hearkee! Have you a mind to have a good laugh against Joseph?

CHARLES. I should like it of all things—

SIR PETER. Then efaith we will—[*Aside*] *I'll be quit with him for discovering me*—[*To him*] he had a girl with him when I called—

CHARLES. What Joseph! You jest—

SIR PETER. Hush! A little—French milliner—and the best of the jest is—she's in the room now—

CHARLES. The devil she is—

SIR PETER. Hush—I tell you—[*Points.*

CHARLES. Behind the screen—'slife, let us unveil her—

SIR PETER. No—no! He's coming you shan't indeed—

CHARLES. O, egad! We'll have a peep at the little milliner—

SIR PETER. Not for the world—Joseph—will never forgive me.

CHARLES. I'll stand by you—

SIR PETER. [*Struggling with* Charles] Odds! Here he is . . .

[Surface *enters just as* Charles *throws down the screen.*

CHARLES. Lady Teazle! By all that's wonderful!

SIR PETER. Lady Teazle! By all that's horrible[!]

CHARLES. Sir Peter—This is one of the smartest French milliners I ever saw—Egad you seem all to have been diverting yourselves here at hide and seek—and I don't see who is out of the secret—shall I beg your Ladyship to inform me—not a word!—Brother! Will you please explain this matter?—What—morality dumb too!—Sir Peter tho' I found you in the dark—perhaps you are not so now. All mute! Well tho' *I* can make nothing of the affair I suppose you perfectly understand one another—so I leave you to yourselves [*Going*] Brother I'm sorry to find you *have given that worthy man so much uneasiness!* Sir Peter there's *nothing in the world so noble as a man of sentiment!* [*Exit* Charles.

[*Stand for some time looking at each other.*

SURFACE. Sir Peter—notwithstanding I confess that appearances are against me—if you will afford me your patience—I make no doubt but I shall explain every thing to your satisfaction.

SIR PETER. If you please—

SURFACE. The fact is Sir—that Lady Teazle knowing my pretentions to your ward Maria—I say Sir Lady Teazle being apprehensive of the jealousy of your temper, and knowing my friendship to the family—She Sir I say call'd here, in order that I might explain those pretensions—but on your coming being apprehensive—as I said of your jealousy—she withdrew—and this you may depend on't is the whole truth of the matter—

SIR PETER. A very clear account upon my word, and I dare swear the lady will vouch for every article of it—

LADY TEAZLE. [*Coming forward*] For not one word of it Sir Peter.

SIR PETER. How! Don't you even think it worth while to agree in the lie—

LADY TEAZLE. There is not one syllable of truth in what that gentleman has told you—

SIR PETER. I believe you upon my soul Ma'am.

SURFACE. [*Aside*] *'Sdeath Madam will you betray me*—

LADY TEAZLE. Good Mr. Hypocrite by your leave, I will speak for myself—

SIR PETER. Aye—let her alone Sir—you'll find she'll make out a better story than *you* without prompting—

LADY TEAZLE. Hear me Sir Peter—I came hither on no matter relating to your ward, and even ignorant of this gentleman's pretensions to her—but I came seduced by his insidious arguments, at least to listen to his pretended passion if not to sacrifice *your* honor to his baseness—

SIR PETER. Now I believe the truth *is* coming indeed—

SURFACE. The woman's mad!

LADY TEAZLE. No Sir, she has recover'd her sences, and your own arts have furnish'd her with the means—Sir Peter—I do not expect you to credit me—but the tenderness you expressed for me, when I am sure you could not think I was a witness to it, has penetrated to my heart, and had I left the place without the shame of this discovery my future life should have spoke the sincerity of my gratitude! As for that smooth tongue hypocrite, who would have seduced the wife of his too credulous friend while he affected honourable addresses to his ward—I behold him now in a light so truly despicable—that I shall never again respect myself for having listen'd to him—[*Exit.*

SURFACE. Notwithstanding all this Sir Peter—Heav'n knows—

SIR PETER. That you are a villain!—And so I leave you to your conscience—

SURFACE. You are too rash Sir Peter—you shall hear me! The man who shuts out conviction by refusing to—

SIR PETER. Oh!—

[*Exeunt,* Surface *following and speaking.*

V.i

[*The library. Enter* Surface & Servant.]

SURFACE. Mr. Stanley! Why should you think I would see him? You *must* know he comes to ask something!

SERVANT. Sir, I should not have let him in, but that Mr. Rowley came to the door with him.

SURFACE. Pshaw! Blockhead! To suppose that I should *now* be in a temper to receive visits from poor relations! Well why don't you shew the fellow up?

SERVANT. I will Sir—why Sir, it was not my fault that Sir Peter discover'd my Lady—

SURFACE. Go fool! [*Exit* Servant] Sure fortune never played a man of my policy[134] such a trick before—my character with Sir Peter, my hopes with Maria! destroyed in a moment!—I'm in a rare humour to listen to other people's distresses! I shan't be able to bestow even a benevolent sentiment on Stanley. So! Here he comes, and Rowley with him—I must try to recover myself—and put a little charity into my face however. . . [*Exit.*

[*Enter* Sir Oliver & Rowley.

SIR OLIVER. Why does he avoid us?—That was he, was it not?

ROWLEY. It was Sir—but I doubt you are come a little too abruptly;—his nerves are so weak, that the sight of a poor relation may be too much for him—I should have gone first to break you to him.

SIR OLIVER. A plague of his nerves!—Yet this is he whom Sir Peter extols as a man of the most benevolent way of thinking!—

ROWLEY. As to his way of thinking—I cannot pretend to decide; for to do him justice he appears to have as much speculative[135] benevolence as any private gentleman in the kingdom—tho' he is seldom so sensual as to indulge himself in the exercise of it.

SIR OLIVER. Yet has a string of charitable sentiments I suppose at his fingers'[136] ends!

ROWLEY. Or rather at his tongue's and Sir Oliver, for I believe there is no sentiment he has more faith in, than that charity begins at home.

SIR OLIVER. And his I presume is of that domestic sort which never stirs abroad at all—

ROWLEY. I doubt you'll find it so—but he's coming—I mustn't seem to interrupt you—and you know immediately as you leave him—I come in to announce your arrival in your real character.

SIR OLIVER. True—and afterwards you'll meet me at Sir Peters.

ROWLEY. Without losing a moment. [*Exit* Rowley.

SIR OLIVER. So! I don't like the complaisance of his features.

[*Re-enter* Surface.

SURFACE. Sir, I beg you ten thousand pardons, for keeping you a moment waiting—Mr. Stanley I presume—

SIR OLIVER. At your service—

SURFACE. Sir—I beg you will do me the honour to sit down, I intreat you Sir—

SIR OLIVER. Dear Sir, there's no occasion—[*Aside*] *Too civil by half!*

SURFACE. I have not the pleasure of knowing you Mr. Stanley—but I am extreamly happy to see you look so well—you were nearly related to my mother I think, Mr. Stanley.

SIR OLIVER. I was Sir—so nearly that my present poverty I fear may do discredit to her wealthy children—else I should not have presum'd to trouble you.

SURFACE. Dear Sir—there needs no apology—He that is in distress tho' a stranger has a right to claim kindred with the wealthy;—I am sure I wish *I* was of that class, and had it in my power to offer you even a small relief.

SIR OLIVER. If your uncle Sir Oliver were here—I should have a friend.

SURFACE. I wish he were Sir, with all my heart—you should not want an advocate with him—believe me Sir.

SIR OLIVER. I should not *need* one—my distresses would recommend me; but I imagin'd his bounty, had enabled *you* to become the agent of his charity.

SURFACE. My dear Sir—you were strangely misinformed; Sir Oliver is a worthy man—a very worthy sort of man—but—avarice Mr. Stanley is the vice of age—I will tell you my good sir in confidence—what he has done for me, has been a mere nothing, tho' people I know have thought otherwise, and for my part I never chose to contradict the report.

SIR OLIVER. What has he never transmitted you bullion! rupees! pagodas!

SURFACE. O dear Sir nothing of the kind—no—no—a few presents now and then—china—shawls—Congo tea—avadavats and India crackers[137]—little more believe me.

SIR OLIVER. [*Aside*] *Here's gratitude for twelve thousand pounds—avadavats and Indian crackers!*

SURFACE. Then my dear Sir—you have heard I doubt not of the extravagance of my brother, there are very few would credit what I have done for that unfortunate young man.

SIR OLIVER. [*Aside*] *Not I for one?*

SURFACE. The sums I have lent him—indeed I have been exceedingly to blame—it was an amiable weakness; however—I don't pretend to defend it—and now I feel it doubly culpable since it has depriv'd me of the power of serving *you* Mr. Stanley as my heart directs.

SIR OLIVER.—[*Aside*] *Dissembler!*—[*To him*] Then Sir you cannot assist me.

SURFACE. At present it grieves me to say I cannot, but whenever I have the ability, you may depend upon hearing from me.

SIR OLIVER. I am extreamly sorry.

SURFACE. Not more than I am believe me, to pity without the power to relieve, is still more painful than to ask and be denied.

SIR OLIVER. Kind Sir your most obedient humble servant.

SURFACE. You leave me deeply affected Mr. Stanley—William be ready to open the door—

SIR OLIVER. O, dear Sir, no ceremony.

SURFACE. Your very obedient.

SIR OLIVER. Sir, your most obsequious.

SURFACE. You may depend upon hearing from me, whenever I can be of service.

SIR OLIVER. Sweet Sir, you are too good.

SURFACE. In the mean time I wish you health, and spirits.

SIR OLIVER. Your ever grateful and perpetual humble servant.

SURFACE. Sir, yours as sincerely.

SIR OLIVER. [*Aside*][138] *Now I am satisfied!* [*Exit.*

SURFACE. [*Solus*] This is one bad effect of a good character, it invites applications from the unfortunate; and there needs no small degree of address to gain the reputation of benevolence without incurring the expence: the silver ore ofpure charity is an expensive article in thecatalogue of a man's good qualities—whereas the sentimental French plate I use instead of it, makes just as good a shew, and pays no tax.[139]

[*Enter* Rowley.

ROWLEY. Mr. Surface your Servant—I was apprehensive of interrupting you—tho' my business demands immediate attention—as this note will inform you.

SURFACE. Always happy to see Mr. Rowley—[*Reads*] How! "*Oliver Surface!*" my uncle arrived!

ROWLEY. He is indeed—we have just parted—quite well—after a speedy voyage, and impatient to embrace his worthy nephew.

SURFACE. I am astonish'd! William,—stop Mr. Stanley—if he's not gone—

ROWLEY. Oh he's out of reach—I believe.

SURFACE. Why didn't you let me know this when you came in together?

ROWLEY. I thought you had particular business, but I must be gone to inform your brother, and appoint him here to meet his uncle. He will be with you in a quarter of an hour.

SURFACE. So he says—well—I am strangely overjoy'd at his coming.—[*Aside*] *Never to be sure was any thing so damn'd unlucky!*

ROWLEY. You will be delighted to see how well he looks.

SURFACE. Oh, I am rejoiced to hear it—[*Aside*] *Just at this time!*

ROWLEY. I'll tell him how impatiently you expect him.

SURFACE. Do—do—Pray give my best duty and affection—indeed I cannot express the sensations I feel at the thought of seeing him![140]—[*Aside*] *Certainly his coming just at this time is the cruellest piece of of ill fortune . . .* [*Exit.*

V.ii

[*At* Sir Peter*'s. Enter* Mrs. Candour *and* Maid.]

MAID. Indeed Ma'am my Lady will see nobody at present.

MRS. CANDOUR. Did you tell her it was her friend Mrs. Candour—

MAID. Yes Madam, but she begs you will excuse her—

MRS. CANDOUR. Do go again—I shall be glad to see her, if it be only for a moment—for I am sure she must be in great distress . . . [*Exit* Maid] Dear heart, how provoking!—I'm not mistress of half the circumstances!—We shall have the whole affair in the news papers with the names of the parties at length, before I have dropt the story at a dozen houses. [*Enter* Sir Benjamin] Oh dear Sir Benjamin you have heard I suppose—

SIR BENJAMIN. Of Lady Teazle and Mr. Surface—

MRS. CANDOUR. And Sir Peter's discovery—

SIR BENJAMIN. O, the strangest piece of business to be sure!—

MRS. CANDOUR. Well I never was so surpris'd in my life: I am so sorry for all parties indeed I am.

SIR BENJAMIN. Now I don't pity Sir Peter at all—he was so extravagantly partial to Mr. Surface.

MRS. CANDOUR. Mr. Surface! Why, 'twas with Charles Lady Teazle was detected—

SIR BENJAMIN. No such thing—Mr. Surface is the gallant—

MRS. CANDOUR. No—no—Charles is the man—'twas Mr. Surface brought Sir Peter on purpose to discover them.

SIR BENJAMIN. I tell you I have heard it from one—

MRS. CANDOUR. And I have it from one—

SIR BENJAMIN. Who had it from one—who had it—

MRS. CANDOUR. From one immediately—but here's Lady Sneerwell—perhaps she knows the whole affair.

[*Enter* Lady Sneerwell.

LADY SNEERWELL. So my dear Mrs. Candour! Here's a sad affair of our friend Lady Teazle—

MRS. CANDOUR. Aye! My dear friend who could have thought it!

LADY SNEERWELL. Well there's no trusting appearances, tho' indeed she was always too lively for me—

MRS. CANDOUR. To be sure her manners were a little too free—but she was very young.

LADY SNEERWELL. And *had* indeed some good qualities—

MRS. CANDOUR. So she had indeed—but have you heard the particulars[?]

LADY SNEERWELL. No—but every body says that Mr. Surface—

SIR BENJAMIN. Aye there I told you—Mr. Surface was the man—

MRS. CANDOUR. No—no—indeed—the assignation was with Charles.

LADY SNEERWELL. With Charles!—You alarm me Mrs. Candour.

MRS. CANDOUR. Yes, yes, he was the lover—Mr. Surface—do him justice—was only the informer.

SIR BENJAMIN. Well I'll not dispute with you Mrs. Candour, but be it which it may—I hope that Sir Peter's would wound will not—

MRS. CANDOUR. Sir Peter's wound!—O mercy! I didn't hear a word of their fighting—

LADY SNEERWELL. Nor I a syllable.

SIR BENJAMIN. No—what no mention of the duel[?]

MRS. CANDOUR. Not a word.

SIR BENJAMIN. O Lord—yes, yes—they fought before they left the room.

LADY SNEERWELL. Pray let us hear.

MRS. CANDOUR. Aye do oblige us with the duel.

SIR BENJAMIN. Sir says Sir Peter—immediately after the discovery—you are a most ungrateful fellow.

MRS. CANDOUR. Aye, to Charles.

SIR BENJAMIN. No—no, to Mr. Surface—a most ungrateful fellow, and old as I am Sir says he I insist on immediate satisfaction.

MRS. CANDOUR. Aye that must have been to Charles for 'tis very unlikely Mr. Surface should go to fight in his house—

SIR BENJAMIN. Gad's life Ma'm not at all—giving me immediate satisfaction—on this—Madam—Lady Teazle seeing Sir Peter in such danger—ran out of the room in strong hysterics—and Charles after her calling out for hartshorn and water![141]—Then Madam they began to fight with swords—

[*Enter* Crabtree.

CRABTREE. With pistols Nephew—I have it from undoubted authority.

MRS. CANDOUR. O Mr. Crabtree! Then it is all true!

CRABTREE. Too true indeed Ma'am! And Sir Peter's dangerously wounded—

SIR BENJAMIN. By a thrust in secónde[142] quite thro' his left side.

CRABTREE. By a bullet lodged in the thorax—

MRS. CANDOUR. Mercy on me, poor Sir Peter!

CRABTREE. Yes Ma'am—tho' Charles would have avoided the matter if he could—

MRS. CANDOUR. I knew Charles was the person.

SIR BENJAMIN. O my uncle I see, knows nothing of the matter.

CRABTREE. But Sir Peter tax'd him with the basest ingratitude—

SIR BENJAMIN. That I told you, you know.

CRABTREE. Do Nephew let me speak—and insisted on an immediate—

SIR BENJAMIN. Just as I said.

CRABTREE. Odds! Life! Nephew allow others to know something too—a pair of pistols lay on the bureau, for Mr. Surface it seems had come the night before late from Salt-Hill, where he had been to see the Montem with a friend who has a son at Eton;[143] so unluckily the pistols were left charged.

SIR BENJAMIN. I heard nothing of this.

CRABTREE. Sir Peter forced Charles to take one, and they fired it seems pretty nearly together—Charles's shot took place as I told you,—and Sir Peter's miss'd;—but what is very extraordinary, the ball struck against a little bronze Pliny[144] that stood over the chimney piece—grazed out of the window at a right angle, and wounded the postman, who was just coming to the door with a double letter[145] from Northhamptonshire!

SIR BENJAMIN. My uncle's account is more circumstantial I must confess, but I believe mine is the true one for all that.

LADY SNEERWELL. [*Aside*] *I am more interested in this affair than they imagine and must have better information.* [*Exit* Lady Sneerwell.

SIR BENJAMIN. [*After a pause looking at each other*] Ah—Lady Sneerwell's alarm is very easily accounted for—

CRABTREE. Yes, yes, they certainly *do* say—but that's neither here nor there.

MRS. CANDOUR. But pray where is Sir Peter at present?

CRABTREE. Oh! They brought him home, and he is now in the house, tho' the servants are ordered to deny it.

MRS. CANDOUR. I believe so, and Lady Teazle I suppose—attending him. . .

CRABTREE. Yes, yes, I saw one of the faculty[146] enter just before me.

SIR BENJAMIN. Hey!—Who comes here?

CRABTREE. O this is he—the physician depend on't—

MRS. CANDOUR. O certainly, it must be the physician—and now we shall know—

[*Enter* Sir Oliver.

CRABTREE. Well Doctor—what hopes?

MRS. CANDOUR. Aye Doctor! How's your patient?

SIR BENJAMIN. Now Doctor isn't it a wound with a small sword?

CRABTREE. A bullett lodg'd in the thorax, for a hundred!

SIR OLIVER. Doctor!—A wound with a small sword! And a bullet in the thorax! Oons! Are you mad good people?

SIR BENJAMIN. Perhaps Sir, you are not a Doctor.

SIR OLIVER. Truly I am to thank you for any degree if I am.

CRABTREE. Only a friend of Sir Peter's then I presume; but Sir you must have heard of this accident—

SIR OLIVER. Not a word!

CRABTREE. Not of his being dangerously wounded?

SIR OLIVER. The devil he is!

SIR BENJAMIN. Run thro' the body—

CRABTREE. Shot in the breast—

SIR BENJAMIN. By one Mr. Surface—

CRABTREE. Aye the younger—

SIR OLIVER. Hey! What the plague! You seem to differ strangely in your accounts—however you agree that Sir Peter is dangerously wounded—

SIR BENJAMIN. O yes, we agree there—

CRABTREE. Yes, yes, I believe there can be no doubt of that.

SIR OLIVER. Then upon my word, for a person in that situation he is the most imprudent man alive—for here he comes walking as if nothing at all were the matter. [*Enter* Sir Peter] Odd's heart Sir Peter—you are come in good time I promise you, for we had just *given you over.*[147]

SIR BENJAMIN. 'Egad Uncle this is the most sudden recovery!

SIR OLIVER. Why man, what do you do out of bed with a small sword thro' your body, and a bullet lodged in your thorax!

SIR PETER. A small sword and a bullet—

SIR OLIVER. Aye these gentlemen would have kill'd you without law or physic—and wanted to dubb me a doctor—to make me an accomplice.

SIR PETER. Why! What is all this?

SIR BENJAMIN. We rejoice Sir Peter, that the story of the duel is not true—and are sincerely sorry for your other misfortunes—

SIR PETER. [*Aside*] *So—so—all over the town already—*

CRABTREE. Tho' Sir Peter, you were certainly vastly to blame to marry at all, at your years.

SIR PETER. Sir, what business is that of yours?

MRS. CANDOUR. Tho' indeed as Sir Peter made so good a husband he's very much to be pitied!

SIR PETER. Plague on your pity Ma'am, I desire none of it.

SIR BENJAMIN. However Sir Peter, you must not mind the laughing and jests, you will meet with on the occasion—

SIR PETER. Sir, I desire to be master in my own house.

CRABTREE. 'Tis no uncommon case, that's one comfort.

SIR PETER. I insist on being left to myself, without ceremony, I insist on your leaving my house directly.

MRS. CANDOUR. Well, well, we are going, and depend on't we'll make the best report of you we can—

SIR PETER. Leave my house!

CRABTREE. And tell how hardly you have been treated.

SIR PETER. Leave my house!

SIR BENJAMIN. And how patiently you bear it.

SIR PETER. Fiends—Vipers!—Furies!—Oh that their own venom would choak them—

[*Exeunt* Mrs. Candour, Sir Benjamin, Crabtree, etc.

SIR OLIVER. They are very provoking indeed Sir Peter.

[*Enter* Rowley.

ROWLEY. I heard high words[148]—what has ruffled Sir Peter?

SIR PETER. Pshaw what signifies asking—do I ever pass a day without my vexations?

SIR OLIVER. Well I'm not inquisitive—I come only to tell you that I have seen both my nephews in the manner we proposed.

SIR PETER. A precious couple they are!

ROWLEY. Yes and Sir Oliver is convinced—that your judgment was right Sir Peter—

SIR OLIVER. Yes I find *Joseph* is indeed the man after all—

ROWLEY. Yes as Sir Peter says, he's a man of sentiment.

SIR OLIVER. And acts up to the sentiments he professes.

ROWLEY. It certainly is edification to hear him talk.

SIR OLIVER. Oh he's a model for the young men of the age!—But how's this Sir Peter—you don't join in your friend Joseph's praise as I expected.

SIR PETER. Sir Oliver, we live in a damn'd wicked world and the fewer we praise the better.

ROWLEY. What do *you* say so, Sir Peter! who were never mistaken in your life—

SIR PETER. Pshaw! Plague on you both—I see by your snearing you have heard the whole affair—I shall go mad among you.

ROWLEY. Then to fret you no longer Sir Peter—we are indeed acquainted with it all—I met Lady Teazle coming from Mr. Surface's, so humbled that she deigned me to request me, to be her advocate with you.

SIR PETER. And does Sir Oliver know all too?

SIR OLIVER. Every circumstance—

SIR PETER. What of the—closet—and the screen, hey?

SIR OLIVER. Yes, yes, and the little French milliner—O I have been vastly diverted with the story—ha! ha!

SIR PETER. 'Twas very pleasant!

SIR OLIVER. I never laugh'd more in my life I assure you, ha! ha!

SIR PETER. Vastly diverting—ha! ha!

ROWLEY. To be sure Joseph with his sentiments—ha! ha!

SIR PETER. Yes, yes, his sentiments—ha! ha! A hypocritical villain!

SIR OLIVER. Aye—and that rogue Charles to pull Sir Peter out of the closet—ha! ha!

SIR PETER. Ha! ha! 'Twas devilish entertaining to be sure.

SIR OLIVER. Ha! ha! Egad Sir Peter I should like to have seen your face when the screen was thrown down ha! ha!

SIR PETER. Yes, yes, my face when the screen was thrown down! ha! ha! O I must never shew my head again—

SIR OLIVER. But come—come—it isn't fair to laugh at you neither my old friend—tho' upon my soul I can't help it.

SIR PETER. O pray don't restrain your mirth on my account—it does not hurt me at all—I laugh at the whole affair myself—yes, yes—I think being a standing jest for all one's acquaintances—a very happy situation—O yes, and then of a morning to read the paragraphs about Mr. S—Lady T—and Sir P—will be so entertaining!

ROWLEY. Without affectation Sir Peter you may dispise the ridicule of fools—but I see Lady Teazle going towards the next room—I am sure you must desire a reconciliation as earnestly as she does—

SIR OLIVER. Perhaps my being here, prevents her coming to you—well I'll leave honest Rowley to mediate between you—but he must bring you all presently to Mr. Surface's—where I am now returning—if not to reclaim a libertine—at least to expose hypocrisy—

SIR PETER. Ah!—I'll be present at your discovering yourself there with all my heart—tho' tis a vile unlucky place for discoveries!

ROWLEY. We'll follow—

SIR PETER. She is not coming, here you see Rowley—

ROWLEY. No but she has left the door of that room open you perceive—see she is in tears!

SIR PETER. Certainly a little mortification appears very becoming in a wife!—Don't you think it will do her good to let her pine a little?

ROWLEY. Oh, this is ungenerous in you!

SIR PETER. Well I know not what to think—you remember Rowley the letter I found of hers, evidently intended for Charles?

ROWLEY. A mere forgery Sir Peter—laid in your way on purpose—this is some of the point which I intend *Snake* shall give you conviction on.

SIR PETER. I wish I were once satisfied of that—she looks this way, what a remarkable elegant turn of the head, she has!—Rowley I'll go to her—

ROWLEY. Certainly—

SIR PETER. Tho' when it is known, that we are reconciled, people will laugh at one ten times more!

ROWLEY. Let them laugh and retort their malice only by shewing them you are happy in spite of it—

SIR PETER. 'Efaith so I will—and if I'm not mistaken we may yet be the happiest couple in the country.

ROWLEY. Nay Sir Peter—he who once lays aside suspicion—

SIR PETER. Hold my dear Rowley—if you have any regard for me—never let me hear you utter any thing like a sentiment—I have had enough of them to serve me the rest of my life!

[*Exit* Sir Peter & Rowley.

V.iii

[*The Library.* Surface *and* Lady Sneerwell.]

LADY SNEERWELL. Impossible; will not Sir Peter immediately be reconciled to Charles, and of consequence no longer oppose his union with Maria?—The thought is distraction to me!

SURFACE. Can passion furnish a remedy?

LADY SNEERWELL. No: nor cunning either—O! I was a fool! an ideot—to league with such a blunderer.

SURFACE. Sure Lady Sneerwell *I* am the greatest sufferer—yet you see I bear the accident with calmness.

LADY SNEERWELL. Because the disappointment doesn't reach your *heart*—your *interest* only attached you to Maria—had you felt for *her*, what *I* have for that *ungrateful* libertine, neither your temper nor hypocrisy could prevent your shewing the sharpness of your vexation.

SURFACE. But why should your reproaches fall on *me* for this disappointment?

LADY SNEERWELL. Are not you the cause of it?—What had you to do to bate in your pursuit of Maria, to pervert Lady Teazle by the way? Had you not a sufficient field for your roguery in blinding Sir Peter, and supplanting your brother? I hate such an avarice of crimes—'tis an unfair monopoly and never prospers—

SURFACE. Well I admit I have been to blame—I confess I deviated from the direct road of wrong, but I don't think we're so totally defeated neither—

LADY SNEERWELL. No.

SURFACE. You tell me, you have made a trial of Snake since we met, and that you still believe him faithful to us—

LADY SNEERWELL. I do believe so—

SURFACE. And that he has undertaken—should it be necessary—to swear and prove that Charles is at this time contracted by vows and honor to your Ladyship—which some of his former letters to you will serve to support.

LADY SNEERWELL. This indeed might have assisted.

SURFACE. Come, come, it is not too late yet, but hark! This is probably my Uncle Sir Oliver, retire to that room—We'll consult farther when he's gone—

LADY SNEERWELL. Well!—But if *he* should find you out too—

SURFACE. Oh! I have no fear of that—Sir Peter will hold his tongue for his own credit sake, and you may depend on't, I shall soon discover Sir Oliver's weak side!

LADY SNEERWELL. I have no diffidence of your abilities—only be constant to one roguery at a time . . . [*Exit.*

SURFACE. I will—I will—So! 'Tis confounded hard, after such bad fortune, to be baited by one's confederate in evil—Well, at all events my character is so much better than Charles's—that I certainly—Hey! What! This is not *Sir Oliver*—but *Old Stanley* again! Plague on't! That he should return to teize me, just now—we shall have Sir Oliver come and find him here and—[*Enter* Sir Oliver] Gads life! Mr. Stanley, why have you come back to plague me just at this time! You must not stay now upon my word—

SIR OLIVER. Sir—I hear your uncle Oliver is expected here, and tho' he has been so penurious to *you*—I'll try what he'll do for *me*.

SURFACE. Sir, 'tis impossible for you to stay now—so I must beg—come any other time and I promise you, you shall be assisted.

SIR OLIVER. No—Sir Oliver and I must be acquainted.

SURFACE. Zounds Sir, then I insist on your quitting the room directly—

SIR OLIVER. Nay Sir!

SURFACE. Sir, I insist on't—here William—Shew this gentleman out. Since you compel me Sir—not one moment—this is such insolence! [*Going to push him out.*

[*Enter* Charles.

CHARLES. Hey dey! What's the matter now?—What the devil have you got hold of my little broker here? Zounds Brother—don't hurt little Premium—What's the matter my little fellow?

SURFACE. Soh! he has been with you too has he?

CHARLES. To be sure he has! Why 'tis as honest a little—but sure Joseph you have not been borrowing money too, have you?

SURFACE. Borrowing, no!—But Brother you, know here we expect Sir Oliver—every—

CHARLES. O Gad that's true Noll mustn't find the little broker there to be sure—

SURFACE. Yet *Mr. Stanley* insists.

CHARLES. Stanley! Why his name is *Premium*.

SURFACE. No—no—*Stanley*—

CHARLES. No—no—*Premium*—

SURFACE. Well no matter which but—

CHARLES. Aye, aye, Stanley or Premium 'tis the same thing as you say, for I suppose he goes by half hundred names, besides *A.B.'s* at the coffee houses—[149]

[*Knocking.*

SURFACE. Death here's Sir Oliver at the door. [*Knock*] Now I beg Mr. Stanley—

CHARLES. Aye, and I beg Mr. Premium—

SIR OLIVER. Gentlemen—

SURFACE. Sir by Heaven you shall go—

CHARLES. Aye, out with him certainly—

SIR OLIVER. This violence—

SURFACE. 'Tis your own fault—

CHARLES. Out with him to be sure—

[*Both forcing* Sir Oliver *out. Enter* Sir Peter, Lady Teazle, Maria *and* Rowley.

SIR PETER. My old friend Sir Oliver!—Hey!—What in the name of wonder! Here are dutifull nephews!—Assault their uncle at the first visit—

LADY TEAZLE. Indeed Sir Oliver 'twas well we came in to rescue you.

ROWLEY. Truly it was—for I perceive Sir Oliver the character of Old Stanley was no protection to you.

SIR OLIVER. Nor of Premium either—the necessities of the *former* couldn't extort a shilling from *that* benevolent gentleman—and now Egad, I stood a chance of faring worse than my ancestors, and being knock'd down without being bid for!

[*After a pause* Joseph *and* Charles *turning to each other.*

SURFACE. Charles!

CHARLES. Joseph!

SURFACE. 'Tis now compleat!

CHARLES. Very!

SIR OLIVER. Sir Peter, my friend, and Rowley too—look on that elder nephew of mine—you know what he has already received from my bounty,—and you know also, how gladly I would have regarded half my fortune, as held in trust for him—judge then my disappointment in discovering him to be destitute of truth—charity—and gratitude.

SIR PETER. Sir Oliver! I should be more surprized at this declaration if I had not myself found him selfish, treacherous, and hypocritical!

LADY TEAZLE. And if the gentleman pleads not guilty to these, pray let him call *me* to his character—

SIR PETER. Then I believe we need add no more—if he knows himself, he will consider it as the most perfect punishment, that he is known by the world.

CHARLES. [*Aside*] *If they talk this way to* honesty—*what will they say to me bye and bye?*

SIR OLIVER. As for that prodigal his brother there—

CHARLES. [*Aside*] *Aye, now comes my turn—the damn'd family pictures will ruin me—*

SURFACE. Sir Oliver! Uncle!—Will you honour me with a hearing?

CHARLES. [*Aside*] *Now if Joseph would make one of his long speeches—I might recollect*[150] *myself a little—*

SIR PETER. I suppose you would undertake to justify yourself entirely.

SURFACE. I trust I could.

SIR OLIVER. Pshaw! [*To* Charles] Well Sir, and *you* could justify yourself too I suppose?

CHARLES. Not that I know of Sir Oliver—

SIR OLIVER. What little Premium—has been let too much into the secret I presume—

CHARLES. True Sir—but they were family secrets—and should never be mentioned again you know.

ROWLEY. Come Sir Oliver, I know you cannot speak of Charles's follies with anger—

SIR OLIVER. Odds heart no more I can—nor with gravity either, Sir Peter, do you know the rogue bargain'd with me for all his ancestors—sold me judges and generals by the foot—and maiden aunts as cheap as broken china—

CHARLES. To be sure Sir Oliver I did make a little free with the family canvas that's the truth on't; my ancestors may certainly raise in evidence against me, there's no denying it.—But believe me sincere when I tell you, and upon my soul I would not say it if I was not, that if I do not appear mortified at the exposure of my follies it is because I feel at this moment the warmest satisfaction in seeing you my liberal benefactor—

SIR OLIVER. Charles—I believe you—give me your hand again; the ill looking little fellow over the settee has made your peace—

CHARLES. Then Sir, my gratitude to the original is still increased.

LADY TEAZLE. [*Pointing to* Maria] Yet I believe Sir Oliver, here is one whom Charles is still more anxious to be reconcil'd to.

SIR OLIVER. O I have heard of this attachment there, and with the young lady's pardon, if I construe right, that blush—

SIR PETER. Well child, speak your sentiments—

MARIA. Sir, I have little to say, but that I shall rejoice to hear that he is happy—for me, whatever claim I had to his affection, I willingly resign it to one who has a better title.

CHARLES. How Maria!

SIR PETER. Hey, dey! What's the mystery now? While he appeared an incorrigible rake, you would give your hand to no one else and now that he is likely to reform, I warrant you won't have him.

MARIA. His own heart—and Lady Sneerwell knows the cause.

CHARLES. Lady Sneerwell!

SURFACE. Brother, it is with great concern, I am oblig'd to speak on this point, but my regard to justice compels me—and Lady Sneerwell's injuries can no longer—be concealed [*Goes to the door.*

[*Enter* Lady Sneerwell.

SIR PETER. Soh! Another French milliner!—Egad he has one in every room in the house I suppose.

LADY SNEERWELL. Ungrateful Charles!—Well may you be surprized and feel for the indelicate situation which your perfidy has forced me into.

CHARLES. Pray Uncle, is this another plot of yours? For as I have life, I don't understand it—

SURFACE. I believe Sir, there is but the evidence of one person more necessary to make it extreamly clear.

SIR PETER. And that person I imagine is Mr. Snake—Rowley, you were perfectly right to bring him with us, and pray let him appear.

ROWLEY. Walk in Mr. Snake. [*Enter* Snake] I thought his testimony might be wanted, however it happens unluckily, that he comes to confront Lady Sneerwell, and not to support her.

LADY SNEERWELL. Villain! Treacherous to me at last!—[*Aside*] *Speak fellow have you too conspired against me?*

SNAKE.[151] I beg your Ladyship ten thousand pardons—you paid me extreamly liberally for the lie in question but I have unfortunately been offered double to speak the truth.

SIR PETER. Plot and counter plot egad. I wish your Ladyship joy of the success of your negotiation.

LADY SNEERWELL. The torments of shame and disappointment on you all—

LADY TEAZLE. Hold—Lady Sneerwell—before you go, let me thank you for the trouble you, and that gentleman have taken in writing letters to me from Charles, and answering them yourself—and let me also request you, to make my respects to the scandalous college of which you are president—and inform them that Lady Teazle, licentiate, begs leave to return the diploma they granted her—as she leaves off practice and kills characters no longer.—

LADY SNEERWELL. You too Madam—provoking! —Insolent!—May your husband live these fifty years! [*Exit.*

SIR PETER. Oons what a fury—

LADY TEAZLE. A malicious creature indeed!

SIR PETER. Hey! Not for her last wish.

LADY TEAZLE. O no—

SIR OLIVER. Well Sir and what have you to say now?

SURFACE. Sir, I am so confounded to find that Lady *Sneerwell* could be guilty of suborning[152]—Mr. *Snake* in this manner to impose on us all, that I know not what to say; however lest her revengfull spirit should prompt her to injure my brother, I had certainly better follow her directly— [*Exit.*

SIR PETER. Moral to the last drop—

SIR OLIVER. Ay and marry her Joseph if you can—oil and vinegar egad! You'll do very well together—

ROWLEY. I believe we have no more occasion for Mr. Snake at present—

SNAKE. Before I go—I beg pardon once for all, for whatever uneasiness I have been the humble instrument of causing to the parties present.

SIR PETER. Well, well, you have made atonement by a good deed at last—

SNAKE. But I must request of the company that it shall never be known.

SIR PETER. Hey!—What the plague—are you asham'd of having done a right thing once in your life[?]

SNAKE. Ah, Sir,—consider I live by the badness of my character, I have nothing but my infamy to depend on! And if it were once known that I had been betrayed into an honest action, I should lose every friend I have in the world—

SIR OLIVER. Well, well, we'll not traduce you by saying any thing to your praise never fear— [*Exit* Snake.

SIR PETER. There's a precious rogue—yet that fellow is a writer and a critic!

[Charles *and* Maria *apart.*

LADY TEAZLE. See Sir Oliver there needs no persuasion now to reconcile your nephew and Maria.

SIR OLIVER. Aye, aye, that's as it should be, and egad we'll have the wedding tomorrow morning.

CHARLES. Thank you my dear Uncle!

SIR PETER. What you rogue don't you ask the girl's consent first?

CHARLES. O I have done that a long time above a minute ago—and she has look'd, yes—

MARIA. For shame—Charles—I protest Sir Peter there has not been a word—

SIR OLIVER. Well then the fewer the better—may your love for each other never know abatement—

SIR PETER. And may you live as happily together as Lady Teazle and I—intend to do—

CHARLES. Rowley my old friend—I am sure you congratulate me and I suspect that I owe you much.

SIR OLIVER. You do indeed Charles.

ROWLEY. If my efforts to serve you had not succeeded, you would have been in my debt for the attempt—but deserve to be happy—and you over pay me—

SIR PETER. Aye honest Rowley always said you would reform.

CHARLES. Why as to reforming Sir Peter I'll make us no promises, and that I take to be a proof that I intend to set about it—But here shall be my monitor, by gentle guide—Ah! Can I leave the virtuous path those eyes illumine?

Tho'—thou, dear maid; shoulds't wave thy *Beauty's* sway,
—Thou still must rule—because I *will* obey;
An humbled fugitive from Folly view
No sanctuary near—but *Love* and *you*;
[*To the audience*] *You*, can indeed each anxious Fear remove,
—For even *Scandal* dies if *you* approve.

FINIS.

Epilogue.

[*Written by G. Colman, Esq. Spoken by Mrs. Abington in the character of Lady Teazle.*]

I, who was late so volatile and gay,
Like a trade-wind must now blow all one way,
Bend all my cares, my studies, and my vows,
To one old rusty weathercock—my spouse!
So wills our virtuous bard—the motley Bayes[153]
Of crying epilogues and laughing plays!

Old batchelors, who marry smart young wives,
Learn from our play to regulate your lives!
Each bring his dear to Town—all faults upon her—
London will prove the very source of honor.
Plung'd fairly in, like a cold bath, it serves,
When principles relax, to brace the nerves.

Such is my case—and yet I might deplore
That the gay dream of dissipation's o'er;
And say, ye fair, was ever lively wife,
Born with a genius for the highest life,
Like me, untimely blasted in her bloom,
Like me condemned to such a dismal doom?
Save money—when I just knew how to waste it!
Leave London—just as I began to taste it!
Must I then watch the early-crowing cock?
The melancholy ticking of a clock?
In the lone rustic hall for ever pounded,
With dogs, cats, rats, and squalling brats surrounded?
With humble Curates can I now retire,
(While good Sir Peter Boozes with the Squire)
And at Back-gamon mortifying my soul,
That pants for lue,[154]—or flutters at a vole?
Seven's the main! dear sound!—that must expire,
Lost at Hot Cockles, round a Christmas fire!
The transient hour of Fashion, too soon spent,
Farewell the tranquil mind, farewell content!
Farewell the plumed head—the cushion'd Tète[155]
That takes the cushion from its proper seat!
The spirit stirring Drum—Card Drums I mean,[156]
Spadille, Odd trick, Pam, Basto, King and Queen![157]
And you, ye knockers, that with brazen throat,
The welcome visitor's approach denote,
Farewell!—All quality of high Renown
Pride, pomp, and circumstance of glorious Town,
Farewell! Your Revels I partake no more,
And Lady Teazle's occupation's o'er.
All this I told our Bard. He smil'd and said 'twas clear,
I ought to play deep Tragedy next year:[158]
Meanwhile he drew wise morals from his play,
And in these solemn periods stalk'd away.
[']Blest were the Fair like you, her faults who stopt,
And Clos'd her Follies, when the curtain dropt!
No more in Vice or Error to Engage,
Or play the Fool at large, on Life's great Stage.[']

17.2 *THE TOWN AND COUNTRY MAGAZINE*, "HISTORY OF THE TÊTE-À-TÊTE OR MEMOIRS OF THE HON. CAPT. H____Y AND MRS. N______T"

Scandal in the Periodical Press

From *The Town and Country Magazine,* vol. 7 (January 1775), 9–12. "History of the Tête-à-Tête or Memoirs of the hon. Capt. H____y[159] and Mrs. N______t[160]"

EXTRAORDINARY EVENTS USUALLY BRING FORTH extraordinary characters, and open many avenues to secret anecdotes, which would otherwise probably never have been explored. The truth of this assertion was never more forcibly evinced than by some late transactions that have made every one inquisitive to know the secret histories of all the interested parties. To this cause may, in a great degree, be ascribed our presenting at this juncture our readers with the following memoirs.

Our hero is allied to a noble family, and brother to an earl. His inclination early led him to a maritime life, and he gradually rose to the rank of captain in the navy. In this honourable station he distinguished himself the war before last in the Mediterranean, where he commanded; and has upon every occasion approved himself a brave and gallant officer. After the conclusion of the peace, in 1748, he returned to England greatly honoured and caressed, and soon after made an acquaintance with the celebrated Miss C_____,[161] then a reigning toast, and who gave the *ton* in dress and conversation.

This lady is the daughter of an officer, at whose demise, her mother was appointed housekeeper to one of the palaces, which with her pension as widow, enabled her to make a genteel appearance, and figure in her usual circle of acquaintance. Miss C_____ was placed at a capital boarding school, where she acquired the usual female accomplishments of dancing, music, and French, in which she was a great proficient. She was particularly noticed by a very great personage and he prevailed upon his consort to put her upon the list of her maids of honor. In this elevated station, she had an opportunity of displaying her accomplishments, the circle of which she daily extended.

A beautiful young woman, endowed with uncommon personal and mental qualifications, placed in so conspicuous a point of view in a gay and gallant court, could not fail attracting many admirers. She was addressed from pages almost up to monarchs. She was the meteor of L—c-st-r house, and every one viewed her with admiration. She rallied their compliments with poignant vivacity, and seemed to be a salamander insensible in the midst of the flames; but when she was upon the point of being pronounced a most accomplished coquette, she was compelled to acknowledge herself a woman with all her natural feelings. Amongst the most ardent of her admirers was lord B_____; he was the only one that she had particularly distinguished, and for whom she felt every sensible *penchant.* He had paid his addresses to her upon the most honorable terms, and his billets breathed the purest effusions of love. In a word, the treaty was brought to such a crisis that the nuptial day was actually appointed. In the interim his lordship made a visit to a relation's in the country, where he formed an acquaintance with a young lady of very considerable fortune, to whom he gave his hand in a short time. The news of this match no sooner reached Miss C_____, than it had the most violent effect upon her—it threw her into all the agonies of despair, and in a fit of phrenzy, she took a dose of arsenic, with the intent of destroying herself: fortunately it was not sufficient to battle the effects of the antidotes that were speedily administered: but it, nevertheless, threw her into a very languid state, which, added to the disordered situation of her mind, had nearly proved fatal. By degrees, however, with the help of an excellent constitution, she recovered, and being once more emerged in the polite world, she resumed her gaiety, and had the fortitude to despise her faithless lover.

It was about this period that our hero returned from the Mediterranean, when Miss C_____, was in the meridian of her charms, and the general toast of all the fine fellows of the time. Capt. H_____ now paid his addresses to her, which she listened to, and being sensible that it was a very advantageous match, she yielded to his intreaties. A marriage ensued, which was, however, kept as secret as possible: the reason then assigned for that privacy was, that if it were divulged she must give up her post of maid of honor, which she still held. Though this does not seem a very cogent reason, it was admitted amongst her particular acquaintance.

Mr. and Mrs. H_____ did not long remain together; a rupture almost immediately ensued, and they were separated ere the honey moon was accomplished. The censorious public, who by this time had penetrated the secret, reasoned variously upon this occasion, and as usual the censure fell by turns, as interest or partiality prevailed, on the husband or the wife. Capt. H_____ being appointed to a ship, soon after went abroad, and left his consort to roam at large free and unrestrained in the wilds of love.

Being now a *femme couverte*, she thought herself authorized to be *découverte* upon many occasions, and in this respect she particularly signalized herself at a jubilee masquerade, at Ranelagh, where she appeared in the character of Iphigenia. She copied her dress from a picture of the sacrifice of Iphigenia in the possession of Sir Henry Cheere, which she obtained permission to view. The upper part of her body to her waist was covered only with a thin gauze; and a single petticoat very short was drawn up on one side, whereby she displayed a well turned leg to the greatest advantage. She was particularly noticed upon this occasion by the late duke of Cumberland, who archly said, "he always thought Miss C_____ had a warm constitution, but was never till now convinced of the great ardency of her feelings." It is indeed astonishing, how thus apparelled all night she avoided a violent cold, which often caught by the most athletic constitutions, when far less wantonly courted. The next day she received a very severe rebuke from a great princess, who was upon the point of striking her off the list of maids of honor, which she would have done, had not the P. strongly solicited in her favour.

This ridiculous appearance, to call it by no harsher name, brought many sarcasms upon her, as well in private as public: the news paper satyrists made very free with her, in this dress, to the public. The tea tables pronounced this step as the test of her conduct, and accordingly stamped the title of *demi-rep* upon her.

When once a woman undergoes this sentence, the most reserved conduct will not rescue her from slander, and the slightest indiscretion will be construed to criminality. We need not, therefore, be surprised to find that many intrigues were allotted her, of which probably she was innocent, though her conduct gave some grounds for suspicion. However, one soon after manifested itself, that erased every doubt. This connexion was with the late D____ of K_____, who had lately lost a much admired mistress in madame La T______e. This lady was the wife of a Farmer General, and one of the richest financiers in France; he had married her entirely for love, he indeed doated upon, and she lived in the magnificence and splendor of a princess; but there was an union of hearts still wanting, which gratitude could not create, to make her happy. This union, however, she found in his grace, and she readily agreed to decamp with him to England. In consequence of this excursion, a criminal process was instituted against the parties, and his G. was sentenced to be hung in effigy. Dear as the D. paid for this intrigue, it no way diminished his fondness for madame La T____e, and they were judged for several years the most faithful lovers in the environs of St. James.

Having settled Miss C_____ or Mrs. H______ with the D. of K______, we must enquire after our hero. He was now in the Mediterranean, and heard of his wife's exploits, with the greatest philosophic indifference; he wished the duke joy of his conquest, and drank Miss C_____ as an accomplished demi-rep. We cannot suppose that in a soil so fruitful as Italy for beauty, he did not taste of the luscious banquets that were every where spread before him. A succession of temporary mistresses occasionally amused him, without his making any lasting connexion either at Leghorn or Genoa. His attention was chiefly engaged in the service of his country, which he had much at heart, and in which he displayed great maritime knowledge, and uncommon bravery. Upon his return to England, finding Miss C_____ completely happy in the possession of the D____ of K_____, he did not disturb their tranquility, but meeting with a very agreeable companion in Miss L_____, he furnished a small retreat for her near Richmond, where he passed the moments of his amorous dalliance.

Miss C_____, whose ambition was unlimited, finding the influence she had over her paramour, resolved to avail herself of it, and to grasp a ducal coronet. There seemed one insurmountable obstacle in the way, which was her former marriage; but she thought to obviate this by destroying the register of it, which she did with the assistance of an old nurse, who was the only living witness of her nuptials. Notwithstanding this manœuvre, the duke's pride could not let him yield to give his hand to a woman, whose character was very problematical before his acquaintance with her, and who had convinced him of the probability of her yielding to a lover, without the intervention of a priest. Piqued at this refusal, she went abroad, and visited several courts in Germany, particularly Dresden, where she remained some time, and received great attentions, and civility. The duke till now was unacquainted with the extent of her influence; he grew melancholy, company was irksome to him, books he could not enjoy; in fine, every thing had lost its relish but his dear Miss C_____. He wrote to her a penitential letter, and offered her a *carte blanche*. Her dissembled resentment, but real policy, was so great that she did not immediately return, in order to rivet the chains of her captive still more permanently.

It was necessary, however, before the celebration of their nuptials, notwithstanding the demolition of the register, and the only evidence was properly secured, that another party should also be silenced, lest he should lay his claim to the fair fat duchess, and convict her of bigamy. Overtures were accordingly made and listened to, and it is assured the sum of nine thousand guineas was stipulated as a valuable consideration for hush money.

In the mean while our hero formed an acquaintance with the celebrated Mrs. N___b___t, whose exploits in the republic of Gallantry have made some noise east and west of the Temple-bar. This lady, whose origin may be traced to a wheelbarrow, was taken notice of by a celebrated Mercury belonging to the Bedford arms Tavern, and he had rhetoric sufficient, with the auxillary of a second-hand silk sack to persuade her to enroll in his list. She had not long been mustered, ere she made acquaintance with Mr. N____b____t,[162] a worthy young gentleman, then in partnership in the banking business. She doubtless had many female attractions, which being now properly tutored by an avaricious mother, she soon levied heavy contributions on Mr. N______t, who being of an easy docile temper, gave into all the little snares that were laid for him. Indeed, he was wrapt up in a kind of enthusiastic phrenzy for her, and has been known in the height of the most important business, to wait booted in his shop with eager expectation for his horse, to fly to his charmer at some spot of appointed rendezvous. Finding him so tractable she resolved to push her point to the ultimate extreme—in a word, she refused her company, unless he would comply with her most honorable terms, MATRIMONY!

We shudder at the word, and yet so complete was her dominion over him, that he complied, and in a short time she became *really* Mrs. N______t. Her ambition thus dilated, and in a great degree gratified, she resolved upon making herself entirely independent, and to this end she obtained a genteel settlement from him. The necessary drafts for this purpose from the house, alarmed the partnership, and it was agreed by the rest to strike him off the Firm.

In the mean while, however, he had purchased for her a neat villa by Norwood, (where she still resides) and where he was her constant companion, when the most urgent business did not detain him in town. Here, like Anthony, he for a woman lost the world and himself. Distress brought him to recollection, and despair drove him to distraction. Sorry we are to conclude his history, in saying that he died insane, in a mean lodging near Black Friar's Bridge.

Callous to all the fine feelings of humanity, Mrs. N______ triumphed in her husband's misery. She laughed at his folly, ridiculed his weakness, and satirized his personal defects. The last expression may, perhaps, carry our readers beyond our meaning—His figure was agreeable, his structure manly, his sentiments noble and generous—he had, however, some small impediment in his speech, which *virtuous, candid, faithful,* and *grateful* Mrs. N____b____t took the greatest pains to expose.

No sooner had she thrown off the shackles of connubial restraint, than she once more gave a full loose to her most wanton passions, and ran riot at every man that pleased her eye. Amongst the rest the captain particularly attracted her; his atheletic form, his generous disposition, his rank, in fine, his *tout en semble*, struck her so forcibly, that she relinquished a long catalogue of lovers, to be blessed in the arms of *Augustus*.

We need only add with respect to Mrs. N______t's memoirs, that she still resides in the villa, which her husband purchased for her near Norwood: that here the captain often visits her, where the luxuriant moments of reciprocal bliss pass without alloy, and where interest seems to have lost its magnetic power, in mutual affection.

Something farther is due to so exalted and extraordinary a character as the duchess of K_____. Her life, however enigmatical, can now be solved. At the demise of her husband, finding the secrets of her former marriage disclosed, and that the duke's heirs intended a criminal prosecution against her, she *cautiously* disposed of all his moveables, and made a retreat to the Continent, still more ambitiously inclined, to become a queen, in the arms of a Polish monarch. It being, however, necessary to return, she appeared once more in the metropolis of England, from whence (after having laid hands upon all her husband's effects that were *tangible*) she judged it absolutely necessary ⋆ to retire *à la jourdine*, and is said now to be at Rome, to assist at the election of a Pope.

⋆The following paragraphs, which have appeared in the papers, will throw some additional lights upon this extraordinary affair.

A very extraordinary prosecution has been carrying on against the dowager D_____ of K_____. The accusation is for having two husbands; being, as it is said to the hon. Capt. H_____, at the time she wedded the late D______ of K______.

A motion was made in the Court of Chancery, for an injunction, to stop the payment of a sum of money in the hands of Mr. T_____all, from being paid to the trustees of the D_____ of K_____, which arose from the late D___e's horses, dogs, &c. on the ground of her being an executor by false pretences, and being now indicted of felony; when the Lord Chancellor remarked, that as a noble Lord had made it appear, that there was no indictment against her, as it had been brought against Elizabeth C_____h, and there being no such person, he ordered the money to be paid into the hands of the trustees, for payment of funeral expences, debts, and legacies.

17.3 *SCENE FROM* SCHOOL FOR SCANDAL *BEING PERFORMED IN DRURY LANE THEATRE, LONDON*

Scene from School for Scandal *being performed in Drury Lane Theatre, London*; four actors on stage, the audience watching from boxes on either side, etching and engraving, 1778. Trustees of the British Museum.

Notes

1 *The School for Scandal* was first performed on May 8, 1777 at Drury Lane Theatre. Editing Sheridan's play poses significant challenges because he did not authorize the printing of the script in his lifetime. By keeping the play out of print Sheridan effectively controlled performance of the most successful play in the late-century repertoire. The version of the play presented here is based on an elegant presentation manuscript—basically a gift—to Sheridan's mistress Frances Anne Crewe. The Crewe manuscript is held in the Georgetown Rare Books Library and we kindly acknowledge their permission to reproduce the text. Aside from minor changes in punctuation and spelling, every effort has been made to offer a precise transcription of the manuscript.

2 Frances Anne Crewe (1748–1818) was Sheridan's mistress in the late 1770s and early 1780s, and the recipient of the presentation manuscript from which this edition of *The School for Scandal* has been transcribed. This poem appears to have accompanied the leather bound copy of the play.

3 Both Elizabeth Sheridan and Charles James Fox appear to have addressed Frances Crewe as Amoret in separate private panegyrics.

4 The painter Sir Joshua Reynolds painted three portaits of Frances Crewe.

5 The renowned beauties Mary Isabella, wife of the Marquis of Granby, and Georgiana, the Duchess of Devonshire, were also painted by Reynolds.

6 *quantum sufficit:* "as much as suffices".

7 Wormwood: playing on the bitter aromatic plant, Mrs. Wormwood embodies bitterness, and the newspaper will play on her name below.

8 *poz*: slang for "positively".

9 *Dash and Star*: stars and dashes were used to hint at names in scandalous reports. Lisp is being asked to look for the juicy bits.

10 *Grosvenor Square*: the fashionable aristocratic neighbourhood.

11 Sheridan compares himself to Cervantes' hero, but the playwright goes in hunt of Scandal.

12 In Greek mythology, the Hydra's many heads grew back as fast as they were severed.

13 In eighteenth-century newspapers stories were only separated by indentations. Snake has paid for a paragraph to be inserted into the paper. Editors would charge both for inserting paragraphs and for suppressing them.

14 *matches*: intended marriages.

15 *close confinements*: secret births.

16 *separate maintenances*: the financial support a husband paid his wife after they were formally separated.

17 Divorces were extraordinarily difficult to attain and usually required proof of adultery.

18 *The Town and Country Magazine* was a monthly periodical infamous for its scandal-mongering. Every month featured a *tête-à-tête*: a lightly-veiled account of sexual scandal complete with a two-headed engraving of the people in question.

19 *Character*: reputation.

20 *city knight*: the knight in question is being looked down upon because his background is in the City—i.e. he is a merchant.

21 *jointure*: the estate settled upon a wife after her husband's death.

22 *close with*: make an arrangement, here implying a betrothal.

23 *confidential*: in one another's confidence.

24 *man of sentiment*: equally a man of deep feeling and a man who expresses strong moral views. The latter need not imply the former, but Sir Peter collapses the two.

25 *sensibility*: "quickness and acuteness of apprehension or feeling; the quality of being easily and strongly affected by emotional influences" (OED).

26 *lover*: suitor.

27 The Town refers both to people of fashion and the west-end neighbourhoods in which they resided.

28 The fast stage-coach to York. They are presumably en route to Scotland where marriage laws were more lax.

29 They are now bickering like other married couples.

30 An allusion to pregnancy.
31 *a house of no extraordinary fame*: a house of ill repute.
32 All these names invoke gambling: Spindle (roulette), Splint (horseracing), Quinze and Nickit (cards).
33 bankrupt.
34 A rhebus or a charade was a coded rhyme or puzzle for private circulation. Perhaps the most famous literary example is from Austen's *Emma.*
35 *conversationé*: from the Italian word for a literary salon held in a private residence.
36 Petrarch's sonnets are addressed to Laura. Likewise, Sacharissa was the addressee of Edmund Waller's love poems. Both are examples of unrequited or unconsummated desire.
37 Sir Benjamin's description of the wide-margined quarto page implies both expensive printing and very little substance.
38 *bespoke*: ordered to be made.
39 Tunbridge Wells, like Bath, was a fashionable spa town.
40 Fashionable women frequently had their children nursed by working class women. It was often seen as a reason for high infant mortality.
41 That Sir Oliver has an East Indian career is extremely important. Members of the East India Company often made vast sums during their Indian service and the influx of money upon their return often destabilized rank and class.
42 This implies that Charles is in debt to Jewish money-lenders.
43 *Old Jewry*: a street near the Bank of England that was home to many Jews.
44 The Irish Tontine was a lottery that paid annuities to its winners. It was designed as a scheme to pay down the national debt.
45 *securities*: friends who have vouched for Charles in loans and notes of credit.
46 *doubt*: fear.
47 Sir Oliver has not married.
48 *Noll*: Sir Oliver.
49 The Pantheon, opened in 1772, was the most fashionable place of entertainment in London. It was the site of masquerades, balls and other diversions. By the time of this play it was synonymous with intrigue and scandal.
50 *fête-champêtre*: a country entertainment. The term was popularized by an extravagant entertainment hosted by General John Burgoyne in 1774 at The Oaks, Lord Edward Stanley's estate in Surrey. The Fête Champêtre was also the subject of a highly successful play by Burgoyne, *The Maid of the Oaks*, that not only starred Fanny Abington, but also explored the propagation of scandal in the press.
51 *tambour:* "a species of embroidery in which patterns are worked with a needle of peculiar form on material stretched in a circular frame" (OED).
52 *fruits in worsted of your own working*: home made wall hangings.
53 *Pope Joan*: a card game.
54 A spinnet was an early keyboard instrument.
55 *vis-à-vis*: "a light carriage for two persons sitting face to face" (OED).
56 Kensington Gardens was a fashionable park in the vicinity of Kensington Palace.
57 Reputation is being compared to money by invoking forgery, counterfeiting ("coiners") and the clipping of coins. Because they were seen as offences against the King, all of these financial infractions were held to be treasonous and were capital crimes in Sheridan's day.
58 *curricle*: a light, open two-wheeled carriage drawn by a pair of matched horses.
59 Hyde Park was another fashionable site for riding and promenading. Sheridan is joking on the phrase "taking the air."
60 Duodecimo paper is smaller than a quarto or octavo page, thus a duodecimo phaeton is a small, open carriage.
61 A macaroni was an extravagantly dressed young man of fashion. Adopting effeminate modes of dress, the macaronis were satirized as barometers of social dissipation.
62 The skirts of a macaroni's jacket were often cut high in the front and very low in the back.
63 Phoebus Apollo rode the chariot of the sun from horizon to horizon.

64 inserted.
65 Caulking and painting refer to the excessive application of cosmetics.
66 A poor's box, typically placed in a church, had a narrow slot for the insertion of alms.
67 *acids*: could refer simultaneously to juices and rancour.
68 The Ring was a fashionable horse promenade in Hyde Park.
69 This extends the joke on excessive make-up: Lady Stucco is like a marzipan "fruit," a confection frequently wrapped around a paper motto.
70 "Caledonian locks" indicates long hair; a "Dutch nose" is flat; an "Austrian lip" is a protuberant lower lip associated with the Habsburg emperors; a "Spanish complexion" is dark implying Moorish background; and Chinese teeth were ostensibly stained black. The meaning of an Irish forehead is unclear.
71 table d'hôte.
72 Spa was a fashionable resort where visitors took the waters and carried on illicit affairs.
73 As war became an increasingly global matter, peace negotiations, such as the Peace of Paris in 1763, involved delegations from a large number of nations.
74 *united*: married.
75 Poaching was a capital offence throughout the eighteenth century.
76 *law merchant*: "body of rules regulating trade and commerce between different countries" (OED).
77 A series of puns linking scandal and financial infractions. "Currency" simultaneously signifies the circulation of scandal and money as a medium of exchange. "Drawer" is both one who invents the lie and one who withdraws money on a bill of exchange. "Endorsers" are both those who give credit to slander by repeating it and those who legitimate a bill of exchange by putting their name to it. "Come on" means both attack and demand repayment.
78 There's no earlier direction for Surface to kneel.
79 A cicibeo was an escort who took the public place of the husband in some European societies.
80 Politics here means scheming.
81 *stool of repentance*: "a stool formerly placed in a conspicuous position in some Scottish churches, on which was seated a person required to make a public display of repentance for a sin, esp. a sin involving extramarital sex" (OED).
82 *compound*: settle his debts and liabilities.
83 *cross accident*: adversity or adverse events.
84 *jet*: "the real ground or point of an action at law, hence the substance of any matter" (OED).
85 He has been imprisoned for debt.
86 He has obtained permission from his gaolers.
87 Shakespeare, *2 Henry IV*, 4.3.31–32. Rowley is comparing Charles to the dissolute Prince Hal.
88 Because the financial system depended on paper credit, forgery was a capital offence.
89 "A continuation of Jewry Street, running from Aldgate to Mark Lane" (Price).
90 *represent*: impersonate.
91 Legislation passed just prior to the opening of the play. It "protected minors from paying more than 10 shillings per L100 per annum to moneylenders" (Cordner 399). According to Price, the character of Moses was reputed to be a caricature of Benjamin Hopkins, who was believed to be making usurious loans to minors. He was standing for re-election as the Government's candidate for the Chamberlain of the City of London, and the parallel almost scuttled the license for Sheridan's play.
92 Lady Teazle plays on Sir Peter's joking demand for a bond by offering her hand to be kissed and referring to the gesture as a "note of hand."
93 A financial arrangement that would allow Lady Teazle to live separately from her husband.
94 Joseph is Charles's older brother and thus he inherited the house. And the implication is that he burdened his own brother in the sale.
95 *bags and bouquets*: perks.
96 Manuscript does not mark Aside.
97 Brush is Charles's valet.
98 This refers again to the Annuity Bill. See note 91.

99 Trip expects to be given some of his master's clothing and this opens a string of jokes on investment and inheritance. A reversion was money paid in anticipation of inheritance and a post obit is a bond given by a borrower that is payable after the death of a specified person—in this case a bond given to a moneylender by an expectant heir promising to pay when his benefactor dies.
100 *play*: gambling.
101 He is living only on the game of hazard, a particularly volatile dice game.
102 *peers*: equals.
103 *sentiment*: aphorism or, in this context, a toast.
104 Charles is not indulging in flattery or preliminary rituals.
105 *connections*: relatives.
106 This indication of Aside does not appear in manuscript.
107 See note 99.
108 *principal*: the original amount of a loan before interest.
109 Charles insinuates that "*Mr. Premium*" is afraid that Sir Oliver will have a long life.
110 *plate*: silver.
111 *race cups and corporation bowls*: cups or prizes won at horse races and silver bowls awarded to recognize public or civic service.
112 Shakespeare, *The Merchant of Venice*, 1.3.143–50.
113 Back to the Norman Conquest (1066).
114 *volunteer graces*: no excess ornamentation, implying that the countenances are beautiful of themselves.
115 *your modern Raphael*: Sir Joshua Reynolds's portrait practice was renowned for subordinating likeness to overall pictorial effects.
116 Richard Brinsley Sheridan was heir to Thomas Sheridan.
117 Charles's actions would kill his father if he were not already dead.
118 A ravelin was a fortification.
119 The Duke of Marlborough led the British forces in Europe during the War of Spanish Succession.
120 Battle of Malplaquet (1709) was one of the bloodiest battles in the War of Spanish Succession. Although Marlborough and Prince Eugene of Savoy technically won the battle, the massive loss of life made it a phyrric victory. Reaction to the battle turned public opinion against the war.
121 The uniforms of modern officers were considerably less ornate than those of the early eighteenth century.
122 There are no asides marked through this section.
123 Sir Godfrey Kneller was the pre-eminent portrait painter in England in the late seventeenth and early eighteenth centuries. He painted all the major figures of Augustan England, but his work was considered formulaic by the time of Sheridan's play.
124 Judges rode around the countryside to hear cases. The western circuit was one of six circuits in England and Wales.
125 The Woolsack refers to the seat occupied by the Lord Chancellor who administered the circuit courts.
126 "These gentlemen" refers to the paintings.
127 *nabob*: a pejorative term used to describe wealthy merchants and military men who made their fortunes in the employ of the East India Company. In the 1770s they were seen as class interlopers and as a threat to the landed gentry.
128 Moses takes one third of the money as a commission.
129 *so deep*: for such large sums.
130 Fourth in the MS, but it is third.
131 Someone with a plethora was believed to have too much blood.
132 *trapan*: to entrap.
133 Genesis, 39:12. The Biblical Joseph rejected the explicit advances of his master's wife.
134 *policy*: strategic acumen.
135 *speculative*: theoretical.
136 The manuscript has "finger's" here.
137 Black tea from China; songbirds and firecrackers from India.

138 This indication of Aside does not appear in manuscript.
139 According to the Plate Tax of 1756 a household that owned more than 100 ounces of real silver had to pay a tax to the government. Joseph states that in the face of such a law it is better to own imitation silver, thus it is better to appear charitable than actually perform charitable acts.
140 Although not noted in the MS, Rowley must exit here.
141 *hartshorn*: ammonium smelling salts.
142 A fencing term denoting second position wherein one's blade is thrust below the blade of the opponent.
143 Students at Eton conducted a procession called the Montem on Whit Tuesday.
144 Bust of the Roman letter writer. It is apt that the bullet rebounds off of the bust and wounds the letter-carrier.
145 *double letter*: "a letter written on two sheets and charged double postage" (OED).
146 *one of the faculty*: a doctor.
147 *given you over*: given you up for dead.
148 *high words*: expressions of anger.
149 Newspaper advertisements were frequently signed A. B. and transactions were carried out at specified coffee houses.
150 *recollect*: compose.
151 "Sneak" in the manuscript.
152 *suborning*: abetting.
153 Bayes is the inept playwright made famous in Buckingham's *The Rehearsal*. Buckingham was satirizing Dryden, but in this period it was one of Garrick's most renowned roles.
154 *loo*: a card game. "Seven's the main" refers to the dice game of hazard.
155 the cushion'd Tête: Georgian hair styles often attained height by pinning hair to a small cushion on the head.
156 *Card-drum*: card parties at a private residence associated with suspect forms of domiciliary sociability.
157 These are all card terms.
158 Abington was only ever cast in comedy.
159 Augustus Hervey, 3rd Earl of Bristol (1724–1779) had a distinguished naval career during the Seven Years' War and went on to have an active career in Parliament.
160 Mary Nesbitt (1742/3–1825) started her career as a model for Sir Joshua Reynolds and became a notable courtesan or demi-rep.
161 The fashionable Elizabeth Chudleigh (1721–88) secretly married Hervey in 1744 but they quickly separated. Since the marriage was secret it did not seem necessary to dissolve the union. Both Hervey and Chudleigh went on to have numerous high profile affairs: he with the demi-rep Mary Nesbitt and she with a series of admirers. Chudleigh eventually attracted the favors of the Duke of Kingston. This scandalous account tracks Chudleigh's career up to the point of her trial for bigamy. She was tried as a peer in Westminster Hall in 1776 and found guilty of bigamy by 116 peers without dissent. She quickly fled the country to France. Samuel Foote satirized her in *A Trip to Calais*, but the Lord Chamberlain prevented its production.
162 Alexander Nesbitt (1730–1772) was a merchant banker in the City.

18. *The Belle's Stratagem*

THE BELLE'S STRATAGEM. **HANNAH COWLEY.**
FIRST PERFORMED 22 FEBRUARY 1780 AND FIRST PUBLISHED 1782

18.1 *THE BELLE'S STRATAGEM*[1]

Hannah Cowley

First Performed 22 February 1780 and First Published 1782

As WITH APHRA BEHN AND SUSANNAH CENTLIVRE, we are now at a moment when Hannah Cowley's stature as a playwright can be recognized.[2] She sent her first play *The Runaway* (1776) to David Garrick anonymously. Staged at Drury Lane with Sarah Siddons in the lead role, the play was a huge financial success, in part because of its controversial rejection of arranged marriages. Cowley spent her entire career attacking the injustice of British marriage law and gender relations more generally. Her comedies went head-to-head with Sheridan's great work of the 1770s and she emerged as both his greatest competitor and arguably his most trenchant critic. Both Sheridan, in his role as manager of Drury Lane, and Thomas Harris, the manager at Covent Garden, made a pact to impede her rise. Sheridan prevented a second run of *The Runaway* and both Sheridan and Harris turned down her first tragedy *Albina*. *Albina* was eventually produced at the Haymarket in 1779, but the play became involved in a different kind of controversy. Shortly after *Albina* opened, Drury Lane staged not one but two plays by Hannah More that bore "wonderful resemblances" to Cowley's play. The ensuing conflict regarding the plagiarism flooded the newspapers and prompted much commentary on the propriety of women's place in the public sphere.

In many ways the controversy was the perfect precursor for Cowley's masterpiece, *The Belle's Stratagem*. The play is a thorough meditation on the politics of female sociability and the gendering of public space. Yet the play's feminist analysis of marriage and gender performance is itself a virtuoso critique of the theatrical tropes used to regulate gender norms. As Gillian Russell has argued, her complex comedies are often explicit re-workings of Sheridan's material.[3] In *The Belle's Stratagem* Cowley incorporates one of Sheridan's more controversial inventions, the Jew Isaac Mendoza from *The Duenna*, into the great masquerade scene. Audiences would have immediately understood that her agonistic relation to Sheridan was not only a function of theatrical rivalry, but also a matter of substantial concern for the politics of gender in the Georgian period. Both *The Belle's Stratagem* and its sequel of sorts *Which is the Man?* explicitly scrutinize the efficacy of British masculinity during a period when the empire's political and military leaders were at a loss as to how to deal with the American crisis. In this regard, Cowley's plays from the period of the American war need to be read in relation to this great political and social upheaval. Cowley met the challenge of imagining British theatrical practice in the wake of American decolonization with another great comedy *A Bold Stroke for a Husband* (1783). Like *The Belle's Stratagem*, *A Bold Stroke* not only reworked key scripts from the past, in this case Centlivre's *A Bold Stroke for a Wife*, but also re-activated the cross-dressed heroine for a new era. Cowley's post-war plays remained commercially successful and since Sheridan had retired from playwriting she was deprived of her primary male competitor. In the late 1780s and 1790s, the market for new five act comedy was dominated for the first time by two women: Cowley's work was now competing with that of Elizabeth Inchbald. In spite of strong receipts, *A School for Greybeards* (1786), *The Fate of Sparta* (1788), *A Day in Turkey, or, The Russian Slaves* (1791), and *The Town Before You* (1794) all generated controversy in the press. Each in their own way challenged received notions of female decorum. And each struggled to assert the primacy of spoken theatre against the increasing taste for spectacle, pantomime, and comic opera.

The Belle's Stratagem exhibits all the hallmarks of Cowley's practice. Like much of her work, the comedy directly addresses women's agency in the sexual marketplace, but its real innovation lies in the exploration of how Georgian society gendered spaces of social interaction. The proliferation of sites of leisure throughout the 1760s and 1770s was met with enthusiastic participation on the part of patrons and with increasing unease among constituencies with a moral and/or commercial interest in the status quo. Among the most resistant to these new forms of entertainment were the theatrical establishment, whose monopoly was now challenged by a wide variety of venues featuring music, dancing, masquerade, gambling, and other social practices. The resistance to these changes in leisure was almost always staged in terms of sexual and social decorum. The incorporation of the Pantheon—one of the most notorious and innovative entertainment ventures of the time—into *The Belle's Stratagem* is crucial to its politics and to its dramaturgy. By naming the space and by insisting on the recreation of the Pantheon's famous decorations, Cowley directly engaged with the controversy concerning new forms of sociability. But even more importantly, the staging of a masquerade within the play itself allowed for an exploration of all manner of social performance. Letitia Hardy's masquerade is an enabling act and proves instrumental to the reform of Doricourt's masculinity. At a time when masquerade was being routinely critiqued as a suspect practice, Cowley's validation of performance not only argued for the necessity of female autonomy and agency, but also for the importance of performance itself as a way to think about social relations.

This is why Cowley continually re-works past plays or texts. Her entire oeuvre can be seen as a remediation or critique of prior theatrical practice. This intervention is often signaled by the play's titles: *The Belle's Stratagem* modifies George Farquhar's *The Beaux' Stratagem* and by a simple substitution declares that women can control their social and sexual destiny. But in a more complex fashion her plays are often directly in dialogue with recent or concurrent theatrical productions. The productive struggle with Sheridan's success meant that London theatregoers in the 1770s and 1780s were continually asked to evaluate their own investment in the misogyny of comedy and of eighteenth-century society at large. It is perhaps this deep engagement with received theatrical practice that has made it so difficult to recognize her genius and her audacity.

To The Queen[4]

Madam,

In the following comedy, my purpose was, to draw a female character, which with the most lively sensibility, fine understanding, and elegant accomplishments, should unite that beautiful reserve and delicacy which, whilst they veil those charms, render them still more interesting. In delineating such a character, my heart naturally dedicated it to Your Majesty; and nothing remained, but permission to lay it at Your feet. Your Majesty's graciously allowing me this high honour is the point to which my hopes aspired, and a reward, of which without censure I may be proud.

Madam,

With the warmest wishes for the continuance of your Majesty's felicity, I am Your Majesty's most devoted and most dutiful Servant,

H. Cowley.

Dramatis Personæ

Men

Doricourt	Mr. Lewis
Hardy	Mr. Quick[5]
Sir George Touchwood	Mr. Wroughton
Flutter	Mr. Lee Lewes
Saville	Mr. Aickin
Villers	Mr. Whitfield
Courtall	Mr. Robson
Silvertongue	Mr. W. Bates
Crowquill	Mr. Jones
First Gentleman	Mr. Thompson
Second Gentleman	Mr. L'Estrange
Mountebank	Mr. Booth
French Servant	Mr. Wewitzer
Porter	Mr. Fearon
Dick	Mr. Stevens

Women

Letitia Hardy	Miss Younge
Mrs. Racket	Mrs. Mattocks
Lady Frances Touchwood	Mrs. Hartley
Miss Ogle	Mrs. Morton
Kitty Willis	Miss Stewart
Lady	Mrs. Poussin

Masqueraders, Tradesmen, Servants, &c.

I.i

[*Lincoln's-Inn.*[6] *Enter* Saville, *followed by a* Servant, *at the top of the stage, looking round, as if at a loss.*]

SAVILLE. Lincoln's-Inn!—Well, but where to find him, now I am in Lincoln's-Inn?—Where did he say his master was?

SERVANT. He only said in Lincoln's-Inn, Sir.

SAVILLE. That's pretty! And your wisdom never enquired at whose chambers?

SERVANT. Sir, you spoke to the servant yourself.

SAVILLE. If I was too impatient to ask questions, you ought to have taken directions, blockhead! [*Enter* Courtall *singing*] Ha, Courtall!—Bid him keep the horses in motion, and then enquire at all the chambers round. [*Exit* Servant] What the devil brings you to this part of the town?—Have any of the Long Robes,[7] handsome wives, sisters or chambermaids?

COURTALL. Perhaps they have;—but I came on a different errand; and, had thy good fortune brought thee here half an hour sooner, I'd have given thee such a treat, ha! ha! ha!

SAVILLE. I'm sorry I miss'd it: what was it?

COURTALL. I was informed a few days since, that my cousins Fallow were come to town, and desired earnestly to see me at their lodgings in Warwick-Court, Holborn. Away drove I, painting them all the way as so many Hebes.[8] They came from the farthest part of Northumberland, had never been in town, and in course were made up of rusticity, innocence, and beauty.

SAVILLE. Well!

COURTALL. After waiting thirty minutes, during which there was a violent bustle, in bounced five fallow damsels, four of them maypoles;—the fifth, Nature, by way of variety, had bent in the Æsop style.[9]—But they all opened at once, like hounds on a fresh scent:—"Oh, cousin Courtall! —How do you do, cousin Courtall! Lord, cousin, I am glad you are come! We want you to go with us to the park, and the plays, and the opera, and Almack's,[10] and all the fine places!"—The devil, thought I, my dears, may attend you, for I am sure I won't.—However, I heroically stayed an hour with them, and discovered, the virgins were all come to town with the hopes of leaving it—Wives:—their heads full of knight-baronights, fops,[11] and adventures.

SAVILLE. Well, how did you get off?

COURTALL. Oh, pleaded a million engagements. — However, conscience twitched me; so I reakfasted with them this morning, and afterwards 'squired them to the gardens here, as the most private place in town; and then took a sorrowful leave, complaining of my hard, hard fortune, that obliged me to set off immediately for Dorsetshire, ha! ha! ha!

SAVILLE. I congratulate your escape!—Courtall at Almack's, with five aukward country cousins! ha! ha! ha!—Why, your existence, as a man of gallantry, could never have survived it.

COURTALL. Death, and fire! had they come to town, like the rustics of the last age, to see Paul's, the Lions, and the Wax-work[12]—at their service;—but the cousins of our days come up ladies—and, with the knowledge they glean from magazines and pocket-books, fine ladies; laugh at the bashfulness of their grandmothers, and boldly demand their *entrées* in the first circles.

SAVILLE. Where can this fellow be!—Come, give me some news—I have been at war with woodcocks and partridges these two months, and am a stranger to all that has passed out of their region.

COURTALL. Oh! enough for three gazettes.[13] The ladies are going to petition for a bill, that, during the war,[14] every man may be allowed two wives.

SAVILLE. 'Tis impossible they should succeed, for the majority of both houses know what it is to have one.

COURTALL. Gallantry was black-ball'd at the *Coterie*[15] last Thursday, and Prudence and Chastity voted in.

SAVILLE. Ay, that may hold 'till the camps break up.[16]—But have ye no elopements? No divorces?

COURTALL. Divorces are absolutely out, and the commons-doctors[17] starving; so they are publishing trials of *Crim. Con.*[18] with all the separate evidences at large; which they find has always a wonderful effect on their trade, actions tumbling in upon them afterwards, like mackerel at Gravesend.[19]

SAVILLE. What more?

COURTALL. Nothing—for weddings, deaths, and politics, I never talk of, but whilst my hair is dressing. But prithee, Saville, how came you in town, whilst all the qualified gentry are playing at pop-gun on Coxheath, and the country over-run with hares and foxes?[20]

SAVILLE. I came to meet my friend Doricourt, who, you know, is lately arrived from Rome.

COURTALL. Arrived! Yes, faith, and has cut us all out!—His carriage, his liveries, his dress, himself, are the rage of the day! His first appearance set the whole *Ton* in a ferment, and his valet is besieged by *levées* of taylors, habit-makers, and other Ministers of Fashion, to gratify the impatience of their customers for becoming *à la mode de Doricourt*. Nay, the beautiful Lady Frolic, t'other night, with two sister countesses, insisted upon his waistcoat for muffs; and their snowy arms now bear it in triumph about town, to the heart-rending affliction of all our *beaux garçons*.[21]

SAVILLE. Indeed! Well, those little gallantries will soon be over; he's on the point of marriage.

COURTALL. Marriage! Doricourt on the point of marriage! 'Tis the happiest tidings you could have given, next to his being hanged—Who is the bride elect?

SAVILLE. I never saw her; but 'tis Miss Hardy, the rich heiress—the match was made by the parents, and the courtship begun on their nurses' knees; Master used to crow at Miss, and Miss used to chuckle at Master.

COURTALL. Oh! then by this time they care no more for each other, than I do for my country cousins.

SAVILLE. I don't know that; they have never met since thus high, and so, probably, have some regard for each other.

COURTALL. Never met! Odd!

SAVILLE. A whim of Mr. Hardy's; he thought his daughter's charms would make a more forcible impression, if her lover remained in ignorance of them 'till his return from the Continent.

[*Enter* Saville*'s* Servant.

SERVANT. Mr. Doricourt, Sir, has been at Counsellor Pleadwell's,[22] and gone about five minutes.

[*Exit* Servant.

SAVILLE. Five minutes! Zounds! I have been five minutes too late all my life-time!—Good morrow, Courtall; [*Going*] I must pursue him.

COURTALL. Promise to dine with me to-day; I have some honest fellows. [*Going off on the opposite side.*

SAVILLE. Can't promise; perhaps I may.—See there, there's a bevy of female Patagonians coming down upon us.

COURTALL. By the Lord, then, it must be my strapping cousins.—I dare not look behind me—Run, man, run. [*Exit, on the same side.*

I.ii

[*A hall at* Doricourt*'s. A gentle knock at the door. Enter the* Porter.]

PORTER. Tap! What sneaking devil art thou? [*Opens the door. Enter* Crowquill] So! I suppose *you* are one of Monsieur's customers too? He's above stairs, now, overhauling all his Honour's things to a parcel of 'em.

CROWQUILL. No, Sir; it is with you, if you please, that I want to speak.

PORTER. Me! Well, what do you want with me?

CROWQUILL. Sir, you must know that I am—I am the gentleman who writes the *tête-à-têtes* in the magazines.[23]

PORTER. Oh, oh!—What, you are the fellow that ties folks together, in your sixpenny cuts,[24] that never meet any where else?

CROWQUILL. Oh, dear Sir, excuse me!—We always go on *foundation*; and if you can help me to a few anecdotes of your master, such as what marchioness he lost money to, in Paris—who is his favourite lady in town—or the name of the girl he first made love to at college—or any incidents that happened to his Grandmother, or Great aunts—a couple will do, by way of supporters—I'll weave a web of intrigues, losses, and gallantries, between them, that shall fill four pages, procure me a dozen dinners, and you, Sir, a bottle of wine for your trouble.

PORTER. Oh, oh! I heard the butler talk of you, when I lived at Lord Tinket's. But what the devil do you mean by a bottle of wine!—You gave him a crown for a retaining fee.

CROWQUILL. Oh, Sir, that was for a lord's amours; a commoner's are never but half. Why, I have had a baronet's for five shillings, though he was a married man, and changed his mistress every six weeks.

PORTER. Don't tell me! What signifies a baronet, or a bit of a lord, who, may be, was never further than sun and fun round London? *We* have travelled, man! My master has been in Italy, and over the whole island of Spain; talked to the

Queen of France, and danced with her at a masquerade. Ay, and such folks don't go to masquerades for nothing; but mum—not a word more—Unless you'll rank my master with a lord, I'll not be guilty of blabbing his secrets, I assure you.

CROWQUILL. Well, Sir, perhaps you'll throw in a hint or two of other families, where you've lived, that may be worked up into something; and so, Sir, here is one, two, three, four, five shillings.

PORTER. [*Pocketing the money*] Well, that's honest. To tell you the truth, I don't know much of my master's concerns yet;—but here comes Monsieur and his gang: I'll pump them: they have trotted after him all round Europe, from the Canaries to the Isle of Wight.

[*Enter several foreign* Servants *and two* Tradesmen. *The* Porter *takes one of them aside.*

TRADESMAN. Well then, you have shew'd us all?

FRENCHMAN. All, *en vérité, Messieurs!* you *avez* seen every ting. *Serviteur, serviteur.* [*Exeunt* Tradesmen] Ah, here comes one *autre* curious Englishman, and dat's one *autre* guinea *pour moi.* [*Enter* Saville] *Allons, Monsieur,* dis way; I will shew you tings, such tings you never see, begar, in England!—velvets by Le Mosse, suits cut by Verdue, trimmings by Grossette, embroidery by Detanville—[25]

SAVILLE. Puppy!—where is your master?

PORTER. Zounds! you chattering frog-eating dunderhead, can't you see a gentleman?—'Tis Mr. Saville.

FRENCHMAN. Monsieur Saville! *Je suis mort de peur.*—Ten thousand pardons! *Excusez mon erreur,* and permit me you conduct to Monsieur Doricourt; he be too happy *à vous voir.* [*Exeunt* Frenchman *and* Saville.

PORTER. Step below a bit;—we'll make it out some-how!—I suppose a slice of sirloin won't make the story go down the worse. [*Exeunt* Porter *and* Crowquill.

I.iii

[*An apartment at* Doricourt*'s. Enter* Doricourt.]

DORICOURT. [*Speaking to a servant behind*] I shall be too late for St. James's; bid him come immediately.

[*Enter* Frenchman *and* Saville.

FRENCHMAN. Monsieur Saville. [*Exit* Frenchman.

DORICOURT. Most fortunate! My dear Saville, let the warmth of this embrace speak the pleasure of my heart.

SAVILLE. Well, this is some comfort, after the scurvy reception I met with in your hall.—I prepared my mind, as I came up stairs, for a *bon jour,* a grimace, and an *adieu.*

DORICOURT. Why so?

SAVILLE. Judging of the master from the rest of the family. What the devil is the meaning of that flock of foreigners below, with their parchment faces and snuffy whiskers? What! can't an Englishman stand behind your carriage, buckle your shoe, or brush your coat?

DORICOURT. Stale, my dear Saville, stale! Englishmen make the best soldiers, citizens, artizans, and philosophers in the world; but the very worst footmen. I keep French fellows and Germans, as the Romans kept slaves; because their own countrymen had minds too enlarged and haughty to descend with a grace to the duties of such a station.

SAVILLE. A good excuse for a bad practice.

DORICOURT. On my honour, experience will convince you of its truth. A Frenchman neither hears, sees, nor breathes, but as his master directs; and his whole system of conduct is compris'd in one short word, *obedience*! An Englishman reasons, forms opinions, cogitates, and disputes; he is the mere creature of your will: the other, a being, conscious of equal importance in the universal scale with yourself, and is therefore your judge, whilst he wears your livery, and decides on your actions with the freedom of a censor.

SAVILLE. And this in defence of a custom I have heard you execrate, together with all the adventitious manners imported by our travell'd gentry.

DORICOURT. Ay, but that was at eighteen; we are always *very* wise at eighteen. But consider this point: we go into Italy, where the sole business of the people is to study and improve the powers of music: we yield to the fascination, and grow enthusiasts in the charming science: we travel over France, and see the whole kingdom composing ornaments, and inventing fashions: we condescend to avail ourselves of their industry and adopt their modes: we return to England, and find the nation intent on the most important objects; polity, commerce, war, with all the liberal arts, employ her sons; the latent sparks glow afresh within our bosoms; the sweet follies of the Continent imperceptibly slide away, whilst senators, statesmen, patriots and heroes, emerge from the *virtû* of Italy, and the frippery of France.

SAVILLE. I may as well give it up! You had always the art of placing your faults in the best light; and I can't help loving you, faults and all: so, to start a subject which must please you, when do you expect Miss Hardy?

DORICOURT. Oh, the hour of expectation is past. She is arrived, and I this morning had the honour of an interview at Pleadwell's. The writings were ready; and, in obedience to the will of Mr. Hardy, we met to sign and seal.

SAVILLE. Has the event answered? Did your heart leap, or sink, when you beheld your mistress?

DORICOURT. Faith, neither one nor t'other; she's a fine girl, as far as mere flesh and blood goes.—But—

SAVILLE. But what?

DORICOURT. Why, she's *only* a fine girl; complexion, shape, and features; nothing more.

SAVILLE. Is not that enough?

DORICOURT. No! she should have spirit! fire! *l'air enjoué!*[26] that something, that nothing, which every body feels, and which no body can describe, in the resistless charmers of Italy and France.

SAVILLE. Thanks to the parsimony of my father, that kept me from travel! I would not have lost my relish for true unaffected English beauty, to have been quarrell'd for by all the belles of Versailles and Florence.

DORICOURT. Pho! thou hast no taste. *English* beauty! 'Tis insipidity; it wants the zest, it wants poignancy, Frank! why, I have known a Frenchwoman, indebted to nature for no one thing but a pair of decent eyes, reckon in her suite as many counts, marquisses, and *petits maîtres*,[27] as would satisfy three dozen of our first-rate toasts. I have known an Italian *marquizina* make ten conquests in stepping from her carriage, and carry her slaves from one city to another, whose real intrinsic beauty would have yielded to half the little *grisettes* that pace your Mall on a Sunday.[28]

SAVILLE. And has Miss Hardy nothing of this?

DORICOURT. If she has, she was pleased to keep it to herself. I was in the room half an hour before I could catch the colour of her eyes; and every attempt to draw her into conversation occasioned so cruel an embarrassment, that I was reduced to the necessity of news, French fleets, and Spanish captures, with her father.

SAVILLE. So Miss Hardy, with only beauty, modesty, and merit, is doom'd to the arms of a husband who will despise her.

DORICOURT. You are unjust. Though she has not inspir'd me with violent passion, my honour secures her felicity.

SAVILLE. Come, come, Doricourt, you know very well that when the honour of a husband is *locum-tenens*[29] for his heart, his wife must be as indifferent as himself, if she is not unhappy.

DORICOURT. Pho! never moralise without spectacles. But, as we are upon the tender subject, how did you bear Touchwood's carrying Lady Frances?

SAVILLE. You know I never look'd up to her with hope, and Sir George is every way worthy of her.

DORICOURT. *A la mode Angloise*, a philosopher even in love.

SAVILLE. Come, I detain you—you seem dress'd at all points, and of course have an engagement.

DORICOURT. To St. James's. I dine at Hardy's, and accompany them to the masquerade in the evening: but breakfast with me to-morrow, and we'll talk of our old companions; for I swear to you, Saville, the air of the Continent has not effaced one youthful prejudice or attachment.

SAVILLE.—With an exception to the case of ladies and servants.

DORICOURT. True; there I plead guilty:—But I have never yet found any man whom I could cordially take to my heart, and call Friend, who was not born beneath a British sky, and whose heart and manners were not truly English. [*Exit* Doricourt *and* Saville.

I.iv

[*An apartment at* Mr. Hardy*'s.* Villers *seated on a sopha, reading. Enter* Flutter.]

FLUTTER. Hah, Villers, have you seen Mrs. Racket?— Miss Hardy, I find, is out.

VILLERS. I have not seen her yet. I have made a voyage to Lapland since I came in [*Flinging away the book*] A lady at her toilette is as difficult to be moved, as a Quaker[30] [*Yawning*]. What events have happened in the world since yesterday? Have you heard?

FLUTTER. Oh, yes; I stopt at Tattersall's[31] as I came by, and there I found Lord James Jessamy, Sir William Wilding, and Mr.—. But, now I think of it, you sha'n't know a syllable of the matter; for I have been informed you never believe above one half of what I say.

VILLERS. My dear fellow, somebody has imposed upon you most egregiously!—Half! Why, I never believe one tenth part of what you say; that is, according to the plain and literal expression: but, as I understand you, your intelligence is amusing.

FLUTTER. That's very hard now, very hard. I never related a falsity in my life, unless I stumbled on it by mistake; and if it were otherwise, your dull matter-of-fact people are infinitely oblig'd to those warm imaginations which soar into fiction to amuse you; for, positively, the common events of this little dirty world are not worth talking about, unless you embellish 'em!—Hah! here comes Mrs. Racket: Adieu to weeds, I see! all life! [*Enter* Mrs. Racket] Enter, Madam, in all your charms! Villers has been abusing your toilette for keeping you so long; but I think we are much oblig'd to it, and so are you.

MRS. RACKET. How so, pray? Good-morning t'ye both. Here, here's a hand a-piece for you. [*They kiss her hands*.

FLUTTER. How so! because it has given you so many beauties.

MRS. RACKET. Delightful compliment! what do you think of that, Villers?

VILLERS. That he and his compliments are alike—shewy, but won't bear examining.—So you brought Miss Hardy to town last night?

MRS. RACKET. Yes, I should have brought her before, but I had a fall from my horse, that confined me a week.—I suppose in her heart she wished me hanged a dozen times an hour.

FLUTTER. Why?

MRS. RACKET. Had she not an expecting lover in town all the time? She meets him this morning at the lawyer's.—I hope she'll charm him; she's the sweetest girl in the world.

VILLERS. Vanity, like murder, will out.—You have convinced me you think yourself more charming.

MRS. RACKET. How can that be?

VILLERS. No woman ever praises another, unless she thinks herself superior in the very perfections she allows.

FLUTTER. Nor no man ever rails at the sex, unless he is conscious he deserves their hatred.

MRS. RACKET. Thank ye, Flutter—I'll owe ye a *bouquet* for that. I am going to visit the new-married Lady Frances Touchwood.—Who knows her husband?

FLUTTER. Every body.

MRS. RACKET. Is there not something odd in his character?

VILLERS. Nothing, but that he is passionately fond of his wife;—and so petulant is his love, that he open'd the cage of a favourite Bullfinch, and sent it to catch Butterflies, because she rewarded its song with her kisses.

MRS. RACKET. Intolerable monster! Such a brute deserves—

VILLERS. Nay, nay, nay, nay, this is your sex now—Give a woman but one stroke of character, off she goes, like a ball from a racket; sees the whole man, marks him down for an angel or a devil, and so exhibits him to her acquaintance.—This monster! this brute! is one of the worthiest fellows upon earth; sound sense, and a liberal mind; but doats on his wife to such excess, that he quarrels with every thing she admires, and is jealous of her tippet and nosegay.

MRS. RACKET. Oh, less love for me, kind Cupid! I can see no difference between the torment of such an affection, and hatred.

FLUTTER. Oh, pardon me, inconceivable difference, inconceivable; I see it as clearly as your bracelet. In the one case the husband would say, as Mr. Snapper said t'other day, Zounds! Madam, do you suppose that *my* table, and *my* house, and *my* pictures!—*A-propos, des bottes*.[32] There was the divinest Plague of Athens sold yesterday at Langford's![33] the dead figures so natural, you would have sworn they had been alive! Lord Primrose bid five hundred—Six, said Lady Carmine.—A thousand, said Ingot the Nabob.[34]—Down went the hammer.—A *rouleau* for your bargain, said Sir Jeremy Jingle. And what answer do you think Ingot made him?

MRS. RACKET. Why, took the offer.

FLUTTER. Sir, I would oblige you, but I buy this picture to place in the nursery: the children have already got Whittington and his Cat;[35] 'tis just this size, and they'll make good companions.

MRS. RACKET. Ha! ha! ha! well, I protest that's just the way now—the Nabobs and their wives outbid one at every sale, and the creatures have no more taste—

VILLERS. There again! You forget this story is told by Flutter, who always remembers every thing but the circumstances and the person he talks about:—'twas Ingot who offer'd a *rouleau* for the bargain, and Sir Jeremy Jingle who made the reply.

FLUTTER. Egad, I believe you are right.—Well, the story is as good one way as t'other, you know. Good morning. I am going to Mrs. Crotchet's concert, and in my way back shall make my bow at Sir George's. [*Going.*

VILLERS. I'll venture every figure in your taylor's bill, you make some blunder there.

FLUTTER. [*Turning back*] Done! My taylor's bill has not been paid these two years; and I'll open my mouth with as much care as Mrs. Bridget Button, who wears cork plumpers[36] in each cheek, and never hazards more than six words for fear of shewing them. [*Exit* Flutter.

MRS. RACKET. 'Tis a good-natur'd insignificant creature! let in every where, and cared for no where.—There's Miss Hardy return'd from Lincoln's-Inn:—she seems rather chagrin'd.

VILLERS. Then I leave you to your communications. [*Enter* Letitia, *followed by her* Maid] Adieu! I am rejoiced to see you so well, Madam! but I must tear myself away.

LETITIA. Don't vanish in a moment.

VILLERS. Oh, inhuman! you are two of the most dangerous women in town.—Staying here to be cannonaded by four such eyes is equal to a *rencontre* with Paul Jones, or a midnight march to Omoa![37]—[*Aside*] *They'll swallow the nonsense for the sake of the compliment.* [*Exit* Villers.

LETITIA. [*Gives her cloak to her maid*] Order Du Quesne never to come again; he shall posi-tively dress my hair no more. [*Exit* Maid] And this odious silk, how unbecoming it is!—I was bewitched to chuse it. [*Throwing herself on a sopha, and looking in a pocket-glass,* Mrs. Racket *staring at her*] Did you ever see such a fright as I am to-day?

MRS. RACKET. Yes, I have seen you look much worse.

LETITIA. How can you be so provoking? If I do not look this morning worse than ever I look'd in my life, I am naturally a fright. You shall have it which way you will.

MRS. RACKET. Just as you please; but pray what is the meaning of all this?

LETITIA. [*Rising*] Men are all dissemblers! flatterers! deceivers! have I not heard a thousand times of my air, my eyes, my shape—all made for victory! and to-day, when I bent my whole heart on one poor conquest, I have proved that all those imputed charms amount to nothing;—for Doricourt saw them unmov'd.—A husband of fifteen months could not have examined me with more cutting indifference.

MRS. RACKET. Then you return it like a wife of fifteen months, and be as indifferent as he.

LETITIA. Aye, there's the sting! The blooming boy, who left his image in my young heart, is at four and twenty improv'd in every grace that fix'd him there. It is the same face that my memory, and my dreams, constantly painted to me; but its graces are finished, and every beauty heightened. How mortifying, to feel myself at the same moment his slave, and an object of perfect indifference to him!

MRS. RACKET. How are you certain that was the case? Did you expect him to kneel down before the lawyer, his clerks, and, your father, to make oath of your beauty?

LETITIA. No; but he should have look'd as if a sudden ray had pierced him! he should have been breathless! speechless! for, oh! Caroline, all this was I.

MRS. RACKET. I am sorry you was such a fool. Can you expect a man, who has courted and been courted by half the fine women in Europe, to feel like a girl from a boarding-school? He is the prettiest fellow you have seen, and in course bewilders your imagination; but he has seen a million of pretty women, child, before he saw you; and his first feelings have been over long ago.

LETITIA. Your raillery distresses me; but I will touch his heart, or never be his wife.

MRS. RACKET. Absurd, and romantic! if you have no reason to believe his heart pre-engaged, be satisfied; if he is a man of honour, you'll have nothing to complain of.

LETITIA. Nothing to complain of! Heav'ns! shall I marry the man I adore, with such an expectation as that?

MRS. RACKET. And when you have fretted yourself pale, my dear, you'll have mended your expectation greatly.

LETITIA. [*Pausing*] Yet I have one hope. If there is any power whose peculiar care is faithful love, that power I invoke to aid me.

[*Enter* Mr. Hardy.

HARDY. Well, now; wasn't I right? Aye, Letty! aye, Cousin Racket! wasn't I right? I knew 'twould be so. He was all agog to see her before he went abroad; and, if he had, he'd have thought no more of her face, may be, than his own.

MRS. RACKET. May be, not half so much.

HARDY. Aye, may be so:—but I see into things; exactly as I foresaw, to-day he fell desperately in love with the wench, he! he! he!

LETITIA. Indeed, Sir! how did you perceive it?

HARDY. That's a pretty question! How do I perceive every thing? How did I foresee the fall of corn, and the rise of taxes? How did I know, that if we quarrelled with America, Norway deals would be dearer? How did I foretell that a war would sink the funds? How did I forewarn Parson Homily, that if he didn't some way or other contrive to get more votes than Rubrick, he'd lose the lectureship? How did I—But what the devil makes you so dull, Letitia? I thought to have found you popping about as brisk as the jacks of your harpsichord.

LETITIA. Surely, Sir, 'tis a very serious occasion.

HARDY. Pho, pho! girls should never be grave before marriage. How did you feel, Cousin, beforehand? Aye!

MRS. RACKET. Feel! why exceedingly full of cares.

HARDY. Did you?

MRS. RACKET. I could not sleep for thinking of my coach, my liveries, and my chairmen; the taste of clothes I should be presented in, distracted me for a week; and whether I should be married in white or lilac, gave me the most cruel anxiety.

LETITIA. And is it possible that you felt no other care?

HARDY. And pray, of what sort may your cares be, Mrs. Letitia? I begin to foresee now that you have taken a dislike to Doricourt.

LETITIA. Indeed, Sir, I have not.

HARDY. Then what's all this melancholy about? A'n't you going to be married? And, what's more, to a sensible man? And, what's more to a young girl, to a handsome man? And what's all this melancholy for, I say?

MRS. RACKET. Why, because he *is* handsome and sensible, and because she's over head and ears in love with him; all which, it seems, your fore-knowledge had not told you a word of.

LETITIA. Fye, Caroline!

HARDY. Well, come, do you tell me what's the matter then? If you don't like him, hang the signing and sealing, he sha'n't have ye:—and yet I can't say that neither; for you know that estate, that cost his father and me upwards of fourscore thousand pounds, must go all to him if you won't have him: if he won't have you, indeed, 'twill be all yours. All that's clear, engross'd upon parchment, and the poor dear man set his hand to it whilst he was a dying.—"Ah!" said I, "I foresee you'll never live to see 'em come together; but their first son shall be christened Jeremiah after you, that I promise you."— But come, I say, what is the matter? Don't you like him?

LETITIA. I fear, Sir—if I must speak—I fear I was less agreeable in Mr. Doricourt's eyes, than he appeared in mine.

HARDY. There you are mistaken; for I asked him, and he told me he liked you vastly. Don't you think he must have taken a fancy to her?

MRS. RACKET. Why really I think so, as I was not by.

LETITIA. My dear Sir, I am convinced he has not; but if there is spirit or invention in woman, he shall.

HARDY. Right, girl; go to your toilette—

LETITIA. It is not my toilette that can serve me: but a plan has struck me, if you will not oppose it, which flatters me with brilliant success.

HARDY. Oppose it! not I indeed! what is it?

LETITIA. Why, Sir—it may seem a little paradoxical; but, as he does not like me enough, I want him to like me still less, and will at our next interview endeavour to heighten his indifference into dislike.

HARDY. Who the devil could have foreseen that?

MRS. RACKET. Heaven and earth! Letitia, are you serious?

LETITIA. As serious as the most important business of my life demands.

MRS. RACKET. Why endeavour to make him dislike you?

LETITIA. Because 'tis much easier to convert a sentiment into its opposite, than to transform indifference into tender passion.

MRS. RACKET. That may be good philosophy, but I am afraid you'll find it a bad maxim.

LETITIA. I have the strongest confidence in it. I am inspired with unusual spirits, and on this hazard willingly stake my chance for happiness. I am impatient to begin my measures. [*Exit* Letitia.

HARDY. Can you foresee the end of this, Cousin?

MRS. RACKET. No, Sir; nothing less than your penetration can do that, I am sure; and I can't stay now to consider it. I am going to call on the Ogles, and then to Lady Frances Touchwood's, and then to an auction, and then—I don't know where—but I shall be at home time enough to witness this extraordinary interview. Good-bye. [*Exit* Mrs. Racket.

HARDY. Well, 'tis an odd thing—I can't understand it—but I foresee Letty will have her way, and so I sha'n't give myself the trouble to dispute it.

[*Exit* Hardy.

II.i

[*Sir* George Touchwood*'s. Enter* Doricourt *and* Sir George.]

DORICOURT. Married, ha! ha! ha! you, whom I heard in Paris say such things of the sex, are in London a married man.

SIR GEORGE. The sex is still what it has ever been since *la petite morale*[38] banished substantial virtues; and rather than have given my name to one of your high-bred fashionable dames, I'd have crossed the line in a fire-ship, and married a Japanese.

DORICOURT. Yet you have married an English beauty, yea, and a beauty born in high life.

SIR GEORGE. True; but she has a simplicity of heart and manners, that would have become the fair Hebrew damsels toasted by the Patriarchs.

DORICOURT. Ha! ha! Why, thou art a downright matrimonial Quixote.[39] My life on't, she becomes as mere a Town Lady in six months as though she had been bred to the trade.

SIR GEORGE. [*Contemptuously*] Common—common—No, Sir, Lady Frances despises high life so much from the ideas I have given her, that she'll live in it like a salamander in fire.

DORICOURT. Oh, that the circle *dans la place Victoire*[40] could witness thy extravagance! I'll send thee off to St. Evreux this night,[41] drawn at full length, and coloured after nature.

SIR GEORGE. Tell him then, to add to the ridicule, that Touchwood glories in the name of husband; that he has found in one Englishwoman more beauty than Frenchmen ever saw, and more goodness than Frenchwomen can conceive.

DORICOURT. Well—enough of description. Introduce me to this phœnix;[42] I came on purpose.

SIR GEORGE. Introduce!—oh, aye, to be sure—I believe Lady Frances is engaged just now—but another time.—[*Aside*] *How handsome the dog looks to-day!*

DORICOURT. Another time!—but I have no other time. 'Sdeath! this is the only hour I can command this fortnight!

SIR GEORGE.—[*Aside*] *I am glad to hear it, with all my soul.*—[*To him*] So then, you can't dine with us to-day? That's very unlucky.

DORICOURT. Oh, yes—as to dinner—yes, I can, I believe, contrive to dine with you to-day.

SIR GEORGE. Psha! I didn't think on what I was saying; I meant supper—You can't sup with us?

DORICOURT. Why, supper will be rather more convenient than dinner—But you are fortunate—if you had ask'd me any other night, I could not have come.

SIR GEORGE. To-night!—Gad, now I recollect, we are particularly engaged to-night.—But to-morrow night—

DORICOURT. Why look ye, Sir George, 'tis very plain you have no inclination to let me see your wife at all; so here I sit [*Throws himself on a sopha*].—There's my hat, and here are my legs.—Now I sha'n't stir till I have seen her; and I have no engagements: I'll breakfast, dine, and sup with you every day this week.

SIR GEORGE. Was there ever such a provoking wretch! but, to be plain with you, Doricourt, I and my house are at your service: but you are a damn'd agreeable fellow, and ten years younger than I am; and the women, I observe, always simper when you appear. For these reasons, I had rather, when Lady Frances and I are together, that you should forget we are acquainted, further than a nod, a smile, or a how-d'ye.

DORICOURT. Very well.

SIR GEORGE. It is not merely yourself in *propriâ personâ*[43] that I object to; but, if you are intimate here, you'll make my house still more the fashion than it is; and it is already so much so, that my doors are of no use to me. I married Lady Frances to engross her to myself; yet such is the blessed freedom of modern manners, that, in spite of me, her eyes, thoughts, and conversation, are continually divided amongst all the flirts and coxcombs of Fashion.

DORICOURT. To be sure, I confess that kind of freedom is carried rather too far. 'Tis hard one can't have a jewel in one's cabinet, but the whole town must be gratified with its lustre.—[*Aside*] *He sha'n't preach me out of seeing his wife, though.*

SIR GEORGE. Well, now, that's reasonable. When you take time to reflect, Doricourt, I always observe you decide right, and therefore I hope—

[*Enter* Servant.

SERVANT. Sir, my Lady desires—

SIR GEORGE. I am particularly engaged.

DORICOURT. Oh, Lord, that shall be no excuse in the world [*Leaping from the sopha*]. Lead the way, John.—I'll attend your Lady. [*Exit, following the* Servant.

SIR GEORGE. What devil possessed me to talk about her!—Here, Doricourt! [*Running after him*] Doricourt!

[*Enter* Mrs. Racket, *and* Miss Ogle, *followed by a* Servant.

MRS. RACKET. Acquaint your Lady, that Mrs. Racket, and Miss Ogle, are here.

[*Exit* Servant.

MISS OGLE. I shall hardly know Lady Frances, 'tis so long since I was in Shropshire.

MRS. RACKET. And I'll be sworn you never saw her *out* of Shropshire.—Her father kept her locked up with his caterpillars and shells; and loved her beyond any thing—but a blue butterfly, and a petrified frog!

MISS OGLE. Ha! ha! ha!—Well, 'twas a cheap way of breeding her:—you know he was very poor, though a lord; and very high-spirited, though a virtuoso.[44]—In town, her Pantheons, operas, and *robes de cour*,[45] would have swallowed his sea-weeds, moths, and monsters, in six weeks!—Sir George, I find, thinks his wife a most extraordinary creature: he has taught her to despise every thing like fashionable life, and boasts that example will have no effect on her.

MRS. RACKET. There's a great degree of impertinence in all that—I'll try to make her a fine lady, to humble him.

MISS OGLE. That's just the thing I wish.

[*Enter* Lady Frances.

LADY FRANCES. I beg ten thousand pardons, my dear Mrs. Racket.—Miss Ogle, I rejoice to see you: I should have come to you sooner, but I was detained in conversation by Mr. Doricourt.

MRS. RACKET. Pray make no apology; I am quite happy that we have your Ladyship in town at last.—What stay do you make?

LADY FRANCES. A short one! Sir George talks with regret of the scenes we have left; and as the ceremony of presentation[46] is over, will, I believe, soon return.

MISS OGLE. Sure he can't be so cruel! Does your Ladyship wish to return so soon?

LADY FRANCES. I have not the habit of consulting my own wishes; but, I think, if they decide, we shall not return immediately. I have yet hardly form'd an idea of London.

MRS. RACKET. I shall quarrel with your Lord and Master, if he dares think of depriving us of you so soon. How do you dispose of yourself to-day?

LADY FRANCES. Sir George is going with me this morning to the mercer's, to chuse a silk; and then—

MRS. RACKET. Chuse a silk for you! ha! ha! ha! Sir George chuses your laces too, I hope; your gloves, and your pincushions!

LADY FRANCES. Madam!

MRS. RACKET. I am glad to see you blush, my dear Lady Frances. These are strange homespun ways! If you do these things, pray keep 'em secret. Lord bless us! If the Town should know your husband chuses your gowns!

MISS OGLE. You are very young, my Lady, and have been brought up in solitude. The maxims you learnt among the wood-nymphs in Shropshire, won't pass current here, I assure you.

MRS. RACKET. Why, my dear creature, you look quite frighten'd!—Come, you shall go with us to an exhibition, and an auction.—Afterwards, we'll take a turn in the Park, and then drive to Kensington;[47]—so we shall be at home by four, to dress; and in the evening I'll attend you to Lady Brilliant's masquerade.

LADY FRANCES. I shall be very happy to be of your party, if Sir George has no engagements.

MRS. RACKET. What! Do you stand so low in your own opinion, that you dare not trust yourself without Sir George! If you chuse to play Darby and Joan,[48] my dear, you should have stay'd in the country;—'tis an exhibition not calculated for London, I assure you!

MISS OGLE. What I suppose, my Lady, you and Sir George, will be seen pacing it comfortably round the Canal, arm and arm, and then go lovingly into the same carriage;—dine *tête-à-tête*, spend the evening at picquet,[49] and so go soberly to bed at eleven!—Such a snug plan may do for an attorney and his wife; but, for Lady Frances Touchwood, 'tis as unsuitable as linsey-woolsey,[50] or a black bonnet at the *Festino!*[51]

LADY FRANCES. These are rather new doctrines to me!—But, my dear Mrs. Racket, you and Miss Ogle must judge of these things better than I can. As you observe, I am but young, and may have caught absurd opinions.—Here is Sir George!

[*Enter Sir* George.

SIR GEORGE. [*Aside*] *'Sdeath! another room full!*

LADY FRANCES. My love! Mrs. Racket, and the Miss Ogle.

MRS. RACKET. Give you joy, Sir George.—We came to rob you of Lady Frances for a few hours.

SIR GEORGE. A few hours!

LADY FRANCES. Oh, yes! I am going to an exhibition, and an auction, and the Park, and Kensington, and a thousand places!—It is quite ridiculous, I find, for married people to be always together—We shall be laughed at!

SIR GEORGE. I am astonished!—Mrs. Racket, what does the dear creature mean?

MRS. RACKET. Mean, Sir George!—what she says, I imagine.

MISS OGLE. Why, you know, Sir, as Lady Frances had the misfortune to be bred entirely in the country, she cannot be supposed to be versed in fashionable life.

SIR GEORGE. No; heaven forbid she should!—If she had, Madam, she would never have been my wife!

MRS. RACKET. Are you serious?

SIR GEORGE. Perfectly so.—I should never have had the courage to have married a well-bred fine lady.

MISS OGLE. [*Sneeringly*] Pray, Sir, what do you take a fine lady to be, that you express such fear of her?

SIR GEORGE. A being easily described, Madam, as she is seen every where, but in her own house. She sleeps at home, but she lives all over the town. In her mind, every sentiment gives place to the lust of conquest, and the vanity of being particular. The feelings of wife, and mother, are lost in the whirl of dissipation. If she continues virtuous, 'tis by chance—and if she preserves her husband from ruin, 'tis by her dexterity at the card-table!—Such a woman I take to be a perfect fine lady!

MRS. RACKET. And you I take to be a slanderous cynic of two-and-thirty.—Twenty years hence, one might have forgiven such a libel!—Now, Sir, hear my definition of a fine lady:—She is a creature for whom Nature has done much, and education more; she has taste, elegance, spirit, understanding. In her manner she is free, in her morals nice. Her behaviour is undistinguishingly polite to her husband, and all mankind;—her sentiments are for their hours of retirement. In a word, a fine lady is the life of conversation, the spirit of society, the joy of the public!—Pleasure follows where ever she appears, and the kindest wishes attend her slumbers.—Make haste, then, my dear Lady Frances, commence fine lady, and force your husband to acknowledge the justness of my picture!

LADY FRANCES. I am sure 'tis a delightful one. How can you dislike it, Sir George? You painted fashionable life in colours so disgusting, that I thought I hated it; but, on a nearer view, it seems charming. I have hitherto lived in obscurity; 'tis time that I should be a woman of the world. I long to begin;—my heart pants with expectation and delight!

MRS. RACKET. Come, then; let us begin directly. I am impatient to introduce you to that society, which you were born to ornament and charm.

LADY FRANCES. Adieu! my love!— [*Going*] We shall meet again at dinner.

SIR GEORGE. Sure, I am in a dream!—Fanny!

LADY FRANCES. [*Returning*] Sir George?

SIR GEORGE. Will you go without me?

MRS. RACKET. "Will you go without me!"—ha! ha! ha! what a pathetic address! Why, sure you would not always be seen side by side, like two beans upon a stalk. Are you afraid to trust Lady Frances with me, Sir?

SIR GEORGE. Heaven and earth! with whom can a man trust his wife, in the present state of society? Formerly there were distinctions of character amongst ye: every class of females had its particular description; grandmothers were pious, aunts, discreet, old maids censorious! but now aunts, grandmothers, girls, and maiden gentlewomen, are all the same creature;—a wrinkle more or less is the sole difference between ye.

MRS. RACKET. That maiden gentlewomen have lost their censoriousness, is surely not in your catalogue of grievances.

SIR GEORGE. Indeed it is—and ranked amongst the most serious grievances.—Things went well, Madam, when the tongues of three or four old virgins kept all the wives and daughters of a parish in awe. They were the dragons that guarded the Hesperian fruit;[52] and I wonder they have not been oblig'd, by act of parliament, to resume their function.

MRS. RACKET. Ha! ha! ha! and pension'd, I suppose, for making strict enquiries into the lives and conversations of their neighbours.

SIR GEORGE. With all my heart, and impowered to oblige every woman to conform her conduct to her real situation. You, for instance, are a widow: your air should be sedate, your dress grave, your deportment matronly, and in all things an example to the young women growing up about you!—instead of which, you are dress'd for conquest, think of nothing but ensnaring hearts; are a coquette, a wit, and a fine lady.

MRS. RACKET. Bear witness to what he says! A coquette! a wit! and a fine Lady! Who would have expected an eulogy from such an ill-natur'd mortal!—Valour to a soldier, wisdom to a judge, or glory to a prince, is not more than such a character to a woman.

MISS OGLE. Sir George, I see, languishes for the charming society of a century and a half ago; when a grave 'squire, and a still graver dame, surrounded by a sober family, form'd a stiff groupe in a mouldy old house in the corner of a park.

MRS. RACKET. Delightful serenity! undisturb'd by any noise but the cawing of rooks, and the quarterly rumbling of an old family-coach on a state-visit; with the happy intervention of a friendly call from the parish apothecary, or the curate's wife.

SIR GEORGE. And what is the society of which you boast?—a meer chaos, in which all distinction of rank is lost in a ridiculous affectation of ease, and every different order of beings huddled together, as they were before the creation. In the same *select party*, you will often find the wife of a bishop and a sharper, of an earl and a fidler. In short, 'tis one universal masquerade, all disguised in the same habits and manners.

SERVANT. Mr. Flutter. [*Exit* Servant.

SIR GEORGE. Here comes an illustration. Now I defy you to tell from his appearance, whether Flutter is a Privy Counsellor or a Mercer, a Lawyer, or a Grocer's 'Prentice.

[*Enter* Flutter.

FLUTTER. Oh, just which you please, Sir George; so you don't make me a Lord Mayor. Ah, Mrs. Racket!—Lady Frances, your most obedient; you look—now hang me, if that's not provoking!—had your gown been of another colour, I should have said the prettiest thing you ever heard in your life.

MISS OGLE. Pray give it us.

FLUTTER. I was yesterday at Mrs. Bloomer's. She was dress'd all in green; no other colour to be seen but that of her face and bosom. So says I, "My dear Mrs. Bloomer! you look like a carnation, just bursting from its pod."

SIR GEORGE. And what said her husband?

FLUTTER. Her husband! Why, her husband laugh'd, and said a cucumber would have been a happier simile.

SIR GEORGE. But there *are* husbands, Sir, who would rather have corrected than amended your comparison; I, for instance, should consider a man's complimenting my wife as an impertinence.

FLUTTER. Why, what harm can there be in compliments? Sure they are not infectious; and, if they were, you, Sir George, of all people breathing, have reason to be satisfied about your Lady's attachment; every body talks of it: that little bird there, that she killed out of jealousy, the most extraordinary instance of affection, that ever was given.

LADY FRANCES. I kill a bird through jealousy!—Heavens! Mr. Flutter, how can you impute such a cruelty to me?

SIR GEORGE. I could have forgiven you, if you had.

FLUTTER. Oh, what a blundering fool!—No, no—now I remember—'twas your bird, Lady Frances—that's it; your bullfinch, which Sir George, in one of the refinements of his passion, sent into the wide world to seek its fortune.—He took it for a knight in disguise.

LADY FRANCES. Is it possible! O, Sir George, could I have imagin'd it was you who depriv'd me of a creature I was so fond of?

SIR GEORGE. Mr. Flutter, you are one of those busy, idle, meddling people, who, from mere vacuity of mind, are the most dangerous inmates in a family. You have neither feelings nor opinions of your own; but, like a glass in a tavern, bear about those of every blockhead, who gives you his;—and, because you *mean* no harm, think yourselves excus'd, though broken friendships, discords, and murders, are the consequences of your indiscretions.

FLUTTER. [*Taking out his tablets*] Vacuity of mind!—What was the next? I'll write down this sermon; 'tis the first I have heard since my grandmother's funeral.

MISS OGLE. Come, Lady Frances, you see what a cruel creature your loving husband can be; so let us leave him.

SIR GEORGE. Madam, Lady Frances shall not go.

LADY FRANCES. *Shall* not, Sir George?—This is the first time such an expression—[*Weeping*.

SIR GEORGE. My love! my life!

LADY FRANCES. Don't imagine I'll be treated like a child! denied what I wish, and then pacified with sweet words.

MISS OGLE [*Apart*] The bullfinch! that's an excellent subject; never let it down.

LADY FRANCES. I see plainly you would deprive me of every pleasure, as well as of my sweet bird—out of pure love!—Barbarous man!

SIR GEORGE. 'Tis well, Madam;—your resentment of that circumstance proves to me, what I did not before suspect, that you are deficient both in tenderness and understanding.—Tremble to think the hour approaches, in which you would give worlds for such a proof of my love. Go, Madam, give yourself to the public; abandon your heart to dissipation, and see if, in the scenes of gaiety and folly that await you, you can find a recompence for the lost affection of a doating husband. [*Exit* Sir George.

FLUTTER. Lord! what a fine thing it is to have the gift of speech! I suppose Sir George practises at Coachmakers-hall,[53] or the Black-horse in Bond-street.[54]

LADY FRANCES. He is really angry; I cannot go.

MRS. RACKET. Not go! foolish creature! you are arrived at the moment, which some time or other was sure to happen; and everything depends on the use you make of it.

MISS OGLE. Come, Lady Frances! don't hesitate!—the minutes are precious.

LADY FRANCES. I could find in my heart!—and yet I won't give up neither.—If I should in this instance, he'll expect it for ever.

[*Exeunt* Lady Frances, *and* Mrs. Racket.

MISS OGLE. Now you act like a woman of spirit. [*Exit* Miss Ogle.

FLUTTER. A fair tug, by Jupiter—between duty and pleasure!—Pleasure beats, and off we go, *Iö! Triumphe*![55] [*Exit* Flutter.

II.ii

[*Scene changes to an auction room.—Busts, pictures, &c. &c. Enter* Silvertongue *with three* Puffers.]

SILVERTONGUE. Very well,—very well.—This morning will be devoted to curiosity; my sale begins to-morrow at eleven. But, Mrs. Fagg, if you do no better than you did in Lord Fillagree's sale, I shall discharge you.—You want[56] a knack terribly: and this dress—why, nobody can mistake you for a gentlewoman.

FAGG. Very true, Mr. Silvertongue; but I can't dress like a lady upon half-a-crown a day, as the saying is.—If you want me to dress like a lady, you must double my pay.—Double or quits, Mr. Silvertongue.

SILVERTONGUE.—*Five shillings* a day! what a demand! why, woman, there are a thousand parsons in the town, who don't make five shillings a day; though they preach, pray, christen, marry, and bury, for the good of the community.—Five shillings a day!—why, 'tis the pay of a lieutenant in a marching regiment, who keeps a servant, a mistress, a horse; fights, dresses, ogles, makes love, and dies upon five shillings a day.

FAGG. Oh, as to that, all that's very right. A soldier should not be too fond of life; and forcing him to do all these things upon five shillings a day, is the readiest way to make him tir'd on't.

SILVERTONGUE. Well, Mask, have you been looking into the antiquaries?—have you got all the terms of art in a string—aye?

MASK. Yes, I have: I know the age of a coin by the taste; and can fix the birth-day of a medal, *Anno Mundi* or *Anno Domini*,[57] though the green rust should have eaten up every character. But you know, the brown suit and the wig I wear when I personate the antiquary, are in limbo.[58]

SILVERTONGUE. Those you have on, may do.

MASK. These!—Why, in these I am a young travell'd *cognoscento*: Mr. Glib bought them of Sir Tom Totter's valet; and I am going there directly. You know his picture-sale comes on today; and I have got my head full of Parmegiano, Sal Rosa, Metzu, Tarbaek, and Vandermeer. I talk of the relief of Woovermans, the spirit of Teniers, the colouring of the Venetian School, and the correctness of the Roman. I distinguish Claude by his sleep, and Ruysdael by his water. The rapidity of Tintoret's pencil strikes me at the first glance; whilst the harmony of Vandyk, and the glow of Correggio, point out their masters.[59]

[*Enter company.*

1ST LADY. Hey-day, Mr. Silvertongue! what, nobody here?

SILVERTONGUE. Oh, my Lady, we shall have company enough in a trice; if your carriage is seen at my door, no other will pass it, I am sure.

1ST LADY.—[*Aside*] *Familiar monster!*—[*To him*] That's a beautiful Diana, Mr. Silvertongue; but in the name of wonder, how came Actæon to be placed on the top of a house?

SILVERTONGUE. That's a David and Bathsheba, Ma'am.[60]

LADY. Oh, I crave their pardon!—I remember the names, but know nothing of the story.

[*More company enters.*

1ST GENTLEMAN. Was not that Lady Frances Touchwood coming up with Mrs. Racket?

2ND GENTLEMAN. I think so;—yes, it is, faith.—Let us go nearer.

[*Enter* Lady Frances, Mrs. Racket, *and* Miss Ogle.

SILVERTONGUE. Yes, Sir, this is to be the first lot:—the *Model of a City*, in wax.

2ND GENTLEMAN. The *Model of a City*! What city?

SILVERTONGUE. That I have not been able to discover; but call it Rome, Pekin, or London, 'tis still a city: you'll find in it the same jarring interests, the same passions, the same virtues, and the same vices, whatever the name.

GENTLEMAN.[61] You may as well present us a map of *Terra Incognita.*

SILVERTONGUE. Oh, pardon me, Sir! a lively imagination would convert this waxen city into an endless and interesting amusement. For instance —look into this little house on the right-hand; there are four old prudes in it, taking care of their neighbours' reputations. This elegant mansion on the left, decorated with Corinthian pillars—who needs be told that it belongs to a court lord, and is the habitation of Patriotism, Philosophy, and Virtue? Here's a city hall—the rich steams that issue from the windows nourish a neighbouring work-house. Here's a church—we'll pass over that, the doors are shut. The parsonage-house comes next;—we'll take a peep here, however.—Look at the doctor! he's asleep on a volume of Toland; whilst his lady is putting on *rouge* for the masquerade.—Oh! oh! this can be no English city; our parsons are all orthodox, and their wives the daughters of Modesty and Meekness.

[Lady Frances *and* Miss Ogle *come forward, followed by* Courtall.

LADY FRANCES. I wish Sir George was here.—This man follows me about, and stares at me in such a way, that I am quite uneasy.

MISS OGLE. He has travell'd, and is heir to an immense estate; so he's impertinent by patent.

COURTALL. You are very cruel, Ladies. Miss Ogle—you will not let me speak to you. As to this little scornful beauty, she has frown'd me dead fifty times.

LADY FRANCES. Sir—[*Confus'd*] I am a married woman.

COURTALL.—[*Aside*] *A married woman! a good hint.*—[*To her*] 'Twould be a shame if such a charming woman was not married. But I see you are a Daphne just come from your sheep, and your meadows; your crook, and your waterfalls. Pray now, who is the happy Damon, to whom you have vow'd eternal truth and constancy?

MISS OGLE. 'Tis Lady Frances Touchwood, Mr. Courtall, to whom you are speaking.

COURTALL. Lady Frances!—[*Aside*] *By Heaven, that's Saville's old flame.*—[*To her*] I beg your Ladyship's pardon. I ought to have believed that such beauty could belong only to your name——a name I have long been enamour'd of; because I knew it to be that of the finest woman in the world.

[Mrs. Racket *comes forward.*

LADY FRANCES. [*Apart*] My dear Mrs. Racket, I am so frighten'd! here's a man making love to me, though he knows I am married.

MRS. RACKET. Oh, the sooner for that, my dear; don't mind him. Was you at the *Cassino* last night, Mr. Courtall?

COURTALL. I look'd in.—'Twas impossible to stay. No body there but antiques. You'll be at Lady Brilliant's to-night, doubtless?

MRS. RACKET. Yes, I go with Lady Frances.

LADY FRANCES. [*To* Miss Ogle] Bless me! I did not know this gentleman was acquainted with Mrs. Racket.—I behaved so rude to him!

MRS. RACKET. Come, Ma'am; [*Looking at her watch*] 'tis ha' past one. I protest, if we don't fly to Kensington, we sha'n't find a soul there.

LADY FRANCES. Won't this gentleman go with us?

COURTALL. [*Looking surpris'd*] To be sure, you make me happy, Madam, beyond description.

MRS. RACKET. Oh, never mind him—he'll follow.

[*Exeunt* Lady Frances, Mrs. Racket, *and* Miss Ogle.

COURTALL. Lady *Touchwood*! with a vengeance! But, 'tis always so;—your reserved ladies are like ice, 'egad!—no sooner begin to soften, than they melt. [*Following.*

III.i

[Mr. Hardy's. *Enter* Letitia *and* Mrs. Racket.]

MRS. RACKET. Come, prepare, prepare; your lover is coming.

LETITIA. My lover!—Confess now that my absence at dinner was a severe mortification to him.

MRS. RACKET. I can't absolutely swear it spoilt his appetite; he eat as if he was hungry, and drank his wine as though he liked it.

LETITIA. What was the apology?

MRS. RACKET. That you were ill;—but I gave him a hint, that your extreme bashfulness could not support his eye.

LETITIA. If I comprehend him, aukwardness and bashfulness are the last faults he can pardon in a woman; so expect to see me transform'd into the veriest maukin.[62]

MRS. RACKET. You persevere then?

LETITIA. Certainly. I know the design is a rash one, and the event important;—it either makes Doricourt mine by all the tenderest ties of passion, or deprives me of him for ever; and never to be his wife will afflict me less, than to be his wife and not be belov'd.

MRS. RACKET. So you wo'n't trust to the good old maxim—"Marry first, and love will follow"?

LETITIA. As readily as I would venture my last guinea, that good fortune might follow. The woman that has not touch'd the heart of a man before he leads her to the altar has scarcely a chance to charm it when possession and security turn their powerful arms against her.—But here he comes.—I'll disappear for a moment.—Don't spare me.

[*Exit* Letitia. *Enter* Doricourt, *not seeing* Mrs. Racket.

DORICOURT. So! [*Looking at a picture*] this is my mistress, I presume.—*Ma foi*! the painter has hit her off.—The downcast eye—the blushing cheek—timid—apprehensive—bashful.—A tear and a prayer-book would have made her *La Bella Magdalena*.[63]—

Give *me* a woman in whose touching mien
A mind, a soul, a polish'd art is seen;
Whose motion speaks, whose poignant air can move.
Such are the darts to wound with endless love.

MRS. RACKET. Is that an impromptu? [*Touching him on the shoulder with her fan.*

DORICOURT. [*Starting*] Madam!—[*Aside*] *Finely caught!*—[*To her*] Not absolutely—it struck me during the dessert, as a motto for your picture.

MRS. RACKET. Gallantly turn'd! I perceive, however, Miss Hardy's charms have made no violent impression on you.—And who can wonder?—the poor girl's defects are so obvious.

DORICOURT. Defects!

MRS. RACKET. Merely those of education.—Her father's indulgence ruin'd her.—Mauvaise honte[64]—conceit and ignorance—all unite in the lady you are to marry.

DORICOURT. Marry!—I marry such a woman!—Your picture, I hope, is overcharged.—I marry mauvaise honte, pertness and ignorance!

MRS. RACKET. Thank your stars that ugliness and ill temper are not added to the list.—You must think her handsome?

DORICOURT. Half her personal beauty would content me; but could the Medicean Venus[65] be animated for me, and endowed with a vulgar soul, I should become the statue, and my heart transform'd to marble.

MRS. RACKET. Bless us!—We are in a hopeful way then!

DORICOURT.—[*Aside*] *There must be some envy in this!—I see she is a coquette.*—[*To her*] Ha, ha, ha! and you imagine I am persuaded of the truth of your character? Ha, ha, ha! Miss Hardy, I have been assur'd, Madam, is elegant and accomplished:—but one must allow for a lady's painting.

MRS. RACKET.—[*Aside*] *I'll be even with him for that.*—[*To him*] Ha! ha! ha! and so you have found me out!—Well, I protest I meant no harm; 'twas only to increase the *éclat* of her appearance, that I threw a veil over her charms.—Here comes the lady;—her elegance and accomplishments will announce themselves.

[*Enter* Letitia, *running.*

LETITIA. La! Cousin, do you know that our John—oh, dear heart!— [*Hanging down her head, and dropping behind* Mrs. Racket] I didn't see you, Sir.

MRS. RACKET. Fye, Letitia! Mr. Doricourt thinks you a woman of elegant manners. Stand forward, and confirm his opinion.

LETITIA. No, no; keep before me.—He's my sweetheart; and 'tis impudent to look one's sweetheart in the face, you know.

MRS. RACKET. You'll allow in future for a lady's painting, Sir. Ha! ha! ha!

DORICOURT. I am astonish'd!

LETITIA. Well, hang it, I'll take heart.—Why, he is but a man, you know, Cousin;—and I'll let him see I wasn't born in a wood to be scar'd by an owl. [*Half apart; advances, and looks at him through her fingers*] He! he! he! [*Goes up to him, and makes a very stiff formal curtesy*]—[*He bows*]—You have been a great traveller, Sir, I hear?

DORICOURT. Yes, Madam.

LETITIA. Then I wish you'd tell us about the fine sights you saw when you went over-sea.—I have read in a book that there are some countries where the men and women are all horses.[66]—Did you see any of them?

MRS. RACKET. Mr. Doricourt is not prepared, my dear, for these enquiries; he is reflecting on the importance of the question, and will answer you—when he can.

LETITIA. When he can! Why, he's as slow in speech as Aunt Margery when she's reading Thomas Aquinas;—and stands gaping like mum-chance.[67]

MRS. RACKET. Have a little discretion.

LETITIA. Hold your tongue!—Sure I may say what I please before I am married, if I can't afterwards.—D'ye think a body does not know how to talk to a sweetheart? He is not the first I have had.

DORICOURT. Indeed!

LETITIA. Oh, Lud! He speaks!—Why, if you must know—there was the curate at home:—when Papa was a-hunting, he used to come a-suitoring, and make speeches to me out of books.—No body knows what a *mort* of fine things he used to say to me;—and call me Venis, and Jubah, and Dinah![68]

DORICOURT. And pray, fair Lady, how did you answer him?

LETITIA. Why, I used to say, "Look you, Mr. Curate, don't think to come over me with your flim-flams;[69] for a better man than ever trod in your shoes, is coming over-sea to marry me;"—but, ifags![70] I begin to think I was out.—Parson Dobbins was the sprightfuller[71] man of the two.

DORICOURT. Surely this cannot be Miss Hardy!

LETITIA. Laws! why, don't you know me! you saw me to-day—but I was daunted before my father, and the lawyer, and all them, and did not care to speak out:—so, may be, you thought I couldn't;—but I can talk as fast as any body, when I know folks a little:—and now I have shewn my parts, I hope you'll like me better.

[*Enter* Hardy.

HARDY. I foresee this won't do!—Mr. Doricourt, may be you take my daughter for a fool; but you are mistaken: she's a sensible girl, as any in England.

DORICOURT. I am convinced she has a very uncommon understanding, Sir.—[*Aside*] *I did not think he had been such an ass.*

LETITIA. My Father will undo the whole.—Laws! Papa, how can you think he can take me for a fool! when every body knows I beat the potecary[72] at conundrums[73] last Christmas-time? And didn't I make a string of names, all in riddles, for the Lady's Diary?[74]—There was a little river, and a great house; that was Newcastle.—There was what a lamb says, and three letters; that was *Ba*, and *k-e-r*, ker, baker.—There was—

HARDY. Don't stand ba-a-ing there. You'll make me mad in a moment!—I tell you, Sir, that for all that, she's dev'lish sensible.

DORICOURT. Sir, I give all possible credit to your assertions.

LETITIA. Laws! Papa, do come along. If you stand watching, how can my sweetheart break his mind, and tell me how he admires me?

DORICOURT. That would be difficult, indeed, Madam.

HARDY. I tell you, Letty, I'll have no more of this.—I see well enough—

LETITIA. Laws! don't snub me before my husband—that is to be.—You'll teach him to snub me too,—and I believe, by his looks, he'd like to begin now.—So, let us go, Cousin; you may tell the gentleman what a genius I have—how I can cut watch-papers, and work cat-gut; make quadrille-baskets with pins, and take profiles in shade; ay, as well as the lady at N°. 62, South Moulton-street, Grosvenor-square.[75]

[*Exit* Hardy *and* Letitia.

MRS. RACKET. What think you of my painting, now?

DORICOURT. Oh, mere water-colours, Madam! The Lady has caricatured your picture.

MRS. RACKET. And how does she strike you on the whole?

DORICOURT. Like a good design, spoiled by the incapacity of the artist. Her faults are evidently the result of her father's weak indulgence. I observed an expression in her eye, that seemed to satyrise the folly of her lips.

MRS. RACKET. But at her age, when education is fixed, and manner becomes nature—hopes of improvement—

DORICOURT. Would be as rational, as hopes of gold from a jugler's crucible.[76]—Doricourt's wife must be incapable of improvement; but it must be because she's got beyond it.

MRS. RACKET. I am pleased your misfortune sits no heavier.

DORICOURT. Your pardon, Madam; so mercurial was the hour in which I was born, that misfortunes always go plump to the bottom of my heart, like a pebble in water, and leave the surface unruffled.—I shall certainly set off for Bath,[77] or the other world, to-night;—but whether I shall use a chaise with four swift coursers, or go off in a tangent—from the aperture of a pistol, deserves consideration; so I make my *adieus*. [*Going*.

MRS. RACKET. Oh, but I intreat you, postpone your journey 'till to-morrow; determine on which you will—you must be this night at the masquerade.

DORICOURT. Masquerade!

MRS. RACKET. Why not?—If you resolve to visit the other world, you may as well take one night's pleasure first in this, you know.

DORICOURT. Faith, that's very true; ladies are the best philosophers, after all. Expect me at the masquerade. [*Exit* Doricourt.

MRS. RACKET. He's a charming fellow!—I think Letitia sha'n't have him. [*Going*.

[*Enter* Hardy.

HARDY. What's he gone?

MRS. RACKET. Yes; and I am glad he is. You would have ruined us!—Now, I beg, Mr. Hardy, you won't interfere in this business; it is a little out of your way. [*Exit* Mrs. Racket.

HARDY. Hang me, if I don't though. I foresee very clearly what will be the end of it, if I leave ye to your selves; so, I'll e'en follow him to the masquerade, and tell him all about it: let me see.—What shall my dress be? A Great Mogul? No.—A Grenadier?[78] No;—no, that, I foresee, would make a laugh. Hang me, if I don't send to my favourite little Quick, and borrow his Jew Isaac's dress:[79]—I know the dog likes a glass of good wine; so I'll give him a bottle of my forty-eight, and he shall teach me. Aye, that's it—I'll be cunning little Isaac! If they complain of my want of wit, I'll tell 'em the cursed Duenna wears the breeches, and has spoilt my parts. [*Exit* Hardy.

III.ii

[Courtall*'s. Enter* Courtall, Saville, *and three others, from an Apartment in the back Scene.* (*The last three tipsey*)

COURTALL. You shan't go yet:—Another catch, and another bottle!

FIRST GENTLEMAN. May I be a bottle, and an empty bottle, if you catch me at that!—Why, I am going to the masquerade. Jack—, you know who I mean, is to meet me, and we are to have a leap at the new lustres.

SECOND GENTLEMAN. And I am going too—a Harlequin—[*Hiccups*] Am not I in a pretty pickle to make Harlequinades?—And Tony, here—he is going in the disguise—in the disguise—of a gentleman!

FIRST GENTLEMAN. We are all very disguised; so bid them draw up—D'ye hear!

[*Exeunt the three* Gentlemen.

SAVILLE. Thy skull, Courtall, is a lady's thimble:—no, an egg-shell.

COURTALL. Nay, then you are gone too; you never aspire to similes, but in your cups.

SAVILLE. No, no; I am steady enough—but the fumes of the wine pass directly through thy egg-shell, and leave thy brain as cool as—Hey! I am quite sober; my similes fail me.

COURTALL. Then we'll sit down here, and have one sober bottle.—Bring a table and glasses.

SAVILLE. I'll not swallow another drop; no, though the juice should be the true Falernian.[80]

COURTALL. By the bright eyes of her you love, you shall drink her health.

SAVILLE. Ah! [*Sitting down*] Her I loved is gone [*Sighing*].—She's married!

COURTALL. Then bless your stars you are not her husband! I would be husband to no woman in Europe, who was not dev'lish rich, and dev'lish ugly.

SAVILLE. Wherefore ugly?

COURTALL. Because she could not have the conscience to exact those attentions that a pretty wife expects; or, if she should, her resentments would be perfectly easy to me, nobody would undertake to revenge her cause.

SAVILLE. Thou art a most licentious fellow!

COURTALL. I should hate my own wife, that's certain; but I have a warm heart for those of other people; and so here's to the prettiest wife in England—Lady Frances Touchwood.

SAVILLE. Lady Frances Touchwood! I rise to drink her [*Drinks*]. How the devil came Lady Frances in your head? I never knew you give a woman of chastity before.

COURTALL. That's odd, for you have heard me give half the women of fashion in England.—[*Sneeringly*] But, pray now, what do you take a woman of chastity to be?

SAVILLE. Such a woman as Lady Frances Touchwood, Sir.

COURTALL. Oh, you are grave, Sir; I remember you was an adorer of hers—Why didn't you marry her?

SAVILLE. I had not the arrogance to look so high—Had my fortune been worthy of her, she should not have been ignorant of my admiration.

COURTALL. Precious fellow! What, I suppose you would not dare tell her now that you admire her?

SAVILLE. No, nor you.

COURTALL. By the Lord, I have told her so.

SAVILLE. Have! Impossible!

COURTALL. Ha! ha! ha!—Is it so?

SAVILLE. How did she receive the declaration?

COURTALL. Why, in the old way; blushed, and frowned, and said she was married.

SAVILLE. What amazing things thou art capable of! I could more easily have taken the Pope by the beard, than prophaned her ears with such a declaration.

COURTALL. I shall meet her at Lady Brilliant's to-night, where I shall repeat it; and I'll lay my life, under a mask, she'll hear it all without blush, or frown.

SAVILLE. [*Rising*] 'Tis false, Sir!—She won't.

COURTALL. She will! [*Rising*] nay, I'd venture to lay a round sum, that I prevail on her to go out with me—only to taste the fresh air, I mean.

SAVILLE. Preposterous vanity! From this moment I suspect that half the victories you have boasted are false and slanderous, as your pretended influence with Lady Frances.

COURTALL. Pretended!—How should such a fellow as you, now, who never soared beyond a cherry-cheeked daughter of a ploughman in Norfolk, judge of the influence of a man of my figure and habits? I could shew thee a list, in which there are names to shake thy faith in the whole sex!—and, to that list I have no doubt of adding the name of Lady—

SAVILLE. Hold, Sir! my ears cannot bear the profanation;—you cannot—dare not approach her!—For your soul you dare not mention love to her! Her look would freeze the word, whilst it hovered on thy licentious lips!

COURTALL. Whu! whu! well, we shall see—this evening, by Jupiter, the trial shall be made—If I fail—I fail.

SAVILLE. I think thou darest not!—But my life, my honour on her purity. [*Exit* Saville.

COURTALL. Hot-headed fool! [*Musing*] but since he has brought it to this point, by Gad I'll try what can be done with her Ladyship [*Musing, rings*] She's frost-work, and the prejudices of education yet strong: *ergo*, passionate professions will only inflame her pride, and put her on her guard.—For other arts then! [*Enter* Dick] Dick, do you know any of the servants at Sir George Touchwood's?

DICK. Yes, Sir; I knows the groom, and one of the house-maids: for the matter-o'-that, she's my own cousin; and it was my mother that holp'd her to the place.

COURTALL. Do you know Lady Frances's maid?

DICK. I can't say as how I know she.

COURTALL. Do you know Sir George's Valet?

DICK. No, Sir; but Sally is very thick with Mr. Gibson, Sir George's Gentleman.

COURTALL. Then go there directly, and employ Sally to discover whether her master goes to Lady Brilliant's this evening; and, if he does, the name of the shop that sold his habit.

DICK. Yes, Sir.

COURTALL. Be exact in your intelligence, and come to me at Boodle's.[81] [*Exit* Dick] If I cannot otherwise succeed, I'll beguile her as Jove did Alcmena, in the shape of her husband. The possession of so fine a woman—the triumph over Saville, are each a sufficient motive; and united, they shall be resistless. [*Exit* Courtall.

III.iii

[*The street. Enter* Saville.]

SAVILLE. The air has recover'd me! what have I been doing! perhaps my petulance may be the cause of *her* ruin, whose honour I asserted:—his vanity is piqued;—and where women are concerned, Courtall can be a villain. [*Enter* Dick. *Bows, and passes hastily*] Ha! that's his Servant!—Dick!

DICK. [*Returning*] Sir.

SAVILLE. Where are you going, Dick?

DICK. Going! I am going, where my master sent me.

SAVILLE. Well answer'd;—but I have a particular reason for my enquiry, and you must tell me.

DICK. Why then, Sir, I am going to call upon a cousin of mine, that lives at Sir George Touchwood's.

SAVILLE. Very well.—There, [*Gives him money*] you must make your cousin drink my health.—What are you going about?

DICK. Why, Sir, I believe 'tis no harm, or elseways I am sure I would not blab.—I am only going to ax if Sir George goes to the masquerade to-night, and what dress he wears.

SAVILLE. Enough! now, Dick, if you will call at my lodgings in your way back, and acquaint me with your cousin's intelligence, I'll double the trifle I have given you.

DICK. Bless your honour, I'll call—never fear. [*Exit* Dick.

SAVILLE. Surely the occasion may justify the means: —'tis doubly my duty to be Lady Frances's protector. Courtall, I see, is planning an artful scheme; but Saville shall out-plot him. [*Exit* Saville.

III.iv

[*Sir* George Touchwood*'s. Enter* Sir George *and* Villers.]

VILLERS. For shame, Sir George! you have left Lady Frances in tears.—How can you afflict her?

SIR GEORGE. 'Tis I that am afflicted;—my dream of happiness is over.—Lady Frances and I are disunited.

VILLERS. The Devil! why, you have been in town but ten days: she can have made no acquaintance for a Commons affair yet.[82]

SIR GEORGE. Pho! 'Tis our minds that are disunited: she no longer places her whole delight in me; she has yielded herself up to the world!

VILLERS. Yielded herself up to the world! why did you not bring her to town in a cage? Then she might have taken a peep at the world!—But, after all, what has the world done? A twelvemonth since you was the gayest fellow in it:—If any body ask'd who dresses best?—Sir George Touchwood.—Who is the most gallant man? Sir George Touchwood.—Who is the most wedded to amusement and dissipation? Sir George Touchwood.—And now Sir George is metamorphosed into a sour censor; and talks of fashionable life with as much bitterness, as the old crabbed fellow in Rome.[83]

SIR GEORGE. The moment I became possessed of such a jewel as Lady Frances, every thing wore a different complexion: that Society in which I liv'd with so much *éclat*, became the object of my terror; and I think of the manners of polite life, as I do of the atmosphere of a pest-house.—My Wife is already infected; she was set upon this morning by maids, widows, and bachelors, who carried her off in triumph, in spite of my displeasure.

VILLERS. Aye, to be sure; there would have been no triumph in the case, if you had not oppos'd it:—but I have heard the whole story from Mrs. Racket; and I assure you, Lady Frances didn't enjoy the morning at all;—she wish'd for you fifty times.

SIR GEORGE. Indeed! Are you sure of that?

VILLERS. Perfectly sure.

SIR GEORGE. I wish I had known it:—my uneasiness at dinner was occasioned by very different ideas.

VILLERS. Here then she comes, to receive your apology; but if she is true woman, her displeasure will rise in proportion to your contrition;—and till you grow careless about her pardon, she won't grant it:—however, I'll leave you.—Matrimonial duets are seldom set in the style I like. [*Exit* Villers.

[*Enter* Lady Frances.

SSIR GEORGE. The sweet sorrow that glitters in these eyes, I cannot bear [*Embracing her*]. Look chearfully, you rogue.

LADY FRANCES. I cannot look otherwise, if you are pleas'd with me.

SIR GEORGE. Well, Fanny, to-day you made your *entrée* in the fashionable world; tell me honestly the impressions you receiv'd.

LADY FRANCES. Indeed, Sir George, I was so hurried from place to place, that I had not time to find out what my impressions were.

SIR GEORGE. That's the very spirit of the life you have chosen.

LADY FRANCES. Every body about me seem'd happy—but every body seem'd in a hurry to be happy somewhere else.

SIR GEORGE. And you like this?

LADY FRANCES. One must like what the rest of the World likes.

SIR GEORGE. Pernicious maxim!

LADY FRANCES. But, my dear Sir George, you have not promis'd to go with me to the Masquerade.

SIR GEORGE. 'Twould be a shocking indecorum to be seen together, you know.

LADY FRANCES. Oh, no; I ask'd Mrs. Racket, and she told me we might be seen together at the Masquerade—without being laugh'd at.

SIR GEORGE. Really?

LADY FRANCES. Indeed, to tell you the truth, I could wish it was the fashion for married people to be inseparable; for I have more heart-felt satisfaction in fifteen minutes with you at my side, than fifteen days of amusement could give me without you.

SIR GEORGE. My sweet Creature! How that confession charms me!—Let us begin the Fashion.

LADY FRANCES. O, impossible! We should not gain a single proselyte; and you can't conceive what spiteful things would be said of us.—At Kensington to-day a Lady met us, whom we saw at Court, when we were presented; she lifted up her hands in amazement!—Bless me! said she to her companion, here's Lady Frances without Sir Hurlo Thrumbo![84]—My dear Mrs. Racket, consider what an important charge you have! for Heaven's sake take her home again, or some enchanter on a flying dragon will descend and carry her off.[85]—Oh, said another, I dare say Lady Frances has a clue at her heel, like the peerless Rosamond:[86]—her tender swain would never have trusted her so far without such a precaution.

SIR GEORGE. Heav'n and earth!—How shall innocence preserve its lustre amidst manners so corrupt!—My dear Fanny, I feel a sentiment for thee at this moment, tenderer than love—more animated than passion.—I could weep over that purity, expos'd to the sullying breath of Fashion, and the *Ton*, in whose latitudinary vortex Chastity herself can scarcely move unspotted.

[*Enter* Gibson.

GIBSON. Your Honour talk'd, I thought, something about going to the Masquerade?

SIR GEORGE. Well.

GIBSON. Isn't it?—Hasn't your Honour?—I thought your Honour had forgot to order a Dress.

LADY FRANCES. Well consider'd, Gibson.—Come, will you be Jew, Turk, or Heretic; a Chinese Emperor, or a Ballad-Singer; a Rake, or a Watchman?[87]

SIR GEORGE. Oh, neither, my Love; I can't take the trouble to support a character.

LADY FRANCES. You'll wear a Domino then:—I saw a pink Domino trimm'd with blue at the shop where I bought my habit.—Would you like it?

SIR GEORGE. Any thing, any thing.

LADY FRANCES. Then go about it directly, Gibson.—A pink Domino trimm'd with blue, and a Hat of the same—Come, you have not seen my Dress yet—it is most beautiful; I long to have it on.

[*Exeunt* Sir George *and* Lady Frances.

GIBSON. A pink Domino trimm'd with blue, and a hat of the same—What the devil can it signify to Sally now what his Dress is to be?—Surely the slut has not made an assignation to meet her master! [*Exit* Gibson.

IV.i

[*A Masquerade. A Party dancing Cotillons*[88] *in front—a variety of Characters pass and repass. Enter* Folly *on a Hobby-Horse, with Cap and Bells.*[89]]

MASK. Hey! Tom Fool! what business have you here?

FOLLY. What, Sir! Affront a prince in his own dominions! [*Struts off.*

MOUNTEBANK.[90] Who'll buy my nostrums? Who'll buy my nostrums?

MASK. What are they? [*They all come round him.*

MOUNTEBANK. Different sorts, and for different customers. Here's a Liquor for Ladies—it expels the rage of gaming and gallantry; Here's a Pill for Members of Parliament—good to settle consciences. Here's an Eye-Water for Jealous Husbands—it thickens the visual membrane, through which they see too clearly. Here's a Decoction for the Clergy—it never sits easy, if the patient has more than one living. Here's a Draught for Lawyers—a great promoter of modesty. Here's a Powder for Projectors—'twill rectify the fumes of an empty stomach, and dissipate their airy castles.

MASK. Have you a nostrum that can give patience to young heirs, whose uncles and fathers are stout and healthy?

MOUNTEBANK. Yes; and I have an Infusion for Creditors—it gives resignation and humility, when fine gentlemen break their promises, or plead their privilege.

MASK. Come along:—I'll find you customers for your whole cargo.

[*Enter* Hardy, *in the Dress of Isaac Mendoza.*[91]

HARDY. Why, isn't it a shame to see so many stout, well-built young fellows, masquerading, and cutting *Couranta's* here at home—instead of making the French cut capers to the tune of your Cannon—or sweating the Spaniards with an English *Fandango*?—I foresee the end of all this.

MASK. Why, thou little testy Israelite! back to Duke's Place;[92] and preach your tribe into a subscription for the good of the land on whose milk and honey ye fatten.—Where are your Joshuas and your Gideons, aye? What! all dwindled into Stockbrokers, Pedlars, and Rag-Men?

HARDY. No, not all. Some of us turn Christians, and by degrees grow into all the privileges of Englishmen! In the second generation we are patriots, rebels, courtiers, and husbands.[93] [*Puts his fingers to his forehead.*

[*Two other Masks advance.*

3D MASK. What, my little Isaac!—How the Devil came you here? Where's your old Margaret?[94]

HARDY. Oh, I have got rid of her.

3D MASK. How?

HARDY. Why, I persuaded a young Irishman that she was a blooming plump Beauty of eighteen; so they made an Elopement, ha! ha! ha! and she is now the Toast of Tipperary. Ha! there's Cousin Racket and her Party; they sha'n't know me. [*Puts on his Mask.*

[*Enter* Mrs. Racket, Lady Frances, Sir George, *and* Flutter.

MRS. RACKET. Look at this dumpling Jew; he must be a Levite by his figure. You have surely practised the flesh-hook[95] a long time, friend, to have raised that goodly presence.

HARDY. About as long, my brisk Widow, as you have been angling for a second Husband; but my hook has been better baited than yours.—[*Pointing to* Flutter] You have only caught Gudgeons, I see.

FLUTTER. Oh! this is one of the Geniuses they hire to entertain the Company with their *accidental* sallies.—Let me look at your Common-Place Book, friend.—I want a few good things.

HARDY. I'd oblige you, with all my heart; but you'll spoil them in repeating—or, if you shou'd not, they'll gain you no reputation—for no body will believe they are your own.

SIR GEORGE. He knows ye, Flutter;—the little Gentleman fancies himself a Wit, I see.

HARDY. There's no depending on what *you* see—the eyes of the jealous are not to be trusted.—Look to your Lady.

FLUTTER. He knows ye, Sir George.

SIR GEORGE. [*Aside*] *What! am I the Town-talk?*

HARDY. [*Aside*] *I can neither see Doricourt nor Letty.—I must find them out.* [*Exit* Hardy.

MRS. RACKET. Well, Lady Frances, is not all this charming? Could you have conceived such a brilliant assemblage of objects?

LADY FRANCES. Delightful! The days of enchantment are restor'd; the columns glow with Sapphires and Rubies. Emperors and Fairies, Beauties and Dwarfs, meet me at every step.

SIR GEORGE. How lively are first impressions on sensible minds! in four hours, vapidity and languor will take place of that exquisite sense of joy, which flutters your little heart.

MRS. RACKET. What an inhuman creature! fate has not allow'd us these sensations above ten times in our lives; and would you have us shorten them by anticipation?

FLUTTER. O Lord! your Wise Men are the greatest Fools upon earth:—they reason about their enjoyments, and analyse their pleasures, whilst the essence escapes. Look, Lady Frances: D'ye see that Figure strutting in the dress of an Emperor? His Father retails Oranges in Botolph Lane. That Gypsey is a Maid of Honour, and that Rag-man a Physician.

LADY FRANCES. Why, you know every body.

FLUTTER. Oh, every creature.—A Mask is nothing at all to me.—I can give you the history of half the people here. In the next apartment there's a whole family, who, to my knowledge, have lived on Water-Cresses this month, to make a figure here to-night;—but, to make up for that, they'll cram their pockets with cold Ducks and Chickens, for a Carnival to-morrow.

LADY FRANCES. Oh, I should like to see this provident Family.

FLUTTER. Honour me with your arm.

[*Exeunt* Flutter *and* Lady Frances.

MRS. RACKET. Come, Sir George, you shall be *my* Beau.—We'll make the *tour* of the rooms, and meet them. Oh! your pardon, you must follow Lady Frances; or the wit and fine parts of Mr. Flutter may drive you out of her head. Ha! ha! ha! [*Exit* Mrs. Racket.

SIR GEORGE. I was going to follow her, and now I dare not. How can I be such a fool as to be govern'd by the *fear* of that ridicule which I despise! [*Exit Sir* George.

[*Enter* Doricourt, *meeting a* Mask.

DORICOURT. Ha! my Lord!—I thought you had been engaged at Westminster on this important night.[96]

MASK. So I am—I slipt out as soon as Lord Trope got upon his legs; I can *badiner*[97] here an hour or two, and be back again before he is down.—There's a fine figure! I'll address her. [*Enter* Letitia] Charity, fair Lady! Charity for a poor Pilgrim.

LETITIA. Charity! If you mean my prayers, Heaven grant thee Wit, Pilgrim.

MASK. That blessing would do from a Devotee: from you I ask other charities;—such charities as Beauty should bestow—soft Looks—sweet Words—and kind Wishes.

LETITIA. Alas! I am bankrupt of these, and forced to turn Beggar myself.—[*Aside*] *There he is!—how shall I catch his attention?*

MASK. Will you grant me no favour?

LETITIA. Yes, one—I'll make you my Partner—not for life, but through the soft mazes of a minuet.—Dare you dance?

DORICOURT. Some spirit in that.

MASK. I dare do any thing you command.

DORICOURT. Do you know her, my Lord?

MASK. No: such a woman as that, would formerly have been known in any disguise; but Beauty is now common—Venus seems to have given her *Cestus* to the whole sex.[98]

[*A Minuet.*

DORICOURT. [*During the Minuet*] She dances divinely.—[*When ended*] Somebody must know her! Let us enquire who she is. [*Exit.*

[*Enter* Saville *and* Kitty Willis, *habited like* Lady Frances.

SAVILLE. I have seen Courtall in Sir George's habit, though he endeavoured to keep himself conceal'd. Go, and seat yourself in the tea-room, and on no account discover your face:—remember too, Kitty, that the Woman you are to personate is a Woman of Virtue.

KITTY. I am afraid I shall find that a difficult character: indeed I believe it is seldom kept up through a whole Masquerade.

SAVILLE. Of that *you* can be no judge—Follow my directions, and you shall be rewarded.

[*Exit* Kitty. *Enter* Doricourt.

DORICOURT. Ha! Saville! Did you see a Lady dance just now?

SAVILLE. No.

DORICOURT. Very odd. No body knows her.

SAVILLE. Where is Miss Hardy?

DORICOURT. Cutting Watch-papers, and making Conundrums, I suppose.

SAVILLE. What do you mean?

DORICOURT. Faith, I hardly know. She's not here, however, Mrs. Racket tells me.—I ask'd no further.

SAVILLE. Your indifference seems increas'd.

DORICOURT. Quite the reverse; 'tis advanced thirty-two degrees towards hatred.

SAVILLE. You are jesting?

DORICOURT. Then it must be with a very ill grace, my dear Saville; for I never felt so seriously: do you know the creature's almost an Ideot?

SAVILLE. What!

DORICOURT. An Ideot. What the devil shall I do with her? Egad! I think I'll feign myself mad—and then Hardy will propose to cancel the engagements.

SAVILLE. An excellent expedient. I must leave you; you are mysterious, and I can't stay to unravel ye.—I came here to watch over Innocence and Beauty.

DORICOURT. The Guardian of Innocence and Beauty at three and twenty! Is there not a cloven foot under that black gown, Saville?

SAVILLE. No, faith. Courtall is here on a most detestable design.—I found means to get a knowledge of the Lady's dress, and have brought a girl to personate her, whose reputation cannot be hurt.—You shall know the result to-morrow. Adieu. [*Exit* Saville.

DORICOURT. [*Musing*] Yes, I think that will do.—I'll feign myself mad, see the Doctor to pronounce me incurable, and when the parchments are destroyed—

[*As he stands in a musing posture,* Letitia *enters, and sings.*

SONG.

I.
Wake! thou Son of Dullness, wake!
From thy drowsy senses shake
All the spells that Care employs,
Cheating Mortals of their joys.

II.
Light-wing'd Spirits, hither haste!
Who prepare for mortal taste
All the gifts that Pleasure sends,
Every bliss that youth attends.

III.
Touch his feelings, rouze his soul,
Whilst the sparkling moments roll;
Bid them wake to new delight,
Crown the magic of the night.

DORICOURT. By Heaven, the same sweet creature!

LETITIA. You have chosen an odd situation for study. Fashion and Taste preside in this spot:—they throw their spells around you:—ten thousand delights spring up at their command;—and you, a Stoic—a being without senses, are wrapt in reflection.

DORICOURT. And you, the most charming being in the world, awake me to admiration. Did you come from the Stars?

LETITIA. Yes, and I shall reascend in a moment.

DORICOURT. Pray shew me your face before you go.

LETITIA. Beware of imprudent curiosity; it lost Paradise.

DORICOURT. Eve's curiosity was rais'd by the Devil;—'tis an Angel tempts mine.—So your allusion is not in point.

LETITIA. But *why* would you see my face?

DORICOURT. To fall in love with it.

LETITIA. And what then?

DORICOURT. Why, then—[*Aside*] *Aye, curse it! there's the rub.*

LETITIA. Your Mistress will be angry;—but, perhaps, you have no Mistress?

DORICOURT. Yes, yes; and a sweet one it is!

LETITIA. What! is she old?

DORICOURT. No.

LETITIA. Ugly?

DORICOURT. No.

LETITIA. What then?

DORICOURT. Pho! don't talk about *her*; but shew me your face.

LETITIA. My vanity forbids it;—'twould frighten you.

DORICOURT. Impossible! your Shape is graceful, your Air bewitching, your Bosom transparent, and your Chin would tempt me to kiss it, if I did not see a pouting red Lip above it, that demands—

LETITIA. You grow too free.

DORICOURT. Shew me your face then—only half a glance.

LETITIA. Not for worlds.

DORICOURT. What! you will have a little gentle force? [*Attempts to seize her Mask.*

LETITIA. I am gone for ever! [*Exit.*

DORICOURT. 'Tis false;—I'll follow to the end. [*Exit.*

[Flutter, Lady Frances, *and* Saville *advance.*

LADY FRANCES. How can you be thus interested for a stranger?

SAVILLE. Goodness will ever interest; its home is Heaven: on earth 'tis but a Wanderer. Imprudent Lady! why have you left the side of your Protector? Where is your Husband?

FLUTTER. Why, what's that to him?

LADY FRANCES. [*To* Flutter] Surely it can't be merely his habit;—there's something in him that awes me.

FLUTTER. [*To her*] Pho! 'Tis only his grey beard.—I know him; he keeps a Lottery-office on Cornhill.[99]

SAVILLE. My province, as an Enchanter, lays open every secret to me. Lady! there are dangers abroad—Beware! [*Exit.*

LADY FRANCES. 'Tis very odd; his manner has made me tremble. Let us seek Sir George.

FLUTTER. He is coming towards us.

[Courtall *comes forward, habited like* Sir George.

COURTALL. There she is! If I can but disengage her from that fool Flutter—crown me, ye Schemers, with immortal wreaths.

LADY FRANCES. O my dear Sir George! I rejoice to meet you—an old Conjuror has been frightening me with his Prophecies.—Where's Mrs. Racket?

COURTALL. In the dancing-room.—I promis'd to send you to her, Mr. Flutter.

FLUTTER. Ah! she wants me to dance. With all my heart. [*Exit.*

LADY FRANCES. Why do you keep on your mask?—'tis too warm.

COURTALL. 'Tis very warm—I want air—let us go.

LADY FRANCES. You seem quite agitated.—Sha'n't we bid our company adieu?

COURTALL. No, no;—there's no time for forms. I'll just give directions to the carriage, and be with you in a moment. [*Going, steps back*] Put on your mask; I have a particular reason for it. [*Exit.*

[Saville *advances with* Kitty.

SAVILLE. Now, Kitty, you know your lesson. Lady Frances, [*Takes off his mask*] let me lead you to your Husband.

LADY FRANCES. Heavens! is Mr. Saville the Conjuror? Sir George is just stept to the door to give directions.—We are going home immediately.

SAVILLE. No, Madam, you are deceiv'd: Sir George is this way.

LADY FRANCES. This is astonishing!

SAVILLE. Be not alarm'd: you have escap'd a snare, and shall be in safety in a moment.

[*Exit* Saville *and* Lady Frances. *Enter* Courtall, *and seizes* Kitty's *Hand.*

COURTALL. Now!

KITTY. 'Tis pity to go so soon.

COURTALL. Perhaps I may bring you back, my Angel—but go now, you must. [*Exit.*

[*Music.* Doricourt *and* Letitia *come forward.*

DORICOURT. By Heavens! I never was charm'd 'till now.—English beauty—French vivacity—wit—elegance. Your name, my Angel!—tell me your name, though you persist in concealing your face.

LETITIA. My name has a spell in it.

DORICOURT. I thought so; it must be *Charming*.

LETITIA. But if reveal'd, the charm is broke.

DORICOURT. I'll answer for its force.

LETITIA. Suppose it Harriet, or Charlotte, or Maria, or—

DORICOURT. Hang Harriet, and Charlotte, and Maria—the name your Father gave ye!

LETITIA. That can't be worth knowing, 'tis so transient a thing.

DORICOURT. How, transient?

LETITIA. Heav'n forbid my name should be *lasting* till I am married.

DORICOURT. Married! The chains of Matrimony are too heavy and vulgar for such a spirit as yours.—The flowery wreaths of Cupid are the only bands you should wear.

LETITIA. They are the lightest, I believe: but 'tis possible to wear those of marriage gracefully.—Throw 'em loosely round, and twist 'em in a True-Lover's Knot for the Bosom.

DORICOURT. An Angel! but what will you be when a Wife?

LETITIA. A Woman.—If my Husband should prove a Churl, a Fool, or a Tyrant, I'd break his heart, ruin his fortune, elope with the first pretty Fellow that ask'd me—and return the contempt of the world with scorn, whilst my feelings prey'd upon my life.

DORICOURT.—[*Aside*] *Amazing!*—[*To her*] What if you lov'd him, and he were worthy of your love?

LETITIA. Why, then I'd be any thing—and all!—Grave, gay, capricious—the soul of whim, the spirit of variety—live with him in the eye of fashion, or in the shade of retirement—change my country, my sex,—feast with him in an Esquimaux hut, or a Persian pavilion—join him in the victorious war-dance on the borders of Lake Ontario, or sleep to the soft breathings of the flute in the cinnamon groves of Ceylon—dig with him in the mines of Golconda,[100] or enter the dangerous precincts of the Mogul's Seraglio—cheat him of his wishes, and overturn his empire to restore the Husband of my Heart to the blessings of Liberty and Love.

DORICOURT. Delightful wildness! oh, to catch thee, and hold thee for ever in this little cage! [*Attempting to clasp her.*

LETITIA. Hold, Sir! Though Cupid must give the bait that tempts me to the snare, 'tis Hymen[101] must spread the net to catch me.

DORICOURT. 'Tis in vain to assume airs of coldness—Fate has ordain'd you mine.

LETITIA. How do you know?

DORICOURT. I feel it *here*. I never met with a Woman so perfectly to my taste; and I won't believe it form'd you so, on purpose to tantalize me.

LETITIA. [*Aside*] *This moment is worth a whole existence.*

DORICOURT. Come, shew me your face, and rivet my chains.

LETITIA. To-morrow you shall be satisfied.

DORICOURT. To-morrow! and not to-night?

LETITIA. No.

DORICOURT. Where then shall I wait on you to-morrow?—Where see you?

LETITIA. You shall see me in an hour when you least expect me.

DORC. Why all this mystery?

LETITIA. I like to be mysterious. At present be content to know that I am a Woman of Family and Fortune. Adieu!

[*Enter* Hardy.

HARDY. Adieu! [*Aside*] *Then I am come at the fag end.*

DORICOURT. Let me see you to your carriage.

LETITIA. As you value knowing me, stir not a step. If I am follow'd, you never see me more. [*Exit.*

DORICOURT. Barbarous Creature! she's gone! what, and is this really serious?—Am I in love?—Pho! it can't be—O Flutter! do you know that charming Creature?

[*Enter* Flutter.

FLUTTER. What charming Creature? I pass'd a thousand.

DORICOURT. She went out at that door, as you enter'd.

FLUTTER. Oh, yes;—I know her very well.

DORICOURT. Do you, my dear Fellow? Who?

FLUTTER. She's kept by Lord George Jennett.

HARDY. [*Aside*] *Impudent Scoundrel!*

DORICOURT. Kept!!!

FLUTTER. Yes; Colonel Gorget had her first;—then Mr. Loveill;—then—I forget exactly how many; and at last she's Lord George's. [*Talks to other* Masks.

DORICOURT. I'll murder Gorget, poison Lord George, and shoot myself.

HARDY. Now's the time, I see, to clear up the whole. Mr. Doricourt!—I say—Flutter was mistaken; I know who you are in love with.

DORICOURT. A strange *rencontre!* Who?

HARDY. My Letty.

DORICOURT. Oh! I understand your rebuke;—'tis too soon, Sir, to assume the Father-in-law.

HARDY. Zounds! what do you mean by that? I tell you that the Lady you admire is Letitia Hardy.

DORICOURT. I am glad *you* are so well satisfied with the state of my heart.—I wish *I* was. [*Exit.*

HARDY. Stop a moment.—Stop, I say! What, you won't? Very well—if I don't play you a trick for this, may I never be a Grand-father! I'll plot *with* Letty now, and not against her; aye, hang me if I don't. There's something in my head, that shall tingle in his heart.—He shall have a lecture upon impatience, that I foresee he'll be the better for as long as he lives. [*Exit.*

[Saville *comes forward with other* Masks.

SAVILLE. Flutter, come with us; we're going to raise a laugh at Courtall's.

FLUTTER. With all my heart. "Live to Live," was my Father's motto: "Live to Laugh," is mine.

[*Exit.*

IV.ii

[Courtall*'s. Enter* Kitty *and* Courtall.]

KITTY. Where have you brought me, Sir George? This is not our home.

COURTALL. 'Tis *my* home, beautiful Lady Frances! [*Kneels, and takes off his Mask*] oh, forgive the ardency of my passion, which has compell'd me to deceive you.

KITTY. Mr. Courtall! what will become of me?

COURTALL. Oh, say but that you pardon the Wretch who adores you. Did you but know the agonizing tortures of my heart, since I had the felicity of conversing with you this morning—or the despair that now—[*Knock.*

KITTY. Oh! I'm undone!

COURTALL. Zounds! my dear Lady Frances. I am not at home. Rascal! do you hear?—Let no body in; I am not at home.

SERVANT. [*Without*] Sir, I told the Gentlemen so.

COURTALL. Eternal curses! they are coming up. Step into this room, adorable Creature! *one* moment; I'll throw them out of the window if they stay there.

[*Exit* Kitty; *through the back scene. Enter* Saville, Flutter, *and* Masks.

FLUTTER. O Gemini! beg the Petticoat's pardon.—Just saw a corner of it.

1ST MASK. No wonder admittance was so difficult. I thought you took us for Bailiffs.

COURTALL. Upon my soul, I am devilish glad to see you—but you perceive how I am circumstanc'd. Excuse me at this moment.

2ND MASK. Tell us who 'tis then.

COURTALL. Oh, fie!

FLUTTER. We won't blab.

COURTALL. I can't, upon honour.—Thus far—She's a Woman of the first Character and Rank. Saville, [*Takes him aside*] have I influence, or have I not?

SAVILLE. Why, sure, you do not insinuate—

COURTALL. No, not insinuate, but swear, that she's now in my bed-chamber:—by gad, I don't deceive you.—There's Generalship, you Rogue! Such an humble, distant, sighing Fellow as thou art, at the end of a six-month's siege, would have *boasted* of a kiss from her glove.—I only give the signal, and—pop!—she's in my arms.

SAVILLE. What, Lady Fran—

COURTALL. Hush! You shall see her name tomorrow morning in red letters at the end of my list. Gentlemen, you must excuse me now. Come and drink chocolate at twelve, but—

SAVILLE. Aye, let us go, out of respect to the Lady:—'tis a Person of Rank.

FLUTTER. Is it?—Then I'll have a peep at her. [*Runs to the door in the back Scene.*

COURTALL. [*Trying to prevent him*] This is too much, Sir.

1ST MASK. By Jupiter, we'll all have a peep.

COURTALL. Gentlemen, consider—for Heaven's sake—a Lady of Quality. What will be the consequences?

FLUTTER. The consequences!—Why, you'll have your throat cut, that's all—but I'll write your Elegy. So, now for the door! [*Part open the door, whilst the rest hold* Courtall]—Beg your Ladyship's pardon, whoever you are: [*Leads her out*] emerge from darkness like the glorious Sun, and bless the wond'ring circle with your charms. [*Takes off her Mask.*

SAVILLE. Kitty Willis! ha! ha! ha!

OMNES. Kitty Willis! ha! ha! ha! Kitty Willis!

1ST MASK. Why, what a Fellow you are, Courtall, to attempt imposing on your friends in this manner! A Lady of Quality—an Earl's daughter—Your Ladyship's most obedient.—Ha! ha! ha!

SAVILLE. Courtall, have you influence, or have you not?

FLUTTER. The man's moon-struck.

COURTALL. Hell, and ten thousand Furies, seize you all together!

KITTY. What! me, too, Mr. Courtall? Me, whom you have knelt to, prayed to, and adored?

FLUTTER. That's right, Kitty; give him a little more.

COURTALL. Disappointed and laugh'd at!—

SAVILLE. Laugh'd at and despis'd. I have fullfilled my design, which was to expose your villainy, and laugh at your presumption. Adieu, Sir! Remember how you again boast of your influence with Women of Rank; and, when you next want amusement, dare not to look up to the virtuous and to the noble for a Companion. [*Exit, leading* Kitty.

FLUTTER. And, Courtall, before you carry a Lady into your bed-chamber again, look under her mask, d'ye hear? [*Exit.*

COURTALL. There's no bearing this! I'll set off for Paris directly. [*Exit.*

V.i

[*Hardy*'s. *Enter* Hardy *and* Villers.]

VILLERS. Whimsical enough! dying for her, and hates her; believes her a Fool, and a Woman of brilliant Understanding!

HARDY. As true as you are alive;—but when I went up to him last night, at the Pantheon[102], out of downright good-nature to explain things—my Gentleman whips round upon his heel, and snapt me as short as if I had been a beggar-woman with six children, and he Overseer of the Parish.

VILLERS. Here comes the Wonder-worker.—[*Enter* Letitia] Here comes the Enchantress, who can go to Masquerades, and sing and dance, and talk a Man out of his wits!—But pray, have we Morning Masquerades?

LETITIA. Oh, no—but I am so enamour'd of this all-conquering Habit, that I could not resist putting it on, the moment I had breakfasted. I shall wear it on the day I am married, and then lay it by in spices—like the miraculous Robes of St. Bridget.[103]

VILLERS. That's as most Brides do. The charms that helped to catch the Husband, are generally *laid by*, one after another, 'till the Lady grows a downright Wife, and then runs crying to her Mother, because she has transform'd her *Lover* into a downright Husband.

HARDY. Listen to me.—I ha'n't slept to-night, for thinking of plots to plague Doricourt;—and they drove one another out of my head so quick, that I was as giddy as a goose, and could make nothing of 'em.—I wish to goodness you could contrive something.

VILLERS. Contrive to plague him! nothing so easy. Don't undeceive him, Madam, 'till he is your Husband. Marry him whilst he possesses the sentiments you labour'd to give him of Miss Hardy—and when you are his Wife—

LETITIA. Oh, Heavens! I see the whole—that's the very thing. My dear Mr. Villers, you are the divinest Man.

VILLERS. Don't make love to me, Hussey.

[*Enter* Mrs. Racket.

MRS. RACKET. No, pray don't—for I design to have Villers myself in about six years.—There's an oddity in him that pleases me.—He holds Women in contempt; and I should like to have an opportunity of breaking his heart for that.

VILLERS. And when I am heartily tired of life, I know no Woman whom I would with more pleasure make my Executioner.

HARDY. It cannot be—I foresee it will be impossible to bring it about. You know the wedding wasn't to take place this week or more—and Letty will never be able to play the Fool so long.

VILLERS. The knot shall be tied to-night.—I have it all here [*Pointing to his forehead*], the licence is ready. Feign yourself ill, send for Doricourt, and tell him you can't go out of the world in peace, except you see the ceremony performed.

HARDY. I feign myself ill! I could as soon feign myself a Roman Ambassador.—I was never ill in my life, but with the tooth-ach—when Letty's Mother was a breeding I had all the qualms.

VILLERS. Oh, I have no fears for *you*.—But what says Miss Hardy? Are you willing to make the irrevocable vow before night?

LETITIA. Oh, Heavens!—I—I—'Tis so exceeding sudden, that really—

MRS. RACKET. That really she is frighten'd out of her wits—lest it should be impossible to bring matters about. But *I* have taken the scheme into my protection, and you shall be Mrs. Doricourt before night. Come, [*To* Mr. Hardy] to bed directly: your room shall be cramm'd with phials, and all the apparatus of Death;—then heigh presto! for Doricourt.

VILLERS. [*To* Letty] You go and put off your conquering dress, and get all your aukward airs ready—[*To* Hardy] And you practise a few Groans—[*To Mrs.* Racket] And you—if possible—an air of gravity. I'll answer for the plot.

LETITIA. Married in jest! 'Tis an odd idea! well, I'll venture it.

[*Exit* Letitia *and* Mrs. Racket.

VILLERS. Aye, I'll be sworn! [*Looks at his watch*] 'Tis past three. The Budget's to be open'd this morning. I'll just step down to the House.[104]—Will you go?

HARDY. What! with a mortal sickness?

VILLERS. What a Blockhead! I believe, if half of us were to stay away with mortal sicknesses, it would be for the health of the Nation. Good-morning.—I'll call and feel your pulse as I come back. [*Exit.*

HARDY. You won't find 'em over brisk, I fancy. I foresee some ill happening from this making believe to die before one's time. But hang it—a-hem!—I am a stout man yet; only fifty-six—What's that? In the last Yearly Bill there were three lived to above an hundred. Fifty-six!—Fiddle-de-dee! I am not afraid, not I. [*Exit.*

V.ii

[Doricourt*'s.* Doricourt *in his Robe-de-Chambre. Enter* Saville.]

SAVILLE. Undress'd so late?

DORICOURT. I didn't go to bed 'till late—'twas late before I slept—late when I rose. Do you know Lord George Jennett?

SAVILLE. Yes.

DORICOURT. Has he a Mistress?

SAVILLE. Yes.

DORICOURT. What sort of a creature is she?

SAVILLE. Why, she spends him three thousand a year with the ease of a Duchess, and entertains his friends with the grace of a *Ninon*.[105] *Ergo*, she is handsome, spirited, and clever. [Doricourt *walks about disordered*] In the name of caprice, what ails you?

DORICOURT. You have hit it—*Elle est mon Caprice*—The mistress of Lord George Jennett is my caprice—Oh, insufferable!

SAVILLE. What, you saw her at the Masquerade?

DORICOURT. *Saw* her, *lov'd* her, *died* for her—without knowing her—And now the curse is, I can't hate her.

SAVILLE. Ridiculous enough! all this distress about a kept woman, whom any man may have, I dare swear, in a fortnight—They've been jarring some time.

DORICOURT. Have her! the sentiment I have conceived for the Witch is so unaccountable, that, in that line, I cannot bear her idea. Was she a Woman of Honour, for a Wife, I cou'd adore her—but, I really believe, if she should send me an assignation, I should hate her.

SAVILLE. Hey-day! This sounds like Love. What becomes of poor Miss Hardy?

DORICOURT. Her name has given me an ague. Dear Saville, how shall I contrive to make old Hardy cancel the engagements! The moiety of the estate which he will forfeit, shall be his the next moment, by deed of gift.

SAVILLE. Let me see—Can't you get it insinuated that you are a dev'lish wild fellow; that you are an Infidel, and attached to wenching, gaming, and so forth?

DORICOURT. Aye, such a character might have done some good two centuries back.—But who the devil can it frighten now? I believe it must be the mad scheme, at last.—There, will that do for the grin?

SAVILLE. Ridiculous!—But, how are you certain that the Woman who has so bewildered you, belongs to Lord George?

DORICOURT. Flutter told me so.

SAVILLE. Then fifty to one against the intelligence.

DORICOURT. It must be so. There was a mystery in her manner, for which nothing else can account. [*A violent rap*] Who can this be? [Saville *looks out.*

SAVILLE. The proverb is your answer—'tis Flutter himself. Tip him a scene of the Mad-man, and see how it takes.

DORICOURT. I will—a good way to send it about town. Shall it be of the melancholy kind, or the raving?

SAVILLE. Rant!—rant!—Here he comes.

DORICOURT. Talk not to me who can pull comets by the beard, and overset an island! [*Enter* Flutter] There! This is he!—this is he who hath sent my poor soul, without coat or breeches, to be tossed about in ether like a duck-feather! Villain, give me my soul again!

FLUTTER. [*Exceedingly frightened*] Upon my soul I hav'n't got it.

SAVILLE. Oh, Mr. Flutter, what a melancholy sight! —I little thought to have seen my poor friend reduced to this.

FLUTTER. Mercy defend me! what's he mad?

SAVILLE. You see how it is. A cursed Italian Lady—Jealousy—gave him a drug; and every full of the moon—

DORICOURT. Moon! who dares talk of the Moon? The patroness of genius—the rectifier of wits—the—Oh! here she is!—I feel her—she tugs at my brain—she has it—she has it—Oh! [*Exit.*

FLUTTER. Well! this is dreadful! exceeding dreadful, I protest. Have you had Monro?[106]

SAVILLE. Not yet. The worthy Miss Hardy—what a misfortune!

FLUTTER. Aye, very true.—Do they know it?

SAVILLE. Oh, no; the paroxysm seized him but this morning.

FLUTTER. Adieu! I can't stay [*Going in great haste*].

SAVILLE. [*Holding him*] But you must. Stay, and assist me:—perhaps he'll return again in a moment; and, when he is in this way, his strength is prodigious.

FLUTTER. Can't indeed—can't upon my soul. [*Exit.*

SAVILLE. Flutter—Don't make a mistake, now;—remember 'tis Doricourt that's mad. [*Exit.*

FLUTTER. Yes—you mad.

SAVILLE. No, no; Doricourt.

FLUTTER. Egad, I'll say you are both mad, and then I can't mistake.

[*Exeunt severally.*

V.iii

[Sir George Touchwood*'s. Enter* Sir George*, and* Lady Frances.]

SIR GEORGE. The bird is escaped—Courtall is gone to France.

LADY FRANCES. Heaven and earth! have ye been to seek him?

SIR GEORGE. Seek him! Aye.

LADY FRANCES. How did you get his name? I should never have told it you.

SIR GEORGE. I learnt it in the first Coffee-house I entered.—Every body is full of the story.

LADY FRANCES. Thank Heaven! he's gone!—But I have a story for you—The Hardy family are forming a plot upon your Friend Doricourt, and we are expected in the evening to assist.

SIR GEORGE. With all my heart, my Angel; but I can't stay to hear it unfolded. They told me Mr. Saville would be at home in half an hour, and I am impatient to see him. The adventure of last night—

LADY FRANCES. Think of it only with gratitude. The danger I was in has overset a new system of conduct, that, perhaps, I was too much inclined to adopt. But henceforward, my dear Sir George, you shall be my constant Companion, and Protector. And, when they ridicule the unfashionable Monsters, the felicity of our hearts shall make their satire pointless.

SIR GEORGE. Charming Angel! You almost reconcile me to Courtall. Hark! [*Stepping to the door*] here's company 'tis your lively Widow—I'll step down the back stairs, to escape her. [*Exit* Sir George.

[*Enter* Mrs. Racket.

MRS. RACKET. Oh, Lady Frances! I am shock'd to death.—Have you received a card from us?

LADY FRANCES. Yes; within these twenty minutes.

MRS. RACKET. Aye, 'tis of no consequence.—'Tis all over—Doricourt is mad.

LADY FRANCES. Mad!

MRS. RACKET. My poor Letitia!—Just as we were enjoying ourselves with the prospect of a scheme that was planned for their mutual happiness, in came Flutter, breathless, with the intelligence:—I flew here to know if you had heard it.

LADY FRANCES. No, indeed—and I hope it is one of Mr. Flutter's dreams. [*Enter* Saville] A-propos; now we shall be informed. Mr. Saville, I rejoice to see you, though Sir George will be disappointed: he's gone to your lodgings.

SAVILLE. I should have been happy to have prevented Sir George. I hope your Ladyship's adventure last night did not disturb your dreams?

LADY FRANCES. Not at all; for I never slept a moment. My escape, and the importance of my obligations to you, employed my thoughts. But we have just had shocking intelligence—Is it true that Doricourt is mad?

SAVILLE.—[*Aside*] *So; the business is done*—[*To her*] Madam, I am sorry to say, that I have just been a melancholy witness of his ravings: he was in the height of a paroxysm.

MRS. RACKET. Oh, there can be no doubt of it. Flutter told us the whole history. Some Italian Princess gave him a drug, in a box of sweetmeats, sent to him by her own page; and it renders him lunatic every month. Poor Miss Hardy! I never felt so much on any occasion in my life.

SAVILLE. To soften your concern, I will inform you, Madam, that Miss Hardy is less to be pitied than you imagine.

MRS. RACKET. Why so, Sir?

SAVILLE. 'Tis rather a delicate subject—but he did not love Miss Hardy.

MRS. RACKET. He did love Miss Hardy, Sir, and would have been the happiest of men.

SAVILLE. Pardon me, Madam; his heart was not only free from that Lady's chains, but absolutely captivated by another.

MRS. RACKET. No, Sir—no. It was Miss Hardy who captivated him. She met him last night at the Masquerade, and charmed him in disguise—He professed the most violent passion for her; and a plan was laid, this evening, to cheat him into happiness.

SAVILLE. Ha! ha! ha!—Upon my soul, I must beg your pardon; I have not eaten of the Italian Princess's box of sweetmeats, sent by her own page; and yet I am as mad as Doricourt, ha! ha! ha!

MRS. RACKET. So it appears—What can all this mean?

SAVILLE. Why, Madam, he is at present in his perfect senses; but he'll lose 'em in ten minutes, through joy.—The madness was only a feint, to avoid marrying Miss Hardy, ha! ha! ha!—I'll carry him the intelligence directly. [*Going.*

MRS. RACKET. Not for worlds. I owe him revenge, now, for what he has made us suffer. You must promise not to divulge a syllable I have told you; and when Doricourt is summoned to Mr. Hardy's, prevail on him to come—madness, and all.

LADY FRANCES. Pray do. I should like to see him shewing off, now I am in the secret.

SAVILLE. You must be obeyed; though 'tis inhuman to conceal his happiness.

MRS. RACKET. I am going home; so I'll set you down at his lodgings, and acquaint you, by the way, with our whole scheme. *Allons!*

SAVILLE. [*Leading her out*] I attend you.

MRS. RACKET. You won't fail us?

[*Exit* Saville, *and* Mrs. Racket.

LADY FRANCES. No; depend on us. [*Exit.*

V.iv

[Doricourt*'s.* Doricourt *seated, reading.*]

Doricourt. [*Flings away the book*] What effect can the morals of fourscore have on a mind torn with passion? [*Musing*] Is it possible such a soul as hers, can support itself in so humiliating a situation? A kept woman! [*Rising*] Well, well—I am glad it is so—I am glad it is so!

[*Enter* Saville.

SAVILLE. What a happy dog you are, Doricourt! I might have been mad, or beggar'd, or pistol'd myself, without its being mentioned—But you, forsooth! the whole Female World is concerned for. I reported the state of your brain to five different women—The lip of the first trembled; the white bosom of the second heaved a sigh; the third ejaculated, and turned her eye—to the glass; the fourth blessed herself; and the fifth said, whilst she pinned a curl, "Well, now, perhaps, he'll be an amusing Companion; his native dullness was intolerable."

DORICOURT. Envy! sheer envy, by the smiles of Hebe!—There are not less than forty pair of the brightest eyes in town will drop crystals, when they hear of my misfortune.

SAVILLE. Well, but I have news for you:—Poor Hardy is confined to his bed; they say he is going out of the world by the first post, and he wants to give you his blessing.

DORICOURT. Ill! so ill! I am sorry from my soul. He's a worthy little Fellow—if he had not the gift of foreseeing so strongly.

SAVILLE. Well; you must go and take leave.

DORICOURT. What! to act the Lunatic in the dying Man's chamber?

SAVILLE. Exactly the thing; and will bring your business to a short issue: for his last commands must be, that you are not to marry his Daughter.

DORICOURT. That's true, by Jupiter!—and yet, hang it, impose upon a poor fellow at so serious a moment!—I can't do it.

SAVILLE. You must, 'faith. I am answerable for your appearance, though it should be in a strait waistcoat. He knows your situation, and seems the more desirous of an interview.

DORICOURT. I don't like encountering Racket.—She's an arch little devil, and will discover the cheat.

SAVILLE. There's a fellow!—Cheated Ninety-nine Women, and now afraid of the Hundredth.

DORICOURT. And with reason—for that hundredth is a Widow.

[*Exeunt.*

V.v

[Hardy*'s. Enter* Mrs. Racket, *and* Miss Ogle.]

MISS OGLE. And so Miss Hardy is actually to be married to-night?

MRS. RACKET. If her Fate does not deceive her. You are apprised of the scheme, and we hope it will succeed.

MISS OGLE. [*Aside*] *Deuce, take her! she's six years younger than I am.—Is Mr. Doricourt handsome?*

MRS. RACKET. Handsome, generous, young, and rich.—There's a Husband for ye! Isn't he worth pulling caps[107] for?

MISS OGLE.—[*Aside*] *I' my conscience, the Widow speaks as though she'd give cap, ears, and all for him.*—[*To her*] I wonder you didn't try to catch this wonderful Man, Mrs. Racket?

MRS. RACKET. Really, Miss Ogle, I had not time. Besides, when I marry, so many stout young fellows will hang themselves, that, out of regard to society, in these sad times, I shall postpone it for a few years.—[*Aside*] *This will cost her a new lace—I heard it crack.*

[*Enter* Sir George, *and* Lady Frances.

SIR GEORGE. Well, here we are.—But where's the Knight of the Woeful Countenance?[108]

MRS. RACKET. Here soon, I hope—for a woeful Night it will be without him.

SIR GEORGE. Oh, fie! do you condescend to pun?

MRS. RACKET. Why not? It requires genius to make a good pun—some men of bright parts can't reach it. I know a Lawyer who writes them on the back of his briefs; and says they are of great use—in a dry cause.

[*Enter* Flutter.

FLUTTER. Here they come!—Here they come!—Their coach stopped, as mine drove off.

LADY FRANCES. Then Miss Hardy's fate is at a crisis.—She plays a hazardous game, and I tremble for her.

SAVILLE. [*Without*] Come, let me guide you!—This way, my poor Friend! Why are you so furious?

DORICOURT. [*Without*] The House of Death—to the House of Death! [*Enter* Doricourt, *and* Saville] Ah! this is the spot!

LADY FRANCES. How wild and fiery he looks!

MISS OGLE. Now, I think, he looks terrified.

FLUTTER. Poor creature, how his eyes work!

MRS. RACKET. I never saw a Madman before—Let me examine him—Will he bite?

SAVILLE. Pray keep out of his reach, Ladies—You don't know your danger. He's like a Wild Cat, if a sudden thought seises him.

SIR GEORGE. You talk like a Keeper of Wild Cats—How much do you demand for shewing the Monster?

DORICOURT.—[*Aside*] *I don't like this—I must rouse their sensibility.*—[*To them*] There! there she darts through the air in liquid flames! Down again! Now I have her—Oh, she burns, she scorches!—Oh! she eats into my very heart!

OMNES. Ha! ha! ha!

MRS. RACKET. He sees the Apparition of the wicked Italian Princess.

FLUTTER. Keep her Highness fast, Doricourt.

MISS OGLE. Give her a pinch, before you let hergo.

DORICOURT. I am laughed at!

MRS. RACKET. Laughed at—aye, to be sure; why, I could play the Madman better than you.—"There! there she is! Now I have her!" Ha! ha! ha!

DORICOURT. I knew that Devil would discover me.—[*Aside*] *I'll leave the house:—I'm covered with confusion.* [*Going.*

SIR GEORGE. Stay, Sir—You must not go. 'Twas poorly done, Mr. Doricourt, to affect madness, rather than fulfill your engagements.

DORICOURT. Affect madness!—Saville, what can I do?

SAVILLE. Since you are discovered, confess the whole.

MISS OGLE. Aye, turn Evidence, and save Yourself.

DORICOURT. Yes; since my designs have been so unaccountably discovered, I will avow the whole. I cannot love Miss Hardy—and I will never—

SAVILLE. Hold, my dear Doricourt! be not so rash. What will the world say to such—

DORICOURT. Damn the world! What will the world give me for the loss of happiness? Must I sacrifice my peace, to please the world?

SIR GEORGE. Yes, every thing, rather than be branded with dishonour.

LADY FRANCES. Though *our* arguments should fail, there *is* a Pleader, whom you surely cannot withstand—the dying Mr. Hardy supplicates you not to forsake his Child.

[*Enter* Villers.

VILLERS. Mr. Hardy requests you to grant him a moment's conversation, Mr. Doricourt, though you should persist to send him miserable to the grave. Let me conduct you to his chamber.

DORICOURT. Oh, aye, any where; to the Antipodes—to the Moon—Carry me—Do with me what you will.

MRS. RACKET. Mortification and disappointment, then, are specifics in a case of stubbornness.—I'll follow, and let you know what passes.

[*Exeunt* Villers, Doricourt, Mrs. Racket, *and* Miss Ogle.

FLUTTER. Ladies, Ladies, have the charity to take me with you, that I may make no blunder in repeating the story. [*Exit* Flutter.

LADY FRANCES. Sir George, you don't know Mr. Saville. [*Exit* Lady Frances.

SIR GEORGE. Ten thousand pardons—but I will not pardon myself, for not observing you. I have been with the utmost impatience at your door twice to-day.

SAVILLE. I am concerned you had so much trouble, Sir George.

SIR GEORGE. Trouble! what a word!—I hardly know how to address you; I am distressed beyond measure; and it is the highest proof of my opinion of your honour, and the delicacy of your mind, that I open my heart to you.

SAVILLE. What has disturbed you, Sir George?

SIR GEORGE. Your having preserved Lady Frances, in so imminent a danger. Start not, Saville; to protect Lady Frances was my right. You have wrested from me my dearest privilege.

SAVILLE. I hardly know how to answer such a reproach. I cannot apologize for what I have done.

SIR GEORGE. I do not mean to reproach you; I hardly know what I mean. There is one method by which you may restore peace to me; I cannot endure that my Wife should be so infinitely indebted to any man who is less than my Brother.

SAVILLE. Pray explain yourself.

SIR GEORGE. I have a Sister, Saville, who is amiable; and you are worthy of her. I shall give her a commission to steal your heart, out of revenge for what you have done.

SAVILLE. I am infinitely honoured, Sir George; but—

SIR GEORGE. I cannot listen to a sentence which begins with so unpromising a word. You must go with us into Hampshire; and, if you see each other with the eyes I do, your felicity will be complete. I know no one, to whose heart I would so readily commit the care of my Sister's happiness.

SAVILLE. I will attend you to Hampshire, with pleasure; but not on the plan of retirement. Society has claims on Lady Frances, that forbid it.

SIR GEORGE. Claims, Saville!

SAVILLE. Yes, claims; Lady Frances was born to be the ornament of Courts. She is sufficiently alarmed, not to wander beyond the reach of her Protector;—and, from the British Court, the most tenderly-anxious Husband could not wish to banish his Wife. Bid her keep in her eye the bright Example who presides there;[109] the splendour of whose rank yields to the superior lustre of her Virtue.

SIR GEORGE. I allow the force of your argument. Now for intelligence!

[*Enter* Mrs. Racket, Lady Frances, *and* Flutter.

MRS. RACKET. Oh! Heav'ns! do you know—

FLUTTER. Let me tell the story—As soon as Doricourt—

MRS. RACKET. I protest you sha'n't—said Mr. Hardy—

FLUTTER. No, 'twas Doricourt spoke first—says he—No, 'twas the Parson—says he—

MRS. RACKET. Stop his mouth, Sir George—he'll spoil the tale.

SIR GEORGE. Never heed circumstances—the result—the result.

MRS. RACKET. No, no; you shall have it in form.—Mr. Hardy performed the Sick Man like an Angel—He sat up in his bed, and talked so pathetically, that the tears stood in Doricourt's eyes.

FLUTTER. Aye, stood—they did not drop, but stood.—I shall, in future, be very exact. The Parson seized the moment; you know, they never miss an opportunity.

MRS. RACKET. Make haste, said Doricourt; if I have time to reflect, poor Hardy will die unhappy.

FLUTTER. They were got as far as the Day of Judgement, when we slipped out of the room.

SIR GEORGE. Then, by this time, they must have reached *Amazement*,[110] which, every body knows, is the end of Matrimony.

MRS. RACKET. Aye, the Reverend Fathers ended the service with that word, Prophetically—to teach the Bride what a capricious Monster a Husband is.

SIR GEORGE. I rather think it was Sarcastically—to prepare the Bridegroom for the unreasonable humours and vagaries of his Help-mate.

LADY FRANCES. Here comes the Bridegroom of to-night.

[*Enter* Doricourt *and* Villers.—Villers *whispers* Saville, *who goes out.*

OMNES. Joy! joy! joy!

MISS OGLE. If *he*'s a sample of Bridegrooms, keep me single!—A younger Brother, from the Funeral of his Father, could not carry a more fretful countenance.

FLUTTER. Oh!—Now, he's melancholy mad, I suppose.

LADY FRANCES. You do not consider the importance of the occasion.

VILLERS. No; nor how shocking a thing it is for a Man to be forced to marry one Woman, whilst his heart is devoted to another.

MRS. RACKET. Well, now 'tis over, I confess to you, Mr. Doricourt, I think 'twas a most ridiculous piece of Quixotism, to give up the happiness of a whole life to a Man who perhaps has but a few moments to be sensible of the sacrifice.

FLUTTER. So it appeared to me.—But, thought I, Mr. Doricourt has travelled—he knows best.

DORICOURT. Zounds! Confusion!—Did ye not all set upon me?—Didn't ye talk to me of Honour—Compassion—Justice?

SIR GEORGE. Very true—You have acted according to their dictates, and I hope the utmost felicity of the Married State will reward you.

DORICOURT. Never, Sir George! to Felicity I bid adieu—but I will endeavour to be content.

Where is my—I must speak it—where is my *Wife?*

[*Enter* Letitia, *masked, led by* Saville.

SAVILLE. Mr. Doricourt, this Lady was pressing to be introduced to you.

DORICOURT. [*Starting*] Oh!

LETITIA. I told you last night, you shou'd see me at a time when you least expected me—and I have kept my promise.

VILLERS. Whoever you are, Madam, you could not have arrived at a happier moment.—Mr. Doricourt is just married.

LETITIA. Married! impossible! 'Tis but a few hours since he swore to me eternal Love: I believ'd him, gave him up my Virgin heart—and now!—Ungrateful Sex!

DORICOURT. Your Virgin heart! No, Lady—my fate, thank Heaven! yet wants that torture. Nothing but the conviction that you was another's, could have made me think one moment of Marriage, to have saved the lives of half Mankind. But this visit, Madam, is as barbarous as unexpected. It is now my duty to forget you, which, spite of your situation, I found difficult enough.

LETITIA. My situation!—What situation?

DORICOURT. I must apologise for explaining it in this company—but, Madam, I am not ignorant, that you are the companion of Lord George Jennet—and this is the only circumstance that can give me peace.

LETITIA. I—a Companion! Ridiculous pretence! No, Sir, know, to your confusion, that my heart, my honour, my name is unspotted as hers you have married; my birth equal to your own, my fortune large—That, and my person, might have been yours.—But, Sir, farewell! [*Going.*

DORICOURT. Oh, stay a moment—Rascal! is she not—

FLUTTER. Who, she? O Lard! no—'Twas quite a different person that I meant.—I never saw that Lady before.

DORICOURT. Then, never shalt thou see her more. [*Shakes* Flutter.

MRS. RACKET. Have mercy upon the poor Man!—Heavens! he'll murder him.

DORICOURT. Murder him! Yes, you, myself, and all Mankind. Sir George—Saville—Villers—'twas you who push'd me on this precipice;—'tis you who have snatch'd from me joy, felicity, and life.

MRS. RACKET. There! now, how well he acts the Madman!—This is something like! I knew he would do it well enough, when the time came.

DORICOURT. Hard-hearted Woman! enjoy my ruin—riot in my wretchedness. [Hardy *bursts in.*

HARDY. This is too much. You are now the Husband of my Daughter; and how dare you shew all this passion about another Woman?

DORICOURT. Alive again!

HARDY. Alive! aye, and merry. Here, wipe off the flour from my face. I was never in better health and spirits in my life.—I foresaw t'would do—. Why, my illness was only a fetch, Man! to make you marry Letty.

DORICOURT. It was! Base and ungenerous! Well, Sir, you shall be gratified. The possession of my heart was no object either with You, or your Daughter. My fortune and name was all you desired, and these—I leave ye. My native England I shall quit, nor ever behold you more. But, Lady, that in my exile I may have one consolation, grant me the favour you denied last night;—let me behold all that mask conceals, that your whole image may be impress'd on my heart, and chear my distant solitary hours.

LETITIA. This is the most awful moment of my life. Oh, Doricourt, the slight action of taking off my Mask, stamps me the most blest or miserable of Women!

DORICOURT. What can this mean? Reveal your face, I conjure you.

LETITIA. Behold it.

DORICOURT. Rapture! Transport! Heaven!

FLUTTER. Now for a touch of the happy Madman.

VILLERS. This scheme was mine.

LETITIA. I will not allow that. This little stratagem arose from my disappointment, in not having made the impression on you I wish'd. The timidity of the English character threw a veil over me, you could not penetrate. You have forced me to emerge in some measure from my natural reserve, and to throw off the veil that hid me.

DORICOURT. I am yet in a state of intoxication—I cannot answer you.—Speak on, sweet Angel!

LETITIA. You see I *can* be any thing; chuse then my character—your Taste shall fix it. Shall I be an *English* Wife?—or, breaking from the bonds of Nature and Education, step forth to the world in all the captivating glare of Foreign Manners?

DORICOURT. You shall be nothing but yourself—nothing can be captivating that you are not. I will not wrong your penetration, by pretending that you won my heart at the first interview; but you have now my whole soul—your person, your face, your mind, I would not exchange for those of any other Woman breathing.

HARDY. A Dog! how well he makes up for past slights! Cousin Racket, I wish you a good Husband with all my heart. Mr. Flutter, I'll believe every word you say this fortnight. Mr. Villers, you and I have manag'd this to a T. I never was so merry in my life—'Gad, I believe I can dance. [*Footing*.

DORICOURT. Charming, charming creature!

LETITIA. Congratulate me, my dear friends! Can you conceive my happiness?

HARDY. No, congratulate me; for mine is the greatest

FLUTTER. No, congratulate me, that I have escaped with life, and give me some sticking plaster—this wild cat has torn the skin from my throat.

SIR GEORGE. I expect to be among the first who are congratulated—for I have recovered one Angel, while Doricourt has gained another.

HARDY. Pho! pho! Don't talk of Angels, we shall be happier by half as Mortals. Come into the next room; I have order'd out every drop of my Forty-eight, and I'll invite the whole parish of St. George's, but what we'll drink it out—except one dozen, which I shall keep under three double locks, for a certain Christening, that I foresee will happen within this twelvemonth.

DORICOURT. My charming Bride! It was a strange perversion of Taste, that led me to consider the delicate timidity of your deportment, as the mark of an uninform'd mind, or inelegant manners. I feel now it is to that innate modesty, English Husbands owe a felicity the Married Men of other nations are strangers to: it is a sacred veil to your own charms; it is the surest bulwark to your Husband's honour; and cursed be the hour—should it ever arrive—in which *British* Ladies shall sacrifice to *foreign Graces* the Grace of Modesty!

FINIS.

EPILOGUE.

Nay, cease, and hear me—I am come to scold—
Whence this night's plaudits, to a thought so old?
To gain a Lover, hid behind a Mask!
What's new in that? Or where's the mighty task?
For instance, now—What Lady Bab,[111] or Grace,
E'er won a Lover—in her natural Face?
Mistake me not—French red, or blanching creams,
I stoop not to—for those are hackney'd themes;
The arts I mean, are harder to detect,
Easier put on, and worn to more effect;—
As thus—
Do Pride and Envy, with their horrid lines,
Destroy th' effect of Nature's sweet designs?
The Mask of Softness is at once applied,
And gentlest manners ornament the Bride.
  Do thoughts too free inform the Vestal's eye,
Or point the glance, or warm the struggling sigh?
Not Dian's brows more rigid looks disclose;
And Virtue's blush appears, where Passion glows.
  And you, my gentle Sirs, wear Vizors too;
But here I'll strip you, and expose to view
Your hidden features—First I point at you.
That well-stuff'd waistcoat, and that ruddy cheek;
That ample forehead, and that skin so sleek,
Point out good-nature, and a gen'rous heart—
Tyrant! stand forth, and, conscious, own thy part:
Thy Wife, thy Children, tremble in thy eye;
And Peace is banish'd—when the Father's nigh.
  Sure 'tis enchantment! See, from ev'ry side
The Masks fall off!—In charity I hide
The monstrous features rushing to my view—
Fear not, there, Grand-Papa—nor you—nor you:
For should I shew your features to each other,
Not one amongst ye'd know his Friend, or Brother.
'Tis plain, then, all the world, from Youth to Age,
Appear in Masks—Here, only, on the Stage,
You see us as we are: Here trust your eyes;
Our wish to please, admits of no disguise.

18.2 "AN ACCOUNT . . . THE MASQUERADE AT THE PANTHEON"

"An Account of, with Observations upon, the Masquerade at the Pantheon, on Thursday, Feb. 18, 1773," *The Gentleman's and London Magazine*, (March 1773), 177–79.

THE ENGLISH ARE OF ALL OTHER PEOPLE the least calculated for Masquerades. There is a phlegmatic dullness about them, that when they put on a dress they never reflect what is required to support that character: therefore, whenever they have a witticism addressed to the mask, they are splenetic and pettish.—The English, in general, are not happy at bon mot or repartee; which again makes a Masquerade dull and insipid. It was observed by many people, that the last company which attended the Pantheon were churlish before supper; but, true John Bull-like, they were more affable after full filling of their bellies. Many houses receive Masks with great impropriety, particularly Mr. Tuffnell in Cavendish-square, whose company were all *unmasked*; which is destroying the very nature and existence of a Masquerade. Besides, Mr. Tuffnell, in a true military stile, had procured a serjeant and a party of the foot-guards to protect his house—very unbecoming the constitution of this country! Lord Darlington's method was infinitely superior:–it is not the elegance, it is the mode of doing any thing that gives it a consequence.

The doors of the Pantheon were opened about half after ten. By supper-time, 1800 people, as near as can be computed, were in the rooms; and the brilliancy of their dresses, added to the rich display of lamps and illuminations in every part of the Pantheon, gave the place an air of uncommon splendor and gaiety. A prodigious number of the first nobility were in Dominos. Among the character Masks were, Lord Stanley, and Mr. Stanley, in Grecian dresses of that kind which the French term *selon l'ordre de Matelót*. Sir Richard Adams, a Vandyke. Sir Watkin Williams Wynne, a St. David, mounted on a goat: he afterwards put on a Domino, and walked with his lady, who also wore a Domino. Mrs. Shepherd, Diana. Mrs. Becher, a Polonese lady; by much the finest figure in the room, having 20,000 l. worth of jewels on her. Sir William Prideaux, in an elegant Turkish dress of a peculiar stile. Miss Gower and another lady, in beautiful Fancy Dresses. Mr. Farrer, a Chimney-sweeper. Mr. Andrews, a Dutchman. Mr. Stroud, a Procuress. Mr. Guyon, an Hussar. Mr. Colman, a Scythian. Mr. Fisher, a Witch. Mr. Dawson and Mr. Ashley; one a fine Vandyke, the other a French Paysan. Captain Thompson, a Conjuror. Mr. Dawes, a Black Messenger to the Morning Post. Miss West, a Magician. Two gentlemen who walked on the late installation of the Knights of the Bath, in their Esquires' dresses. Clara Haywood, in a Fancy Dress. Fanny Herbert, a Waggoner. The other Masks, whom we did not know, were Three Sybils. A woman with a tall Head-dress and a Ladder to it, after Darley's print. Three Watchmen, very troublesome with their rattles. A Noble Newmarket Jockey, with Star on his waistcoat breast. A Groupe of Gypsies. A Blue coat Boy. A Mungo. A Merlin. A Fish-girl. Angria the Pirate, a good

Mask. A Merry-Andrew to a Mountebank. A Waterman. Lady Pentweazle. A Macaroni Tallow-chandler. The lady of the French Ambassador in a Fancy Dress, with the Ambassador's Star, and other jewellery ornaments on. An Alderman. A Lawyer, having one side of his face black, with the word "Plaintiff" written on it; the other white, with the word "Defendant". A Wooden-legg'd Sailor. A Coachman. Four fine tall Grenadiers. A Poet and his Footman. A Double Mask: one side an Old Woman, the other a Young one. A Somebody. A Nobody. A Bacchanal. Two Girls with live Chickens. A Foreigner with a Squirrel. A Harlequin, who might from his nimbleness have been taken for Lewes, of Covent-Garden Theatre, if he had not spoken in the language of Punch all evening. A dull Mercury. Two more Harlequins, who bore no more resemblance to the character than having party-coloured coats and black Masks on. A School-master. Friars, Nuns, Shepherdesses, Chinese, Nabobs, Old Women and Servant Maids in abundance, with the following Theatrical Masks: An Elfrida, her first Virgin, Kitely, Momus, Henry the Sixth, Cyrus, Jachimo, Falstaff, Touchstone, a wretched Richard, and several Pierrots and Pantaloons. Mrs. Thompson, in the character of a Haymaker, supported with ease and vivacity. Mr. Bristow, a Gurderius. The beautiful Miss Thompson, in a black Domino. Mr. Prescot, with two black Petticoats; one on the shoulders, the other on the hips. A Country Clown, Mr. Bryer. Sir Sampson Gideon, a senseless Cyrus. A Nymph, Miss Mills. A Shepherdess, Mrs. Blaquiere. Mr. and Mrs. Kelly, in Fancy Dresses. A Roman Punch.

After the various accounts given, it will appear a vanity to attempt a new mode of describing a Masquerade: but as we mean to give our country readers, who are far removed from the follies of fashion, an idea of such a whimsical entertainment, that they may enjoy what they are deprived of seeing; we have annexed a repetition of the liveliest witticisms, as addresses to the characters.

Mr. Franks the Jew, in a Domino, was importuned greatly by a lady to converse, or to answer her questions; but he being dully silent, she observed, *That the Fathers of the Synagogue had certainly made a mistake, and had unhappily circumcised him in the tongue.*— Four Gentlemen in black Masks and Dominos addressed a Conjuror to know, Which of their shoulders itched? The Conjuror replied, *Anum.*—Mr. Wynn, and two Gentlemen of the Fiddle, asked the Conjuror if he could smell them out. *Yes*, replied the Seer, *the rosin is very powerful.*—A *thin* Macaroni Cook teasing a pretty Haymaker, and asking her repeatedly if she knew what he wanted—*Yes*, replied she, *very well*; *you want a fop in the pan.*—The Devil went up to Mr. Colman (in the character of the Scythian), and asked him, How he came not to be as much a Soldier when he was attacked in Drury-lane? *Because*, replied Colman, *the Church have power even over you—much more over tiny mortals!*

Miss West (who is very handsome), being in the character of a Magician, asked Captain Thompson the Conjuror, if his magic powers were superior? *No*, replied the military Magi, *your Circean incantations, and most bewitching charms, are far excelling mine*—The Devil coming up to a Conjuror in a violent rage, roared out, Who made you a Conjuror? He answered, *You*. Damn such a Conjuror? He answered, *You*. Damn such a Conjuror, says the Devil. *Sir*, replied the Seer, *I always knew the Devil to be a Gentleman: therefore, as you are not one, you must be a most diabolical imposter.*—An old Courtesan (in the character of Night) addressed the Conjuror to have her fortune told. *Madam*, replied the Sage, *Night, you have had your Day.* And to a Widow in the character of Diana he observed, *That she was truly in Masquerade; for the Goddess of Chace was celebrated only for her virginity.*—Four Officers of the English Guards personated Officers of the Swiss Guards, and spoke in French; (they were fine figures, dressed in blue, with red cloth stocks) which a Wag observed, *made them look like Norfolk Turkies with their throats cut.*—A Courtesan, in the character of a Market Girl with eggs in a basket, asked the Conjuror to tell her her fortune. He replied, *A crack'd Egg and a crack'd Maid can never be mended.*—A talkative Mungo pestered the Conjuror to know his fate. He replied, *Tyburn.*—And when the same question was asked by Captain Constantine Phipps, he answered, *Glory, and a Nation's praises.*

Lord E_____e, in the character of an Old Woman, desired to know her end. He replied, *You will die the death of Tantalus—craving drink without being able to swallow it.* Why so? Says the Old Woman. *Because,* says the Sage, *you drink at your own table good wines, and give sour to your guests.*

A Man and Woman, not of the most pure characters, pestering the Conjuror to know his opinion of them though masked, he answered,

Many a Rogue, and many a Jade,
Come unto a Masquerade.

There were two Gardeners and two Eves—the men dull, the women handsome; which made a Wag observe, *That there was no wonder that Eve was tempted by a Serpent, if the original Adam was but half as stupid.*—A Gentleman cloathed in Canvass called himself a Roman Punch; and disputing about the originality and propriety of the characters with the Conjuror, the Sage replied, *that if Foote's Punch was half as dull, he would burn him for a log in his kitchen, to boil his kettle.*—A heavy dull youth in the character of Falstaff, kept repeating, "Care blows a man up like a bladder!" *True,* says a Wag; *and you're quite as empty.*—Mr. Astly (who was rather indecent in the character of a Procuress) asked a Gentlemen in the garb of a Watchman, if he should procure him a Girl? The Watchman observed, *If you don't mend your manners, Mrs. Cole, I'll procure you a Round-house.*—A Cyrus being asked by a Haymaker how Mandane did, answered, You should enquire after Aspasia. *No*, replied the Lady, *you look as if you wanted your Mother more than a Mistress.*—Mr. Kelly being in a superb Eastern dress, a Lady observed, *if he made his Comedies as well as his Cloaths, he would be the first dramatic Genius living.* Cætera desiderantur.

18.3 REVIEW OF *THE BELLE'S STRATAGEM, MORNING CHRONICLE AND LONDON ADVERTISER*

Morning Chronicle and London Advertiser 23 Feb. 1780.

Theatrical Intelligence

A NEW COMEDY, called *The Belle's Stratagem*, was performed last night (for the first time) at Covent-Garden Theatre . . . [cast of characters omitted]

This piece, which is the avowed production of Mrs. Cowley, author of the comedy of the *Runaway*, the farce of *Who's the Dupe?* And the tragedy of *Albina*, was honoured with strong marks of applause by a very crouded audience in the course of its representation, and at the conclusion of it was stamped with as loud and as general a seal of approbation as has been bestowed on any one comedy, presented of late years, from either of our stages.

The story of it is full of incident, bustle, and situation . . . [plot summary omitted]

This comedy affords much ground for commendation, and some for censure. It does great credit to the fertility of the author's genius, but it does not prove that her judgment is matured in proportion as her ability has increased. The fable is more artful than natural, and the dialogue is exceptionable in some particulars, but on the whole it is more brilliant than characteristic. The incidents are in general contrived very plausibly, and the business of the plot, though it is obviously matter of invention, connects well, and excites curiosity, while it affords satisfaction.

The characters are for the most part well drawn and well sustained, and though not originals, are so used that they acquire the merit of originality from their exercise and employment. Lady Frances is by much the best portrait in the groupe; her figure is correctly designed, and coloured with great delicacy and truth. The character of Letitia is boldly drawn and finished in a very high stile. Sir George exhibits a warm picture of a man rendered uneasy from the excess of his love for the object in his possession, and Old Hardy's humour is very pleasantly managed. Flutter affords much entertainment, and Saville interests the heart in his favour.

In many of the scenes there is a strength and shrewdness of observation, a pleasantry of turn, a propriety and a prettiness of diction, and some strokes of wit and humour that would do honour to any dramatist; but then it must be observed, that there is too studied an affectation of [the] power of writing, an unnecessary larding of the dialogue with French phrases, a frequency of images either unapposite or inelegant, and occasionally a low allusion and expression which disgrace the characters they come from. The piece interests the spectator early, but the effect of the difficulties and embarrassments is much lessened, not only from their being contrived in the sight of the audience, but in consequence of the means, by which they are to be done away, being discovered too soon. The play is abundantly too long in representation; a defect that may easily be remedied, as the greatest part of the auction scene may well be spared, and other scenes require to be much shortened. That, in which Sir George so satirically describes the old virgins of the last age, would be considerably benefited by curtailment, since the force of his excellent remarks, is almost spent by the same thought's being too often repeated. One matter in particular, calls for the author's pruning knife, and that is, the vulgar expression of "Don't think to come over me with your flams," which Letitia uses to Doricort, when speaking in her assumed character; no lady of the smallest delicacy could use such language on any pretence; and though she is to be supposed to talk as an ignorant person, there is a main difference between simplicity and vulgarity.

We forbear to point out the many obvious resemblances in the characters, situations, and incidents of *The Belle's Stratagem* to those of preceding comedies, because we are aware of the great difficulty of creating a drama perfectly original in all its parts; and, if the manner in which a resemblance to what has before been seen on the stage, be new, and produce a good effect, we think the author's ingenuity ought, at least, to be admitted as a protection from censure, if not considered as a warrantable claim to applause.

Upon the whole, this play, though liable to the objections we have made, (and we have made them because we have the satisfaction to know that the piece is too firmly established in the public favour, to be hurt by the severest criticism, and rather with a view to induce the author to take more care in her future productions, than to chill her merit or check her progress as a writer,) affords great entertainment in the theatre, and it will afford still more, when the necessary [alterations] are made.

18.4 REVIEW OF *THE BELLE'S STRATAGEM, MORNING POST AND DAILY ADVERTISER*

Morning Post and Daily Advertiser 23 Feb, 1780.

Theatrical Intelligence. Covent-garden.

LAST NIGHT A NEW COMEDY was performed here for the first time, called the *Belle's Stratagem* . . . [cast and plot summary omitted]

The *Belle's Stratagem* is the avowed production of Mrs. Cowley, and tho' a more unequal performance than her *Runaway*, will not, on due examination, be found inferior to that comedy.—Many of the scenes are well written, and therefore we wish they were more connected with the main business of the piece. Indeed the principal defect is in the very limited foundation on which the story is built; from whence naturally arises all that extraneous matter, which disproportions, as it increases the superstructure.—To the same cause we may attribute the want of incident and situation, so essential in dramatic compositions, and the confusion with which the denouement is brought about. If the pruning knife should be found necessary, we would recommend, that unpromising excrescence of the auction-room to be totally cut away. Indeed we think the whole may be much improved by a variety of curtailings.—Miss Hardy's character is in itself well drawn, but we dislike its affinity to Maria in the *Citizen*, though it be intended to produce a contrary effect.—Old *Hardy*'s notions of *prescience* are humorous, and give him a turn of originality; but we cannot account for his acquired wit when he appears at the masquerade. On the whole, however, the play was very warmly, and in many places deservedly applauded by a numerous audience.

The performers acquitted themselves very ably in their several lines; Miss Young however not content with the common exertions of her procession, *danced a grand minuet,—and sung a die-away air*; we were told indeed that she intended also to have rode down the stage upon three of *Astley's* horses, and afterwards to have stood upon her head on the top-most round of a high ladder; but those achievements we found, for some managerial reason or other, were postponed to another evening!

18.5 CHAS. WHITE, *A MASQUERADE SCENE IN THE PANTHEON*

Chas. White, *A Masquerade Scene in the Pantheon,* engraving, March 13, 1773. Trustees of the British Museum.

18.6 JOHN DIXON, *INSIDE VIEW OF THE PANTHEON*

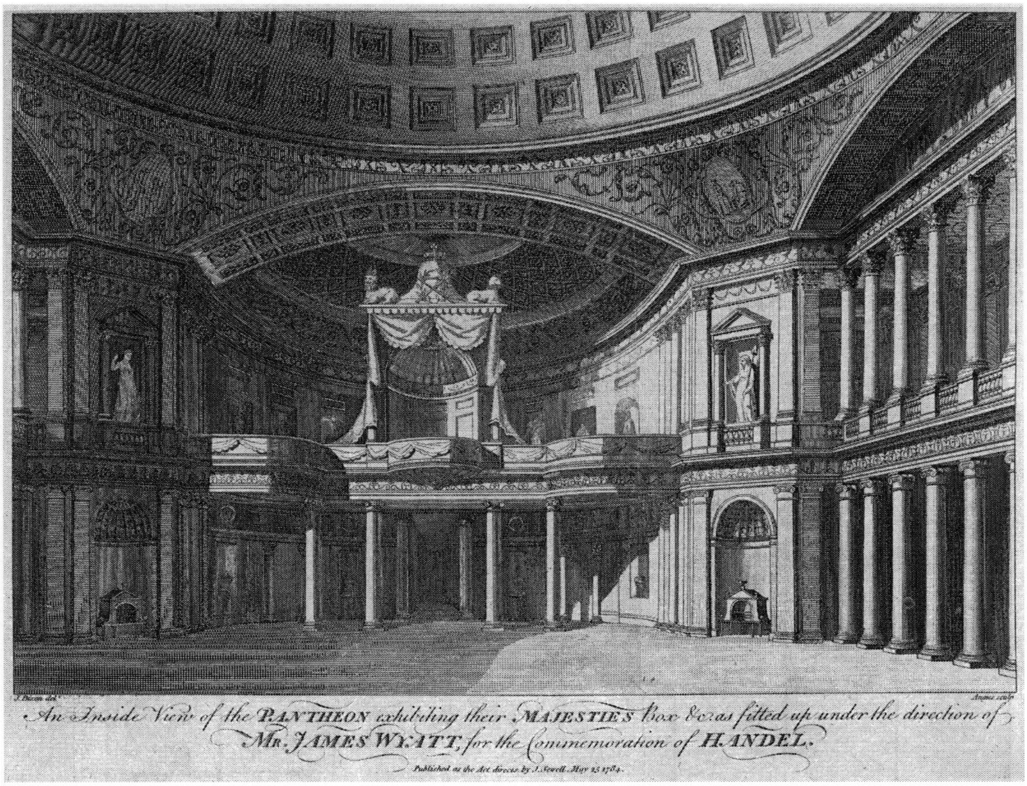

John Dixon, *Inside View of the Pantheon,* etching, May 25, 1784. Victoria and Albert Museum, London.

18.7 *PORTRAIT OF HANNAH COWLEY*

COMEDY unveiling to Mrs COWLEY.
by Mr Heath, From a Painting by R. Cosway Esq. R.A. in the Possession of M^rs Co

James Heath (after Richard Cosway), *Comedy unveiling herself to Mrs. Cowley*, stipple etching, c. 1784. Trustees of the British Museum.

Notes

1 The copy text is *The Belle's Stratagem, A Comedy as acted at the Theatre Royal in Covent Garden,* by Mrs. Cowley, London, printed for T. Cadell in the Strand, 1782.
2 Cowley was born in 1743 and died in 1809.
3 Gillian Russell, *Women, Sociability and Theatre in Georgian London.* Cambridge: Cambridge University Press, 2007, 220–4.
4 Queen Charlotte (1744–1818), consort of George III (1738–1820).
5 As we will see in the masquerade of IV.i, casting John Quick in this role was important for Cowley's satire on Sheridan's *The Duenna.* See notes 78 and 88 below. For more on Quick see the headnote and notes for *She Stoops to Conquer.*
6 One of the four Inns of Court. It is immediately opposite the Royal Courts of Justice in Holborn and is composed of numerous buildings and courtyards.
7 *Long Robes*: Judges.
8 *Hebes*: the youthful Hebe was the cupbearer to the gods and renowned for her innocence, but here the term also may mean barmaids.
9 *in the Æsop style*: according to legend Aesop was physically deformed.
10 *Almack's*: Opened in 1765 by William Almack, Almack's Assembly Rooms was an elite social club and one of the first to admit women. It was the chief rival to Teresa Cornelys' mixed entertainments at Carlisle House. Both establishments were synonymous with fashion and with gambling.
11 *Fops*: fashionable men who affected the manners of the continent. As represented in numerous plays and novels, they were both effeminate and vain.
12 *Paul's, the Lions, and the Wax-work*: St. Paul's Cathedral, the lions kept in the Royal Menagerie at the Tower of London and the "Moving Wax Works of the Royal Court of England," a museum or exhibition of 140 life-size figures, some apparently with clockwork moving parts, opened by Mrs. Mary Salmon in Fleet Street in the late seventeenth century.
13 *Gazette*: a supplement to the daily paper carrying important news.
14 *War*: The American Revolutionary War.
15 *Coterie*: The "Female Coterie" was a group of "ladies of quality" that met at Almack's Assembly Rooms. To blackball someone was to reject the application of a candidate to private club usually by a secret ballot—sometimes the actual casting of a black ball.
16 *'till the camps break up*: After the French entered the American War in 1778, military camps were established in south-east England to prepare for possible French invasion. They were the subject of much satire because fashionable men played at being officers and women of fashion would tour the camps. The point here is that the Town is depleted of men.
17 *Commons-doctors*: lawyers at Doctor's Commons, where lawyers trained in Roman-based civil law practiced. This was especially pertinent for ecclesiastical law relating to divorce.
18 *Crim. Con.*: short for criminal conversation, the legal term for the crime of adultery. According to the law, the husband was entitled to civil damages from the man who seduced his wife. Women could not bring a similar action against their husbands.
19 *Mackerel at Gravesend*: situated on the Thames estuary, Gravesend was famous for runs of mackerel.
20 Coxheath was the most famous of the Army camps and ruthlessly satirized by Richard Brinsley Sheridan in *The Camp* (1778).
21 Doricourt is just returned from the Grand Tour of France and Italy and people of fashion—i.e. the *Ton*—are imitating his affected style.
22 *Counsellor Pleadwell*: A barrister.
23 *The Town and Country Magazine* featured scandalous stories, called *tête-à-têtes,* about the affairs of fashionable people. See Contextual Materials for *The School for Scandal.*
24 *six-penny cuts*: Tête-à-têtes usually featured a pair of woodcuts of the scandalous lovers. The prints were sometimes sold separately.
25 Le Mosse, Verdue, Grossette and Detanville were all prominent French clothiers.
26 *l'air enjoué*: a playful nature.
27 *petits maîtres*: lesser gentry.

28 The Mall was a tree-lined promenade in St. James's Park. A *grissette* is a working class French woman.
29 *locum-tenens*: Latin for representative.
30 In Quaker services, members of the congregation were silent until someone was "moved" to speak.
31 Founded in 1766 near Hyde Park Corner, Tattersall's was the home of the Jockey Club. Because it was a site for selling and wagering on horses, it had private "Subscription Rooms" frequented by sporting and betting men.
32 *Á propos, des bottes*: by way of nothing.
33 According to Thucydides, Athens was beset by a horrible plague in the second year of the Peloponnesian War (430 BC). A typical subject for history painting, the picture referred to here would have been a copy of paintings of plague in classical cities by artists such as Poussin, Sweerts and Caroselli. Langfords was a prominent auction house.
34 *Nabob*: a former merchant of the East India Company who has returned to Britain with sufficient wealth to buy his way into upper echelons of society.
35 Dick Whittington and his Cat: both a tale from English folklore and a popular pantomime, it told the tale of how the Dick escaped poverty and became Mayor of London due to the ratting abilities of his cat. That the purchasers see the paintings as a matching pair based on their similar size is a sign of the general devolution of taste.
36 Poor dental care meant that many people were missing teeth and thus had hollow cheeks. Cork was stuffed between the gums and cheek to attain a full-looking face. These "plumpers" made it exceedingly difficult to talk.
37 John Paul Jones (1747–92) was a heroic naval commander in the American war. His actions in British waters were renowned. Omoa, a fortress on the Bay of Honduras, was the site of pyrrhic victory of the British over the American's Spanish allies. Despite taking the fort after a siege, the British troops were decimated by illness and eventually evacuated.
38 *la petite morale*: protocols of politeness and courtesy.
39 *Quixote*: a person characterized by romantic idealism, but here it also has the connotation of naïve.
40 *dans la place Victoire*: the Place de la Victoire in Paris featured a famous statue celebrating the military victories of Louis XIV.
41 The cathedral at St. Evreux was famous for its stained glass.
42 According to legend, only one of these birds can exist at a time.
43 *propria persona*: in legal terms, in his own person without the assistance of an attorney. Sir George is using legal jargon to object to the presence of Doricourt and all young men of fashion like him.
44 *virtuoso:* a scientist or natural philosopher, especially a member of the Royal Society. Lady Frances's father's botanical and geological interests parallel those of the natural philosophers whose works were adapted for the stage as the *Wonders of Derbyshire* in 1779. Covent Garden's spectacular production dominated receipts for the period immediately prior to *The Belle's Stratagem*.
45 The *robe de cour*, or grand habit, was the formal court wear worn throughout Europe from as far back as the 1680s. It was composed of stiff, boned bodice, a full skirt and a separate train.
46 *ceremony of presentation*: formal introductions at Court were regularly reported in the press.
47 Hyde Park is immediately adjacent to Kensington Palace. Mrs. Racket is sketching a popular open carriage ride.
48 *Darby and Joan*: a devoted elderly couple content to live in quiet retirement. The song *The Joys of Love Never Forgot*, published in *The Gentleman's Magazine*, goes as follows: "Old Darby, with Joan by his side, / You've often regarded with wonder: / He's dropsical, she is sore-eyed, / Yet they're never happy asunder."
49 *picquet*: a card game not usually associated with gambling.
50 *linsey-woolsey*: a plain woven fabric with a linen warp and a woolen weft valued for its warmth not its beauty.
51 *Festino*: a feast or entertainment. Sheridan's *The Camp* (1778) refers to "Festino tents and opera pavilions."
52 *Hesperian fruit*: the Garden of Hesperides, Hera's garden, contained trees that bore golden apples that would confer immortality on those who ate them. Atlas's daughters, the Hesperides, were charged with guarding the apples, but Hera had to introduce a hundred-headed dragon to protect

the trees from these very guardians. One of these apples was stolen by Eris, the goddess of discord, and it led to the Trojan War.

53 *Coachmaker's Hall*: The home of the coachmakers guild. In 1780, Lord George Gordon, commenced the Gordon Riots by staging an incendiary speech outside the hall protesting against the Papists Act of 1778, legislation intended to reduce religious discrimination against Catholics. The sectarian riots went on for days and deeply unsettled the metropolis.

54 The Black Horse Tavern was a noted site for public oratory and debating societies.

55 *Io Triumphe*: in a Roman Triumph, the phrase chanted by the principal celebrant of the religious procession celebrating past or present victories.

56 *want*: need.

57 *Anno Mundi* or *Anno Domini*: the former refers to the year of creation and the latter to the year of Christ's birth.

58 An antiquary is someone who studies and collects antiquities.

59 Mask litters his speech with names of Italian, Flemish and Dutch Old Masters in order to appear knowledgeable about painting.

60 Old Master paintings and their copies represented a small repertoire of Biblical and classical stories. The inability to discern the difference between a rendering of Diana and Actæon and a painting of David and Bathsheba carries a serious moral implication because it means that she can't differentiate between Actæon's inadvertent incursion on Diana's privacy and David's calculated act of seduction and adultery.

61 Copy text does not indicate 1st or 2nd Gentleman.

62 *maukin*: malkin, a servant or country girl.

63 The penitent Magdalen was a favourite subject for Renaissance Italian painting.

64 *Mauvaise honte*: bashfulness.

65 The *Venus de Medici*, now as then, was a classical sculpture on view in the Tribuna of the Uffizi Gallery in Florence. It was deemed the epitome of female beauty and artistic accomplishment.

66 An allusion to Jonathan Swift, *Gulliver's Travels*, Book 4.

67 *Mumchance*: a silent stupid person.

68 The misspellings here indicate that Letitia is mispronouncing Venus, Jubal and Diana (perhaps Dinah, but unlikely in this context).

69 *Flim-flams*: nonsense.

70 *Ifags*: I'fegs, short for the oath "in faith" or "by my faith."

71 sprightfuller: more sprightly.

72 *Pothecary*: a corruption of apothecary.

73 *Conundrums*: riddles in the form of a question the answer to which is a pun or play on words (*OED*).

74 *The Lady's Diary: Or Women's Almanack* was an annual that supplemented its calendar with stories and riddles often submitted by readers. Letitia's name riddles are typical of the kind used to fill out the latter pages of the volume.

75 These are all women's accomplishments. Cutting watch-papers refers to the practice of making intricate paper or silk circles to replace the papers that kept dust out of pocket-watches. In order to prepare strings for harps and other instruments, women would need to know how to work catgut. Letitia is also claiming expertise in decorating baskets and making silhouettes of equal merit to "the lady at N°. 62, South Moulton-street, Grosvenor-square." In doing so she is comparing her skills to that of a professional whose advertisement she would have read in the papers. It may well correspond to a commonly read advertisement.

76 *jugler's crucible*: alchemist's crucible.

77 *Bath*: a popular retreat and spa.

78 Both typical masquerade costumes. See Contexts for a detailed description of a Pantheon masquerade.

79 Quick, who plays Hardy in this play, famously played Isaac Mendoza in Richard Brinsley Sheridan's *The Duenna*, one of the most successful musical plays of the eighteenth-century. Mendoza's character is a study in anti-Semitism, so part of Cowley's point here is to send Quick to revive his part in order to critique Sheridan's work.

80 *Falernian*: a celebrated Italian wine from Campania.

81 *Boodles*: A prestigious gentleman's club on Pall Mall founded by Lord Shelburne, a prominent critic of Lord North's American policies and a critic of the American war.

82 Commons affair: adultery was prosecuted as criminal conversation at Doctor's Commons. Villers implies that Lady Touchwood has had insufficient time to take a lover.

83 *the old crabbed Fellow in Rome*: This is likely Cato the Elder, whose capacity to subordinate all private attachment to the greater glory of Rome was celebrated in Joseph Addison's eponymous play.

84 From the burlesque *Hurlo Thrumbo* by Samuel Johnson (1691–1773).

85 A reference to Rich's *The Necromancer.* Dr. Faustus flies off with Helen on a dragon.

86 According to legend, Rosamond Clifford was beloved by King Henry II. In order to hide her from his wife the King secreted Rosamond away in an intricate labyrinth; however, the Queen penetrated the labyrinth and forced Rosamond to poison herself.

87 All common masquerade costumes.

88 *Cotillons*: cotillions, a dance, usually of French origin, with a variety of steps and figures.

89 Folly wears the Jester's cap and the figure of a horse, made of wicker or a similar light material, around his waist.

90 A mountebank was a travelling salesman who sold quack medicines.

91 See note 78 above.

92 The Great Synagogue of London was in Duke's Place, north of Aldgate.

93 In *The Duenna*, Mendoza converts thus Hardy is playing his role according to script.

94 In *The Duenna*, Mendoza is forced to marry Margaret, the eponymous duenna or chaperone, so Hardy is being asked about her whereabouts. Guests would often come to masquerades in sets, but Hardy's response opts in favour of ridiculing the tendency of stage Irishmen to favour older women.

95 *Flesh-hook*: a hook for removing meat from the pot. There is a meat and fish joke underway here.

96 Doricourt is splitting time between parliament and the masquerade.

97 For *bandiner*, to jest or banter.

98 In *The Iliad*, Aphrodite makes Hera irresistible by giving her her *cestus*, or belt.

99 There was a State Lottery Office at No. 57 Cornhill, nearly opposite Bishopsgate-Street. Lottery loans, in which investors bought bonds whose size was determined by a draw, were frequently issued to raise funds, especially for military campaigns.

100 *Golconda*: the fortress in Hyderabad, India where some of the world's largest diamonds were mined.

101 The god of marriage ceremonies.

102 The reading of the budget is one of the most important events in parliament.

103 St. Bridget's cloak ostensibly had healing powers.

104 The reading of the budget in the House of Commons is one of the most important events in the Parliamentary calendar.

105 *Ninon*: The witty French courtesan Anne de Lenclos (1620–1705) was known by this nickname. She had many prominent lovers and maintained an important literary salon.

106 The physician John Monro (1715–91) specialized in mental illness and was the chief doctor at Bethlem Hospital, later known as Bedlam.

107 Pulling caps denotes fighting between women.

108 *Knight of the Woeful Countenance*: Don Quixote.

109 *the bright Example who presides there*: Queen Charlotte (1744–1818), consort of George III (1738–1820).

110 "Day of Judgment" appears near the beginning of the wedding ceremony in the Church of England; and "amazement" is uttered near the end.

111 Lady Bab Lardoon, a famous woman of fashion from John Burgoyne's play *The Maid of the Oaks* (1774). See note 51 for *The School for Scandal*. Fanny Abington made the most of the role's scandalous qualities.

---

19. *Inkle and Yarico*

***INKLE AND YARICO*. GEORGE COLMAN.**
FIRST PERFORMED 4 AUGUST 1787 AND FIRST PUBLISHED 1787

19.1 *INKLE AND YARICO*[1]

George Coleman

First Performed 4 August 1787 and First Published 1787

THERE ARE CERTAIN STORIES that a culture seems to need to tell itself over and over again. The Inkle and Yarico tale is one such story. Across the seventeenth and eighteenth centuries, this simple story of love and betrayal between the English merchant Inkle and the indigenous woman Yarico was published and circulated in a wide range of forms. Starting out as a brief digression in the travel writings of Jean Mocquet and Richard Ligon, the story achieved widespread notoriety when Richard Steele adapted it as a cautionary tale regarding female constancy for an early number of *The Spectator.* All subsequent versions of the tale are in dialogue with Steele's version, and versions of the story from, respectively, Inkle's and Yarico's perspective became the subject of sentimental verse. It was not until 1787 that the tale was adapted for the stage by George Colman the Younger (1762-1836). Considering the subject matter—interracial love, betrayal and enslavement—one would expect an adaptation to come in the form of a sentimental tragedy, but Colman chose to embed the story of Inkle and Yarico's love in a rather boisterous comic opera. That generic decision is important because much of *Inkle and Yarico*'s success on the London stage is directly attributable to Samuel Arnold's music and to the singing and dancing of the play's low characters Trudge and Wowski. Colman's play actually tells the story of three couples: a naval officer Captain Campley and his betrothed Narcissa, the merchant Inkle and the Native American woman who saves him, and their servants Trudge and Wowski. When listed in this fashion what we see among the men is a steady descent through the ranks. A similar change is registered among the women characters, only this time it is marked by racial difference: Narcissa is so white she is barely visible, Yarico operates in a state of noble savagery, while her servant Wowski exhibits all the traits of stage blackness. Thus *Inkle and Yarico* is one of the most instructive examples of what Michael Ragussis calls a multi-ethnic spectacle:[2] a play whose schematic deployment of the signs of rank and race tell us a great deal about British notions of difference in the years after the American War. As Christopher Leslie Brown has argued, the popularization of anti-slavery sentiment in the 1780s and 1790s was part of a larger movement to render Britons morally superior to their slave-holding brethren in the former colonies.[3]

The relationship between Colman's play and the abolitionist movement is ambiguous. Looking back on the play in her "Introduction" for the *British Theatre*, Elizabeth Inchbald clearly read the play through this lens:

> This is a drama, which might remove from Mr. Wilberforce his aversion to theatrical exhibitions, and convince him, that the teaching of moral duty is not

> confined to particular spots of ground; for, in those places, of all others, the doctrine is most effectually inculcated, where exhortation is the most required – the resorts of the gay, the idle, and the dissipated . . . [The opera] was popular before the subject of abolition of the slave trade was popular. It has the peculiar honour of preceding that great question. It was the bright forerunner of alleviation of the hardships of slavery.[4]

The ascription of abolitionist intent should give us pause because at the time of the composition of Inchbald's remarks the general approbation of the moral argument against slavery was at its height and hence Inchbald was making yet another argument for the moral value of the theatre. But this attempt to make *Inkle and Yarico* morally exemplary is strained by the critical contortions required to direct Colman's play at the African slave trade. As she notes:

> A fault more important, is – that the scene at the commencement of the opera, instead of Africa, is placed in America. It would undoubtedly have been a quick passage, to have a fourth part of the western globe, during the interval between the first and second acts; still, as the hero and heroine of the drama are compelled to go to sea – imagination, with but little more exertion, might have given them fair wind as well from the coast whence slaves are *really* bought, as from the shore where no such traffic is held*.
>
> > * No doubt the author would have ingenuity to argue away this objection – but that, which requires argument for its support in a dramatic work, is a subject for complaint. As slaves are imported from Africa, and never from America, the audience, in the two last acts of this play, feel as if they had been in the wrong quarter of the globe during the first act. Inkle could certainly steal a native from America, and sell her in Barbadoes, but this is not so consonant with that nice imitation of the order of things as to rank above criticism.[5]

These claims were complicated further by the fact that the play's most significant cultural legacy lay in the representation of Trudge's working class subjectivity and Wowski's highly sexualized racial difference. Indeed Wowski became a character with a life separate from the play, showing up in satirical prints, poems, and the popular press as the name for black femininity.

From our perspective the play's highly unstable treatment of gender, race, and class is perhaps suitable to a moment when competing notions of identity and sociability were sweeping through European society. By projecting these volatile categories outward, Colman was able to turn cultural anxiety into profit in the playhouse. As Julie Carlson has argued, it was not the first time nor will it be the last when anxieties about identity, and specifically colour, will be used to keep theatre in the black.[6]

Persons Represented

Inkle	Mr. Bannister, jun.
Sir Christopher Curry	Mr. Parsons.
Medium	Mr. Baddeley.
Campley	Mr. Davies.
Trudge	Mr. Edwin.
Mate	Mr. Meadows.
Yarico	Mrs. Kemble.
Narcissa	Mrs. Bannister.
Wowski	Miss George.
Patty	Mrs. Forster.

Prologue[7]

Again we venture, cheer'd by summer skies,
To bring in plain array and usual guise,
Scenes you have oft view'd here with gracious eyes.
No airs of foreign opera we borrow,
But Yarico resumes her genuine sorrow;
And, as the scene commands in various places,
Our ladies lay by rouge, and *black* their faces.

Yet you'll behold tonight—nor think it strange!
Before the piece concludes some little change.
A change not made to damp the glow of youth,
But "To set passion on the side of truth."
Here first, not following the stale narration,
In Inkle's heart was wrought a reformation.
But how shou'd he, all guilt, for pardon plead?
How prove his penitence sincere indeed?
Unwise to aggravate offences past,
Struggling on others own shame to cast,
And even a father's reverend name to blast.
Here then, yet not in spleen or anger done,
An anxious parent's hand corrects a son.
Nature, with culture not quite unrefin'd,
And growing years matur'd his youthful mind,
While you well pleas'd, to hail a muse-struck child,
Upon his earliest efforts partial smil'd.
Ah! think not then that arrogant and vain,

We boast to add new graces to the scene;
Or now, with pedant chymistry[8] design,
The sterling ore of genius to refine;
No! we but claim the charter of the stage,
'Gainst vice and folly constant war to wage;
To teach young poets the first rule of art,
To charm the fancy, and improve the heart.
Awhile with patience yet attention bend!
Your sentence a brief hour or two suspend!
Then judge impartially our little cause
We dread your censure! but ask no applause.

Scene—First on the main of America: *afterwards in* Barbadoes.

I.i

[*An American forest.*]

MEDIUM. [*Without*] Hilli ho! ho!

TRUDGE. [*Without*] Hip! hollo! ho! ho!—Hip!—

[*Enter* Medium *and* Trudge.

MEDIUM. Pshaw! it's only wasting time and breath. Bawling won't persuade him to budge a bit faster. Things are all alter'd now; and whatever weight it may have in *some* places, bawling, it seems, don't go for argument here. Plague on't! we are now in the wilds of America.

TRUDGE. Hip, hillio—ho—hi!—

MEDIUM. Hold your tongue, you blockhead, or—

TRUDGE. Lord! Sir, if my master makes no more haste, we shall all be put to sword by the knives of the natives. I'm told they take off heads like hats, and hang 'em on pegs in their parlours. Mercy on us! My head aches with the very thoughts of it. Hollo! Mr. Inkle! master; hollo!

MEDIUM. [*Stops his mouth*] Head aches! Zounds, so does mine, with your confounded bawling. It's enough to bring all the natives about us; and we shall be stript and plunder'd in a minute.

TRUDGE. Aye; stripping is the first thing that wou'd happen to us; for they seem to be woefully off for a wardrobe. I myself saw three, at a distance, with less clothes than I have, when I get out of bed: all dancing about in black buff; just like Adam in mourning.[9]

MEDIUM. This is to have to do with a schemer! a fellow who risques his life, for a chance of advancing his interest.—Always advantage in view! trying, here, to make discoveries, that may promote his profit in England. Another Botany Bay scheme,[10] mayhap. Nothing else could induce him to quit our foraging party, from the ship; when he knows every inhabitant here is not only as black as a pepper-corn, but as hot into the bargain—and *I*, like a fool, to follow him! and then to let him loiter behind.—[*Calling*] Why, nephew;—Why, Inkle.—

TRUDGE. Why, Inkle—Well! only to see the difference of men! he'd have thought it very hard, now, if I had let him call so often after me. Ah! I wish he was calling after me now, in the old jog-trot way, again. What a fool was I to leave London for foreign parts!—That ever I should leave Threadneedle-street,[11] to thread an American forest, where a man's as soon lost as a needle in a bottle[12] of hay!

MEDIUM. Patience, Trudge! patience! if we once recover the ship—

TRUDGE. Lord, Sir, I shall never recover what I have lost in coming abroad. When my master and I were in London, I had such a mortal snug birth of it! Why, I was *factotum*.[13]

MEDIUM. Factotum to a young merchant is no such sinecure, neither.

TRUDGE. But then the honour of it. Think of that, Sir; to be clerk as well as *own man*. Only consider. You find very few city clerks made out of a man, now-a-days. To be king of the counting-house, as well as lord of the bed-chamber. Ah! if I had him but now in the little dressing-room behind the office; tying his hair, with a bit of red tape,[14] as usual.

MEDIUM. Yes, or writing an invoice in lampblack, and shining his shoes with an ink-bottle, *as usual*, you blundering blockhead!

TRUDGE. Oh, if I was but brushing the accounts or casting up the coats! mercy on us! what's that?

MEDIUM. That! what?

TRUDGE. Didn't you hear a noise?

MEDIUM. Y—es—but—hush! Oh, heavens be praised! here he is at last. [*Enter* Inkle] Now nephew!

INKLE. So, Mr. Medium.

MEDIUM. Zounds, one wou'd think, by your confounded composure, that you were walking in St. James's Park,[15] instead of an American forest: and that all the beasts were nothing but good company. The hollow trees, here, sentry boxes, and the lions in 'em, soldiers; the jackalls, courtiers; the crocodiles, fine women; and the baboons, beaus. What the plague made you loiter so long?

INKLE. Reflection.

MEDIUM. So I should think; reflection generally comes lagging behind. What, scheming, I suppose; never quiet. At it again, eh? What a happy trader is your father, to have so prudent a son for a partner! Why, you are the carefullest co.[16] in the whole city. Never losing sight of the main chance; and that's the reason, perhaps, you lost sight of us, here, on the main of America.

INKLE. Right, Mr. Medium. Arithmetic, I own, has been the means of our parting at present.

TRUDGE. [*Aside*] *Ha! A sum in division, I reckon.*

MEDIUM. And pray, if I may be so bold, what mighty scheme has just tempted you to employ your head, when you ought to make use of your heels?

INKLE. My heels! Here's pretty doctrine! Do you think I travel merely for motion? A fine expensive plan for a trader truly. What, wou'd you have a man of business come abroad, scamper extravagantly here and there and every where, then return home, and have nothing to tell, but that he has *been* here and there and every where? 'Sdeath,[17] Sir, would you have me travel like a lord?

MEDIUM. No, the Lord forbid! but I am wrong perhaps! There is something in the air of this forest, I believe, that inclines people to be hasty.

INKLE. Travelling, uncle, was always intended for improvement; and improvement is an advantage; and advantage is profit; and profit is gain. Which in the travelling translation of a trader, means, that you shou'd gain every advantage of improving your profit.

MEDIUM. How—gain, and advantage, and profit? Zounds, I'm quite at a loss.

INKLE. You've hit it Uncle! so am I. I have lost my clue by your conversation; you have knock'd all my meditations on the head.

MEDIUM. It's very lucky for you, no-body has done it before me.

INKLE. I have been comparing the land, here, with that of our own country.

MEDIUM. And you find it like a good deal of the land of our own country—cursedly encumbered with black legs,[18] I take it.

INKLE. And calculating how much it might be made to produce by the acre.

MEDIUM. You were?

INKLE. Yes; I was proceeding algebraically upon the subject.

MEDIUM. Indeed!

INKLE. And just about extracting the square root.

MEDIUM. Hum!

INKLE. I was thinking too, if so many natives cou'd be caught, how much they might fetch at the West India markets.

MEDIUM. Now let me ask you a question, or two, young cannibal catcher, if you please.

INKLE. Well.

MEDIUM. Arn't we bound for Barbadoes; partly to trade, but chiefly to carry home the daughter of the governor, Sir Christopher Curry, who has till now been under your father's care, in Threadneedle-street, for polite English education?

INKLE. Granted.

MEDIUM. And isn't it determin'd, between the old folks, that you are to marry Narcissa, as soon as we get there?

INKLE. A fix't thing.

MEDIUM. Then what the devil do you do here, hunting old hairy negroes, when you ought to be obliging a fine girl in the ship? Algebra, too! you'll have other things to think of when you are married, I promise you. A plodding fellow's head, in the hands of a young wife, like a boy's slate, after school, soon gets all its arithmetic wip'd off: and then it appears in its true simple state: dark, empty, and bound in wood, Master Inkle.

INKLE. Not in a match of this kind. Why, it's a table of interest from beginning to end, old Medium.

MEDIUM. Well, well, this is no time to talk. Who knows but, instead of sailing to a wedding, we may get cut up, here, for a wedding dinner, toss'd up for a dingy duke perhaps, or stew'd down for a black baronet, or eat raw by an inky commoner?

INKLE. Why sure you aren't afraid?

MEDIUM. Who, I afraid? Ha! ha! ha! no, not I! what the deuce should I be afraid of? Thank Heaven I have a clear conscience, and need not be afraid of any thing. A scoundrel might not be quite so easy on such an occasion; but it's the part of an honest man not to behave like a scoundrel: I never behav'd like a scoundrel—for which reason I am an honest man, you know. But come—I hate to boast of my good qualities.

INKLE. Slow and sure, my good, virtuous Mr. Medium! our companions can be but half a mile before us: and, if we do but double their steps, we shall overtake 'em at one mile's end, by all the powers of arithmetick.

MEDIUM. Oh curse your arithmetick! How are we to find our way?

INKLE. That, Uncle, must be left to the doctrine of chances.

[*Exeunt.*

I.ii

[*Another part of the forest.—A ship at anchor in the bay at a small distance.*[19] *Enter* Sailors *and* Mate, *as returning from foraging.*]

MATE. Come, come, bear a hand, my lads. Tho' the bay is just under our bowsprits, it will take a damned deal of tripping to come at it—there's hardly any steering clear of the rocks here. But do we muster all hands? All right, think ye?

SAILORS. All, all my hearty.

MATE. What Nick Noggin—Ralph Reef—Tom Pipes—Jack Rattlin—Dick Deck—Mat Mast—Sam Surf—Ten water casks and a hog?

1ST. SAILOR. Ey eye—All to a man—besides yourself, and a monkey—the three land lubbers, that edg'd away in the morning, goes for nothing, you know—they're all dead, may-hap, by this.

MATE. Dead! you be—Why they're friends of the captain; and if not brought safe aboard to-night, you may all chance to have a salt eel for your supper—that's all—Moreover the young plodding spark, he with the grave, foul weather face, there, is to man the tight little frigate, Miss Narcissa—what d'ye call her? that is bound with us for Barbadoes. Rot'em for [not] keeping under way, I say.

2ND SAILOR. Foolish dogs! suppose they're met by the Natives.

MATE. Why then the Natives would look plaguey black upon 'em, I do suppose. But come, let's see if a song will bring 'em too. Let's have a full chorus to the good merchant ship, the Achilles,[20] that's wrote by our captain. Where's Tom Pipes?

SAILOR. Here.

MATE. Come then, Pipe all hands. Crack the drums of their ears, my tight fellow. Hail 'em with your singing trumpet.

SONG (Sailors and Mate)

I.
The Achilles, tho' christen'd, good ship, 'tis surmis'd,
From that old man of war, great Achilles, so priz'd,
Was he, like our vessel, pray fairly baptiz'd?
Ti tol lol, &c.

II.
Poets sung that Achilles—if, now, they've an itch
To sing this, future ages may know which is which;
And that one rode in Greece—and the other in pitch.
Ti tol lol, &c.

III.
What tho' but a merchant ship—sure our supplies:
Now your men of war's gain in a lottery lies,
And how blank they all look, when they can't get a prize![21]
Ti tol lol, &c.

IV.
What are all their fine names? when no rhino's[22] *behind,*
The Intrepid, *and* Lion, *look sheepish you'll find;*
Whilst, alas! the poor Æolus *can't raise the wind!*
Ti tol lol, &c.

V.
Then the Thunderer*'s dumb; out of tune the* Orpheus*;*
The Ceres *has nothing at all to produce;*
And the Eagle[23] *I warrant you, looks like a goose.*
Ti tol lol, &c.

VI.
But we merchant lads, tho' the foe we can't maul,
Nor are paid, like [fine] king-ships, to fight at a call,
[Why] we pay [ourselves] well, without fighting at all.
Ti tol lol, &c.

1ST. SAILOR. Avast! look a-head there. Here they come, chased by a fleet of black devils.

MIDSHIPMAN. And the devil a *fire* have I to give them. We han't a grain of powder left. What must we do, lads?

2ND. SAILOR. Do? Sheer off to be sure.

MIDSHIPMAN. What, and leave our companions behind?

1ST SAILOR. Why not? They left us before; so it comes to the same thing.

MIDSHIPMAN. No damn it—I can't—I can't do that neither.

3RD. SAILOR. Why then we'll leave you; who the plague is to stand there, and be peppered by a parcel of savages?

MIDSHIPMAN. Why, to be sure as it is so—plague on't. [*Reluctantly.*

1ST SAILOR. Paw mun, they're safe as we. Why we're scarce a cable's length asunder, and they'll keep in our wake now I warrant 'em.

MIDSHIPMAN. Why, if you will have it so—It makes a body's heart yearn to leave the poor fellows in distress too.

ALL. Come bear a hand, Master Marlinspike.

MIDSHIPMAN. [*Reluctantly*] Well, if I must, I must. [*Going to the other side, and holloing to* Inkle, *&c*] Yoho, lubbers! Crowd all the sail you can, d'ye mind me!

[*Exeunt* Sailors. *Enter* Medium, *running across the stage, as pursued by the* Blacks.

MEDIUM. Nephew! Trudge! run—scamper! Scour—fly! Zounds, what harm did I ever do to be hunted to death by a pack of black bloodhounds? Why nephew! Oh, confound your long sums in arithmetick! I'll take care of myself; and if we must have any arithmetick, dot and carry one for my money. [*Exit.*

[*Enter* Inkle *and* Trudge, *hastily.*

TRUDGE. Oh! that ever I was born, to leave pen, ink, and powder for this!

INKLE. Trudge, how far are the sailors before us?

TRUDGE. I'll run and see, Sir, directly.

INKLE. Blockhead, come here. The savages are close upon us; we shall scarce be able to recover our party. Get behind this tuft of trees with me; they'll pass us, and we may then recover our ship with safety.

TRUDGE. [*Going behind*] Oh! Threadneedle-street, Thread—

INKLE. Peace.

TRUDGE. [*Hiding*]—Needle-street.

[*They hide behind trees.* Natives *cross. After a long pause,* Inkle *looks from the trees.*

INKLE. Trudge.

TRUDGE. [*In a whisper*] Sir.

INKLE. Are they all gone by?

TRUDGE. Won't you look and see?

INKLE. [*Looking round*] So all's safe at last. [*Coming forward*] Nothing like policy in these cases; but you'd have run on, like a booby![24] A tree, I fancy, you'll find, in future, the best resource in a hot pursuit.

TRUDGE. Oh, charming! It's a retreat for a king, Sir: Mr. Medium, however, has not got up in it; your uncle, Sir, *has run on like a booby*; and has got up with our party by this time, I take it; who are now most likely at the shore. But what are we to do next, Sir?

INKLE. Reconnoitre a little, and then proceed.

TRUDGE. Then pray, Sir, proceed to reconnoitre; for the sooner the better.

INKLE. Then look out, d'ye hear, and tell me if you discover any danger.

TRUDGE. Y—Ye—s—Yes. But [*Trembling*]. As you understand this business better than I Sir, suppose you stick close to my elbow to give me directions.

INKLE. Cowardly scoundrel! Do as you are order'd, Sir. Well, is the coast clear?

TRUDGE. Eh! Oh lord!—Clear! [*Rubbing his eyes*] oh dear! oh dear! the coast will soon be clear enough now, I promise you—The ship is under sail, Sir!

INKLE. Death and damnation!

TRUDGE. Aye, death falls to *my* lot. I shall starve and go off like a pop-gun.

INKLE. Confusion! my property carried off in the vessel.

TRUDGE. All, all, Sir, except me.

INKLE. Treacherous villains! My whole effects lost.

TRUDGE. Lord, Sir! any body but you wou'd only think of effecting his safety in such a situation.

INKLE. They may report me dead, perhaps, and dispose of my property at the next island.

[*The vessel appears under sail.*

TRUDGE. Ah! there they go. [*A gun fir'd*]—That will be the last report we shall ever hear from 'em I'm afraid.—That's as much as to say, good bye to ye. And here we are left—two fine, full-grown babes in the wood!

INKLE. What an ill-timed accident! Just too, when my speedy union with Narcissa, at Barbadoes, wou'd so much advance my interests. [*Thinking*] Something must be hit upon, and speedily; but what resource?

TRUDGE. The old one—a tree, Sir.—'tis all we have for it now. What wou'd I give, now, to be perched upon a high stool, with our brown desk squeez'd into the pit of my stomach—scribbling away on an old parchment!—But all my red ink will be spilt by an old black pin of a negro.

SONG (Trudge) [*Last Valentine's Day*]

I..

A voyage over seas had not enter'd my head,
Had I known but on which side to butter my bread,
Heigho! sure I—for hunger must die!
I've sail'd like a booby; come here in a squall,
Where, alas! there's no bread to be butter'd at all!
Oho! I'm a terrible booby!
Oh, what a sad booby am I!

II.

In London, what gay chop-house[25] *signs in the street!*
But the only sign here is of nothing to eat.
Heigho! that I—for hunger shou'd die!
My mutton's all lost; I'm a poor starving elf!
And for all the world like a lost mutton myself.
Oho! I shall die a lost mutton!
Oh! what a lost mutton am I!

III.

For a neat slice of beef, I cou'd roar like a bull;
And my stomach's so empty, my heart is quite full.
Heigho! that I—for hunger should die!
But, grave without meat, I must here meet my grave,
For my bacon, I fancy, I never shall save.
Oho! I shall ne'er save my bacon!
I can't save my bacon, not I!

TRUDGE. Hum! I was thinking—

INKLE. Well, well, what? Something to our purpose, I hope?

TRUDGE. I was thinking, Sir—if so many natives could be caught, how much they might fetch at the West India markets!

INKLE. Scoundrel! is this a time to jest?

TRUDGE. No, faith, Sir! hunger is too sharp to be jested with. As for me, I shall starve for want of food. Now you may meet a luckier fate: you are able to extract the square root, Sir; and that's the very best provision you can find here to live upon. But I! [*Noise at a distance*] Mercy on us! here they come again.

INKLE. Confusion! Deserted on one side, and press'd on the other, which way shall I turn?—This cavern may prove a safe retreat to us for the present. I'll enter, cost what it will.

TRUDGE. Oh Lord! no, don't, don't—We shall pay too dear for our lodging, depend on't.

INKLE. This is no time for debating. You are at the mouth of it: lead the way, Trudge.

TRUDGE. What! go in before your honour! I know my place better, I assure you—[*Aside*] *I might walk into more mouths than one, perhaps.*

INKLE. Coward! then follow me.

[*Noise again.*

TRUDGE. I must, Sir; I must! Ah, Trudge, Trudge! what a damned hole are you getting into!

[*Exeunt into a Cavern.*

I.iii

[A cave, decorated with skins of wild beasts, feathers, &c. In the middle of the scene, a rude kind of curtain, by way of door to an inner apartment. Enter Inkle *and* Trudge*, as from the mouth of the cavern.]*

TRUDGE. Why Sir! Sir! you must be mad to go any farther.

INKLE. So far, at least, we have proceeded with safety. Ha! no bad specimen of savage elegance. These ornaments would be worth something in England.—We have little to fear here, I hope: this cave rather bears the pleasing face of a profitable adventure.

TRUDGE. Very likely, Sir! But for a pleasing face, it has the cursed'st ugly month I ever saw in my life. Now do, Sir, make off as fast as you can. If we once get clear of the natives' houses, we have little to fear from the lions and leopards: for by the appearance of their parlours, they seem to have kill'd all the wild beast in the country. Now pray, do, my good master, take my advice, and run away.

INKLE. Rascal! Talk again of going out, and I'll flea[26] you alive.

TRUDGE. That's just what I expect for coming in.—All that enter here appear to have had their skin stript over their ears; and ours will be kept for curiosities—We shall stand here, stuff'd, for a couple of white wonders.

INKLE. This curtain seems to lead to another apartment: I'll draw it.

TRUDGE. No, no, no, don't; don't. We may be call'd to account for disturbing the company: you may get a curtain-lecture,[27] perhaps, Sir.

INKLE. Peace, booby, and stand on your guard.

TRUDGE. Oh! what will become of us! Some grim, seven foot fellow ready to scalp us.

INKLE. By heaven! a woman.

[As the curtain draws, Yarico *and* Wowski *discovered asleep.*

TRUDGE. *[Aside] A woman!—[Loud] But let him come on; I'm ready—dam'me, I don't fear facing the devil himself—Faith it is a woman—fast asleep too.*

INKLE. And beautiful as an angel!

TRUDGE. And egad! there seems to be a nice, little plump bit in the corner; only she's an angel of rather a darker sort.

INKLE. Hush! keep back—she wakes.

[Yarico *comes forward*—Inkle *and* Trudge *retire to opposite sides of the scene.*

SONG (Yarico)

I.
When the chace of day is done,
And the shaggy lion's skin,
Which for us our warriors win,
Decks our cell at set of sun;
Worn with toil, with sleep oppress't,
I press my mossy bed, and sink to rest.

II.
Then, once more, I see our train,
With all our chace renew'd again:
Once more 'tis day,
Once more our prey
Gnashes his angry teeth, and foams in vain.
Again, in sullen haste, he flies,
Ta'en in the toil, again he lies,
Again he roars—and in my slumbers dies.

INKLE. Our language!

TRUDGE. Zounds, she has thrown me into a cold sweat.

YARICO. Hark! I heard a noise! Wowski, awake! whence can it proceed?

[She awakes Wowski*, and they both come forward—* Yarico *towards* Inkle; Wowski *towards* Trudge.

TRUDGE. Madam, your very humble servant.

YARICO. Ah! what form is this?—Are you a man?

INKLE. True flesh and blood, my charming heathen, I promise you.

YARICO. What harmony in his voice! *[Gazing]* What a shape! How fair his skin too—

TRUDGE. This must be a lady of quality, by her staring.

YARICO. Say, stranger, whence come you?

INKLE. From a far distant island; driven on this coast by distress, and deserted by my companions.

YARICO. And do you know the danger that surrounds you here? Our woods are fill'd with beasts of prey—my countrymen too—(yet, I think they cou'd'nt find the heart)—might kill you.—It would be a pity if you fell in their way—I think I shou'd weep if you came to any harm.

TRUDGE. O ho! It's time, I see, to begin making interest with the chambermaid. *[Takes* Wowski *apart.*

INKLE. How wild and beautiful! sure there's magic in her shape, and she has rivetted me to the place. But where shall I look for safety? Let me fly and avoid my death.

YARICO. Oh! no, but—[*As if puzzled*] well then die stranger, but don't depart. I will try to preserve you; and if you are killed, Yarico must die too! yet, 'tis I alone can save you; your death is certain, without my assistance; and, indeed, indeed you shall not want it.

INKLE. My kind Yarico! what means, then, must be used for my safety?

YARICO. My cave must conceal you: none enter it, since my father was slain in battle. I will bring you food by day, then lead you to our unfrequented groves by moonlight, to listen to the nightingale. If you should sleep, I'll watch you, and awake you when there's danger.

INKLE. Generous maid! then, to you will I owe my life; and whilst it lasts, nothing shall part us.

YARICO. And shan't it, shan't it indeed?

INKLE. No, my Yarico! for when an opportunity offers to return to my country, you shall be my companion.

YARICO. What! cross the seas!

INKLE. Yes, help me to discover a vessel, and you shall enjoy wonders. You shall be deck'd in silks, my brave maid, and have a house drawn with horses to carry you.

YARICO. Nay, do not laugh at me—but is it so?

INKLE. It is indeed!

YARICO. Oh wonder! I wish my countrywomen cou'd see me—But won't your warriors kill us?

INKLE. No, our only danger on land is here.

YARICO. Then let us retire further into the cave. Come—your safety is in my keeping.

INKLE. I follow you—Yet, can you run some risk in following me?

DUETT [*O say, Bonny Lass*]

INKLE. *O say, simple maid, have you form'd any notion*
Of all the rude dangers in crossing the ocean?
When winds whistle shrilly, ah! won't they remind you,
To sigh with regret, for the grot left behind you?

YARICO. *Ah! no, I cou'd follow, and sail the world over,*
Nor think of my grot, when I look at my lover;
The winds, which blow round us, your arms for my pillow,
Will lull us to sleep, whilst we're rock'd by each billow.

INKLE. *Then say, lovely lass, what if haply espying*
A rich gallant vessel with gay colours flying?

YARICO. *I'll journey, with thee, love, to where the land narrows,*
And sling all my cares at my back with my arrows.

BOTH. *O say then my true love, we never will sunder,*
Nor shrink from the tempest, nor dread the big thunder:
Whilst constant, we'll laugh at all changes of weather,
And journey all over the world both together.

[*Exeunt thro' the cut of the rock. Manent* Trudge *and* Wowski.

TRUDGE. Why, you speak English as well as I, my little Wowski.

WOWSKI. Iss.

TRUDGE. Iss! and you learnt it from a strange man, that tumbled from a big boat, many moons ago, you say?

WOWSKI. Iss—Teach me—teach good many.

TRUDGE. Then, what the devil made 'em so surpriz'd at seeing us! was he like me? [Wowski *shakes her head*] Not so smart a body, mayhap. Was his face, now, round and comely, and—eh! [*Stroking his chin*] Was it like mine?

WOWSKI. Like dead leaf—brown and shrivel.

TRUDGE. Oh, ho! an old shipwreck'd sailor, I warrant. With white and grey hair, eh, my pretty beauty spot?

WOWSKI. Iss; all white. When night come, he put it in pocket.

TRUDGE. Oh! wore a wig. But the old boy taught you something more than English, I believe.

WOWSKI. Iss.

TRUDGE. The devil he did! What was it?

WOWSKI. Teach me put dry grass, red hot, in hollow white stick.

TRUDGE. Aye, what was that for?

WOWSKI. Put in my mouth—go poff, poff!

TRUDGE. Zounds! did he teach you to smoke?

WOWSKI. Iss.

TRUDGE. And what became of him at last? What did your countrymen do for the poor fellow?

WOWSKI. Eat him one day—Our chief kill him.

TRUDGE. Mercy on us! what damn'd stomachs, to swallow a tough old Tar! Though, for the matter of that, there's many of our captains, would eat all they kill I believe! Ah, poor Trudge! your killing comes next.

WOWSKI. No, no—not you—no—[*Running to him anxiously*.

TRUDGE. No? Why what shall I do, if I get in their paws?

WOWSKI. I fight for you!

TRUDGE. Will you? Ecod she's a brave good-natur'd wench! she'll be worth a hundred of your English wives.—Whenever they fight on their husbands' account, it's *with* him instead of *for* him, I fancy. But how the plague am I to live here?

WOWSKI. I feed you—bring you kid.

SONG (Wowski) [*One day, I heard Mary say*]

I.
White man, never go away—
Tell me why need you?
Stay, with your Wowski, stay:
Wowski will feed you.
Cold moons are now coming in;
Ah, don't go grieve me!
I'll wrap you in leopard's skin:
White man, don't leave me.

II.
And when all the sky is blue,
Sun makes warm weather,
I'll catch you a cockatoo,
Dress you in feather.
When cold comes, or when 'tis hot,
Ah, don't go grieve me!
Poor Wowski will be forgot—
White man, don't leave me!

TRUDGE. Zounds! leopard's skin for winter wear, and feathers for a summer's suit! Ha, ha! I shall look like a walking hammer-cloth,[28] at Christmas, and an upright shuttlecock, in the dog-days.[29] And for all this, if my master and I find our way to England, you shall be part of our travelling equipage; and, when I get there, I'll give you a couple of snug rooms, on a first floor, and visit you every evening, as soon as I come from the counting-house. Do you like it?

WOWSKI. Iss.

TRUDGE. Damme, what a flashy fellow I shall seem in the city! I'll get her a white boy to bring up the tea-kettle.[30] Then I'll teach you to write and dress hair.

WOWSKI. You great man in your country?

TRUDGE. Oh yes, a very great man. I'm head clerk of the counting-house, and first valet-de-chambre of the dressing-room. I pounce[31] parchments, powder hair, black shoes, ink paper, shave beards, and mend pens. But hold! I had forgot one material point—you ar'n't married, I hope?

WOWSKI. No: you be my chum-chum!

TRUDGE. So I will. It's best, however, to be sure of her being single; for Indian husbands are not quite so complaisant as English ones, and the vulgar dogs might think of looking a little after their spouses. Well, as my master seems king of this place, and has taken his Indian Queen already, I'll e'en be usher of the black rod here. But you have had a lover or two in your time; eh, Wowski?

WOWSKI. Oh, iss—great many—I tell you.

DUETT

WOWSKI. *Wampum, Swampum, Yanko, Lanko,*
Nanko, Pownatowski,
Black men—plenty—twenty—fight for me,
White man, woo you true?
TRUDGE. *Who?*
WOWSKI. *You.*
TRUDGE. *Yes, pretty little Wowski!*
WOWSKI. *Then I leave all, and follow thee.*
TRUDGE. *Oh then turn about, my little tawny tight one!*
Don't you like me?
WOWSKI. *Iss, you're like the snow!*
If you slight one—
TRUDGE. *Never, not for any white one;*
You are beautiful as any sloe.
WOWSKI. *Wars, jars, scars, can't expose ye,*
In our grot—
TRUDGE. *So snug and cosey!*
WOWSKI. *Flowers, neatly*
Pick'd, shall sweetly
Make your bed.
TRUDGE. *Coying, toying,*
With a rosy
Posey,
When I'm dozey,
Bearskin nightcaps too shall warm my head.
BOTH. *Bearskin nightcaps, &c. &c.*

II.i

[*The quay at* Barbadoes, *with an inn upon it. People employed in unloading vessels, carrying bales of goods, &c. Enter several* Planters.]

1ST PLANTER. I saw her this morning, gentlemen, you may depend on't. My telescope never fails me. I popp'd upon her as I was taking a peep from my balcony. A brave tight ship, I tell you, bearing down directly for Barbadoes here.

2ND PLANTER. Ods, my life! rare news! we have not had a vessel arrive in our harbour these six weeks.

3RD PLANTER. And the last brought only Madam Narcissa, our governor's daughter, from England; with a parcel of lazy, idle, white folks about her. Such cargoes will never do for our trade, neighbour.

2ND PLANTER. No, no; we want slaves. A terrible dearth of 'em in Barbadoes, lately! but your dingy passengers for my money. Give me a vessel like a collier, where all the lading tumbles out as black as my hat. [*To* 1st Planter] But are you sure now you aren't mistaken?

1ST PLANTER. Mistaken! 'sbud,[32] do you doubt my glass? I can discover a gull by it six leagues off: I could see every thing as plain as if I was on board.

2ND PLANTER. Indeed! and what were her colours?

1ST PLANTER. Um! why English—or Dutch—or French—I don't exactly remember.

2D PLANTER. What were the sailors aboard?

1ST PLANTER. Eh! why they were English too—or Dutch—or French—I can't perfectly recollect.

4TH PLANTER. Your glass, neighbour, is a little like a glass too much: it makes you forget every thing you ought to remember.

[*Cry without,* "A sail, a sail!"

1ST PLANTER. Egad, but I'm right though. Now, gentlemen!

ALL. Aye, aye; the devil take the hindmost.

[*Exeunt hastily. Enter* Narcissa *and* Patty.

SONG (Narcissa)

Freshly now the breeze is blowing,
As yon ship at anchor rides;
Sullen waves, incessant flowing,
Rudely dash against the sides.
So my heart, its course impeded,
Beats in my perturbed breast;
Doubts, like waves by waves succeeded,
Rise, and still deny it rest.

PATTY. Well, ma'am, as I was saying—

NARCISSA. Well, say no more of what you were saying—Sure, Patty, you forget where you are; a little caution will be necessary now, I think.

PATTY. Lord, madam, how is it possible to help talking? We are in Barbadoes here, to be sure—but then, ma'am, one may let out a little in a private morning's walk by ourselves.

NARCISSA. Nay, it's the same thing with you in doors.

PATTY. Why, to say the truth, ma'am, tho' we do live in your father's house, Sir Christopher Curry, the grand governor that governs all Barbados—and yet a terrible positive governor he is to be sure; yet, he'll find it a difficult matter to govern a chambermaid's tongue, I believe.

NARCISSA. That I am sure of, Patty; for it runs as rapidly as the tide which brought us from England.

PATTY. Very true, ma'am, and like the tide it stops for no man.

NARCISSA. Well, well, let it run as you please, only for my sake, take care it don't run away with you.

PATTY. Oh, ma'am, it has been too well train'd in the course of conversation, I promise you; and if ever it says any thing to your disadvantage, my name is not Patty Prink—I never blab, ma'am, never, as I hope for a gown.

NARCISSA. And your never blabbing, as you call it, depends chiefly on that hope, I believe. The unlocking of my chest, locks up all your faculties. An old silk gown makes you turn your back on all my secrets; a large bonnet blinds your eyes, and a fashionable high handkercheif covers your ears, and stops your mouth at once, Patty.

PATTY. Dear ma'am, how can you think a body so mercenary. Am I always teasing you about gowns and gew-gaws, and [f]allals[33] and finery? Or do you take me for a conjuror, that nothing will come out of my mouth but ribbons? I have told the story of our voyage, indeed, to old Guzzle, the butler, who is very inquisitive; and, between ourselves, is the ugliest old quiz I ever saw in my life.

NARCISSA. Well, well, I have seen him; pitted with the small-pox and a red face.

PATTY. Right, ma'am. It's for all the world like his master's cellar, full of holes and liquor; but when he asks me what you and I think of the matter, why I look wise, and cry like other wise people who have nothing to say—All's for the best.

NARCISSA. And thus, you lead him to imagine I am but little inclin'd to the match.

PATTY. Lord, ma'am, how cou'd that be? Why I never said a word about Captain Campley.

NARCISSA. Hush! hush! for heaven's sake.

PATTY. Aye! there it is now.—There, ma'm, I'm as mute as a mack'rel—That name strikes me dumb in a moment. I don't know how it is, but Captain Campley somehow or other has the knack of stopping my mouth oftener than any body else, ma'am.

NARCISSA. His name again!—Consider.—Never mention it, I desire you.

PATTY. Not I, ma'am, not I. But if our voyage from England was so pleasant, it wasn't owing to Mr. Inkle, I'm certain. He didn't play the fiddle in our cabin, and dance on the deck, and come languishing with a glass of warm water in his hand, when we were sea-sick. Ah, ma'am, that water warm'd your heart, I'm confident. Mr. Inkle! No, no; Captain Cam—there, he has stopped my mouth again, ma'am.

NARCISSA. There is no end to this! Remember, Patty, keep your secrecy, or you entirely lose my favour.

PATTY. Never fear me, ma'am. But if somebody I know is not acquainted with the governor, there's such a thing as dancing at balls, and squeezing hands when you lead up, and squeezing them again when you cast down,[34] and walking on the quay in a morning.

NARCISSA. No more of this!

PATTY. O, I won't utter a syllable. [*Archly*] I'll go and take a turn on the quay by myself, if you think proper. But remember, I'm as close as a patch box.[35] Mum's the word, ma'am, I promise you.

SONG (Patty)

I.
This maxim let ev'ry one hear,
Proclaim'd from the north to the south,
Whatever comes in at your ear,
Should never run out at your mouth.
We servants, like servants of state,
Should listen to all, and be dumb;
Let others harangue and debate,
We look wise—shake our heads—and are mum.

II.
The judge, in dull dignity drest,
In silence hears barristers preach,
And then, to prove silence is best,
He'll get up, and give 'em a speech.
By saying but little, the maid
Will keep her swain under her thumb;
And the lover that's true to his trade
Is certain to kiss, and cry mum. [*Exit.*

NARCISSA. This heedless wench, every time she speaks, I dread a discovery of my sentiments. How awkward is my present situation! promis'd to one, who, perhaps, may never again be heard of; and who, I am sure, if he ever appears to claim me, will do it merely on the score of interest—press'd too by another, who has already, I fear, too much interest in my heart—what can I do? What plan can I follow?

[*Enter* Campley.

CAMPLEY. Follow my advice, Narcissa, by all means. Enlist with me under the best banners in the world. General Hymen[36] for my money! little Cupid's his drummer: he has been beating a round rub-a-dub on our hearts, and we have only to obey the word of command, fall into the ranks of matrimony, and march through life together.

NARCISSA. Halt! halt, Captain! You march too quick; besides, you make matrimony a mere parade.

CAMPLEY. Faith, I believe, many make it so at present; be we are volunteers, Narcissa and I am for actual service, I promise you.

NARCISSA. Then consider our situation.

CAMPLEY. That has been duly consider'd. In short, the case stands exactly thus—your intended spouse is all for money; I am all for love. He is a rich rogue; I am rather a poor honest fellow. He wou'd pocket your fortune; I will take you without a fortune in your pocket.

NARCISSA. But where's Mr. Inkle's view of interest? Hasn't he run away from me?

CAMPLEY. And I am ready to run away *with* you; you won't always meet with such an offer on an emergency.

NARCISSA. Oh! I am sensible of the favour, most gallant Captain Campley; and my father, no doubt, will be very much oblig'd to you.

CAMPLEY. Aye, there's the devil of it! Sir Christopher Curry's confounded good character—knocks me up at once. Yet I am not acquainted with him neither; not known to him even by sight; being here only as a private gentleman, on a visit to my old relation, out of regimentals, and so forth; and not introduc'd to the governor, as other officers of the place. But then, the report of his hospitality—his odd, blunt, whimsical friendship—his whole behaviour—

NARCISSA. All stare you in the face; eh, Campley?

CAMPLEY. They do, till they put me out of countenance. But then again, when I stare *you* in the face, I can't think I have any reason to be asham'd of my proceedings.—I stick here between my love and my principle, like a song between a toast and a sentiment.

NARCISSA. And if your love and your principle were put in the scales, you doubt which wou'd weigh most?

CAMPLEY. Oh, no! I shou'd act like a rogue, and let principle kick the beam: for love, Narcissa, is as heavy as lead, and like a bullet from a pistol, cou'd never go thro' the heart, if it wanted weight.

NARCISSA. Or rather like the pistol itself, that often *goes off* without any harm done. Your fire must end in smoke, I believe.

CAMPLEY. Never, whilst—

NARCISSA. Nay, a truce to protestations at present. What signifies talking to *me*, when you have such opposition from others? Why hover about the city, instead of boldly attacking the guard? Wheel about, Captain! face the enemy! March! Charge! Rout 'em!—Drive 'em before you, and then—

CAMPLEY. And then—

NARCISSA. Lud ha' mercy on the poor city!

SONG *(rondeau,* Narcissa*)* [*Since 'tis Vain to Think of Flying*]

I.
Mars wou'd oft, his conquest over,
To the Cyprian Goddess[37] *yield;*
Venus gloried in a lover,
Who, like him, cou'd brave the field.
Mars would oft, &c.

II.
In the cause of battles hearty,
Still the god wou'd strive to prove,
He who fac'd an adverse party,
Fittest was to meet his love.
Mars wou'd oft, &c.

III.
Hear then, Captains, ye who bluster,
Hear the God of War declare,
Cowards never can pass muster,
Courage only wins the fair.
Mars would oft, &c.

[*Enter* Patty, *hastily.*

PATTY. Oh lud, ma'am, I'm frighten'd out of my wits! sure as I'm alive, ma'am, Mr. Inkle is not dead; I saw his man, ma'am, just now, coming ashore in a boat, with other passengers, from the vessel that's come to the island. [*Exit.*

NARCISSA. Then one way or other I must determine.

PATTY. But pray ma'am, don't tell the captain; I'm sure he'll stick poor Trudge in his passion, and he's the best-natur'd, peaceable, kind, loving soul in the world. [*Exit* Patty.

NARCISSA. [*To* Campley] Look'ye, Mr. Campley, something has happened which makes me wave ceremonies.—If you mean to apply to my father, remember, that delays are dangerous.

CAMPLEY. Indeed!

NARCISSA. [*Smiling*] I mayn't be always in the same mind, you know.

CAMPLEY. Nay, then—Gad, I'm almost afraid too —but living in this state of doubt is torment. I'll e'en put a good face on the matter; cock my hat; make my bow; and try to reason the governor into compliance. Faint heart never won a fair lady.

SONG (Campley)

I.
Why shou'd I vain fears discover,
Prove a dying, sighing swain?
Why turn shilly-shally lover,
Only to prolong my pain?

II.
When we woo the dear enslaver,
Boldly ask, and she will grant;
How should we obtain a favour,
But by telling what we want?

III.
Should the nymph be found complying,
Nearly then the battle's won;
Parents think 'tis vain denying,
When half our work is fairly done. [*Exeunt*

[*Enter* Trudge *and* Wowski, *(as from the ship) with a dirty* Runner[38] *to one of the inns.*

RUNNER. This way, Sir; if you will let me recommend—

TRUDGE. Come along, Wows! Take care of your furs, and your feathers, my girl!

WOWSKI. Iss.

TRUDGE. That's right.—Somebody might steal 'em, perhaps.

WOWSKI. Steal!—What that?

TRUDGE. Oh Lord! see what one loses by not being born in a Christian country.

RUNNER. If you wou'd, Sir, but mention to your master, the house that belongs to my master; the best accommodations on the quay.—

TRUDGE. What's your sign, my lad?

RUNNER. The Crown, Sir.—Here it is.

TRUDGE. Well, get us a room for half an hour, and we'll come: and harkee! let it be light and airy, d'ye hear? My master has been us'd to your open apartments lately.

RUNNER. Depend on it.—Much oblig'd to you, Sir. [*Exit.*

WOWSKI. Who be that fine man? He great prince?

TRUDGE. A prince—Ha! ha!—No, not quite a prince—but he belongs to the Crown.[39] But how do you like this, Wows? Isn't it fine?

WOWSKI. Wonder!

TRUDGE. Fine men, eh?

WOWSKI. Iss! all white; like you.

TRUDGE. Yes, all the fine men are like me. As different from your people as powder and ink, or paper and blacking.

WOWSKI. And fine lady—Face like snow.

TRUDGE. What! the fine lady's complexions? Oh, yes, exactly; for too much heat very often dissolves 'em! then their dress, too.

WOWSKI. Your countrymen dress so?

TRUDGE. Better, better a great deal. Why, a young flashy Englishman will sometimes carry a whole fortune on his back. But did you mind the women? [*Pointing before and behind*] All here—and there; they have it all from us in England.—And then the fine things they carry on their heads, Wowski.

WOWSKI. Iss. One lady carry good fish—so fine, she call every body to look at her.

TRUDGE. Pshaw! an old woman bawling flounders. But the fine girls we meet, here, on the quay—so round and so plump!

WOWSKI. You not love me now?

TRUDGE. Not love you! Zounds, have not I given you proofs?

WOWSKI. Iss. Great many: but now you get here, you forget poor Wowski!

TRUDGE. Not I. I'll stick to you like wax.

WOWSKI. Ah! I fear! what make you love me now?

TRUDGE. Gratitude, to be sure.

WOWSKI. What that?

TRUDGE. Ha! this it is, now, to live without education. The poor dull devils of her country are all in the practice of gratitude, without finding out what it means; while we can tell the meaning of it, with little or no practice at all.—Lord, Lord, what a fine advantage Christian learning is! Hark'ee, Wows!

WOWSKI. Iss.

TRUDGE. Now we've accomplish'd our landing, I'll accomplish you. You remember the instructions I gave you on the voyage?

WOWSKI. Iss.

TRUDGE. Let's see now—What are you to do, when I introduce you to the nobility, gentry, and others—of my acquaintance?

WOWSKI. Make believe sit down; then get up.

TRUDGE. Let me see you do it. [*She makes a low courtesy*] Very well! and how are you to recommend yourself, when you have nothing to say, amongst all our great friends?

WOWSKI. Grin—show my teeth.

TRUDGE. Right! they'll think you've liv'd with people of fashion. But suppose you meet an old shabby friend in misfortune, that you don't wish to be seen speak to—what would you do?

WOWSKI. Look blind—not see him.

TRUDGE. Why wou'd you do that?

WOWSKI. 'Cause I can't bear see good friend in distress.

TRUDGE. That's a good girl! and I wish every body cou'd boast of so kind a motive for such cursed cruel behaviour.—Lord! how some of your flashy bankers' clerks have *cut* me in Threadneedle-street.—But come, tho' we have got among fine folks, here, in an English settlement, I won't be asham'd of my old acquaintance: yet, for my own part, I shou'd not be sorry, now, to see my old friend with a new face.—Odsbobs! I see Mr. Inkle—Go in, Wows;—call for what you like best.

WOWSKI. Then, I call for you—ah! I fear I not see you often now. But you come soon—

SONG (Wowski)

I.
Remember when we walk'd alone,
And heard so gruff the lion growl:
And when the moon so bright it shone,
We saw the wolf look up and howl;
I led you well, safe to our cell,
While tremblingly,
You said to me,

—And kiss'd so sweet—dear Wowski tell,
How cou'd I live without ye?

II.
But now you come across the sea,
And tell me here no monsters roar;
You'll walk alone, and leave poor me,
When wolves to fright you howl no more.
But ah! think well on our old cell,
Where tremblingly,
You kiss'd poor me—
Perhaps you'll say—dear Wowski tell,
How can I live without ye? [*Exit* Wowski.

TRUDGE. Eh! oh! my master's talking to somebody on the quay: who have we here!

[*Enter* First Planter.

PLANTER. Hark'ee, young man! Is that young Indian of yours going to our market?

TRUDGE. Not she—she never went to market in all her life.

PLANTER. I mean, is she for our sale of slaves? Our black fair?

TRUDGE. A black fair, ha! ha! ha! You hold it on a brown green, I suppose.

PLANTER. She's your slave, I take it?

TRUDGE. Yes; and I'm her humble servant, I take it.

PLANTER. Aye, aye, natural enough at sea.—But at how much do you value her?

TRUDGE. Just as much as she has sav'd me—My own life.

PLANTER. Pshaw! you mean to sell her?

TRUDGE. [*Staring*] Zounds! what a devil of a fellow! Sell Wows!—my poor, dear, dingy, wife!

PLANTER. Come, come, I've heard your story from the ship.—Don't let's haggle; I'll bid as fair as any trader amongst us. But no tricks upon travellers, young man, to raise your price.—Your wife, indeed! Why she's no Christian!

TRUDGE. No; but I am; so I shall do as I'd be done by, Master *Black-Market*; and if you were a good one yourself, you'd know, that fellow-feeling for a poor body, who wants your help, is the noblest mark of our religion.—I wou'dn't be articled clerk to such a fellow for the world.

PLANTER. Hey-day! the booby's in love with her! Why, sure, friend, you wou'd not live here with a black?

TRUDGE. Plague on't; there it is. I shall be laugh'd out of my honesty, here.—But you may be jogging, friend; I may feel a little queer, perhaps, at shewing her face—but, dam'me, if ever I do any thing to make me asham'd of shewing my own.

PLANTER. Why, I tell you, her very complexion—

TRUDGE. Rot her complexion—I'll tell you what, Mr. *Fair-trader*, if your head and heart were to change places, I've a notion you'd be as black in the face as an ink-bottle.

PLANTER. Pshaw! the fellow's a fool—a rude rascal—he ought to be sent back to the savages again. He's not fit to live among us Christians. [*Exit* Planter.

TRUDGE. Christians! Ah tender souls they are to be sure.

SONG (Trudge) [*American Tune*]

I.
Christians are so good, they say,
Tender souls as e'er can be!
Let them credit it who may;
What they're made of let us see.

II.
Christian drovers, charming trade!
Who so careful cattle drive;
And the tender Christian maid,
Sweetly skinning eels alive.

III.
Tender tonish dames, who take
Whip in hand, and drive like males;
Have their ponies nick'd—to make
The pretty creatures cock their tails.

IV.
Christian boys will shy at cocks,
Worry dogs, hunt cats, kill flies;
Christian Lords will learn to box,
And give their noble friend black eyes.

TRUDGE. Oh, here he is at last.

[*Enter* Inkle, *and another* Planter.

INKLE. Nay, Sir, I understand your customs well; your Indian markets are not unknown to me.

2ND PLANTER. And, as you seem to understand business, I need not tell you, that dispatch is the soul of it. Her name you say is—

INKLE. Yarico: but urge this no more, I beg you; I must not listen to it: for, to speak freely, her anxious care of me demands, that here,—though here it may seem strange—I should avow my love for her.

PLANTER. Lord help you for a merchant!—What a pretty figure you would cut upon Change—It's the first time I ever heard a trader talk of love;

except, indeed, the love of trade, and the love of the *Sweet Molly*, my ship.

INKLE. Then, Sir, you cannot feel my situation.

PLANTER. Oh yes, I can! we have a hundred such cases just after a voyage; but they never last long on land. It's amazing how constant a young man is in a ship! But, in two words, will you dispose of her, or no?

INKLE. In two words, then, meet me here at noon, and we'll speak further on this subject: and lest you think I trifle with your business, hear why I wish this pause. Chance threw me, on my passage to your island, among a savage people, deserted,—defenceless,—cut off from my companions,—my life at stake—to this young creature I owe my preservation;—she found me, like a dying bough, torn from its kindred branches; which, as it drooped, she moisten'd with her tears.

PLANTER. Nay, nay, talk like a man of this world.

INKLE. Your patience.—And yet your interruption goes to my present feelings; for on our sail to this your island—the thoughts of time mispent—doubt—fears—or call it what you will—have much perplex'd me; and as your spires arose, reflections still rose with them; for here, Sir, lie my interests, great connections, and other weighty matters—which now I need not mention—

PLANTER. But which her presence here will mar.

INKLE. Even so—And yet the gratitude I owe her—

PLANTER. Pshaw! so because she preserv'd your life, your gratitude is to make you give up all you have to live upon.

INKLE. Why, in that light indeed—This never struck me yet, I'll think on't.

PLANTER. Aye, aye, do so—Why, what return can the wench wish more than taking her from a wild, idle, savage people, and providing for her, here, with reputable hard work, in a genteel, polish'd, tender, Christian country?

INKLE. Well, Sir, at noon—

PLANTER. I'll meet you—but remember, young gentleman, you must get her off your hands—you must, indeed.—I shall have her a bargain, I see that—your servant!—Zounds, how late it is—but never be put out of your way for a woman—I must run—my wife will play the devil with me for keeping breakfast. [*Exit.*

INKLE. Trudge.

TRUDGE. Sir!

INKLE. Have you provided a proper apartment?

TRUDGE. Yes, Sir, at the Crown[40] here; a neat, spruce room they tell me. You have not seen such a convenient lodging this good while, I believe.

INKLE. Are there no better inns in the town?

TRUDGE. Um—Why there is the Lion, I hear, and the Bear, and the Boar—but we saw them at the door of all our late lodgings, and found but bad accommodations within, Sir.

INKLE. Well, run to the end of the quay, and conduct Yarico hither. The road is straight before you: you can't miss it.

TRUDGE. Very well, Sir. What a fine thing it is to turn one's back on a master, without running into a wolf's belly! One can follow one's nose on a message here, and be sure it won't be bit off by the way. [*Exit.*

INKLE. Let me reflect a little. This honest planter councils well. Part with her.—What is there in it which cannot easily be justified? Justice!—Pshaw—My interest, honour, engagements to Narcissa, all demand it. My father's precepts too—I can remember, when I was a boy, what pains he took to mould me!—School'd me from morn to night—and still the burthen of his song was—Prudence! Prudence, Thomas, and you'll rise.—Early he taught me numbers; which he said—and he said rightly,—wou'd give me a quick view of loss and profit, and banish from my mind those idle impulses of passion, which mark young thoughtless spendthrifts; his maxims rooted in my heart, and as I grew—*they* grew; till I was reckon'd, among our friends, a steady, sober, solid, good young man; and all the neighbours call'd me *the prudent Mr. Thomas*. And shall I now, at once, kick down the character which I have rais'd so warily?—Part with her—sell her!—The thought once struck me in our cabin, as she lay sleeping by me; but, in her slumbers, she passed her arm around me, murmur'd a blessing on my name, and broke my meditations.

[*Enter* Yarico *and* Trudge.

YARICO. My love!

TRUDGE. I have been shewing her all the wigs and bales of goods we met on the quay, Sir.

YARICO. Oh! I have feasted my eyes on wonders.

TRUDGE. And I'll go feast on a slice of beef, in the inn, here. [*Exit.*

YARICO. My mind has been so busy, that I almost forgot even you; I wish you had staied with me—You wou'd have seen such sights!

INKLE. Those sights have become familiar to *me*, Yarico.

YARICO. And yet I wish they were not—You might partake my pleasures—but now again, methinks, I will not wish so—for, with too much gazing, you might neglect poor *Yarico*.

INKLE. Nay, nay, my care is still for you.

YARICO. I'm sure it is: and if I thought it was not, I'd tell you tales about our poor old grot—bid you remember our palm-tree near the brook, where in the shade you often stretch'd yourself, while I wou'd take your head upon my lap, and sing my love to sleep. I know you'll love me then.

SONG (Yarico)

I.
Our grotto was the sweetest place!
The bending boughs, with fragrance blowing,
Wou'd check the brook's impetuous pace,
Which murmur'd to be stopt from flowing.
'Twas there we met, and gaz'd our fill:
Ah! think on this, and love me still.

II.
'Twas then my bosom first knew fear,
Fear to an Indian maid a stranger;
The war-song, arrows, hatchet, spear,
All warn'd me of my lover's danger.
For him did cares my bosom fill:—
Ah! think on this, and love me still.

III.
For him, by day, with care conceal'd,
To bring him food I climb'd the mountain;
And when the night no form reveal'd,
Jocund we sought the bubbling fountain.
Then, then wou'd joy my bosom fill;
Ah! think on this and love me still. [*Exeunt.*

II.ii

[*An apartment in the house of* Sir Christopher Curry. *Enter* Sir Christopher *and* Medium.]

SIR CHRISTOPHER. I tell you, old Medium, you are all wrong. Plague on your doubts! Inkle shall have my Narcissa. Poor fellow! I dare say he's finely chagrin'd at this temporary parting—Eat up with the blue devils,[41] I warrant.

MEDIUM. Eat up by the black devils, I warrant; for I left him in hellish hungry company.

SIR CHRISTOPHER. Pshaw! he'll arrive with the next vessel, depend on't—besides, have not I had this in view ever since they were children? I must and will have it so, I tell you. Is not it, as it were, a marriage made above? They *shall* meet, I'm positive.

MEDIUM. Shall they? Then they must meet where the marriage was made; for hang me, if I think it will ever happen below.

SIR CHRISTOPHER. Ha!—and if that is the case—hang me, if I think you'll ever be at the celebration of it.

MEDIUM. Yet, let me tell you, Sir Christopher Curry—my character is as unsullied as a sheet of white paper.

SIR CHRISTOPHER. Well said, old fool's-cap![42] and it's as mere a blank as a sheet of white paper. It bears the traces of neither a bad or a good hand upon it! Zounds! I had rather be a walking libel on honesty, than sit down a blank in the library of the world.

MEDIUM. Well, it is not for me to boast of virtues: that's a vice I never get into.

SIR CHRISTOPHER. Your virtues! Zounds, what are they?

MEDIUM. I am not addicted to passion—that at least, Sir Christopher—

SIR CHRISTOPHER. Is like all your other virtues—A negative one. You are honest, old Medium, by comparison, just as a fellow sentenc'd to transportation is happier than his companion condemn'd to the gallows—Very worthy, because you are no rogue, a good friend, because you never bear malice.—Tender hearted because you never go to fires and executions;[43] and an affectionate father and husband, because you never pinch your children, or kick your wife out of bed.

MEDIUM. And that, as the world goes, is more than every man can say for himself. Yet, since you force me to speak my positive qualities—but, no matter,—you remember me in London; and know, there was scarcely a laudable institution in town without my name in the list. Hav'n't I given more tickets to recommend the lopping off legs than any governor of our hospital? And didn't I, as member of the Humane Society,[44] bring a man out of the New River,[45] who, it was afterwards found, had done me an injury?

SIR CHRISTOPHER. And, dam'me, if I wou'd not kick any man into the New River that had done me an injury. There's the difference of our honesty. Oons![46] if you want to be an honest fellow, act from the impulse of nature. Why, you have no more gall than a pigeon.[47]

MEDIUM. That, I think, is pretty evident in my private life.—Patience, patience, you must own, Sir Christopher, is a virtue. And I have sat and heard my best friends abus'd, with as much quiet patience as any Christian in Christendom.

SIR CHRISTOPHER. And I'd quarrel with any man, that abus'd my friend in my company. Offending my ears is as bad as boxing them.

MEDIUM. Ha! You're always so hasty; amongst the hodge-podge of your foibles, passion is always predominant.

SIR CHRISTOPHER. So much the better.—A natural man unseason'd with passion is as uncommon as a dish of hodge-podge without pepper, and devilish unsipid too, old Medium. Foibles, quotha?[48] foibles are foils that give additional lustre to the gems of virtue. You have not so many foils as I, perhaps.

MEDIUM. And, what's more, I don't want 'em, Sir Christopher, I thank you.

SIR CHRISTOPHER. Very true; for the devil a gem have you to set off with 'em.

MEDIUM. Well, well; I never mention errors; that, I flatter myself, is no disagreeable quality.—It don't become me to say you are hot.

SIR CHRISTOPHER. 'Sblood! but it does become you: it becomes every man, especially an Englishman, to speak the dictates of his heart.

SONG (Sir Christopher)

I.
O give me your plain dealing fellows,
Who never from honesty shrink;
Not hinking on all they shou'd tell us,
But telling us all that they think.

II.
Truth from man flows like wine from a bottle,
His free spoken heart's a full cup;
But when truth sticks half way in the throttle,
Man's worse than a bottle cork'd up.

III.
Compliance, is a gingerbread creature,
Us'd for shew, like a watch by each spark;
But truth is a golden repeater,[49]
That sets a man right in the dark.

MEDIUM. But suppose his heart dictates to any one to knock up your friend, Sir Christopher?

SIR CHRISTOPHER. Eh!—why—then it becomes me to knock him down.

MEDIUM. Mercy on us! If that was the consequence of scandal in England now-a-days, all our fine gentlemen wou'd cut each others' throats over a bottle; and if it be extended to the card tables, our routs wou'd be fuller of black eyes, than black aces.

[*Enter* Servant.

SERVANT. An English vessel, Sir, just arriv'd in the harbour.

SIR CHRISTOPHER. A vessel! Od's my life!—Now for the news—If it is but as I hope—Any dispatches?

SERVANT. This letter, Sir, brought by a sailor from the quay. [*Exit.*

SIR CHRISTOPHER. Now for it! If Inkle is but amongst 'em—Zounds! I'm all in a flutter; my hand shakes like an aspin leaf; and you, you old fool, are as stiff and steady as an oak. Why ar'n't you all tiptoe—all nerves?

MEDIUM. Well, read, Sir Christopher.

SIR CHRISTOPHER. [*Opening the letter*] Huzza! here it is. He's safe—safe and sound at Barbadoes. [*Reading*]— *Sir, My master, Mr. Inkle, is just arriv'd in your harbour,* Here, read, read! old Medium—

MEDIUM. [*Reading*] Um'—*Your harbour;—we were taken up by an English vessel, on the 14th ult^{o}.*[50] *He only waits till I have puff'd his hair, to pay his respects to you, and Miss Narcissa: In the mean time, he has order'd me to brush up this letter for your honour, from Your humble Servant, to command,* Timothy Trudge.

SIR CHRISTOPHER. Hey day! Here's a stile! the voyage has jumbled the fellow's brains out of their places; the water has made his head turn round. But no matter; mine turns round, too. I'll go and prepare Narcissa directly; they shall be married slap-dash, as soon as he comes from the quay. From Neptune to Hymen: from the hammock to the bridal bed—Ha! old boy!

MEDIUM. Well, well; don't flurry yourself—you're so hot!

SIR CHRISTOPHER. Hot! blood, ar'n't I in the West Indies? Ar'n't I governor of Barbadoes? He shall have her as soon as he sets his foot on shore. But, plague on't, he's so slow.—She shall rise to him like Venus out of the sea.[51] His hair puff'd? He ought to have been puffing, here, out of breath, by this time.

MEDIUM. Very true; but Venus's husband is always supposed to be lame,[52] you know, Sir Christopher.

SIR CHRISTOPHER. Well, now do, my good fellow, run down to the shore, and see what detains him. [*Hurrying him off.*

MEDIUM. Well, well; I will, I will. [*Exit.*

SIR CHRISTOPHER. In the mean time I'll get ready Narcissa, and all shall be concluded in a second. My heart's set upon it.—Poor fellow! after all his rumbles, and tumbles, and jumbles, and fits of despair—I shall be rejoic'd to see him. I have not seen him since he was that high.—But, Zounds! he's so tardy!

[*Enter* Servant.

SERVANT. A strange gentleman, Sir, come from the quay, desires to see you.

SIR CHRISTOPHER. From the quay? Od's my life!—'Tis he—'Tis Inkle! Show him up directly. [*Exit* Servant] The rogue is expeditious after all.—I'm so happy. [*Enter* Campley] My dear fellow! [*Shakes hands*] I'm rejoiced to see you. Welcome; welcome here, with all my soul!

CAMPLEY. This reception, Sir Christopher, is beyond my warmest wishes—Unknown to you—

SIR CHRISTOPHER. Aye, aye; we shall be better acquainted by and by. Well, and how, eh! tell me!—But old Medium and I have talk'd over your affair a hundred times a day, ever since Narcissa arrived.

CAMPLEY. You surprise me! Are you then really acquainted with the whole affair?

SIR CHRISTOPHER. Every tittle.

CAMPLEY. And, can you, Sir, pardon what is past?—

SIR CHRISTOPHER. Pooh! how cou'd you help it?

CAMPLEY. Very true—sailing in the same ship—and—

SIR CHRISTOPHER. Aye, aye; but we have had a hundred conjectures about you. Your despair and distress, and all that—Yours must have been a damn'd situation, to say the truth.

CAMPLEY. Cruel, indeed, Sir Christopher! and I flatter myself will move your compassion. I have been almost inclin'd to despair indeed, as you say,—when you consider the past state of my mind—the black prospect before me.—

SIR CHRISTOPHER. Ha! ha! Black enough, I dare say.

CAMPLEY. The difficulty I have felt in bringing myself face to face to you.

SIR CHRISTOPHER. That I am convinc'd of—but I knew you wou'd come the first opportunity.

CAMPLEY. Very true: yet the distance between the governor of Barbadoes and myself. [*Bowing.*

SIR CHRISTOPHER. Yes—a devilish way asunder.

CAMPLEY. Granted, Sir: which has distressed me with the cruellest doubts as to our meeting.

SIR CHRISTOPHER. 'Twas a toss up.

CAMPLEY.—[*Aside*] *The old gentleman seems devilish kind.—Now to soften him.*—[*To him*] Perhaps, Sir, in your younger days, you may have been in the same situation yourself.

SIR CHRISTOPHER. Who? I! 'sblood! no, never in my life.

CAMPLEY. I wish you had, with all my soul, Sir Christopher.

SIR CHRISTOPHER. Upon my soul, Sir, I am very much obliged to you. [*Bowing.*

CAMPLEY. As what I now mention might have greater weight with you.

SIR CHRISTOPHER. Pooh! pr'ythee! I tell you I pitied you from the bottom of my heart.

CAMPLEY. Indeed! Had you been but kind enough to have sent to me, how happy shou'd I have been in attending your commands!

SIR CHRISTOPHER. I believe you wou'd, egad—ha! ha! sent to you! Very well! ha! ha! ha! A dry rogue! You'd have been ready enough to come my boy, I dare say. [*Laughing.*

CAMPLEY. But now, Sir, if, with your leave, I may still venture to mention Miss Narcissa—

SIR CHRISTOPHER. An impatient, sensible young dog! like me to a hair! Set your heart at rest, my boy. She's yours; yours before to-morrow morning.

CAMPLEY. Amazement! I can scarce believe my senses.

SIR CHRISTOPHER. Zounds! you ought to be out of your senses: but dispatch—make short work of it, ever while you live, my boy. [*Enter* Narcissa *and* Patty. *To* Narcissa] Here girl: here's your swain.

CAMPLEY. I just parted with my Narcissa, on the quay, Sir.

SIR CHRISTOPHER. Did you! ah, sly dog—had a meeting before you came to the old gentleman.—But here—Take him, and make much of him—and, for fear of further separations, you shall e'en be tack'd together directly. What say you, girl?

CAMPLEY. Will my Narcissa consent to my happiness?

NARCISSA. I always obey my father's commands, with pleasure, Sir.—[*Aside to* Patty] Steal out, Patty, as soon as you can, and prevent Mr. Inkle's appearance. My father has mistaken Campley, I am confident.

PATTY. It is not for his daughter, ma'am, to tell him of his mistakes, you know.

SIR CHRISTOPHER. Od! I'm so happy, I hardly know which way to turn; but we'll have the carriage directly; drive down to the quay; trundle old Spintext[53] into church, and hey for matrimony!

CAMPLEY. With all my heart, Sir Christopher; the sooner the better.

SONG (Sir Christopher, Campley, Narcissa, Patty)

SIR CHRISTOPHER. *Your Colinettes, and Arriettes,*
Your Damons[54] *of the grove,*
Who like fallals,[55] *and pastorals,*
Waste years in love;
But modern folks know better jokes,
And, courting once begun,
To church they hop at once—and pop—
Egad, all's done!

ALL. *In life we prance a country dance,*
Where every couple stands;
Their partners set—a while curvett[56]*—*
But soon join hands.

NARCISSA. *When at our feet, so trim and neat,*
The powder'd lover sues,
He vows he dies, the lady sighs,
But can't refuse.
Ah! how can she unmov'd e'er see
Her swain his death incur?
If once the squire is seen expire,
He lives with her.

ALL. *In life, &c. &c.*

PATTY. *When John and Bet are fairly met,*
John boldly tries his luck;
He steals a buss,[57] *without more fuss,*
The bargain's struck.
Whilst things below are going so,
Is Betty pray to blame?
Who knows up stairs, her mistress fares
Just, just the same.

ALL. *In life we prance, &c. &c.* [*Exeunt.*

III.i

[*The quay. Enter* Patty.]

PATTY. Mercy on us! what a walk I have had of it! well, matters go on swimmingly at the governor's—The old gentleman has order'd the carriage, and the young couple will be whisk'd here, to church, in a quarter of an hour. My business is to prevent young sober-sides, young Inkle, from appearing to interrupt the ceremony.—Ha! here's the Crown, where I hear he is hous'd: so now to find Trudge, and trump up a story, in the true stile of a chambermaid. [*Goes into the house. Within*] I tell you it don't signify, and I will come up.

TRUDGE. [*Within*] But it does signify, and you can't come up.

[*Re-enter* Patty *with* Trudge.

PATTY. You had better say at once, I shan't.

TRUDGE. Well then, you shan't.

PATTY. Savage! pretty behaviour you have pick'd up amongst the Hottypots![58] Your London civility, like London itself, will soon be lost in smoke, Mr. Trudge: and the politeness you have studied so long in Threadneedle-street, blotted out by the blacks you have been living with.

TRUDGE. No such thing; I practis'd my politeness all the while I was in the woods. Our very lodging taught me good manners; for I could never bring myself to go into it without bowing.

PATTY. Don't tell me! a mighty civil reception you give a body, truly, after a six weeks parting.

TRUDGE. Gad, you're right; I am a little out here, to be sure. [*Kisses her*] Well, how do you do?

PATTY. Pshaw, fellow! I want none of your kisses.

TRUDGE. Oh! very well—I'll take it again. [*Offers to kiss her.*

PATTY. Be quiet. I want to see Mr. Inkle, I have a message to him from Miss Narcissa. I shall get a sight of him, now, I believe.

TRUDGE. May be not. He's a little busy at present.

PATTY. Busy—ha! plodding! what he's at his multiplication table again?

TRUDGE. Very likely; so it would be a pity to interrupt him, you know.

PATTY. Certainly;—[*Aside*] *and the whole of my business was to prevent his hurrying himself*—[*To* Trudge] Tell him, we shan't be ready to receive him, at the governor's, till to-morrow, d'ye hear?

TRUDGE. No?

PATTY. No! Things are not prepared. The place isn't in order; and the servants have not had proper notice of the arrival.

TRUDGE. Oh! let me alone to give the servants notice—Rat—Fat—Tat—It's all the notice we had in Threadneedle-street of the arrival of a visitor.

PATTY. Threadneedle-street! Threadneedle non-sense! I'd have you know we do everything with an air. Matters have taken another turn—Stile! Stile, Sir, is required here, I promise you.

TRUDGE. Turn—Stile! And pray what stile will serve your turn now, Madam Patty?

PATTY. A due dignity and decorum, to be sure; Sir Christopher intends Mr. Inkle, you know, for his son-in-law, and must receive him in public form, (which can't be till to-morrow morning) for the honour of his governorship: why the whole island will ring of it.

TRUDGE. The devil it will!

PATTY. Yes; they've talk'd of nothing but my mistress's beauty and fortune for these six weeks. Then he'll be introduc'd to the bride, you know.

TRUDGE. O, my poor master!

PATTY. Then a public breakfast; then a procession; then—if nothing happens to prevent it, he'll get into church, and be married in a crack.

TRUDGE. Then he'd get into a damn'd scrape, in a crack.

PATTY. Hey-day! a scrape! The holy state of matrimony!

TRUDGE. Yes; it's plaguey holy; and many of its votaries, as in other holy states, live in repentance and mortification.—[*Half aside*] *Ah! Poor Madam Yarico! My poor pilgarlick*[59] *of a master, what will become of him?*

PATTY. Why, what's the matter with the booby?

TRUDGE. Nothing, nothing—he'll be hang'd for poli-bigamy.

PATTY. Polly who?

TRUDGE. It must out—Patty!

PATTY. Well!

TRUDGE. Can you keep a secret?

PATTY. Try me.

TRUDGE. Then. [*Whispering*] My master keeps a girl.

PATTY. Oh, monstrous! another woman?

TRUDGE. As sure as one and one make two.

PATTY.—[*Aside*] *Rare news for my mistress!*—[*To him*] Why I can hardly believe it: the grave, sly, steady, sober Mr. Inkle, do such a thing!

TRUDGE. Pooh! it's always your sly, sober fellows, that go the most after the girls.

PATTY. Well; I should sooner suspect *you*.

TRUDGE. Me? Oh Lord! he! he!—[*Conceitedly*] Do you think any smart, tight, little, black-eyed wench, would be struck with my figure?

PATTY. Pshaw! never mind your figure. Tell me how it happen'd?

TRUDGE. You shall hear: when the ship left us ashore, my master turn'd as pale as a sheet of paper. It isn't every body that's blest with courage, Patty.

PATTY. True.

TRUDGE. However, I bid him cheer up; told him, to stick to my elbow: took the lead, and began our march.

PATTY. Well?

TRUDGE. We hadn't gone far, when a damn'd one-eyed black boar, that grinn'd like a devil, came down the hill in jog trot! My master melted as fast as a pot of pomatum![60]

PATTY. Mercy on us!

TRUDGE. But what does I do, but whips out my desk knife, that I us'd to cut the quills with at home; met the monster, and slit up his throat like a pen—The boar bled like a pig.

PATTY. Lord! Trudge, what a great traveller you are!

TRUDGE. Yes; I remember we fed on the flitch for a week.

PATTY. Well, well; but the lady.

TRUDGE. The lady! Oh, true. By and by we came to a cave—a large hollow room, under ground, like a warehouse in the Adelphi.[61]—Well; there we were half an hour, before I could get him to go in; there's no accounting for fear, you know. At last, in we went, to a place hung round with skins, as it might be a furrier's shop, and there was a fine lady, snoring on a bow and arrows.

PATTY. What, all alone?

TRUDGE. Eh!—No—no.—Hum—She had a young lion, by way of a lap-dog.

PATTY. Gemini![62] what did you do?

TRUDGE. Gave her a jog, and she open'd her eyes—she struck my master immediately.

PATTY. Mercy on us! with what?

TRUDGE. With her beauty, you ninny, to be sure: and they soon brought matters to bear. The wolves witness'd the contract—I gave her away—The crows croak'd amen; and we had board and lodging for nothing.

PATTY. And this is she he has brought to Barbadoes?

TRUDGE. The same.

PATTY. Well; and tell me, Trudge;—she's pretty, you say—Is she fair or brown? Or—

TRUDGE. Um! she's a good comely copper.

PATTY. How! a tawny?

TRUDGE. Yes, quite dark; but very elegant; like a Wedgwood tea-pot.[63]

PATTY. Oh! the monster! the filthy fellow! Live with a black-a-moor!

TRUDGE. Why, there's no great harm in't, I hope.

PATTY. Faugh! I wou'dn't let him kiss me for the world: he'd make my face all smutty.

TRUDGE. Zounds! you are mighty nice all of a sudden; but I'd have you to know, Madam Patty, that Blackamoor ladies, as you call 'em, are some of the very few whose complexions never rub off![64] S'bud, if they did, Wows and I should have changed faces by this time—But mum; not a word for your life.

PATTY. Not I!—[*Aside*] *except to the governor and family. But I must run*—[*To him*] and, remember, Trudge, if your master has made a mistake here, he has himself to thank for his pains.

SONG *(Patty)*

I.
Tho' lovers, like marksmen, all aim at the heart,
Some hit wide of the mark, as wenches all know;
But of all the bad shots, he's the worst in the art
Who shoots at a pigeon, and kills a crow—O ho!
Your master has kill'd a crow.

II.
When younkers[65] *go out, the first time in their lives,*
At random they shoot, and let fly as they go;
So your master unskill'd how to level at wives,
Has shot at a pigeon, and kill'd a crow—O ho!
Your master has kill'd a crow.

III.
Love and money thus wasted, in terrible trim!
His powder is spent, and his shot running low:
Yet the pigeon he miss'd, I've a notion with him
Will never, for such a mistake, pluck a crow.[66]*—*
No! No!
Your master may keep his crow. [*Exit Patty.*

TRUDGE. Pshaw! these girls are so plaguy proud of their white and red! but I won't be shamed out of Wows, that's flat.—[*Enter* Wowski] Ah! Wows, I'm going to leave you.

WOWSKI. For what you leave me?

TRUDGE. Master says I must.

WOWSKI. Ah, but you say in your country, women know best; and I say you not leave me.

TRUDGE][67] Master, to be sure, while we were in the forest, taught Yarico to read, with his pencil and pocket-book. What then? Wows comes on fine and fast in her lessons. A little awkward at first, to be sure—Ha! ha!—She's so used to feed with her hands, that I can't get her to eat her victuals, in a genteel, Christian way, for the soul of me; when she has stuck a morsel on her fork, she don't know how to guide it, but pops up her knuckles to her mouth, and the meat goes up to her ear. But, no matter—After all the fine, flashy London girls, Wowski's the wench for my money.

SONG (Trudge)

I.
A clerk I was in London gay,
Jemmy linkum feedle,
And went in boots to see the play,[68]
Merry fiddlem tweedle.
I march'd the lobby, twirl'd my stick,
Diddle, daddle, deedle;
The girls all cry'd, "He's quite the kick."
Oh, Jemmy linkum feedle.

II.
Hey! for America I sail,
Yankee doodle, deedle;
The sailor-boys cry'd, "Smoke his tail!"
Jemmy linkum feedle.
On English belles I turn'd my back,
Diddle, daddle, deedle;
And got a foreign Fair, quite black,
O twaddle, twaddle, tweedle!

III.
Your London girls, with roguish trip,
Wheedle, wheedle, wheedle,
May boast their pouting under lip,

Fiddle, faddle, feedle.
My Wows would beat a hundred such,
Diddle, daddle, deedle,
Whose upper lip pouts twice as much,
O, pretty double wheedle!

IV.
Rings I'll buy to deck her toes;
Jemmy linkum feedle;
A feather fine shall grace her nose,
Waving sidle seedle.
With jealousy I ne'er shall burst;
Who'd steal my bone of bone-a?
A white Othello, I can trust
A dingy Desdemona.[69]

[*Exeunt.*

III.ii

[*A room in* The Crown. *Enter* Inkle.]

INKLE. I know not what to think—I have given her distant hints of parting; but still, so strong her confidence in my affection, she prattles on without regarding me. Poor Yarico! I must not—cannot quit her. When I would speak, her look, her mere simplicity disarms me; I dare not wound such innocence. Simplicity is like a smiling babe, which, to the ruffian that wou'd murder it, stretching its little naked, helpless arms, pleads, speechless, its own cause. And yet, Narcissa's family—

[*Enter* Trudge.

TRUDGE. There he is; like a beau bespeaking a coat—doubting which colour to choose—Sir—

INKLE. What now?

TRUDGE. Nothing unexpected, Sir:—I hope you won't be angry.

INKLE. Angry!

TRUDGE. I'm sorry for it; but I am come to give you joy, Sir!

INKLE. Joy!—of what?

TRUDGE. A wife, Sir! a white one.—I know it will vex you, but Miss Narcissa means to make you happy, to-morrow morning.

INKLE. To-morrow!

TRUDGE. Yes, Sir; and as I have been out of employ, in both my capacities, lately, after I have dressed your hair, I may draw up the marriage articles.

INKLE. Whence comes your intelligence, Sir?

TRUDGE. Patty told me all that has pass'd in the governor's family, on the quay, Sir. Women, you know, can never keep a secret. You'll be introduc'd in form, with the whole island to witness it.

INKLE. So public, too!—Unlucky!

TRUDGE. There will be nothing but rejoicings in compliment to the wedding, she tells me; all noise and uproar! married people like it, they say.

INKLE. Strange! that I shou'd be so blind to my interest, as to be the only person this dis-tresses!

TRUDGE. They are talking of nothing else but the match, it seems.

INKLE. Confusion! How can I, in honour, retract?

TRUDGE. And the bride's merits—

INKLE. True!—A fund of merits!—I wou'd not—but from necessity—a case so nice as this—I—wou'd not wish to retract.

TRUDGE. Then they call her so handsome.

INKLE. Very true! so handsome! the whole world wou'd laugh at me; they'd call it folly to retract.

TRUDGE. And then they say so much of her fortune.

INKLE. O death! it would be *madness* to retract. Surely, my faculties have slept, and this long parting from my Narcissa has blunted my sense of her accomplishments. 'Tis this alone makes me so weak and wavering. I'll see her immediately. [*Going.*

TRUDGE. Stay, stay, Sir; I am desired to tell you, the governor won't open his gates to us till to-morrow morning, and is now making preparations to receive you at breakfast, with all the honours of matrimony.

INKLE. Well, be it so; it will give me time, at all events, to put my affairs in train.

TRUDGE. Yes; it's a short respite before execution; and if your honour was to go and comfort poor Madam Yarico—

INKLE. Damnation! Scoundrel, how dare you offer your advice?—I dread to think of her!

TRUDGE. I've done, Sir, I've done—But I know I should blubber over Wows all night, if I thought of parting with her in the morning.

INKLE. Insolence! begone, Sir!

TRUDGE. Lord, Sir, I only—

INKLE. Get down stairs, Sir, directly.

TRUDGE. [*Going out. Aside*] *Ah! you may well put your hand to your head; and a bad head it must be, to forget that Madam Yarico prevented her countrymen from peeling off the upper part of it.* [*Exit.*

INKLE. 'Sdeath, what am I about? How have I slumbered! Rouse, rouse, good Thomas Inkle! Is it I?—I—who, in London, laugh'd at the younkers of the town—and, when I saw their chariots, with some fine, tempting girl, perk'd in the corner, come shopping to the city, wou'd cry—Ah!—there sits ruin—there flies the greenhorn's money! then wondered with myself how men could trifle time on women; or, indeed, think of any women without fortunes. And now, forsooth, it rests with me to turn romantic puppy, and give up All for Love.[70]—Give up!—Oh, monstrous folly!—thirty thousand pounds!

TRUDGE. [*Peeping in at the door*] May I come in, Sir?

INKLE. What does the booby want?

TRUDGE. Sir, your uncle wants to see *you*.

INKLE. Mr. Medium! Shew him up directly. [*Exit* Trudge] He must not know of this. To-morrow! I must be blunt with Yarico. I wish this marriage were more distant, that I might break it to her by degrees: she'd take my purpose better, were it less suddenly deliver'd. Women's weak minds bear grief as colts do burdens: Load them with their full weight at once, and they sink under it, but every day add little imperceptibly to little, 'tis wonderful how much they'll carry.

[*Enter* Medium.

MEDIUM. Ah! here he is! give me your hand, nephew! welcome, welcome to Barbadoes, with all my heart.

INKLE. I am glad to meet you here, Uncle!

MEDIUM. That you are, that you are, I'm sure. Lord! Lord! when we parted last, how I wish'd we were in a room together, if it were but the black hole![71] I have not been able to sleep o'nights for thinking of you. I've laid awake, and fancied I saw you sleeping your last, with your head in the lion's mouth, for a night-cap! and I've never seen a bear brought over to dance about the street, but I thought you might be bobbing up and down in its belly.[72]

INKLE. I am very much oblig'd to you.

MEDIUM. Aye, aye, I am happy enough to find you safe and sound, I promise you. Why I've been hunting you all over the quay, and been in half the houses upon it, before I cou'd find you; I should have been here sooner else. Whew!—I'm so warm, I've run as fast—

INKLE. As you did in the forest—Eh! Mr. Medium?

MEDIUM. Well, well; thank heaven we are both out of the forest! Hounslow-heath at dusk is a trifle to it. I shall never see a tree without shaking; and, I cou'd not walk in a grove again with comfort, tho' it were in the middle of Paradise. But, you have a fine prospect before you now, young man. I am come to take you with me to Sir Christopher, who is impatient to see you.

INKLE. To-morrow, I hear, he expects me.

MEDIUM. To-morrow! directly—this moment—in half a second.—I left him standing on tip-toe, as he calls it, to embrace you; and he's standing on tiptoe now in the great parlour, and there he'll stand till you come to him.

INKLE. Is he so hasty?

MEDIUM. Hasty! he's all pepper—and wonders you are not with him, before it's possible to get at him. Hasty, indeed! why, he vows you shall have his daughter this very night.

INKLE. What a situation!

MEDIUM. Why, it's hardly fair just after a voyage. But come, bustle, bustle, he'll think you neglect him. He's rare and touchy, I can tell you; and if he once takes it into his head that you shew the least slight to his daughter, it wou'd knock up all your schemes in a minute.

INKLE. [*Aside*] *Confusion! If he should hear of Yarico!*

MEDIUM. But at present you are all and all with him; he has been telling me his intentions these six weeks; you'll be a fine warm husband, I promise you.

INKLE. [*Aside*] *This cursed connection!*

MEDIUM. It is not for me, though, to tell you how to play your cards; you are a prudent young man, and can make calculations in a wood. I need not tell you that the least shadow of affront disobliges a testy old fellow: but, remember, I never speak ill of my friends.

INKLE. [*Aside*] *Fool! fool! fool!*

MEDIUM. Why, what the devil is the matter with you?

INKLE. [*Aside*] *It must be done effectually, or all is lost; mere parting wou'd not conceal it.*

MEDIUM. Ah! now he's got to his damn'd square root again, I suppose, and Old Nick[73] would not move him.—Why, nephew!

INKLE. [*Aside*] *The planter that I spoke with cannot be arriv'd—but time is precious—the first I meet—common prudence now demands it. I'm fix'd; I'll part with her.* [*Exit.*

MEDIUM. Damn me, but he's mad! The woods have turned the poor boy's brains; he's scalp'd, and gone crazy! Hoho! Inkle! Nephew! Gad, I'll spoil your arithmetick, I warrant me. [*Exit.*

III.iii

[*The quay. Enter* Sir Christopher Curry.]

SIR CHRISTOPHER. Ods, my life! I can scarce contain my happiness. I have left 'em safe in church, in the middle of the ceremony. I ought to have given Narcissa away, they told me; but I caper'd about so much for joy, that Old Spintext advised me to go and cool my heels on the quay, till it was all over. Ods I'm so happy; and they shall see, now, what an old fellow can do at a wedding.

[*Enter* Inkle.

INKLE. Now for dispatch! [*To the* governor] Hark'ee, old gentleman!

SIR CHRISTOPHER. Well, young gentleman?

INKLE. If I mistake not, I know your business here.

SIR CHRISTOPHER. 'Egad, I believe half the island knows it, before this time.

INKLE. Then to the point—I have a female, whom I wish to part with.

SIR CHRISTOPHER. Very likely; it's a common case, now a-days, with many a man.

INKLE. If you could satisfy me you wou'd use her mildly, and treat her with more kindness than is usual—for I can tell you she's of no common stamp—perhaps we might agree.

SIR CHRISTOPHER. Oho! a slave! faith, now I think on't, my daughter may want an attendant or two extraordinary; and as you say she's a delicate girl, above the common run, and none of your thick-lip'd, flat-nos'd, squabby, dumpling dowdies, I don't much care if—

INKLE. And for her treatment—

SIR CHRISTOPHER. Look ye, young man; I love to be plain: I shall treat her a good deal better than you wou'd, I fancy; for though I witness this custom every day, I can't help thinking the only excuse for buying our fellow creatures is to rescue 'em from the hands of those who are unfeeling enough to bring them to market.

INKLE. Somewhat too blunt, Sir; I am no common trafficker, dependent upon proud rich planters. Fair words, old gentleman; an Englishman won't put up an affront.

SIR CHRISTOPHER. An Englishman! more shame for you! Let Englishmen blush at such practices. Men, who so fully feel the blessings of liberty, are doubly cruel in depriving the helpless of their freedom.

INKLE. Confusion!

SIR CHRISTOPHER. 'Tis not my place to say so much; but I can't help speaking my mind.

INKLE. I must be cool. Let me assure you, Sir, it is not my occupation; but for a private reason—an instant pressing necessity—

SIR CHRISTOPHER. Well, well, I have a pressing necessity too; I can't stand to talk now; I expect company here presently; but if you'll ask for me to-morrow, at the castle—

INKLE. The castle!

SIR CHRISTOPHER. Aye, Sir, the castle; the governor's castle; known all over Barbadoes.

INKLE.—[*Aside*] *'Sdeath this man must be on the governor's establishment: his steward, perhaps, and sent after me, while Sir Christopher is impatiently waiting for me. I've gone too far; my secret may be known—As 'tis, I'll win this fellow to my interest.*—[*To him*] One word more, Sir: my business must be done immediately; and as you seem acquainted at the castle, if you should see me there—and there I mean to sleep to-night—

SIR CHRISTOPHER. [*Aside*] *The devil you do!*

INKLE. Your finger on your lips; and never breathe a syllable of this transaction.

SIR CHRISTOPHER. No! why not?

INKLE. Because, for reasons, which, perhaps, you'll know to-morrow, I might be injured with the governor, whose most particular friend I am.

SIR CHRISTOPHER.—[*Aside*] *So! here's a particular friend of mine, coming to sleep at my house, that I never saw in my life. I'll sound this fellow.*—[*To him*] I fancy, young gentleman, as you are such a bosom friend of the governor's, you can hardly do any thing to alter your situation with him? I shou'dn't imagine any thing cou'd bring him to think a bit worse for you than he does at present.

INKLE. Oh! pardon me; but you'll find that hereafter—besides, you, doubtless, know his character?

SIR CHRISTOPHER. Oh, as well as I do my own. But let's understand one another. You may trust me, now you've gone so far. You are acquainted with his character, no doubt, to a hair?

INKLE. I am—I see we shall understand each other. You know him too, I see, as well as I—A very touchy, testy, hot old fellow.

SIR CHRISTOPHER.—[*Aside*] *Here's a scoundrel! I hot and touchy! Zounds! I can hardly contain my passion!—But I won't discover myself. I'll see the bottom of this*—[*To him*] Well now, as we seem to have come to a tolerable explanation—And, as you may be assur'd I'm incapable of whispering all this in the governor's ear, let's proceed to business—Bring me the woman.

INKLE. No; there you must excuse me. I rather wou'd avoid seeing her more; and wish it to be settled without my seeming interference. My presence might distress her—You conceive me?

SIR CHRISTOPHER.—[*Aside*] *Zounds! what an unfeeling rascal!—The poor girl's in love with him, I suppose.*—[*To him*] No, no, fair and open. My dealing is with you and you only: I see her now, or I declare off.

INKLE. Well then, you must be satisfied: yonder's my servant—ha—a thought has struck me. Come here, Sir. [*Enter* Trudge] I'll write my purpose, and send it her by him—It's lucky that I taught her to decypher characters; my labour now is paid. [*Takes out his pocket book, and writes*]—[*To himself*] This is somewhat less abrupt; 'twill soften matters. [*To* Trudge] Give this to Yarico; then bring her hither with you.

TRUDGE. I shall, Sir. [*Going.*

INKLE. Stay; come back. This soft fool, if uninstructed, may add to her distress. When she has read this paper, seem to make light of it; tell her it is a thing of course, done purely for her good. I here inform her that I must part with her. D'ye understand your lesson?

TRUDGE. Pa—part with Ma—Madam Ya-ri-co!

INKLE. Why does the blockhead stammer!—I have my reasons. No muttering—And let me tell you, Sir, if your rare bargain were gone too, 'twou'd be the better: she may babble our story of the forest, and spoil my fortune.

TRUDGE. I'm sorry for it, Sir; I have lived with you along while; I've half a year's wages too, due the 25th *ulto.* for dressing your hair, and scribbling your parchments; but take my scribbling; take my frizzing; take my wages; and I and Wows, will take ourselves off together—she sav'd my life, and rot me, if any thing but death shall part us.

INKLE. Impertinent! Go, and deliver your message.

TRUDGE. I'm gone, Sir. Lord, Lord! I never carried a letter with such ill will in all my born days. [*Exit.*

SIR CHRISTOPHER. Well—shall I see the girl?

INKLE. She'll be here presently. One thing I had forgot: when she is yours, I need not caution you, after the hints I've given, to keep her from the castle. If Sir Christopher should see her, 'twou'd lead, you know, to a discovery of what I wish conceal'd.

SIR CHRISTOPHER. Depend upon *me*—Sir Christopher will know no more of our meeting, than he does at this moment.

INKLE. Your secrecy shall not be unrewarded; I'll recommend you particularly to his good graces.

SIR CHRISTOPHER. Thank ye, thank ye; but I'm pretty much in his good graces, as it is; I don't know anybody he has a greater respect for.—

[*Re-enter* Trudge.

INKLE. Now, Sir, have you perform'd your message?

TRUDGE. Yes, I gave her the letter.

INKLE. And where is Yarico? did she say she'd come? didn't you do as you were ordered? Didn't you speak to her?

TRUDGE. I cou'dn't, Sir, I cou'dn't—I intended to say what you bid me—but I felt such a pain in my throat, I cou'dn't speak a word, for the soul of me; and so, Sir, I fell a crying.

INKLE. Blockhead!

SIR CHRISTOPHER. 'Sblood, but he's a very honest blockhead. Tell me, my good fellow—what said the wench?

TRUDGE. Nothing at all, Sir. She sat down with her two hands clasped on her knees, and look'd so pitifully in my face, I cou'd not stand it. Oh, here she comes. I'll go and find Wows: if I must be melancholy, she shall keep me company. [*Exit.*

SIR CHRISTOPHER. O here she comes. Ods my life, as comely a wench, as ever I saw!

[*Enter* Yarico, *who looks for some time in* Inkle*'s face, bursts into tears, and falls on his neck.*

INKLE. In tears! nay, Yarico! why this?

YARICO. Oh do not—do not leave me!

INKLE. Why, simple girl! I'm labouring for your good. My interest, here, is nothing: I can do nothing from myself, you are ignorant of our country's customs. I must give way to men more powerful, who will not have me with you. But see, my Yarico, ever anxious for your welfare, I've found a kind, good person who will protect you.

YARICO. Ah! why not you protect me!

INKLE. I have no means—how can I?

YARICO. Just as I shelter'd you. Take me to yonder mountain, where I see no smoke from tall, high houses, fill'd with your cruel countrymen. None of your princes, there, will come to take me from you. And should they stray that way, we'll find a lurking place, just like my own poor cave; where many a day I sat beside you, and bless'd the chance that brought you to it—that I might save your life.

SIR CHRISTOPHER. His life! Zounds! my blood boils at the scoundrel's ingratitude!

YARICO. Come, come, let's go. I always fear'd these cities. Let's fly and seek the woods; and there we'll wander hand in hand together. No cares will vex us then—We'll let the day glide by in idleness; and you shall sit in the shade, and watch the sun-beam playing on the brook, while I sing the song that pleases you. No cares, love, but for food—and we'll live cheerily I warrant—In the fresh, early morning, you shall hunt down our game, and I will pick you berries—and then, at night I'll trim our bed of leaves, and lie me down in peace—Oh! we shall be so happy!—

INKLE. This is mere trifling, the trifling of an unenlighten'd Indian. Hear me, Yarico. My countrymen and yours differ as much in minds as in complexions. We were not born to live in woods and caves—to seek subsistence by pursuing beasts—We Christians, girl, hunt money, a thing unknown to you. But, here, 'tis money which brings us ease, plenty, command, power, every thing; and of course happiness. You are the bar to my attaining this; therefore 'tis necessary for my good—and which, I think, you value—

YARICO. You know I do; so much, that it would break my heart to leave you.

INKLE. But we must part; if you are seen with me, I shall lose all.

YARICO. I gave up all for you—my friends—my country: all that was dear to me: and still grown dearer since you shelter'd there.—All, all, was left for you—and were it now to do again—again I'd cross the seas, and follow you, all the world over.

INKLE. We idle time; Sir, she is yours. See you obey this gentleman; 'twill be the better for you. [*Going.*

YARICO. O barbarous! [*Holding him*] Do not, do not abandon me!

INKLE. No more. I'm fix'd.

YARICO. Stay but a little. I shan't live long to be a burden to you: your cruelty has cut me to the heart. Protect me but a little—or I'll obey this man, and undergo all hardships for your good; stay but to witness 'em.—I soon shall sink with grief; tarry till then, and hear me bless your name when I am dying; and beg you now and then, when I am gone, to heave a sigh for your poor Yarico.

INKLE. I dare not listen. You, Sir, I hope, will take good care of her. [*Going.*

SIR CHRISTOPHER. Care of her!—that I will—I'll cherish her like my own daughter; and pour balm into the heart of a poor, innocent girl, that has been wounded by the artifices of a scoundrel.

INKLE. Hah! 'Sdeath, Sir, how dare you!—

SIR CHRISTOPHER. 'Sdeath, Sir, how dare you look an honest man in the face?

INKLE. Sir, you shall feel—

SIR CHRISTOPHER. Feel!—It's more than ever you did, I believe. Mean, sordid, wretch! dead to all sense of honor, gratitude, or humanity—I never heard of such barbarity! I have a son-in-law, who has been left in the same situation; but, if I thought him capable of such cruelty, dam'me if I would not turn him to sea with a peck-loaf in a cockle shell—Come, come, cheer up, my girl! [*Taking* Yarico *by the hand*] You shan't want a friend to protect you, I warrant you.

INKLE. Insolence! The governor shall hear of this insult.

SIR CHRISTOPHER. The governor! liar! cheat! rogue! impostor! breaking all ties you ought to keep, and pretending to those you have no right to. The governor had never such a fellow in the whole catalogue of his acquaintance—the governor disowns you—the governor disclaims you—the governor abhors you; and to your utter confusion, here stands the governor to tell you so. Here stands old Curry, who never talk'd to a rogue without telling him what he thought of him.

INKLE. Sir Christopher!—Lost and undone!

MEDIUM. [*Without*] Holo! young Multiplication! Zounds! I have been peeping in every cranny of the house. Why, young Rule of Three![74] [*Enters from the inn*] Oh, here you are at last—Ah, Sir Christopher! What are you there! too impatient to wait at home. But here's one that will make you easy, I fancy. [*Clapping* Inkle *on the shoulder.*

SIR CHRISTOPHER. How came you to know him?

MEDIUM. Ha! ha! well, that's curious enough too. So you have been talking here, without finding out each other.

SIR CHRISTOPHER. No, no; I have found him out with a vengeance.

MEDIUM. Not you. Why this is the dear boy. It's my nephew; that is, your son-in-law, that is to be. It's Inkle!

SIR CHRISTOPHER. It's a lie; and you're a purblind old booby,—and this dear boy is a damn'd scoundrel.

MEDIUM. Hey-day! what's the meaning of this? One was mad before, and he has bit the other, I suppose.

SIR CHRISTOPHER. But here comes the dear boy—the true boy—the jolly boy, piping hot from church, with my daughter.

[*Enter* Campley*,* Narcissa*, and* Patty.

MEDIUM. Campley!

SIR CHRISTOPHER. Who? Campley?—It's no such thing.

CAMPLEY. That's my name, indeed, Sir Christopher.

SIR CHRISTOPHER. The devil it is! And how came you, Sir, to impose upon me, and assume the name of Inkle? A name which every man of honesty ought to be ashamed of.

CAMPLEY. I never did, Sir.—Since I sailed from England with your daughter, my affection has daily encreased: and when I came to explain myself to you, by a number of concurring circumstances, which I am now partly acquainted with, you mistook me for that gentleman. Yet had I even then been aware of your mistake, I must confess, the regard for my own happiness would have tempted me to let you remain undeceiv'd.

SIR CHRISTOPHER. And did you, Narcissa, join in—

NARCISSA. How could I, my dear Sir, disobey you?

PATTY. Lord your honour, what young lady could refuse a captain?

CAMPLEY. I am a soldier, Sir Christopher. Love and war is the soldier's motto; tho' my income is trifling to your *intended* son-in-law's, still the chance of war has enabled me to support the object of my love above indigence. Her fortune, Sir Christopher, I do not consider myself by any means entitled to.

SIR CHRISTOPHER. 'Sblood! but you must tho'. Give me your hand, my young Mars, and bless you both together!—Thank you, thank you for cheating an old fellow into giving his daughter to a lad of spirit, when he was going to throw her away upon one, in whose breast the mean passion of avarice smothers the smallest spark of affection or humanity.

INKLE. Confusion!

NARCISSA. I have this moment heard a story of a transaction in the forest, which I own would have rendered compliance with your former commands very disagreeable.

PATTY. Yes, Sir, I told my mistress he had brought over a Hotty-pot gentlewoman.

SIR CHRISTOPHER. [*To* Narcissa] Yes, but he would have left her for you; and you for his interest; and sold you, perhaps, as he has this poor girl to me, as a requital for preserving his life.

NARCISSA. How![75]

[*Enter* Trudge *and* Wowski.

TRUDGE. Come along, Wows! take a long last leave of your poor mistress: throw your pretty, ebony arms about her neck.

WOWSKI. No, no;—she not go; you not leave poor Wowski. [*Throwing her arms about* Yarico.

SIR CHRISTOPHER. Poor girl! a companion, I take it!

TRUDGE. A thing of my own, Sir. I cou'dn't help following my master's example in the woods—*Like master, like man.*

SIR CHRISTOPHER. But you wou'd not sell her, and be hang'd to you, you dog, would you?

TRUDGE. Hang me, like a dog, if I wou'd, Sir.

SIR CHRISTOPHER. So say I to every fellow that breaks an obligation due to the feelings of a man. But, old Medium, what have you to say for your hopeful nephew?

MEDIUM. I never speak ill of my friends, Sir Christopher.

SIR CHRISTOPHER. Pshaw!

INKLE. Then let me speak: hear me defend a conduct—

SIR CHRISTOPHER. Defend! Zounds! plead guilty at once—it's the only hope left of obtaining mercy.

INKLE. Suppose, old gentleman, you had a son?

SIR CHRISTOPHER. 'S'blood! then I'd make him an honest fellow, and teach him, that the feeling heart never knows greater pride than when it's employ'd in giving succour to the unfortunate. I'd teach him to be his father's own son to a hair.

INKLE. Even so my father tutor'd me: from my infancy, bending my tender mind, like a young sapling, to his will—Interest was the grand prop round which he twin'd my pliant green affections; taught me in childhood to repeat old sayings—all tending to his own fix'd principles, and the first sentence that I ever lisp'd, was—*Charity begins at home.*

SIR CHRISTOPHER. I shall never like a proverb again as long as I live.

INKLE. As I grew up, he'd prove—and by example—were I in want, I might e'en starve, for what the world cared for their neighbours; why then shou'd I care for the world? Men now liv'd for themselves. These were his doctrines: then, Sir, what wou'd you say, should I, in spite of habit, precept, education, fly in my father's face, and spurn his councils?

SIR CHRISTOPHER. Say! why, that you were a damn'd honest, undutiful fellow. O curse such principles! Principles which destroy all confidence between man and man—Principles which none but a rogue cou'd instil, and none but a rogue cou'd imbibe.—Principles—

INKLE. Which I renounce.

SIR CHRISTOPHER. Eh!

INKLE. Renounce entirely. Ill-founded precept Barbadoes too long has steel'd my breast—but still 'tis vulnerable—this trial was too much—Nature, 'gainst habit combating within me, has penetrated to my heart; a heart, I own, long callous to the feelings of sensibility; but now it bleeds—and bleeds for my poor Yarico. Oh, let me clasp her to it, while 'tis glowing, and mingle tears of love and penitence. [*Embracing her.*

TRUDGE. [*Capering about*] Wows, give me a kiss! [Wowski *goes to* Trudge.

YARICO. And shall we—shall we be happy?

INKLE. Aye; ever, ever, Yarico.

YARICO. I knew we shou'd—and yet I feared—but shall I still watch over you? Oh! love, you surely gave your Yarico such pain, only to make her feel this happiness the greater.

WOWSKI. [*Going to* Yarico] Oh Wowski so happy! —and yet I think I not glad neither.

TRUDGE. Eh, Wows! How!—why not!

WOWSKI. 'Cause I can't help cry—

SIR CHRISTOPHER. Then, if that's the case—curse me, if I think I'm very glad either. What the plague's the matter with my eyes?—Young man, your hand—I am now proud and happy to shake it.

MEDIUM. Well, Sir Christopher, what do you say to my hopeful nephew now?

SIR CHRISTOPHER. Say! Why, confound the fellow, I say, that is ungenerous enough to remember the bad action of a man who has virtue left in his heart to repent it—[*To* Trudge] As for you, my good fellow, I must, with your master's permission, employ you myself.

TRUDGE. O rare!—Bless your honour!—Wows! you'll be lady, you jade, to a governor's factotum.

WOWSKI. Iss—I Lady Jacktotum.

SIR CHRISTOPHER. And now, my young folks, we'll drive home, and celebrate the wedding. Od's my life! I long to be shaking a foot at the fiddles, and I shall dance ten times the lighter, for reforming an Inkle, while I have it in my power to reward the innocence of a Yarico.

FINALE [*La Belle Catharine*]

CAMPLEY. *Come, let us dance and sing,*
While all Barbadoes bells[76] *shall ring:*
Love scrapes the fiddle string,
And Venus plays the lute;
Hymen gay, foots away,
Happy at our wedding day,
Cocks his chin, and figures in,
To tabor, fife, and flute.

CHORUS. *Come then dance and sing,*
While all Barbadoe's bells shall ring, &c.

NARCISSA. *Since thus each anxious care*
Is vanish'd into empty air,
Ah! how can I forbear
To join the jocund dance?
To and fro, couples go,
On the light fantastic toe,
White with glee, merrily,
The rosy hours advance.

CHORUS. *Come then, &c.*

YARICO. *When first the swelling sea*
Hither bore my love and me,
What then my fate would be,
Little did I think—
Doom'd to know care and woe,

Happy still is Yarico;
Since her love will constant prove,
And nobly scorns to shrink.

CHORUS. *Come then, &c.*

WOWSKI.[77] *Whilst all around, rejoice,*
Pipe and tabor raise the voice,
It can't be Wowski's choice,
Whilst Trudge's to be dumb.
No, no, dey blithe and gay,
Shall like massy, missy play.
Dance and sing, hey ding, ding,
Strike fiddle and beat drum.

CHORUS. *Come then, &c.*

TRUDGE. *'Sbobs! now, I'm fix'd for life,*
My fortune's fair, tho' black's my wife,
Who fears domestic strife—
Who cares now a souse![78]
Merry cheer my dingy dear
Shall find with her factotum here;
Night and day, I'll frisk and play
About the house, with Wowski.

CHORUS. *Come then, &c.*

INKLE.[79] *Love's convert here behold,*
Banish'd now my thirst of gold,
Bless'd in these arms to fold
My gentle Yarico.
Hence all care, doubt, and fear,
Love and joy each want shall cheer,
Happy night, pure delight,
Shall make our bosoms glow.

CHORUS. *Come then, &c.*

PATTY. *Let Patty say a word—*
A chambermaid may sure be heard—
Sure men are grown absurd,
Thus taking black for white;
To hug and kiss a dingy miss,
Will hardly suit an age like this,
Unless, here, some friends appear,
Who like this wedding night.

CHORUS. *Come then, &c.*

19.2 EXTRACT FROM RICHARD LIGON, *HISTORY OF THE ISLAND OF BARBADOES*

From the second edition (1673)

AS FOR THE *INDIANS*, we have but few, and those fetched from other countries; some from the neighbouring islands, some from the Main, which we make slaves: the women who are better vers'd in ordering the cassavie[80] and making bread than the *negroes* we imploy for that purpose, as also for making mobbie:[81] the men we use for footmen and killing fish, which they are good at; with their own bows and arrows they will go out; and in a day's time, kill as much fish, as will serve a family of a dozen persons, two or three days, if you can keep the fish so long. They are very active men, and apt to learn any thing, sooner than the *negroes*; and as different from them in shape, almost as in colour; the men very broad shoulder'd, deep breasted, with large heads, and their faces almost three square, broad about the eyes and temples, and sharp at the chin, their skins some of them brown, some a bright bay. They are much craftier, and subtler th[a]n the *negroes*, and in their nature falser; but in their bodies more active. Their women have very small breasts, and have more of the shale of the *Europeans* than the *negroes*, their hair black and long, a great part whereof hangs down upon their backs, as low as their haunches, with a large lock hanging over either breast, which seldom or never curls: clothes they scorn to wear, especially if they be well shap'd; a girdle they use of tape, covered with little smooth shells of fishes, white, and from their flank of one side, to their flank on the other side, a fringe of blue *bugle*;[82] which hangs so low as to cover their privities. We had an *Indian* woman, a slave in the house, who was of excellent shape and colour, for it was a pure bright bay;[83] small breasts, with the nip[p]les of a porphyry colour, this woman would not be woo'd by any means to wear clothes. She chanc'd to be with child, by a Christian servant, and lodging in the *Indian*-house, amongst other women of her own country, where the Christian servants, both men and women came; and being very great, and that her time was come to be delivered, loath to fall in labour before the men, walk'd down to a wood, in which was a pond of water, and there by the side of the pond, brought her self a bed; and presently washing her child in some of the water of the pond, lap'd it up in such rags, as she had begg'd of the Christians; and in three hours' time came home, with her child in her arms, a lusty boy, frolick and lively.

This *Indian* dwelling near the sea-coast, upon the Main, an *English* ship put in to a bay, and sent some of her men ashore, to try what victuals or water they could find, for in some distress they were: but the *Indians* perceiving them to go up so far into the country, as they were sure they could not make a safe retreat, intercepted them in their return and fell upon them, chasing them into a wood, and being dispersed there, some were taken, and some kill'd: but a young man amongst them straggling from the rest, was met by this *Indian* maid, who upon the first sight fell in love with him, and hid him close from her countrymen (the *Indians*) in a cave, and there fed him, till they could safely go down to the shore, where the ship lay at anchor, expecting the return of their friends. But at last, seeing them upon the shore, sent the long-boat for them, took them aboard, and brought them away. But the youth, when he came ashore in the *Barbadoes*, forgot the kindness of the poor maid, that had ventured her life for his safety, and sold her for a slave, who was as free born as he: and so poor *Yarico* for her love, lost her liberty . . .

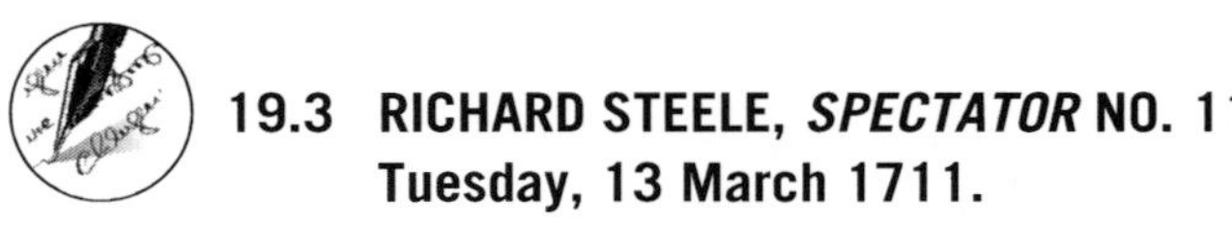

19.3 RICHARD STEELE, *SPECTATOR* NO. 11 Tuesday, 13 March 1711.

Dat veniam corvis, vexat censura columbas. Juv.[84]

ARIETTA IS VISITED BY ALL PERSONS of both sexes, who have any pretence to wit and gallantry. She is in that time of life which is neither affected with the follies of youth, or infirmities of age; and her conversation is so mixed with gaiety and prudence, that she is agreeable both to the young and the old. Her behaviour is very frank, without being in the least blameable; and as she is out of the tract of any amorous or ambitious pursuits of her own, her visitants entertain her with accounts of themselves very freely, whether they concern their passions or their interests. I made her a visit this afternoon, having been formerly introduced to the honour of her acquaintance, by my friend *Will. Honeycomb*, who has prevailed upon her to admit me sometimes into her assembly, as a civil, inoffensive man. I found her accompanied with one person only, a common-place talker, who, upon my entrance, rose, and after a very slight civility sat down again; then turning to *Arietta*, pursued his discourse, which I found was upon the old topic, of constancy in love. He went on with great facility in repeating what he talks every day of his life; and, with the ornaments of insignificant laughs and gestures, enforced his argument by quotations out of plays and songs, which allude to the perjuries of the fair, and the general levity of women. Methought he strove to shine more than ordinarily in his talkative way, that he might insult my silence, and distinguish himself before a woman of *Arietta*'s taste and understanding. She had often an inclination to interrupt him, but could find no opportunity, 'till the larum ceased of its self; which it did not 'till he had repeated and murdered the celebrated story of the *Ephesian* Matron.[85]

Arietta seemed to regard this piece of raillery as an outrage done to her sex, as indeed I have always observed that women, whether out of a nicer regard to their honour, or what other reason I cannot tell, are more sensibly touched with those general aspersions, which are cast upon their sex, than men are by what is said of theirs.

When she had a little recovered her self from the serious anger she was in, she replied in the following manner.

Sir, When I consider how perfectly new all you have said on this subject is, and that the story you have given us is not quite two thousand years old, I cannot but think it a piece of presumption to dispute with you: but your quotations put me in mind of the Fable of the Lion, and the Man.[86] The man walking with that noble animal, showed him, in the ostentation of human superiority, a sign of a man killing a lion. Upon which the lion said very justly, *We lions are none of us painters, else we could show a hundred men killed by lions, for one lion killed by a man.* You men are writers, and can represent us women as unbecoming as you please in your works, while we are unable to return the injury. You have twice or thrice observed in your discourse, that hypocrisy is the very foundation of our education; and that an ability to dissemble our affections, is a professed part of our breeding. These, and such other reflections, are sprinkled up and down the writings of all ages, by authors, who leave behind them memorials of their resentment against the scorn of particular women, in invectives against the whole sex. Such a writer, I doubt not, was the celebrated *Petronius*, who invented the pleasant aggravations of the frailty of the *Ephesian* lady; but when we consider this question between the sexes, which has been either a point of dispute or raillery ever since there were men and women, let us take facts from plain people, and from such as have not either ambition or capacity to embellish their narrations with any beauties of imagination. I was the other day amusing myself with *Ligon*'s account of *Barbadoes*; and in answer to your well-wrought tale, I will give you (as it dwells upon my memory) out of that honest traveller, in his fifty fifth age, the history of *Inkle* and *Yarico*.

Mr. *Thomas Inkle* of *London*, aged 20 years, embarked in the *Downs* on the good ship called the *Achilles*, bound for the *West-Indies*, on the 16th of *June* 1647, in order to improve his fortune by trade and merchandize. Our adventurer was the third son of an eminent citizen, who had taken particular care to instill into his mind an early love of gain, by making him a perfect master of numbers, and consequently giving him a quick view of loss and advantage, and preventing the natural impulses of his passions, by prepossession towards his interests. With a mind thus turned, young *Inkle* had a person every way agreeable, a ruddy vigour in his countenance, strength in his limbs, with ringlets of fair hair loosely flowing on his shoulders. It happened, in the course of the voyage, that the *Achilles*, in some distress, put into a creek on the main of *America*, in search of provisions: the youth, who is the hero of my story, among others, went ashore on this occasion. From their first landing they were observed by a party of *Indians*, who hid themselves in the woods for that purpose. The *English* unadvisedly marched a great distance from the shore into the country, and were intercepted by the natives, who slew the greatest number of them. Our adventurer escaped among others by flying into a forest. Upon his coming into a remote and pathless part of the wood, he threw himself, tired and breathless, on a little hillock, when an *Indian* maid rushed from a thicket behind him: after the first surprize, they appeared mutually agreeable to each other. If the *European* was highly charmed with the limbs, features, and wild graces of the naked *American*; the *American* was no less taken with the dress, complexion and shape of an *European*, covered from head to foot. The *Indian* grew immediately enamoured of him, and consequently solicitous for his preservation: she therefore conveyed him to a cave, where she gave him a delicious repast of fruits, and led him to a stream to slake his thirst. In the midst of these good offices, she would sometimes play with his hair, and delight in the opposition of its colour, to that of her fingers: then open his bosom, then laugh at him for covering it. She was, it seems, a person of distinction, for she every day came to him in a different dress, of the most beautiful shells, bugles and bredes. She likewise brought him a great many spoils, which her other lovers had presented to her; so that his cave was richly adorned with all the spotted skins of beasts, and most party-coloured feathers of fowls, which that world afforded. To make his confinement more tolerable, she would carry him in the dusk of the evening, or by the favour of moon-light, to unfrequented groves and solitudes, and show him where to lie down in safety, and sleep amidst the falls of waters, and melody of nightingales. Her part was to watch and hold him in her arms, for fear of her country-men, and wake him on occasions to consult his safety. In this manner did the lovers pass away their time, till they had learn'd a language of their own, in which the voyager communicated to his mistress, how happy he should be to have her in his country, where she should be clothed in such silks as his waistcoat was made of, and be carried in houses drawn by horses, without being exposed to wind or weather. All this he promised her the enjoyment of, without such fears and alarms as they were there tormented with. In this tender correspondence these lovers lived for several months, when *Yarico*, instructed by her lover, discovered a vessel off the coast, to which she made signals, and in the night, with the utmost joy and satisfaction accompanied him to a ship's-crew of his countrymen, bound for *Barbadoes*. When a vessel from the main arrives in that island, it seems the planters come down to the shore, where there in an immediate market of the *Indians* and other slaves as with us of horses and oxen.

To be short, Mr. *Thomas Inkle*, now coming into *English* territories, began seriously to reflect upon his loss of time, and to weigh with himself how many days' interest of his money he had lost during his stay with *Yarico*. This thought made the young man very pensive, and careful what account he should be able to give his friends of his voyage. Upon which considerations, the prudent and frugal young man sold *Yarico* to a *Barbadian* merchant; notwithstanding that the poor girl, to incline him to commiserate her condition, told him that she was with child by him: but he only made use of that information, to rise in his demands upon the purchaser.

I was so touch'd with this story, (which I think should be always a counterpart to the *Ephesian* Matron) that I left the room with tears in my eyes; which a woman of *Arietta*'s good sense did, I am sure, take for greater applause, than any compliments I could make her.

19.4 ROBERT POLLARD (AFTER HENRY SINGLETON), *THE YOUNG ENGLISH MERCHANT INKLE*

Robert Pollard (after Henry Singleton), *Inkle and Yarico*, plate 1, aquatint engraving, 1788. Trustees of the British Museum. Inkle and Yarico's first encounter in the cave. Trudge is to the right of Inkle and Wowski is in the shadows.

19.5 ROBERT POLLARD (AFTER HENRY SINGLETON), *INKLE DELIVERS THE UNHAPPY BLACK GIRL*

INKLE AND YARICO. Plate 2d

Robert Pollard (after Henry Singleton), *Inkle and Yarico*, plate 2, aquatint engraving, 1788. Trustees of the British Museum.

19.6 JAMES GILLRAY, *WOUSKI*

James Gillray, *Wouski*, 23 January 1788, hand-coloured etching. Trustees of the British Museum.

As this satire on the profligate Prince of Wales indicates, Wowski went on to have a life of her own in the racial imaginary of Georgian England.

Notes

1 The copy text is George Colman, *Inkle and Yarico: an Opera in Three Acts as Performed at the Theatre-Royal in the Haymarket, on Saturday, August 11, 1787*. London: G.C.J. and J. Robinson, 1787.
2 Michael Ragussis, *Theatrical Nation: Jews and Other Outlandish Englishmen in Georgian England*. Philadelphia, PA: University of Pennsylvannia Press, 2010, 24 and 43–5.
3 Christopher Leslie Brown, *Moral Capital: Foundations of British Abolitionism*. Chapel Hill, NC: University of North Carolina Press, 2006.
4 Elizabeth Inchbald, *The British Theatre; or A Collection of Plays which Are Acted at the Theatres Royal Drury Lane, Covent Garden and Haymarket vol. 20*. London, 1808, 3.
5 Inchbald, 4. See Frank Felsenstein, *English Trader, Indian Maid: Representing Gender, Race, and Slavery in the New World: An Inkle and Yarico Reader*. Baltimore, MD: The Johns Hopkins University Press, 1999, 18–19 for copious examples in the play that confuse the conventional visual and discursive distinctions between Africans and Native Americans.
6 Julie Carlson, "Race and Profit in Romantic Theatre," in Jane Moody and Daniel O'Quinn, *Cambridge Companion to British Theatre, 1730–1830*. Cambridge: Cambridge University Press, 2007, 175–88.
7 This Prologue appears in the Larpent version of the play.
8 *pedant chymistry*: alchemy.
9 *mourning:* mourning clothes.
10 Various proposals had been made to establish a colony at Botany Bay prior to the performance of Colman's play. In 1783, James Matra proposed that it be populated by American loyalists in the wake of the American war. The proposal was rejected and the colony was eventually populated by transported convicts.
11 *Threadneedle-street*: a prominent street in the City, London's financial district, and home to the Bank of England.
12 *bottle:* bundle. Colman is playing on "a needle in a haystack."
13 *factotum*: domestic servant.
14 Playing on Inkle's name which refers to "a kind of linen tape" (OED).
15 *St. James's Park*: Situated in Westminster adjacent to Buckingham House (acquired by George III for his wife in 1761 it would be remodeled into Buckingham Palace), St. James's Park is the oldest of the Royal Parks in London. The Mall was a favorite site for promenading and the park itself was a notable pleasure ground.
16 *co.*: Company.
17 *'Sdeath*: contraction of "God's Death."
18 *black legs*: swindlers, and in this context, Native Americans.
19 Elizabeth Inchbald's widely circulated version of the play adds "—*Mouth of a cave*" to this description of scenery.
20 In all of the versions of the Inkle and Yarico tale extending back to Ligon (see Contexts), the name of the shape remains constant.
21 *prize*: plunder or booty captured by force.
22 *rhino*: eighteenth century slang for money.
23 The *Intrepid, Lion, Æolus, Thunderer, Orpheus, Ceres*, and *Eagle* are ostensible names of British ships.
24 *booby*: fool.
25 *chop-house*: a low restaurant that specializes in grilled meat, usually muttonchops and beefsteaks.
26 *flea*: flay.
27 According to Johnson's *Dictionary*, a *curtain-lecture* is "A reproof given by a wife to a husband in bed."
28 *hammer-cloth*: A cloth covering the driver's seat in a carriage.
29 *dog-days*: the hottest part of the summer.
30 This joke plays a reverse on the fashionable practice of employing young black boys to serve at the tea table. The second plate of Hogarth's *The Harlot's Progress* famously depicts such a scene of domestic racism.

31 *pounce*: to prepare parchment for writing—often this involved dusting the surface with a fine powder to prevent ink from running.

32 *'sbud*: short for "God's blood."

33 *fallals*: frippery.

34 In country dancing a couple leads up past the others holding hands and again joins hands when casting down the room.

35 *Patch-box:* "a box for holding decorative patches for the face" (*OED*).

36 *Hymen:* The Roman god of marriage.

37 *Cyprian Goddess*: Venus, the goddess of love and Mars's lover.

38 *runner*: "one whose business it is to solicit custom for a hotel" (*OED*).

39 Trudge is making a pun on the name of the inn.

40 A common name for an inn.

41 *blue devils*: despondency.

42 A multi-layered joke invoking the jester's cap and punning on foolscap, the type of paper associated with business transactions.

43 Both fires and executions tended to draw the mob.

44 The Humane Society, founded in 1774 by Dr. William Hawes (1736–1806) and Dr. Thomas Cogan (1736–1818) for the purpose of saving victims from drowning, had just been renamed the Royal Humane Society in 1787, the year of *Inkle and Yarico*'s first performance.

45 The New River was a 36-mile long channel designed to bring fresh water into London from Hertfordshire.

46 *Oons*!: Zounds!

47 *pigeon:* a coward (*OED*).

48 *quotha*: an ironic or sarcastic way of repeating the words of someone else. Sir Christopher is ridiculing Medium's euphemistic use of "foibles".

49 A watch or clock that chimes the hours.

50 *ulto.*: abbreviation for ultimo, meaning the final point or limit.

51 According to Greek and Roman mythology, Venus was borne of the sea foam.

52 Venus's husband Vulcan, the God of Fire, was lame. Vulcan was cuckolded by Mars so the physical disability also has sexual connotations.

53 *Spintext*: a humorous name for a long-winded parson.

54 Colman is adapting conventional names of the shepherds who populate pastoral verse. "Arriette" may be derived from "Arrieta," the character who tells the tale of Inkle and Yarico in Steele's version for *The Spectator* (see Contexts).

55 *fallals*: excessive finery or adornment (*OED*).

56 *curvet*: to leap about, a term adapted from horsemanship.

57 *buss:* a kiss.

58 Hottentot was a derogatory terms for Africans. In the early nineteenth century, the term was applied to Sarah Baartman, who was displayed as the Hottentot Venus, and then took on more general usage.

59 A man looked on with contempt or false pity.

60 *pomatum*: ointment for the skin or hair (*OED*).

61 *The Adelphi*: A fashionable set of residences designed by Robert and James Adam that overlooked the Thames. David Garrick was a famous resident.

62 *Gemini*: slang for Jesu Domine.

63 Josiah Wedgwood's jasperware and basaltware replicated ancient cameo glass. The reference is significant here because in 1787 Wedgwood became one of the most active voices in the British abolitionist movement. His anti-slavery medal was an icon for the movement.

64 Actors playing blackface roles used burnt cork to darken their complexions. This is an intriguing meta-theatrical moment because of course Wowski's complexion not only could, but probably had worn off on Trudge himself.

65 *younkers*: young men.

66 *proverb*: Have a crow to pluck = Have a fault to find.

67 The material from Wowski's entrance to this point in Trudge's speech is not presented in the copy text. All other editions of the play include this material.
68 The behavior of servants in the theatre was of concern because their presence blurred the separation of ranks.
69 Referring to Shakespeare's *Othello*.
70 Because it is capitalized in the copy text, Colman seems to be referring to Dryden's play.
71 Colman is referring to the 1758 incident of the Black Hole of Calcutta. According to the narrative of John Zephaniah Holwell, the troops of Siraj ud-Dawlah, the Nawab of Bengal closely confined 146 British soldiers in a small dungeon in Fort William; Holwell stated that of these 123 died.
72 Referring to the common entertainment of exhibiting dancing bears. It was also possible at this time to still see fighting animals for entertainment.
73 *Old Nick*: the devil.
74 *Rule of Three*: a mathematical method of deducing a fourth number from three given proportionate numbers. Medium is satirizing Inkle's proclivity for numerically reckoning his advantage at all times.
75 From this point onward we know that Colman significantly altered the ending. Fragments of the original ending are in the Larpent manuscript.
76 *Barbadoe's bells*: refers equally to wedding bells and to the practice of ringing bells to call slaves to work.
77 Wowski's verse is not printed in the 1787 text, but appears in the widely circulated Inchbald edition of 1789.
78 *souse*: sou; a coin of insignificant value.
79 Inkle's verse is not printed in the 1787 text, but appears in the widely circulated Inchbald edition of 1789.
80 *Cassava*: a crucial staple.
81 Mauby was a bitter liquor.
82 beads.
83 *bay*: reddish brown.
84 "judgement acquits the ravens and condemns the doves" (Juvenal, *Satires, Book I*, ed. Braund, 138).
85 Petronius's story of the Ephesian matron was widely known through La Fontaine's *conte*. The matron was celebrated for her chastity but after the death of her husband succumbed to the entreaties of a soldier guarding her husband's tomb.
86 Referring to Aesop's *Fables*.

20. *Every One Has His Fault*

EVERY ONE HAS HIS FAULT. ELIZABETH INCHBALD. FIRST PERFORMED 29 JANUARY 1793 AND FIRST PUBLISHED 1793

20.1 *EVERY ONE HAS HIS FAULT*[1]

Elizabeth Inchbald

First Performed 29 January 1793 and First Published 1793

BY ANY MEASURE ELIZABETH INCHBALD (1753–1821) was Britain's pre-eminent playwright for the last 20 years of the eighteenth century. Over the course of 16 five-act comedies and three afterpieces, Inchbald explored not only the volatile politics of the Revolutionary era, but also the transformations in the sex/gender system in a fashion that consistently engaged theatrical audiences.[2] The success of her plays can in many ways be attributed to experience on the stage as a player. She was a regular performer at Covent Garden before writing her first afterpiece *The Mogul Tale* in 1784; and her influence was felt well after her retirement as a playwright in 1800 because she edited *The British Theatre*, 25 vols. (1806–09), *Collection of Farces and Afterpieces*, 7 vols. (1809) and *The Modern Theatre*, 10 vols. (1811). The headnotes to the selected plays in these anthologies constitute a major contribution to theatrical criticism. Her novels *Nature and Art* and *A Simple Story* are now canonical texts of British Romanticism.

Every One Has His Fault was both the most controversial and most successful of Inchbald's comedies. Inchbald typically intertwined highly topical plots that referenced the politics of the day with complex sexual plots that challenged conventional understandings of normative femininity. Marriage was crucial to eighteenth-century comedy, but in Inchbald's plays the institution's legal, social, and ethical dimensions were challenged head on. What is more she revived the practice of using the power dynamics inherent to the institution of marriage to allegorize the changing nature of sovereignty and politics for a period of revolution and reform. Thus marriages in earlier comedies that would have signaled the stability of the Crown through the strong validation of paternal authority are often used by Inchbald to figure tyranny and anti-democratic sentiment. In other words, the historical movement toward increasingly equitable marriage practices afforded Inchbald the opportunity to allegorize political change. And that dramatization of reform, both sexual and political, was extensive: it included important scrutiny of Britain's colonial practices in India (*Such Things Are*, *The Wise Man of the East*), as well as the government's domestic policies and its prosecution of war in this play.

Needless to say this level of political engagement and feminist intervention required a deft hand both to preserve Inchbald's own reputation and to maintain her audience. *Every One Has His Fault* is particularly interesting in this regard because its initial performance generated a firestorm of controversy in the press. This was perhaps inevitable. The play was originally scheduled to open at Covent Garden on January 23, 1793 but was postponed by Thomas Harris for fear of coinciding with the French regicide. The play was in rehearsal when the Edict of Fraternity was passed, and opened on January 29, 1793: eight days after the execution of Louis XVI and three days prior to the declaration of war with France. The *Anti-Jacobin* picked up on the audience's reaction to the repeated phrase "Provisions are so scarce" and denounced Inchbald as a supporter of the French Revolution and the Jacobin cause at home. The *Contexts* section for this play presents the denunciation and the ensuing debate in its entirety because it offers a crucial window not only into the politics of the era, but also into the challenges for the woman playwright in the public sphere. The controversy surrounding the play did not abate quickly. When the play opened in Brighton Theatre, military officers in the audience successfully ejected the Reverend Vicessimus Knox from the house for his opposition to the war with France.[3]

What is curious about this controversy is that Inchbald chose to examine the politics of revolution and war through an extremely important displacement. The political plot of the play concerns the destitution and insults sustained by Irwin, a veteran of the American war. In many ways, the Revolution in France was grounded on the same principles as successful decolonization in America and the build up to the war with Revolutionary France would have seemed very similar to the acrimony and political maneuvering of the mid 1770s. Irwin's desolation and his ensuing actions were a very disturbing evocation both of Britain's failure to fully deal with the loss of the American colonies and of the troubling status of Liberty for British identity. As a figure for the failed claims of British military power, Irwin's plight and his resistance seem to imply that Liberty was perhaps more at home elsewhere. By collapsing Irwin's resentment with reformist and revolutionary claims for autonomy, Inchbald was simultaneously opening a recent wound and making a subtle prediction about the Ministry's bellicose intentions towards France.[4]

Despite, or perhaps because of, this controversy, *Every One Has His Fault* was Inchbald's most frequently performed comedy. Its longevity on the stage is likely a result of its remarkably sparkling dialogue and its complex treatment of women's relation to the marriage market. Throughout the period of the play's popularity Anglophone societies in Britain and America were witnessing a fundamental realignment in the structure and importance of the domestic sphere. This play, like many of Inchbald's plays, pits earlier forms of sexual ideology, here represented by Lord Norland's excessive paternalism and Sir Robert Random's libertinism, against emergent notions of conjugal matrimony. But unlike many other plays of the era, Inchbald is extremely attentive to those women at the margins of the marital economy. In this play there are four categories of women: maid (i.e. women of marriageable age), wife, spinster, and widow. For Lord Norland's strict commodification of women, only maids and wives are of value; widows and spinsters amount to little more than societal excess. Inchbald's attention to these figures, and to the even more problematic category of divorced women, is remarkable. As Misty Anderson has argued, *Every One Has His Fault* is one of the most thorough and important analyses of divorce in the period.[5] She explores the varying laws around divorce in the British Isles, the hypocrisy surrounding the law and its interpretation in England, and most importantly, the emotional turmoil exacted on women by husbands, parents and guardians.

Prologue

By the Reverend Mr. Nares.[6] *Spoken by Mr. Farren*

Our Author, who accuses great and small,
And says so boldly, there are faults in all;
Sends me with dismal voice, and lengthen'd phiz,[7]
Humbly to own one dreadful fault of *his*:
A fault, in modern Authors not uncommon,
It is,—now don't be angry—He's—*a woman.*

Can you forgive it? Nay, I'll tell you more,
One who has dar'd to venture here before;
Has seen your smiles, your frowns—tremendous sight!
O, be not in a frowning mood to-night!
The play, perhaps, has many things amiss:
Well, let us then reduce the point to this,
Let only those that have no failings, hiss.

The Rights of Women,[8] says a female pen,
Are, to do every thing as well as men,
To think, to argue, to decide, to write,
To talk, undoubtedly—perhaps, to fight.
(For females march to war, like brave commanders,
Not in old authors only—but in Flanders.)[9]

I grant this matter may be strain'd too far,
And maid 'gainst man is most uncivil war:
I grant, as all my City friends will say,
That men should rule, and women should obey:
That nothing binds the marriage contract faster,
Than our—"Zounds, Madam, I'm your Lord and Master."
I grant their nature, and their frailty such.
Women make too free—and know too much.
But since the Sex at length has been inclin'd
To cultivate that useful part—the mind;—
Since they have learnt to read, to write, to spell;—
Since some of them have wit—and use it well;—
Let us not force them back with brow severe,
Within the pale of ignorance and fear,
Confin'd entirely to domestic arts,
Producing only children, pies, and tarts.

The fav'rite fable of the tuneful Nine,[10]
Implies that female genius *is divine*.
Then, drive not, Critics, with tyrannic rage,
A supplicating fair-one from the stage;
The Comic Muse perhaps is growing old,
Her lovers, you well know, are few and cold.
'Tis time then freely to enlarge the plan,
And let all those write comedies—that can.

Dramatis Personæ

Men

Lord Norland	Mr. Farren
Sir Robert Ramble	Mr. Lewis
Mr. Solus	Mr. Quick
Mr. Harmony	Mr. Munden
Mr. Placid	Mr. Fawcett
Mr. Irwin	Mr. Pope
Hammond	Mr. Powell
Porter	Mr. Thompson
Edward	Miss Grist

Women

Lady Eleanor Irwin	Mrs. Pope
Mrs. Placid	Mrs. Mattocks
Miss Spinster	Mrs. Webb
Miss Wooburn	Mrs. Eston
Servants, &c.	

Scene—London.

I.i

An apartment at Mr. Placid*'s. Enter* Mr. Placid[11] *and* Mr. Solus.

PLACID. You are to blame.

SOLUS. I say the same by you.

PLACID. And yet your singularity pleases me; for you are the first elderly bachelor I ever knew, who did not hug himself in the reflection, that he was not in the trammels of wedlock.

SOLUS. No; I am only the first elderly bachelor who has truth and courage enough to confess his dissatisfaction.

PLACID. And you really wish you were married?

SOLUS. I do. I wish still more, that I had been married thirty years ago. Oh! I wish a wife and half-a-score children would now start up around me, and bring along with them all that affection, which we should have had for each other by being earlier acquainted. But as it is, in my present state, there is not a person in the world I care a straw for; and the world is pretty even with me, for I don't believe there is a creature in it who cares a straw for me.

PLACID. Pshaw! you have in your time been a man of gallantry; and, consequently, must have made many attachments.

SOLUS. Yes, such as men of gallantry usually make. I have been attached to women who have purloined my fortune, and to men who have partaken of the theft: I have been in as much fear of my mistress, as you are of your wife.

PLACID. Is that possible?

SOLUS. Yes; and without having one of those tender, delicate ties of a husband, an excuse for my apprehension.—I have maintained children—

PLACID. Then why do you complain for the want of a family?

SOLUS. I did not say, I ever had any children; I said I had *maintained* them; but I never believed they were mine; for I could have no dependence upon the principles of their mother—and never did I take one of those tender infants in my arms, that the forehead of my valet, the squint eye of my apothecary, or the double chin of my chaplain, did not stare me in the face, and damp all the fine feelings of the parent, which I had just called up.

PLACID. But those are accidents, which may occur in the marriage state.

SOLUS. In that case, a man is pitied—in mine, he is only laughed at.

PLACID. I wish to heaven I could exchange the pity which my friends bestow on me, for the merriment which your ill fate excites.

SOLUS. You want but courage to be envied.

PLACID. Does any one doubt my courage?

SOLUS. No; if a prince were to offend you, you would challenge him, I have no doubt.

PLACID. But if my wife offend me, I am obliged to make an apology.—Was not that her voice? I hope she has not overheard our conversation.

SOLUS. If she have, she'll be in an ill humour.

PLACID. That she will be, whether she have heard it or not.

SOLUS. Well, good day. I don't like to be driven from my fixed plan of wedlock; and, therefore, I won't be a spectator of your mutual discontent. [*Going.*

PLACID. But before you go, Mr. Solus, permit me to remind you of a certain concern, that, I think, would afford you much more delight than all you can, at this time of life propose to yourself in marriage. Make happy, by your beneficence, a near relation, whom the truest affection has drawn into that state, but who is denied the blessing of competency to make the state supportable.

SOLUS. You mean my nephew, Irwin? But do not you acknowledge he has a wife and children? Did not he marry the woman he loved, and has he not, at this moment, a large family, by whom he is beloved? And is he not, therefore, with all his poverty, much happier than I? He has often told me, when I have reproached him with his indiscreet marriage, "that in his wife he possessed kingdoms!" Do you suppose I will give any part of my fortune to a man who enjoys such extensive domains? No:—let him preserve his territories, and I will keep my little estate for my own use. [*Exit.*

PLACID. John! John! [*Enter* Servant] has your mistress been inquiring for me?

JOHN. Yes, Sir:—My Lady asked, just now, if I knew who was with you?

PLACID. Did she seem angry?

JOHN. No, Sir;—pretty well.

PLACID. [*In anger*] You scoundrel, what do you mean by "pretty well"?

JOHN. Much as usual, Sir.

PLACID. And do you call that "pretty well"? You scoundrel, I have a great mind—

[*Enter* Mrs. Placid, *speaking very loud.*

MRS. PLACID. What is the matter, Mr. Placid? What is all this noise about? You know I hate a noise. What is the matter?

PLACID. My dear, I was only finding fault with that blockhead.

MRS. PLACID. Pray, Mr. Placid, do not find fault with any body in this house. But I have something which I must take *you* very severely to task about, Sir.

PLACID. No, my dear, not just now, pray.

MRS. PLACID. Why not now?

PLACID. [*Looking at his watch*] Because dinner will be ready in a few minutes. I am very hungry, and it will be cruel of you to spoil my appetite. John, is the dinner on table?

MRS. PLACID. No, John, don't let it be served yet—Mr. Placid, you *shall* first hear what I have to say. [*Sitting down.*

[*Exit* Servant.

PLACID. But then I know I sha'n't be able to eat a morsel.

MRS. PLACID. Sit down. [Placid *sits*]—I believe Mr. Placid, you are going to do a very silly thing. I am afraid you are going to lend some money?

PLACID. Well, my dear, and suppose I am?

MRS. PLACID. Then, I don't approve of people lending their money.

PLACID. But, my dear, I have known you approve of borrowing money: and, once in our lives, what should we have done, if every body had refused to lend?

MRS. PLACID. That is nothing to the purpose.—And, now, I desire you will hear what I say, without speaking a word yourself.

PLACID. Well, my dear.

MRS. PLACID. Now, mind you don't speak, till I have done.—Our old acquaintance, Captain Irwin, and Lady Eleanor, his wife (with whom we lived upon very intimate terms, to be sure, while we were in America), are returned to London; and, I find, you have visited them very frequently.

PLACID. Not above two or three times, upon my word, for it hurts me to see them in distress, and I forbear to go.

MRS. PLACID. There! you own they are in distress; I expected as much. Now, own to me that they have asked you to lend them money.

PLACID. I do own it—I do own it. Now, are you satisfied?

MRS. PLACID. No: for I have no doubt but you have promised they shall have it.

PLACID. No, upon my word, I have not promised.

MRS. PLACID. Then promise me they shall not.

PLACID. Nay, my dear, you have no idea of their distress!

MRS. PLACID. Yes, I have; and 'tis that which makes me suspicious.

PLACID. His regiment is now broken; all her jewels, and little bawbles are disposed of; he is in such dread of his old creditors, that, in the lodging they have taken, he passes by the name of Middleton[12]—They have three more children, my dear, than when we left them in New England; and they have, in vain, sent repeated supplications, both to his uncle, and her father, for the smallest bounty.

MRS. PLACID. And is not Lord Norland, her father, a remarkable wise man, and a good man? and ought you to do for them, what he has refused?

PLACID. They have offended him, but they have never offended me.

MRS. PLACID. I think 'tis an offence to ask a friend for money, when there is no certainty of returning it.

PLACID. By no means: for, if there *were* a certainty, even an enemy might lend.

MRS. PLACID. But I insist, Mr. Placid, that they shall not find a friend in you upon this occasion.—What do you say, Sir?

PLACID. [*After a struggle*] No, my dear, they shall not.

MRS. PLACID. Positively shall not?

PLACID. Positively shall not—since they have found an enemy in you.

[*Enter* Servant.

SERVANT. Dinner is on table.

PLACID. Ah! I am not hungry now.

MRS. PLACID. What do you mean by that, Mr. Placid? I insist on your being hungry.

PLACID. Oh, yes! I have a very excellent appetite. I shall eat prodigiously.

MRS. PLACID. You had best. [*Exeunt.*

I.ii

[*An apartment at* Mr. Harmony*'s. Enter* Mr. Harmony, *followed by* Miss Spinster.]

MISS SPINSTER. Cousin, cousin Harmony, I will not forgive you, for thus continually speaking in the behalf of every servant whom you find me offended with. Your philanthropy becomes insupportable; and, instead of being a virtue, degenerates into a vice.

HARMONY. Dear Madam, do not upbraid me for a constitutional[13] fault.

MISS SPINSTER. Very true; you had it from your infancy. I have heard your mother say, you were always foolishly tender-hearted, and never shewed one of those discriminating passions of envy, hatred, or revenge, to which all her other children were liable.

HARMONY. No: since I can remember, I have felt the most unbounded affection for all my fellow creatures. I even protest to you, dear Madam, that as I walk along the streets of this large metropolis, so warm is my heart towards every person who passes me, that I long to say, "How do you do?" and, "I am glad to see you," to them all. Some men, I should like even to stop, and shake hands with;—and some women, I should like even to stop, and kiss.

MISS SPINSTER. How can you be so ridiculous!

HARMONY. Nay, 'tis truth: and I sincerely lament, that human beings should be such strangers to one another as we are. We live in the same street, without knowing one another's necessities; and oftentimes meet and part from each other at church, at coffee-houses, playhouses, and all public places, without ever speaking a single word, or nodding "Good bye!" though 'tis a hundred chances to ten we never see one another again.

MISS SPINSTER. Let me tell you, kinsman, all this pretended philanthropy renders you ridiculous. There is not a fraud, a theft, or hardly any vice committed, that you do not take the criminal's part, shake your head, and cry, "Provisions are so scarce!"[14] and no longer ago than last Lord Mayor's Day,[15] when you were told that Mr. Alderman Ravenous was ill with an indigestion, you endeavoured to soften the matter, by exclaiming, "Provisions are so scarce!"—But, above all, I condemn that false humanity, which induces you to say many things in conversation, which deserve to stigmatize you with the character of deceit.

HARMONY. This is a weakness I confess. But though my honour sometimes reproaches me with it as a fault, my conscience never does: for it is by this very failing that I have frequently made the bitterest enemies friends—Just by saying a few harmless sentences, which, though a species of falsehood and deceit, yet, being soothing and acceptable to the person offended, I have immediately inspired him with lenity and forgiveness; and then, by only repeating the self-same sentences to his opponent, I have known hearts cold and closed to each other, warmed and expanded, as every human creature's ought to be.

[*Enter* Servant.

SERVANT. Mr. Solus. [*Exit* Servant.

MISS SPINSTER. I cannot think, Mr. Harmony, why you keep company with that old bachelor; he is a man, of all others on earth, I dislike; and so I am obliged to quit the room, though I have a thousand things to say. [*Exit angrily*.

[*Enter* Solus.

HARMONY. Mr. Solus, how do you do?

SOLUS. I am very lonely at home; will you come and dine with me?

HARMONY. Now you are here, you had better stay with me: we have no company; only my cousin Miss Spinster and myself.

SOLUS. No, I must go home; do come to my house.

HARMONY. Nay, pray stay: what objection can you have?

SOLUS. Why, to tell you the truth, your relation, Miss Spinster, is no great favourite of mine; and I don't like to dine with you, because I don't like her company.

HARMONY. That is, to me, surprising!

SOLUS. Why, old bachelors and old maids never agree: we are too much alike in our habits: we know our own hearts so well, we are apt to discover every foible we would wish to forget, in the symptoms displayed by the other. Miss Spinster is peevish, fretful, and tiresome, and I am always in a fidget when I am in her company.

HARMONY. How different are her sentiments of you! for one of her greatest joys is to be in your company. [Solus *starts and smiles*] Poor woman! she has, to be sure, an uneven temper—

SOLUS. No, perhaps I am mistaken.

HARMONY.—But I will assure you, I never see her in half such good humor as when you are here: for I believe you are the greatest favorite she has.

SOLUS. I am very much obliged to her, and I certainly *am* mistaken about her temper—Some people, if they look ever so cross, are good natured in the main; and I dare say she is so. Besides, she never has had a husband to sooth and soften her disposition; and there should be some allowance made for that.

HARMONY. Will you dine with us?

SOLUS. I don't care if I do. Yes, I think I will. I must however step home first:—but I'll be back in a quarter of an hour.—My compliments to Miss Spinster, if you should see her before I return. [*Exit*.

[*Enter* Servant.

SERVANT. My lady begs to know, Sir, if you have invited Mr. Solus to dine? Because if you have, she shall go out. [*Exit* Servant.

[*Enter* Miss Spinster.

HARMONY. Yes, Madam, I could not help inviting him; for, poor man, his own house is in such a state for want of proper management, he cannot give a comfortable dinner himself.

MISS SPINSTER. And so he must spoil the comfort of mine.

HARMONY. Poor man! poor man! after all the praises he has been lavishing upon you.

MISS SPINSTER. What praises?

HARMONY. I won't tell you: for you won't believe them.

MISS SPINSTER. Yes, I shall.—Oh no—now I recollect, this is some of your invention.

HARMONY. Nay I told him it was *his* invention; for he declared you looked better last night, than any other lady at the Opera.

MISS SPINSTER. No, this sounds like truth:— and, depend upon it, though I never liked the manners of Mr. Solus much, yet—

HARMONY. Nay, Solus has his faults.

MISS SPINSTER. So we have all.

HARMONY. And will you leave him and me to dine by ourselves?

MISS SPINSTER. Oh no, I cannot be guilty of such ill manners, though I talked of it. Besides, poor Mr. Solus does not come so often, and it would be wrong not to show him all the civility we can. For my part, I have no dislike to the man; and, if taking a bit of dinner with us now and then can oblige either you or him, I should be to blame to make any objection.—Come, let us go into the drawing-room to receive him.

HARMONY. Ay! this is right: this is as it should be.

[*Exeunt.*

I.iii

[*A room at the lodgings of* Mr. Irwin. Mr. Irwin *and* Lady Eleanor Irwin *discovered.*]

LADY ELEANOR. My dear husband, my dear Irwin, I cannot bear to see you thus melancholy. Is this the joy of returning to our native country, after a nine years' banishment?

IRWIN. Yes: For I could bear my misfortunes, my wretched poverty, with patience, in a land where our sorrows were shared by those about us; but here, in London, where plenty and ease smile upon every face; where, by birth you claim distinction, and I by services:—here to be in want,—to be obliged to take another name in shame of our own,—to tremble at the voice of every stranger, for fear he should be a creditor,—to meet each old acquaintance with an averted eye, because we would not feel the pang of being shunned.—To have no reward for all this, even in a comfortable home; but there, to see our children looking up to me for that support I have not in my power to give—Can I,—can I love them and you, and not be miserable?

LADY ELEANOR. And yet I am not so. And I am sure you will not doubt my love to you or them.

IRWIN. I met my uncle this morning, and was mean enough to repeat my request to him:— he burst into a fit of laughter, and told me my distresses were the result of my ambition, in marrying the daughter of a nobleman, who himself was too ambitious ever to pardon us.

LADY ELEANOR. Tell me no more of what he said.

IRWIN. This was a day of trials:—I saw your father too.

LADY ELEANOR. My father! Lord Norland! Oh Heavens!

IRWIN. He passed me in his carriage.

LADY ELEANOR. I envy you the blessing of seeing him! for, oh!—Excuse my tears—he is my father still.—How did he look?

IRWIN. As well as he did at the time I used to watch him from his house, to steal to you.—But I am sorry to acquaint you, that, to guard himself against all returning love for you, he has, I am informed, adopted a young lad, on whom he bestows every mark of that paternal affection, of which you lament the loss.

LADY ELEANOR. May the young man deserve his tenderness better than I have done—May he never disobey him—May *he* be a comfort, and cherish his benefactor's declining years—And when his youthful passions teach him to love, may they not, like mine, teach him disobedience!

[*Enter a* Servant *with a letter.*

IRWIN. What is that letter?

SERVANT. It comes from Mr. Placid, the servant, who brought it, said, and requires no answer. [*Exit.*

IRWIN.—[*Aside*] *It's strange how I tremble at every letter I see, as if I dreaded the contents. How poverty has unmann'd me!*—[*To her*] I must tell you, my dear, that finding myself left this morning without a guinea, I wrote to Mr. Placid, to borrow a small sum: This is his answer; [*Reading the superscription*] "*To Mr. Middleton*"—That's right;—he remembers the caution I gave him. I had forgot whether I had, for my memory is not so good as it was. I did not even now recollect this hand, though it is one I am so well acquainted with, and ought to give me joy rather than sorrow. [*Opens the letter hastily, reads, and lets it drop*] Now I have not a friend on earth.

LADY ELEANOR. Yes, you have me. You forget me.

IRWIN. [*In a transport of grief*] I would forget you—you—and all your children.

LADY ELEANOR. I would not lose the remembrance of you or of them, for all my father's fortune.

IRWIN. What am I to do? I must leave you! I must go, I know not where! I cannot stay to see you perish. [*Takes his hat, and is going.*

LADY ELEANOR. [*Holding him*] Where would you go? 'Tis evening—'tis dark—Whither would you go at this time?

IRWIN. [*Distractedly*] I must consider what's to be done—and in this room my thoughts are too confined to reflect.

LADY ELEANOR. And are London streets calculated for reflection?

IRWIN. No;—for action. To hurry the faint thought to resolution.[16]

LADY ELEANOR. You are not well—Your health has been lately impaired.—Your temper has undergone a change too:—I tremble lest any accident—

IRWIN. [*Wildly*] What accident?

LADY ELEANOR. I know your provocations from an ungrateful world: but despise it, as that despises you.

IRWIN. But for your sake, I could.

LADY ELEANOR. Then witness, Heaven! I am happy.—Though bred in all the delicacy, the luxury of wealth and splendour; yet I have never murmured at the change of fortune, while that change has made me wife to you, and mother of your children.

IRWIN. We *will* be happy—if possible. But give me this evening to consider what plan to fix upon.—There is no time to lose; we are without friends—without money,—without credit.—Farewell for an hour.—I will see Mr. Placid, if I can; and though he have not the money to lend, he may, perhaps, give me some advice.

LADY ELEANOR. Suppose I call on *her*?—Women are sometimes more considerate than men, and—

IRWIN. Do you for the best, and so will I.—Heavens bless you! [*Exeunt separately.*

II.i

[*A coffee or club-room at a tavern. Enter* Sir Robert Ramble—Mr. Solus *and* Mr. Placid *at the opposite side.*]

SOLUS. Sir Robert Ramble, how do you do?

SIR ROBERT RAMBLE. My dear Mr. Solus, I am glad to see you. I have been dining by myself, and now come into this public room, to meet with some good company.

SOLUS. Ay, Sir Robert, you are now reduced to the same necessity which I frequently am—I frequently am obliged to dine at taverns and coffee-houses, for want of company at home.

SIR ROBERT RAMBLE. Nay, I protest I am never happier than in a house like this, where a man may meet his friend without the inconvenience of form, either as a host or a visitor.

SOLUS. Sir Robert, give me leave to introduce to you Mr. Placid: he has been many years abroad; but I believe he now means to remain in his own country for the rest of his life. This, Mr. Placid, is Sir Robert Ramble.

SIR ROBERT RAMBLE. [*To* Mr. Placid] Sir, I shall be happy in your acquaintance; and I assure you, if you will do me the honour to meet me now and then at this house, you will find every thing very pleasant. I verily believe that since I lost my wife, which is now about five months ago, I verily believe I have dined here three days out of the seven.

PLACID. Have you lost your wife, Sir? And so lately?

SIR ROBERT RAMBLE. [*With great indifference*] Yes, Sir; about five months ago—Is it not, Mr. Solus? You keep account of such things better than I do.

SOLUS. Oh! ask me no questions about your wife, Sir Robert; if she had been mine, I would have had her to this moment.

PLACID. What, wrested her from the gripe of death?

SIR ROBERT RAMBLE. No, Sir; only from the gripe of the Scotch lawyers.

SOLUS. More shame for you. Shame! to wish to be divorced from a virtuous wife.

PLACID. Was that the case? Divorced from a virtuous wife! I never heard of such a circumstance before. [*Very anxiously*] Pray, Sir Robert, will you indulge me, by letting me know in what manner you were able to bring about so great an event?

SIR ROBERT RAMBLE. It may appear strange to you, Sir; but my wife and I did not live happy together.

PLACID. Not at all strange, Sir; I can conceive—I can conceive very well.

SOLUS. Yes, he can conceive that part to a nicety.

SIR ROBERT RAMBLE. And so, I was determined on a divorce.

PLACID. But then her character could not be unimpeached.

SIR ROBERT RAMBLE. Yes, it was, Sir. You must know, we were married in Scotland, and by the laws there, a wife can divorce her husband for breach of fidelity; and so, though my wife's character was unimpeached, mine was not—and she divorced me.[17]

PLACID. And is this the law in Scotland?

SOLUS. It is. Blessed, blessed country! that will bind young people together before the years of discretion,[18] and, as soon as they have discretion to repent, will unbind them again!

PLACID. I wish I had been married in Scotland.

SOLUS. But, Sir Robert, with all this boasting you must own that your divorce has greatly diminished your fortune.

SIR ROBERT RAMBLE. [*Taking* Solus *aside*] Mr. Solus, you have frequently hinted at my fortune being impaired; but I do not approve of such notions being received abroad.

SOLUS. I beg your pardon; but every body knows that you have played very deep lately, and have been a great loser: and every body knows—

SIR ROBERT RAMBLE. No, Sir, every body does not know it, for I contradict the report wherever I go. A man of fashion does not like to be reckoned poor, no more than he likes to be reckoned unhappy. We none of us endeavour to *be* happy, Sir, but merely to be *thought* so; and for my part, I had rather be in a state of misery, and envied for my supposed happiness, than in a state of happiness, and pitied for my supposed misery.

SOLUS. But, consider, these misfortunes, which I have just hinted at, are not of any serious nature, only such as a few years' economy—

SIR ROBERT RAMBLE. But were my wife and her guardian to become acquainted with these little misfortunes, they would triumph in my embarrassments.

SOLUS. Lady Ramble triumph! [*They join* Mr. Placid] She, who was so firmly attached to you, that I believe nothing but a compliance with your repeated request to be separated, caused her to take the step she did.

SIR ROBERT RAMBLE. Yes, I believe she did it to oblige me, and I am very much obliged to her.

SOLUS. As good a woman, Mr. Placid—

SIR ROBERT RAMBLE. Very good—but very ugly.

SOLUS. She is beautiful.

SIR ROBERT RAMBLE. [*To* Solus] I tell you, Sir, she is hideous. And then she was grown so insufferably peevish.

SOLUS. I never saw her out of temper.

SIR ROBERT RAMBLE. Mr. Solus, it is very uncivil of you to praise her before my face. Lady Ramble, at the time I parted with her, had every possible fault both of mind and person, and so I made love to other women in her presence; told her bluntly, that I was tired of her; that "I was very sorry to make her uneasy, but that I could not love her any longer."—And was not that frank and open?

SOLUS. Oh! that I had but such a wife as she was!

SIR ROBERT RAMBLE. I must own I loved her myself when she was young.

SOLUS. Do you call her old?

SIR ROBERT RAMBLE. In years I am certainly older than she, but the difference of sex makes her a great deal older than I am. For instance, Mr. Solus, you have often lamented not being married in your youth; but if you had, what would you have now done with an old wife, a woman of your own age?

SOLUS. Loved and cherished her.

SIR ROBERT RAMBLE. What, in spite of her loss of beauty?

SOLUS. When she had lost her beauty, most likely I should have lost my eye-sight, and have been blind to the wane of her charms.

PLACID. [*Anxiously*] But, Sir Robert, you were explaining to me—Mr. Solus, give me leave to speak to Sir Robert—I feel myself particularly interested on this subject.—And, Sir, you were explaining to me—

SIR ROBERT RAMBLE. Very true: where did I leave off? Oh! at my ill usage of my Lady Ramble. Yes, I did use her very ill, and yet she loved me. Many a time, when she has said to me,—"Sir Robert, I detest your principles, your manners, and even your person,"—often at that very instant, I have seen a little sparkle of a wish, peep out of the corner of one eye, that has called out to me, "Oh! Sir Robert, how I long to make it up with you!"

SOLUS. [*To* Mr. Placid] Do not you wish that your wife had such a little sparkle at the corner of one of her eyes?

SIR ROBERT RAMBLE. [*To* Mr. Placid] Sir, do you wish to be divorced?

PLACID. I have no such prospect. Mrs. Placid is faithful, and I was married in England.

SIR ROBERT RAMBLE. But if you have an unconquerable desire to part, a separate maintenance[19] will answer nearly the same end—for if your lady and you will only lay down the plan of separation, and agree—

PLACID. But, unfortunately, we never do agree!

SIR ROBERT RAMBLE. Then speak of parting as a thing you dread worse than death; and make it your daily prayer to her, that she will never think of going from you—She will determine upon it directly.

PLACID. I thank you; I'm very much obliged to you: I thank you a thousand times.

SIR ROBERT RAMBLE. Yes, I have studied the art of teasing a wife; and there is nothing vexes her so much as laughing at her. Can you laugh, Mr. Placid?

PLACID. I don't know whether I can; I have not laughed since I married.—But I thank you, Sir, for your instructions—I sincerely thank you.

SOLUS. And now, Sir Robert, you have had the good nature to teach this gentleman how to get rid of his wife, will you have the kindness to teach me how to procure one?

[*Enter* Mr. Irwin.

SIR ROBERT RAMBLE. Hah! sure I know that gentleman's face?

SOLUS. [*Aside*] *My nephew! Let me escape his solicitations.—Here, waiter!* [*Exit.*

PLACID. [*Starting*] Irwin!—[*Aside*] *Having sent him a denial, I am ashamed to see him. Here, Mr. Solus!*—[*Exit, following* Mr. Solus.

IRWIN. [*Aside*] *More cool faces! my necessitous visage clears even a club-room.*

SIR ROBERT RAMBLE. My dear Captain Irwin, is it you? Yes, 'faith it is—After a nine years' absence, I most sincerely rejoice to see you.

IRWIN. Sir Robert, you shake hands with a cordiality I have not experienced these many days, and I thank you.

SIR ROBERT RAMBLE. But what's the matter? You seem to droop—Where have you left your usual spirits? Has absence from your country changed your manners?

IRWIN. No, Sir; but I find some of my countrymen changed. I fancy them less warm, less friendly, than they were; and it is that which, perhaps, has this effect upon me.

SIR ROBERT RAMBLE. Am I changed?

IRWIN. You appear an exception.

SIR ROBERT RAMBLE. And I assure you, that instead of being grown more gloomy, I am even more gay than I was seven years ago; for then, I was upon the point of matrimony—but now, I am just relieved from its cares.

IRWIN. I have heard as much. But I hope you have not taken so great an aversion to the marriage state as never to marry again.

SIR ROBERT RAMBLE. Perhaps not: but then it must be to some rich heiress.

IRWIN. You are right to pay respect to fortune. Money is a necessary article in the marriage contract.

SIR ROBERT RAMBLE. As to that—that would be no great object at present. No, thank Heaven, my estates are pretty large; I have no children; I have a rich uncle, excellent health, admirable spirits;—and thus happy, it would be very strange if I did not meet my old friends with those smiles which never for a moment quit my countenance.

IRWIN. In the dispensation of the gifts of Providence, how few are blest like you! [*Sighing.*

SIR ROBERT RAMBLE. And I assure you, my dear Mr. Irwin, it gives me the most serious reflections, and the most sincere concern, that they are not.

IRWIN. I thank you, Sir, most heartily: I thank you for mankind in general, and for myself in particular. For after this generous, unaffected declaration (with less scruple than I should to any man in the world) I will own to you, that I am at this very time in the utmost want of an act of friendship.

SIR ROBERT RAMBLE. [*Aside*] *And so am I— Now must I confess myself a poor man; or pass for an unfeeling one; and I will choose the latter.* [*Bowing with great ceremony and coldness*] *Any thing that I can command, is at your service.*

IRWIN. [*Confounded, and hesitating*] Why then, Sir Robert—I am almost ashamed to say it—but circumstances have been rather unfavourable—My wife's father [*Affecting to smile*] is not reconciled to us yet—My regiment is broke—My uncle will not part with a farthing.—Lady Eleanor, my wife, [*Wipes his eyes*] has been supported as yet, with some little degree of tenderness, elegance; and—in short, I owe a small sum, which I am afraid of being troubled for; I want a trifle also for our immediate use, and if you would lend me an hundred pounds—though, upon my honour, I am not in a situation to fix the exact time when I can pay it.

SIR ROBERT RAMBLE. My dear Sir, never trouble yourself about the time of paying it, because it happens not to be in my power to lend it you.

IRWIN. Not in your power? I beg your pardon; but have not you this moment been saying you are rich?

SIR ROBERT RAMBLE. And is it not very common to be rich without money? Are not half the town rich! and yet half the town has no money. I speak for this end of the town, the West End. The Squares, for instance, part of Piccadilly, down St. James's-Street, and so home by Pall Mall.[20] We have all, estates, bonds, drafts, and notes of hand without number; but as for money, we have no such thing belonging to us.

IRWIN. I sincerely beg your pardon. And be assured, Sir, nothing should have induced me to have taken the liberty I have done, but the necessities of my unhappy family, and, having understood by your own words, that you were in affluence.

SIR ROBERT RAMBLE. I *am* in affluence, I am, I am; but not in so much, perhaps, as my hasty, inconsiderate account may have given you reason to believe. I forgot to mention several heavy incumbrances, which you will perceive are great drawbacks on my fortune.—As my wife sued for the divorce, I have her fortune to return; I have also two sisters to portion off—a circumstance I totally forgot. But, my good friend, though I am not in circumstances to do what you require, I will do something that shall be better. I'll wait upon your father-in-law, (Lord Norland) and entreat him to forgive his daughter: and I am sure he will if I ask him.

IRWIN. Impossible.

SIR ROBERT RAMBLE. And so it is, now I recollect: for he is no other than the guardian of my late wife, and a request from me will be received worse than from any other person.—However, Mr. Irwin, depend upon it, that whenever I have an opportunity of serving you, I will. And whenever you shall do me the favour to call upon me, I shall be heartily glad to see you. If I am not at home, you can leave your card, which, you know, is all the same, and depend upon it, I shall be extremely glad to see you, or that, at any time. [*Exit.*

IRWIN. Is this my native country? Is this the hospitable land which we describe to strangers? No—We are savages to each other;[21] nay, worse—The savage makes his fellow-savage welcome; divides with him his homely fare; gives him the best apartment his hut affords, and tries to hush those griefs that are confided in his bosom—While in this civilized city, among my own countrymen, even among my brother officers in the army, and many of my nearest relations, so very civilized they are, I could not take the liberty to enter under one roof, without a ceremonious invitation, and that they will not give me. I may leave my card at their door, but as for me, or any one of mine, they would not give us a dinner; unless, indeed, it was in such a style, that we might behold with admiration their grandeur, and return still more depressed to our own poverty.—Can I bear this treatment longer? No, not even for you, my Eleanor. And this [*Takes out a pistol*] shall now be the only friend to whom I will apply—And yet I want the courage to be a villain.

[*Enter* Mr. Harmony, *speaking as he enters.*—Irwin *conceals the pistol instantly.*

HARMONY. Let me see half a dozen newspapers—every paper of the day.

[*Enter* Waiter.

WAITER. That is about three dozen, Sir.

HARMONY. Get a couple of porters, and bring them all.

[*He sits down; they bring him papers and he reads*— Irwin *starts, sits down, leans his head on one of the tables, and shows various signs of uneasiness; then comes forward.*

IRWIN. Am I a man, a soldier?—And a coward? Yes, I run away, I turn my back on life—I forsake the post, which my commander, Providence, has allotted me, and fly before a banditti[22] of rude misfortunes. Rally me, love, connubial[23] and parental love, rally me back to the charge! no, those very affections sound the retreat. [*Sits down with the same emotions of distraction as before.*

HARMONY. [*Aside*] *That gentleman does not seem happy. I wish I had an opportunity of speaking to him.*

IRWIN. [*Coming forward and speaking again*] But oh! my wife, what will be your sufferings, when I am brought home to your wretched habitation!—And by my own hand!

HARMONY. I am afraid, Sir, I engross all the news here. [*Holding up the papers.*

IRWIN. [*Still apart*] Poor soul, how her heart will be torn!

HARMONY. [*After looking steadfastly on him*] Captain Irwin, till this moment I had not the pleasure of recollecting you!—It is Mr. Irwin, is it not?

IRWIN. [*His mind deranged by his misfortunes*] Yes, Sir: but what have you to say to him more than to a stranger?

HARMONY. Nothing more, Sir, than to apologize to you, for having addressed you just now in so familiar a manner, before I knew who you were; and to assure you, that although I have no other knowledge of you than from report, and having been once, I believe, in your company at this very house before you left England; yet, any services of mine, as far as my abilities can reach, you may freely command.

IRWIN. Pray, Sir, do you live at the West End of the town?

HARMONY. I do.

IRWIN. Then, Sir, your services can be of no use to me.

HARMONY. Here is the place where I live, here is my card. [*Gives it to him.*

IRWIN. And here is mine. And now I presume we have exchanged every act of friendship, which the strict forms of etiquette, in this town, will admit of.

HARMONY. By no means, Sir. I assure you my professions never go beyond my intentions; and if there is any thing that I can serve you in—

IRWIN. Have you no sisters to portion off? No lady's fortune to return? Or, perhaps, you will speak to my wife's father, and entreat him to forgive his child.

HARMONY. On that subject, you may command me; for I have the honour to be intimately acquainted with Lord Norland.

IRWIN. But is there no reason you may recollect, "why you would be the most unfit person in the world to apply to him?"

HARMONY. None. I have been honoured with marks of his friendship for many years past: and I do not know any one who could, with less hazard of his resentment, venture to name his daughter to him.

IRWIN. Well, Sir, if you should see him two or three days hence, when I am set out on a journey I am going, if you will then say a kind word to him for my wife and children, I'll thank you.

HARMONY. I will go to him instantly. [*Going.*

IRWIN. No, do not see him yet; stay till I am gone. He will do nothing till I am gone.

HARMONY. May I ask where you are going?

IRWIN. No very tedious journey; but it is a country, to those who go without a proper passport, always fatal.

HARMONY. I'll see Lord Norland to-night: perhaps I may persuade him to prevent your journey. I'll see him to-night, or early in the morning, depend upon it.—I am a man of my word, Sir; though I must own I do live at the West End of the town. [*Exit.*

IRWIN. 'Sdeath![24] am I become the ridicule of my fellow-creatures? or am I not in my senses?—I know this is London—this house a tavern—I know I have a wife—Oh! 'Twere better to be mad than to remember her!—She has a father—he is rich and proud—that I will not forget. [*Furiously*] But I will pass his house, and send a malediction as I pass it. No; breathe out my last sigh at his inhospitable door, and that sigh shall breathe—forgiveness. [*Exit.*

II.ii

[*The lodgings of* Mr. Irwin. *Enter* Mrs. Placid, *followed by* Lady Eleanor Irwin.]

LADY ELEANOR. I am ashamed of the trouble I have given you, Mrs. Placid. It has been sufficient to have sent me home in your carriage; to attend me yourself was ceremonious.

MRS. PLACID. My dear Lady Eleanor, I was resolved to come home with you, as soon as Mr. Placid desired I would not.

LADY ELEANOR. Was that the cause of your politeness? I am sorry it should.

MRS. PLACID. Why sorry? It is not proper he should have his way in every thing.

LADY ELEANOR. But I am afraid you seldom let him have it at all.

MRS. PLACID. Yes, I do.—But where, my dear, is Mr. Irwin?

LADY ELEANOR. [*Weeping*] I cannot hear the name of Mr. Irwin, without shedding tears: his health has been so much impaired of late, and his spirits so bad—sometimes I even fear for a failure in his mind. [*Weeps again.*

MRS. PLACID. Is not he at home?

LADY ELEANOR. I hope he is. [*Goes to the side of the scenes*] Tell your master, Mrs. Placid is here.

[*Enter* Servant.

SERVANT. My master is not come in yet, Madam.

LADY ELEANOR. Not yet? I am very sorry for it;—very sorry indeed.

MRS. PLACID. Bless me, my dear, don't look thus pale. Come, sit down, and I'll stay with you till he returns. [*Sits down herself.*

LADY ELEANOR. My dear, you forget that Mr. Placid is in the carriage at the door all this time.

MRS. PLACID. No, I don't. Come, let us sit, and have half an hour's conversation.

LADY ELEANOR. Nay, I insist upon your going to him, or desiring him to walk in.

MRS. PLACID. Now I think of it, they may as well drive him home, and come back for me. [*Enter* Mr. Placid] Why, surely, Mr. Placid, you were very impatient! I think you might have waited a few minutes longer.

PLACID. I would have waited, my dear, but the evening is so damp.

LADY ELEANOR. Ah! 'Tis the evening—which makes me alarmed for Mr. Irwin.

PLACID. Lady Eleanor, you are one of the most tender, anxious, and affectionate wives, I ever knew.

MRS. PLACID. There! now he wishes he was your husband—he admires the conduct of every wife but his own, and envies every married man of his acquaintance. But it is very ungenerous in you.

PLACID. So it is, my dear, and not at all consistent with the law of retaliation; for I am sure, there is not one of my acquaintance who envies me.

MRS. PLACID. Mr. Placid, your behaviour throughout this whole day has been so totally different to what it ever was before, that I am half resolved to live no longer with you.

PLACID. [*Aside*] *It will do—It will do.*

LADY ELEANOR. Oh, my dear friends, do not talk of parting: how can you, while every blessing smiles on your union? Even I, who have reason to regret mine, yet, while that load of grief, a separation from Mr. Irwin, is but averted, I will think every other affliction supportable. [*A loud rapping at the door*] That is he!

MRS. PLACID. Why, you seem in raptures at his return.

LADY ELEANOR. I know no greater rapture. [*Enter* Irwin, *pale, trembling, and disordered*] My dear, you are not well, I see.

IRWIN. [*Aside to her in anger*] Yes—Why do you speak of it?

PLACID. How do you do, Irwin?

IRWIN. I am glad to see you. [*Bows.*

MRS. PLACID. But I am sorry to see you look so ill.

IRWIN. I have only been taking a glass too much.

[Lady Eleanor *weeps.*

PLACID. Pshaw! Don't I know you never drink.

IRWIN. You are mistaken: I do, when my wife is not by. I am afraid of her.

PLACID. Impossible.

IRWIN. What! to be afraid of one's wife?

PLACID. No; I think that very possible.

MRS. PLACID. But it does not look well when it is so; it makes a man appear contemptible, and a woman a termagant. Come, Mr. Placid, I cannot stay another moment. Good night. [*To* Lady Eleanor] Heaven bless you!— Good night, my dear Mr. Irwin; and now, pray take my advice and keep up your spirits.

IRWIN. I will, Madam.—[*Shaking hands with* Placid] And do you keep up your spirits. [*Exeunt* Mr. *and* Mrs. Placid. Irwin *shuts the door with care after them, and looks round the room, as if he feared to be seen or overheard*] I am glad they are gone.—I spoke unkindly to you just now, did I not? My temper is altered lately; and yet I love you.

LADY ELEANOR. I never doubted it, nor ever will.

IRWIN. If you did, you would wrong me; for there is no danger I would not risk for your sake; there is not an infamy I would not be branded with to make you happy, nor a punishment I would not undergo, with joy, for your welfare.—But there is a bar to this; we are unfortunately so entwined together, so linked, so rivetted, so cruelly, painfully fettered to each other, you could not be happy unless I shared the self same happiness with you—But you will learn better—now you are in London, and amongst fashionable wives; you must learn better. [*Walks about and smiles, with a ghastly countenance.*

LADY ELEANOR. Do not talk, do not look thus wildly—Indeed, indeed, you make me very uneasy.

IRWIN. What! uneasy when I come to bring you comfort; and such comfort as you have not experienced for many a day? [*He pulls out a pocket-book*] Here is a friend in our necessity,—a friend that brings a thousand friends; plenty and—no, not always—peace.

[*He takes several papers from the book, and puts them into her hands—She looks at them, then screams.*

LADY ELEANOR. Ah! 'Tis money! [*Trembling*] These are bank notes!

IRWIN. Hush! for Heaven's sake, hush! We shall be discovered. [*Trembling and in great perturbation*] What alarms you thus?

LADY ELEANOR. What alarms you?

IRWIN. Do you say I am frightened?

LADY ELEANOR. A sight so new has frightened me.

IRWIN. Nay, they are your own: by heaven, they are! No one on earth has a better, or a fairer right than you have. It was a laudable act, by which I obtained them.—The parent bird had forsook its young, and I but forced it back, to perform the rites of nature.

LADY ELEANOR. You are insane, I fear. No, no, I do not *fear*—I *hope* you are.

[*A loud rapping at the street door—He starts, takes the notes from her, and puts them hastily into his pocket.*

IRWIN. Go to the door yourself; and if 'tis any one who asks for me, say I am not come home yet.

[*She goes out, then returns.*

LADY ELEANOR. It is the person belonging to the house; no one to us.

IRWIN. My dear Eleanor, are you willing to quit London with me in about two hours' time?

LADY ELEANOR. Instantly.

IRWIN. Nay, not only London, but England.

LADY ELEANOR. This world, if you desire it. To go in company with you, will make the journey pleasant; and all I loved on earth would still be with me.

IRWIN. You can, then, leave your father without regret, *never, never,* to see him more?

LADY ELEANOR. Why should I think on him, who will not think on me? [*Weeps.*

IRWIN. But our children—

LADY ELEANOR. We are not to leave them?

IRWIN. One of them we must; but do not let that give you uneasiness. You know he has never lived with us since his infancy, and cannot pine for the loss of parents whom he has never known.

LADY ELEANOR. But I have *known him.* He was my first; and, sometimes, I think, more closely wound around my heart, than all the rest. The grief I felt on being forced to leave him when we went abroad, and the constant anxiety I have since experienced lest he should not be kindly treated, have augmented, I think, my tenderness.

IRWIN. All my endeavours to-day, as well as every other day, have been in vain, to find into what part of the country his nurse has taken him.—Nay, be not thus overcome with tears; we will (in spite of all my haste to be gone) stay one more miserable day here, in hopes to procure intelligence, so as to take him with us; and then smile with contempt on all we leave behind. [*Exeunt.*

III.i

[*A library at* Lord Norland*'s.*]

[*Enter* Lord Norland, *followed by* Mr. Harmony.

LORD NORLAND. [*In anger*] I tell you, Mr. Harmony, that if an indifferent person, one on whom I had never bestowed a favour in my life, were to offend me, it is in my nature never to forgive. Can I then forgive my own daughter, my only child, on whom I heaped continually marks of the most affectionate fondness? Shall she dare to offend me in the tenderest point, and you dare to suppose I will pardon her?

HARMONY. Your child, consider.

LORD NORLAND. The weakest argument you can use. As my child, was not she most bound to obey me? As my child, ought she not to have sacrificed her own happiness to mine? Instead of which, mine has been yielded up for a whim, a fancy, a fancy to marry a beggar; and, as such is her choice, let her beg with him.

HARMONY. She does by me;—pleads hard for your forgiveness.

LORD NORLAND. If I thought she dared to send a message to me, though dictated on her knees, she should find, that she had not yet felt the full force of my resentment.

HARMONY. What could you do more?

LORD NORLAND. I have done nothing yet. At present, I have only abandoned her;—but I can persecute.

HARMONY. I have no doubt of it: and, that I may not be the means of aggravating your displeasure, I assure you, that what I have now said has been entirely from myself, without any desire of hers; and, at the same time, I give you my promise, I will never presume to introduce[25] the subject again.

LORD NORLAND. On this condition (but on no other) I forgive you now.

HARMONY. And now, then, my Lord, let us pass from those who have forfeited your love, to those who possess it.—I heard, some time ago, but I presumed to mention it to you, that you had adopted a young man as your son.

LORD NORLAND. "A young man!" Pshaw! No; a boy—a mere child, who fell in my way by accident.

HARMONY. A chance child! ho! ho!—I understand you.

LORD NORLAND. Do not jest with me, Sir. Do I look—

HARMONY. Yes, you look as if you would be ashamed to own it, if you had one.

LORD NORLAND. But this boy I am not ashamed of:—he is a favourite—rather a favourite.—I did not like him so well at first;—but custom,—and having a poor creature entirely at one's mercy, one begins to love it merely from the idea of—What would be its fate if one did not?

HARMONY. Is he an orphan then?

LORD NORLAND. No.

HARMONY. You have a friendship for his parents?

LORD NORLAND. I never saw the father: his mother I had a friendship for once. [*Sighing.*

HARMONY. Ay, while the husband was away?

LORD NORLAND. [*Violently*] I tell you, no.—But ask no more questions. Who his parents are, is a secret, which neither he, nor any one (that is now living) knows, except myself; nor ever shall.

HARMONY. Well, my lord, since 'tis your pleasure to consider him as your child, I sincerely wish you may experience more duty from him, than you have done from your daughter.

LORD NORLAND. Thank Heaven, his disposition is not in the least like hers—No: [*Very much impassioned*] I have the joy to say, that never child was so unlike its mother.

HARMONY. [*Starting*] How! his mother!

LORD NORLAND. Confusion!—what have I said?—I am ashamed—

HARMONY. No,—be proud.

LORD NORLAND. Of what?

HARMONY. That you have a lawful heir to all your riches; proud, that you have a grandson.

LORD NORLAND. I would have concealed it from all the world; I wished it even unknown to myself. And let me tell you, Sir, (as not by my design, but through my inadvertency, you are become acquainted with this secret) that, if ever you breathe it to a single creature, the boy shall answer for it; for, were he known to be hers, though he were dearer to me than ever *she* was, I would turn him from my house, and cast him from my heart, as I have done her.

HARMONY. I believe you;—and, in compassion to the child, give you my *solemn promise*, never to reveal who he is. I have heard that those unfortunate parents left an infant behind when they went abroad, and that they now lament him as lost. Will you satisfy my curiosity, in what manner you sought and found him out?

LORD NORLAND. Do you suppose I searched for him? No;—he was forced upon me. A woman followed me, about eight years ago, in the fields adjoining to my country seat, with a half-starved boy in her hand, and asked my charity for my grand-child: the impression of the word made me turn round involuntarily; and, casting my eyes upon him, I was rejoiced not to find a feature of his mother's in all his face; and I began to feel something like pity for him. In short, he caught such fast hold by one of my fingers, that I asked him carelessly, "if he would go home and live with me?" On which, he answered me so willingly "Yes," I took him at his word.

HARMONY. And did never your regard for him, plead in his mother's behalf?

LORD NORLAND. Never. For, by Heaven, I would as soon forgive the robber, who met me last night at my own door, and, holding a pistol to my breast, took from me a sum to a considerable amount, as I would pardon her.

HARMONY. Did such an accident happen to you?

LORD NORLAND. Have you not heard of it?

HARMONY. No.

LORD NORLAND. It is amazing we cannot put a stop to such depredations.

HARMONY. Provisions are so scarce![26]

[*Enter* Servant.

SERVANT. Miss Wooburn, my lord, if you are not engaged, will come and sit an hour with you.

LORD NORLAND. I have no company but such as she is perfectly acquainted with, and shall be glad of her visit. [*Exit* Servant.

HARMONY. You forget I am a stranger, and my presence may not be welcome.

LORD NORLAND. A stranger! what, to my ward? To Lady Ramble? For that is the name which custom would authorize her to keep; but such courtesy she disdains, in contempt of the unworthy giver of the title.

HARMONY. I am intimate with Sir Robert, my lord: and, though I acknowledge that both you and his late wife have cause for complaint, yet Sir Robert has still many virtues.

LORD NORLAND. Not one. He is the most vile, the most detestable of characters. He not only contradicted my will in the whole of his conduct, but he seldom met me that he did not give me some personal affront.

HARMONY. It is, however, generally held better to be uncivil in a person's presence, than in his absence.

LORD NORLAND. He was uncivil to me in every respect.

HARMONY. That I will deny; for I have heard Sir Robert, in your absence, say such things in your praise!

LORD NORLAND. Indeed!

HARMONY. Most assuredly.

LORD NORLAND. I wish he had sometimes done me the honour to have spoken politely to my face.

HARMONY. That is not Sir Robert's way;—he is no flatterer. But then no sooner has your back been turned, than I have heard him lavish in your praise.

LORD NORLAND. I must own, Mr. Harmony, that I never looked upon Sir Robert as incorrigible. I could always discern a ray of understanding, and a beam of virtue, through all his foibles; nor would I have urged the divorce, but that I found his wife's sensibility could not bear his neglect; and, even now, notwithstanding her endeavour to conceal it, she pines in secret, and laments her hard fortune. All my hopes of restoring her health rest on one prospect—that of finding a man worthy my recommendation for her second husband, and, by thus creating a second passion, expel the first—Mr. Harmony, you and I have been long acquainted—I have known your disposition from your infancy—Now, if such a man as you were to offer—

HARMONY. You flatter me.

LORD NORLAND. I do not—would you venture to become her husband?

HARMONY. I cannot say I have any particular desire; but if it will oblige either you or her,—for my part, I think the short time we live in this world, we should do all we can to oblige each other.

LORD NORLAND. I should rejoice at such an union myself, and, I think I can answer for her.—You permit me then, to make overtures to her in your name?

HARMONY. [*Considering*] This is rather a serious business—However, I never did make a difficulty, when I wished to oblige a friend.—But there is one proviso,[27] my lord; I must first mention it to Sir Robert.

LORD NORLAND. Why so?

HARMONY. Because he and I have always been very intimate friends; and to marry his wife without even telling him of it, will appear very uncivil!

LORD NORLAND. Do you mean, then, to ask his consent?

HARMONY. Not absolutely his consent; but I will insinuate the subject to him, and obtain his approbation in a manner suitable to my own satisfaction.

LORD NORLAND. You will oblige me then if you will see him as early as possible; for it is reported he is going abroad.

HARMONY. I will go to him immediately;—and, my Lord, I will do all in my power to oblige you, Sir Robert, and the Lady—[*Aside*] *but as to obliging myself, that was never one of my considerations*. [*Exit*.

[*Enter* Miss Wooburn.

LORD NORLAND. I am sorry to see you thus; you have been weeping? Will you still[28] lament your separation from a cruel husband, as if you had followed a kind one to the grave?

MISS WOOBURN. By no means, my Lord. Tears from our sex are not always the result of grief; they are frequently no more than little sympathetic tributes, which we pay to our fellow beings, while the mind and the heart are steeled against the weakness which our eyes indicate.

LORD NORLAND. Can you say, your mind and heart are so steeled?

MISS WOOBURN. I can: my mind is as firmly fixed against Sir Robert Ramble, as at our first acquaintance it was fixed upon him. And I solemnly protest—

LORD NORLAND. To a man of my age and observation, protestations are vain.—Give me a proof, that you have rooted him from your heart.

MISS WOOBURN. Any proof you require, I will give you without a moment's hesitation.

LORD NORLAND. I take you at your word; and desire you to accept a gentleman, whom I shall recommend for your second husband. [Miss Wooburn *starts*]—You said, you would not hesitate a moment.

MISS WOOBURN. I thought I should not;—but this is something so unexpected—

LORD NORLAND. You break your word then; and still give cause for this ungrateful man to ridicule your fondness for him.

MISS WOOBURN. No, I will put an end to that humiliation; and whoever the gentleman is whom you mean to propose—Yet, do not name him at present—but give me the satisfaction of keeping the promise I have made to you (at least for a little time) without exactly knowing how far it extends; for, in return I have a promise to ask from you, before I acquaint you with the nature of your engagement.

LORD NORLAND. I give my promise. Now name your request.

MISS WOOBURN. Then, my Lord, [*Hesitating and confused*]—the law gave me back, upon my divorce from Sir Robert, the very large fortune which I brought to him.—I am afraid, that in his present circumstances, to enforce the strict payment of this debt would very much embarrass him.

LORD NORLAND. What if it did?

MISS WOOBURN. It is my entreaty to you (in whose hands is invested the power to demand this right of law) to lay my claim aside for the present. [Lord Norland *offers to speak*] I know, my lord, what you are going to say; I know Sir Robert is not *now*, but I can never forget that he *has been*, my husband.

LORD NORLAND. To shew my gratitude for your compliance with the request I have just made you [*Goes to a table in the library*], here is the bond by which I am empowered to seize on the greatest part of his estates in right of you; take the bond into your own possession, till your next husband demands it of you; and, by the time you have called him husband for a few weeks, this tenderness, or delicacy to Sir Robert, will be worn away.

[*Enter* Harmony, *hastily*.

HARMONY. My lord, I beg pardon; but I forgot to mention—

MISS WOOBURN. Oh, Mr. Harmony, I have not seen you before, I know not when: I am particularly happy at your calling just now, for I have—[*Hesitating*]—a little favour to ask of you.

HARMONY. If it were a great favour, Madam, you might command me.

MISS WOOBURN. But—my lord, I beg your pardon—but the favour I have to ask of Mr. Harmony must be told to him in private.

LORD NORLAND. Oh! I am sure I have not the least objection to you and Mr. Harmony having a private conference. I'll leave you together. [Harmony *appears embarrassed*] You do not derange my business—I'll be back in a short time. [*Exit*.

MISS WOOBURN. Mr. Harmony, you are the very man on earth whom I most wanted to see. [Harmony *bows*] I know the kindness of your heart, the liberality of your sentiments, and I wish to repose a charge to your trust, very near to me indeed—but you must be secret.

HARMONY. When a lady reposes a trust in me, I should not be a man if I were not.

MISS WOOBURN. I must first inform you, that Lord Norland has just drawn from me a promise, that I will once more enter into the marriage state: and without knowing to whom he intends to give me, I will keep my promise—But it is in vain to say, that though I mean all duty and fidelity to my second husband, I shall not experience moments when my thoughts—will wander on my first.

HARMONY. [*Starting*] Hem!—hem!—[*To her*]—Indeed!

MISS WOOBURN. I must always rejoice in Sir Robert's successes, and lament over his misfortunes.

HARMONY. If that is all—

MISS WOOBURN. No, I would go one step further: [Harmony *starts again*] I would secure him from those misfortunes, which to hear of, will disturb my peace of mind. I know his fortune has suffered very much, and I cannot, *will not*, place it in the power of the man, whom my Lord Norland may point out for my next marriage, to distress him farther.—This is the writing, by which that gentleman may claim the part of my fortune from Sir Robert Ramble, which is in landed property; carry it, my dear Mr. Harmony, to Sir Robert instantly; and tell him, that, in separating from him, I meant only to give him liberty; not make him the debtor, perhaps the prisoner, of my future husband.

HARMONY. Madam, I will most undoubtedly take this bond to my friend; but will you give me leave to suggest to you, that the person on whom you bestow your hand may be a little surprised to find, that while he is in possession of you, Sir Robert is in the possession of your fortune?

MISS WOOBURN. Do not imagine, Sir, that I shall marry any man, without first declaring what I have done—I only wish at present it should be concealed from Lord Norland—When this paper is given, as I have required, it cannot be recalled; and when that is past, I shall divulge my conduct to whom I please; and first of all, to him, who shall offer me his addresses.

HARMONY. And if he is a man of my feelings, his addresses will be doubly importunate for this proof of liberality to your former husband.—But are you sure, that in the return of this bond, there is no secret affection, no latent spark of love?

MISS WOOBURN. None. I know my heart; and if there was, I could not ask you, Mr. Harmony (nor any one like you), to be the messenger of an imprudent passion. Sir Robert's vanity, I know, may cause him to judge otherwise; but undeceive him; let him know, this is a sacrifice to the golden principles of duty, and not an offering to the tinselled shrine of love.

[*Enter* Lord Norland.

MISS WOOBURN. Put up the bond.—

[Harmony *conceals it.*

LORD NORLAND. Well, my dear, have you made your request?

MISS WOOBURN. Yes, my Lord.

LORD NORLAND. And has he granted it?

HARMONY. Yes, my Lord. I am going to grant it.

LORD NORLAND. I sincerely wish you both joy of this good understanding between you. But, Mr. Harmony, [*In a whisper*] are not you going to Sir Robert?

HARMONY. Yes, my Lord, I am going this moment.

LORD NORLAND. Make haste, then, and do not forget your errand.

HARMONY. No, my Lord, I sha'n't forget my errand: it won't slip my memory—Good morning, my Lord:—good morning, Madam. [*Exit.*

LORD NORLAND. Now, my dear, as you and Mr. Harmony seem to be on such excellent terms, I think I may venture to tell you (if he has not yet told you himself), that he is the man, who is to be your husband.

MISS WOOBURN. He! Mr. Harmony!—No, my lord, he has not told me; and I am confident he never will.

LORD NORLAND. What makes you think so?

MISS WOOBURN. Because—because—he must be sensible he would not be the man I should choose.

LORD NORLAND. And where is the woman who marries the man she would choose? You are reversing the order of society; men only have the right of choice in marriage. Were women permitted theirs, we should have handsome beggars allied to our noblest families, and no such object in our whole island as an old maid.

MISS WOOBURN. But being denied that choice, why forbid to remain as I am?

LORD NORLAND. What are you now? Neither a widow, a maid, nor a wife. If I could fix a term to your present state, I should not be thus anxious to place you in another.

MISS WOOBURN. I am perfectly acquainted with your friendly motives, and feel the full force of your advice.—I therefore renew my promise—and although Mr. Harmony (in respect to the marriage state) is as little to my wishes as any man on earth, I will nevertheless endeavour—whatever struggles it may cost me—to be to him, if he prefers his suit, a dutiful, an obedient—but, for a loving wife, that I can never be again. [*Exeunt severally.*

III.ii

[*An apartment at* Sir Robert Ramble*'s. Enter* Sir Robert, *and* Mr. Harmony.]

SIR ROBERT RAMBLE. I thank you for this visit. I was undetermined what to do with myself. Your company has determined me to stay at home.

HARMONY. I was with a gentleman just now, Sir Robert, and you were the subject of our conversation.

SIR ROBERT RAMBLE. Had it been a lady, I should be anxious to know what she said.

HARMONY. I have been with a lady likewise; and she made you the subject of her discourse.

SIR ROBERT RAMBLE. But was she handsome?

HARMONY. Very handsome.

SIR ROBERT RAMBLE. My dear fellow, what is her name? What did she say, and where may I meet with her?

HARMONY. Her name is Wooburn.

SIR ROBERT RAMBLE. That is the name of my late wife.

HARMONY. It is her I mean.

SIR ROBERT RAMBLE. Zounds, you had just put my spirits into a flame, and now you throw cold water all over me.

HARMONY. I am sorry to hear you say so, for I came from her this moment; and what do you think is the present she has given me to deliver to you?

SIR ROBERT RAMBLE. Pshaw! I want no presents. Some of my old love-letters returned, I suppose, to remind me of my inconstancy?

HARMONY. Do not undervalue her generosity: this is her present; this bond, which has power to take from you three thousand a year, her right.

SIR ROBERT RAMBLE. Ah! this is a present, indeed. Are you certain you speak truth? Let me look at it:—Sure my eyes deceive me!—No, by Heaven it is true! [*Reads*][29] The very thing I wanted, and will make me perfectly happy. Now I'll be generous again; my bills shall be paid, my gaming debts cancelled, poor Irwin shall find a friend; and I'll send her as pretty a copy of verses as ever I wrote in my life.

HARMONY. Take care how you treat with levity a woman of her elevated mind. She charged me to assure you, "that love had no share whatever in this act, but merely compassion to the embarrassed state of your affairs."

SIR ROBERT RAMBLE. Sir, I would have you to know, I am no object of compassion. However, a lady's favour one cannot return; and so, I'll keep this thing. [*Puts it in his pocket.*[30]

HARMONY. Nay, if your circumstances are different from what she imagines, give it me back, and I will return it to her.

SIR ROBERT RAMBLE. No, poor thing! it would break her heart to send it back—No, I'll keep it—She would never forgive me, were I to send it back. I'll keep it. And she is welcome to attribute her concern for me to what she pleases. But surely you can see—you can understand—But Heaven bless her for her love! and I would love her in return—if I could.

HARMONY. You would not talk thus, if you had seen the firm dignity with which she gave me that paper—"Assure him," said she, "no remaining affection comes along with it, but merely a duty which I owe him, to protect him from the humiliation of being a debtor to the man, whom I am going to marry."

SIR ROBERT RAMBLE. [*With the utmost emotion*] Why, she is not going to be married again!

HARMONY. I believe so.

SIR ROBERT RAMBLE. But are you sure of it, Sir? Are you sure of it?

HARMONY. Both she and her guardian told me so.

SIR ROBERT RAMBLE. That guardian, my Lord Norland, is one of the basest, vilest of men.—I tell you what, Sir, I'll resent this usage.

HARMONY. Wherefore?—As to his being the means of bringing about your separation, in that he obliged you.

SIR ROBERT RAMBLE. Yes, Sir, he did, he certainly did;—but though I am not in the least offended with him on that head (for at that I rejoice), yet I will resent his disposing of her a second time.

HARMONY. And why?

SIR ROBERT RAMBLE. Because, little regard as I have for her myself, yet no other man shall dare to treat her so ill as I have done.

HARMONY. Do not fear it—Her next husband will be a man, who, I can safely say, will never insult, or even offend her; but sooth, indulge, and make her happy.

SIR ROBERT RAMBLE. And do you dare to tell me, that her next husband shall make her happy? Now that is worse than the other—No, Sir, no man shall ever have it to say "he has made her either happy or miserable," but myself.

HARMONY. I know of but one way to prevent it.

SIR ROBERT RAMBLE. And what is that?

HARMONY. Pay your addresses to her, and marry her again yourself.

SIR ROBERT RAMBLE. And I would, rather than she should be happy with any body else. The devil take me if I would not.

HARMONY. To shew that I am wholly disinterested in this affair, I will carry her a letter from you, if you like, and say all I can in your behalf.

SIR ROBERT RAMBLE. Ha! ha! ha! now, my dear Harmony, you carry your good-natured simplicity too far. However, I thank you, I sincerely thank you—But do you imagine I should be such a blockhead, as to make love to the same woman I made love to seven years ago, and who for the last six years I totally neglected?

HARMONY. Yes: for if you have neglected her six years, she will now be a novelty.

SIR ROBERT RAMBLE. Egad, and so she will. You are right.

HARMONY. But being in possession of her fortune, you can be very happy without her.

SIR ROBERT RAMBLE. Take her fortune back, Sir. [*Taking the bond from his pocket, and offering it to* Harmony] I would starve, I would perish, die in poverty and infamy, rather than owe an obligation to a vile, perfidious, inconstant woman.

HARMONY. Consider, Sir Robert, if you insist on my taking this bond back, it may fall into the husband's hands.

SIR ROBERT RAMBLE. Take it back—I insist upon it. [*Gives it him, and* Harmony *puts it up*] But, Mr. Harmony, depend on it. Lord Norland shall hear from me, in the most serious manner, for his interference—I repeat, he is the vilest, the most villainous of men.

HARMONY. How can you speak with such rancour of a nobleman, who speaks of *you* in the highest terms?

SIR ROBERT RAMBLE. Does he, 'faith?

HARMONY. He owns you have some faults.

SIR ROBERT RAMBLE. I know I have.

HARMONY. But he thinks your good qualities are numberless.

SIR ROBERT RAMBLE. Now, dam'me if ever I thought so ill of *him* as I have appeared to do!—But who is the intended husband, my dear friend? Tell me, that I may laugh at him, and make you laugh at him.

HARMONY. No, I am not inclined to laugh at him.

SIR ROBERT RAMBLE. Is it old Solus?

HARMONY. No.

SIR ROBERT RAMBLE. But I will bet you a wager it is somebody equally ridiculous.

HARMONY. I never bet.

SIR ROBERT RAMBLE. Solus is mad for a wife, and has been praising mine up to the heavens;—you need say no more—I know it is he.

HARMONY. Upon my honour, it is not. However, I cannot disclose to you at present the person's name; I must first obtain Lord Norland's permission.

SIR ROBERT RAMBLE. I shall ask you no more. I'll write to her, she will tell me;—or I'll pay her a visit, and ask her boldly myself. [*Anxiously*] Do you think—do you think she would see me?

HARMONY. You can but try.

[*Enter* Servant.

SERVANT. Mr. Solus.

SIR ROBERT RAMBLE. Now I will find out the secret immediately.—I'll charge him with being the intended husband.

HARMONY. I will not stay to hear you. [*Enter* Solus] Mr. Solus, how do you do? I am extremely sorry that my engagements take me away as soon as you enter. [*Exit* Harmony *running, to avoid an explanation.*

SOLUS. Sir Robert, what is the matter? Has any thing ruffled you? Why, I never saw you look more out of temper, even while you were married.

SIR ROBERT RAMBLE. Ah! that I had never married! never known what marriage was! for, even at this moment, I feel its torments in my heart.

SOLUS. I have often heard of the torments of matrimony; but I conceive, that at the worst, they are nothing more than a kind of violent tickling, which will force the tears into your eyes, though at the same time you are bursting your sides with laughter.

SIR ROBERT RAMBLE. You have defined marriage too favourably; there is no laughter in the state: all is melancholy, all gloom.

SOLUS. Now I think marriage is an excellent remedy for the spleen. I have known a gentleman at a feast receive an affront, disguise his rage, step home, vent it all upon his wife, return to his companions, and be as good company as if nothing had happened.

SIR ROBERT RAMBLE. But even the necessary expenses of a wife should alarm you.

SOLUS. I can then retrench some of my own. Oh! my dear Sir, a married man has so many delightful privileges to what a bachelor has;—An old lady will introduce her daughters to you in a dishabille[31]—"It does not signify, my dears, it's a married man"—One lady will suffer you to draw on her glove—"Never mind, it's a married man"—Another will permit you to pull on her slipper; a third will even take you into her bedchamber—"Pshaw, it's *nothing* but a married man."

SIR ROBERT RAMBLE. But the weight of your fetters will overbalance all these joys.

SOLUS. And I cannot say, notwithstanding you are relieved from the bond, that I see much joy or brightness here.

SIR ROBERT RAMBLE. I am not very well at present; I have the head-ache; and, if ever a wife can be of comfort to her husband, it must be when he is indisposed. A wife, then, binds up your head, mixes your powders, bathes your temples, and hovers about, in a way that is most endearing.

SOLUS. Don't speak of it; I long to have one hover about me. But I will—I am determined I will, before I am a week older. Don't speak, don't attempt to persuade me not. Your description has renewed my eagerness—*I* will be married.

SIR ROBERT RAMBLE. And without pretending not to know who you mean to make your wife, I tell you plainly, it is Miss Wooburn, it is my late wife.—I know you have made overtures to my Lord Norland, and that, he has given his consent.

SOLUS. You tell me a great piece of news—I'll go ask my Lord if it be true; and if he says it is, I shall be very glad to find it so.

SIR ROBERT RAMBLE. That is right, Sir; marry her, marry her;—I give you joy,—that's all.—Ha! ha! ha! I think I should know her temper.—But if you will venture to marry her, I sincerely wish you happy.

SOLUS. And if we are not, you know we can be divorced.

SIR ROBERT RAMBLE. Not always. Take my advice, and live as you are.

SOLUS. You almost stagger my resolution.—I had painted such bright prospects in marriage:—Good day to you. [*Going, returns*]—You think I had better not marry?

SIR ROBERT RAMBLE. You are undone if you do.

SOLUS. [*Sighing*] *You* ought to know from experience.

SIR ROBERT RAMBLE. From that I speak.

SOLUS. [*Going to the door, and returning once or twice, as unstable in his resolution*] But then, what a poor, disconsolate object shall I live, without a wife to hover about me; to bind up my head, and bathe my temples! oh! I am impatient for all the chartered rights, privileges, and immunities of a married man. [*Exit.*

SIR ROBERT RAMBLE. Furies! racks! torments!—I cannot bear what I feel, and yet I am ashamed to own I feel any thing!

[*Enter* Mr. Placid.

PLACID. My dear Sir Robert, give me joy. Mrs. Placid and I are come to the very point you advised; matters are in the fairest way for a separation.

SIR ROBERT RAMBLE. I do give you joy, and most sincerely.—You are right; you'll soon be as happy as I am [*Sighing*]. But, would you suppose it? That deluded woman, my wife, is going to be married again! I thought she had had enough of me!

PLACID. You are hurt, I see, lest the world should say she has forgot you.

SIR ROBERT RAMBLE. She cannot forget me; I defy her to forget me.

PLACID. Who is her intended husband?

SIR ROBERT RAMBLE. Solus, Solus. An old man—an ugly man. He left me this moment, and owned it—owned it! Go after him, will you, and persuade him not to have her.

PLACID. My advice will have no effect, for you know he is bent upon matrimony.

SIR ROBERT RAMBLE. Then could not you, my dear Sir (as you are going to be separated), could not you recommend him to marry your wife?— It will be all the same to him, I dare say, and I shall like him much better.

PLACID. Ours will not be a divorce, consider, but merely a separate maintenance. But were it otherwise, I wish no man so ill, as to wish him married to Mrs. Placid.

SIR ROBERT RAMBLE. That is my case exactly—I wish no man so ill, as to wish him married to my Lady Ramble; and poor old Solus in particular, poor old man! a very good sort of man—I have a great friendship for Solus.—I can't stay a moment in the house—I must go somewhere— I'll go to Solus—No, I'll go to Lord Norland— No, I will go to Harmony; and then I'll call on you, and we'll take a bottle together; and when we are both free [*Takes his hand*] we'll join, from that moment we'll join, to laugh at, to contemn, to despise, all those who boast of the joys of conjugal love. [*Exeunt.*

IV.i

[*An apartment at* Mr. Harmony*'s. Enter* Mr. Harmony.]

HARMONY. And now for one of the most painful tasks that brotherly love ever draws upon me; to tell another the suit, of which I gave him hope, has failed.—Yet, if I can but overcome Captain Irwin's delicacy so far, as to prevail on him to accept one proof more of my good wishes towards him;—but to a man of his nice sense of obligations, the offer must be made with caution.

[*Enter* Lord Norland.

LORD NORLAND. Mr. Harmony, I beg your pardon: I come in thus abruptly, from the anxiety I feel concerning what passed between us this morning in respect to Miss Wooburn. You have not changed your mind, I hope?

HARMONY. Indeed, my lord, I am very sorry that it will not be in my power to oblige you.

LORD NORLAND. [*In anger*] How, Sir? Did not you give me your word?

HARMONY. Only conditionally, my lord.

LORD NORLAND. And what were the conditions?

HARMONY. Have you forgot them? Her former husband—

[*Enter* Servant.

SERVANT. Sir Robert Ramble is in his carriage at the door, and, if you are at leisure, will come in.

HARMONY. Desire him to walk up. I have your leave, I suppose, my lord? [*Exit* Servant.

LORD NORLAND. Yes; but let me get out of the house without meeting him. [*Going to the opposite door*] Can I go this way?

HARMONY. Why should you shun him?

LORD NORLAND. Because he used his wife ill.

HARMONY. He did. But I believe he is very sorry for it.—And as for you, he said to me only a few hours ago—but no matter.

LORD NORLAND. What did he say? I insist upon knowing.

HARMONY. Why then he said, "that if he had a sacred trust to repose in any one, *you* should be the man on earth, to whom he would confide it."

LORD NORLAND. Well, I am in no hurry; I can stay a few minutes.

[*Enter* Sir Robert Ramble.

SIR ROBERT RAMBLE. Oh! Harmony! I am in such a distracted state of mind—[*Seeing* Lord Norland, *he starts, and bows with the most humble respect.*

LORD NORLAND. Sir Robert, how do you do?

SIR ROBERT RAMBLE. My lord, I am pretty well.—I hope I have the happiness of seeing your Lordship in perfect health.

LORD NORLAND. Very well, Sir, I thank you.

SIR ROBERT RAMBLE. Indeed, my Lord, I think I never saw you look better.

LORD NORLAND. Mr. Harmony, you and Sir Robert may have some business—I wish you a good morning.

HARMONY. No, my Lord, I fancy Sir Robert has nothing particular.

SIR ROBERT RAMBLE. Nothing, nothing, I assure you, my Lord.

LORD NORLAND. However, I have business myself in another place, and so you will excuse me. [*Going.*

SIR ROBERT RAMBLE. [*Following him*] My Lord—Lord Norland,—I trust you will excuse my inquiries.—I hope, my Lord, all your family are well?

LORD NORLAND. All very well.

SIR ROBERT RAMBLE. Your little eléve,—Master Edward,—the young gentleman you have adopted—I hope he is well—[*Hesitating and confused*] And—your ward, Sir—Miss Wooburn—I hope, my Lord, she is well?

LORD NORLAND. Yes, Sir Robert, Miss Wooburn is tolerably well.

SIR ROBERT RAMBLE. Only tolerably, my Lord? I am sorry for that.

HARMONY. I hope, my Lord, you will excuse my mentioning the subject; but I was telling Sir Robert just now of your intentions respecting a second marriage for that Lady; but Sir Robert does not appear to approve of the design.

LORD NORLAND. What objection can *he* have?

SIR ROBERT RAMBLE. My Lord, there are such a number of bad husbands; there are such a number of dissipated, unthinking, unprincipled men!—And—I should be extremely sorry to see any lady with whom I have had the honour of being so closely allied, united to one, who would undervalue her worth.

LORD NORLAND. Pray, Sir Robert, were you not then extremely sorry for her, while she was united to you?

SIR ROBERT RAMBLE. Very sorry for her, indeed, my Lord. But, at that time, my mind was so taken up with other cares, I own I did not feel the compassion which was her due; but, now that I am single, I shall have leisure to pay her more attention; and should I find her unhappy, it must, inevitably, make me so.

LORD NORLAND. Depend upon it, that, on the present occasion, I shall take infinite care in the choice of her husband.

SIR ROBERT RAMBLE. If your Lordship would permit me to have an interview with Miss Wooburn, I think I should be able at least—

LORD NORLAND. You would not sure insult her by your presence?

SIR ROBERT RAMBLE. I think I should at least be able to point out an object worthy of her taste—I know what she will like better than any one in the world.

LORD NORLAND. Her request has been, that I may point her out a husband the reverse of you.

SIR ROBERT RAMBLE. Then, upon my honour, my Lord, she won't like him.

LORD NORLAND. Have not you liked women the reverse of her?

SIR ROBERT RAMBLE. Yes, my Lord, perhaps I have, and perhaps I still do. I do not pretend to love *her*; I did not say I did; nay, I positively protest I do not; but this indifference I acknowledge as one of my faults; and, notwithstanding all my faults, give me leave to acknowledge my gratitude that your Lordship has nevertheless been pleased to declare you think my virtues are numberless.

[Lord Norland *shows surprise.*

HARMONY. [*Aside to* Sir Robert] Hush, hush!—Don't talk of your virtues now.

LORD NORLAND. Sir Robert, to all this incoherent language, this is my answer, this is my will: the Lady, to whom I have had the honour to be guardian, shall never (while she calls me friend) see you more.

[Sir Robert, *at this sentence, stands silent for some time, then, suddenly recollecting himself.*

SIR ROBERT RAMBLE. Lord Norland, I am too well acquainted with the truth of your word, and the firmness of your temper, to press my suit one sentence farther.

LORD NORLAND. I commend your discernment.

SIR ROBERT RAMBLE. My Lord, I feel myself a little embarrassed.—I am afraid I have made myself a little ridiculous upon this occasion—Will your Lordship do me the favour to forget it?

LORD NORLAND. I will forget whatever you please.

HARMONY. [*Following him, whispers*] I am sorry to see you going away in despair.

SIR ROBERT RAMBLE. I never did despair in my life, Sir; and while a woman is the object of my wishes, I never will. [*Exit.*

LORD NORLAND. What did he say?

HARMONY. That he thought your conduct that of a just and an upright man.

LORD NORLAND. To say the truth, he has gone away with better manners than I could have imagined, considering his jealousy is provoked.

HARMONY. Ah! I always knew he loved his wife, notwithstanding his behaviour to her; for, if you remember, he always spoke well of her behind her back.

LORD NORLAND. No, I do not remember it.

HARMONY. Yes, he did; and that is the only criterion of a man's love, or of his friendship.

[*Enter* Servant.

SERVANT. A young gentleman is at the door, Sir, inquiring for Lord Norland.

LORD NORLAND. Who can it be?

HARMONY. Your young gentleman from home, I dare say. Desire him to walk in. Bring him here.

[*Exit* Servant.

LORD NORLAND. What business can he have to follow me?

[*Enter* Edward.

EDWARD. Oh, my Lord, I beg your pardon for coming hither, but I come to tell you something you will be glad to hear.

HARMONY. Good Heaven, how like his mother!

LORD NORLAND. [*Taking him by the hand*] I begin to think he is—but he was not so when I first took him. No, no, if he had, he would not have been thus near me now;—but to turn him away because his countenance is a little changed, I think would not be right.

EDWARD. [*To* Harmony] Pray, Sir, did you know my mother?

HARMONY. I have seen her.

EDWARD. Did *you* ever see her, my Lord?

LORD NORLAND. I thought you had orders never to inquire about your parents?—Have you forgot those orders?

EDWARD. No, my Lord;—but when this gentleman said I was like my mother—it put me in mind of her.

HARMONY. You do not remember your mother, do you?

EDWARD. Sometimes I think I do. I think sometimes I remember her kissing me, when she and my father went on board of a ship; and so hard she pressed me—I think I feel it now.

HARMONY. Perhaps she was the only lady that ever saluted you?

EDWARD. No, Sir; not by many.

LORD NORLAND. But, pray, young man, (to have done with this subject,) what brought you here? You seem to have forgot your errand?

EDWARD. And so I had, upon my word. Speaking of my mother, put it quite out of my head—But, my Lord, I came to let you know, the robber, who stopped you last night is taken.

LORD NORLAND. I am glad to hear it.

EDWARD. I knew you would; and therefore I begged to be the first to tell you.

HARMONY. [*To* Lord Norland] Should you know the person again?

LORD NORLAND. I cannot say I should; his face seemed so much distorted.

HARMONY. Ay, wretched man! I suppose, with terror.

LORD NORLAND. No; it appeared a different passion from fear.

HARMONY. Perhaps, my Lord, it was *your* fear, that made you think so.

LORD NORLAND. No, Sir, I was not frightened.

EDWARD. Then, why did you give him your money?

LORD NORLAND. It was surprise caused me to do that.

EDWARD. I wondered what it was! you said it was not fear, and I was sure it could not be love.

HARMONY. How has he been taken?

EDWARD. A person came to our steward, and informed against him;—and, oh! my Lord, his poor wife told the officers, who took him, they had met with misfortunes, which she feared had caused a fever in her husband's head; and, indeed, they found him too ill to be removed; and so, she hoped, she said, "that as a man not in his perfect mind, you would be merciful to him."

LORD NORLAND. I will be just.

EDWARD. And that is being merciful, is it not, my lord?

LORD NORLAND. Not always.

EDWARD. I thought it had been.—It is not *just* to be unmerciful, is it?

LORD NORLAND. Certainly not.

EDWARD. Then it must be *just*, to have mercy.

LORD NORLAND. You draw a false conclusion. Great as the virtue of *mercy*, *justice* is greater still.—*Justice* holds its place among those cardinal virtues, which include all the lesser.—Come, Mr. Harmony, will you go home with me? And before I attend to this business, let me persuade you to forget there is such a person in the world as Sir Robert, and suffer me to introduce you to Miss Wooburn, as the man who—

HARMONY. I beg to be excused—Besides the consideration of Sir Robert, I have another reason why I cannot go with you. The melancholy tale, which this young gentleman has been telling, has cast a gloom on my spirits, which renders me unfit for the society of a lady.

LORD NORLAND. Now I should not be surprised were you to go in search of this culprit and his family, and come to me to intreat me to forego the prosecution; but, before you ask me, I tell you it is in vain—I will not.

HARMONY. Lord Norland, I have lately been so unsuccessful in my petitions to you, I shall never presume to interpose between your rigour and a weak sufferer more.

LORD NORLAND. Plead the cause of the good, and I will listen; but you find none but the wicked for your compassion.

HARMONY. The good in all states, even in the very jaws of death, are objects of envy; it is the bad who are the only sufferers: there, where no internal consolation cheers, who can refuse a little external comfort?—[*Speaking with unaffected compassion*] And, let me tell you, my Lord, that amidst all your authority, your state, your grandeur, I often pity you.

LORD NORLAND. Good-day, Mr. Harmony; and when you have apologized for what you have said, we may be friends again. [*Exit, leading off* Edward.

HARMONY. Nay, hear my apology now. I cannot —no, it is not in my nature to live in resentment, nor under the resentment of any creature in the world. [*Exit, following* Lord Norland.

IV.ii

[*An apartment at* Lord Norland's.]

[*Enter* Sir Robert Ramble, *followed by a* Servant.

SIR ROBERT RAMBLE. Do not say who it is—but say, a gentleman, who has some very particular business with her.

SERVANT. Yes, Sir. [*Going.*

SIR ROBERT RAMBLE. Pray,—[Servant *returns*] You have but lately come into this service, I believe?

SERVANT. Only a few days, Sir.

SIR ROBERT RAMBLE. You don't know me, then?

SERVANT. No, Sir.

SIR ROBERT RAMBLE. I am very glad of it. So much the better. Go to Miss Wooburn, with a stranger's compliments who is waiting, and who begs to speak with her, upon an affair of importance.

SERVANT. Yes, Sir. [*Exit.*

SIR ROBERT RAMBLE. I wish I may die, if I don't feel very unaccountably! how different are our sensations towards our wives, and all other women! this is the very first time she has given me a palpitation since the honey-moon.

[*Enter* Miss Wooburn, *who starts on seeing* Sir Robert; *—he bows in great confusion.*

MISS WOOBURN. [*Aside*] *Support me, Heaven!*

SIR ROBERT RAMBLE. [*Bows repeatedly, and does not speak till after many efforts. Aside*] *Was ever man in such confusion before his wife!*

MISS WOOBURN. Sir Robert, having recovered in some measure, from the surprise into which this intrusion first threw me, I have only to say, that, whatever pretence may have induced you to offer me this insult, there are none to oblige me to bear with it. [*Going.*

SIR ROBERT RAMBLE. Lady Ramb—[*Recalling himself*] Miss Woo—[*She turns*] Lady Ramble—[*Recalling himself again*] Miss Wooburn—Madam—You wrong me—There was a time when I insulted you, I confess: but it is impossible that time should ever return.

MISS WOOBURN. While I stay with you, I incur the danger. [*Going.*

SIR ROBERT RAMBLE. [*Holding her*] Nay, listen to me as a friend, whom you have so often heard as an enemy.—You offered me a favour by the hands of Mr. Harmony—

MISS WOOBURN. And is this the motive of your visit—this the return—

SIR ROBERT RAMBLE. No, Madam, that obligation was not the motive which drew me hither—The real cause of this seeming intrusion is—you are going to be married once more, and I come to warn you of your danger.

MISS WOOBURN. That you did sufficiently in the marriage-state.

SIR ROBERT RAMBLE. But now I come to offer you advice that may be of the most material consequence, should you really be determined to yield yourself again into the power of a husband.

MISS WOOBURN. Which I most assuredly am.

SIR ROBERT RAMBLE. Happy, happy man! how much is he the object of my envy! none so well as I know how to envy him, because none so well as I, know how to value you. [*She offers to go*] Nay, by Heaven, you shall not go till you have heard all that I came to say!

MISS WOOBURN. Speak it then instantly.

SIR ROBERT RAMBLE. No, it would take whole ages to speak; and should we live together, as long as we *have* lived together, still I should not find time to tell you—how much I love you.

[*A loud rapping at the street door.*

MISS WOOBURN. That, I hope, is Lord Norland.

SIR ROBERT RAMBLE. And what has Lord Norland to do with souls free as ours? Let us go to Scotland again; and again bid defiance to his stern commands.

MISS WOOBURN. Be assured, that through him only, will I ever listen to a syllable you have to utter.

SIR ROBERT RAMBLE. One syllable only, and I am gone that instant.

MISS WOOBURN. Well, Sir?

[*He hesitates, trembles, seems to struggle with himself; then approaching her slowly, timidly, and, as if ashamed of his humiliation, kneels to her—She turns away.*

SIR ROBERT RAMBLE. [*Kneeling*] Maria, Maria, look at me!—Look at me in this humble state—Could you have suspected this, Maria?

MISS WOOBURN. No: nor can I conceive what this mockery means.

SIR ROBERT RAMBLE. It means, that, now you are no longer my wife, you are my goddess; and thus I offer you my supplication, that (if you are resolved not to live single) amongst the numerous train who present their suit, you will once more select me.

MISS WOOBURN. You!—You, who have treated me with cruelty; who made no secret of your love for others; but gloried, boasted of your gallantries?

SIR ROBERT RAMBLE. I did, I did—But here I swear, only trust me again—do but once more trust me, and I swear by all I hold most sacred, that I will, for the future, carefully conceal all my gallantries from your knowledge—though they were ten times more frequent than they were before.

[*Enter* Edward.

EDWARD. Oh, my dear Miss Wooburn—What! Sir Robert here too! [*Goes to* Sir Robert, *and shakes hands*] How do you do, Sir Robert? Who would have thought of seeing you here? I am glad to see you, though, with all my heart; and so, I dare say, is Miss Wooburn, though she may not like to say so.

MISS WOOBURN. You are impertinent, Sir.

EDWARD. What, for coming in? I will go away then.

SIR ROBERT RAMBLE. Do, do—there's a good boy—do.

EDWARD. [*Going, returns*] I cannot help laughing, though to see you two together!—For you know you never were together when you lived in the same house.

SIR ROBERT RAMBLE. Leave the room instantly, Sir, or I shall call Lord Norland.

EDWARD. Oh, don't take that trouble; I will call him myself. [*Runs to the door*] My Lord! my Lord! pray come hither this moment—As I am alive, here is Sir Robert Ramble along with Lady Ramble!

[*Enter* Lord Norland. Sir Robert *looks confounded*—Lord Norland *points to* Edward *to leave the room. Exit* Edward.

LORD NORLAND. Sir Robert, on what pretence do you come hither?

SIR ROBERT RAMBLE. On the same pretence as when I was, for the first time, admitted into your house; to solicit this lady's hand. And, after having had it once, no force shall compel me to take a refusal.

LORD NORLAND. I will try, however—Madam, quit this room instantly.

SIR ROBERT RAMBLE. My Lord, she shall not quit it.

LORD NORLAND. I command her to go.

SIR ROBERT RAMBLE. And I command her to stay.

LORD NORLAND. Which of us will you obey?

MISS WOOBURN. My inclination, my Lord, disposes me to obey you;—but I have so lately been accustomed to obey him; that *custom* inclines me to obey him still.

SIR ROBERT RAMBLE. There! there! there, my Lord! Now I hope you will understand better for the future, and not attempt to interfere between a man and his wife.

LORD NORLAND. [*To* Miss Wooburn] Be explicit in your answer to this question—Will you consent to be his wife?

MISS WOOBURN. No, never.

SIR ROBERT RAMBLE. Zounds, my Lord, now you are hurrying matters.—You should do it by gentle means;—let me ask her gently—[*With a most soft voice*] Maria, Maria, will you be my wife once again?

MISS WOOBURN. Never.

SIR ROBERT RAMBLE. So you said seven years ago, when I asked you, and yet you consented.

LORD NORLAND. And now, Sir Robert, you have had your answer; leave my house. [*Going up to him.*

SIR ROBERT RAMBLE. Yes, Sir; but not without my other half.

LORD NORLAND. "Your other half?"

SIR ROBERT RAMBLE. Yes; the wife of my bosom —the wife, whom I swore at the altar "to love and to cherish, and, forsaking all others, cleave only to her as long as we both should live."

LORD NORLAND. You broke your oath, and made the contract void.

SIR ROBERT RAMBLE. But I am ready to take another oath, and another after that, and another after that—And, oh, my dear Maria, be propitious to my vows, and give me hopes you will again be mine. [*He goes to her, and kneels in the most supplicating attitude.*

[*Enter* Edward, *showing in* Mr. Solus *and* Mr. Placid; Edward *points to* Sir Robert *(who has his back to them) and goes off.*

SIR ROBERT RAMBLE. [*Still on his knees, and not perceiving their entrance*] I cannot live without you.—Receive your penitent husband, thus humbly acknowledging his faults, and imploring you to accept him once again.

SOLUS. [*Going up to* Sir Robert] Now, is it wonderful that I should want a wife?

PLACID. And is it to be wondered at, if I should hesitate about parting with mine?

SIR ROBERT RAMBLE. [*Starts up in great confusion*] Mr. Solus, Mr. Placid, I am highly displeased that my private actions should be thus inspected.

SOLUS. No one shall persuade me now, to live a day without a wife.

PLACID. And no one shall persuade me now, not to be content with my own.

SOLUS. I will procure a special licence, and marry the first woman I meet.

SIR ROBERT RAMBLE. Mr. Solus, you are, I believe, interested in a peculiar manner, about the marriage of this lady.

SOLUS. And, poor man, you are sick, and want somebody to "bathe your temples," and to "hover about you."

MISS WOOBURN. You come in most opportunely, my dear Mr. Solus, to be a witness—

SIR ROBERT RAMBLE. "My dear Mr. Solus!"

SOLUS. To be a witness, Madam, that a man is miserable without a wife. I have been a fatal instance of that, for some time.

MISS WOOBURN. Come to me, then, and receive a lesson.

SIR ROBERT RAMBLE. No, Madam, he shall not come to you; nor shall he receive a lesson. No one shall receive a lesson from you, but me.

LORD NORLAND. Sir Robert, one would suppose, by this extraordinary behaviour, you were jealous.

SIR ROBERT RAMBLE. And so I am, my lord; I have cause to be so.

LORD NORLAND. No cause to be jealous of Mr. Solus—He is not Miss Wooburn's lover, I assure you.

SIR ROBERT RAMBLE. Then, my Lord, I verily believe it is yourself. Yes, I can see it is; I can see it by her eyes, and by every feature in your face.

MISS WOOBURN. Oh! my good friend, Mr. Placid, only listen to him.

SIR ROBERT RAMBLE. And why "my good friend, Mr. Placid"?—[*To* Placid] By Heavens, Sir, I believe that you only wished to get rid of your own wife, in order to marry mine.

PLACID. I do not wish to part with my own wife, Sir Robert, since what I have just seen.

SIR ROBERT RAMBLE. [*Going up to* Solus *and* Lord Norland] Then, pray, gentlemen, be so good as to tell me, which of you two is the happy man, that I may know how to conduct myself towards him?

MISS WOOBURN. Ha, ha, ha!

SIR ROBERT RAMBLE. Do you insult me, Maria?— Oh! have pity on my sufferings.

SOLUS. If you have a mind to kneel down again, we will go out of the room.

PLACID. Just as I was comforting myself with the prospect of a divorce, I find my instructor and director pleading on his knees to be remarried.

[*Enter* Mrs. Placid.

MRS. PLACID. What were you saying about a divorce?

SIR ROBERT RAMBLE. Now, down on your knees, and beg pardon.

MISS WOOBURN. My dear Mrs. Placid, if this visit is to me, I take it very kind.

MRS. PLACID. Not absolutely to you, my dear. I saw Mr. Placid's carriage at the door, and so I stepped in to desire him to go home. Go home directly.

PLACID. Presently, my dear; I will go presently.

MRS. PLACID. Presently won't do; I say, directly. There is a lady at my house in the greatest possible distress—[*Whispers him*]—Lady Eleanor —I never saw a creature in such distraction; [*Raising her voice*]—therefore go home this moment; you sha'n't stay an instant longer.

SOLUS. Egad, I don't know whether I will marry or no.

MRS. PLACID. Why don't you go, Mr. Placid, when I bid you?

SOLUS. No;—I think I won't marry.

PLACID. But, my dear, will not you go home with me?

MRS. PLACID. Did not I tell you to go by yourself?

[Placid *bows, and goes off.*

SOLUS. No;—I am sure I won't marry.

LORD NORLAND. And now, Mr. Solus and Sir Robert, these ladies may have some private conversation. Do me the favour to leave them alone.

MISS WOOBURN. My Lord, with your leave *we* will retire. [*Turns when she gets to the door*] Sir Robert, I have remained in your company, and compelled myself to the painful talk of hearing all you have had to say, merely for the satisfaction of exposing your love, and then enjoying the triumph of bidding you farewell for ever. [*Exit with* Mrs. Placid.

SOLUS. [*Looking steadfastly at* Sir Robert] He turns pale at the thoughts of losing her. Yes, I think I'll marry.

LORD NORLAND. Come, Sir Robert, it is vain to loiter; your doom is fixed.

SIR ROBERT RAMBLE. [*In a melancholy musing tone*] Shall I then never again know what it is to have a heart like hers, to repose my troubles on?

SOLUS. Yes, I am pretty sure I'll marry.

SIR ROBERT RAMBLE.—A friend in all my anxieties, a companion in all my pleasures, a physician in all my sicknesses—

SOLUS. Yes, I *will* marry.

LORD NORLAND. Come, come, Sir Robert, [*Leading him towards the door*] do not let you and I have any dispute.

SIR ROBERT RAMBLE. Senseless man, not to value those blessings—Not to know how to estimate them, till they were lost. [Lord Norland *leads him off.*

SOLUS. [*Following*] Yes,—I am determined;—nothing shall prevent me—I will be married. [*Exit.*

V.i

[*An apartment at* Lord Norland's. *Enter* Hammond, *followed by* Lady Eleanor.]

HAMMOND. My lord is busily engaged, Madam; I do not suppose he would see any one, much less a stranger.

LADY ELEANOR. I am no stranger.

HAMMOND. Your name then, Madam?

LADY ELEANOR. That I cannot send in—But tell him, Sir, I am the afflicted wife of a man, who, for some weeks past, has given many fatal proofs of a disordered mind. In one of those fits of phrensy, he held an instrument of death, meant for his own destruction, to the breast of your Lord (who by accident that moment passed,) and took from him, what he vainly hoped might preserve his own life, and relieve the wants of his family. But his paroxysm over, he shrunk from what he had done, and gave the whole he had thus unwarrantably taken, into a servant's hands, to be returned to its lawful owner. The man, admitted to this confidence, betrayed his trust, and instead of giving up what was so sacredly delivered to him, secreted it; and to obtain the promised reward, came to this house, but to inform against the wretched offender; who now, only resting on your Lord's clemency, can escape the direful fate he has incurred.

HAMMOND. Madam, the account you give, makes me interested in your behalf, and you may depend, I will repeat it all with the greatest exactness. [*Exit* Hammond.

LADY ELEANOR. [*Looking round*] This is my father's house! it is only through two rooms and one short passage, and there he is sitting in his study. Oh! in that study, where I (even in the midst of all his business) have been so often welcome; where I have urged the suit of many an unhappy person, nor ever urged in vain. Now I am not permitted to speak for myself, nor have one friendly voice to do that office for me, which I have so often undertaken for others.

[*Enter* Hammond, Edward *following.*

HAMMOND. My Lord says, that any petition concerning the person you come about, is in vain. His respect for the laws of his country demands an example such as he means to make.

LADY ELEANOR. Am I, am I to despair then? [*To* Hammond] Dear Sir, would you go once more to him, and humbly represent—

HAMMOND. I should be happy to oblige you, but I dare not take any more messages to my lord; he has given me my answer.—If you will give me leave, Madam, I'll see you to the door. [*Crosses to the other side, and Exit.*

LADY ELEANOR. Misery—Distraction!—Oh, Mr. Placid! Oh, Mr. Harmony! Are these the hopes you gave me, could I have the boldness to enter this house? But you would neither of you undertake to bring me here!—neither of you undertake to speak for me!

[*She is following the* Servant;[32] Edward *walks softly after her, till she gets near the door; he then takes hold of her gown, and gently pulls it; she turns and looks at him.*

EDWARD. Shall I speak for you, Madam?

LADY ELEANOR. Who are you, pray, young Gentleman?—Is it you, whom Lord Norland has adopted for his son?

EDWARD. I believe he has, Madam; but he has never told me so yet.

LADY ELEANOR. I am obliged to you for your offer; but my suit is of too much consequence for *you* to undertake.

EDWARD. I know what your suit is, Madam, because I was with my Lord when Hammond brought in your message; and I was so sorry for you, I came out on purpose to see you—and, without speaking to my Lord, I could do you a great kindness—if I durst.

LADY ELEANOR. What kindness?

EDWARD. But I durst not—No, do not ask me.

LADY ELEANOR. I do not. But you have raised my curiosity; and in a mind so distracted as mine, it is cruel to excite one additional pain.

EDWARD. I am sure I would not add to your grief for the world.—But then, pray do not speak of what I am going to say.—I heard my Lord's lawyer tell him just now, "that, as he said he should not know the person again, who committed the offence about which you came, and as the man who informed against him is gone off, there could be no evidence that he did the action, but from a book, a particular pocket-book, of my Lord's, which he forgot to deliver to his servant with the notes and money to return, and which was found upon him at your house: and this Lord Norland will affirm to be his."—Now, if I did not think I was doing wrong, this is the very book—[*Takes a pocket-book from his pocket*] I took it from my Lord's table;—but it would be doing wrong, or I am sure I wish you had it [*Looking wishfully at her.*

LADY ELEANOR. It will save my life, my husband's, and my children's.

EDWARD. [*Trembling*] But what is to become of me?

LADY ELEANOR. That Providence, who never punishes the deed, unless the *will* be an accomplice, shall protect you for saving one, who has only erred in a moment of distraction.

EDWARD. I never did any thing to offend my Lord in my life;—and I am in such fear of him, I did not think I ever should.—Yet, I cannot refuse *you;*—take it.— [*Gives her the book*] But pity me, when my Lord shall know of it.

LADY ELEANOR. Oh! should he discard you for what you have done, it will embitter every moment of my remaining life.

EDWARD. Do not frighten yourself about that.—I think he loves me too well to discard me quite.

LADY ELEANOR. Does he indeed?

EDWARD. I think he does!—for often, when we are alone, he presses me to his bosom so fondly, you would not suppose—And, when my poor nurse died, she called me to her bedside, and told me (but pray keep it a secret)—she told me I was—his grand-child.

LADY ELEANOR. You are—you are his grand-child—I see,—I feel you are;—for I feel that I am your mother. [*Embraces him*] Oh! take this evidence back [*Returning the book*]—I cannot receive it from thee, my child;—no, let us all perish, rather than my boy, my only boy, should do an act to stain his conscience, or to lose his grand-father's love.

EDWARD. What do you mean?

LADY ELEANOR. The name of the person with whom you lived in your infancy, was Heyland?

EDWARD. It was.

LADY ELEANOR. I am your mother; Lord Norland's only child, [Edward *kneels*] who, for one act of disobedience, have been driven to another part of the globe in poverty, and forced to leave you, my life, behind. [*She embraces and raises him*]

Your father, in his struggles to support us all, has fallen a victim;—but Heaven, which has preserved my child, will save my husband, restore his senses, and once more—

EDWARD. [*Starting*] I hear my Lord's step,—he is coming this way:—Begone, mother, or we are all undone.

LADY ELEANOR. No, let him come—for though his frown should kill me, yet must I thank him for his care of thee. [*She advances towards the door to meet him.* [*Enter* Lord Norland. Lady Eleanor *falls on her knees*] You love me,—'tis in vain to say you do not. You love my child; and with whatever hardships you have dealt, or still mean to deal by me, I will never cease to think you love me, nor ever cease my gratitude for your goodness.

LORD NORLAND. Where are my servants? Who let this woman in?

[*She rises, and retreats from him, alarmed and confused.*

EDWARD. Oh, my Lord, pity her.—Do not let me see her hardly treated—Indeed I cannot bear it.

[*Enter* Hammond.

LORD NORLAND. [*To* Lady Eleanor] What was your errand here? If to see your child, take him away with you.

LADY ELEANOR. I came to see my father;—I have a house too full of such as he already.

LORD NORLAND. How did she gain admittance?

HAMMOND. With a petition, which I repeated to your lordship. [*Exit* Hammond.

LORD NORLAND. Her husband, then, it was, who—[*To* Lady Eleanor] But let him know, for this boy's sake, I will no longer pursue him.

LADY ELEANOR. For that boy's sake you will not pursue his father; but for whose sake are you so tender of that boy? 'Tis for mine, for my sake; and by that I conjure you—[*Offers to kneel.*

LORD NORLAND. Your prayers are vain—[*To* Edward] Go, take leave of your mother *for ever*, and instantly follow me; or shake hands with me for the last time, and instantly begone with her.

EDWARD. [*Stands between them in doubt for some little time; looks alternately at each with emotions of affection; at last goes to his grandfather, and takes hold of his hand*] Farewell, my Lord,—it almost breaks my heart to part from you;—but if I have my choice, I must go with my mother.

[*Exit* Lord Norland *instantly.*—Lady Eleanor *and her son go off on the opposite side.*

V.ii

[*Another apartment at* Lord Norland*'s. Enter* Miss Wooburn *and* Mrs. Placid.]

MRS. PLACID. Well, my dear, farewell.—I have stayed a great while longer than I intended—I certainly forgot to tell Mr. Placid to come back after he had spoken with Lady Eleanor, or he would not have taken the liberty not to have come.

MISS WOOBURN. How often have I lamented the fate of Lord Norland's daughter! but, luckily, I have no personal acquaintance with her, or I should probably feel a great deal more on her account than I do at present.—She had quitted her father's house before I came to it.

[*Enter* Mr. Harmony.

HARMONY. My whole life is passed in endeavouring to make people happy, and yet they won't let me.—I flattered myself, that after I had resigned all pretensions to you, Miss Wooburn, in order to accommodate Sir Robert—that, after I had told both my lord and him, in what high estimation they stood in each other's opinion, they would of course be friends; or, at least, not have come to any desperate quarrel:—instead of which, what have they done, but, within this hour, had a duel!—and poor Sir Robert—

MISS WOOBURN. For Heaven's sake, tell me of Sir Robert—

HARMONY. You were the only person he mentioned after he received his wound; and such encomiums as he uttered—

MISS WOOBURN. Good Heaven! if he is in dan-ger, it will be vain to endeavour to conceal what I shall suffer. [*Retires a few paces to hide her emotions.*

MRS. PLACID. Was my husband there?

HARMONY. He was one of the seconds.

MRS. PLACID. Then he shall not stir out of his house this month, for it.

HARMONY. He is not likely; for he is hurt too.

MRS. PLACID. A great deal hurt?

HARMONY. Don't alarm yourself.

MRS. PLACID. I don't.

HARMONY. Nay, if you had heard what he said!

MRS. PLACID. What did he say?

HARMONY. How tenderly he spoke of you to all his friends—

MRS. PLACID. But what did he say?

HARMONY. He said you had imperfections.

MRS. PLACID. Then he told a falsehood.

HARMONY. But he acknowledged they were such as only evinced a superior understanding to the rest of your sex;—and that your heart—

MRS. PLACID. [*Bursting into tears*] I am sure I am very sorry that any misfortune has happened to him, poor, silly man! but I do not suppose [*Drying up her tears at once*] he will die.

HARMONY. If you will behave kindly to him, I should suppose not.

MRS. PLACID. Mr. Harmony, if Mr. Placid is either dying or dead, I shall behave with very great tenderness; but if I find him alive, and likely to live, I will lead him such a life as he has not led a long time.

HARMONY. Then you mean to be kind?—But, my dear Miss Wooburn, [*Going to her*] why this seeming grief? Sir Robert is still living; and should he die of his wounds, you may at least console yourself, that it was not your cruelty which killed him.

MISS WOOBURN. Rather than have such a weight on my conscience, I would comply with the most extravagant of his desires, and suffer *his* cruelty to be the death of me.

HARMONY. If those are your sentiments, it is my advice that you pay him a visit in his affliction.

MISS WOOBURN. Oh no, Mr. Harmony, I would not for the universe. Mrs. Placid, do you think it would be proper?

MRS. PLACID. No, I think it would not—Consider, my dear, you are no longer a wife, but a single lady, and would you run into the clutches of a man?

HARMONY. He has no clutches, Madam; he is ill in bed, and totally helpless.—But, upon recollection, it would, perhaps, be needless to go; for he may be too ill to admit you.

MISS WOOBURN. If that is the case, all respect to my situation, my character, sinks before the strong desire of seeing him once more. Oh! were I even married to another, I feel, that, in spite of all my private declarations, or public vows, I should fly from him, to pay my duty where it was first plighted.

HARMONY. My coach is at the door; shall I take you to his house? Come, Mrs. Placid, wave all ceremonious motives, on the present melancholy occasion, and go along with Miss Wooburn and me.

MISS WOOBURN. But, Mrs. Placid, perhaps poor Mr. Placid is in want of your attendance at home.

HARMONY. No, they were both carried in the same carriage to Sir Robert's.

MISS WOOBURN. [*As* Harmony *leads her to the door*] Oh! how I long to see my dear husband, that I may console him!

MRS. PLACID. Oh! how I long to see my dear husband, that I may quarrel with him!

[*Exeunt.*

V.iii

[*The hall at* Sir Robert Ramble*'s. The* Porter *discovered asleep. Enter a* Footman.]

FOOTMAN. Porter, porter, how can you sleep at this time of the day?— It is only eight o'clock.

PORTER. What did you want, Mr. William?

FOOTMAN. To tell you my master must not be disturbed and so you must not let in a single creature.

PORTER. Mr. William, this is no less than the third time I have received those orders within this half hour;—First from the butler, then from the valet, and now from the footman.—Do you all suppose I am stupid?

FOOTMAN. I was bid to tell you. I have only done what I was desired; and mind you do the same. [*Exit.*

PORTER. I'll do my duty, I warrant you. I'll do my duty. [*A loud rapping at the door*] And there's a rap to put my duty to the trial. [*Opens the door.*

[*Enter* Harmony, Miss Wooburn, *and* Mrs. Placid.

HARMONY. These ladies come on a visit to Sir Robert. Desire one of the servants to conduct them to him instantly.

PORTER. Indeed, Sir, that is impossible—My master is not—

HARMONY. We know he is at home, and therefore we can take no denial.

PORTER. I own he is at home, Sir; but, indeed, he is not in a situation—

MISS WOOBURN. We know his situation.

PORTER. Then, Madam, you must suppose he is not to be disturbed. I have strict orders not to let in a single soul.

HARMONY. This lady, you must be certain, is an exception.

PORTER. No lady can be an exception in my master's present state; for I believe, Sir, but—perhaps, I should not speak of it—I believe my master is nearly gone.

MISS WOOBURN. Oh! support me, Heaven!

MRS. PLACID. But has he his senses?

PORTER. Not very clearly, I believe.

MISS WOOBURN. Oh, Mr. Harmony, let me see him before they are quite lost.

PORTER. It is as much as my place is worth, to let a creature farther than this hall; for my master is but in the next room.

MRS. PLACID. That is a dining room. Is not he in bed?

HARMONY. [*Aside to the ladies*] In case of wounds, the patient is often propped up in his chair.

MISS WOOBURN. Does he talk at all?

PORTER. Yes, Madam, I heard him just now very loud.

MISS WOOBURN. [*Listening*] I think I heard him rave.

HARMONY. No, that murmuring is the voice of other persons.

MRS. PLACID. The doctors in consultation, I apprehend.—Has he taken any thing?

PORTER. A great deal, I believe, madam.

MRS. PLACID. No amputation, I hope?

PORTER. What, Madam?

HARMONY. [*To* Miss Wooburn] He does not understand you.—Come, will you go back?

PORTER. Do, my Lady, and call in the morning.

MISS WOOBURN. By that time he may be totally insensible, and die without knowing how much I am attached to him.

MRS. PLACID. And my husband may die without knowing how much I am enraged with him!—Mr. Harmony, never mind this foolish man, but force your way into the next room.

PORTER. Indeed, Sir, you must not. Pray, Mr. Harmony, pray, ladies, go away.

MISS WOOBURN. Yes, I must go from my husband's house for ever, never to see that, or him again! [*Faints on* Mr. Harmony.

MRS. PLACID. She is fainting—open the windows—give her air.

PORTER. Pray go away:—There is plenty of air in the streets, Ma'am.

HARMONY. Scoundrel! your impertinence is insupportable. Open these doors; I insist upon their being opened. [*He thrusts at a door in the centre of the stage; it opens and discovers* Sir Robert *and* Mr. Placid *at a table, surrounded by a company of gentlemen.*

SIR ROBERT RAMBLE. A song—a song—another song [Miss Wooburn, *all astonishment, is supported by* Mr. Harmony *and* Mrs. Placid—*The* Porter *runs off*] Ah, what do I see!—Women!—Ladies!—Celestial beings we were talking of.—Can this be real? [Sir Robert *and* Mr. Placid *come forward*—Sir Robert, *perceiving it is* Miss Wooburn, *turns himself to the company*] Gentlemen, gentlemen, married men and single men, hear me thus publicly renounce every woman on earth but this: and swear henceforward to be devoted to none but my own wife. [*Goes to her in raptures.*

PLACID. [*Looking at* Mrs. Placid, *then turning to the company*] Gentlemen, gentlemen, married men and single men, hear me thus publicly declare, I will henceforth be master; and from this time forward, will be obeyed by my wife.

[Sir Robert *waves his hand, and the door is closed on the company of gentlemen.*

MRS. PLACID. Mr. Placid—Mr. Placid, are you not afraid?

PLACID. No, Madam, I have consulted my friends, have drank two bottles of wine, and I never intend to be afraid again.

MISS WOOBURN. [*To* Sir Robert] Can it be, that I see you without a wound?

SIR ROBERT RAMBLE. No, my life, that you do not; for I have a wound through my heart, which none but you can cure. But, in despair of your aid, I have flown to wine, to give me a temporary relief by the loss of reflection.

MRS. PLACID. Mr. Placid, you will be sober in the morning.

PLACID. Yes, my dear; and I will take care that you shall be dutiful in the morning.

HARMONY. For shame! how can you treat Mrs. Placid thus? You would not, if you knew what kind things she has been saying of you: and how anxious she was when I told her you were wounded in a duel.

MRS. PLACID. Was not I, Mr. Harmony? [*Bursting into tears.*

PLACID. [*Aside to* Harmony *and* Sir Robert] I did not know she could cry;—I never saw it before, and it has made me sober in an instant.

MISS WOOBURN. Mr. Placid, I rely on you to conduct me immediately from this house.

SIR ROBERT RAMBLE. That I protest against: and will use even violent measures to prevent it.

[*Enter* Servant.

SERVANT. Lord Norland.

[*Enter* Lord Norland.

MISS WOOBURN. He will protect me.

SIR ROBERT RAMBLE. Who shall protect you in my house but I? My Lord, she is under my protection; and if you offer to take her from me, I'll exert the authority of a husband, and lock her up.

LORD NORLAND. [*To* Miss Wooburn] Have you been deluded hither, and wish to leave the place with me? Tell me instantly, that I may know how to act.

MISS WOOBURN. My Lord, I am ready to go with you, but—

HARMONY. But you find she is inclined to stay;—and do have some compassion upon two people, that are so fond of you.

[*Enter* Mr. Solus, *dressed in a suit of white clothes.*

SOLUS. I am married!—I am married!—Wish me joy! I am married!

SIR ROBERT RAMBLE. I cannot give you joy, for envy.

SOLUS. Nay, I do not know whether you will envy me much when you see my spouse—I cannot say she was exactly my choice. However, she is my wife now; and that is a name so endearing, I think I love her better since the ceremony has been performed.

MRS. PLACID. And pray, when did it take place?

SOLUS. This moment. We are now returning from a friend's house, where we have been joined; and I felt myself so happy, I could not pass Sir Robert's door without calling to tell him of my good fortune. And, as I see your Lady here, Sir Robert, I guess you are just married too; and so I'll hand my wife out of the carriage, and introduce the two brides to each other. [*Exit* Solus.

SIR ROBERT RAMBLE. You see, my Lord, what construction Mr. Solus has put on this Lady's[33] visit to me. And by Heaven, if you take her away, it will be said, that she came and offered herself to me, and that I rejected her!

MISS WOOBURN. Such a report would kill me.

[*Enter* Solus, *leading on* Miss Spinster.

SOLUS. [*Introducing her*] Mistress Solus.

HARMONY. [*Starting*] My relation! dear Madam, by what strange turn of fortune do I see you become a wife?

MRS. SOLUS. Mr. Harmony, it is a weakness, I acknowledge; but you can never want an excuse for me, when you call to mind "the scarcity of provisions."[34]

SOLUS. Mr. Harmony, I have loved her ever since you told me she spoke so well of me behind my back.

[*Enter* Servant, *and whispers* Mr. Harmony, *who follows him off.*

LORD NORLAND. I agree with you, Mr. Solus, that this is a most excellent proof of a person's disposition; and in consideration, Sir Robert, that throughout all our many disagreements, you have still preserved a respect for my character in my absence, I do at last say to that lady, she has my consent to trust you again.

SIR ROBERT RAMBLE. And she will trust me: I see it in her smiles. Oh! unexpected ecstasy!

[*Enter* Mr. Harmony.

HARMONY. [*Holding a letter in his hand*] Amidst the bright prospects of joy, which this company are contemplating, I come to announce an event that ought to cloud the splendour of the horizon.—A worthy, but an ill-fated, man, whom ye were all acquainted with, has just breathed his last.

LORD NORLAND. Do you mean the husband of my daughter?

SOLUS. Do you mean my nephew?

PLACID. Is it my friend?

SIR ROBERT RAMBLE. And my old acquaintance?

HARMONY. Did Mr. Irwin possess all those titles you have given him, gentlemen? [*To* Lord Norland] Was he your son? [*To* Solus] Your nephew? [*To* Mr. Placid] Your friend? [*To* Sir Robert] And your old acquaintance? How strange, he did not know it!

PLACID. He did know it.

HARMONY. Still more strange, that he should die for want, and not apply to any of you?

SOLUS. What! die for want in London! starve in the midst of plenty!

HARMONY. No; but he seized that plenty, where law, where honour, where every social and religious tie forbade the trespass; and, in punishment of the guilt, has become his own executioner.

LORD NORLAND. Then my daughter is wretched, and her boy involved in his father's infamy.

SOLUS. The fear of his ghost haunting me will disturb the joys of my married life.

PLACID. Mrs. Placid, Mrs. Placid, my complying with your injunctions, in respect of Mr. Irwin, will make me miserable for ever.

MISS WOOBURN. I wish he had applied to me.

SIR ROBERT RAMBLE. And as I refused him his request, I would give half my estate he had *not* applied to me.

HARMONY. And a man who always spoke so well of you all behind your backs!—I dare say, that, in his dying moments, there was not one of you whom he did not praise for some virtue.

SOLUS. No, no—when he was dying, he would be more careful of what he said.

LORD NORLAND. Sir Robert, good-day. Settle your marriage as you and your Lady shall approve; you have my good wishes. But my spirits have received too great a shock to be capable of any other impression at present.

MISS WOOBURN. [*Holding him*] Nay, stay, my Lord.

SOLUS. And, Mrs. Solus, let me hand you into your carriage to your company; but excuse my going home with you. *My* spirits have received too great a shock, to be capable of any other impression at present.

HARMONY. [*Stopping* Solus] Now, so loth am I to see any of you, only for a moment, in grief, while I have the power to relieve you, that I cannot help—Yes, my philanthropy will get the better of my justice. [*Goes to the door, and leads in* Lady Eleanor, Irwin, *and* Edward.

LORD NORLAND. [*Runs to* Irwin, *and embraces him*] My son! [Irwin *falls on his knees*] I take a share in all your offences—The worst of accomplices, while I impelled you to them.

IRWIN. [*On his knees*] I come to offer my returning reason; to offer my vows, that, while *that* reason continues, so long will I be penitent for the phrensy which put your life in danger.

LADY ELEANOR. [*Moving timidly to her father, leading* Edward *by the hand*] I come to offer you this child, this affectionate child; who, in the midst of our caresses, droops his head, and pines for your forgiveness.

LORD NORLAND. Ah! there is a corner of my heart left to receive him. [*Embraces him.*

EDWARD. Then, pray, my Lord, suffer the corner to be large enough to hold my mother.

LORD NORLAND. My heart is softened, and receives you all. [*Embraces* Lady Eleanor, *who falls on her knees; he then turns to* Harmony]—Mr. Harmony, I thank you, I most sincerely thank you for this, the joyfullest moment of my life. I not only experience release from misery, but return to happiness.

HARMONY. [*Goes hastily to* Solus, *and leads him to* Irwin; *then turns to* Mr. *and* Mrs. Placid] And now, that I see all you reconciled, I can say—there are not two enemies, in the whole circle of my acquaintance, that I have not within these three days made friends.

SIR ROBERT RAMBLE. Very true, Harmony; for we should never have known half how well we all love one another, if you had not told us.

HARMONY. And yet, my good friends, notwithstanding the merit you may attribute to me, I have one most tremendous fault; and it weighs so heavy on my conscience, I would confess what it is, but that you might here after call my veracity in question.

SIR ROBERT RAMBLE. My dear Harmony, without a fault, you would not be a proper companion for any of us.

LORD NORLAND. And whilst a man like you, may have (among so many virtues) some faults; let us hope there may be found in each of us, (among all our faults) some virtues.

HARMONY. Yes, my Lord,—and notwithstanding all our numerous faults, it is my sincere wish, that the world may speak well of us—behind our backs.

Epilogue

By M.P. Andrews, Esq.

"Each has his fault," we readily allow,
To this decree, our dearest friends must bow;
One is too careless, one is too correct,
All, save our own sweet self, have some defect:
And characters to ev'ry virtue dear,
Sink from a hint, or suffer by a sneer.

"Sir Harry Blink! Oh, he's a worthy man,
"Still anxious to do all the good he can;
"To aid distress, wou'd share his last poor guinea,
"Delights in kindness—but then, what a ninny!"
Lady Doll Primrose says to Lady Sly,
"You know Miss Tidlikins? Yes—looks awry—
"She's gone to be married—that won't mend it;—
"They say she'll have a fortune—and she'll spend it.
"I hope your La'aship visits Lady Hearty,
"We meet to-night—a most delightful party.
"I don't like Dowagers, who *would* be young,
"And 'twixt ourselves they say—She has a tongue."

If such the general blame that all await,
Say, can our Author 'scape the general fate?
Some will dislike the saucy truths she teaches,
Fond bachelors, and wives who wear the breeches.

"Let me be wedded to a handsome youth,"
Cries old Miss Mumblelove, without a tooth.
"These worn-out beaux, because they've heavy purses,
Expect us, spinsters, to become their nurses.
To love, and be beloved is the happy wife,
A mutual passion is the charm of life."

"Marriage is Heaven's best gift, we must believe it,
Yet some with weak ideas can't conceive it.—
Poor Lady Sobwell's grief, the town wou'd stun;
Oh, Tiffany! Your mistress is undone.
Dear Ma'am—I hope my Lord is well—don't cry—
Hav'n't I cause?—The monster will not die—
The reason why I married him, is clear,
I fondly thought he cou'd not live a year:
But now his dropsy's[35] better, and his cough—
Not the least chance for that to take him off.
I, that could have young husbands now in plenty,
Sha'n't be a widow till I'm one-and-twenty—
No lovely weeds—No sweet dishevell'd hair—
Oh! I cou'd cry my eyes out in despair." [*Sobbing and crying.*

Sir Tristram Testy, worn with age and gout;
Within, all spleen, and flannel all without;
Roars from his elbow-chair, "Reach me my crutches,
Oh! if Death had my wife within his clutches,
With what delight her funeral meats[36] I'd gobble,
And tho', not dance upon her grave, I'd hobble;
No longer then, my peace she could unhinge,
I shou'd cut capers[37] soon, [*Tries to jump, and stumbles*]
Zounds! What a twinge!"

These playful pictures of discordant life,
We bring to combat discontent and strife.
And, by the force of contrast, sweetly prove
The charm that waits on fond and faithful love:
When suited years, and pliant tempers join,
And the heart glows with energy divine,
As the lov'd offspring of the happy pair
Oft climb the knee, the envied kiss to share.

Such joys this happy country long has known,
Rear'd in the cot, reflected from the throne;
Oh! may the glorious zeal, the loyal stand
Which nobly animate this envied land,
Secure to every breast, with glad increase,
The heartfelt blessings of domestic peace!

20.2 *THE MORNING HERALD*, 30 JANUARY 1793

COVENT GARDEN. A new Comedy, called 'Every One Has His Fault', was presented at this theatre, last night. [The review, as is the norm, list actors, characters and provides a synopsis of the plot.] It will appear from this recapitulation, that some parts of the story, are rendered interesting, by the show of probable misery; and some are ludicrous, more than was intended, by the course of events, perhaps, too far incongruous and improbable.—But though the scenes are not all naturally produced, there are few, which do not compensate for a faulty introduction, by a dialogue abounding with interesting sentiment, or lively repartee. Some of the scenes between Captain *Irwin*, and his family or friends, are very tenderly wrought; and those, in which Sir *Robert Ramble* appears, have a sort of gaiety, which if it does not reach the purity of wit, is never debased by buffoonery.

The characters, except that of *Placid*, which is from Foote, have at least, as much novelty, as can be expected at the present day; and that of *Harmony* is, perhaps, entirely new. In the general conduct of the play there is this distinguishing merit, that the incidents are not produced, or heightened by any mechanic contrivances or efforts of *manual wit*, without which so few comedies have of late been ventured upon the stage. Upon the whole, this is a piece, with some scenes of forceful interest, some of elegant manners, and some of well-tempered ridicule;—a polite comedy, after the mode, which was called French, while any thing like literature, or manners remained in France.

The house was filled with a very fashionable audience, who received it with unanimous and frequent applause; so that it promises to be the favourite comedy of the season. The author, we understand, is Mrs. Inchbald, who gave it a prologue and epilogue, which were very well spoken by Farren and Mrs. Mattocks.

20.3 *THE STAR*, 30 JANUARY 1793

COVENT GARDEN. A new comedy, called *Every One has his Fault*, was presented at this theatre last night. [The conventional list of actors and characters is omitted]. This piece may more properly be called a dramatized novel than a comedy. It has much distress, much fine sentiment, and some interest, but little nature and less humour.

There is little originality of character in the comedy, if we except the part given to Munden, which is that of a whimsical philanthropist, the sole business of whose life it is to reconcile his jarring friends towards one another, by the means of little insinuations behind the other's back.—Though this sort of character may not be found very frequently in nature,—it may furnish out a good moral hint to such as are of a quite contrary disposition—"More studious to divide than to unite."[38]

And we give the author credit for the sketch, though made from fancy than reality. Munden played it, as he does every thing, admirably. The part given to Quick he made the most of, but he could not make much. The rest of the good acting was with Mr. and Mrs. Pope, Lewis, Mrs. Mattocks, Farren, and Mrs. Esten.—Fawcett, though a good player, was not well suited with a character.

The play was received with applause by a very full house. The company in the boxes and pit was almost entirely in mourning.[39]

The prologue and epilogue were delivered by Mr. Farren and Mrs. Mattocks.

20.4 *THE TRUE BRITON* NO. 26, 30 JANUARY 1793

[List of actors, characters and the plot synopsis have been omitted]

THE PIECE, WELL AS IT WENT OFF, is very exceptionable. Can it be conceived that a military officer, whose detestation of cowardice, under his supposed insanity, made him shudder at the commission of suicide, would become a foot-pad, with the instrument of self-destruction in his hand, and commit a robbery in the street?

It has another tendency, and that highly objectionable. Allusions are made to the dearness of provisions in the metropolis; and in several sentences the *Democrat* displays a cloven foot.

The audience are kept alive throughout the whole of the performance, alternately moved either by the pathetic or the ludicrous, which were most unaccountably blended. The emotion excited by a tender scene had not time to subside, when the spectator was half convulsed with laughter by a new effort of the Comic Muse.

We are at a loss what to term this new species of composition; 'tis neither comedy, nor tragi-comedy, but something anomalous in which the two are jumbled together.

The performers were very successful, and more perfect than could have been expected at a first representation.

The Margrave and Margravine of Anspach, made a part of a very crowded and respectable audience.[40]

20.5 *THE WORLD*, 30 JANUARY 1793

WE HAVE BEEN SO LONG BEEN ACCUSTOMED to behold our theatres disgraced by performances under the false title of comedy, that we sit down with the greater pleasure to recommend the production of last night, which, if its success be equivalent with its merit, must be beneficial, in a very extraordinary degree, to the interest of the manager.

Mrs. Inchbald had amused, and what redounds more to her honour, instructed the town in more instances than one. To her pen we are indebted for the present comedy, which she has introduced to the public under the title of *Every One has his Fault*. . . .

Mr. *Harmony* is a character as singular as it is benevolent. Totally regardless of his own advantages or felicities, he seeks only to comfort the dejected, reconcile those at variance, and make every body happy he has any concern with: his mode of burying animosity, by expressing to the opposite parties the respect which they secretly entertain for each other, is whimsical enough; but from so frequent a repetition it becomes stale and insipid.

Solus and *Placid* are well opposed—the one made to *enter*, the other eager to *retire* from the marriage state; the eccentricities of the former contrive to keep the audience in an uninterrupted roar of laughter the whole time he is on stage.

Lord *Norland*, stern, haughty, and inflexible, comes directly from *Dorriforth*, in the "*Simple Story*";[41]—and indeed the circumstances of his taking under his particular protection the son of Lady *Elinor*, cannot be disputed to derive its source from the same novel. Plagiarism is always a fault—but perhaps not quite so enormous when the author robs only herself.

Character, Mrs. Inchbald has evidently taken great pains to delineate—and it must be confessed she has not missed her aim. Mrs. *Placid* is the only one we cannot acknowledge to take its exact origin from nature—it certainly is rather overdrawn.

The distresses of *Irving*, are such as *told*, if we may use the expression, to the feelings of every one present, not absolutely dead to pity and humanity—the absurd and dangerous tendency to overstrained etiquette and ceremony, are very well, and very properly exposed. Many an honest man has sunk beneath its rigour—and when the punctilios of form are suffered to crush the indigent and worthy—who is there that will not unite to remedy their increase?

The language is what might be expected from so elegant an author—but if it were deprived of a few expressions which *may* be converted into a *double entendre*, we should like it the better. We say *may*, because there are a set of beings, who, to the disgrace of British gallantry, grasp at any thing; which by the horrible additions of their conceit, may be rendered matter of imputation on the decency of the female author. These literary *monsters*, for nothing else can they be called, seem to glory in attempting the disrepute of the fair part of our countrymen; but to their confusion be it spoken, the talents of a Barbauld, a Cowley, a More, and an Inchbald, will be the ornament and boast of Great Britain; not withstanding the mean and unjust attacks of ignorance and envy.[42]

The performers we have not time to mention. The prologue and epilogue were well delivered by Farren, and Mrs. Mattocks.

POLLIO

20.6 *CRITICAL REVIEW*, NEW SERIES 7, FEBRUARY 1793: 223–4

A MINUTE ACCOUNT OF THIS COMEDY would lead to a disquisition of too much length for the limits of our review; and, perhaps, a general criticism will be much more satisfactory. We might select some of the striking scenes, in order to exhibit the dramatic art with which they are constructed, and the elegant, yet natural, turn of the dialogue. That method, however, seems to us too much hackneyed; and besides, all specific beauties, either of plot or composition, are relative, depending entirely upon their place, their connection, their relation to what preceded; and the consequences, which follow like effects from their causes. For this reason it is that detached scenes seldom make the impression for the sake of which they are selected. We shall, therefore, content ourselves with stating, upon the whole, what sort of a play Mrs. Inchbald has presented to the public.

The very title develops her subject, and indicates a dramatic genius. Comedy, it must be observed, has been distinguished into different classes, arising from the practice of modern poets. The critics have enumerated the several species, such as comedy of intrigue, comedy of character, the pathetic comedy (*comedie larmoyante*), genteel comedy, and the lower comedy (*comedy bourgeose*). The comedy of intrigue, depending upon surprize, and a rapid succession of incidents, has often succeeded on the stage. Of late years it seems to have been chiefly cultivated by our present race of authors. It is unnecessary to mention the pieces that have given *a cheap* delight in the representation, but have left in the mind of the loudest applauders not one trace of sentiment or observation on the manners. Of such performances we may say, with Horace, that they are addressed to the eye, not to the ear.—Mrs. Inchbald, undismayed by the reigning taste, has had the courage to aim at useful mirth and moral instruction. She has produced a variety of characters, well marked, and well contrasted, all tending to explain and prove the maxim which forms the title of her play. She has cultivated the noblest province of the drama, which consists in true delineation of character. She has not selected her dramatis personae from books written for circulating libraries. She has looked at life, and, to use Dryden's expression, her play is the theft of a comic writer from mankind.[43] The piece before us is a comedy of character, with an intermixture of that, which has been called pathetic comedy. Irwin has his fault, but a fault that springs from delicate sensibility and a generous disposition. It must be acknowledged that his producing a pistol, as the instrument which is to relieve him from misery, is a circumstance that shocks even in the reading; but he atones for it when he says, "And yet I want the courage to be a villain." Mrs. Irwin is a beautiful specimen of true affection and conjugal fidelity. Comic humour and the pathetic are happily blended in this play, and are so managed as to succeed each other with the most pleasing vicissitude. The man who, after his career of folly, has seen the merit of a valuable woman, from whom he had been divorced, has occurred in the course of human transactions. Mr. Solus, who is tired of solitude, and wishes to enter into the married state, but is deterred by the imperious spirit of Mrs. Placid, is an agreeable compound of sense and folly, or, properly speaking, of the ridiculous absurd.—The play, upon the whole, is a picture of life; the fable is well conducted, and the plot is artfully brought to a conclusion. It must, therefore, be said of Mrs. Inchbald, that the praise of aiming at the true ends of comedy, must be fairly allowed to her. Her success in so arduous an undertaking needs not to be mentioned; the public suffrage is loud in her favour at every repetition of her play.

20.7 *THE THESPIAN MAGAZINE* 1, MARCH 1793: 234–5

IN THE DECLINE OF DRAMATIC GENIUS, the world is indebted to Mrs. Inchbald for contributing her share of support; and it is a powerful argument in favour of female capability, that at present, the soft sex are the chief support: it is the argument of experience. The present piece is not a strict comedy. It has a double—we had almost said a triple plot; at least there are three separate interests. . . The characters are well conceived and such as nature may own. The peer and the philanthropist form a fine contrast, and the more so as it does not appear a studied one: they are placed in such different situations that it is not till towards the close that we are permitted to view them in conjunction; then indeed we are surprised. The man of fashion we pronounce to be the best and nearest to real life, that has been drawn for some time; we may recognize the original every day. The philanthropist presents an amiable moral; had his mode of reconciliation been better correspondent with veracity, it might have been more so. These with the batchelor, are the characters the author may claim. We give her great credit for her representation of Irvin after he has committed the robbery; it is the scene of nature and of feeling, and shows a wonderful knowledge of the human heart. The language is perspicuous and just; wit has no share in the piece. There is an error which the general of our plays abound with, and which has not entirely escaped: it is conceived that comedy should represent eccentricities, which is encroaching on farce: this we think is done in the answer of Placid to Mrs. Placid; he had said that he had lost his appetite; she insists he shall be hungry, and he answers: "O yes, I have an excellent appetite, I shall eat prodigiously."—It is not consistent with the character of the peer that he should be so easily softened by the flattery which the philanthropist offers him: we may almost say of him that "his is too proud to be vain." Some of the others are easier wrought upon than we conceive to be natural. We do not approve of making the names of the persons expressive of their characters: it anticipates novelty. Upon the whole this piece has so much to praise and so little to censure that we think it is a considerable acquisition to the fame of the fair author, and the drama of her country.

CENSOR DRAMATICUS.

20.8 GEORGE DANCE, *ELIZABETH INCHBALD*

George Dance, *Elizabeth Inchbald*, pencil, 1794. National Portrait Gallery, London.

Notes

1 Inchbald's stranding of "One" in the title is significant. This is a play where society's (and comedy's) derogation of a solitary condition—especially for women—is put under intense scrutiny. The copy-text is *Every One Has His Fault: A Comedy in five acts, as it is performed at the Theatre Royal, Covent Garden*. 3rd Edition. London: G.G.J. and J. Robinson, 1793.

2 Eighteen of Inchbald's plays were published, though she may have written as many as 23.

3 See Gillian Russell, *The Theatres of War: Performance, Politics and Society, 1793–1815*. Oxford: Clarendon Press, 1995, 11.

4 See O'Quinn, "Bread."

5 See Misty G. Anderson, *Female Playwrights and Eighteenth-Century Comedy: Negotiating Marriage on the London Stage*. London: Palgrave, 2002, 171–200.

6 Edward Nares (1762–1841) was an Anglican vicar who lived as librarian at Blenheim Palace from 1788 to 1797. During this period he wrote many minor works such as this prologue and was an avid performer, along with the daughters of the Duke of Marlborough, in private theatricals at the Palace. He scandalously eloped with Lady Charlotte Spencer (1769–1802), the Duke's third daughter in 1797.

7 *phiz*: face.

8 Referring to Mary Wollstonecraft's *Vindication of the Rights of Woman* (1792).

9 When Parisian women marched on Versailles on October 5, 1789 a portion of the Flanders Regiment, charged with guarding the palace, joined the women's cause.

10 Referring to the nine Muses.

11 In the Larpent Version, Mr. Placid is "Colonel Placid," thus Inchbald appears to have cast Placid and Irwin as military men. This has important implications for how we consider Irwin's plight and Placid's name.

12 The Larpent version adds, "for fear of being dunn'd" at this point.

13 The pun on "constitutional" signals Mr. Harmony's democratic politics.

14 "Provisions are so scarce!": This speech generated a fire-storm of political objections in the press and considerable reaction in the playhouse [see Contexts for the ensuing debate]. Harmony's remarks on scarcity evoke a long history of food rioting among the working poor in which protestors carried loaves of bread wrapped in black cloth to take control of the market place and set the price of provisions. But Harmony's remark resonates specifically with the conjunction of scarcity and anti-war sentiment in the lead-up to war with Revolutionary France that was itself a re-play of anti-war activism prior to the American War. This phrase returns again in Act III and in a modified form in the resolution of Act V.

15 *Lord Mayor's Day*: On November 9 the Lord Mayor of London proceeded via coach and flotilla with the Alderman from the Guildhall in the City of London to Westminster to swear his allegiance to the Crown and to receive the assent of Lord Chancellor. On its return to the City, the pageant ended up at Mansion House for a vast entertainment. It was one of the most spectacular events of the urban calendar.

16 The Larpent version follows Irwin's speech with two further speeches:

> LADY ELEANOR. Oh! Do not throw yourself into the way of such temptation as London Streets yield to the unfortunate.
> IRWIN. What do you apprehend?

17 The laws around marriage and divorce were less stringent in Scotland than England especially following Hardwicke's Marriage Act of 1753, which only recognized marriages performed within the physical confines of the Church of England. Hardwicke did not apply in Scotland where it had been historically easier to both marry and divorce. Sir Robert likely went to Scotland to be married without the consent of either his father or the father/guardian of his intended wife. In Scotland divorce was permissible on the grounds of adultery or desertion and it is clear that Lady Ramble divorced Lord Robert for his infidelity. In England no Act of Parliament was ever passed granting divorce on the grounds of a husband's adultery.

18 *years of discretion*: Giles Jacob's *A New-Law Dictionary* (1729) handles this issue as follows: "A Man . . . at Fourteen, which is his *age of Discretion,* may consent to Marriage, and chuse his Guardian; . . . A Women . . . at Twelve . . . may consent to Marriage; at Fourteen she is at Years of Discretion, and may chuse a Guardian" (4). The age of consent was fourteen for men *and* women in Scotland, so Solus's ensuing remarks are confused.

19 In England, where divorce was extremely difficult to obtain, it was not uncommon for a formal separation to be arranged whereby the husband supported the wife's financial needs in exchange for de facto "liberty." These private agreements enabled husbands to live apart from wives whom they had no adequate grounds to divorce. As Sir Robert seems to imply and Susan Staves has shown, judges often interpreted these agreements after the fact to the wife's disadvantage by reverting to pre-1660 notions of marital property.

20 Sir Robert is alluding to fashionable promenades in the West End of London.

21 As a veteran of the American War, Irwin's charge had significant political purchase. The invocation of "savage" hospitality resonates with Rousseau's notion of the "noble savage", but the speech also mobilizes the anxious rhetoric surrounding the misgovernment of colonial and military affairs. The common metaphorical link between "American" and "savage" suggests that Americans may well be the "True Britons" Irwin is yearning for and that the Britain Irwin fought for has become a perversion of civil society far more dangerous than the new nation across the Atlantic. Deploying the discourse of savagery, Inchbald appears to agree with Edmund Burke and Charles James Fox's assessment of the American War in the late 1770s and perhaps suggests, like many prominent Whigs in the early 1790s (Burke excluded), that a similar set of miscalculations was driving Pitt's policy towards Revolutionary France.

22 *banditti*: plural for bandit; outlaws.

23 *connubial*: of or relating to marriage.

24 *'Sdeath*: "God's death."

25 Corrected from "Intrude" in the Robinson edition.

26 The repetition of this phrase is notable. The political import of the phrase can be gathered from the Larpent version which inserts the following speeches after Harmony's remark:

> LORD NORLAND. How! Do you take the part of public ruffians.
> HARMONY. No. I wish them still extirpated—But if there are persons who, by their oppression provoke those outrages, I wish them punished first.

27 *proviso*: a condition or stipulation attached to an agreement. All of the language in this passage pitches Harmony's contractual understanding of marriage against Norland's obsession with property.

28 In the Larpent version this speech reads as follows:

> I am sorry to see you thus; you have been weeping? Surely your pride should teach you to overcome this continual sorrow. You appear to lament your separation from a cruel husband, as if you had followed a kind one to the grave.

29 Larpent adds "*Estate Entail*". In English common law an entail is a form of trust established by deed or settlement that restricts the sale or inheritance of an estate in order to ensure that it automatically passes to the heir pre-determined by the settlement deed.

30 i.e. Sir Robert appropriates the bond.

31 *dishabille*: not technically in a state of undress, rather clothing intended to be worn informally. In this context, the married man gains a familiarity that would be deemed licentious were he unattached.

32 Hammond.

33 i.e. Miss Wooburn.

34 This is a re-working of the "Provisions are so scarce!" speeches in Acts 1 and 3. Solus's remarks on starvation and plenty in the ensuing speeches bring this trope to its conclusion.

35 *dropsy*: edema, a condition where soft tissues swell due to the accumulation of excess water. If unchecked it could be fatal.

36 *funeral meats*: the favorite dishes of the deceased usually presented at the funeral reception.

37 *cut capers*: dance.

38 Alexander Pope, *An Essay on Man*, Epistle 2, line 72.

39 Louis XVI was executed on January 21, 1793. The news had only just reached England when Inchbald's play opened.

40 Although her second marriage to Christian Frederic, the Margrave of Anspach partially restored her reputation, Elizabeth Craven (1750–1828) had long been associated both with the theatre and with sexual scandal. The latter history adds a certain irony to this sentence.

41 Dorriforth is the principle male character in Inchbald's novel *A Simple Story* (1791).

42 The reviewer invokes the poet Anna Laetitia Barbauld, the playwright, essayist and novelist Hannah More, the poet and playwright Hannah Cowley and the novelist and playwright Elizabeth Inchbald.

43 "For to write humour in Comedy (which is the theft of Poets from mankind) little of fancy is requir'd; the Poet observes only what is ridiculous, and pleasant folly, and by judging exactly what is so, he pleases in the representation of it." John Dryden, Preface to *An Evening's Love* (1671).

Index